## FIFTH EDITION

# THE HUMAN VENTURE

## From Prehistory to the Present

### COMBINED EDITION

## Anthony Esler

*College of William and Mary*

Upper Saddle River, New Jersey 07458

A CIP catalog record for this book can be obtained from the Library of Congress.

Editorial Director: *Charlyce Jones Owen*
Senior Acquisition Editor: *Charles Cavaliere*
Associate Editor: *Emsal Hason*
Senior Managing Editor: *Jan Stephan*
Production Liaison: *Fran Russello*
Project Manager: *Patty Donovan/Pine Tree Composition*
Prepress and Manufacturing Buyer: *Tricia Kenny*
Art Director: *Jayne Conte*
Cover Designer: *Kiwi Design*
Cover Art: Safavid Shah Tahmasp, "Reception of Mughal Shah Humayun" depicts a meeting of the medieval Persian king.
   Mural from Chehel Sutun Palace, Isfahan, Iran.
Director, Image Resource Center: *Melinda Lee Reo*
Manager, Rights & Permissions: *Zina Arabia*
Interior Image Specialist: *Beth Boyd-Brenzel*
Cover Image Specialist: *Karen Sanatar*
Image Permission Coordinator: *Fran Toepher*
Photo Researcher: *Kathy Ringrose*
Marketing Manager: *Claire Bitting*

F or my father, Jamie Arthur Esler, who wrote the history of the world on one page many years ago.

This book was set in 10/12 Times by Pine Tree Composition, Inc.
and was printed and bound by RR Donnelly & Sons Company
The cover was printed by Phoenix Color Corp.

 © 2004, 2000, 1996, 1992, 1986 by Pearson Education, Inc.
Upper Saddle River, New Jersey 07458

Printed in the United States of America
10  9  8  7  6  5

ISBN 0-13-183481-9

Pearson Education Ltd., *London*
Pearson Education Australia Pty. Limited, *Sydney*
Pearson Education Singapore, Pte. Ltd.
Pearson Education North Asia Ltd., *Hong Kong*
Pearson Education Canada, Ltd., *Toronto*
Pearson Educación de Mexico, S.A. de C.V.
Pearson Education—Japan, *Tokyo*
Pearson Education Malaysia, Pte. Ltd.
Pearson Education, *Upper Saddle River, New Jersey*

# CONTENTS

# A Global History Since 1500

# PREFACE

Prefaces are always challenging, and the prefaces to this book seem to get more challenging with each new edition. For a preface is at least in part a look ahead. And in the opening years of the twenty-first century, the global prospect before us looks less predictable than ever.

This fifth edition of *The Human Venture*, like its predecessors, attempts to provide a historical background to the changing world of today. Like earlier editions, this one tries to offer a genuinely global perspective, rather than a European history with add-ons about other cultures. It still aims at the broadest possible coverage—coverage of women as well as of men, of preurban as well as of urban-imperial peoples, of culture as well as of politics. It still tries to humanize the past with emphasis on the historical roles of individual human beings, from ancient emperors to laboring peasants. And this particular version of our global past still builds on a strong narrative line that reflects the nature of history as the author sees it—as a story going somewhere, obscure though that somewhere may still be to the principal historical actors—us.

A major goal of this new edition has been to adapt the book more closely to the requirements of classroom teaching and learning. The number of chapters, for instance, has been reduced from fifty to thirty—roughly the number of weeks in many academic years. This change, I hasten to add, has been largely accomplished by combining chapters, not by cutting! All chapters have again been revised, and each now has a new theme-setting "Glance Ahead" opener and a substantially updated bibliography.

There are also some new maps, some new pictures, and a new emphasis on the "Voices from the Past" boxes—one for each chapter now. The "Overviews" introducing each of the six large sections into which the book is divided have also been revised, and a new big-picture time line appended to each. And the book as a whole has been redesigned in a "trade-book" format that I hope will be easier for the reader to hold while absorbing the carefully digested insights of twenty-five centuries of historians from many times and lands.

Once more, I have included the odd anecdote and I hope some new insights picked up during the three months or more I spend overseas each year. Several weeks each on the upper Amazon, across the Outback and the Top End of Australia, in the Northwest Frontier Province of Pakistan, and among the ethnic minority villages of western China have certainly added to my respect for the indigenous peoples of the world. And annual visits to familiar neighborhoods in favorite European cities serve as a healthy reminder that the peoples of the developed world have a lot to teach each other too.

A key function of the preface, finally, remains to express proper gratitude to the many people without whom there would be no book at all. Here a primary debt must be to Charles Cavaliere, the new Prentice Hall history editor, for injecting a surge of youthful dynamism into this particular venture into the human past. Many thanks also to Emsal Hasan and Patty Donovan for getting me through the hard part—finishing—and to Adrienne Paul for handling every unlikely request of mine effectively and expeditiously.

Without the shared insights and shrewd criticisms of scholarly readers, of course, a synthesis as broad as this would be impossible. My thanks, then, to Kenneth Wilburn, East Carolina University; Louis McDermott, California Maritime Academy; Trevor Getz, University of New Orleans; Robert Garfield, DePaul University; and Pamela McVay, Ursuline College.

Thanks for past critical readings should also go to Akanmu G. Adebayo, Kennesaw State University; Alana Cain Scott, Morehead State University; Elizabeth C. George, Southern Illinois University; Farid Mahdavi-Izadi, San Diego State University; Linda L. Taber, Wayne State University; Joe Gowaskie, Rider College; John Voll, University of New Hampshire; Penny S. Gold, Knox College; Walter S. Hanchett, SUNY/Cortland; Donald L. Layton, Indiana State University; Melvin E. Page, Murray State University; Susan Fitzpatrick, Lindenwood College; Curtis Anderson, Oakland Community College; Dorothy Zeisler-Vralsted, University of Wisconsin, La Crosse; Ed Balog and James Hood, Lindenwood College; James Weland and Nancy R. Northrup, Bentley College; Thomas Anderson, Eastern Connecticut State University; Howard A. Barnes, Winston Salem University; Olwyn M. Blouet, Virginia State University; Robert Garfield, De Paul University; W. Scott Jessee, Appalachian State University; Gerald Newman, Kent State University; and John A. Phillips, University of California-Riverside.

Thanks again to scholars who have patiently labored to educate me over the years, including Marjorie W. Bingham of Women in World Area Studies; Mario D. Mazzarella and the Department of History at Christopher Newport College; J. F. Watts and the faculty of the trailblazing World Civilization course at City College of New York; Richard Snyder, William Pemberton, and the landmark World History program at the University of Wisconsin, La Crosse; and Bill Alexander, Cassandra Newby, and Jeanne Zeidler of Hampton University.

As always, my thanks must go to friends and colleagues here at William and Mary, who do their best to correct the sweeping generalizations I bring to the acid test of their expertise. For many years of help, my thanks to Ismail Abdalla, Berhanu Abegaz, Jim Axtell, Craig Canning, John Carroll, Ed Crapol, Judy Ewell, A. Z. Freeman, Phil Funigiello, Dale Hoak, Ward Jones, Kris Lane, Gil McArthur, Jim McCord, Leisa Meyer, Ed Pratt, Abdul Karim Rafeq, Ernie Schwintzer, John Selby, Tom Sheppard, Rich Sigwalt, George Strong, Cam Walker, and Jim Whittenburg.

For introductions to some fascinating corners of the world, my thanks to Steve and Peggy Brush, for Peru when things were much too exciting to be saddled with a guest as well; to Professor Dong Leshan, of the Chinese Academy of Social Sciences; to Chris Drake, for showing me how to look at the African land; to Carol Clemeau Esler, for all the village-level sojourns in Europe; to Marcia Davidson Field, for her insights into Latin America over many years; to Richard Goff, for caustic comments and sage council along the Atlantic; to Professor Isaria N. Kimambo, of the University of Dar es Salaam, for insights into African historiography; to Ross Kreamer for Java, Sumatra, and Vietnam; to Chris Mullen Kreamer, for sharing her remarkable "African destiny"; to Steve and Ann Marlowe, for expat Europe and much more; to Don Meyer, for Benares, the Ganges, and the border roads of India; to Ernie Schwintzer and Alice Davenport for Jakarta in tense times; and to Jerry Weiner, for running a tight ship from Abidjan to Zanzibar.

And thanks again to Cam Walker, who keeps coming up with amazing places we haven't ever been—two different versions of Shangri-la so far!—but never lets anything get in the way of that evening trip to the corner café.

*Anthony Esler*

# ABOUT THE AUTHOR

Anthony Esler has taught history at the College of William and Mary in Williamsburg, Virginia, for most of his sixty-odd years. But he has also lived in many parts of the United States, accumulated several years of living and travel in Europe, and visited every inhabited continent several times. He spends a minimum of three months overseas each year, sampling the wine, exploring the streets and the ruins, and checking to see if the rainforests are still there. Esler's books reflect his enthusiasms. These include a fascination with generational conflict nurtured in the streets of the sixties, a passion for story-telling, and a preference for panoramic "big picture" history—like *The Human Venture*.

Esler on the road to the ruins of Tsaparang in western Tibet.

# INTRODUCTION

# VENTURE INTO HISTORY

## AN UNDERTAKING OF UNCERTAIN OUTCOME

## HISTORY AND CIVILIZATION

## FROM ROME TO MACHU PICCHU

## An Undertaking of Uncertain Outcome

History does not happen—it is made by human beings. It is made by people of differing opinions, of varied degrees of knowledge and control, of more or less good will. It is the work of all the peoples of this world, down all the human centuries. History is, has been, and will continue to be the common venture of us all.

The word *venture* derives from an old word for *adventure*—and history is surely that.

It is too easy in writing (or reading) a textbook to lose sight of the great adventure that is the human story. The long wanderings of our prehistoric predecessors over land and sea, peopling the continents, are epics of adventure that will never be written. The struggles of our ancestors with each other, sometimes savage and often tragic, are nonetheless tales of human heroism too. Even the silent inner struggles of the poet, the philosopher, or the prophet may be great adventures of the human spirit.

Nor are all the historic adventurers famous names in history books. The cabin boy who signed on to sail with Ferdinand Magellan and returned alive—one of seventeen to do so, the first human beings to circumnavigate the globe—was as much an adventurer as Magellan himself, whose bones whitened on a far Pacific shore. The peasant girl who never traveled ten miles from her medieval village but heard the voices of angels in the church bells ringing was as much an adventurer of the spirit as Joan of Arc, who rallied armies and left her name to history.

We are all of us part of the human venture. Bantus trekking across Africa, Amerindians descending the length of the Americas, builders of the ancient cultures of Egypt or India or China—we are all adventurers in history. The future may well look upon our highways and skyscrapers, our tumultuously expanding global computer network, our miles-high jets and rockets drifting among the stars, and see all of us today as a race of heroes.

A *venture*, according to *Webster's* dictionary, is "an undertaking involving chance, risk, or danger," an attempt fraught with "peril" and "jeopardy." We may be spared the great plagues, the long hungers, the slowly descending ice that pressed inexorably upon our ancestors. But the threats of sudden economic collapse, of faiths and ideologies in conflict, of wars open and secret are with us as much today as they ever were. And overpopulation, poverty, and famine, pollution, dwindling resources, and climatic change may be even more dangerous.

*Webster's* further defines a venture as "an undertaking of uncertain outcome." Here, too, history clearly qualifies. Even the most clearsighted historian would hesitate to say much about where we are all going—let alone whether we will ever get there.

There have been those who thought they saw the outcome. Chinese scholars saw history following a pattern of endless cycles. Medieval Christians and medieval Muslims sought meaning in history as the will of God. Enlightenment philosophers and the ideologues of the last two centuries have offered various versions of the gospel of progress as the road to utopia. But we do not know that any of these patterns imposed upon the human story accurately describes the primary direction in which history is moving. We do not know for certain that history is moving in any particular direction at all!

What does seem evident from the historical record is that we are trying. The outcome may be unsure, but human beings have been laboring for many centuries to give direction to the human story. In this sense, at least, our human venture into history is a purposeful one. We may frequently be blind to our true destination. We may often be operating at vigorous crosspurposes with one another, one nation or one people against another. We may fail of our endeavors; some of the most promising historic drives have broken down in the end, collapsing from internal rot or overwhelmed by external enemies. But they have been conscious drives. Launched in the names of whatever false gods or faltering causes, group follies or individual egotism, every great movement, every great civilization has nonetheless been, at least in significant part, a deliberate effort to impose human will upon the world.

## HISTORY AND CIVILIZATION

The perilous course of human history is thus something more than an adventure. It is a great commitment.

To our ancestors several centuries ago, the word *venture* could mean simply an investment, a risking of capital in hopes of a golden return. The human venture into history may also be seen as such an investment—a commitment of energy, purpose, and generations of human lives to the great undertaking called civilization.

Civilization as it is usually defined began more than five thousand years ago in western Asia and northeastern Africa. From these beginnings in the river valleys of Mesopotamia and Egypt, this form of human society has since spread around the earth.

Definitions of the term *civilization* have varied down the centuries. One view, which goes back to ancient Greece and probably still farther back in China, would define civilizations like their own as "the higher culture," to be contrasted with the primitive ways of peasants, savage peoples, and other barbarians. The opposite approach, also of ancient lineage, would apply the term to virtually any society, with special emphasis on preurban peoples, whose ways of life are seen as every bit as complex and subtle, considerably more in synch with the natural world, and perhaps possessing ancient wisdom lost to the city-based cultures. Here, the word *civilization* will be used, along with more neutral terms like *urban* or *urban-imperial,* to mean a style of human life rooted in the city and larger political units, and in the material and cultural forms that historically have tended to go with these political structures.

The pattern has looked much the same everywhere and ever since. Civilization means cities and larger states, centralized and bureaucratic governments, classes and castes, technological advance and the growth of trade, the magical craft of writing, and increasingly sophisticated arts and sciences, religions, and philosophies. Not all of these are found in all cases, but the overall picture is similar and clearly recognizable wherever it appears.

Civilizations make possible larger and more complex human endeavors than could be undertaken by less developed societies. The larger resources and shared assumptions of a great civilization make possible great buildings, marvelous engineering works, and the integration of large numbers of people into a single system of administration and law. Civilization produces elaborate systems of thought, art of unexcelled subtlety and grandeur, and longer, healthier, less circumscribed lives for millions of people. Major civilizations, in short, substantially enhance the human capacity for achieving human goals.

Yet there are those who regard this entire enterprise as pointless, illusory, or even downright dangerous, and their objections are not to be lightly dismissed by the serious student of history.

As far back as ancient times, for instance, some students of the human past saw civilization as a pointless trajectory of rise and fall. Rome and Babylon, mighty once, are ruins today. What purpose, then, in laboring to build anew, if such desolation is the end of all constructive labor?

Others have pointed out that great crimes have been committed in the name of civilization. Narrow definitions of good and evil have led highly civilized peoples to deal savagely with others whose definitions differed from their own. Medieval Christian and Muslim societies, for all the glory of their cathedrals and mosques, fought each other for centuries in bloody crusades and *jihads*. Twentieth-century industrial civilization, while providing more material goods and human freedom to more people than ever before in human history, also invented total war and totalitarian tyranny, generated widespread economic exploitation, and did unprecedented damage to our natural environment.

Heavy charges, then, may be laid against the human enterprise we call civilization.

Perhaps the best response to all these criticisms lies in the historical record itself—in the long record of human commitment to the rearing of complex and far-reaching civilized societies. At least as striking as the pattern of rise and fall in the history of cultures is the eternal recurrence of the drive to build and build again, to raise civilization once more from its own ruins. Among the earliest styles of life, both hunting and gathering and pastoral nomadism are rapidly nearing extinction today. Even the self-supporting agricultural village is undergoing rapid assimilation into an urban-dominated order as peoples the world around rush to join the latest wave of civilized societies, those built on the culture of the machine.

On the whole, then, human beings seem to value what more sizable and complex societies can give them more than they fear the abuses of power that go with civilization. Preurban Germans and Mongols fought to get into ancient Rome and Han China, and village people the world around continue to flood into the cities of the developed world today.

## FROM ROME TO MACHU PICCHU

In this book, then, the mainstream of history will thus be the story of the city builders, the empire builders. The peoples who undertook the greatest of human enterprises appeared in all corners of the earth, on almost every habitable continent. Isolated at first, they slowly expanded the areas of their domination at the expense of their neighbors who did not know how to build great walls or make the magic signs that spoke on stone or clay or paper. By C.E. 1500, as we shall see, the tide was turning decisively against other forms of the human

venture. At the beginning of modern history, the road was open to the final victory of the city-based civilizations.

Victory justifies much, and history, as we are often told, is always written by the winners. But there is more than simply victory to justify our focus on what this book sees as the great enterprise of civilization building. The builders of great civilizations have, after all, been constructing something of value.

The ruins of vanished civilizations strew the earth—evidence not so much of the inevitability of human failure as of the grandeur of the great enterprise at its best. The lengthening shadows of the Roman Colosseum, once the tourists have gone and the little old lady who feeds the cats is alone among the looming arches and the empty seats where crowds once cheered or turned thumbs down, remind us of the achievements of vanished Western empires. Chinese archaeologists are still exhuming the buried army of Huangdi, thousands of life-size statues of men, horses, even chariots that tell us much about that driven man and the laboring generations who built the Great Wall of China. The glooms and glimmers of St. Peter's in Rome, aglow with marble and pigment and bronze—room after room, acre after acre of art—remind us at every visit of what splendid things the European spirit has been capable. The towering Khmer temples of Angkor in Cambodia, the mysterious African ruins of Great Zimbabwe, and the roofless stone city of Machu Picchu, heaved high on a mountain peak above the Peruvian jungles, stir feelings of awe and wonder in even the most jaded tourist.

Socrates and Muhammad speaking in their market squares, Christ and Buddha wandering the dusty roads of Galilee or the banks of the Ganges, Confucius preaching common decency to a war-torn world—all had, at one level, a single message. It was the message of all the storytellers and praise singers, the shapers and singers of dreams, who have immortalized human heroism and human love, great leaders and great souls. It was a word the preachers and the poets shared: We can do better. We can be more.

With all the crimes and follies of past ventures into civilization on our consciences, we are thinkers, doers, builders. And the great enterprise continues. If the past is any guide at all to what lies ahead, we will probably go on constructing ever more elaborate attempts at civilization, as we have done for more than fifty centuries. The good society may still elude us, but we will not stop trying.

The crimes and follies, the labors, exploits, and achievements of first fifty centuries of human civilization are the subject of the first volume of this book.

# CHAPTER 1

# THE WORLD BEFORE HISTORY
## Stone Age People
## (5,000,000–3500 B.C.E.)

**A GLANCE AHEAD: HISTORY BUILDS ON PREHISTORY**

**THE PREHISTORIC WORLD**
Beginnings
Setting the Stage
Ecology and History

**HUMAN DEVELOPMENT**
The Bone Hunters
Biological Evolution
The Prehistoric Migrations
The Human Races

**PALEOLITHIC HUNTERS AND GATHERERS**
The Foraging Band
Stone Age Women
Beginnings of Religion and Art

**NEOLITHIC FARMERS**
The Discovery of Agriculture
Crops and Flocks
Life in the Neolithic Village
Alternate Lifestyles

**THE TRANSITION TO CIVILIZATION**
The First Civilizations
Monarchy, Hierarchy, and Patriarchy
Economics, Technology, Culture

## A Glance Ahead: History Builds on Prehistory

The hairy, beetle-browed cavemen and cavewomen you see in museum dioramas usually don't look as if they would rate very high on anybody's scale of civilization. In fact, however, prehistoric people played an essential and immensely innovative role in world history. It took millions of years of prehistoric biological development and cultural evolution to lay the foundations for the few thousand years of city-based history we have enjoyed thus far.

It was our prehistoric ancestors who discovered such basic skills as walking on two legs and manipulating things with their hands. It was they who learned how to make tools, how to herd animals and cultivate the soil, how to settle in villages and develop even more skills there. They explored the first forms of artistic expression and formulated some basic religious ideas. And they migrated restlessly around the globe, until all the habitable continents and countless islands had their scattered settlements of hominids.

And then, at the end of this long, slow progression, prehistoric humanity raised the walls and gates of the first cities and walked through them into history.

## The Prehistoric World

### Beginnings

Perhaps the most familiar version of the beginning of human life on earth is that given in the Judeo-Christian Old Testament:

> But there went up a mist from the earth, and watered the whole face of the ground
>
> And the Lord God formed man of the dust of the ground, and breathed into his nostrils the breath of life; and man became a living soul.[1]

And more familiar still:

> So God created man in his own image, in the image of God created he him: male and female created he them.[2]

One of the most vivid modern Western representations of the creation is surely the series of pictures painted by Michelangelo on the ceiling of the Sistine Chapel in the Vatican at Rome. Thousands of tourists daily crane their necks to gaze up at the magnificently muscled, hugely bearded figure of Jehovah dividing light from darkness with a gesture, rolling the sun and the moon into being, extending his powerful right hand to bestow upon Adam the ultimate gift of life.

An African version of the creation says that Doondari made humankind out of the "five elements"—fire, water, air, iron, and stone. The oldest of all creation stories, that of the "Memnite theology" carved in stone at Memphis on the Nile almost five thousand years ago, calls the creator Ptah and says that he made the first sentient beings with weapons in their hands! Down the centuries and around the world, "first things" have thus been matters of profound concern for many peoples.

---

[1]*Genesis* 2:6–7
[2]*Genesis* 1:27

Our own modern version of the beginnings of things is as exotic as any, though it seems (to many of us, at least) rather more likely to be true.

## Setting the Stage

In the beginning, modern science tells us, the solid earth beneath our feet was not solid at all, but a ring of glowing, superheated gases swirling around the searing core of our sun. There was a cooling and a condensing, and where only the gaseous outreach of a spinning star had been, there were separate whirling chunks of slowly cooling matter. Several billions of years in the future people would call these "planets."

The cooling and settling continued, with dramatic changes in what became our world. This third planet out from the sun cooled and hardened on the surface, though the core has remained molten and seething. Water spread over much of the globe, and an atmosphere that we would find breathable slowly formed to a height of several miles above the surface. In this strange world of exploding volcanoes, flickering lightning, and bombarding cosmic rays, matter miraculously quickened into life in the primal seas.

From single-celled bacteria and "blue-greens" to shapeless jellies and shelled creatures in the sea, from shellfish to insects, from backboned fish to reptiles, birds, and beasts, animal life evolved. Vegetable life developed also over the uncountable hundreds of millions of years, from moss and horsetails to conifers and broad-leafed trees, from ferns to fruits and flowers. Long before the first identifiable hominid squinted into the sun, our Eden was prepared.

Change continued in the world around us even after the human race had begun to take shape. Shifts in the surface structures of the earth caused "continental drift" as the continental masses drifted slowly apart. The oceans grew and shrank, rose and fell. The climate changed drastically from one geological epoch to the next, caking the northern zone with ice, turning forests into grasslands, grasslands into deserts. Nevertheless, by the time history began, a recognizable geography had taken shape. Since, with some continuing changes, this was to be the stage for all our subsequent adventures, we should survey it briefly before going on to the actors and the story.

More than two thirds of the earth—the oceans, seas, lakes, and rivers of the world—was covered with water. The large expanses of dry land that protruded from this world-ocean formed seven continents. One of these, Antarctica, the frozen land around the South Pole, was all but uninhabitable. Of the other six, two were actually a single land mass, the great world island of Eurasia, divided for historical reasons into Europe in the west and the far larger expanse of Asia to the east. South of Europe, Africa, the largest continent after Asia, stretched southward across the equator and on toward the southern pole.

The other three continents lay farther away, cut off by seas and oceans from Eurasia and Africa. Australia lay at the far edge of Southeast Asia, in the western Pacific. North and South America, linked by the narrow isthmus of Central America, were isolated even more thoroughly from the rest of the world by the ocean barriers of the Atlantic and the Pacific.

Each of these continental land masses, and many of the islands that lay between them, had a range of climate and topography that provided a great variety of environments for human beings. These varying niches would in turn foster a variety of styles of life and help shape a number of historic societies.

## Ecology and History

The twentieth century just past developed a strong awareness of the ecological dimensions of human society. Ecologists focus on the interrelatedness of all species of living things with each other and with the rest of their material environment. Historians have begun to find this approach useful too, especially in their attempts to understand the "big picture" of human life on earth.

Ecologists look upon all plants and animals—including people—as parts of chains, webs, cycles, interlocking niches, and other patterns of relationship. Our place in this

# PROBING THE PAST

The excitement of digging up the past is vividly illustrated by this first-hand account of the 1974 discovery by paleo-anthropologist Donald Johanson and his colleague Tom Gray of the skeleton of a pre-human hominid, Lucy, believed to have lived three and a half million years ago.

What problems of identifying such bones are indicated by Gray's remarks? What can you deduce about the particular importance of the find from Johanson's thoughts? Maitland Edey, Johanson's co-author, is a distinguished writer on scientific subjects for nonscientific readers. What do you think he may have contributed to this dramatic account? (Assume Johanson and Gray did not happen to have a tape recorder running when they made their discovery.)

*"The gully in question was just over the crest of the rise where he had been working all morning. . . . But as we turned to leave, I noticed something lying on the ground partway up the slope.*
*"That's a bit of a hominid arm," I said.*
*"Can't be. It's too small. Has to be a monkey of some kind."*
*We knelt to examine it.*
*"Much too small," said Gray again.*
*I shook my head. "Hominid."*
*"What makes you so sure?" he said.*
*"That piece right next to your hand. That's hominid too."*
*"Jesus Christ," said Gray. He picked it up. It was the back of a small skull. A few feet away was part of a femur: a thighbone. "Jesus Christ," he said again. We stood up, and began to see other bits of bone on the slope: a couple of vertebrae, part of a pelvis—all of them hominid. An unbelievable, impermissible thought flickered through my mind. Suppose all these fitted together. Could they be parts of a single, extremely primitive skeleton? No such skeleton had ever been found—anywhere.*
*"Look at that," said Gray. "Ribs."*
*A single individual?*
*"I can't believe it," I said. "I just can't believe it."*
*"By God, you'd better believe it!" shouted Gray. "Here it is. Right here!" His voice went up into a howl, I joined him. In that 110-degree heat we began jumping up and down. With nobody to share our feelings, we hugged each other, sweaty and smelly, howling and hugging in the heat-shimmering gravel, the small brown remains of what now seemed almost certain to be parts of a single hominid skeleton lying all around us."*

---

Donald Johanson and Maitland Edey. *Lucy: The Beginnings of Humankind* (New York: Warner Books, 1981), pp. 16–17.

complex tangle of mutual dependency and interaction has undoubtedly had its impact, both on our development as a species and on the histories of the tribes, peoples, and other subdivisions into which we have divided ourselves.

As we will see, various of our prehuman ancestors evolved first in dense forests, moved on to open grasslands, and still later found themselves living in the shadows of ice-age glaciers. Each of these ecological niches had its impact on the way these ancestral prehumans lived, on their biological evolution, and on the course of prehistory. The first great change in the lifeways of prehistoric peoples—the shift from food gathering and hunting to settled agriculture—would come where it did because of a climate conducive to particularly valuable grains.

A similar level of significant interaction between peoples and their environments will be detected as we move on into history itself. Climatic change can drive peasants to rebellion and topple emperors who are seen as having lost the favor of the gods. The sedentary, agricultural settlements of people who lived on fertile soil; the hardy, nomadic lives of herders on sparse grasslands; the venturesome, violent, or mercantile societies of island or seacoast peoples all reflect the responses of a single species to a wide range of environmental niches.

Ecological interaction, however, is a two-way street. Throughout our span, humans and prehumans have been part of the ecological environment of other creatures too. As early predators, we played our part in the extinction of entire species. Most recently, technological exploitation of our world on a scale undreamed of before has apparently threatened to exhaust basic resources, polluted our living space, punched holes in our protective atmosphere, and generally shaken up the network of ecological linkages that have been shaping our world throughout its history.

Many factors, of course, have had a hand in shaping human cultures in history. For the time being, the fact of regional and cultural differences and the fact that geography and ecology helped determine them need only be noted here. There were, however, many ways in which our common humanity also determined our destiny as a species on this planet. It is to the emergence of that common human nature that we must now turn.

## HUMAN DEVELOPMENT

### The Bone Hunters

Almost all we know about the earliest stages of human life on earth has been uncovered during the last century and a half. The first Neanderthal bones clearly identified as belonging to prehistoric "cave men" were found by workers building a railway in the Neander Valley of Germany in 1856. Since then, archaeologists, anthropologists, and other professional "bone hunters" have dug up whole races of our human and prehuman ancestors. They have also stirred up considerable controversy in so doing.

Their discoveries have pushed the human story back far into the prehistoric past. In Olduvai Gorge in Tanzania, East Africa, Mary and Louis Leakey uncovered the skull that established the African origins of the human species. The skeleton of Don Johanson's "Lucy," found scattered over a hillside in Ethiopia, pushed prehuman origins back several million years. Hominid or humanlike bones from more recent times include those of the

Neanderthal Man—as reconstructed from bone fragments by a modern researcher—squints into an uncertain future. Some authorities now suspect that the Neanderthal subdivision of the hominid family did not die out before breeding with <u>Homo</u> <u>sapiens</u> <u>sapiens</u>. Modern people may thus carry some of the genes of this long-vanished race. (American Museum of Natural History)

Cro-Magnon and Neanderthal types first found in France and Germany and their kin Peking Man and Java Man discovered at the other end of Eurasia. With many of these finds, rude stone tools and later pots, pictures, and bits of clothing have been unearthed.

Experts in many fields have contributed to our understanding of these remains. Geologists and laboratory scientists have learned to date the finds by analyzing the rock strata in which they are found or by carbon dating, which measures the dwindling carbon radiation of the finds themselves. Biologists link the surviving bits of bone to ourselves by comparing anatomical structures, blood groups, and chromosome patterns. Ethologists and anthropologists make more controversial comparisons with the behavior of other animals and of surviving food-gathering peoples like the Khoi-San of Africa or the Australian Aborigines.

Though they usually consist only of bones and stones, these discoveries have sometimes been much more sensational. The famous "Ice Man," an intact human corpse discovered frozen in the Alpine ice in 1991, came complete with deerskin coat, fur hat, stone dagger, bow and arrows, and a crude copper ax. Scientific theories can also be astonishing. Comparisons of genetic material from contemporary humans around the world, for instance, have led some scientists to claim that all of us can trace our ancestry to an "African Eve." This single early hominid—if the theory proves correct—lived in Africa 200,000 years ago.

The experts have come up with many such theories to explain the connections between these prehistoric remains, and between prehistoric people and ourselves. The pattern of evolutionary development favored by most scientists is outlined very generally in the next section. But how many earlier human-related species there were, how they related to each other, whether we have a "family tree" or a confusing evolutionary bush with many branches rather than a single central stem—all these questions await final answers.

## Biological Evolution

A few simple numbers may help to put the story that begins here in at least rough chronological perspective. Dates have that value, at least, in history. And these dates are easy enough to remember, since all of them begin with five.

What is usually taught in school as modern history—from the world of Christopher Columbus and Leonardo da Vinci, Babur the Great and Suleiman the Magnificent, to the present age of Einstein and atomic power—covers a span of some five hundred years. The entire history of civilized humanity, from the first clay cities in ancient Sumer to the present, goes back more than five thousand years. The prehistoric line of human evolutionary development extends at least five million years into the past. It is this immense span of time with which we shall be primarily concerned in the present chapter.

Our most ancient detectable ancestors actually go considerably farther back than that. Scarcely recognizable as our kin to any but the informed scientific imagination, these small, furry creatures had huge nocturnal eyes and long tails. They balanced on high branches and snatched at insects in the primeval rain forests of the earliest age of mammals, not long after the passing of the dinosaurs. From these *prosimian* ancestors who lived tens of millions of years ago, there evolved several lines of mammals called *primates:* lemurs and their kin, Old and New World monkeys, and apes, the family to which the human race belongs. Among these ancient apes—whose other descendants today include orangutans, chimpanzees, and gorillas—there emerged as long as five million years ago the line of development known as *hominids,* of which the humans of our own time are the only surviving descendants.

Over this vast tract of time, from the first prosimian to the most developed hominid, the ancestors of humanity changed both biologically and culturally. These changes first enabled them to survive and then gave them increasing mastery of their environment. For biological evolution, a few paragraphs will suffice; for the story of our cultural evolution, the rest of the chapter will be required.

The biological changes over tens of millions of years were certainly striking. The eyes of that first tree dweller, for instance, evolved dramatically, developing both stereoscopic (depth) vision and color sightedness, very useful capacities for leaping from branch to branch or distinguishing brightly colored fruit from the green canopy that was the prosimian's world.

When our progenitors abandoned the shrinking primeval forest for the open grasslands five million years ago, more changes followed. Their legs and feet changed to permit erect bipedal walking on the African savannas. This in turn freed the hands for carrying game and foraged nuts and berries back to the family circle. The hands developed too, producing the most efficient opposable thumb for fine manipulation of any primate's. Most important, the hominid brain grew, doubling and tripling in size and evolving a neural capacity that gave human beings their most valuable biological advantage: the capacity to go beyond biology to culture.

Down the long evolutionary road, a number of hominid species developed, flourished for a time, and then died out. The earliest Australopithecines, of three and a half million years ago, were perhaps four feet tall and had brains about a third the size of a modern human's. Hominids of the Neanderthal line, who appeared perhaps 125,000 years ago, were close enough to ourselves, it is sometimes said, to pass for modern people in a crowd today.

These species left their bones on the African grasslands, in the caves of North China, or among the glaciers of ice-age Europe. But those hominids who survived were making delicate stone tools, burying their dead with ceremony, and decorating the walls of their caves with paintings of the animals they hunted as the last glaciers withdrew to the north. These survivors, who emerged approximately thirty-five thousand years ago, were the Cro-Magnon people, a subspecies of the hominid family called *Homo sapiens sapiens* ("wise people"). They were in fact the last of the hominid line. Biologically, they were indistinguishable from ourselves.

## The Prehistoric Migrations

While it evolved physically, the human race was also spreading to almost every corner of the earth.

The earliest hominid species first evolved toward humanity in southern and eastern Africa. Fossil bones going back several million years testify to our long residence on that continent; the chromosomes in our DNA suggest all of us can trace our ancestry to a single "African Eve" in prehistoric times. And then, perhaps half a million years ago, human beings began to move northward. Both the motive for this greatest of human migrations and the means to make these journeys were provided by the most disturbing natural phenomenon of the period: the ice ages.

A rather modest drop in average temperatures in the Northern Hemisphere—no more than a few degrees—was enough to prevent the winter's snows from melting the following summer, so that next winter's snows piled on top of them. By 500,000 B.C.E. the ice stood thick over northern Europe and had intruded deep into North America. In time, however—forty thousand to sixty thousand years—the cooling trend reversed itself, and warmer weather pushed the edge of the ice cap back into the Arctic. This advance and retreat of the ice took place several times over the last half million years of the Old Stone Age.

The descent and withdrawal of the glacier turned Europe and other parts of the Northern Hemisphere from relatively barren areas to well-watered comparatively lush forests and grasslands, the latter especially capable of supporting deer, bison, hairy elephants, and other large game for hominid hunters. The freezing over of the north had a second great effect, however; by locking up a significant percentage of the earth's surface water in colossal ice sheets, the glaciers lowered the level of the world's oceans, creating temporary land bridges between large land areas that were otherwise cut off from each other by sea.

Perhaps two million years ago, then, our hominid forebears moved north out of Africa and up through the Near East into Eurasia. From the Near East, some drifted west into Europe, others eastward across Asia. A skull recently found in China indicates that our ancestors reached East Asia two hundred thousand years ago.

Migration beyond the Old World—Africa, Europe, and Asia—had to wait for the land bridges. Between 70,000 and 40,000 B.C.E., however, human beings reached Australia, going most of the way by land and improvising some sort of boats for perhaps only fifty miles or so. Between 40,000 and 20,000 B.C.E., other groups of humans followed their prey across another land bridge at what is today the Bering Strait to the Americas. Cana-

# GLOBAL DISTRIBUTION OF HOMINIDS AND HOMO SAPIENS

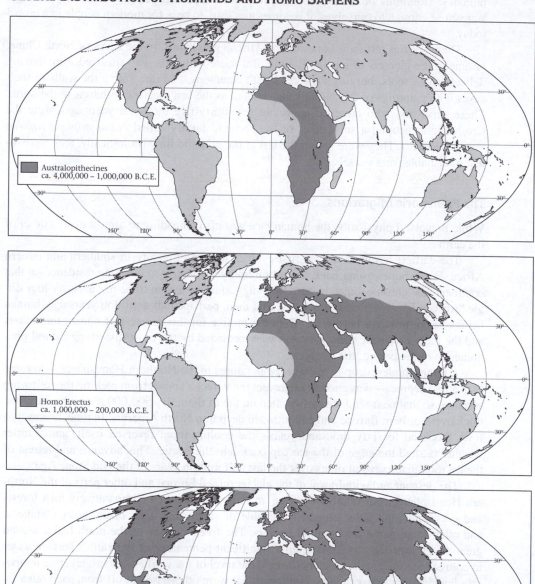

Australopithecines
ca. 4,000,000 – 1,000,000 B.C.E.

Homo Erectus
ca. 1,000,000 – 200,000 B.C.E.

Homo Sapiens
appears ca. 200,000 B.C.E.

Essentially modern by
35,000 B.C.E.

Range is for 10-15,000 B.C.E.
(Classic Neanderthal Man
of Western Europe is
included in Homo Sapiens)

dian glaciation may have held them up for a considerable time, but once a corridor had opened southward, hunting and gathering humanity flooded south to feed upon whole new species of food plants and game. In a short time, perhaps no more than a few thousand years, the human race had colonized North and South America too.

The great migrations were neither as purposive nor as direct as this schematic account may sound. Quite likely, humans advanced and retreated as the glaciers did, hunting and gathering in the shadow of the ice. Whole branches of the evolving half-human race were caught in culs-de-sac and became extinct, along with the plants and animals they fed on. Others adapted to new conditions and drifted on, reacting to shifts in climate and vegetation, following the herds.

We should not imagine anything like the picturesque migrations of historic nomads, whole tribes and peoples trundling across the steppes with beasts and baggage. It might take a tiny hunting band several lifetimes to decide to move on to the next valley. But then, even at an average pace of no more than ten miles a generation, it would have taken early hominids only fifteen thousand years to travel from East Africa to North China.[3] Even with endless back-tracking and aimless wandering—since after all they had no plans for reaching North China, or anywhere else in particular—it is not surprising that our prehistoric ancestors were able to spread around the world in half a million years.

## The Human Races

Closely related to these primal folk wanderings is another often-noticed aspect of our humanness: the racial differences that distinguish some groups of human beings from others.

They are very modest differences. No human type differs as strikingly from another as a St. Bernard does from a Chihuahua, or a tiger from an alley cat. But there are detectable physical differences among the three major racial groups—caucasoid, mongoloid, and negroid—and among such surviving racial remnants as the bushmanoid and pygmoid peoples of Africa and the australoids who were the original inhabitants of Australia. And these differences do go back to the great migrations of prehistoric times.

Racial differences seem to have evolved like other human adaptations, in order that subdivisions of the species might survive under the drastically differing conditions humanity encountered in various parts of the world. For instance, Eskimos tended toward stocky builds, which retain body heat in the arctic cold. Equatorial peoples developed high concentrations of skin-darkening melanin, which protect them from the sun's heat.

We thus became hardy and versatile animals indeed. Some of us developed immunities to the ever-present infectious parasites of tropical rain forests. Others built lungs capable of breathing the thin air of the Andes and the Himalayas. We have adapted physically as well as culturally to deserts where only a few spiny growths of vegetation and a handful of insects and reptiles can survive, and to arctic wastelands where houses must be built of snow and the sun does not rise above the horizon for half the year. We have learned to live in a wider range of physical environments than any other species on the face of the planet—and some of this versatility is due to racial variations.

Two or three other points should be briefly made about the racial diversity that is part of our heritage from prehistory.

---

[3]Richard E. Leakey and Roger Lewin, *Origins* (New York: E. P. Dutton, 1977), pp. 120–121.

First and most important, we are in fact not many but one single human race. Only one branch of the hominid line has survived—*Homo sapiens sapiens*—and we are all members of that species. Beneath all minor differences of lip thickness, inner eyefold, texture of hair, skin pigmentation, and proportion of leg length to length of trunk, we remain one breeding group, one people biologically.

Second, the various subdivisions of the species we have come to call *races* have historically become inextricably mixed almost everywhere—with generally excellent results. The exchange of cultural know-how that comes with the mixing of peoples made the polyglot, often turbulent Near East perhaps the most culturally productive corner of the globe. The historic isolation of a place such as Australia, by contrast, produced little in the way of social change and cultural development.

Finally, it scarcely needs to be mentioned that no one of the world's peoples has shown any intrinsic superiority to any other. There have been barbarians of every color, and enviable civilizations have been built by people of all racial stocks. In the end, it is the course of cultural evolution that distinguishes one people from another historically—not biological evolution. And it is to that cultural evolution that we must turn now.

## PALEOLITHIC HUNTERS AND GATHERERS

### The Foraging Band

In terms of cultural development, the evolving lifeways of the species, almost all of this first five million years is called the *Paleolithic period,* or Old Stone Age. This was the period when our human and prehuman ancestors survived by hunting and gathering with stone tools and weapons.

Like their prehuman ancestors, early hominids were both vegetarian and carnivorous. They were gatherers of nuts, roots, berries, and other vegetable food. They were also hunters of all sorts and sizes of game—from the huge, hairy mammoth and vast herds of deer to a wide range of smaller animals, birds, and fish. Their style of living and the whole course of their cultural evolution were significantly shaped by this fundamental activity of prehistoric people: the collection of sufficient food to keep them alive.

Humans seem to have learned quite far back that survival is a cooperative venture. Food gathering alone, the collection of primarily vegetable food, can be undertaken on an individual basis. Hunting, however, particularly the hunting of large animals, is practiced most efficiently by groups working in close cooperation. Prehistoric hominids, like wolves or lions, worked together to pull down animals as large as the giant sloth or the elephant-sized mammoth. Almost uniquely even among hunting animals, furthermore, hominids seem to have shared their food on a regular basis, dividing up game and vegetable food among all the members of the group.

From very early times, then, human beings were social animals, living and working together in the tight-knit community of a band of hunters and gatherers. In prehistoric times, as among Pygmies, Bushmen, or Eskimos today, a typical band probably numbered five or six nuclear families—no more than two or three dozen individuals altogether. These small groups developed some ingenious hunting techniques, inventing pits and other traps or using brush fires to drive whole herds of game over cliffs or into swamps where they might be easily killed. At certain seasons of the year, when major herds were due in the neighborhood, a number of such bands, adding up to several hundred hunters, might come together for a large-scale cooperative hunting expedition and a great gorge afterward.

The technology that accompanied this social evolution—and made much of it possible—included a large "kit" of tools and weapons. Rudely split rocks were apparently being used for cutting and scraping by prehuman creatures a couple of million years ago. During the hundreds of thousands of years that followed, hand axes and knives, scrapers and spears, and finally spear-throwers and bows and arrows were chipped out of flint or carved from wood all over Africa, Europe, and Asia. Long after Europeans with more complex metallurgical skills had landed in the New World, stone arrowheads, some exquisitely shaped, were still serving American Indians as well as they had all our ancestors.

Fire, clothing, and rude shelters also appeared well before history began. Our forebears met the millennial cold of recurring ages of ice, first by wrapping themselves in animal hides, then by sewing the hides into sleeves and pantlegs, coats and hoods. They took shelter in caves and under rocky outcroppings, then in tents and shelters made primarily of bone. They tamed fire perhaps half a million years ago, first using it where they found it, then learning to kindle it through friction. The warm yellow-orange flame, used for both heating and cooking, became the center of the developing group life of the prehistoric band.

It was a simple society, rude and dangerous. For several millions of years, from the African savannas to glacier-prone Eurasia, this was the lifestyle of all our ancestors. Around such fires, it has been suggested, the monkey jabber of earlier hominids may have become speech as hunters and gatherers laid plans for the next day's labors or tried to explain more clearly than grunts and gestures could about the one that got away.

Social relations within the hunter-gatherer community may also be deduced from what we know about surviving preagricultural peoples and from some basic facts of all human life. Thus it has been suggested that these small prehistoric bands, like hunter-gatherer societies of our own time, were probably roughly egalitarian. They had little of the division into castes and classes, the powerful sense of hierarchy that was to come with organization into larger social units.

Like foraging peoples still surviving in deserts and rain forests from Africa to Australia, prehistoric hominids probably recognized degrees of family kinship. They perhaps shared the meat of a large kill on the basis of elaborate social categories of their own, as hunting peoples still do. But in groups as small as two or three dozen, possessing so little in the way of material things, class divisions on the basis of power or wealth seem exceedingly unlikely.

## Stone Age Women

Sexual distinctions probably did exist among our earlier prehistoric ancestors; but there is no reason to assume that prehistoric sex roles resembled those of any particular historic people, including our own. The female half of the human race has played many roles in a wide variety of societies down the centuries. This is quite likely to have been true in prehistoric times also.

There is some general agreement that among Stone Age hunter-gatherers, as among such peoples today, women were almost always the gatherers. Whereas hunting might involve more teamwork, gathering probably provided a more reliable source of food most of

A Venus figurine, found in Austria, of the sort that made earlier researchers see these cult objects as fertility symbols. What reasons can you think of for the omission of the individualizing face entirely? (Museum of Natural History, Vienna)

the time. Fruit, berries, nuts, roots, grubs, and shellfish were more stable and dependable sources of nutriment than the large or middle-sized game that might or might not show up at the water hole. Except in the depths of winter, then, Stone Age women—again, like hunter-gatherer women today—probably brought in most of the Paleolithic family's steady diet.

A few more generalizations may be risked about the role of women in prehistoric societies—some obvious, some rather more debatable. Women were, of course, the producers of new Paleolithic people and therefore essential to the survival of the band, indeed of the species. In addition, it seems likely that roughly monogamous pair bonding—close personal and social relations between individual men and women that provided a stable environment for rearing children—goes far back into our human and prehuman past. Women may also have been early recognized as custodians of the camp, the band's home base, while men and boys predominated in the hunting terrain.

Overall, women probably enjoyed more freedom and more influence in hunting and gathering societies than they often have in later civilizations. In surviving food-gathering cultures, at least, domestic chores and child-rearing duties are more equally shared between women and men. Within the band, women as foragers often have as much mobility and initiative as the male hunters do.

It is also possible, finally, that women were considered to have mysterious powers, perhaps on the order of those attributed to witches, prophetesses, and priestesses in later times. Almost all the sculptured figures that survive from Paleolithic times—the so-called Venus figurines—are of women. The figurines are by no means all of pregnant women, as was once thought, but range from virginal maidens to full-breasted mothers and withered crones.[4] Why these tiny figures were carved we do not know, but cult or religious purposes seem likely. In any event, these carved figures do seem to reflect the crucial place of women in the Stone Age world.

## Beginnings of Religion and Art

If it is difficult to reconstruct the social life of the Old Stone Age, it would seem downright foolhardy to try to guess what went on inside the skulls of our hominid ancestors. Yet even here we can do some conjecturing, at least about our more recent forebears of later Paleolithic times.

There is at least some evidence that some sort of supernatural belief—the seeds of religion—existed as far back as 100,000 B.C.E. At that time prehistoric hunters appear to have set up the skulls of cave bears, early humans' fiercest challengers for the rock shelters they both needed, as though to worship these huge rivals. By 50,000 B.C.E., Neanderthal people were burying their dead with a care and ceremony that points to a belief in some sort of life after death. Corpses were painted with red ocher, positioned carefully with the knees drawn up, provided with flint weapons, and in one famous case—at Shanidar in Iraq—strewn with fresh flowers from the surrounding hills. Finally, Cro-Magnon cave paintings of game animals indicate the possibility, by 30,000 B.C.E., of magical rites aimed at controlling the game supply. It is about this time also that the Venus

The Ring of Brodgar, an impressive stone circle dating back to stone-age times, still looms over the heather of the Orkney Islands, off the northern coast of Scotland. Stone pit-houses and burial places reveal a thriving community who gathered here for ceremonies we can only guess at. Have you heard of megalithic monuments like this elsewhere in the world? (Anthony Esler)

---

[4]Patricia C. Rice, "Prehistoric Venuses: Symbols of Motherhood or Womanhood?" *Journal of Anthropological Research,* 37 (1981), 402–414.

figurines appear, quite possibly indicating not only respect for womanhood but special reverence for female divinities.

Bear skulls and burial customs, hunting rites, and rude statuettes are clues rather than proof. Still, they point to religion as one of the earliest detectable achievements of human abstract thought.

There is no question, however, about the early emergence of another basic impulse toward higher cultural expression: the invention of art.

As we noted previously, Cro-Magnon people—our own direct forebears—seem to have been the inventors of the arts. They engraved recognizable animals on bone. They produced the small stone Venus figures, rudely made, armless, but clearly representational and clearly intended to be feminine. Prehistoric musical instruments have been discovered, including bone drums, rattles, whistles, pipes, and "bull roarers." Still used by Aboriginal Australians on ceremonial occasions, bull roarers are attached to a string and swung around the head to produce a terrifying booming sound.

The most celebrated examples of prehistoric art are the paintings of bulls, bison, deer, horses, and other animals on the walls of caves. The most famous of them, including the dazzling painted caves at Lascaux in southern France, have been closed to the hordes of visitors whose very breath damaged pigments tens of thousands of years old. But you can go into the dark, cold caverns at nearby Les Eyzies for a glimpse of the leaping animals that filled the imaginations—and the lives—of Europe's prehistoric hunters. Thousands of miles to the south, you can see other prehistoric creatures, including some very realistic red giraffes, marching around the walls of caves in the sunny Motopo hills of southern Zimbabwe.

These prehistoric cave paintings have been interpreted in a number of ways: as hunting-cult ritual objects, as tribal totems, and even as art for art's sake. Whatever the artists' motive for making them, these naturalistic renderings of the game animals that were life itself to our ancestors certainly reveal a startling level of artistic skill.

What totems these people believed in, what taboos they practiced must remain largely objects of speculation. But we know from their graves that they talked seriously about life and death around their glowing fires. We know that bone music echoed from those painted caves tens of thousands of years before civilization as we know it was born.


## NEOLITHIC FARMERS

### The Discovery of Agriculture

Group life, rudimentary technology, and the beginnings of high culture thus flourished by the end of the Paleolithic period, or Old Stone Age, the immensely long period of human development that began several million years in the past and ended no more than twelve thousand years ago. The *Neolithic period* or New Stone Age was the age of the Agricultural Revolution, the final link in the long chain of cultural evolution that led to history proper.

The common designation of the period from 10,000 to perhaps 3500 B.C.E. as the New Stone Age refers to the new, ever more expertly crafted stone implement produced during this period. Metalworking remained undiscovered, but the polished stone tools and weapons of these last centuries of prehistory are a notable step beyond the flaked flints of earlier generations, and many steps beyond the split pebbles of our earliest precursors. The great event of the Neolithic period, however, was not the advance in stoneworking but a much more fundamental step forward in the material culture of the human race: the discovery of agriculture.

The original Agricultural Revolution was in fact the climax of prehistory—and the essential foundation upon which civilization itself would be built.

This great change from the moving life of hunting and gathering to the settled life of the farmer may have been made independently in a number of places, including several parts of Eurasia, West Africa, and Mesoamerica, but it was in the Near East that the best documented and historically most significant shift from following game to growing crops came first. It was a crucial change in the life of the race. Nothing as sweeping would occur again until the Industrial Revolution of the last two centuries.

Because the Agricultural Revolution was primarily a change in human methods of exploiting vegetable food, it is likely that this breakthrough was the work of women. As the primary gatherers of vegetable food, women would have been most likely to understand the cycle of growth, to see how human ingenuity might seize control of this natural cycle from seed to edible plant. Thus an annual visit to harvest wild grain could lead to watering, weeding, and finally scattering of seeds, perhaps in a religious ceremony to encourage a bumper crop the following year.

A number of explanations have been offered for this basic shift from hunting and gathering to agriculture. One likely cause may have been the simple exhaustion of game animals in a particular region, forcing humanity to seek other means of subsistence. Another primary cause may have been the development of new wild grains in warmer postglacial times, enabling people to settle down and live off these cereals and the animals who fed on them without having to do much cultivation at all. Recent archaeological finds do in fact reveal such transitional phases between food gathering and food producing. Thus Old Stone Age Russian hunters built semipermanent shelters of mammoth bone twenty thousand years ago, and the Natufian food-gathering people of what is today Israel lived in rude stone huts thirteen thousand years back.

Perhaps the earliest fully agricultural societies emerged east of the Mediterranean Sea in what is today Turkey. There climatic conditions favored particularly nutricious grain—einkorn and emmer wheat—which could, in turn, support a growing human population. The same grains could feed grazing animals, such as cattle, sheep, and later horses, which would provide food, clothing, and fellow laborers for the peoples who built early villages, towns, and cities.

On such foundations, then, the first agricultural villages rose in the Near East twelve thousand years ago.

## Crops and Flocks

Agriculture most likely began with the simple practice of harvesting edible grains found growing wild, part of the normal food-gathering procedures of Old Stone Age people. Alert gatherers might sometimes encourage the ripening of the crop by extra care—for instance, by watering plants at the end of a dry summer. But the great break-through came when bands of *Homo sapiens sapiens* learned to plant some of the grain in order to guarantee a harvest the following year. Wherever this occurred—with wheat and barley in the Near East, millet in North China, corn in Central America—the wandering days of the hunting band were numbered and a new way of life was set in train.

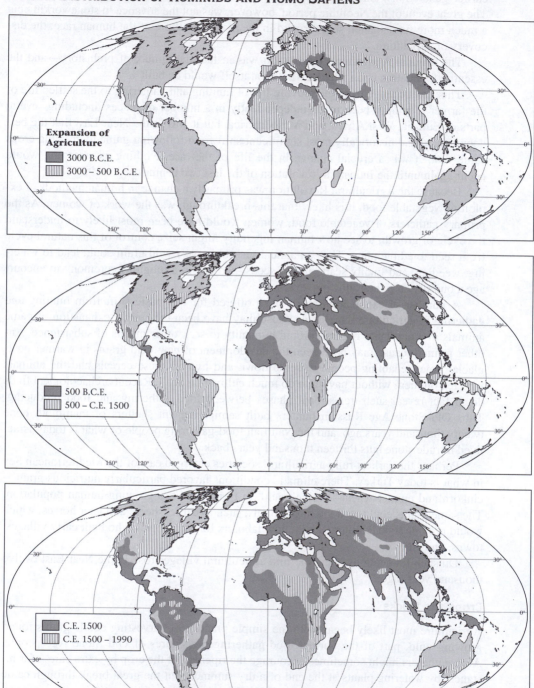

## GLOBAL DISTRIBUTION OF HOMINIDS AND HOMO SAPIENS

**Expansion of Agriculture**

- 3000 B.C.E.
- 3000 – 500 B.C.E.

- 500 B.C.E.
- 500 – C.E. 1500

- C.E. 1500
- C.E. 1500 – 1990

Besides the growing of crops, another important aspect of the Agricultural Revolution was the domestication of animals. Again, transition stages have been hypothesized, including perhaps the herding and riding of reindeer, a comparatively docile game animal that is both ridden and herded in northern Asia today. From this success, Neolithic people could have moved naturally to herding other animals or to keeping them in pens and enclosed fields. Cattle, sheep, goats, and pigs were early domesticated in this way, horses only much later.

For some early peoples, the herding of animals became the center of their posthunting cultures. These peoples became pastoralists rather than cultivators of the soil. They did not settle, but followed their herds of deer, cattle, or horses from summer to winter pasturage, sometimes migrating across hundreds of miles of savanna, steppe, or even less attractive desert land in search of water and grass. Pastoral peoples remained closer to the lives of the hunting ancestors than farmers did. In historical times, at least, nomadic pastoralists came to covet the material goods accumulating among more settled peoples, with sometimes violent results.

Life thus grew in complexity as the Neolithic centuries rolled on. The settled agricultural peoples of the Near East, like their fellows in many parts of the globe, learned to cultivate their crops with care, to weed and irrigate, to use the manure produced by their stock to fertilize their croplands. They discovered how to breed stock for meat or for strength, how to use milk, milk products, and other animal and vegetable products seldom utilized by their hunting-and-gathering predecessors. First in the rain-watered hills, then in the river valleys that provided the most fertile land, these prehistoric farmers reaped a greater bounty than nature had normally provided for their Paleolithic ancestors.

Above, all, they grew in numbers. Farming was hard work, probably more demanding than hunting and gathering had been. But agriculture had the great advantage of feeding many more people from the same tract of land than could be fed by hunting and gathering. One estimate suggests that whereas the foraging economy could support one person per square kilometer, even primitive farming could feed fifty persons from a single square kilometer. From this population growth came the Neolithic agricultural village and—in time—the city, the political state, and all their history.

## Life in the Neolithic Village

Prehistoric handicraft technology also improved significantly during the New Stone Age. As we noted previously, Neolithic people learned to make polished stone tools and weapons that eclipsed even the most impressive chipped flints of their forebears. They also developed such basic agricultural equipment as a simple stick plow, pulled first by a man and later by an animal, and a flint-bladed sickle with which they harvested grain.

Other crafts were probably the work of women. In their hands, the loosely woven net gave rise to baskets for carrying and storing and then to the weaving of cloth. Neolithic clothing progressed from animal hides to woven fabrics, first of all wool from the backs of newly domesticated sheep. The complex technology of ceramics—pots for storage, cooking, and other purposes—also simplified the lives of prehistoric peoples, and was probably also developed by women. And there is increasing evidence of trade, or perhaps of ritual exchanges of gifts, between one agricultural community and another.

Most striking, the New Stone Age produced the Neolithic village, and with it a revolution in the ways of life of the race.

About ten thousand years ago the caves and tent shelters of roving hunters were replaced by permanent collections of huts. These were simple structures, usually made of sun-dried mud, clay brick, or stone. You can visit a Stone Age village at Skara Brae in the Orkney Islands north of Scotland. Walking among the now roofless stone huts, you will find each equipped with a central cooking area, roughly partitioned sleeping spaces, and even stone shelves. Fish hooks and stone-edged scythes give clues to an economy that still included fishing even while the people learned to plant and harvest grain.

Class distinctions were probably still modest in the Neolithic period, but gender roles remained clearly defined. As in preurban cultures in historic times, women were primarily responsible for the raising of the children. In settled New Stone Age communities, however, they probably had more of them and devoted more time to child care. Farming required more hands than food gathering, and laborers lost to the contagious diseases that came with settled living had to be replaced.

Like their Paleolithic foremothers, some Neolithic women may also have been believed to possess supernatural powers. Women shamans have often served as channels or mediums in preurban societies, bringing the voices of the gods or of the dead to rapt audiences. From Neolithic times also come mysterious wall paintings showing women disguised as giant birds performing funeral rites.

## Alternate Lifestyles

The human venture into history has taken many forms. Its most amazing enterprise, as we shall see, has been the series of essays in civilization that began in various parts of the world more than five thousand years ago. But 99 percent of the human story thus far was played out before civilization began. And even during the historical period, most of the world remained in the hands of people who were neither literate nor urban, who did not build states or litter the earth with massive ruins, people who, though they lived in historic times, lived pretty much as their prehistoric ancestors had.

Some of this continuing precivilized majority of the human race were village agriculturalists, living in many ways as Neolithic farmers did. Some would become pastoralists, nomads following their herds of sheep or cattle in an unending search for grass and water. Some would remain hunters and gatherers, living off game and fish, fruits, roots, and vegetables, as their Paleolithic forebears did before civilization began.

Climate and geography tended to determine the distribution of these basic styles of life—agricultural, pastoral, hunter-gatherer—around the globe during the first three thousand years of history. Thus, cultivators of such cereal crops as maize, wheat, millet, and rice were concentrated in the world's temperate zones. They flourished across central Eurasia—in Europe, the Middle East, China, and India—and in the middle parts of the Americas, from the southern reaches of North America to the northern highlands of South America. The cultivation of root crops, such as yams and manioc, was most common in the tropics, including the rain forests of South America, Central Africa, and Southeast Asia. In all these areas, agricultural villages were scattered over the land. But it was only in the temperate grain-growing regions that urban power centers eventually emerged.

Pastoral nomads wandered the steppes of Eurasia and the savannas of Africa. Their flocks of sheep and cattle were here one month and gone the next. In their journeyings they not infrequently brushed—often violently—against the new city-based civilizations of the Old World.

Finally, surviving hunter-gatherers were increasingly limited to the northern and southern extremities of the world's landmasses and the most arid corners of the earth. Hunting tribes as vigorous as their ice-age ancestors still stalked deer and other large game in the arctic regions of both the Old and New Worlds. Thinning populations of hunters and gatherers scraped a living out of much smaller game and meager vegetation in the desiccated southern reaches of South America and Africa and in Australia. Living thus primarily on the last frontiers, far from the fertile temperate zones, primordial hunters and food gatherers were unlikely to have any knowledge that such a thing as civilization existed in the world.

## THE TRANSITION TO CIVILIZATION

### The First Civilizations

For a period as long as all recorded history since, the agricultural village was the most complex form of human social organization, and the chiefdom and the primitive monarchy the most elaborate political structure. Then, sometime around 3500 B.C.E., small segments of the human family stumbled into a new and even more elaborate way of life. This new stage of human group life was achieved in the city-states and empires of ancient times. It is frequently described as the birth of civilization.

As noted in the Introduction to this volume, the term *civilization* has had a number of meanings. The definition employed here is essentially a technical one, like such descriptive terms as *food-gathering band* or *agricultural village*. Civilization is a complex amalgam of centralized government, expanded economic and technological capacities, and more elaborate social and cultural structures. Monument building, metal working, and writing are identifiable elements in some (though not all) civilizations.

Like the Neolithic village, cities and empires emerged in different places over a span of several thousand years. Beginning not much more than five thousand years ago, civilization appeared first in Mesopotamia, Egypt, northern India, and northeastern China. Later still, urban life and imperial structures evolved in Europe, parts of Africa and the Americas, Southeast Asia, Japan, and elsewhere.

These unprecedented developments in the cultural evolution of the race have been explained in a number of ways. Some attribute the rise of larger political units to climatic change; the gradual drying out of marshes along major rivers left firm but extremely fertile land capable of supporting much larger populations. Others describe the early states as "hydraulic empires," emphasizing the need for a central political authority to tame great rivers such as the Nile, the Tigris and Euphrates, the Indus, and the Huanghe (Yellow River) of China.[5] Imperial power, according to this view, was needed to maintain the elaborate systems of dams, canals, and rules for water use that were necessary if agriculture was to realize its immense productive potential along these waterways. Still others see the expansion of political power as fundamentally a matter of greed for dominion, wealth, and glory leading to military conquest. Certainly "conquest empires" arose in many parts of the world as a result of self-aggrandizing wars—the winners absorbing the lands of the losers in larger and larger imperial domains.

---

[5]Karl A. Wittfogel, *Oriental Despotism* (New Haven, Conn.: Yale University Press, 1957).

As noted previously, not all civilizations exhibit all these features. But all reveal a scale and complexity that distinguish them from hunter-gatherer bands, pastoral nomads, or agricultural villages. *Civilization* may be hard to define, but you will know one when you see one—whether it is in ancient Egypt or ancient Greece, China before Confucius, or pre-Columbian Mexico.

### Monarchy, Hierarchy, and Patriarchy

Three organizational principles dominated most early civilizations. We may call them monarchy, hierarchy, and patriarchy.

*Monarchy* was a form of government in which political power was exercised by monarchs—kings, queens, emperors, or other powerful individual rulers. Monarchs passed on their power through hereditary succession, so that a single family might govern for generations, even centuries. Almost everywhere monarchs ruled in close alliance with gods and the priests who tended them. This divinely sanctioned political authority was commonly exercised through proliferating bodies of officials. These early scribal bureaucrats collected royal taxes, administered royal justice, kept the irrigation ditches in repair or the armies in the field, and ruled in the sovereign's name as far as his cohorts could reach or his justice prevail.

The society over which monarchs ruled was increasingly organized according to the principle of *hierarchy*. Society was divided up into groups based on the function they performed, on the prestige they enjoyed, or simply on how many material things they possessed. Those with highly valued functions, traditional prestige, or material wealth were ranked higher than other people. Thus, a priest, an aristocratic landowner, or a wealthy merchant would outrank an artisan, a peasant, or a slave in the new social hierarchy. This system of classes, castes, or social orders, which originated at the beginning of our history, is with us still today.

The term *patriarchy* refers to a family structure in which husbands and fathers exercise authority over other members. In a more general sense, patriarchy means male dominance of society as a whole. As we will see, women have always played a variety of roles in civilized societies. Nevertheless, it does seem to be true that the rough gender equality of food-gathering bands faded in early villages and cities. Men emerged as heads of the family, plowers of fields, soldiers, priests. Women were increasingly identified with household responsibilities and child rearing, with the "private sphere" of life, while men dominated the "public sphere"—the palace, the temple, and the battlefield.[6]

### Economics, Technology, Culture

Crucial economic and cultural changes also characterized early civilizations. The city emerged as a uniquely powerful economic unit, the home of vast public buildings, specialized crafts, organized systems of religion, and elaborate fine arts.

The economic foundations of city-based civilizations that emerged about 3500 B.C.E. were broader and more complex than at any earlier stage. Urban centers were the focus of economic innovation as well as political development during the first two or three millennia of civilization—the Bronze and Iron Ages. It was in the cities that metallurgy and other advanced crafts developed, and from these centers of wealth and population that

---

[6]On this complex subject, see Gerda Lerner, *The Creation of Patriarchy* (New York: Oxford University Press, 1986).

long-distance trade reached out to similar urban areas, some of them hundreds of miles away. The hinterland, by contrast, was typically composed of agricultural villages much like those of Neolithic times, though their methods of cultivation were now more efficient and they were now firmly integrated into the larger city-centered economic unit.

In the earliest historic centuries, ancient artisans—builders, carvers of stone, workers in precious metals—joined painters, poets, philosophers, and prophets of many faiths in producing a high culture that still has the power to amaze and move us today. Vast structures such as the pyramids of Egypt or Mexico, the palace at Knossos, and the white temples on the Athenian Acropolis still draw tourists in the thousands. Jades and bronzes from the earliest periods of Chinese history have been treasured by collectors for hundreds of years.

Literature was highly developed as an art form long before any of our modern languages even existed. Early systems of writing, including Mesopotamian cuneiform, Egyptian hieroglyphics, Indian Sanskrit, Chinese characters, the Phoenician alphabet, and the Greek and Roman scripts derived from it, made it possible to preserve at least some of the wisdom and belief, the legend and poetry, of these dawn ages of human civilization.

## SUMMARY

The human venture actually began several million years before history did. Humankind passed through a complex development long before city life, civilization—and with them, history—finally emerged. Crucial aspects of these first five million years included evolution, migration, and racial differentiation. The human species evolved biologically from prehuman forms to *Homo sapiens sapiens,* its present incarnation. At the same time, humankind evolved culturally, adapting to its changing environment with an ingenious series of technological and social inventions. During prehistoric times also, human beings migrated from their original home in Africa to all the other habitable continents: Europe and Asia, the Americas, and Australia. Racial differences developed as additional biological adaptations to these varied habitats.

The first stage of human cultural evolution was the Paleolithic or Old Stone Age, the hunting and gathering phase of human cultural evolution, which began several million years ago. The Paleolithic era brought such fundamental discoveries as fire, clothing, basic techniques of hunting game and gathering vegetable food, and the simple social organization of the hunting band. Women played an important role in Old Stone Age society. Forms of art and religious beliefs also took shape, probably toward the end of this period.

The second stage of human social development was the Neolithic agricultural phase, which began twelve thousand years ago. Having perhaps exhausted the game in a given area, some humans settled down to cultivate crops and domesticate animals. Over a few thousand years their stone tools improved drastically, and they learned to make textiles and pottery. They also lived a more settled life in small villages, with women, the probable discoverers of agriculture, playing an important part.

A third stage of human social evolution—and the beginning of civilization—was reached when villages evolved into cities. This happened for the first time more than five thousand years ago, around 3500 B.C.E. in the Middle East. The same transition occurred over the next two or three thousand years elsewhere in Eurasia, in northern Africa, and in Middle and South America. The more complex urban-imperial cultures that resulted were distinguished by such skills and trends as city- and empire-building, metal-working, monumental architecture, literacy, bureaucratic centralized government, class structure, and a tendency toward patriarchy. The unfolding of this final stage over the past fifty-five hundred years will be the central concern of this book.

## Suggested Reading

Bettinger, P. L. *Hunter-Gatherers.* New York: Plenum Press, 1991. Contributions of archaeology and biology to our understanding of early human society.

Bogucki, P. *The Origins of Human Society.* Oxford: Blackwell, 1999. Argues that individual ambitions and decisions by prehistoric hominids led to the emergence of elites and social inequalities.

Borenhult, G., ed. *The First Humans.* San Francisco: Harper, 1993. Authoritative coverage of the Old Stone Age. See also the archaeological perspectives in P. Mellars, ed., *The Emergence of Modern Humans* (Ithaca, N.Y.: Cornell University Press, 1990), and essays in G. L. Isaac's *The Archaeology of Human Origins* (New York: Cambridge University Press, 1989).

Chambers, F.M., ed. *Climate Change and Human Impact on the Landscape.* London: Chapman and Hall, 1993. Studies of the complex relationship between humans and their environment.

Clive, G. *Timewalkers: The Prehistory of Global Colonization.* Cambridge, Mass.: Harvard, 1994. Valuable account of prehistoric human migration.

Diamond, J. *Guns, Germs, and Steel: The Fates of Human Societies.* New York: W. W. Norton, 1997. Widely discussed analysis, focusing on material environment as the key force shaping civilizations.

Ehrenberg, M. *Women in Prehistory.* Norman: University of Oklahoma Press, 1989. Women in prehistoric Europe. See also J. M. Gero and M. W. Conkey, eds., *Engendering Archaeology: Women and Prehistory* (Oxford: Blackwell, 1991), for papers on women in preurban societies in both the Old and New Worlds, and F. Dahlberg, ed., *Woman, the Gatherer* (New Haven, Conn.: Yale University Press, 1983), for essays on women in Paleolithic times.

Goudsblom, J. *Fire and Civilization.* London: Allen Lane, 1992. Emphasizes the contribution made by human control of a single basic force—fire—to the emergence of more complex societies.

Henry, D. O. *From Foraging to Agriculture: The Levant at the End of the Iron Age.* Philadelphia: University of Pennsylvania Press, 1989. A detailed study of the first such transition. See also B. Bender, *Farming in Prehistory: From Hunter-Gatherer to Food Producer* (London: J. Baker, 1975).

Johanson, D., and M. Edey. *Lucy: The Beginnings of Humankind.* New York: Warner Books, 1981. Highly readable account of an important discovery. See also D. Johanson, D. L. Johanson, and B. Edgar, *Ancestors: In Search of Human Origins* (New York: Villard Books, 1994).

Lerner, G. *The Creation of Patriarchy.* New York: Oxford University Press, 1986. A classic on the interaction of class and gender in the shaping of early society.

Lewis, M. W., and K. E. Wigan. *The Myth of Continents: A Critique of Metageography.* Berkeley: University of California Press, 1997. Explores the degree to which the six habitable continents are defined more by history and historians than by clear geographical boundaries.

Melko, M., and L. R. Scott. *The Boundaries of Civilizations in Space and Time.* Lanham, Md.: University Press of America, 1987. The concept of "civilization" defined by historians, social scientists, philosophers, and others. See also R. J. Wenke, *Patterns in Prehistory,* 3rd ed. (New York: Oxford University Press, 1990).

Simmons, I. G. *Changing the Face of the Earth: Culture, Environment, and History.* Oxford: Blackwell, 1989. Human impact on the world we live in.

Please refer to the document CD-ROM for primary sources related to this chapter.

# OVERVIEW I

# ANCIENT CIVILIZATIONS

## (3500–200 B.C.E.)

Civilization was born not once, but many times. Each of the earth's historic regions has in fact produced its own ancient civilizations, its own historic beginnings around the world.

Mostly in the fertile river valleys of the north temperate zone, elaborate structures of stone and wood and clay heaved up above the surrounding landscape. There were towers and labyrinthine palaces, massive city walls, and tangled warrens of city streets. And scuttling through those urban mazes were human beings with heads full of new questions and new ambitions. Living together in large numbers now, challenging and stimulating each other, some among them at least began to wonder how to build a better brick—how to get a larger share of the irrigated fields beyond the gates—and what to do about the new town rising only a few miles away.

Sometimes the wider goals and ambitions of which humans were now capable led them to attack their neighbors, forging large states and empires in the process. Sometimes the whole urban-imperial venture failed, falling before alien invaders or through the follies of their own builders.

But once they had invented civilization, humans never abandoned it for long. Sooner or later the glimmer of ambition would flicker once more across the faces of human beings. And then the walls would rise again, the labyrinths and towers.

An early cluster of the city-based societies we call civilizations emerged near the point where the continents of Europe, Asia, and Africa come together. These three linked continents are often referred to as the Old World, thus contrasting it with the New World of the Americas. The region where these three giant land masses join around the eastern end of the Mediterranean Sea became the cultural crossroads of this half of the inhabited world. Here four early centers of civilization emerged, interacting with and influencing each other in many ways. These were the ancient Mesopotamian peoples, the Egyptians, the Hebrews, and—just across a corner of the Mediterranean—the ancient Greeks.

Other city-based civilizations also emerged in ancient times in both the Old and the New Worlds. But isolation rather than interaction defined most of these more far-flung experiments in living beyond the agricultural village. Almost all the ancient civilizations of India and China, Mexico and Peru thus developed without guides or models, uninfluenced by either the developed peoples of the continental crossroads or by each other.

There were many differences among both groups of early civilizations. Some were essentially differences of style, in ways of achieving a common end. It is easy to distinguish between Greek temples and Indian *stupas* or shrines, between the two dozen letters of the Greek alphabet and the thousands of characters of written Chinese. But the differences are essentially stylistic ones: religious centers and written languages are common among civilized peoples.

There were more fundamental differences as well, of course. The small, squabbling, determinedly independent city-states of Greece, for instance, would seem to contrast fundamentally with the vast, relatively centralized empire of China. Here and there, high civilizations even emerged without benefit of key elements in the standard definition of a civilization. Neither the Olmecs nor the Chavín developed the art of writing, for example, and the pharaohs of Old Kingdom Egypt raised their awesome pyramids without having yet discovered the wheel.

Similarities, however, undoubtedly outweigh the differences among these ancient civilizations. A wander through their ruins reveals something of what all urban-imperial peoples were capable of doing. In a world where most human beings still lived in the one-room huts of tiny agricultural villages or in the tents of nomadic herders, such monumental achievements as the Egyptian pyramids or the Athenian Acropolis, the cities of Harappan India or the Great Wall of China clearly represented a major change in the lifeways of the human race.

Whether they raised their first walls and towers in the close-clustering crossroads of the Old World or at the farther reaches of the Old and New Worlds, these ancient peoples had taken a decisive step. It was the step that took the human race from preurban living to urban civilization, from prehistory into history.

# ANCIENT CIVILIZATIONS

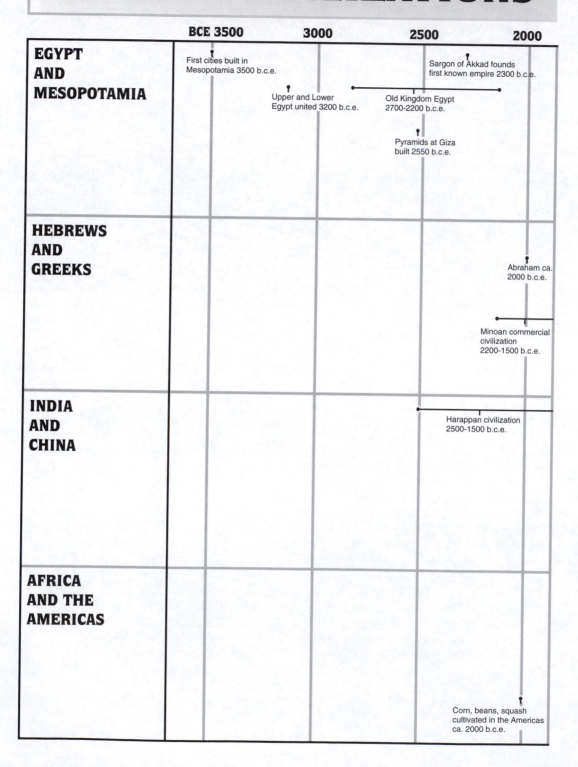

| | BCE 3500 | 3000 | 2500 | 2000 |
|---|---|---|---|---|
| **EGYPT AND MESOPOTAMIA** | First cities built in Mesopotamia 3500 b.c.e. | Upper and Lower Egypt united 3200 b.c.e. | Old Kingdom Egypt 2700-2200 b.c.e. / Pyramids at Giza built 2550 b.c.e. | Sargon of Akkad founds first known empire 2300 b.c.e. |
| **HEBREWS AND GREEKS** | | | | Abraham ca. 2000 b.c.e. / Minoan commercial civilization 2200-1500 b.c.e. |
| **INDIA AND CHINA** | | | Harappan civilization 2500-1500 b.c.e. | |
| **AFRICA AND THE AMERICAS** | | | | Corn, beans, squash cultivated in the Americas ca. 2000 b.c.e. |

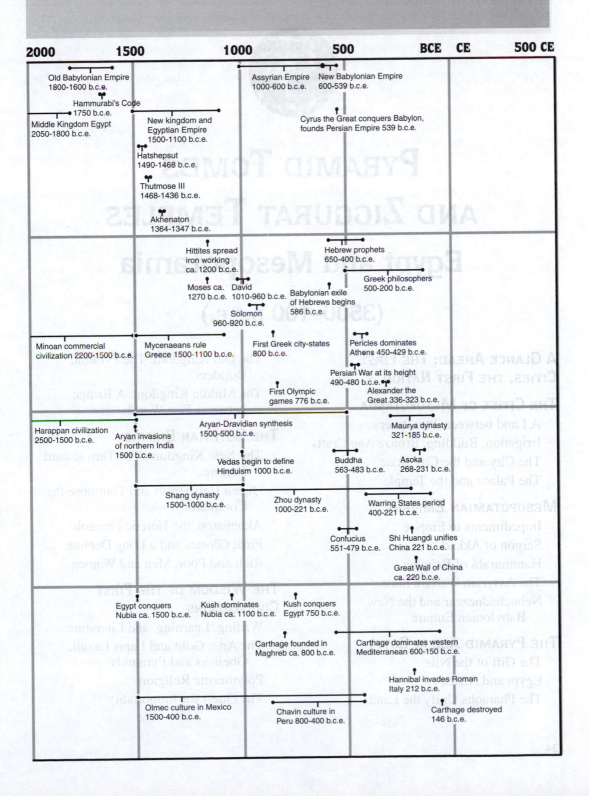

| 2000 | 1500 | 1000 | 500 | BCE | CE | 500 CE |
|---|---|---|---|---|---|---|

Old Babylonian Empire
1800-1600 b.c.e.

Assyrian Empire
1000-600 b.c.e.

New Babylonian Empire
600-539 b.c.e.

Hammurabi's Code
1750 b.c.e.

New kingdom and
Egyptian Empire
1500-1100 b.c.e.

Middle Kingdom Egypt
2050-1800 b.c.e.

Cyrus the Great conquers Babylon,
founds Persian Empire 539 b.c.e.

Hatshepsut
1490-1468 b.c.e.

Thutmose III
1468-1436 b.c.e.

Akhenaton
1364-1347 b.c.e.

Hittites spread
iron working
ca. 1200 b.c.e.

Hebrew prophets
650-400 b.c.e.

Moses ca.
1270 b.c.e.

David
1010-960 b.c.e.

Babylonian exile
of Hebrews begins
586 b.c.e.

Greek philosophers
500-200 b.c.e.

Solomon
960-920 b.c.e.

Minoan commercial
civilization 2200-1500 b.c.e.

Mycenaeans rule
Greece 1500-1100 b.c.e.

First Greek city-states
800 b.c.e.

Pericles dominates
Athens 450-429 b.c.e.

Persian War at its height
490-480 b.c.e.

First Olympic
games 776 b.c.e.

Alexander the
Great 336-323 b.c.e.

Harappan civilization
2500-1500 b.c.e.

Aryan invasions
of northern India
1500 b.c.e.

Aryan-Dravidian synthesis
1500-500 b.c.e.

Maurya dynasty
321-185 b.c.e.

Vedas begin to define
Hinduism 1000 b.c.e.

Buddha
563-483 b.c.e.

Asoka
268-231 b.c.e.

Shang dynasty
1500-1000 b.c.e.

Zhou dynasty
1000-221 b.c.e.

Warring States period
400-221 b.c.e.

Confucius
551-479 b.c.e.

Shi Huangdi unifies
China 221 b.c.e.

Great Wall of China
ca. 220 b.c.e.

Egypt conquers
Nubia ca. 1500 b.c.e.

Kush dominates
Nubia ca. 1100 b.c.e.

Kush conquers
Egypt 750 b.c.e.

Carthage founded in
Maghreb ca. 800 b.c.e.

Carthage dominates western
Mediterranean 600-150 b.c.e.

Hannibal invades Roman
Italy 212 b.c.e.

Olmec culture in Mexico
1500-400 b.c.e.

Chavin culture in
Peru 800-400 b.c.e.

Carthage destroyed
146 b.c.e.

# CHAPTER 2

# PYRAMID TOMBS AND ZIGGURAT TEMPLES
## Egypt and Mesopotamia
### (3500–100 B.C.E.)

## A Glance Ahead: The First Cities, the First Nation

The range of ancient civilizations mentioned in the Overview spans three thousand years and much of the globe. Two of the most intriguing, however, have a special interest for us moderns, with our passion for priority, our enthusiasm for being first. As far as we know, the city-states of Mesopotamia, in what is today Iraq, were the first real cities built anywhere. And the kingdom of Egypt winding down the Nile—ancient Egypt of the pharaohs—was probably the first real country in history.

These patterns of political organization laid down by ancient Near Easterners and North Africans would play a crucial part in the future history of humankind.

Civilization emerged in cities. It spread across the earth in the larger and more complex units we call variously countries, nations, kingdoms, and republics. All these primary political units, furthermore, were capable of conquering their neighbors and creating even larger polities called empires. In the following pages, we will see these patterns emerging over and over as humankind discovers these basic forms of political organization thousands of years ago.

## The Cities of Mesopotamia

### A Land between Two Rivers

Nobody, of course, ever set out to build the first civilizations. They happened, like the growth of families or feuds between clans, like droughts or animal migrations or somebody learning from somebody else a better way to weave cloth or chip stone.

Gods demanded houses and servants, just as the heads of powerful families did, so temples and their attendant priesthoods emerged. Vendettas against neighbors or stock rustling raids threw up war leaders, and war leaders became hereditary rulers. Villages absorbed neighboring villages, and then a victorious local warlord threw a wall around them all, and a city emerged. People started counting their animals and making marks on clay to remind themselves how many there were, and writing was born.

Thousands of years in the future, learned people would look back and call it the birth of civilization.[1] They would tick off the elements of the new lifestyle: "urbanization . . . political institutions . . . organized religious beliefs . . . job specialization . . . social ranking . . . visual arts . . . a network of public works . . ." and of course "writing." But we do not need to postulate any conscious drive toward civilization-building to admire the remarkable consequences of these lives lived long ago.

We will begin this look at the oldest civilizations with the cities of ancient Mesopotamia. The first of these cities probably emerged a few brief centuries before the pharaohs united Egypt into the beginnings of a nation. This initial breakthrough into urban living came in the middle of the fourth millennium B.C.E. in Sumeria, in the southeastern corner of what is today Iraq.

*Mesopotamia* means "Between the Rivers" in Greek, and "Land of the Two Rivers" is as adequate a label as we are likely to get for a place where so many political states have come and gone. Geographically speaking, it is the swath of alluvial plain and patches of

---

[1] See Gregory G. Guzman, "A Working Definition of the Term 'Civilization' " in the *World History Bulletin*, Volume 7, No. 1 (1991) for a handy summary.

bordering hills that run northwestward along the banks of the Tigris and Euphrates rivers from the head of the Persian Gulf to the edge of the Anatolian uplands of modern Turkey. It is an arid region now. Where the land once blew golden with grain in the palm-lined fields along the ancient canals, the earth cracks in the sun today or smoulders with the ruins of recent wars. Where the cities of Mesopotamia once stood, shapeless mounds called *tells* remain, from which the archaeologist's spade can bring forth no more than a rough sense of the shape and scale of the achievement of these first builders.

Over a span of some three thousand years, from perhaps 3500 to 539 B.C.E., the center of Mesopotamian civilization moved slowly up the two rivers. Cities and empires first emerged in Sumeria, or Sumer, in the marshy delta at the head of the Persian Gulf. Civi-

## ANCIENT CIVILIZATIONS OF EURASIA, 3500–1500 B.C.E.

lization flourished next in Akkadian Babylon, farther up the rivers, and came to a violent climax in the northwest, in Assyria, during the first millennium B.C.E.

## Irrigation, Building, Bronze Age Crafts

It may have been the gradual drying out of the sea-covered delta at the mouths of the two rivers, producing marshy but highly fertile land, that first drew Neolithic farmers. They came down from the rain-watered hills, where they had already learned to cultivate the land, pasture animals, and live in villages, into Sumer. We do not really know. A pre-Sumerian people were there already; they have left us only a few stone tools and some non-Sumerian names on the land. We do know that during the fourth millennium before Christ, two groups met and merged along the lower Tigris and Euphrates. There was a Sumerian-speaking people from somewhere to the north, perhaps around the Caspian Sea, and the first of many waves of people who spoke Semitic languages, drifting in from Syria or Arabia to the west. From the fertile fusion of these two groups, a vastly productive little society emerged as early as 3500 B.C.E.

The members of this society built reed huts in the marshes of a sort that may still be seen in the delta of southern Iraq today. They hunted birds and speared fish from graceful canoes with high prows and sterns that glided through the marsh grass with scarcely a ripple. But they were farmers as well as hunters and gatherers, and the rich alluvial soil favored agriculture. Out of the reeds and the mud of the delta, then, the ancient Sumerians built over centuries a small prototype of all the larger civilizations that would follow.

Their first great discovery was how to tame the erratic rivers of Mesopotamia. The sluggish Euphrates and the faster-moving Tigris crested late for planting. They frequently brought unmanageable quantities of rain water and melting snow down from the northern mountains to flood the land and sweep away homes and topsoil. Only with discipline and ingenuity did the Sumerians learn the proper combination of dikes, canals, and irrigation ditches for turning destructive floods into a source of ever more complex life.

By so doing they were able to raise enough food to support much larger populations than had been possible in the Neolithic villages of earlier times. The Sumerians grew barley as the staple grain of the south; wheat would flourish later, in northern Mesopotamia. They cultivated the date palm for fruit and for palm wine. They grew onions and garlic and garnished meals of unleavened barley bread with the oil of the sesame seed. Sumerian shepherds watched flocks of sheep and goats, from whose wool and hair clothing was made. They learned to use oxen to pull their plows, and patient donkeys became their primary beasts of burden. Only later, when Mesopotamian kings went forth to make war upon their neighbors, were camels and horses brought home from foreign parts and domesticated along the two rivers.

The Sumerians and their successors in the Land of the Two Rivers developed many crafts with great skill—textiles, pottery, and stone carving, the smelting of copper and the alloying of bronze. They even invented that archetype of human ingenuity, the wheel—solid and spoked—and the carts and wagons that went with it. Theirs is the first form of writing to come down to us. But their most important invention was the Mesopotamian city itself. The city became the center of this first of civilizations. And urban complexes, whatever their shortcomings as living spaces, have been the center of civilized society ever since.

## The City and the City-State

Walls, high and thick, pierced with monumental gateways, were the most prominent feature of Mesopotamian cities. Within the walls the typical large town was divided into four quarters by main streets that entered the city through four main gates, one in the middle of each wall. The developing power structure of the city and the city-state was architecturally embodied in the king's palace, the temples of the gods, and the large houses of the leading citizens. Palaces and houses tended to be built around a succession of courtyards, meandering labyrinths of cool, thick-walled rooms, some of which were elaborately decorated with painting or colored tiles. Temples were characterized most strikingly by *ziggurats*—pyramidal, terraced towers visible from far beyond the city walls. The streets were mostly narrow and winding, crowded with shopkeepers and artisans, jostling slaves and citizens, priests in fluted skirts, and the majestic sedan chairs of the wealthy.

These first cities already contained a clear aristocracy and a detectable middle class. Handicraft industries, including the manufacture of textiles and metalwork in copper and bronze, produced a middle class of skilled artisans. Other bourgeois citizens included the merchants, especially the most wealthy among them, and the long-distance traders, whose caravans transported raw materials and luxury goods from one city to another. Above this stratum was a thin layer of aristocrats, royal officials, members of the royal family, and perhaps the chief priests of the major temples.

Few of the people who worked the fields outside the walls of these urban complexes were free peasants. Some were tenant farmers, holding their land in return for payment in kind to an absentee landlord who lived in the city. Others were serfs or even slaves, working the large tracts owned by the royal family and the chief gods of the city-state. All were subject to the rules laid down and the authority wielded by the officials who supervised the elaborate irrigation system that made the life of the city-state possible.

The developed irrigation systems of these first Mesopotamian hydraulic empires involved massive dikes and levees that protected the croplands of large parts of the valley from the often destructive annual floods. Canals carried the runoff water, ditches distributed it to individual fields, and everywhere the *shaduf*—a long pivoted pole with a weight at one end and a bucket of some sort at the other—lifted the water from larger channels into the furrows where the seeds were planted. Levees had to be constantly strengthened, canals and ditches redredged to prevent silting up, and large-scale drainage efforts made in the south to slow the salinization of the soil by the salt water of the Persian Gulf. Elaborate regulations, rigid authority, and a good deal of cooperation were necessary if such elaborate group labors were to be successful.

If class distinctions were much clearer in these early civilizations, gender differences seem to have been considerably more complicated. There is no denying the generally patriarchal tone of society and the state. Rulers, officials, priests, merchants, and heads of families were normally male. In the warlike Assyrian society described below, respectable women were veiled, prevented from owning property, married off by their fathers to establish business alliances, and could be sold into slavery and savagely punished for sexual offenses.

On the other hand, many Mesopotamian women did work outside the confines of the family as weavers, pottery makers, and even farm workers and manual laborers. In Sumer and Babylon, women could own property, sign legal contracts, and engage in business themselves. It is a complex picture, as gender relations will prove to be down the centuries.

## The Palace and the Temple

The central institutions of Sumerian society were the monarchies and the cults of the gods.

The temple came first. The pyramidal ziggurats and broad temple complexes of the gods and goddesses—Anu and Enlil, Enki and Ninhursag and Innana (the last known later as Ishtar)—dominated the skyline of the Sumerian city. Each city had its own patron among the heavenly assembly, who was believed to bring rising rivers and rich harvests, to keep the barbarian from the gate, and to maintain order in the land.

Elaborate priesthoods served the major deities. Reverent hands dressed the cult statues daily, wafted food before their nostrils to feed them, played music to delight their ears. City dwellers could see their gods through the open doors of temple courtyards, dim and awesome in their niches. On great festival days such as the New Year, the gods and goddesses

---

# PROBING THE PAST

This letter from an Assyrian courtier to Assurbanipal (668 – 627 B.C.E.) was written with a very practical purpose having little to do with historical interpretation. Yet his petition does offer an excellent brief summary of what good government and good times meant in ancient Mesopotamia.

What sanction for Assurbanipal's rule is stressed? What political and economic benefits has his rule conferred on his people? How does this courtier describe the "good life" for Mesopotamian women? Would a woman have agreed?

*"To the king, my lord (Assurbanipal), from your servant Adad-šumi-usur:*

*Good health to Your Majesty! May the gods Nabû and Marduk give many, many blessings to Your Majesty.*

*When Aššur, the king of the gods, designated Your Majesty to rule Assyria as king, and when the gods Samaš and Adad confirmed by reliable oracles that Your Majesty should rule as king over all the countries, the great gods of the entire cosmos brought about during the reign of Your Majesty a happy rule with days and years in which law and order prevail: there are copious rains, abundant flooding of the rivers, favorable prices, and reconciliation of the gods; there is much piety and the temples of the gods are well provided. Old men dance with joy, young men sing happy songs, women and young girls happily learn to do what women do; they go into confinement and bring forth boys and girls, and the births are easy.*

*Why, then, since Your Majesty has pardoned persons condemned to death for their crimes, and has released those who for many years had been imprisoned, and since . . . the hungry have been sated with food . . . and those who had been destitute have been clad in sumptuous garments—why then should I and my son Arad-Gula, among all those happy people, remain restless and in low spirits? Only recently has Your Majesty shown his love for Nineveh by telling the prominent citizens: "Bring me your sons, they shall become servants at my court!" If this son of mine, Arad-Gula, could become a servant at the court of Your Majesty, serving together with these same people, then we too would be as happy as all other people are; we would dance and bless Your Majesty."*

A. Leo Oppenheim, ed. and trans., *Letters from Mesopotamia* (Chicago and London: University of Chicago Press, 1967), pp. 149–150.

---

of the land of the Two Rivers, gorgeously robed, their dark saucer-like eyes staring, were carried up the avenue in procession above the heads of their reveling worshipers.

Veneration of the gods predated the birth of the city: the power of the king grew more slowly in Sumer. Initially, the growing city was probably ruled by a city governor and war leader called the *ensi,* who governed in conjunction with an assembly of the city's free adult male citizens. As war leader, however, the *ensi* accumulated emergency powers that he did not surrender. He thus emerged in time as a hereditary monarch, still general in wartime but responsible also for maintaining the irrigation system, regulating prices and wages, and implementing other welfare measures. The assemblies—no doubt legacies from earlier, smaller-scale social organizations—faded, and the power of the kings grew. By the days of the Assyrian hegemony, the king had absorbed many religious functions, and the power of the palace clearly exceeded that of the temples of even the most ancient gods.

## MESOPOTAMIAN EMPIRES

### Impediments to Empire

Beyond the city-states of early times, the most common larger form of political organization was the empire. Empires were most often created when one people conquered others, absorbing them into a single larger political unit ruled by foreigners.

Successful efforts at empire-building in the Tigris-Euphrates valley occurred less than half a dozen times over a period of nearly three thousand years. There was the Sumerian Empire of Sargon of Akkad in the twenty-third century B.C.E. There was the Old Babylonian Empire founded by Hammurabi in the eighteenth century before Christ. There was the fierce Assyrian predominance of the eighth and seventh centuries B.C.E. and the short-lived New Babylonian Kingdom of the sixth century B.C.E. After that, Cyrus the Persian swept down from the mountains, and Mesopotamia found unity at last—as a satrapy or province of the Persian Empire.

Many factors militated against unification in the Land of the Two Rivers during the three thousand years between the rise of the first Sumerian cities and the final fall of Babylon in the days of Belshazzar. Most obviously, the rich valley lay open to nomadic incursion from east, west, and north. Barbaric invaders such as the Akkadians, Gudians, Kassites, and Persians might in time be civilized by the enduring culture of Sumer. Nonetheless, such onslaughts from the deserts or the mountains repeatedly frustrated the best efforts of a Sargon or a Hammurabi to impose a single imperium on Mesopotamia.

A second challenge to larger unity was the appearance of a fragmented feudal order in much of Mesopotamia. As in medieval Europe many centuries later, feudalism in the Near East meant the division of a large measure of power among a landowning aristocracy. Such a divided socioeconomic structure evidently did not make for political unity.

A third force was what has been called *petty-statism*—a tendency of the region to break up into a number of middle-sized states, each enjoying local hegemony but none strong enough to overpower the others and impose a larger order on all of Mesopotamia.

A final roadblock to political unity was polarization. When one of the feuding Mesopotamian city-states did grow powerful enough to reach for supremacy, it was repeatedly confronted by the rise of a great rival. Polarization could clearly be as powerful an obstacle as barbarian invasions, feudalization, or petty-statism to unification in the Land of the Two Rivers.

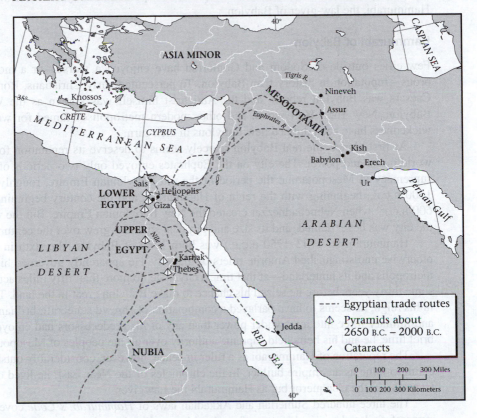

When unity did come, albeit temporarily, it came as centralized political authority has normally come to disunited peoples. It was imposed by blood and violence and attended with toppling walls and corpses steaming in the roadways, with kings struck down and gods carried off into exile. Yet such a larger order, however imposed, could bring with it a better life for all the divided peoples of the wide valley.

## Sargon of Akkad

The most celebrated of Sumerian kings was Sargon of Akkad, who founded a dynasty around 2300 B.C.E. that governed much of Mesopotamia for almost a hundred years.

Having begun his career as a Semitic royal official of one of the lesser Sumerian city-states, Sargon replaced his royal master on the throne, overthrew the mighty dynasty of neighboring Uruk, and subsequently conquered most of the Tigris and Euphrates valley. He garrisoned his conquests with Akkadian troops and built himself a new capital, the rich and powerful city of Agade. His son and grandson ruled after him. But volcanic ash from an eruption may have brought drought to the region. And then the violent Gutians swept down from the neighboring hills to destroy the city and its imperial Mesopotamian domain. The powerful bronze head traditionally identified as Sargon shows a strong, curly-bearded face with heavy lips and a hawklike nose—the face of the world's first empire builder.

Perhaps the most famous of all attempts at Mesopotamian unity, however, was that of Hammurabi, the law-giver of Babylon.

## Hammurabi of Babylon

Few cities outside of Sodom and Gomorrah have enjoyed a worse—or a more glamorous—reputation in history than Babylon. To persecuted early Christians, Rome of the Caesars was Babylon reborn, and the Antichrist himself was known as the Whore of Babylon. New York, Hollywood, and other modern metropolises famed for wealth and wickedness have been dubbed new Babylons in their turn.

At first glance, the real Babylon scarcely seems to deserve its reputation for wealth, worldliness, and power. The city on the Euphrates enjoyed only two periods of genuine supremacy in Mesopotamia: the period of the old Babylonian Empire, roughly 1800 to 1600 B.C.E., beginning with the reign of Hammurabi, and the century beginning around 600 B.C.E., when Nebuchadnezzar created the New Babylonian Empire. But the wealth of the city was never denied, and its size and physical splendor grew over the centuries.

Hammurabi (c. 1792–1750 B.C.E.) was born King of Babylon, the sixth in a line of otherwise undistinguished Amorite rulers of that city. He apparently governed his modest metropolis and its hinterland—at that time a city-state no more than fifty miles across—for some thirty years before he seized his chance to make Babylon great in the land. Then, late in his reign, he seems to have parlayed a combination of shrewd statecraft, brilliant timing, and military force into a far wider power than any of his predecessors had enjoyed. For a brief time, he and his heirs held supreme authority over all the peoples of Mesopotamia.

The reputation of Hammurabi as a ruler in peace, however, considerably outshines his claim to fame as an empire builder. In the chronicles of the Near East, he lived on not as Hammurabi the Conqueror but as Hammurabi the Lawgiver.

The three hundred Sumerian and Akkadian laws of *Hammurabi's Code* cover a wide range of civil and criminal matters, from land law and business law to regulation of family relations, from personal injury to military service, from witchcraft to taxes. Many of the principles promulgated in the code seem harsh to the modern reader. The principle of an eye for an eye, a life for a life, is here commonly invoked, centuries before Moses. Mutilation and death are repeatedly prescribed as fair and fitting punishments. And a clear sense of social hierarchy is reflected throughout; there is one law for slaves, another for their masters.

Yet the Code of Hammurabi does reveal a society with a highly developed belief in social justice. Even harsh punishment imposed by the state may be seen as an advance over the random retaliation of feuding clans that it replaced. And if the life of the slave is not rated as high in shekels of compensation as the life of a freeman, by the same token a nobleman may be punished more rigorously for the same offense than his social inferiors. Perhaps most important, there is a clear conviction that might does not make right, that the law has a fundamental obligation to protect the weak from the strong. It was not the worst foundation for this early attempt at a larger social order, which reached beyond the city-state to govern a whole people.

When the great king died, his heirs could not hold what he had won. New waves of preurban peoples appeared at the gates, most formidably the Kassites from the east, and within a century and a half, the brief Babylonian unification of Mesopotamia had crumbled away.

The next unifiers of the valley of the Tigris and Euphrates emerged still farther to the north, in the region that came to be known as Assyria.

Assyrian warriors in combat, vividly depicted on the walls of the royal palace at Nineveh. Charging troops, slaughtered foes, and severed heads all reflect the ferocity of the Assyrian war machine. (Erich Lessing/Art Resource)

## The Assyrian Warfare State

The world has seen more than its share of frightfulness over the fifty-five hundred years since civilization was born in ancient Sumer. But the Assyrians were among the most savage of civilized peoples, even by modern standards of violence.

The source of the endless brutal military campaigns that are the very texture of Assyrian history has been sought in various aspects of this last great Mesopotamian culture.

One approach is simply to point out that geographically, Assyria was highly vulnerable, more open even than southern Mesopotamia to foreign invasion. The Assyrians may thus have treated their foes more savagely than usual in order to replace nonexistent natural frontiers with a wall of fear. There may also have been, at the royal palace and among the priesthood of their chief god, Assur, a sense of imperial and religious duty to impose and reimpose order on the chaos of the Near East in the second and first millennia B.C.E. There was, in addition, almost certainly a normal human lust for something for nothing, for the loot and tribute that made wars a paying proposition for the powerful Assyrian military machine. There may well have been, finally, more subtle economic motives at work. Some historians have detected behind Assyrian imperialism the need for copper and stone and timber, or the desire to control trade routes.

For whatever reason, the story of the rise and fall of the Assyrians is a story of almost unending war.

According to their own records, at least, they began to win wars with the barbarians in the fourteenth century B.C.E., during the Babylonian dark age that followed the decline of the heirs of Hammurabi. By the latter part of the eighth century, they were incorporating their victims into a large and growing empire. In the seventh century, under Sennacherib and Assurbanipal, Assyrian power overwhelmed Egypt and most of Mesopotamia. In the reign of the redoubtable Assurbanipal, Assyria thus stood briefly as master of the band of civilized states that ran from the Nile to the Persian Gulf.

Everywhere they went, they brought devastation. "I built a pillar over against his city gate," reported a ninth-century Assyrian ruler, "and I flayed all his chief men . . . and I covered the pillar with their skins. . . ."[2] Whole populations were deported, cities leveled, their gods—and sometimes their citizens—given over to the flames. And the tribute of a terrorized world rolled in.

But the lust for loot and victory of even the most martial people may be sated in time. Sennacherib built an aqueduct that pleased him perhaps as much as the looting of the land of the Hebrews.

It was perhaps a softening. And it brought its reward. Chaos closed over the Assyrian Empire in the last years of the seventh century. In 612 B.C.E., an allied force of Chaldeans from Babylon and Medes from the eastern mountains broke into the heart of Assyria, ringed Nineveh, and crushed it.

The punishment imposed upon the erstwhile terror of the world was as thorough as any inflicted by the Assyrians in their pride. Mighty Nineveh was leveled so efficiently that when the Greek general Xenophon passed that way two centuries later, no one could even identify the site for him.

## Nebuchadnezzar and the New Babylonian Empire

The New Babylonian Empire, which briefly succeeded Assyrian power in Mesopotamia, was very much the creation of one man: Nebuchadnezzar II (605–562 B.C.E.), notorious in Bible history as the Chaldean ruler who carried off the Hebrews into their Babylonian captivity. Nebuchadnezzar was a conqueror and an empire builder in the by now time-honored Mesopotamian tradition. Seven years after the fall of Nineveh, while still crown prince of Babylon, he commanded the Babylonian army that crushed the forces of the Egyptian pharaoh at Carchemish in 605 B.C.E. As king, he led repeated expeditions down into Palestine, destroying Jerusalem, and carrying much of the population of Judea off into exile. At its brief height, the New Babylonian empire of the sixth century rivaled its Assyrian predecessor in size and splendor, governing once more from a single center all the land from the Persian Gulf to the Mediterranean.

Nebuchadnezzar built more than a mighty empire, however. He was celebrated in antiquity not as the man who took torch and crowbar to Solomon's Temple but as the rebuilder of the city of Babylon.

Just as Hammurabi was before him at Babylon, Nebuchadnezzar II was a great builder of canals and caravan roads, temples and palaces. He raised huge new crenellated walls around his capital, eleven miles long and so wide that a chariot could turn around on

---

[2]Samuel Noah Kramer, *Cradle of Civilization* (New York: Time-Life Books, 1967), p. 58.

the roadway that ran along the top. He opened the broad Processional Way through the heart of the city to the famous Ishtar Gate. He built the Hanging Gardens of Babylon—a towering ziggurat featuring terraces planted with trees and exotic plants—to please his Median wife, who missed the hills of her mountainous home.

But the Babylon of Nebuchadnezzar was a brief, final flowering. Its conqueror was one of history's great empire builders—Cyrus the Great. This half-barbarian king, called Cyrus the Shepherd by his Persian and Median troops, had already overrun all the kingdoms of the north and east, from rich Lydia on the Mediterranean to the far frontiers of India. Then in 539 B.C.E., he turned his leather-clad horsemen toward the richest plum of all—Babylon.

He found the ancient city ripe for the plucking. Nebuchadnezzar's successors had not ruled well, and there were powerful men within the walls who felt that their interests would be better served by a change of dynasty than by a protracted struggle with as famous a soldier as Cyrus the Persian. Cyrus's troops, with the help of a quisling governor, entered the city without resistance. And his victory marked the beginning of a new era in the Near East.

Just a caravan journey to the west, meanwhile, another remarkable center of civilization had been keeping pace with developments in Mesopotamia. This was the ancient African civilization of Egypt, to which we now turn.

# THE PYRAMID AGE IN EGYPT

## The Gift of the Nile

Civilization apparently emerged a few centuries later in the Nile valley than it did on the banks of the Tigris and the Euphrates, perhaps around 3200 B.C.E. But the Egyptians very quickly moved ahead of their neighbors beyond the Arabian Desert, in one area at least. Egypt early developed a powerful centralized government, whereas Mesopotamia remained a land of city-states and short-lived empires throughout its long history. Egypt thus enjoyed a high degree of unity, stability, and cultural continuity through much of its three thousand years of independent life.

As is so frequently the case, the course of Egyptian historical development was in large part set by the geographical framework within which Egypt evolved. "Egypt," reported the ancient Greek historian Herodotus, "is the gift of the Nile." The river was clearly central to the daily life of the Egyptians. The heart of the land was that part of the river from the first cataract at Aswan to the fan-shaped delta where it flowed into the Mediterranean. (The Nile, incidentally, flows northward to the Mediterranean, so that *Upper* Egypt is in the south, *Lower* Egypt in the north.) The river winds six hundred miles from the cataracts to the delta, gouging out a valley that is seldom more than a few miles wide. Only over the last hundred miles or so does the valley open up into the flat, triangular delta spread along the sea. The traditional "two lands" of Egypt were defined by this difference: Upper Egypt, with its sacred city at Thebes, covered most of the river valley; Lower Egypt, with its even more ancient capital at Memphis, comprised mostly the delta.

The great river's annual rise and fall were crucial for the life of Egypt. The Nile has its sources far to the south, in the mountains of Ethiopia and the lake country of equatorial Africa. Each year spring rains in these far-off regions sent high water surging north across the Sudan and the lands of ancient Nubia, thrashing through the cataracts, and rolling on at a more majestic pace through the sandstone- and limestone-walled valley of Upper

Egypt. Here the rising waters overflowed their banks and deposited over the narrow valley a layer of rich black mud, alluvium picked up along all the hundreds of miles from central Africa. It was this rich gift of fertile soil and life-giving water that enabled the Nile valley to bloom and made Egypt the most favored land in the ancient world.

## Egypt and Africa

The African location of Egypt brought the kingdom of the Nile more than fertile soil, however. Some cultural influences also flowed north from inner Africa into Egypt.

As we will see, scholars have long seen Mesopotamian influences at work in Egyptian civilization. More recently, historians like Cheikh Anta Diop have urged the importance of African influences on the shaping of Egyptian culture. Evidence of inner African influence on the emerging Egyptian kingdom includes political, social, and cultural similarities.

Culturally, Egyptians shared both myths and individual gods—including an important jackal-headed god of the dead—with other African peoples. Among similar artifacts, you can see wooden headrests like those used in ancient Egypt still in use in parts of rural Africa today. Social customs common to this ancient civilization and later African cultures include circumcision and totemic animals symbolizing a clan or people. There are also parallels between Egyptian and other African languages.

Similar political patterns also suggest closer ties than was once thought between Egypt and the rest of Africa. Matrilineal descent—the inheritance of property and power through the female side of the family—was common in Africa and crucial in Egypt, where even pharaohs often married their sisters to guarantee their hereditary power over the land. Specific forms and rituals of divine kingship also link the pharaohs with kings and chiefs from farther south.

We will see later contacts, often initiated by the Egyptians, in later centuries. For now, it will suffice to plant the kingdom of the pharaohs firmly in African soil before going on to survey Egypt's own development and its key role in the history of the Near East and the Eastern Mediterranean.

## The Pharaohs Unify the Land

Perhaps as early as the fifth millennium B.C.E., the hunters and nomadic pastoralists who had gravitated to the well-watered river valley had discovered the agricultural potential of the endlessly replenished black earth along the Nile. Like their Neolithic fellows farther east, they settled into agricultural villages. There were differences, of course. The cereal on which Egyptian agriculture was based was wheat instead of barley, and the Egyptians grew flax for clothing instead of depending on sheep's wool. Like preurban peoples in many places, the Egyptians organized themselves into clans having animal totems, such as the crocodile or the hippopotamus. They probably worshiped these animals as well, since many of the gods of later Egyptian times were depicted with animal heads on their otherwise anthropomorphic—human-headed—bodies.

Along the Nile, as along the Tigris and Euphrates, it took slow centuries and many generations for village life to evolve into something more complex. Nevertheless, the outlines of a distinctly Egyptian culture were clear before the Old Kingdom ever began.

Sometime between 3500 and 3000 B.C.E., cooperative economic effort appeared as the Egyptians began to try to control the great river with dikes and catch basins. Copper was used more widely. The population grew. There was, however, less of the bustling urban life that had flourished in early Sumeria. Nor did trade play such an important part in Egypt; the Nile valley was so nearly self-sufficient that there was apparently little felt need for exotic foreign imports.

There were some influences from outside, even this early. Mesopotamian-style cylinder seals have been found in Egypt. Sumerian pictograms appear among the earliest Egyptian hieroglyphics. But there was one great difference: Because there was less urban commercial culture in Egypt, the city-state also failed to appear. Instead, Egypt seems to have moved relatively early directly into the centralized monarchical state.

There was one intermediate stage, however. After the villages along the river, there were the two lands of Upper and Lower Egypt. We do not know a great deal about these two lands before they became one. We know that the vulture of the goddess Nekhbet was sacred in Upper Egypt, the cobra of Wadjet in Lower Egypt. We know that the kings of the upper valley wore a white crown, the kings of the delta a red one. And we know that their two peoples fought each other.

We do not need to follow the struggle of the cobra and the vulture, the white crown and the red. After generations, maybe centuries, the warriors of Upper Egypt fought their way northward from inner Africa to the Mediterranean. A new capital was founded at Memphis, and the crowns of Upper and Lower Egypt were combined into the double crown of the pharaohs. By 3000 B.C.E., Egypt stood as a united land.

## The Old Kingdom: The Pyramid Builders

*Old Kingdom* Egypt—the stable, monumentally impressive first period of Egyptian history—was not a large nation by today's standards. It covered about the same area that Mesopotamia did—approximately ten thousand square miles. But in 3000 B.C.E. there was no nation in the world as large or half as centralized.

There was resistance, of course. Egyptians of the valley and Egyptians of the delta did not lose a sense of their differentness. The pharaoh was always officially "the King of Upper and Lower Egypt," "the Lord of the Two Ladies" (the vulture and the cobra), and as such was crowned and symbolically buried in each of the two lands. There were separate treasuries for the two halves of his kingdom and much duplication of officials.

More challenging still to the fundamental unity of the state was the tendency toward fragmentation embodied in the *nomes,* the provinces of pharaonic Egypt. Independent totemic tribes or clans prior to unification, the nomes could become centers of disunity under ambitious governors.

To hold the nation together, the early pharaohs, like the princes of Mesopotamia, forged a powerful alliance with the temples and the priests. Mesopotamian kings ruled as stewards or bailiffs of the gods; the pharaohs claimed that they themselves were incarnations of divinity.

Pharaoh was believed to be the son of the sun god Re. The reigning pharaoh was also Horus the sky god, symbolized by the falcon. On his death, "the falcon flew to the horizon," and the dead pharaoh became Osiris, king of the underworld. "What is the king of Upper and Lower Egypt?" a statesman of a later dynasty rhetorically inquired. "He is a god by whose dealings one lives, the father and mother of all men, alone by himself, without an equal."[3]

---

[3]Milton Covensky, *The Ancient Near Eastern Tradition* (New York: Harper & Row, 1966), p. 51.

Above all, he was "the good god." Every year he performed religious ceremonies that guaranteed the rising of the river. He and his officials ruled the land in the spirit of *Ma'at*, a combination of truth, justice, and order that was for the Egyptians the highest of virtues. In the underworld, the souls of the dead were weighed against *Ma'at*. In this world, pharaoh himself was its living embodiment and the guarantee that the land would be ruled in its spirit.

To carry out the will of the god-king, the Egyptians developed an elaborate administrative system as early as the Old Kingdom. The chief administrative officer under the pharaoh was the vizier, whose roles included chief judge, superintendent of public works, and general right hand to the king. Under the vizier an impressive array of bureaus emerged, including the treasuries, the ministry of agriculture, the officials in charge of the irrigation system, and a secretariat that piled up an immense volume of public records.

There was also a provincial administration charged with governing the nomes. The rulers of these provinces, the *nomarchs,* exercised considerable local authority. In particular, they controlled the local militia, the source of most of the military strength of the kings of Upper and Lower Egypt.

The body of the Egyptian bureaucracy—and subsequently the top spots as well—was staffed by scribes, the masters of the sacred art of writing. If the records they left behind are any indication, Egyptian scribes were busy bureaucrats. They conducted censuses of land and people, estimated the size of the harvest, and collected taxes in kind. They supervised the vital irrigation system, organized the care and feeding of the pharaohs and the building of the royal tombs. Next to the divinity of pharaoh himself, these scribal administrators were the glue that held ancient Egypt together in a genuine national state built many centuries before its time.

Old Kingdom Egypt was a thoroughly ordered state. Society was organized hierarchically, as it would be almost everywhere in the increasingly complex cultures of the civilized world. Peasant farmers were the backbone of the nation—and the bottom of the social pyramid. Many of them were serfs on royal or noble lands, required to labor on building projects as well as to till the soil. Above these peasant *fellahin* were the royal officials, the priesthoods of the temples, the nobles, the princes, and the incarnate god upon the throne.

This hierarchy was symbolized most massively by the pyramid tombs of the pharaohs of the famous fourth dynasty—the dynasty of Khufu (known to Western history as Cheops), builder of the great pyramid at Giza, ca. 2550 B.C.E. Today the tombs of the pharaohs loom in splendid isolation above the sands. Originally the royal pyramids of Khufu, Khafre, Menkaure, and the rest stood not alone but as centers of ordered necropolises, cities of the dead. Each pyramid was surrounded by the smaller pyramids of queens and princes of the blood and by row after row of the flat-roofed *mastaba* tombs of high officials. The total effect of these ranks of tombs laid out along straight-ruled streets must have been somberly impressive. It expressed to perfection the order of the living state. In death as in life, the "good god" ruled, and his people slept around him.

## The Middle Kingdom: A Bridge between Two Worlds

The Middle Kingdom and the intermediate periods before and after it may be seen as a historic transition, a bridge between two worlds. During these half-dozen centuries Egypt moved from the self-contained, intensely conservative land of the pyramid builders to the more dynamic—and more turbulent—New Kingdom. Therefore, this entire period, from the collapse of the Old Kingdom around 2200 B.C.E. to the emergence of the New Kingdom about 1550, will be considered here as a whole.

The initial phase of this great transition is what historians have called the First Intermediate. We do not know what triggered this great disruption. There may have been a series of low Niles, or a succession of weak rulers. There was clearly a good deal of political turbulence, particularly among the nomarchs. There was famine in the land of the bountiful Nile, and marauding desert bedouin appeared in the delta. The poor cried out for justice—so the scribes lamented—and all Egyptians longed for a return to the immemorial order of past centuries.

What they got was not a return to the past but a dynamic new direction in national life. Ambitious dynasts from the new city of Thebes in Upper Egypt wrested the kingdom from the last royal house to rule in Memphis. During the twentieth and nineteenth centuries before Christ, the powerful twelfth dynasty restored prosperity and order along the Nile.

The Middle Kingdom thus inaugurated brought what seems to many historians a new concern for the governed on the part of twelfth-dynasty pharaohs. Contemporary scribes talked of a new sense of civic responsibility among the governed themselves during this briefest of the three Egyptian kingdoms.

But the most striking new dimension was the outward reach of the pharaohs of the twelfth dynasty. Trade expanded rapidly in the prosperous new era. Egyptian merchants traded with Palestine and Syria, satellite civilizations of ancient Mesopotamia, and even sailed to Minoan Crete, the island kingdom where the first European civilization was just emerging. Egyptian arms pushed south along the Nile into Nubia, the land of the nearest black African people, and on into the Sudan.

Thus for the first time Egypt became involved on a large scale with the busy life of the Near East and north-eastern Africa. From Middle Kingdom days on, the pharaohs were to play a key role in the history of both Africa and the Near East.

Contact with the outside world could flow two ways, however. The dynasties that followed the twelfth seem to have produced less capable rulers. Tendencies toward dissolution of the union, no longer restrained by a firm hand, reasserted themselves. And covetous strangers from overseas, attracted by the wealth and increasingly visible weakness of Egypt at the end of the Middle Kingdom, began to appear once more in the delta.

Shortly before 1700 B.C.E.—in the middle of the Second Intermediate—the gathering storm burst over Egypt in what ancient Egyptians regarded as their greatest catastrophe: the invasion of the Hyksos.

The priest Manetho described the onslaught of this mysterious Semitic-speaking people as "a blast of God." The seizure of power by the Hyksos may not have been quite that dramatic. The Hyksos influx was part of a general reshuffling of nomadic peoples during the second millennium B.C.E., to be discussed in the next chapter. These folk migrations were slow infiltrations as often as they were invasions. The invaders of Egypt actually spent several generations settling in the delta. Once they had seized power from the enfeebled pharaohs of the Second Intermediate, the Hyksos found nobles and nomarchs quite willing to collaborate with their leadership.

As often happens when a less sophisticated people overpowers a more developed culture, the newcomers soon became culturally assimilated, taking the names of the people they ruled, worshiping their gods, following all the traditional royal rites to the letter. For a century, perhaps a century and a half, they remained the predominant force in the Egypt of the Second Intermediate.

Governing the delta, dominating the valley, the Hyksos were also responsible for some valuable innovations. The use of bronze instead of the softer copper became widespread at this time. New weapons of war invented on the distant steppes were probably introduced by the intruders—notably the two-wheeled horse-drawn war chariot.

Then, as had happened twice already in Egyptian history, a powerful force surged out of the south to restore the direction of that history to Egyptian hands once more.

## THE EGYPTIAN EMPIRE

### The New Kingdom: The Turn toward Empire

The spearhead of this northward drive was the princely house of Thebes and its current head, Ahmose I, founder of the eighteenth and most powerful of Egyptian dynasties. His father and his brother had rallied noble opposition to the Hyksos before him. Around 1550 B.C.E., Ahmose led an army up the Nile, mastered the delta, captured the Hyksos capital, and harried the foreigner out of the land. He even pursued the Hyksos into Palestine, where they were conspiring with local chieftains for help, and destroyed their base there.

Returning to Egypt, the liberator crushed rebellions by some of the nobility and the Nubian princes who had collaborated with the Hyksos. He heaped the loot of all his victories at the feet of Amon, the sun god of Thebes. The priesthood of Amon thus became the most powerful in Egypt, and Thebes the new capital.

Thebes and the Theban princes were now at the head of an Egypt cleansed of foreign power. Egyptians had also had a taste of foreign conquest themselves, and of the loot and tribute that flowed from it. It was a heady experience, and it was to sweep Egypt into its last great age, the *New Kingdom* and the *Empire* (1550–1100 B.C.E.), when for four centuries Egyptian power would dominate the civilized peoples of the ancient Near East.

### Queen Hatshepsut and Thutmose the Conqueror

The kings and queens of the New Kingdom seem to stand out in bold relief against the background of the centuries. These rulers of the last half of the second millennium B.C.E. were shapers of the history of their times. They also vividly illustrate those times, in all their strange ambitions and exotic grandeur. It will therefore be in order to slow the pace now and look into a royal lifetime or two as it was lived thirty-five hundred years ago.

Lying across the river from Thebes, the mortuary temple of Pharaoh Hatshepsut (ca. 1490–1468 B.C.E.)—wide and many-pillared, the cliffs of Deir el-Bahari looming dramatically behind it—is one of the most splendid sights in Egypt. And Hatshepsut was unique among pharaohs. She was a woman.

There were other powerful queens in Egypt, especially during the eighteenth dynasty. But Hatshepsut governed the land, not as pharaoh's wife, but as sole ruler.

The daughter of one pharaoh and the widow of another, she began her reign as regent for the male heir to the throne. Soon, however, she went beyond this quite legal role. Unprecedentedly, she declared herself the child of Re and the god's designated ruler, had herself crowned with the double crown, and seated herself on the golden throne of the pharaohs.

Hatshepsut's most lifelike surviving statue shows an attractive, slightly built woman wearing the clothing and headdress of the king of Upper and Lower Egypt. She is known to have surrounded herself with brilliant and ambitious advisors, and to have lavished wealth on the powerful priesthood of Amon at Thebes. She trumpeted her deeds from temple wall and obelisk in true pharaonic fashion. It was a bravura performance, and we would like to know more about it.

The reign of Hatshepsut, however, is more than a startling historical anomaly. It illustrates a crucial aspect of New Kingdom history: the commercial development and widespread prosperity that made this one of the most pleasant times in Egypt's long history.

Under Hatshepsut, as under other pharaohs, high-prowed "Byblos travelers" plowed the gentle swells of the Mediterranean north to the cities of Phoenicia and beyond, while tinkling Egyptian caravans followed the great military roads north and east to Mesopotamia. Nubia and Sinai poured their copper and gold into the coffers of Egypt. Hatshepsut's most renowned commercial venture, however, was the expedition she dispatched down the Red Sea to the Terraces of Incense, the legendary land of Punt, where the natives had beards like Egyptian gods and lived in grass houses built on pilings. The Egyptian fleet returned laden with ebony and ivory, perfumes and spices, apes, monkeys, leopard skins, slaves, and thirty-one live myrrh trees, which were ceremoniously replanted in front of the queen's temple at Deir el-Bahari.

She was a great ruler. But greatness sometimes kindles greatness in its rivals, and Hatshepsut had a great rival indeed. Prince Thutmose, the royal heir she had supplanted, grew into a restless young man. He was a skilled archer and charioteer, the darling of the militaristic elements among the aristocracy who longed for a more aggressive foreign policy. Thutmose himself seems to have chafed in his powerful aunt's leading strings, and to have resented the ambitious "new men" with whom she filled her court.

And then one year, as our meager records run, the young man had become Pharaoh Thutmose III, the new king of the two lands, and was preparing his chariots for war. Hatshepsut simply disappears from the records, and presumably from this world. It has been suggested—though there is no firm evidence—that the great queen did not "go gently into that good night."

Thutmose III (ca. 1468–1436 B.C.E.) the "Napoleon of Egypt," embodied another and even more typical aspect of the history of the imperial New Kingdom: the unending military campaigns that fill the annals of the epoch. Thutmose himself fought seventeen campaigns, and he did more than anyone else to establish the bounds and form of Egypt's New Kingdom empire. From his time on, the pharaoh as god was complemented, if not replaced, by the pharaoh as hero and empire builder in the minds of the Egyptians.

Thutmose III was a short, thick-chested, bull-necked man with a large nose and immense physical strength and courage. His famous victories—the siege of Megiddo, the battle of Kadesh, the crossing of the Euphrates into the lands of the Mitanni—and the defeated princes who groveled in the dust before him to "beg breath for their nostrils" are long forgotten. But he did construct a genuine empire for Egypt that stretched over much of the ancient Fertile Crescent, from the Euphrates to the fourth cataract of the Nile. "I let you trample down the far corners of the lands," chanted the great god Amon on the granite of Karnak, "the circle of the ocean was caught in your fist."[4]

There was more to it, of course, than the favor of the gods. The soldiers of Thutmose III, battle-hardened veterans after a few campaigns, were equipped with the latest swords, bows, and armor of the late Bronze Age and led by the light, beautifully constructed chariots that

---

[4]George Steindorff and Keith C. Seele, *When Egypt Ruled the East* (Chicago: University of Chicago Press, 1957), p. 55; Pierre Montet, *Lives of the Pharaohs* (Cleveland, Ohio: World, 1968), p. 102.

the Hyksos had bequeathed to Egypt. Thutmose carefully established garrison towns, local governors, and a sophisticated system of puppet kings to control what he had conquered.

Thutmose III raised obelisks as far south as the fourth cataract to thunder his imperial greatness to the world. They still stand today—in Rome, Istanbul, London, and New York's Central Park—loot for later empires larger by far than his.

## Akhenaton, the Heretic Pharaoh

Perhaps the most fascinating of all the New Kingdom pharaohs was Akhenaton (ca. 1364–1347 B.C.E.), described by later scholars as the heretic pharaoh, a religious visionary, or the doom of his dynasty. Akhenaton was in fact everything to intrigue the historian—and the romancer. He was abnormally ugly, but he had a beautiful wife, the swan-necked Nefertiti. He loved his family and his own version of religious truth. His unique contribution to Egyptian history consisted in his effort to impose monotheism upon the people of the Nile valley thirteen and a half centuries before Christ.

The son of one of the later pharaohs of the famous eighteenth dynasty, the prince apparently became fascinated in his youth with one of the smaller solar cults, the worship of Aton, the sun disk itself. This fascination led the grown man to change his own name from Amenhotep IV (Amon Is Satisfied) to Akhenaton (Spirit of Aton). It drove him to move the capital of Egypt from Thebes, the stronghold of the priesthood of Amon, to a new city

The heretic pharaoh Akhenaton, prophet of a lost religion. From the grotesquely exaggerated features and the encumbering royal regalia, an intensely human face looks out upon the world. (Hirmer Fotoarchiv)

that he reared in the wilderness halfway between Thebes and Memphis, a city he christened Akhetaton ("Horizon of Aton"). His zealous faith, finally, apparently led him to launch a campaign to destroy all the other cults and replace them with the worship of the one true god, Aton the sun disk, throughout Egypt.

In this fantastic venture, Akhenaton shook up Egypt as it had not been shaken since the days of the Hyksos. The great Aton was represented not in human form, like the other gods, but simply by the solar disk. Rays spread down from it, and at the ends of the rays there were hands. Temples of Aton were built without roofs, so that the worshiper might commune directly with the god and feel in return the light and heat of the great creative force sailing majestically through the sky above. An Atonist hymn sometimes attributed to Akhenaton himself declares the glory of the one god, "beautiful, great, dazzling, and exalted over every land."[5]

The new city dedicated to the one god rose in a few years beneath the cliffs along the river near the present-day village of El-Amarna—hence the label Amarna Period for the whole unlikely adventure. Temples and palaces, fine homes for high officials, pleasure gardens and lovely courtyards grew up at the new cult center. Akhenaton may have been a fanatic, but there is an idyllic quality to those years at Horizon of Aton, cut off from the world and the gathering storm, that can scarcely fail to charm.

But it was not possible to transform the faiths of two thousand years in a single generation, and it took no more than the premature death of the pharaoh to destroy his new religion. The authority of the old cults was restored soon after Akhenaton's passing. Horizon of Aton was abandoned to the lizard and the jackal, and Akhenaton's very name was chiseled from the monuments and obliterated from the king list, as though he had never been. His youthful heir, Tutankhamun, returned to the faith of his ancestors and became a worshiper of Amon.

## Final Glories and a Long Decline

Egypt had powerful pharaohs and pleasant times to come. But the empire grew harder to hold as its enemies grew more numerous and powerful. Despite intermittent high points, then, the last centuries of ancient Egypt are a story of long decline.

Pharaohs like Ramses II fought the Hittites to a standstill and watched the short-lived Hittite Empire crumble while life went on along the Nile. They repelled the attacks of the Sea People (the biblical Philistines), the greatest plague to descend upon the delta since the Hyksos. They built great temples and huge statues of themselves, and perhaps made Egyptians of the twelfth century B.C.E. think that the eternal life of Egypt would never end.

Royal women and women of the priestly classes achieved great wealth and power during this last millenium of Egyptian history. Pharaoh's daughters became chief priests of Amon at Karnak and de facto rulers of Upper Egypt. Their wealth and the battalions of administrators who served under them were proverbial.

But weak kings, overmighty priests, and continuing waves of invaders undermined the state. During the thousand years that followed the end of the New Kingdom in the eleventh century, Theban priests, Libyan mercenaries, Nubian kings, Assyrians, Persians, Macedonians, and Romans ruled Egypt in turn. The notorious Cleopatra, who welcomed Julius Caesar to Egypt, was as much Macedonian as she was Egyptian, and the most famous Egyptian city of her day was the thoroughly hellenized metropolis of Alexandria. The Egypt of the Pyramid Age and the Empire had long since passed into history.

---

[5]Steindorff and Seele, *When Egypt Ruled the East*, p. 214.

### Rich and Poor, Men and Women

The lives of ancient Egyptians, like those of many other peoples, depended very largely on their place in the social hierarchy. We have many pictures of Egyptian *fellahin* hard at work in the fields, following a light plow or scattering seed in the furrows, harvesting wheat and barley, herding cattle in the delta, or fishing in the Nile. There was steady work also on the dikes and channels and basins that controlled the river, as well as compulsory labor on the tombs, temples, palaces, and public building projects of the pharaohs. But these projects depended for their success more on plenty of time and careful planning than on the flogged and sweated labor of the Hollywood epics. What records we have indicate a less than oner-ous work schedule: two four-hour work stints daily with a long noon siesta in between.

The condition of women was equally ambiguous among the Egyptians. Poor women worked as hard as their husbands, grinding grain at home and gleaning in the fields, with minimal time off to bear children. On the other hand, in contrast with many societies, Egyptians seem to have welcomed daughters as enthusiastically as they did sons.

The Greek historian Herodotus was struck by the freedom of Egyptian women to work and move freely in society. "The Egyptians," he wrote, "in their manners and cus-toms, seem to have reversed the ordinary practices of mankind. For instance, women at-tend market and are employed in trade, while men stay at home and do the weaving."[6] A woman was allowed to go into business for herself if she could demonstrate that she had had three children and could read and write. Among the professions filled by women were midwifery, mourning, dancing, music, some important priesthoods and—Herodotus to the contrary—weaving. The women of the royal harem in fact ran the state cloth manufac-tures and oversaw women weavers in the temples. Women are also recorded as running wig shops, dining halls, and other establishments.

As noted previously, Egypt was a matrilineal society from top to bottom. All property was inherited in the female line. Even pharaoh frequently had to marry a sister in order to be sure of the crown. The leverage this gave the Egyptian woman must have been considerable.

The pictures we have of Egyptians at feasts seem to reveal a convivial people. They sat on reed mats with finger bowls and jars of wine at hand, while servants bore the festival meats around. The company was cheerfully mixed, men and women sitting easily together, crowned alike with garlands and entertained by the music of lutes and tambourines.

## THE WISDOM OF THE FIRST CIVILIZATIONS

### Writing, Learning, and Literature

Writing is one of the most important of the skills that would distinguish the peoples within the walls from many of their neighbors. Both the Egyptians and the Mesopotamian peoples developed forms of writing, though their approaches differed significantly from one another.

The true inventors of writing were probably the nameless precursors of the Sumerians in the marshy delta of the two rivers. Sometime during the later fourth millennium B.C.E., however, Sumerian scribes were making lists of goods and produce, flocks and harvested grain. They did so by scratching crude *pictograms* (pictorial representations) of the items in question on a small clay tablet with a reed stylus. The strokes of the triangular reed came to

---

[6]B. Waterson, *Women in Ancient Egypt* (New York: St. Martin's Press, 1991), p. 25.

be known as *cuneiform* (wedge-shaped) script. Over the centuries these signs began to be used simply to represent the *sound* of the names of the original articles. Several of these sound-symbols or *phonograms,* could then be combined to represent other words. The result was an exceedingly complicated system of writing that combined pictograms and phonograms and required a long course of specialized training in the scribal schools.

Only professional scribes could read in ancient Mesopotamia, and the only "libraries"—collections of classic texts—were in the scribal schools and perhaps the temples. Such science and philosophy as there was is frequently closer to folk sayings and fortune-telling than to the complex systematic thought of later ages. Nevertheless, the Mesopotamians left some mathematical insights and astronomical observations that still impress us. They based their number system on six rather than on ten; to them we owe the sixty-minute hour and the division of the circle into 360 degrees. The Babylonians charted the movements of the planets and predicted eclipses of the sun and the moon. Their knowledge of the night skies was so celebrated, in fact, that the word *Chaldean* became a synonym for *astronomer* in the ancient world.

The most famous literary product of ancient Mesopotamia is the *Epic of Gilgamesh,* the half-legendary Sumerian king who is sometimes called the Mesopotamian Hercules. The surviving fragments of this long poem tell how Gilgamesh and his friend Enkiddu, the wild man of the desert, killed the monster Huwawa and the Wild Bull of Heaven; how Gilgamesh scorned the advances of the goddess Ishtar; how he lost the faithful Enkiddu; and how he set out on his last and greatest adventure, the search for eternal life. His dreamlike journey to the twilight realm of Utnapishtim, sole survivor of the great flood that once destroyed humankind, climaxes with his discovery—and loss—of the plant that confers everlasting life, and with his final realization that death is the appointed end of every human life—even the life of a hero.

Among the Egyptians, as among the Mesopotamians, the discovery of the art of writing began quite literally as picture writing, as cuneiform had. But whereas the Mesopotamians soon reduced their little pictures to a collection of quick strokes of the stylus, the official Egyptian hieroglyphic writing never completely abandoned the pictographic element. In the hands of conservative Egyptians literacy remained to a considerable degree "picture writing" from one end of Egyptian history to the other.

Carved on stone monuments, this ancient priestly and official writing looked extremely impressive. But it proved a bit cumbersome for busy scribes scrawling with reed pens on papyrus, the paper Egyptians made from the pith of the papyrus stem found along the Nile. As a working script, therefore, hieroglyphic writing evolved over centuries into a cursive script called *hieratic,* which looked more like modern Arabic than like pictograms.

Egyptian observation of nature could be remarkably precise also. This was certainly the case in astronomy, one of the fields of scientific inquiry in which they were most successful. They divided the night sky into separate constellations, compiled detailed records of the nightly positions of some heavenly bodies, and constructed on this basis a calendar that is remarkably close to the solar one in use today. They used mathematics in a practical way as well, to survey and reestablish boundary lines after the annual inundation had washed out line markers up and down the Nile. They used measurement and calculation for architecture and engineering, for predicting harvests and totaling royal tax receipts.

Egyptian medicine, which enjoyed great renown among other ancient peoples, also operated on the basis of experience and rules of thumb—plus a sizable dollop of magic. Nevertheless, Egyptian doctors did show genuine clinical concern with symptoms, diagnosis, and treatment. And some of the prescribed remedies include drugs, such as castor oil, that may even have done the patient some good.

Over the thirty-odd centuries of ancient Egypt, writing became a craft and a career ladder for government or temple scribes, a device for communicating at a distance and for keeping records. Like most early written languages, however, it was not originally intended as an instrument for literary expression.

Egyptian literature includes hymns such as Akhenaton's song of praise to the sun and epic accounts of the victories of Thutmose III, which have the qualities of religious and patriotic literature from many times and lands. We have poetry too, especially from the New Kingdom, sad poems on the brevity of human life and happy poems of love. Perhaps the most impressive literary products of ancient Egypt, however, were to be found in the philosophical "wisdom literature" and the lively prose of Egyptian stories and tales.

Wisdom literature, common throughout the ancient Near East, includes collections of proverbs like those attributed to Solomon in the Old Testament. Here they are attributed to sages and pharaohs. These "instructions" urge youth to obey and respect their elders and betters and to sing the praises of old ways and ancient institutions.

If the Egyptians loved anything more than a good maxim for life, it was a good story. The most famous tale by far is the Middle Kingdom *Story of Sinuhe,* a first-person account of a noble Egyptian who, having been exiled from his native land, fights his way to fame and fortune among the bedouin of Syria. Yet Sinuhe's greatest joy—and no doubt the profoundest satisfaction of his readers—comes when he is summoned home to Egypt in his declining years by pharaoh himself. Egyptians loved to hear about wanderings in distant lands, but in the end they couldn't imagine anyone being happy far from the sound of the wind in the reeds along the Nile.

## The Arts: Gold and Lapis Lazuli, Obelisks and Pyramids

The Mesopotamian palaces and temples that have been excavated from the mounded earth have a simplicity of design and detail that could have produced an effect of monumental grandeur above the arid plain. Palaces, like private homes, were constructed around a series of courtyards. Monumental gateways, square towers, and crenellated walls provided some exterior variety, and glazed tile and wall paintings of animals and men enlivened cool, dim interiors. In Babylonian and Assyrian times, sculptured columns, stone reliefs on walls, and huge human-headed bulls and other creatures added an air of imperial magnificence to the Mesopotamian palace.

The temple, however, was the Mesopotamian city's dominant feature. The most striking element in the temple complex was the pyramidal terraced tower, or ziggurat. Wide stairways, much like those of the later pyramid temples of the Mayans and the Aztecs, led to the flat top of the ziggurat, where a special shrine to the god or goddess stood. A simple, open structure, it was nonetheless god's house to the ancient Mesopotamians.

The sculpture of ancient Mesopotamia does not catch the modern imagination as immediately as that of some other cultures. Yet there is a convincing vitality in the smooth round face of a five-thousand-year-old Sumerian woman, bright-eyed and smiling still, her simple gown cut to leave the right arm and shoulder free for work. A rare wall painting of Assyrian officials brings these civilized savages to life, with their looped gold earrings, their black hair and beards oiled and dressed in ringlets. There is even a tense realism in the famous Lion Hunt Frieze: the horse of Assurbanipal charging with mouth open and tendons taut, and the dying lioness, arrows buried half their length in its flanks, dragging paralyzed hindquarters behind it, yet rearing up to roar in final defiance at the king of kings.

The cylinder seal, the most distinctive of Mesopotamian art forms, was carved in intaglio on a small stone cylinder, then rolled over soft clay to leave a unique identifying mark on anything from a merchant's goods to a private letter. On these carved seals, animals, gods, and men mingle freely with symbolic objects, the owner's name in cuneiform script, and other sculptured space fillers. The endless ingenuity of the carvers as they fill these tiny friezes with gracefully balanced figures rearing up, wrestling, sometimes seeming almost to dance across the clay, can stir the sense of beauty in the observer still.

The same may be said of the gold of Ur. A treasure trove of necklaces, helmets, cups, and other artifacts exhumed from royal tombs, they are all as directly accessible to us in their intricate beauty as anything from Cartier's or Tiffany's. The smooth golden sheen of a bull's head or a dagger blade plays beautifully against the beard or the hilt, made of the blue stone called lapis lazuli of which Mesopotamians were so fond. The monumental power of the vastly winged, human-headed bulls that once guarded the palace of Khorasabad still stops museum visitors in their tracks and draws their eyes inevitably upward.

The Egyptians were even greater builders than the Mesopotamian peoples—and they built in stone.

It is the immense age and the colossal size of the Old Kingdom pyramids that have awed posterity. The forty-five hundred years and the two and half million cubic yards of solid stone in the great pyramid of Khufu add up to one of the most awesome of human engineering feats. Many of the gigantic masonry blocks had to be quarried at Aswan, five hundred miles up the Nile, floated down the river, and moved by sledge, levers, ropes, and straining human muscle across the desert and up immense temporary earthen ramps to their places in the rising structure. And all this without benefit of the wheel!

Obelisks were another Egyptian architectural specialty. These tall, thinly tapering stone spires cut in a single block sometimes stood almost a hundred feet high. Their hieroglyphic inscriptions described the achievements of the pharaohs who erected them, as the gold that gilded their pointed tips proclaimed the glory of Hatshepsut or Thutmose III.

Temples to the gods also challenged the Egyptians to build greatly. Hordes of tourists gape daily at the eighty-foot columns at Karnak, raised by the celebrated New Kingdom warrior Ramses II, elaborately carved with hieroglyphics, and crowned with the characteristic papyrus-bud capitals of ancient Egypt. The facade of the temple at Abu Simbel, carved out of the living rock of the cliffs along the Nile, was flanked by four sixty-five-foot-tall statues of the powerful New Kingdom pharaoh Ramses seated on his throne.

The gold of King Tut's tomb—the famous tomb of Tutankhamun, discovered practically intact in 1922—has shown us how dazzling the luxury art of the Egyptians could be. The golden sarcophagus of King Tut has symbolized the splendor of the pharaohs to generations of museum goers, though Tutankhamun himself, Akhenaton's unhappy successor, was a pharaoh of no particular distinction.

The conservative genius of the Egyptians is nowhere better revealed than in their representations of the human figure in paint and stone. In bas-relief sculpture and wall painting, the famous Egyptian "canon" included such exotic requirements as representing the head and limbs in profile while showing the eyes, shoulders, and torso in a full-face view. The pharaoh, of course, was always to be painted or sculpted several times the size of his servants, soldiers, or defeated foes.

The softer, more human style of the Amarna period, which was centered in Akhenaton's new city dedicated to Aton, depicted that unfortunate pharaoh not as the wide-shouldered, lean-hipped superman of yore but as the pot-bellied, long-headed, downright ugly figure he apparently was. The Amarna style also gave us the long-necked beauty of his queen, Nefertiti, much as she must have been in life, and painted their small daughters playing in their gardens, large-eyed and oddly sweet despite their shaved heads and thin, gracefully posed limbs.

## Polytheistic Religions

The sources of religion have been sought in many places. Among them surely are the need our ancestors felt for supernatural help to ensure a supply of game, growing herds, rich harvest. Other sources no doubt include the desire of people for divine support when they deal with life transitions such as birth, initiation, and death and with such special afflictions as war, pestilence, famine, and oppression.

But a developed religion seems to require more than these. It requires an encounter with the numinous. The word comes from the Latin *numen,* meaning divine power. A numinous experience is defined by students of the history and nature of religion as a sense of the presence of something "wholly other," something totally different in kind from all the material realities of everyday living. One may have a sudden sense of the presence of divine power in nature itself—in running water, the whispering leaves of a giant tree, the knee-buckling immensity of the sky above. It may come in the lifting of the sun's disk above the horizon, in a circle of standing stones, in a carven idol, in an icon or a crucifix.

At this deepest level of experience, the origin of all religious belief is the same. As far as we can tell, the meditating Hindu, the Muslim Sufi, and the Christian saint all experience much the same thing at this transcendent moment: In their own minds, at least, they are all in the presence of the Lord.

To express the inexpressible, religious leaders have had to turn to metaphor. They have tried to say what that awesome encounter with the numinous was *like* in the everyday material world the prophet and his people all know. Inevitably, however, this expedient has brought religious discourse from the level of the universal down to the historically conditioned realities of a particular time and place. God is white and male in a white man's world; Shiva is a high-caste Indian; the sun god rides across the sky in a chariot in ancient Greece and sails down a celestial Nile in the mind of the Egyptian.

The peoples of ancient Sumeria, Babylonia, and Assyria, like most peoples in most times and places, were believers in polytheism—the existence of many gods and goddesses. They felt themselves to be surrounded by spiritual presences. There were gods and goddesses associated with practically everything—gods of earth and sky, storm and bountiful harvest, brick mold and irrigation ditch. Most of these divinities were thoroughly anthropomorphic; they were depicted in sculpture as awesome figures with the long hair and square-cut beards of many Mesopotamian peoples and with the saucer-sized eyes that make them instantly recognizable in any museum.

In early Sumer the chief divinities in the numerous pantheon included Anu, the lord of heaven; Enlil, the water god; the earth mother, Ninhursag; the gods of the sun and moon, Utu and Sin; and the powerful goddess of love, Ishtar. Other leading divinities emerged over the centuries, notably Marduk, the chief god of imperial Babylon, and Assur, the sun god of the Assyrians.

Around these many divinities elaborate rites grew up. The great gods were believed to dwell within the ritually crafted and consecrated cult statues that the priests tended so

Isis on the left and Osiris on the right watch the weighing of a princess's heart against the symbol of Ma'at. This picture of a judgment in the underworld is from a New Kingdom papyrus copy of the Book of the Dead that was buried with a royal mummy. (Funerary Papyrus of the Princess Entiuny [ca. 1025 B.C.E.]. From the tomb of Queen Meryet-Amun at Deir el-Bahari, Thebes. The Metropolitan Museum of Art, Museum Excavations, 1928–1929, and Rogers Fund, 1930)

carefully in the temples. Around these figures a year-round succession of ceremonies, processions, sacred drama and other liturgical observances developed. Mythologies, sacred texts, and theological literature added to the richness of Mesopotamian religion.

There were also subtle changes in the religious conceptions held by the Mesopotamians over the three thousand years of their history. In the earliest times, gods and goddesses were conceived of as "indwelling wills and powers," divine presences *within* the natural forces, crops, and flocks necessary for human survival.[7] These early divinities embodied the mysterious power that made the barley grow or the palm produce plentiful clusters of dates.

By the time of Sargon of Akkad, however, a political metaphor is increasingly used to describe the reality of the divine. Gods are *rulers* of humanity. They protect the citizens of a particular city-state, or they lead the people to imperial conquest of their neighbors. And as the monarchy grew among the Mesopotamians, so a single god came to be honored as the king of the divine assembly, just as the *ensi* governed on earth.

During the last Mesopotamian centuries, divinities seemed more and more like parents. The gods became as concerned about the behavior and the well-being of their worshipers as parents are for their children. In hard times, it was comforting to know that higher powers cared.

Toward the very last, in the days of the Assyrian terror and of unchecked barbarian incursions, religion seems to have degenerated into the rankest superstition. There was "a

---

[7]Thorkild Jacobsen, *The Treasures of Darkness: A History of Mesopotamian Religion* (New Haven, Conn.: Yale University Press, 1976), p. 21.

coarsening and barbarization of the idea of divinity . . . witchcraft and sorcery were sus- pected everywhere; demons and evil spirits threatened unceasingly."[8] In the worst of times, perhaps, it was hard to believe that there *were* any higher powers.

The Egyptians had the reputation of being the most religious and other-worldly of peoples. It is easy for moderns to imagine the Egyptians as a darkly superstitious race who worshiped monstrous animal-headed gods and were obsessed with mummies and tombs, with death and what comes after it. In fact, as we have seen, most Egyptians seem to have been thoroughly materialistic about most things, to have loved gardens and chil- dren and the hot African sun. But like their Near Eastern neighbors, they did worship many gods, some of whom retained more than a trace of their animal origins. And of all the earlier civilizations, the Egyptians seem to have been the most concerned with the uni- versal fact of death and the dream of life eternal.

More than two thousand gods were worshiped by the people who lived along the Nile. The chief of these was always a god of the sun—first Re, the sun god of Memphis, later Amon of Thebes. There were other widely worshiped divinities, including Horus the sky god, represented as a falcon; Thoth the ibis-headed god of wisdom and of scribes; Hathor the cow, the Egyptian goddess of beauty; and Anubis the jackal-headed god of the tomb.

## The Quest for Immortality

The most popular of Egyptian myths—particularly from the Middle Kingdom onward— was the sacred story of Isis the merciful and her husband Osiris, the god who rose from the dead. Many an Egyptian mother told her children how Osiris, son of the sky and the earth, married his sister Isis and ruled over all the gods, until their jealous brother Set murdered Osiris, tore him to pieces, and scattered the dismembered divinity up and down the land. But the story had a happy ending. Before mother put out the lamp she would tell how Isis, grieving but determined, hunted over the world to recover her husband's body and bring it back to life, perhaps with a touch of the *ankh,* the looped cross that Egyptian mothers wore as amulets round their necks. Osiris lived still, as king of the underworld, with the loyal and compassionate Isis at his right hand. Egyptians fully expected to meet the divine pair when they too passed to the land of silence.

Mummification was a fine art in ancient Egypt. The corpse was washed with expen- sive oils, debrained through the nostrils, eviscerated through an incision in the abdomen, and dried for some weeks in a packing of natron, a crystalline substance with a special ca- pacity to absorb moisture. It was then massaged and washed again, stuffed with amulets, more natron, and sometimes sand, sawdust, or other filling, wrapped carefully in endless strips of white linen, and returned at last to the mourning relatives for burial.

The spiritual parts, meanwhile, were believed to be undergoing their own transition from this life to the next.

To guide the soul through the underworld to its final judgment, the survivors inserted a collection of spells and ritual responses in the sarcophagus before interment. This so-called *Book of the Dead* depicts many aspects of the afterlife, climaxing in the final weighing of the soul against the principle of righteousness, *Ma'at.* This last judgment took place in the Hall of the Double Law under the eyes of twelve sceptered gods. The ape of Thoth crouched on the balance beam, jackal-headed Anubis adjusted the scale, and the hideous Devourer of

---

[8]Ibid.

the Dead crouched below, crocodile jaws agape for the soul found wanting. The soul that had not sinned against the gods, however, became "an Osiris," was led into the presence of the great king of the underworld, and was received into the company of the immortals.

## SUMMARY

Civilization was born fifty-five centuries ago around the eastern end of the Mediterranean Sea, in Mesopotamia and Egypt. It produced a growing network of cities in the Near East, the first real nation in Egypt, a number of small empires, and two of history's most impressive cultures.

Mesopotamia—present-day Iraq—was the site of the first urban imperial culture. Mesopotamian peoples built elaborate irrigation works and walled cities in the valley of the Tigris and Euphrates rivers. They also developed the city-state, a polity centered on the new urban complex but including the hinterland of villages around it. These city-states were dominated by priests in early times, later by kings.

Though normally divided into separate city-states, ancient Mesopotamia also produced several early empires. The earliest such empire was that of the Sumerian ruler Sargon of Akkad in the twenty-third century B.C.E. The most famous was that of Hammurabi the Lawgiver of Babylon, founder of the Old Babylonian Empire in the eighteenth and seventeenth centuries B.C.E. The most oppressive was the Assyrian Empire (eighth and seventh centuries); the most admired in antiquity was the short-lived new Babylonian Empire of Nebuchadnezzar in the sixth century.

Egyptian civilization developed along the fertile banks of the Nile. Separate kingdoms first took shape in Upper and Lower Egypt but were unified by the first pharaohs around 3000 B.C.E. The Old Kingdom, or Pyramid Age (twenty-seventh to twenty-second centuries B.C.E.), was an extremely stable, strongly conservative society held together by pharaohs who were believed to be divine and by a busy scribal bureaucracy. The Middle Kingdom that followed (twentieth to eighteenth centuries B.C.E.) witnessed a transition to a more dynamic culture that interacted commercially and militarily with the rest of the Middle East.

The New Kingdom (sixteenth to twelfth centuries B.C.E.) saw the pharaohs of the powerful eighteenth dynasty building a large and impressive Egyptian Empire. Under Hatshepsut, the only female pharaoh, Egypt grew rich in trade. The successful general Thutmose III and his successors conquered most of the crescent from Nubia around through Palestine to Mesopotamia. And Pharaoh Akhenaton, a religious zealot, attempted to impose a monotheistic religion on the nation, though his unique cult only lasted Akhenaton's lifetime.

From about 1100 B.C.E. on, Egypt underwent a long decline. During this period the ancient land was frequently ruled by foreigners, and after the first century B.C.E. it disappeared into the vastly larger empire of the Romans.

Both Egypt and Mesopotamia were rooted in the polytheistic religion most common everywhere in the ancient world. Mesopotamians developed the first writing, cuneiform, and were skilled at astronomy and mathematics. They built truncated pyramidal temples called ziggurats and carved stone cylinder seals with which they left their mark on clay.

The Egyptians produced the best-known early form of writing, the system of pictograms known as hieroglyphics. They erected massive pillared temples to their animal-headed gods, proclaimed their pharaohs' achievements on gold-tipped obelisks, and left as their most famous monuments the huge pyramid tombs of the Old Kingdom.

# SUGGESTED READING

Bottéro, J. *Religion in Ancient Mesopotamia.* trans. T. L. Fagan. Chicago: University of Chicago Press, 2001. Scholarly study of early polytheism.

Clayton, P. A. *Chronicle of the Pharaohs.* New York: Thames and Hudson, 1994. Narrative of reigns and dynasties.

Crawford, H. E. W. *Sumer and the Sumerians.* New York: Cambridge University Press, 1991. Good overview, with helpful illustrations.

Diakonoff, H. E. W., ed. *Early Antiquity.* Chicago: University of Chicago Press, 1991. Essays on early civilizations from Sumer to China.

Diop, C. A. *The African Origin of Civilization: Myth or Reality?* trans. Mercer Cook. New York: Lawrence Hill, 1974. Provocative study, including discussion of the influence of other African cultures on Egyptian civilization. More recent is M. Bernal's widely discussed multivolume study, *Black Athena: The Afroasiatic Roots of Classical Civilization* (New Brunswick, N.J.: Rutgers University Press, 1987–1991), which also emphasizes the African roots of Egyptian civilization.

El Mahdy, C. *The World of the Pharaohs.* New York: Thames and Hudson, 1990. Illustrated guide to ancient Egypt.

Kubba, S. A. A. *Mesopotamian Architecture and Town Planning.* Oxford: B. A. R., 1987. Agricultural villages evolve toward cities.

Lepre, J. P. *The Egyptian Pyramids.* Jefferson, N.C.: McFarland, 1990. Solid introduction to the tombs of the pharaohs. See also A. R. David, *The Pyramid Builders of Ancient Egypt* (London: Routledge and Kegan Paul, 1986), which focuses on "pharaoh's workforce," the people who physically built these monuments.

Moorey, P. R. S. *Ancient Mesopotamian Materials and Industries.* New York: Clarendon Press, 1994. Scholarly examination of archaeological evidence.

Potts, D. T. *Mesopotamian Civilization: The Material Foundation.* Ithaca, N.Y.: Comell University Press, 1997. Valuable overview of material culture, drawing also on the cuneiform record.

Redford, D. B. *Egypt, Canaan, and Israel in Ancient Times.* Princeton, N.J.: Princeton University Press, 1992. A scholarly, sometimes provocative study. For an introduction to disputes over the chronology of the ancient history of the region, see P. James, *Centuries of Darkness: A Challenge to the Conventional Chronology of Old World Archaeology* (New Brunswick, N.J.: Rutgers University Press, 1993).

Redman, C. W. *Human Impact on Ancient Environments.* Phoenix: University of Arizona Press, 1999. Examines the ways in which ancient peoples impacted the world they lived in.

Robins, G. *The Art of Ancient Egypt.* Cambridge, Mass.: Harvard University Press, 1997. Brief but scholarly overview.

———. *Women in Ancient Egypt.* Cambridge, Mass.: Harvard University Press, 1993. Scholarly discussion illustrated by well-chosen art. A good introduction to the subject is B. Waterson, *Women in Ancient Egypt* (New York: St. Martin's Press. 1991).

Saggs, H. W. F. *Babylonians.* Norman: University of Oklahoma Press, 1995. Society in the ancient Mesopotamian city-state.

Silver, M. *Economic Structures in the Ancient Near East.* Totowa, N.J.: Barnes & Noble, 1985. Uses modern economic theory applied to Mesopotamian clay tablets to explain the economic organization of the region.

Simpson, W. K., ed. *The Literature of Ancient Egypt: An Anthology of Stories, Instructions, and Poetry.* Includes examples of all of the literary forms.

Spenser, A. J. *The Rise of Civilization in the Nile Valley.* London: British Museum Press, 1993.

Taylor, J. H. *Death and the Afterlife in Ancient Egypt.* Chicago: University of Chicago Press, 2001. Explorations of immortality as this ancient African people understood it.

Walker, C. B. F. *Reading the Past: Writing from Cuneiform to the Alphabet.* London: British Museum, 1990. Stimulating introduction to early forms of writing.

# CHAPTER 3

# PROPHETS AND PHILOSOPHERS
## The Hebrews and the Greeks

## (1500–200 B.C.E.)

# A Glance Ahead: Small Peoples with Large Ideas

While Mesopotamian peoples raised their walled cities and Egyptians built mightily along the Nile, others also brought remarkable contributions to the new style of life called civilization. Among these, two other peoples from the eastern end of the Mediterranean, the Hebrews and the Greeks, generated a dazzling range of new ideas. Their religious, moral, philosophic, and artistic insights would provide the intellectual underpinnings for many future societies—including our own.

Neither of these two small peoples, the ancient Greeks and Hebrews, conquered many of their neighbors or built great empires. In time, both were scattered across the world. Greek ships still plow the seas and oceans of the globe, while descendants of the ancient Hebrews have settled into many lands down the centuries. But in the *Torah* and the rest of the *Old Testament,* in the philosophy of Plato and Aristotle and the art of ancient Greece, they have left intellectual monuments every bit as imposing as the pyramids of Egypt or the walls of Babylon.

## Turbulent Centuries

### The Near East in Tumult

When civilizations first emerged in Mesopotamia and Egypt in the fourth millennium B.C.E., they were solitary flowers blooming alone in a world of Paleolithic hunter-gatherers, Neolithic villages, and wandering pastoralists. By the second millennium B.C.E., however, when Hammurabi ruled in Babylon and the powerful twelfth dynasty in Egypt, a number of other islands of civilization had come into existence around the globe. The ships of the Minoans, precursors of the ancient Greeks, were sailing the blue Mediterranean. In northwestern India—Pakistan today—an impressive center of civilized living had emerged around the great cities of Harappa and Mohenjodaro. Still farther to the east, the states of North China were about to be drawn together into a loose-knit Bronze Age civilization dominated by the Shang dynasty. And beyond the wide Atlantic, metals were being worked in Peru.

Civilization had also emerged among other Near Eastern peoples on the frontiers of the Mesopotamian world. The turbulent centuries between 2000 and 1000 B.C.E. were particularly fecund producers of new centers of civilized living. During these centuries, nomadic peoples from the great Eurasian steppes or the deserts of Arabia and North Africa buffeted the city-based cultures of the Near East. In so doing, they helped bring about a fertile mixture of cultures and traditions. They brought skills with them from their earlier wandering lives, and they learned from the more settled peoples whom they frequently conquered.

The invaders thus contributed largely to the emergence of such satellite cultures at the periphery of the cultural zone around Mesopotamia and Egypt as the Hittites and the Phoenicians. And this tumultuous little world at the eastern end of the Mediterranean sea was the world of the ancient Hebrews.

Culturally, this was an immensely productive corner of the globe. From this time and place came such achievements as Hittite ironworking and the Phoenician alphabet. And it was here that the Hebrews developed their astonishing new religious ideas, leading the world definitively beyond polytheism to the worship of one God in the first successful monotheistic religion.

## The Hittites and the Iron Age

The Hittites were Indo-Europeans, speakers of languages ancestral to those of modern India, Iran, and most of Europe. The Hittite subdivision of this great steppe-dwelling people wandered down into Asia Minor, subdued the natives of the hill and mountain country north of Mesopotamia, and evolved a powerful empire in the second millennium B.C.E. For roughly two hundred years, 1400 to 1200 B.C.E. the Hittites ruled the eastern end of the Mediterranean, collected tribute from the Egyptians, and raided Babylon. For several centuries, at least, they were a power to be reckoned with in the Near East.

Like most less developed cultures, the Hittites borrowed heavily from the more complex civilizations with which they came in contact. From the Land of the Two Rivers they carried home such cultural booty as cuneiform writing, Mesopotamian myths, and the concept of a codified system of laws. The charioteers from the steppes retained much of their own culture too, legends and styles of art that looked back to their days as nomads of the great northern grasslands. Hittite religion particularly reminds us that they were a people whose culture had developed on the edge of the civilized world: There is, for instance, evidence of human sacrifice among them.

From the Hittites, however, came one great contribution to the civilization of the ancient Near East: the working of iron.

Bronze, alloyed usually of copper and tin, had been the hard metal since civilization first appeared in Sumeria. Now, in the smithies of Hittite towns and villages and the double-walled mountain capital of Hattusas, brawny Hittite metalworkers discovered that iron ore, more plentiful than bronze, might also be used for hard-edged tools and weapons. The secret, which may have reached the Hittites from their old steppe homeland, involved much pounding of the heated but not melted ore to remove impurities, followed by a sudden quenching in cold water. The result was a sort of semisteel more readily available and cheaper than the alloy of copper and tin on which older, more aristocratic Bronze Age cultures had been built.

Understandably, the Hittites did not distribute the secret of the new metal widely. But when new waves of invaders swept down across Asia Minor and tumbled Hattusas into ruin, skilled ironworkers were widely scattered. The working of iron would have a significant impact on societies all across the Old World. It gave ordinary people weapons to match the bronze of the aristocrats. It also opened up land which could not readily be cultivated with stone, wood, or bronze-edged plows. The Hittites themselves vanished from the historical record until modern archaeologists unearthed their lost civilization. But their technological contribution was so important that some historians still date a new age of world history from the Hittites' twelfth-century prime—the Iron Age.

## The Far-Trading Phoenicians

The Phoenicians were a Semitic-speaking people who settled the harbors and inshore islands along the coast of what is today Lebanon and Syria. They rose to prominence at the end of the second millennium, following the collapse of Hittite power, and flourished from 1100 to 800 B.C.E. They became the most famous traders on the sea before the Greeks and the chief bearers of developed Near Eastern culture to other peoples around the Mediterranean.

Politically, the Phoenicians were city-state dwellers, like the Mesopotamians. Failing to achieve political unity of their own, they were frequently absorbed into the larger polities of such powerful neighbors as the Egyptians, Hittites, and Assyrians. They borrowed Babylonian business methods and weights and measures and used Babylonian astronomy as a navigational aid. Their mythology was replete with Mesopotamian echoes, though their religion harked further back. Like the Hittites, the Phoenicians sometimes sacrificed human beings on the altars of their gods.

In one way, however, the Phoenicians made a major break with the practices of their Near Eastern neighbors. Unable to feed their numbers on the thin strip of mountain-girt coastline they inhabited, they turned gradually from agriculture to manufacturing and above all to trade.

The Phoenicians seem to have turned to profit everything their 120-mile stretch of coastline had to offer. The famous cedars of Lebanon provided them with a valuable early export item. After learning glassmaking from the Mesopotamians, they used a fine local sand to produce glass gewgaws that sold well to simpler folk around the Mediterranean. Even a tiny shellfish called the murex was used to make perhaps the most famous dye of all times, the Tyrean purple that would color the robes of emperors in centuries to come.

The location of the Phoenician cities—on the Mediterranean and astride the main trade route between Mesopotamia and Egypt—encouraged the Phoenicians to become traders as well as handicraft manufacturers. Byblos, Tyre, Sidon, and other cities were famous commercial centers in Old Testament times. The Phoenicians founded colonies on the islands of Cyprus and Sicily and on the coasts of Spain and North Africa. Among these Phoenician colonies was the North African metropolis of Carthage, Rome's great rival in later centuries. Other adventurous Phoenician sailors even passed out of the Mediterranean through the Strait of Gibraltar, the "Pillars of Hercules," beyond which few ancient seamen dared to venture. There is evidence that their little vessels braved the heavier swells and rougher winds of the Atlantic to trade for tin in western Britain.

The Phoenicians were *carriers of culture,* transplanters of ideas, styles, and folkways, rather than cultural originators. Their impact, however, was not small. Their city of Byblos, which became famous for the export of Egyptian papyrus, gave its name to the Greek word for *book*—and our word *Bible.* And whether the Phoenicians developed their own written language or borrowed it from their neighbors, they passed that too on to the Greeks. The twenty-two consonants of the Phoenician alphabet, together with the vowels added by the Greeks, would evolve down the centuries into all the written languages of the Western World.

## The Ancient Hebrews

### The Wandering Years

The Hebrew people of Palestine never produced an empire to rival that of the Hittites, nor did they wander as far as the Phoenicians, at least in ancient times. Yet they too left a great legacy to future ages, a heritage at least as valuable as either iron or the alphabet: monotheistic religion.

At the beginning of the second millennium before Christ, the Hebrews were part of the nomadic population of Semitic-speaking peoples that wandered and settled along the edges of the Arabian Desert, between the developed civilizations of Mesopotamia and Egypt. Abraham, the patriarch of the Hebrew tribes, trudges into history heading west from Ur with his wives and children, servants, shepherds, and flocks around him. The twelve Hebrew tribes apparently settled for a time in Palestine—or Canaan—between the Jordan River and the sea. Some of these, perhaps driven by drought, drifted on southward into Egypt, the great pillar of civilization at the other end of the fertile crescent from Mesopotamia. Oppressed—according to tradition actually enslaved in New Kingdom Egypt—they burst out once more in the thirteenth century B.C.E. to resume their wanderings.

Their liberator, and the leader of the folk migration known in the Bible as the Exodus, was a fiery preacher named Moses. Moses managed to hold his people together for forty years in the scorching deserts of Sinai. To accomplish this feat, he seems to have rallied the Hebrew tribes around a single divine being, Yahweh. By the 1200s B.C.E., then, the Hebrews had become monotheists—believers in one God, sworn to obey the commandments of the divine Lord whose laws Moses had brought down from the mountain to Yahweh's chosen people.

According to tradition, Moses was the author of the *Torah,* also called the *Pentateuch,* the first five books of the Bible. In a gesture known to every Western schoolchild, he is believed to have descended from Mount Sinai with the *Ten Commandments,* binding his people to a high standard of moral conduct, engraved on two stone tablets. Even his death was dramatic, coming within sight of the promised land he was never to enter. Leader, law-giver, and shaper of one of the world's great religions, this liberator of a small Near Eastern people became through the power of the word a world-historical figure.

## The Kingdom of David

The wanderings of this pastoral nomadic people had taken them back to Palestine, which they now saw as the homeland promised to them by Yahweh. A hilly barren land along the Mediterranean Sea, Palestine nevertheless looked good after two generations in the wilderness. The region, however, was already settled by the Canaanites, a people who had built modest cities and established laws on the Mesopotamian model. Furthermore, in the second millennium B.C.E. this area was still subject to incursions by other nomadic peoples besides the Hebrews, including the powerful, iron-armed Philistines. To conquer and hold their promised land, then, the twelve tribes evolved once more, this time politically rather than religiously. In the fires of combat the Hebrew kingdom was forged.

Despite their monotheistic faith, the Hebrew tribes had frequently been disunited. A clan-based as well as an extremely religious society, they were guided by leaders called "judges" and sometimes by charismatic prophets who claimed divine inspiration for their warnings and injunctions. Shortly before 1000 B.C.E., however, all the tribes agreed to follow a single king, a war leader who might bring them final victory over their foes. Thus was the kingdom of Saul, David, and Solomon born.

The first of these rulers, Saul, was an impressive fighter, but he proved unable to win the definitive victories his people demanded. When he fell in battle, King David (ca. 1010–960 B.C.E.) took his place. And under David and his son Solomon (ca. 960–920 B.C.E.), the new state of Israel flourished as it would not do again until the twentieth century C.E.

A gifted military leader, David crushed the Philistines and completed the conquest of Canaan. He cemented the political unity of the twelve tribes, established a Hebrew state, and began to build a Hebrew capital at Jerusalem. Generally recognized as the mightiest

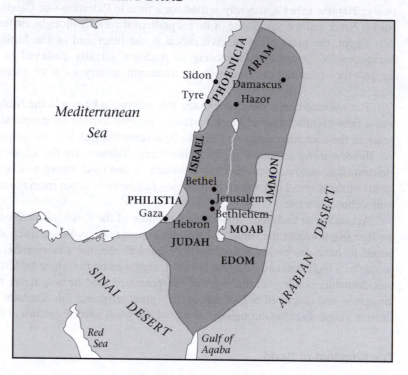

of Hebrew rulers, David became the center of an admiring body of biblical legend and literature chronicling his rise from shepherd lad to war hero and finally to founder of a centralized Near Eastern monarchy, the tenth-century B.C.E. kingdom of Israel.

## The Splendor of Solomon

David was the founder, but Solomon brought a genuine splendor to the newly united Hebrew state. His reign would leave almost as deep a mark on the minds of future generations as the heroic achievements of the nation's first ruler.

Celebrated in the Bible for his wisdom, Solomon was apparently a shrewd diplomat and a great builder. His harem, his huge stables, the palace he built for himself, and the temple he raised to the glory of Yahweh were all in the most opulent Near Eastern style. He strengthened his army and equipped it with chariots and new iron-age weapons. He built, rebuilt, and fortified a number of cities. He constructed ships and traded with the Phoenicians and even down the Red Sea.

In the powerful imagery of the Old Testament, Solomon looms as the wisest and wealthiest of kings. Symbolically, he plays as important a role in the historical memory of Jews and Christians as Asoka does in the Indian past, the Duke of Zhou in early China, or Plato's philosopher kings in the classical tradition of the West—all to be discussed below. He embodies the governmental ideal of wisdom and power in the service of the people.

But tensions and divisions underlay the success of the Hebrew kingdom. The work of Saul, David, and Solomon would be undone within a single generation. And the Hebrew

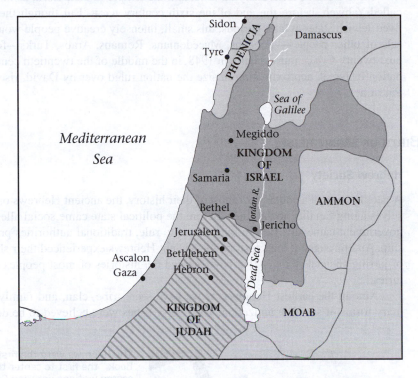

people, divided once more, would soon fall victim to larger and more aggressive neighboring peoples.

## Division and Disaster

Solomon's efforts to make the Hebrew kingdom a powerful player on the Near Eastern chessboard of nations cost huge amounts of labor and money. Oppressive taxation, forced labor, and other expedients made Solomon increasingly unpopular among his own people. Differences between the more sophisticated, urban, and commercial northern reaches of the kingdom and the pastoral, agricultural, more pious south further weakened the monarchy. Simmering rebellion split the kingdom after Solomon's death.

The result was the creation of two smaller nations: Judah in the south, inhabited by two of the Hebrew clans and still ruled from Jerusalem; and the new nation of Israel in the north, including ten of the original dozen tribes. Neither half of the old kingdom proved viable in the shark-infested waters of ancient Near Eastern politics. In the eighth century B.C.E., Israel fell to the powerful Assyrian Empire; in the sixth century B.C.E., Judah was overwhelmed by the New Babylonian Empire of Nebuchadnezzar. At the time of the latter cataclysm, in 586 B.C.E., Jerusalem and Solomon's great temple were leveled and many Hebrews were carried off into captivity in Babylon. Others scattered to Egypt and beyond, beginning the *diaspora,* or dispersal, of the people who became the Jews across the Western world.

Some returned from Babylon to rebuild the temple to their Lord, as they increasingly called Yahweh, before the end of the sixth century B.C.E. But though there were short-lived Jewish states at later periods, this small, intensely creative people would remain vassals of other peoples—Persians, Macedonians, Romans, Arabs, Turks—for most of the next twenty-five centuries. Only in 1948, in the middle of the twentieth century, did a new nation of Israel, approximating in size the nation ruled over by David, rise once again in Palestine.

## THE BIRTH OF MONOTHEISM

### Hebrew Society

A people without a country for most of their history, the ancient Hebrews organized themselves along familiar social lines. Before the political state came social allegiance. Before government came law. Before kings came to rule, traditional authorities provided leadership. And throughout their history, the ancient Hebrews experienced their share of the sort of jarring societal changes that have marked the histories of most peoples down the centuries.

Among the earliest Hebrews, as we have seen, tribe, clan, and family were the primary forms of social organization. The twelve tribes were believed to be descended from

The Hebrews were the first "People of the Book," the first to center their faith on sacred writings detailing God's will toward his people. The Torah, illustrated here, provides the same sort of religious inspiration for modern Jews that it offered to their spiritual ancestors in ancient times. (S. Meltzer/Getty Images, Inc.)

the twelve sons of the patriarch Abraham. Within the basic family unit, patriarchy—domination by the father—prevailed, giving male heads of families great power over wives and children. Polygamy was allowed for men wealthy enough to support several wives. Only sons could inherit property, since daughters would become the responsibility of the families into which they married. A wife retained control of the dowry she brought with her to her marriage, but had few other property rights. Divorce was easy for men but very difficult for women to secure.

It is a familiar pattern among earth's earlier civilizations. Yet here as elsewhere, there are mitigating points to be made. The Book of Proverbs in the Old Testament praises the righteous and God-fearing woman who feeds, clothes, and supervises a sizable household in terms that suggest larger responsibilities:

> She considereth a field and buyeth it; with the fruit
> of her hand she planteth a vineyard.
> She girdeth her loins with strength, and
> strengtheneth her arms.
> She perceiveth that her merchandise is good . . .[1]

Some women, furthermore, clearly stepped outside the family-centered system entirely. Some exercised political power as judges or religious authority as prophetesses. Some, like Judith, who slew the commander of an invading host, were even hailed as national heroes for their deeds.

Religion played a central role in Hebrew life, and the many ancient Hebrew laws recorded in the Old Testament had a deep religious core. These traditional rules of life, however, were also rooted in the Hebrew sense of identity and, to some extent, in the influences of the older and larger peoples among whom they lived.

Thus it is easy to see such principles as letting the punishment fit the crime—"an eye for an eye"—in the collections of laws sanctioned by both Moses and Hammurabi. Both formulations probably reflected a popular sense of fairness and equivalence among these ancient peoples. Yet the Hebrew tribes also accepted distinctive laws that prescribed what one might eat, whom one might marry, and what punishments might be meted out for violations of these taboos. And both dietary regulations and practices like endogamy—marriage only within the Hebrew community—forged a strong Hebrew sense of identity long before the Hebrew state emerged.

On top of this structure of traditional society and law, a changing cast of recognized authority figures led the chosen people down the centuries. In early nomadic times, as noted above, charismatic personalities called "judges" took the lead. These influential individuals, often claiming divine inspiration, included women, like the wise Deborah or the heroic Judith. With the emergence of the kingdom, however, patriarchal male dominance was established at all levels. The Hebrew kings claimed a hereditary right to rule, appointed officials to impose their will, and governed by royal fiat like other Near Eastern monarchs.

The society of David and Solomon's day, finally, was as much divided by social tensions as any other complex society. Rural people soon came to resent the wealth and sophistication of their urban fellows living in Jerusalem and other Hebrew cities. The rough

---

[1]Proverbs 31: 16–18.

egalitarianism of earlier, less affluent times gave way to class conflicts between landowner and laborer, aristocrat and commoner, rich and poor. Socially speaking, at least, the Hebrews who were carried off to captivity in Babylon in the first millennium B.C.E. had little in common with those who had followed Abraham out of Mesopotamia well over a thousand years before.

## The Worship of the One God

The Hebrew story was in many ways a paradigm case, a history and a society like many another in the long dawn age of human history. In one area, however, the ancient Hebrews stood out. The remarkable development of their religious beliefs would take them—and many generations yet unborn—to a new plateau of spiritual understanding.

The Hebrews seem to have been particularly concerned with religion, even by Near Eastern standards. Hebrew prophets in goatskins wandered among them like loin-clothed holy men in Hindu India, preaching an ever more rigorous faith. The Hebrews carried the words of their god Yahweh carved on two stone tablets in a chest, and they believed that they were divinely ordained to rule a promised land somewhere in Palestine. Over the millennium and a half between Abraham and the return to Jerusalem from Babylon, the Hebrews evolved a unique conception of divinity and of humanity's relationship to it.

The Hebrews of Abraham's day prayed and sacrificed to their own god much as Babylonians worshiped Marduk or as ancient Greeks might have venerated Athena—as their special patron among the many gods who ruled above. By the time of Moses, however, Hebrew spiritual leaders began to insist that Yahweh demanded exclusive worship in return for his special patronage—and then that he was the *only* real God in the universe.

During the course of the second millennium B.C.E., then, the ancient Hebrews came to believe that their God demanded an exclusive devotion from Hebrews that other Near Eastern gods did not. A Mesopotamian or an Egyptian could sacrifice to any number of divinities, but Yahweh was a jealous god and would tolerate no others. From this early Judaic view it was only a step further—albeit an immensely significant one—to the denial of the existence of other gods altogether.

Over the centuries the Hebrews added to this startling monotheism a powerful emphasis on the spiritual aspects of religion. Like Allah after him, Yahweh allowed no graven images of himself. He thus remained a purely spiritual presence, lacking the carven habitations where the gods of other peoples dwelt. Though the God of the Old Testament "spoke" to his human creations, from Adam to the prophets and beyond, he had few of the human feelings or relations of such widely worshiped gods and goddesses as the Egyptian Isis and Osiris, India's Shiva and Vishnu, or the familiar Greco-Roman pantheon—Jupiter, Mars, Venus, and the rest. He remained an incarnation of such suprahuman qualities as all knowledge, absolute power, and benevolent caring who had, miraculously, selected the ancient Hebrews as his chosen people.

In addition, Yahweh's prophets of the first millennium B.C.E. preached a strongly ethical monotheism, stressing the moral dimension of the worship of the one God. In passionate sermons to the Hebrews, preachers like Samuel, Jeremiah, and Isaiah insisted that Yahweh had imposed strict ethical requirements on his people. Sacrifice was not enough: Believers must rigorously obey the commandments that forbade murder, theft, lying, covetousness, and a whole array of sins. Beyond personal morality, furthermore, the prophets

# PROBING THE PAST

This portion of the biblical book of Isaiah was probably composed by a Hebrew prophet living at the time of the captivity in Babylon (550 – 538 B.C.E.). During this period, when the Hebrew states of Judah and Israel had been absorbed by Assyrian and Babylonian conquerors and many Hebrews were living in exile in the New Babylonian Empire, the future of this small band of people must have seemed very dim indeed. At such a time, the powerful preaching of Isaiah revived their confidence that their God would save them in the end.

To what does Isaiah compare Yahweh when he wants to emphasize God's care for his chosen people? Why was this comparison likely to move his hearers? How is the greatness of the Lord expressed here? Who are the "nations" and "princes" whom the Lord "maketh as nothing?" Why would claims that worldly power is vain and that divine power will strengthen true believers appeal to the Hebrews in Babylon? To Christians in Rome centuries later?

*"O Zion, that bringest good tidings, get thee up into the high mountain; O Jerusalem, that bringest good tidings, lift up thy voice with strength; lift it up, be not afraid; say unto the cities of Judah, Behold your God!*

*Behold, the Lord God will come with strong hand, and his arm shall rule for him, and his work before him.*

*He shall feed his flock like a shepherd: he shall gather the lambs with his arm, and carry them in his bosom, and shall gently lead those that are young.*

*Who hath measured the waters in the hollow of his hand, and meted out heaven with the span, and comprehended the dust of the earth in a measure, and weighed the mountains in scales, and the hills in a balance? . . .*

*Behold, the nations are as a drop of a bucket. . . . All nations before him are as nothing; and they are counted to him less than nothing, vanity. . . .*

*It is he that sitteth upon the circle of the earth . . . that bringeth the princes to nothing; he maketh the judges of the earth as vanity. . . .*

*But they that wait upon the Lord shall renew their strength; they shall mount up with wings as eagles; they shall run, and not weary; and they shall walk and not faint."*

Isaiah 40: 9–15, 17, 22–23, 31. *The Holy Bible* (Cambridge, England: Cambridge University Press).

insisted that the one God demanded social justice from his people. The rich should not oppress the poor, nor the powerful trample the humble underfoot.

God had made a special agreement, or *Covenant*, with the Hebrews, their prophets told them. When they fell into sin, God punished them with such historical calamities as the enslavement in Egypt or the captivity in Babylon. But if they remained loyal to him alone and kept his commandments, God's covenant promised them a land of their own and a place of respect among the nations.

Monotheistic, highly spiritual, and rigorously moralistic, the religion of the Hebrews would maintain the cultural distinctness of this vital people through a long and often tragic history. The Hebrews may have borrowed their flood story from Mesopotamia, proverbs from Egyptian wisdom literature, and psalms from both of these developed civilizations; but the faith of the children of Yahweh was distinctly their own, and a major contribution to the spiritual history of the world.

## The Hebrew Heritage

Some Hebrews at least were called *Yehudim*—whence, via a Greek intermediary, the English *Jew* is derived—even before the sixth-century B.C.E. Babylonian captivity. The *Judaic* religion as it has evolved since that time was clearly built on these ancient foundations of ethical monotheism, emphasis on the spirituality of God, and belief in the historicity of his manifest will in the world. In the first century C.E., Jesus Christ, born and raised in the Jewish community of northern Palestine, became the founder of the Christian faith, a creed that would spread around the world. And in the seventh century C.E., the Prophet Muhammad, an Arabian merchant conversant with both Judaism and Christianity, founded the third major world religion to emerge in this region—Islam. Down through the centuries, Hebrew leaders like Moses and Solomon would be honored, not only in later Judaism but also in the Christian Old Testament and the Muslim Quran.

The walls that enclose the narrow, winding lanes and crowded *souks* (markets) of Old Jerusalem today are mostly Ottoman Turkish battlements, built in the sixteenth century by Suleiman the Magnificent. Pass in through the Damascus Gate, however, and you can visit in fifteen minutes three of the most sacred sites of the great religions that emerged in the western portion of Eurasia: the golden Dome of the Rock, built on the spot from which Muhammad is believed by Muslims to have ascended into heaven; the Church of the Holy Sepulcher, allegedly encompassing the site of the Crucifixion of Christ; and the Wailing Wall, all that is left of Solomon's long-vanished temple, the holy of holies for Jews the world over. Amid the tensions and explosive violence of this long-fought-over corner of the globe, it is chastening to remember that all three of these militant faiths derive in large part from the spiritual intimations that first took shape in the minds of a single people three thousand years ago.

# EARLY GREECE

## Mountains and the Sea

> The mountain looks on Marathon—
> And Marathon looks on the sea;
> And musing there an hour alone,
> I dream'd that Greece might still be free.[2]

Lord Byron's famous lines tell us as much about Greek geography as they do about the continuing Greek dream of freedom. Greece *is* mountains and the sea. Greece is a jagged peninsula protruding some 350 miles southward from the Balkans into the Mediterranean, the central sea of European ancient history. The land of the Hellenes, as the Greeks called themselves, was all mountains and narrow valleys, capes, blue bays, strings and clusters of rocky islands—a place very different from the vast continental expanses of China and India, or the inward-looking Near Eastern river valleys of Mesopotamia and Egypt.

Greek civilization—the first of European civilizations—thus developed in a naturally fragmented little world. Each mainland city-state was walled off by mountains from its

---

[2]George Gordon, Lord Byron, "The Isles of Greece," from *Don Juan,* ed. Leslie A. Marchand (Boston: Riverside Press, 1958), p. 127.

# ANCIENT GREECE

Athenian Empire, 450 B.C.E.
■ Battle sites

*Black Sea*

T H R A C E

Byzantium
*Propontis*
*(Sea of Marmora)*

M
A
C
E
D
O
N
I
A

CHALCIDICE

Aegospotami

■ Troy

EPIRUS

▲ *Mt. Olympus*

Dodona

*Aegean*
*Sea*

THESSALY

LESBOS

ARGINUSAE IS.

LYDIA

PHRYGIA

Thermopylae ■

*ITHACA*

EUBOEA

Delphi

Thebes

CHIOS

Sardis

*Gulf of*
*Corinth*

Athens

*SAMOS*

Mycenae
Corinth

Olympia

Argos

■ Miletus

PELOPONNESUS

*DELOS*

*Ionian*
*Sea*

Sparta
LACONIA

■ Halicarnassus

*COS*

See Inset
Below

*MELOS*

*THERA*
*(SANTORIN)*

*Cretan*
*Sea*

RHODES

*CYTHERA*

CRETE

Knossos

*Mediterranean Sea*

## Inset (Peloponnesus/Attica)

PHOCIS

Chaeronea

EUBOEA

Delphi

BOEOTIA

Thebes

Delium

*Gulf of Corinth*

Leuctra

Plataea

Marathon

ATTICA

Eleusis

Megara

Athens

Piraeus

Corinth

*Saronic Gulf*

Mycenae

*AEGINA*

Mantinea

Argos

Tiryns

Epidaurus

## Inset (Mediterranean)

Areas of Greek settlements

*A L P S*

ILLYRIA

CRIMEA
Panticapaeum

PYRENEES

Massilia
(Marseilles)

*Adriatic*

*Black Sea*

IBERIA

*CORSICA*

Rome
ITALY

*Sea*

Trebizond

*SARDINIA*

Neapolis
(Naples)

Paestum

Byzantium

ASIA

Cadiz

*MAGNA*

Apollonia
GREECE

MINOR

*Strait*
*of Gibraltar*

Segesta

*SICILY*

Croton

Corinth

Athens

IONIA

Selinus

Syracuse

*GRAECIA*

Carthage

*MELITA*

*CRETE*

*RHODES* *CYPRUS*

*PHOENICIA*

*SYRIA*

AFRICA

*Mediterranean Sea*

Cyrene

LIBYA

EGYPT

neighbors. Many Greeks, furthermore, lived on islands in the Aegean or in colonies along the nearby coasts of Asia Minor (Turkey today).

The institutions of the Greek city-states, taking shape in isolated valleys, on islands, or in colonies along the coasts of other peoples' countries, were deeply influenced by this geographical fragmentation. The passionate sense of independence that was the glory and the downfall of the Greeks emerged quite naturally in this divided land. Fiercely independent toward other nationalities and even other Hellenes, the Greeks also developed a powerful sense of loyalty to their own isolated communities.

## The Minoans

We know very little about the first people to drift into this sunny, sea-washed world of gray rock and gray-green islands. We believe that they filtered in from Asia Minor as early as 3000 B.C.E., while pyramids were rising in Egypt and ziggurats in Mesopotamia. By about 1800 B.C.E., however, a great palace had been built at the city of Knossos on Crete, the largest of the islands. Around this center, a pre-Greek seaborne civilization briefly flourished.

The civilization of Minoan Crete and its scattering of trading posts around the Aegean were clearly built on commercial exchange. Minoans traded in Egypt and the Levant, exporting pottery and bronze, olive oil and timber, and bringing back, among other things, the forms of writing we call Linear A and Linear B. Minoan culture, in turn, dominated the islands and much of the mainland of Greece.

The kings who ruled at Knossos lived in considerable splendor in the vast, labyrinthine palace excavated by archaeologists thirty-five centuries later. There were scribes and bureaucrats in attendance and an elegant court life. But there were few soldiers, if we are to judge from archaeological evidence. Theirs was a network of trade, not a military or political imperium.

Life at the center of this small island world, the frivolous, fragile, lovely court life of the Minoan sea kings, comes vividly to us across the centuries in the brightly colored wall paintings of the royal palace at Knossos. In these murals, bare-breasted, bejeweled court ladies stroll in gardens full of flowers, and bronzed youths lift goblets of Cretan wine to a future that must have seemed as unlimited to them as our own does to us—and as pleasant as the life of any civilization we know.

The end seems to have come swiftly. They lived, traded, and prospered for a few short centuries: the standard dating of Middle Minoan, the heyday of Cretan civilization, is from 2200 to 1500 B.C.E. Then they vanished, swept away in a series of catastrophes perhaps partially the work of nature—earthquakes and volcanic eruptions have been suggested—but almost surely in part the work of humans. The first Greeks had lived among them and learned to read and write and worship their gods. But other Greeks came later, perhaps around 1500 B.C.E., from the mainland city of Mycenae, bringing fire and sword.

## The Mycenaeans

The Mycenaeans who next dominated this Aegean world were part of the great wave of migrating barbarian conquerors who intruded upon most of the main Eurasian enclaves of civilization during the second millennium B.C.E. These so-called Indo-Europeans— "tamers of horses" as Homer called them, chariot fighters, speakers of the lost Indo-

European tongue that would father all the major languages of Europe—constituted one of the most terrible of all barbarian onslaughts on civilization.

But the Mycenaeans were builders too. There was a structure of authority within the typical Mycenaean city-state—rule by an independent kinglet, rather than by council and assembly as in later centuries—and some records were kept in Minoan script. Their economic life is sometimes dismissed as little more than piracy and conquest, but they were traders too, exchanging goods around the Near East as the Minoans had done, pressing in where the declining Hittites and Egyptians gave way. Mycenae was a rich city, if we are to judge by the gold unearthed from the tombs of their nobles and kings.

Most noticeable from the distance of many centuries, they built walled cities and stone castles to garrison the lands they conquered. They raised the Lion Gate and the beehive-shaped *tholos* tombs of Mycenae. Sometimes they built on Minoan foundations; and Greek cities would rise in turn on the sites of Mycenaean ones.

But they were warriors above all, ruling the blue seas and rock promontories by the strength of their arms and the power of their bronze-tipped spears. Their most celebrated exploit was the great armada of ships and soldiers that descended on Troy, a wealthy Near Eastern city on the shores of the Hellespont. That famous conquest, probably undertaken by a loose confederation of warlords bent on plunder and headed by the king of Mycenae, would provide the half-legendary basis for the first great monument of Greek literature, the *Iliad* of Homer.

## The Greek Dark Age

After the Mycenaeans, the mists close almost totally over the life of this southeastern corner of Europe where Western civilization began. Other tribes and clans of northern barbarians followed the Mycenaeans and crushed them in their turn. For at least three centuries—from around 1100 B.C.E., when the city of Mycenae itself fell to new invaders, to approximately 800—a genuine dark age settled over Greece.

Wave after wave of Indo-European peoples drifted down the valleys and on to the neighboring islands and the shores of Asia Minor beyond. There were rude Dorians, who settled in the Peloponnesus and became the ancestors of the militaristic Spartans of later centuries. There were Ionians, who moved on to the islands and the Asian coast of the Aegean, where, fertilized by contact with the older civilizations of the Near East, the Greek intellect would soon kindle into life with particular vigor.

But wherever these people came during the dark centuries, they blighted what remained of the wealth and culture of Minoan-Mycenaean times. The kings of the Mycenaeans disappeared, monumental architecture ceased, pottery grew cruder, the use of the Minoan script was forgotten.

It was not all dark, of course. Toward the end of this period, in the eighth century, two of the most famous of Greek poets, Homer and Hesiod, composed their works—or, more likely, sang or chanted them before gatherings of Greeks in rude halls or village squares. The more basic arts of agriculture were not forgotten; settlers old and new went on scraping a meager living out of the dry, light Mediterranean soil. The petty Mycenaean kingdoms were destroyed, but this may have been an advantage in the long run, since imperial, divine-right monarchies like those of the ancient East were thus prevented from gaining a firm foothold in Greece, leaving the way open for wider participation in government during the next age.

# CLASSICAL GREECE

## Wealth and Colonies

One thing that did continue to grow during the Greek dark ages was the population. And one consequence of population growth was the spread of Greek-speaking people still further around the Mediterranean world.

The dry soil of Greece simply could not support all the newcomers. Many Greeks were thus driven to emigrate by pure Malthusian pressure; their numbers were pressing too hard upon the food supply. Others, especially after the revival of the city-state around 800 B.C.E., emigrated as traders or as mercenary soldiers.

This surge of expansion, which was especially intense from about 750 to 600 B.C.E., carried Greek-speaking people much further than their Mycenaean or Minoan predecessors had gone. Greek colonies were established not only on nearby islands and along the Ionian coasts of Asia Minor, but farther to the east around the Black Sea, and much farther to the west—in southern Italy and Sicily, in Libya and France, and on the coast of Spain at the far end of the Mediterranean.

The Greeks maintained a loose cultural unity wherever they traveled and settled. No matter how great a colony became in its own right, it tended to retain ties with the city-state that had fathered it. All Greeks spoke dialects of the same language. They worshiped the same gods and goddesses, some brought down from the north, some found among the older peoples of the eastern Mediterranean. Early on they gathered for athletic competitions in honor of their gods. Among these contests were the first Olympic Games, traditionally believed to have been held as far back as 776 B.C.E.

At home the Greeks produced elegant pottery, olive oil, and wine for sale overseas. From more lavishly endowed lands they brought back staples such as grain, essentials such as copper and tin and iron, and—from the Near East, for the second time—a written language. The characters were Phoenician in origin, but the language was Greek. The earliest surviving written record of the language in which Homer had already sung and in which Plato was to write appears on a Greek pot dating from perhaps 750 B.C.E., the early days of the great Greek diaspora.

## The Greek City-State

The Greek form of city-state, the *polis,* was one of the wonders of human social organization, a delicate balance that could not and did not long endure. But while it lasted, it gave some selected human beings more say in their own lives than some peoples know even today.

Physically speaking, the *polis* was two cities: a lower city, where the people lived, and an *acropolis* (high city) on a hill in the center of town, where the gods had their temples. In fact, however, the whole of the *polis* became in classical times the possession of the Greek citizenry. The all-too-human gods, glorified in white temples, were more objects of civic pride than sources of superstitious awe. The citizens owned the *polis,* and the city itself, with its unique political, social, economic, and military structure, governed and shaped the lives of its people.

The Greek-speaking invaders from the north brought with them the tribal and clan organization of the distant steppes. The typical *polis* thus took shape initially as an alliance of such tribes, governed by a council of leading families. This aristocracy, tribal in origin

The Acropolis of ancient Athens, with its white-columned temples, still rises above rocky, tree-fringed slopes. The Parthenon, dedicated to Athena, is right of center in this picture. Despite the carefully chosen angle from which this photograph was taken, the Acropolis actually sits in the center of the modern city of Athens, where the ancient stone is seriously threatened by pollution. (Source © 2002 by Benaki Museum Athens/Dimitris Harissiadis)

and now commonly including the leading landowners, sometimes tolerated a chief or petty king for a time, "a first among equals" like the kings of the ancient Mycenaeans. But real power lay with the landowners and the tribal leaders, and the last generation of Greek kings seems to have faded away without much struggle, transformed into elected magistrates or simply expiring as an institution.

In the seventh and sixth centuries, however, the aristocracy soon followed the monarchy into decline, opening the way to an astonishing degree of freedom among the Greek cities. A number of factors contributed to the decline of the aristocrats. One was the continuing growth of trade, which raised the social status of merchants as well as of farmers and potters, who produced wine, oil, and jars for overseas sale. Another cause was a radical change in military tactics, the replacement of the chariot-fighting aristocracy by a heavily armed phalanx of citizen infantry. The phalanx, composed of all who could afford the sword, spear, shield, helmet, and basic body armor of a *hoplite* (infantryman), rapidly replaced the Homeric charioteer as the backbone of Greek armies.

Land, money, and military service simply could not be excluded forever from political power. A military assembly of hoplites—the farmers, merchants, and craftsmen who could afford the weapons—was one road to political involvement for these solid citizens. Frequently also, men called "tyrants" (without the negative connotation of later times) became their spokesmen. These extra-legal rulers, often former military leaders, proceeded to modify political institutions in order to strengthen their citizen-supporters. Tyrannies tended to last only a generation or two. But the citizen assemblies they fostered survived, establishing the predominance of the middle ranks in the Greek *polis*.

By 500 B.C.E., in fact, the evolving Greek city-state was on the verge of producing the prosperous, comparatively democratic Athens of Pericles.

Not everyone strolled the streets discoursing about public policy, of course. Greek women were largely excluded from the public sphere of social and political life. Confined instead to the private sphere of the home, respectable women were honored for such traditional skills as feeding and clothing their families, raising children, and supervising sometimes quite large house-holds full of relatives, servants, and slaves.

The images of powerful or heroic Greek women which have come down to us were thus for the most part mythical. They were goddesses like Athena, Aphrodite, queen of love, or the warlike Amazons. Or they were heroines in plays or poems like the beautiful Helen of Troy, the witch woman Medea, or Antigone, who defies political authority for a higher cause.

There were exceptions. Spartan women exercised as their men did and owned most of the property. The exercise, however, was intended to help them bear strong sons, and they cared for the family property in order to free their husbands for a higher calling—war. Aspasia, consort of the Athenian statesman Pericles, was famed for her wit and wisdom. But she was also a foreigner and a courtesan—hardly a respectable woman at all by orthodox Athenian standards.

The famous "Greek democracy" was thus far from democratic by any modern definition of the term. The total population of Athens and its surrounding villages in the fifth century B.C.E. was perhaps two hundred thousand—of whom thirty thousand were free citizens. Only native-born free adult males of a certain economic standing—hoplite material—could be citizens. The rest—women and children, slaves, resident foreigners, and the lower orders generally—had no voice in the state or any place in the philosophical conversations of thinkers like Socrates.

Nevertheless, this is still a long way from the autocratic rule of pharaohs or Near Eastern kings. Greek citizens did meet in political assemblies to thrash out public policy. They did elect their own magistrates, war leaders, even a surviving electoral monarch here and there. They were citizens, not subjects. And it made a difference.

## The Persian War

Against this small, bustling people, the biggest empire in the western half of Eurasia came awesomely in arms at the beginning of the fifth century B.C.E. The Persian Empire, built by Cyrus the Great less than half a century before, stretched from the eastern Mediterranean to the banks of the Indus, from the mountains of the Caucasus to the shores of the Arabian Sea. Cyrus and his son had overrun Mesopotamia and Egypt and pushed their frontiers eastward to the nearest of the rivers of India. Darius I, who had inherited this vast realm in the late sixth century, built roads and canals, divided his domain into twenty more or less efficiently governed satrapies, adopted the enlightened faith of Zoroaster, and reigned in civilized splendor from his great palaces at Persepolis and Susa.

Darius, of course, suppressed rebellion wherever it emerged among his many peoples. It was the suppression of one such insurrection, among the Greek city-states of Ionia, that triggered the Greek Persian War, a struggle that lasted decades but ended in a totally unexpected Greek victory.

The Ionian city-states of Asia Minor revolted in 499 B.C.E., under the leadership of the famous trading city of Miletus. Like others before them, the Milesians and their allies were crushed. But before they fell, the Ionians sent pleas for help to the Greeks of the mainland; and some small assistance was sent, most notably by the Athenians. For this act of defiance, Darius of Persia resolved to punish the mainland Greeks.

Of all the cities of the Hellenes, two were already prominent at the beginning of the fifth century: Athens, the largest and the most civilized, and Sparta, the most militaristic and most disciplined. These two were to dominate the history of that turbulent and splendid century. It was the Athenians, however, who bore the brunt of the Persian War and carried off the rewards of victory.

The first Persian punishment force drew their ships ashore at the edge of the small plain of Marathon, north-east of Athens, in 490 B.C.E. The mere sight of the iron-armed hosts of the Medes and the Persians, twenty thousand of them, with their royal guard of "Immortals" in the van, was enough to shake most enemies. The Athenian phalanx, outnumbered probably two to one, charged them at a dead run. The Athenian center broke, and the Persians poured through. But the Greek wings overwhelmed the Persian flanks, closed upon the Asian center, and drove the invaders in disarray back to their ships.

Retribution, however, was sure. Darius died before he could take further action, but his son Xerxes spent four years preparing a huge fleet and a massive army to avenge his father's humiliation and to add the lands of the Hellenes to his already swollen empire.

The new Persian host arrived in 480. They swarmed into northern Greece in unstoppable numbers, perhaps sixty thousand strong: Medes and Persians in leather breeches and fishtail iron jerkins, with their short, powerful bows; Assyrians with their bronze helmets and long lances; Arabs in long robes; Ethiopians in leopard and lion skins; and many more. The Spartans headed a coalition army that tried to halt them at a narrow northern pass called Thermopylae—the Hot Gates—and died almost to the last man when a Greek traitor showed the invaders a way to take the defenders in the rear. The Persians moved on southward, like locusts over the land, while a Persian fleet closed in on southern Attica by sea. Athens was taken and burned. All northern Greece lay open to Persian arms, and the defense of the south seemed no more than a forlorn hope.

But the Greeks bred brilliant leaders as well as soldiers who knew how to die for their homeland. Themistocles the Athenian had for years urged his countrymen to pin their faith on their fleet. Hundreds of new *triremes*—the long, oar-driven warships of the Mediterranean—had been built. These vessels, with their contingents of disciplined Greek hoplites, now turned the tide against the Persian host.

The turning point came at Salamis. Between this small island off the port of Athens and the shore, the Athenians tricked the larger Persian fleet into giving battle. Ramming and swarming aboard the demoralized Persian vessels, the Athenians once more routed their enemies. "No longer could we see the water," a Persian in a Greek play later lamented, "charged with ship's wrecks and men's blood."[3]

The Persian army was thus left without the support of its fleet. They wintered in Thessaly and marched south again the following year, 479. But this time a large Greek force led by a Spartan general met them at the village of Plataea, northwest of Athens, and shattered them on land as the Athenians had by sea. What was left of the Persian army stumbled home in defeat.

The war was not over. It dragged on nominally for some thirty years. But after Salamis in 480 and Plataea in 479, the struggle took the form of annual plundering raids by Greek fleets on the shores of the Persian Empire. The Persians never came again to Greece.

## The Athens of Pericles

The history of Athens was in some ways similar to that of other Greek city-states. Its kings were replaced by a government of aristocratic councils early in the seventh century B.C.E. At the beginning of the sixth century the *archon* (magistrate) Solon—a member of the city's chief elected council—became Athens' most famous lawgiver. The laws of Solon freed poor farmers from debt slavery and opened up public office to citizens of less than aristocratic birth. Later in the sixth century the tyrant Pisistratus destroyed the residual power of the old clan-based aristocracy and transferred land from the aristocrats to the landless farmers who supported him. Pisistratus also encouraged handicraft manufacture and foreign trade and began the vast program of temple building that Pericles would carry to a triumphant climax.

Paradoxically, it was the aristocratic Cleisthenes who, during the last decade of the sixth century, brought participatory democracy to Athens. Winning popular support in 508, Cleisthenes instituted a Council of Five Hundred, chosen by lot, which was given sweeping authority to guide foreign and domestic affairs, to control government finances, and to prepare the crucial agenda for assembly meetings. The assembly of citizens still elected archons, passed all new laws, voted on questions of peace and war. A citizen-jury system began to edge out the aristocratic Areopagus court in judicial power. *Demokratia,* the rule of the citizens, was from this time on—a dozen years before the onset of the Persian War—the basic political reality of Athens.

Pericles, who dominated Athenian politics between 450 and 429 B.C.E., was another of those descendants of the old aristocracy who seemed to flourish under Athenian democracy. The sculptured head that has come down to us, bearded and helmeted, the eyes gazing out calm and blank like those of all Greek gods and heroes, gives us only an idealized notion of what he was like. The Athenian historian Thucydides says he was famous for financial integrity and enormously popular among the people. Beyond these bare facts, Pericles seems to have been a man with a vision of Athenian greatness, a policy of *grandeur* that carried Athens to the climax of the Greek golden age.

Pericles put the finishing touches on the democratic constitution of Athens. He also presided over the conversion of Athens' victory over the Persian Empire into an Athenian empire among the Greeks.

---

[3] Aeschylus, *The Persians,* trans. Seth G. Benardete, in *The Complete Greek Tragedies,* Vol. 1, eds. David Grene and Richmond Lattimore (Chicago: University of Chicago Press, 1959), pp. 234–235.

Pericles, the most celebrated statesman of ancient Greece, broods on the fate of nations in this idealized funerary sculpture. Is this a "realistic" representation? Look particularly at the hair, beard, and eyes. (Copyright The British Museum)

The decades of naval warfare against Persia that followed Salamis added a new element to the turbulent mix of Athenian politics. The Athenian sailors, fundamentally oarsmen whose straining backs propelled Athenian triremes into battle, were typically landless city dwellers too poor to afford arms and armor. Thanks to their military contribution, this less affluent group now acquired a share of power in the assembly comparable to that of the hoplite class. Their growing participation in government represented a clear gain for *demokratia* in the Athens of Pericles.

Meanwhile, to keep up the pressure on the Persians and to bring home as much of the pillage of Asia as their arms could win, the Greeks organized the Delian League. This military alliance, originally voluntary, was gradually transformed into an Athenian empire. Under the leadership of Pericles, membership in the league became compulsory for some fifty Greek city-states. The headquarters—and the treasury—of the league were moved from the sacred island of Delos to Athens. Free contributions became required tribute. And the funds contributed by all the members began to be spent to build temples on the Athenian acropolis.

Under such leadership Athens flourished. Trade boomed, and the docks at the Athenian port of Piraeus were jammed with long ships and jars of wine and oil. There was plenty of work in the city—laboring on the public works on the acropolis or producing goods for export. And the city itself was a joy to live in. Philosophers such as Socrates disputed in the agora; the hands of Phidias sculptured stone among the columns of the Parthenon; Aeschylus and Sophocles produced moving tragedies for the annual festival of Dionysus.

Loyalty to the *polis* had never been greater. An aging Pericles appealed to it when he urged his hearers to "draw strength . . . from the busy spectacle of our great city's life as we have it before us day by day, falling in love with her as we see her."[4] These men of ancient Athens, with all their faults, had come as close to genuine self-government as any ancient people ever would. And they had found uses for their freedom that would seldom be matched, perhaps never exceeded.

## The Peloponnesian War

The Greeks were always a rivalrous, contentious people. The war between Athens and Sparta that brought the fifth century B.C.E. to its disastrous close was more than a typical Greek feud, however. It was a clash of principle, a conflict between two irreconcilable ways of life.

Sparta had retained the virtues of virile Homeric warrior heroes, the stress on personal courage, and the conservative institutions of an earlier day. As late as the fifth century the Spartans still had not one but two kings, and their politics was dominated by an old-fashioned council of elders. Military service was normal for full citizens of any *polis*, but in Sparta all males lived in barracks till the age of thirty.

There was more to all this than conservative sentiment, of course. The fields of Sparta were worked not by Spartan citizens but by subject peoples called *helots*. Since the helots vastly outnumbered the Spartans, every Spartan had to be a soldier simply to keep the helots in their place. This need to dominate by force had also led the Spartans to impose their will on their neighbors in the Peloponnesus, the sprawling peninsula of southern Greece, through a compulsory alliance called the Peloponnesian League. In the last decades of the fifth century, the Peloponnesian League and the Delian League—the land-based Spartan coalition and the seaborne empire of the Athenians—came to an all but inevitable conflict.

The rise of Athenian power was bound to cause concern in Sparta. When the Athenians began to interfere in the affairs of Spartan allies, the leaders of the southern alliance responded violently. The Peloponnesian War, 431–404 B.C.E., dragged on for more than a quarter of a century. It was a civil war, pitting Greeks against Greeks, and it was the Hellenes as a whole who suffered.

From the beginning the Athenians had the worst of it. Sparta, located in the interior of the Peloponnesus, was safe from the Athenian navy, which had been Athens' most powerful military arm ever since Themistocles. Athens, by contrast, lay open to repeated incursions by the redoubtable Spartan army. Other misfortunes fell upon the Athenians. In the second year of the war, a plague ravaged the city, costing many lives, including that of Pericles.

There were battles without number, bloody massacres and shocking betrayals, tangled alliances involving even the Persians, the old enemies of all Greeks. In the end, the Spartans emerged victorious in 404 B.C.E. Athens was humiliated, stripped of its navy, deprived of its empire. The city was forced to raze the "long walls" connecting it with the Piraeus and the sea, which had been the source of its wealth and power. The Spartans im-

---

[4]George Willis Botsford and Charles Alexander Robinson, Jr., *Hellenic History,* 3rd ed. (New York: Macmillan, 1950), p. 202.

posed upon the city the notorious Thirty Tyrants—a council of Athenian collaborators—and returned home in triumph.

Athens was the loser, but no one gained permanently. The Athenians regained their freedom almost at once, but other wars and intrigues followed, dragging on into the fourth century. Peace was at last imposed from without—by a half-barbaric northern power called Macedon. Long before the Macedonian conquest, however, the Greeks had sacrificed their freedom on the altar of their own eternal contentiousness.

## Alexander the Great: Long March to Glory

Philip and Alexander of Macedon, father and son, composed a strange, brief dynasty of power. Philip's triumph brought unity to Greece at least. Alexander's unrivaled string of victories spread at least an approximation of Greek ways and Greek culture from the Nile to the Indus.

Philip II seized the throne of the northern kingdom of Macedon from his own ward in the middle of the fourth century. He built up a powerful army of hard-bitten Macedonians, conquered his more barbarous neighbors, and soon became involved in the tangled wars and alliances of the Greeks. In 338 B.C.E., Philip's soldiers smashed the combined armies of Athens and Thebes on the brutal field of Chaeronea. Two years later Philip was dead, murdered by his own officers.

His son, Alexander, replaced him as king and warrior lord. He was apparently a youth of more subtlety than his father. Having been tutored by the Athenian philosopher Aristotle, he was perhaps capable of imagining a more sophisticated world order than conquest and pillage. But he was a warrior first and always. He began at once a twelve-year trek across western Eurasia seldom matched in the annals of warfare.

The tale of Alexander's victories reads like a gazeteer of the ancient Middle East. He crossed the Hellespont into Persia in 334, repeatedly defeated the Persians, swung south into ancient Egypt, and founded Alexandria in the delta of the Nile. Plunging back into Asia Minor, he finally crushed the Persian emperor Darius II at the Battle of Gaugamela in 331 B.C.E., and then marched farther and farther east across the far-flung Persian satrapies. He passed south of the Caspian Sea, crossed what is today Afghanistan, and went beyond the reach even of the Persians, into northern India. After tracing the Indus south to the Indian Ocean, Alexander turned back across the great desert to bring his odyssey to an end in Babylon. Here, his destiny accomplished, he died suddenly of a fever in 323 B.C.E. He was thirty-three years old.

For good or ill, Alexander's long march accomplished more than can ever have been imagined in his narrow Macedonian skull. He himself had "gone native" on the long road east, adopting Persian garb, marrying a Persian princess, declaring himself a king and a god after the Oriental manner. But he had also founded twenty-five Greek city-states along his march, and married off thousands of his Macedonian officers and soldiers to native women. Henceforth Greek administrators, Greek traders, Greek ways of living, thinking, and carving stone would become part of the life of this half of Asia.

A new and wider world was opened up by Philip of Macedon and Alexander the Great. But an old world died too—the untidy little world of craggy mountains, blue water, and white cities where a small, combative, immensely energetic people had brought to a climax one of the great human efforts at civilized living.

# THE LEGACY OF GREECE

## The Art of the Acropolis

Greek sculpture apparently began, as the Greek dark age ended and the city-state emerged, with models borrowed from immemorial Egypt. The stiff frontality of Greek archaic statuary—the gowns like a fluted column, the fixed "archaic smile"—seem to look back to Memphis and Karnak. However, these stiff sixth-century Apollos and skirted female figures probably also reflect the limitations of the log from which earlier figures were fashioned by Greek woodcarvers.

Yet from these crude beginnings developed the perfect physical proportions and idealized shapes of fifth-century sculpture. The classic simplicity of the head of Pericles or Phidias's *Athena Lemnia* became a model for later ages. The calm strength of the *Apollo* from the Temple of Zeus at Olympia and the incarnate majesty of the great bronze *Zeus* from the sea off Euboea have a power that challenges all efforts at emulation since.

But the restless mind of the ancient Greeks appears never to have been content, even with classic perfection. Greek sculptors of the fourth, third, and second centuries went on to more intricate, more violent, and perhaps more human things. Hellenistic sculpture included the tangled draperies of the *Winged Victory,* which stands in the Louvre today, and the writhing bodies of the muscular *Laocoön* and his sons in the serpent's coils. It also included the living flesh of perfect Hellenistic Aphrodite—the Greek goddess of beauty—and the wrinkled skin, taut tendons, and swollen veins of the *Old Market Woman.* Realism, melodrama, and sentiment thus replaced classic idealized forms as human concerns replaced ideal ones among the ever-changing Greeks.

Greek building, for all its subtlety of proportion, was very simple. Post-and-lintel structure—pillars and pediments and a gently sloping roof—made a Greek temple. The plain Doric order predominated, at least through the fifth century: a flat abacus at the head of the column and no base at all below. Yet ruined beauty of the Parthenon, the Temple of Athena Parthenos (Athena the Virgin), on the Athenian acropolis testifies to what could be done with such economy of means.

A city crowned with such beauty—marble temples against the mountains and the sky—was a city that any people could, as Pericles said, fall in love with day by day.

## Homer's Epics and Athenian Tragedy

"Sing, goddess, the wrath of Achilles," begins Homer's *Iliad,* the oldest and for many still the greatest of Greek poems. It dates from the Greek dark ages—perhaps 800 B.C.E.—and harks back for its warlike theme to the wars of Mycenaean times. But it was as close to a Bible as the worldly Greeks ever got, even in the vastly more sophisticated centuries after 500 B.C.E.

The strength of Homer's twin epics, the *Iliad* on the Trojan War and the *Odyssey* on the wanderings of the hero Odysseus, would not be easily equaled. The *Iliad* in particular stands alone in the classical canon as a powerful poem of men at war. The long hexameter lines boom with the rolling of the sea and the clash of battle on that distant Asian coast where Bronze Age Greeks and Trojans fought before Troy. The story of the wrath of Achilles—vain of honor, grieving terribly for the friend who dies in his place, and exploding at last, a blood-stained meteor across the battle-field—brings back with unparalleled power a savage age long gone.

Later Greek times produced lovely poetry as well. There are the fragile lyrics of Sappho, the Greek poet of the islands. Only fragments of her verse remain, yet they combine with unmatched beauty the poet's love of other women with a sensitive awareness of the legends of her people and the loveliness of the Greek isles. There are Pindar's famous odes, celebrating the transient glory of the heroes of his day and later imitated by many Western poets.

The ancient Greek theater apparently began with primitive hymn-singing and dancing in honor of Dionysus, god of the grape in particular and of fertility and generation in general. By the fifth century B.C.E., this simple celebration of divine beneficence had evolved into a complex dramatic form. In this classic Greek tragedy, characters in stylized masks acted out the story while a chorus danced, sang, and chanted a commentary between the "acts" of the play. The stories themselves normally derived from Greek mythology, but the old tales of gods and heroes often emerged with universal reference in the work of the fifth-century Athenian playwrights Aeschylus, Sophocles, and Euripides.

The dramatic heroes of Sophocles perhaps best embody what Aristotle considered the perfect tragic type: the noble character marred by a single tragic flaw. Thus *Oedipus the King* attempts to discover the crime against the gods that has brought divine retribution in the form of a plague upon the city he rules. The dramatic tension of the play grows out of the inability of this great king to see what would be obvious to the audience even if they did not know the story: that Oedipus himself is the criminal, the man who in defiance of all the laws of gods and humans has inadvertently murdered his father and married his own mother.

There was laughter in ancient Greece as well, evidently, and a comic theater to stimulate it. Most celebrated is the so-called Old Comedy of fifth-century Athens, embodied in the plays of Aristophanes. A comedy such as *The Clouds,* which lampoons the generation gap, the teachings of the philosopher Socrates, and much else, is typical. Aristophanes offers a rich mixture of social satire and personal innuendo, of bawdy farce and lyric flights of great beauty. We would expect nothing less complex and subtle of the Age of Pericles. Even Greek laughter was a many-splendored thing.

## Philosophy: Socrates, Plato, Aristotle

From ancient Greece, as from Confucian China and ancient India, however, it is not shaped stone or patterns of words that have survived the longest, but the ideas of Greek teachers. These equivalents of the Hebrew prophets or the sages and gurus of the East are called the Greek philosophers, "lovers of wisdom."

In the cosmopolitan city-states of the Ionian coasts in particular, a handful of choice spirits among the Hellenes went beyond mythology to ask themselves, "What is the universe *really* made of?" The answers Thales, Anaximander, Pythagoras, and others came up with—water, the four elements, fire, number, and so on—are of largely antiquarian interest. But from them descended both the philosophy of the fifth and fourth centuries and the Hellenistic science of the fourth century and after.

The most famous of Greek philosophers were Socrates in the fifth century B.C.E. and Plato and Aristotle in the fourth.

Socrates called himself the "gadfly" of Athens, an intellectual horsefly stinging Athenians into questioning traditional values, examining their own lives, thinking seriously about the real meaning of life itself. More of a crackerbarrel philosophizer than a systematic thinker, Socrates buttonholed his fellow citizens in the agora, asking judges what justice was, querying poets about the function of art, discussing with the young people who gathered around him how society ought to be organized, how the good life ought to be lived. "The unexamined life" he told his disciples, "is not worth living." In the terrible years after the Peloponnesian War, Socrates was tried and executed by his fellow countrymen, less for his words than for his insistence on his right to speak them.

One of the admirers who mourned Socrates was a broad-shouldered, poetic young man called Plato. For the rest of his life, this most influential of all Western philosophers would immortalize his teacher in a series of *Dialogues* expounding first the views of Socrates and later Plato's own mature notions of the nature of reality, of the good society, of the ideal life, and much more.

This most famous of Greek philosophers insisted that there is more to reality than meets the eye. There are two levels to the universe, said Plato, a lower world of matter, or "particulars," and a higher, nonmaterial realm of Ideas, Forms, or Absolutes. A triangle drawn in the dust by a Greek geometer is a particular triangle, and it ceases to exist with a sweep of a sandaled foot. The Form of the Triangle—the definition of a triangle, we might say—is an Idea, invisible, immaterial, and eternal. The courage you show in a tight spot, your sense of justice, whatever wisdom you may have—all these are temporary, finite, bounded by one imperfect human heart and mind. The Idea of Courage, of Justice, of Wisdom would survive even if there were not one wise or just or brave person left alive to think such thoughts, or to embody them. Ultimate reality, then, is not material at all but rather is pure, transcendental Idea. The Idea of Man, the Form of the Good, Absolute Beauty—these Platonic formulations would be powerful shapers of Western minds for centuries to come.

Plato's ethical teachings stressed one of these capitalized abstractions especially: Reason. The goal of life, Plato said, was happiness. But happiness comes from the practice of virtue, and the highest of virtues is wisdom. Since wisdom is achieved through reason, the best possible life is a life dedicated wholly to rational inquiry and the pursuit of truth. Philosophy ("love of wisdom") is thus itself the highest of human activities, and the philosophical life is the best life.

The good society, in turn, would be one in which philosophers were kings, or kings philosophers, and in which the rest of us performed the functions to which we are best suited by nature, class, or profession. Plato was no democrat: His family was an ancient aristocratic one, and it was the popular demagogues who had executed Socrates. Let the best minds guide the state, said Plato, as the brain rules the body. It was a beguiling notion, one that can tantalize us even today.

Other Greek sages proposed other theories of the ultimate nature of things, and of the good life for human beings. For Plato's disciple Aristotle—himself "the master of those who know" to later ages—the Forms are real enough but exist only *within* the particulars that derive their structure from them—not in some transcendental realm of nonmaterial being. On ethical and political matters, Aristotle took an eminently practical view. After studying the constitutions of more than 150 Greek city-states, he classified them under three heads—monarchy, aristocracy, and democracy—and found strengths and weaknesses in all three. In the realm of personal morality, Aristotle agreed with Plato that the truth-seeking life of the philosopher was the best life possible. Recognizing, however, that most people were not capable of such a life, he urged that for the average person, virtuous conduct is a "golden mean" between two extremes. The good person, he believed, avoids excess and seeks moderation in all things.

Aristotle's wide-ranging mind left Western people ideas on every subject, from metaphysics, politics, and morality to science and the arts. He meticulously catalogued biological species and left theories that dominated physics until modern times. His writing on poetry and drama explained the "cathartic" effect, the sense of psychological purging and relief, that comes from great drama. Aristotle also laid out the means of constructing a "well-made play," methods still taught in drama and film schools today.

## History and Science

The eager Greek intellect explored this world as well as the transcendental realm of the philosophers. Both Western science and Western history were founded by the ancient Greeks.

The two most honored of Greek historians were Herodotus and Thucydides, chroniclers of the two great fifth-century B.C.E. wars that bracketed the age of Pericles. Herodotus's *Persian War,* perhaps the first real history book ever written, recounted in colorful detail the epic struggle between the Greek city-states and the huge Persian Empire. Breaking with the ancient tradition of mythic and poetic accounts of the past in which gods and goddesses always played important parts, Herodotus sought to explain how human beings, Greeks and Persians, settled their differences by a resort to arms. Though he was not above inventing inspiring speeches for kings and generals and reading sententious morals into past events, Herodotus did travel widely, seeking evidence and talking to eyewitnesses, conducting a genuine historical investigation for the first time.

Thucydides' history of the grim and disillusioning *Peloponnesian War* offers subtler analysis and more thoughtful syntheses than his predecessor. Thucydides' account of the cruelty, corruption, follies, and defeats of Athens at war is all the more moving when we remember that he was himself an Athenian commander. Exiled by his fellow citizens for an early failure in the struggle, he gave the rest of his life, not to justifying himself, but to compiling an unbiased yet deeply moving history of the great conflict.

There seemed to be no end to the intellectual curiosity of the Hellenes. By Hellenistic times much of the Greek thirst for ultimate understanding had shifted from philosophy to science. Here the Greeks made more substantial contributions than did any Western people before the Scientific Revolution of Copernicus and Newton.

The names of some of the early Greek scientists are well known still. Pythagoras is most familiar as a mathematician. His famous theorem about the squares of the sides of a right-angle triangle is part of the bric-a-brac of every school-child's mind today. Aristotle's researches in biology and physics were so impressive that later ages would revere even his mistakes. Euclid's *Elements* of geometry remained standard for more than twenty centuries, and doctors to this day begin their careers with the Oath of Hippocrates, most renowned of ancient Greek physicians, to "do no harm" to any patient. Archimedes's promise to move the world itself if you could give him a lever long enough and a place to stand has the ring of Greek speculative daring at its best.

Perhaps as far back as Pythagoras, Greek astronomers recognized that the earth is a ball. They calculated its size by mathematics and used trigonometry to estimate its distance from the sun and the moon. They made one fundamental error; in the end they agreed with Ptolemy's earth-centered theory of the structure of the universe rather than with Aristarchus's sun-centered view. For Ptolemy's elaborate cosmological explication and mathematical calculation—it took some doing to present so erroneous a theory convincingly—carried the best scientific minds of Roman, Byzantine, Arab, and medieval Christian times along with him, till Copernicus in the sixteenth century set them right.

Reason was the heart of it, the core of Greek achievement in the linked fields of philosophy and science. When they set their minds to work, this ancient Mediterranean people produced a body of rational speculation and calculation that is a major human effort to explain the meaning of it all, the nature of things.

## SUMMARY

The first age of human history saw the emergence of other peoples besides the Mesopotamian states and ancient Egypt. Around the eastern end of the Mediterranean and on across western Asia, new cities, kingdoms, and empires bubbled up, many of them during the turbulent second millennium B.C.E. Among these, the Hittites added iron to civilization's repertoire of workable metals, while the Phoenician city-states of what is today Lebanon traded the length of the Mediterranean and left the Western world its basic alphabet.

Much more influential in the long run were the ancient Hebrews and the ancient Greeks. The Hebrews were a small but immensely significant people who entered history as a group of pastoral nomads shortly after 2000 B.C.E. They established the short-lived kingdom of Israel under David and Solomon around 1000 B.C.E. The kingdom soon split into two halves, the northern half falling to Assyrian conquerors in the eighth century, the southern half to the Babylonians in the sixth century B.C.E.

Through these trials and tribulations, however, the Hebrews developed a unique religion. Focused on a divine Covenant between themselves and their God, the faith of the Hebrews was monotheistic, highly spiritual, and fostered both personal morality and a sense of social justice. This ancient faith survives today as modern Judaism. It also became the direct ancestor of both Christianity and Islam.

European history began in southern Europe, in the islands and mountainous mainland of Greece, where a series of cultures flourished between 2200 and 200 B.C.E. climaxing in the fifth century with the Age of Pericles.

The first two societies to develop in this area were those of the Minoans and the Mycenaeans. The Minoans (2200–1500 B.C.E.) migrated from the Near East to the large island of Crete, which they made the center of a city-based, seaborne, commercial hegemony over neighboring islands and coasts. The Mycenaeans (1500–1100 B.C.E.), Indo-European nomads from the north, overran this first European urban culture and became pirates, traders, and builders of rude cities.

As early as the eighth century B.C.E., Greek traders also took to the sea. The Greek city-state, or *polis,* ruled by a popular assembly with elected magistrates and other officials, became perhaps the most democratic of ancient urban institutions. The history of the celebrated fifth century B.C.E. began with Greece's victorious war against the huge Persian Empire. The century centered on the rich and culturally brilliant age of Pericles in Athens, and it ended with the self-destructive civil war between Athens and Sparta in which Sparta won but all Greece was the loser. In the fourth century the Greek peninsula fell under the military domination of Philip and Alexander of Macedon. Alexander brought the long feud with Persia to a climax by over-running the empire and scattering Greek cities across much of western Asia.

Greek culture, like that of the ancient Hebrews, provided a vital legacy to later peoples. Greek literature—from Homer's epics the *Iliad* and the *Odyssey* to the delicate lyrics of Sappho or the dramas of Sophocles—provided models for later writers. Greek sculpture idealized the human form in lifelike figures of gods and famous citizens.

Above all, the philosophy of Greek thinkers like Socrates, Plato, and Aristotle left the West a legacy of daring ideas. From Socrates's challenge to "know thyself," through Plato's belief in absolute Ideas like Truth and Beauty, to Aristotle's conviction that ethics is a golden mean between extremes, their views have shaped Western thinking ever since.

## SUGGESTED READING

Ahlstrom, G. W. *The History of Ancient Palestine.* Minneapolis, Minn.: Fortress Press, 1993. Massive scholarly study.

Ben-Tor, A. *The Archaeology of Ancient Israel.* New Haven, Conn.: Yale University Press, 1992. Trans. R. Greenberg. From the Neolithic through the Bronze and Iron Ages.

Bernal, M. *Black Athena.* London: Free Association Press, 1987. Controversial study emphasizing Egyptian influence on Greece.

Bryce, T. *The Kingdom of the Hittites.* New York: Clarendon Press, 1998. Strong on political and military history.

Cantor, N. F., *The Sacred Chain: The History of the Jews.* New York: HarperCollins, 1994. Sweeping overview.

Chadwick, J. *The Mycenaean World.* Cambridge: Cambridge University Press, 1976. Overview by a scholar known for his exposition of the Minoan script, Linear B.

Dothan, T. K., and M. Dothan. *People of the Sea: The Search for the Philistines.* New York: Macmillan, 1992. Archaeological investigation of the Hebrews' great enemies.

Flanders, H. J., R. W. Crapps, and D. A. Smith. *People of the Covenant.* New York: Oxford University Press, 1988. Hebrew history through the Old Testament.

Freeman, C. *Egypt, Greece, and Rome: Civilizations of the Ancient Mediterranean.* Oxford: Oxford University Press, 1996. Greek and Roman history set against an Egyptian background.

Grene, D., and R. Lattimore, eds. *The Complete Greek Tragedies* (4 vols.). Chicago: University of Chicago Press, 1959–1960. All the surviving plays by the three greatest Greek tragic dramatists—Aeschylus, Sophocles, and Euripides—translated by various hands.

Hammond, C. L. *Alexander the Great: King, Commander, and Statesman.* London: Chatto and Windus, 1980. Combines deep classical learning with first-hand knowledge of the lands Alexander traversed.

Herodotus. *The History of Herodotus,* trans. G. Rawlinson. Chicago: Encyclopaedia Britannica, 1955. The first Western historian's account of the Persian War and of the Near East in his own time.

Homer. *The Iliad,* trans. R. Lattimore. Chicago: University of Chicago Press, 1951. Excellent rendering by an experienced translator and poet. See also *The Odyssey.*

Just, R. *Women in Athenian Law and Life.* London: Routledge, 1991. Illuminating anthropological approach.

Lefkowitz, M., and M. B. Fant. *Women's Life in Greece and Rome.* Baltimore, Md.: Johns Hopkins University Press, 1982. Perhaps the best description, but see also the highly praised S. Pomeroy, *Goddesses, Whores, Wives and Slaves: Women in Classical Antiquity* (New York: Schocken Books, 1975).

Podlecki, A. J. *Perikles and His Circle.* New York: Routledge, 1998. Useful new life based on re-reading of the very limited evidence available.

Seltzer, R. M., ed. *Judaism: A People and Its History.* New York: Macmillan, 1989. The Jews and the evolution of their faith.

Shanks, H. *Jerusalem: An Archaeological Biography.* New York: Random House, 1995. Illustrated history of the holy city.

Smith, M. S. *The Early History of God.* San Francisco: Harper & Row, 1990. Early Hebrew beliefs about God. See also K. Armstrong, *A History of God* (New York: Knopf, 1994), which takes the story into Christian and Islamic times.

Taylor, C. C. W., ed. *From the Beginning to Plato.* London: Routledge, 1997. Development of Greek philosophy.

Walbank, F. W. *The Hellenistic World.* Cambridge, Mass.: Harvard University Press, 1982. Scholarly introduction to the fascinating later Greek centuries.

 Please refer to the document CD-ROM for primary sources related to this chapter.

# CHAPTER 4

# BRAHMAN, BUDDHA, AND THE AGE OF THE SAGES
## The Emergence of India and China
### (2500–200 B.C.E.)

# A Glance Ahead: Two Giants Emerge in the East

While Egyptians and Mesopotamians were building cities, kingdoms, and even small empires, while Hebrews and Greeks were enriching the cultural life of the world around the Mediterranean, great civilizations were also taking shape much farther to the east. Much larger empires—and cultures as profound—emerged in the states that would become the India and China of later centuries.

Both are enormous. China is as wide as all Europe, and India is often called "the subcontinent" of Asia. Between them, China and India are home to one third of the population of the earth today.

Historic India generated not one but two of the major world religions—Hinduism and Buddhism. China was a unified superstate many centuries before the modern great powers were dreamed of. These two civilizations dominated their zones of civilized living down the centuries as no single people did in Europe, Africa, or the Americas. And while most of the ancient empires discussed in this book are honored names in history today, India and China are here still—and likely to make more history in years to come.

# Lost Civilization of the Indus

## The Indian Subcontinent

The raw physical reality of India is mud in the monsoon, dust in the dry season. It is the high thin cold of the Hindu Kush and the glittering snowfields of the Himalayas, the lush green valley of the Ganges, the dry hills of the south. It is a mixture of peoples, a babble of many languages, a meeting place of some of the world's greatest religions. To Westerners today it is a richly physical world of hot curries and importunate bazaars from which, mysteriously, has emerged the profound spiritual tradition of the yogi and the guru, enlightenment and Nirvana.

Indian civilization, like the civilizations of the Near East, was born in its river valleys, but it expanded inexorably thereafter, till it encompassed the entire subcontinent. On the map, this Indian subcontinent is one of the most readily recognizable of global features. It is a vast triangle, two thousand miles from north to south, about half the size of the United States. Like Arabia to the west and Indochina to the east, India is a gigantic peninsula jutting down from the underside of Asia.

Within this huge triangle, three main geographical subdivisions stand out. In the north the colossal ranges loom—the Hindu Kush and the snow-shrouded Himalayas. Just south of the mountains run India's most celebrated rivers: the arid basin of the Indus in the northwest, the five rivers of the Punjab and the long green valley of the Ganges in the northeast, flowing from the Himalayas to the Bay of Bengal. South of the rivers, finally, lies the wedge-shaped Deccan, a dry, hilly plateau fringed by narrow coastal plains as it runs down to Cape Comorin at the southern tip of the subcontinent.

Each of the major regions of India has its distinctive and historic features. But the first center of Indian civilization was along the low, intensively cultivated banks of the great northern rivers, especially the sacred Ganges. It is along the shores of these rivers, then, that any history of India must begin.

## Harappan Culture

The first of the Indian civilizations may well have been the work of speakers of Dravidian languages like those spoken today in southern India. This ancient culture emerged, however, in the northwest, in what is now Pakistan.

Here, not long after the appearance of civilization in Mesopotamia and Egypt, the culture centered in the twin cities of Harappa and Mohenjodaro took shape.

The origins and development of Harappan culture, as the civilization that flourished along the banks of the Indus between 2500 and 1500 B.C.E. is called, remains to a large degree mysterious. We know that Harappan culture dominated an area larger than present-day Pakistan, leaving ruins scattered up and down the Indus basin and along the coast of the Arabian Sea. We know that it endured as long as a thousand years, from roughly 2500 to about 1500 B.C.E. We know nothing of Harappan kings and dynasties and wars, or even if they had kings or central government at all. But we can learn a good deal from the remains about the lives, the social organization, and even the attitudes of the people who produced them.

Harappan culture was built on agriculture, as most ancient civilizations were. As in Egypt and Mesopotamia, a system of dikes and drains enabled Harappan villagers to cultivate grain, especially wheat and barley, along the Indus and its tributaries. A considerable portion of this produce found its way down the rivers to the granaries of Harappa and Mohenjodaro, probably as taxes or tribute.

This ancient people worked copper and bronze, though stone tools continued to be used even after Neolithic times. They knew how to build bullock carts and small boats for transport. They exchanged goods, not only up and down the rivers of northern India but around the shores of the Arabian Sea and up the Persian Gulf to Mesopotamia. The rectangular Harappan seals inscribed with their distinctive script have in fact been found as far away as Persia and Egypt.

Both Mohenjodaro and Harappa seem to have been planned cities, with straight, right-angled streets and a remarkable system of underground drains and sewers. There were also citadels for defense, city granaries, and large public pools, perhaps intended for ceremonial washing in connection with religious observances.

Earlier suggestions that the two cities were the twin capitals of a Harappan empire now seem less convincing. Religious authority, however, may well have been combined with some degree of political control in Harappan India. It now seems likely that priests occupied the citadels, directed artisans and farmers at their labors, and even imposed their authority on the merchant families who lived in the large two-story houses in the cities. The chief god of this ruling elite may have been the horned male figure whose likeness has been found in many places, while the masses worshiped a female divinity heavy with jewelry and an elaborate hairstyle. Animals also seem to have been venerated, including particularly a long-horned bull that would retain its position as an object of religious worship in India thereafter.

Above all, perhaps, an overwhelmingly conservative cast of mind is indicated by what we know of Harappan civilization. For hundreds of years, the cities of the Indus were built and rebuilt on precisely the same rectilinear ground plan, and new houses were raised on the foundations of old. Foreign ideas seem to have been consciously rejected. Harappan merchants must have seen the elaborate irrigation works and the records on clay

The ruins of ancient Mohenjodaro shimmer beneath the blistering sun of the Punjab. Built of clay brick, the walls, streets, and stairs still follow the carefully laid-out plans of their vanished builders. (Anthony Esler)

tablets developed in the Tigris-Euphrates valley, for instance, yet these valuable innovations were apparently never introduced along the Indus.

## The Aryan Invasions

The passing of Harappan culture is in some ways as obscure as its origins. Shifts in the course of the Indus or repeated flooding of the cities may have contributed to its decline. But the final fall of the Harappan world was almost certainly due to the intrusion of a new people into northwestern India: the Aryans.

The Aryan invaders who broke in upon the peaceful Indian world of 1500 B.C.E. were drifting tribes of Indo-European pastoralists and intermittent agriculturalists. They traveled like many nomadic peoples, seeking water and pasturage for their herds of cattle, horses, and sheep. Their gradual filtering through the passes of the Hindu Kush and down into northwest India was a folk migration lasting several centuries, not an organized military campaign like those of Mongols and other later nomads. But the impact of the Aryans was every bit as devastating.

We have no detailed contemporary accounts of the Aryan conquest. The Hindu Vedas, a collection of Aryan hymns to their northern gods, give us our best information, but they tend to be couched in highly figurative language. We do know that the newcomers charged into battle in chariots against Harappan foot soldiers, and there is good evidence that at least some of the Aryan tribes wielded iron weapons against the native bronze. We know that Indra, the Aryan war god, proudly styled himself *Purandara*, "Breaker of Cities," and that his followers left the corpses of their foes to rot in the streets of Mohenjodaro.

# KINGDOMS OF THE GANGES

## Cities, Family, and Caste

The period of the Aryan predominance in India, roughly 1500 to 500 B.C.E., thus began with the destruction of a civilization. Cities were abandoned for hundreds of years. Writing was forgotten. Much of Vedic India—the Aryan-dominated northern India described in the Vedas—returned to the village life that had characterized pre-Harappan, Neolithic India. Then, during the first half of the first millennium B.C.E., urban culture did reemerge—and its primary architects were the barbarian conquerors themselves.

The process began with an eastward migration by the restless Aryans from the Indus into the valley of the Ganges. The heavy rain forest there, which had resisted the bronze tools of Harappan times, yielded to the iron of the Aryans. The result was the opening up of rich soil for cultivation. The broad Ganges also contributed significantly to the economic development of the region, emerging as a busy avenue of trade.

Another aspect of the new India was the mingling of peoples and blending of cultures known as the Aryan-Dravidian synthesis. This subtle interpenetration of everything from religious beliefs to modes of production eventually turned the nomadic Aryans into settled farmers and their worship of anthropomorphic nature gods into the sophisticated concepts of Hinduism.

Accompanying the eastward migrations and the cultural synthesis of later Aryan centuries was the transformation of society. Some Aryans became sedentary landowners along the fertile Ganges valley, the more powerful of them using Dravidian farm laborers to work their land. Other Aryans became traders on the river itself. Crafts increased in complexity, providing heavy iron plows, trade goods, and the rough luxury items favored by the new, primarily Aryan aristocracy of landed and commercial wealth.

Here and there along the Ganges valley, finally, cities reappeared. Mere clearings in the jungle initially, these stockaded villages expanded into recognizable urban centers with substantial populations of artisans, traders, resident landowners, priests, warriors, and kings. Thus emerged such rude metropolises as Patna, the future capital of the Mauryan Empire, and Benares on the Ganges, still the holy city of the Hindus and perhaps the oldest continuously functioning city in the world.

Other institutions dominated Indian life in villages and cities—and from that day to this. The ancient Indian family seems to have been originally rather more open to power and prestige for women than would later be the case. Dravidian traditions, at least, were often matriarchal and matrilineal and allowed women to accumulate great wealth and enjoy high status in society. Among the invading Aryans, on the other hand, patriarchy prevailed. Wives were required to move to their husbands' families, bring substantial dowries, and accept their husbands' authority.

Even in the Aryan north, however, women could own property and run businesses. Some even became famous as philosophers or renowned for their religious piety in the Hindu or Buddhist traditions. Others found relative independence as temple dancers, prostitutes, or skilled courtesans, admired for their wit and gracious companionship as much as for their physical charms.

The caste system would play at least as important a role in Indian society. The word for caste was *varna,* meaning "color" and clearly referring to the old racial differences between conquerors and conquered. But the actual basis of caste divisions was social and economic rather than racial. These divisions represented a clear shift from color bar to social classes in Indian society.

The four original castes were *kshatriyas,* the warrior nobility; *brahmans,* the priests; *vaisyas,* landowners and merchants, and *sudras,* cultivators of the land and other manual laborers. As warfare became less perpetual and religion more complex and important, the ranking of the top two castes was reversed; priests came to be regarded as the highest caste, followed by warriors.

The caste system grew more complicated and more rigid, however, with the passing of the centuries. In time the system would subdivide into hundreds of occupational categories. The religious sanctions would grow more strict, forbidding all forms of social interaction between castes, from eating together to intermarriage. Even the touch of the "untouchables" at the bottom of Indian society would come to be thought of as polluting to a high-caste Indian.

But there was also an open-ended quality to the caste system that made it remarkably easy for later immigrants—and there were many of them—to be absorbed into Indian society. Newcomers in later centuries would be assigned a place in the structure of castes based on their traditional skill, craft, or occupation. Paradoxically, this undemocratic system of traditional classes thus made India a very tolerant society into which newcomers could be accepted with minimal social tension.

## The Rise of the Rajas

Politically, the Aryan invaders had been loosely organized into tribes, clans, and families. Tribes were headed by chiefs or kings called *rajas,* most of them elected or chosen by rotation among the leading families. Councils of elders and assemblies of adult males normally shared political power with their kings. But the centuries of social evolution that carried India out of the dark ages following the Aryan conquest also transformed these simple tribal political institutions.

Most important, two new forms of state emerged in northern India: republics and kingdoms. The republican form retained many tribal institutions, including powerful councils and an oligarchy of leading families. In the developing kingdoms, however, the power of the *rajas* grew steadily at the expense of councils and assemblies. The new monarchies frequently became hereditary. They also developed administrative systems, headed by chief priests and military leaders, that exercised some degree of central control over the villages that composed the state.

As the caste system acquired religious support, so too did the institution of the monarchy. The brahmans conducted elaborate sacrifices, sometimes lasting as long as a year, to consecrate each new *raja.* The *rajas* in turn supported the evolving Hindu priesthood, establishing a close relationship between throne and altar. In India as elsewhere, the odor of sanctity thus hovered early over the kings of the Ganges, augmenting their growing authority over their people.

By the sixth century B.C.E. there were at least sixteen separate little states—many monarchies and some surviving republics—in the Ganges valley. These states retained some of their ties with the more traditional Aryan societies left behind in the Indus region to the west. They also continued the long-established Aryan tradition of incessant warfare among themselves and against the Dravidian peoples of the Deccan to the south.

Increasingly, however, one principality loomed larger than any of the others in the little world of the Ganges—the kingdom of Magadha. Its rulers, the Nanda clan, had by the fifth century B.C.E. expanded its power at the expense of its neighbors, pushing their way down the delta of the Ganges to the head of the Bay of Bengal. Domination of the Ganges valley thus came into the hands of a single state. From this power base the dynasty that followed the Nanda to the throne of Magadha would provide the foundation for the first genuine Indian empire—that of the Mauryas.

## The Mauryas: Chandragupta

The Mauryan dynasty (321–185 B.C.E.) was the first to bring almost the entire subcontinent under a single government. And the earlier Mauryas—Kings Chandragupta and Asoka in particular—seem to have presided over one of those rare occurrences in human history: a genuine golden age.

Legend—which must here make do for history—has it that Chandragupta Maurya (321–297 B.C.E.) was the son of a concubine at the Nanda court. He is supposed to have seized the throne of Magadha from the last of the Nandas with the help of his mentor and evil genius, a shrewd but unscrupulous brahman named Kautilya. With their authority thus firmly established along the Ganges, Chandragupta and Kautilya turned their eyes to a field of operations much larger than any of the princelings of the Ganges had ever dreamed of—the whole of India.

Chandragupta first led the large and powerful army of Magadha back to the old Aryan heartland on the Indus for a confrontation with the Greek forces of Alexander's heir in that part of the world, the shrewd general Seleucus. The founder of the Seleucid dynasty, however, chose not to fight for his distant Indian satrapies. He ceded to Chandragupta not only the Indus and the five rivers of the Punjab, but also much of what is today Afghanistan.

Thus strengthened, the Mauryan leader turned back eastward and pushed the frontiers of his growing domain all the way to the mouth of the Ganges in Bengal. He thus came to rule an empire that stretched some two thousand miles across northern India, from the head of the Bay of Bengal in the east to the high passes of the Hindu Kush in the west.

We know little of Chandragupta Maurya personally. He is said to have been a severely autocratic ruler, and indeed he would almost surely have had to be to hold such an expanse of recently conquered territory together. A Greek ambassador records that the self-made emperor, who had seized the throne by force, employed a notoriously efficient secret police, and was heavily guarded in his palace at Patna.

Chandragupta's heir Bindusara expanded the Mauryan empire southward almost to the tip of the continent. Most of India thus acknowledged the overlordship of the Mauryas when the third of that redoubtable line came to the throne—Asoka, the most famous of them all.

The governing of such vast lands and peoples evidently required some doing in the third century before Christ. Some historians have suggested a rough system of more or less feudal allegiance on the part of local *rajas* to the Mauryan ruler at Patna. There is also some evidence of appointed Mauryan officials governing sizable chunks of the empire. However it was ruled, the Mauryan Empire was an amazing accomplishment, one of the most impressive feats of empire-building in all of ancient history.

## Asoka, the Philosopher King

The reign of Asoka (ca. 268–231 B.C.E.) was an even more astonishing achievement than that of Chandragupta. Like the Greek Age of Pericles or the Augustan Age in Rome, the Age of Asoka seems to have been one of the high points of human governance.

Asoka's royal lion capital once crowned a seventy-foot-tall column at Sarnath, on the site of Buddha's first sermon. The style shows Persian influence, but the symbolism and the inspiration are distinctly Indian. Can you think of other cultures in which the lion was the royal beast? (Lauros-Giraudon/Art Resource)

Specific facts about the life of the celebrated Asoka are very hard to come by. He is reputed to have had to fight for his throne, a struggle that may have involved an older brother. He almost certainly completed the conquest of the eastern coastal region of Kalinga, on the Bay of Bengal. And he was beyond doubt a very pious king. On this thin scaffolding of fairly well-attested fact, an awesome edifice of tradition, elaboration, and symbolic truth has been raised.

It seems to have been the bloody Kalinga campaign that changed Asoka's life. Before he saw the heaped-up corpses and heard the wailing of women seeking their kindred among the dead, he was a Mauryan sovereign, wielding power and expanding the empire as his predecessors had. After the horrors of Kalinga, he was a man determined to live and rule in a different spirit.

That spirit was not that of Brahmanical Hinduism, but of Buddhism, a religion then two and a half centuries old in India. Asoka became a convert and apparently dedicated much of the rest of his life to the pursuit of *dharma,* the saving truth of the Buddha. He founded many shrines, sponsored a Buddhist council that dispatched missionaries to spread the faith as far as Tibet and Ceylon, and devoted the rest of his reign to Buddhist virtues, public service, and the spiritual unification of his vast empire.

Asoka declared his new principles in an extraordinary series of public inscriptions carved on the walls of caves and on stone pillars erected along high roads from the Northwest Frontier to Mysore in the south, from the Arabian Sea to the Bay of Bengal. Some of these sermons in stone clearly reflected Asoka's conversion, urging upon his people such Buddhist virtues as reverence for parents and teachers, compassion, religious piety, and *dharma*. Others declared the emperor's larger public policies, a firm intent to see that his government would follow righteousness and serve the people.

Asoka particularly advocated the distinctly Indian virtue of *ahimsa*—nonviolence—and promised to live by this principle as king. He would be mild toward his own subjects and would refrain from foreign conquests—as in fact he did. He renounced violence even toward animals, curtailed the mass animal sacrifices of Vedic days, and imposed a vegetarian regimen upon himself and his court.

A good deal of more practical public service accompanied Asoka's edicts. He dug public wells, built rest houses for weary travelers and clinics for the sick, and lined the roads of his empire with shade and fruit trees for the use of passersby. His masterpiece was the Grand Trunk Road, the commercial artery of North India, which ran many hundreds of miles from Patna to the Northwest Frontier and was still in use more than two thousand years later.

## THE SOUL OF INDIA

### The Lost Arts of Ancient India

Nature and history have not been kind to the earliest achievements of Indian art. The cities of Harappan India were built of clay, those of Mauryan times of wood, and only the faintest traces of either have survived. Yet enough fragments remain to give us some idea at least of the high levels of artistic accomplishment reached by the earliest dwellers along the Indus and the Ganges. This is especially so of the Harappan and Mauryan high points of India's ancient history.

The geometrical beauty of what we know of the "planned cities" of Harappa and Mohenjodaro, with their rectilinear street patterns and public bathing places, has already been mentioned. The meticulously laid-out blocks with water gurgling under the streets of residential structures rising two or more stories above them must have made an imposing spectacle in a world of Neolithic villages and tent-dwelling nomads.

The pieces of Harappan sculpture that remain—hundreds of carven seals and small figurines of terracotta, stone, or copper—reveal even more sophisticated traditions. The small rectangular seals usually depict animals, beautifully chiseled in low relief, as well as inscriptions in the unknown Harappan tongue. There are also examples of much more sophisticated sculpture, such as a lovely limestone torso only three and a half inches high, yet so exquisitely and naturalistically carved that it is often compared with the classic sculpture of Hellenic Greece. The lost civilization of the Indus would indeed have been a world worth seeing before the breakers of cities swept down from the north.

But the new civilization that eventually emerged in the Ganges valley to the east, the jungle-girt world of the first *rajas,* also nurtured builders of great skill. The palace of Chandragupta at Patna was described by Greek envoys as more splendid than the Persian cities of Susa and Ecbatana. Its pillared audience hall echoed the columns of Persian Persepolis. Patna itself stretched for miles along the river. Contemporary Buddhist bas-reliefs show high walls, many towers, and railed balconies over the streets. But all of it was made of wood cut from the great rain forests, and today only sections of the palisaded teak walls remain.

Among the Mauryan carvings that survive, most famous are the large animal figures—lions, bulls, and others—that top Asoka's famous inscribed pillars. In particular the conventionalized lion capitals of these smoothly polished forty- to fifty-foot freestanding columns show clear Persian influence. But they are nonetheless triumphs of Indian art.

There was a more completely Indian style in Mauryan sculpture, however, a style notably embodied in the massive statues of *yakshas,* or nature spirits. These big-bellied, larger-than-life figures are depicted naked to the waist, their powerful legs swathed in what looks like the *dhoti* that Indian men still wear in the villages. The *yakshis,* the female of this spiritual species, clearly reveal the supple, swaying stance, the narrow waist, and the swollen breasts that would be hallmarks of the female figure in Indian sculpture for centuries to come.

## Epic Poetry: The Song of God

The literature that survives from these early Indian centuries is also sparse. There are, however, three literary peaks in that dawn age of Indian civilization. Two of these are epic poems: the *Mahabharata* and the *Ramayana.* The third is a hard-boiled treatise on statecraft called the *Arthasastra.*

The *Mahabharata* is, at 100,000 verses, the longest poem in the world. It is a Homeric saga of the struggle between two powerful Indian clans, the five Pandava brothers—particularly Prince Arjuna, the famous bowman—and their cousins the Kuravas. It clearly reflects the Aryan age of chariot fighters and kinship loyalties, of great archers, wild gamblers, and pious holy men wandering in the uncut Gangetic forest. Gods and other supernatural beings also play their part in a story that has a cosmic as well as a human dimension. The final victory of the Pandavas comes only after a colossal battle that, in the final version at least, seems to pit half the peoples of India against the other half.

The other great Indian epic, the *Ramayana,* is the more romantic story of how Prince Rama of one of the settled Ganges states rescues his lovely wife, Sita, from Ravana, the demon king of Ceylon. There is plenty of excitement in the adventures of Rama, Sita, and the friendly general of the apes, Hanuman, first exiled in the northern forests, then fighting epic battles in the south. But the original adventure story has been thoroughly reworked by brahman editors, so that Rama emerges as the ideal Hindu man, Sita as the perfect woman, and their relationship a model of the sort of conjugal loyalty and devotion expected in the settled agricultural states of the middle of the first millennium B.C.E.

The political commentary called the *Arthasastra,* attributed to Kautilya, Chandragupta's unscrupulous chief advisor, is a tract for a ruthless time of territorial statebuilding. For Kautilya, as apparently for his royal master, efficiency and success are the sole criteria of princely governance; morality is never taken into account. The people are to be kept in line by any means that work, including draconian laws vigorously enforced, hordes of bureaucrats, and battalions of what we would today call secret police.

A hard-nosed realist, Kautilya advises the shrewd *raja* to consider all his neighbors as enemies and all states beyond that inner ring as potential allies against the future victims between them. The *Arthasastra* thus projects a grimly convincing image of political and diplomatic affairs among the raw new states along the Ganges.

Before pious brahmans had done with the *Mahabharata* and the *Ramayana,* on the other hand, central figures in both these epic adventures had turned out to be incarnations of the god Vishnu or of Brahman, the spiritual foundation of the universe. This is illustrated most vividly in the section of the *Mahabharata* called the *Bhagavadgita,* the famous Indian *Song of God.* This best-loved of all Hindu texts is a dialogue between Arjuna the archer, youngest of the Pandava brothers, and his divine charioteer Krishna. Its climax comes when Krishna reveals that he is actually the incarnation of Brahman, the divine ground of all things, in a vision that dazzles Arjuna like "a thousand suns":

> O Lord of the universe [cries Arjuna] I see You without beginning, middle or end . . . endowed with numberless hands, having the moon and the sun for Your eyes and the blazing fire for Your mouth, and scorching the universe with Your radiance.[1]

The great victories of Prince Rama, the god-hero of the *Ramayana,* have become major festivals in the Hindu religious calendar. The feast of Diwali, a night of lights, candy, and toys for children rather like Christmas in the West, celebrates the victorious return of Rama and Sita to their kingdom in this ancient epic, which is still widely read. Even Hanuman the monkey prince has his share of temples and festivals over the length and breadth of India.

## Hinduism: From the Sacred Cow to Brahman

We know little or nothing about the religion of Harappan India. Worship of a mother goddess, mentioned earlier, seems a likely explanation for the many small female cult figures found in Harappa and Mohenjodaro. Harappan seals point to some veneration of animals, and one in particular may indicate a Harappan origin for the cult that was to grow up around the great god Shiva as Lord of the Beasts.

The Aryans brought to India the gods of the northern steppes, gods of thunder and sun—Indra, the god of war; Agni, the spirit of the sacrificial fire; and Varuna, lord of the big sky over the endless Eurasian plains. Aryans sacrificed to these divinities, slaughtering dozens or even hundreds of animals, and sometimes human beings too. The hymns, prayers, and rituals committed to memory syllable by syllable by the brahman priests were passed down to become the core of the oldest Hindu scriptures, the Vedas (1000–500 B.C.E.).

Hinduism as it developed in Vedic times involved a merging of the pantheons of the Aryan invaders and the conquered Dravidians, and perhaps even a certain gentling of the brawling gods of the breakers of cities. Most important, there was a striking evolution from naïve anthropomorphic divinities to a profound philosophic search for the deepest spiritual principle of the universe, the Brahman of later Hindu thought.

For ancient Hindus, there were many nature spirits like the *yakshas* and *yakshis* mentioned above, while hordes of demons lurked in the shadows, ready to tear and rend the souls of the unwary. Living among the teeming life of the Ganges rain forest, early Hindus saw some of their gods in the shape of monkeys, snakes, or the sacred cow, which was the measure of wealth and source of life for their pastoral Aryan ancestors. To this day sacred cows browse more or less unopposed in the lanes and market squares of Indian villages. Grocers shoo them away from the vegetables and pedestrians step around the piles of dung they leave in their wake, but no one would deny them the streets.

The most important of all the gods were—and are—Brahma, the rather hazy creator god; Vishnu, the preserver of the universe; and Shiva, the four-armed dancing divinity who is often presented simplistically as the destroyer of all things. These three were in

---

[1]*The Bhagavadgita or The Song Divine* (Gorakhpur, India: Gita Press, 1975), pp. 233–235.

time subsumed theologically under the persona of Brahman, the universal spiritual principle underlying all that exists. Brahman is not a personal god at all, but the unimaginable spiritual essence permeating the entire cosmos, "the One . . . hidden in all things."

The fabric of Hindu belief generated such peculiarly Indian concepts as the brotherhood of all living beings, reincarnation, karma, and *ahimsa*. For Hindus, all life is one and all living things have souls. This view was amplified by a later belief, first expressed around 500 B.C.E. in the philosophical dialogues called the Upanishads, in reincarnation, the transmigration of the soul. The Hindu doctrine of transmigration holds that each human soul is reincarnated, or reborn, in the body of some other creature—human, animal, or even supernatural—over and over again. In precisely what form one is reincarnated depends on *karma*, the "actions" one takes during one's present life. If you lead a good and pious life, you may be reborn as a brahman or other high-caste Indian; if you wallow in self-indulgence and sin, you may live your next life in the body of a rooting hog or a worm to be crushed by any passing sandal. From belief in reincarnation and the brotherhood of all life, finally, sprang the doctrine of *ahimsa*, or nonviolence. Arising first among Buddhists and Jains (see below), it eventually permeated all of Indian society.

# VOICES FROM THE PAST

This discussion from the Hindu *Upanishads*—religious speculations on the philosophical dimensions of the faith—depict a teacher and a pupil discussing a key point for a religion whose temples swarm with gods and demons: How many gods are there, really? How would an ancient Egyptian or Greek have answered such a question? An ancient Hebrew?

*1. Then Vadagdha Sakalya asked him: "How many gods are there, O Yajnavalkya?" He replied with this very Nivid: "As many as are mentioned in the Nivid of the hymn of praise addressed to the Visvedevas, viz. three and three hundred, three and three thousand."*
*"Yes," he said, and asked again: "How many gods are there really, O Yajnavalkya?"*
*"Thirty-three," he said.*
*"Yes," he said, and asked again: "How many gods are there really, O Yajnavalkya?"*
*"Six," he said.*
*"Yes," he said, and asked again: "How many gods are there really, O Yajnavalkya?"*
*"Three," he said.*
*"Yes," he said, and asked again: "How many gods are there really, O Yajnavalkya?"*
*"Two," he said.*
*"Yes," he said, and asked again: "How many gods are there really, O Yajnavalkya?"*
*"One and a half (adhyardha)," he said.*
*"Yes," he said, and asked again: "How many gods are there really, O Yajnavalkya?"*
*"One," he said.*
*"Yes," he said, and asked: "Who are these three and three hundred, three and three thousand?"*
*2. Yajnavalkya replied: "They are only the various powers of them . . .*
*He asked: "Who is the one god?"*
*Yajnavalkya replied: "Breath (prana), and he is Brahman (the Sutratman), and they call him That (tyad)."*

S. E. Frost, *The Sacred Writings of the World's Great Religions* (New York: McGraw-Hill, 1972, pp. 23–24.)

The heart of developing Hinduism, however, lay not in its ceremonies and scriptures but in the central role of the mystical element in Indian religion. As early as the first millennium B.C.E., Hindus decided that they might escape the endless round of lives filled with human suffering through the mystical concentration of their psychic forces known as meditation.

The goal of the yogi's meditation is not "life everlasting" for the individual soul but rather the submergence of the ego in the supreme unity of Brahman. This mystic merging of the self with the spiritual oneness of the universe is sometimes compared to the dissolving of a drop of water in the ocean. It is to be achieved through spiritual enlightenment—the simple realization that all differences are illusions, or *maya,* that all that really exists is the totality of Brahman.

## The Naked Philosophers

Hinduism as it emerged in the first millennium B.C.E. had already established itself as a basic social cement for evolving Hindu society. The ancient faith sanctified the caste system and sanctioned the rule of the *rajas.* The brahmans were the highest caste in society and could demand rich rewards for putting their ritualistic expertise at the service of rulers and people.

But the middle of the first millennium B.C.E. was a time of many changes and strains in Indian society. Out of these tensions a restless new impulse toward spiritual exploration emerged in northern India. In particular, this spirit produced the gurus (spiritual teachers) of the sixth century whom Western envoys would later describe as *gymnosophists*—the "naked philosophers."

Some of these wandering holy men were in fact naked, going unclothed in monsoon rains and under the Indian sun to discipline the flesh. Others starved themselves for long periods or engaged in exhausting exercises that would soon develop into the sacred discipline of yoga. A few sought to rediscover ancient sorceries in backwoods tribes, or even attempted spiritual growth through alcohol and orgiastic sexual practices. Of all the gurus of this age of intellectual ferment, however, two left by far the most important imprints on the Indian mind—Mahavira and Gautama Buddha.

Mahavira (ca. 540–476 B.C.E.), the founder of the religion of the Jains ("Conquerors") actually accepted a broad range of conventional Hinduism, from the caste system to reincarnation. But he did have some extreme notions—such as complete celibacy, total honesty, and the rejection of all earthly possessions. Like the most extravagant seekers of his generation, he practiced rigorous asceticism, meditated intensively, and went naked in rain and sun.

His major contribution to Indian thought, however, was the doctrine of *ahimsa,* which he defined as the nonviolent refusal to take a life. In pursuit of *ahimsa,* the Jains carried brooms to sweep insects from under their feet, fed ants, and filtered the water they drank and the air they breathed in order to avoid accidentally extinguishing some minute form of life. Their piety took extreme forms. But it sometimes takes extremists to get a hearing for a new doctrine, and the notion of nonviolence was clearly thrust into the mainstream of Indian thought by the extravagant commitment of the followers of Mahavira.

## Buddhism: The Teachings of Prince Siddartha

One approaches the historic Siddartha, or Gautama Buddha (563–483 B.C.E.), through a thick incrustation of image and legend. And the fairy-tale version of Siddartha's life has an undeniable charm. He grew up in splendor as a king's son, protected from any sight of human suffering. On one fatal day in his youth, however, he beheld a sick man, an old man, and finally a dead man—and learned that such evils came in time to all human beings. The stricken prince thereupon left his young wife and infant son and set out to find a way to escape the wheel of human misery. After many years of self-denial, he found enlightenment at last under the great bodhi (or bo) tree at Gaya, and devoted the rest of his life to spreading his new gospel.

He was not actually a *raja*'s son: His Sakya people were an undeveloped hill tribe among whom the headship rotated, his father being one of a number of sturdy *kshatriyas*—farmers who had a right to a turn as chief. But the rest of the legend—the years of rigorous asceticism, the meditation under the bo tree at Gaya, the famous first sermon in the deer park at Sarnath outside Benares, the monkish order he founded, and the long lifetime of wandering the roads of India with his disciples—all these are likely enough, given the spiritual ferment of the times.

Gautama Buddha found the fundamental cause of all suffering in one great human failing: desire, the almost universal human attachment to the good things of this world. Desire in turn fosters the central human illusion: that the things of this world are real. The Buddha agreed with orthodox Hinduism that worldly things are a grand illusion, a fantasy world of *maya*. Behind this illusory separateness of things, he further agreed, lies an ineffable spiritual unity—what the Hindus called Brahman. Buddha himself tended not to call it anything. His goal was to get there. Escape from desire, from the wheel of life and the *maya* world, was to be found along the eight-fold path that Buddha preached for half a century in the growing cities and along the jungle trails of Gangetic India.

The eight steps to Nirvana—union with the ultimate spiritual reality of things—begin with the recognition and rejection of selfish worldly desires as the blind follies they are. Next comes the cultivation of unselfishness, compassion, and honesty; then rejection of such injury to others as murder, theft, and adultery; and finally the choice of a source of livelihood that does not bring harm to other living things. The path leads through a turning away from evil thoughts and all physical concerns to deep meditation and final escape from the wheel of unending lives through Buddhahood—that is, enlightenment—and Nirvana, the extinction of the suffering ego in the great ocean of eternal peace.

Buddha and his followers wore only the simplest of robes, owned nothing but their begging bowls and staves, traveled always on foot, and never slept under a roof—a striking contrast with the patrician, sometimes greedy and worldly brahmans. The Buddha presented his faith to live by in simple language that the layperson could understand, without the elaborate theology of developed Hinduism. Perhaps most radically, he accepted people of all castes as equals on the eightfold path.

Men joined him to escape the chains of caste, women to break with the exhausting load of family obligations. Men and women both shaved their heads and donned the saffron robes of the mendicant in search of the higher truth he preached. His orders of monks and nuns would carry his doctrines far across the eastern half of Asia over the next thousand years.

The results are still visible today. You can still see Buddhist temples in the People's Republic of China or at Kamakura in businesslike modern Japan. And in Tibetan monasteries beyond the Himalayas, the gold-painted Buddhas of the Past, the Present, and the Future gaze down at you over flickering candles of yak butter.

Paradoxically, after becoming royal orthodoxy under sovereigns such as Asoka, Buddhism would all but die out in India in later centuries. But there are temples in all the architectual styles of the East in the Buddhist shrine at Bodh Gaya on the Ganges today. There pilgrims from many lands remove their shoes and pass reverently under the shadow of the giant bo tree where Prince Siddartha found enlightenment and into the hall where a huge gold statue of the Buddha still meditates on human folly and desire.

## THE FIRST CHINESE DYNASTIES

### The Middle Kingdom of East Asia

Sprawling across the far end of Eurasia, China is the world's third largest nation today. It has the largest population: Well over a billion strong, the Chinese constitute a fifth of the population of the earth. A great power and a powerful influence on all its neighbors, China is to East Asia what India is to South Asia—and then some.

Nor is China's preeminence a new thing in the world: It has probably been the most populous of nations since its first unification in the third century B.C.E. Cut off from other centers of civilization by formidable barriers such as the Gobi Desert, the jungles of Southeast Asia, and the Pacific, the giant of East Asia has inevitably emerged as the predominant force in its own very substantial corner of the globe, from Tibet to Korea and Japan.

Isolation and cultural supremacy have bred a strong belief in China's uniqueness, a sense of being "the Middle Kingdom," the center of civilization, indeed the only civilized people in a barbarous world. This conviction—which China shares with many other peoples—would help to hold together a huge nation marked by great geographical diversity over many centuries.

China today is slightly larger than the United States, stretching, like America, roughly three thousand miles from west to east and two thousand north to south. The land stairsteps down from the inhospitable Tibetan Plateau, the world's highest landmass, to the densely populated sea-level plains along the Pacific rim. North to south, China is divided into three main regions, two of them defined by great rivers. The Huanghe (Yellow River) of north China, with its light yellow loess soil blown south from the Gobi, has been the political core of Chinese development. Beijing, the political capital, is the metropolis of north China today. The Yangzi River of central China is the main artery of a spreading web of tributaries and lakes that water some of the nation's most fertile farm land. Central China, with its wheat fields and rice paddies, bamboo groves and mulberry trees, has a major outlet at Shanghai today. The more mountainous south is monsoon-drenched and semitropical, rich in rice and tea production, the nation's historic commercial center and not infrequently the center of revolt. Guangzhou (Canton) and Hong Kong are its gateways to the world.

In the northeastern corner of this huge and ancient land, then, another center of civilization emerged sometime in the second millennium B.C.E.

Neolithic Chinese still hunted and fished along the Yellow River, but they also farmed, cultivating millet and vegetables with the aid of hoes and other polished-stone tools. They domesticated dogs and pigs—both for meat—and oxen and horses for their labor. They made pottery much like that of other Neolithic people all across Eurasia.

These Stone Age farmers and hunters, squatting before their round mud houses along the Huanghe and its tributaries, did not of course see themselves as precursors of anyone. It is barely possible, however, that they did recognize the crucial change that they had pioneered: the invention of agriculture in the Far East. For it was on the backs of laboring Chinese farmers down the centuries, and with the leisure that labor made possible for a favored few, that one of the great world civilizations would be built.

MONGOLIA

*GOBI DESERT*

*NAN SHAN*

(Beijing)

Anyang
*Yellow R.*

SHENSI
Xian

*SHAN TUNG*

Birthplace of
Confucius, 551 B.C.E.

Luoyang

Site of Capital of Western
Zhou, 1127–770 B.C.E.

*Wei R.*

Nancheng

Chengtu

SZECHWAN *Yangtze R.*

*Mekong R.*

*Yangzi R.*

Sea
of
Japan

KOREA

JAPAN

*Yellow
Sea*

(Shanghai)

(Hangzhou)

*East
China
Sea*

TRIBAL AND
LOCAL GROUPS

TAIWAN

*Pearl R.*

(Canton)

(Hong Kong)
(Br.)

(BURMA)

Hanoi

(THAILAND)

(VIETNAM)

*South
China
Sea*

| | |
|---|---|
| ▨ | Shang States 1520–1027 B.C.E. |
| ▦ | Zhou Kingdom ca. 300 B.C.E. |
| ▩ | Qin Empire ca. 220 B.C.E. |
| ⌁ | Great Wall |
| | Modern place names in parentheses |

0    200    400 Miles

0   200   400 Kilometers

110°                          120°

40°

30°

20°

## The Shang State

Traditionally, Chinese history begins with the Three Dynasties—the Xia, the Shang, and the Zhou. Of these, the Xia may have been mythical; the Shang, once dismissed as legendary also, has been proved real enough; and the Zhou, China's longest historic dynasty, is as thoroughly documented as any age so far back is likely to be. It was in the wake of the Zhou, finally, that China for the first time found genuine unity under the short-lived dynasty of Qin—the climax of China's early history.

As far as we presently know, then, Chinese civilization began with the hazily documented Shang dynasty, roughly 1500 to 1000 B.C.E. This was the period when northeastern China moved from Neolithic agricultural villages along the banks of the Huanghe to cities and kingdoms. It also saw the emergence of some of China's most ancient traditions.

Granted, most subjects of the Shang kings still lived in pit houses or similarly simple dwellings and worked their fields with stone tools. But there were other classes of society too. There were skilled artisans, workers in bronze and silk as well as in stone and ceramics. There was an embryonic merchant class that traded at some distance in salt and shells and the metals needed by the bronze workers, especially copper and tin. At the top of Shang society, finally, there was an aristocracy who hunted, fought, and enjoyed the finer things of Shang life—jade jewelry, bronze weapons and ritual vessels, silken robes, leather armor, and four-horse chariots from which to direct their frequent wars.

Presiding over this developing society were kings who, despite their titles, enjoyed only very limited powers. Shang kings were above all military leaders, defending northeastern China from border raids or embarking upon campaigns for loot or tribute. In peacetime, the monarch performed essential religious rituals and sacrifices on behalf of his people, entreating the gods for victory or good harvests. In performing these narrowly defined but important functions, rulers were aided by a still modest number of officials. These included expert scribes and diviners, the earliest specialists in the Chinese administration.

This Shang state was thus probably a loose confederation of clan states. The clans acknowledged the Shang king as leader in war and as a special intermediary with the gods. Beyond that, the power of the monarchy was almost certainly circumscribed by that of the more ambitious nobles. Royal authority probably seldom extended very far beyond the capital.

## Families, Cities, Culture

The core of Chinese society has always been the traditional Chinese family, and the roots of this institution probably go back at least this far. The Shang father ruled with patriarchal authority, owning all property, arranging marriages, dictating to all other members. "Filial piety"—reverent obedience to the father—was the highest of virtues.

Women were expected to obey their fathers in childhood, their husbands after marriage, and their sons as they grew older. Men could take more than one wife, but women could not even remarry if their husbands died. Sons were valued more than daughters, because only males could perform the all-important religious ceremonies in honor of ancestors discussed below.

As we will see, an older woman might have considerable influence over a son who had inherited headship of the family. But in the ideal Chinese family, at least, woman's lot was not an enviable one.

Shang cities were substantial if in some ways rudimentary accomplishments. The city walls, sometimes as high as thirty feet, were made of pounded earth and must have involved the regimented labor of thousands of workers. Within the walls were the large houses of nobles and kings and the temples of the gods, all constructed of wattle and daub hung on a framework of heavy timber.

Yet this newly civilized folk also produced the beginnings at least of one of the most sophisticated cultures the world has seen. Shang artisans, for instance, learned very early to alloy bronze out of copper, tin, and sometimes other metals. Writing also developed early, as a means of recording prophecies. Religion was polytheistic, embracing a welter of nature gods, goddesses, and other spiritual beings. These included the ancestral sky god Shangdi, later referred to as Tian (Heaven), and the Dragon Woman, as well as countless local spirits of earth and air and water. Among Shang aristocrats, however, one other element of Chinese religious belief began to take shape: the worship of ancestors.

The elite seem to have believed that Shangdi in particular was too awesome and elevated to be approached directly. Therefore they prayed to their own most celebrated ancestors, now transported to that spirit world where Shangdi reigned, to intercede with the god on behalf of living generations here below. This procedure had the practical advantage of giving the aristocracy, who alone *had* celebrated ancestors, exclusive access to the greatest of the gods. Ancestor worship thus effectively excluded all other classes from any concern with public affairs.

The veneration of ancestors was therefore a powerful conservative force from the beginning. It was not the least important legacy from the Shang period of Chinese history.

## The Kings of the Western Zhou

The Zhou dynasty, which seized power in the eleventh century B.C.E., would carry China from its first civilization to the age of Confucius, China's most revered philosopher.

According to the traditional dynastic histories, the house of Shang reigned, and sometimes ruled, for more than five hundred years during the second half of the second millennium B.C.E. The last Shang king, however, was a royal monster, a man steeped in crimes against gods and humanity. Then, out of the west, came two brothers, King Wu and the famous Duke of Zhou, at the head of a great army. These two princes of the western tributary state of Zhou are the heroes of this version of the change of dynasties.

The Zhou dynasty did in fact come to power in north China shortly before the year 1000 B.C.E. This house was to be recognized as at least the nominal overlord of China's political heartland until the year 221 B.C.E. Within this broad tract of time, two major periods are customarily distinguished: the comparatively successful Western Zhou comprising the first two and a half centuries of the period, and the long debacle of the Eastern Zhou, five hundred years of anarchy under a house that reigned in name only. And yet, paradoxically, the turbulent later-Zhou centuries may have seen more progress than the more renowned reigns that began the dynasty.

The Western Zhou is so called from the fact that the early Zhou kings continued to rule from their hereditary lands in the west. Here in the mountain-girt Wei River valley, on the edge of civilization, they were able to retain the martial spirit of border lords while profiting from the more advanced institutions of the principalities they had conquered to the east. Their nominal rule reached as far north as the future site of Beijing, as far south as the Yangzi valley of central China.

## Zhou Feudalism

Zhou China was essentially a feudal state, as Shang China had been. The kings of the Western Zhou did, however, boast a more elaborate bureaucracy than those of Shang times. They also propounded a far more ingenious—and influential—set of justifications for the power they had seized with the sword.

At the top of the Zhou administration was a chief advisor who could sometimes be the actual formulator of royal policies. The prototype of this traditional chief minister was the Duke of Zhou, who labored by his brother King Wu's side through the long struggle that led to Zhou supremacy. The best of later-Zhou ministers strove to emulate this spirit of selfless dedication to the welfare of the monarchy. The worst of them exploited their power for their own benefit.

Beneath the king and his chief minister, six administrative departments, charged with such matters as agriculture, war, public works, and religious observances, developed under the Zhou. These administrators collected tribute and issued communiqués, though the tributary princes were often too involved with their own affairs to pay much attention to royal officials.

Zhou kings, or their shrewder advisors, did, however, evolve what became the standard Chinese rationalization for their rule: the Mandate of Heaven. As Sons of Heaven, Zhou rulers claimed to govern by a special mandate, a divine charge to govern the land. They further claimed that it was the heinous crimes of the last Shang king that had led Heaven to dispatch the princes of Zhou to replace the Shang. This ingenious doctrine had only a single drawback. Any failing of moral force in the Zhou themselves—or any striking series of public calamities, from earthquakes to invasions—could lead to the charge that the Zhou in their turn had lost the Mandate of Heaven. And without the clearly perceived divine right to rule, how long would the descendants of the Zhou continue to govern China?

The doctrine of the Mandate of Heaven thus introduced by apologists for the Zhou dynasty remained an essential feature of Chinese political theory. The chaotic rise and fall of later Chinese dynasties was explained by this cosmic pattern of interrupted harmony and reestablished order. It was a pattern that would be repeated over and over again throughout the long history of the Middle Kingdom.

## The Eastern Zhou: Progress in a World at War

In the eighth century a military disaster signaled a fundamental turn in the fortunes of the dynasty—but this one a turn for the worse. Barbarians broke through into the Wei valley and sacked the Zhou capital. The monarchy thereupon prudently moved the capital eastward to Luoyang, in the civilized heart of northeast China. It was, apparently, a mistake.

From that time on, the authority of the Eastern Zhou—as the royal house is henceforth called—declined to the merest nominal allegiance. Feudal barons frequently failed in their tribute payments, sometimes refused even to respond when summoned to support the king in arms. During the latter part of the Eastern Zhou—the so-called Warring States period (fourth and third centuries B.C.E.)—this loose feudal empire dissolved entirely into a patchwork of separate states and clashing ambitions.

The Eastern Zhou has traditionally been considered a long decline after the more coherently ordered Western Zhou. More recently, however, historians have discovered some strikingly progressive elements in the politically anarchic later-Zhou centuries.

Veterans of the last wars of the Warring States, this soldier and his horse helped bring the Qin dynasty to power and unify China for the first time. These figures were among the hundreds of life-sized clay statues excavated from the underground tomb of China's First Emperor, Shi Huangdi. (Courtesy of the Cultural Relics Bureau, the People's Republic of China, and the Metropolitan Museum of Art, New York. Photograph by Seth Joel.)

Perhaps most obvious—but no less important—the population grew substantially. By the third century the civilized areas of northeastern and central China had the largest population of any center of civilization in the world. The dynasty that succeeded in unifying the warring states would thus emerge as master of the world's most populous nation, a rank China would continue to hold down to the present.

Economic development seems to have accompanied demographic growth. For one thing, China moved from the Bronze Age to the Iron Age during the later Zhou, producing iron axes, scythes, plows, and swords from approximately 500 B.C.E. on. New crops such as soybeans were introduced, and large-scale irrigation works sponsored by later-Zhou princes are mentioned for the first time. The merchant class particularly seems to have prospered during the Warring States period, making use of new military roads, and the first real Chinese coins, copper "cash" with holes in the center. Strung on cords, copper cash was from that time on China's most common medium of exchange.

Some historians have also detected a decline in the nobility and the rise of a new, self-made social type in the more fluid society of the Eastern Zhou. Men of humble background could rise at the courts of competing princes on the basis of energy, intelligence, and expertise in war or politics. This was especially so if the ambitious new man also possessed the winning social grace and air of spiritual force called *shi*. Shi was a debonair mastery of gentlemanly forms, religious ritual, and traditional wisdom that seems to have gained the pushiest social climber an entrée at the courts of the warring states.

Finally, the later Zhou was one of China's cultural golden ages. The book was invented during these centuries, and learning came to be respected for the first time in China. Princes and barons supported schools at their capital cities that would teach an aristocratic elite reading and music as well as archery and chariot fighting. From court to court, finally, there wandered not only unemployed officials and military commanders but sages as well. For the later Zhou was also, as we shall see, the Age of Confucius.

## THE QIN DYNASTY UNIFIES CHINA

### The Rise of the House of Qin

The state of Qin was located in modern Shaanxi in the mountain-walled valley of the Wei River, where the old Zhou capital had been. But the kings of Qin, rising to prominence eight hundred years later in China's social evolution, developed along very different lines from the loose feudalism of Zhou.

The Qin began with much of the border-lord military spirit that had distinguished their predecessors. They too evolved as a society on the dangerous edge, between the barbarian intruders from the north and west and the heart-land of Chinese civilization to the east. To this militant heritage they added a rigorous new approach to governance—a philosophy known as Legalism. The result was a potent mix of military toughness and authoritarian control that carried the Qin state to mastery of China in the third century B.C.E.

Defending the mountainous northwestern frontiers of Chinese civilization against raiders on horseback from the northern steppes, Qin warriors became expert cavalrymen themselves. During the fourth century B.C.E., the Qin kings used this cavalry arm to conquer a number of neighboring states in the northwest. In the third century, finally, they turned their powerful cavalry and the large armies recruited from their new subject states upon the civilized Zhou states to the east.

Discussion of the theory of Legalism may be deferred to a later section on the philosophical schools. In practice, however, Qin Legalism meant emphasis on law and punishment, rationalization and strengthening of the bureaucracy, and autocratic control from the center. Legalist administrators made appointments and promotions exclusively on the basis of merit and pushed policies that would keep the whole nation productively at work for the good of the state. They also put heavy stress on the military, planted secret police across the land to spy on the populace, and inflicted savage—if rigorously impartial—punishments for infractions of their draconian laws.

In the middle of the third century B.C.E., then, this militarily powerful, rigorously authoritarian state marched east against the collection of separate little kingdoms that still formally acknowledged the primacy of the decaying house of Zhou. The King of Qin was a young and aggressive prince surrounded by cadres of ambitious advisors, most prominent among them Li Si, a latter-day Legalist. The Qin army was ready, the rival Zhou monarchy moribund. Luoyang fell, and with it the house of Zhou.

One by one thereafter the other major states were overwhelmed, gobbled up, as a famous Chinese historian later put it, "like a silkworm devouring a mulberry leaf." In 221 B.C.E., the last of them fell. The King of Qin assumed a new throne, and Chinese chroniclers later gave him a new name and title to go with it—Qin Shi Huangdi, the First Emperor.

## Shi Huangdi: The First Emperor

Shi Huangdi is one of those larger-than-life figures who sometimes erupt into history, wrenching events out of their time-worn course, dazzling and often horrifying their contemporaries. "Cracking his long whip," even a hostile Chinese historian admitted, "he drove the universe before him, swallowing up the eastern and the western Zhou and overthrowing the feudal lords. He ascended to the highest position and ruled the six directions, scourging the world with his rod, and his might shook the four seas."[2]

Certainly Shi Huangdi was a man of feverish energy. By 221 B.C.E. he ruled the largest part of modern China. But he did not stop there. His armies hurled back the nomadic barbarians of the northern steppes and pushed far south into what is today Vietnam. His archers and spearmen in their bronze and leather armor, his lumbering chariots and light cavalry clattered back and forth across the land, garrisoned the passes, held princes and people alike in awe. He was by far the greatest conqueror China had yet seen.

Yet it is the domestic achievements of Huangdi that most boggle the historical imagination. In the decade left him after unification, the First Emperor seems almost to have lifted the land out of one path and set it upon another.

Almost at a stroke he abolished both the warring states and the feudal system that had spawned them. The strongholds of the defeated princes were destroyed, and the nobles of the old order were decimated or compelled to live in the new Qin capital under the watchful eye of the emperor. The new China was divided into thirty-six districts, each with a military and a civil governor, and into many more country-sized subdistricts, each with its appointed administrator. A centralized bureaucracy thus for the first time genuinely governed a united nation in East Asia.

Within the nation Shi Huangdi labored to effect a degree of uniformity never attempted before. He standardized weights and measures for the whole of China, issued a uniform coinage, and commissioned scholars to produce a simplified standard set of Chinese characters for writing in all parts of the empire. Even the length of cart axles was made uniform by decree, so that cart wheels could all follow the same ruts in the soft loess soil of north China.

## The Great Wall of China

Like kings and conquerors in other lands, the First Emperor also embarked upon an astonishing number of large-scale building projects. Roads crisscrossed the empire as never before, facilitating troop movements but also encouraging merchants to ply their trade once more. Canals were dug or refurbished, both for inland transport and to irrigate cropland. The emperor constructed elaborate palaces in his capital, including one allegedly large

[2]Theodore de Bary, Wing-tsit Chan, and Burton Watson, eds., *Sources of Chinese Tradition,* Vol. 1 (New York: Columbia University Press, 1960), p. 151.

enough to house ten thousand people. And he built himself a tomb at Chang'an—modern Xi'an—which traditional Chinese historians described as one of the miracles of the age. And in fact it awed a later age when parts of it were excavated in the 1970s.

All this, and still more. Somewhere between conquest and unification, among irrigation projects, royal palaces, and tombs, the First Emperor found time to build the Great Wall of China. In its final form, this amazing monument would stretch for fifteen hundred miles across China's northern frontier. It would average twenty-five feet in height over all those hundreds of miles, with watchtowers every two or three hundred yards. Huangdi did not build it all, of course. Sections had already been constructed by the lords of the northernmost Zhou states, and much of the emperor's work consisted of joining up these sections into a continuous barrier. Later rulers and dynasties revamped and added to the marvel, and most of the ramparts up which tourists toil and camera-toting Chinese teenagers mill today were actually raised in the sixteenth century C.E. rather than the third century B.C.E. Yet the Great Wall remains a monument to the will and vision of Shi Huangdi, and one of the undoubted wonders of the world.

To accomplish so much in so little time, the First Emperor had to drive his people mercilessly. Heavy taxes were laid on the peasant population. Forced labor was utilized for his enormous building projects. Whole populations were moved from one part of the country to another to carry out the emperor's orders. It was a triumph of the will unparalleled in China's ancient history—and one that many laboring Chinese probably could just as well have done without.

Legalists like Li Si particularly urged Huangdi to clamp down on intellectuals, the Confucian officials and other philosophers who objected to the rigors of the new regime. The books of philosophers who disagreed with the Legalists were collected and burned. Dissidents were imprisoned or executed, sometimes by the hundreds. They were harsh measures, but the men around the emperor justified them by the most powerful of Legalist arguments: success.

And then, when the first empire died suddenly in 210 B.C.E., the vaunted Legalist order collapsed like a house of cards.

Huangdi's chief ministers turned upon his heirs and then upon each other. Intrigue, executions, and royal suicide turned the dreamlike pleasure palaces of the First Emperor's capital into a nightmare world. Popular uprisings broke out among a people pushed to the breaking point and beyond. Within four years of Huangdi's death the dynasty of Qin followed its founder into extinction.

The unifier and his house perished; his capital was ravaged and looted, his tomb defiled. The Mandate of Heaven passed on to new hands. But the First Emperor's greatest achievement, the united China to which the Qin (Ch'in) dynasty had given its name, lived on.

## ART AND THOUGHT OF ANCIENT CHINA

### Art: Bronze Dragons and Clay Soldiers

There was much that was harsh and violent about the history of the first three Chinese dynasties. But even a sketchy survey of the architecture and sculpture, the poetry and philosophy of the first millennium and a half of Chinese history will strikingly brighten the perhaps too grim political picture thus far presented.

A serious problem arises at the outset for the student of Shang, Zhou, and Qin architecture. Since it was built primarily of wood, like Indian architecture of that period, there is simply none of it left to study. Yet it is possible, on the basis of surviving postholes and poetic descriptions, to reconstruct at least the shape and color of those vanished cities.

We read of luxurious noble residences set in large courtyards and raised on high platforms reached in many cases by a double ceremonial staircase. Spacious halls and chambers are mentioned, as well as pergolas, terraces, galleries, and balconies. Gardens and lotus pools and banks of blooming flowers glimmer through the pages of Zhou poetry. Descriptions of scarlet-painted pillars, carved and polished rafters, and similar princely indulgences are convincing evidence that these kings and barons of the Chinese Bronze and Iron ages built splendidly in their own way.

Where sculpture is concerned, we need no convincing. Considerable quantities of cast bronze in particular remain, collectors' items in China for hundreds of years. The archetypal Shang bronze is not a human figure but a vessel for holding meat, grain, or wine at a religious sacrifice. These ritual vessels stand on three or four legs and are typically covered with curvilinear or rectilinear designs in low or high relief, representing schematically the faces and bodies of animals. These animal-mask or monster-mask patterns became increasingly abstract and geometrical, until little remained but the eyes, polished bosses still peering out of the rhythmic interweaving of the sculptured bronze.

Fully figural sculpture still survives, some in marble or jade, but most elegantly cast in bronze. Animal motifs again are most common, including the water buffalo and rhinoceros as well as birds, horses, and dragons. The Chinese dragon shape in particular is fully developed by late Zhou times, with its undulating reptilian body, its wings and dorsal spines, and a scalelike patterning over its metal skin.

All this carved and cast sculpture from early China is small in size, and most of it is more decorative than realistic in style. But in 1974 the fabled tomb of the First Emperor of the Qin was discovered at Xi'an, and the emperor's fantastic army of life-size terracotta soldiers saw the light of day for the first time in twenty-two hundred years. There are reputed to be seven thousand of these clay statues—men, horses, even chariots—all life-size. Lined up in proper military formation, armed with real weapons, they were buried in underground tunnels to protect the emperor's subterranean tomb. Each figure is individualized and precisely detailed, from leather or bronze armor and intricate coiffure to the furrowed brow of an officer or the smooth-faced good looks of an infantry recruit.

These clay figures in their silent hundreds, idealized though they may be, give some indication of how convincingly these ancient Chinese could model the human figure when they wished to. They bring us as close as we will probably ever get to the living faces of the human beings who built the Great Wall of China.

## Literature: Chinese Characters and the Book of Songs

Writing was invented in China during the Shang period as a means of communicating with spirits. During the Zhou dynasty, when writing began to be directed to human readers, books appeared—slips of bamboo or wood fastened along one edge. Under the First Emperor the characters were standardized. They have changed very little since—another instance of the remarkable continuity that is so central a feature of Chinese civilization.

The Chinese characters thus established are very different from any Western written language. Each character stands not for an alphabetical sound but for an entire word. The shapes themselves, executed with brush and ink, have a beauty of line that has made calligraphy a major art in China. Most striking, perhaps, there is a distinctly pictorial quality to many Chinese characters. Thus the symbol for *dragon* originally looked like a dragon; the character for *good* resembled a picture of a mother and child.

The sheer difficulty of learning these thousands of complex written signs—by contrast with the twenty-six letters required for written English, for example—severely limited the number of people who would become literate in China. The prestige of the scholar and the powerful place of the mandarin administrator in Chinese government are among the most important results of this elaborate Chinese system of writing.

There is no literature beyond oracle bones from the Shang, but the eight centuries of the Zhou dynasty were seen by subsequent generations of Chinese as a literary golden age. Perhaps the most immediately appealing products of this first great age of Chinese literature are poems, most notably the three-hundred-odd lyrics of the *Book of Songs,* first collected around 600 B.C.E.

The *Book of Songs* includes a variety of material, from elegant poems on the deeds of kings and courtiers to simple folk songs illustrating the lives of Chinese peasants. The latter, composed most commonly in short, rhymed lines comparable to those of European folk ballads, deal with many aspects of life in the fields and villages of ancient China. Farmers complain of the eternal tax collector. Soldiers lament the hardships of military service. Young people glow to the first tremor of love in an idyllic setting of pasturelands and country gardens:

> Mid the bind-grass on the plain
> that the dew makes wet as rain
> I met by chance my clear-eyed man,
> > then my
> > > joy began.[3]

There are human misfortunes to complain of, and much talk of millet and rice, mulberry leaves, and the farmer's year. But after the hard work is over, there always seems to be a bountiful harvest, with country music and baskets full of food.

> . . . guests to feasting
> strike lute and blow
> pipes to show how
> feasts were in Chou [Zhou]
> > drum up that basket-lid now.[4]

Like Huangdi's soldiers in clay, these lines present an idealized version of ancient Chinese reality—but a salutary reminder too of the good times that, though perhaps rarer than the songs allow, were nonetheless a part of life in old China.

## The Sages: The Teachings of Confucius

Nothing undercuts the stereotyped Western image of the mysterious East more sharply than Chinese philosophy. To plunge into the writings of these Chinese sages after an immersion in the religious teaching of ancient India, for example, is to move from mysticism

---

[3]Cyril Birch and Donald Keene, *Anthology of Chinese Literature from Early Times to the Fourteenth Century* (New York: Grove Press, 1965), p. 8.

[4]Ibid., p. 12.

to humanism, from metaphysical to social thought, even—dismayingly—from a longing for the infinite to a pious emphasis on good manners. It can be a disturbing experience; for a Westerner hungering for mystical insights, it can even be a bit of a let-down.

It should not be. The sages of China, like the philosophers of Greece, were concerned above all with *human* relations, with life in the world of living, breathing men and women. Considering how human affairs have commonly been managed down the centuries, this was surely no ignoble concern.

The sages and schools of the period between the sixth and third centuries B.C.E. left a mark on the mind of China that no subsequent school of thought could match. And the first and greatest of them, at least in the admiring eyes of later generations, was Kongfuzi—"Master Kong"—known to the West by the Latinized name of Confucius (551–479 B.C.E.).

The Founder of Confucianism, China's national philosophy in later centuries, was born in what is now Shandong province in northeastern China, apparently in humble circumstances, though of aristocratic descent. He became one of the gentlemanly seekers after posts of authority at the courts of the kings of the later Zhou. Failing in this quest, he fell back upon teaching. Like Socrates and Jesus, he does not seem to have written anything himself, but his discussions with his students were preserved in the collection called the *Analects*. Respected in his own day, he was to be China's most honored sage in later centuries.

There is a deceptively conventional sound to many of Confucius's teachings. He earnestly urged such commonplaces of his day as respect for one's social superiors, reverence for one's elders and ancestors, pious observation of traditional religious rites, and formal courtesy. But Confucius had more startling things to say to his contemporaries. In a land where petty wars were more the rule than the exception, he was a pacifist. In a society still dominated by an arrogant hereditary aristocracy, he declared that the true gentleman was the man of wisdom and virtue, whatever his social origin. And in a Middle Kingdom ravaged by official exploitation, Confucius insisted that the care of the people should be the primary concern of their rulers.

His overall goal seems to have been social harmony. He dreamed of an ordered society in which each individual recognized his place and each group performed its proper function. In such a world, the loyal subject and the benevolent ruler would complement and support one another. The family would be the linchpin of society. And on the individual level, all would live by a maxim that has a certain resonance for Christians: "What you do not want done to yourself, do not do to others."

## The Hundred Flowers

The later Zhou period, for all its social and political misfortunes, was hailed in later centuries as the age of the "hundred schools" of thought, the time when a "hundred flowers" of wisdom bloomed across the Middle Kingdom.

Mencius, a Confucianist who lived a couple of generations after Confucius, was a philosophic optimist. Mencius declared that human nature is fundamentally good, all appearances to the contrary. He urged self-perfection, the cultivation of virtue through study directed at bringing out our innate capacity for human decency. He was a political utopian as well, proposing the redivision of the land of China on a basis of eight parts for the people, one for the king. The voice of the people, he suggested, is the real voice of the gods, since it is they who will finally decide by their actions whether a ruler possesses the Mandate of Heaven or not. There were enough rebellions in China's history to give this last point more of a realistic edge than some of Mencius's other ideas.

Han Faizi (died 233 B.C.E.) and the Legalists declared by contrast that human nature is basically selfish and undisciplined. To govern such people required rigorous laws rigorously applied, as in the authoritarian state of Qin. "A 'tender mother,' " said Han Faizi, "has spoiled the children!" There is a grimly Machiavellian ring to maxims like "When a sage governs the state, he does not count on the people to do what is beneficial to him. Instead, he sees to it that [they] can do him no harm."[5] Ironically, this most celebrated of Legalist sages died in the dungeons of the Qin, according to tradition imprisoned and compelled to commit suicide by his most illustrious pupil—the First Emperor's Legalist chief minister, Li Si.

Perhaps the most influential of all the hundred flowers to bloom after Confucius's day, however, was Daoism, a school that was more a religion than a philosophy. It was a mystical view of the human condition whose founder may himself have been a myth.

The name Laozi, the legendary founder of Daoism (Taoism) means simply "Old Master." According to tradition, he was a sage of Confucius's own day, a keeper of the archives in the state of Zhou. Confucius once met him, so the story goes, and later told his pupils that he had seen that day a being that was neither fish nor fowl—but a dragon. At the end of his life Laozi, seeing Zhou China collapsing around him, left by the western gate and disappeared, leaving behind him only one short book, the *Daodejing (Tao Te Ching, The Classic of Virtue and the Way)* the most commented upon and most widely translated of all the Chinese classics.

*Dao* means *the Way*—but what the Way means is a mystery wrapped in an enigma. The Way is the way of virtue; it is the way of nature. And it is something more. It is the ultimate ground of all being, the way things work, the way things are.

Virtue for many Daoists was to do nothing at all but relax and get in tune with the universe, with nature and the ultimate. Confucianists and Legalists argued incessantly, labored interminably to change things. Daoists tended to feel that the best society was a simple preliterate life synchronized with the rhythms of nature, and they would rather go fishing than argue about it.

Chinese hermits, nature poets, and landscape painters of later centuries would all practice in their various ways this philosophy of simplicity, acceptance, and harmony with the larger natural forces of the universe. Pressed to define the Way, the philosophical Daoist could only join the muted chorus of mystics down the ages in asserting that

> those who know do not talk
> and talkers do not know.[6]

## SUMMARY

City-based civilization emerged in both India and China between 2500 and 200 B.C.E., reaching a first climax under the Mauryan dynasty in India, the brief Qin dynasty in China.

India's first civilization, that of Harappa, was born in the Indus River valley around 2500 B.C.E. The Harappans built gridlike cities and had an integrated agricultural society.

---

[5]Han Fei Tzu [Faizi], *The Complete Works,* vol. 2, trans. W.K. Liao (London: A. Probsthain, 1959), pp. 306–307.
[6]Lao Tsu [Laozi], *The Way of Life,* trans. R. B. Blakney (New York: The New American Library, 1955), p. 109.

The Aryans, nomadic Indo-European cattle-herders from the northern steppes, destroyed the cities of the Indus and drove most of their Dravidian builders southward into the Deccan around 1500 B.C.E.

Civilization reemerged between 1000 and 500 B.C.E. in the Ganges River valley, east of the Indus. During this period the Aryans merged with the more settled Dravidians. Aryan iron tools succeeded in opening up the dense jungles of the Ganges valley and in rebuilding urban society once more. Although the institution of caste erected rigid barriers among races, classes, and occupations, it also made a place for future newcomers as new castes.

Magadha, one of the small kingdoms ruled by divinely sanctioned *rajas* along the Ganges, unified much of the Indian subcontinent under the Mauryan dynasty (322–185 B.C.E.). But the greatest of the Mauryas, the Buddhist Asoka, rejected the use of force and ruled as an Indian philosopher king.

Hinduism, the complex faith of most Indians, evolved during the Aryan-Dravidian synthesis shortly after 100 B.C.E. It developed a range of religious sects and practices ranging from veneration of sacred cows to the mystical meditations of Indian gurus. Buddhism emerged as part of a new religious ferment around 500 B.C.E. Prince Gautama the Buddha and his monks preached escape from earthly suffering and desire through spiritual enlightenment. Even India's most famous epic poems, the *Mahabharata* and the *Ramayana,* reflect not only the warlike ways of the Aryans but the spiritual insights of the brahmans who edited them as well.

Shang China (1500–1000 B.C.E.) was really a collection of separate states in northeastern China.

The Zhou dynasty (1000–221 B.C.E.), a clan of border lords from the rugged northwest, conquered Shang China in the eleventh century. Their claim that they had the Mandate of Heaven helped them to govern in a loose feudal fashion longer than any other royal house. But it was the short-lived Qin dynasty (221–206 B.C.E.) that first imposed a centralized imperial order on all the Chinese states under the hard-driving First Emperor Huangdi. Huangdi linked the nation's northern defenses against nomadic invasion in the Great Wall of China.

Shang bronzes, the sculptured metal dragons of Zhou times, and the astonishing life-size clay soldiers from Huangdi's tomb are marvelous artistic achievements. The poetry of the *Book of Songs* has been beloved in China for more than two thousand years.

Most important, however, the philosophers of the later-Zhou period, around 500 B.C.E., played a central part in Chinese cultural tradition. Confucius's call for good government and human decency would echo down the Chinese centuries. So would Mencius's faith in human virtue and self-improvement, the Legalists' demand for rigor and justice, and the gentle urgings of Laozi to follow "the Way" of nature, goodness, and the cosmos.

## SUGGESTED READING

Allan, S. *The Shape of the Turtle: Myth, Art, and Cosmos in Early China.* Albany: State University of New York Press, 1991. Intriguing analysis of Shang beliefs and art.

Burton, T. R. *Hindu Art.* Cambridge, Mass.: Harvard University Press, 1993. Brilliantly illustrated survey.

Chakravarti. *The Social Dimensions of Early Buddhism.* New York: Oxford University Press, 1987. Useful focus on social teachings and consequences. See also C.-S. Yu, *Early Buddhism and Christianity* (Delhi: Motilal Banarsidass, 1981), comparing Christ and the Buddha in terms of authority, community, and the discipline they taught.

Confucius. *The Analects of Confucius,* trans. A. Waley. London: G. Allen and Unwin, 1938. Two valuable recent studies are R. L. Taylor, *The Religious Dimension of Confucianism* (Albany: State University of New York Press, 1990), and W.M. Tu, *War, Learning, and Politics: Essays on the Confucian Intellectual* (Albany: State University of New York Press, 1993).

Corless, R. *The Vision of Buddhism: The Space Under the Tree.* New York: Paragon, 1989. Good introduction to the life and teachings of the Buddha. Two readable lives of the Buddha are R. A. Mitchell, *The Buddha: His Life Retold* (New York: Paragon, 1989), and D. J. Kalupahana, *The Way of Siddhartha: A Life of the Buddha* (Lanham, Md.: University Press of America, 1987).

Cotterell, A. *The First Emperor of China.* Harmondsworth, U.K.: Penguin, 1989. Readable life of Shi Huangdi.

Fu, Z. *China's Legalists: The Earliest Totalitarians and Their Art of Ruling.* Armonk, N.Y.: M. E. Sharpe, 1996. Strong Chinese condemnation of Legalist rigor by a Chinese who has lived under modern totalitarianism.

Kostermeier, K. K. *A Survey of Hinduism.* Albany: State University of New York Press, 1989. Expert overview of the world's oldest religion. See also D. M. Knipe, *Hinduism: Experiments in the Sacred* (San Francisco: Harper, 1991), and D. R. Kingsley's brief but penetrating *Hinduism, a Cultural Perspective* (Englewood Cliffs, N.J.: Prentice Hall, 1982).

Lewis, M. E. *Writing and Authority in Early China.* Albany: State University of New York Press, 1999. How the unifying power of the written word in the minds of a classically educated ruling class shaped a united China.

Li, H. C. *Eastern Zhou and Qin Civilization,* trans. K. C. Chang. New Haven, Conn.: Yale University Press, 1985. Emphasizes the emergence of centralized imperial government in a feudal world.

Li, Y.-N. *Chinese Women Through Chinese Eyes.* Armonk, N.Y.: W. E. Sharpe, 1992. Chinese essays, including studies of ancient China.

Loewe, M., and E. L. Shaughnessy, eds. *The Cambridge History of Ancient China: From the Origins of Civilization to 221 B.C.* New York: Cambridge University Press, 1999. Wide variety of views in a rapidly expanding field as Chinese scholarship piles up new evidence.

Pruthi, R., and B. R. Sharma, eds. *Buddhism, Jainism, and Women.* New Delhi: Anmol Publications, 1997. Considerations of women's role.

Quigley, D. *The Interpretation of Caste.* Oxford: Clarendon Press, 1993. Anthropological analysis of India's "peculiar institution." On the origins of caste, see B. K. Smith, *Classifying the Universe: The Ancient Indian Varna System and the Origins of Caste* (New York: Oxford University Press, 1994), and H. A. Gould, *The Hindu Caste System: The Sacralization of a Social Order* (Delhi: Chanakya, 1987).

Roy, K. *The Emergence of Monarchy in North India.* New York: Oxford University Press, 1994. Theoretical social analysis of a complicated subject.

Strong, J. S. *The Legend of King Asoka.* Princeton, N.J.: Princeton University Press, 1983. Translation and analysis of the *Asokavadana,* an early account of the Buddhist philosopher king.

Thapar, R. *Asoka and the Decline of the Mauryas,* rev. ed. New York: Oxford University Press, 1997. Critical look at the philosopher king.

Waldron, A. *The Great Wall of China: From History to Myth.* New York: Cambridge University Press, 1989. Carefully researched history of the wall, debunking many myths.

Willier, R. "Confucian Ideal of Womanhood," *Journal of the China Society,* 13 (1976). An apologia for the Confucian view of women.

Wiltshire, M. G. *Ascetic Figures Before and in Early Buddhism.* New York: Mouton de Gruyter, 1990. Scholarly study of the religious framework.

 Please refer to the document CD-ROM for primary sources related to this chapter.

# CHAPTER 5

# THE FURNACES OF MEROE AND THE OLMEC HEADS

## Ancient Civilizations of Africa and the Americas

### (1500–150 B.C.E.)

# A Glance Ahead: Lost Civilizations across Three Continents

Early civilization happened elsewhere besides the places we have visited already. Ancient cities rose in other parts of Africa besides Egypt. Across the Atlantic in the Americas, long-vanished peoples laid the foundations of future civilizations too.

In North Africa, Kushite kings conquered ancient Egypt, and Carthage was Rome's most powerful rival for mastery of the Mediterranean. In Middle and South America, thousands of years before the more familiar Aztecs and Incas, the Mexican Olmecs carved huge stone heads and the ancient Chavín culture raised towering temples in Peru.

All that is left today are scattered artifacts, ruined structures, and the accounts of travelers many centuries ago. Archaeologists, anthropologists, and other scholars add to our knowledge of these long-vanished cultures. But until they can tell us more, historians can only poke admiringly through the ruins of these lost civilizations.

# Nubia, Kush, and Inner Africa

## The Second Largest Continent

There was once a predisposition—rooted perhaps in too many old Tarzan movies—to imagine Africa as one vast jungle inhabited by "natives" who lived in grass huts and were constantly being devoured by tigers and crocodiles. Even people with some knowledge tended to fall in with this "dark continent" image, claiming that Africa had been cut off from progress through lack of intercourse with other peoples throughout its history. The reality, as usual, is a good deal more complex and interesting than the myth.

The world's second largest continent—only Asia is larger—covers a little less than twelve million square miles. More than two fifths of that vast area is covered with grassy plains. Another two fifths is arid-to-desert land. Less than one fifth is forested, and only a small part of that is genuine tropical rain forest, most of it in the Congo River basin and along the Guinea coast of West Africa.

The geography of the continent falls into a series of clearly definable bands: fertile Mediterranean coastal lands in the north, the wider swath of the barren Sahara, the sudannic belt of grasslands, the equatorial rain forests, then grassy plains again, the Kalahari Desert, and finally the fertile uplands of South Africa. This simplified pattern of east-to-west bands is complicated by a curving north-to-south trench composed of the Nile and the Great Rift Valley with its attendant lakes, running almost the length of East Africa.

Historically speaking, the peoples and cultures of Africa have been as varied as those of any other continent. Black Africans have apparently always been important, constituting 70 percent of the population today. But there are also Arabs and Berbers in large numbers in the north and in recent centuries influential immigrations from Europe and Asia. Even the "black" majority is normally subdivided into a variety of culturally diverse peoples and language groups, from the Bantu-speaking agricultural people of the central and southern portions of the continent to the food-gathering Khoi-San and Mbuti peoples still to be found in the deserts and deep woods.

For Western explorers and imperialists as recently as a century ago, Africa was the dark continent, a symbol of the unknown and the primitive. In fact, Africa was making crucial contributions to the human story long before civilization was dreamed of.

## Early Contributions

As the evidence now runs, the earliest hominids first evolved into human beings in Africa. Africa probably maintained a long lead in the production of basic stone tools throughout the Old Stone Age. One of the oldest civilizations, that of ancient Egypt, took shape in northeastern Africa, though as we saw in the last chapter, the history of the lower Nile was also closely bound up with the early history of the Near East. Civilization, however, emerged, in parts of Africa besides Egypt, and it is with these historic beginnings that the following sections will be concerned.

The existence of these early African cultures argues strongly against the notion that Africa was cut off from progressive outside influences. Several of the early cultures to be considered here—Nubia and Kush on the upper Nile and Carthage on the western Mediterranean—developed in fruitful interchange with other areas. Their stories clearly illustrate the process of sociocultural development in the usual historical web of influences and interchange of goods and ideas.

Edgar Rice Burroughs, the creator of Tarzan and his fairy-tale Africa, once said that the best way to get ahead as a writer was to write about something you know absolutely nothing about. His vision of a dark continent thick with jungle, peopled by Hottentots, and stalked by man-eating tigers (who don't live in Africa at all) would seem to illustrate his theory to perfection. But that fictional vision does not tell us much about Africa. As a

Swahili-speaking East African might put it, shaking his head over this Wild West legend of his own land: "More *Wazungu* lies!"

## The Nubian Corridor

Out of the south they came, by river and by caravan into Egypt: gold, ivory, ebony, ostrich feathers, slaves. And more: cattle, grain, leopards (and their skins), giraffes (whose tails were used as fly whisks), oils and perfumes, "amazon stone," carnelian, gum, and red ocher and ostrich eggs. Century after century the largesse of the mysterious lands beyond the cataracts of the Nile came north—in booty, in tribute, and in trade goods. Sometimes, especially during Egypt's long decline, African armies came down the Nile to smite Thebes and Memphis, and African kings from the south to sit on the throne of the pharaohs, to negotiate with the Greeks or fight the Romans.

For at least two thousand years there were rich lands south of Egypt, in that part of northeastern Africa once called Nubia, today straddling the border between Egypt and Sudan. From the eleventh century B.C.E. to the fourth century C.E., these lands were ruled by the powerful African state of Kush.

Nubia, or the Nubian corridor, has become a catchall geographical term for the area between the First Cataract of the Nile and the bifurcation of that immense river into the Blue and White Niles. On a map of modern Africa, it is the region of the cataracts and the enormous S-curve of the river between Egypt's Aswan High Dam and the Sudanese capital of Khartoum.

Before the beginning of history, the Nubians lived much as other Paleolithic or Neolithic peoples did along the banks of the Nile. From the Mediterranean in the north to the Ethiopian highlands and the Great Lakes of Central Africa, these early Africans hunted and fished and learned to grow crops and herd animals as other peoples did around the globe. Like other African peoples, they lived in small groups, in nomadic bands or agricultural villages. Some of the same tools and styles of pottery were produced in Nubia, south of the First Cataract, as in Egypt, north of it.

Then, around 3000 B.C.E. came the great change in Egypt. Led by the first pharaohs, centralized government mobilized the villages to bring the Nile under control. The resulting system of levees, catch basins, and irrigation ditches turned the Nile River north of the cataracts into one of the most productive agricultural zones in the world. Bureaucratic government, social classes, monumental building, and other elements of a developed civilization followed.

Life in Nubia, just south of the emerging Egyptian kingdom, could not help but be affected. In time, as we will see, many of the characteristics of Egyptian civilization would spread up the Nile into Nubia. Soon also, indigenous Nubian kingdoms—including Kush and Meroe—would emerge in the south and begin to play a key part in the history of the Nile valley as a whole.

Perhaps most important, however, Nubia continued to serve as the most important link between Egypt and the Mediterranean world in the north and inner Africa to the south. Though the cataracts required that boats be transported overland around them, the long river remained the easiest north-south route across the desert.

It is not surprising, then, that Egyptian rulers, eager for ivory, ebony, incense, and other products, sent trading expeditions up the Nile toward the heart of Africa. Up and down the Nubian corridor, goods, ideas, and power thus flowed for many centuries. As early as the Egyptian Old Kingdom, a pharaoh gratefully accepted a Pygmy dancer from Central Africa,

Women of ancient Kush, illustrated in a black stone relief sculpture from Meroe. The figure on the left is a Kushite queen. Note the elaborate headdresses, necklaces, bracelets, and decorated skirts, as well as the impressive throne on which the sovereign sits. (Werner Forman Archive/Art Resource)

sent to him as a gift from Nubia. As late as Roman times, Kushite raiders carried off a carved head of Augustus Caesar from an attack on an Egypt that had become a Roman province. Nubia was thus a vital link in the chain that bound the civilizations of the Old World together.

## The Kingdom of Kush

From the beginning, Egyptian influences were of paramount importance in the development of these southern lands. The pharaohs of the Middle Kingdom went south of the first cataract and raided the region of the upper Nile. Around 1500 B.C.E., the aggressively expansionist pharaonic empire builders of the New Kingdom overran the area, and made the wealth—and the fearless bowmen—of the region prime resources in Egypt's most ambitious bid to master the Fertile Crescent.

During these centuries of northern domination, Egyptian governors and garrisons, priests, and artisans left an indelible mark on the lands and peoples of the upper Nile. The sons of Kushite kings were educated at the Egyptian royal court at Thebes. Egyptian temples and gods, Egyptian royal rituals, and Egyptian hieroglyphics were all transplanted to the Sudan. The Egyptian religious complex at Napata in particular became a center for the spread of Egyptian culture among the Africans beyond the cataracts.

When the long decline of Egypt began around 1100 B.C.E., the kingdom of Kush regained its independence and flourished as the master of the Upper Nile. But the black kings of Kush still followed Egyptian ways and worshiped Egyptian gods. They glorified their own deeds in hieroglyphic inscriptions and were buried under pyramids like those of the Old Kingdom. It was a new Egypt—upriver.

As old Egypt fell under foreign domination during the first millennium B.C.E., the Kushites may well have seen themselves as the true guardians of the old ways and ancient values they had shared with their neighbors down the river for so many centuries. Around

750 B.C.E., the Kushite kings Kashta and Piankhi marched north to liberate Egypt from its Libyan rulers, the mercenary North African princes who had seized the throne. For more than half a century thereafter, the Kushite pharaohs of the twenty-fifth Egyptian dynasty ruled a dual kingdom that stretched perhaps fourteen hundred miles from the Blue Nile to the shores of the Mediterranean.

But the future of Kush lay in the Sudan. Within sixty years the savage Assyrians had expelled the twenty-fifth dynasty and replaced the Kushite kings in Egypt. Assyrian predominance would be succeeded by that of other peoples, including the Greek Ptolemies and the Roman Caesars. Upriver, beyond the cataracts, Kush went its independent way.

## The Furnaces of Meroe

The golden age of Kushite civilization was the period of the ascendancy of the city of Meroe, from the third to the first century B.C.E. Much of what follows will refer to these centuries.

The centers of Kushite civilization were populous cities, built from sun-dried brick, like those of Egypt and Mesopotamia, and garnished with palaces and temples. But there were differences too. The Kushite kings lived like Egyptian pharaohs, but the succession in Kush was decided by consensus among the royal princes, and the queen mother was uniquely powerful among the Kushites. There were powerful Kushite queens as well, though we know little about them. One, called Candace, attacked the Romans in Egypt, and another Kushite Candace earned a mention in the Bible.

Egyptian-style priesthoods, notably that of the sun god Amon, were extremely influential, but Amon's central place was later usurped by the Kushite lion god Apedemek, whose graven image is frequently found among the ruins of Kushite cities.

The wealth of Kush lay in its land, its location, and its energetic people. The Kushite capital of Meroe was watered not only by the Nile but by a significant annual rainfall. The result was a broad expanse of pasture and cropland, a green island in the desert where cattle grazed and grain stood tall. There were minerals of great value under the soil of Kush as well, including gold and iron. Kush was fortunate also in its locale, up the river from Egypt and on the trade routes that wound east through the Ethiopian up-lands to the Red Sea. From these advantages a vigorous people—farmers and herders, soldiers, traders, builders—made a very good life indeed for several hundred years.

Kushite artisans in particular exploited the iron ore of southern Kush so industriously that Meroe became the greatest center for the production of iron in Africa. Its surviving heaps of slag have led some Africanists to see Meroe as the Birmingham—or Pittsburgh—of the continent.

Culture seems to have flourished too in the inner African world of Kush. Carven images of Kushite victories in nameless wars are still to be seen in low relief across ruined walls. There are long lines of prisoners and royal processions parading in Egyptian silhouette, though their royal figures are more solidly built than the leaner, more sinuous people downriver, and the jewelry they wear is of Kushite make. There are animal gods and royal beasts, the lion and the elephant soon replacing the Egyptian vulture and cobra.

The wars the Kushites fought remain for the most part nameless because just about the time that the independent greatness of Kush began, the Kushites evolved their own form of writing—and we cannot read it. They developed a true alphabet, like that of the Phoenicians or the Greeks. But there is no Rosetta stone for Kushite; we can pronounce the words, but we cannot tell their meanings.

Gradually over the centuries, Kush lost touch with the Mediterranean world to the north. The passing of Kushite glory during the first centuries of what was elsewhere the Christian era has been explained in various ways. The limited land was probably over-grazed and perhaps dried out by the slow southward creep of the Sahara. Kush's best customers in Egypt were ruined by Rome's insatiable demands upon this breadbasket of empire, and business in Meroe suffered as poverty spread along the Nile. Trade to the east was taken over by new Red Sea powers. And around C.E. 350 one of these East African states, the Kingdom of Axum, put an end to what had been the greatest early civilization of inner Africa: "I made war on them [the Axumite king Ezana declared]. . . . I burnt their towns . . . and my army carried off their food and copper and iron . . . and destroyed the statues in their temples, their granaries and cotton trees and cast them into the [Nile]."[1]

The traveler approaching Meroe by train from Cairo today sees a scattering of ruined temples, huge broken pyramids, and heaps of slag from the famous ironworks. There is little left of the royal city at the center, the baths, the processional way running through row on row of rectangular roofs and courtyards up to the Kushite temple of the sun.

## CARTHAGE: EMPIRE OF THE WESTERN SEAS

### The Phoenician Diaspora

At the other end of North Africa from Egypt, and facing the Mediterranean Sea rather than inner Africa, stood the great city of Carthage and its seaborne empire. Founded by Near Eastern immigrants from Phoenicia—discussed in Chapter 3—Carthage became an independent African empire strong enough to challenge both the Greeks and the Romans for mastery of the western Mediterranean. Modern historians have tended to see the founding of Carthage as part of a larger, primarily economic Phoenician diaspora. In this view, the far-trading Phoenicians first came ashore at the site of the future Carthage to establish a way station—one of many—on the road to Spain. On Spain's Atlantic coast, beyond the Pillars of Hercules—now called the Straits of Gibraltar—they had established a major base at Gades, modern Cadiz. There they traded with the indigenous Spanish population for silver mined nearby and for tin imported from France and England.

It was a profitable trade. But the Atlantic coast of Spain was 2,000 miles from Lebanon, a long voyage even for the intrepid Phoenicians. The merchants of Tyre needed way stations along the North African coast where they could get food and water and repair their ships. It was probably for this purpose that Phoenician ships first anchored in the sheltered harbor where Carthage would later be built.

For the rest of the story of the rise of imperial Carthage, we must depend on legends that may well contain a kernel of fact. For legend has it that the city that became the capital of a vast commercial empire was built by a Near Eastern queen in the ninth century B.C.E. Elissa—known to the Greeks and Romans as Dido—was the royal sister of the king of Tyre, a wealthy Phoenician trading city on the coast of Lebanon. Caught up in a bloody feud in her Phoenician home, she fled the city at the head of many Tyrian nobles. Gathering support from other Phoenician cities as they moved westward, she and her followers settled at last on the coast of what is today Tunisia, where she built her city.

---

[1]Robert W. July, *A History of the African People* (New York: Scribner's, 1970), p. 38.

By all accounts, Elissa's "New City"—*Qart Hadash,* later Latinized to "Carthage"—was a splendid piece of work. In his epic poem, the *Aeneid,* the Roman poet Vergil described the exiled queen—here called Dido—raising her palaces and temples. Vergil's own hero, Aeneus, future founder of Rome, dawdles and watches, falling in love with the builder of the city that would become Rome's greatest rival. Legends also tell of Elissa's tragic end, dying by her own hand for love of Aeneus. These latter tales are probably poetic inventions. But the city she built was a concrete and powerful reality.

## Peoples of the Maghreb

The Tyrian immigrants built their city on land bought or leased from the African people who already lived there. The peoples of this northern bulge of North Africa, later known as the Maghreb, would play an important part in the history of this African commercial empire.

The ancient peoples of North Africa west of Egypt have traditionally been called Libyans. We have no way of knowing what they called themselves, and they may have had little sense of being one people at all. We know, however, that they spoke one language and shared a precarious living space between the scorching Sahara and the Mediterranean Sea. Ethnically, they were probably the ancestors of the modern Berber population who share the land today with the later Arab conquerors of North Africa.

The Libyans were farmers and herders, growing grain and herding oxen, sheep, and goats. They rode horses and used them to pull carts and war chariots. They worked their land with stone tools, though some Libyans wore copper bracelets, anklets, and other metal items of personal adornment. Their religion, like that of ancient Egypt, seems to have focused on animal-headed gods and goddesses, especially on a ram-headed sun god called Ammon. Politically, they were originally organized into tribes and clans. In Carthaginian times, as we will see, some Libyan peoples developed hereditary kingdoms in the Maghreb.

These were the people, then, who agreed to sell a strip of coastal land to a handful of immigrants from the east in the eighth century B.C.E. In the centuries that followed, the lives of both the indigenous population and the intruders would be transformed by this fertile fusion of cultures.

## The Carthaginian Empire

From the eighth to the second century B.C.E., the naval and commercial power of Carthage grew till it dominated the western Mediterranean and the seas beyond.

The Phoenician cities from which Carthage sprang foundered and fell in the welter of near Eastern peoples. On its own, the commercial empire or trading zone dominated by Carthage emerged by the sixth century as mistress of its own seaborne domain. Its power dominated all the other surviving Phoenician settlements of the west. The Carthaginian Empire included territories across the Mediterranean in southern Europe—parts of Spain and the islands of Sardinia, Corsica, and Sicily. In time it embraced trading centers on the Atlantic, from settlements in Britain and French Brittany through Cadiz in Spain down to the west coast of Africa.

Closer to home, the nearby peoples of the Maghreb, including the sizable Berber states of Numidia and Mauritania, were subject to or allied with Carthage. Even desert tribes such as the Garamantes fed the insatiable hunger of the Carthaginians for trade, bringing goods by the Saharan ways only they could follow from the oases of Fezzan.

A laughing mask from vanished Carthage reminds us that ancient peoples also saw the comic side of life. Power and wealth, conquest and defeat filled their history, but some may see more life in a face like this than in many pages of historical heroics. (Anthony Esler)

From this western, largely maritime empire the Carthaginians derived such valuable goods as pottery and glass, textiles and ivory, tin, silver, and gold. Much of this trade was by barter. The famous "silent trade" in African gold, described by the tireless Greek historian Herodotus, is perhaps not atypical of the trade that took place without money or a common language in these early times. The Greek explained how the Carthaginians, when trading with a certain African nation "beyond the pillars of Hercules," laid out their trade goods on the beach and then withdrew to their ships until the local people had brought forth sufficient gold to pay for what they wanted. No words were exchanged, only Mediterranean goods for West African gold. Herodotus added that "neither party deals unfairly with the other," as if it were rather an oddity in that world of shrewd horse traders.

There is evidence of voyages even farther down the coasts of Africa in ancient times. The most important of these was apparently undertaken by the respected Carthaginian Hanno, who set out with a large fleet on a voyage around West Africa in the fifth century B.C.E. According to descriptions copied from the walls of a Carthaginian temple, Hanno's ships slowly rounded the great bulge of West Africa, founding colonies, trading with the local people, and discovering strange lands. There were rivers filled with hippopotamuses and crocodiles and coasts lined with fires and drums in the night. There were people dressed in animal skins who pelted them with stones and hairy "savages" called Gorillas who resisted capture by clawing, biting, and climbing up trees. There were mysterious islands and erupting volcanoes with lava flowing down into the sea.

Hanno may have got as far as the modern country of Cameroon, at the inner angle of West Africa. If he did, it was a feat that would not be duplicated for almost two thousand years.

## Rivals of the Greeks and Romans

Carthage was governed by an oligarchy of increasingly wealthy commercial families. These plutocrats sat on the Carthaginian ruling councils and held the main magistracies, called *sufets,* which apparently were similar to the Roman consuls. These civilian authorities kept close watch over the military in particular, so that Carthaginian generals seldom challenged the civil government, as happened so often in Rome.

As seen by their rivals across the Mediterranean, these empire builders of northern Africa were a dour and grasping lot, possessing a streak of cruelty that even the Romans professed to be shocked by. And there does seem to be some substance to the charge that the lords of Carthage sacrificed even their children to the gods who brought the city its wealth and power. For human sacrifice was practiced among them, as among other Phoenician colonists, and the burned bones of children have been found in special tombs in the Carthaginian holy place, the *tophet,* close by the harbor.

Carthage in its prime in many ways resembled a Tunisian town of today. The whitewashed walls of the multistory tenements of the lower city must have been crammed with humanity, since estimates of the population run higher than half a million. Nicer homes and gardens lay in the northern suburbs. On the high city, or Byrsa, stood the temples of Baal the sun god, the even more popular goddess Tanit, and other divinities. A wall sixty feet high stretched across the neck of the peninsula on which the city stood, protecting Carthage from attack by land, while its fleet guarded it by sea.

To maintain its supremacy on the western seas, Carthage fought a long series of wars, particularly with the Greeks and the Romans on the other side of the Mediterranean. A brief glance at these conflicts may round out this overview of Africa's most celebrated early empire.

The Greeks were the great trade rivals first of the Phoenicians and later of the Carthaginians. Greek colonies in the western Mediterranean early ran afoul of Carthage's trade monopoly, and the two peoples fought intermittently through the fifth and fourth centuries B.C.E. Greeks even invaded the Maghreb and for a short time threatened the very survival of Carthage, only to be turned back in the end by Carthaginian forces.

During the third and second centuries, the rising power of Rome, almost due north of Carthage across the narrow waist of the Mediterranean, collided with this rich nation of traders. The results were the three Punic Wars, the most desperate struggles of Rome's own violent climb to mastery of the Mediterranean world.

The two empires first fell out with each other in the third century B.C.E. over rival claims in Sicily. Roman arms triumphed in the long run, but Carthage accepted only a temporary setback. The Second Punic War dealt the Romans a shock from which they did not recover for generations: the sudden descent of the Carthaginian general Hannibal's war elephants, come round by way of Spain, through the Alpine passes and into northern Italy. The armies of the great North African power ravaged the Roman heartland almost at will during the last years of the third century. But the Romans, fighting on their home ground, finally wore the invaders down once more. And fifty years later, in the middle of the second century, they launched the war of revenge that destroyed Carthaginian power forever.

It must have been a laborious as well as a bloody business to burn and topple into ruins a significant portion of a city that had once held half a million people. But the soldiers of Scipio the Younger managed it. Today the outer promontory of the double harbor is a dangerous underwater reef, and the line of the sixty-foot wall that once crossed the peninsula is detectable only from the air. The best that modern archaeology can muster has found very little of old Carthage in between.

## THE FIRST NORTH AMERICANS

### The Americas Before Columbus

The geography of the Americas is of course familiar in broad outline to all Americans; we have seen the globe turned our way all our lives. We have some notion of the mountainous spine that runs down the western side of the new World, the Rockies and the Andes. We know about the great plains and icy tundras of Canada, the plains and deserts of the western United States, and the dark forests that once covered eastern North America. We should know more than we do of the mountains and jungles of Central America and the Caribbean, of the world's largest rain forest in Brazil, of the southward-flowing pampas of Argentina, and of the howling seas and bitter winds around Cape Horn.

As recently as five centuries ago, this vast and varied sweep of continents and islands was inhabited by a single people, known through Columbus's fundamental error of geographical judgment as Indians. Among these Native Americans, a series of civilizations had arisen long before Columbus came.

Highly developed cultures emerged in two parts of the New World especially, in what are today Mexico and Peru. They are usually represented in the modern imagination by their final formulations, those that the European conquerors encountered—the Aztecs and

## ANCIENT AMERICAN CIVILIZATIONS

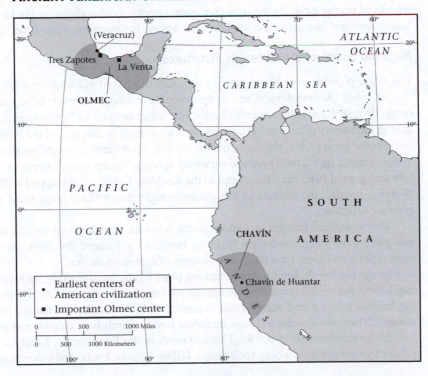

the Incas. But civilizations far older than these flourished and faded in the Americas hundreds and even thousands of years before the coming of the conquistadores. It is with these beginnings of civilization in the New World—with the long-vanished Olmec people of Mexico and the Chavín culture of Peru—that this chapter must finally concern itself.

We will begin, however, with a look at the earlier Amerindian cultures from which these first American civilizations emerged—the food-gatherers and farmers of Stone Age America.

## Hunters and Farmers

In 3500 B.C.E. the great hunts on the western plains of North America were already thousands of years in the past. When the first Paleolithic hunters had passed through the gap in the Canadian ice sheet into what is today the western United States, they had found a hunter's paradise of big game. Endless herds of mammoths and mastodons, camels, prehistoric horses, giant bison, lion-sized cats, and many other creatures roamed the grasslands. The hunting bands from Asia had grown fat in this Eden of raw meat on the hoof. They had also spread rapidly southward, as we have seen, occupying both continents of the New World in no more than a millennium or two.

Then things began to change.

The last ice age drew to a close. The retreat of the glacier and the resulting changes in temperature and vegetation transformed the New World environment. The warmer, drier climate substantially diminished the variety and numbers of the great herd animals of earlier times. In addition, the growing numbers and increasing skill of human hunting bands may have led to vast overkill and the extinction of whole species. Most of the big game, the so-called megafauna of the Americas, was thus wiped out thousands of years ago.

A changing environment inevitably led to changes in the ways of life of the people who lived on the land. By the time civilization began to take shape on the far-off plains of Sumer, cultural change was also under way among the peoples of the Americas.

## Regional Economies and Family Structures

The native population of North America was once dismissed as a uniformly primitive collection of tribes. Archaeological and anthropological studies, however, have emphasized the range, diversity, and achievements of even the earliest peoples of North America. This is evident in the variety of regional economies which emerged in this part of the New World.

On the great plains, the extinction of most of the American megafauna led the Indians to concentrate increasingly on one surviving species: the enormous herds of bison or buffalo that grazed from the Mississippi to the Rockies. Using spears tipped with deadly new "Folsom points," the hunters of the plains brought down these large meat animals with growing efficiency.

The woodland hunters of eastern North America prowled vast forests of hardwoods and pine. Like hunter-gatherers in many lands, they foraged for fruit, nuts, and roots, hunted deer, and fished the rivers and streams of eastern America.

In the Far North, Inuit peoples, lacking plant foods, lived entirely by hunting and fishing, killing bears, seals, and other mammals for food and clothing. In the Pacific Northwest, the Indians killed forest animals and depended heavily on the rich harvest of the salmon streams. They also developed boats, including kayaks, birch-bark canoes, and log dugouts.

In the deserts west of the Rockies and north of the Rio Grande, finally, a surprisingly productive foraging economy took shape, killing lizards, birds, and other small game and collecting prickly pear in the lowlands, berries and nuts on the flat-topped mesas. These desert gatherers lived in caves and rock shelters, made early baskets, nets, and traps, and, like most of their fellow Native Americans, chipped tools out of stone. It was to these foraging peoples of the American southwest that agriculture would first spread up from Mexico around 2000 B.C.E.

Among those many peoples, a remarkable variety of gender and family relations developed. Some evolved small nuclear families composed only of parents and children. Others developed extended families, uniting several generations and the nuclear families of grown siblings. In some cultures, men ruled with a heavy patriarchal hand. In others, matrilineal and matrilocal patterns made succession through the woman's side the rule. In these cultures, the husband was required to move into the wife's family, giving women the whip hand.

A similar variety prevailed in the assigning of traditional roles and tasks. Among northern Indians, where clothing was mostly made of animal hides and leather, men were primarily responsible for making it. In the south, where cotton and other vegetable fibers were used, women were the weavers. In some areas, including the far north, gender roles were sometimes scarcely defined at all, leaving men and women free to divide up the work as they pleased!

## Harmony with Nature

The religious views of these first Americans are almost entirely inferred from beliefs that survived into modern times and from parallels with preurban peoples elsewhere in the world. In North America, as in South America, Africa, and indeed, almost everywhere in early times, people had a strong sense of the oneness of the natural world and of the need to live in harmony with nature. Like animists elsewhere, early Native Americans attributed life to all things and sought only to take their fair share of nature's plenty.

Modern examples must suffice. Thus, for instance, a twentieth-century Papago woman, digging in the Arizona earth for clay to make a pot, expresses her gratitude to the clay. "I take only what I need," she declares. "It is to cook for my children."[2] Far to the east, in the forests along the Mississippi, a Fox Indian explains his people's attitude toward the timber they use for many things:

> We do not like to harm the trees. Whenever we can, we always make an offering of tobacco to the trees before we cut them down. We never waste the wood, but use all that we cut down. If we did not think of their feelings . . . all the other trees in the forest would weep, and that would make our hearts sad too.[3]

# MEXICO: THE OLMECS

## Origins of the Olmecs

The geography of Mesoamerica ("Middle America"—Mexico plus Central America) is confusing at first glance. It appears to be a twisting line of mountains and lowland plains choked with tropical rain forest that winds between the continents. A cross-sectional view,

---

[2]Ruth M. Underhill, *Red Man's Religion: Beliefs and Practices of the Indians North of Mexico* (Chicago: University of Chicago Press, 1965), p. 116.

[3]Ibid.

however, reveals an underlying symmetry. There are frequently coastal plains on both Pacific and Caribbean shores, inland mountain walls, and, especially in Mexico, high plateaus among the mountains. Civilization developed toward the center of this three-thousand-mile isthmus, in the region that today comprises southern Mexico, Guatemala, and Honduras, in areas that included both highlands and the coastal plains.

Mexico's jungle-shrouded Yucatán Peninsula, home of the Maya, and the fertile Mexican plateau called the Mesa Central, the center of the Aztec Empire, are the sites of the most famous Mesoamerican civilizations. But they were not the oldest.

America's first civilization emerged in southern Mexico between 1500 and 400 B.C.E. It did not develop in the highlands, as the more celebrated cultures of the Aztecs and the Peruvian Incas did, but on the coastal lowlands around present-day Veracruz. This oldest American civilization is called Olmec culture, after the Aztec name for the tribes who lived there at the time of the Spanish conquest. We have no idea what the people who created that ancient civilization called themselves.

We know that much of the Old World pattern of cultural evolution was duplicated in Mesoamerica. We have stone tools left by hunter-gatherers who drifted south twenty thousand years ago. We have archaeological remains of the villages of their Neolithic descendants in Mexico, settled village-dwellers who were making the delicate transition from foraging to agriculture. We know that the population grew, here as elsewhere, until it reached numbers sufficient to produce more complex forms of social organization. And we have the beginnings of Mexican art and religion in the thousands of small figurines—almost always female, as in the Old World—found among the hearths and burial sites of these vanished village peoples.

## Olmec Culture

And then, out of the mists of the first millennium before Christ, looms the high culture of the Olmecs, ancient Mexico's first civilization.

The head is nine feet high, carved from solid stone, and weighs perhaps fifteen tons. It stands on the grass, bodiless, neckless, wearing a round, close-fitting helmet, staring back at you. This is not some Easter Island primitive, but a startlingly realistic face. It is one of a number of similar monumental heads unearthed so far, carved by the Olmec Indians while Greece still languished in its dark age and before Rome existed.

The famous Olmec heads are only part of a growing archaeological treasure of sculpture and architecture, all clearly linked by the Olmec style, the best of it dated between 800 and 400 B.C.E. Most of the finds are clustered in such tropical lowland sites on the Caribbean shore of Mexico as La Venta, in the Veracruz region. These sites include ruins that clearly point ahead to Mayan and Aztec culture. And they have yielded up artifacts that would not be bettered by these later civilizations—that would not in fact be matched by them, for their realistic mode was developed by the Olmecs alone in Middle America.

La Venta and similar sites are usually described not as true cities but as ceremonial centers for the surrounding villages. Typical architectural finds include large pyramidal earthern mounds, precursors of the stone pyramids of the Mayans and Aztecs. There are also engraved stone altars, stelae, and sarcophagi. Such complexes are quite large and must have required the labor of all the surrounding peoples to build.

Besides the great carved heads there are smaller heads and figurines in clay, jade, serpentine, and other stone. Some of these are masks, as lifelike as the great heads, or perhaps even idealized portraits. Some are either infants or dwarfs, the latter freighted with

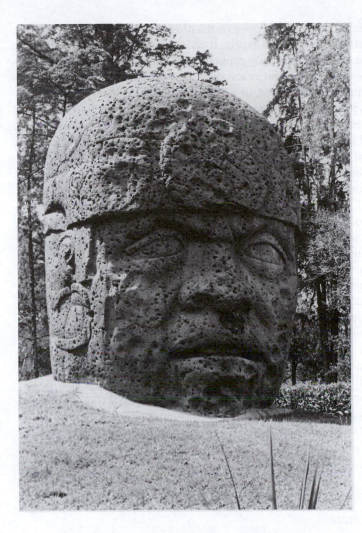

An Olmec head. The realistic modeling was rare in pre-Columbian American art. The flattened nose and ears may have been carved this way to avoid breakage when the sculptured heads were drawn overland from the deposits of basaltic rock where they were carved to the Olmec ceremonial center where they were displayed. (Museo Nacional de Antropología)

supernatural significance for Mesoamerican Indians. There are lifesize clay "tomb watchers," some of them sinister enough to suit their grim task admirably.

The most common motif of all, however, is that of the jaguar, which was probably a rain god, and the strangest of these are the half-human, half-cat were-jaguars. So pervasive is this feline presence that one authority has called his study of the Olmecs simply *The Jaguar's Children.* Were-jaguars in the form of children are a particularly common—and startling—form of this sculptural type. We do not know what a smoothly sculptured, soft-fleshed infant with jaguar claws on its little hands and jaguar teeth just showing between softly parted baby lips may have meant to the ancient people of Mesoamerica. But we can be properly terrified ourselves.

## Olmec Society

What then can we say with any confidence about the builders of Olmec culture?

Much more can be deduced with some certainty about socioeconomic and even intellectual achievements than about the precise political organization or history of the Olmec people. Olmec culture seems to emerge full-blown on the Mesoamerican scene; there is little evidence of the slow development we would expect. It ends as suddenly, around 400 B.C.E., when the great complex at La Venta apparently expired in violence. Whether it was a rebellion against priestly overlords or an invasion by less developed peoples we do not know.

What political structure the Olmecs had, or whether any large political unit existed at all, also remains controversial. Some archaeologists have suggested that an Olmec empire, headed perhaps by priests or warlike traders, linked the Veracruz centers with more distant Olmec-influenced areas as far away as central Mexico and even Guatemala. Others have postulated the spread of a new religion centering in the worship of the jaguar god, or the simple exchange of Olmec goods in distant parts of Middle America.

More can be said about the economic aspects of Olmec life. Most Olmecs, to begin with, seem to have lived in pole-and-thatch houses in the tropical lowlands along the Caribbean, or in adobe-and-stone huts on the highland fringes. They grew corn and beans and other vegetables and wore clothing made of cotton and maguey. They made clay pots and small figurines by hand.

Social classes higher than peasant agriculturists are also indicated. Priests ran great ritual centers like La Venta. Richly furnished tombs indicate an aristocratic elite, as does the depiction at one site of a man kneeling before another, a much more gorgeously clad person. Farmers, artisans, priests, and perhaps nobility, then, existed in the Olmec world.

Something more, finally can be said about the highest expressions of the culture. The religion of the Olmecs was evidently of primary importance to them; no palace ruins have been found, only the remains of temples. Their cults very probably included sky gods and earth gods, a female fertility goddess, the jaguar divinity, and the strange jaguar people who were perhaps that rain god's human representatives. Gods are also shown in bas relief hovering over clubwielding soldiers locked in combat, indicating that war too had its divine patrons in this oldest of Middle American civilizations.

## PERU: CHAVÍN CULTURE

### Origins of the Chavín Culture

The condor is the largest of all flying birds. Balancing on ten-foot wings, it cruises above the longest mountain range in the world, from Patagonia in the far south to the peaks that loom above the Amazon. It is an ugly bird close up, vulture-headed and ungainly on the ground. But riding on the icy winds that whistle among the crags, it is the sovereign of the Andes skies.

A condor's-eye view of the Peruvian Andes, where civilization first appeared in South America, would reveal a rather simpler topography than the tangled mountains and jungles of Mesoamerica. To the east of the north–south mountain chain, the jungles of the Amazon basin flow eastward beneath mist and rolling clouds two thousand miles to the Atlantic. To the west the Andean foothills descend to a narrow strip of desert between the mountains and the Pacific shore. Rain is rare, but river valleys carve their way through the arid land to the ocean. The mountainous highlands are much less fertile than the high plateaus of Mexico. Corn will not grow there naturally, though flocks may be grazed on the slopes.

Tropical jungles, forbidding heights, and a strip of rock and sand along the sea—it seems an unlikely area for civilization to emerge in. But that is precisely what happened on the western slopes of the Peruvian Andes and the arid Pacific coastlands early in the first millennium B.C.E.

In the end, civilized societies were to evolve over a large part of the central Andean region of South America, including portions of what are today Peru, Bolivia, Ecuador, and northern Chile and Argentina. But it began with the Chavín culture of Peru, named for the highlands site of Chavín de Huantar and usually dated between 800 and 400 B.C.E. Like Olmec culture in Mexico, Chavín culture was to spread widely and to be hailed by later archaeologists as a mother culture for the entire region.

The cruising condor probably paid no particular attention to the first people to appear in Peru, filtering southward through the Andean gorges perhaps twenty thousand years ago. These Paleolithic people hunted deer and llamas in the mountains and hauled in huge catches of fish along the shore. Within ten or twelve thousand years, they had settled into the universal Neolithic village. Soon they were raising potatoes and herding woolly llamas and alpacas in the highlands, growing cotton and making fishnets on the coast. They learned, probably as late as the second millennium B.C.E., to make ceramic pottery and to grow corn.

Corn cultivation required elaborate irrigation and terracing procedures, and these soon appeared in both the dry coastal valleys and the highlands. Regional exchange also developed, with potatoes, meat, and wood flowing down the mountains, and corn and cotton coming up from the lowlands.

Then, early in the first millennium B.C.E., came the oldest of Peruvian civilizations, Chavín culture.

## Ruins in the Andes

Chavín de Huantar is not the center of the culture that is named for it. Indeed, Chavín culture seems to have had no single center. But the Chavín site, almost 9,000 feet up in the Cordillera Blanca of northern Peru, is a splendid example of the style that would impose itself on much of the central Andes over succeeding centuries.

This extremely old temple complex of truncated pyramids, plazas, and raised platforms impressed the conquistadores in the sixteenth century and continues to impress archaeologists in the twentieth. Perhaps the best brief description is still that of a Spanish chronicler who was closer to the living reality than we are. The temple at Chavín de Huantar, wrote Vasquez de Espinosa, was "a large building of huge stone blocks, very well wrought . . . one of the most famous heathen sanctuaries, like Rome or Jerusalem with us." The Indians, he said, "used to come and make their offerings and sacrifices, for the Devil pronounced many oracles from here, and so they repaired here from all over the kingdom."[4] That was written in the days of the Inca Empire; two millennia before, there was very probably no "kingdom." But the ceremonial center was there, and flourishing.

From the battered walls and chambers of dry stone-masonry that remain, here and elsewhere, a lost way of life may still be reconstructed today.

Agricultural terracing had become extremely elaborate by the first millennium B.C.E., and the multilevel stone terraces followed many winding rivers through the mountains and down to the sea. Large numbers of disciplined workers labored on the temple complexes. Common textiles and ceramics still flourished on the coast, where the temples tended to be built of sundried adobe brick instead of stone. In the uplands, the llama and the alpaca

---

[4]George Bankes, *Peru before Pizarro* (New York: Phaidon Press/E. P. Dutton, 1977), pp. 132–133.

provided meat, wool, and the beast of burden that was so notably lacking elsewhere in the Americas. Trade was well established between regions in Peru, and pilgrims may have threaded the mountain trails to cult centers like Chavín de Huantar, where organized priesthoods served as intermediaries between native American people and their gods.

## Chavín Religion and Art

Beyond such concrete details, however, early Peruvian society, even more than that of Mexico, is generally the object of speculation or dispute. Was there a Chavín polity, an empire coextensive with the reach of the culture? It seems extremely unlikely, given the broken country and the size and resources of the population. How then, was that culture disseminated over so wide an area of the central Andes? Opinion inclines to a spreading religious cult that perhaps included a feline god like the Olmec jaguar. It has recently been suggested that the new religion spread together with a new form of corn, which provided the caloric intake to support larger populations and a more diversified society of specialists.

As with Olmec culture, finally, art and religion are the heart of what we know or guess about Chavín.

Chavín religion, like that of the Olmecs, probably involved nature and animal divinities, gods of earth and air and water, and deities who manifested themselves primarily as great cats with snaky hair and monstrous fangs. Sacrifice was also important: one gallery at Chavín de Huantar is heaped with the bones of sacrificial beasts and with fragments of exquisite ceramic ritual vessels. Goods found buried with the dead indicate some hope for an afterlife. Beyond such basic guesses we can know little about the rites, myths, and theologies of the people in the long fringed shirts and simple loincloths who came down the mountain paths to the temple, or of the priests who met them at the gates.

The stone itself remains, as does the ceramic ware and, on the dry coast of Peru, some remarkably preserved textiles and rudely worked gold. All tell us something of the artistic sensibilities of the people who created the Chavín culture.

Unlike the La Venta and other Olmec temples, those of Chavín de Huantar are not solid but are honeycombed with rooms and passages. The largest of them, nicknamed the Castillo (Castle), was originally a three-story structure 250 feet square. Inside, it was a maze of chambers, narrow corridors and galleries, ramps, stairways, and an intricate system of air shafts that brought the bracing air down to the lowest level. It was decorated inside and out with carved heads of eagles, cats, and other creatures—many of them, puzzlingly, native to the Amazon jungles rather than to the mountains or the coast.

These examples of Chavín sculpture look much more like the highly stylized, symbolic carving we associate with pre-Columbian America than does the precocious realism of the Olmec. It is mostly flat bas-relief on stone, though there are some decorative heads, human and animal, protruding from the exteriors of the more elaborate temples. It is as hard to see the falcons in the symmetrical lines and curves and scrolls of a low relief at Chavín de Huantar as it is to pick out the animal masks in a Shang bronze. But the space is as full of restless movement, and the sense of design is as strong in America as it is in the first Chinese culture five hundred or a thousand years before.

Distinctive "stirrup-spout" pottery, woven cloth with painted designs and representations of the cat god, gold beaten into sheets and worked by the technique of *repoussage* into the familiar snarling feline face—all reveal the presence of the common culture we call Chavín.

Then as now, the mountains changed color in the sunset, the wind cried among the peaks, and the big bird floated on the wind. From the height of the drifting condor, the changes in the world below could not have looked like much. Stone terraces along the rivers, temples in isolated valleys or on far coastlines, perhaps larger clusters of dry-stone or wattle-and-daub huts here and there. But in the large cult centers, in the restless patterning of stone and clay and cloth, in the cat god and the unknown prayers of Chavín people, there was something new in the Andean world. There was a shared spirit, a common culture, the beginning of a pan-Andean civilization before any documentable political union had yet emerged on the wrinkled land below.

## SUMMARY

Civilization emerged beyond Eurasia in these early centuries as well. Parts of both Africa and the Americas still have their share of shards and ruins dating from this period more than twenty centuries ago.

Egypt, discussed in an earlier chapter, was the oldest of these early African civilizations. Others were Kush, located in Nubia south of Egypt, and the commercial empire of Carthage.

Both the Kingdom of Kush and the Carthaginian Empire were at their height during the later first millennium B.C.E. Kush evolved under Egyptian influence farther up the Nile, in what is today Sudan. Kushite kings even ruled Egypt for a time in the eighth century B.C.E. During the golden age of Kush (third to the first centuries B.C.E.), the furnaces of Kushite Meroe may have spread iron and ironworking across much of Africa, enabling that continent to skip the Bronze Age entirely.

Carthage established a commercial empire including most of the western Mediterranean, with trading posts beyond Gibraltar on the Atlantic coasts of Europe and Africa. At its height in the middle of the first millennium, Carthage repelled the Greeks, but it fell at last to the Romans in the middle of the second century B.C.E.

The first Native American peoples to make their way from the Old World to the New settled in America north of the Rio Grande. After thousands of years as hunters and gatherers, they moved toward the settled life of predominantly agricultural villages.

The larger Amerindian populations south of the Rio Grande moved still further from their food-gathering beginnings. The mother cultures of Middle and South America were those of the Olmecs and the Chavín, both of which flourished during the first millennium B.C.E.

Olmec culture, which produced the famous giant stone Olmec heads, developed on the Caribbean coast of Mexico around modern Veracruz. Sites like La Venta were probably religious ceremonial centers rather than cities. But the structured society and uniquely naturalistic art of the Olmecs indicate a highly sophisticated culture.

The Peruvian culture named for the elaborate stone temples at Chavín de Huantar was also socially complex. Elaborately terraced fields and large stone structures reveal an impressive material culture. As with the Olmecs, however, there is no evidence of centralized political institutions.

## SUGGESTED READING

Adams, R. E. W. *Ancient Civilizations of the New World.* Boulder, Colo.: Westview Press, 1997. Brief survey of both Mesoamerican and South American civilizations.

Ben Khader, A. B.A., and D. Soren, eds. *Carthage: A Mosaic of Ancient Tunisia.* New York: American Museum of Natural History and W. W. Norton, 1987. Western and North African perspectives, beautifully illustrated by many color photographs.

Burger, R. L. *Chavín and the Origins of Andean Civilization.* New York: Thames and Hudson, 1992. Brief illustrated overview of the oldest South American civilization.

Burstein, S., ed. *Ancient African Civilizations: Kush and Axum.* Princeton: Markus Wiener, 1998. Useful introduction to these two successive East African states.

Clark, J. E., and M. E. Pye. *Olmec Art and Archaeology in Mesoamerica.* Washington, D.C.: National Gallery of Art, 2000. Authoritative discussions of the Olmec achievement.

Coe, M. D. *Mexico: From the Olmecs to the Aztecs,* 4th ed. New York: Thames and Hudson, 1994. Short, readable overview.

Hansberry, W. L. *Africa and Africans as Seen by Classical Writers,* ed. J. E. Harris. Washington, D.C.: Howard University Press, 1981. Discussion of references to Africa by Greek and Roman scholars, poets, and others.

Hassig, R. *War and Society in Ancient Mesoamerica.* Berkeley and Los Angeles: University of California Press, 1992. Sophisticated examination of empire-building and war-making capacities.

Hurt, R. D. *Indian Agriculture in America: Prehistory to the Present.* Lawrence: University of Kansas Press, 1987. Includes some emphasis on pre-Columbian agriculture.

Krech, S. *The Ecological Indian: Myth and History.* New York: W. W. Norton, 1999. Challenges the view that Native Americans consciously acted to preserve their environment.

Lazenby, J. F. *Hannibal's War: A Military History of the Second Punic War.* Warminster, England: Aris and Phillips, 1978. Detailed narrative account of the great African general's long struggle against Rome. See also his account titled *The First Punic War: A Military History* (Stanford: Stanford University Press, 1996).

Shinnie, M. *Ancient Nubia.* New York: Kegan Paul, 1996. A leading archaeologist's summary account. See also her *Ancient African Kingdoms* (New York: New American Library, 1970), a quick overview.

Soren, D. *Carthage: Uncovering the Mysteries and Splendors of Ancient Tunisia.* New York: Simon & Schuster, 1990. Recent illustrated view.

Taylor, J. H. *Egypt and Nubia.* Cambridge, Mass.: Harvard University Press, 1991. The British Museum's excellent holdings illustrate many aspects of Nubian life.

Welsby, D. A. *The Kingdom of Kush: The Napatan and Meroitic Empires.* Princeton, N.J.: Markus Wiener, 1998. Brief but scholarly treatment.

Yamauchi, E. M., ed. *Africa and Africans in Antiquity.* East Lansing: Michigan State University Press, 2001. Up-to-date papers on ancient Kush and Meroe, Nubia, Carthage, and the Maghreb.

 Please refer to the document CD-ROM for primary sources related to this chapter.

## Overview II

# The Classic Age

## (500 B.C.E.–C.E. 500)

*Classic* is a word with a ring to it. It conjures up the polished enamel and gleaming chrome of ancient automobiles, or orchestras tuning up. A classic age should be something splendid.

What makes the half-dozen centuries centering upon the time of Christ so distinctive as to earn them such a label?

In the first place, there is a certain scale and grandeur to them. Both the Roman Empire and Han China were about the size of the United States today. The Guptas ruled the subcontinent of India, and successive Persian empires filled most of the Middle East most of the time. Important political units of this second age of human history were thus considerably larger than those of earlier times.

A special feature of the so-called classic age of world history is an increased level of contact between neighboring societies, particularly between the formerly islanded civilizations of Eurasia. Goods could travel from China to Rome in the time of Christ.

Still, there is more to the claim that these centuries constitute a classic age than the size of empires and the reach of trade. There is a breadth and depth of accomplishment here too that is hard to match in even the most brilliant of the earlier cultures.

The civilizations of the classic age had, after all, the advantage of being able to draw upon the cultural, political, economic, and technological heritage of their predecessors—and go on from there. The Classical Maya, for instance, had hundreds of years of Mesoamerican experience in monumental architecture, stone carving, even mathematics and astronomy, to build upon. The people of Axum brought with them into East Africa the skills at building and trading developed over centuries in their Yemeni homeland.

To some degree, it is perhaps a matter of tone—a tone of confident supremacy that few before or since can match. Like the rich, full tones of a symphony orchestra, the civilizations of the classic age radiated a powerful confidence that they knew what they were doing.

Roman poets or Han historians spoke with confidence of their place in the world as one of absolute supremacy—of Rome as "the City and the World" or of China as the "Middle Kingdom" ringed by hopelessly inferior barbarians.

A grand scale of political organization, sustained trade and communication between peoples, breadth and depth of cultural achievement, and a tone of confident certainty about it all are perhaps as close as we can come to defining the classic age. Yet there is an undeniable feel of cultural climax to these centuries immediately before and after Christ—we can scarcely be more precise—that other ages of civilization can only envy.

# CLASSICAL CIVILIZATIONS

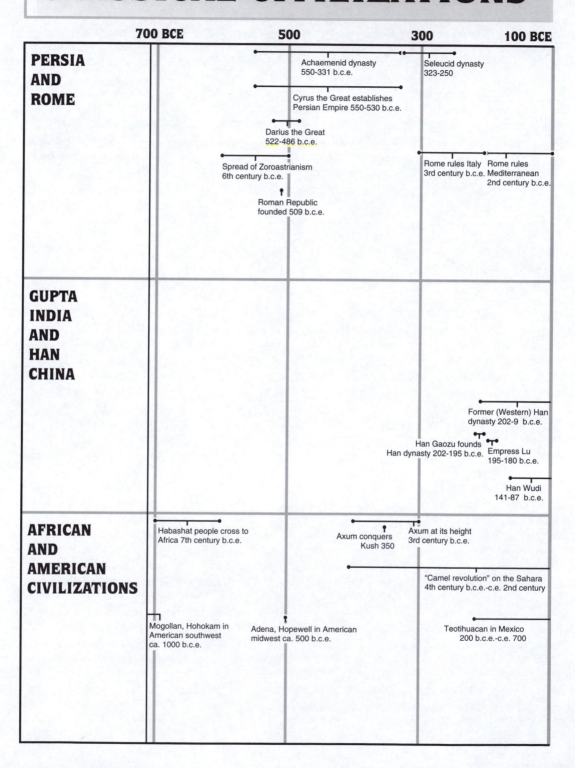

|  | 700 BCE | 500 | 300 | 100 BCE |
|---|---|---|---|---|

**PERSIA AND ROME**

Achaemenid dynasty
550-331 b.c.e.

Seleucid dynasty
323-250

Cyrus the Great establishes
Persian Empire 550-530 b.c.e.

Darius the Great
522-486 b.c.e.

Spread of Zoroastrianism
6th century b.c.e.

Rome rules Italy
3rd century b.c.e.

Rome rules
Mediterranean
2nd century b.c.e.

Roman Republic
founded 509 b.c.e.

**GUPTA INDIA AND HAN CHINA**

Former (Western) Han
dynasty 202-9 b.c.e.

Han Gaozu founds
Han dynasty 202-195 b.c.e.

Empress Lu
195-180 b.c.e.

Han Wudi
141-87 b.c.e.

**AFRICAN AND AMERICAN CIVILIZATIONS**

Habashat people cross to
Africa 7th century b.c.e.

Axum conquers
Kush 350

Axum at its height
3rd century b.c.e.

"Camel revolution" on the Sahara
4th century b.c.e.-c.e. 2nd century

Mogollan, Hohokam in
American southwest
ca. 1000 b.c.e.

Adena, Hopewell in American
midwest ca. 500 b.c.e.

Teotihuacan in Mexico
200 b.c.e.-c.e. 700

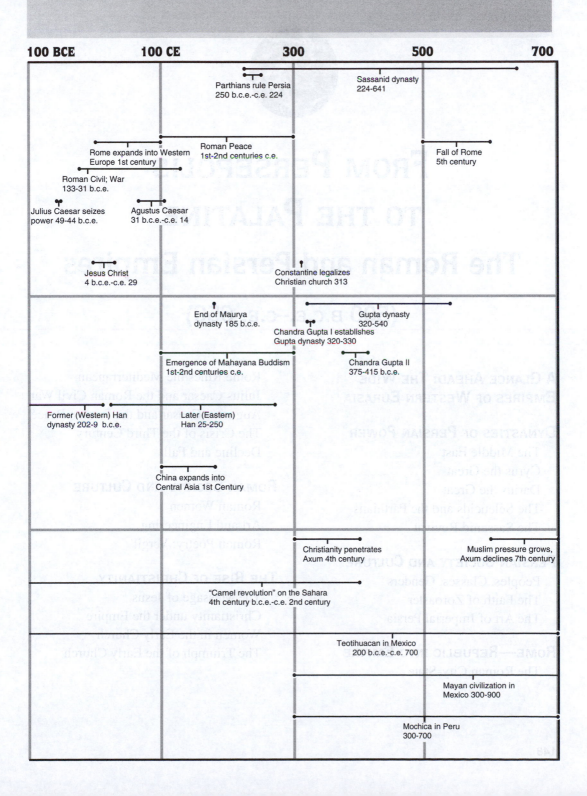

100 BCE | 100 CE | 300 | 500 | 700

Parthians rule Persia
250 b.c.e.-c.e. 224

Sassanid dynasty
224-641

Rome expands into Western
Europe 1st century

Roman Peace
1st-2nd centuries c.e.

Fall of Rome
5th century

Roman Civil; War
133-31 b.c.e.

Julius Caesar seizes
power 49-44 b.c.e.

Agustus Caesar
31 b.c.e.-c.e. 14

Jesus Christ
4 b.c.e.-c.e. 29

Constantine legalizes
Christian church 313

End of Maurya
dynasty 185 b.c.e.

Gupta dynasty
320-540

Chandra Gupta I establishes
Gupta dynasty 320-330

Emergence of Mahayana Buddism
1st-2nd centuries c.e.

Chandra Gupta II
375-415 b.c.e.

Former (Western) Han
dynasty 202-9 b.c.e.

Later (Eastern)
Han 25-250

China expands into
Central Asia 1st Century

Christianity penetrates
Axum 4th century

Muslim pressure grows,
Axum declines 7th century

"Camel revolution" on the Sahara
4th century b.c.e.-c.e. 2nd century

Teotihuacan in Mexico
200 b.c.e.-c.e. 700

Mayan civilization in
Mexico 300-900

Mochica in Peru
300-700

# CHAPTER 6

# FROM PERSEPOLIS TO THE PALATINE
## The Roman and Persian Empires
### (500 B.C.E.–C.E. 650)

## A Glance Ahead: The Wide Empires of Western Eurasia

Rome and Persia were wide empires indeed. The Roman Empire encompassed Western Europe, plus slices of North Africa and the Near East. At its height, the empire of the Persians reached from the Middle East to Central Asia.

The Roman Empire, whose ruins dot the landscape of Western Europe, is as well known as any slice of ancient history is to modern Western people. The Persian Empire is less familiar—yet it was unified earlier and lasted longer than Rome did. Between them, these two sprawling dominions brought order to roughly half of civilized Eurasia.

The thousand years of Roman history break down into two five-hundred-year chunks, the Republic and the Empire. Persia's twelve hundred years are subdividable into a series of ruling dynasties. Yet both preserved a remarkable unity and continuity across their broad swathes of the globe. It was a unity that would never be matched again in either Europe or the Middle East, two regions that have been notable for divisiveness and violence for most of their history since.

## Dynasties of Persian Power

### The Middle East

To many Westerners, the Middle East means mostly oil—or oil and bloody little wars that never seem to settle anything. It is a tangle of states, middling or small in size but almost uniformly underpopulated, barren, and of interest only because of the oceans of petroleum beneath their sun-baked soil. Historically, the region is much more interesting than that. Geographically, it is certainly more complicated.

Even by a conservative definition, the Middle East is a huge slice of land.[1] It stretches from Arabia in the west to modern Afghanistan in the east, from the Black and Caspian seas in the north to the Red Sea, the Persian Gulf, and the Arabian Sea in the south. It is as far from one end of this region to the other as it is from New York to California.

The region is also much more heterogeneous topographically than the popular impression of a desert floating on oil might indicate. The northern tier of large Middle Eastern nations—Turkey, Iran, and Afghanistan—consists of high plateaus ringed by protecting mountains. The southerly tangle of states including Israel, Jordan, Lebanon, Syria, Arabia, the states of the Persian Gulf, and Iraq have their share of rolling sands; but they also have such important rivers as the Tigris, the Euphrates, and the Jordan.

North or south, however, most of the Middle East is low on both rainfall and population. The region has produced more than its share of nomads moving their flocks from one oasis or stubbly pasturage to the next. From the deserts of Arabia to the rugged Anatolian Plateau of Turkey and on to the mountains of Afghanistan, the area has bred hard people leading hard lives. Perhaps for this reason they have taken special pleasure in each historic Middle Eastern metropolis, from ancient Thebes and Babylon to Persian Persepolis and Islamic Damascus and Baghdad.

---

[1]The terms *Middle East* and *Near East* are frequently used almost interchangeably. In this book, *Near East* means primarily the states and regions of the eastern end of the Mediterranean, from Mesopotamia up through Palestine and the Levant to Constantinople and the Straits connecting the Mediterranean and the Black Sea. The term *Middle East* will usually be used to denote the considerably larger area described in this section.

During the millennium centering roughly on the time of Christ, this diversified region enjoyed a period of intermittent unity presided over by a series of powerful Persian dynasties. Of these, the first unifiers of the Middle East were the Achaemenids (550–331 B.C.E.), the royal house founded by Cyrus the Great.

## Cyrus the Great

Cyrus the Persian (550–530 B.C.E.)—Cyrus the Shepherd, as they called him in his own time—was a self-made emperor if there ever was one. He seems to have been shrewdly merciful with defeated foes, judiciously tolerant of all religions, and automatically and totally courageous. He lived, fought, and died with the modest simplicity we would expect of a man who might have had trouble making his own mark on a Babylonian clay tablet. The fact that he devoted nearly all of his life, as far as we know it, to fighting with his fellow men is all the staunchest modern moralist could hold against him. And that, as they say, was a vice of the times rather than of the man.

The Persians and their overlords the Medes were Indo-Europeans, descendants of steppe nomads who had drifted south onto the Iranian Plateau hundreds of years before. In the sixth century B.C.E., they were still a warlike, semipastoral people living in the mountains of what is today western Iran. There they were within easy striking distance of the rich valley of the Tigris and Euphrates. The Medes had in fact participated prominently in the destruction of the penultimate Mesopotamian empire, that of the Assyrians.

By the middle of the sixth century B.C.E., however, the Medes had grown soft. This apparently put ideas into the head of Cyrus, hereditary chief of the tributary Persian tribes, in his mountain city of Pasagardae. In 550 B.C.E. Cyrus marched on the last Medean king, overthrew him, and made himself king of the Medes and the Persians. The twenty years of victories that followed constitute one of the most astonishing careers of blood and glory in the history of western Eurasia.

Cyrus's horse soldiers wore leather breeches and heavy felt boots, sat upon their rugged mountain ponies like centaurs, and were armed with the short, powerful compound bows of their steppe ancestors. They had a leader of genius in Cyrus. In his reign and that of his two successors, the Persians made themselves masters of the largest empire the sixth-century world had seen.

Three years after seizing control of the Median confederacy, Cyrus crossed the Taurus Mountains into what is today Turkey and there overthrew King Croesus of Lydia. The Lydians may have been the inventors of coinage, and Croesus was widely believed to be the richest king in the world. With the fabled wealth of Croesus at his command, Cyrus swung eastward, accepting submission from most of the tribes and peoples of modern-day Iran and Afghanistan. Only then, with a huge army and many victories behind him, did Cyrus turn south for the richest prize of all: Babylon.

The New Babylonian Empire was in decay and disarray. The unworthy heirs of Nebuchadnezzar, feuding with the powerful priesthoods of the city, had lost their authority over the people. With the help of a shrewd propaganda campaign, a Babylonian collaborator, and a well-placed victory or two, Cyrus was able to take possession of Babylon in 539 B.C.E. without even a token siege. It was the end of Mesopotamian independence and the beginning of Persian greatness in the Middle East.

Cyrus died in the saddle nine years later, struck down in a war with the queen of a nomadic tribe in eastern Iran. His son Cambyses conquered the other earliest center of civilization, Egypt. Cambyses' successor, Darius I, extended the power of the Persians still further. His armies crossed both the Indus River into northwestern India and the straits of Bosporus and Dardanelles into southeastern Europe, where he accepted the submission of Macedonia, on the northern frontiers of Greece.

By 500 B.C.E. the Persian Empire was thus the master of the Middle East, the great power between Europe and farther Asia. For a thousand years, the Persians and their successors would maintain that position. Persia would be a powerful threat to its neighbors east and west and a crucial link in the chain of commerce and cultural influences that would connect the Roman and the Han Chinese empires in the days of the Caesars.

Cyrus the Shepherd was buried in a simple, house-shaped tomb on the grounds of his palace in mountain-girt Pasagardae. The Persian Empire itself was a far more splendid monument to the barbarian king.

## Darius the Great

But Cyrus was first and last a soldier. It was his successors Cambyses and particularly Darius I who transformed a patchwork of conquered tributary states into the most impressive political structure—and the most physically impressive empire—in the western Eurasia of that time.

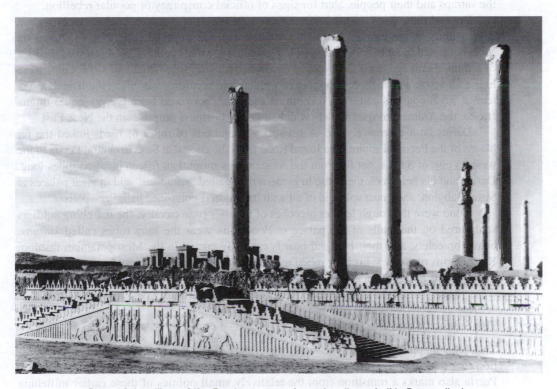

Some of the pillars of the Persian emperor's royal audience hall in Persepolis, in modern Iran, still tower against an evening sky. If you had only the destruction of this palace by Alexander the Great to go by, whom would you judge more "civilized"—the Greeks or the Persians? (The Oriental Institute, the University of Chicago)

Darius I (522–486 B.C.E.), also sometimes called the Great, ruled a huge realm. He had to govern a considerable variety of peoples, from sophisticated Egyptians and Babylonians and businesslike Lydians and Greeks to his own vigorous Persians and Medes and the wilder steppe peoples, such as the Scythians and Parthians, with a handful of Indians from beyond the Hindu Kush thrown in. And he and those who followed him on the throne of Cyrus had to hold this vast empire together without the benefit of modern technology, modern bureaucracy, or the faintest shadow of modern national feeling. That they were able to do it at all is a tribute to the ingenuity and organizing ability of these barbarians turned empire builders.

Achaemenid Persia—so called after a revered ancestor of Cyrus—was divided into a couple of dozen provinces called satrapies. Each of these was headed by an appointed satrap, or governor, often a member of the imperial family or a prestigious local nobleman. The satraps were normally granted wide-ranging political, military, and financial autonomy. Indeed, as long as a satrapy paid its tribute on time and provided its share of recruits for the army, the province could pretty much go its own way in matters of local concern.

This loose-reined autonomy was balanced, however, by an ingenious array of imperial controls. There were garrisons of royal troops at strategic points across the empire. There were also royal agents, known as "the king's eyes and ears," who kept tabs on both the satraps and their people, alert for signs of official conspiracy or popular rebellion.

Beyond these coercive measures, a more subtle web of common institutions brought a deeper unity to the empire. Darius formulated a single imperial code of laws, based on Mesopotamian models going back to Hammurabi, for all his peoples. He borrowed the idea of a minted coinage from the Lydia of Croesus, and soon royal gold and silver coins were in use all across Persia. A common set of weights and measures was also established, a system of royal couriers and mail, a common calendar (borrowed from Egypt), and a lingua franca, the Aramaic tongue already widely used for business purposes in the Near East.

Darius built extensively too. A network of hundreds of miles of roads linked the far places of the Persian Empire. The Royal Road from the capital at Susa in central Persia to the western city of Sardis, not far from the Aegean, was more than fifteen hundred miles long. Darius and his heirs took their ease in gardens they called "paradises" and in great palaces at Susa, Babylon, and, most splendid of all with its hundred-columned hall, Persepolis.

Gone were the rough leather breeches of Cyrus's rude cavalry; the marching soldiers sculptured on the walls of the palace at Persepolis wear the long robes called *kaftans*, heavy bracelets, and their hair and beards carefully curled in the Mesopotamian fashion. King Darius or Xerxes, his heir, robed in Tyrean purple, heavy with gold embroidery, gold jewelry, and a high tiara of gold, awed his prostrate nobles into the conviction that they were "in very truth . . . looking upon the lord of all the earth."[2]

## The Seleucids and the Parthians

The Achaemenid Persian Empire marks the climax of the strain of urban-imperial civilization that had first emerged in Mesopotamia and Egypt three thousand years before. But Persia also marks a transition from the relatively small polities of these earlier millennia to the much larger empires of later ages. And the Persian Empire itself remained at least an intermittent player on the great-power stage for more than a thousand years.

---

[2]A.T. Olmstead, *History of the Persian Empire* (Chicago: University of Chicago Press, 1948), pp. 282–283.

At the beginning of the fifth century B.C.E. a handful of Ionian Greek city-states on the Aegean coast revolted against Darius and found support from the newly emergent Greek city of Athens. Darius suppressed the Ionian Greeks, but the punitive expeditions he and his successor Xerxes sent against Athens and the other Greek cities of the West were decisively defeated. As the fifth century advanced, palace intrigues and harem plots undermined the power of the kings of kings. Persian women took the lead in such conspiracies, proving as ruthlessly ambitious as the men who had founded the dynasty. And in the fourth century B.C.E., as we have seen, the young Macedonian king Alexander the Great led the forces of the Greek West in a counterattack that shattered the Achaemenid empire.

Later dynasties labored with varying success to rebuild the greatness of Persia. Two of these were dynasties of foreign kings, the Greek Seleucids and the Parthians, another wave of intruders from the northern steppes. The third was a new Persian dynasty, the Sassanids. Among them they carried the history of this ancient empire throughout the classic age.

The Seleucids (323–250 B.C.E.) were the Greek dynasty who ruled Persia for the better part of a century after Alexander the Great conquered it. Seleucus was one of Alexander's chief lieutenants. Within a decade or so after the Macedonian conqueror's death in Babylon in 323 B.C.E., his generals had parceled out his vast empire among themselves. Seleucus got the best of it—most of the Persian domain, minus Egypt. He and his successors were great builders of cities and great Hellenizers, spreading the Greek way of life at least to urban enclaves across the Middle East.

The Parthians replaced the Seleucids around 250 B.C.E. and ruled till C.E. 224, five long and tumultuous centuries. A warrior people from east of the Caspian Sea, the Parthians challenged the Romans for dominance of the ancient Near East. Their cavalry attacks and volleys of arrows combined with the blistering sun of the region to swallow up whole Roman legions.

These rugged fighters also played a more constructive role in the establishment of trade across the Eurasian continent. As we will see in a later chapter, this series of trade routes linked China in the east with the Roman Empire in the west. In so doing, the Great Silk Road curved down from the mountains of Central Asia into Persia. In Persia, Parthian and later Sassanid rulers guaranteed merchants safe passage—and took their share of the profits of this legendary road.

But the Parthians seem to have lacked the organizing ability of the Persians. They let much power go by default into the hands of local nobility, the Iranian barons who would play such an important part in Persian history from this time on.

## The Sassanid Revival

The Sassanids, finally, expelled the Parthians in C.E. 224 and ruled the empire until 641, several centuries after the fall of Rome. The Sassanids—the word originally meant simply "Commanders"—were of Iranian stock, like the first Persians, and they claimed an Achaemenid connection. The four-hundred-year reign of the Sassanids is thus often seen as a restoration of the realm's legitimate rulers. Of the three dynasties, it certainly came the closest to equaling the splendor of the days of Cyrus and Darius.

During their four centuries on the Persian throne, the Sassanids constructed an elaborate system of power. It was a system based on a carefully structured bureaucracy and on two influential groups—the Iranian barons and the magi, or priests of Zoroaster.

A cluster of state officials directed the affairs of this most developed of Persian governments. In most periods, the chief of these was the grand vizier, the king's right hand

and the operational head of the state. Other powerful officials were the chief priest, head scribe, and general of the armies. Below this exalted level, appointed officials spread out to the four main provinces, the lesser satrapies and other districts.

The Iranian barons, or Persian nobility, granted estates along the frontiers of the empire, and provided a flexible border defense. In defending their own lands, these Iranian barons protected the Sassanid Empire as well. The ancient Zoroastrian priesthood, whose religious ideas will be discussed below, also served the state well. The magi collected the crucial peasant land tax on which government finances depended and provided religious sanction for Sassanid imperial power.

Under the Sassanids, that power was great enough to challenge the West once more, as Persia had done in the days of Darius and Xerxes. Under these rulers, Persia expanded until it briefly matched the vast extent of the original Persian Empire of the Achaemenids. At its greatest extent, Sassanid power reached from today's Pakistan in the east to Egypt in the west and northward into Central Asia, and up to the suburbs of Constantinople.

The building of this vast empire, however, brought Persia once more into conflict with Western powers, first with ancient Rome, then with the medieval Byzantine Empire, whose capital was Constantinople. In later Sassanid times, when Rome and Byzantium were Christian states, the struggle acquired overtones of a religious clash between Zoroastrian and Christian. Exhausted by these wars, the Sassanid regime fell in its turn to the first wave of Muslim conquerors to come galloping out of Arabia.

The Persian achievement was a monumental one indeed, with a geographical and historical dimension that reaches through classic and even into the medieval period of Western history. It is a powerful illustration of the scope of human political achievement across the western end of Asia.

## PERSIAN SOCIETY AND CULTURE

### Peoples, Classes, Genders

The Persian Empire, like most large ancient empires, made no effort to homogenize its diverse populations into a single people. Instead, Persia remained a land of many peoples, a hierarchy of classes, and a variety of patterns of gender relations.

At its height, the empire included such ancient peoples as Mesopotamians and Egyptians, as well as citizens of newly emerging Greek city-states. It encompassed both sophisticated Mediterranean peoples and Central Asian tribes. As a result, the satraps who governed these very different provinces enjoyed a large degree of autonomy to deal with local problems appropriately.

In terms of class, there is a certain similarity. At least within the wealthy urban societies of the empire, aristocrats, officials, priests, merchants, artisans, peasants, laborers, and slaves were to be found. The imperial government could relate to such groups much as their former governments had—again, probably a source of stability.

Gender relations could, however, differ significantly from one part of the empire to another. In Mesopotamia, for instance, a rise in the slave population undercut the traditional claim of women workers to jobs in handicraft industries. In Egypt, by contrast, we have documents testifying to the persistence of many legal rights for women. A marriage contract, for instance, guaranteed the bride not only the return of her dowry in the event of the marriage's dissolution, but also a third of her husband's earnings.

## ACHAEMENID PERSIAN EMPIRE

Like the Roman Empire, then, the Persian Empire of the classic age was a complex assemblage of communities and groups. That these groups were able to function in tandem at all is a testimony to the success of the succession of dynasties who ruled Persia for more than a thousand years.

## The Faith of Zoroaster

The earliest religion of the Persians was probably the sort of polytheistic worship of natural forces that was common among ancient peoples. Indo-European Persians prayed to the powerful Anahita, goddess of the life-giving waters, and to Mithra, god of the sun. They sensed the presence of the numinous, the wholly other, the divine in the forces of light and darkness, earth and wind. Sacrificial fire played a central part in the religion of the early Persians, as it did among their Aryan relatives in India. There was a caste or tribe of priests among them—the magi—who like Indian brahmans performed all religious ceremonies.

Then, in the same sixth century that saw the emergence of the Persian Empire under Cyrus and Darius, a new and startlingly different religion appeared in Persia. Its founder was a prophet called Zoroaster, a mysterious figure about whom almost nothing is known with certainty. There are legends in plenty, of course, as there are surrounding most religious leaders. There are stories of his miraculous birth, his visions, his ten years' labor to find his first convert; of the Persian satrap who became his first patron, of his temporary happiness and later misfortunes, even of his murder by barbarous nomads while he prayed before the sacred flame. In actual fact, we scarcely know where or even when he lived, though best-informed guesses seem to be eastern Iran and sixth century. We do have his words, however, in *Avesta,* the Zoroastrian Bible, and we know what effect they had upon the Persians.

Six hundred years before Christ, Zoroaster preached a religion that had many of the elements of developed Christianity. There was, he said, not a multiplicity of gods but one god: Ahura Mazda, the Wise Lord, god of light, goodness, and truth. Ahura Mazda was the creator of all things, the judge of all people, the rewarder of virtue with an infinity of spiritual bliss.

It was a splendid vision. But, as in the later faith of the Christians, there was a dark side too. Zoroastrianism saw a principle of evil in the world also—the cosmic Liar, the prince of darkness, called Ahriman in developed Zoroastrianism. The universe itself was the battleground between Ahura Mazda and his chief lieutenant Mithra on the one side, and Ahriman on the other. All human beings, said Zoroaster, must take a stand in this eons-long struggle between light and darkness, good and evil. For in the end Ahura Mazda must win, and on that day his followers will enter rejoicing into paradise, while those who have served the Liar will be cast from the Bridge of Judgment into a pit of darkness and torment.

It was a creed suited to a militant people, and from the days of Darius the Great it was the faith of Persian royalty and nobility. The symbol of Ahura Mazda—a small human figure in profile, framed by vast horizontal wings—can still be seen carved in the ruined stone of Persepolis.

The Persians seldom sought converts to Zoroastrianism, and it remained largely the religion of an aristocratic elite. But even so carefully preserved a faith underwent change, as all faiths do. The fire sacrifice and the priestly role of the magi were annexed to Zoroastrianism from the beginning. Particularly under the Sassanids, every village had its sacred fire and two magi to tend it and perform all sacrifices. Other gods clustered around Ahura Mazda in popular folk belief. And Mithra, the Wise Lord's champion, became the protagonist of a growing cult of his own.

The Persians' Zoroastrian vision had its influence on neighboring peoples too. The faith spread eastward into India, where the Parsi sect comprises the largest body of Zoroastrians in the world today. The cult of Mithra the sun god, champion of light against darkness, spread westward to become a popular mystery religion in Rome and the favorite cult of Roman soldiers all over the empire. Even the Zoroastrian Liar found a place in foreign pantheons as the Satan of the Christians—the Father of Lies whose pit of fiery punishment carries more than an echo of the pit of Ahriman.

## The Art of Imperial Persia

The pillars of Persepolis are the best-known relics of Persia's early glories. On a huge stone-faced platform projecting from a wall of cliffs, Darius the Great and his son Xerxes raised an intricate complex of palaces, monumental portals, harems, and audience halls in the fifth century B.C.E. Here was the celebrated hall of a hundred columns where Darius sat in state—the hall that Alexander and his drunken generals gave over to the flames a century and a half later.

One may climb the broad double stairway today, with its flanking bas-reliefs of marching soldiers and subjects bearing tribute, and pass through surviving doorways and porticos carved with the royal figures of massive human-headed bulls. There is a huge fallen capital crowned with back-to-back bulls' heads that would be echoed centuries later on the pillars of Asoka in far-off India. And there are the soaring columns, sixty-five feet high, that once supported the lofty roofbeams of Achaemenid palaces.

Achaemenid glazed brick from Susa shows Persian soldiers in long embroidered kaftans, bows and quivers on their backs, long spears held vertically before them. Such figures give an idea at least of the blaze of color that once dazzled the eye of a Herodotus—or an Alexander—approaching a Persian royal residence for the first time. Persian treasure troves include gold and silver jewelry, cups of bronze and ivory, chased daggers, and plates of silver. From such exquisite work we may get an idea of life at the top among the most ancient Persians.

There is a monumental, formal, ceremonial quality to much of this art of ancient Persia that clearly derives from the Mesopotamian provinces of the empire. It is an art of audience halls and throne rooms, of silhouetted soldiers in embroidered robes. But there is a flowing freedom of movement to the bronze and gold and silver animals, the lions and griffins, a winged ibex leaping into space. There is a freshness and vitality here that breathes the cooler air of the Iranian Plateau—or the winds of the distant steppes.

And from time to time a living face looks out. From Susa the marble head of a Parthian queen, smooth-cheeked and calm, carved in polished stone in the Greco-Roman manner, gazes thoughtfully upon the world. From the distant Asiatic province of Tajikistan, a clay-sculpted head of a man, short-bearded and warmly capped, eyebrows raised, mustache tilted in a smile, radiates a sense of life. Such faces remind us that life did in fact once beat between the ribs of men and women who moved through the streets of even such exotic places as Persepolis and Susa.

## ROME—REPUBLIC INTO EMPIRE

### The Roman City-State

The Romans have an image in history very different from that of the creative, liberty-loving, self-destructive Greeks who preceded them as the dominant European people in the Mediterranean world. In fact, however, these two strikingly dissimilar peoples were descended from common Indo-European origins somewhere on the Caucasian steppes. Speakers of various Italic dialects, including Latin, probably drifted into the Mediterranean basin at roughly the same time—early in the first millennium B.C.E.—as the Greek speakers to the east. Their histories were to be closely linked from then on.

Other peoples lived and flourished in the Italian peninsula before Rome rose, of course, most prominent among them the Etruscans. But, like the Minoans and Mycenaeans, whose civilizations preceded that of the Greeks in the Aegean, the ancient Etruscans are a people all but lost in the mists of history.

The Etruscans probably came, like the Minoans, from somewhere in Asia Minor. They imposed their rule upon the Iron Age natives living north of the Tiber River in central Italy sometime early in the first millennium B.C.E. They built a loose league of fortified cities, made lovely pottery, and furnished their tombs with grave goods of bronze. They learned to read and write from Greek colonies established in southern Italy and Sicily, and they passed this skill on to the Romans. By 500 B.C.E., however, Etruscan sovereignty over central Italy was drawing to a close. In the fourth century a decadent Etruria was absorbed by Rome; in the third the Greek colonies of the south followed the Etruscans into the Roman maw. It was a fate that awaited many other peoples then tilling their tiny fields and fighting their petty wars around the Mediterranean in blissful ignorance of the powerhouse that was building on the Tiber.

The core of Roman power lay for centuries in the hard-fisted Roman peasantry and their grim patrician overlords. Between them they provided the backbone of the Roman army. They were a hardy people, practical, disciplined, and traditionally brave. They were, above all, an intensely conservative lot. Not for these Romans the restless political experiments of the Athenians, or the Greek delight in the free play of the intellect. As their Roman forefathers had done, so would they do. "This thing, Rome," the Roman historian Ennius said "is simply men who know what their past means."

They were, in their own judgment, a people made to rule. "Others, I know," wrote Vergil, the most famous of all Roman poets, "will mould the breathing brass with a finer touch; in marble trace the features to the life." But "these shall be your arts, [Romans:] to rule the subject nations with imperial sway . . . to impose the arts of peace, to spare the humbled, and to crush the proud."[3] In time, much of the Western world would come to accept that judgment—and that imperial sway.

There were many myths of Roman origins, among them Aeneas's flight from burning Troy, and Romulus and Remus suckled by a wolf. In fact the city of Rome seems to have been founded by descendants of a number of tribes—Latins, Sabines, Etruscans—living among the seven hills, meeting in the little valley that would become the Forum. Among these Latin tribes there were two important classes: *patricians,* who were the better-off farmers, and *plebeians,* the poorer. The real centers of authority among them remained for a long time the old tribes and clans, whose heads were the chief men in the emerging Roman state.

Under the Etruscans Rome became a sizable city, important for trade and a power in that part of Italy. Probably sometime around 509 B.C.E., the traditional date of the founding of the Roman Republic, the Latin tribes overthrew their Etruscan kings. The constitution they established to replace the old Etruscan monarchy was dominated by the Senate, a patrician council composed of elder statesmen, former magistrates, and other leaders of the old clans. The magistrates, especially two executive officials called *consuls,* were chosen for short terms by assemblies of the free male fighting men.

Roman women did have more freedom than Greek women did. Upperclass women joined their husbands at the theater, the circus, and the banquet table. Working-class women labored as servants, artisans, shopkeepers, garment workers, nurses, midwives, doctors, entertainers, actresses, dancers, prostitutes, and servers in restaurants and taverns.

The Romans settled their domestic disputes, between patrician and plebeian in particular, with comparatively little violence. The "struggle of the orders" in Rome was settled by a striking conservative compromise. The championship of the interests of the lower social orders was vested in elected officials called *tribunes of the people*—who more often than not supported the will of the patrician Senate. The Roman Republic was to have its share of destructive domestic conflict, but that lay centuries in the future.

The city on the Tiber River extended its sway over the entire Italian peninsula quite rapidly. Fear impelled some of the neighboring states to accept the protection and sovereignty of Rome—fear of a resurgence of Etruscan power, or of the barbarian Goths who had once stormed down from the north. The primitive ethnic organization of the other Italian tribes favored the Romans too: The loosely structured tribal societies that surrounded

---

[3]*The Aeneid,* in *The Works of Vergil,* trans. A. Hamilton Bryce (London: Bohn's Classical Library, 1907), pp. 320–321.

# GROWTH OF ROMAN DOMINIONS UNDER THE EMPIRE

MAJOR ROADS
OF THE
ROMAN EMPIRE

Rome

500 MILES
500 KILOMETERS

Wall of
Antoninus
Wall of
Hadrian

North
Sea

HIBERNIA

BRITAIN

Cologne

ATLANTIC
OCEAN

GERMANIA
(INF.)

GERMANIA
(SUP.)

GERMANIA

SARMATIA

LUGDUNENSIS

GAUL

AQUITANIA

RHAETIA

NORICUM

CISALPINE
GAUL

(SUP.)
PANNONIA
(INF.)

DACIA

NARBONENSIS

DALMATIA

UPPER
MOESIA

LOWER
MOESIA

Black Sea

Caspian
Sea

TARRACONENSIS

CORSICA

Rome

ITALY

MACEDONIA

THRACE

Byzantium

BITHYNIA

PONTUS

SPAIN

SARDINIA

ILLYRIA

GREECE

GALATIA

CAPPADOCIA

ARMENIA

LUSITANIA

ACHAEA

PISIDIA

LYCIA

CILICIA

ASIA

ASSYRIA

MESOPOTAMIA

BAETICA

SICILY

CRETE

CYPRUS

PARTHIAN
[PERSIAN]
EMPIRE

Carthage

MAURETANIA

NUMIDIA

AFRICA

CYRENAICA

LIBYA

PALESTINE
Jerusalem

ARABIA PETRAEA

Tigris R.

Euphrates R.

Persian
Gulf

EGYPT

Red Sea

C.E. 14 – Death of Augustus

C.E. 98 – Acquisitions,
Augustus to Trajan

C.E. 98–117 – Acquisitions During
the Reign of Trajan

500 MILES
500 KILOMETERS

Rome offered little resistance to the imposition of Roman authority. By the end of the third century, Rome was the undisputed master of the Italian peninsula. And the centuries of the Roman conquest were just beginning.

## Rome Rules the Mediterranean

During the last three centuries before Christ, then, Rome became the political center of the Mediterranean world.

The empire that grew up around the Mediterranean Sea in the later centuries of the Republic was an oddly improvised, ramshackle, even reluctant affair. The Romans fought a good deal during those centuries, but most commonly in defense of their own interests or those of their allies and their expanding provinces. The rule was unenthusiastic involvement—followed by famous victories—and an expanding empire that led the Romans into more foreign involvements, more wars, more provinces to rule.

Reluctant imperialists though they might be, the Romans were extremely good at empire-building. Italy was Roman by 285 B.C.E. Carthage, Rome's powerful North African rival, which had come to dominate the western Mediterranean, had been decisively defeated by 200 B.C.E. and was destroyed shortly after 150 B.C.E. Macedon and Greece also fell to Roman arms in the middle of the second century, western Persia and Ptolemaic Egypt in the first.

The Romans earned their place in history. Roman discipline and the Roman short sword, the eagle standards, and the tramping legions had a fierce implacability, tenacity of purpose. The epic wars with Hannibal's Carthage illustrate this determination as well as any in the long litany of Roman victories.

There were three Punic Wars, stretching from the middle of the third to the middle of the second century B.C.E. The first was a struggle over Sicily (264–241), where the Carthaginians had replaced the Greeks as the predominant power. The Africans were driven from the island only at the cost of fearsome Roman casualties. The second was the Hannibalic war (212–202), begun when that brilliant general brought an African army down from the Alps on the backs of elephants to take the Romans in the rear. Hannibal was dislodged from Italy only when the Romans, after suffering repeated defeats on their home ground, turned the tables by invading North Africa to shatter the Carthaginians at Zama in 202. The Third Punic War (149–146) was a bitter piece of Roman chauvinism. Carthage was taken, pillaged, and much of it burned. The stubborn Roman refusal to admit defeat despite Hannibal's victories and the pragmatic shrewdness of the Roman general Fabius "the Delayer" in wearing out the Carthaginians by refusing to give battle were typical of the builders of the Roman Empire.

## Julius Caesar and the Roman Civil War

The greatest danger to the Roman polity during the last centuries of the Republic, however, lay not in foreign wars but in the threat of civil war.

The conquest of the eastern Mediterranean in particular made some Romans very rich. Opportunities multiplied for pillage in war and for corruption among the *proconsuls,* who governed conquered provinces. Land was cheap, tens of thousands of slaves were there for the taking, taxes and tribute flowed into the hands of the few. They spent their new wealth on broad estates and large houses, on Greek culture and Asiatic luxuries, and forgot the spartan virtues of earlier centuries.

The poor, by contrast, rapidly grew poorer as Roman power spread. Hannibal's campaigns in Italy ravaged the countryside, and long service in the East left farms untenanted. Rich men bought out small holdings, combined them into great estates called *latifundia,* and worked them with slave labor. Roman farmers, landless and unemployed, swarmed to Rome, where the Senate and the consuls now governed in splendor from the white-columned buildings that rose around the ancient Forum. Generals and proconsuls built themselves palaces on the Palatine Hill in Rome; the poor sweltered in multistoried tenements and lived on the grain dole taken in tribute from Sicily and Egypt.

The resulting bitterness of the masses was exacerbated by the increasingly violent political ambitions of the mighty. The very generals whose victories turned the Roman Republic into an empire brought their armies home with them and became a menace to domestic tranquility, indeed to the very existence of the state.

The result of this unhappy mix of social pressures and political ambition was a turbulent century of tension and recurrent violence called the Roman Civil War (roughly 133–31 B.C.E.).

The history of those troubled decades is studded with the names of famous politicians. But it is well to remember that beneath the surface of high politics and military challenge there rumbled the bewilderment, bitterness, and sudden furies of a whole people caught in the grip of trends and currents that were as far beyond their understanding as the political and economic pressures of our own times often beyond our comprehension.

The reforming brothers Tiberius and Gaius Gracchus, tribunes of the people in 133 and 123, respectively, stirred up the popular assemblies, passed laws to provide land for the landless at the expense of the *latifundia,* and were hounded to violent deaths by the Senate. A series of victorious generals next took the center of the stage, mobilizing conservative sentiment and factional political support in the capital to slaughter their enemies. This penultimate round of the Roman Civil War nearly tore the empire apart. It was a savage time, dominated by the powerful personalities of the generals Pompey the Great and Julius Caesar, the latter the only one of them all whose name is a watchword to this day.

As a general, Pompey won many victories for Rome. As a politician, he organized the so-called First Triumvirate, a loose political alliance including a rich nonentity and a much younger but equally ambitious man named Julius Caesar. Caesar spent most of a decade conquering Gaul—most of modern France. Then, feeling threatened by both allies and enemies at home, he turned back toward Rome to face more deadly enemies there than he had found among the Gallic barbarians.

In 49 B.C.E. Caesar crossed the Rubicon River into Italy with the famous remark that "the die is cast"—and all his future hung on that cast. In Rome he smashed an alliance of convenience between Pompey and the Senate. He thereafter drove Pompey from the Italian peninsula and crushed him for good in Greece. He pursued his foes around the Mediterranean, enjoyed a brief liaison with Cleopatra in Egypt, and returned triumphantly to Rome in 46 B.C.E.

He was the undisputed master of the Roman world. He had a little more than two years to live.

Julius Caesar seems to have been a somewhat more complex person than such pithy communiqués as the celebrated *Veni, vidi, vici*—"I came, I saw, I conquered"—might lead us to expect. A famous portrait head of him shows what appears to be a rather thoughtful man, half smiling, shadowed at the temples. He was as ambitious as other victorious Roman generals had been. He may also have had a touch of the reforming Gracchus brothers in his makeup. He claimed at least to be the people's champion, and the aristocratic Senate was terrified of him. The Republic, he said, was a hollow sham.

What exactly he might have done about it if he had lived we cannot know. What he did do was make himself dictator for life, packing the Senate with his officers, and give land to his soldiers. He also inaugurated a program of public works, reorganized the administration of Italy, reformed taxation in the provinces, extended Roman citizenship to at least some conquered peoples, lowered the debt burden, and reformed the calendar. His enemies said he planned to make himself king of Rome.

On the Ides of March, 44 B.C.E., he was stabbed to death in the Senate house by a group of senatorial conspirators led by two of his own lieutenants. Caesar thus died as he had lived—dramatically.

The battered shell of the Republic survived him by a dozen years. The wars and intrigues that followed were complicated and brutal, the last bloody gasp of the Roman Civil War. Caesar's assassins and his old commanders fought while champions of the old order such as the eloquent orator Cicero labored to save the Republic. In the end, they were all out-smarted by a young man who was only nineteen when Julius Caesar died: his grandnephew and adopted son Octavian, known to history as Augustus Caesar.

The year after his uncle's assassination, Octavian and his allies of the Caesarian faction formed the Second Triumvirate and forced the Senate to grant them—and their legions—the power to restore order to the state. In the year 42 B.C.E. at Philippi in northern Greece, they defeated the men who had murdered Caesar. Octavian then fell out with his own allies, most importantly with Caesar's old friend (and Cleopatra's new lover) Antony. In 31 B.C.E. Octavian's forces destroyed Antony's in a naval battle off Actium, and the Roman Civil War was over.

From the reign of Augustus Caesar, we date the most successful and prosperous period of Roman rule: the Principate at home and the Roman Peace over the length and breadth of their wide empire.

## Augustus Caesar and the Roman Peace

Gaius Julius Caesar Octavianus, holder of the *imperium* (military command) and of the tribunician power (and hence spokesman for the people), *pontifex maximus* (chief priest), *princeps* (which then meant not "prince" but simply "first citizen"), voted the title of *Augustus* (the Fortunate and Blessed) during his lifetime and "the Divine" after his death, was never officially emperor of Rome at all. Nor were his successors during the most successful centuries of what we call the Empire, as contrasted with the Republic. The purple robe and the diadem, the bowing and scraping as before a Near Eastern potentate, were adopted at Rome only in the fourth century C.E. by rulers desperate to hold the empire together. Augustus had no need for such trappings.

Augustus, Rome's "second founder." The armor, the pose, the upraised arm all embody the force of character and confident authority that made Augustus not merely another successful general and shrewd politician, but the first ruler of Rome's golden age. This idealized portrait, however, probably bears little physical resemblance to the real Octavian. (Library of Congress)

Historians call the order he established the Principate—rule by the princeps. It was a typical conservative Roman compromise, yet it amounted to little less than a second founding of Rome after a century of civil strife.

During the forty-five years of Augustus's rule (31 B.C.E.–C.E. 14), the Senate and the popular assemblies still met. But the former was filled with friends of the first citizen's, and the assemblies seem to have lost all political function. Consuls, proconsuls, tribunes, and other officials were still elected, but only after securing Augustus's political blessing. He ruled the vast empire, whose frontiers now reached to the Rhine and the Danube, as commander of the Roman armies. He dominated Rome on the strength of his great-uncle Julius Caesar's name, his own military triumphs, and the simple fact that he had brought peace and order after decades of civil war. He earned a reputation for piety as the rebuilder of the temples and refurbisher of the cults of the Olympian gods, but he also built temples to the "divine" Julius Caesar and to "Rome and Augustus," thus surrounding the name of the emperor with the faint aura of divine right. He did not go beyond that. But then he did not need to.

The peace and prosperity fashioned by Augustus Caesar lasted for the better part of two hundred years. These were the centuries of the *Pax Romana,* the Roman Peace, an achievement Europe would not see again.

The "good emperors"—Claudius and Trajan, Hadrian, Marcus Aurelius, and others—who reigned during the first and second centuries C.E. perpetuated and expanded the Augustan heritage. They completed the building of the splendid city on the seven hills that future generations would revere as the Rome of the Caesars. They brought the protection of Roman power to more and more of their subjects. And they expanded the empire beyond anything the West had seen before.

Among the material benefits of the empire, three deserve special attention: Roman administration, Roman citizenship, and Roman law.

Roman administration under the Republic had been relatively simple, a matter of the short-term proconsuls, who not infrequently milked their provinces mercilessly. Under the

# Voices from the Past

Roman emperors like Claudius, as the author of this book points out, used spectacles in the Colosseum to "become 'one with the people.'" Do modern politicians ever give the impression that they share the popular tastes of the masses of the voting public?

*[The Emperor] Titus noisily supported the Thracians and apostrophised their adversaries with gibes worthy of a bargee. Claudius proved himself, through simplicity it is true and not by calculation, a model in this respect:*

*'There was no respectable [situation] . . . in which he appeared more affable and more gay [than at gladiatorial combats]; he could be seen, in the manner of the vulgar, counting on his fingers at the top of his voice the gold pieces offered to the victor. He would urge all the spectators to enjoy themselves, calling them his 'masters' from time to time, and larding his remarks with jokes in fairly bad taste. . . . But what was liked above all was that he wrote notices addressed to the crowd on tablets and had these circulated among the spectators, instead of having them transmitted by means of heralds as was customary.'"*

Roland Auguet, *Cruelty and Civilization: The Roman Games* (London: Allen and Unwin, 1972), p. 186.

emperors of the first two centuries C.E., however, a much more elaborate system of imperial administration was carried out by paid permanent officials closely supervised by their superiors. It was a system that provided lower taxes and more effective government than most parts of the Roman world had ever known before.

Roman citizenship was also extended far more widely by Augustus and his successors; by approximately C.E. 200, all free provinces had been granted citizenship, making them equal in every way to their conquerors. The army, the bureaucracy, and even the higher reaches of the government were thoroughly opened up to Gauls and Spaniards, Near Easterners and North Africans.

Roman law, finally, embodied the benefits of Roman government more concretely and longlastingly than almost any other aspect of the Roman predominance. The first laws of the Romans had been inscribed on the famous Twelve Tablets as early as the fifth century B.C.E. Over the following centuries, Roman civil and criminal law grew through legislation by the assemblies and decrees promulgated by the emperors, but above all through precedents established by Roman magistrates down the years. The resulting system of justice was among the most impressive bodies of law ever produced.

"Let justice be done," the Roman maxim ran, "though the heavens fall." Mercy was not a Roman strongpoint; stern justice seems to have been.

The sheer size of the empire, as well as the complexity of its government, grew significantly under the *imperators* who followed Augustus. Roman legions pushed farther east into former Persian lands, north across the Danube into central and eastern Europe, north across the Channel to overrun most of Britain. There were setbacks and withdrawals, especially in what was to become Germany, but the legions were generally victorious. At its height, the Roman Empire covered more than three million square miles, only slightly less than the size of the United States today. Recent estimates of the population of the empire run to eighty million, about a third that of modern America.

## The Crisis of the Third Century

There were breakdowns, of course, as there are in any human institution, even during the early centuries of the empire. There was the increasing interference of the Praetorian Guard—the elite troops who served as the emperor's bodyguard and policed the city of Rome—in selection of each new emperor. There were tyrants even among the good emperors, men such as the insane Caligula and Nero, who crucified the Christians and drove all Gaul to revolt. And there was plain brutality: the severed hands of those who took up arms against Rome, the enslavement of whole armies of her foes, the popular savagery of gladiatorial contests and public executions.

Neither anarchy nor tyranny, however, was new to either Europe or the Mediterranean. What was unprecedented was the level of general prosperity, the long years of peace. It was when these began to fail seriously that the decline and fall of the Roman Empire began.

It came in two stages. There was a first major breakdown in the third century C.E. This was followed by recovery under an increasingly autocratic regime in the fourth century. But the recovery was only temporary. In the fifth century came the collapse.

The good times seem to have ended with the reign of Marcus Aurelius (161–180), the celebrated Stoic emperor, last of the benevolent successors of Augustus. The next hundred years, the disastrous third century C.E., saw a bewildering series of short-term rulers, many of them provincial generals who were elevated by their troops and then killed by their own or rival legions. Standards of living declined sharply. The countryside was depopulated, the cities swollen with poor people living on the government grain dole, the solid middle classes of society shrinking under the pressures of government exactions. There were rebellious rumblings in the provinces—Gaul, Spain, North Africa—and new pressure on the frontiers from Germanic peoples in Europe and a revived Persian Empire in the East.

This century of disasters was ended by the reforms of the emperors Diocletian and Constantine, who between them at least temporarily restored the Roman order on a more autocratic basis than ever before.

Diocletian (284–305), a strong-willed Balkan peasant from Illyria who had risen through the army, attempted to quell anarchy by the installation of the so-called Tetrarchy. Imperial power was shared among four rulers, two senior *Augusti* and two junior men called *Caesars*. Diocletian strengthened the bureaucracy, reformed taxation in the direction of greater equality—and rigor—and even attempted to fix prices. In his last years he embarked upon the last major persecution of the Christian church, in whose growing power he apparently detected a threat to the restored authority of the state.

The Tetrarchy collapsed after Diocletian, and Constantine (306–337), son of one of the tetrarchs, fought his way to sole mastery of Rome. Constantine carried Diocletian's bureaucratic reforms to even greater lengths. He established two capitals, one at Rome and one at Byzantium (renamed Constantinople in his honor) in the east, where a Byzantine (or East Roman) Empire would survive for another thousand years. He set up an elaborate centralized system of administration involved four huge imperial prefectures, a dozen dioceses, and 120 separate provinces from Britain to Egypt. He also shrewdly separated civil government from the military and encouraged a series of army reforms in order to strengthen the frontiers.

At home the autocratic Constantine prescribed fixed hereditary membership in the crafts and professions. He levied taxes for defense that were so oppressive that free farmers had to be reduced to near slavery if they were to be kept on the land. Only the Christians had obvious cause to love him, for he finally legalized the Christian church in Rome in 313.

## Decline and Fall

The fall of Rome in the fifth century C.E., the destruction of one of history's most impressive political achievements, still challenges historians. It clearly involved both internal weakening and external assault.

Of all Rome's preurban neighbors to the north—Germans, Celts, Slavs, and others—the Germanic tribes along the Rhine-Danube frontiers had generally been the most important. Half-Romanized Germans had infiltrated the empire for centuries, as settlers on deserted lands and as mercenary soldiers. Late in the fourth century, however, these Germanic peoples were thrust more violently against Roman frontiers by the onslaught of warlike East Asian nomads following the steppe gradient westward. Thus pressured from the rear, armies of Visigoths, Ostrogoths, Vandals, Franks, and others crashed through the Roman boundaries in force in the fifth century. Barbarian cavalry broke the Roman phalanxes, ravaged whole provinces, and twice sacked Rome itself, the Visigoths in 410, the Vandals in 455. The invaders ended by establishing kingdoms of their own all across the western half of the Roman Empire.

There is little argument about the unhappy sequence of events that Edward Gibbon, in perhaps the most famous of Western histories, christened *The Decline and Fall of the*

*Roman Empire.* What fills the pages of more recent historical studies are attempts to explain the underlying causes of this mighty fall.

Before the barbarians came, so most modern historians believe, the empire had been fatally weakened from within. It is these internal weaknesses that have preoccupied students of Roman history since Gibbon.

There were obviously political factors at work. The lack of orderly procedures for the transfer of power, thanks to Augustus's shying away from hereditary monarchy, clearly opened the door to political turmoil. After Diocletian and Constantine, there was also the increasing remoteness of government—of emperors in purple and gold glittering with jewels, of elaborate court ceremonies, of corrupt and arrogant bureaucrats.

A wide range of social and economic problems also existed. There was the widening gap between rich and poor, the heavy cost of bread and circuses to keep the poor properly docile, the squeezing of the middle classes of society by government regulation and economic pressure. And there were more technical problems: the diminishing quantities of silver available for coinage, the exhaustion of soil, the abandonment of farmlands. They all added up to a substantial decline in the prosperity that had been one of the empire's chief claims on the loyalty of its subjects.

Demographic factors have been stressed in some analyses. The "barbarization" of the army and much of the bureaucracy that took place when Romans refused to serve seems a major weakness to some. Population decline, especially among the millions of slaves who did much of the work of the empire, may also have weakened the empire seriously.

Cultural and ideological causes may also have played a part. A general malaise, or failure of nerve, as the center failed to hold and things fell apart may have further undermined Rome's will to fight. Gibbon himself put some of the blame on the subversive influence of early Christianity, which siphoned off the best minds for the church and encouraged pacifist and antistate attitudes among its other-worldly followers.

There are historians who throw up their hands at this complex array of causes and simply blame the colossal difficulty of governing so vast an assemblage of lands and peoples with the limited personnel and resources available in Roman times. The wonder was not that Rome fell, this school declares, but that it lasted as long as it did.

Other historians urge that what took place was less the "decline and fall" of a great civilization than the transformation of one society into another one. They emphasize the fact that the Germanic invaders of the Roman Empire had been living on its borders and infiltrating the empire itself for centuries. German chiefs had become landowners, married Roman ladies, taken Roman names, and tried to take part in Roman public life. Even the Germanic invaders of the fifth century sought less to destroy the sophisticated society they had long admired than to take it over and live as the Romans did. Their alien ideas and customs led to the failure of this effort; but the result was less a savage destruction than a slow change from ancient to medieval civilization in the West.

Nevertheless, by the end of the fifth century, there were barbarian kingdoms where once Roman eagles stood, from North Africa to Britain. And in centuries to come, though Rome later became the city of the popes and the center of western Christianity, the teeming metropolis of half a million souls shrank to tens of thousand. The villas of a ruder nobility were built within the gigantic shells of public baths, and goats grazed on the Palatine Hill where palaces had once stood. Difficult as it is to define or explain the end of an era, one surely ended here.

# ROMAN SOCIETY AND CULTURE

## Roman Women

Ancient Rome, aggressively militaristic and imperialistic as it was, might seem a thoroughly male-dominated society. Yet women played a crucial part in Roman history—and often got some credit for it too.

During the period of the Republic—the first five centuries of Rome's history—women were nominally under the complete control of their fathers. Among the upper classes, at least, the *paterfamilias* or "father of the family" exercised life-and-death power over every member of it, from younger siblings, women, and children to slaves. Even after his daughter married, his power over her was officially greater than that of her husband.

This legal authority, however, seems not to have been much exercised in practice. More important was the belief that a "Roman matron" should be a worthy partner to her stern-faced husband. Virtue, character, and sheer competence were key qualities of the Roman matron. She was expected to be capable, not only of running a large household, but also of exercising political authority while her husband was away at the wars.

Roman women could also legally inherit and manage property, a right that gave them real leverage in society. During the late Republic and the centuries of imperial rule that began with Augustus, ruling-class women significantly expanded their range of independent activity. Moralists professed to be shocked when aristocratic women showed up at banquets, theaters, and horse races, attended gladiatorial combats in the Colosseum, and even took lovers. Poets, on the other hand, sang the praises of these emancipated women and sometimes even fell in love with them themselves.

In some periods, women also exercised significant political power in Rome. Emperor Augustus's wife Livia carved out a place for herself as empress, complete with a substantial staff. Imperial women of the second and third centuries C.E. sometimes actually ruled the empire through weak male emperors. The third-century empress Julia Domna was a powerful ally for her imperial husband Septimius Severus and became known as Julia the Philosopher in the intellectual circle she founded.

The arches of a Roman aqueduct still tower over the city of Segovia in Spain, once a province of the Roman Empire. Like Roman roads and Roman law, Roman cities—with their aqueducts, theaters, and other amenities—were major benefits of the only period of political unity in European history. Can you think of any structures in modern America that will probably still be standing two thousand years from now? (Barbara Rios/Photo Researchers, Inc.)

In Rome as elsewhere, then, the position of women as conventionally defined was considerably different from the positions some women at least were able to carve out for themselves.

## Art and Engineering

Roman official religion, literature, art, and philosophy were all based to a considerable degree on Greek mythology, writing, carving, and thought. Over centuries of emulation, the Romans did succeed in absorbing much of Greek culture, in making its conventions theirs, even in going beyond their brilliant neighbors in some areas. But the overall consequence was as clearly derivative as, say, much of modern American culture is derived from that of Europe. Roman culture, therefore, cannot be discussed without repeated backward glances at the cultural achievements of the first of Western civilizations, that of the ancient Greeks.

The Greeks had produced highly idealized representations of gods and great leaders in the Hellenic fifth century B.C.E. and extremely realistic statues in the later, Hellenistic period. Both the ideal and the realistic legacy in sculpture were taken over wholesale by the Romans.

Many Greek statues, for instance, exist today only as stone copies preserved in Rome. But the Romans used Greek styles for their own purposes too. Portrait heads of Roman citizens from the late Republic were as hyperrealistic as any Hellenistic achievement. Yet Roman statuary projects a special force of its own. The strength of a Roman *paterfamilias*—the strength of character that befits the head of an old Republican clan—shows through the craggy features. The whole figure of *Augustus* in armor, one arm upraised, radiates idealized authority as effectively as any fifth-century Greek god—as the image of the refounder of the Roman Empire should.

Nowhere was that spirit expressed more powerfully than in Roman building. The Romans had vast spaces to cover, public baths and basilicas (law courts), palaces and temples built on an imperial scale. To roof such buildings they introduced the arch, the vault, and the dome. They embellished these great buildings with scrolled Ionic and complicated Corinthian columns, with carving and tile and gold leaf. Most of that ornate splendor is gone today. But even the ruins of the Baths of Caracalla and the Basilica of Constantine have a spaciousness and a grandeur not to be found in the Greek world.

In engineering, finally, the pragmatic Roman spirit found one of its truest expressions. The Romans criss-crossed Europe with more than fifty thousand miles of stone-paved roadway, a system not equaled until modern times. The soaring arches of Roman aqueducts awed and baffled the peoples who came after them; the one built to supply Segovia with water was known as the Devil's Bridge to medieval Spaniards. Into the city of Rome itself a total of fourteen aqueducts brought 100 million gallons of water every day.

## Roman Poetry: Vergil

The Roman cultural debt to Greece is nowhere clearer than in Roman literature. Again, though, there are distinctive Roman accomplishments to admire.

Most of the common elements in the literature of the two peoples—style, themes, mythological foundations, literary conventions—were the result of conscious modeling of Roman work upon Greek. Thus, if Homer opens his epic *Iliad* by calling upon the gods for divine inspiration, Roman Vergil will not go many lines before he calls upon his Muse for inspiration too. If there is a catalogue of the ships that brought the Greeks to Troy with all their colorful crews in Homer's epic, there will be a catalogue of the peoples that followed Aeneas to Italy in the later poem. And so on, through much of Latin literature. The literary genres are the same for the two peoples: epic and lyric poems, tragedy and comedy, pastoral and satirical modes flourish among them both. There is similarly bawdy humor on both their stages, a common nostalgia for a simpler, pastoral past in much of their verse.

Roman poetry, however, needs no excuses: It clearly matched the best of its Greek precursors and left an influential legacy. There is a barbaric strength to Homer not to be found in later epics, but Vergil's *Aenid,* the Augustan epic of the founding of Rome, has a perhaps subtler power of its own. Vergil's Aeneas is a man with a mission, driven by a Roman sense of duty, yet he is tempted by very human feelings along the way. The mythic core of the story was simple enough: the ancient tale that Rome had been founded by the last Trojan, the hero Aeneas, escaped from flaming Troy and charged by the gods to found a new city in a new land. But it took the genius of Vergil to ask: How would the future founder of Rome feel when his wanderings took him to North Africa and he was welcomed by Queen Dido, busy raising the walls of her own city—Carthage? How would he react, and how would she, when the founders of the two great imperial rivals of Roman times fell passionately in love?

There is much more to the *Aeneid.* But the love of Aeneas and Dido has enthralled readers over the almost two thousand years since Vergil wrote it, in the days of Caesar Augustus.

## THE RISE OF CHRISTIANITY

### The Message of Jesus

"And it came to pass in those days," the second chapter of the third Gospel informs us, "that there went out a decree from Caesar Augustus, that all the world should be taxed." So Jesus of Nazareth was born in Bethlehem, where his parents had gone to render unto Caesar, around the year 4 B.C.E.

He was thus born at a time when the Roman Republic was turning into the Empire, and a time when Greek ideas had been thoroughly assimilated by the Romans. His story sits oddly in the middle of Roman history, so largely secular and practical in spirit. Yet the religion that grew up around the name and teachings of Jesus Christ constitutes a crucial part of the legacy of those times. Modified by Greek ideas, adopted as the Roman state religion, Christianity would survive the Greco-Roman world to become the dominant religion of the West.

We do not know what Jesus looked like—there are no dependable contemporary likenesses—but the traditional medieval image of a gaunt man with long hair and a beard is likely enough, given the styles of his time and province. The Bible does offer a vivid picture of his wandering ministry, of his style of preaching in vigorous parables, of his ability to move the hearts of his hearers. He was clearly a charismatic figure, whatever he looked like.

According to the Testament of his followers in the first and second centuries C.E., his birth was heralded by angels, his life replete with miracles, his passing accompanied by storms and earthquakes and climaxed by the greatest miracle of all, his rising from the dead and ascending to heaven. Jesus began his active ministry—which apparently was limited to the last three years of his life—at the age of thirty, when he became a wandering holy man in the far Roman province where he was born and put to death. Here his messianic claims—that he was the Messiah prophesied of old, come to save the world—led to his arrest at the instigation of the Hebrew priestly hierarchy in Jerusalem and his execution by the Roman authorities. And here in the eastern provinces of the empire, the Christian church began to grow.

The moral passion of Jesus had gone straight to the heart, and it would reach many others in the Roman Empire whose needs were like those of his first hearers: "Blessed are the poor in spirit, for theirs is the kingdom of heaven" (*Matthew* 5:3). His commandments had a scope that would stir even the skeptics of a later age:

> Thou shalt love the Lord thy God with all thy heart, and with all thy soul, and with all thy mind. This is the first and great commandment. And the second is like unto it. Thou shalt love thy neighbor as thyself. On these two commandments hang all the laws and the prophets. (*Matthew* 23: 37–40)

The new religion thus began with the law and the prophets of the ancient Hebrews and looked at first like a schismatic form of Judaism. From his Hebrew heritage Jesus derived the monotheism that had long distinguished the Jews and the ethical emphasis brought to their faith by the prophets of earlier centuries. But Jesus added his own unique beliefs to the faith of his fathers, and it was these additions that were to carry Christianity from obscurity and persecution to the top of the Roman world.

The two distinguishing features of the Christian message, as early Christians understood it, were, first, the assertion that he was not a mere prophet, like his predecessors, but the Son of God himself, and, second, that he came to bring to his followers the supreme gift of eternal life. "Dost thou believe in the Son of God?" he asked the man that was born blind. "Thou hast seen him, and it is he that talketh with thee" (*John* 9:35, 37). And to Martha: "I am the resurrection and the life: he that believeth in me, though he were dead, yet he shall live: and whosoever liveth and believeth in me shall never die" (*John* 11:25–36).

## Christianity Under the Empire

This message was spread by the twelve disciples who had followed Jesus during his lifetime. But the new faith was carried outside the Hebrew community most effectively by a man who had never seen Jesus of Nazareth in life—Saint Paul. This Greek-trained Hebrew was able to preach the message of Christ to the Greek-speaking Eastern Roman Empire particularly. More than anyone else, he saw Christianity not merely as a Hebrew sect but as a religion open to all believers. Through his endless travels, his letters to Christian communities around the eastern end of the Mediterranean, and his total conviction of the truth of the Christian message, Paul became almost a second founder of the new religion.

There is no doubt that Jesus believed in his own divinity and in his mission to bring salvation to suffering humankind. Nor is there any doubt of the spark these messianic claims of divinity and salvation kindled in the souls of the faithful. The sign of the fish, under which Christians met in secret in the early years, was used because the letters that spelled *fish* in Greek—the lingua franca of the Roman East—were also the initials of the key words in the Christian message: "Jesus Christ—Son of God—Savior."

Various eastern "mystery cults" had made a similar offer of eternal life, and indeed had practiced some of the same rites and rituals that emerged in the early church. The cults of Dionysus, Demeter, the Egyptian Isis and Osiris, and others had promised life after death.

Osiris and Dionysus had returned from the dead themselves. Magna Mater—the Great Mother—and Mithras, the Zoroastrian god of light, required baptism of initiates. Dionysus, the Great Mother, and Isis and Osiris all offered a communion feast. But the Christian forms of these practices and promises, rooted in a claim of recent historicity rather than ancient myth, had a special appeal. Christianity gradually outdistanced all the rest.

The spread of the new cult was also fostered by men of learning who took up the new ideas, interpreted them in the familiar light of Greek philosophy, and thus made them acceptable to respectable Romans. In this way, the Greek doctrine of the *Logos* (the Word, or the spiritual manifestation of the World Soul) was used to explain Christ's coming into this world: "And the Word [*Logos* in the original Greek of the New Testament] was made flesh, and dwelt among us . . ." (*John* 1:14). Thus also Saint Augustine, writing in the last days of the Roman Empire, explained the problem of evil in a world made by a beneficent and all-powerful God by referring to well-known Neoplatonic doctrines of the distance between spirit and matter. From Paul in the first century to Augustine around 500, the simple story and dramatic claims of Jesus were supported and elaborated by men imbued with the rational spirit of Greco-Roman culture, till Christ's message emerged as the core of a formidable system of theology.

## Women in the Early Church

Women also played a significant part in the rise and spread of Christianity. They seem in fact to have been rather more prominent in early Christian times than they would be in many later Christian centuries.

Jesus himself had included a number of women among his early followers, and the Apostles who took up his work also found many women converts. Wealthy women welcomed traveling preachers, accepted conversion for themselves and their households, and then turned their homes into "house churches" where fellow Christians might worship in safety. If persecution followed, women as well as men went heroically to their martyrdom, glorifying the new faith.

As church institutions took shape, women often served as deaconesses, converting and baptizing women and administering church charities. Some, feeling seized by the Holy Spirit, preached and prophesied themselves. Once the Christian church was legalized by Constantine, rich and powerful women like his mother Helena went on pilgrimages, brought home holy relics, and built churches to house them.

Without these dedicated women, it is difficult to imagine Christianity surviving through those early centuries, or taking the shape it did in generations to come.

## The Triumph of the Early Church

The rise of Christianity was not as rapid as that of Islam seven hundred years later. The early Christians were accused of atheism as the Jews had been—they did reject all but *one* of the gods, after all—and were rumored to practice abominable rites in secret. There were brutal persecutions in the first three centuries, mob violence in provincial cities and mass executions in Rome. Saint Paul and other spreaders of the new faith were martyred for their beliefs.

Slowly but surely, however, the church found social and political recognition. Its own institutions were strengthened and systematized as its doctrine was. The isolated, persecuted Christian communities of the early centuries grew into a structure of episcopal sees, each headed by a big-city bishop. Even this early, furthermore, there was a tendency to defer on doctrinal matters to the bishop of Rome, the head of the Christian community at the imperial capital.

After one final round of savage persecutions under Diocletian at the beginning of the fourth century, then, the Christian church was finally recognized by the emperor Constantine in the Edict of Milan (313 B.C.E.). At the end of the fourth century, under Theodosius, the pagan temples were closed at last and Christianity became the state church of the Roman Empire.

The Greco-Roman world was a shell of its former self by then, deeply split and ready to crumble. But when the superstructures of the state fell away under the hammerblows of the barbarians, the Christian church would stand. It would go on alone into the darkness that lay ahead.

## SUMMARY

Two vast empires divided much of Western Eurasia between them in the classic age. Rome dominated the Mediterranean and Western Europe, while Persia ruled Western Asia.

The Persian Empire, the largest in history up to that time, emerged with dramatic suddenness in the sixth century B.C.E., temporarily unifying the entire Middle East—western Asia—by 500 B.C.E. The founders and the most celebrated of Persia's four successive ruling houses were the Achaemenids (539–331 B.C.E.). Cyrus the Great and his rough, leather-clad Persian cavalry conquered most of the empire in the later sixth century B.C.E. Cyrus's heirs added to their inheritance, till by 500 the Persia of Darius the Great stretched from Egypt and Mesopotamia to the northwest frontier of India. Persian imperial administration of this sprawling system of satrapies, Persian roads, and palaces all set a new standard for western Eurasia.

The inheritors of the Persian imperial tradition were a diverse line of dynasties—the Seleucids, the Parthians, and the Sassanids.

Persian high culture was significantly influenced by neighboring peoples, east and west, but produced lasting monuments that were distinctly Persian. The militant religion of Zoroaster—preaching life as a struggle between light and darkness, good and evil—influenced Persia's neighbors in their turn. And Persian palaces like those at Persepolis were magnificent embodiments of Persian imperial achievement.

Farther to the west, the ancient Romans were also among the world's most successful empire builders—and the only ones ever to bring Europe under a single government.

Beginning around 500 B.C.E., the city of Rome in central Italy grew into another vast Eurasian empire. But Rome's endless wars and vast imperial holdings corrupted its aristocracy and tempted its generals to use their armies to advance their own political ambitions. Around the time of Christ, two remarkable men, Julius and Augustus Caesar, ended this civil strife, imposed order, and left Rome united, powerful, and prosperous.

The period of the Roman peace—the first two centuries C.E.—saw Roman power established all around the Mediterranean Sea and over most of Western Europe. The third century, however, saw political chaos in the capital once more. Diocletian and Constantine reestablished order during the fourth century. But Rome was decaying economically, socially, culturally, and in other ways; and in the fifth century, the Western Roman Empire collapsed under waves of invasion by less developed peoples who lived on its frontiers.

During their centuries of power, the Romans developed practical arts like engineering and architecture themselves, building roads, aqueducts, theaters, and temples across Europe. Roman administration was efficient, Roman law a major cultural accomplishment. Rome's great writers left an unexcelled literary heritage to the West.

Jesus Christ was born during the reign of Augustus Caesar and preached in Palestine at the beginning of Rome's golden age. Though persecuted in its early centuries, Christianity spread across the empire, won official recognition in the fourth century, and survived the fall of Rome to shape the civilization of medieval Europe.

## SUGGESTED READING

Balsdon, J. P. V. D. *Roman Women.* Westport, Conn.: Greenwood Press, 1975. The best place to start. Equally scholarly are M. Lefkowitz and M. B. Fant, *Women's Life in Greece and Rome* (Baltimore, Md.: Johns Hopkins University Press, 1982). See also J. P. Hallett, *Fathers and Daughters in Roman Society: Women and the Elite Family* (Princeton, N.J.: Princeton University Press, 1984), impressionistic discussion of women's influence on society, exercised through family connections.

*Cambridge History of Iran* (7 vols.). Cambridge: Cambridge University Press, 1983. Volumes 2 and 3 deal with the first four dynasties of Persia in scholarly detail.

Cherry, D. *Frontier and Society in Roman North Africa.* New York: Clarendon Press, 1998. Challenges claims that native North Africans were effectively "Romanized" during the Roman period.

Cook, J. M. *The Persian Empire.* New York: Schocken Books, 1983. Achaemenid Persia in the light of recent archeological discoveries.

Curtis, J. *Ancient Persia.* Cambridge Mass.: Harvard University Press, 1990. Brief but authoritative introduction to the subject.

Deschesne-Guillemin, J. *Hymns of Zarathustra.* Boston: Beacon Press, 1963. Valuable introduction and commentaries accompany these translations of the Zoroastrain hymns, or *gathas.*

Evans, K. K. *War, Women and Children in Ancient Rome.* London: Routledge, 1991. Studies of the legal, familial, and workday problems of Roman women.

Ferrier, R. W., ed. *The Arts of Persia.* New Haven, Conn.: Yale University Press, 1989. Solid overview of the arts in ancient Persia.

Garnset, P., and R. Saller. *The Roman Empire: Economy, Society, and Culture.* Berkeley and Los Angeles: University of California Press, 1987. Particularly useful on government administration and social relations.

Giardina. A. *The Romans,* trans. L. G. Cochrane. Chicago: University of Chicago Press, 1993. Intriguing collection of essays on Roman social types, from citizens and priests to bandits and slaves.

Grainger, J. D. *The cities of Seleukid Syria.* New York: Oxford University Press, 1990. Scholarly account of the cities of this part of the Persian Empire under Alexander's successors.

Gruen, E. S. *Cultural and National Identity in Republican Rome.* Ithaca, N.Y.: Cornell University Press, 1992. Analysis of the republican ideology before the rise of the Caesars.

Harris, W. V. *War and Imperialism in Republican Rome 327–70 B.C.* New York: Oxford University Press, 1985. Scholarly account of Roman expansion around the Mediterranean Sea.

Jenkyns, R., ed. *The Legacy of Rome: A New Appraisal.* New York: Oxford University Press, 1992. New collection based on a classic anthology of scholarly essays on Rome's cultural legacy to later ages.

Lintott, A. *The Constitution of the Roman Republic.* New York: Clarendon Press, 1999. Analytical overview of the evolving Roman political system in the centuries before Augustus.

Meeks, W. A. *The First Urban Christians: The Social World of the Apostle Paul.* New Haven, Conn.: Yale University Press, 1983. Sees leading converts to Christianity as socially isolated people—wealthy women, Jews, freedmen—in need of a sense of spiritual community.

Stambaugh, J. E. *The Ancient Roman City.* Baltimore, Md.: Johns Hopkins University Press, 1988. Physical and social parameters of Roman urban life, based on literary sources as well as historical and archaeological materials.

Sherwin-White, S., and A. Kuhrt. *From Samarkand to Sardis.* Berkeley: University of California Press, 1992. Survey of Hellenistic Persia. See also their edited collection, *Hellenism in the East* (Berkeley: University of California Press, 1987).

Wells, P. *The Barbarians Speak: How the Conquered Peoples Shaped Roman Europe.* Princeton, N.J.: Princeton University Press, 1999. Focus on resistance to Roman imperialism, especially on the social and cultural side. See also G. Woolf, *Becoming Roman: The Origins of Provincial Civilization in Gaul* (New York: Cambridge University Press, 1998), for an archaeologist's view of Roman influence on conquered peoples.

Wiesehöfer, J. *Ancient Persia: From 550 B.C. to 650 A.D.* trans. A. Azodi. London: I. B. Tauris, 1998. Broad synthesis of Persian history from Cyrus to the Arab conquest.

 Please refer to the document CD-ROM for primary sources related to this chapter.

# CHAPTER 7

# FROM THE GANGES TO THE GOBI
## Gupta India and Han China
### (200 B.C.E.–C.E. 500)

## A Glance Ahead: Evolving Empires of Eastern Eurasia

Due east of Rome and Persia in the classic age lay two more remarkable empires: those of Gupta India and Han China. The striking qualities of historic India often seem to lie in its capacity for generating spiritual insights, religions that have spread far across Asia. China's genius, on the other hand, has seemed to be more political, a capacity for building—and repeatedly rebuilding—political unity over a vast tract of eastern Asia.

The weaknesses of the two giants also complement each other. India was politically divided for most of its history, a collection of peoples united by commerce and culture. Han China, by contrast, established a political unity that would be replicated by succeeding dynasties. When it came to religion, the global faith that made the profoundest impact on China was Buddhism—which had to be imported from India.

Different in many ways, but alike in vast reach and historical longevity, India and China stand second to none among the giants of the classic age.

## The Many Peoples of India

### Invaders of the Punjab: The Kushans

From the fall of the Maurya dynasty in 185 B.C.E. to the rise of the Guptas in C.E. 320, India was without even a shadow of a central government. During this period of five centuries, foreign invaders shouldered their way down through the Northwest Frontier once more. Separate kingdoms rose and fell in the Deccan. But a tough nucleus of cultural elements, from religion to caste, was already binding India together. And even the foreign invaders of this period would enrich rather than undermine the traditional culture that was the heart of India.

During these centuries foreign invaders thrust far beyond the Punjab, the region of the five rivers that branch out of the Indus. Over several hundred years, these foreign intruders set up kingdoms of their own over various parts of northwestern India. The mongoloid Kushan Empire, in particular, stretched for a time all the way from the frontiers of Parthian Persia into the heart of the Ganges valley. But all the newcomers followed one of two patterns. Some adopted Indian names, religions, and culture, and were absorbed into a population that was already becoming adept at absorbing foreigners. Some were eventually dislodged and went their way. In either case, India survived the onslaught of each new intruder in turn.

Most of the invaders of these five centuries, however, left something of their own to add its tang to the rich mix of Indian tradition. The Greeks brought coinage to India, and helped develop trade between India and the Mediterranean. The Kushans patronized Buddhism and presided over the emergence of a new form, the Mahayana Buddhism that would spread far across Asia.

### Kingdoms of the Deccan: The Tamils

Indian history thus far had centered in the north, in the valleys of the Indus and the Ganges, in the shadow of the Himalayas.

But there were also cities and kingdoms in the south during these centuries around the time of Christ—highly developed Dravidian cultures in the great southward-reaching triangle of peninsular India called the Deccan.

The Deccan was cut off from the north by the Narmada River and by ranges of thickly forested hills. But the hills of the Deccan stairstep down to fertile coastal plains on

Map legend:
- Mauryan Empire, ca. 250 B.C.E.
- Kushan Empire, ca. C.E. 100
- Gupta Empire, ca. C.E. 400

Map labels: KASHMIR, [AFGHANISTAN], PUNJAB, TIBET, Indus R., [PAKISTAN], [New Delhi], HIMALAYA MOUNTAINS, Brahmaputra R., BALUCHISTAN, GULF OF OMAN, Madras, SIND, Ganges R., Patna, Sarnath, Benares, Nalanda, [Calcutta], Sanchi, Narbada R., MAGADHA, ORISSA, Ajanta, [Bombay], Elephanta, Godavari R., Karli, ARABIAN SEA, DECCAN, BAY OF BENGAL, Amaravati, TAMILS, [Madras], Cauvery R., Tanjore, Muziris, PANDYAS, Cape Comorin, Anuradhpura, CEYLON, INDIAN OCEAN

Scale: 0 300 600 Miles / 0 300 600 Kilometers

both sides of the peninsula, and these plains became increasingly prosperous centers of both agriculture and trade in the first centuries C.E.

The peoples of the south were still almost purely Dravidian stock, as yet little affected by the long-established Aryan predominance in the north. The southerners spoke their own languages and had their own culture and social patterns. Trade, both overseas and with north India, appeared and grew during this period. Commercial contacts with the cities of the Indus and Ganges began to bring such northern cultural characteristics as Hinduism and the caste system into the south. In the first centuries after Christ, there were southern kingdoms that could challenge the most powerful northern principalities.

The most important peoples of the further south were the Tamils. Their language was the most widely spoken southern tongue, and they dominated the whole region from what is today Madras down to Cape Comorin, at the tip of the subcontinent.

During the first centuries C.E. the Tamil peoples were just moving from village culture into larger political units—chiefdoms and monarchies. Village councils were still central decision-making bodies, even after hereditary monarchy was introduced. The people still prayed to commemorative "hero stones" or made sacrifices of blood and rice to ancient gods of fertility, regarding the elaborate Vedic rituals—so ancient in the north—as modern novelties.

But change came rapidly to the shrewd Tamils. The source was growing prosperity as they developed the agricultural potential of their converging coastal plains and above all the mushrooming trade that flourished on both coasts. Southern India thus became a booming center of commerce and handicraft industries, and the land along the southern rivers bloomed.

Political and cultural evolution came with economic growth. Matrilineal succession prevailed in many parts of the south. The queen of the Pandyas, a powerful Tamil people, could field an army of thirteen thousand infantrymen, four thousand cavalry, and five hundred elephants. Tamils for a time conquered and occupied northern Ceylon (Sri Lanka)—where they are still a revolutionary force today—and they fought epic battles among themselves. Poetry also flowered among them very early, and the songs of the Tamil bards are among the treasures of India's literary heritage.

## Nations of Shopkeepers

The lack of a strong central government during the five hundred years between the Maurya and Gupta empires seems in no way to have handicapped the rapid growth of hand manufacturing, trade, and cities in both northern and southern India. Indeed, the half-envious label applied to industrial Britain many centuries later—"a nation of shopkeepers!"—would seem almost equally appropriate to India in the last centuries before Christ and the first centuries C.E.

Over a region approximately half the size of the continental United States, Indians found raw materials in considerable quantity. Iron and copper, gold and silver and precious stones were mined. The subcontinent's still abundant forests provided woods of all sorts, from teak to aromatic sandalwood. Cotton was widely grown and silk introduced. Even the sea contributed, providing pearls for Indian jewelry and for export.

These materials were processed by a complicated array of guilds, most of them organized by castes or subcastes who traditionally practiced particular hereditary crafts. Guilds of carpenters, metalworkers, and ceramicists were especially powerful in many urban areas. Like guilds in medieval Europe centuries later, Indian guilds regulated quality, prices, and competition, contributed substantially to religious foundations—especially Buddhist and Jain—and made the streets of Indian cities colorful with banners and processions on their feast days.

Trade also boomed during these centuries. North and south were linked by sea trade along the coasts and by a more modest system of roads begun in Asoka's day. Flotillas of coastal trading vessels, caravans of mules, oxen, and camels bound all the regions from the Himalayas to Cape Comorin. Foreign trade also prospered as Greek and Kushan states in the northwest encouraged Indian trade with the Mediterranean and China. And

Indian merchants searching for the spices that brought such good prices in the West increasingly traded and even settled in Southeast Asia, where Indian religious influence was also growing.

It was, in sum, a bustling, prosperous time in the cities of India. Coinage replaced barter in the urban centers; gold, silver, and copper coins of many kinds were minted, and even Roman *sesterces* circulated freely. The literature of the age describes a colorful urban population of guild craftsmen, wealthy caravan masters, and shipowners mingling with Hindu brahmans and Buddhist monks, prostitutes and poets, in narrow city streets. The courts of the *rajas* and of kings with even more exalted titles borrowed from Persia or China were centers of luxurious living and cultivated taste.

## THE GUPTA GOLDEN AGE

### Chandra Gupta I: The Raja Of the Rajas

India was a highly literate society by this time, one with several written languages. But the destruction in later centuries of what records might have survived leaves us with almost as little detailed knowledge of the reigns of the Guptas (C.E. 320–540) as we have of their Maurya predecessors half a millennium earlier. Enough is known, however, to piece together some striking parallels between these two Indian empires.

To begin with, both centered in northern India, specifically in the Ganges valley, which had been the center of Indian development since the Aryan conquest. Both the Maurya and Gupta dynasties, in fact, rose to power first in the same Ganges state of Magadha. Both expanded westward from there to incorporate the old pre-Aryan heartland on the Indus and the five rivers of the Punjab. Both pushed much more tentatively southward. The greatest of the Guptas actually controlled less of the Deccan than Asoka had. The Mauryas ruled for only about a century and a half (321–185 B.C.E.), the Guptas nominally for two centuries (C.E. 320–540). But in both cases the first three reigns were the glory days, and then the empire began to fragment and decline.

The first of the Guptas, Chandra Gupta I, even had the same name as the founder of the earlier dynasty, Chandragupta Maurya, though they were not related. The second of the Gupta clan, Samudra Gupta, was the great conqueror. The third, Chandra Gupta II, presided, like Asoka, over the dynasty's golden age.

Chandra Gupta I (320–330) seems to have been either a minor princeling or a wealthy landowner in the Ganges valley who married well. His bride, Princess Kumara Devi of the powerful Lichchhavi tribe, brought him an alliance powerful enough to make him ruler of the state of Magadha. From its now ancient capital of Patna, Chandra Gupta expanded his suzerainty over enough of the surrounding territories to kindle dreams of empire. In C.E. 320 he took the grandiloquent title of *maharajadhiraja,* "great king of kings." Ten years later he left this title, with all its implied aspirations, to his son Samudra Gupta, who made good on them with a vengeance.

### Samudra and Chandra Gupta II

Samudra Gupta (330–375) is shown on some of the gold coins he minted with the profits of his wars reflectively strumming a lute, and he is supposed to have loved poetry. The most important single record of his reign, however, is a record of his conquests. According to this eulogy, Samudra broke many kings in the field, forcing some to accept his overlordship and pay tribute and others to do homage. He brought most of northern India under Gupta rule and raided hundreds of miles into the southern jungles, returning laden with glory and plunder. He imposed direct Gupta government, collected tribute, or exercised a paramount influence from the mountains to a point well south of the Narmada. He became what his father had dreamed of being: *raja* of the *rajas,* great king of kings.

Chandra Gupta II (375–415), a grandson of the founder, fought his share of campaigns too. He completed the conquest of the northwest, so that Gupta power stretched all across northern India, from the Indus valley to the head of the Bay of Bengal. He also negotiated a shrewd series of marriage alliances with the preeminent princes of the south that cemented Gupta influence in the Deccan. An additional advantage of his wars and marriage diplomacy was that it gave the Guptas control of valuable west-coast seaports and their trade with the West.

Chandra Gupta II is most famous, however, for the cultural life of his reign and for his own patronage of the arts. Kalidasa the poet lived at his court, and literature and art flourished while he ruled. When we reflect that his forty years on the throne generally constituted a time of peace and prosperity, despite his celebrated conquest of the northwest, the "golden age" label so often affixed to the reign is easy to understand.

The first century of Gupta rule (the fourth century C.E.) was thus a time of expanding power, growing prosperity, and cultural splendor. The second Gupta century, however, was increasingly darkened by new invaders moving down from central Asia across the Northwest Frontier: the White Huns.

The White Huns were probably kin to those Huns who, under the notorious Attila, had reached the walls of Rome a hundred years before. Now, in the fifth century, while Rome foundered and fell to half-civilized Germanic invaders, the White Huns battered at the gates of Gupta India.

Gupta leaders succeeded in turning them back until late in the century. By 500, however, the Huns ruled the northwest and the Guptas were drawing back once more upon their Ganges base. They were a local power thereafter, and one that would disappear from the skimpy records in a few decades more.

## Life in Gupta India

Government was probably less centralized and less intrusive in Gupta India than in Maurya times. Most of the day-to-day authority was in the hands of the provincial viceroys, district officers, and even the headmen and elders of the individual villages. The councils of major cities were chosen by local people—especially merchants and craft guildsmen— rather than appointed from the center, as was apparently done in Maurya times. Nor was there anything in the India of Chandra Gupta II to correspond to the secret police of Chandragupta Maurya's day.

Economically, the trends of more recent centuries continued. Indian farmers labored in fields of wheat and sugar cane in the west, rice in the east, and in orchards and vegetable gardens everywhere. Craftspeople in bustling Indian cities continued to produce large quantities of pottery, metal goods, and textiles for home and foreign consumption. Trade with the west, by caravan and ship, dwindled in Gupta times as Rome declined. But Indian merchants were still frequently seen in East African ports, and they increased their activities in Southeast Asia. Spices, gems, perfumes, and sandalwood were exported; silk from China, ivory from Africa, and horses from Arabia and Persia flowed in.

Women's lives in general were varied. Upper-class girls were given some education, and girls of all classes were married young. Outside of marriage and motherhood, the only ways of life commonly open to women were withdrawal to a Buddhist nunnery, acting in a theatrical company, or prostitution. There were women who were teachers and even philosophers. On the other hand, the sixth century saw the first recorded case of widow burning: pious self-immolation by a high-case Hindu widow who believed she would thereby become a *sati*, or woman of great virtue. This supreme act of loyalty was considered to prove the widow's faithfulness to her husband and to guarantee their reunion after death. Widows also occupied a very low social status, which may have encouraged some to commit suicide in this way.

A Chinese Buddhist pilgrim who visited northern India in the reign of Chandra Gupta II described the Indians as on the whole a fortunate people. The land was prosperous, yet the people, he said, religiously refrained from both meat and wine. Charity hospitals were provided for the poor by pious citizens. Even the untouchables, the caste at the bottom of society, knew their place. These pariahs never entered a city without beating on a piece of wood so that their betters might avoid being polluted by contact with them.

Even allowing for the exaggerations of an enthusiastic visitor, it was a model society by the standards of its time.

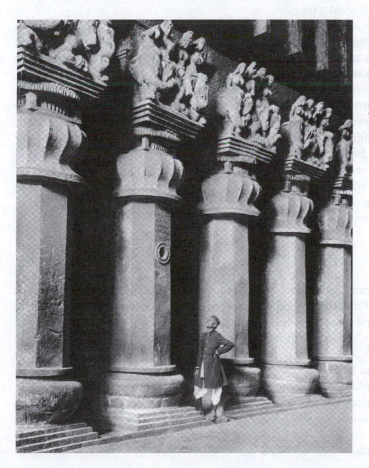

The sanctuary at Karli. The dimness, the heavy polygonal columns, and capitals thronged with spiritual presences generate the profoundly religious atmosphere for which India has been known for three thousand years. Note the balance of horizontals and verticals, circles and rectangles, in each column. (Library of Congress)

## The Hindu Renaissance

Hinduism, meanwhile, underwent even more impressive transformations, both before and during the Gupta era. Some of these changes paralleled those in Buddhism. Hinduism too saw a turning away from older texts toward more popular religion, and a widespread belief in a divine incarnation as savior. But the Hindu Renaissance, as it is often called, was a unique series of developments within India's oldest and always majority religion. These developments involved the priesthood, the scriptures, and the basic beliefs of Hinduism.

The brahmans, the hereditary priestly caste, remained widely respected and essential for ceremonial occasions. But the public turned more and more to a new collection of religious literature. These were the Puranas, popular myths and chronicles of Indian dynasties infused with religious significance and a prophetic framework by brahman authors.

The many gods, or *devas,* of the Vedic tradition remained, but there was a trend toward monotheism, the ancient sun god Vishnu or the fertility god Shiva emerging as the one true God in the thinking of his followers. Thus Shiva *nataraj,* "lord of the dance," embodied the cosmic rhythms of the universe. Depicted as a four-armed deity dancing in a ring of fire, crushing the demon of ignorance underfoot, he was seen as the cyclic force that both created and destroyed worlds.

There was also a tendency to group three of the most prominent old divinities as a sort of Trinity, embodying the three main forces in the universe. In this Hindu tradition, Brahma was the Creator of the universe; Vishnu was the Preserver, frequently appearing in human incarnation to save the virtuous; and Shiva was the Destroyer who brings a deserved end to all things when evil has corrupted the cosmos beyond hope of salvation. The process is cyclical, however, and Brahma soon creates heaven and earth anew.

The richness of this evolved Hinduism made a wide variety of religious experience available to Indians. An individual might worship the *lingam* (phallus) in the temples of Shiva or practice one of the many forms of *bakhti* (personal piety) encouraged by the cult of Vishnu.

The Gupta rulers were Hindus: Chandra Gupta II was even a theologian of sorts. Yet religious toleration prevailed, as it had under the Buddhist Asoka. Comparative tolerance of other people's beliefs would continue to characterize Indian religion until the coming of more militant faiths from the western end of Eurasia in later centuries.

## Mahayana Buddhism

The Buddhist visitor from China, cited above, noticed particularly the intense religious feeling of Gupta India. From the first century C.E., in fact, both Buddhism and Hinduism had been undergoing vital changes in the land of their birth.

The crucial changes in Buddhism took place in the centuries between the empires, particularly during the first two centuries C.E. It was in this period that Buddhist belief divided into the two great traditions that have characterized it ever since. This division, comparable to the Catholic-Protestant split in Christianity or the division between Shiite and Sunni Islam, produced two separate communities in international Buddhism. The older form, *Hinayana* ("Little Vehicle") Buddhism remained perhaps closer to the precise words and ideas of the founder. But the newer form, *Mahayana* ("Big Vehicle") Buddhism, was to reach much further, spreading in the end over most of East Asia.

Hinayana Buddhists saw Prince Siddartha the Buddha as the greatest teacher who had ever lived. He was the man who showed how an individual might, through right living, right thought, and assiduous meditation, escape from the endless wretched wheel of life into that blissful extinction of the self called Nirvana. It was a practical if profound message, from one enlightened human to those others, most commonly monks and nuns, who were capable of following him on the rigorous path of spiritual enlightenment.

Mahayana Buddhism expanded this conception drastically, and by so doing reached much larger numbers of people. Mahayana Buddhists saw the Buddha not merely as a wise teacher but as an incarnation of God. His goal, they asserted, was also larger: not only individual escape from the wheel, but the salvation of all humanity through the self-sacrificing labor of the spiritually enlightened few.

In the Mahayana theology there was in fact not one Buddha but a whole series of such incarnations of divinity, "blessed Buddhas . . . equal in number to the sands of the river" come to save humankind.[1] Before and after the historic Buddha there had lived, or would live, many other *bodhisattvas,* people who attained enlightenment but deliberately rejected escape into Nirvana in order to continue their pious work in this world, showing others the way to salvation. In addition, hosts of lesser gods clustered around the central figure of the Buddha in the art and thought of Mahayana Buddhism. Even Nirvana looked different to followers of the newer path, who envisioned a hierarchy of heavens and hells awaiting the faithful or the unbeliever after death.

Like Confucius, the historic Buddha had apparently refused even to speculate about gods; unlike Christ, he had never claimed to be divine himself. Seven centuries after Siddartha's death, many of his followers went further than the founder ever had, transforming Buddha into the central god of an immensely popular religion. His worship became a spectacle of impressive proportions, replete with huge temples and elaborate rituals. The Chinese visitor quoted earlier described a Buddhist festival in which towering floats were dragged through the streets, decorated with devas and spirits, Buddhas and bodhisattvas, canopies and streamers, and accompanied by singers, musicians, monks, and throngs of worshipers expressing their devotion with "flowers and incense."[2]

The larger conception of salvation for the multitude was splendid, but one wonders what the simply dressed man who had walked the dusty roads of the Gangetic states in the sixth century B.C.E. would have thought of the temples and the ritual, the incense and the bells.

## The Art of Caves and Stupas

The classic art of the half-dozen centuries climaxing in the Gupta age is the architecture and, above all, the sculpture of Buddhism. It is the art of the cave temple and the stupa, and it shows what beauty Buddhism could inspire even in this dawning of the Hindu Renaissance.

The *stupa,* a center of worship that goes back before the time of Christ, was a large domed mound with a relic of the Buddha buried at the center of it. Around this masonry-covered mound ran a circular paved path where monks walked, murmuring their devotions. Enclosing the entire precinct was a circular railing with four ornamental gateways set at the four cardinal points of the compass.

---

[1] *The Smaller Sukhavati-Vyuha in Buddhist Mahayana Texts,* trans. E. B. Cowell (New York: Dover, 1969), p. 99.

[2] Fa Hsien, *A Record of Buddhist Kingdoms Being an Account by the Chinese Monk Fa-Hsien of His Travels in India and Ceylon,* A.D. 399–414, trans. James Legge (Oxford: Clarendon Press, 1886), p. 79.

It is on these high, elaborately carved stone gateways that we see for the first time the interwoven tangle of figures that will be so typical of later Indian temples of many faiths. Thus, the three transverse panels that top the gateways of the Great Stupa at Sanchi, in the northern Deccan, are already bursting with sculptured life—elephants and lions, peacocks and lotuses, kings and surging crowds. The gods are there too; benevolent bodhisattvas and fullbreasted, narrow-waisted *yakshis* (nature spirits) swaying under mango trees. Buddha himself is never shown, but the stone is thick with Buddhist symbols, from the glowing footprints left by Prince Gautama's departure from his father's palace to the bo tree—the throne of his enlightenment—and the great spoked wheel of life.

Perhaps even more striking to Western eyes are the "cave temples," rock-cut sanctuaries where the western hills stairstep down to the coastal plains above Bombay. These temples, complete with facade, long interior nave, flanking pillars, side aisles, and a mounded stupa at the far end, are carved entirely out of the living rock of the cliffs. They were sculpted, even to the obviously nonfunctional ribbed vaults overhead, in perfect imitation of the wooden, thatch-roofed temples then in use in the world outside.

In the dim light of the most imposing of these sanctuaries, the one at Karli, the rows of close-set polygonal pillars with their lotus and elephant capitals give one a dizzy sense of moving in a world where nothing is what it ought to be. All that would be needed to catapult the viewer back a score of centuries would be the murmur of shaved, saffron-robed monks moving down the shadowy aisle beyond the sixteen-sided pillars.

Nowhere does Buddha himself appear in these earlier monuments to Hinayana purity. Soon, however, the traditional figure of the more popular religion of later centuries begins to show. The Indo-Greek sculptors of the Gandhara school in the northwest offer an almost Hellenic Buddha, replete with acanthus leaves and even cupids. Farther south, however, the Mathura school presents a more convincingly Indian figure—the round face, the shaved crown, the bump of enlightenment, the right hand raised in a gesture not of blessing but of fearlessness. Here if anywhere the classic simplicity and calm strength of Gupta art look out at us.

To see the best of what remains of Gupta painting, finally, one would have to go to the famous Ajanta caves in the mountains of the Deccan. Here, on the walls of some thirty cave temples and monks' cells hollowed out over several hundred years, the lives of the aristocracy of that long-vanished age live on in faintly glowing colors. Here lovers lounge eternally on the veranda of an elegantly pillared palace. A prince and princess stroll among the palms and flowers. And a bodhisattva, his handsome head bowing under the weight of a high jeweled crown, gazes beneath half-lowered lids into his divine destiny. The smoky modeling of cheeks and lips, the glimmering colors on the cave walls, illuminate that forgotten world of sensuality and mystic faith with a somber beauty.

## Beast Fables and Courtly Love

The age of the Guptas was the great age of Indian literature as well. It was the age of Kalidasa, frequently described as the Indian Shakespeare, of the final versions of the great Indian epics, and of the triumph of literary Sanskrit in plays, poetry, and prose.

The great technical breakthrough was the adoption of a version of Sanskrit, the language of the ancient Vedas and other Hindu religious texts, as the language of a brilliant living literature. Kalidasa and other playwrights and poets of this Indian "nest of singing birds" used this two-thousand-year-old tongue with refined and courtly elegance. They also used the vernacular Prakrit language in plays for the speeches of the lower-class characters.

If Buddhism shaped the painting and sculpture of the Gupta age, the Hindu Renaissance inspired much of its literature. It was at this time that the ancient epics—the *Ramayana* and the *Mahabharata*—were put into the versions we have today under the judicious guidance of brahmanical scholars. Thus interpreted, these old poems of war and adventure acquired heavy religious overtones: the *Song of God* episode, with its revelations of princely duty and the nature of the godhead, was added to the *Mahabharata* at this time. The *Panchatantra,* the widely popular collection of Indian beast fables and fairy tales, was also assembled during this period. The wisdom here is more worldly, but this world of talking animals, of beast and human life commingled, seems distinctly Hindu in spirit.

There is even a substantial mythological framework to the romantic plays and poems of Kalidasa, the most celebrated secular writer of the Gupta age. Shiva and Vishnu, the two ancient epics, and the even older Indian myths of gods and nature spirits hover over his works as Greek mythology informs Greek tragic drama. Kalidasa's most famous play, *Shakuntala,* is based on an incident from the *Mahabharata,* and gods move freely in and out of the story.

As writers have learned in many lands, however, much can be done with sacred material. *Shakuntala,* the story of a king's love for the lovely daughter of a pious hermit, is as romantic a piece as a Gupta court audience could have wished. The lyric passages, which were apparently sung, give the performance something of the air of a modern musical comedy. But the depth and endless variety of emotional tones, the joy in nature, the humanity of the middle-aged king, and the shy eagerness of Shakuntala herself have earned Kalidasa's masterwork a high place in Indian literature ever since.

## Mathematics, Medicine, and Science

Religion seems to infuse so much of the Indian consciousness that it is perhaps surprising that some of the most impressive achievements of the Gupta age came not in mystic insight or theology but in science. As it happens, no great conflict was felt between science and religion in Gupta India. Buddhist monasteries and Hindu schools taught mathematics and medicine as well as philosophy and their respective sacred texts. The Buddhist college at Nalanda, the largest institution of higher learning in India, taught medicine and physics along with languages, literature, and metaphysics.

Gupta medicine was based too little on empirical observation to make much progress. Gupta astrology was very popular, but it is hard to establish progress in a pseudoscience. In astronomy and mathematics, however, Indian scientists clearly rivaled the Greeks and the Chinese.

The great leap forward made by Indian mathematicians was the development of what Westerners came to call Arabic numerals—a vast improvement over the Roman numerals that remained standard in the West for another thousand years. With nine numerical symbols and that wonderful little invention, the zero, India immensely simplified the process of mathematical calculation. With the decimal system and the concept of place value, new spheres of mathematical operation were opened up. The value of pi and the beginnings of algebra were also developed here.

Greek astronomy was in circulation among Indian scientists, and Greek scientific terminology was absorbed into Indian texts. But the astronomers of the subcontinent discovered for themselves that the earth was a rotating sphere and learned the causes of lunar eclipses. They also calculated the length of the solar year to the seventh decimal place.

The life of the scientific mind, at any rate, has never been limited to any one corner of this spinning globe.

# THE HAN DYNASTY OF CHINA

## The Exalted Founder: Han Gaozu

On the great eastward bulge of Asia, the first attempt at a unified China had collapsed in ruins in 207 B.C.E. The awesome First Emperor, Shi Huangdi, had scarcely been placed in his fantastic tomb when court intrigue, peasant rebellion, and rival warlord armies tore his empire apart. From the Great Wall in the north to the warm, typhoon-swept south, the river valleys and tile-roofed cities were tumbled into chaos once more. With the collapse of the Qin dynasty after a single reign, China seemed to be sliding back into Zhou feudalism and the anarchy of the Warring States.

But this was not what happened. When the Mauryas succumbed in India, no new unifying power emerged for five centuries. In China the violence burned itself out, and a new dynasty took up the task of unification in less than twenty years. The Han dynasty (202 B.C.E.–C.E. 220) would in fact be one of China's greatest—and most admired—ruling houses, a model to those that followed.

Two strikingly different rivals for supreme power emerged in the chaos of feuding warlords that followed the death of Huangdi. One was a dashing southern aristocrat named Xiang Yu. Xiang Yu was willing to leave other princes and warlords in possession of their own lands in return for the sort of semifeudal suzerainty that had been wielded by the Zhou kings. The other contender was a rare type in Chinese imperial annals: a one-time village official and former bandit turned rebel general named Liu Bang. Liu Bang was not an aristocrat or even a gentleman, and his ambitions went considerably beyond feudal suzerainty.

Liu Bang seems to have had a good deal of peasant cunning and more than his share of dogged determination. He was no great military leader; at one point he was even captured and held for ransom by the Xiongnu barbarians from beyond the Great Wall. In his protracted struggle with Xiang Yu, he won only one battle—the last one.

Surrounded, outmaneuvered, and outlasted, the aristocratic Xiang Yu committed suicide—and has lived on ever since as a tragic figure in Chinese opera. Liu Bang got on with the business of organizing power in China.

The Han dynasty he founded was to rule, with a single brief interregnum, for more than four hundred years, from 202 B.C.E. to C.E. 220. The Liu family took their dynastic name from the river Han, which flowed through the territory that had been Liu Bang's home base. The peasant emperor himself was posthumously awarded a new name by the historians of his reign. He is officially known to history as Han Gaozu, "Exalted Founder" of the Han dynasty. It was a dynasty that would be so honored in Chinese history that to this day the Chinese call themselves "people of Han."

In the few years left to him after his long struggle for power (he died in 195 B.C.E.), Gaozu set the dynasty on the basic political course it would follow thereafter. He chose to reject Zhou feudalism and to continue instead the centralizing policies of the Qin. But he also had the common sense to proceed with less rigor and more moderation than the hard-driving First Emperor had used. Taxes were easier to bear under Gaozu, punishments less savage than they had been under Huangdi's Legalist advisers. Some elements of the feudal order were preserved temporarily by the pragmatic Exalted Founder—notably, feudal domains for some of his own supporters and relatives.

The Chinese people, exhausted by Huangdi's grand schemes and by the years of civil war thereafter, responded to this more temperate course by conferring their support on the

# VOICES FROM THE PAST

Sima Qian (Ssu-ma Ch'ien) (145–90 B.C.E.), the "Grand Historian" of Han China, was famous for his dramatic style and for his ability to bring historical figures to life. Here Gaozu, the founder of the Han dynasty, faces the difficult problem of rewarding his chief supporters after their victory and accession to power. Which does the new emperor seem to value more, military or administrative skills? From what you know about Gaozu, does this homely parable sound like something he might actually have said? Do you get a sense of his character from this anecdote?

> *The king of Han, now emperor, considered that Hsiao Ho had achieved the highest merit, and hence enfeoffed him as marquis of Tsuan with the revenue from a large number of towns. But the other distinguished officials objected, saying, "We have all buckled on armor and taken up our weapons, some of us fighting as many as a hundred or more engagements, the least of us fighting twenty or thirty. Each, to a greater or lesser degree, has engaged in attacks upon cities or seizures of territory. And yet Hsiao Ho, who has never campaigned on the sweaty steeds of battle, but only sat here with brush and ink deliberating on questions of state instead of fighting, is awarded a position above us. How can this be?"*
>
> *"Gentlemen," the emperor asked, "do you know anything about hunting?"*
>
> *"We do," they replied.*
>
> *"And do you know anything about hunting dogs?"*
>
> *"We do."*
>
> *"Now in a hunt," the emperor said, "it is the dog who is sent to pursue and kill the beast. But the one who unleashes the dog and points out the place where the beast is hiding is the huntsman. You, gentlemen, have only succeeded in capturing the beast, and so your achievement is that of hunting dogs. But it is Hsiao Ho who unleashed you and pointed out the place, and his achievement is that of the huntsman. Also in your case only you yourselves, or at most two or three of your family, joined in following me. But Hsiao Ho dispatched his whole family numbering twenty or thirty members to accompany me. This is a service I can hardly forget."*

Ssu-ma Ch'ien, *Records of the Grand Historian of China: The Shih Chi*, trans. Burton Watson (New York: Columbia University Press, 1961), pp. 127–128.

new dynasty. The Han rulers, in turn, brought the Chinese a period of relative peace and prosperity comparable to that enjoyed by Romans after Augustus or Indians in the Gupta age. It established traditions that would shape the lives of generations far into China's future.

### The Sustainer: Empress Lü

Life was easier along the Yellow River, the Yangzi, and their webs of tributaries wandering among the misty mountains of China. Labor in the millet fields of the north and the rice paddies of the south brought the peasant farmer a large share at least of his just reward, thanks to the dynasty established by the peasant emperor. But at the imperial capital at Chang'an (modern Xi'an), politics was still full of intrigue and violence.

After Gaozu's death, someone was desperately needed to carry on the work, to sustain the drive for unification and conciliation he had begun. Fortunately for China—if not for her court rivals—there was such a person: the empress dowager Lü.

Empress Lü was not Gaozu's only wife, nor was her son the late emperor's oldest or even his favorite. But Lü was well known to Gaozu's old comrades in the long struggle for power, now the chief ministers of the Han Empire. Two of her brothers had been generals in the wars, and she herself had contributed substantially to the successful struggle and suffered in the cause. When her undeniable intelligence, firmness of purpose, and driving ambition are added to this record, the rise of the empress to power has almost a ring of inevitability about it.

In fact, she rose through a court struggle as devious and cruel as anything the Hans had faced in the field. Lü ruled first through her son, a well-meaning but unaggressive sixteen-year-old. When the boy emperor suffered a nervous collapse, allegedly out of horror at his mother's brutal treatment of her defeated rivals, the dowager empress governed directly. There was no doubt of her vindictiveness toward rivals. There was no doubt either that hordes of ambitious members of the Lü clan descended on Chang'an during the years of her supremacy, challenging even the old fighters for the empress's favor.

Precisely because of her need for supporters, however, Dowager Empress Lü endeavored to earn the support of the people through moderate and humane policies. Like Gaozu, she eased the tax burden. She allowed the substitution of fines for physical punishments, and she rescinded the Qin book-burning laws. Her rule was strong and beneficent enough to earn the grudging admiration even of those of the old guard who objected to the growing power of the Lü clan.

Despite all the feuding of the factions, then, the great Han historian Ban Gu wrote approvingly of her reign:

> During the times of [Empress Lü] the world had succeeded in putting behind it the sufferings [during the period of] Contending States. . . . the world was quiet, [mutilating] punishments and other penalties were seldom used, the people were busy in sowing and harvesting, and clothing and food multiplied and were abundant.[3]

But the years rapidly grew heavy on the empress, who was not young when she acceded to power, and her strength waned as her years advanced. She appointed favorite nephews to supreme civil and military authority, advanced her family in the crucial tables of precedence—and then quite suddenly died. The cause of death was the bite of a black dog, which Lü swore on her deathbed was the spirit of a long-defeated rival come back to take its revenge.

Like the First Emperor of the Qin, the great sustainer of the Han could do nothing to impose her will from beyond the grave. Within weeks of her death, old fighters and members of Gaozu's clan had joined with leading officials and military men to massacre the entire Lü family and to put another of the Exalted Founder's line on the dragon throne of China.

### The Martial Emperor: Han Wudi

The greatest of the Han emperors came to the throne half a century after the founder's death. Han Wudi, "the Martial Emperor" (141–187 B.C.E.), believed totally in the Mandate of Heaven and the mystique of the emperor. To fortify his claim to absolute sovereignty, he revived or instituted what became traditional imperial prayers and sacrifices to Heaven, to Earth, and to many other supernatural powers. To strengthen the developing system of

---

[3]Ban Gu, *The History of the Former Han Dynasty,* trans. Homer H. Dubs (Baltimore, Md.: Waverly Press, 1938), p. 210.

imperial administration, he recruited, trained, and appointed a pyramidal bureaucracy of tens of thousands of officials.

Wudi's economic policies built consciously on the prosperity of the earlier Han. To encourage continued economic growth, he expanded the transportation system through an extensive program of canal building. He established a system of imperial granaries to store grain for resale in time of bad harvest—a system that both stabilized agricultural prices and provided a tidy profit for the imperial treasury. To pay for his large-scale foreign and domestic projects, however, Wudi tapped the growing wealth of the empire through expanded taxation on trade, handicraft industry, and agriculture and through state monopolies on the sale of such essentials as iron, salt, and liquor.

The Martial Emperor's most obsessive concern, however, was with foreign wars, both defensive and expansionist. Perhaps his greatest military efforts were lavished on a series of campaigns against the nomadic Xiongnu north of the Great Wall. Wudi sent huge armies north to push the intrusive nomads back across the Gobi. He extended the Great Wall itself and set up military colonies to keep watch over the northern frontiers. He also developed what became a traditional Chinese policy of "using barbarians to control barbarians." This involved an intricate combination of marriage alliances, tributary relationships, and hostage taking in the guise of providing court education for the children of Xiongnu chieftains.

Besides these defensive measures, Wudi also embarked on a grandiose program of Chinese imperial expansion. Following in the footsteps of the First Emperor, the Martial Emperor pushed into both Korea and north Vietnam. His reaffirmation of Chinese authority made Vietnam a Chinese colony for most of the next millennium. His aggressiveness

## CHINESE EMPIRES THROUGH THE CLASSIC AGE

also helped transform Korea into the cultural base from which the offshore islands of Japan would later be reshaped in China's image.

But the ambitions of Wudi did not stop with domination of East Asia. He sent expeditions far across the northwestern frontiers as well, into the heart of Eurasia. His expeditions had several goals: alliances with western barbarians against the Xiongnu, acquisition of the famed war-horses of Ferghana in Central Asia, and quite possibly control of the east-west trade routes across Eurasia as well. These military campaigns established Chinese power from Mongolia to the borders of Tibet, pushed over the Pamirs into central Asia, and established Chinese control over crucial oases on the caravan roads around the Tarim Basin.

China's interest in westward expansion was to continue, and Chinese armies were to push westward still farther. But the Martial Emperor had done his share for Chinese territorial expansion north, south, and west. By the time of his death in 87 B.C.E., the borders of the Middle Kingdom were beginning to look a good deal like those of modern China.

## Wang Mang and the Interregnum

In traditional Chinese historiography, the four centuries of Han rule are divided into two halves: the Former or Western Han, from 202 B.C.E. to C.E. 9, and the Later or Eastern Han, from C.E. 25 to 220. The thirty-five years in between constitute the brief, colorful period of the usurping emperor Wang Mang.

The emperors of the Former Han fell victim to what was to become a familiar combination of peasant unrest and weakness at the center. Peasant revolts broke out during the last two decades of the first century B.C.E., partly because of excess taxation, partly because of population growth that outstripped the land available to feed the people. At the same time, the government faced dwindling tax revenues as once-taxable peasant farmers became farm laborers on the traditionally untaxed estates of large noble landowners.

Amid this crisis, Wang Mang, nephew of a reigning empress, assumed power, proposing radical surgery to cure the ailing state. In the process he temporarily replaced the Han dynasty with his own imperial house.

The usurper claimed that he was reviving traditional policies of pre-Han rulers. In fact, some of his reforms look rather like revivals of some of the most extravagant policies of his great Han predecessor Wudi. Thus Wang also expanded government monopolies, strengthened the system of imperial granaries, and even indulged in inflationary coinage to put more money into circulation. His most drastic innovation, however, was a scheme to boost government revenues—and benefit the peasantry—by nationalizing the great estates of the aristocracy and parceling them out among taxable peasant proprietors.

Needless to say, this plan quickly alienated the great landowners from the new government. Bad harvests and terrible flooding by the Yellow River then triggered a new wave of peasant rebellions—the bloody revolt of the Red Eyebrows. Crusading for vaguely Daoist ideals, this group adopted red as its symbolic color because this was the color of the Hans, whose restoration they championed. They rose first in Shandong, China's great northeastern peninsula and the site of its most sacred mountain, and were soon ravaging the central plains. When nomads from beyond the Wall broke through the depleted border garrisons, it was clear to all that the Mandate of Heaven had not passed to Wang Mang after all.

Wang was slaughtered by rampaging rebels in his own capital in C.E. 23. Two years later the head of a branch of the ruling house of the Han Empire seized power, and the Han began two more centuries of rule over China.

## New Frontiers

The first century of the Later Han dynasty—the first century C.E.—was a period of internal recovery and renewed external expansion. The restored Han moved the capital from Chang'an eastward, down to the city of Luoyang and reestablished the strong centralized administration of earlier Han times. Prosperity was revived across the country and relative peace reigned.

The Later Han, however, also saw a revival of Han imperial expansion. Armies from Luoyang reestablished Han authority over South China and north Vietnam, and Chinese influence grew in Korea. The first respectful embassy from one of the "hundred tribes" of Japan was received during Later Han times. The Xiongnu were dealt so crushing a defeat toward the end of the first century C.E. that they began the long westward drift across the steppes that would eventually bring them up against the walls of Rome—under the name of Huns.

Most striking, however, was the renewed westward drive under the Later Han emperors. The leading spirit in this expansion was Ban Chao, one of China's most celebrated proconsuls of empire. In two major expeditions he reestablished Chinese authority over the Tarim Basin and pushed on over the Pamirs and across central Asia as far as the region of the Caspian Sea. At the moment of Han China's farthest westward penetration, only the Parthian Empire of Persia lay between the great Empire of the East and the Roman Empire of the West. And the Later Han emperors actively encouraged trade with the West over the Silk Road—a connection that would continue for some time even after the fall of the dynasty.

## The Mandate Passes

The second century of Later Han rule—the fourth of the dynasty's total tenure of power—was far less successful. As usual, the troubles were both political and economic, focusing in the court and in the country as a whole.

A special political difficulty was one that had surfaced as early as the reign of Empress Lü in Former Han times: the ambitious families of empresses. In the feudal times of the Shang and the Zhou, before unification was achieved, the kings of the various affiliated Chinese states could marry each other's daughters—their equals in rank. But under the unified empire of the Han, there were no other monarchs in China, and the neighboring peoples were dismissed as barbarians, unsuitable sources of Han empresses. Han emperors therefore had to marry the daughters of aristocratic subjects. The multitudinous kin of the empress invariably flocked to court to take advantage of the family's good fortune by establishing themselves in as many positions of power as possible. When an empress outlived her imperial husband and governed as regent for a minor emperor, the power drive of her clan could tear the Luoyang court apart. This in fact happened more than once under the Later Han.

Other centers of factional rivalry existed at the imperial court as well. These included the large numbers of eunuchs, whose power extended far beyond the imperial harem; the most successful generals; and the chief ministers of state. All these groups contributed to the downfall of this and more than one later dynasty.

Finally, economic factors and peasant upheavals once more played crucial parts in the coming catastrophe. Rich landowners, recovered from the disasters of Wang Mang's regime, once more acquired tax exemptions for their large estates. Buckling under the increased tax burden thus shifted to their shoulders, peasants sought to escape the tax collectors by fleeing into South China or by rebelling against the state.

Like the Red Eyebrows, the Yellow Turbans of the later second century C.E. had Daoist sympathies and social grievances. They also had the usual share of peasant superstitions; the yellow cloth they wore wrapped around their heads symbolized the color of Chinese earth, which would quench the red fire of Han. Like the Eyebrows, the Turbans rose first in the great northern peninsula of Shandong and were soon terrorizing much of North China.

The collapse of the Later Han thus came in a typical turmoil of court conspiracy, peasant revolt—and finally warlord generals carving up the crumbling empire into their own separate fiefdoms. By C.E. 220 China was once more divided, this time into the Three Kingdoms. The generals who headed these successor states began four centuries of political fragmentation and disarray in China. The first and one of the greatest of Chinese experiments in empire, that of the Qin and the Han, was over.

In a sense, the Han Empire was the victim of its own success. The centralized administration that was one of its greatest achievements could not work without close ties with the landed aristocracy. But the landed magnates milked this special relationship so successfully that they became too rich and powerful to control and created autonomous power centers all over the empire. Again, the very peace and prosperity of Han times seem to have led to an unprecedented growth in the peasant population—until there were simply more people than the government could support or control. Nevertheless, the Han dynasty had fathered a sense of political unity that would reassert itself time and again in centuries to come.

## THE STRUCTURE OF HAN CHINA

### The Imperial Mystique

China under the Han was the great empire of the east, as Rome—at almost exactly the same time—was the empire of the western end of Eurasia. The two had much in common: vast size and population; increasing power in the hands of the emperors; increasingly centralized bureaucratic administration; a sense of being the only truly civilized people, surrounded by barbarians; even an important breakdown of authority midway in their history, in both cases about the time of Christ. The two were aware of each other's existence and traded through intermediaries from one end of the world island to the other.

The Han emperors built a significant bastion of imperial authority on the Zhou doctrine of the Mandate of Heaven. It was under the Han that this doctrine of divine right to rule became associated not with a weak feudal regime like the Zhou but with a powerful centralized monarchy. From Han times the Chinese tended to believe that legitimate government meant strong rule by a single benevolent despot—a fatherly, authoritarian emperor whose governance was both virtuous and divinely sanctioned.

That the facts of political life at the Chinese court seldom corresponded to this pious theory was much less important for China's subsequent history than was the impact of the theory itself. This imperial mystique, the belief in paternal, virtuous, and divinely mandated governmental authority, was a powerful unifying and centralizing force in Chinese life. Reinforced by a common written language, shared traditions, and—as will be emphasized presently—Confucian beliefs and a classically educated centralized bureaucracy, this image of the emperor helped to weld China's tens of millions of people into something that Rome and India could never be: not a polyglot empire but a gigantic unified nation.

There were major breakdowns of Chinese unity still to come. But the centralizing rule of the Han set China on the road to national unity and strong central government infused with a sense of its own righteousness and right to rule. China has followed this road ever since, despite all that its huge size, vast population, and strong regional loyalties did to pull it apart.

## The Scholar Bureaucrats

The Han period also saw a crucial institutional development that made the authority of the imperial government much more than a theory. For in Han times, China's famous system of scholar bureaucrats began to evolve.

The great shift from government by an autonomous feudal aristocracy to government by appointed officials of the central government had had a brief, violent trial run under the Qin. But the Legalist rigor of Qin administrators had made the system too brutal for widespread acceptance. Infused with the more moderate spirit of Confucianism—and with due concessions to the existing social elite of the countryside—China's administration under the Han dynasty became the most impressive in the world.

At the center of the Han administrative system were a small number of powerful court officials. These included a chancellor who chaired meetings and wielded substantial authority under the emperor; a director of the secretariat, whose power came from his control over what documents actually reached the emperor for signature; and a commandant of the Chinese armed forces. There were also nine ministers of state charged with the daily business of government, with running the huge imperial palace, and with the crucial religious rituals required of the Son of Heaven.

Outside the capital at Chang'an or Luoyang, the nation was divided and subdivided into administrative districts. There were a dozen main regions, 20 princedoms (holdovers from the feudal system), more than 100 commanderies, 240 marquisates, and 1,300 counties in Han China—all governed by officials appointed by the emperor. In the Han period, as noted above, most of these officials were still members of wealthy landowning families.

Also under the Han, however, the system of civil-service examinations that would eventually undermine the remaining power of the landed magnates slowly took shape. Exams on Confucian principles and classics were given annually at Chang'an to young gentlemen nominated for office. To prepare them, an imperial university was established at the capital. Again, the children of the wealthy, who had money for books and tutors, were evidently the ones most likely to succeed. Nevertheless, the result was to produce a ruling elite of government administrators who had a common family background and whose heads were filled with common Confucian theories, shared historical understanding, and the same basic values—a powerful force for stability in the ancient Middle Kingdom.

Around 100 B.C.E. China's governmental bureaucracy, divided into eighteen civil-service ranks, included upwards of 130,000 people—not many to govern tens of millions of Chinese, but an astonishing number of educated, centrally appointed officials for those days, when most of the world was still ruled by village elders, hereditary clan chieftains, and local princes.

## Sixty Million Chinese—and Counting

The land they administered was large, populous, and generally prosperous in spite of some startling social and economic changes over the four centuries of Han rule. The size of the Han Empire, with the cementing of Chinese authority over northern Vietnam and the addition of Xinjiang—China's far west—was close to the size of twentieth-century China. The population, according to tax censuses taken around the middle of the dynasty, ran higher than sixty million people. We are thus dealing with a nation approaching the geographical size of the United States today, though with a population approximately one quarter that of the present United States.

Han society, however, underwent significant changes. Han China was particularly affected by the destruction of the ancient pattern of provincial feudalism by Gaozu and his successors. Gaozu abolished most of the autonomous states upon his seizure of power, leaving only a few such feudal enclaves to reward his own followers. Later Han emperors undermined even those few by edicts requiring feudal landholders to divide their estates equally among their male offspring. Within a few generations, this procedure had so thoroughly fragmented the great feudal holdings that they easily came under imperial control.

From this change emerged the basic social structure of China from Han times to the twentieth century. When feudal landholding was replaced by freehold property, three main classes quickly developed across the vast expanse of China's countryside. There was a class of locally powerful, often very wealthy large landowners. There was a larger class of peasant freeholders who often had to struggle to keep enough land to feed themselves. And there was an even larger class of tenant farmers and farm laborers. The interaction among these social classes, who composed the bulk of China's population, would determine much of its subsequent history.

The relative peace and prosperity of the Former Han transformed the nation economically as well. A true money economy, for example, was established for the first time. The widespread use of coins instead of barter brought with it such exotic problems as inflation and the need for a firm governmental monetary policy. But the growing wealth of China also filled the government's treasury with strings of copper cash, revenues that accumulated through so many reigns that the strings actually rotted away—an enviable situation for any government.

Under the expansionist Han emperors, furthermore, foreign trade expanded significantly. China traded, in the first instance, with the less developed tributary peoples around it. More important, Chinese goods moved westwards across Eurasia along the great Silk Road to India or to Rome, where Chinese silk became a major luxury import. Chinese merchants themselves did not travel that far. But the trade overland through central Asia or by sea through the archipelagoes of Southeast Asia became one of the basic ties that bound the world island into a single, if loosely linked, unit during the classical period.

## The Women of Han China

The Han dynasty is commonly characterized as one of China's most splendid periods. In the lives of the female half of the huge Chinese population, it was also a time of considerable variety and significant achievement.

During this age in which much of the traditional Chinese way was first established, the position of women was also apparently set. Widely accepted maxims and popular anecdotes illustrating admired feminine qualities came into circulation: Like so much else, these precepts were sanctified in Han times by attribution to Confucian sages. They added up to a prescription for ideal womanhood that would prevail in China through most of its history.

According to this Confucian view—as in Christian, Muslim, and other groups in later centuries—women's virtues were family virtues. Chinese women were expected to be devoted to their parents in childhood and youth, to their husbands thereafter. Care of their

Chinese court ladies, hair elaborately dressed, hands concealed in long sleeves. The well-fed self-assurance of the Middle Kingdom in one of its greatest ages is eloquently captured in these clay figurines, which have survived remarkably undamaged over twenty centuries. (Library of Congress)

family and children was to be their central preoccupation as adults. Fidelity, chastity, and modesty were the ideal female qualities.

In actuality, however, Han China produced a number of women who transcended this image. Women of several important classes became highly educated and much respected for their learning during the Han dynasty. At the top of the social pyramid, Han empresses and imperial concubines were sometimes celebrated for their culture, as were the wives and daughters of some of the landowning aristocracy. Daoist and later Buddhist nuns might be both educated and relatively independent in traditional China. A few at least of the courtesan class were also highly cultured, as *geishas* would be in Japan at a later date.

We shall meet all these groups of learned ladies in later periods of Chinese history. But the Han period—the very time when the constricting Confucian ideal of womanhood was taking shape—was also a time of relative success, for the elite at least, of China's female population.

## THE MIND AND ART OF THE HAN

### The Triumph of Confucianism

If Shang bronzes were the glory of that dynasty, and if the supreme cultural achievement of the Zhou lay in philosophy and poetry, then Han China's major cultural monuments are to be found in the somewhat less exalted fields of scholarship and history. But Confucian scholarship and the study of the great dynastic cycle of Chinese history also had their contributions to make to the many-splendored culture and the amazing longevity of Chinese civilization.

The triumph of Confucianism in Chinese thought during the Han period was a complicated and in some ways rather unedifying spectacle. But that triumph would make a great difference to China's future.

All the schools of philosophy that had survived the "burning of the books" under the Qin had their place under the Han. The Qin Legalist tradition itself, with its justification of ruthless efficiency and rigorous punishment, was often the actual policy of Han emperors, even those who paid reverent lip service to Confucius. The romantic mysticism of Daoism became in Han times the basis of a widely popular farrago of nature worship, dietary regimen, research into methods of preserving life indefinitely and transmuting base metals into gold, and plain magic.

Nevertheless, the Confucian tradition did become the predominant philosophy of China during the Han period. Han emperors, from the classically uneducated Exalted Founder to the ruthlessly Legalistic Martial Emperor, filled their edicts with Confucian invocations of government for the good of the people, respect for the sages, and other pieties. The official examinations were based on the Confucian classics, so that all government administrators had at least studied the master's writings. Official sacrifices were made to his immortal spirit, and the classics themselves were engraved in stone and set up for all to see. From Han times on, Confucian philosophy was the national philosophy of the Chinese people.

In some ways the Confucianism thus established bore little resemblance to the social and ethical doctrine preached by Master Kong five hundred years before. Confucian scholars of the Han period attributed to their founder many views he never held. He was presented as a supporter of harsh punishments, as the author of a book on fortune-telling, and as an ardent champion of the doctrine that the emperor was the Son of Heaven. Like Buddha in India, Confucius was thus transformed at the moment of his triumph. Yet Confucius's canonization as the nation's official philosopher did bring a strong emphasis on learning and virtue as inextricably linked in human society.

A surprising product of this emphasis was the work of ancient China's most admired woman writer, Pan Chao. A member of an aristocratic family and educated in the Chinese classics, Pan Chao composed her widely admired verses, essays, and treatises—sixteen volumes in all—during the Han period. Pan Chao's classic *Precepts for Women* became the basis of Chinese women's education for most of the next two thousand years. Her *Precepts* included an idealistic view of marriage as "the fusion of Yin and Yang"—the male and female principles of the universe.[4]

Her main emphasis, however, was on the value of serious education for women. Only through equal access to knowledge, Pan Chao declared, could women and men ever find true equality in this world. It was a view that defenders of women's rights would take up with vigor in later centuries.

A broader consequence of this linking of learning and virtue was that many Confucian sages did not take official jobs or become pedantic scholars but remained poor men—and social critics—all their lives. Such men could still speak for the people whose ragged robes and torn sandals they shared. Official doctrines attributed to Confucius still included much of the master's spirit, including his insistence that virtue should rule, and even his radical notion that government should serve the people rather than exploit them. The endless repetition of these views over many centuries, by everyone from the emperor to the raggediest Confucian student, gave these principles of duty and decency, harmony and order, some weight at least in shaping the policies that ruled China.

---

[4]Pan Chao, *Nu Chieh: Precepts for Women,* in Florence Ayscough, *Chinese Women Today and Yesterday* (New York: Da Capo, 1975), pp. 240–241.

## The Grand Historian

The study of history was another area in which the Han dynasty made significant contributions to Chinese culture and political understanding. Han China actually nurtured not one but two of the greatest historians Chinese civilization has ever produced. In addition, Han historical scholarship developed a central concept of Chinese social thought: the idea of the dynastic cycle.

Sima Qian lived during the Former, Ban Gu during the Later Han. Both men were close to great events and the great men of the age—Sima Qian as court historian to Wudi the Martial Emperor, and Ban Gu as the twin brother of Ban Chao, the most famous of Han empire builders. Their books followed what became a Chinese historiographical tradition by incorporating large amounts of source material, from government documents to snatches of poetry, into their texts. Otherwise, however, the two historians and their histories were very different.

Sima Qian's *Records of the Grand Historian* was a monumental attempt at a universal history of China, from the age of the mythical sages through the Shang, Zhou, and Qin to his own time. He passed judgments, told colorful stories, invented speeches for his historical figures, and generally filled his ten thousand or so pages with fascinating and thoroughly humanized history.

Ban Gu's *History of the Former Han* was more restrained in tone and more restricted in scope. But it became a model for a standard form of Chinese history thereafter: the history of a single dynasty, from vigorous beginnings to final collapse.

The interpretation of China's past as a series of such more or less uniform dynastic cycles became the core of traditional Chinese historiography—and the Former Han the great exemplar of this pattern. Each of the great dynasties thereafter was seen as beginning vigorously, rising to great achievement, then settling into a long decline and fall as the Mandate of Heaven passed on to strong new hands.

A more modern approach sees the dynastic cycle as a pattern of institutional, social, and economic development and decline. Thus, the success of a new dynasty is seen in its centralizing policies as much as in its personalities, and factional feuds built into the structure of the court contribute to its downfall. All dynasties build grandly, send out great armies, and in so doing overspend, leading to pressure on the tax-paying peasantry that will finally drive them to rebel. As revenues dry up, inadequately maintained dikes and border garrisons are likely to give way, leading to natural disasters and barbarian invasions. These catastrophes indicate that the Mandate of Heaven has been withdrawn—and yet another dynasty is swept away.

There seems to be truth in the concept of the dynastic cycle itself—one form of the eternal recurrence of rise and fall that plays over the history of all civilization. In China's case, however, we can chart the cycle in remarkable detail, thanks to the scrupulous efforts of Chinese historians to record the histories of their dynasties over the two thousand years since the Former Han.

## Art in the Palace of Han

Surprisingly little remains of the art and architecture of Han China. The Han Chinese left us no crumbling Forum like that of ancient Rome, no Ajanta caves full of wonders. Their magnificent palaces were built of wood, and the paintings that literary sources describe have vanished with the plastered walls that held them. From such literary ac-

The vigor and dynamism of the Han Empire are powerfully conveyed by this beautiful bronze horse, dating from the second century C.E. Note the "flying gallop" pose. What conveys the sense of rapid motion in this statue? (Library of Congress)

counts, however, and from surviving fragments of metalwork and lacquerware, pottery, pressed tile, and the walls of tombs, we may get some idea at least of the subjects and styles of Han art.

The subjects are human, social, and historical: laborers in the fields, banqueters at the table, dignitaries parading in their parasol-shaded chariots, ancient sages, famous kings. There are few gods and no heavens, hells, or judgment halls of the dead, even in Chinese tombs. The style is simple, vigorous, and full of energy. Human figures are clearly outlined, rather flat, almost cartoonlike at first glance. But they move, gesture, reach out— their horses prance or charge at a flying gallop—with the dash and vigor that made the Han age great.

For the architecture of Han, we have some small pottery models, a few sketchy pictures, and the usual extravagant literary descriptions. From the models we get a sense of multistory tile- or thatch-roofed houses, walled courtyards, pig-pens and kitchens, balconies, people sitting in open doorways. From the written descriptions of Han palaces, we get a picture of something much more splendid.

The scale of Han public building clearly matched and even exceeded that of Huangdi. Gaozu's palace complex at Chang'an was more than a mile square and filled one ninth of the capital city. One of Wudi's even larger palaces, located outside the city walls, was connected to a royal residence inside the ramparts by an overpass that soared across the city moat as well as the walls. Inside a royal compound were many sumptuous buildings with ornamental gates and towers, mazes of courtyards, and vast audience halls, the whole surrounded by extensive parklands dotted with artificial lakes and stocked with exotic plants, beasts, and birds. Interiors of palaces or mansions were bright with plaster, paint, and gilt, bronze, and lacquer.

Gaozu, a peasant's son long used to field and camp, may have felt faintly ill at ease moving through such newly painted splendor in his elaborate silk robes. But the great Wudi surely strode with perfect confidence across an audience hall apparently larger than the one that graced the royal palace in twentieth-century Beijing. For the Han emperors built to their own measure, and that scale was often significantly larger than life.

## SUMMARY

As in Persia and Rome, powerful centralizing dynasties ruled both India and China in the classic age.

India's second golden age, the reign of the Guptas, came as the climax of a long period of turbulence and growth in the subcontinent. After the disintegration of the unified Maurya Empire in the second century B.C.E., India did not know unity again for more than five tumultuous but prosperous centuries. During this period repeated waves of invaders swept down through the passes of the Northwest Frontier.

But prosperous cities and kingdoms also grew in southern India, which now rivaled the north in wealth and power for the first time. Increased urbanization, sophisticated crafts, and the expansion of trade both within and beyond the subcontinent made this prosperous period for the many peoples of India.

A true golden age came with unification under the Gupta dynasty (C.E. 320–540). The two earliest of these maharajas, Chandra Gupta I and Samudra Gupta, repeated the Maurya feat of conquering much of the land between the Himalayas and the southern cape. Chandra Gupta II gave India a Hindu Renaissance when order and prosperity pervaded the land, and the arts flourished. Then new invaders swept down across the Northwest Frontier, and the Gupta supremacy too passed into history.

Religious piety continued to be central to the high culture of India. Buddhism divided into two historic traditions, the Hinayana and Mahayana schools, and completed its evolution into an elaborate popular religion. Hinduism grew even more dramatically, tending toward monotheism and popular diversity and undergoing a genuine spiritual revival all across India.

Architectural remains reveal Indian piety, and sculpture projects a sense of the many forms of life. The plays of Kalidasa flourished in sophisticated princely courts and Indian scholars invented the zero and compiled a calendar very similar to our own.

China under the Han dynasty (206 B.C.E.–C.E. 220) laid the foundations for an imperial unity that would be reestablished again and again over the next two thousand years.

Gaozu, "Exalted Founder" of the dynasty, was a tough, hard-driving peasant who imposed order by force on the anarchy that had followed the death of Huangdi, the first unifier of China. His successor, the Empress Lü, established the new order firmly all across the Middle Kingdom. The empress's grandson and the most famous of all the Hans, Wudi, the "Martial Emperor," expanded China's frontiers by conquest, pushed back the Xiongnu nomads, built immense public works, and encouraged the establishment of a Confucian administrative system that would long outlast his dynasty.

Lesser Han rulers were briefly displaced around the time of Christ by the short-lived reforming regime of the usurper Wang Mang; but the Hans of the first century C.E. were again vigorous and successful. China's wealth and empire grew once more, until Chinese armies almost confronted Roman armies on the distant steppes of central Asia. Internal decay, rebellious generals, and invasions by northern peoples finally brought the Han dynasty down in the third century C.E.

Under this vigorous ruling house, the imperial mystique was honored, and the astonishing system of highly trained Confucian scholar bureaucrats, which would make China perhaps the best governed of all nations for many centuries, took shape. The population of China passed sixty million, and the wealth of the land supported such growth.

Confucius became the empire's official philosopher and the core of China's educational system under the Hans, and history writing emerged as one of China's major cultural achievements. Han emperors patronized art and literature on a scale suited to the wealth and splendor of the Middle Kingdom during one of its greatest ages.

## Suggested Reading

Altekar, A. S. *The Position of Women in Hindu Civilization.* Banares: Motilal Banarsidass, 1956. Recommended survey of the subject; especially useful for earlier periods.

Champakalakshmi, R. *Trade, Ideology, and Urbanization: South India 300 B.C. to A.D. 1300.* New York: Oxford University Press, 1996. Scholarly study of city life in the south of the subcontinent.

Chattopadhyaya, B. *The Making of Early Medieval India.* New York: Oxford University Press, 1994. Useful summary.

De Bary, W. T., ed. *Sources of Indian Tradition.* New York: Columbia University Press, 1958. Valuable collection of source materials.

Dutt, N. *Mahayana Buddhism.* Calcutta: Firma K. L. Mukhopadhyay, 1973. Older but solid, exploring contrasts with the Hinayana tradition.

Flood, G. *An Introduction to Hinduism.* New York: Cambridge University Press, 1996. Balanced treatment.

Ganguly, D. K. *The Imperial Guptas and Their Times.* New Delhi: Abhinav Publications, 1987. Concise study of the dynasty and its achievements.

Juneja, M., ed. *Architecture in Medieval India: Forms, Contexts, Histories.* Delhi: Permanent Black, 2001. Substantial collection of studies of the age of the temple builders.

Kalidasa. *Shakuntala and Other Writings,* trans. W. Ryder. New York: Dutton, 1959. Highly praised translation of the Gupta dramatist.

Loewe, M. *Crisis and Conflict in Han China.* London: Allen and Unwin, 1974. Breakdown of the Former Han.

———. *Divination, Mythology, and Monarchy in Han China.* New York: Cambridge University Press, 1994. How supernatural beliefs supported imperial authority.

Needham, J. *Science and Civilization in China,* 6 vols. New York: Cambridge University Press, 1986. Massive ongoing study directed by a scholar who has given his life to examining China's scientific and technological achievements.

Nilakanta Sastri, K. A. *Development of Religion in South India.* New Delhi: Munshiram Manoharlal Publications, 1992. Brief survey of spread of Hinduism into the south.

Paul, D. Y. *Women in Buddhism: Images of the Feminine in Mahayana Tradition.* Berkeley: Asian Humanities Press, 1979. Cultural analysis.

Sima Qian. *Historical Records,* trans. R. Dawson. New York: Oxford University Press, 1994. Brief selections from China's Grand Historian.

Thani Nayagam, X. S., ed. *Tamil Culture and Civilization: Readings.* New York: Asia Publishing House, 1971. Anthology of classical Tamil writing.

Yang, L. "Female Rulers in Imperial China," *Harvard Journal of Asiatic Studies,* 23 (1960–1961), 47–61. Includes empresses during the Han, when women rulers were particularly prominent. For a contemporary life of Empress Lü, see Ban Gu's *History of the Former Han Dynasty,* Vol. 1, trans. H. H. Dubs (Baltimore, Md.: Waverly Press, 1938), chaps. 2 and 3.

Please refer to the document CD-ROM for primary sources related to this chapter.

# CHAPTER 8

# FROM THE SAHARA TO PERU
## The Classic Age in Africa
## and the Americas
### (600 B.C.E.–C.E. 900)

# A Glance Ahead: Kingdoms and Cultures of Africa and the Americas

No other region could match the sheer size and scope of Rome, Persia, India, and China in the classic age. But old civilizations developed further and notable new ones emerged across Africa and the Americas as well.

North Africa made major contributions to Mediterranean culture with its fertile fields and famous cities like Alexandria. Down the east coast of Africa, ancient Kush was swallowed up by Axum—which also played an important part in the trade of the Indian Ocean. Across the Atlantic, great cities like Teotihuacán bloomed in what would become Mexico and Peru.

You can see classic grandeur in the towering obelisks of African Axum—in the immense stone pyramids of the classical Mayans in Middle America—or in the huge brick pyramids built by the Peruvian Mochica. There is impressive scale in the far-spread Amerindian trade routes or in the Camel Revolution that swept across the Sahara. Sit on top of the Huaca del Sol on the coast of Peru, or cruise the Saharan dunes on camelback, and you will feel some of the sense of mastery that is the hallmark of the classic age.

## Africa North and East

### Greek and Roman Africa

The centers of most of the world's more developed cultures during the classic age remained on the linked continents of Asia and Europe. On this huge landmass complex cultures interacted in ways that fostered comparatively rapid growth and development. But civilization had already begun outside the world island, and there were further developments on other continents during this period too.

Africa, closest to Eurasia and the home of one of the earliest civilizations, that of Egypt, continued to be integrated into the large patterns of Old World civilization. But sophisticated societies emerged outside the older cultural areas as well.

North Africa's ties to the Near East and the Mediterranean world remained strong in the classic age. Thus, Egypt was ruled first by the Ptolemies, heirs of one of Alexander the Great's generals, then by the Romans. The Romans especially squeezed the Egyptian peasantry unmercifully to ring all the grain possible out of the fertile Nile valley to feed the populous cities across the Mediterranean. Egypt's monuments and reputation for deep wisdom survived, however. Alexandria, in the Nile delta, became, as we will see, one of the great Mediterranean centers of learning.

By the time of Christ, all the rest of North Africa had also been incorporated into the Roman Empire. From the mouths of the Nile to the site of ancient Carthage and on west to the Strait of Gibraltar, Roman soldiers maintained domestic order and turned desert raiders back into the Sahara. The Romans also sowed the fertile strip along the Mediterranean coast with ordered farms and public wells, aqueducts and cities. The ruins are still there today, villas and temples, colosseums and aqueducts as impressive as any to be found in Italy or Greece, here on the northern edge of Africa.

### Alexandria

The Egyptian city of Alexandria was famed for its harbor in Greek and Roman times. Its towering Pharos, a 400-foot lighthouse, was hailed as one of the wonders of the ancient world. Visitors from Africa, Asia, and Europe gazed in awe at the great Delta city's commercial wealth, palaces, and temples. Even more important, however, was the central part played by Alexandrian culture in the history of the classic age.

Alexandria's cultural institutions in particular were unrivaled. Its zoological and botanical gardens drew throngs of citizens. Its museum was true to its name, a temple of learning dedicated to the Muses. Most celebrated of all was the great library of Alexandria, which may have contained as many as 400,000 books. Here Egypt's Ptolemaic dynasty supported scholars, scientists, and other learned people, freeing them for study and writing in an atmosphere like that of a modern research institution.

Many writers and thinkers flocked to this new Athens on the southern shores of the Mediterranean. The geographer and astronomer Ptolemy worked here, assembling the theory of the structure of the universe that would dominate Western thought down to the time of Copernicus. The philosopher Plotinus, founder of the Neo- or New Platonism, probed the metaphysical limits of human understanding in the shadow of these brightly painted, multistoried buildings. The Greek-speaking Ptolemaic dynasty gave way to Roman emperors, but Egypt's reputation for wisdom continued to draw the best minds from Hellenistic into early Christian times.

The intellectual brilliance of Alexandria owed much to the city's Egyptian setting. Egypt's ancient skill at surgery and medicine, for instance, helped make Alexandria a leading medical center. There, thanks to the prevailing intellectual freedom, doctors conducted valuable anatomical studies by dissecting corpses. Greek and Egyptian styles of art and architecture began to blend and mingle here.

Greek and Egyptian taste for artistic representations of black Africans has left us a particularly valuable legacy of statuettes in marble, bronze, and terra cotta clay. Here these people of the Upper Nile are shown riding elephants, battling crocodiles, wrestling, dancing, juggling, making speeches, or playing musical instruments. These small figures are a vivid reminder that Hellenistic and Roman Alexandria was still an African city.

## VOICES FROM THE PAST

This North African proudly described his own successful climb from rags to riches and community respect in the second century C.E. Does this inscription from ancient Africa remind you of any more recent attitude of "self-made men" toward their own success?

*I was born of humble parentage. My father possessed neither money nor house of his own. Almost from the day of my birth I have lived by working on the land. I gave my plot of land no rest; nor did I spare my own labour. Came harvest time, when gangs of itinerant labourers set out on their rounds going as far afield as Cirta in Numidia and the Plains of Jupiter, I was always in the lead. For twelve years I toiled on these rounds under a broiling sun. From labourer I rose to the position of a contractor of labour, and for eleven years I led my troop of harvesters all over the Numidian plains. Hard work and thrift made me the owner of a house and a well equipped farm. My house lacks nothing in the way of material comforts. My life has earned its reward of distinction. I was co-opted to a seat on our local municipal Council by the Council's own decree, and from poor peasant I have risen to the position of municipal censor.*

L. Thompson and J. Ferguson, *Africa in Classical Antiquity* (Ibadan: Ibadan University Press, 1969), p. 148.

Meanwhile, an impressive African civilization flourished far from the intersecting cultures of the Mediterranean during this period. This was the East African empire of Axum, south and east of Egypt on the shores of the Red Sea.

## Axum and the Red Sea

Axum rose to supremacy in northeastern Africa on the ruins of ancient Kush and its capital, Meroe. The Axumite troops of King Ezana ravaged this ancient African kingdom on the upper Nile around C.E. 350. But Kush may already have been tributary to the kings of Axum when Ezana's armies desecrated its temples, for Axum was nearing the apogee of its power in the fourth century C.E. Axumite civilization, in fact, had its complex origins the better part of a thousand years before.

Axum was located southeast of the Sudan, in an area that straddles both the high Ethiopian plateau and the sun-bleached coast of the Red Sea. Perhaps as early as the seventh century B.C.E., Semitic-speaking Arab people had crossed the southern end of the Red Sea from Yemen to Africa. The newcomers, known as the Habashat people, settled both on the African shore and in the high country back from the coast. Here they met, dominated, and merged with a farming, herding Kushite-speaking people to produce the Axumites of the first millennium C.E.

The intruders came with experience in agriculture, trade, and other skills. The Habashat had already made southern Arabia bloom through the judicious deployment of dams and aqueducts. They had for generations been trading along the Red Sea and around the Indian Ocean. They were literate in their own Ge'ez tongue, and they knew how to build with stone.

## Axumite Society

The new land the Habashat came to combined one of the hottest strips of territory on earth—the African Red Sea shore—with the mile-high mountains, deep gorges, and rushing rivers of the Ethiopian highlands inland. The Kushite people they found there lived in farming villages or followed their herds through the hills down to Lake Tana or the wide bend of the blue Nile. The Habashat blended with this older people on the land, as Aryans had with Dravidians in India, to produce a new African people—the people of Axum.

Such inland African products as ivory, hides, rhinoceros horn, and gold passed to the outside world through their highland capital, the city of Axum itself. Adulis, their port city in the lowlands, became a collecting point for goods from further down the coast of East Africa, or from as far away as India and Ceylon, across the Indian Ocean. From Axum and Adulis these African and Asian goods would flow north up the Red Sea to the eastern Mediterranean, to the Near East, Greece, Rome, and beyond.

During its most prosperous time, from the third century B.C.E. to the fourth century C.E.—the heart of the classical age—these Axumite cities were thriving centers of trade. Greek, Arab, and Jewish merchants mingled in its port cities, and caravans from the Sudan and beyond jostled each other in the streets of its capital. This bustling nation of traders became a key juncture in the flow of goods and ideas between the three continents of the Old World.

With wealth from overseas, furthermore, there came power in Africa. The Habashat invaders did not originally have a centralized political structure. Priests were important among them in the early days, and there were governors who collected tribute from local areas. Like so many others around the world, they were one people culturally but not yet a

A carved megalith from Axum, in today's Ethiopia, dwarfs the tiny human figure standing at its base. Notice the false door inscribed in the solid stone at the base of the structure. Where else have we seen inscribed vertical shafts set up as commemorative and decorative structures? (Library of Congress)

political nation. More centralized political institutions, however, evolved with time. By the first century C.E. the written guide to the Red Sea used by Greek traders reported that there was a king at Axum—and that he had some Greek education. A traveler of a later century described the Axumite ruler progressing in splendor, clad in gold-embroidered linen and standing in a four-wheeled chariot drawn by four elephants. Both the king and his counselors were armed with gilded spears and shields, and flutes made music for them as they passed.

## The Culture of Axum

The soldiers of the kings of Axum carried the power of the coastal kingdom inland. Axumite armies pushed north through the Ethiopian mountains as far as the frontiers of Egypt. They thrust west across the grasslands of the Sudan to ravage Kush and Meroe. For a time they controlled all the land from the Ethiopian uplands to the Horn of Africa, dominated a long stretch of the Red Sea coast, policed the interior caravan trails, and kept all the neighboring pastoral peoples in awe.

The city of Axum itself, settled in the well-watered highlands some days' journey back from the coast, developed a unique material culture under the Axumite kings. The ruins that remain remind the traveler of no place else on earth. There are crenelated castles and thrones of carven stone. There are "stepped walls" and the giant obelisks of Axum, sixty-five feet high and carefully sculptured to look like towers with false doors and windows and strange round arches at the top.[1]

---

[1]G. W. B. Huntingford, "The Kingdom of Axum," in *The Dawn of African History,* Roland Oliver, ed. (London: Oxford University Press, 1961), p. 23.

In pagan Axum there were temples to the old gods of Arabia—gods of earth and war and the blazing sun—and blood sacrifices to these deities, even of humans. But in the fourth century C.E. the celebrated King Ezana accepted conversion to Christianity at the hands of his old tutor, an Eastern Orthodox priest. Thereafter churches began to rise in Axum. Thereafter also the fortunes of the Axumites began to change.

In Christian Axum, many things changed. The blood sacrifices ended, if they had not ended before, and commercial ties with the Christian Near East grew still stronger. But conversion also had a powerful isolating effect on Axum, which became the only Christian country in this part of the world. This effect was intensified in the seventh century C.E., when Islam swept like a prairie fire across North Africa and down through Arabia. The Christian Axumites then found themselves alone indeed, between the pagan peoples south and west of them and the Muslims to the north and east.

These enemies encroached slowly upon the greatness of Axum. Adulis was taken by the Arabs, and other Axumite harbors by neighboring African peoples. The herdsmen that king Ezana had held in check now raided at will across the croplands of the Axumites. There were kings in the city of Axum for another century or two; then they too disappeared from history.

The survivors of once proud and prosperous Axum clung to the faith of Ezana, if they could not keep his wealth and power. Christianity persisted and strengthened them in their long isolation. They survived to become the ancestors of Africa's oldest continuously independent people, the Ethiopians of today.

# AFRICA SOUTH OF THE SAHARA

## Saharan and Sub-Saharan Societies

During the thousand years before and after Christ, Africa south of the Sahara desert developed at its own pace. There were as yet no Alexandrias or Axums in these regions, any more than there were in Europe north of the Alps or Asia north of the Great Wall of China. Nevertheless, archaeological research reveals technological and economic progress and suggests the emergence of more complex political forms in the western and southern parts of Africa during the classic age.

Social structures for most of Africa remained solidly traditional during this period. The family, as in so many other places, was the foundation of all group life. Extended families grouped several generations and the families of several siblings in a single sizable compound. These family units in turn evolved into villages. Within the village, gender and age further organized society. Specific social roles were assigned to men and women, and special prominence and power went to village elders, whose long experience was deemed valuable to the community as a whole.

There was variety within these common patterns, particularly within the area of gender relations. Some African societies were patriarchal and patrilineal, recognizing power and inheritance in the male line, others matriarchal and matrilineal. Everywhere, however, family ties were the ties that bound African societies together.

## Technology: Metals and Salt

Many African peoples of this period continued to shape stone into hard-edged tools for everyday use. Some of them also learned to work copper, iron, and gold and to mine salt during these centuries.

Of the chief metals, copper was mined in Mauretania in northwestern Africa in pre-Christian times. Copper ornaments and use objects have been found in tombs in this area. The West Africans of Senegal and the central and southern Africans of today's Zaire, Zimbabwe, and Zambia also worked copper, though we know less about these regions.

Ironworking, as we have seen, may have radiated from ancient Meroe or may have emerged spontaneously in several parts of Africa. Some authorities believe Africans outside of the Nile valley both mined and worked iron during the first millennium after Christ. Khoi-San peoples may have mined iron in southern Africa as Bantu-speaking Africans did in West Africa. Certainly, the great Bantu migrations, to be discussed in a later chapter, spread iron far across central and southern Africa.

Gold, which would emerge as a key African export in the next stage of African history, also came into use south of the Sahara this early. Far up the Senegal and Niger rivers of West Africa, people probably panned and mined for gold as early as the first millennium C.E.

The lowly mineral called salt became increasingly valuable as more and more Africans settled down in agricultural villages. Hunting peoples got plenty of salt from the animals they killed, but people dependent on crops had little salt in their diets. Living as they did in an increasingly hot climate, Saharan and equatorial Africans also lost much salt each day through perspiration. While archaeologists still have much digging to do, salt works from the first millennium C.E. have been found in the Sahara itself as well as in East Africa.

You can pick up the white, crusty stuff today in the salt pans of the northern Sahara, or buy lumps of it wrapped in plastic along the Niger south of Timbuktu. It is still as essential as ever to human survival in these dessicated lands.

The camel, which reached Africa from Asia in the early centuries of the Common Era, could carry heavy loads of trade goods through arid lands where horses or mules could not survive. Here camels are being loaded with salt in the modern West Africa state of Niger for the journey across the Sahara to the populations of the tropical African lands to the South. (James L. Stanfield/National Geographic)

## Trade: The Camel Revolution

Commercial exchange, as we have seen, goes back a long way in Africa. Both food-gathering and agricultural peoples traded stone and metal for tools, decorative beads, meat, grain, dried fish, and many other things. Most of this exchange, however, was local and small in scale. Only with the spreading use of metals and the introduction of the camel into Africa did long-distance trade emerge.

Metal deposits were found only in widely scattered sites. As peoples began to work them, however, metals became the most widely valued of trade goods. Evidence of exchange includes the discovery of copper ingots in South Africa and of ornaments made of metals not locally available in West African graves. Other things were widely traded too, including salt from the Sahara and glass beads, which may have been made as far away as India.

A key development that made wider trade possible was the Camel Revolution. This major improvement in transportation spread westward from Asia during the centuries around the time of Christ. Capable of carrying as much as 500 pounds for many days with little water and only the scantiest grass, camels were ideally suited for desert travel across northern Africa. The hardy beasts were probably introduced from the Near East into Egypt by the Greek Ptolemies and to the rest of North Africa under the Romans. The African Berbers quickly adopted camels, using them for travel across the Sahara to the Western Sudan and the forests of the Guinea coast.

Camels are not friendly animals, and there seems to be little love lost between them and their keepers. Riding a camel up and down real Saharan dunes is rather like hanging onto a small boat bucking through heavy seas. But their introduction into North Africa by C.E. 200 revolutionized travel and transport across the northern half of the continent.

## NORTH AMERICAN CULTURES

### The Desert Southwest: Mogollon and Hohokam

Agriculture replaced hunting and gathering in Mexico thousands of years before Christ. Slowly, this pattern of life, with its settled villages and increasingly structured society, spread north of the Rio Grande.

An early such shift north of Mexico occurred in what became the American south-west before C.E. 1000. In Arizona and New Mexico, a hotter, drier climate menaced the stable foraging society that had taken root there. Threatened with extinction, the Mogollon and Hohokam peoples moved toward settled farming.

The Mogollon people used digging sticks to cultivate the basic trio of crops that had first developed in Mexico: corn or maize, beans, and squash. They built permanent pit houses that were cool in summer and warm in winter. They also constructed underground storage rooms for harvested food.

The Hohokam were themselves immigrants from Mexico. One thoroughly excavated Hohokam site reveals a hundred pit houses. The site also includes perhaps the first irrigation system constructed in America, here used to bring river water to arid fields several miles away. The Hohokam grew not only the basic food crops mentioned above but cotton and tobacco as well.

## The Eastern Woodlands: Adena and Hopewell

Farming began to spread to eastern North America about this time also, though it complemented rather than replaced hunting and gathering. This was particularly so in the eastern woodlands of what would later become the United States.

On the Ohio River, the Adena culture emerged earlier than the Mogollon tradition—before C.E. 500. The existence of settled villages shows that the Adena people spent a large part of the year in one place, probably tending crops. They combined pumpkins and other food plants with nuts, fish, and game gathered or hunted in the forest.

Around the first century C.E., the much more widespread Hopewell culture emerged in the Mississippi and the Ohio River valleys. Like their Adena predecessors, the Hopewell people combined foraging with limited farming. But maize was not yet effectively adapted to the colder northern environment. Further development would await both new strains of corn and some crucial technological advances.

## Society and Culture

During the thousand years around the birth of Christ, however, these Native American peoples of the classic age did make some remarkable social and cultural breakthroughs. The people of the southwest, for instance, learned to weave cotton into cloth and to make pottery. Besides their impressive irrigation works, the Hohokam people mined for turquoise. This they traded with the city-dwellers of Mexico for copper bells and earrings, rubber balls, and other handcrafted products. They also imported from Mexico such cultural practices as mounds for religious ceremonies and large outdoor ball courts.

The eastern forest people traded even further and built even more impressively. The Hopewell culture constructed large and elaborate burial mounds for their most honored dead. These graves have yielded trade goods accumulated by Hopewell people, sometimes from halfway across the continent. Among these were shells from the Gulf Coast, copper from the Great Lakes, and obsidian from the Rocky Mountains. Their Adena predecessors were even greater builders. The Great Serpent Mound in southern Ohio, winding for some 1,300 feet, is the largest representational earthwork in the world.

The artistic achievements of these peoples could be striking. Human figures dance around an elaborately decorated Hohokam pot dating from the first millennium C.E. Hopewell artisans shaped a flat sheet of mica into a startlingly lifelike silhouette of a

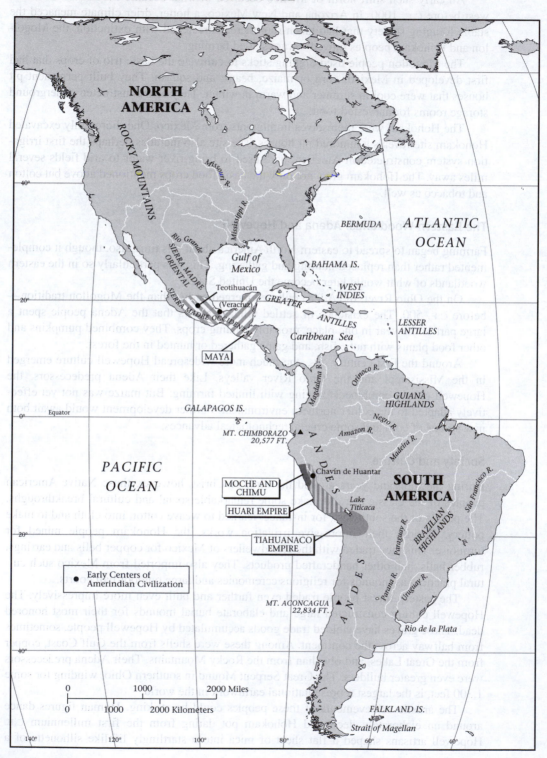

NORTH AMERICA

ROCKY MOUNTAINS

Missouri R.

Mississippi R.

Rio Grande

SIERRA MADRE ORIENTAL

SIERRA MADRE OCCIDENTAL

Gulf of Mexico

Teotihuacán

(Veracruz)

MAYA

GREATER ANTILLES

Caribbean Sea

BERMUDA

BAHAMA IS.

WEST INDIES

LESSER ANTILLES

ATLANTIC OCEAN

Magdalena R.

Orinoco R.

GUIANA HIGHLANDS

Negro R.

Amazon R.

Madeira R.

São Francisco R.

SOUTH AMERICA

BRAZILIAN HIGHLANDS

GALAPAGOS IS.

Equator

MT. CHIMBORAZO 20,577 FT.

Chavín de Huantar

MOCHE AND CHIMU

HUARI EMPIRE

TIAHUANACO EMPIRE

Lake Titicaca

A N D E S

PACIFIC OCEAN

• Early Centers of Amerindian Civilization

MT. ACONCAGUA 22,834 FT.

Paraguay R.

Paraná R.

Uruguay R.

A N D E S

Rio de la Plata

0          1000          2000 Miles

0     1000     2000 Kilometers

FALKLAND IS.

Strait of Magellan

40°

20°

0°

20°

40°

140°          120°          100°          80°          60°          40°

human hand around C.E. 500. The great traditions of Native American art thus began to take shape even before many of these people had settled into fully agricultural societies.

## SOUTH AMERICAN SOCIETIES

### Growing Populations

The rise of the United States to prominence over the past two centuries has fostered a completely unhistorical sense of "natural" North American predominance in the western hemisphere. For most of the history of civilization in the New World, Middle and South America have in fact been the leaders, and North America the less developed continent of our hemisphere.

Population densities in the pre-Columbian Americas are an intensely debated subject, but there does seem to be some agreement that the south was much more heavily populated than the north. In both Middle America and northwestern South America, intensive advanced agriculture centering in corn, beans, squash, and, in South America, potatoes had produced a population base adequate to support societies more elaborate than any to be found north of the Rio Grande.

The Olmec culture of Mexico and the Chavín culture of Peru had begun the social evolution of Mesoamerica and South America during the first millennium before Christ. During the first thousand years C.E., that process of cultural evolution continued in Mexico and Central America on the one hand, and in northwestern South America on the other.

In both these areas the process of state formation was a key element in this development. From agricultural villages linked by religion and culture, there evolved states with populations of tens and hundreds of thousands, specialization of labor, structured systems of social classes, and sometimes true cities and central governments as well. Unification into larger empires like those of the Aztecs and Incas of later centuries was rare. Nevertheless, during the classical period areas of advanced culture were scattered all over the highlands and lowlands of Mexico, Honduras, Guatemala, and through the central Andes and neighboring coastal lowlands of Peru.

While North America remained the preserve of hunting-and-gathering tribes and agricultural villages dominated by hereditary chiefs, impressive civilizations had thus emerged in Middle and South America. Three of the better known of these societies will be dealt with here, including perhaps the most sophisticated of all Amerindian cultures, that of the Classical Maya.

### The Mochica Pottery Makers

We will begin with South America and the continuing evolution of civilization in the shadow of the Andes.

The first highly developed culture in Peru, the Chavín culture of the first millennium B.C.E., had faded several centuries before Christ. But its influence lingered on, giving rise to several successor cultures during the first millennium C.E. One among these has particularly impressed the archaeologists, who are once more our primary sources of understanding: the Mochica culture of the Moche River region of northern Peru.

The cult centers of the old Chavín culture had been in the Andes. Mochica culture, like most of the successor cultures to Chavín, developed on the coastal strip along the Pacific and in the river valleys that spread through the foothills of the Andes down to the sea. Like most of the classical American cultures, they flourished rather later than the classic civilizations of the Old World: Mochica culture was probably at its height between C.E. 300 and 700.

Although they were preliterate, the Mochica people have left us a great deal of concrete information about themselves in their unique pottery. In the naturalistically sculptured forms of many of their ceramic works and in the pictures with which they decorated them, a whole vanished culture comes to life. These, coupled with huge clay-brick ruins, reveal one of the most sophisticated South American societies before the Inca.

The Mochica civilization was almost surely that of an organized state, and one that dominated the coastal valleys of much of Peru. The ruling elite must have included a priestly class that supervised the large temple complexes. It must also have involved a warrior class, since the Mochica were a warlike people who built their empire, as empires have generally been built, by force.

The bulk of the population were farmers, though they supplemented their diet with game and fish. The Mochica were, in fact, very advanced agriculturists, cultivating maize, beans, potatoes, and other crops on the narrow green patches along the rivers. These they irrigated by elaborate systems of ditches and fertilized with bird dung fetched on large seagoing rafts from offshore guano islands.

The Mochica were also large-scale builders, mostly in adobe brick. They constructed genuine cities and raised massive step-pyramids in their religious ceremonial centers. One of these pyramids, the Huaca del Sol in the Moche Valley, towers 150 feet high and required as many as fifty million clay bricks for its construction.

Beyond all this, the Mochica became some of the most skilled artists and artisans in the Americas. Their metalworkers made masks of copper, headdresses of gold, and jewelry of various metals. Mochica women specialized in textiles, doing both the spinning and the weaving of cloth. They produced richly embroidered, elaborately decorated tunics, shirts, and mantels—most of them worn by men. Mochica potters manufactured the sculptured ceramic ware that has provided information about their culture and the gems of many ceramics collections since.

Many Mochica pots and jars are fully sculptured and as realistically representational as the Olmec heads of Mexico. There are actual portrait heads on these Peruvian jars.

Other ceramic works and the painted images on them show Moche warriors swinging their clubs in battle or leading home long lines of prisoners with ropes around their necks, probably for sacrifice. They depict reed boats on voyages to guano islands or peasant farmers laboring in shorts or even naked in the fields. And they provide detailed documentation of the rich sexual lives of Moche men and women in a ceramic record as vivid as India's *Kama Sutra* or any Japanese "pillow book."

This Mochica people of the north coast of Peru are only one of several Peruvian societies that developed on the Pacific coast and in the Andes between the ancient Chavín and the awesome achievement of the Incas. But thanks to their artistic and architectural accomplishments, they illustrate Peruvian civilization during the classical age more vividly and more impressively than most of the other societies of northwestern South America.

## Peruvian Culture

Other cultures flourished in Peru, both on the coast and in the mountains, during this period. Archaeologists have a plentiful supply of ruins to explore, tombs to excavate, and surviving artifacts to evaluate. Partly because of the lack of a written script, however, firm

Teotihuacán's immense Temple of the Sun, larger than the largest pyramid at Egyptian Giza, dominates this revered Mesoamerican"city of the gods." A four-chambered cave recently discovered under the huge pyramid may have been dedicated to a primordial Mother Goddess believed to dwell underground. (Jim Fox/Photo Researchers)

conclusions are hard to come by. A brief survey of some of the remarkable remains of these vanished peoples will perhaps be more useful than a summary of debatable conclusions.

In the Peruvian highlands, multistoried stone buildings gaze out over the mountains, their purpose unknown. Statues of warriors or women and pottery decorated with hunting scenes give haunting glimpses of vanished civilizations. More striking are the gorgeous textiles discovered wrapped around mummies found on the arid south coast of Peru. Thanks to the dry climate, fabric thousands of years old has been perfectly preserved. Woven of a variety of threads—wool, cotton, even human hair—and dyed with more than a hundred different colors, the textiles of Paraca Necropolis have been described as among the most beautiful in the world. Yet we know almost nothing of the society that produced them.

Perhaps most tantalizing of all are the famous Nazca lines. These marks inscribed in the dry earth of southern Peru were discovered by accident when a plane flew over them in the first half of the twentieth century. Seen from that height, it was clear that many of the lines sketched out animals and birds, while others defined geometrical shapes or ran straight across the desert pointing at the horizon.

Those who have studied the enigmatic lines have seen astronomical significance in some, which point toward solstice or equinox points. The pictures, undetectable on the ground, must have been intended for the gods to contemplate.[2]

---

[2]Alternative explanations relating the Nazca lines to flying saucers have not found favor with archaeologists.

# MIDDLE AMERICAN CIVILIZATION

## The Pyramids of Teotihuacán

There are more huge stone pyramids in Mesoamerica than there are in Egypt—striking testimony to the centuries of organized society and the sophisticated cultural heritage of Mexico and Central American before the conquistadores came. Some of the most impressive of these monuments are to be found not in the coastal Caribbean lowlands where Olmec and later Mayan culture flourished, but in the upland valleys of central Mexico. Of these peoples of the high plateau, the earliest and one of the most revered were the builders of the great city of Teotihuacán, the "sacred center . . . of the Mesoamerican world" around the time of Christ.[3]

The civilization of Teotihuacán emerged perhaps as early as 200 B.C.E. and expired in violence around C.E. 700. As usual, lacking significant documentary evidence, we know virtually nothing of the political history of this early Mesoamerican people and can do no more than speculate on their political institutions. But there is plenty of information—including, once more, pictorial evidence—concerning the economic life, social structure, and artistic capabilities of the people of Teotihuacán.

There is an aggressive tone to surviving Teotihuacán mural paintings—warriors with human hearts skewered on their blades—suggesting a predatory foreign policy similar to that of the Aztecs of later centuries. Evidence of Teotihuacán's cultural predominance is found as far afield as Guatemala. Whether this evidence proves trade and cultural contacts or actual conquest and rule must remain uncertain. We know only that we are dealing with a powerful people whose influence was widespread.

The best evidence of their greatness is, of course, the city of Teotihuacán itself. Several square miles in area with a population of well over one hundred thousand, this was one of the true cities—as opposed to ceremonial religious centers—in pre-Columbian America. It was a planned city, designed probably by priestly administrators. Its grid of streets and avenues provided space for the temples, palaces, and market plazas, the courtyards and arcades of the rich, and the single-story, flat-roofed "apartment houses" of the less affluent.

The arts of Teotihuacán included elegant ceramics, beautiful stone masks, and the carefully carved stone faces of the gods. There are also paintings, here in the form of thousands of murals found in houses and palaces throughout the city. The chief divinities of Teotihuacán were Tlaloc the rain god and Quetzalcoatl, the feathered serpent of later Aztec times. But the great monuments in the city are the gigantic pyramids of the Moon and the Sun. The Pyramid of the Sun, seven hundred feet long and more than two hundred feet high, built of stone over an earthen core, is one of the largest structures to be found anywhere in Amerindian Mexico.

Teotihuacán was a thriving place for nine hundred years before it perished by fire, perhaps in war or revolution, between C.E. 650 and 750. Eight centuries later the vast ruins of this dead city drew the Aztec emperor Moctezuma to pray and consult with the gods among its empty avenues and tumbled stones. But the gods of Teotihuacán, who could not save their own people from the common fate of empires, could not save the Aztecs either.

---

[3]Jill Leslie Furst and Peter T. Furst, *Pre-Columbian Art of Mexico* (New York: Ableville Press, 1980), p. 43.

## The Mayan City-States

The Classic Maya of Mesoamerica, who flourished between C.E. 300 and 900, produced what many scholars consider the most brilliant of all pre-Columbian Amerindian civilizations. Every enthusiast for "lost civilizations" knows their huge step-pyramids, bursting vertically out of the jungle, vines and bushes sprouting picturesquely from the ancient stone. Fewer know their faces, the convincingly modeled middle-aged cheeks, hooked noses, heavy lids of men in ceremonial headdresses reproduced in ceramic figurines, or the painted figures of priests, nobles, and warriors in fantastic regalia marching across the walls of temples. But it is only when we begin to penetrate the minds of the Maya that we glimpse the true dimensions of their accomplishment.

There are many mysteries about Mayan civilization. We know that the Mayans lived in the lowlands of the Mexican Gulf Coast and in parts of Guatemala, Honduras, and El Salvador in the first millennium after Christ. We know that in some ways their culture derived from that of the ancient Olmecs—but even Olmec antecedents cannot explain mathematical insights that had not yet occurred to Europeans at that time. We know that after centuries of dynamic cultural development Mayan civilization withered and died. But we have only informed guesses as to why.

Even basic facts about the Mayan economy are debated. They were certainly a fully agricultural people, cultivating maize, beans, squash, and other foods and feeding a population of upwards of two million people. One of the long-standing puzzles of Mayan history has been how the Mayans managed to feed so many people using old-fashioned slash-and-burn agricultural methods. Recent research employing aerial photographs, however, seems to have detected intricate patterns of irrigation canals beneath the brush and forest that blanket the region today. So one Mayan mystery at least may be on its way to a solution.

The political and social organization of the Mayans is clearer than that of any Amerindian culture we have glanced at so far. The Maya region was divided into a number of small states, all speaking related but not always mutually intelligible languages. Warfare was common among these states, and prisoners were brought home and ritually sacrificed to the gods of the victors.

Like Mesopotamian or Greek city-states, the lands of the Mayans shared a similar hierarchic social and political structure. They were normally ruled by a hereditary elite of priests and nobles. There was an intermediate social class of artisans and artists, traders and civil servants. And there was a majority population of peasant farmers and a smaller number of serfs and slaves.

Among the peasant masses, men and women worked hard with stone tools clearing the jungle for planting. Their standard of living, however, seems to have been relatively high, perhaps higher than that of the Indians of Yucatan or Chiapas today. Their pole-and-thatch houses were built on platforms. Their cotton clothing included skirts and shirts for women, knee-length trousers for men. More aristocratic families flaunted jade and feather ornaments and pierced ears, noses, and lips for further decoration. Marriages were monogamous among the peasantry, polygamous among the upper classes, and if things didn't work out, divorce was easy.

## Mayan Religion and Art

Like other lowland Mesoamerican peoples, the Mayans were not yet a truly urban culture. But they did build huge ceremonial centers with the famous stone step-pyramids, multistory palaces, wide plazas, ceremonial ball courts, intricately carved stone stelae, and other impressive structures and carvings. Thousands of people could live at centers like those of Tikal in northern Guatemala, with its 230-foot pyramid, or at Palenque in eastern Mexico, with its great palace towering over the surrounding jungle. Tens of thousands of others would live in wattle-and-daub thatched huts around the periphery of such a place. And countless more would come for the great celebrations before the temples of the gods.

Even experienced archaeologists can get dizzy climbing the steep, narrow steps of a Mayan pyramid—let alone descending! Sitting outside the temple you will find perched on top, gazing down at the hazy green of bush or jungle below, you are likely to develop a deep respect for what these Native Americans could do. This is especially true when you remember that under the green canopy, or in those hills and valleys on the horizon, countless other ruins remain, choked in roots or vines or rubble, still waiting for the excavator's pick.

In stone and plaster sculpture as well as in multicolored wall paintings, the Mayans have left even more detailed information about their daily lives than did the Mochica or the people of Teotihuacán. In these images from the past, a colorful aristocracy of warriors in jaguar skins and plumed headdresses and ladies in long white robes watch costumed dancers spin to the music of drums, rattles, and trumpets. Crowds cheer the young players of ceremonial ball games or watch the bloody sacrifices of prisoners from the last war. The excitement of these vanished spectacles lives still in moving limbs, an upraised hand.

But there were minds at work here whose concerns went far beyond such common pastimes as sports, music, and war. There was, for instance, as bewildering a pantheon of gods as we have encountered anywhere in the world. The chief of these was Itzamná, creator of humankind, inventor of the arts and sciences—a toothless old man often represented as a lizard, a crocodile, or a serpent. There was Ah Kinchil, god of the sun, and Ah Puch, lord of death, with his spotted body and protruding spine. There were gods who protected the interests of all sorts and conditions of people in this complex Mayan world. There were patrons of traders, travelers, farmers, hunters, fishermen, and beekeepers; gods of poetry and music, of war, sacrifice, and suicide; gods of the rain and the life-giving corn.

All of these divinities mingled traits of humans and animals, reptiles, or birds in monstrous, sometimes changing shapes. In the complicated Mayan theology, they presided over thirteen heavens above the earth and nine hells below it. Like gods in many other lands, they made the corn grow, the women fertile, and the warriors victorious.

## Mayan Mathematics, Science, and Writing

Once again, however, we make them seem too simple. For the Classic Mayans are most famous not for theology but for science, mathematics, and their unique system of writing.

Mayan mathematical thinking was in some ways at least as advanced as that of the Old World. Their system was based on the number twenty—rather than ten, as in the later metric system. Like Gupta Indian mathematicians, the Mayans also understood the concept of zero. They were thus able to undertake calculations reaching into the millions.

Mayan astronomers were also remarkably accurate, both as observers and as calculators. Astronomer-priests recorded detailed observations of the movements of the moon and the planet Venus over generations. They were able to predict both solar and lunar eclipses. Temples were aligned with the heavenly bodies, and some temples may have been intended primarily as astronomical observatories. On the foundation of this astronomical knowledge, Mayan priests designed a 365-day calendar that came considerably closer to measuring the earth's actual annual revolution around the sun than the contemporary Julian calendar in use in Europe.

The Mayans, finally, developed the most advanced system of hieroglyphic writing in the Americas. Though all but a handful of their bark-paper codices (books) were destroyed by their Spanish conquerors in the sixteenth century, subjects of special literary concern seem to have included religion, science, and the political achievements of their rulers. Religious texts included sacred songs and spells, horoscopes and prophecies. Among subjects of political interest were the victories of their rulers in the many wars between the separate Mayan city-states.

A related document is the famous Mayan *Popol Vuh,* written after the conquest in a Mayan language but using European letters rather than Mayan glyphs. This book preserves a Mayan informant's view of history, from the creation of the world to the last Mayan kings, mingling the deeds of gods and men in a narrative that still fascinates modern students of this ancient people.

## SUMMARY

Advanced societies continued to develop in Africa and the Americas during the classic age. North Africa continued to flourish as part of the Mediterranean culture that surrounded the world's largest inland sea. Alexandria, in Egypt, became a great intellectual center of the Mediterranean world during Hellenistic and Roman times. The fertile North African shores played an important role in the larger Roman imperium of these centuries.

Eastward in Africa, on the blistering Red Sea shore and in the cool Ethiopian highlands, the Kingdom of Axum (third century B.C.E. to fourth century C.E.) built its independent place in the commercial life of the Old World. Serving as a meeting place for goods from inner Africa, the Mediterranean, the Indian Ocean, and the lands beyond, Axum enjoyed many prosperous centuries before succumbing to isolation and conquest early in the Christian era. The Sahara itself, finally, was criss-crossed with trade routes as camel caravans transported goods between the Mediterranean and the southern half of West Africa.

Agriculture spread widely across North, Middle, and South America during the classic age. In the North American southwest, the Hohokam and Mogollon cultures drew from neighboring Mexico to build their own village societies. In the eastern woodlands, the Mississippi Valley produced the Adena and Hopewell cultures with trade links to distant parts of the continent.

Among a number of local cultures that rose in the Peruvian Andes on the foundations laid by the ancient Chavín "mother culture," the society of the Mochica people has perhaps most intrigued historians, archaeologists, and art collectors. These makers of some of the New World's most famous pottery also built a powerful state with a structured society and a brutally successful military class.

The metropolis of Teotihuacán in upland Mexico represented an urban achievement of the first order. Perhaps the most impressive of American cultures during the classic age, however, was that of the Mayans (C.E. 300–900) of Middle America. Mayan society, like that of ancient Greece, never evolved politically beyond the city-state. But Mayan art, religion, and intellectual achievement, from early writing to mathematics and astronomy, were dazzling. Mayan culture provided a cultural reservoir for later civilizations in Middle America.

## SUGGESTED READING

Adams R. E. W. *Ancient Civilizations of the New World.* Boulder, Colo.: Westview Press, 1997. Brief overview of Mexican and Peruvian civilizations.

Alva, W., and C. B. DONNAN. *Royal Tombs of Sipan.* Los Angeles: University of California Press, 1993. Golden burial of Peru's Lord of Sipan.

Anfray, F. "The Civilization of Aksum from the First to the Seventh Century," in *Ancient Civilizations of Africa,* Vol. 2 of the *UNESCO General History of Africa,* G. Mokhtar, ed. London: Heinemann, 1981. By a leading excavator of Ethiopian ruins.

Bawden, G. *The Moche.* Cambridge, Mass.: Blackwell, 1996. Solid study of Mochica society and history.

Bulliet, R. W. *The Camel and the Wheel.* Cambridge, Mass.: Harvard University Press, 1975. Spread of the camel revolution from the Middle East to North Africa. See also H. Gauthier-Pilters and A. I. Dagg, *The Camel: Its Evolution, Ecology, Behavior, and Relationship to Man* (Chicago: University of Chicago Press, 1981).

Canfora, L. *The Vanished Library.* Berkeley: University of California Press, 1989. Alexandria's vanished treasure trove of ancient learning.

Carrasco, D., L. Jones, and S. Sessions, eds. *Mesoamerica's Classical Heritage: From Teotihuacán to the Aztecs.* Boulder, Colo.: University Press of Colorado, 2000. New studies of the meaning of the classical tradition in Middle America.

Clancy, F. S. *Sculpture in the Ancient Maya Plaza: The Early Classic Period.* Albuquerque: University of New Mexico Press, 1999. Formative period in Maya carving.

Coe, M. D. *The Maya,* 5th ed. New York: Thames and Hudson, 1995. One of the best surveys of this much discussed ancient Mesoamerican people.

Ehret, C. *An African Classical Age: Eastern and Southern Africa in World History 1000 B.C. to 400 A.D.* Charlottesville: University Press of Virginia, 1998. Impressive attempt to use linguistic evidence to construct an overview of East African history over this long period.

Haas, C. *Alexandria in Late Antiquity.* Baltimore, Md.: Johns Hopkins University Press, 1997. Social conflict in the context of urban topography.

Joyce, R. A. *Gender and Power in Prehistoric America.* Austin: University of Texas Press, 2000. Thoughtful analysis, with some emphasis on the Maya. See also T. Ardren, ed., *Ancient Maya Women* (Walnut Creek, Calif.: AltaMira Press, 2002), for more studies of gender in Maya society and culture.

Lovejoy, P. E. *Salt of the Desert: A History of Salt Production and Trade in the Central Sudan.* New York: Cambridge University Press, 1986. Solid study of this key item in Saharan trade.

Munro-Hay, S. C. *Aksum: African Civilization of Late Antiquity.* Edinburgh: Edinburgh University Press, 1991. Scholarly and up-to-date.

Pillsbury, J., ed. *Moche Art and Archaeology in Ancient Peru.* Washington, D.C.: National Gallery of Art, 2001. Studies of the intriguing Mochica material culture that survives.

Schele, L., and M. E. Miller. *The Blood of Kings: Dynasty and Ritual in Maya Art.* Fort Worth, Tex.: Kimbell Art Museum, 1986. Mayan art in its social context.

Snowden, F. M. *Before Color Prejudice: The Ancient View of Blacks.* Cambridge, Mass.: Harvard University Press, 1983. Classic study of Greco-Roman views of Africa. See also W. L. Hansberry, *Africa and Africans as Seen by Classical Writers,* J. E. Harris, ed. (Washington, D.C., 1981).

Tedlock, D. *Popol Vuh: The Mayan Book of the Dawn of Life and the Glories of Gods and Kings.* New York: Random House, 1985. Translation of a Mayan religious classic.

Wolf, E. R. *Sons of the Shaking Earth.* Chicago: University of Chicago Press, 1959. Ecologically based poetic evocation of Mesoamerican cultures.

 Please refer to the document CD-ROM for primary sources related to this chapter.

# OVERVIEW III

# EXPANDING CULTURAL ZONES

## (500–1500)

Civilization survived, despite the widespread destruction that brought the classic age to an end. Out of the ruins, as so often before, areas of order, prosperity, and high culture emerged once more.

If anything, the new cultures—or the reconstituted older ones—were larger and more impressive than those that had collapsed during the middle centuries of the first millennium C.E. For civilization had grown until it transcended the reach of political authority. The result was a series of *zones* of culture, harder to define historically than any nations and empires, but real nonetheless.

Several types of cultural zone are detectable during the thousand years between C.E. 500 and 1500. The most obvious, perhaps, are the satellite civilizations that appeared around the fringes of great empires. In China's East Asian sphere, for example, related civilizations developed during these years in Korea, Vietnam, and, most important, Japan. Indian culture reached almost all of Southeast Asia, scattering trade and temples from Java to Vietnam.

A second sort of cultural zone was that created by the rise and spread of a new international religion. Medieval Christianity, in both its Roman Catholic and Greek Orthodox forms, completed the process of civilizing Europe that the Roman Empire had begun. Islam, born in the seventh century, spread so rapidly that by the fifteenth century a series of Islamic states stretched from West Africa to Southeast Asia. In each case, the particular forms of urban, literate culture that developed clearly reflected the shaping power of the religious faiths that dominated these two wide swathes of the Old World.

A third type of cultural zone was that created by the far-reaching conquests of a single people—the Mongols. And even when the Mongol Empire crumbled, a zone of Mongol culture still reached from the steppes of western Russia to the Pacific.

Larger cultural zones had by this time also emerged in the New World and in Africa south of the Sahara. The kingdoms and empires of the West African savanna constituted a zone of related cultures even before the shaping influence of Islam began to be felt there. The peoples of Mesoamerica and Peru manifested common cultural traits well before the unifying power of the Aztecs and the Incas welded them into empires in the fifteenth century. In these cases, similar geographical environment—the West African grasslands or the Andes, for instance—might help to explain the phenomenon.

Of course, cultural zones were not new in the world. A common civilization had infused the separate states of ancient Greece, of Shang China, even of ancient Mesopotamia. But the new zones of culture that flourished between 500 and 1500 had a size and a dynamism that pointed toward something still more impres-sive: the beginning of a truly global culture in centuries to come.

The major cultural zones remained separate for the most part during the period under consideration here. Except for the brief Mongol interlude, even Eurasia was without the unifying exchange of goods and ideas that had tentatively linked east and west during the classic age. But the new zones of culture were growing. And the time would come when one among them, around 1500, would launch a drive for dominion that would threaten to turn the whole world into a single cultural zone—the emerging global culture of our own time.

# EXPANDING CULTURAL ZONES

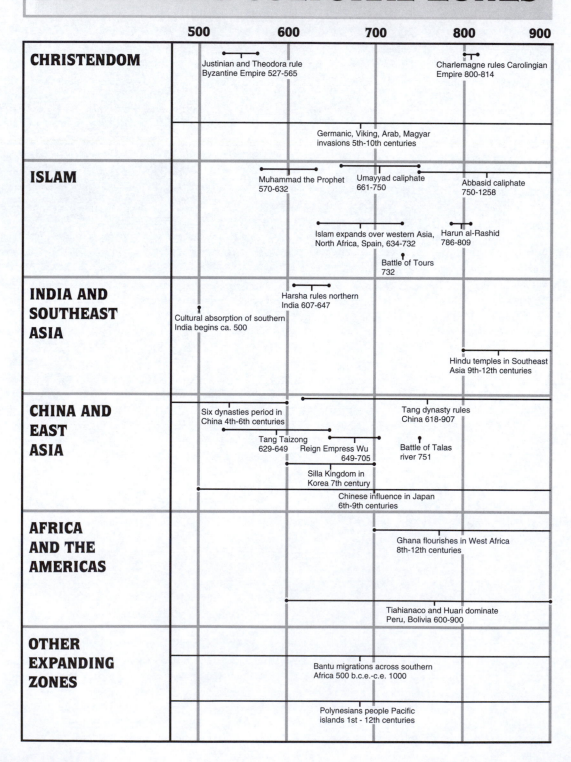

|  | 500 | 600 | 700 | 800 | 900 |
|---|---|---|---|---|---|
| **CHRISTENDOM** | Justinian and Theodora rule Byzantine Empire 527-565 | | | Charlemagne rules Carolingian Empire 800-814 | |
| | | Germanic, Viking, Arab, Magyar invasions 5th-10th centuries | | | |
| **ISLAM** | | Muhammad the Prophet 570-632 | Umayyad caliphate 661-750 | Abbasid caliphate 750-1258 | |
| | | | Islam expands over western Asia, North Africa, Spain, 634-732 | Harun al-Rashid 786-809 | |
| | | | Battle of Tours 732 | | |
| **INDIA AND SOUTHEAST ASIA** | Cultural absorption of southern India begins ca. 500 | Harsha rules northern India 607-647 | | | |
| | | | | Hindu temples in Southeast Asia 9th-12th centuries | |
| **CHINA AND EAST ASIA** | Six dynasties period in China 4th-6th centuries | | Tang dynasty rules China 618-907 | | |
| | | Tang Taizong 629-649 | Reign Empress Wu 649-705 | Battle of Talas river 751 | |
| | | Silla Kingdom in Korea 7th century | | | |
| | | Chinese influence in Japan 6th-9th centuries | | | |
| **AFRICA AND THE AMERICAS** | | | | Ghana flourishes in West Africa 8th-12th centuries | |
| | | | Tiahianaco and Huari dominate Peru, Bolivia 600-900 | | |
| **OTHER EXPANDING ZONES** | | Bantu migrations across southern Africa 500 b.c.e.-c.e. 1000 | | | |
| | | Polynesians people Pacific islands 1st - 12th centuries | | | |

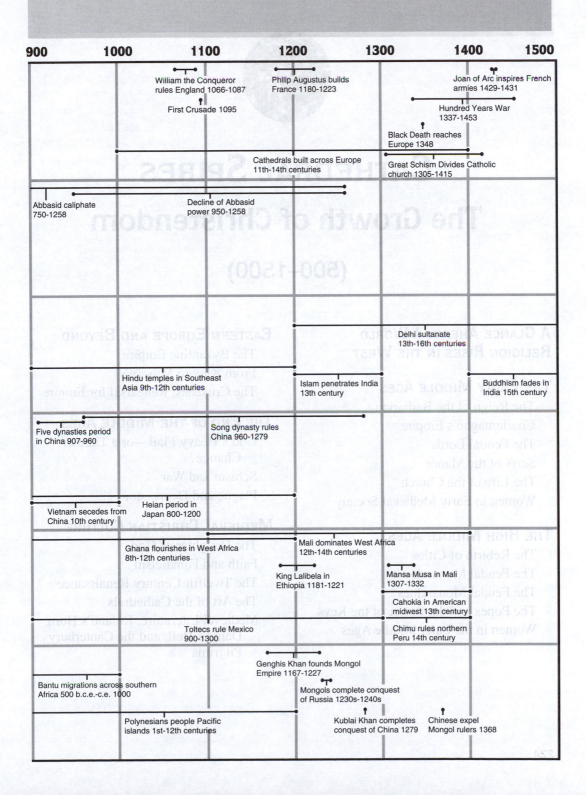

| 900 | 1000 | 1100 | 1200 | 1300 | 1400 | 1500 |
|-----|------|------|------|------|------|------|

William the Conqueror
rules England 1066-1087

First Crusade 1095

Philip Augustus builds
France 1180-1223

Joan of Arc inspires French
armies 1429-1431

Hundred Years War
1337-1453

Black Death reaches
Europe 1348

Cathedrals built across Europe
11th-14th centuries

Great Schism Divides Catholic
church 1305-1415

Abbasid caliphate
750-1258

Decline of Abbasid
power 950-1258

Delhi sultanate
13th-16th centuries

Hindu temples in Southeast
Asia 9th-12th centuries

Islam penetrates India
13th century

Buddhism fades in
India 15th century

Five dynasties period
in China 907-960

Song dynasty rules
China 960-1279

Vietnam secedes from
China 10th century

Heian period in
Japan 800-1200

Ghana flourishes in West Africa
8th-12th centuries

Mali dominates West Africa
12th-14th centuries

King Lalibela in
Ethiopia 1181-1221

Mansa Musa in Mali
1307-1332

Cahokia in American
midwest 13th century

Toltecs rule Mexico
900-1300

Chimu rules northern
Peru 14th century

Genghis Khan founds Mongol
Empire 1167-1227

Bantu migrations across southern
Africa 500 b.c.e.-c.e. 1000

Mongols complete conquest
of Russia 1230s-1240s

Polynesians people Pacific
islands 1st-12th centuries

Kublai Khan completes
conquest of China 1279

Chinese expel
Mongol rulers 1368

# CHAPTER 9

# CATHEDRAL SPIRES
## The Growth of Christendom

### (500–1500)

# A Glance Ahead: A World Religion Rises in the West

Jesus Christ had lived in Roman times, but most of the citizens of Roman Europe were still pagans when Rome fell. The Christianization of most of Europe was the work of the thousand years of European history we call the Middle Ages.

Medieval Europe was a patchwork quilt of kingdoms and fiefdoms, city-states, and even smaller political entities. But similar political structures, common economic institutions, and above all the Christian Church united them all in a single vast zone of Christian culture.

This chapter will trace the rise of Christian civilization out of the ruins of Rome. It will outline the emergence of new European nations and their long feud with nearby Muslim powers. We will analyze the Gothic climax of the High Middle Ages and the series of cataclysms, from the Black Death to the Hundred Years War, which brought this cycle of European history to an end.

Medieval Europe was history by 1500, and western Christendom was on the verge of the greatest schism in its history. But the European nations shaped over the preceding millennium were poised to play an unprecedented role in the coming age.

# The Early Middle Ages

## The Reign of the Barbarian

Bordered by the glittering cultures of Byzantium and Islam, sharing the Eurasian land mass with the great civilization of India and China, Europe in the Middle Ages looks like a very backward cultural zone indeed. But medieval Europe did flower, briefly and brilliantly, in the High Middle Ages—the eleventh, twelfth, and thirteenth centuries. And its future greatness may be traced back this far at least, to the crusading religion, the increasingly productive agriculture, the enterprising merchants, the militaristic aristocracy, and the increasingly powerful kingdoms of the medieval centuries.

We must begin, however, where the story does, with a very different Europe from that of the High Middle Ages—with a Europe lying broken and helpless in the ruins of its greatest historic catastrophe.

From the fifth century to the tenth, barbarian kingdoms divided Europe among themselves, fought one another and each new wave of barbarian invaders, and gradually transformed life on the western end of Eurasia.

They came in two great surges. The first, composed mostly of semicivilized Germanic peoples, shouldered their way into the empire they had long admired and established themselves as early as the fifth century. They set up an Ostrogothic kingdom in Italy, a Visigothic one in Spain, Franks in what would become France, Angles and Saxons in Britain, and Alemanni in Germany. A second, more varied wave of invasions began in the eighth century. Vikings pressed down from the north by sea, Magyars from the eastern steppes, and Muslim Arabs up from the south across Spain and the Mediterranean.

Some of the intruders took what they could carry and headed home. Others settled among the peoples of the broken empire or the unstable barbarian kingdoms that replaced it. Some of those who stayed became Europe's new masters, a military aristocracy distinguished by cavalry skills and increasingly heavy arms and armor—the mounted knights of the new age.

# DARK AGE INVASIONS OF THE WEST

The process of transition from the civilization of the ancient Romans to the culture of the early Middle Ages was more gradual than was once imagined, more evolutionary than revolutionary in nature.

The new peoples brought some new ways of life with them, of course. The German royal entourage, a war band called the *comitatus,* would provide the germ of the new feudal political order, based on personal allegiance to an overlord. The proclivity of the Germans for country rather than urban living would contribute to the disintegration of the network of cities that had dominated ancient Greco-Roman civilization. Yet when towns reappeared in the later Middle Ages, German social brotherhoods called *guilds* would evolve into the merchant and craft guilds that played a central role in the medieval urban economy.

But there were Roman roots for medieval civilization too. Roman estates called *villas* worked by slave labor probably evolved in some places into medieval manors with their labor force of serfs. The cities the Romans had built were abandoned slowly, over generations, but the Roman Catholic Church, with its structure of episcopal administration and its communities of monks and nuns who preserved some vestiges of Latin culture, would reach new heights in the Middle Ages.

A mingling of folkways accompanied by a slow merging of peoples thus lay at the root of the new society of medieval Europe. Germanic chiefs intermarried with Roman aristocrats, while German freemen settled beside Celtic or other indigenous peasant cultivators. The Vikings who descended from Scandinavia established themselves in parts of northern Europe, including Normandy (in modern France) and northern England. Muslims from the other side of the Mediterranean colonized Spain, Sicily, and other places along the southern fringes of the continent, producing enclaves of civilized living along the southern margins of Europe. From the glory of Augustus in his far-off city of marble, it was a long comedown to the "do-nothing" kings of the Merovingian Franks, who, according to a contemporary chronicler, were sometimes trundled along the rutty lanes of the kingdom in a farm wagon while a servant trotted ahead blowing a ram's horn.

## Charlemagne's Empire

Here and there, however, strength and capacity existed even in Dark Age Europe. The most impressive attempt to restore order and unity to the Continent was led by perhaps the most famous of medieval monarchs, the Frankish king Charles the Great, known to history as Charlemagne.

Charlemagne (768–814) was a half-literate giant, six feet and several inches in height, a tremendous toper, trencherman, and womanizer, and a mighty warrior in a war-battered age. The greatest of the ambitious Carolingian kings of the Franks who succeeded the do-nothing Merovingians in the eighth century, Charlemagne spent most of his long reign fighting. He hammered together a rude but sizable empire, with modern France at its core and chunks of Spain, northern Italy, western Germany, and neighboring regions as outlying provinces. On Christmas day, 800, a pope, grateful for his help against barbarian intruders and the pope's political enemies in Rome, placed a crown on Charlemagne's head, hailing him "Pious Augustus, crowned by God," and heir of all the Caesars.[1]

He was scarcely that, this huge, thick-bearded man who spoke vulgar Latin as well as the Frankish tongue and kept a slate beside his bed so that he could practice tracing the letters of the alphabet in rare quiet moments. His endless campaigns spread Roman Christianity and Frankish rule far across western Europe. He organized his empire into a loose

---

[1]Robert S. Hoyt and Stanley Chodorow, *Europe in the Middle Ages* (New York: Harcourt Brace Jovanovich, 1976), p. 160.

provincial structure of *counties*—each headed by a count—and tried to keep tabs on them, both in person and through royal inspectors sent out from his court at Aachen near the Rhine. He even presided over a temporary revival of learning, the Carolingian Renaissance, which at least made a virtue of Latin literacy and theological scholarship at Aachen. Charlemagne's scholars both preserved much of Rome's literary heritage for the future and developed a new form of writing—*Carolingian minuscule,* the small or lower-case letters we still use, along with Roman capitals, today.

But Charlemagne's heir had none of his strength of will, and his three grandsons divided the Carolingian Empire among them less than thirty years after his death. The Carolingian Renaissance too proved to be a false dawn in the Dark Ages. But it did at least halt the long decline and point out one way in which peace and prosperity might be restored to Europe. To the extent that they accepted this obligation, the strong kings of centuries to come were all Charlemagne's heirs.

## The Feudal Lords

The forces that pulled Charlemagne's empire apart were rooted more deeply in medieval society than in the rivalries of feuding heirs. For the real rulers of Europe in the Dark Ages were not the kings of the barbarian states but the powerful dukes, counts, knights, and other warrior lords of medieval Europe linked in a loose structure of power called *feudalism.*

Feudalism was a system of military service and land tenure that bound Europe's ruling classes into an elaborate pyramid of political and military power. Under this system

Charlemagne, looking almost larger than his horse in this bronze representation, wears the crown and holds the orb of imperial authority. Note the heavy sword under his cloak, a symbol of his many victories and conquests. Notice also the monumental feel of this representation, which is in fact only a small figurine. (Courtesy of the Library of Congress)

the less powerful knights—called *vassals*—sought political protection and economic support, commonly in the form of a grant of land, from the more powerful, who became their feudal lords, or *seigneurs*. In return, feudal overlords required military service, money payments, and general support from their vassals.

The ceremony of feudal vassalage was solemn and symbolic. The vassal knelt, placed his hands between those of his lord, and took an oath of *fealty,* or allegiance. He pledged perhaps forty days of military service each year, plus money payments when the lord's son was knighted, his daughter married, or the lord himself captured and in need of ransom. In return the seigneur handed the vassal a clod of earth or a sprig from a tree, and with it conferred on him a *fief,* a parcel of land replete with villages of serfs to cultivate it.

This structure of interlocking obligations was quite suitable to a violent age in which only local authority was strong enough to offer any real protection. In time, however, the system became immensely complex and sometimes self-defeating. Loyal vassals might find themselves with a number of overlords, some of whom might feud with each other, creating embarrassing conflicts of interest. The strong kings of later centuries sometimes came into conflict with the most powerful of feudal overlords, "overmighty subjects" who could rival even kings for power. The royal rulers of the High Middle Ages would thus often prefer to depend on hired mercenary companies, whose services could be depended on as long as the monarch's money lasted.

Throughout the Middle Ages in Europe, the feudal lords would hold much of the Continent's political power. In the early Middle Ages—the first half of the thousand years of medieval history—the military leaders were the real rulers of the land.

## Serfs of the Manor

If feudalism constituted the political power structure of Europe in the early Middle Ages, the manor system was the heart of the earlier medieval economy. In a world reduced to isolated, county-sized political units, subsistence agriculture was essential. The manor system fed the farm laborers themselves, the feudal aristocracy, the priests, the kings. And it provided at least a modicum of protection for masses of people who could no longer look to garrisoned legions or civil authorities for defense against violence or help in hard times.

The typical medieval manor consisted of a village surrounded by arable land, usually with the manor house or castle overlooking it. A dozen, perhaps several dozen, stone or mud huts clustered along a single unpaved village street. A small, rude church might occupy one end of the street, and perhaps a mill, bakehouse, smithy, and other adjuncts were mixed in among the houses of the peasants. The surrounding land would include, besides the arable for spring and autumn planting, a third field left fallow in rotation each year so that it could recover its strength. These three fields were typically divided into strips so that all might have a share of the best as well as the worst land. Beyond the three-field system of strips were blocks of common pastureland for farm animals and portions of uncut forest for firewood and foraging pigs.

Medieval peasants were totally subservient to the lord of the manor. They paid portions of their produce to support the lord. They also worked the lord's land for him and did other manual labor around the estate—the *corvée* work on roads, bridges, and so on. The blacksmith's shop, the bakehouse, and similar amenities were the lord's, and the peasants paid to use them. Peasants were tried for all but the most serious crimes in the baron's court, and married outside the manor only with his consent. They were not chattel slaves, as in the ancient world. But they were serfs, bound to the land and the village for life—and thus to the lord, for as long as he held that land.

Life in the village under the hill during the early Middle Ages was a hard and narrow round. The typical peasant family—that is, the large majority of Europeans—lived in a meagerly furnished, earth-floored, one-room hut. They moved by day in a clutter of chickens and animals who shared the hut with them, slept whole families curled together for warmth on a straw-covered sleeping floor at night. They plowed with horses or oxen and a heavy wheeled plow, harvested and threshed their grain with rough homemade tools.

There had been such breakdowns of the great enterprise many times in many parts of the world. But this was probably the worst that Europe ever had to endure.

## The Life of the Church

In this harsh, subsistence-level world, one institution worked still for higher ends and provided islands of culture in a backward Europe. The Christian Church survived the Fall of Rome and actually expanded and grew more powerful through the medieval centuries.

As we shall see, Christianity spread north from two radiant centers in the Mediterranean world during the Middle Ages. The popes of Rome sponsored the vast expansion of Roman Catholicism over Western Europe, while the patriarchs of Constantinople, capital of the Byzantine or Eastern Roman Empire, spread Greek Orthodox Christianity across much of Eastern Europe. Even in the early Middle Ages, daring missionaries converted pagan kings and queens, and through them their peoples. Churchmen like Charlemagne's advisor Alcuin preserved some Latin learning, produced beautifully decorated hand-written books, and presided over such heroic attempts at cultural revival as the Carolingian Renaissance.

Humbler monks and nuns sought refuge from worldly temptation behind the walls of monasteries and convents. There they lived according to the strict religious rules of St. Benedict, which prescribed poverty, chastity, and obedience to their superiors in the order. Alternating hard work in the fields or cloisters with religious meditation and prayer, they created islands of order, charity, and often relatively efficient agriculture in the medieval world.

Monastic establishments planted among non-Christian populations also provided centers from which these pagans might be converted to Christianity. Monks and nuns were also among the few literate Europeans during this period. By copying Latin works— partly to learn their letters, partly as discipline—these pious Christians preserved the classics of pagan Rome for later generations.

How many medieval villages had their own priests and little churches, or even a cross on a hill around which to pray, we do not know. Many probably did not, especially during the earlier medieval centuries. In many parts of Europe, old religions worshiping the forces of nature, pre-Christian cults, folk beliefs, and superstitions undoubtedly survived. But the Christian Church remained the most determined and dynamic of Western institutions even during this grim time.

## Women in Early Medieval Society

The role of women at all levels of medieval life, finally, was extremely important. In a time when Western civilization struggled simply to maintain itself, women may in fact have played a particularly important part in society.

In a world reduced to fundamentals, the family was a central institution. The peasant household, which included the large majority of medieval people, was the basic unit of production, one in which women carried at least their half of the common burden. Caring for farm animals and children, tending vegetables near the house, preparing food, making all clothing by hand, and often doing a share of sowing or harvesting crops in distant fields as well, medieval peasant women needed nimble fingers and strong backs.

Higher up the social ladder, women of noble families often shared in the ruling functions and responsibilities of the upper classes. The structure of power and prestige, like the system of economic production, was based on the family, on inheritance and marriage. Women born of great families could inherit vast estates. As wives of fighting barons, they were often called on to administer and sometimes defend their lands and manor houses while their husbands were away at the frequent wars.

Women, finally, could also make an independent place for themselves, and even exercise considerable authority, within the Church. Women who found the burdens of family life oppressive could dedicate their lives to God by "taking the veil" and entering a convent. Women with large estates could even establish and run their own convents. Within these holy institutions, they could wield the absolute authority of a mother superior or an abbess. Women as well as men, finally, might lead lives so pious that they achieved the ultimate medieval accolade of saint-hood. Hildegarde of Bingen, whose convents carried Christianity to the Germanic peoples, was famed for her learning and visionary insights. The pope himself wrote to her that "We are filled with admiration, my daughter . . . for the new miracles that God has shown you in our time, filling you with his spirit so that you see, understand, and communicate many secret things."[2]

## THE HIGH MIDDLE AGES

### The Rebirth of Cities

In the year C.E. 1000, Europe was a cramped and drafty fortress on a hill, a dozen families huddled in huts along a muddy street below, and all around, a world of fen and forest stretching to an empty horizon. It was as though the Greek city-states and the metropolis on the seven hills of Rome had never existed.

A century later, two centuries, and it was a world transformed.

Once again the gates of cities swung wide, and to the braying of donkeys and the baaing of sheep, country folk could pass through an arched gateway into crowded cobblestoned streets. Steep-roofed multistory houses pressed close above. There were market squares and gingerbready guildhalls, street after street of artisans and merchants, and rising against a misty gray sky, the half-finished towers of a cathedral. This was the twelfth century, or the thirteenth—the greatest of centuries, medieval enthusiasts have insisted since. Paris was the cultural capital of one of Europe's great ages—the Athens of the age of faith.

But where did it come from, this new urban sprawl, this urban splendor reborn? Among the causes most commonly credited, three stand out: agricultural improvements, population growth, and perhaps most important, the revival of trade.

The medieval European manor, primitive as it was in many ways, produced several crucial agricultural innovations. These included the three-field system, the heavy wheeled plow

---

[2]*Patrologia Latina,* Vol. 197, Col. 145, quoted in F. and J. Gies, *Women in the Middle Ages* (New York: Crowell, 1978), p. 81.

(both mentioned above), the horseshoe and the horse collar, and the windmill for grinding grain where no river was available for a water mill. After the year 1000 there was also a significant expansion in the amount of land under cultivation, due to the clearing of woodlands, the draining of swamps, and the movement of productive western European lords and peasants into less developed eastern Europe. Because of this increase in food production, the population began to grow, after centuries of stagnation, And some of these additional people concentrated in islands of dense population in which cities rapidly took shape.

The heart of the medieval cities, however, was commercial exchange and skilled handicraft manufacturing. The revival of trade in Europe in the eleventh, twelfth, and thirteenth centuries is thus a central cause of the rebirth of cities.

Trade grew up in Europe once more, partly because of the increased demand for goods created by the expanding population. Another cause was the taste for Eastern luxury goods encouraged by the Crusades, which began at the end of the eleventh century. And a prime stimulus was the expanded commercial exchange between the Near East and Italian trading cities such as Venice, which had survived the Dark Ages because of their connection with the powerful Byzantine Empire, Rome's heir to the east. The merchants who participated in this commercial revival became the builders and rulers of the medieval cities.

The trading cities were dominated first by merchant and craft guilds—trade associations of dealers in or makers of particular products, from cloth to goldsmith work. In time cities acquired independent political authorities—magistrates and city councils elected by this oligarchy of business people. Around the leading merchants and the master craftsmen, a colorful urban population soon gathered. The craft guilds included journeymen assistants and apprentices to the trade as well as masters. Merchants required stevedores, porters, muleteers, and other adjuncts. Priests, students, lawyers, runaway serfs, and other masterless men sought the protection of the city's walls.

In this stimulating environment—a world within the walls once more—what is sometimes called the commercial revolution of the High Middle Ages took place. The robed and ermined merchants of the twelfth and thirteenth centuries revived the use of coins after long centuries of barter and payment in kind. They began once more to lend money at interest and to develop such important modern business practices as double-entry bookkeeping and letters of credit. They began the pooling of capital for large-scale economic investments through the joint-stock company—an institution pointing ahead to all the stock markets of the modern world. Modern Western capitalism was thus born well before modern history began, in the cathedral-dominated cities of the age of faith.

## The Feudal Monarchs

This burgeoning economic revival was accompanied and encouraged by the equally striking resurgence of centralized political power in the hands of medieval kings.

They were a varied lot. William the Conqueror of England still signed his name with an X; Frederick II, the German emperor, spoke half a dozen languages fluently. France's Philip Augustus was bald, one-eyed, and crafty. Nor were their lives textbook models of selfless statesmanship. They hunted, wenched, squeezed their subjects for funds, and fought endless wars. They feuded with each other, with the popes, with their own barons, and embarked on futile crusades and extremely successful programs of state-building with indiscriminate enthusiasm. In the end it was this last mentioned effort that has earned most of them their places in history.

Not all even of these famous names succeeded. None of the so-called Holy Roman Emperors of the Germans—not even the redoubtable Frederick Barbarossa—were able to impose genuine unity on the many German-speaking states of central Europe over which they held feudal suzerainty. Throughout most of its history the Holy Roman Empire would remain a ramshackle collection of separate principalities giving only minimal allegiance to its emperor. England and France, by contrast, were among the best examples of the centralized monarchy in medieval Europe.

Duke William the Bastard of Normandy overwhelmed Anglo-Saxon England in 1066, thus earning the more dignified sobriquet of William the Conqueror (1066–1087). He brought developed Norman-French feudalism with him to backward Britain. By asserting his position as king of England at the top of the feudal pyramid of power, he gave the country stronger centralized rule than it had ever had. His successors, including Henry I and Henry II, developed such governmental institutions as the royal council, the exchequer (treasury), and a system of royal justice based on English common law. By the end of the twelfth century—less than a century and a half after the conquest—England had the strongest monarchical government in Europe.

Close behind was the thirteenth-century French monarchy of Philip Augustus (1180–1223) and Saint Louis—Louis IX (1226–1270). Personally unprepossessing, Philip emerged as France's most successful medieval monarch. Like the English kings, he used his place at the apex of the feudal system to increase his power over the nobility. Like English rulers also, he developed an independent royal administrative system, including a more effective chamber of accounts, or treasury, and a stronger legal system. He did not conquer a new country for himself, like William of Normandy, but he did launch a calculated crusade against the heretical barons of southern France that tripled the size of the royal domain, and he took from the heirs of Henry II some important English holdings in France.

Under Philip Augustus thirteenth-century France replaced the Holy Roman Empire as the most powerful nation on the European continent. Under Louis IX the French monarchy acquired the prestige of having a duly canonized saint in its roster of kings. Louis was no weakling: He increased royal power over French towns, dared to issue royal edicts without consulting his baronial vassals, and strengthened the French system of law courts, or *parlements*. But he was also a paragon of medieval Christian and chivalric virtues, washing the feet of lepers, meting out justice under an oak tree, and earning such a reputation for fairness and piety that he was known as Louis the Just in his own time and was canonized only thirty years after his death. In the age of faith, a saintly life was no small contribution to the power of the French monarchy over its people.

It was a long step up from the "do-nothing" Merovingian kings of the Dark Ages to the power and vitality of William the Conqueror or Philip Augustus. And even the conflicts and competitiveness of Europe's kings helped to generate a dynamism that would prove in later centuries more than a match for the great empires of other parts of the globe.

## The Feudal Monarchies

Undergirding the achievements of individual feudal monarchs, medieval government itself was evolving. The *feudal monarchy* as a set of political institutions and relationships would survive the Middle Ages and continue to develop through early modern times. In the end, modern bureaucratic government is a distant descendant of the monarchical institutions of the Middle Ages.

Basic problems for medieval rulers who truly wished to rule their lands included the need to impose the royal will on powerful vassals, the necessity of replacing a ragbag of feudal law with some sort of royal law, and perhaps most important, the need to get the right to tax the nation. Where these goals were met, as they were to a considerable degree in England and France, monarchs had to pay for their growing power by recognizing the rights of representatives bodies speaking for the chief estates or classes of medieval society—the nobility, the church, and the wealthy new towns.

The Norman feudalism that William the Conqueror imposed on England was the most developed in Europe. William claimed all the land in England for his own after the conquest: What he distributed as fiefs to his followers came with stringent feudal obligations. All the new vassals were actually required to gather on Salisbury Plain and take a mass oath of allegiance to their king. The legal reforms of William's successors began the process of replacing feudal law with the traditional English common law, which had been evolving for centuries before the Norman Conquest.

The right of English kings to tax their people, finally, was acquired with much more difficulty and in return for significant concessions. During the later Middle Ages, the English Parliament claimed the right to have the nation's grievances redressed before voting the monarch customs duties, taxes, or other sources of government revenue. Granted, Parliament met only when the monarch summoned it and represented only the elites of medieval society—ecclesiastical institutions, the nobility and country gentry, and the urban middle classes—not the masses of the people. But Parliament would in later centuries challenge royal authority and finally bring modern democracy to Britain.

The royal rulers of France had to deal with nobles whose claims went back many centuries and who saw the monarch as merely "first among equals" in the feudal structure. Great landed magnates whose holdings were sometimes larger than the king's would prove very hard to bring under royal control. The royal law the French kings strove to impose was Roman law, which had reached the West from the Byzantine Empire in the eleventh century. This strongly centralized code of laws, with its origins outside feudalism altogether, did significantly strengthen royal claims to overarching authority.

In France as in England, finally, the royal right to collect revenues outside the ruler's own lands was challenged. Again, a body representing the three estates emerged and demanded to be consulted. The French estates general would not prove as successful as the English Parliament in limiting royal power; indeed, in early modern times it would become moribund for the better part of two centuries. But it would be revived in time to trigger the great French Revolution, which would turn that nation toward democracy.

## The Popes and the Power of the Keys

The power of barons in the countryside, business oligarchies in the cities, and the stronger kings in the nation as a whole could be great. But in some ways the power of the Catholic church—the power of the keys of heaven—was greater still. And the wielders of that vast power were the popes of Rome, the heads of the Roman Catholic church.

Because Saint Peter, the "rock" on whom Christ had said he would build his church, had been martyred in Rome, the popes, as bishops of Rome, claimed to be Peter's heirs. As successors to Peter, to whom the keys to heaven's gate had traditionally been confided, the popes wielded the vast power of spiritual life and death over Western Christians.

Some Roman popes even asserted a double legacy of authority, declaring themselves to be the custodians of the "two swords" of spiritual and secular sovereignty. They thus claimed supremacy not only in the Church but also over any earthly sovereign—a claim hotly contested, of course, by earthly sovereigns. On the basis of this religious supremacy, the papacy over the centuries built the most impressive of all medieval European institutions: the Roman Catholic church.

The papal administration of the High and later Middle Ages was larger and more sophisticated than that of any king or emperor. The wealth of the Church, which had been collecting tithes, fees, and contributions and receiving gifts and bequests from the faithful for centuries, was greater than that of any landed magnate, merchant prince, or monarch. The Church owned a good percentage of the land of western Europe, and cathedral spires dominated the skylines of medieval cities. Indeed, a significant proportion of the population of medieval Europe held holy orders or otherwise worked for the Church.

Popes contended on roughly equal terms with kings and emperors. Their weapons were the spiritual powers of excommunication and interdict—exclusion from membership in the Church and prohibition of the performance of essential religious ceremonies. Powerful popes such as Gregory VII in the eleventh century and Innocent III in the thirteenth could bring sovereigns as powerful as Philip Augustus to their knees by threatening to excommunicate them or by absolving their vassals of their feudal oaths of loyalty.

Not every hamlet and manor village had its priest, but most probably did. There were also thousands of monasteries and convents scattered over Europe, to which brotherhoods of monks and groups of nuns had withdrawn from worldly temptation to give their lives wholly to prayer and good works. Beginning in the High Middle Ages, Franciscan and Dominican friars wandered the roads begging their bread and helping with the Church's mission of saving souls.

The priests were frequently illiterate, the monasteries sometimes wealthy, and the Church's rule of celibacy not always obeyed. Yet despite endless satire and sermons aimed at Church abuses, the people of the Middle Ages valued their religion as no other Western society has. The most prominent architectural feature of any medieval city, after all, was neither the battlements of its baronial citadel nor its Gothic guildhall, but the towers and soaring spires of its cathedral.

## Women in the Later Middle Ages

In later medieval society as a whole, some scholars believe, women lost many of the independent opportunities and positions of authority that had earlier been theirs. This seems to have been so despite the presence of some immensely celebrated individual women in the annals of the High Middle Ages.

Some noblewomen still administered and defended large feudal holdings in later medieval times. Such queens as Eleanor of Aquitaine might accompany their royal husbands on crusades or govern their own realms. And aristocratic and royal ladies played a central role in the emergence of the elaborate code of chivalry that was supposed to govern the conduct of the knightly classes.

In its earliest formulation, chivalry meant mostly such warrior virtues as courage, skill with weapons, fairness to one's foes, and loyalty to one's feudal superior. Church leaders urged protection of noncombatants, including women and of course the Church. Medieval ladies, however, guided the development of the most striking element of the chivalric code—the cult of courtly love. The truly chivalrous knight was thus encouraged, not only to protect women, but to love, serve, and revere a particular lady, usually from a distance. Troubadours and minstrels, medieval entertainers whose reward came from the lady who ran the noble household, were responsive to the tastes of their patronesses, singing songs of love and praising knights who served their ladies well.

At a less elevated level, middle-class women shared in the works and profits of the evolving urban guilds. Indeed, some guilds, including some devoted to the cloth and clothing industries, were actually run by women. In other guilds, women sometimes inherited and continued to operate their husbands' handicraft workshops. At the same time, in the agricultural villages where most people lived, women continued to bear their share of the burden of feeding the medieval world.

Some historians, however, have detected a decline in the independent power of women in later medieval times. As the Church strove to assert its authority over religious appointments and institutions, for instance, wealthy noblewomen lost their right to run the monastic institutions they founded or supported. In the realm of high politics, modifications in feudal practice required even queens and noblewomen to surrender control of their landed property to husbands or male guardians. Among the middle classes, dowries, which had once given women of the burgher class some leverage in a marriage, were increasingly turned over entirely to their husbands.

The image of women in the Middle Ages, finally, was strikingly ambiguous. Eve and Mary, two women from the Bible, were seen as embodying women's extravagant potential for both good and evil. Thus theologians, preachers, and composers of crude popular tales endlessly described women as lustful and treacherous, prone to betray their husbands as Eve had betrayed Adam. Yet church leaders and preachers never tired of extolling the piety of saintly, virginal women like Mary—convents multiplied across the land—and the vast majority of medieval cathedrals were dedicated to the Mother of God.

## EASTERN EUROPE AND BEYOND

### The Byzantine Empire

All this time, of course, there was another side of Christendom. In Western Europe Christianity spoke Latin, and Christians looked for spiritual guidance to the pope of Rome. But in Eastern Europe during the Middle Ages the language of the Church was Greek, and the fount of Christian consolation was the patriarch of Constantinople. To the eastern half of Christendom and the Byzantine Empire that was its heart we must now turn.

In many ways, medieval Byzantium and Western Christendom were historically opposite and complementary. Western Europe in the Middle Ages was comparatively practical, noisily disunited, and increasingly dynamic. The Byzantine Empire—or Eastern Roman Empire, as it was officially called—was more mystical, united by a rigid autocracy, and intensely conservative. Western Europe began the medieval period in the depths of a dark age and slowly evolved to a twelfth-century apogee. Byzantium's greatest age came at the beginning of the medieval period, during the sixth-century reign of the Emperor Justinian, and the later medieval centuries saw its greatest misfortunes.

The high point of Byzantine power and cultural creativity came under Emperor Justinian (527–565) and his formidable empress, Theodora, a former courtesan who put steel into the emperor's backbone when he needed it. Justinian's greatest effort went into a massive drive to reclaim the West from the barbarian. After decades of campaigning, his generals succeeded in overthrowing the Ostrogothic kingdom in Italy, the Visigoths in southern Spain, and the Vandals in North Africa. For a short time a "Roman" empire—this one ruled from Constantinople—almost girdled the Mediterranean once more.

Justinian is probably best known, however, for his sponsorship of an immense collection, abridgment, and codification of Roman law. Justinian's Code, as it is commonly called, passed Roman law on to medieval and modern Europe, where it proved extremely influential in shaping the law codes of many modern nations.

Justinian's greatest passion after the reconquest of the empire in the West was the Eastern Orthodox church. He built the largest church in Christendom in its honor—Hagia Sophia, the Church of the Holy Wisdom. With its marble and mosaics and its great dome, Hagia Sophia has for fourteen centuries been an awesome symbol of the splendor of Byzantium in the days of Justinian and Theodora.

For the next five hundred years, the Byzantine Empire remained proverbial for wealth, power, and military strength. Its emperor, served by a large and efficient bureaucracy, dominated his church, his nobility, and his people. So great was the power of the Byzantine emperors that one of their titles, *autokrator,* has come into modern languages as a synonym for absolute power—*autocrat.* The Byzantine army and navy, well trained and organized and equipped with such technological innovations as "Greek fire" (a flammable chemical substance sprayed on enemy ships) threw back wave after wave of would-be conquerors—Persians, Arabs, Turks, and many others. In so doing, Byzantium incidentally protected Western Europe from foreign invasion during its weakest centuries.

Constantinople, controlling the bottleneck of east-west trade across Eurasia, became perhaps the richest city in the world during those centuries. From its famous harbor, the Golden Horn, Byzantine goldsmith work, Chinese silks, and Persian carpets reached Europe through the Italian trading cities. The Byzantine capital teemed with shrewd Greek and Levantine merchants and skilled artisans—a profit-hungry business community whose most popular leaders were monks!

With its palaces and churches rich with mosaic and gold leaf, Constantinople flourished down the medieval centuries, while Western Europe was slowly pulling itself out of mud huts and manor villages. Byzantines called their capital, located on a narrow peninsula protected by water and heavy walls, "the city protected by God." For many centuries it seemed that it was so.

Then in the early 1200s, an army of Norman Crusaders, encouraged by Venetians envious of the city's wealth, captured and looted Constantinople. And in 1453 the Ottoman Turkish sultan, Muhammad II, breached the ancient walls, killed the last emperor, and turned the Church of the Holy Wisdom into a mosque. The Eastern Roman Empire had finally fallen—a thousand years after the fall of the Empire of the West.

## From Kiev to Muscovy

The history of Eastern Europe is commonly neglected by European historians—a serious mistake, especially in a world that was divided for much of the twentieth century along a line that split Europe precisely into eastern and western halves. A few words, then, about Eastern Europe in these earliest centuries will be in order here.

Even in medieval times, Eastern Europe was never the land of cossacks, gypsies, and Transylvanian vampires of the popular Western imagination. Yet there were distinctive differences between the two halves of Europe long before the Cold War divided the continent. A primary source of these differences was the influence of Byzantine and later of

Mongol culture on the Slavic population of Russia in particular. Slavic origins and Byzantine influences will be glanced at here, and Mongol influences deferred to Chapter 14.

The Slavs settled much of the eastern half of the continent from the Balkans to the Baltic, from predominantly German-speaking central Europe to what became European Russia. These Slavic herders and farmers soon came to be ruled by more warlike minorities—Bulgars and Avars from Asia and Vikings coming down the Russian rivers from the fjords of Scandinavia. The East Slavs, who had settled in what became Russia, were governed by a loose confederation of Viking princes known as Varangians. From their metropolis at Kiev, Varangians and Slavs voyaged down the Dnieper to the Black Sea and on to Byzantium to trade their wheat and honey, furs and amber for the luxury goods to be had in the bazaars of Constantinople.

From Constantinople, then, Eastern Europe in general and Russia in particular received the first impress of a more complex civilization toward the end of the early Middle Ages. But it was a set of cultural influences very different from those Rome had imprinted on Western Europe.

Byzantine missionaries carried Christianity to pagan Slavs, Varangians, and other East European peoples. Thus, the faith to which Russia was converted was the mystical, liturgical Greek Orthodox form of Christianity, with its particular reverence for monks and the lovely little sacred images called *ikons,* and its Byzantine sense of the emperor as head of the church as well as the state. Russia learned to write in the Greek-based Cyrillic alphabet devised by Byzantine missionaries rather than the Roman alphabet used in Western Europe, and Russian art echoed that of the Byzantines. And when the czarist Russian state began to take shape centuries later around Moscow, far to the north, the czars took upon themselves all the autocratic claims of Byzantine emperors in their prime.

The shift in the center of Russian power from Kiev in the southern grasslands to Moscow in the darkly forested north was precipitated by one of Russia's greatest historic catastrophes—the Mongol conquest of the thirteenth and fourteenth centuries. The impact of the Golden Horde on Russian development will be dealt with presently. One key consequence, however, should be stressed here. The primacy of Kiev, already weakened by feuds among the princes, was ended with its destruction by the Mongols. Leadership passed from the open steppes to the more defensible northern woodlands, and finally to the palisaded river city of Moscow. And Moscow, far from a now rapidly declining Constantinople, oriented its policy toward the Baltic and Western Europe, rather than the Black Sea and Byzantium, in centuries to come.

Yet the Byzantine influence lingered on. The Russian Orthodox church continued in the Byzantine pattern: Monasteries owned huge tracts of land; the church supported the evolving monarchy (instead of feuding with it, as the popes did in Western Europe); and the people prayed devoutly before their ikons. The grand dukes—later czars—of Muscovy shaped their new nation on a hazily conceived model of Byzantine autocracy—with a dash of Mongol rigor. And when Constantinople fell to the Turks in 1453, the Moscow rulers took for their own state the title of "third Rome," the heir to both Byzantine civilization and the imperial tradition of the ancient Caesars.

## The Crusades: Rehearsal for Empire

Medieval Christian civilization was in general a more dynamic, expansive culture than is often realized. Its growth was by no means as spectacular as that of Islam—whose story will begin in the next chapter—yet Christendom also spread outward from its Mediter-

**THE HOLY LAND**

SULTANATE OF ROUM

BYZANTINE EMPIRE

SARACENS

Edessa
Antioch
Tripoli
Acre
Jerusalem
Alexandria

CYPRUS
CRETE

Tigris R.
Euphrates R.

BLACK SEA

Constantinople

MEDITERRANEAN SEA

Volta R.
Astrakhan

Moscow

R U S S I A

Novgorod

Kiev

Dnieper R.

Dniester R.

Danube R.

Vienna

Ratisbon

Odra R.

Elbe R.

Rhine R.

Lübeck
Danzig
Bremen

BALTIC SEA

SWEDES

NORTH SEA

ENGLAND
London

NORMANDY

FRANCE
Clermont-Ferrand
Loire R.
Vézelay
Lyons
Rhône R.
Toulouse
Marseilles

Bruges
Metz

HOLY ROMAN EMPIRE

Venice
Milan
Genoa
Pisa
Rome
ITALY
Naples

CORSICA
SARDINIA
SICILY
MALTA

Tunis
Ceuta

SARACENS

ATLANTIC OCEAN

IBERIA
Lisbon
Toledo
Granada

Zara

Normans from Normandy
Normans to Italy

Swedes convert the Finns, ca. 1150

Infidels defeated temporarily and the Latin States were created 1099-1244

**Conquests and Reconquests by Christendom**

| | Reconquest of Iberia from the Moors, 1000-1492 |
|---|---|
| 1029-1096 | Norman Conquest of South Italy and Sicily, 1042-1147 |
| 1097-1186 | Major routes of the Crusaders to the Holy Land, 1097-1250 |
| After 1200 | Teutonic Order, 1100-1250 |

0    50    100 Miles
0    50    100 Kilometers

ranean and Western European base during the Middle Ages. It constituted not a single state or a static region of cultural predominance but an expanding zone of culture.

Christianity had spread to the limits of the Roman Empire during its last centuries. When Rome fell, the Roman and the Byzantine churches continued to reach out for new souls to save, converting new waves of barbarians and reaching well beyond the Rhine-Danube line into areas the Romans had never penetrated. The new kingdoms that emerged in Europe also expanded, carrying developing medieval civilization with them. During the High Middle Ages, finally, international Christian Crusades marched on the Muslim lands of the eastern Mediterranean. Pious Christian missionaries and aggressive monarchs, land-hungry barons and peasants, Crusaders driven by piety or greed, and merchants seeking commercial footholds in the Levant—all contributed to the beginnings of a European expansion that would one day astonish the world.

The medieval European Crusades actually accomplished little in the way of territorial expansion. But they did set in motion a Western outreach that would in later centuries swell into the greatest wave of imperial conquest in history.

The beginnings were small enough. The First Crusade began in 1095, sending tens of thousands of Christian holy warriors swarming into the Near East to liberate from Islam the lands where Christ had lived. The movement was triggered by a plea from the Byzantine emperor for help against the Muslim Turks, and was encouraged by Pope Urban II's assurances that the liberation of the Holy Land from the infidels was a good work in God's eyes. Other important causes included such nonreligious factors as population pressures in Europe, the restless ambitions of European nobles, and the desire of Italian commercial cities to establish trading posts across the Mediterranean.

The First Crusaders did "liberate" Jerusalem, massacring most of its Jewish and Muslim population in the process. They then set up a series of Crusader States stretching along the eastern end of the Mediterranean from Gaza through Lebanon. European pilgrim traffic, Italian trading colonies, and a steady flow of men and money maintained this Western toehold in the Near East for two hundred years (though Jerusalem fell to the famous Muslim leader Saladin in less than a century). European taste for Asian spices and other luxury goods and Christian zeal for spreading the faith by force of arms were both whetted by the Crusades. The Western money economy of the High Middle Ages was stimulated by the expanded trade with the East, and Europeans learned to tax themselves and to organize large-scale overseas ventures while mounting these international military campaigns.

All the later Crusades were costly failures, however, and the movement dwindled to talk and minor skirmishes after 1250. It would be another two and a half centuries before Europeans would again reach out for spices and converts, land and booty, beyond the confines of their own end of Eurasia. But the dynamism, the organizing ability, the ruthlessness, courage, and greed of the West had been demonstrated in this first rehearsal for empire.

## THE END OF THE MIDDLE AGES

### God's Heavy Flail—or a Time of Change?

After the splendid achievements of the High Middle Ages in the twelfth and thirteenth centuries, the next century and a half looked to medieval people like "God's heavy flail," a terrible divine punishment. Disaster struck all major segments of society, decimated the population, plunged the economy into a long depression. It was, in many important ways the end of an era, and the modern age that emerged from its ashes would be a different world.

Yet in dealing with the end of the Middle Ages, as with its beginnings, recent scholarship has come to see this period as a time of transition rather than one of cataclysm. Between 1300 and 1500, important medieval institutions suffered massive setbacks, often accompanied by traumatic experiences for large segments of the population. Plagues, wars, popular rebellions, economic turmoil, and struggles between rival claimants to the papacy itself scarred the lives of generations of Europeans. But there was a revival too, a recovery from these disasters that was well under way by 1500, when the modern world was clearly emerging. What must have felt like divine punishment to many also stimulated a surge of creative restructuring that produced the modern age.

## Schism and War

The papacy fell into the deepest decline of its history during this period. The linked crises of the Babylonian Captivity and the Great Schism filled the century from 1305 to 1415.

The Babylonian Captivity—the name deriving from a fancied parallel with the Hebrews' ancient captivity in Babylon—was the Avignon papacy of the fourteenth century. During this period the popes, once so powerfully independent, fell under the influence of French kings, lived at Avignon in southern France, and became a byword in Christendom for extortionate greed. The Schism followed soon after. For several decades around 1400, there were two and even three claimants at a time to the throne of St. Peter, each excommunicating his rivals, and further degrading the Church in the eyes of bewildered and increasingly cynical Christians.

There were other disasters during this long season of Europe's discontent.

For more than a century England and France, the most successful of the medieval monarchies, mired themselves in the long agony of the Hundred Years War (1337–1453). The great early victories won by the English longbow—Crécy, Poitiers, Agincourt—go into every English schoolchild's notebook, as Joan of Arc's later heroism does on the French side of the Channel. In fact, the protracted conflict devastated France in the fourteenth century and drained England in the fifteenth. In the end, the English kings' efforts to retain control of large parts of the French kings' lands failed. The success of the longbow—which could pierce a knight's chain mail at a hundred yards—marked the beginning of the end of the baronial cavalry as masters of European battlefields. The marauding of mercenary companies and of rebellious peasants added to the havoc of this worst of medieval wars.

## Plague and Depression

In the middle of the fourteenth century, meanwhile, an even more terrible calamity befell Europe as a whole. It came with the shiny little fleas that infested a species of black ship rat brought up the Mediterranean from Byzantium or the Black Sea. It was the Black Death.

The Black Death was an excruciatingly painful, almost inevitably fatal, and extremely contagious disease, technically known as bubonic plague. After ravaging the cities of China and traveling west along the caravan routes, the plague struck Europe first in 1348 and ravaged its populations repeatedly for three centuries thereafter. During this first horrifying visitation at the end of the Middle Ages, the plague may have killed a quarter of Europe's people. The population growth of the preceding centuries ended with a crash.

Add to all these catastrophes the deep Europe-wide depression that began in the middle of the fourteenth century, in part as a result of the wars and the plague. The economic hard times shattered the boom of the high-medieval commercial revolution and plunged the European economy into turmoil for a hundred years.

Drastic reduction in the size of the population raised the cost of labor, cut production, and thus inflated the prices of the goods that were produced. Landowners suffered from the high cost of labor, consumers from rising prices. In response, landholders often turned from farming to less labor-intensive sheep raising, while governments at all levels tried to fix both wages and prices. Another expression of this conservative reaction was the organization of protective associations of cities like the German Hanseatic League, dedicated to defending their own economic interests in a shrunken economic arena.

There was a more positive response to the economic upheaval as well, however. The workers who survived the plagues and famines, for example, earned much higher wages than before; merchants profited from rising prices; and sheep raising proved quite lucrative for many landowners. Some alert entrepreneurs, furthermore, adapted to changing times with more flexible business organization and with real technological innovations. In mining, metallurgy, printing, and ship building, lost labor was replaced with labor-saving devices that made these industries considerably more efficient. A new economic order would thus take shape in early modern times. But the upheaval itself must have been enormously painful for most who experienced it.

## MEDIEVAL CHRISTIAN CULTURE

### The Daughter of God

The Christian religion was the pulsing heart of medieval European culture. And there is no better illustration of the power of religious belief in medieval life than the briefly glorious but tragic career of Jeanne d'Arc—Joan of Arc—one of the most amazing of medieval saints.

The familiar story can be retold in a couple of paragraphs. Born in a small village in northeastern France early in the fifteenth century, Saint Joan grew up illiterate and pious in the middle of the Hundred Years War. In 1429, at the age of seventeen, she began to hear the voices of angels telling her to go forth and save her country from the unending ravages of the wars. With the simplicity of total belief, she thereupon set off for the court of Charles VII, where she miraculously picked that unimpressive—and as yet uncrowned—monarch out of a crowd of his own courtiers. Even more astonishing, she then convinced the unhappy French king that she should be allowed to ride off with the troops currently gathering for a major confrontation with the English.

Inspired by the Maid, as she was universally called, the disheartened French rallied. Joan's soldiers lifted the siege of Orleans—a key French bastion—defeated the English repeatedly, and swept triumphantly through to Reims. There, in the heart of English-held territory, in July of 1429, Charles VII was at last formally crowned King of France in a traditional ceremony in Reims cathedral.

Thus anointed with holy oil by the Church, Charles could look forward to a new loyalty from his people, who everywhere began to flock to the king's support against the English. Joan deemed her mission accomplished and wanted to return home, but she was too potent a symbol to be let go. And not long after her triumph, she was captured, tried for witchcraft by a subservient ecclesiastical court, and burned at the stake in Rouen in 1431.

Joan of Arc's brief, meteoric career did not include time out to sit for portraits. This modern rendering, however, tries to give a sense of the youth, vigor, and naïve piety of this most beloved of medieval French saints. Can you imagine this Joan as an athlete today, or an officer in a modern army? (Powell Gulick/Bettmann)

Joan of Arc believed completely in her voices—Saint Catherine and the archangel Michael—and in the unheard-of task they called her to perform. In this, at least, she was completely typical of her time. The English called her "a disciple and limb of the Fiend"; she insisted that her voices called her a "daughter of God."[3] But no one in that far distant century questioned the reality of the supernatural presences that urged her on.

## Faith and Fanaticism

The mind of the Middle Ages was as thoroughly dominated by religion as were the minds of ancient Egyptians, Hindu Indians, or Europe's own Muslim neighbors.

The doctrines of the developed medieval church went far beyond the simple teachings of Jesus of Nazareth. Jesus's basic message remained central: Christ the Son of God still offered eternal life to those who believed. The Pauline virtues of faith in Christ, hope of salvation, and charity toward one's neighbor were still preached. But there was much more now.

Medieval priests catechized Christians on more elaborate creeds established by Church councils over the centuries. God was the Three-in-One—Father, Son, and Holy Ghost. There were seven deadly sins—pride, greed, envy, sexual self-indulgence, violence, laziness, and gluttony. Heaven, hell, and purgatory (a halfway house for purging away modest quantities of sin) were minutely anatomized, with all their angelic and demonic caretakers.

Religious duties were central to every human life. The seven sacraments brought religion into the lives of Christians at crucial points in the life cycle, sanctifying birth with

---

[3]Joseph R. Strayer and Dana C. Munro, *The Middle Ages: 395–1500* (New York: Appleton-Century-Crofts, 1959), p. 486.

baptism, coming-of-age with confirmation, marriage with matrimony, and death with extreme unction. The sacraments also provided penance and absolution for sins freely confessed, conferred spiritual powers on priests through ordination, and celebrated the communion of believers with their Savior in the central Christian mystery of the Mass.

But there was another side to the age of faith. There was the fanaticism that produced popular persecution of Jews, heretics, witches, and others believed to be in league with Satan. The Holy Office of the Inquisition, which was charged with maintaining the purity of Christian thought, used the most unscrupulous methods, including torture, to get confessions from those accused of heresy. Incorrigible enemies of Christ were turned over to the secular authorities to be burned alive in public marketplaces.

A faith founded on the love of God thus sponsored the cruel persecution of all who rejected its tenets. It was a feature of many creeds, past and yet to come, which claimed to offer universal truths to humankind.

## The Twelfth-Century Renaissance

It is evident that medieval religion was far from a simple matter. The Christian leaders of the High Middle Ages, in fact, devoted their most intense intellectual efforts to making sense out of their immense and complex religious heritage. And they produced one of the major intellectual triumphs of Western history: the scholastic synthesis of the Twelfth-Century Renaissance.

Dubbed a *renaissance*, or "rebirth," by historians after the more famous cultural revival of the fifteenth century, this medieval cultural flowering was actually a remarkably original synthesis. It took ancient materials—Greek philosophy and science, Roman law, and above all the revealed truths of the Judeo-Christian religious tradition—and wove them into something original and profound.

Paradoxically, this first recovery of Greco-Roman ideas came to Christian Europeans mostly by way of their archenemies, the Muslims. The culture of Islam had flowered several centuries before that of Christendom and had absorbed the wisdom of the restless Greek mind during the Muslim conquest of Byzantine territories in the Near East. Greek books had then traveled across North Africa to Muslim Spain at the other end of the Mediterranean. Here, in the flourishing cultural centers of Córdoba and Toledo, Christian scholars from Western Europe had come to study the pre-Christian philosophy of Aristotle at the feet of learned followers of the non-Christian Prophet Muhammad!

European scholars thus recovered the mathematics, astronomy, and medical ideas of the ancient Greeks and—from Byzantium directly—Justinian's Code of Roman law. Most important, they immersed themselves in the encyclopedic writings of Aristotle, "the master of those who know" in medieval times. From these varied sources St. Anselm drew arguments for the primacy of Christian faith, while Abelard raised probing questions that strengthened the structure of belief it subjected to challenge. The beloved St. Bernard condemned the immoralities of the times, and St. Thomas Aquinas summed up the knowledge of his age in a vast structure of Christian thought.

To study and spread this newly acquired knowledge, medieval scholars invented the Western university. Other cultures had developed their own centers of higher learning, from the informal Greek "schools" of philosophy to such religious institutions as the Buddhist school at Nolanda in India and the Sankore mosque in Timbuktu. In the twelfth and

# VOICES FROM THE PAST

Medieval students at the west's first universities were often no more enthusiastic about their studies than many modern students are. These "Goliard" ("sheep-stealer" or "vagabond") songs were written in Latin, the language of university instruction as it was of the church that provided it. They were the work of disreputable wandering scholars who hung around the emerging universities and were sung by real students in real taverns eight hundred years ago.

### Philosopher's Holiday

*Lay aside our studies,*
*It's well to be unwise,*
*Gather all the sweetness*
*Of youth as it flies;*
*Leave it to the old men*
*To ponder and advise. . . .*

*Swift age, it overtakes us*
*While study holds us down;*
*It's young blood that makes us*
*Frolic through the town. . . .*

*Live then like immortals!*
*Worthy is the aim:*
*To seek at love's portals*
*Heart's ease without blame.*
*Young likings are entrancing,*
*Why check them with a frown?*
*Outside the girls are dancing,*
*O hurry, hurry down!*

*The Goliard Poets: Medieval Songs and Satires,* trans. George F. Whicher (New York: New Directions, 1949), p. 177.

---

thirteenth centuries, similar associations of teachers and students, operating in rented halls or in churches, sprang up in many cities in Western Europe.

These medieval universities taught undergraduates rhetoric, law, and above all Aristotle's logic, while graduate faculties gave professional training in law, medicine, and the queen of the sciences, theology. For it was in theological speculation, explored with the help of Aristotelian logic, that medieval thinkers made their greatest contributions to the history of Western thought.

By applying Aristotelian rigor to their inherited Christian insights, these Christian theologians achieved a remarkable synthesis of faith and reason. Even more impressive, they produced a coherent view of the world that was rationally and emotionally acceptable—indeed inspiring—to the simplest peasant and the deepest doctor of theology. They anatomized in convincing detail a world made by God's fiat, guided by God's providence, yet comprehensible by human minds and deeply moving to the human heart.

Chartres Cathedral was one of the most beautiful of the hundreds of great churches built to the glory of Mary the Mother of God during the later medieval centuries. It is seen here as it must have looked then, towering above the cobbled streets and peaked roofs of a medieval town. The two towers flanking the portals in front, built at different times, are very different in design. (Bernard P. Wolff/Photo Researchers, Inc.)

## The Art of the Cathedrals

Between 1050 and 1350 no less than eighty cathedrals and hundreds of churches of comparable size and grandeur were built in France alone. They were not built by the people themselves, exalted mobs of true believers with kings and commoners pulling together on the ropes, as romantic historiography once believed. The cathedrals were raised over long, slow decades by master builders, skilled architects who called themselves masons and who hired the best medieval artists to make God's house a thing of beauty. These towering Christian temples, dedicated to the Virgin Mary, still constitute the finest expression we have of the religious spirit of the age of faith.

The image of Paris's Notre Dame leaps quickly to mind, of course. But it is well to remember that not all the great churches of the Middle Ages were gothic, like Notre Dame de Paris. There were many lovely romanesque cathedrals in the earlier medieval centuries, built with round instead of pointed arches, mural paintings instead of stained-glass windows. There were also Eastern Orthodox churches, from Constantinople to Kiev and Moscow, built with wide domes instead of spires, gold leaf and mosaic decorating their labyrinthine interiors. And there is as much beauty and spirituality in Constantinople's Church of the Holy Wisdom as there is in Paris's more familiar Church of Our Lady.

Nevertheless, the great gothic churches built in Western Europe in the High Middle Ages remain the most celebrated artistic achievements of the age. Rising hundreds of feet above the rooftops and the cobblestoned streets of the medieval city below, gothic cathedrals such as those of Paris or Chartres, Salisbury or Cologne (not completed until the nineteenth century) were marvels of architectural skill and daring.

Lofty verticality was the keynote of the gothic style. Pointed gothic arches, clustered pillars, and ribbed vaulting support a thin fabric of stone and glass many stories high. This immense height and the weight of the roof was supported by graceful external braces called flying buttresses. All of it, finally—towers and buttresses, inside and out—was thick with restless gothic decoration: statuary, carved wood, stained glass, finials and spires, kings, saints, and gargoyles. This too was a hallmark of the gothic—abhorence of empty space, so that every inch is filled with intricately interwoven shapes.

The other arts of the medieval period clustered about the churches. Stone figures flanking the deepset portals combine convincingly real faces with robes whose folds blend into the verticality of the surrounding pillars. Along the walls, high arched windows ablaze with stained glass trace scenes from the Bible or the lives of the saints. Under the seats in the choir, animals and humans, bunches of grapes and leering demons show what the art of the wood-carver could do. Even the great handmade Bible in the lectern was bright with illuminated capitals and glowing illustrations of events that happened long ago and far away in fairy-tale places with names such as Jerusalem and Bethlehem, Golgotha and Galilee.

## Medieval Literature: Roland's Horn, Dante's Hell, and the Canterbury Pilgrims

Most of the serious religious literature of the Middle Ages, in Western Europe at least, was written in Latin and thus inaccessible to most medieval people. But in the High and later Middle Ages, some impressive popular literature began to appear in the vernaculars—the living languages of modern Europe. Most of this writing was in verse, and the religious element was often powerfully present (two strikes against it for many modern readers). Nevertheless, there is a life to the work of Chaucer or Dante or the unknown author(s) of *The Song of Roland* that is hard to find in the staider, more respectable writing of the time.

*The Song of Roland* is one of many French "songs of deeds," long epic war poems sung in the halls of medieval barons, much as Homeric bards sang of the deeds of Greek and Trojan heroes to the warlords of an earlier age. It is the story of the heroic death of Roland, one of Charlemagne's mythic paladins, the French equivalent of King Arthur's knights of the round table. Almost to the last moment the chivalrous Roland, though surrounded by enemies, refuses to blow his great horn Olifant, whose high clear note would bring Charlemagne and the French host galloping to the rescue. When Roland's horn is blown at last, it summons the Christian cavalry only to bury their dead—and guarantee chivalric immortality for Roland and his horn.

With the Italian poet Dante Alighieri, we follow the medieval spirit to the other side of death, into the Christian other-worlds beyond the grave. Dante's *Divine Comedy,* an epic poem on the afterlife, traces the poet's imaginary descent into hell, the inferno at the center of the earth, up the steep slopes of purgatory on the other side of the world, and on beyond the stars into the radiance of paradise. It is a journey thick with history and symbol, told in musical Italian verse. Yet it is Dante's inferno, that "nation of the lost," that has always fascinated modern readers.[4] It is a lurid vision of living souls wrapped in agony, punctuated with vivid flashbacks to the world above and the sins that have doomed these men and women to their eternal torment. Even in our calloused age, this plunge into the nightmare geography of the pit, the deepest netherworld of the medieval imagination, is not to be undertaken lightly.

But there was a world above, birdsong and spring flowers glittering with dew along the road to Canterbury—the world of the English poet Geoffrey Chaucer's *Canterbury Tales.* Among the company that assemble at the Tabard Inn in the London suburb of Southwark for the short spring pilgrimage to the cathedral at Canterbury are representatives of all walks of medieval life. The merchant, the friar, and the Oxford university stu-

---

[4]Dante Alighieri, *The Divine Comedy,* trans. Thomas G. Bergin (New York: Appleton-Century-Crofts, 1955), p. 8.

dent, the nun and the much-married wife of Bath, the earthy miller and the "gentle, perfect knight" all have their characteristic tales to tell to help pass the journey. The wit, variety, and high good humor of the whole remind us finally that there was more in the medieval mind than crusades and hellfire. There were bawdy tales, high ideals, and busy worldly lives to be led, even in the shadow of cathedral spires.

## SUMMARY

The European Dark Age that followed immediately upon the Fall of Rome was admittedly a hard time of political and social disintegration, poverty, and violence. To deal with waves of invasion, Europeans developed the feudal system, a loose structure of political power based on military service in return for land. To survive after the collapse of Western trade, Europeans evolved the manor system of subsistence agriculture. Rude empires even emerged from time to time, the most famous being the Carolingian Empire of Charlemagne, who was crowned on Christmas Day, 800.

During the High Middle Ages—the eleventh, twelfth, and thirteenth centuries—European society and culture experienced a brilliant revival. Thanks in large part to the reemergence of trade by land and sea, great cities appeared in Europe once more. Kings, by imposing their will on the feudal barons, began the building of modern nation-states in France, England, Spain, and elsewhere. And the Roman Catholic church, led by powerful popes and fueled by the passionate belief of many medieval people, became the most impressive single institution in Western Christendom.

In East Europe and on the fringes of the Middle East, both autocratic imperial government and Greek Orthodox Christianity were centered in Constantinople. This strongly centralized Byzantine Empire spread Christianity and civilization in East Europe, provided economic stimulation, and survived for a thousand years, from the fifth to the fifteenth century. Muscovy, the core of the future Russian state, emerged at the end of the Middle Ages, modeling its political and religious institutions on those of fallen Byzantium.

The Crusades of the High Middle Ages represented Europe's first rehearsal for the great overseas imperial expansion of modern times. But in the fourteenth and fifteenth centuries, medieval society collapsed in a welter of economic disaster, plague, wars, and religious schism.

At its peak, however, medieval Christendom was an impressive cultural achievement in its own right. Built on a mixture of ardent faith and sometimes savage fanaticism, the culture of the Middle Ages was as intensely religious as any the world has seen. The Twelfth-Century Renaissance provided rigorous intellectual underpinnings for medieval Christianity in the scholastic philosophy of Thomas Aquinas. The great church builders of the age raised cathedral spires over hundreds of European cities. The poetry of Dante, Chaucer, and other medieval writers reflected a culture in which this world and the Christian "other world" met and mingled in the minds of western people.

## SUGGESTED READING

Allmand, C. *The Hundred Years War: England and France at War, ca. 1300–ca. 1450.* New York: Cambridge University Press, 1988. Concise topical treatment, including a clear and brief summary of the military campaigns.

Bartlett, R. *The Making of Europe: Conquest, Colonization, and Cultural Change 950–1350.* Princeton: Princeton University Press, 1993. Impressive social and cultural overview of the High Middle Ages.

Cohen, M. R. *Under Crescent and Cross: The Jews in the Middle Ages.* Princeton: Princeton University Press, 1994. Student-oriented survey.

Cowdrey, H. E. J. *Pope Gregory VII: 1073–1085.* New York: Clarendon Press, 1998. Stresses the inspirational role of Pope Gregory in the growth of papal power.

Duby, G. *A History of Private Life,* Vol. 2: *Revelation of the Medieval World.* trans. A. Goldhammer. Cambridge, Mass.: Belknap Press, 1988. Social and cultural aspects of the private lives of French and Italian people, lavishly illustrated.

Duggan, A. J., ed. *Queens and Queenship in Medieval Europe.* Rochester, N.Y.: Boydell, 1997. Papers tending to see women's political power as rooted in family connections. But see studies in T. Evergates, ed., *Aristocratic Women in Medieval France* (Philadelphia: University of Pennsylvania Press, 1999), stressing independent power of these women in the High Middle Ages.

Fletcher, R. *The Barbarian Conversion: From Paganism to Christianity.* New York: Holt, 1998. Medieval Christianization of Europe, emphasizing the causes and process of conversion.

France, J. *Victory in the East: A Military History of the First Crusade.* New York: Cambridge University Press, 1994. Sees disorganized early Crusader forces evolving into an effective fighting force. See also his *Western Warfare in the Age of the Crusades 1000–1300* (Ithaca: Cornell University Press, 1999), on all aspects, from recruitment and logistics to castle design and combat tactics, and P. Partner, *God of Battles: Holy Wars of Christianity and Islam* (Princeton: Princeton University Press, 1998), which sees crusading as a key feature of both religious communities.

Franklin, S., and J. Shepard. *The Emergence of Rus 750–1200.* New York: Longman, 1996. Broader socioeconomic interpretation of Russian origins.

Freedman, P. *Images of the Medieval Peasant.* Stanford: Stanford University Press, 1999. Social theory and social reality of life among European peasantry.

Le Goff, J. *The Medieval Imagination,* trans. A. Goldhammer. Chicago: University of Chicago Press, 1988. Challenging probe of the medieval mind through analysis of changing words and conflicting intellectual structures.

Menuge, N. D., ed. *Medieval Women and the Law.* Rochester, N.Y.: Boydell and Brewer, 2000. Essays on ways in which medieval law defined women's place—and ways women used the law for their own purposes.

Treadgold, W. *A History of the Byzantine State and Society.* Stanford: Stanford University Press, 1997. Sweeping narrative treatment of the history of the medieval Eastern Christian empire.

Wright, N. *Knights and Peasants: The Hundred Years War in the French Countryside.* Rochester, N.Y.: Boydell, 1996. Grim evocation of the ways in which chivalric idealism failed to prevent the ravaging of the French countryside.

 Please refer to the document CD-ROM for primary sources related to this chapter.

# CHAPTER 10

# DOMES AND MINARETS
## The Spread of Islam
## (600–1300)

## A Glance Ahead: A New Religion Reaches across the Old World

South and east of medieval Christian Europe, a second great world religion emerged during this age of expanding cultural zones: Islam, the faith of the Prophet Muhammad. Islam would be the last religion with truly global reach. During this period, the Islamic faith would in fact spread much farther than Christianity did.

Born of the visions of the trader Muhammad in the Arabian city of Mecca, the Muslim faith was spread far and wide by the Prophet's successors. Hard-riding true believers burst out of Arabia in a holy war that carried Islam—and Arab rule—up into the Middle East, west across North Africa, and even into southern Europe. And wherever the Islamic faith spread, so did Islamic law and flourishing Islamic trade routes, shared beliefs, and forms of worship.

By the fifteenth century, the Islamic cultural zone thus loomed as a massive rival to the Christian zone. And Islam was on the eve of a new golden age of its own as the modern period began in Europe.

## The Prophet

### Muhammad, the Messenger of God

Muhammad the Messenger of God (570–632) lived six centuries after Jesus Christ, twelve centuries after Gautama Buddha. He became the prophet of Islam, the last of the great world religions to emerge in history thus far.

Muhammad was born in Mecca, an oasis city on the caravan routes of western Arabia about forty miles from the Red Sea. It was a busy town, full of merchants, handicraft artisans, and pilgrims. The caravans came and went, carrying silks and spices, frankincense, and other luxury products to and from Damascus, Byzantium, Basra. But Mecca was also a

The Shah-i-Zinda, a burial place for Muslim saints and rulers outside Samarkand. Built on the site of the old city, it has been a focus for pilgrimage and worship since the Muslim conquest. (Anthony Esler)

religious center. Its central temple, the odd cubical structure called the Kaaba, contained a mysterious black stone that God—*Allah* in Arabic—was believed to have cast down from heaven, as well as idols dedicated to a number of other gods, to *jinn* and desert demons.

Beyond Mecca, with its gardens and bustling markets, the sea of sand began: shifting sand hills, dry *wadis,* and the desolate crags of the Najd, the Exhausted Land. Here roamed restless tribes of bedouin—the desert Arabs, herding their flocks, conducting their blood feuds, swooping down on hapless caravans.

It was a world not much changed from Jesus's time, or the time of the Hebrew prophets. It was about to produce a third great religion, and one integrally related to Judaism and Christianity. Muhammad never claimed to be the first Prophet—only the last.

Muhammad, the son of Abdullah, son of Abdul Muttalib, of the tribe of Qureysh, was orphaned early in life and had to make his own way in the marketplaces of Mecca. He probably traveled with the caravans, perhaps as far as Palestine, and picked up the rudiments of the religions of Moses and Jesus there. At twenty-five he married a wealthy and intelligent woman fifteen years older than himself, who gave him a modest place among the Meccan merchants, to whom he was known as *Al Amin,* the Trustworthy. According to Islamic tradition, he was a husky man with a black beard and fair skin, a hooked nose and black, luminous eyes. An upright, sometimes melancholy man, he was given to long silences.

At the age of forty, meditating in a cave outside the town, he had his first vision. "Read!" a voice thundered. "I cannot read," replied Muhammad, who was apparently illiterate. "Read!" the voice intoned twice more. And then, beyond the cave mouth, the Arab saw standing in the sky an angelic figure who spoke once more: "O Muhammad! Thou art Allah's Messenger, and I am Gabriel."[1] The "reading" of the divine message to the world ("recitation" or even "speaking forth" are perhaps better renderings of the original Arabic) occupied Muhammad for the rest of his life and was preserved for the Islamic world in the verses of the Quran (Koran). For countless millions of Muslims, the visions of Muhammad would constitute God's final Message to humankind.

He was at first a prophet without honor in his own country, ridiculed and dismissed as mad or possessed. Some of the poor listened to his revelations, and his wife, Khadijah, stood staunchly behind her husband. He also won the support of a wealthy merchant named Abu Bakr, and Omar, a leading citizen of Mecca. A persecutor of Muhammad in the early days, Omar was to become his most effective successor as leader of Arabic Islam.

## The *Hijrah* and the Return

For the time being, however, his enemies prevailed. In 622 Muhammad left Mecca, taking his prophecies north to the oasis city known today as Medina. He was then a man in his fifties, and the black beard must have been at least flecked with gray.

The *Hijrah,* as the move from Mecca to Medina is called, was a great success. At Medina, Muhammad won many converts to his doctrines of *Islam,* "submission" to the will of Allah as it had been revealed to him. He preached an end to idolatry, monotheistic worship of Allah, prayer five times a day, fasting from dawn to dusk through the month of Ramadan, paradise for the faithful, and hellfire for the wicked. He recognized Moses and Jesus as earlier prophets and seems to have expected Jews and Christians to accept him as

---

[1] Mohammed Marmaduke Pickthall, *The Meaning of the Glorious Koran* (New York: New American Library, 1953), p. x.

God's Messenger too. When the Jews of Medina refused to do so, he exercised his new-found ascendancy by expelling them from the city.

There were external enemies of the new faith to deal with as well. Whereas Jesus's three-year ministry was strewn with miracles, Muhammad's career was punctuated with battles. The aging merchant turned holy man personally led some two dozen campaigns during his last ten years. His struggles with his most obdurate foes, the Meccans, climaxed in 630 with his victorious return to his birthplace. There the Prophet cleansed the Kaaba of its idols, prayed before the Black Stone, and forgave his enemies.

He died two years later, the founder of a new religion whose phenomenal spread over the coming centuries would perhaps have awed even Muhammad, the Trustworthy, the Prophet, the Messenger of God.

## The Social Message of the Prophet

Like other prophets before him, Muhammad also had a social message for his followers. Like Confucius and the Buddha, like the Hebrew prophets and Christian preachers, the Prophet of Islam urged believers to seek the path of virtue in this world.

Poverty Muhammad saw as a great social evil. To improve the economic lot of Muslims, he urged such reforms as charitable alms-giving and the sharing of inheritances rather than conferring all on the first-born son. In at least one place, he condemned the unearned profit that comes from interest on loans, saying that all income should be earned by honest toil. Some Muslim communities, like some medieval Christian theologians, therefore tried to exclude banking as we know it from economic life.

On the condition of women, Muhammad also urged significant changes. In a society where women were often treated like property, where the birth of a daughter was widely regarded as a disaster, and where female infanticide was not uncommon, the Prophet's teachings substantially improved women's lot. Muslim women, he declared, were to share rights with men, to enjoy a portion of any inheritance, to be married only with their consent, and to be able to initiate divorce proceedings if the marriage failed.

Muhammad also supported the right of a man to as many as four wives if he could support them. And he did encourage the harem system, confining wives and children to the private sphere of the home. These changes, however, could be regarded as a considerable improvement in a world where women had often been treated with promiscuous contempt in times past.

Muhammad also sought to end the curse of blood feuds among Arabs and to improve treatment of slaves. He showed his openness to all peoples by taking Hagar, a black African woman, as his second wife. He even urged more humane conduct of the inevitably brutal business of warfare. Both he and his successors would have plenty of experience of this widespread social practice.

## The Islamic World

The force unleashed by the Arab prophet dreaming in the marketplace in Mecca was to have a genuinely seismic impact on history. Yet this militant faith, spreading over substantial portions of all three continents of the Old World, was less focused and considerably more complex than some of those we have examined thus far.

We are not dealing here with a single empire, a territorial polity like ancient Egypt or the Roman Empire. Islam was a living, growing organism, dividing into separate and sometimes antagonistic states, spreading ever farther across Eurasia and beyond. Its extent became in time so vast that it is quite unlikely that the Muslim kings of Sokoto in West Africa, for instance, were even aware of the existence of the Islamic coastal states of Borneo. Yet there are fundamental historical patterns to be detected in this vast intercontinental sprawl that we call Islam.

Islam was above all a religious community, bound together in the first instance by the Holy Quran, the "reading" that Gabriel had enjoined upon Muhammad and that Allah had inspired in his Messenger. This volume of sacred verses, read and memorized in Arabic all across the Muslim world, served as a powerful cultural cement. So did the Muslim Law, a detailed body of religious strictures and traditions professed by holy men sitting in dusty market squares from Spain to Samarkand. Paradoxically, finally, the religious unity of Islam was actually strengthened by the sectarian upheavals that swept through it from time to time. Initially divisive, such challenges to orthodoxy as the mystic Sufi movement or the Sunni–Shiite split—to be examined in a later section—stirred new fervor in the faithful and sometimes, as in the case of the Sufis, contributed significantly to the further expansion of Islam.

Submission to Allah was thus a religious submission first of all. But Islam was also a human dominion, and its bearers, while a diverse lot, fitted a pattern nonetheless. Typically, the ruling peoples of the Muslim world began their rise to predominance as rude converts—hard-fighting, comparatively barbarous warriors of Allah. They ended as cultivated Oriental princes, more worldly and more sophisticated than the founder of their

## MUSLIM EXPANSION TO 750

faith had ever been. The Arabs first, then Turks, Mongols, Africans, and others followed this historic cycle, rejuvenating Islam and reaching out for new converts and new dominions each in turn.

Islam is, finally, a variegated and brilliant civilization, a pattern of culture as distinctive in its way as those of China or the Greco-Roman Mediterranean. Mosque and minaret and the Arabic script of the Quran flourished all across this broad swath of Africa, Europe, and Asia. Men of Muslim beliefs and ways of life traded on all the caravan routes across Eurasia and rode the monsoon winds across the Indian Ocean. Their rulers lived cultivated court lives in Damascus or Baghdad, Córdoba or Constantinople, Samarkand or Timbuktu.

A complex entity, Islam was thus not only a religion but also a succession of political hegemonies and a variety of linked cultures. For a thousand years, from the seventh century to the seventeenth, Muslim power reached out, winning converts from the Russian steppes to the African savannas, thrusting into Christian Europe, conquering most of Hindu India, and reshaping the lives of millions of human beings. But there was order beneath the tumult. Islam bound all its millions to a religion, a civilization, and a pattern of history.

## THE HOLY WAR

### Jihad: The Holy Struggle

When Muhammad died, he had left his mark upon most of the oasis towns and primitive bedouin of northern Arabia. In the centuries that followed the Prophet's death in 632, his followers were to seize with the sword an area larger than the Roman Empire, all in the name of Allah and his Messenger. A survey of Arab Islamic expansion during the first few centuries after Muhammad will give us some idea of the realm with which we will be dealing in subsequent pages and chapters, and of the general pattern of Islamic expansion across the Old World.

The ragged bedouin from the Exhausted Land of Arabia were a proud, tough people, but they had little of this world's goods. They wore clothing and lived in tents made of the hides of their beasts, milked and slaughtered them for food, and warmed themselves around small fires of dried camel dung under the brilliant stars. The simple pressure of overpopulation in their arid land has often been seen as a spur that drove the Arabs on to conquest of other lands.

A key concept from the new religion of Muhammad, however, also contributed significantly to the great wave of Arab conquests of the seventh and eighth centuries. This was the complex Islamic concept of *jihad*, or religious struggle.

The term is often presented as the Muslim equivalent of the Christian crusade, or religious war. In fact, both terms have had wider applications down the centuries, and *jihad* was a more complicated idea from the beginning. It refers to sacred struggle on more than one level. On the individual or personal level, *jihad* is the intense spiritual effort of the believer to live by his or her Islamic beliefs. It is the inner struggle to be worthy of salvation. On the larger, communal level, however, *jihad* has traditionally meant "holy war," struggle to defend or expand the realm where the Prophet is honored, his teachings available to guide people—as Muslims believe—on the path that leads to salvation.

Historically, the religion of Muhammad had been a crusading faith from the beginning. Struggle against ungodly forces, both within themselves and in the outside world, early became a central Islamic duty. And the communal form of *jihad*—holy war against the unbeliever—became the most important form of struggle. It was in a sense a deal the Arabs couldn't refuse. If they won, they came home laden with more booty than any caravan raid provided. If they died in the attempt, they would come home to Paradise: "What though ye be slain or die," the glorious Quran declared, "when unto Allah ye are gathered?" (*The Quran*, III, 158).

## The Arab Conquests

When the Prophet died in 632, his old companion Abu Bakr was hailed as *caliph* ("successor") in the cities of Arabia. Some of the desert sheiks resisted, but Abu Bakr brought them around, sometimes by force, before he died, two years after Muhammad.

Omar, the Prophet's earlier persecutor and first official patron, became the second caliph. A man of vision and organizing skill and the best general among the Muslims, Omar fused the desert tribes into an army and turned their first tentative probes into the great *jihad.*

The Arabs were not vastly numerous or well equipped. But by sticking to the barren wilderness they knew, and to their camel cavalry and hit-and-run tactics, they proved quite effective. Their fierce traditional pride and their new faith gave a sharp edge to their swords. As with true believers in other times and lands, their strength would sometimes seem the strength of ten because their hearts were, if not purer than other men's, at least more passionate.

The neighboring lands turned out to be plums ripe for the plucking. The Persian and Byzantine empires northeast and northwest of Arabia were old and worn out with fighting each other. The Berbers of North Africa, otherwise much like their Arab assailants, had no *jihad* to unify them. And once the holy war was well begun, the warriors of Allah developed a momentum that would take some stopping, even by more formidable rivals.

Under Omar (634–644), the ragtag army took the provinces of Syria and Palestine from the Byzantine Empire, occupied most of Sassanid Persia, and conquered Egypt. Under the Umayyad dynasty that followed, despite internal divisions and civil strife, the Arabs swept on westward across North Africa, crossed the Straits of Gibraltar, overwhelmed the Visigothic kingdom in Spain, and swarmed over the Pyrenees into western France. There they were finally stopped by a Frankish army under Charles Martel at the Battle of Poitiers (Tours) in 732. In the eastern Mediterranean, meanwhile, Arab warriors had built themselves ships, destroyed the fleet of the Byzantines, and mounted a massive siege of Constantinople. Here again they met with a substantial check, and in 718 they abandoned the assault on the impregnable walls of the Byzantine capital.

But these reverses at Constantinople and Poitiers did not stop the far-ranging soldiers of the Prophet. In the early eighth century, roving bands were already pushing northeast into the Caucasus and Central Asia and east beyond Persia into the valley of the Indus.

## The Long Reach of Islam

The scale of the Islamic zone a century after the Prophet's death was truly amazing. On a map of Muslim lands in the early 700s C.E., you can see a cultural zone that combines most of the Mediterranean core of the former Roman Empire with the Middle eastern sweep of the Persian Empire. Western Asia, North Africa, and significant portions of southern Europe had been overrun in a couple of lifetimes.

During this period, furthermore, the cultural zones on either side of Islam—Europe and the Indian subcontinent—were fragmented. Only Tang China, at the far end of Eurasia, could match the scale of the Islamic achievement. And only the first stage of Muslim expansion was ended. Indeed, the Arab conquest had laid the foundation for a predominance that would fill the center of Eurasia with Islamic power by the beginning of the modern period.

The victorious Arabs tended to be less fanatical then Christian legend long believed. Christians and Jews in particular, as followers of earlier prophets in Muhammad's line, were usually allowed the freedom of their religion, though they paid a special tax for the privilege. Persians and Byzantines, with their long experience of government, were soon managing conquered territories for the victorious but administratively unsophisticated Arabs.

Yet the legend of that first eruption out of Arabia lived on—above all, perhaps, for their most persistent enemies, the Christian peoples still sunk in the depths of the early Middle Ages on the other side of the Mediterranean. Muhammad became Mahound, the Devil himself, to medieval Christians, and "Lord, save us from the Saracens" their most fervent prayer.

## THE ARAB EMPIRE

### The Caliphs: Successors to the Prophet

The Arab Empire founded by Omar would flourish for some three centuries. Thereafter Islam would march on under other banners than those of its Arab founders. But the development of the two Arab caliphates, the Umayyads (661–750) and the Abbasids (750–1258), was typical of much that was to come.

Under Muhammad's early successors—the "rightly guided" caliphs who immediately followed him and the Umayyad dynasty thereafter—Arabs came to rule vast tracts of the Near East, North Africa, and parts of southern Europe. In attempting to govern their new conquests, they found that their ancient desert heritage of tribal life and their new power in the world interacted to produce unforeseen social and economic problems and some sanguinary political history. However, the Arab Empire also fashioned an integrated society and a brilliant flowering of Islamic culture. These aspects of their history deserve as much attention as the dazzling conquests that carried the Arabs with such rapidity to the mastery of their substantial corner of the globe.

The problems began at the heart of Islam, with the religious leadership of the faithful, which was vested from the beginning in the caliphs.

The institution of the caliphate was intended to be at least partially theocratic. The *caliphs,* as successors to the Prophet, were initially the religious as well as the political heads of Islam, as Muhammad had been. In Islamic thinking there was no difference between these two spheres of activity, secular and ecclesiastical, sacred and profane. As the caliphs became more worldly and luxury-loving, however, their spiritual leadership was harder and harder to reconcile with the style of life their political ascendancy brought them. Under these circumstances they allowed their spiritual authority to pass largely into the hands of the *ulama*—the experts on the life and teachings of the Prophet, the shapers and masters of the Muslim Law. While retaining their nominal headship of the faithful in religious matters, the caliphs thus became concerned more and more exclusively with politics.

Abu Bakr, the first caliph, was chosen by the acclaim of the believers, at least in the Arabian cities. After the first four caliphs, however, the dynastic principle came into play. During both of the two main Arab caliphates, family succession determined the leadership of Islam. The dynastic succession was punctuated, however, by some of the bloodiest high politics since third-century Rome.

## The Umayyads

Of the four "rightly guided" caliphs, only Abu Bakr died peacefully in bed. Omar was assassinated in 644; so was his successor, in 656; and so was the next in line, Muhammad's son-in-law Ali, in 661. Nor did the establishment of the Umayyad clan that year put an end to fratricide among the Arab rulers. There was civil strife again in the last decades of the seventh century, and the Umayyad dynasty expired finally in a massacre that all but wiped out their house.

The sources of this sanguinary political history lay in a number of unresolved problems that plagued the Umayyads throughout that first century of Islam. There was the traditional bedouin penchant for clan vendettas that a century of common victories did not abolish. There was the inevitable tendency of recently conquered peoples to revolt, producing recurring civil wars in the Arab Empire. And there was the appearance of the sectarian spirit within the body of the Muslim faithful as early as the death of Ali, whose dissident Shiite followers constitute to this day a sometimes violent minority in the Islamic world.

We have already noticed the emergence of new interpretations and doctrines—often declared heretical by mainstream believers—in Hinduism, Buddhism, and Christianity. Among Muslims, the Shiites remain the largest dissident faction today.

Shiites were originally "the party of Ali," militant supporters of the third of the Rightly Guided Caliphs who followed Muhammad. Personally a man of great piety, Ali was also married to the prophet's daughter Fatima and—Shiites believed—Muhammad's chosen successor. His assassination in 661 should in their view have brought one of Ali's own sons to the caliphate. When the Umayyad dynasty succeeded instead, Shiites refused to recognize the political or religious authority of these new leaders. Over the centuries, the ten or fifteen percent of Muslims who still comprise the party of Ali have developed distinctive religious beliefs and have been bitterly persecuted. The Islamic world, like Christendom, had its fanatics in this age of the temple builders.

## A Changing Style of Life

Other transformations, less violent but more far-reaching, were also going on beneath the surface of victorious conquest and self-destructive civil conflict that characterized the rule of the Umayyads.

In the first place, there were transformations in the conquered peoples. The Arabs did not give much attention to conversion of unbelievers during the early years. They collected taxes and tribute regularly, making effective use of the existing Persian or Byzantine bureaucratic structures for these purposes, and otherwise asking—and offering—little more. Before the end of the Umayyad century, however, this policy began to change. The defeated peoples, impressed with the theology and military success of Islam, slowly began to seek conversion to the religion of the victors. This process was no doubt encouraged by the fact that by converting to Islam non-Muslims escaped the taxes levied on infidels. At the same time, the Arabs began to fraternize more with the natives, so that the Arabic language came into increasingly common use all across the Muslim world. The spread of Arabic was also hastened by the spread of the faith, since the Quran could be read and prayers addressed properly to Allah only in the language in which he had spoken to the Prophet.

The spread of the Islamic religion and the Arabic language provided the basis for a slow but extensive change in the peoples the Arabs had overwhelmed during the century after the Prophet's death. It was a process that would continue under later dynasties and other regimes, imposing a far-reaching cultural unity on the Islamic world.

Changes also came about in the Arab conquerors themselves during this early period. Once they had abandoned their isolated garrisons and mingled with the peoples they ruled, Arabs everywhere gradually became part of the indigenous ruling classes. Some of them turned into wealthy landowners, adopted the luxurious lifestyles of their former enemies, and increasingly left the fighting to new, non-Arab converts to Islam. Arab viceroys and governors built themselves palaces and even whole new cities, where they lived in opulence, cut off from the people they ruled. The Umayyad caliphs transferred the capital of Islam from its old center of Mecca to the rich city of Damascus, where a more imperial style of life might be lived more easily. In their new capital, they created a court to rival the most luxurious of earlier Near Eastern emperors.

By the end of its first century, then, the Arab Empire had produced a style of life very different from the desert wandering of Muhammad's day. Under the Abbasid dynasty, which seized the caliphate in 750, Arab rule was to reach its apogee of grandeur. It was also to undergo one final metamorphosis before slipping slowly and lingeringly out of the pages of history.

## The Abbasids

The founder of the new dynasty was a powerful and ruthless man named Abu al-Abbas. He had himself proclaimed the true caliph in Persia in 749 and marched at once on Damascus. With him marched the disaffected of the Arab Empire. There were, as always, poor men hoping to better their lot under the new regime. There were Shiites who, believing that only blood ties with Muhammad could confer legitimacy on a caliph, were duly impressed by Abu al-Abbas's assertion of kinship with the Prophet. There was, finally, a group with a powerful future in Islam: the new, non-Arab converts to the faith who had been relegated to second-class status among the faithful.

The new dynasty would not make poor men rich, nor would it turn the Shiite heresy into orthodoxy. But over the two centuries of their actual supremacy—and the five centuries of their nominal rule—the Abbasids would preside over a complete transformation of the ruling class of Islam. The Arab conquerors would merge with the ancient aristocracy of Persia, and with Turks and even Mongols, vigorous new converts from the nomadic northern steppes.

With this support from the disaffected, Abu al-Abbas seized Damascus in 750. He invited all the princes of the defeated Umayyad clan to a conciliatory banquet—and sent the executioners in. Afterwards, according to legend, the victorious Abbasids enjoyed the meal themselves.

Among the Abbasids there were names more famous than that of the founder. The most celebrated was the legendary Harun al-Rashid, the wealthy, sophisticated caliph immortalized in *The Arabian Nights,* who ruled in the decades around 800. The most beneficent was perhaps his cultivated son, Mamun the Great. There were still fighters among them too—the pleasure-loving Harun fought many military campaigns. But the political history of the dynasty during its first two centuries—the period of its real power—was dominated by three new trends: centralization, secession, and the gradual decline of Arab supremacy at the center of the web.

Some sort of centralization of government power was clearly necessary if the Abbasids were to rule so vast a realm at all. By the time of Abu al-Abbas, the Arabs nominally governed territories that stretched from Spain to Afghanistan. Building on Umayyad beginnings and drawing as their predecessors had on the long experience of the Persians in particular, the Abbasid dynasty constructed an elaborate system of administration.

Persian influence became crucially important to the emerging Arab Empire. Persian aristocrats converted to Islam and continued to form an important part of Baghdad's Islamic elite. Besides staffing the emerging administration of the Arab Empire, Persians also helped reorganize a guerrilla Arab army into a more tightly structured military machine.

Baghdad, the new Abbasid capital, thus became the center of an impressive bureaucratic structure. At its head, just beneath the caliph himself, stood the grand vizier (chief counselor), a position that might also have become hereditary if Harun al-Rashid had not shrewdly decided to root out the family that had come to dominate the office in his reign. Beneath the vizier, the will of the caliph was to be carried out by provincial governors all across the empire. Governorships did become hereditary, and the central authority did not always reach effectively into distant provinces dominated by local dynasties. Yet there was a structure of authority, which in the person of the *qadi,* the judge and authority on Muslim law in almost every town and city, reached even to the local level. It was a governmental system far superior to that of contemporary Europe, then struggling out of the earliest Middle Ages into the uncertain light of the Carolingian Renaissance.

A structure of power thus grew up under the Abbasids. But not all the caliph's far-flung realms accepted his authority. Secession also spread, fragmenting the western portions of the empire in particular. Only one of the Umayyad princes escaped Abu's executioners in 750; five years later he founded an independent Umayyad caliphate in Spain. Other secessionist regimes established themselves across North Africa: in Morocco in 788, in Tunis in 800, and the Fatimid dynasty, which traced its lineage back to Muhammad's daughter Fatima, in Egypt in 868. A separatist movement even succeeded in eastern Persia in 820. All these remained part of the great body of Islamic religion, civilization, and commerce, but politically they were lost to the Arab government in Baghdad.

An even more dangerous threat to the Arab predominance, finally, was nourished within the empire itself. As the descendants of the Arab conquerors settled into splendor in Baghdad, other peoples came to the fore. Persian power predominated increasingly in council and among the cadres of lesser officials. At the same time, a new wave of hardy nomads infiltrated the empire from the Eurasian steppes. Among them the Seljuk and Ottoman Turks and the Mongols were to be the most important for the future of Islam.

The Turks infiltrated the frontier cities first, often coming as mercenary soldiers. Sometimes whole tribes of them accepted conversion. By the middle of the ninth century, less than a hundred years after the Abbasids had seized power, Turkish guards were providing the caliph with the heart of his standing army. They proved their value as willing repressers of disorders among the native peoples of the caliphate. In time they became as powerful in Arab affairs as the Praetorian Guard had been in Rome.

The Persians, however, were the first to profit from the decline of Arab vitality and power. In 946 a Persian general unmade one caliph and made another a puppet, content to live in Persia and rule as his masters willed. The Abbasids would reign in name only for three more centuries, till 1258. But Persians and Turks dominated the empire in the east, and secessionist regimes still flourished in the west. Abbasid splendor was not diminished, but Abbasid power was a shadow of what the Arabs had once wielded. The peoples of the northern steppe soon replaced the people of the southern desert as the masters and builders of Islam.

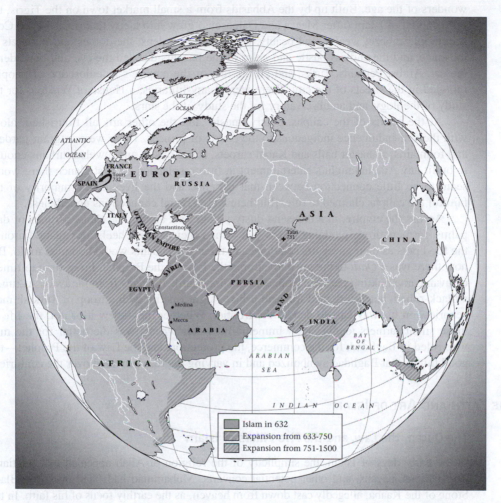

ARCTIC
OCEAN

ATLANTIC
OCEAN

FRANCE
Tours
732
SPAIN
EUROPE
RUSSIA
ITALY
Constantinople
OTTOMAN EMPIRE
SYRIA
EGYPT
Medina
Mecca
ARABIA
AFRICA
ARABIAN
SEA
ASIA
Talas
751
CHINA
PERSIA
SIND
INDIA
BAY
OF
BENGAL
INDIAN   OCEAN

Islam in 632
Expansion from 633-750
Expansion from 751-1500

## The Splendors of Baghdad

Through all the conflicts and transformations outlined above, the Arab Empire in general and the Abbasid caliphate in particular did much to advance the welfare of their subjects. The Arab peace fostered agriculture in Egypt and Persia, in Muslim Sicily and Spain. Most important, the spread of a common culture across a wide swath of the Old World encouraged trade, by caravan and swift Arab dhow, from Spain to India.

A common language and religion, a Muslim law code based on the life of the merchant and the caravan town all encourage commercial development. And commerce in turn contributed to the development of handicraft industry; Damascus steel, Córdoba leather, and silks and cottons from the East were all internationally known. The tales of *The Arabian Nights* include mouthwatering descriptions of Baghdad bazaars heaped with good things, from Syrian apples and Arabian peaches to perfumes and incense, aloewood, musk, and candles of Alexandria wax.

Baghdad itself—"City of Peace, Gift of God, Paradise on Earth"—was one of the wonders of the age. Built up by the Abbasids from a small market town on the Tigris, the third capital of Islam (after Mecca and Damascus) grew into a city that rivaled even Constantinople in size, wealth, and beauty. Palaces and gardens, the domes and minarets of mosques, and the endless bustle and color of the bazaars dazzled the eye and bewildered the ear. Arabs, Persians, Turks, and all the rest of the empire's kaleidoscope of peoples mingled in the streets of the city. There were many libraries, a House of Wisdom for the study of theology, and an observatory for the study of the stars.

At the courts of the caliphs, poetry, music, and the other arts all flourished, along with the self-indulgence indigenous to the courts of princes. There were fragrant gardens and fountains, alabaster halls and Kabul carpets, robes of silk and jeweled turbans enough to outfit any Arabian night's entertainment in fitting splendor. At first glance there would seem to be little connection between that paradise and the lives of the majority of the faithful the caliphs claimed to rule. But there were crucial connections nonetheless.

Across the empire, in a thousand dusty villages set among the slender trunks of date palms, farmers drove plodding beasts that turned their water wheels, or squatted around the food pots as their ancestors had done and their descendants would continue to do. But now there was a *Qadi* in the town to enforce the Law of the Prophet. From time to time a caravan came tinkling past and stopped to display unlikely wares from far away. At times, a black-robed, black-turbaned Abbasid prince might ride by with a troop of Turkish mercenaries, on his way east to defend the frontier. Whether they knew it or not, the life of those silent farmers tending their immemorial water wheels was the better for the men who ruled in Baghdad, for the commerce, the protection, and the Law of the Prophet—the good things that Baghdad symbolized and in varying degrees provided over the centuries.

## THE FAITH AND ART OF ISLAM

### The Quran, the Law, and the Five Pillars of Islam

In the early days of Islam, the simplicity of the religion of Allah appealed to Christians, Zoroastrians, pagans, and other potential converts. Muhammad had fixed upon the Black Stone of the Kaaba, allegedly cast down from heaven, as the earthly focus of his faith. In the beginning any enclosed area with a clearly designated side facing Mecca seems to have done for a mosque. Beyond that there was only the Book, the Law, and the worship they enjoined.

The Quran, the sacred book of Islam, was spoken aloud by Muhammad in oracular, poetic verse in a series of revelations over a period of more than twenty years. These prophecies and injunctions, taken down by disciples, were assembled within a few years of the Prophet's death into a book about the size of the Christian New Testament. Its 114 *suras,* or chapters, are composed in Arabic poetry so moving that Muslims regard this alone as evidence of its divine origin. Small boys memorize its thousands of verses entire, and grown men weep when it is chanted in the mosque.

The faith whose essence is Submission (*Islam*) to the will of God (Allah) begins with a *sura* often described as the Lord's Prayer of Islam:

In the name of Allah, the Beneficent, the Merciful.
Praise be to Allah, Lord of the Worlds,
The Beneficent, the Merciful.

Owner of the Day of Judgment,
Thee (alone) we worship; Thee (alone) we ask
for help. (*The Quran*, I, 1–5)

The briefest summary of the faith, offered daily in the mosque, goes simply: "There is no God but Allah, and Muhammad is his prophet."

The most obvious differences between Islam and the Christian tradition lies in the part played by Muhammad himself in the Islamic revelation. The Muslim Prophet claimed no divinity, performed no miracles save the one great miracle of bringing God's will to humanity. The Quran was thus believed to embody God's final revelation, and to be superior to any other holy book.

But the Quran was the beginning, not the end, of the development of the Islamic faith. Theology came to Islam a century after Muhammad's death. Muslims argued like theologians of other religions over such abstruse points as predestination, major and minor sins, the role of reason in expounding the faith. But it was in the Muslim Law that the theological genius of Islam was expressed most strikingly.

The Islamic Law is an attempt to bring the Islamic faith to bear on every aspect of the life of the believer. The Arab compilers of the Law sought to explicate God's will toward people in such detail that the faithful need never be in doubt about how a good Muslim ought to act in any situation. Experts in the Law—the *qadis*—sat in the market squares of all Muslim towns, adjudicating civil disputes and ruling in criminal cases on the basis of their detailed knowledge of the words of the Prophet and the traditions of his faith.

The compilation of Islamic Law was a monumental effort undertaken in the earlier Muslim centuries by the *ulama,* the body of Muslim scholars. These learned men drew upon four sources of divine truth: the Quran, the traditions, consensus, and analogy.

The Quran itself stood first in authority, of course. When the Quran provided no clear direction, the *ulama* turned to the *hadith,* the traditional accounts of the Prophet's deeds and opinions expressed outside the Quran. The scholarly study of these traditions occupied generations of Islamic scholarship.

Where neither the *hadith* nor the Quran offered sufficient insight, the Law was based on the consensus of the Islamic community, on the theory that God would not allow the faithful to be in error about any important matter down the centuries. Finally, where all else failed, the makers of the Islamic Law undertook to reason by analogy; if the Prophet forbade wine, for instance, this prohibition might be extended to other intoxicants as well.

The result was an immense body of *Sunna,* or traditional requirements and prohibitions concerning religion, personal morality, social conduct, and political behavior. Business and marital relations, criminal law, ritual practices, and much more were covered in this vast system. Even where central government broke down, Islamic Law provided an effective framework for living for peoples all across the Islamic world.

Besides the Quran and the Law, lifelong routines of worship welded Islam into a cultural unity. From the earliest centuries the Islamic faith had five essential practices, the Five Pillars of Islam: witnessing to one's belief that there is no God but God, and Muhammad is his Prophet; praying in the mosque five times each day; alms-giving and other forms of charity for the less fortunate; fasting from dawn to dusk during the holy month of Ramadan; and pilgrimage, particularly the great pilgrimage to Mecca that every Muslim dreams of making at least once in a lifetime.

The Book, the Law, and the life of Islam thus blended to produce one of the most successful of all the major religions of humankind. But like all religions, the Muslim faith had its divisions and revisions. And these too are part of the story of the intercontinental reach of Islam.

### Shiites and Sufis

Sectarian divisions broke out early in Islamic history. Theology, history, and the mystical impulses to which all religions are liable all helped to divide the faith of the Prophet.

The most historically important sectarian outbreaks, however, were rooted in the political realities of the early Muslim centuries. The most long-lived and devastating of these Muslim religious schisms was the Shiite revolt, which began in the first century after

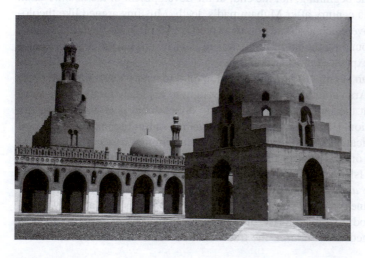

The ninth-century mosque of Ibn Tulun in Cairo shows the open Abbasid form, with minarets and an arcade around the central court. Like the cathedral shown in the preceding chapter and the temples in the next chapter, this thousand-year-old mosque is still in use today. (Carolyn Brown/Photo Researchers, Inc.)

Muhammad's death and has persisted to the present. It began with the murder of the fourth caliph, Ali, son-in-law to the Prophet, and the accession of the Umayyad dynasty. The Shiites were those Muslims who objected to the Umayyad succession on the grounds that only descendants of Ali and Muhammad's daughter Fatima—Ali's wife—could be legitimate successors to the Prophet. In time the Shiites became opponents of the whole orthodox, traditional approach taken by the Sunni majority. Habituated to martyrdom at the hands of the orthodox, Shiite Muslims remain today a powerful movement, particularly in that part of ancient Persia that is now Iran.

The most successful new direction in the Islamic religion, however, was the Sufi movement. The Sufis were Muslim mystics, seekers after Islamic truth through direct spiritual experience. Like Buddhist or Christian monks, Sufis reacted to the increasing worldliness of the caliphate by stressing self-denial. They saw asceticism as the beginning of the arduous road to mystical union with Allah.

They began their preaching in the seventh century, the first century of Islam. For some time the oddness and immediacy of Sufi religious experience brought them into conflict with the keepers of the Book and the Law. One of the most famous of all Sufi seekers, al-Hallaj, was crucified in the tenth century for asserting, "I am the Absolute Truth."[2] In time, however, Sufism found its place and became an immense influence in Islam. By the twelfth century there were orders of Sufis all across the Muslim world, each with its revered masters and saints, its diverse practices and doctrines, its own version of the mystic way to union with Allah.

These ceremonies included chanting, rhythmic motion, and sometimes the singing of Sufi poems to musical accompaniment. In a murky atmosphere of incense and ritual, prayers, incantations, and invocations of angelic beings, these Sufi performance could bring the adept into a state of religious exaltation.

The Sufis were among the most effective propagators of the faith to unbelievers. Their direct, emotional approach could touch the hearts of potential converts. Later would come Arabic and the Quran, the *qadi* and the Law. But simple faith, a call to the heart, ecstasies and trances were a quicker way to win new converts to the teachings of a Prophet who had himself been summoned to his task by angelic voices.

## Islamic Art: Mosques and Minarets

In the Arab Empire, as wherever the faith of the Prophet spread, religious experience and theological prescriptions profoundly influenced the practice of the arts. The most obvious example of this influence is the Muslim ban on the depiction of the human figure in art. This prohibition, honored particularly in the broad spectrum of religious art, all but abolished sculpture and severely limited the figurative element in painting. This rejection of the representational also contributed to the highly abstract nature of Islamic design. Muslim art thus stressed geometric shapes, arabesque curvilinear patterns abstracted from floral designs, and religious maxims in angular or flowing Arabic scripts used as decorative motifs.

The overwhelming influence of religion also made itself felt in more positive ways. Like the cathedral in medieval Christendom, the mosque became the most characteristic artistic achievement of the Muslim peoples, and architecture generally their central art.

---

[2]Annemarie Schimmel, *Mystical Dimensions of Islam* (Chapel Hill: University of North Carolina Press, 1975), p. 72.

A muezzin calls the faithful to prayer from the minaret that is part of every mosque complex. A recorded call has replaced the muezzin in many modern mosques, but the call still goes out five times every day. (Photographer: Omnia, Getty Images, Inc.)

The mosque was the center of any Arab town. Its essential features as a place of worship include a large court with a fountain for ceremonial ablutions; a prayer hall with a wall facing Mecca; a decorated niche in that wall providing a focus for the devotions of the faithful; and a pulpit near this niche for readings from the Quran and for sermons. The most readily recognizable element, however, is the tall, often slender tower called a minaret, from which the faithful are called to prayer five times daily.

This simple pattern of court and hall, with inner and outer adjuncts, proved capable of immense elaboration. Typical Arab extrapolations included the addition of an impressive facade flanked by towering minarets, roofed galleries around the courtyard, and forests of pillars in the prayer hall itself. The Great Mosque of Córdoba, built by the Umayyad caliphs of Spain, and the Fatimid Mosque of El-Hakim in Cairo follow this elaborated model.

Other characteristic types of Muslim architecture include the *madrasah,* or Muslim seminary, the mausoleums of sultans and saints, bazaars, and royal palaces. Of the few palaces that survive, the late medieval Alhambra with its famous Lion Court, located in the Spanish city of Granada, is by far the best known. The immense "desert castles," such as that of Ukhaydir in the sea of sand south of Baghdad, give us only the roughest idea of what Abbasid Baghdad itself must have been like in its glory.

Muslims were masters of all the decorative arts—ceramics and tiles, metalwork and textiles, calligraphy, the art of miniature, and many more. A gilded and illuminated copy of the Quran is a thing of beauty to set beside any medieval Christian Bible. But nowhere did the decorative artistry of the Muslim peoples stand out more clearly than in their efforts to express "the experience of the infinite" in the Muslim house of prayer, the mosques that are the glory of Islam.

### Arab Literature: Poems and Tales

The mosque is a luminous artistic achievement accessible in some degree, at least, even to the non-Muslim. The same cannot be said for the literature and thought of Islam. Poetry, fiction, history and biography, philosophy, and the sciences all seem to date more rapidly than the direct formal statements of architectural design and decorative motif. Between the modern Western reader and the words and ideas of the medieval Arab Empire lies a gap as great in time as that which separates us from our own Middle Ages—and an even greater cultural divide. Nevertheless, a glimpse must be attempted, particularly into Arab literature, which is one of the great literatures of the world.

Arabic literature began as verse, the oral poetry of the desert Arabs. Arab bards celebrated the greatness of their clans and the perfidy of their enemies; they described the harsh beauty of their desert world and the joys of fighting and fast riding. By the time Muhammad came, Arabic poetry was a highly developed art, and it was the poetic language of the desert Arabs that the Prophet used in speaking the revelations of the Quran.

Arab experience of the world changed drastically after Muhammad, however, and in the centuries that followed, both the subjects and the forms of Arabic literature expanded dramatically. Wine songs, love songs, and poems of a markedly mystical tone replaced the older verses devoted to horses and camels and the pride of the clan. Verse forms became more complex still, and poets reached for more ingenious metaphors, more complicated tropes and figures than before. From the celebration of a hard ride over the desert, they moved to al Masudi's famous ode to the banquet table or Ibn Hazm's frequently erotic *Ring of the Dove:*

> Her body was a jasmine rare,
> Her perfume sweet as amber scent
> Her face a pearl beyond compare,
> Her all, pure light's embodiment. . . .[3]

Arabic prose was as varied and ingenious as Arabic poetry. This was the golden age of the professional Arab storyteller, whose repertoire of popular romantic tales was often arranged in cycles like that of *The Arabian Nights.* Collections of brief anecdotes were also popular, ranging in content from the most pious to downright bawdy tales. Styles varied from the easy flow of the teller of tales to the most elaborate rhetorical devices. The Arabs appreciated a flow of literary eloquence, whether it was the simple tale of the desert bard or the ornate literary construct of a court poet.

## Philosophy and Science: Knowledge Lights the Way to Heaven

More substantial genres flourished during the centuries of Arab greatness. Biographies of Muhammad and of Muslim saints and scholars, histories of the caliphs and their wars, of the great cities of the Islamic world—Mecca, Damascus, Baghdad—and general accounts of the history of the Arabs and the civilization of Islam all appeared from the eighth century on. Travel books and geographies surveyed the Mediterranean world and took readers as far afield as central Europe and East Asia. Collections and encyclopedias multiplied on the bookshelves of Arabic scholars.

In all this array of learning, Arabic philosophy and science were perhaps the fields known and admired the most widely.

Arab philosophy, like medieval European theology, drew upon translations of the works of ancient Greek thinkers. Aristotle, Plato, and the Neoplatonists were all still readily available in the Greek-speaking Byzantine region when the Arabs swept in. Much of

---

[3]Ibn Hazm, *The Ring of the Dove,* in A. J. Arberry, *Aspects of Islamic Civilization* (Ann Arbor: University of Michigan Press, 1967), p. 186.

the Arabs' own philosophizing, therefore, took the form of commentaries on the ancients. Avicenna's vast encyclopedias of philosophic knowledge and Averroes's commentaries on Aristotle, both monuments to Arab scholarship, were clearly rooted in the thinking of the ancient Greeks.

Arab philosophers of the ninth and tenth centuries, however, embarked upon some daring speculative paths of their own. Muslim philosophers meditate more boldly than medieval Christian thinkers on such matters as the creation and nature of the universe, divine providence, and even the relative value of rational philosophy and revealed religion as roads to an understanding of the world. From the end of the eleventh century on, however, such speculations came under fire from religious fundamentalists, and philosophical originality and daring declined in the Arab world thereafter.

The sciences bloomed among the Arabs as they had nowhere else in the western half of Eurasia since Hellenistic times. Arab scientists excelled particularly in astronomy and mathematics, where they made important contributions to algebra and trigonometry. They added significantly to the world's store of knowledge in optics, pharmacology, and other branches of natural science. Arab alchemy and astrology—recognized sciences everywhere in those days—were considered authoritative in Europe. The reputation of Arab medical expertise was so high in the West that Christian kings preferred Saracen physicians to Christian doctors.

"Knowledge," the Prophet had said, "enables its possessor to distinguish what is forbidden from what is not; it lights the way to Heaven."[4] It led at least some of its devotees to other sources than the revelations of the Arab merchant of Mecca. During the Arab golden age, however, the faith of Muhammad and the ideas of ancient Greeks and Hindu Indians were able to coexist within Islam, a striking testimony to the flexibility of this world religion.

## SUMMARY

The first half-dozen centuries after the coming of the Prophet Muhammad—the period of the Arab predominance in the Muslim world—was one of the great ages of Islamic history.

Muhammad preached his gospel in Arabia in the seventh century of the Christian calendar—the first century of the Muslim one. Muhammad's inspiration turned a rabble of desert bedouin and a scattering of oasis traders into an Arab army embarked upon a holy war. This first great *jihad* carried Muslim power across North Africa, up into Europe, and back across the Middle East in less than a century.

The Arab Empire that resulted was ruled by two successive dynasties of caliphs ("successors to the Prophet"), the Umayyads (661–750) and the Abbasids (750–1258). From the seventh through the tenth century, this first Muslim empire brought a degree of political order, real commercial prosperity, and unparalleled spiritual unity to this broad central swath of the Old World. Baghdad was one of the world's great metropolises, and even humble villagers benefited from Islamic Law and Arab protection.

The history of the Arab Empire after 1000 saw a decline in its material strength. Western provinces from Egypt to Spain seceded. In the east, Persians and Turks became

---

[4]Syed Ameer Ali, *The Spirit of Islam* (London: Chatto & Windus, 1964), p. 360.

the real political powers under the later Abbasids. The rise of medieval Christian power raised the possibility of a serious challenge to Islam in western Eurasia. The faith of the Prophet, however, continued to generate one of the greatest of world cultures.

Islam, built on the Quran, Islamic tradition, and the Islamic Law, provided a framework for living throughout the Arab domains. Sects of Sufi mystics offered a more emotional expression of Islam and were particularly effective as missionaries for the faith.

Muslim art produced beautiful mosques, while Arab scholarship explored and expanded Islamic theology as well as Greek philosophy and science. Arab literature, building on a poetry that predated the Prophet and was incarnated in the verse of the Quran itself, found expression in a glittering spectrum of sophisticated poetry and prose.

The cultivated and worldly court of Harun al-Rashid in ninth-century Baghdad was a far cry from the marketplace at Mecca where Muhammad had preached. But Islam, like medieval Christendom, remained a profoundly religious hegemony.

## SUGGESTED READING

Armstrong, K. *Muhammad: A Biography of the Prophet.* San Francisco: Harper, 1992. Useful account of a life too unfamiliar in the West. See also W. E. Phipps, *Muhammad and Jesus: A Comparison of the Prophets and Their Teachings* (New York: Continuum, 1996).

Bonner M. *Aristocratic Violence and Holy War: Studies in the Jihad and the Arab-Byzantine Frontier.* New Haven, Conn.: American Oriental Society, 1996. Political and theoretical forces within the Islamic world forge the concept of holy war.

Crone, P., and M. Hinds. *God's Caliph: Religious Authority in the First Centuries of Islam.* New York: Cambridge University Press, 1986. Challenges the view that the caliphs early abandoned their religious role in Islam for purely political functions.

Dunn, R. E. *The Adventures of Ibn Battuta: A Muslim Traveler of the Fourteenth Century.* Berkeley and Los Angeles: University of California Press, 1986. Scholarly, thoroughly readable account of the life and voyages of the great Muslim traveler.

Ettinghausen, R. *Islamic Art and Architecture, 650–1250.* New Haven: Yale University Press, 2001. New edition of a valuable survey. See also R. Hillenbrand, *Islamic Architecture: Form, Function, and Meaning* (New York: Columbia University Press, 1994), in which Islamic architecture is described, particularly in terms of religious function.

Ghazzali, A. H. M. *The Alchemy of Happiness,* trans. C. Field. New York: Sharpe, 1991. Eleventh-century Arab summary of Islamic values, with emphasis on the Sufi way.

Grube, Ernest J. *The World of Islam.* New York: McGraw-Hill, n.d. Clearly written, very well-illustrated coverage of Islamic arts and architecture by region and period.

Gutas, D. *Greek Thought, Arabic Culture: The Graeco-Arabic Translation Movement in Baghdad and Early Abbasid Society.* London and New York: Routledge, 1998. The rescue of ancient Greek thought by medieval Arab scholars.

Guthrie, S. *Arab Social Life in the Middle Ages.* London: Saqi Books, 1995. Brief, broad, and scholarly.

Hawting, G. R. *The First Dynasty of Islam: The Umayyad Caliphate A.D. 661–750.* London: Routledge, 2000. Brief introduction to the caliphs who succeeded the Prophet's own contemporaries and relatives.

Hill, D. R. *Studies in Medieval Islamic Technology.* Brookfield, Vt.: Ashgate, 1998. A grabbag of studies, including many on Arabs and early machinery.

Hodgson, M. G. S. *The Venture of Islam: Conscience and History in a World Civilization* (3 vols.), Chicago: University of Chicago Press, 1974. An impressive interpretive study of Islamic history, beliefs, and values.

Keddie, N. R., and B. Baron, eds. *Women in Middle Eastern History.* New Haven, Conn.: Yale University Press, 1991. Scholarly papers on Muslim women in various times and places, including the Arab Empire.

Kennedy, H. *The Armies of the Caliphs: Military and Society in the Early Islamic State.* London and New York: Routledge, 2001. Part of a valuable series on warfare and history, a subject too often neglected by historians.

Lassner, J. *The Shaping of Abbasid Rule.* Princeton, N.J.: Princeton University Press, 1980. Scholarly recent account of the Baghdad caliphate.

Mernissi, F. *The Veil and the Male Elite: A Feminist Interpretation of Women's Rights in Islam.* Reading, Mass.: Addison Wesley, 1991. A less positive interpretation than many of the status of women in Islamic societies. But see also Mernissi's *The Forgotten Queens of Islam* (Minneapolis: University of Minnesota Press, 1993), which sees women playing an important part in the politics of the Islamic world.

Peters, F. E. *Allah's Commonwealth: A History of Islam in the Near East A.D. 600–1100.* New York: Simon and Schuster, 1973. A good overview of the subject.

Rahman, F. *Islam.* 2nd ed. Chicago: University of Chicago Press, 1979. Excellent concise summary of Islamic ideas and institutions: a good place to begin.

 Please refer to the document CD-ROM for primary sources related to this chapter.

# CHAPTER 11

# MERCHANTS AND MISSIONARIES OF THE INDIES

## India and Southeast Asia

## (600–1500)

## A Glance Ahead: India's Domination of Southern Asia

Like Christian Europe and the Islamic zone, "India" was a culturally defined region rather than a single country during this period of its history. The Gupta Empire had crumbled, and the Mughal Empire would not reunify India until after 1500. The many Indian states, however, shared a religious culture based on Hinduism, Buddhism, or, toward the end of this period, Islam. Much of India also accepted the ancient caste system, rule by hereditary rajas, and roads and harbors full of energetic traders.

Indian merchants and missionaries had already spread this culture to South Asian neighbors from the Himalayas to Ceylon. Now they moved on to the next great southward bulge of land to the east—the enormous peninsula and thousands of islands we call Southeast Asia today.

You can still find Hindu temples, Buddhist monasteries, and countless Muslim mosques across that zone today. And much of the money that paid for these pious works came from the network of regional trade developed by Indian merchants in this age of expanding cultural zones.

## India Between the Guptas and the Mughals

### Attempts at Unity: Harsha and the Delhi Sultanate

The political history of India for much of the thousand years between the decline of Gupta rule in the fifth century and the coming of the Mughal dynasty not long after 1500 is a tangle of short-lived states, foreign invasions, and power struggles leading nowhere. Some of the peoples of this millennium, such as the chivalric Rajput princes in the north and the ambitious Cholas in the south, left a mark on India's history. There were also two significant attempts at national conquest: the empire of King Harsha and the Turkish regime called the Delhi Sultanate. But none of these matched the political achievements of the Mauryas and Guptas before them or the Mughal Empire to come.

The seventh-century reign of King Harsha (607–647) saw a brief futile attempt to impose order on the peoples and kingdoms of the subcontinent. The cultured warrior King Harsha conquered all of northern India from the Himalayas to the river Narmada, the traditional divide between northern India and the Deccan. Between campaigns, he—like Charlemagne two centuries later—patronized religion and the arts and gave lavishly to the poor. Considerably more literate than the great Frankish king, Harsha may actually have written the plays and poems that are attributed to him.

He moved his capital from Patna, the traditional center of political unification since the Mauryas, to the city of Kanauj farther up the Ganges valley. But—again like Charlemagne—he controlled his north Indian empire primarily by moving about it at the head of his army. The empire itself was probably no more than a loose collection of kingdoms and principalities, and most Indians could have been little affected by the transitory power at Kanauj. With Harsha's death, his empire crumbled and political division reasserted itself.

The second significant effort to impose order on the subcontinent was the work of foreigners—the Turkish Afghan regime known as the Delhi Sultanate, which dominated much of northern India from the thirteenth into the sixteenth century. It was an impressive span of years, but the size of the realm the newcomers ruled varied drastically from reign to reign. For a few years in the fourteenth century, Sultan Jalal ud-din Khalji held at least feudal suzerainty over most of the kingdoms of the south as well as northern India. But this was exceptional, and during the fifteenth and early sixteenth centuries the Turkish sultans really governed little beyond the immediate environs of the city of Delhi itself.

They did make this city, still farther up the Ganges, into the third political center of northern India—and New Delhi is the nation's capital today. But the Delhi sultans had only a rudimentary system of administration, and their rule was essentially feudal. Provincial governors were really soldiers granted control of villages or larger territories in return for military service. These local rulers governed only as far as their troops could reach. Again, most Indians had little significant contact with those who claimed to govern them.

## Challenge from the South: The Cholas

More effective governance may have emerged in southern India, the home of several Tamil-speaking Dravidian kingdoms in this period. The kingdom of the Cholas in particular apparently had a more centralized administrative system based on unions of villages. It

## THE DELHI SULTANATE AND ITS NEIGHBORS

also produced powerful rulers like Rajaraja I (985–1014) and Rajendra I (1014–1042). Great conquerors as well as effective governors, these men extended Chola rule both north and south, from Bengal to Ceylon. For a time it seemed possible that the Cholas would reverse the historic pattern by conquering northern India from a southern base. More striking still in this age of expanding zones of power, Rajendra I dispatched fleets east across the Bay of Bengal to impose temporary Chola rule in parts of Burma, Malaya, and the country-sized island of Sumatra.

Chola dominance in the south lasted the better part of three centuries before its thirteenth-century decline and fall. And despite effective individual rulers and administrative skills, village autonomy remained great. Its major achievements, as we will see, were once again economic and cultural.

### Invasions and Divisions

Besides political disunity, another disturbing feature of the history of those centuries of disarray was the unending series of invasions from without and power struggles within the subcontinent.

Among the foreign invaders who took advantage of India's weakness to push down through the passes of the Northwest Frontier were the White Huns who undermined the Guptas, the Arabs, the Rajputs who became India's military aristocracy, the Muslim Turks who established the Delhi Sultanate, Tamerlane and his Tatars, and finally the Muslim Mughals who reunified India at last in the sixteenth century. This succession of nomadic invasions made things lively along the frontier. Most of them, however, made scarcely a ripple on the steady flow of Indian life that went on as it always had beneath the marching of armies and the feuding of princes.

When there were no new hordes swarming down the Afghan passes, there was still princely feuding to contend with. Two major power struggles within the subcontinent should at least be mentioned here.

In the north, during the centuries following the brief meteoric passage of Harsha, three separate kingdoms struggled to dominate his short-lived empire. There was no decisive outcome but only the gradual decline and fragmentation of the contenders.

### Rajputs and Dravidians

But there was order to the Indian experience, even during these disordered centuries. Beneath the aimlessness of politics, profound social and cultural changes were taking place. Many of these changes represent continuations of earlier trends. But they reached a climax of sorts during the millennium of political disarray between the Guptas and the Mughals.

The greatest social transformation, a continuation of a much older tradition, was the absorption of new peoples into the already complex fabric of Indian society. This was basically the result of creative compromise by Hindu India's brahman elite, who found room in the ancient caste system for the newcomers. Thus, when nomadic invaders such as the Rajputs actually settled in India, their leaders would be accepted as *kshatriyas* (the ancient Aryan warrior caste), less prominent tribesmen as *sudras* (farmers), and even their priests as brahmans of a sort. Like Mongols in China or Germans in the Roman world, these steppe peoples were typically seduced by life in the host culture's rich cities and princely courts and were glad to be part of it. As caste allegiances grew among the new peoples, old loyalties to tribe and clan decreased, until the newcomers were thoroughly assimilated into the polyglot Indian population.

The patterned movement of Shiva Nataraja, Lord of the Dance, symbolizes the pulsing cosmic energy of the universe. This famous figure of the multiarmed god, grinding the demon of ignorance underfoot as he dances the universe into being, is a product of the Dravidian Hindu imagination of southern India. The god holds an hourglass-shaped drum in one of his four hands, fire in another, symbols of his power to awaken the natural world to life and to destroy it at the end of a cosmic cycle. ("Shiva Nataraja" 13th-Century Scultpure-Bronze-Indian, 34.25 × 27.5 × 13 inches [87 × 69.9 × 33 cm]). (The Nelson–Atkins Museum of Art, Kansas City, Missouri (Purchase: Nelson Trust 34-7. Photo by Robert Newcombie)

The fiercely proud Rajputs—"Sons of Kings"—in particular provided ruling houses for many north and central Indian kingdoms. They fought chivalric wars with one another, provided the strongest military force India could muster against subsequent invaders, and still compose an important part of the Indian army's officer corps today. As *kshatriyas,* their warlike proclivities were thus channeled into the service of the ancient Indian society that had absorbed them.

A similar process of assimilation went on in south India. The great triangle of peninsular India had been the haven of the Dravidian peoples driven south by the conquering Aryans many centuries before. Dravidians, particularly the Tamil-speaking people of the far south, had built a flourishing city-based society on foreign trade and agriculture during the preceding half-dozen centuries. The absorption of the Dravidian south into a single cultural zone with northern India, however, dates from approximately the year 500.

Again, the vehicle was the spread of Hinduism and the caste system. The worship of the great Hindu divinities Vishnu and Shiva grew in the south, and Sanskrit began to challenge Tamil as the literary language. Above all, a modified caste system—almost excluding the warrior *kshatriyas* but containing many "untouchable" groups—was gradually imposed upon Dravidian society.

Henceforth, the Indian subcontinent would constitute a single zone of culture, though there would continue to be significant regional differences. The north would remain politically dominant; the south would be a center of artistic and intellectual development.

### Caste and Sex

Another important change during this period—again a continuation of an older trend—was the rigidification of the caste system. The number of castes continued to grow far beyond the four original divisions generated at the time of the Aryan-Dravidian synthesis. Categories and subcategories multiplied, and the obligations imposed by membership in a given caste grew more elaborate—and more rigorous. Respect for caste grew especially as Buddhism—which had ignored caste distinctions—declined in India. And new recruits, among northern tribesmen or in the Dravidian south, took up the system with the fervor of converts.

There was still some freedom of choice in occupation, and marriages across caste lines could occur, if perhaps uncommonly. But the direction of development toward a caste-bound society was clearly established during these centuries before 1500.

The freedom of women in society, which would come to be curtailed more rigorously in India than in many other places, was considerably less constrained during this millennium. The strict seclusion of respectable women was not common yet. And the cruel practice of self-immolation by widows was still rare; some widows even remarried without losing popular respect. Ladies of the upper classes seem generally to have been educated and cultured during this period. They enjoyed music and dancing and shared freely in the pleasures of life at the courts of the *rajas*.

## A FERMENT OF RELIGIONS

### Land of Many Faiths

Religion, as we have seen, is one of the great perennials of world history. It would be extremely difficult to find a people in most times and places who did not believe in higher powers and seek supernatural support. Political authority has repeatedly claimed divine sanction, calculating merchants have frequently prayed or consulted their astrologers before setting sail, and both sides in wars have traditionally claimed that God was on their side.

The role of religion in India's long history, however, seems to loom particularly large. Certainly the rich variety of India's religious heritage continued to flourish in this period.

A thousand years ago, while Christians and Muslims burned and crucified famous heretics across their zones of the Old World, there were in the sprawling subcontinent of India separate but generally tolerant communities of Hindus, Buddhists, Jains, animists, Parsis, Muslims, and even some Christians and Jews. But the religious history of the centuries between 500 and 1500 is really concerned with only three of these religions. It is the story of a continued Hindu flowering, of the virtual disappearance of Buddhism in the land of its birth, and of the coming of Islam to India in force.

### Hindu Mysticism

Hinduism, as we have seen, played a large part in the assimilation of new peoples into the mainstream of Indian life. In so doing, the Vedic tradition and the dominance of the brahmans were increasingly identified with that Indian mainstream. The brahmans also consecrated new generations of monarchs, conferring the status of *devaraja,* "god-king," and suitably divine ancestors on princes all over India. In the process, the status of the brahmans rose still further, till they were commonly accorded the same sort of spiritual standing and powers that Christian priests enjoyed in Europe. Waves of new converts, royal patrons, and the increasingly exalted spiritual status of the brahmans all helped to advance the cause of India's oldest religion.

Main trends in Hinduism during this period included a variety of mystical paths to salvation. The most important of these mystical schools of religious thought, called Vedanta, was the work of a brahman named Sankaracharya. Seeking to purge traditional Vedic thought of its tangled and sometimes obscure theology, the prophet of Vedanta Hinduism declared the true goal of religion to be quite simple: it was the mystic union of the individual soul of the worshiper with the Absolute Soul of the universe. It was vigorous assertion of an ancient emphasis in Hinduism, and it would be an even more central theme thereafter.

## The Decline of Buddhism in India

The decline of Buddhism in the Buddha's own country is perhaps harder to understand. It is sometimes explained by the scarcity of powerful royal patrons to advance the Buddhist cause. Kings in search of sacred support for their right to govern turned increasingly to Hinduism. There were more divine ancestors available in the elaborate pantheon of the brahmans, who had been providing religious sanctions for society and its rulers since Vedic times.

Persecution also undoubtedly played a part, particularly in the Muslim-dominated north. The massacres of Buddhist monks and the burning of monasteries at the time of the establishment of the Delhi Sultanate dealt a fatal blow to Buddhism in the northeast, as well as depriving India as a whole of one of its most vital centers of religious culture.

A more subtle but nonetheless important development was the slow convergence of the Buddhist and Hindu traditions in India. Hinduism became more and more monotheistic in all but name, though the one true god might be Vishnu or Shiva, depending on the cult one belonged to. Since Buddhism was already monotheistic, transferral of allegiance from one faith to the other was made that much easier. Buddha himself was absorbed into some versions of Hinduism as an incarnation of Brahma, like Krishna or Rama in earlier Hindu mythology.

Given the growing prestige of the brahmans, the lack of powerful patrons for Buddhist monks, and the acceptance of Buddhist insights by the older faith, it is not surprising that the number of Buddhist believers dwindled. By 1500 Buddhism was essentially dead in India, while—as we shall see below—it flourished all across Southeast and East Asia.

## The Spread of Islam

Islam descended upon northern India in waves during the later centuries of this period. There were Muslim Arabs in the far northwest before 1000, and Muslim Turkish raiders pushed still further into the north in the eleventh century. But it was the Turko-Afghan regime of the Delhi Sultanate in the thirteenth century that made Islam a vital force from the Punjab in the west to the frontiers of Bengal in the east.

In subsequent centuries Islam was to replace Buddhism as India's second religion, until in the first half of the twentieth century a quarter of India's huge population was Muslim. The process began, however, under the Delhi sultans. Some Indians were converted by the sword during the Turkish invasions. More probably accepted Islam as the high road to political advancement, once the sultanate was established. Many, finally, were drawn to the faith of the Prophet by the Sufis, whose mystical approach to religion appealed to the hearts of Indians even when their heads rejected the rigor of Muslim theology and law.

At the upper levels of Indian society, Hindus and Muslims found it quite possible to live in intellectual and religious harmony in these early days. Fifteenth-century Indian religious leaders argued that there were no spiritual differences between Allah and Vishnu. Intellectuals of both faiths sought to understand the Supreme without theological hairsplitting and undue attention to labels. But at the level of worship and ritual, the masses of north Indians had already drawn the line. Music in front of a mosque (where music was forbidden) or a Muslim beef feast (the cow still being sacred to Hindus) could trigger a riot in an Indian town at any time over the past eight centuries.

Tolerance thus had its limits, even in India. To this most religious of peoples, religion has never been a matter of lip service and formal ceremonies. Religious beliefs are woven into their lives. To this day they have remained a source of potentially explosive interaction with other aspects of Indian history.

## THE ARTS OF INDIA

### The Age of the Temple Builders

The high culture of India during the millennium 500–1500 was thus, as usual, profoundly shaped by religion, and particularly by the renascent Hindu faith. The most striking art forms of this age were religious architecture and sculpture, as combined in the stone temples then beginning to rise all over India. Just as cathedrals and mosques were being built during this period across western Eurasia, this was the age of the temple builders in India.

A Westerner's first impression of an Indian temple is likely to be one of confusion. Here is none of the simplicity of a Greek temple, or even the underlying structure of a gothic cathedral. Buddhist, Jain, and especially Hindu temples of this and later periods, with their beehive-shaped or pyramidal towers and courtyards alive with sculpture, look at first glance rather more like organic growths than human constructs.

In fact, these Indian temples are designed very carefully according to intricate architectural—and metaphysical—principles. The ground plan is a complex of *mandalas,* or squares enclosed in circles, intended to reflect the shape of the world as it was theologically understood at the time. The tower (or *shikara,* meaning "mountain") is the image of the "world mountain," the pillar between heaven and earth, pointing to God. In the north the typical Indo-Aryan *shikara* is shaped rather like a cucumber, or one of the finger-length bananas vendors sell in the streets. In the south, the Dravidian *shikara* is a pyramidal series of terraces of decreasing size, each dedicated to a different god. Over all available surfaces, intricate decorative motifs and the swaying, dancing figures of gods and mortals, animals and plants move round and round the terraces, friezes, bases, and towers.

Whole cities of these great temples—some of them all but deserted now—were built during the centuries between the Guptas and the Mughals across the vast land of India. Perhaps the finest in the Indo-Aryan style is Khajuraho in central India, a score of huge towers (where more than eighty once stood) looming above the plain. Built by Rajput sovereigns a thousand years ago, each mountain of stone, seen closer up, is a mass of detailed, if time-worn, carving.

### The Dance of Shiva

This highly developed civilization did produce a complex secular culture over these centuries, ranging from royal biographies and histories of the various Indian kingdoms to popular tales and erotic poetry. Courtly poetry and elaborate critical commentaries on earlier Indian literature also emphasized the sophistication of India's high culture.

Indian culture during this age also combines devotional poems with poems of sexual passion in a wash of sensuality. In the very secular and languorously sexual *Gita Govinda* of Jayadeva, a woman overwhelmed with desire calls upon the god Krishna, manifesting

The <u>Descent of the Ganges</u>. India's sacred river, from heaven to earth is depicted in this celebrated sculpture at Mamallapuram. All earth's teeming life—animal, human, and divine—gathers to give thanks for the divine gift in this awesome life-size granite carving, only a detail of which is shown here. A lush plenitude of figures and detail is as typical of Indian as of European gothic religious art. (Information Service of India)

himself as a very physical lover, as "the joy of her heart," sweet as sugar and mango and wine.[1]

Painters decorated Buddhist manuscripts with vivid illustrations, as medieval European artists illuminated Christian manuscripts. And Indian sculpture continued to bring all the gods and goddesses to vivid life across the subcontinent.

Many different styles developed in the various parts of India, from the elaborate, ornate stone carving of the west to the spare yet elegant bronzes of the south. Yet all projected the sense of burgeoning life characteristic of the art of South Asia. The famous *Descent of the Ganges,* a gigantic bas-relief put from living rock at a temple complex near Madras, shows the sacred river, which once flowed only through heaven, descending at last to earth, to the admiration of all its creatures. Gods and spirits, men and women, graceful deer and lumbering elephants converge upon the holy spot in the great stone panorama.

Even more famous are the widely imitated and worshiped south Indian bronze sculptures of the *Dance of Shiva.* In this vivid pose, the Destroyer is shown dancing the universe back into being. Often wreathed with a ring of fire, trampling the demon of

---

[1]J. D. Yohannan, *A Treasury of Asian Literature* (New York: New American Library, 1956), pp. 298–299.

ignorance, Shiva deploys his four arms gracefully as he moves to the cosmic measure that makes worlds—and destroys them.

## Tamil Culture

An outstanding illustration of the minority cultures of divided India during this period is that of the Tamils of southern India. A Dravidian people and the builders of such powerful southern states as that of the Cholas, they also produced a distinctive and brilliant body of literature and art of their own.

Tamil literature is the oldest written literature in India after the classical Sanskrit of the north. Early Tamil poetry evoked heroic deeds going back well before Gupta times. The later Tamil poet Kampan made the ancient *Ramayana* available in the vernacular to Tamil speakers in the southern region where Rama had come to seek his kidnaped bride in the ancient epic. Later Tamil literature also included collections of wise sayings on subjects ranging from love and morality to princely politics.

But religious poetry perhaps flamed more passionately across the Tamil south than any other form. *Bakhti*—emotional personal piety—early challenged more traditional and formal types of worship in the hot south. *Bakhti,* like earlier Buddhism, made religion available to true believers regardless of caste or gender. These Hindu believers, hearts overflowing with love for the god—usually Vishnu, but particularly incarnated as Rama or Krishna—sang ardent hymns and made arduous pilgrimages in his honor. And gifted *bakhti* poets created a vivid literature of devotion.

These songs and hymns often described their religious feelings in terms of such intense human affection as love for a parent, a friend, or a lover. Some of these Tamil poets and musicians expressed their piety so movingly that their hymns were incorporated into the official ceremonies in the temples. Some of them were themselves worshiped as saints in later centuries.

# THE INDIAN SPHERE OF INFLUENCE: SOUTHEAST ASIA

## Indian Outreach

This churning center of economic development and religious and cultural ferment inevitably had an impact on neighboring peoples. Even without a single political center, Indian influence on its neighbors was great.

We have seen how Chola rulers from southern India sent naval expeditions to neighboring peoples to the east. The Muslim invasion that established the Delhi Sultanate in the north drove many Buddhist monks out of that part of India, and some of these crossed the Himalayas into Tibet. On that high, desolate plateau, their teachings replaced traditional local shamanism with the distinctive derivative of Buddhism called lamaism, a monkish faith still struggling to survive-and reaching out to a religion—starved world—today.

The most important zone of Indian influence between 600 and 1500, however, was Southeast Asia.

## A Pattern of Village Life

We have touched down in Southeast Asia before, usually on our way somewhere else. This collection of islands and peninsulas at the southeastern corner of Asia was the way station for prehistoric immigrants passing on out through the islands toward Australia and Oceania. We have mentioned the beginnings of Chinese imperial penetration into Vietnam and will have more to say about that directly. In the present chapter, we focus on the profound influence of Indian culture on the region as a whole.

Geographically, Southeast Asia juts south between India and China, pointing roughly toward Australia, Mainland Southeast Asia is Myanmar (Burma), Thailand, Cambodia, Laos, Vietnam, and the long curving peninsula of Malasia, with Singapore today at its southern tip. Island Southeast Asia is mostly Indonesia now, including Java where most of the population live, Sumatra, the large central island of Borneo, the heavily touristed island paradise of Bali, and part of New Guinea, just off the Australian coast. Add the Philippines for the eastern flank—and some 13,000 smaller islands scattered between the Indian Ocean and the China seas—and you have a substantial zone of culture indeed.

But the region had its own culture before the foreigner came. The mountains and rain forests, the rich, fertile river valleys, and the waters full of fish have sheltered human life for many centuries. Bamboo villages on stilts, water buffalo, and rice paddies were all in place before the first Chinese soldier or Indian merchant came marching through the jungle or poking up the muddy rivers. Dong-Son culture developed its special combination of agriculture, trading, and piracy with minimal foreign input. If bronze working filtered down from China, the unique bronze drums that symbolize the Dong-Son achievement are a Southeast Asian artifact.

Perhaps most important, the pattern of Southeast Asian village life—the life of most Southeast Asians to this day—was firmly established long before civilized Indians and Chinese, Muslims and Christians came to bring the splendors and miseries of urban-imperial culture to this substantial corner of the world.

It is too easy to slip into the dismissive frame of mind that sees one peasant as much like another, an agricultural village in Java as really no different from one in Nigeria or Peru. But there are differences, some of them extremely important still.

Southeast Asian villagers were still animists, worshiping natural objects and the forces of nature, while Indian peasants were adopting the larger and more complex creeds of Hinduism, Buddhism, and later Islam. Many parts of Southeast Asia built societies around the small nuclear family of parents and children—as most modern societies do—rather than the extended family prevalent in India and China. Perhaps most striking, Southeast Asians from early times accorded a higher degree of equality to women than their neighbors did.

Women in Southeast Asian villages shared more than labor with their men. In ancient times they were often priestesses and even chiefs. Women sometimes chose their husbands (instead of the other way around), and matrilineal descent—inheritance through the wife's rather than the husband's side—was common. Against this ingrained tradition of relative female equality, such later influences as the Indian drift toward seclusion for married women or such Muslim institutions as harem isolation and the veil could make little progress. Today you are considerably more likely to see young women jogging in the streets of Indonesia's capital Jakarta, for instance, than in New Delhi or any Arab city.

Most of what follows concerns the absorption of Southeast Asia into a larger zone of culture whose radiant center was India. But it should be remembered that the glories of Angkor Wat or Borobudur were built by the labor of village people whose hearts and lives were still shaped to a large extent by an older world where such incongruous beliefs as nature worship and female equality lived on in perfect harmony.

# INDIA AND ITS SPHERE OF INFLUENCE

PACIFIC OCEAN

BORNEO

JAVA
Borobudur
Prambanan

SUMATRA

VIET KINGDOM

CHAMPA KINGDOM

Angkor
KHMERS

Malacca

MALAYA

THAIS

PUNDRAVARDHANA

BURMA
Pagan

KAMARUPA

DAVAKA

LICCHAVI

NEPALA

Vaisali
Pataliputra

BAY OF BENGAL

Vengi

LANKA (SIMHALA)

PANDYA
PALLAVAS
CHOLAS

INDIAN OCEAN

NAGAS
Delhi
Ayodhya
Mathura
Padmavati
Airikina (Eran)
Ujjayini
Sanchi
Ajanta
Nandivardhana

SAKAS
Dasapura (Mandasor)
Girinagara (Girnar)

KUSHANS AND SAKAS

SASANIAN EMPIRE

ARABIAN SEA

1000 Miles

1000 Kilometers

500

500

0

0

## Missionaries and Merchants

Indian influence in Southeast Asia goes back to the classic period, the age of the Guptas and before, but it reached its peak during the thousand years between 500 and 1500. As a source of cultural influence, India substantially outweighed China, whose impact during these centuries seldom reached much further than northern Vietnam. Indian influence, by contrast, spread to most of the mainland peoples, from Burma into southern Vietnam, and to a number of the larger islands, including Sumatra, Java, and Borneo.

This Indian influence differed strikingly from the looming Chinese presence. When the Chinese did come south, it was as conquerors, the organized political and military agents of the world's most populous and powerful nation. Indians, by contrast, filtered into the region primarily as merchants and missionaries. In the end, the cultural impact of Indian civilization, built on mutually beneficial trade and on the emotional and spiritual appeal of India's religions, penetrated Southeast Asian culture as Chinese political influence seldom did.

Indian traders settled into the port towns of Malaya, Java, and Sumatra, even Thailand and south Vietnam, as easily as they did along the coasts of East Africa, far to the west. They gave village chiefs impressive gifts, the products of an Indian handicraft industry that local artisans could only envy. They exchanged textiles, jewels, jars of oil, and perfume for spices and timber, gold and tin. In time they married the daughters of local dignitaries and became influential citizens of communities that grew increasingly prosperous thanks to Indian trade.

Indian missionaries came to spread all three of the greatest Indian religions. Buddhist monks brought a simple, caste-free faith that had a great appeal to ordinary villagers. Brahmans brought a Hinduism that sanctioned *rajas* in Southeast Asia as easily as it did in India and that soon became a common cult among rulers and aristocrats. Islam, when it came, came often in the simple straight-from-the-heart Sufi form. But Indian Muslims came frequently as conquerors too, and some prudent Southeast Asians accepted Islam as a rapid road to success in Muslim-controlled areas.

Sometimes Indians taught techniques of land irrigation and terraced hillside agriculture, though these skills had been developed in many areas before they came. In many places Indians helped Southeast Asian rulers to develop bustling port cities for further trade with India and elsewhere. And Indian monks, brahmans, and Islamic mullahs raised temples to Vishnu and Shiva, to Buddha or to Allah, among the palms and paddies of these lands of the eastern seas.

Climbing over the mountain of terraces, statues, carved gateways, and broken stairs of Borobudur, in Java, one has the odd feeling of exploring a gothic cathedral turned inside out. All the stairs and gates and statues are on the outside; there is no inside. But there is the same careful stonework in a carved Buddha meditating on the Javanese jungle as in any sculptured Christ looking down on a gothic nave. The religious symbols and the religious stories are different, but the Buddhist temple at Borobudur is as much a holy mountain reaching up to God as any Notre Dame.

## Lands of a Million Elephants: From Malacca to Angkor Wat

The fusion of traditional ways with Indian influence produced a whole series of kingdoms and empires across Southeast Asia, a number of them comparable in splendor, if not in size, to those of India itself.

Almost every modern Southeast Asian nation can point to some such glorious center of civilization in the past. The islands of today's Indonesia, especially Java and Sumatra, were the sites of briskly feuding Indianized nations between 500 and 1000, a period when Europe was languishing in its Dark Ages. As early as the ninth century, the huge Buddhist temple at Borobudur and the Hindu temple complex at Palambanan had risen over the jungles of central Java. The great Anirudda filled the far-famed Burmese capital of Pagan with temples and shrines dedicated to Buddha in the eleventh century, at about the same time that the gothic cathedrals were beginning to rise in Europe. Laos looks back to the great days of Lan Xang—Land of a Million Elephants.

Malaya remembers the meteoric career of the great port city of Malacca, which under the leadership of Muslim Indian merchants dominated East Indian trade and spread the faith of Muhammad to many parts of Southeast Asia. Dazzled by bazaars heaped with Indian fabrics and Chinese porcelain, spices, aromatic woods, and precious metals, pearls and perfumes and silks, a Portuguese visitor in the 1400s declared that "Men cannot estimate the wealth of Malacca."

In 1511 the Portuguese captured Malacca, and a new era began for Southeast Asia. But the long millennium between the end of the classic age around 500 and the beginning of the modern era around 1500 had produced achievements in civilization second to none. Perhaps the most famous of all was the kingdom of the Khmer in what became Cambodia—the civilization whose most awesome monument is the great lost city of Angkor.

---

# VOICES FROM THE PAST

Even the economic historian who brings us this quote from an early modern observer is impressed by the wonders of medieval Malacca, the commercial crossroads of Asia until the arrival of European imperialists in the sixteenth century. Note that Tomé Pires credits part of the port's prosperity to the local princes, who saw the importance of "favoring" and "not neglecting" it. Would modern economists agree that favorable government policies are essential to economic success?

*At the end of the 15th century hundreds of merchants from Arabia, Persia, India, Further India, and China, as well as from the Indonesian regions closer at hand, flocked together every year in Malacca, which was then the centre of inter-Asian trade. Like a rich and colourful pageant under the blazing tropical sun, this busy eastern market made an indelible impression on the first Europeans who visited Malacca. It is worth while turning to the almost lyrical descriptions of people like Duarte Barbosa and Tomé Pires.[1] "There is no doubt" writes the latter "that the affairs of Malacca are of great importance, and of much profit and great honour. It is a land that cannot depreciate, on account of its position, but must always grow. No trading port as large as Malacca is known, nor any where they deal in such fine and highly-prized merchandise. Goods from all over the East are found here; goods from all over the West are sold here. It is at the end of the monsoons, where you find what you want, and sometimes more than you are looking for." But it is as if Pires already forsees the fate that lies in store for Malacca" "Wherefore a thing of such magnitude and of such great wealth, which never in the world could decline, if it were moderately governed and favoured, should be supplied, looked after, praised and favoured, and not neglected."*

---

[1]Tomé Pires, *Complete Treatise on the Orient* (London: Hakluyt Society, 1944), quoted in M. A. P. Meilink-Roelofsz, *Asian Trade and European Influence in the Indonesian Archipelago* (The Hague: Martinus Nijhoff, 1962).

The Cambodian "lost city" of Angkor Thom built in the twelfth century while the gothic cathedrals were rising in Europe has awed many Western visitors. Closely shaped by Indian artistic and religious influences, the towers and walls and endless sculptured galleries of Angkor remain one of the greatest monuments of ancient Southeast Asian civilization. (Anthony Esler)

The Indianized, Hindu-Buddhist state of Kambuja (Cambodia) flourished from the ninth to the fifteenth centuries. The Khmer peoples who ruled it extended their sovereignty into parts of southern Vietnam and Thailand. Over its half-dozen centuries of splendor, the Khmer Empire learned Sanskrit, mathematics, architecture, and art from the Indians. Khmer rulers became *devarajas* and pious Hindus, while many of their people accepted the less hierarchical Buddhist faith, the religion of most Cambodians today. The ancient Indian epic poems, the *Mahabharata* and the *Ramayana,* were widely known in southern Indochina. And the great temple of Angkor Wat was built to reproduce on earth the Hindu vision of the shape and structure of the cosmos.

The Khmer Empire was never large in size or population. But the Angkor dynasty channeled the wealth of the land and the labor of their million subjects into huge building projects dedicated to the greater glory of their gods and their god-kings. The temple complex of Angkor Wat is the most splendid evocation of the wealth and dedication of this vanished civilization.

Here the moated city of Angkor once stood, several miles around, surrounded by a green plain criss-crossed by irrigation channels and lush with rice paddies and orchards. Within the city swarmed a population many times as large as that of medieval London. The booming business of the city was dominated—like so much else in Southeast Asia— by women. But the city's great centers, clearly visible over the rooftops of the earth or wooden houses of the people, were the bristling stone towers of the royal city of Angkor Thom and the temple complex of Angkor Wat.

Even the ruins that survive today—much of it still overgrown with jungle, discolored by monsoon rains, pocked by the bullets of more recent Southeast Asian wars—are among the most impressive to be found anywhere. Angkor Wat itself, six hundred feet on a side, has been described as the largest temple in the world. Around its courtyards and galleries and up the sides of its *shikara*, hundreds of carven figures retell Hindu myths and glorify the Khmer King—Suryavarman II—who built it in the twelfth century. The style is distinctly that of this great Southeast Asian people, but the images of Vishnu and Shiva and Buddha, the creation myths, and the cosmological design all reflect the cultural influence of India.

## SUMMARY

The thousand years of Indian history between the Guptas and the Mughals were tangled and confused politically, like so much of India's history. But they were also centuries of cultural flowering and of the spread of Indian influence, above all into Southeast Asia.

During this period, from roughly C.E. 500 to 1500, the Northwest Frontier admitted Rajputs, Turks, Tatars, and others to find their place in the polyglot population of India. The Dravidian south merged with the north in a single arena of competitive states. The caste system grew more complex and more rigid, and women's place in society became fixed. Attempts at imposing political unity included the short-lived empire of King Harsha and the longer but no more substantial regime called the Delhi Sultanate.

India's culture, with its roots still deeply planted in the subcontinent's many religions, continued to probe spiritual profundities and to generate artistic splendors.

Hinduism, which had experienced a spiritual revival under the Guptas, still flowered during the following millennium. But Buddhism lost favor in the Buddha's own homeland, expiring finally in the turmoil following the Muslim invasions. The rise of Islam itself, particularly in the north, made the Muslim faith the third main current of Indian religious history during this period, India's second largest religion in later centuries.

As Western Christian art centered on the cathedral and that of Islam on the mosque, so Indian art focused on the countless huge stone temples that were built in all parts of India in this age. Dense with life, myth, and symbol, the temples of Hindu, Buddhist, Jain, and other faiths glorified Indian cities, as churches of Our Lady did the cities of Christendom. Among the many regional cultures of divided India, that of the Tamils glowed with particular brilliance in the south, particularly in the Chola kingdom.

This ancient and complex culture, finally, had an important impact on a large cultural zone comprising almost all of Southeast Asia in this period.

Indian merchants and Buddhist, Hindu, and Muslim missionaries guided the developing cities and empires of these lush islands and peninsulas. Southeast Asian village culture was significantly affected by the new faiths. Kingdoms in Burma, Java, Sumatra, and the famous Angkor Wat of Cambodia all reflected the influence of the timeless culture of India.

## SUGGESTED READING

Chattopadhyaya, B. *The Making of Early Medieval India.* New York: Oxford University Press, 1994. Aspects of Indian social and political development.

Chaudhuri, K. N. *Asia Before Europe: Economy and Civilization of the Indian Ocean from the Rise of Islam to 1750.* Cambridge, England: Cambridge University Press, 1991. Regional study of the ocean and its neighboring peoples. See also K. R. Hall, *Maritime Trade and State Development in Early Southeast Asia* (Honolulu: University of Hawaii Press, 1985).

Jackson, P. *The Delhi Sultanate: A Political and Military History.* New York, Cambridge University Press, 1999. Highly praised recent overview.

Mannikka, E. *Angkor Wat: Time, Space, and Kingship.* Honolulu: University of Hawaii Press, 1996. Inner meanings of the Khmer complex at Angkor.

Michell, G. *The Hindu Temple: An Introduction to Its Meaning and Form.* Chicago: University of Chicago Press, 1988. Religious symbolism in architecture.

Pearson, M. N., ed. *Spices in the Indian Ocean World.* London: Variorum, 1996. Impact of a small but vital commodity on South Asian trade.

Ramusack, B. N., and S. L. Sievers. *Women in Asia: Restoring Women to History.* Bloomington and Indianapolis: Indiana University Press, 1999. Women playing active roles in both South and East Asian history.

Wriggens, S. H. *Xuanzang: A Buddhist Pilgrim on the Silk Road.* Boulder, Colo.: Westview Press, 1996. Highly readable account of the Chinese pilgrim's epic journey in quest of Indian Buddhist texts.

Zimmer, H. *The Art of Indian Asia* (2 vols). New York: Pantheon Books, 1960. Outstanding study, beautifully illustrated, of the art of the Indian zone of culture.

 Please refer to the document CD-ROM for primary sources related to this chapter.

# CHAPTER 12

# THE MIDDLE KINGDOM
## China and East Asia

### (600–1250)

## A Glance Ahead: China's Supremacy in Eastern Asia

Towering over the eastern end of Eurasia, China was still the world's largest country in this period of world history. It passed through two of its certified golden ages during this era, the Tang and the Song dynasties. And its traditional cultural zone continued to include all of East Asia, while Tang armies pushed still farther west across the steppes of Eurasia.

China's main influence, however, continued to be on its nearer neighbors, including Vietnam, Korea, and Japan. Across this vast zone, the ancient "middle kingdom" continued to radiate its cultural imperatives, a mix of Confucian principles and commercial know-how, military power, Buddhist faith, and the sheer weight of its ancient civilization.

A crisis lay in wait toward the end of this period—the catastrophic Mongol conquest. But China would shrug off this disaster too and enter the modern age with an enormous potential to impress its neighbors and resist encroachment from beyond its zone.

## The Tang Dynasty

### The Six Dynasties

There are sober businessmen in Singapore or Hong Kong or Tokyo—and even soberer scholars in America—who will tell you that the twenty-first century will be the century of the Pacific rim. The Atlantic powers have had their day, they will say. The nations that border the Pacific will be the arbiters of the planet's destiny in the new century and East, South, and Southeast Asian nations will lead all the rest.

A traditional Chinese scholar would tell you that the Asian rim of the Pacific has actually been the center of world history for a couple of thousand years already. Since the Qin and Han dynasties united China in the third century B.C.E., creating at a stroke the largest and most populous nation on earth, Chinese primacy has been an article of faith in the land they call the Middle Kingdom.

Basic geography—and basic history—certainly seemed to support the Chinese sense of being the center of human civilization during most of the millennium between the end of the classic age and the beginning of the modern era.

China sprawls massively across the eastward bulge of Asia. For most of its history it has been a large, powerful, centralized state with a proud and ancient culture. During much of the period under consideration here, China basked in the renewed glories of two of its greatest ages, the Tang and Song dynasties.

Over these centuries, which saw the rise of Islam and the climax of the Christian age of faith at the other end of Eurasia, another major zone of civilization thus developed and produced great things along the far Pacific rim.

The four hundred years that elapsed between the collapse of the Han dynasty in 220 and the accession of the Tang in 618 are a hopeless tangle politically. The epoch may be subdivided into the sometimes overlapping periods of the Three Kingdoms, the Six Dynasties, and the brief pre-Tang unification under the Sui dynasty. But the essential elements of this age—which we may refer to for convenience simply as the Six Dynasties—lay not in its political confusion but in other areas of Chinese history and culture.

Perhaps the decisive event was not political but military. It was not so much the third-century collapse of the Han monarchy that shattered Chinese unity but the fourth-century

Li Shimin, known to history as Tang Taizong, the reunifier of China and founder of the great Tang dynasty, looks pardonably self-satisfied in this drawing based on a rubbing from Shensi. Notice the elaborately embroidered robe, the carefully trimmed and curled beard, and the traditional full sleeves. (Courtesy of the Library of Congress)

overrunning of northeastern China by a chaotic flood of preurban nomadic peoples from beyond the Great Wall. The result of this barbarian conquest of the old Chinese heartland was to leave China culturally as well as politically divided between north and south for most of the next three hundred years.

But the impulse toward complete political unification was always there. Toward the end of the sixth century, finally, the brief Sui dynasty (589–618) reunited most of China and began the great unifying works that the Tang emperors were to bring to a triumphant climax.

The two Sui emperors, Yang Jian and his brilliant, unscrupulous son Yang Guang, were northerners with the blood of the Xiongnu in their veins. The armies of the militant Sui broke through the Yangzi demarcation line to conquer the south. Then this vigorous father and son labored successively to rebuild an administrative system for all China. They worked also to extend the Grand Canal system begun by the Han and the Great Wall built by the Qin emperor Huangdi. They strove with considerable success to keep out the barbarians and to impose Chinese rule once more upon the Vietnamese and Chinese influence on the Koreans.

The Sui emperors, like Huangdi, exhausted the country with extravagant building projects at home and costly military campaigns abroad. A nation strained beyond the breaking point rebelled, and the dynasty fell after less than thirty tumultuous years. But like the Qin, the Sui had paved the way for something more long lasting.

### The Founder: Tang Taizong

For some Chinese historians, the Tang dynasty (618–907) was the greatest of dynasties and the three hundred years of Tang rule the most lustrous of China's several golden ages. For others, the Han and Tang stand roughly on a par, twin peaks in China's history.

Like the Han, the Tang combined political and economic strength, imperial expansion, and cultural brilliance in a uniquely successful way. The earlier Tang, like the former Han, was an era of powerful personalities and glittering accomplishment, a period when China's preeminence and influence were unquestioned throughout East Asia. The latter half of the Tang period, like the Later Han, was a time of retrenchment and decline. In both cases, however, a long-reigning dynasty and frequently competent leadership gave China a considerable spell of domestic tranquility and international power.

The first two Tang emperors, like the two Sui, were father and son. But in the case of the Tang founders, the son was so clearly the dominant personality that it is common to see him as the true establisher of the dynasty, though he was its second emperor. This hard-driving second son is in fact often considered the greatest of all China's many emperors.

The father, Li Yuan, was the scion of an ancient northwestern Chinese family who married a daughter of the northern steppes, sired three sons, and became a leading general under the Sui. He seems, however, to have fallen strongly under the influence of his second son, an ambitious young war hero named Li Shimin. When the brief Sui restoration of imperial unity began to crumble, Li Shimin urged his father step by step along the road to power.

The older man was still at the fore when a key alliance was forged with the northern Turks against the crumbling Chinese regime. Father and son took the Sui capital of Chang'an (modern Xi'an) together, and soon thereafter Li Yuan was installed with all due solemnity as the new Son of Heaven, emperor of China. In the eight years of his reign, the new emperor firmly established the Tang regime at Chang'an, crushed several drawn-out rebellions in South China, and repelled an invasion by the new dynasty's former allies, the Turks.

In the end, however, the stronger personality of Li Shimin thrust its way forward. Returning from the wars, where he had spent his youth fighting for his country and his clan, the second son confronted a conspiracy hatched against him by the crown prince and by the third Li brother, both envious of Shimin's fame. The border warrior reacted with the directness of the military commander he was. He took a squad, ambushed his brothers and their retainers outside the palace gates, and shot both the plotters down with bows and arrows. He then compelled his aging father to step down and mounted the throne himself—emperor at the age of twenty-six.

Li Shimin would be listed in the history books as Tang Taizong (629–649), Grand Ancestor of the Tang. Brilliant general, governmental reformer, famous historian, and master of the calligraphy brush, he would be one of the most admired of all Chinese emperors.

Taizong's governmental reforms were in part a restoration of the Han system already partially revived by the Sui, in part a long step beyond these traditional ways. This real founder of the Tang put government in the hands of an administrative system of six central ministries (for state revenues and public works, defense and justice, personnel and religious rites), ten provinces, and hundreds of prefectures and lesser administrative units. He expanded the Confucian examination system for civil servants and established a structure of schools, including a central university at Chang'an that would prepare students for the exams. He promulgated a flexible new law code and a new state-supported court aristocracy in nine graduated ranks. He laid the groundwork, in short, for the whole Tang system of imperial government.

Taizong also launched the reunited Chinese nation on the road to renewed imperial preeminence in East Asia. He led his armies himself, following the trail of westward expansion already blazed by the Han. Taizong's armies pushed the Turks back out of the Tarim Basin and carried Chinese power all the way to the Pamirs and into the valley of the Oxus River beyond. South of the Tarim Basin he imposed Chinese authority on the newly unified mountain kingdom of Tibet. He thus opened the doors to trade with western Eurasia once more—though in the seventh century there was no developed civilization in Europe with which to trade.

Tang Taizong ruled for more than twenty years, building palaces for himself and public granaries for his people, exalting Buddha at his court and establishing temples to the honor of Confucius across the land. He died at the comparatively young age of forty-nine, his health destroyed by a hard military campaign in Korea.

In the end, Taizong's one great failure was that he produced no heir strong enough to hold and build upon this heritage. But even this turned out to be for the best, for weakness at the top allowed his true successor to fight her way up through the cauldron of court politics—his former concubine who became the formidable Empress Wu.

## The Greatest Empress: Wu Zetian

Like the Han empress Lü, Empress Wu Zetian (649–705) of the Tang period owed her initial power to male connections. Concubine of the second Tang emperor, wife of the third, and mother of the next two, Wu finally dispensed with surrogates and ruled in her own right and name. Beautiful and cruel in her early years, she displayed in later life the intelligence, good judgment, and foresight that make a great ruler.

In her climb to the throne of China, Wu Zetian struck down her rivals ruthlessly, exalted her own family, and even tried to establish a new dynasty of her own. She fostered the Buddhist faith as her predecessors had, fell temporarily in love with a Buddhist monk, and even had herself proclaimed a new incarnation of the Enlightened One. In her later years she declared herself emperor, performed the rites, and received the homage due the Son of Heaven. Though other women governed China—from the Han empress Lü to imperial China's last great ruler, Ci Xi in the nineteenth century—Empress Wu was the only woman to hold the titles as well as the power in her strong hands.

This later representation of the Empress Wu Zetian probably does not do justice to the powerful preserver of the Tang order even in her later years. Can you detect winged dragon motifs—symbolic of imperial power—in the empress's headdress? (Library of Congress)

## TANG CHINA

Beneath the gaudy surface of her long tenure of power, however, Wu Zetian governed capably and well. Her chief ministers tended to be men of talent, the provincial officials stayed loyal, and the state prospered. In foreign affairs, she shrewdly supported the unification of Korea—which the Chinese had been trying and failing to conquer for generations—and thus enjoyed cordial relations with the new state throughout her life. In the west, she sent Chinese armies out as her predecessors had to chastise Turks and Tibetans and keep open China's trade routes across the Tarim Basin into western Asia and beyond. She was "perspicacious, and rapid and sure in decision" and enjoyed an international reputation for astuteness and success.[1]

Empress Wu's efforts to establish a new dynasty—her own—finally brought her down. She was deposed at last in her eighties, after more than half a century of ruling China. She left the nation more firmly united, wealthier, and more powerful than it had ever been before. What Tang Taizong had begun, Wu Zetian finished, and she was as much the architect of Tang greatness as he.

### The Brilliant Emperor: Tang Xuanzong

The last in this colorful line of great early Tang rulers was Empress Wu's grandson Tang Xuanzong (713–756). The long reign of Xuanzong, known to history as the Brilliant Em-

---

[1]C. P. Fitzgerald, *The Empress Wu* (Vancouver: University of British Columbia Press, 1968), p. 146.

peror, covered most of the first half of the eighth century and is often seen as the cultural apogee of the Tang period.

Xuanzong's huge palaces and gardens at Chang'an and elsewhere glittered with the work of some of the most famous of Tang poets and painters. Some of the most exquisitely beautiful of Chinese porcelain was produced for him, and he and his courtiers ate off silver dishes that were works of art. The magnificence of his court is often illustrated by his enthusiasm for fine horses, which he reportedly gratified by keeping forty thousand of them in the royal stables.

The Brilliant Emperor made more concrete contributions to the history of China than just living magnificently, however. It was during his reign that the fertile Yangzi River valley of central China was made to produce agriculturally on a scale that substantially increased the wealth of the nation. The imperial armies pushed still farther to the west under Tang Xuanzong, down into Kashmir and on toward the Caspian once more.

But it was here in central Asia that a disastrous encounter with the Arabs, driving eastward as the Chinese pushed west, ended Chinese expansion in that direction forever. China's defeat by Muslim armies at the Talas River near Samarkand in 751 was, in fact, a turning point in Chinese imperial history. It began a centuries-long decline of Chinese power in central Asia.

At home there was a similar turn in the emperor's—and the dynasty's—fortunes. It came in the guise of a September-and-May love affair between the aging Xuanzong and an attractive concubine named Yang Guifei. Yang's influence, that of her family, and finally that of her ambitious young protégé, An Lushan, predominated at court thereafter. When An Lushan openly revolted, the imperial troops demanded the death of the concubine whose influence had raised him so high. Yang Guifei was executed, and the Brilliant Emperor abdicated, a broken king.

The revolt of An Lushan was ultimately suppressed. But there were other revolts and other palace intrigues to come over the next century and a half. And there were no more Taizongs, no more Empress Wus, in the second half of the Tang era. The road, if not downhill all the way, was distinctly bumpier.

## The World's Largest Country

From the administrative capital at Chang'an, a nation as large as all Europe was governed by a handful of courtier-politicans and an army of scholarly civil servants. There were too many bureaucrats, as is frequently the case—secretariats and chancelleries to check every piece of paper the emperor saw. But the six ministries for revenue and public works, justice and defense, personnel and rites and ceremonies did their jobs with relative efficiency. There was a board of censors, who kept tabs on the whole elaborate system and reported inefficiency, malfeasance, and treason directly to the palace. The nation beyond the walls of the capital was administered at three levels, including ten provinces, 360 prefectures, and hundreds of subprefectures or districts.

Office seekers were trained in the unique Chinese educational system of local schools, provincial colleges, and a national university at Chang'an where one could study not only the Confucian classics but science, mathematics, and law. This system of education, keyed to examinations for civil-service jobs, in time perfected the ancient Han system of scholar bureaucrats. Most officeholders henceforth came not from the ranks of the aristocratic large landowners but from the literate gentry class of lesser landholders whose sons qualified for office by study and high marks. It was a system based substantially on merit, awarding the highest posts in government to those most qualified.

The power of this centralized administration was, for the seventh or eighth century C.E., very great indeed. Every ward in the great planned city of Chang'an was locked at midnight, and no one moved around thereafter. Every peasant belonged to a "collective-guarantee" group of neighbors, all of whom were responsible for one another's taxes and general good behavior—and all of whom thus kept an eye on one another for the government. Military service and corvée labor were rigorously imposed and could fall heavily on whole villages.

Responsibility, not freedom, was the keynote of a system of government that became traditional in China—and may sound oppressive to a Western ear. On the other hand, at a time when emperors like Charlemagne in Europe and Harsha in India had to mount many military campaigns to maintain their empires intact, China was ruled in a rather more modern way—by a steady flow of paper from the capital out across the provinces of the world's largest nation.

## Equal Fields and Wide Empire

Tang officialdom developed further the "equal-field" system originated by earlier dynasties, a form of land nationalization that assigned most of China's agricultural land on an equal basis to free peasants. The practice was intended to regularize—and maximize—the land tax. It also had the effect of limiting the amount of land held by wealthy landowners and hence of further undermining their power.

The government, like the governments of many developed nations, involved itself vigorously in the economy. A hundred mints produced strings of copper cash, and government-issued paper money was widely used. Royal roads radiating from Chang'an were equipped with hostels every ten miles and an impressive system of royal posts. Both the roads and the canal system were thronged with domestic traders.

Government incentives also helped turn the huge Yangzi valley into China's rice bowl. The emperor built ten shipyards in central China alone to give China a merchant marine, and entertained foreign merchants in growing numbers at Canton and other southern ports. Tang China was a great deal richer than Han China, and the imperial government played a significant part in this development.

Empire-building and foreign trade, finally, were carried to new highs under the Tang. At the height of their power, the Tang emperors dominated Asia. Their writ ran more or less effectively from the southern margins of Siberia down to Southeast Asia and west from the Pacific to somewhere beyond Ferghana—sometimes even to the neighborhood of the Caspian Sea. Chinese armies intervened in the affairs of northern India and Afghanistan, and China established a temporary protectorate over eastern Persia.

China's network of foreign trade reached out to the whole of Asia, from Japan to Syria. Foreign influences played more freely on Chinese culture than ever before. And China's manifest superiority was admired and imitated by a larger proportion of the human race than ever previously. If it was not China's greatest age, it was certainly a strong candidate for this highly competitive honor.

## THE SONG DYNASTY

### The Five Dynasties

The last years of the Tang seem to have been typical of that cyclic dynastic end game that recurs so frequently in Chinese history. There were fractious governors in the provinces, feuding bureaucrats and eunuchs at court, and underage or ailing emperors trying to hold it all together. Unpaid armies revolted, provinces seceded, short-lived emperors became tools in the hands of scheming subjects. In the 880s the nation slid helplessly into anarchy. In the early 900s the last Tang emperor and all his family were slaughtered, the magnificent capital at Chang'an pillaged and burned.

The period of the Five Dynasties that separates the Tang from the Song lasted only a little more than fifty years (907–960)—a striking contrast with the several hundred years of the Six Dynasties between the Han and the Tang. The five dynasties in question—all in the north—were necessarily brief, usually no longer than the life of the founder. There were at least ten other secession states in the south, all feuding, conniving, dreaming of unity, and destroying any of their number who strove to impose it. Rebellion was endemic, and invaders from beyond the Great Wall once more overran the north. A famous poem of the time, "The Lament of Lady Qi," describes fountains running with blood, palaces in ashes, feet crunching through the calcined bones of court officials.

Yet it ended. In 960 a group of loyal and no doubt ambitious officers threw an embroidered dragon robe around the shoulders of a general named Zhao Kuangyin and told him he should be their emperor or die on the spot. General Zhao, who commanded the armies of one of the northern dynasties, chose to live and reign. He became the founder of the Song.

The Song dynasty (960–1279) would not achieve the universality, the range of achievement of the Han or the Tang; in some areas, however, it would exceed these predecessors. When it came to governing, to getting and spending, and to art and poetry, the Song have seldom been excelled.

### Northern Song, Southern Song

General Zhao Kuangyin (960–976) seems to have been the only one of the twenty Song emperors whose personality stands out in the traditional historiography. He was a scholar as well as a general, an autocrat—and a man who saw that unity had become China's destiny.

As a general, Zhao Kuangyin first unified as much as he could of the north, leaving a wedge of territory still in barbarian hands, and then reconquered the fragmentary kingdoms of central and southern China. As a scholar, he revived the traditional Confucian education and examination system, which had fallen into abeyance during the Five Dynasties period, and fostered culture at his court. As an autocrat by nature, he revived and strengthened the Tang system of provinces and prefectures and strove to concentrate as many functions of government as possible in his own hands. And as a man with a sense of Chinese unity, Zhao Kuangyin benefited from the fact that many educated Chinese had come to believe that the secret of peace, prosperity, and order lay in unity and centralized authority. Many cities opened their gates to Zhao simply on the assurance that unity, not loot, was his object. The Song thus became in a sense the first dynasty established as much by consensus as by conquest.

The Song dynasty lasted about the same length of time as the Tang—three centuries. Like the Han and the Zhou before it, the Song was a clearly divided dynasty. The Northern Song (960–1127) governed from Kaifeng in the northern Yellow River valley; the Southern Song (1127–1279) fell back to the great city of Hangzhou in the valley of the Yangzi, China's great waterway. The whole era, contemporary with the High Middle Ages at the other end of Eurasia, was another high point in Chinese history.

In domestic affairs, the Song period was one of China's golden ages. Song emperors further improved on the Tang administrative structure. They controlled the military more effectively than their predecessors had, and they tried to tax large and small landowners alike. Song China was freer from popular discontent and rebellion than China had ever been before.

The dynasty even produced a great reforming minister of state in Wang Anshi, who in the eleventh century, a hundred years after Zhao Kuangyin, tried to revitalize the Northern Song with innovations in agriculture, trade, education, and the army and navy. Wang's Legalist rigor and his attack on wealth alienated Confucian bureaucrats and wealthy landowners and led to the frustration of many of his reforms. Nevertheless, Wang Anshi was one of a long line of reforming spirits who periodically shook up and infused new vigor into the Confucian system, which otherwise tended to become set in its ways.

China's problems under the Song dynasty—and the nation had serious ones—were rather foreign than domestic in origin. Most of these difficulties were with China's northern neighbors, the external peoples of the steppe. These conflicts climaxed with the loss of North China to the barbarians in the twelfth century.

Throughout the Song period parts of northwestern China were occupied by the Tibetans, and a slice of territory south of the Great Wall in the northeast was controlled by semiagricultural peoples from Mongolia. The Northern Song emperors were never able to dislodge these northern barbarians, who had established themselves during the anarchy of the Five Dynasties. In the first half of the twelfth century, finally, the Ruzhen (Jürchen) people descended from the Manchurian steppes in the far northeast, helped the Song overpower the rulers of the northeast, and then rampaged on south, conquering all of North China and carrying off the last emperor of the Northern Song to live out his life as a prisoner beyond the Great Wall.

The Southern Song, established by a son of that unhappy exile, set up a new capital at Hangzhou and ruled a truncated empire for the next century and a half. China under the Southern Song was vastly wealthy, immensely cultured, peaceful, and well governed. But the Chinese failed in all efforts to expel the Ruzhen and were actually forced to pay them tribute and to recognize China's status as vassal to the northern barbarians.

The Song emperors' deemphasis of the military, while it minimized the risk of warlordism and civil war, thus cost them dearly in the international arena. It was the middle passage of a long decline in China's power in East Asia. That decline, which began with the Brilliant Emperor's defeat on the Talas River in central Asia in 751, would climax in the thirteenth century with the overthrow of the Song and the conquest of the entire nation by the Mongols of Genghis Khan—to be dealt with in the following chapter. Through it all, however, China's wealth, its remarkable administrative institutions, and its cultural brilliance would continue to dominate the life of East Asia—even when Chinese armies could not.

## The First Meritocracy

Despite foreign-policy setbacks and the catastrophic loss of North China, the Song period saw material achievements that deserve further notice. These include the perfection of the scholar bureaucracy and its examination system and the immense wealth of the nation.

China's civil-service examinations and the resulting governmental meritocracy are as uniquely Chinese as the caste system is Indian or the Muslim law and its powerful local judges is Islamic. The examination system, originated by the Han dynasty and developed under the Tang, reached what was essentially its final form under the Song. For the next ten centuries it was to give China a stable administration that for most of that time was the envy of all who observed it.

The people who took the exams were for the most part children of China's gentry class—not aristocrats or holders of large estates, but men whose families were well enough off to spare them from agricultural labor while they devoted their lives to study. They typically spent many years reading the Chinese classics—Confucius above all—memorizing and analyzing every line. The tests required them to write passages from memory, to discuss and explain them, to compose a poem or other literary work in the style of particular masters, and to discuss theoretical problems of government having contemporary relevance.

Examinations were prepared with scrupulous attention to fairness. Papers were identified by number rather than name, and were even recopied before being graded so that the calligraphy might not be recognized by a grader. Exams were taken at several levels, beginning locally, where between 1 and 10 percent passed, and climaxing with the palace examinations, which passed perhaps a couple of hundred men a year into high governmental posts. The average "presented scholar" at this top level was in his middle thirties, well off but not wealthy, immensely learned, and one of a handful chosen out of China's millions to govern.

## Economic Growth—and Problems

The Chinese were also more numerous and wealthier than they had ever been. And two thirds of the population and wealth were for the first time concentrated in central and south China, rather than in the old northeastern heartland.

In Song times, China's population passed the hundred-million mark, twice the number counted in the Han period. This growing population created a huge economic demand, which in turn generated what is sometimes called an economic revolution in the Middle Kingdom.

Agriculture grew rapidly, and its center shifted with the center of population from the millet- and wheat-growing north to the rice paddies of the Yangzi and the southeast, where two crops a year of special strains of rice could be grown. Agricultural reforms included increasing use of fertilizer, improved irrigation, and better iron farming tools.

The iron and related coal industries developed rapidly under the Song, and there was widespread production of fine steel for tools, weapons, stoves, nails, and much more. Other growth industries included shipbuilding, the manufacture of ceramics, silk, and paper, and tea and salt processing. Many of these manufacturing enterprises were small craft-shop operations, but some were much larger in scale, employing hundreds of workers.

Trade flourished in Song China. Domestic traders frequently organized themselves in guilds and set up shops dealing in the same articles in the same streets, as in medieval Europe. Inland trade was carried out more commonly on the nation's elaborate network of waterways, both rivers and canals, than by road. It was a larger country, and water was the cheapest form of transport.

Southern Song cities such as Guangzhou (Canton) carried on long-distance foreign trade, both through foreign merchants—whom the Chinese government, for once in its history, eagerly encouraged to come to China—and its Chinese vessels plying foreign waters. Chinese ships were among the most impressive in the world, large enough to carry hundreds of men and large cargoes. They were equipped with such up-to-the-minute technology as watertight bulkheads, sea anchors, rudders (instead of steering oars), depth-sounding lines, compasses, and gunpowder-powered rockets for use in war or against pirates.

China imported drugs, textiles, and some luxury goods. The nation also exported silk in large quantities, metals, and especially ceramics, an export encouraged by the government. Song Chinese porcelain has been found not only in Southeast Asia and India but in the Middle East and East Africa.

There are, however, no paradises on this earth, and Song China was no exception to this melancholy rule.

There were economic problems even under the Song. Growing population, increasing taxation, and played-out land drove peasants into pauperism even in so wealthy a time. The government's paper money encouraged trade—until too much paper currency was put in circulation, leading to inflation. Government spending grew beyond the capacity of even so wealthy a land to support—especially military expenses, which devoured 80 percent of the budget, supported an unheard-of army of a million men, and still could not defeat the northern barbarians.

## SOCIETY AND CULTURE UNDER THE TANG AND SONG

### The Condition of Women

In some ways, upper-class women at least enjoyed increased freedom during the Tang and Song periods. But there were disturbing trends, particularly in Song times.

Urbanization brought women as well as men into the liberating, often tempting atmosphere of the cities. Only men could immerse themselves freely in the urban pleasures of teahouse and wine shop, theater and brothel, but some wealthy women did take discreet lovers. Imperial wives and concubines indulged in the political pleasures of conspiracy and cabal, seeking to advance their own interests and those of their relatives and political factions. Simpler and healthier pleasures were also apparently open to them: We even have ceramic images of Tang women on horseback, playing polo!

On the other hand, the power of male heads of households seems to have been ever greater during these centuries. From a woman's point of view, a limiting aspect of the neo-Confucian revival (dicussed below) was its emphasis on women's place in the home as a producer of male heirs. The retreat of Buddhism also undercut the place that liberating faith had offered for women as nuns or even scholars. And while men had their pick of multiple wives and—increasingly—concubines too, Song women in particular were confined to the home and forbidden to remarry even after their husbands' deaths.

Most disturbing, however, was the introduction of footbinding among the women of China's elites during Song times. This involved wrapping the feet of young girls with long strips of cloth, which produced a "lily foot" about half normal size. This made women useless for work—hence advertised their husbands' wealth—and gave them an odd, stilted walk that men found intensely attractive. The footbinding itself was also an extremely painful process for the daughters of the aristocracy.

# Voices from the Past

This speech is part of the famous legend of the Chinese Princess Miaoshan, whose dedication to the spiritual life in the end revealed her own Buddhahood as an incarnation of Guanyin, the Chinese Buddha of Compassion. The three conditions she sets for abandoning her religious commitment for a "normal" married life closely echo the experience of the original Buddha, Prince Siddartha, who discovered his vocation when he encountered old age, sickness, and death for the first time.

*The king told his wife, "Our daughter does not (want to marry. Please talk to her and make her change her mind." The mother then tries to persuade Miaoshan, who answered,) "I will obey Mother's command only if it will prevent three misfortunes." The mother asked, "What are the three misfortunes?" she answered, "The first is this: when people are young, their faces are as fair as the jade-like moon, but when they grow old, their hair turns white, their faces are wrinkled; in walking, resting, sitting, or lying down they are in every way worse off than when they were young. The second is this: one's limbs may be strong and vigorous, one may walk as briskly as if flying through the air, but when one suddenly becomes sick, one lies in a bed (without a single pleasure in life. The third is this: a person may have a large group of relatives and) be surrounded by his flesh and blood, but when death comes, even such close kin as father and son cannot take the person's place. If a husband can prevent these three misfortunes, I will marry him. But if he cannot do so, I vow never to marry. People of the world are all mired in these kinds of suffering. If one desires to be free from these sufferings, one must leave the secular world and pass through the gate of Buddhism. Only when one practices religion and obtains its fruit can one deliver all people from suffering. This is why I have undertaken my quest (for enlightenment . . ."*

Susan Mann and Yü-Yin Cheng, *Under Confucian Eyes: Writings on Gender in Chinese History* (Berkeley: University of California Press, 2001), p. 35.

## Missionary Buddhism and the New Confucianism

The great intellectual currents of Tang and Song times were the spread of Buddhism in the earlier period and the resurgence of Confucianism in the latter. Buddhism was brought by missionary monks from northern India to western China over the caravan routes of the great Silk Road. As early as the first century C.E., it was the faith of many foreign merchants resident in China. It appealed to Chinese and other East Asians through its direct dealing with human suffering, from which Buddhist enlightenment promised escape. In addition, evolving Mahayana Buddhism soon offered ritual and music, magic, art, and a variety of heavens and hells for people who couldn't grasp the nonbeing of Nirvana. During the Six Dynasties, Chinese Buddhist monks spread their faith all over China.

There were problems with translating abstract Indian concepts—like Nirvana—into Chinese. And the celibacy of Buddhist monks and nuns clashed jarringly with the Chinese emphasis on continuing the family line. But adaptable Buddhist missionaries in North China outdid the barbarian shamans at magic tricks, while Buddhists in the sophisticated south adroitly mixed religious propaganda with witty worldly conversation. Monasteries blossomed in many places, royal patrons were won, and the poor and unfortunate of the divided land found solace in the new faith.

But the real flowering of Chinese Buddhism came after the nation was reunited in Tang times. Despite the status of Confucianism as China's official philosophy and the penchant of a number of emperors for Daoism, Buddhism enjoyed its golden noon in Tang China. There was a proliferation of sects, providing a form of Buddhist belief for any Chinese. The *Tiantai* (Heavenly Terrace) sect tried to synthesize the conflicting doctrines of northern and southern Chinese Buddhism on various levels of truth, while claiming that all truth could actually be found in a single sermon—Buddha's famous Lotus Sutra. *Qingtu* (Pure Land) Buddhism, widely followed by ordinary Chinese with no head for theology, worshiped Buddha as ruler of a paradise in the west called the Pure Land and offered salvation simply through calling upon his name with a pure and sincere heart. *Chan* Buddhism, better known by its Japanese name of *Zen,* rejected all theology, scripture, and ceremony in favor of pure meditation, which alone would provide a true mystical understanding of the path to enlightenment.

In Tang times Buddhism thus channeled China's spiritual and intellectual impulses in an untypically religious direction. Under the Song, however, the Neo-Confucian revival—like the Hindu renaissance in Gupta India—drew China's educated classes back to an older faith. In China's case, it was a turn from an other-worldly religion back to a more typically Chinese secular philosophy.

Neo-Confucianism produced many commentaries on the Confucian classics. It established the Four Books of Confucian wisdom that were to be China's core curriculum for the next millennium. Confucian scholars and philosophers reinvigorated historical study and revived public and private education. Perhaps most striking, however, they tried to answer the sort of question about the ultimate nature of things that Master Kong himself had always avoided—to provide a metaphysical foundation for Confucian social and ethical thought.

The most famous instance of Neo-Confucian metaphysical theorizing was the work of the philosopher Zhu Xi, a twelfth-century thinker who was to the Confucian revival what his contemporary Thomas Aquinas was to the scholastic theology of the Christian Middle Ages. The best-known philosophical explorations of Zhu Xi involved a Platonic-sounding effort to explain the world in terms of *li* and *qi.* The *li* of anything was its basic form or fundamental principle, its *qi* the substance or stuff of which it is made. The most celebrated application of this doctrine had to do with the ancient dispute as to whether human nature was basically good, as Mencius had asserted, or evil, as the Legalists had always insisted. For the Neo-Confucianists, we are in a sense both. Our *li,* or basic principles are good, but the substance of which we are made, our *qi,* is gross, corruptible, and bound to lead us into evildoing. Self-improvement, the cultivation of our human essence of *li,* is, of course, best accomplished through study of the Confucian classics.

## Science and Technology: From Gunpowder to the Printing Press

The physical sciences were an area in which there was striking progress from the third to the thirteenth centuries. In this as in so many things, the Chinese tended to be practical, to make contributions to technology rather than to pure science.

Thus, the famous trio of inventions of which Europeans would boast during their own Renaissance—the compass, the printing press, and gunpowder—were all discovered many centuries earlier in China. Gunpowder was used more commonly for fireworks than for military purposes by the Chinese, but they did have forms of military rockets, hand grenades, and even explosive shells by Song times. The printing press was used most commonly for wood-block printing—whole sheets reprinted from single blocks—rather than printing with movable type, Gutenberg's great contribution. But this was simply because movable type was impractical where thousands of characters, instead of twenty-six letters, were involved. The compass was a clear advantage; it opened all the eastern seas to Chinese junks.

The Chinese of these centuries studied acoustics, optics, astronomy, and mathematics. Chinese cartographers made elaborate maps of Asia, some with a superimposed grid indicating elevations and trade routes across the Far East. They compiled botanical studies classifying many sorts of plants, from garden herbs to trees. Even such apparently superstitious exercises as alchemical experimentation taught the Chinese a good deal about genuine chemical reactions.

Chinese medical studies included treatises on drugs, diagnosis, and other aspects of disease and its treatment. Tea and hot baths were recommended for many ailments, but quite convincing drug treatments were urged in other cases. Chinese doctors took the pulse as an aid to diagnosis and inoculated people against smallpox. Acupuncture, the famous Chinese practice of sticking needles into patients to anesthetize them for surgery, still puzzles Western doctors, who are unsure whether it impedes the flow of pain signals through the nerves or stimulates the body to secrete its own anesthetic substances. Whatever it does, it apparently often works.

The list of practical Chinese inventions goes on and on, well beyond the celebrated trio of compass, gunpowder, and printing press. Sedan chairs for the wealthy and wheelbarrows for the peasants, water mills and suspension bridges, paper and porcelain, ships' rudders and sea anchors, and many other handy devices were produced by the pragmatic Chinese intellect.

### Poetry: Moon in the Water

Besides Buddhist religious writing, Neo-Confucianist scholarship and philosophy, and China's pace-setting performance in science, the Tang and Song periods produced a flood of literary prose and poetry of all kinds. The literary legacy of these centuries is as rich as any in the history of this immensely literate civilization.

Poetry appeared in massive quantities. We have the names of more than two thousand Tang poets and almost four thousand from the Song period, as well as tens of thousands of surviving poems. Poetry, calligraphy, and painting were the gentlemanly arts, and every gentleman, scholar, or official seemed to feel a social if not an aesthetic compulsion to grind out a few verses at least.

Some of the best-known of these poets are still read today. China's most famous poets, in fact, are the Tang masters Du Fu and Li Bo.

Du Fu, perhaps the most admired of all Chinese poets, was an eighth-century writer who wrote in elaborate verse forms. Yet he expressed a deep involvement with ordinary Chinese people, particularly with the oppressed and exploited. His "A Song of War Chariots," for instance, opens with a stirring call to battle:

> The war-chariots rattle,
> The war-horses whinny.
> Each man of you has a bow and a quiver at his belt.

But it soon moves on to a grimmer assessment of the famous wars of the Tang:

We remember others at fifteen sent forth to guard
    the river. . . .
The mayor wound their turbans for them when they
    started out.
With their turbaned hair white now, they are still at
    the border,
At the border where the blood of men spills like the
    sea—
And still the heart of Emperor Wu is beating for war.[2]

Du Fu wrote with grave Confucian concern of the misfortunes that have afflicted humankind from that day to this.

Du Fu's friend and contemporary Li Bo was as bohemian a poet as ever drank himself under a table or declaimed his verses at the moon. Like Du Fu a minor official, Li was a footloose wanderer, a lover of wine, good company, and nature—all of which he celebrated in his poetry. Actually, he seemed quite capable of conjuring up his own company, given the wine and a suitably romantic slice of nature. According to a famous legend, Li Bo drowned during a drunken boating party when he reached over the side to scoop up the moon from the water.

The poets of the Song period wrote masses of verse on such traditional topics as country life, oppressive officials, friendship, and unhappiness. The most famous of them was probably the eleventh-century writer Su Shi. He and his artistic coterie often combined all three of the gentlemanly arts by writing their poems in elegant calligraphy as part of a painting. Su Shi was also a thoughtful critic of both literature and art. Poems, he once said, are "pictures without form," and paintings "unspoken poems."[3]

## Art: Mountains in the Mist

The arts of the thousand years encompassing the Six Dynasties, the Tang, the Five Dynasties, and the Song created beautiful things in many forms. Of them all, Tang architecture was perhaps the most admired in its day, Song painting today. Of the other arts, the two most distinctively Chinese were probably calligraphy and ceramics.

Song pottery is particularly sought after. The simple, graceful vases and jars, sometimes porcelain and sometimes stoneware, manage to blend the strength of earlier pottery with the elegance and delicacy of later ceramics. One style of decoration popular even in the imperial palace was the crackle design, an array of thin cracks produced by a glaze that cooled and broke over the surface of the vessel as it did so.

Calligraphy is one of the hardest of Chinese arts for a foreigner to understand. Chinese characters, executed with brush and ink on paper or silk have, however, a striking beauty to the cultured Chinese eye. The abstract pattern of the character itself, the strength, dash, fluidity, or grace of the brush stroke, the revelation of the personality behind any particular calligraphic style—all have an endless fascination.

Most of the surviving sculpture of the period is Buddhist in origin and includes Buddhas and bodhisattvas, especially Guanyin, the bodhisattva of mercy. The fullness and

---

[2]"A Song of War Chariots," in Cyril Birch, ed., *Anthology of Chinese Literature from Early Times to the Fourteenth Century* (New York: Grove Press, 1965), pp. 240–241.

[3]Susan Bush, *The Chinese Literati on Painting: Su Shih (1037–1101) to Tung Ch'i-ch'ang (1156–1636)* (Cambridge, Mass.: Harvard University Press, 1971), p. 25.

swaying poses of Indian sculpture frequently merge here with the linear quality of much Chinese art, usually in the folds of clothing. There is some awesome stone statuary, notably the huge figures in the seventh-century Longmen cave temples centering on an immense fifty-foot Buddha. There are many smaller, extremely realistic figures in wood, bronze, or china, including graceful Guanyins seated at ease, one hand extended in gentle blessing. In Song times vivid portrait figures of *lohans,* mountain hermits adept in both Buddhist and Daoist mysticism, give us a close look at the faces of these saints of other faiths.

The most massive and sometimes extravagant architecture of these centuries was that produced during the Sui and the earlier Tang. This age of empire builders was built on an imperial scale that was still admired in Song days. Huge palaces, pavilions, pagodas, and other structures are described in surviving literature, and some surviving pagodas give at least a flavor of the age. Pagoda towers, with their multiple, gracefully sloping eaves curving up at the corners, were built in connection with Buddhist temples or tombs.

Palaces also called for monumental building. Empress Wu Zetian, a great builder, once erected a royal hall three hundred feet on a side and almost three hundred feet high. An earlier ruler caused a pavilion to be constructed in which hundreds of guests could dine, and which could be rotated by machinery while they did so.

Not much remains of these great works except a few pagoda towers. But Song painting survives to delight us still. Painting on wall hangings or hand scrolls (to be unrolled horizontally, giving a gradual exposure to the work) was common from the Six Dynasties on. The most common Chinese word for painting is *hua,* meaning "to define by line," and Chinese painting has always been strongly linear.[4] Done with brush and ink, like calligraphy, it frequently looks more like drawing than painting to Western eyes. By whatever name, it is a major achievement.

Tang painting tended to use more color than was usual later. It also concentrated on the human figure, including some thoroughly convincing portraits and many figures of monks and other religious personages, elegant ladies, and other stock subjects. Other painters specialized in particular genre subjects, such as horses, birds, or flowers.

There was some Tang landscape painting, but this form really came into its own under the Song. Here, landscape painters largely abandoned color to concentrate on poetic line and on the famous Chinese composition that makes empty space an important part of the picture. The subjects define the face of the Chinese land as it looked a thousand years ago: bamboo and water, naked tree branches against snow, and again and again mountains in the mist.

Unrolling a hand scroll such as Gao Keming's eleventh-century *Streams and Hills Under Fresh Snow* is like taking a walk along the wintry river, with here a laden coolie, there a barge, gnarled trees close up, and further off a cozy house along the snowy bank, the master and mistress just glimpsed through an open door as they are served their dinner. Fan Guan's magnificently vertical *Travelers Among Streams and Mountains* shows the travelers in their carriages dwarfed by the pine-crowned hills just behind them, rendered utterly insignificant by the gigantic mountains that rise out of a veil of mist to dominate the picture.

---

[4]Wan go Weng, *Chinese Painting and Calligraphy: A Pictorial Survey* (New York: Dover Publications, 1979), p. xvi.

## CHINA AND ZONE OF INFLUENCE IN THE TANG AND SONG DYNASTIES

Tang building is gone, Song painting survives. Both make it only too clear why Chinese civilization dominated the East a thousand years ago.

## CHINA'S SPHERE OF INFLUENCE: EAST ASIA

### The Borderlands

The Chinese sphere of influence consisted of a ring of states and peoples around the Middle Kingdom. All these cultures were less developed than China's during the ten centuries from the fall of the Han to the fall of the Song. Two distinct regions—and relationships—may, however, be distinguished among these peoples of China's borderlands.

Most of China's inner frontier, facing north and west upon Eurasia, opened onto relatively barren and thinly peopled terrain. The dusty deserts, the thin grass of the steppes, the high cold plateaus of Manchuria, Mongolia, Tibet, and the Tarim Basin encouraged a pastoral nomadic style of life very different from China's intensive agriculture and developed urban society. The languages of the Turko-Mongol peoples beyond the Great Wall were so different that they could not even be written in Chinese characters.

The normal relationships between China and its nomadic neighbors to the north and west was one of conflict. Every dynasty had to deal with "the barbarians," either defensively like the Song or by taking the offensive against them as the Tang emperors did. But large-scale assimilation to the Chinese way would prove very difficult in most of these inner Asian borderlands.

South and east, however, the case was very different. Here settled agricultural peoples had already made a beginning at a more developed culture. And here the impressive Chinese achievement in civilization decisively influenced what became the three most important East Asian nations outside of China itself—Vietnam, Korea, and Japan.

## Vietnam: The Lesser Dragon

Vietnam is a narrow S-shaped country running down the eastern edge of the Indochinese peninsula from South China into Southeast Asia. The country has two "rice bowls," the broad, fertile deltas of the Red River in the north and the Mekong in the south, connected by a long, curving mountain spine. Intruders from China began to push into north Vietnam toward the end of the first millennium B.C.E., just about the time of China's unification under the Qin.

They found a Bronze Age people, recently evolved from hunting and fishing yet already shaping an urban, seafaring society on a narrow agricultural base—the Dong-Son culture whose remains were to be found in many parts of Southeast Asia. Vietnam was no match for its huge neighbor. Shortly before 100 B.C.E., the Han emperors formally annexed the country, which would remain part of South China for the next thousand years.

Particularly under the aggressive Tang dynasty, Chinese rule brought Chinese administration and language, Confucian classics, and Mahayana Buddhism. Chinese influence also brought intensified wet-rice agriculture and a more elaborate urban culture. The Chinese presence, however, also generated a growing sense of national identity and resentment of foreign rule on the part of north Vietnamese officials and aristocrats in particular.

North Vietnam was never simply another Chinese province. The Vietnamese felt the cultural pull of their Indianized Southeast Asian neighbors. They were frequently preoccupied with the beginnings of their own long, slow conquest of southern Vietnam, which was then dominated by the Indianized kingdom of Champa. And resentment of their powerful neighbor to the north grew with every passing generation.

When the Tang dynasty collapsed into anarchy in the tenth century, the Vietnamese seized the chance to secede. After a long millennium as part of China, Vietnam was an independent—and growing—nation.

And yet before that century of independence was out, Vietnam's leaders had prudently accepted a tributary relationship with Song China. The cultural ties—and political enmities—that existed between the two nations would continue down the centuries, even to the present one. The troubled relationship between China and Vietnam, sometimes called the Greater and Lesser Dragons, remains a fact of East Asian life today.

## Korea and Chinese Cultural Hegemony

Korea is a broad, slightly hooked peninsula thrusting down between North China's Yellow Sea and the Sea of Japan. The country is broken up by mountain ranges extending throughout much of its length. The western and southern coasts, however, smooth down into level plains and finally break up into many harbors and islands. The population at the time of the first Chinese intrusion was sparse and not long removed from dependence on hunting and fishing, though the western coastal plains particularly were already under cultivation. The Koreans still lived in tribal societies dominated by hereditary chiefs and female shamans called *mudang*. Their major monuments were stone-walled tombs, or dolmens, of the sort found in many parts of Eurasia, from western Europe to Japan, in earlier centuries.

The expansionist Han Chinese pushed into northern Korea in the last centuries before Christ. Empress Lü temporarily annexed part of the northern peninsula around 100 B.C.E. But Korea itself was moving rapidly ahead with state formation by then, and Chinese political control soon evaporated. Nevertheless, an influential colony of Chinese remained in the northern part of the peninsula for several hundred years.

From about the fourth century C.E. on, the Three Kingdoms divided Korea among them. These three rival Korean powers competed for Chinese skills and cultural innovations to strengthen them in their endless feuds. When the Sui and Tang dynasties reunited China in the seventh century, massive Chinese expeditions were launched against Korea. Once more, the attempt at conquest failed. But Empress Wu's shrewd alliance with the Korean kingdom of Silla, which soon established control over most of the peninsula, enhanced the continuing Chinese influence.

Under Silla in Tang times and under the kingdom of Koryo in the days of the Song, Korea's own rulers set out to turn their recently unified nation into a carbon copy of their huge neighbor. What remained of the old tribal culture was replaced as far as possible by a structure of central bureaus and provincial officials. The Korean economy—particularly the commercial sector—remained comparatively backward by Chinese standards. But the Chinese written language and culture, and most especially Chinese Mahayana Buddhism, were widespread.

Like the Vietnamese, the Koreans traditionally paid tribute to China. But the Korean debt to the Middle Kingdom went far deeper than annual payments. The development of Korean civilization illustrates perfectly the pattern of cultural hegemony that underlay the phenomenon of growing zones of culture around the world.

## The Island Kingdom of Japan

The offshore-island kingdom of Japan provides a variant and even more important example of the impact of Chinese culture. Japan was dramatically affected by its encounters with Chinese civilization, yet a distinctive Japanese form of East Asian culture, contrasting sharply with China's in some ways, evolved in the end.

The reason for China's limited impact on Japan was probably primarily geographic. Japan lies more than a hundred miles east of the Asian mainland—five times as far from Asia as Britain is from Europe. At such a distance China's armed forces, which were spearheads of Chinese influence in Vietnam and even Korea, had no impact on Japan. The Japanese were thus much freer to accept or reject Chinese influences, to seek contact with the giant power to the west or to cut themselves off from it for generations at a time. From this unique circumstance evolved the strikingly selective pattern of China's influence on Japan.

The four main Japanese islands run some 1,300 miles, from jagged Hokkaido in the northeast through the long, indented curve of Honshu to the smaller islands of Kyushu and Shikoku in the southwest.

Four fifths of the island country is too mountainous for agriculture, but intensive rice cultivation in the narrow river valleys and coastal plains has made it possible for today's Japan to support the sixth largest population in the world. The mountains contribute to the nation's picture-postcard beauty and have given it a national symbol, the sacred snow-capped cone of Mount Fuji.

The center of Japan's early history was not in the heart of the large central island of Honshu, where Tokyo sprawls today, but in western Japan, around the narrow Inland Sea framed by Kyushu and Shikoku and the southwesternmost tip of Honshu. Here prehistoric hunting, fishing, and farming bands and settlements developed, matriarchal in social organization, worshiping nature spirits, working bronze and then iron.

During the early centuries of the Christian era, a simple clan-based society evolved around the Inland Sea, each small clan, or *uji*, having its hereditary chief and its ancestral god, often a totemic animal or other nature spirit. By the fifth century a loosely feudal state had appeared, dominated by the powerful Yamato clan; other *uji* were ranked in a rough hierarchy. By this time too, the collection of cults and religious practices called *Shinto* had emerged, along with its simple rites and local shrines dedicated to mountains, waterfalls, ancient trees, and a few sanctified individuals.

## Japan and the Chinese Model

In the sixth century Chinese Buddhism reached Japan through Korea, bringing Chinese culture with it. In the seventh and eighth centuries, reforming Japanese regimes sent repeated embassies, including many students and monks, to Tang China to acquire the skills and learn the ways of the East Asian colossus. Powerful Japanese statesmen encouraged this procedure. The famous Prince Shotoku, in particular, preached centralized government and court hierarchy and even imported the Chinese calendar.

The resulting changes seemed likely to turn Japan into another small version of the Tang state. Japanese rulers and *uji* chiefs, some of whom were more powerful than their sovereign, nevertheless preached centralized rule by an absolute emperor and urged a Confucian sense of duty and Buddhist reverence. Centralized bureaus were established, a Chinese-style law code was promulgated, and attempts were made to establish the equal-field system and centralized taxation of Tang China. A capital city called Nara was built at the eastern end of the Inland Sea, modeled on Changian, with royal palaces and massive monasteries. The Japanese elite learned Chinese and used Chinese script, borrowed Chinese court ceremonials, Chinese styles and entertainments.

Beneath these transformations at the top of Nara society, however, Japan remained in many ways the Japan of old. The *uji* aristocracy preserved much of its former feudal independence despite the emperor's exalted claims. The economy remained comparatively simple; money, for example, was still rare, barter far more common. And the great Chinese invention of an educated civil service based on merit was never adopted at all beyond the Sea of Japan.

Then, as Tang China declined and crumbled into chaos in the ninth century, Japan turned away from its great model and began to develop its own distinctive style of civilization. The Heian period (roughly 800–1200), when the Japanese capital was at Heian (present-day Kyoto) was the period when this return to older ways was strongest. In three dynamic centuries Japan's ruling elite had absorbed all they could learn from China. The following four hundred years were given over to digesting and modifying these cultural acquisitions in terms of Japan's older native heritage.

The core of that heritage was *uji* feudalism, and the Heian period saw a significant resurgence of the power of the landed magnates in the *shoen* (estates) system. The *shoen* typically consisted not of a single estate but a dispersed collection of tracts owned by a single aristocratic proprietor. This proprietor looked up to a patron, usually a powerful figure at the royal court or in the Buddhist establishment. Below the proprietor were his estate managers, the farmers they managed, and the farm laborers the farmers hired. The result was a structure much like the feudal and manorial systems of Europe at that time—and very different from the centralized economy of China.

The chief patrons of the *shoen* system were wealthy court families, such as the Fujiwara, or religious institutions, commonly rich Buddhist monasteries. The great families in particular became the real rulers of Japan, using the royal court as an arena for their endless intrigues. The Fujiwara soon became the most powerful of these great clans, supplying the royal house with most of its empresses, monopolizing high government posts, and holding more *shoen* estates than any other family.

Occasionally feisty emperors challenged Fujiwara dominance, and there were damaging splits in the Fujiwara clan itself. But the real problem was that the authority of the government declined so drastically as to be a prize hardly worth controlling. As the power behind a powerless throne, the Fujiwara slowly went down with the monarchy they had themselves undermined.

## The Culture of Court and Monastery

The Japanese cultural accomplishment during the seven centuries from the Yamoto state to the Heian period reflected even more strikingly the unique Japanese amalgamation of indigenous elements and foreign influences. This mixture is clear whichever of the twin centers of Japan's emergent culture we look at—the Buddhist monasteries or the imperial court.

The imported Buddhist faith comprised a variety of Chinese sects, from the ecclectic *Tendai* (Chinese: *Tiantai*) with its emphasis on the Lotus Sutra, through the popular

A Kyoto temple today, with its curving pagoda roof line, reflecting pool, and setting of trees and flowers beautifully embodies both the Chinese Buddhist influence and the grace and elegance of Heian Japan. Lightness, graceful lines, and the integration of buildings with the natural world around were features of Japanese architecture. (Japan National Tourist Organization)

Pure Land school, to the mystic withdrawal of meditative Zen (*Chan*). Pure Land Buddhism, offering hope of rebirth in the Buddhist paradise, had a particular appeal during the later Heian period, when the decay of central government and accompanying domestic violence made many fear that a Buddhist version of the end of the world was nigh.

Buddhist temples and Buddhist sculpture survive in considerable quantities, and Chinese influences are clear. The graceful lines of multiple pagoda roofs rose above the worldly capitals of Nara and Heian and among the forested mountains where some monks sought refuge from the world. Statues of Buddha, of various bodhisattvas, and of famous monks in meditation were crafted in stone, bronze, wood, and other materials. One of the most famous is the *Portrait of Ganjin,* a Chinese monk who tried six times to reach Japan, survived pirates, storms, and shipwreck to do so, and finally arrived—blind, having lost his vision in the course of his tribulations. There is more than realism in this simple figure seated in the Buddhist posture of meditation; the gentle face, shaved head, and closed eyes blend with the curving folds of the robe to project a feeling of benevolence and great peace.

The secular culture of the Heian period especially was immensely sophisticated for a people only a few centuries removed from the rude life of feudal clans. The court life of that period of intrigue and conspiracy was elegant in the extreme. Fashion, aesthetics, and the most delicate sensibilities governed the dress and decorum, the love life and artistic creativity of these courtiers of old Japan.

Poetry and exquisite prose were produced in substantial quantities, much of it by highly cultured court ladies. The greatest subject was love, the medium a mix of prose and poetry. An unusual literary form was the poetic diary, a first-person account of a journey, a love affair, or simply the daily life of the court, much of it written in verse. Though a core of autobiographical fact was necessary, artistic requirements seem to have determined the shapely contours of the finished work.

The novel also appeared this early in Japanese literary history. The most famous Heian novel—indeed, the most famous and influential of all Japanese novels—was Lady Murasaki's eleventh-century *The Tale of Genji.* Often described as the first psychological novel, this lengthy account of the life and love affairs of Prince Genji gives as much attention to nuances of feeling as to complex plotting and court life. Overlying it all, there is a romantic melancholy, a sense of the fragility of all things human, and of the heightened intensity this sense of transitory humanity gives to life, love, and beauty.

Among the rude barons of the back country, however, devotees of the warrior code of *bushido,* the builders of the next age, were already gathering their forces. The reign of the samurai was fast approaching.

## SUMMARY

Between the third and the thirteenth centuries, many dynasties ruled China, but two loom gigantic in the history books: the empire-building Tang and the brilliant Song.

The Tang dynasty (618–907) was founded by Emperor Tang Taizong—"Grand Ancestor," victorious general, political reformer, scholar, artist, and perhaps the greatest of all Chinese rulers. The greatest of Chinese empresses, the Dowager Empress Wu, left the land richer and more powerful than it had ever been. Overall, China's political centralization, foreign trade, domestic wealth, and conquests beyond its own borders had never been greater than they were during the Tang.

The Song dynasty (960–1279) produced fewer great emperors, no foreign conquest, and diminished commercial exchange with the outside world. Yet the Middle Kingdom was never more brilliant. A population of one hundred million Chinese fed itself and was governed by the world's first meritocracy, the Confucian scholar bureaucrats.

Chinese culture during this millennium from the fall of the Han to that of the Song was varied and colorful. Chinese learning probed the nation's lengthening past and analyzed the classics of Confucius. Buddhist monks carried that Indian religion far across China and beyond. The printing press, the compass, gunpowder, and acupuncture all enriched Chinese culture.

Poetry blossomed in unparalleled quantities, including the lyrics of China's most admired poet, Du Fu, who wrote with Confucian concern for the Chinese underdog. Song ceramics and landscape painting established Chinese traditions that have been admired around the world since.

Under the Tang, furthermore, China's zone of influence among neighboring peoples exceeded even that of the Han. China ruled Vietnam as a loosely held province and exercised a decisive cultural influence on Korea. But Tang China's most important impact was felt by the still undeveloped islands of Japan.

Under Chinese influence, the island nation of Japan evolved from a culture of feuding clans into a Tang-style monarchy. China's impact declined during the inward-looking Song era, when Japan's emperors lost most of their power to its great noble families. Yet Japan remained a sophisticated new nation, where Buddhist monks, court poets, and novels like the famous *The Tale of Genji* reflected the seminal influences of the ancient empire more than a hundred miles away across the Sea of Japan.

## SUGGESTED READING

Bol, P. K. *'This Culture of Ours': Intellectual Transitions in T'ang and Song China.* Stanford: Stanford University Press, 1992. Leading Chinese scholars defend and develop their culture.

Chaffee, J. W. *The Thorny Gate of Learning in Sung China: A Social History of Examinations.* New York: Cambridge University Press, 1985. Widely admired study of the development of China's scholarly elite during a period of rapid growth.

Deng, G. *Chinese Maritime Activities and Socioeconomic Development, c. 2100 B.C.–1900 A.D.* Westport, Conn.: Greenwood Press, 1997. Brief overview of Chinese maritime history, including major achievements in earlier centuries.

Dudbridge, G. *Religious Experience and Lay Society in T'ang China: A Reading of Tai Fu's* Kuang-i chi. New York: Cambridge University Press, 1995. Presents supernatural stories as records of spiritual life in "this-worldly" China.

Ebrey, P. B. *The Inner Quarters: Marriage and the Lives of Chinese Women in the Sung Period.* Berkeley and Los Angeles: University of California Press, 1993. Emphasizes women's initiatives in the limiting context of a patriarchal society.

Fitzgerald, C. P. *The Empress Wu.* Vancouver: University of British Columbia Press, 1968. Readable and scholarly life of the great Chinese empress.

Heng, C. K. *Cities of Aristocrats and Bureaucrats: The Development of Medieval Chinese Cityscapes.* Honolulu: University of Hawaii Press, 1999. Changing urban structures in Tang and Song times.

Lo, W. W. *An Introduction to the Civil Service of Sung China.* Honolulu: University of Hawaii Press, 1987. Personnel and organization.

Murasaki, S. *The Tale of Genji,* trans. E. G. Seidensticker. New York: Knopf, 1976. Accurate translation of this most famous of Japanese novels; Arthur Waley's older translation (London: Allen and Unwin, 1935) still has great literary appeal.

Pollack, D. *The Fracture of Meaning: Japan's Synthesis of China from the Eighth Through the Eighteenth Century.* Princeton: Princeton University Press, 1986. Complex interaction of borrowed ideas from China and indigenous Japanese concepts to produce Japan's own unique traditional culture.

Waley-Cohen, J. *The Sextants of Beijing: Global Currents in Chinese History.* New York and London: W. W. Norton, 1999. Survey of cultural contacts, challenging traditional view of Chinese isolation.

Wechsler, H. J. *Mirror to the Son of Heaven: Wei Cheng at the Court of T'ang T'ai-tsung.* New Haven, Conn.: Yale University Press, 1974. The founder of the Tang and his China.

Weinstein, S. *Buddhism Under the T'ang* (New York: Cambridge University Press, 1987), an examination of shifting government policies toward the spread of Buddhism in China.

Weng, W. *Chinese Painting and Calligraphy: A Pictorial Survey.* New York: Dover, 1978. Beautifully reproduced examples from a famous American collection, including many samples from the Northern and Southern Song.

 Please refer to the document CD-ROM for primary sources related to this chapter.

# CHAPTER 13

# KINGS AND CONQUERING PEOPLES
## Empires of Africa and the Americas

### (600–1450)

## A Glance Ahead: Africa and the Americas

Large cultural zones took shape in Africa and the Americas during this period, too. From the grasslands of the Western Sudan to the Swahili coast of East Africa, from the peaks of the Andes to the banks of the Mississippi, neighboring peoples tended to share common cultural patterns.

Similarly intricate patterns of exchange linked peoples across North America as they did the cities of East Africa's Swahili coast. Toltec conquerors in Mexico, Christian kings in Ethiopia, and South American empire builders all raised cities and temples over broad swathes of the Old and New Worlds.

From common building styles or carvings, from the memories of visitors, and from their own heroic legends, we can reconstruct the common cultures that united each of these regions. We will see the peoples of East and West Africa and of North, Middle, and South America following distinctive styles of life shared with their neighbors, defining ever broader subdivisions of the earth.

## West Africa: Ghana and Mali

### The *Bilad al Sudan*

A number of interrelated factors contributed to the emergence of a distinctively West African civilization on the great westward bulge of Africa well before the year 1000. These linked causal factors included geography, trade, and religion.

While North and East Africa were geographically oriented outward toward the developing civilizations of the Mediterranean and the Indian Ocean, West Africa faced inward. Owing to a lack of natural harbors on the coast of West Africa, transport and trade were largely internal. And since commercial exchange was an essential ingredient in the development of kingdoms in West Africa, these new states emerged primarily in the interior, rather than along the coasts.

The interior of Africa, it will be remembered, is divided into a series of horizontal belts of land and climate. These belts are nowhere more clearly marked than in West Africa, and they are crucial to the emergence of trade in that region. In the north there is the thin strip of fertile land along the Mediterranean—the Maghreb, site of ancient Carthage, home in the year 1000 of Muslim Berber and Arab kingdoms, from Tunisia to Morocco. South of this coastal strip the Sahara Desert stretches the width of Africa, with its scattering of oases and caravan trails. Farther to the south lies the Western Sudan, the western end of the belt of lightly wooded savanna that also runs the width of the continent. Still farther south, finally, the dense rain forest of the Guinea coast extends eastward around the internal angle of Africa into the jungles of the Congo basin.

Trade in West Africa flowed predominantly north and south across these belts of climate and terrain. From the Maghreb in the north, camel caravans crossed the desert southward to the savannas to trade in the cities of the *Bilad al Sudan,* the "Land of the Black People," as the Western Sudan was then called. The goods and products these traders took back with them, including the famous gold of Africa, came mostly not from the Sudan itself but from the forests beyond. It was by building their power in this strategic location

# African Empires and Trade Routes

**Ghana Empire**
Early 11th century

**Mali Empire**
14th century

**Songhai Empire**
Early 16th century

**Trade Routes**

• • • • Donkey caravans

———— Camel caravans

‖‖‖‖ Head porterage

· · · · Lesser routes, head porterage

———— Arabian dhows

| 0 | 250 | 500 | 750 | 1000 Miles |

| 0 | 500 | 1000 Kilometers |

Tangier
Algiers
Tunis
*MEDITERRANEAN   SEA*
Fez
Tlemcen
Tripoli
Marrakech
Barka
Alexandria
Nul
Sijilmasa
Wargla
Cairo
Ghadames
Asyut
Kosseir
Tuat
Zuila
Taghaza
Ghat
*S       A       H       A       R       A*
Bilma
Dongola
Awdoghast
Walata
Timbuktu
Axum
Gondar
Rufisque
Gao
Takedda
Zeila
Ghiarou
Jenne
Manan
Katsina
*Niger R.*
*Lake Chad*
Niani
Kano
Elmina
Benin
*Pepper Coast*
Axim
*Ivory Coast*
*Gold Coast*
*Slave Coast*
*Congo R.*
*Nile R.*
Mogadishu
Brava
*Lake Victoria*
Malindi
Mombasa
Lamu I.
*Equator*
*To India and China*
*ATLANTIC OCEAN*
Zanzibar
Luanda
*Lake Tanganyika*
*To India and China*
Kilwa I.
Benguela
*Lake Nyasa*
*Zambezi R.*
Tete
Victoria Falls
Sena
Sofala
Quelimane
*KALAHARI DESERT*
Zimbabwe
*INDIAN OCEAN*
*Cape of Good Hope*
Asyut

between the Sahara and the forest peoples of the Guinea coast that the Sudanic kingdoms waxed rich and famous as centers of trade.

With the traders from the north there also came the new religion of Islam. Muslim merchants and teachers, Arab or Berber, settled in the growing cities south of the Sahara and contributed their faith and their skills to the new West African states. They brought with them literacy and administrative experience, and they often held high offices under African kings. They also brought one of the great world religions, a faith which, while always that of a minority, helped to integrate the African kingdoms into the larger world of Muslim trade, Islamic pilgrimage, and the hospitality of their coreligionists wherever they traveled. Under these stimuli, the ironworking agricultural villages of the Western Sudan evolved into impressive African empires over the centuries between 600 and 1600.

The typical Sudanese state could be as large as, or larger than, the European nations that were developing about the same time. They were ruled by divine-right kings who served as essential intermediaries between their people and their gods. These rulers governed through a combination of appointed officials and alliances with lesser kings. They also maintained substantial armies for the constant warfare of the region. For long stretches of time the peoples of West Africa seem to have been well governed and prosperous. European as well as North African goods were on sale in the cities of the Sudan, and West African gold contributed significantly to the European economic revival of the High Middle Ages.

There were problems in the Sudanese kingdoms, as in all the efforts at civilization-building we have chronicled so far. These African empires seldom had clearly defined boundaries; they are often represented by circles on maps. And as in their medieval European counterparts, royal power faded rapidly the further one moved from the capital. There were serious problems with succession as well, since succession in West Africa was based not on direct patrilineal hereditary descent, but on a more generalized lineage concept that often produced more than one possible heir to a throne. As in most early civilizations, finally, rebellious generals and revolts by recently conquered peoples were common problems.

All such difficulties notwithstanding, the empires of the Western Sudan did represent a major expansion of urban imperial culture, and as such will be examined here. We shall focus on two of the most famous: Old Ghana and Mali.

## Ghana: The Land of Gold

The Western Sudan before the year 1000 was open grassland dotted with scattered trees and groves. The people lived in villages of round, thatch-roofed earthen huts and granaries, cultivated millet and sorghum, and worked iron. The oldest male in a particular village normally ruled the village or sometimes a collection of villages, often with the strong advice and consent of a queen mother or a council of elders. Spirits dwelt nearby in sacred pools and groves of giant baobab trees, and carefully carved fetishes were kept in a special hut and consulted on all serious problems. It was a life, in short, much like that of other peoples outside the walls of urban culture.

Then, perhaps as early as 600, the walls of cities began to go up in West Africa too.

Ghana, the older of the two medieval West African kingdoms to be discussed here, flourished from the eighth through the eleventh centuries, and Mali, its successor, from the twelfth through the fourteenth. Both Ghana and Mali were dominated and most frequently ruled by Mande-speaking peoples: the Soninke, or northern Mande, and the Mandinke, or southern Mande, the latter the famous Mandingo of later history.

Ghana set the pattern of wealth and power built on trade that its successors would follow. As early as 800, while Charlemagne was being crowned in Rome and most of Europe was sunk in feudal chaos and subsistence agriculture, Ghana was already being described by Arab chroniclers as "the land of gold."

The origins of Old Ghana are lost in the mists of time and scholarly dispute.[1] By the eighth and ninth centuries, however, the Soninke kings of Ghana ruled all the lands bounded by the shallow V formed by the upper Niger and Senegal rivers. They governed many villages and clans through a centralized administrative structure and a powerful army. They claimed divine sanction for their governance; like rulers everywhere, they were the chief link between their subjects and the gods. In fact, however, it was commercial exchange that made them great.

From the north came Tuareg camel caravans down across the desert, navigating from oasis to oasis by sun, stars, and wind patterns on the dunes. The Arab and Berber merchants in these caravans brought cloth, brass, glass, and above all, blocks of salt—essential to life in the tropics—to the metropolises of Ghana. From the south, Ghanaian traders brought back agricultural products, slaves, and most important, gold from the mines of Wangara, just south of the Ghanaian frontier. Both Africa and Arab profited from the exchange. And the kings of Ghana collected heavy customs duties on all the gold and all the salt that crossed their borders. So great was the northward flow of gold that medieval Arab travelers and historians thought the king of Ghana must be the richest ruler in the world.

In the end, it was apparently excessive ambition and the slow southward advance of the Sahara that brought Ghana down.

The ambition of the Soninke kings led them to try to extend their authority northward along the trade routes into the Berber lands on the southern edge of the Sahara. The disunited Berbers fell easy victims at first. But in the eleventh century, unified and filled with crusading zeal by the puritanical Almoravid sect of Islam, they swept north as far as Morocco and on into Spain—and south to overwhelm Old Ghana.

The southward creep of the Sahara completed what the Almoravids had begun. The continuing drying-out of northern Africa parched the former heartland of Ghana. Before the slowly advancing sands, black power retreated farther to the south.

## Mali: Where the King Dwells

The Almoravids broke the back of Ghanaian power, but they were not strong enough to rule for long. The result was to create a power vacuum in the Western Sudan where a number of African kingdoms fought for mastery. Another branch of the Mande-speaking people, the Mandinke, emerged victorious by the early thirteenth century from this anarchic period. They became the builders and rulers of an even larger realm than Old Ghana had been: the Empire of Mali.

*Mali* is an Arab corruption of a southern Mande word meaning simply "Where the King Dwells"—and the Mandinke rulers of Mali were kings indeed. They governed in conscious emulation of their Ghanaian predecessors, with appointed officials—including departments of defense, foreign relations, and finance—and with an effective army to enforce the royal will. They revitalized the trans-Saharan trade in gold and salt and grew

---

[1] "Old Ghana" is sometimes so called to distinguish it from the modern nation of Ghana, which is located some hundreds of miles southeast of the empire discussed here.

# VOICES FROM THE PAST

This famous eleventh-century description of the capital of Ghana clearly reflects both the impact of Islam and the persistence of older African traditions. The Arab chronicler Al-Bakri records that the capital was really two "cities"—or city centers, since houses filled all the space between them. The Arab quarter is dominated by its mosques, while the "king's town," or political center, has its sacred grove consecrated to older gods.

According to this Arab account, the king received visitors in state in his royal pavilion, surrounded by the sons of subordinate chiefs, leading advisors, and governors. Guards with swords and shields stood behind him. The royal turban and robes, the shields of the sentries, and even the collars of guard dogs stationed at the door were all of gold.

What does this description tell you about the economy and political structure of Ghana? What do you deduce about the importance of the Arab traders from the fact that, while his majesty's African subjects were required to prostrate themselves on the ground before him and throw dust on their heads, Muslims were allowed to greet him simply by clapping their hands?

> *"The city of Ghana consists of two towns situated on a plain. One of these towns, which is inhabited by Muslims, is large and possesses twelve mosques, in one of which they assemble for the Friday prayer. There are salaried imams and muezzins, as well as jurists and scholars. In the environs are wells with sweet water, from which they drink and with which they grow vegetables.*
>
> *The king's town is six miles [about 10 km] distant from this one and bears the name of al-Ghāba. Between these two towns there are continuous habitations. The houses of the inhabitants are of stone and acacia wood. The king has a palace and a number of domed dwellings all surrounded with an enclosure like a city wall.*
>
> *In the king's town, and not far from his court of justice, is a mosque where pray such Muslims as pay him formal visits.*
>
> *Around the king's town are domed buildings and groves and thickets where the sorcerers of these people, men in charge of the religious cult, live. In them are their idols and the tombs of their kings. These woods are guarded and none may enter them and know what is there."*

Al-Bakri, *Kitab al-masalik wa'l mamalik,* in Nehemia Levtzion, "The Sahara and the Sudan from the Arab Conquest . . . to the Rise of the Almoravids," in J. D. Fage, ed., *The Cambridge History of Africa* (Cambridge: Cambridge University Press, 1986), Vol. 2, p. 668.

---

richer than the Soninke Mande of Ghana. They turned caravan-route cities like Timbuktu into famous emporiums of trade and centers of culture.

Mali reached its highest point in the fourteenth century under its most famous ruler, Mansa (King) Musa (ca. 1307–1332). Musa expanded the empire to its greatest territorial extent, to the big bend of the Niger. He was celebrated not only in Arab lands to the north but as far away as Europe.

The famous Arab traveler and historian Ibn Batuta, who visited Mali around the middle of the fourteenth century, was impressed with what he saw. He received good medical attention there when he fell ill, and he had respectful words for the scholars he met. Above all, he was struck by the strong sense of justice and the rigorous enforcement of it that he found in Mali. The roads of Mali were safe for travelers, he wrote, as they were in few other parts of the world.

This picture of a well-governed, wealthy, and powerful state has its darker side. There were frequent disputes over the succession to the throne, and factions feuded at the courts of the kings of Mali, as they did in royal courts from China to Britain. Conquered peoples were often restless and ready to rebel. Religion became an important divisive factor too, with Mandinke rulers turning to Islam while their peasant subjects and the neighboring peoples with whom Mali traded remained faithful to the old gods and the spirits of the land.

Like all great nations, the kingdom of Mali had its enemies, rivals awaiting only the opportunity to pull the greatest of West African powers down. In the fifteenth century, as we will see, one of them took advantage of internal weakness to do just that.

## Mansa Musa's Pilgrimage

Like all the kings and increasing numbers of the ruling classes of Mali, Mansa Musa was a Muslim, and his most renowned exploit was a pilgrimage to Mecca. His royal progress across Africa astonished the peoples through whose lands he passed. On this long journey to the north and east across Africa, Musa was accompanied by his wife, his chief officials, thousands of servants, and a hundred camels laden with gold. He was given a palace in Cairo by the Egyptian sultan and spent three months there before continuing on to the holy city. He and his retinue had spent so much gold in Cairo that the price of that precious metal declined because there was so much of it in circulation. As an Egyptian official reported,

> This man spread upon Cairo the flood of his generosity: there was no person, officer of the court, or holder of any office of the Sultanate who did not receive a sum of gold from him. The people of Cairo earned incalculable sums from him, whether by buying and selling or by gifts. So much gold was current in Cairo that it ruined the value of money.[2]

On his return, Mansa Musa glorified his capital city. From his pilgrimage, he brought back artists, scholars, and a famous architect to build him palaces and mosques. He established diplomatic ties with African states as far away as Egypt and Morocco. It was from this time on that European map-makers began to put Musa's picture on their maps of West Africa with a lump of gold in his hand.

# EAST AFRICA: ETHIOPIA AND THE SWAHILI COAST

## The Christian States of Nubia

The influence of Islam was profound across North Africa, West Africa, and—as we will see—down the eastern coast of the continent as well. In one area, however, another great world religion exercised a determining influence. In the northeastern corner of Africa, several Christian kingdoms flourished, including the states of Christian Nubia and the Christian kingdom of Ethiopia.

Nubian civilization already had a long history when Christianity reached the Upper Nile in the sixth century. Nubia had been the home of a flourishing culture in the days of ancient Egypt. Kush and Meroe had flowered there, and Axum had overrun the southern core of the region. But great changes came over Nubia when Greek Orthodox preachers from the north converted first the kings and then the upper classes of the Nubian zone.

---

[2]ál-Omari, in E. Jefferson Murphy, *History of African Civilization* (New York: Crowell, 1972), p. 120.

The political history of Christian Nubia covered eight hundred years, from the sixth to the fourteenth centuries. The most powerful of the Christian kingdoms of Nubia was Makouria, whose chief cities were the royal capital at Old Dongola and the chief religious center at Faras.

At the height of its power, Makouria's King Kyriakos could march up the Nile into Muslim Egypt to force the sultan to release the imprisoned head of Egypt's Christian minority. In its heyday around 800, Makouria was ruled by a hereditary monarch who dictated to a dozen subsidiary kings and commanded a large number of officials.

Converted to Christianity by missionaries from the Greek-speaking Byzantine Empire, the Christian Nubian elite also spoke Greek, used Greek titles for officials, and used Greek as the official language of the church. Pictures of Nubian kings show them wearing golden crowns encrusted with jewels and clad in sumptuously embroidered robes like those worn by Byzantine rulers in Constantinople.

In its best days, Christian Nubia was a lovely land of cities and villages, churches and monasteries. A tenth-century Arab visitor recalled "villages with beautiful buildings, churches, monasteries and many palm trees, vines, gardens, fields and large pastures in which graze handsome and well-bred camels."[3]

By the 1300s, however, royal power had declined, and bloody coups were frequent. A feudal aristocracy with castles scattered across the land divided real power between them. Then Arab tribesmen broke through the frontiers, and Egypt's new rulers, the military aristocracy known as the Mamelukes, interfered repeatedly in Nubian royal politics. Cut off from the main body of medieval Christendom in Europe, Christian Nubia held out as long as it could against the growing power of Islam in Africa. By 1400, however, a Muslim dynasty ruled Makouria, and almost all of Nubia was in Islamic hands.

## The Kingdom of Ethiopia

Southeast of Nubia, the Christian survivors of ancient Axum had withdrawn ever deeper into the mountainous regions of their corner of Africa in the latter part of the first mellennium C.E. A one-time trading people, they were now cut off from their former trading partners in the eastern Mediterranean and the Red Sea. Christian converts from the fourth century, they were surrounded by pagans and, from the seventh century on, by Muslim Arabs. Forgotten by their fellow Christians and by those whose ancient civilization they had shared, the people who would come to be known as Ethiopians struggled to survive in their isolated upland home.

Only in the twelfth century did a fusion of Ethiopian peoples under the Christian Zagwe dynasty bring a new flowering of this African kingdom. Under the Zagwe kings, a uniquely Ethiopian form of Christianity took shape. Heavily imbued with both local pagan and ancient Judaic elements, the Ethiopian church also forged a close alliance with the monarchy, a cooperation that strengthened both. The most striking relics of this era still remaining are the dozen rock-carved churches hacked out of the volcanic stone of the Ethiopian mountains at Roha during the reign of King Lalibela (ca. 1181–1221). According to a later medieval account, the king's stone carvers labored on the churches by day, while angels carried on the work at night.

---

[3]Ibn Selim, quoted in William Y. Adams, *Nubia: Corridor to Africa* (Princeton, NJ.: Princeton University Press, 1984), p. 461.

The Solomonid dynasty succeeded the Zagwe kings in 1270 and at least nominally ruled the land for the next seven centuries. Claiming direct descent from Israel's King Solomon and the Queen of Sheba, the Solomonids reached their apogee under King Zara Jacob (1434–1468). Still depending heavily on religion as a social cement, these Ethiopian rulers suppressed heresy at home and crusaded vigorously against neighboring Muslim peoples. From the fourteenth century, priests and monks generated a literary renaissance that produced hymns, royal chronicles, and biographies of kings and saints. By the beginning of modern times, sixteenth-century Ethiopia was an extensive if still isolated kingdom.

Medieval Europeans told legends of the golden realm of Prester John, a fabulously rich Christian king lost somewhere in the unknown southern lands of Africa. A hardy Portuguese traveler even reached Ethiopia in 1494, two years after Columbus reached the New World. But this and other early contacts came to nothing. Muslim military pressure was renewed in the later sixteenth century, and Ethiopian Christians themselves fell into a bloody schism. By 1600, the Solomonid monarchs were little more than figureheads, the kingdom itself a loose confederation of princes.

## A Capital on the Move, A Mountain of Kings

Medieval Ethiopia's political system, at its apogee under the Solomonids, evolved some unique features all its own. Ruling over a large, geographically fragmented realm, over Christians, Muslims, Jews, and traditional animists, over Africans, Arabs, and other peoples, Ethiopia's kings devised a governmental system combining flexibility with strength. A loose feudal regime of vassal kings and nobles meant that the king of Ethiopia delegated a good deal of authority to regional powers. A large military force, ready to move at the first threat of serious disorder, gave the ruler the final say.

Two other institutions emphasized the flexibility of the Ethiopian system. One was the traveling royal court, the other Ethiopia's unique Mountain of Kings.

The court of the Ethiopian king was not settled in a single capital city but was always on the move. In some ways it resembled the restless monarchies of medieval Europe, moving from one castle or province to the next to keep an eye on feudal vassals whose loyalty was often fickle. In Ethiopia, however, the kings seem to have had no favorite seat. The royal court was a movable camp, ever ready to pull up stakes and move on to the next valley, to march against a rebellious prince or an aggressive neighboring people.

The royal caravan brought all the upper classes, ethnic groups, and religious sects together, while moving majestically from one part of the kingdom to another. Thus, the traveling court of Ethiopia performed a vital integrative function for this extremely heterogeneous society.

Ethiopia's legendary Mountain of Kings combined stability with flexibility in a very different way. King Yikunno-Amlak, who established the Solomonid dynasty in 1270, was determined to avoid future palace coups or revolutions. He therefore sent all his relatives except his designated heirs up to the heights of Mount Geshen, an inaccessible retreat guarded by picked troops garrisoning all the passes below. On Mount Geshen, all the princes of the realm who could be rivals for the throne lived in luxurious isolation. They were free to enjoy all the pleasures that went with their high birth—but cut off from political ties to the world below.

As the years passed, many of these royal exiles turned to religious study, took up poetry or music, became wise or creative spirits. And if ever the direct royal line failed in the kingdom, the wisest of all the denizens of the Mountain of Kings could be summoned down to take his place on the throne of Ethiopia.

## The City-States of Zanj

Down the east coast of Africa, along the shores of the Indian Ocean, a process of commercial growth, Islamicization, and cultural synthesis similar to that in West Africa was taking place. The result was the flourishing string of East African ports and city-states the Arabs called the Land of Zanj—mostly Kenya and Tanzania today.

Wave after wave of migrants had settled along this edge of the continent. The Bantu-speaking Africans were migrants across central Africa to these coasts, bringing iron and agriculture. Other peoples had come by sea. Southeast Asians had been coming for centuries, populating the huge southern island of Madagascar and introducing the ubiquitous banana to Africa. Shirazi Persians, probably moving south from earlier settlements on the Horn of Africa, came as traders. But the most successful immigrants, merchants, builders, and sometimes rulers were the Muslim Arabs we have already met in so many places.

The history of evolving relationships between African animists and agriculturists on the one hand and Arab Muslim traders on the other must be worked out largely from archaeological remains and oral tradition. Arabs, by that time masters of most of the Indian Ocean trade, seem to have settled in East Africa in growing numbers from the twelfth century on. They may have established trading posts alongside African towns, as they did in the Western Sudan, accepting the protection of African kings. Or they may have imposed Arab overlordship, as they would do along these coasts in later centuries.

## Swahili Society

In either case, the Muslim faith spread here as well as in West Africa. A mixed Afro-Islamic Swahili culture developed. A Bantu language, Swahili, continued as the lingua franca of the coast, and African customs persisted even among the rulers of the new city-states that emerged. But there were Arab influences in Swahili too—the word itself means "people of the coast" in Arabic—and the architecture of the new towns was more likely to be Arabic or Persian than African in design.

The wealth of East Africa, like that of the Western Sudan, was based on commerce. Here the trade routes of inner Africa met the sea lanes of the Indian Ocean, linking Africa with the Mediterranean, Arabia, India, Southeast Asia, and China. Ivory, gold, iron, copper, pearl, coral, and slaves left African shores; Indian beads, Chinese porcelain, and silks flowed into Africa from overseas.

The East African cities of Kilwa, south of Zanzibar, and Sofala, still farther to the south beyond the Zambesi, dominated the region. The first Portuguese intruders around 1500 reported a number of such cities, with fine stone buildings, women wearing imported silks and beads, and rich agriculture produce. The houses of Mogadishu in the north were multistory structures, and the palace at Kilwa covered two acres, with courtyards and vaulted chambers on a cliff overlooking the sea.

The quality of life in these coastal cities would later be testified to by the Portuguese. The narrow stone-walled city streets were similar to their own. Doors were elegantly carved, beds sometimes inlaid with ivory, walls inset with Chinese porcelain or Persian ceramics, like the dishes on which the wealthy ate. Early European visitors also noticed the luxurious silk and cotton garments of wealthy Swahili women, their gold and silver bangles and earrings set with precious stones.

Foreigners seldom penetrated the inner courtyards of the homes of the well-to-do. But baked clay lamps lit interior rooms, and one Arab author reported that the elites of these East African towns "take spiritual delight in the study of philosophy."[4]

A stroll down the streets of the island town of Lamu off the coast of Kenya today may give a general impression of that lost world. Close-pressing walls of whitewashed stone, intricately carved doorways, cool courtyards and tangled gardens frame the life of what is now a quiet backwater. The muezzin still wakes you before dawn each morning with his call to prayer. And the old stone pier where you land and leave still shelters Arab dhows in from the Red Sea or the Persian Gulf.

## AFRICAN SOCIETY AND CULTURE

### Urban and Rural Africa

Across the continent, outside influences took root much more rapidly in urban than in rural environments. In both East and West Africa, Muslim traders settled in cities. As we have seen, kings sometimes converted to Islam, built mosques, and invited in Muslim artists, holy men, and scholars. Even where they remained pagan, as in Ghana or a number of trading cities in East Africa, African rulers encouraged the development of a wealthy, literate, and skilled Muslim community.

The countryside, by contrast, preserved old ways of life. Most villagers' religious beliefs remained animistic, with strong emphasis on the cults of their own ancestors. The natural world still spoke to them, and their lives were shaped by communal traditions and the legends and memories of their heroic past. Not infrequently, these traditional Africans resented the innovations that took root in the cities. As we will see, it was a social division that could shake the stability of even the great empires of the Western Sudan.

### Women East and West

Family structures varied significantly across the continent. Though a common African pattern of matrilineal control of property may be detected in early times, it was fading by this period of African history. The spread of Islam, furthermore, strengthened patriarchal authority and patrilineal lines of descent. Islam also brought religious sanction for polygyny, allowing up to four wives for a single man.

The spread of Islam, on the other hand, could have a positive impact on the lives of some African women. Women in some places learned to read Arabic and studied the religious documents of their new faith. Others gained materially from conversion, acquiring rights to property and to inheritance prescribed by Islamic law.

As in most societies, of course, women's lives also differed up and down the social scale. In many parts of Africa, women enjoyed both material wealth and real power. As mothers or chief wives of kings, and as officials and independent local magnates, women could hold places at the top of African society. Especially in West Africa, they were a powerful force in the marketplace. Everywhere, they could raise children, feed and clothe families, and do most of the farm work too.

---

[4]Abu 'l-Kasim al-Andalusi, quoted in V. V. Matviev, "The Development of Swahili Civilization," in D. T. Niane, ed., *General History of Africa* (London: Heinemann, 1984), Vol. 4, p. 457.

Visitors also frequently commented on a generally easy pattern of socializing between the sexes. African women did not traditionally live in harems or *purdah*. They seem to have had more power to choose their own friends, their own activities, and the way they lived their lives than in many other parts of the world.

## Muslim and Christian Cultures

As noted previously, Muslim visitors to West Africa were impressed by the building programs of rulers like Mansa Musa. They saw mosques built of brick as well as traditional "mud mosques" made of traditional pounded earth. They saw Arabic scholars supported by African kings and books for sale in the local bazaars. They heard imams preach the faith of the Prophet and other holy men reciting the Quran for the edification of the multitudes. Cities like Timbuktu and Gao struck such visitors as admirable centers of Islamic culture.

Physical remains from East Africa leave the same impression of a rich, sometimes Christian, heritage. Among these are the beautiful frescos rescued from the Nubian cathedral at Faras and the rock-cut churches built by Lalibela.

In the most famous of the Faras frescos, the three youths cast into the fiery furnace in the Old Testament are shielded from harm by the towering Archangel Michael. The figures, garbed in blue and gold, stand out vividly against a wall of leaping scarlet flames.

The eleven churches of the Lalibela complex were named after structures in Jerusalem. A stream flowing through the center was called after the river Jordan, and a high spot overlooking the churches was labeled "Calvary" after the site of Christ's execution. According to legend, King Lalibela had been mystically transported to Jerusalem, where Christ himself showed him the holy places as they were later duplicated in the king's rock-cut church center. There each year Christ's baptism, crucifixion, and resurrection were reenacted in a passion play at this sacred site high in the mountains of Ethiopia.

## Traditional Culture: Dancing the Mask

Recent studies of the traditional religious life of Africa tend to focus on a profound sense of unity in African life. They stress the continuity of nature and humanity, land and people, the individual and the group, the living and the dead. More commonly than not, this faith is called *animism*—a religion that sees a common *life* in all things.

There is, African animists seem to feel, a spiritual vitality in everything around them. Mountains, streams, wells, trees, the animals they kill, and the plants they grow all live as people do, and many communicate with them as people do with each other. Africans and the world they inhabit are thus, in a deep spiritual sense, one.

The individual is also one with the group, or groups, of which he or she is a part. The family and the clan, the age group into which one is born, the village community as a whole form a living network of relationships. This network absorbs people at birth, nurtures them all their lives, and determines their destinies. The individual is part of the community, as he or she is of nature.

There are, finally, fundamental ties binding the generations, living and dead. The spirits of ancestors are with the living still, to guide, warn, or haunt them as their actions warrant. Past and present, life and death thus merge in the mind of the African animist into a seamless web of spirituality surrounding us all.

The African mask, perhaps the most successful African sculptured form, expresses these spiritual themes with unsurpassed intensity. African masks clearly illustrate the con-

Traditional African dancers embody the powers of nature and celebrate key transitions in human life. These Dogon dancers from West Africa perform the same spectacular steps recorded on film by anthropologists early in the last century. (Anthony Esler)

tinuity of the clan and the people. They are made according to strict tribal traditions, and every West African can tell a Senufo from a Mande mask, the shaman's mask from that of a men's secret society. Carved in wood, painted, decorated with raffia, cowrie shells, and colorful beads, these masks have a life of their own—the vivid, sometimes fearful life of the spirit they personify.

It may look like a finished art product, strikingly carved and intricately decorated, hanging on the wall of a museum. But an African mask is never really experienced until it is seen in motion—in performance—worn by an African dancer as part of the ceremonial activity it was made for.

Dancing the mask still expresses the deep African feeling of oneness, of identity among the dancer, the mask he wears, and its indwelling spirit. It is this spiritual presence that possesses the dancer when he presses the wood against his face, feels the leather thongs behind his head and the raffia mane spreading over his shoulders. And it is this spiritual presence that possesses him as he sees through narrow eye slits the familiar village faces, the hard-packed earth of the dancing place, as they appear in the distorting and exalting vision of the spirit of the mask.

## NORTH AMERICA: THE PUEBLOS AND THE GREAT MOUNDS

### Expanding Zones Beyond the Seas

Africa has been closely linked to other cultures of the Old World for thousands of years—hundreds of thousands if we go back to the first great migrations of early hominids north out of Africa. Trade, religious influences, and other connections are thus not surprising. But the peoples of the Americas—the New World, as Europeans would soon be calling it—continued to develop in isolation from Old World peoples and often from each other. Nevertheless, they too evolved expanding zones of common culture during this period of their development.

## Pueblo Culture

*Pueblo* means "town" in Spanish, and we still apply this label to the unique collections of adobe or masonry houses under the red cliffs of the American southwest that the conquistadores recognized with astonishment as "real towns" in that otherwise barren land. In fact, the Pueblo culture is only one phase of a general regional flowering that made Arizona, New Mexico, and the northern provinces of today's Mexico one of the two most impressive zones of preurban development in North America.

This transition was brought about by the arrival from Mexico of the three basic Amerindian crops—corn, beans, and forms of squash—and by their gradual adaptation to the arid southwest. This was accomplished about the time of the Fall of Rome. As we saw, Indians of several cultures were thus transformed into village agriculturalists. Finally, between 900 and 1300—a period roughly contemporary with the High Middle Ages in Europe—the later "pueblo" phases of what archaeologists call the Anasazi culture produced the most remarkable flowering of this impressive preurban society.

The pueblo culture of the Anasazi—"Ancient Ones" in Navaho—left impressive remains and has been studied thoroughly, perhaps more intensively than any other Native American society. Archaeologists note their dikes and dams for collecting precious water, their woven cotton blankets, their feather robes, their bows and many specialized arrows, and their tiny cult figurines, perhaps related to fertility. Collectors treasure their black-and-white Mesa Verde pottery. But it is the pueblos themselves that impress the more casual visitor.

Constructed originally of mud and sticks, these clustered apartment buildings of the southwest were soon being built of stone instead. They were sometimes erected against cliffs or even under rocky overhangs. Others were laid out in rectangular, L-shaped, or semicircular blocks that were several stories high and contained an enclosed court. There were sometimes towers and usually storage pits for the grain that was the mainstay of the economy. There was almost always a *kiva,* or underground ceremonial chamber. With the passing centuries these residential complexes grew larger, till some had more than a hundred units and scores of families living together.

These remarkable structures were usually built on ledges across steep cliffs or on the flat tops of mesas. The builders cultivated their carefully irrigated fields in the valleys below. When attacked by less settled neighboring peoples, they could retreat to their precipitous cliff or mountain-top dwellings and hold their foes at bay.

Among the most famous of these pueblo settlements were those at Chaco Canyon, probably built as early as the eleventh or twelfth century. Those at Mesa Verde were elaborate multistoried cliff dwellings that flourished during the next couple of centuries. Thereafter, changes in southwestern climatic conditions drove the builders to move to the Hopi mesas and the Rio Grande valley, where their descendants still live today.

## The Mississippi Culture

Another impressive Native American society in North America flourished not in the southwest but in the southeast. The major remains of the Mississippi culture are to be found along the rivers of the Mississippi valley, and its cultural roots lie less in Mexico than in the classic Hopewell culture of the eastern woodlands of the future United States.

Mississippian sites, located usually on river banks, feature flat-topped mounds, a particular sort of pottery made with eggshell, and a collection of exquisite artifacts—jewelry and even metalwork—found in graves and associated with what used to be called a death cult. These remains are found across a wide tract of well-watered, temperate, originally thickly forested land that includes the east coast of the United States, the southern Appalachians, and the whole length of the Mississippi River valley.

During the period between 750 or so and the appearance of the first Europeans in 1540, Native Americans in the southeast shifted slowly from hunting and gathering toward dependence on agriculture. Ceremonial religious centers point to a powerful priestly cult among them. But fortifying walls become more common at later Mississippian sites too, indicating warfare and war leaders. These leaders may even have been hereditary, which would have made the societies that built the great mounds true chiefdoms, only half a step from the bureaucratic political state.

Mississippian societies traded widely on the rivers of North America. They practiced some specialized crafts, whole villages manufacturing stone hoes or mining salt. Their ceremonial pottery included exotic human and animal shapes, and their graves have yielded copper and shell ornaments and flat copper representations of winged human beings.

The famous mounds actually took a number of forms and served a variety of purposes. Some are cone shaped, some pyramidal in form. Some were raised in the shape of animals of various types, including birds and serpents. Most were magnificent burial mounds for local notables. The "effigy" mounds—those shaped like living creatures—were probably intended for religious purposes. But some were used like similar earthen mounds in Mexico—or on the hills of ancient Greece—as foundations for important buildings.

The largest such center so far excavated was at Cahokia, a site near the modern city of St. Louis. Here a string of some 85 mounds stretches for six miles along a river bank. In the 1200s, most of the people of Cahokia worked the hundreds of acres of corn that surrounded the complex, feeding a population of perhaps 30,000 people.

The largest of Cahokia's impressive earthworks was the huge Monks Mound, a hundred feet high and built on a base seventeen acres in area. Constructed entirely by Indian labor equipped with baskets to carry the earth, this mound must have dominated Cahokia as an acropolis did an ancient Greek city-state. Like the mounded temple bases of Mexico, this man-made hill was almost certainly the location of temples and the rude palaces of chiefs. Religious ceremonies on the high mound would feature chiefs and priests in elaborate costumes and dazzling headdresses made of brightly colored feathers.

## The Ritual Ball Game

Ancient peoples of many lands, from classical Greece and Rome to Celtic Britain, engaged in rough competitive team sports involving balls. In the urban-imperial parts of the pre-Columbian Americas, a Great Ball Court was a common feature of both Toltec and later Aztec towns. The ball court at Chichén Itzá was huge, a walled enclosure 270 feet long and 25 feet high. In these Mexican versions of the great game, hard rubber balls were hurled through stone rings in a violent competition, which may have climaxed with the ritual sacrifice of the losers.

Among the preurban peoples of North America, the game was played without a ball court or human sacrifice. But a winning strategy could involve knocking rival players out of the game by breaking limbs or even by killing them. The North American ball game was thus often seen as good training for warfare: The Cherokee called it "the little brother of war." At the same time, there was clearly a religious dimension to the game, which was often surrounded by mystic rites and ritual dancing.

The ball game as played by the Cherokee of the southeastern part of the future United States well illustrates these religious elements. Amerindian peoples, like the African village peoples already discussed, saw themselves as part of the natural world and strove consciously to live in harmony with other natural creatures—animals, plants, and earth itself. Training for the game thus involved not only physical exercise but also invoking the spirits of the natural world. Instead of an athletic coach, the village shaman presided: praying to the spirits of powerful or swift animals (the eagle, the deer) and forbidding tabu foods such as the timorous rabbit. The game itself was preceded by a full night of dancing, invocations, and the ritual "scratching" of the competitors with turkey claws until their legs, arms, and bodies ran with blood. There followed an early morning hike of several miles to the playing field, final prayers to all the forces of the living world, and the game began. Needless to say, the losers immediately demanded a rematch!

## MIDDLE AND SOUTH AMERICA: FROM THE TOLTECS TO CHIMU

### Mexico and Peru: Continuing Centers of American Civilization

Major centers of civilization in the pre-Columbian Americas continued to lie south of the Rio Grande, in Mexico and Peru. By C.E. 1000 both these zones of developed and intermittently urban imperial culture were well established in the Americas.

The complex societies of both regions were built primarily on agriculture.

Mesoamerican culture was built on the traditional agricultural base of maize, beans, chilies, and squash, which supported a comparatively dense population of several million people. Mesoamerican societies were as hierarchical as any in the Old World. Amerindians in this part of the New World were learning the art of effectively governing large empires. They also suffered periodic influxes of skin-clad Indians from the north, attracted as Goths were to Roman Europe or Mongols to China by the seductive charms of civilization.

Agriculture was widely practiced in South America also, but the range of products was greater. Corn, beans, and various kinds of squashes were common in Peru as in Mexico. In addition, potatoes were the upland staple of the Andes, and coca and other tropical products came from the Amazonian interior. Huge flocks of llamas and alpacas were herded in the high country. Hillsides were terraced for agriculture, and irrigation canals and ditches spread water over lowland valleys.

In various parts of Peru, large ceremonial centers and even some true cities featured huge stone buildings, especially temples and palaces. Many crafts were practiced, including the ancient ceramics and textile industries and more working in metal than in Middle America.

### The Toltecs: A Race of Legendary Heroes

The decline of the Mesoamerican civilizations of the classic age—of Teotihuacán and the cities of the Mayans—was apparently accompanied by widespread violence. Preurban, sometimes even preagricultural peoples, particularly from the north, overran central Mexico and the southeastern lowlands. Many of these invaders, like the ancient Aryans in India, did not occupy the cities they conquered but shied away, regarding them as supernatural places. Some used deserted cities as burial places for their dead.

A Toltec pyramid at the Mayan sacred city of Chichén Itzá, in modern Mexico, shows how much the conquerors had absorbed from the subtle minds of the Mayans. The pyramid, for example, has 365 steps, one for each day in the Mayan—and the modern—solar calendar. Its nine levels correspond to the nine levels of the Mayan underworld, while the temple on top is dedicated to the god Kukulcan, the Mayan version of Quetzalcoatl, the Feathered Serpent whose cult went back to ancient Teotihuacán. (Hugh Rogers/Monkmeyer Press)

One famous race of conquerors, however, surged down from the north not to destroy but to reinvigorate the crumbling urban culture of Mesoamerica. These were the legendary Toltecs, the most celebrated of all the precursors of the Aztecs in Middle America.

Like the Aztecs who came after them, the Toltecs were apparently a Nahuatl-speaking, warlike, less developed people from the north. They descended into central Mexico around 900. They may have participated in the destruction of Teotihuacán; they certainly imposed their will on the surviving Mayans of Yucatán—and learned from them. Toltec power extended even into Guatemala.

Everywhere the central feature of their culture was the predominance of a warrior ruling class. Grim-faced soldiers of the orders of the eagle and the jaguar march across the walls of temples in their metropolis of Tula. Priests, who were the highest caste in most Mesoamerican cultures, yielded pride of place to soldiers under the Toltec hegemony.

These invaders were not barbarians, however. They had lived on the northern fringes of Middle American urban culture long enough to be at least partially civilized themselves. And some of their vigor went into other than warlike pursuits.

Far from destroying or abandoning cities, the Toltecs built new ones, like their capital at Tula, or expanded old ones, like Chichén Itzá in Yucatán. Tula included a number of typical Mesoamerican features, such as a central plaza with temples, palaces, and other large buildings around it, as well as such innovations as long roofed colonnades around the square.

Metalworking also developed among the Toltecs, though more commonly for jewelry than for useful objects. Most important, the Toltecs substantially expanded commercial relations within and perhaps beyond Middle America, linking the Mexican highlands with the tropical lowlands and conceivably even with South America.

Especially important trade goods were tropical products with a great appeal to the people of Mexico's central plateau: cocoa, feathers, and cotton. Cocoa was both a favorite drink in Middle America and a common medium of exchange, used as money for buying, selling, and paying debts. Feathers from tropical birds, used as a chief form of personal adornment, became a major medium of artistic expression. Cotton cloth grew in importance during this period and could even be worked into the armor of the warrior elite who dominated the era.

The famous semimythical Toltec ruler Topiltzin, identified with Quetzalcoatl as sage, founder of civilized arts, and spiritual leader, embodied the virtues the Toltecs most admired.

Topiltzin was even alleged to have tried to keep his people from practicing the bloody religious rituals of human sacrifice. In the end, the living embodiment of Quetzalcoatl "went away," promising to return at some distant future time. With his passing, prosperity departed from the Toltecs. After a century of achievement, drought and famine spread over the land, and new waves of more barbarous invaders came down from the north.

## Tiahuanaco and Huari: Cities of the Andes

The postclassical period in the Andean region saw several substantial regional hegemonies emerge. One among them, the Chimu state, was the most impressive political structure erected anywhere in South America before the coming of the Incas. Two other names, however, also help to fill the centuries between the decline of the Mochica and other classical cultures and the rise of the Inca Empire: the linked names of Tiahuanaco and Huari.

Tiahuanaco, on the high Bolivian plateau south of Lake Titicaca, has left behind some huge stone temple ruins and some rare statues of human beings. Huari, in Peru, had dwelling places as well as public buildings and was evidently a true city, rather than a ceremonial center only. The surviving ceramics, textiles, and carvings of these two peoples bear enough resemblance to indicate some relationship between them. But as is usual where written records are lacking, the political history of Tiahuanaco and Huari—and any political ties between them—can only be conjectured.

The two may have been separate conquest empires, one ruling northern Peru, the other southern Peru and parts of Chile and Bolivia, between C.E. 600 and 1000. Or people from Tiahuanaco may have spread north to the Huari area, mixed with coastal peoples to build Huari itself, and then spread a modified Tiahuanaco-Huari culture by conquest over much of pre-Incan Peru.

Under such joint or divided Tiahuanaco-Huari hegemony, in any case, the Andean area saw some changes. The breeding of llamas, for instance, spread down into the valleys, bringing meat, wool, and other advantages. Bronze began to be worked on a modest scale. Most important, a number of small cities sprang up. Many of these were walled and included no temples at all, leading some archaeologists to suggest that here, as in Mexico, a military aristocracy was shouldering the priesthood aside.

It was in the coastal state of Chimu, however, that these tendencies reached their climax.

## Chimu: People of the Coast

According to local legend, the founder of the royal house of Chimu and his entourage came on balsa rafts across the ocean—a story that has led some scholars to postulate an Asiatic origin for this remarkable society with its highly autocratic government. Others point to the elaborate irrigation system that was central to Chimu culture and see in it a typical example of a hydraulic empire requiring strong central authority to regulate the crucial water supply. Whatever its origins, this was a rigorously centralized and militaristic state, and one of the most culturally advanced of pre-Columbian times.

Located in northern coastal Peru, Chimu in the fourteenth century controlled some five hundred miles of coastal valleys along the Pacific. Its geographical and cultural core was the old Mochica region, its economic basis the much expanded irrigation systems of those valleys. The scope of these works, sometimes uniting several valleys in a single hydraulic network, was unprecedented across the region.

This enigmatic statue from Tiahuanaco has some of the "Atlantean" feel of being totally unlike the work of any other culture. The roughly rectilinear decoration generally resembles other pre-Columbian carving, and the figure is no more naturalistic than most early American art. Nevertheless, an overall feeling of strangeness seems to hover over this robot-like survivor of a ruined city on the shores of Lake Titicaca in the stark Andean uplands. (Carolyn Kerson/D. Donnie Bryant Stock Photography)

The cities of Chimu, particularly the capital, Chanchan, were large and rich, with houses and gardens for the warrior nobles, pyramid temples, and administrative centers. Chanchan's walls were thirty feet high and several miles around. The population may have run as high as 100,000. Unlike Mesoamerican cities with their central plazas, however, the Chimu capital was built in ten separate walled wards or precincts, perhaps to house different clans or social classes. Chimu cities were built of adobe brick rather than of stone, but brick so good that surviving examples sell for ten times what a modern brick will bring in Peru today.

## The Power of the Chimu State

It is the government of the Chimu state, however, that arouses the most interest. The scale of irrigation projects and urban construction would have required a central authority with power over large numbers of laborers. The increasing proportion of palaces, fortresses, and other secular structures, as against temple architecture, indicates that here too a warrior elite was replacing a priestly one.

According to Inca evidence, the Chimu state was a kingdom, founded early in the fourteenth century by conquest. The king of Chimu—wherever he came from—was believed to be divine and had immense authority. Each separate valley had its own appointed governor, and a regular structure of government existed in which village headmen, or *curacas,* reported to *curacas* at higher levels up through the governors to the king.

The presence of large buildings, which apparently served as both administrative and religious centers of cities and wards, strengthens our sense of centralized authority. State power also extended to the frontiers, where large fortresses anchored a system of defense against the smaller states of the Peruvian coasts.

Chimu was in fact the most powerful centralized state in South American history before the coming of the Incas, who, like the Aztecs in the north, would put empire-building on a whole new level in the Americas.

## Summary

From West Africa to East Africa, from North to South America, societies and civilizations outside Eurasia continued to evolve during this age of expanding zones of culture around the world.

In Africa, commerce and religion were at the heart of the new zones of urban imperial culture that took shape between C.E. 600 and 1450. The kings of the Western Sudan, located between the Sahara and the deep forests, became middlemen in the lucrative trade between the Arab states of the Maghreb and the forest peoples of the Guinea coast. The kings built powerful states on the grasslands, and Arab merchants brought Islam, literacy, and other innovations to their urban elites.

The most famous of these Sudanic kingdom was Ghana (eighth to eleventh centuries), known to Arab travelers as "the land of gold." Mali (twelfth to fourteenth centuries) emulated earlier Ghanaian practices with even greater success, building such commercial metropolises as Timbuktu and producing one of the most famous of West African rulers in Mansa Musa.

The spread of early Christianity up the Nile strongly influenced the new civilizations that emerged in Nubia and Ethiopia (ancient Axum) between 500 and 1500. Powerful monarchs ruled these countries while churches and monasteries generated new schools of art, architecture, and religious literature. Christian Ethiopia, though declining politically, survived as an independent state on into modern times.

On the East African coasts a number of city-states played an important part in trade on the Indian Ocean between the seventh and the fifteenth centuries. Cities like Kilwa or Sofala had Muslim Arab commercial communities and they traded with Arabia, India, and countries even farther east.

In the New World, new societies continued to emerge north and south of the Rio Grande. In North America, the Pueblo and Mississippi cultures evolved steadily toward the urban economies and centralized governments already developed by their southern neighbors. The Cahokia Mound Builders were closing rapidly on the developed civilizations of Middle and South America when the first Europeans reached the western hemisphere.

Developed civilizations continued to flourish in Mexico and Peru and their neighbors. In both areas warrior elites seem to have been more prominent, priestly predominance less central, than in earlier times.

The Toltecs in Mexico were the most important conquerors before the coming of the Aztecs. Arriving in the ninth century, at the time of the passing of the Classic Maya and Teotihuacán cultures, the Toltecs created several regional states and encouraged trade and city-building in many parts of Middle America.

Among the regional hegemonies of South America, the Tiahuanaco and Huari cultures emerged as early as the seventh century. The most politically integrated was the fourteenth-century Chimu culture of the coast of Peru. With their elaborate cities and huge irrigation works, the Chimu dotted the land with fortresses and created the most impressive centralized government in South America before the coming of the Incas.

# SUGGESTED READING

Adams, R. E. W. *Ancient Civilizations of the New World.* Boulder, Colo.: Westview Press, 1997. Brief but up-to-date account.

Brooks, G. E. *Landlords and Strangers: Ecology, Society, and Trade in Western Africa, 1000–1630.* Boulder, Colo.: Westview Press, 1993. Ecologically rooted study of social and commercial patterns among West African peoples during the period of the great West African empires.

Brose, D. S., J. A. BROWN, and D. W. PENNEY. *Ancient Art of the American Woodland Indians.* New York: Abrams, 1985. Good account of the artistic achievements of these North American peoples.

Coe, M. D. *Mexico: From the Olmecs to the Aztecs,* 4th ed. New York: Thames and Hudson, 1994. Expert overview for the general reader.

Connah, G. *African Civilizations: Precolonial Cities and States in Tropical Africa: An Archaeological Perspective.* Cambridge, England: Cambridge University Press, 1987. Geographical and archaeological analysis of centers of civilization from the Nile to the West African Sudan.

Feidel, S. J. *Prehistory of the Americas,* 2nd ed. New York: Cambridge University Press, 1992. Chronological survey, from the first comers to the emergence of complex societies.

Hassig, R. *War and Society in Ancient Mesoamerica.* Berkeley and Los Angeles: University of California Press, 1992. Theoretically informed study of war and empire-building.

Ibn Battuta, M. *Travels in Asia and Africa, 1324–1354,* trans. H. A. R. Gibb. New York: McBride, 1929. Vivid descriptions of the kingdom of Mali are among the selections translated here.

Josephy, A. M., ed. *America in 1492: The World of the Indian Peoples Before the Arrival of Columbus.* New York: Knopf, 1992. Regional and topical studies of Native American cultures.

Levtzion, N., and J. F. P. HOPKINS. *Corpus of Early Arab Sources for West African History.* New York: Cambridge University Press, 1981. Valuable primary sources.

Marcus, H. G. *A History of Ethiopia.* Berkeley and Los Angeles: University of California Press, 1994. Concise overview of Ethiopian history.

Middleton, J. *The World of the Swahili: An African Mercantile Civilization.* New Haven, Conn.: Yale University Press, 1992. Economic and social history of East African trading communities.

Niane, D. T., ed. *UNESCO General History of Africa,* Vol. 2: *Africa from the Twelfth to the Sixteenth Century.* Berkeley and Los Angeles: University of California Press, 1984. African perspectives on the history of the continent during the centuries before major Western penetration.

Nurse, D., and T. SPEAR. *The Swahili: Reconstructing the History and Language of an African Society, 800–1500.* Philadelphia: University of Pennsylvania Press, 1985. Swahili interaction with Arabs and Persians in the shaping of East African society.

Pearson, M. N. *Port Cities and Intruders: The Swahili Coast, India, and Portugal in the Early Modern Era.* Baltimore: Johns Hopkins University Press, 1998. Explores the African end of the Indian Ocean trade routes.

Smith, R. S. *Warfare and Diplomacy in Pre-Colonial West Africa,* 2nd ed. Madison: University of Wisconsin Press, 1989. The art of war as practiced among the West African kingdoms.

Young, B. W., and M. L. Fowler. *Cahokia: The Great Native American Metropolis.* Champaign: University of Illinois Press, 2000. Outline of archaeological and historical work at the Illinois site.

 Please refer to the document CD-ROM for primary sources related to this chapter.

# CHAPTER 14

# TOWARD A LARGER WORLD
## From the Bantu Migrations
## to the Mongol Empire
### 500 B.C.E.–C.E. 1500

# A GLANCE AHEAD: BEYOND THE CULTURAL ZONE

Over the course of this volume, we have seen cities, nations, and empires rise, expand to classic scale, and give rise to even vaster regional cultural zones. By 1500, there was only one more step to take: the clumsy, cruel, and uncertain lurch toward a global cultural zone.

The second volume of this book will be centrally concerned with the slowly growing rumble of globalization in the modern period. But before moving on to that enormous struggle—in which we are still involved today—we should pause for a look at peoples who pressed against regional barriers in earlier times.

It is a kaleidoscopic story, full of camel caravans and sailing ships, pastoral nomads, migrating peoples, and the astonishing explosion of the Mongol Empire. These early efforts to break through the boundaries of existing cultural zones laid down no lasting boundaries of their own. But their spirit—venturesome, often violent, and sometimes consciously expansionist—will become familiar as we forge ahead into a globalizing future.

# TRADE, MIGRATION, CONQUEST

## Pressing against the Boundaries

In the chapters of Part III, we have seen centers of civilization, new and old, expand and grow. We have seen how these core powers could shape large sections of the inhabited earth in their image, forging impressive cultural zones in many parts of the world. In this final chapter, we will encounter some restless peoples who pressed against these regional barriers—and some who broke through them.

Settled peoples, city-dwellers and empire builders, often seem to dominate history. Yet many historians today would say that real world history is the history of the margins of such cultural zones, of contacts between them, and of the impact of such contacts on the lives of peoples. In the period that emerged in the centuries around 1500, cultural outreach and interaction would certainly play an important role in the global story. Indeed, you can make a good case that the Western empire-builders who set sail with Columbus at the end of the fifteenth century and dominated most of the world by the beginning of the twentieth were the most successful of all these restlessly expansive peoples.

But they were not the first. This chapter will conclude our survey of expanding cultural zones with a look at transregional expansion beyond these spheres of regional influence.

## Forms of Transregional Outreach

We have already seen a number of individual instances of such expansive outreach. Alexander the Great, born in the Greek zone, marched all across western Asia and died in Babylon. The Islamic faith and culture bound impressive slices of three continents into a vast transregional cultural zone. In this and earlier times, however, there were three particular forms of outreach that regularly carried peoples beyond the frontiers of the lands of their birth.

Long-distance traders were among the first to travel the seas and caravan trails of the world. Migrating peoples moved, slowly but inexorable, far beyond the familiar fields of home. And no people had a greater impact on distant populations than history's great conquerors, carrying their cultures on their spears and transforming the regions they overran.

We will look below at half a dozen of these peoples from the two thousand years before 1500. We will survey traders on the Silk Road and the Indian Ocean, at the slow but enormously influential Bantu migrations across Africa and Polynesian reach across the Pacific, and at the stunning impact of the Mongol Empire from one end of Eurasia to the other.

## EURASIAN TRADE ROUTES

### The Horse-Trading Impulse

Commercial exchange has motivated merchants to reach out for many centuries. This horse-trading impulse, originating often in ritual gift-giving and evolving into the classic exchange-for-profit of historic times, seems to be widespread among peoples at all stages of social evolution. Exchange of goods between urban societies and less developed neighboring peoples goes back as far as the city itself. There had been some culturally stimulating exchange between the major early civilizations of western Asia and Africa—the cultures of Mesopotamia, Egypt, and Harappan India. Still, most of the trade in early times was *within* the major civilized areas—back and forth across the Mediterranean, for example, or up and down the Maurya Indian empire.

It was not till the first two centuries C.E.—the heart of the classic age—that the three continents of Asia, Europe, and Africa were linked by highly developed regular trade routes. And even that late, trade between North and South America is hard to prove, and any trade at all between the Americas and the Old World very unlikely indeed.

Western European merchants return from the far end of Eurasia along the Great Silk Road, reopened by the Mongols during the later Middle Ages. What sort of animals are being ridden and used as beasts of burden here? What features seem to be typical of the stylized cities shown on the map below the travelers? (The Bettmann Archive)

## Caravans on the Great Silk Road

The Old World was linked by two great lines of trade during the early centuries C.E. The northern road was the clopping hooves of horses and mules, the tinkle of camel bells, the dust and heat and babble of caravansaries—the land route across Asia. The southern route was the ruffle of lateen sails, the strumming of the monsoon wind in the cordage, gulls calling, and the smell of tar and spices in a foreign port—the sea route from Asia to Africa and the Near East.

The two great empires of the eastern and western ends of Eurasia—Han China and Rome under the heirs of Augustus—were the anchors of the land route. The middlemen were the peoples of the Persian Empire and the Kushans, whose empire included part of northern India but also stretched far up into Central Asia. Particularly when the Romans were not at war with the Persians and when the Chinese controlled the Tarim Basin north of Tibet, goods could flow in an uninterrupted stream from the banks of the Tiber to the Yellow River of North China.

Trade goods were normally carried across China's half-civilized far-west region of Xinjiang to the eastern end of the Takla Maklan Desert in the Tarim Basin, the beginning of the fabled Silk Road linking China and the Middle East across Central Asia. There the route divided, following strings of oases either north or south of the Takla Maklan, north of the Himalayas into the Pamirs. From the western end of the desert, the road wound up through the passes north of the Pamir Knot, where all the great ranges of Eurasia seem to come together, and down into the rich horse country of Ferghana.

From here, the route ran southwest across the Kushan Empire, across the Oxus and into Persia, and then west the length of the Persian Empire. South of the Caspian, south of the Black Sea, the road wound on over the Anatolian plateau and down at last to the warm shores of the Aegean, at the eastern end of the Mediterranean Sea.

## Riding the Monsoon Winds to India

The sea route in the south hinged on India and Southeast Asia and included Africa in the complex equation. Chinese goods entered the flow of international sea trade in the far southeast of the Middle Kingdom, perhaps from Canton, perhaps from Haiphong, in what is today northern Vietnam. Merchandise flowed from there around the southern end of Indochina and through the Indonesian archipelago to Malaya. Goods were either transported by land through the jungles of the Malay Peninsula or carried by ship around the southern tip and northwest again between Malaya and Sumatra. Thence the sea lanes lay west to the southern end of India, or perhaps northwest across the Bay of Bengal to the muddy delta of the Ganges.

From the other side of India, one could follow the shore northwest around to the mouth of the Persian Gulf, up the gulf, and across western Persia to the Mediterranean. Or one could sail due west, riding the seasonal monsoon winds to the mouth of the Red Sea, and thence to the Axumite port of Adulis in East Africa or to one of several Egyptian ports for transshipment to Alexandria and the blue Mediterranean.

Still another flow of goods by sea began in Southeast Asia or in India and crossed directly on the steady monsoon winds to East Africa, perhaps with an intermediate break in the nation-sized island of Madagascar, early settled by Southeast Asian migrants. From East Africa, cargoes were carried by sea up to Axumite or Egyptian Red Sea ports, and from there overland to the Mediterranean.

A reconstruction of one of the ancient lateen-rigged trading vessels that once plied the Indian Ocean, carrying goods from South Asia to East Africa or the Near East. These triangular sails, borrowed by European shipbuilders, would add greatly to the maneuverability of Western ships during Europe's "age of discovery" around the time of Columbus. Arab dhows similarly rigged still make the shorter runs up to the Red Sea or the Persian Gulf today. (Government of India)

The most popular of all the goods that circulated on this interregional trade system was silk from China. Indian muslin and precious stones, spices from Southeast Asia, incense and drugs from Arabia, metals, glass, and pottery from Rome, and many other luxury items, light in proportion to their market value, were exchanged over the caravan trails and sea lanes of the classic age.

A great deal of coin of the realm also traveled from the West to Asia at this time. Europeans prized Asian goods much more highly than Asians valued European products. The Romans, therefore, had to pay cash for the silks and spices of the East. But while it lasted, this long-range commerce at least began the process of drawing the peoples of Eurasia together economically.

## MIGRATION ACROSS AFRICA AND THE PACIFIC

### Whole Peoples on the March

Perhaps the oldest of all forms of linkage among the widely dispersed peoples of the globe has been the continuing human urge to pack up and move on, to see if the grass is really greener on the other side of the fence, the pasture better on the other side of the hill. Such migration from one part of the world to another brings whole peoples together. It may result in war, as so frequently happened with the Eurasian steppe peoples. It may also lead to trade or even a fruitful exchange of ideas. Or it may even result in a merging of peoples and cultures into a new people, a new culture altogether.

## EURASIAN TRADE ROUTES

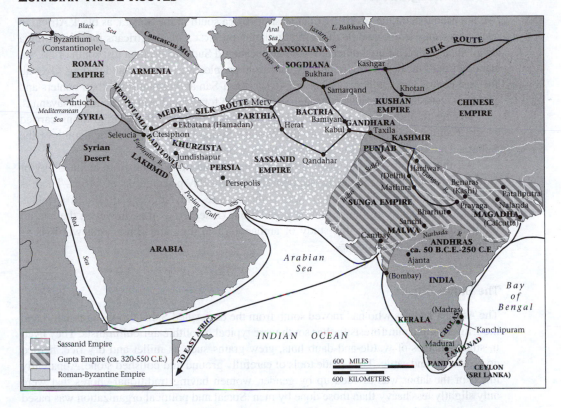

The great migrations of our prehistoric ancestors had peopled almost the entire globe with *Homo sapiens*, the most adaptable of all creatures. In the earliest age of urban culture, nomadic migrations had sometimes destroyed entire civilizations, as we have seen. Migrations had also, however, forged new peoples and new cultures, including those of ancient Sumeria, Gangetic India, and Greece. From the beginning of history, then, migration produced a yeasty mixing and melding of populations and ways of life.

This process continued in the classic age. Migrations and resulting mixtures of bloodlines and basic skills, folk-ways and mythologies, forged most of the great civilizations of this period in Europe, Asia, and Africa. An original mixing of Latin and Etruscan peoples produced the Romans, whose empire was as polyglot a mix as the world has seen. Indian culture was enriched during the classic age by the influx of new peoples—Greeks, Arabs, Kushans, and others—across the Northwest Frontier. Even China, in the most homogeneous end of Eurasia, felt the external pressure of nomadic steppe peoples such as the Xiongnu, and would be overrun by such peoples in the next stage of its history.

We will look in more detail now at two such instances of productive mass migrations: the great Bantu trek across Africa and the seaborne migrations of the island peoples of the Pacific.

## The Bantu Migrations

We are used to thinking of Africa, or at least of Africa south of the Sahara, as black Africa. In fact, as recently as the middle of the first millennium B.C.E., black Africans inhabited only a small slice of their future homeland—the tree-scattered Sudanic savanna just south of the Sahara. North of the desert predominantly caucasoid peoples were herding and trading. Over all the vast central and southern portions of Africa, Khoi-San and diminutive Mbuti hunters and gatherers were thinly distributed through the great rain forests and over the southern savannas.

During the fifteen or more centuries after 500 B.C.E., the Bantu migrations carried black, Bantu-speaking peoples from the Western Sudan over most of Africa south of the Sahara. The secret of their success seems to have been iron.

All that we know of this great southward expansion must come from archaeology or from anthropological or linguistic study of the present-day populations of Africa. There is serious debate about the extent to which the culture and language of Bantu speakers spread independently of the migrating population. Unsettled as it is, however, the overall picture that emerges from this study of archaeological digs and Bantu root words is as dramatic as any written history.

## The Bantu Impact

The African peoples who had moved south from the desiccated Sahara to the grasslands and the fringes of the rain forests farther south were typical Neolithic agriculturalists. They lived in small villages of wattle-and-daub huts, grew grains such as millet and dry rice, herded goats, sheep, and cattle. They made tools of carefully ground and polished stone. Apparently much of the labor was divided up by gender, women having traditional chores that were only slightly less heavy than those done by men. Social and political organization was based on family and clan, as it was in most of the world outside the walls of cities. Some of these peoples, especially in the West African end of the sudanic belt, spoke a language ancestral to the family of Bantu languages that are to be found in many parts of Africa today.

As indicated in an earlier chapter, we do not know for certain how these people learned to smelt and forge hard iron. But whether the new skill was developed independently in West Africa or acquired across the savanna from ancient Meroe, it proved an invaluable aid to the Bantu migrations. Equipped with iron tools and iron weapons, the peoples of the sub-Saharan grasslands pushed through or around the equatorial rain forests into central and southern Africa in a few centuries.

With iron tools came agriculture and a slow but certain withering away of the old hunting-and-gathering life. Cereals from the northern savannas came south with the Bantu cultivators. Another whole range of tropical crops—bananas, coconuts, and yams—were acquired by black settlers in East Africa from Indonesian immigrants. From northeastern Africa cattle and other domesticated animals spread into the south. With all these new peoples came distinctive styles of pottery, distinctive patterns of village life. And with these new things came the Bantu words for them—words that, like Indo-European roots in modern Eurasian languages, tell us much of what we know today about the spread of the culture that produced them.

By C.E. 500 or 1000 at the latest, Bantu-speaking ironworking agriculturalists were almost everywhere south of the Sahara. They still lived in small villages and organized themselves by family and clan. They were probably animists, believers in a multiplicity of nature spirits and in their own close relationship to gods, ghosts, and the rest of the natural world. Little remains of their art, but the famous Nok figurines show what they could do. These terra-cotta figures of animals and human beings, produced by the Nok people of northern Nigeria around the time of Christ, are relatively naturalistic by contrast with the normally nonrealistic traditions of most African art. The human figures are sometimes depicted wearing bracelets, beads, and other indications of a gracious style of life.

## Seaborne Migrations Across the Pacific

We have dealt thus far with the precivilized peoples of the great continental landmasses—Eurasia, Africa, and the Americas. With Oceania we enter a very different world. For Oceania, though it includes the continent of Australia, is largely a world of water.

A remarkably wide variety of environments is encompassed in this fragmented collection of empty landmass, scattered archipelagoes, and open sea. The desiccated Australian Outback contrasts sharply with the steamy rain forests of interior New Guinea; countless barren atolls broiling in the sun differ from such tropical paradises as Tahiti and Hawaii. But the wide Pacific washes all their shores.

The ocean did not completely isolate Oceania from the rest of the world; there was probably considerable communication at least with the islands of Southeast Asia. But the surrounding waters did help shape the distinctive cultures of the region, affecting everything from their economies to their relations with one another. Above all, the Pacific became the pathway for the great Oceanian adventure—the long seaborne migration that is the heart of Oceania's history.

Australia and New Guinea had been reached by human beings during the great prehistoric migrations. The inhabiting of the rest of the jungle-clad volcanoes and coral reefs of the South Pacific would occupy the peoples of Oceania throughout most of their history.

The chronology of these immense seaborne migrations is much disputed by scholars. There seems to be a rough consensus among archaeologists and anthropologists, however, that Melanesia and Micronesia, closer to Southeast Asia, were settled first, during the period of civilization's beginnings. Most of Polynesia would not be explored and occupied by South Sea islanders till much later, during the first dozen centuries C.E.

## From the Outback to Easter Island

The aborigines who had settled Australia thousands of years before had come as Paleolithic hunters and gatherers. The new migrants to the islands of Melanesia and Micronesia were Neolithic agriculturalists, though they hunted and fished as well. Like most of North and South America, then, western Oceania filled up with very successful Stone Age peoples.

The first South Sea islanders hunted animals and birds or speared fish in the rivers of Australia or the lagoons of the islands. They cultivated root crops such as taro and yams and tree fruit such as the coconut. They made tools and weapons tipped with smoothly ground stone or shell, and the remains of their famous Lapita ceramic ware are found today on many widely separated islands.

The Hawaiian Islands, the Society Islands (especially Tahiti), and the original Polynesians of Tonga developed strong chiefdoms, elaborate structures of class and rank, and a material culture that stands out today in museums of indigenous art. The large island of New Zealand fostered the inward-looking society of the Maori, whose carved war canoes were things of beauty. Far-off Easter Island—much closer to South America than to Australia—produced the unique Easter Island statues. These huge heads, probably of former chiefs, make the hearts of true believers in the mythical lands of Atlantis and Mu beat faster to this day.

But the most amazing accomplishment of these long voyagers, these Vikings of the Pacific, as Europeans would call them, was surely the long voyages themselves.

They sailed in outriggers or—for longer inter–island voyages—double canoes, lashed together with braces and a platform. Some of these vessels were reportedly a hundred feet long and could carry food, plants, and livestock for colonizing new islands, as well as a hundred or more Polynesians. They navigated by the stars, by the sun and moon, by the direction of the sea swells and the trade winds, and by the formations of the clouds. Their long double canoes were liable to break apart in heavy seas and were almost impossible to bail when they took in water. But they were "sea-kindly craft," normally stable, and their single triangular sail could carry them a hundred miles in a day of good wind.[1]

They set out in search of new homelands for many reasons. Famine in the home islands, defeat in war, frustrated ambition for political leadership could all impel Polynesians to take to the sea and head east, where experience taught them there were always more islands.

Cross-fertilizing each other's cultures as they voyaged routinely among the islands, hundreds and even thousands of miles between landfalls, theirs is certainly one of the most remarkable achievements of peoples on the move.

# THE MONGOL CONQUESTS

## Herders of the Steppes

While China shaped the societies and destinies of neighboring peoples, some of its most despised neighbors were poised to impact China itself—and the rest of Eurasia—more powerfully than any people ever had. These were the latest wave of steppe-dwelling nomads from the north—the Mongols—and their greatest leader, Genghis Khan.

The nomadic lifestyle adopted by the Mongol tribes had been determined from earliest times by dependence on moving herds of animals. These included goats, sheep, cattle, and even reindeer. The essential animals for riding and for transport were the horse, the ass, and the camel.

Among the Mongols, men traditionally dominated society, but women had a central place as well. Mongol warriors learned to live almost entirely off the milk, blood, and meat, the hides and the wool, of the animals they herded. But girls learned to ride as early as boys did—about the time they learned to walk! Women exercised primary control over

---

[1]Ben R. Finney, "Voyaging," in Jesse D. Jennings, ed., *The Prehistory of Polynesia* (Cambridge, Mass: Harvard University Press, 1979), p. 331.

the camp, and they could at least express opinions in tribal councils, though they apparently had no voice in final decisions.

Three clear patterns of migration guided the ponderous but purposeful progress of the nomads of northern Eurasia in particular.

As a pastoral people, first of all, they followed an established annual round, back and forth across a predefined territory where they knew they would find water and pasturage at each season of the year. As warrior peoples defending—or deliberately invading—unmarked grazing grounds, nomads also frequently clashed with other peoples. If they were defeated, they necessarily retreated from their familiar pasturage and set out in search of new territories—quite often clashing with still other pastoral folk. This jostling tended to flow from east to west, as uprooted nomads turned their horses' heads toward the warmer and moister grasslands of the western steppes.

There were, finally, the predatory southward drives of nomadic peoples into the fat lands of the city-based civilizations. Tempted by the wealth or weakness of the developed societies that stretched from one end of Eurasia to the other, these mobile armies, whole peoples on the move, could have a devastating impact.

Powerful leadership, military skills, and elan, combined with unparalleled mobility and the toughness that went with their rigorous style of life, made nomads formidable opponents for the cities and empires of the civilized zones. Pastoral nomads—as we have seen—left more than one island of urban culture in ruins.

Over the centuries their impact was heaviest on the sedentary populations of western Eurasia. The reason for this nomadic pressure on the West was what is sometimes called the *steppe gradient*—the warmer weather and superior pasturelands of the more southerly western steppes. By 2000 B.C.E., the steppe gradient had already drawn Indo-European nomads into Europe, where they became the ancestors of the Greeks and Romans, the Slavs, Celts, and Germans of later centuries. Other Indo-Europeans in the second and first millennia B.C.E. and Turko-Mongols in the first and early second millennia C.E. followed this historic drift from eastern Asia toward Europe. But they were masters of the eastern steppes as well—and imperial China's most unrelenting foe down the centuries.

### Genghis Khan, Lord of All Men

Genghis Khan (1167?–1227) was born plain Temujin (Ironsmith), son of a minor Mongol chieftain on the chilly steppes northwest of China. While he was still a boy, his father was poisoned by enemies. The heir apparent had to flee from the tents of his own people to wander with a few followers, an outcast among the drifting clans.

He had tremendous physical strength and the physical courage expected of his people. He was also a natural political intriguer and a born military strategist—in both areas patient, cunning, and ruthless when the time to strike finally came. He was a religious man, a believer in the nature gods of the steppe, yet tolerant and eager to have priests of all faiths around him, lest he give offense to any powerful divinity. Perhaps strangest of all in a wandering child of the steppes, he had a remarkable head for organization. He organized his armies and his empire with a rigor that would have done a Chinese or Byzantine bureaucrat proud.

The motives that drove Genghis Khan have been variously represented. To some degree, certainly, it was the simple imperative of many nomadic conquerors before him. He

# VOICES FROM THE PAST

Joveyni (1226–1283) was a cultivated Muslim man of letters; he was also a Persian official in the employ of the Mongol conquerors of Persia. The desecration of the mosque of Bokhara by Genghis Khan and his pagan Mongols described here should be read with an awareness of the author's difficult position as a pious Muslim who served in the government of one of Genghis Khan's descendants.

Does Joveyni try to disguise the blasphemous behavior of the Mongols? How does the remark of the wise imam quoted here try to explain the desecration of Allah's house in terms of Allah's power? Does this explanation seem to mitigate the shocking behavior of the "World Conqueror" Genghis Khan?

> "On the following day when from the reflection of the sun the plain seemed to be a tray filled with blood, the people of Bokhara opened their gates and closed the door of strife and battle. . . . Chingiz-Khan rode into the Friday mosque and pulled up before the maqsura, [where he] asked those present whether this was the palace of the Sultan; they replied that it was the house of God. Then he too got down from his horse, and mounting two or three steps of the pulpit he exclaimed: "The countryside is empty of fodder; fill our horses' bellies." Whereupon [Chingiz-Khan's men] opened all the magazines in the town and began carrying off the grain. And they brought the cases in which the Korans were kept out into the courtyard of the mosque, where they cast the Korans right and left and turned the cases into mangers for their horses. After which they circulated cups of wine and sent for the singing-girls of the town to sing and dance for them; while the Mongols raised their voices to the tunes of their own songs. . . . After an hour or two Chingiz-Khan arose to return to his camp, and as the multitude that had been gathered there moved away the leaves of the Koran were trampled in the dirt beneath their own feet and their horses' hoofs. In that moment, the Emir . . . famous for his piety and asceticism, turned to the learned imam Rukn-ad-Din Imamzada . . . and said: "Maulana, what . . . is this? That which I see do I see it in wakefulness or in sleep, O Lord?" Maulana Imamzada answered: "Be silent: it is the wind of God's omnipotence that bloweth, and we have no power to speak."

'Ala al-Din 'Ata Malek Joveyni, *The History of the World Conqueror,* trans. John Andrew Boyle (Manchester, England: Manchester University Press, 1958), pp. 103–104.

---

led his soldiers into battle, he once said, for the sheer exaltation of winning, the joy of seeing other men break and run before him, of taking their horses, looting their tents and cities. But there was a deeper motive at work as well behind that wind-darkened forehead, those enigmatic eyes—a religious motive. The Eternal Sky—chief of the Mongol gods—had ordered him to take the field against the world.

Drying pasturage and greed for the material luxuries of the cities, common motives for movements of steppe nomads, may also account in part for this greatest onslaught of the steppes against the softer, richer southern lands. But without the uniquely inspired leadership and genius for organization of this most remarkable of nomads, the long ride of the Mongols could never have happened.

In combat the Mongols would circle their enemies, discharging flight after flight of arrows. They might also pretend to flee, drawing their antagonists into yet more devastating barrages. But when enough enemy mounts and men had fallen, they would turn and charge, screaming columns of leather and fur and flashing swords, with always that relentless cloud of armor-piercing arrows driving on before them. That was the last sight many a more civilized soldier ever saw—the charge of the Mongol cavalry—before the dust and blood engulfed him.

In 1206, at a tribal conclave on the Kerulen River in the wastes of Mongolia, the clan chiefs of these Mongol warriors chose Temujin to be their paramount leader. He was neither a boy nor an outcast by then, but a seasoned warrior and a skilled political tactician who had outmaneuvered and destroyed all his rivals among the Mongol tribes. They made him their great khan—Genghis Khan, Lord of All Men.

## The Mongol March Across Eurasia

The Mongol conquests, which began in Genghis Khan's time and lasted through most of the thirteenth century, astonished and horrified all the zones of civilization across Eurasia. Three major centers of urban culture were primary targets of Mongol raids, conquest, and eventual subjugation: Confucian China, the Muslim Middle East, and the eastern part of Christian Europe. Most of the world's largest landmass was thus shaken for a century by the pounding hoofbeats of the Mongol hordes.

Genghis Khan drove first down into North China, where he crushed the Tibetan and Jürched states that shared a divided China with the Song emperors in the south. The Great Wall had been breached and Beijing left a smoldering ruin by 1215, opening the way to the subsequent conquest of all North China and Korea.

After this first assault on China, Temujin turned his horses westward and advanced against the Muslim Middle East. Ancient trading cities like Samarkand and Bokhara were pillaged, their inhabitants slaughtered. By 1220 Afghanistan and Persia lay helpless before the Mongols.

The armies of Genghis Khan pushed on into European Russia, riding through the rich pasturelands of the Ukraine. There a flying column of Mongol horsemen met and overthrew a coalition of Russian princes in 1223. It was only a foreshadowing of what was to come.

To accomplish these feats, Genghis Khan had disciplined his troops as no Mongol horde had been before. He had added military experts from conquered peoples, such as the Turks and Chinese, and more elaborate military technology, such as the catapults and battering rams that now rumbled along in the baggage train. He had developed the process of preliminary intelligence-gathering into a fine art. He had turned the casual terrorism of any nomad campaign into calculated psychological warfare. And his unbeaten cavalrymen were still there, tough, ever-victorious, eager to conquer and loot the rest of the world for his successors.

Mongol armies rode west once more in the 1230s and 1240s. They captured and devastated Kiev, the old southern capital of Russia, and overran a number of northern Russian cities as well, including the still modest town of Moscow. From a base on the Volga, they sent massive raids into Eastern Europe. They ravaged Hungary and Poland and probed Austria before swinging back toward the northern grasslands.

In the 1250s powerful Mongol formations poured into Muslim Persia once more in a campaign that climaxed with the capture of Baghdad. The Abbasid capital was sacked and much of the population put to the sword. The last Abbasid caliph was trampled to death by Mongol ponies.

The conquest of the rest of Song China took the better part of half a century, but that too was accomplished—the first time all of China had ever been overrun by the nomads from beyond the Great Wall. In 1279 Genghis Khan's renowned grandson Kublai Khan overwhelmed the last Song emperor.

## THE MONGOL EMPIRE

### Mongol Mastery of the Eurasian Heartland

The empire the Mongols put together was the largest the world had yet seen. It included both the largest and the most populous of modern nations, China and Russia, as well as much of the Middle East and portions of Southeast Asia. It stretched all across Eurasia, from European Russia to the Far East.

This vast expanse was divided into four khanates, with a splendid capital at Karakorum in the ancestral grasslands of Mongolia. The premier khanate, the realm of the Great Khan, was East Asia, centering in China but including Korea, Tibet, and Mongolia itself. The Jagatai Khanate dominated a vast slice of central Asia. The Ilkhanate ruled the Muslim Middle East. And the Khanate of the Golden Horde governed the rolling expanse of Russia.

The imperial order imposed upon this heartland of the world island was a free-form combination of ancestral ways, military discipline, and borrowed bureaucratic techniques.

The government at Karakorum included administrators from a number of conquered peoples, organized in rough imitation of the developed bureaucracy of China. There were ministries of justice, of the treasury, and of war, and officials were trained by a government academy. Records were kept in a system of Mongolian writing that used Arabic script. A famous system of couriers and post houses carried the word of the Great Khan out across his far-flung realms.

Out in the khanates, however, native officials were generally allowed to continue governing as they had before the Mongols came. They had to pay their tribute regularly and obey all decrees from the khans. Beyond that, the rough feudalism of the nomadic tribes and clans seems to have prevailed.

The final source of Mongol strength, however, remained neither borrowed bureaucracy nor traditional clan structure, but the army. Efficiently organized in groups of tens, hundreds, and thousands, and led by officers promoted on merit, Mongol troops remained ready to ride on the shortest notice. And it was terror of the return of that host that kept the tribute coming and secured obedience to all decrees.

For a time, in the thirteenth and fourteenth centuries, Mongol predominance guaranteed order across northern Eurasia. It certainly opened the road to trade from one end of the world island to the other. Once more, as in the classic age, goods, ideas, and travelers could pass back and forth from Europe to China.

Marco Polo was the most famous merchant traveler to take that long road east and back again. The mere outlining of his route gives some sense of the magnitude of the Mongol achievement.

From Venice the Polos—Marco, his father, and his uncle—sailed to Acre (still a Muslim sultanate) and then plunged into the Ilkhanate, crossing today's Turkey, Iraq, and Iran to the Persian Gulf. They then turned up through Afghanistan and on across the Hindu Kush into the Jagatai Khanate of central Asia. They continued east across the Tarim Basin north of Tibet and on into the Great Khanate, crossed the Great Wall of China, and swung south at last to Beijing.

Later travels took Marco to Burma, to South China, and home by sea via India, the Middle East, Constantinople, and the Adriatic to Venice. The journey, which included much time spent in the service of the Great Khan, took him seventeen years. It was a journey that could not even have been undertaken a hundred years before.

Or a hundred years later. For the precarious Mongol imperium came soon to its end.

## China Under the Mongol Khans

The Mongol Yuan dynasty that reigned in China for a century (1260–1368) was in many ways an interlude rather than a major period in Chinese history. Yet this was the China of the Great Khan Kublai, the "Cathay" that roused the awe and wonder of Western visitors such as Marco Polo, and it should be noticed here.

The conquest itself was a long and bloody business. The Song emperors of South China resisted for decades, depending on rivers and broken country to slow the Mongols and falling back at last on the port cities and their navy. The last Song emperor was killed in a naval battle off Hong Kong in 1279, ending a struggle that had lasted for forty-five years.

Marco Polo's arrival in the palace of the Mongol Khan Kublai is here imaginatively portrayed by a later illustrator. Marco and his older kin do not seem to be kowtowing as they may be presumed to have done before the most powerful ruler in the world, and the architecture and some of the accoutrements make little claim to authenticity. Nevertheless, some sense of pomp and opulence, and of alien cultures encountering each other, does seem to come across. (The National Palace Museum, Taipei, Taiwan, Republic of China. Kublai Khan (1215–1294) ruled lands stretching from the Pacific Ocean to the Black Sea and founded the Yuan Dynasty in China (1279–1368))

Kublai Khan, the victor in the long war with the Southern Song, was the most remarkable Mongol after Genghis Khan. Grandson of the founder, he was also Great Khan, or Khan of Khans, nominal head of the whole sprawling Mongol Empire—though after he moved his capital south of the Great Wall to Beijing, his concerns were largely with his vast Chinese realm.

A Chinese portrait shows a well-padded face with a small, pointed beard and a moustache narrowing to carefully cared-for points. The eyes, under heavy lids, look small, clear, and thoughtful. Marco Polo eulogized him as a giver of alms, builder of public granaries, maintainer of roads, and so on, while allowing him the usual royal vices—overindulgence in food, concubines, and hunting.

Polo found the royal city of Cambaluc, as Beijing was then called, a vast twelve-gated metropolis several miles on each side, laid out foursquare with wide, straight avenues, splendid palaces, gardens, and courts. The royal palace stood in walled parklands a mile square. The central complex was a lofty building on a high platform decorated with gold, silver, and dragons. According to Marco Polo, as many as six thousand people could sit down to dine in the great hall—off gold plate.

The Mongols retained much of the Chinese political system, especially the six central bureaus established by the Tang dynasty and the general division of government into the civil service, the military, and the censors. They even strengthened the system—one of their few lasting innovations—by tightening the links between the central government and the provincial authorities. The result was probably a harsher autocracy than China had seen before.

As elsewhere, the Mongols retained as many natives in power on the local level as possible—here, the large numbers of Chinese clerks and bureaucrats. The new government also paid lip service to Confucian principles of government. But in practice the Mongol Yuan dynasty suspended the civil-service examinations, promoted few Confucian scholars to high positions, and turned most of the top spots in government over to a new, non-Chinese elite of Mongols and hired foreign officials, including Muslims from the Middle East and Christians such as the Polos.

## Russia Under the Golden Horde

But the empire the Yuan dynasty ruled was the dominant component of a Eurasian realm much larger than China. A brief look at the far European edge of the Mongol Empire will emphasize this remarkable period of East Asian power in western Eurasia.

The Mongols who burst into Russia for the second time in 1236 were a whole horde on the move, with wagons, families, and herds, come to stay on the steppes of southern Russia. The Russian princes and city-states, organized in only the loosest of federations, were no match for the Mongols. City after city was sacked and burned, including the old southern capital of Kiev and the new one at Vladimir in the north. By 1240 the Mongols were effectively the masters of European Russia. They would remain so for the next two and a half centuries (1240–1480).

The khans of the Golden Horde—so called from the color of their tents—settled at a new city called Sarai on the lower Volga. Once the initial carnage was ended, the Tatar Yoke, as the Russians call the period of Mongol rule, was less onerous than it might have been. The khans retained control over princely successions and exercised a veto over all major policy decisions. Taxes had to be paid on time and recruits for the Mongol armies sent as ordered. Beyond this, the Russian cities, once they had dug out of their ruins, ordered their affairs pretty much as they wished. A senior Russian prince was even put in charge of tax collection for the Golden Horde, and Mongol officials rigorously punished any profanation of the Orthodox church.

The two and a half centuries of Mongol rule that followed left their mark on Russia. Russian economic growth suffered—from heavy tributes and from a number of punitive expeditions, the Mongol method of maintaining order in Russia. Politically, budding city assemblies that had had some power in the Kievan period withered under the Mongols. Thus, Russia lost the urban merchant oligarchies, the "rising middle classes" that appeared in Western Europe about this time.

A Mongol element may be detected in the Russian population, and some Mongol influence on Russian coinage, military organization, and early administrative practices. But the most significant consequence of the centuries of Russian subservience to the Golden Horde was the impetus it gave to authoritarian rule in czarist Russia.

The Russian people learned to accept harsh discipline under the Mongols. They carried over these habits of obedience into later centuries, making them excellent subjects for future czars. Some have even traced to these early models the seeds of a Russian style of autocracy that would be echoed in the hardfisted regimes of such later Russian rulers as Ivan the Terrible, Peter the Great, and Joseph Stalin.

## The End of the Mongol Adventure

Like the expansion of the Islamic zone eastward across southern Eurasia, the Mongol conquest of most of northern Eurasia was unprecedented. Both would be precursors of the global wave of western imperialism to come. But the Mongol Empire would not last as long as either of these other surges of interzonal expansion.

The Mongol Empire, as indicated previously, depended in the last analysis on the unbeatable Mongol army. When Mongol armies began to fail of their objectives—as inevitably they did—the Mongol predominance was instantly in jeopardy.

Before the thirteenth century was out, a diminished Mongol horde was beaten by the Egyptian Mamelukes in Palestine. Mongol expeditions dispatched to conquer Japan discovered that a lifetime of cavalry warfare on the steppes was no advantage in facing the perils of a seaborne invasion. And thrusts into the dank heat of Southeast Asia, toward Burma, Vietnam, and Sumatra, fell afoul of climate and terrain as well as the tropic seas. There were limits, in short, to what even the Mongol military could do.

The political unity of the Mongol Empire also began to disintegrate within two generations of the death of Genghis Khan. There were too few Mongols to manage so vast a domain, even if they had developed the administrative skills to do so. There were inevitable quarrels among the khans themselves, and they tended to forget their redoubtable founder's warning that due recognition of the primacy of the Great Khan was essential for continued unity. When the Great Khan Kublai moved his capital from Karakorum to Beijing, he turned his attention more and more to Chinese affairs, and the lesser khans went their own ways in their own domains.

Most destructive of unity, finally, was the tendency of the victorious Mongols, like victorious barbarians in many other times, to adopt the culture of the more developed societies they had conquered. But since the Mongols had conquered peoples of so many different cultures, this process of acculturation soon divided the Mongols among themselves.

The fall of the Mongol Yuan dynasty in China followed the ancient Chinese pattern. Mongol rule was never popular there, and Mongols were never socially acceptable to cultivated Chinese. The conquerors dressed in leather and fur instead of silk, ate mutton and mare's milk instead of Chinese cuisine, frequently could not read and write, and had no surnames. Mongol women refused to bind their feet in Chinese fashion, went hunting on horseback with or without their husbands, and sometimes shaped the policies of even the Mongol emperor. Only shrewd leadership and brute force could keep these aliens in power, and after Kublai Khan there were no more great leaders shrewd or strong enough to accomplish this.

In the first half of the fourteenth century, eight lesser Mongol rulers tried to maintain the regime intact. But unbacked paper money led to inflation. The gods indicated their displeasure through repeated destructive flooding of the Yellow River and famine across North China. Secret societies such as the White Lotus proliferated, as in the last days of many dynasties, and rebellion flared in many provinces. During this prolonged crisis the Mongol leaders once more fell to fighting among themselves.

In 1368 a Chinese rebel leader expelled the Mongols from Beijing and declared a new dynasty—the Ming. The Yuan and their followers retreated northward to Mongolia, whence their famous founder had led their ancestors one hundred fifty years before.

Elsewhere, Mongol rule lasted longer. In Russia, a grand duke of newly prominent Moscow finally expelled the Golden Horde more than a century after China had overthrown its Mongol rulers. By 1500, the Mongol adventure was history across most of Eurasia.

In China, the Mongols left only a scattered legacy. They had strengthened the government, as they did elsewhere. They had encouraged further economic growth. They had developed craftwork by fostering the establishment of hereditary crafts within families. They had unintentionally encouraged the arts by driving classically educated people out of government to seek their fortunes where they could find them—even in the arts.

But like the Muslims at the other end of Eurasia, the Mongols had demonstrated the possibility of larger conquests than the world had seen before. Like restless traders on the Great Silk Road or the Indian Ocean, like Bantus drifting across Africa or Polynesians across the Pacific, the Mongols pressed against the traditional regional barriers of their time.

Other restless peoples would follow their example in the age just beginning as the Mongols drifted back to Mongolia. The centuries after 1500 would see vaster intercontinental empires, a genuinely world market emerging, and migrations that would dwarf all earlier such movements of peoples. But the world had confronted new faces in strange lands ever since the first hominids—probably already trading, certainly already fighting—had migrated north out of Africa.

## SUMMARY

Through much of human history, some peoples have pushed restlessly beyond their own lands, beyond familiar boundaries, even beyond the broadest cultural zones. Such restless movement out into a larger world paved the way for the five centuries of genuinely global encounters we call the modern period.

Some of these earlier traveling peoples were long-distance traders, some migrants in search of new places to live, some conquerors of strange and distant peoples. Over the two thousand years between 500 B.C.E. and C.E. 1500, these peoples on the move voyaged, migrated, or imposed their rule on many peoples across a sizable slice of the globe.

Some of the oldest of long-distance trade routes were those across or around Eurasia. The most important or these were the Silk Road from China to Europe and the sea routes from China and India to the Middle East and Africa. Major long-term movements of peoples included the Bantu migrations across Africa and the Polynesian peopling of countless Pacific islands.

The largest land area ever conquered by any people was the stunning if short-lived Mongol conquest of much of Eurasia. Genghis Khan, the founder of the Mongol Empire, welded the nomadic tribes of the eastern steppes into an unstoppable cavalry army. Imposing centralized authority for the first time on the discordant whole, Genghis and successive khans made themselves masters of much of the world island.

In the end, like other conquerors before them, the Mongols reached their limits too. They penetrated only a short distance into Europe and failed to conquer Japan, India, or Southeast Asia. But Russia, China, Persia, and other substantial chunks of the heartland of human civilization fell under the rule of the Mongol hordes for the better part of two centuries.

The Mongols governed as much as possible through local agents and already established institutions. Yet Russia never forgot the Tatar period in its history, which even more than the Byzantine influence shaped the autocratic regime that emerged in Muscovy. And the Chinese Empire, despite much initial devastation, in the end achieved new levels of centralization under Marco Polo's much admired master Kublai Khan.

# SUGGESTED READING

Allsen, T. *Commodity and Exchange in the Mongol Empire: A Cultural History of Islamic Textiles*. Cambridge: Cambridge University Press, 1997. The role of a key trade item in the empire.

Amitai-Preiss, R., and D. O. Morgan, eds. *The Mongol Empire and Its Legacy*. Leiden: Brill, 1999. Essays on the impact of Mongol rule, especially in the Middle East and China.

Bently, J. *Old World Encounters: Cross-Cultural Contacts and Exchanges in Pre-Modern Times*. New York: Oxford University Press, 1993. Excellent brief summary.

Christian, D. *Inner Eurasia from Prehistory to the Mongol Empire*. Oxford: Blackwell, 1998. Struggle between nomads and more settled peoples dominate volume 1 of Christian's *History of Russia, Central Asia, and Mongolia*.

Coleman, S., and J. ELSNER. *Pilgrimage: Past and Present in the World Religions*. Cambridge, Mass.: Harvard University Press, 1995. Multidisciplinary study of the meanings of pilgrimage in major world religions.

Curtin, P. D. *Cross-Cultural Trade in World History*. Cambridge: Cambridge University Press, 1984. Insightful overview of the part played by trade in binding distant cultures together.

Foltz, R. C. *The Religions of the Silk Road: Overland Trade and Cultural Exchange from Antiquity to the Fifteenth Century*. New York: St. Martin's Press, 1999. Spread of major religions, including Buddhism, Islam, and Christianity, along the great inner Asian trade route.

Halperin, C. J. *Russia and the Golden Horde*. Bloomington: Indiana University Press, 1985. The impact of the Mongol conquest on Russian history.

Kirch, P. V. *The Lapita Peoples: Ancestors of the Oceanic World*. Cambridge, Mass.: Blackwell, 1997. Pacific migration and the traces it left.

Langlois. J. D., ed. *China Under Mongol Rule*. Princeton, N.J.: Princeton University Press, 1981. Scholarly essays.

McPherson, K. *The Indian Ocean: A History of People and the Sea*. New York: Oxford University Press, 1993. Commercial and cultural exchanges in a context of international relations.

Ostrowski, D. *Muscovy and the Mongols: Cross-Cultural Influences on the Steppe Frontier, 1304–1589*. Sees the oppressive "Tatar yoke" of traditional Russian historiography as largely mythical.

Polo, M. *Travels of Marco Polo*, trans. R. Latham. New York: Abaris, 1982. Report of the celebrated merchant traveler to Kublai Khan's China.

Rossabi, M. *Khubilai Khan: His Life and Times*. Berkeley: University of California Press, 1988. Authoritative biography of the greatest of the Mongol emperors of China.

Ruysbroeck. *The Mission of Friar William of Rubruck . . . to the Court of the Great Khan Mongke, 1253–1255*, trans. P. Jackson. London: Hakluyt Society, 1990. Classic account of a visit to the Mongol Empire by a Western contemporary.

Severin, T. *In Search of Genghis Khan*. New York: Atheneum, 1992. Illustrated by good photographs.

 Please refer to the document CD-ROM for primary sources related to this chapter.

# INTRODUCTION

# THE CONVERGENCE OF HISTORY

**TRAVELING TO TIBET**

**GLOBAL ENCOUNTERS**

**THE MEANINGS OF GLOBALIZATION**

## Traveling to Tibet

Every journey has a beginning, and most have a destination. The second volume of this global history is a journey too. It begins in the days of Christopher Columbus—perhaps twenty generations ago. It ends in our own time, in a very different world from that in which Columbus sailed.

The terms of travel itself clearly illustrate the astonishing differences between then and now, between Columbus's world and ours. Then, if Columbus wanted to sail from Europe to Asia, he had to spend years begging crowned heads for ships, risk unknown seas and mutinies, and he still ended up in the Caribbean Sea instead of the East Indies. Today, if you should want to visit some ruins in western Tibet, for instance, you could phone trek organizers in London, fly to Lhasa, and connect up with locals who have a four-wheel drive and an old army truck. There could still be problems—rivers to ford, Chinese military bases to talk your way through, nomads whose directions may or may not be sound. But within a couple of weeks out of the States, you could find yourself clambering over the ruins of Tsaparang on a mountaintop in western Tibet.

How the human race moved from a world where even Columbus got lost during his travels to one where almost everywhere can be pinpointed and accessible is the story of this book. It is a story that in a sense begins much earlier than Columbus's day. For most of our time on earth, human beings lived in tiny food-gathering bands, farmed the fields around isolated agricultural villages, or followed their flocks in a narrow, traditional nomadic round. Then, more than five thousand years ago, people began to build the first complicated societies of the sort we call civilizations.

Not long before 3000 B.C.E., these early civilization builders forged the first centralized states with functioning administrative systems. They evolved a variety of social classes and developed remarkable new skills from writing to metalworking to monumental building. Over the millennia that followed, this complex type of human society took many forms in Asia, Africa, Europe, and the Americas. Some of these centers of civilization produced large empires and even larger regional cultures, dominating significant portions of whole continents. Volume One of this book attempted to summarize the diverse histories of these complex societies around the world.

Then, as recently as five hundred years ago, the histories of these various centers of civilization began to converge. This second volume tells the story of that convergence, the five-centuries-long encounter of all the world's peoples with each other.

## Global Encounters

A *convergence* is a coming together, a focusing. *To converge,* according to Webster's Dictionary, is "to tend toward one point, to approach nearer together." As we will see in the later chapters, the world is converging and has in fact never exhibited so high a degree of cultural homogeneity as it does today. Western Tibet is still a way off the beaten track, but there is a Holiday Inn in Lhasa! This volume will outline the steps by which the world's peoples have in fact converged, moved closer to a common human civilization, a genuine global culture, for the first time in our history.

Convergence also means "moving toward union . . . coming together or joining." When peoples encounter each other, the immediate results frequently include misunderstandings and conflict. Global encounters in modern history have in fact all too frequently been violent. Misunderstandings accounted for some of this conflict, but so did greed, fanaticism, perhaps even a determination to dominate on the part of the expanding West as it encountered one foreign people after another around the world.

In time, however, strangers may mix and mingle, exchange goods and ideas. They may even end, generations or centuries later, by joining each other as allies, confederated peoples, or even fellow citizens. It is likely—though by no means certain—that in recent centuries the world as a whole has in fact been converging in this sense too, drifting toward a greater degree of unity than it has ever known before.

In this volume we will begin with a panoramic overview of the half-dozen ancient centers of civilization that flourished around 1500 C.E. We will then survey the centuries of European imperial expansion that followed, during which the civilization that had emerged at the western end of Eurasia began to impose its will upon all the others. By 1800, we will be looking at a world in which Europeans ruled North and South America and had already begun to penetrate the Asian and African continents. By 1900, we will find most of Asia and Africa also swallowed up in European empires, the first genuinely global empires in human history. Between 1900 and 2000, finally, we will see this Western dominion give way to a much more balanced interaction in which everyone's history is inextricably tangled up with everyone else's.

The first five thousand years of history thus scattered cities, states, and empires, cultures and civilizations around the world. The next five hundred years, from approximately the year 1500 to the present, have seen the often painful convergence of these separate human communities. These centuries would see the blending of our histories as the chronicles of Asians and Africans, Europeans and Americans became a single global narrative, a common human story.

## THE MEANINGS OF GLOBALIZATION

The term *globalization* became very trendy as the twentieth century drew to a close. Again, it is a concept with a variety of meanings. To many, globalization has meant primarily the global economic links that have become more visible with every passing century. To others, the concept has included social trends, such as large-scale migration from poor countries to rich ones. To still other observers, globalization is synonymous with the spread of Western culture, most recently of American popular culture, around the globe.

In this book, the term is used in the broadest sense, including all the above significances and more. Here, the *globalization of history* will involve the complex convergence of all aspects of our group lives. In this broad sense, globalization refers to a world-historical process. It is a process that involves more interaction, greater interdependence, and a higher degree of integration of peoples and cultures than the world has ever seen.

The globalization of history thus defined began with the increasing *interaction* among different centers of civilization, triggered by the European intercontinental imperialism that began around 1500. This wave of overseas empire-building created more political, economic, and social connections between peoples than had ever existed before. Greater interaction was clearly a defining characteristic of the colonial relationship.

Over time, furthermore, this forced interaction led to an unprecedented amount of global *interdependence*. Especially in the nineteenth century, widely separated peoples began to depend on each other as never before for raw materials, manufactured goods, profits, military and political support, and many other things.

Here and there, finally, genuine *integration* appeared. Particularly in the twentieth century, a proliferating web of international treaties and organizations, from international charities to the United Nations, affected all countries. Economically also, multinational corporations, international trade and investment, and a widely tapped global labor pool impacted all peoples. Even our problems, from global warming to international crime, have become integrated on a global scale.

Globalization in all these senses has thus become a central—perhaps *the* central—phenomenon of our time. It is also an extremely controversial one.

Many people think we have gone too far already toward "one world." Globalization does in fact have a genuinely terrifying capacity for trampling ancient cultures, undermining local economies, and undercutting national or regional autonomies. And groups thus challenged may lash back. Asian and African Muslims, for instance, may reject Western culture and demand the restoration of traditional Islamic religious law. European or American workers who lose their jobs to people who will work more cheaply in other parts of the world may bitterly oppose the very idea of a globalized market place.

Globalization continues to roar ahead. But so do vigorous counterattacks against it.

Today, a wide variety of human activities, from high politics and big business to sports, entertainment, and popular culture, have to one degree or another "gone global." You may live to see a billion Chinese wearing blue jeans and drinking Coca Cola. You may also see an America with as many Buddhists and Muslims as Protestants and Catholics among its citizens. Or you may see neither, if the world's peoples dig in their heels and say "No!" in thunder to globalization.

What is sure is that in the year 2000 our history is closer than it has ever been to becoming genuinely global history. What you and I do clearly affects people on the other side of the world—and what they do affects us too. We may move on along the road to one world—or we may successfully defend our separateness. It could go either way.

This second volume of *The Human Venture* is the story of how we got to this remarkable turning point in human history.

# OVERVIEW IV

# THE WORLD IN BALANCE

## (1350–1600)

Modern world history is the history of the merging of the histories of the world's diverse peoples into a single human story. In 1500, however, that globalization of history lay in the unthinkable future still.

The world of the fifteenth and sixteenth centuries remained a world of separate zones of culture. Regional societies, great empires, and some of the most impressive civilizations the world has seen shared the earth at the beginning of the modern period. In the next few chapters we will explore each of these zones of culture in turn.

In so doing, we will try to establish a firm sense of the geographical, historical, and cultural identity of each of the main regions and powers. Such a sense of the major cultural zones will be essential when, in later chapters, the global nature of our modern history compels us to move more freely among the continents and cultures.

We will begin, then, with the comparatively familiar continent of Europe around 1500—the tidy little world from which Columbus sailed. Between Columbus's famous voyage in 1492 and the conquest of Aztec Mexico in 1521, the first non-Western empire to fall to Western arms, Leonardo da Vinci painted the *Mona Lisa,* the colorful Henry VIII became king of England, and Martin Luther nailed his Ninety-Five Theses on the church door at Wittenberg. This Western World of the Renaissance and Reformation will be our starting point.

We will then proceed eastward across the double continent of Eurasia—four fifths of which is Asia—into the great Islamic empires of the Muslim center of the Old World. By 1500 the faith of Muhammad the Prophet had spread from West Africa to Southeast Asia. It flourished particularly in the three wealthy and powerful Asian empires of Ottoman Turkey, Safavid Persia, and Mughal India.

Farther still to the east, we will encounter the ancient, immense empire of China and the dynamic island nation of Japan. The Chinese emperors ruled by far the largest country in the world. Chinese civilization, with its Confucian philosophy and its centralized government of scholar bureaucrats, had shaped the cultures of much of the rest of East Asia as well. Of these satellite cultures, vigorously evolving Japan—the Japan of the samurai and the shoguns—will particularly concern us.

Civilization, however, had also grown up outside the world island of Eurasia. There were impressive kingdoms from the grasslands of West Africa to the trading states of the East African coast. To understand these cultures, we will visit a variety of societies, from Songhai to Great Zimbabwe.

The New World—as the Europeans called it—also had its highly developed societies in 1500. The most impressive of all Middle and South American empires had in fact only recently emerged: the Aztec predominance in Mexico and the Inca Empire of Peru. A glimpse of the canals and pyramids of Aztec Tenochtitlán, or the golden temples of Inca Cuzco, was enough to convince even the Spanish conquistadores that high culture was not a European monopoly.

The varied world of many cultures and civilizations of 1500 was thus something none of us has ever seen. It was a world in balance.

For a last few centuries around 1500, genuine cultural diversity prevailed. Many civilizations, many cultures lived together on the surface of the globe in a rough equilibrium. Let us take a last, long look, then, at this world of separate cultures and regional hegemonies, the world all our forebears knew back to the beginning of history. That roughly balanced world deserves our attention for the sake of its own accomplishments. And it was out of this pluralistic world that our own epoch of world history evolved—the period that has seen the emergence of what looks to some observers like a genuinely global culture.

# THE WORLD IN BALANCE

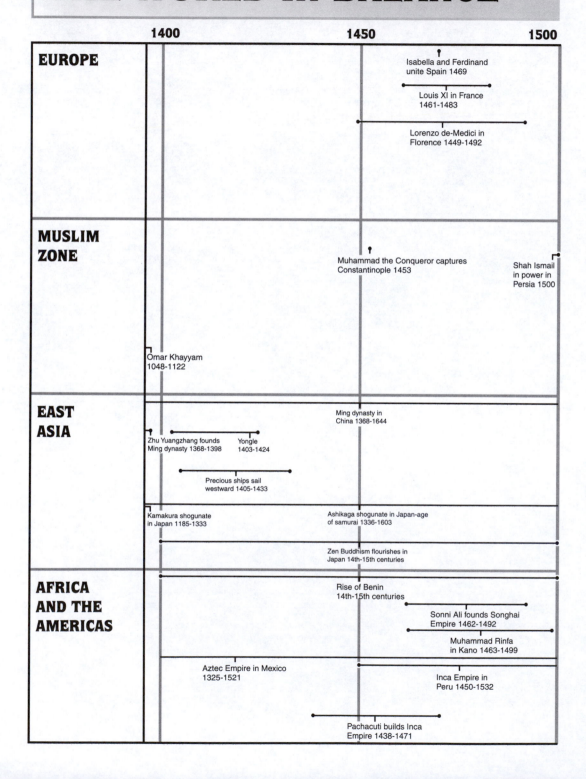

|  | 1400 | 1450 | 1500 |
|---|---|---|---|

**EUROPE**

Isabella and Ferdinand unite Spain 1469

Louis XI in France 1461-1483

Lorenzo de-Medici in Florence 1449-1492

**MUSLIM ZONE**

Muhammad the Conqueror captures Constantinople 1453

Shah Ismail in power in Persia 1500

Omar Khayyam 1048-1122

**EAST ASIA**

Ming dynasty in China 1368-1644

Zhu Yuangzhang founds Ming dynasty 1368-1398

Yongle 1403-1424

Precious ships sail westward 1405-1433

Kamakura shogunate in Japan 1185-1333

Ashikaga shogunate in Japan-age of samurai 1336-1603

Zen Buddhism flourishes in Japan 14th-15th centuries

**AFRICA AND THE AMERICAS**

Rise of Benin 14th-15th centuries

Sonni Ali founds Songhai Empire 1462-1492

Muhammad Rinfa in Kano 1463-1499

Aztec Empire in Mexico 1325-1521

Inca Empire in Peru 1450-1532

Pachacuti builds Inca Empire 1438-1471

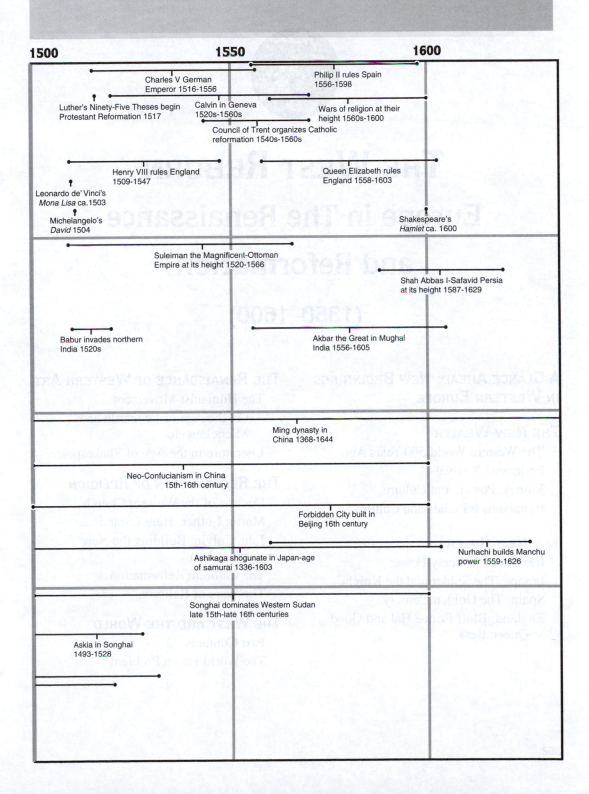

**1500**                          **1550**                          **1600**

Charles V German
Emperor 1516-1556

Philip II rules Spain
1556-1598

Luther's Ninety-Five Theses begin
Protestant Reformation 1517

Calvin in Geneva
1520s-1560s

Wars of religion at their
height 1560s-1600

Council of Trent organizes Catholic
reformation 1540s-1560s

Henry VIII rules England
1509-1547

Queen Elizabeth rules
England 1558-1603

Leonardo de' Vinci's
*Mona Lisa* ca.1503

Michelangelo's
*David* 1504

Shakespeare's
*Hamlet* ca. 1600

Suleiman the Magnificent-Ottoman
Empire at its height 1520-1566

Shah Abbas I-Safavid Persia
at its height 1587-1629

Babur invades northern
India 1520s

Akbar the Great in Mughal
India 1556-1605

Ming dynasty in
China 1368-1644

Neo-Confucianism in China
15th-16th century

Forbidden City built in
Beijing 16th century

Nurhachi builds Manchu
power 1559-1626

Ashikaga shogunate in Japan-age
of samurai 1336-1603

Songhai dominates Western Sudan
late 15th-late 16th centuries

Askia in Songhai
1493-1528

# CHAPTER 15

# THE WEST REBORN
## Europe in The Renaissance and Reformation

## (1350–1600)

## A Glance Ahead: New Beginnings in Western Europe

*Renaissance* means "rebirth," and there was a sense of change, even of cultural rebirth, in the European air around the year 1500. After Europe's late medieval collapse, the European population was growing again, the European economy on the rebound. Aggressive new rulers seized the helm in a number of European nations and began once more to turn loosely structured feudal kingdoms into centralized states. The political power of England, France, and Spain and the wealth of politically divided Italy and the Netherlands made Europe once more a region worth watching.

The European Renaissance is most remembered for its dazzling new directions in the arts, the Reformation as the greatest divide in the history of the Western Christian world. In the end, however, it was the new wealth and the political and military power of the European nations that would have the longest and most jolting impact on the other peoples of this world.

## The New Wealth

### The Western World 500 Years Ago

By most definitions, the Western world today encompasses not only a widespread Atlantic community of nations including most of Europe and North America, but also allied countries as far afield as Israel and Australia. Five hundred years ago, however, the West was Europe only, a cramped little cluster of nations occupying the western one fifth of Eurasia. It was neither the oldest nor the most impressive of world civilizations.

Some of the major modern states had already assumed a rough approximation of today's boundaries by 1500. England and France, Spain and Portugal, even Poland and a truncated version of Russia were all there. Some other areas that would later become unified nations were still disunited regions. Germany was "the Germanies," Italy "the Italian states," the Netherlands a loose confederation, and Switzerland a collection of cantons. Austria presided loosely over the Holy Roman Empire, meaning mostly the three-hundred-odd German states. The Scandinavian countries of Sweden, Norway, and Denmark, on the other hand, temporarily shared a single government.

The lands and peoples of Europe had two thousand years of recorded history behind them in 1500. Western civilization, one of the last Eurasian urban cultures to emerge, had first taken shape in the city-states of ancient Greece, then had swollen to imperial scale in the days of the Roman *imperium*. Europe's Mediterranean phase had ended with the period of internal decay and nomadic invasions that brought Rome down in the fifth century C.E. A new European culture had developed, however, rooted in barbarian vigor and Christian faith. Its political center was north of the Alps, in England, France, and the Germanies. This medieval culture had reached its apogee in the twelfth and thirteenth centuries, the age of the cathedral builders. It was the collapse of this second European civilization that opened the way for the emergence of a third—the vigorous new culture of the modern West.

## Economic Revival

Europe around 1500 was engaged in pulling itself out of the deep trough occasioned by the crumbling of the Christian Middle Ages during the preceding couple of centuries. The great fourteenth-century plague called the Black Death and the depopulation and long economic depression that resulted had been major causes of this medieval collapse. So had the Mongol conquest of Russia, the Hundred Years' War between France and England, the Turkish seizure of Constantinople and invasion of southern Europe, and the civil wars that wracked a number of European nations. The temporary division and spiritual decay of the Roman papacy had put the cap on this continent-wide catastrophe.

The worst period ran from the middle 1300s to the mid-1400s. Thereafter the long recovery was clearly under way. But it had been a major disaster in Europe's history.

A few figures may clarify the scope of the debacle and the strength of the recovery that began modern European history. The population of Europe was more than 70 million in 1300, at the height of the commercial revolution of the High Middle Ages. The Black Death struck for the first time in 1347, and by 1400 the population had tumbled to some 45 million. By 1500, however, there were again almost 70 million Europeans, and by 1600, as Europe paused on the brink of the great population explosion of modern times, almost 90 million.

As a result of this revived demand and the expanded supply of labor to meet that demand, the economy of Europe began to grow once more in the fifteenth and sixteenth centuries. Agriculture expanded as more mouths to feed led to a renewed assault upon waste and marginal lands. More soil was brought under the plow than at any time since

The spirit of Western business enterprise is vividly embodied in this portrait of a banker of the early 1500s by the Flemish painter Jan Gossaert. The watchful eyes, tightly pursed lips, quick pen, and the soberly expensive clothes all reflect the character of the age that forged the first truly global market in the history of the world. (Jan Gossaert [Mabuse] Flemish, ca. 1478–1532. "Portrait of a Merchant." Date: ca. 1530. Wood, 0.636 × 0.475 [25 × 18-3/4 in.]. National Gallery of Art, Washington. Alisa Mellon Bruce Fund 1967)

the High Middle Ages. Improved mining technology, particularly in the extraction of precious metals, significantly increased the amount of silver and gold available for coinage. This in turn put more money in circulation and contributed to both economic growth and inflation.

With coins again available and demand high, trade and handicraft industry boomed once more. Renewed economic growth began in the Mediterranean trading cities of Italy, which enjoyed access to the luxury products of Asia. The commercial cities of the German Hanseatic League, the manufacturing and trading towns of the Netherlands, and great European metropolises such as Paris and London were soon reintegrated into the golden network of commercial exchange.

The medieval commercial revolution of the twelfth and thirteenth centuries and the Renaissance economic revival of the fifteenth and sixteenth laid the foundations of modern capitalism in the West. Key features of the new capitalist economy included private ownership of the means of production (as opposed to feudal landholding in return for military service), production for the market (rather than for mere subsistence, as on the medieval manor), and widespread use of money and credit (by contrast to simple bartering of goods). Other important elements of early capitalism were the development of business law, larger economic organizations, and freedom of economic choice by the individual.

Among the technical innovations that advanced the system from the eleventh to the sixteenth century were expanded minting of coins, double-entry bookkeeping, loans at interest, maritime insurance, bank checks and letters of credit, and above all the joint-stock company, which pooled the capital of many businessmen in a single venture.

Cities were the center of all this business activity. Florence, the most famous of Renaissance cities, had in 1472 some 270 wool merchants' shops, 84 cabinetmakers' establishments, 54 stonecutters' workshops, 44 goldsmiths' shops, and 33 banks. It was not a large city by Asian standards—less than two and a half square miles, with a population of between 50,000 and 70,000. But it was a bustling, vital metropolis, straddling the Arno River in the hills of northern Italy. Woolen cloth, banking, and finance were the core of its prosperity, and the Florentine florin was a gold coin good anywhere in Europe, the dollar of its day. Run by an oligarchy of business wealth, beautified by churches, and distinguished by the palaces of its great financial and commercial families, Florence became the first center of Renaissance art as well as a center of the revived Renaissance economy.

## Money, Power, and Culture

The moneyed aristocracy were certainly among the greatest names of this fifteenth- and sixteenth-century economic revival. There were towering self-made men among them, such as the French tycoon Jacques Coeur, who in his prime negotiated with princes as an equal—and then died broke. There were business dynasties such as the plutocratic Fugger family of Austria, who published an international business newsletter for the far-flung branches of the family firm that was a precursor of today's financial press. Most famous of all, however, was the Medici banking family of Florence.

Generations of the Medici built the family fortune during the fifteenth century, Florence's Renaissance prime. At its height, Medici enterprises included branches in all the major Italian cities—Rome, Milan, Venice, and others—as well as beyond the Alps, in London, Bruges, Lübeck, Avignon, and elsewhere. The Medici were primarily bankers.

processors of woolen cloth, and manufacturers of silk, but they dealt also in sugar and cotton, spices, tapestries and rare manuscripts. They even provided singers from all over Europe for the papal choir.

As the richest bankers in Florence, the Medici soon became the uncrowned political bosses of the city. As the acknowledged rulers of the Florentine Republic, they manipulated the Italian balance of power to keep peace among all the other independent states of the peninsula. In the sixteenth century they became dukes of Florence, popes of Rome, and queens of France—a glittering dynasty of titles and power built on Renaissance money.

As early as the fifteenth century, furthermore, the Medici millions had been put at the service of Renaissance art and culture. The most famous of the clan, Lorenzo the Magnificent (1449–1492), was also the family's most renowned patron of the arts. Under Lorenzo de' Medici, poets like Angelo Poliziano and philosophers like Marsilio Ficino graced the halls of the Medici palace. Artists like Michelangelo learned their craft by sketching ancient Roman statues collected in the Medici gardens. Lorenzo was himself a poet, whose carnival songs are still anthologized in collections of Italian verse.

Self-made men like Jacques Coeur and self-made families like the Medici showed how far brains and ambition could carry a person in the Renaissance business world. Lorenzo the Magnificent—millionaire, political leader, poet, and patron of the arts—also illustrates the multifaceted type we call the Renaissance man.

## Renaissance Ladies and Culture

But there were Renaissance women too. The condition of upper-class Renaissance women at least seems to have been considerably better than that of their medieval predecessors. A few medieval ladies may have been idealized and loved from afar. But some Renaissance ladies were educated and highly cultured, and the admiration they engendered seems to have been based on these genuine accomplishments rather than on the hazy mystique of troubadour romanticism.

Many aristocratic Renaissance women studied Latin, read ancient religious writings, and plunged eagerly into the literary classics of ancient Rome that were the heart of Renaissance intellectual life. Ladies such as Michelangelo's platonic friend Vittoria Colonna, the talented Este sisters, and the famous daughters of England's Sir Thomas More were widely admired for their learning. There were celebrated women poets, such as Christine de Pizan and Louise Labé in France, and women painters, such as Artemisia Gentileschi.

One of the most famous of Italian Renaissance women was Isabella d'Este, "the first lady of the world." Raised in her father's cultivated court at Ferrara, she was married young to the hunting-and-fighting duke of Mantua. She ruled the court at Mantua with grace, firmness, and discriminating culture while her husband enjoyed ruder pleasures elsewhere. Learned in Latin and Greek, a lover of Vergil and other Roman poets, Isabella became a major collector of ancient sculpture, vases, bronzes, coins, and medals. She had her walls decorated with paintings by living Renaissance artists, and she patronized Renaissance poets. Like Lorenzo de' Medici and other patrons of her day, Isabella d'Este thus channeled significant portions of the wealth of the age into the culture that would earn that era its distinctive place in the history books.

# VOICES FROM THE PAST

Well educated by her father, raised at a royal court, and extremely talented, Christine de Pizan found herself widowed and with a family to support in the late 1300s. She therefore turned her hand to literature, composing poems and prose pieces for royal and noble patrons and earning an international reputation in the process. Her most celebrated work, The Book of the City of Ladies, imagines a literary city inhabited by famous women honored in history as strong and faithful helpmates, as rulers and leaders, and as saints and martyrs.

Women in Christine de Pizan's day were traditionally accused of a variety of sins, from being bad-tempered scolds to being easily tempted and sexually insatiable. As she notes, however, most of the literary and learned commentators who accused women of these vices were men. To whom does she turn for an understanding of women's character? Do you think her approach is more or less likely to get at the truth? Do you think men today are more likely to see faults in women than other women are?

*"[A]ll philosophers and poets and . . . all the orators . . . concur in one conclusion: that the behavior of women is inclined to and full of every vice. Thinking deeply about these matters, I began to examine my character and conduct as a natural woman and, similarly, I considered other women whose company I frequently kept, princesses, great ladies, women of the middle and lower classes, who had graciously told me of their most private and intimate thoughts hoping that I could judge impartially and in good conscience whether the testimony of so many notable men could be true. To the best of my knowledge, no matter how long I confronted or dissected the problem, I could not see or realize how their claims could be true when compared to the natural behavior and character of women."[1]*

---

[1]*The Book of the City of Ladies,* in Charity Cannon Willard, *The Writings of Christine de Pizan* (New York: Persea Books, 1994), pp. 171–172.

## THE NEW RULERS

### Revival of Princely Power

During the European Dark Ages following the fall of Rome—roughly the period 500–1000—most of the genuine power in medieval Christendom was in the hands of the feudal aristocracy whose forts, keeps, and finally castles provided what protection there was in an anarchic age. Many of the kings from whom the feudal nobles held their vast estates were do-nothing rulers with little actual authority.

However, during the High Middle Ages—the eleventh, twelfth, and thirteenth centuries—strong kings emerged once more in Europe. Monarchs such as William the Conqueror of England and Philip Augustus of France strove to convert the fiction of royal power into a reality. For a time, at the apogee of medieval civilization, they had in fact tamed if not broken the feudal nobility. They had also expanded the territories under their own direct rule and begun the slow process of reassembling administrative machinery to govern their nations.

The medieval collapse of the fourteenth and earlier fifteenth centuries had brutally interrupted this slow evolution of the European nation-states. In the later fifteenth and sixteenth centuries, however, strong rulers took up the task of their medieval predecessors once more. Europe would remain a divided region, unlike such huge contemporary empires as Ming China and Mughal India. But some of the separate European nation-states would become aggressive political powers capable of challenging their larger imperial rivals around the world.

The new rulers who made this possible were the royal monopolists of power of the later 1400s and the 1500s, the "new monarchs" of the Renaissance.

## France: The Spider and the Knight

The road to the restoration of royal power in France began, properly speaking, when Joan of Arc set the crown on the head of Charles VII at Reims in 1429, reaffirming the legitimacy of the French monarchy then reeling under English assault. The Hundred Years' War dragged on for another quarter of a century, however, and it was not till the accession of Louis XI (1461–1483) that royal authority really began to grow once more in the ravaged French nation.

King Louis, nicknamed "the Spider" for his Machiavellian intrigues, was superstitious, conniving, merciless, and totally unchivalrous. Nevertheless, he left France more powerful, wealthy, and unified than it had been since the High Middle Ages.

Louis ignored other centers of power, such as the *parlements* (regional law courts) and the Estates General, France's embryonic Parliament, while laboring assiduously to make the central administration ever more efficient. Within his growing realm, he actively sought the support of the burghers of the towns by encouraging foreign trade and new industries and by appointing bourgeois advisers. The augmented wealth of the land filled the royal treasuries and paid for an expanded royal standing army, another source of strength for the monarchy.

France would need strong armies in the long series of foreign wars that began in the 1490s and lasted through the 1550s. The great national enemy during this period was the powerful Austrian house of Habsburg—Holy Roman Emperors of the Germanies, rulers of the Netherlands, kings of Spain, and a power in the Italian states. France's most celebrated royal champion in the half-century struggle that followed was Francis I (1515–1547), the most brilliant, knightly, and mercurial of French Renaissance rulers.

Francis preserved his country from encirclement by Habsburg power and established the basic frontiers of the French nation. When he was not leading his armies on the battlefield or dallying with his mistresses, he also directed the continued strengthening of France's central government. A natural autocrat, he increased the power of his royal council and centralized the royal revenues under a single treasury. By so doing, he helped prepare France for an even more brutal challenge than the Habsburg wars: the bloody religious civil wars of the second half of the century.

The wars of religion in France that raged from the 1560s through the 1590s were partly the result of sectarian passions unleashed by the Protestant Reformation. Rivalry for the tottering throne of France, however, led two ambitious noble houses to assume leadership of the two factions—the Guises of the Catholic extremists and the Bourbons of the Protestant Huguenots. Half a dozen civil wars laid the nation waste through the later sixteenth century.

A strong hand took control once more at the end of the sixteenth century when Henry IV restored the authority of the monarchy and founded the powerful Bourbon line. But the Bourbons had something to build on—the foundations of modern French power laid by Louis the Spider and Francis I.

## Spain: The Golden Century

Ferdinand and Isabella are best known to Americans as the sovereigns who financed Columbus. In Spanish history, however, they are the rulers who expelled the last of the Moorish conquerors of Spain, unified the country, and made the new kingdom one of the great powers of Europe.

The marriage of Ferdinand of Aragon and Isabella of Castile in 1469 led to the unification of the two largest portions of Spain, to which lesser territories were added by conquest during their reigns. By driving the last Muslims from Granada, expelling Jews from the country, and turning the notorious Spanish Inquisition on lapsed heretics of either persuasion, the "Catholic Kings," as they were called, strengthened the new nation by religious uniformity—though these brutal policies cost them some of their most industrious subjects. Nevertheless, the founders of Spanish unity made their country perhaps the most powerful in Europe. And when, after long negotiations with Queen Isabella, Columbus sailed in 1492, he laid the foundations for a Spanish New World empire that would grow in the following century into the largest in the world.

The *siglo de oro* ("golden century"), as the sixteenth century is called in Spanish history, owed much of its glitter to that American empire. Charles V (1516–1556), Holy Roman Emperor as well as king of Spain and lord of the Netherlands and large parts of Italy, Mexico, Peru, and other lands beyond the seas, was easily the most powerful of European rulers.

Building on the royal council established by Ferdinand and Isabella, he created a structure of governing councils, which would grow to twelve in number under his successor, Philip II. All these Spanish sovereigns were hard-working rulers: They read reports, presided over councils, and decided government policies themselves rather than delegating authority to ministers of state. The policies they chose—especially their war policies—were not always wise. But Spain was more united and more rigorously governed for their labors.

Philip II (1556–1598) a fervent Catholic, made Spain the sword and shield of the Counter-Reformation. He was also an autocrat by instinct, determined to impress his will on the enormous Spanish domains. The Spain of Philip II had the best armies in Europe and the largest revenues, especially from the Netherlands and the Americas. With the Spanish colossus towering over the West, it looked to rival rulers as if one of the European kings might at last lay a single hegemony upon the whole Western world.

It did not happen, however. The Protestant powers—the England of Elizabeth, the Huguenots in France, and Spain's rebellious Netherlands—allied themselves against Spain in a cause that was as much political as religious. Philip won some great victories, such as the naval battle of Lepanto against the Ottoman Turks, but his greatest military efforts led to defeats. His most famous naval expedition was the attempted invasion of England that climaxed in the humiliating destruction of the Spanish Armada in 1588. His attempt to crush the Protestant revolt in the Netherlands ended, after forty years of bloodshed, in the independence of the Dutch Republic in 1609.

The result of these long wars, furthermore, was to reduce the immensely wealthy Spanish Empire to poverty, to turn its ascendancy into decline. Spain's golden century ended, and from the seventeenth century on, the nation of Ferdinand and Isabella, Charles V, and Philip II was to be a European backwater.

Queen Elizabeth I, looking every inch the Renaissance monarch—something she did very well. This famous "Armada Portrait" by Marcus Gheeraerts is dense with the symbols of the great Queen's wealth (jewels, lace, and velvet), royal power (the crown at the left, her hand resting on the great globe itself), and historic accomplishments (the sinking of the Spanish Armada, shown in the picture behind her). Do modern political leaders also like to project pictorial images associating them with symbols of power and victory? (c. 1588 (oil on panel) (attr. to) George Gower [1540–96], "Elizabeth I—The Armada Portrait." Wooborn Abbey, Bedfordshire/Bridgeman Art Library, London)

## England: Bluff Prince Hal and Good Queen Bess

Tudor England would become for later generations of English-speaking people the very incarnation of "merrie England." Bluff Prince Hal and Good Queen Bess—Henry VIII and Elizabeth I—are perhaps the best known of all British sovereigns. And for such homely things: Every English schoolchild knows that Henry VIII had six wives and threw chicken bones on the floor, that Queen Elizabeth's courtiers spread expensive capes over mud puddles for her.

One of the most successful of the Tudors, however, was the founder of the line, Henry VII (1485–1509)—about whom fewer folk memories survive.

The first Tudor monarch signed trade treaties advancing the cause of English commerce and maintained the "splendid isolation" from European entanglements that was to become England's peacetime trademark.

Henry VII, like the new monarchs elsewhere in Europe, strengthened royal power, using a large royal council and a system of local magistrates called justices of the peace to govern the country. His parliaments were amenable to royal influence, and Henry was his own first minister. When he died, he left the treasury full, the nation at peace, and a popular prince to rule after him as Henry VIII.

Henry VIII (1509–1547), far more famous than his father, is seen by many historians as rather less successful as a ruler. He gave over his earlier years to fun and frolic, hunting, wenching, and an occasional war. He left the real affairs of government during those youthful years to one of the most powerful royal ministers in English history, the intelligent and arrogant Cardinal Wolsey. The latter half of the reign was filled with more serious business for the aging monarch: more wars, the Reformation, and an increasingly desperate effort to provide an heir for the English throne. The wars were, as always, costly. The decision to take Reformation England out of the Roman church—because the pope refused to grant the king a politically necessary divorce—divided the nation religiously. And Henry's six marriages not only failed to produce a healthy male heir but were almost all personal disasters as well.

Yet Henry VIII lived in English memory as a powerful and even admired ruler. This was partly due to the labors of others. An innovative official named Thomas Cromwell strengthened and professionalized the royal bureaucracy during the 1530s. But Henry VIII himself contributed to the growth of central government by making use of Parliament as often as he could. The Parliament, a bicameral assembly of burghers, gentry, and noblemen, was traditionally summoned to vote on taxes. But Parliament also passed laws and sought to influence royal policies—a practice that would have crucial consequences in the next century.

Queen Elizabeth (1558–1603), finally, was the new monarch par excellence, arguably the most successful of any Renaissance ruler. Of all periods of English history, the Elizabethan Age still kindles the warmest feelings in English hearts.

Princess Elizabeth, a slender, athletic, extremely intelligent young woman, received an ideal Renaissance education in Latin, Greek, and modern languages, in history and Scripture. Caught up in the struggle for her father's throne after Henry VIII's death, she also had a very practical education in political intrigue—and the fine art of political survival. She came in 1558 to a royal throne shaken by a decade of misgovernment, religious fanaticism, and economic problems. She proceeded to give England forty-five years of strong government, moderate religious policies, and unexampled prosperity.

Elizabeth was a prudent ruler, avoiding costly wars, seeking religious compromise rather than religious crusades, working through her appointed ministers, and dealing firmly with an increasingly vocal Parliament. She was well served by lifelong royal counselors such as Lord Treasurer Burghley and veteran warriors such as Sir Francis Drake. She was less well supported by dashing younger cavaliers such as Sir Walter Raleigh, whose ardent ambitions got in the way of common sense. Elizabeth herself preferred guile to force. She was a past mistress of public relations, alternately charming and terrifying her friends and her enemies, her ministers, courtiers, and subjects.

Religious extremists found Elizabeth hard to live with, and young men eager for war called her timid. But they called her Gloriana to her face. The whole nation was dazzled by her splendid court and costumes and cowed by the stamp of an indignant royal foot. And she has been Good Queen Bess ever since—England's greatest and best-loved ruler.

# THE RENAISSANCE OF WESTERN ART

## The Humanist Movement

Genuine golden ages are often times of violent conflict; the age of Confucius was also the age of the Warring States in ancient China, and the Periclean Greeks seem to have been almost constantly at war. Golden ages are also not infrequently materialistic times, much concerned with getting and spending the wealth that pays for their culture. Nor are ethical standards always at their highest during such periods, as our own artistically and scientifically brilliant yet morally bewildered century makes clear.

The European Renaissance was as violent, materialistic, and morally questionable as any of the above. But it did leave a cultural legacy that would shape the intellectual and artistic life of the West for the next three centuries at least.

The word *renaissance* means "rebirth," and the age was so called by its own leading intellectual lights, the classical scholars of Renaissance Italy. They thought of their era as one of cultural rebirth, a revival of the wisdom and art of what was for them Europe's greatest age—the ancient world of Periclean Greece and Augustan Rome. The legacy of ancient Rome especially enthralled them. They did a splendid job of imbuing Renaissance culture with Latin literature and Roman history and mythology. Indeed, it is almost impossible to read Renaissance literature or look at much Renaissance art without some knowledge of ancient Rome.

The study of classical culture, in contrast with the study of things divine, was known in the Renaissance as *humanism.* The men who began to read the Latin classics seriously again after a thousand years were called humanists. They were a varied lot of classical scholars—teachers and writers, poets and philosophers, pious Christians and libertines. The first of them, the fourteenth-century Italian poet Petrarch, wrote Renaissance love poems and medieval meditations on death with equal enthusiasm. The most famous sixteenth-century humanist, Erasmus, was equally admired for his editions of the New Testament and for his worldly satires on every aspect of Renaissance life, including the sins of organized religion.

The humanists as a group performed one great service for the modern West. They recovered much of our Western heritage of ancient Greek and Latin literature, lost and moldering in forgotten corners of obscure monastic libraries, unhonored and unread. They also attempted, with more modest success, to "civilize" the sword-swinging medieval nobility by a strong infusion of ancient culture. They did not produce the race of Platonic philosopher-kings they hoped for. But they did produce the first really literate aristocracy Europe had had for ten centuries—a first step at least toward matching the more cultivated courtier classes of the Muslim East or China's Confucian scholar bureaucrats.

Perhaps the most celebrated product of humanist studies was Niccolo Machiavelli, the founder of modern political thought. Machiavelli, well read in Latin literature and history, was also an experienced Florentine diplomat. He fused his knowledge of past and present statecraft in one of the most famous of Renaissance books: *The Prince.* This shrewd, cynical, and brutally realistic commentary on the political style of Renaissance rulers has made the name Machiavelli synonymous with devious political intrigue ever since.

## Art in the Age of Leonardo and Michelangelo

In some areas, Renaissance culture was neither a rebirth nor a revival, but an original creation of the highest order. Among these areas of artistic innovation, Renaissance painting stands out—particularly when we compare it with the brilliant but clearly derivative development of Renaissance architecture and sculpture.

Renaissance Italian architecture was strongly influenced by the Roman ruins that seemed to be everywhere. The architects had no use for the medieval style of architecture they were the first to call "gothic." Instead, Brunelleschi's fifteenth-century dome on the cathedral at Florence and Michelangelo's sixteenth-century one on Saint Peter's in Rome are both modeled on the dome of the Roman Pantheon built by the Caesars.

Renaissance sculpture also showed powerful classical influences. Michelangelo, who called himself a sculptor, learned his trade from Roman statuary, and his own early works included Bacchuses and satyrs. His mature statues of *David* and *Moses*—big-boned, heavy-muscled, with strong features hacked out of the marble—are Old Testament figures, but they look more like Greek or Roman heroes than medieval saints.

Renaissance painting, however, was unique to the age that produced it. No doubt this is partly because there was simply no ancient painting available for copying at that time. But Renaissance painting was also an expression of the creativity of that turbulent time. The epoch that discovered new continents, initiated the Scientific Revolution, and spawned the Reformation was almost bound to produce some striking breakthroughs in the arts as well.

The essence of the Renaissance revolution in the graphic arts was what Renaissance painters themselves frequently called *life-likeness*. Fidelity to nature, or Renaissance naturalism, meant reproducing what the eye actually saw as convincingly as possible. To this end, the artists of the time developed new techniques that would become standard in art schools from that day on. Detailed sketches from nature, study of shadows and highlights, attention to pose, costume, and setting, concealing of brush-strokes, revealing character—all were part of the new approach. The science of perspective became a mania with some Renaissance artists. And anatomically accurate figure drawing—the special achievement of Renaissance painting—became a necessity.

Yet each Renaissance painter had his own distinctive style. They were towering individualists all, and it is their uniqueness and eccentricities of treatment that define their greatness.

Leonardo da Vinci, the eternally restless, many-sided Renaissance mind, was as interested in science and mechanical inventions as he was in art. Experimenting endlessly with everything from pigments to composition, he has left us only a handful of finished paintings. Leonardo's mural of *The Last Supper* depicts the disciples turning toward each other, hands, features, angle of head and trunk expressing their horror as the terrible question runs around the table: "Is it *I* who will betray my Lord?" His portrait of a distinguished patron's wife, the *Mona Lisa*, is perhaps the most famous Western painting in existence. The endlessly debated Mona Lisa smile illustrates one of Leonardo's most delicate and distinctive techniques, the use of "smoky" shadows, here used to define the subtle modeling of the lady's cheeks.

Michelangelo Buonarotti may have thought of himself as a shaper of stone above all, but his paintings on the ceiling of the Sistine Chapel in the Vatican—recently restored to their original brightness—have earned him a place among the greatest painters as well. These scenes from Genesis, running from the Creation of the world to the story of the Flood, are a long parade of heroic Renaissance figures, their heavy limbs and bulging muscles far larger than life size. The most famous of all these scenes is the moment when a white-bearded Jehovah reaches out to pass the gift of life into the limp finger of a just-created Adam—a figure handsome enough to double for Apollo in any classical fresco. That moment in pigment on the Sistine ceiling, combining ancient and medieval inspirations in a uniquely Renaissance way, has for centuries defined the creation of the race in the imagination of Western humanity.

Raphael's seraphic Madonnas and Titian's Renaissance portraits, many of them with the burnished, copper-colored "Titian hair," are also part of our artistic legacy from the Renaissance in Italy. The meticulous bourgeois realism of the Dutch school of Jan and Hubert van Eyck, who produced thoroughly believable portraits of thoroughly believable businessmen, belongs to the artistic heritage of those centuries too. So do Peter Paul Rubens's lush pink goddesses and swirling composition, and the Spanish paintings of El Greco, with their flamelike elongated heads and sour colors.

For the next three hundred years, from 1600 to 1900, Western artists would accept the standards and imitate the techniques of the Renaissance masters. Even on a global scale, the work these masters produced at the dawn of modern history is fit to stand with that of any age and continent.

## Literature in the Age of Shakespeare

The innovative, creative spirit that infused Renaissance art also shaped Renaissance literature.

Literature in the living languages of modern Europe appeared in substantial quantities for the first time during these centuries. The influence of Latin literary forms, Roman mythology, and even the ideas and styles of ancient writers was present in these Italian, French, English, and other literatures. But new forms, new stylistic devices, and great writers of daunting originality flourished in these Renaissance national literatures as well.

Italy, which led Europe into the new age in so many other areas, also had its share of literary pioneers. Francesco Petrarch, the first humanist, was one of the early masters of poetry in the Italian tongue. His collection of love poems, collected as *Sonnets to Laura*, was set to music and sung in Italian taverns during his own lifetime and influenced Renaissance poetry in a number of languages for two hundred years thereafter. His fourteenth-century contemporary Giovanni Boccaccio produced in the *Decameron* perhaps the most famous short-story collection in Western history. In particular the bawdy tales among them were read, enjoyed, and imitated throughout Europe.

France also produced a number of famous Renaissance writers. Christine de Pizan's *The Book of the City of Ladies* defended strong, virtuous women against the common charges that women were the weaker vessel, inferior to men (see page 367). François Rabelais, a former monk, wrote a unique work of fiction about the most famous of all giants, *Gargantua,* and his son *Pantegruel*. Their raw and gaudy adventures satirized all aspects of Renaissance life, including the monasteries from which the author had fled. Michel de Montaigne, a cultivated Renaissance gentleman of the later sixteenth century, invented a whole new literary form to express his thoughts on life and the world—the essay. His three volumes of *Essays* on everything from friendship and education to cannibals and coaches were full of quotes from the wise ancients, but fuller still of the coolly penetrating insights of Michel de Montaigne himself.

A final flowering of Renaissance literature came in the last two decades of the sixteenth century and the early years of the century that followed, in the England of Elizabeth. The "nest of singing birds" of later Elizabethan times included poets and playwrights such as Edmund Spenser, Sir Philip Sidney, Christopher Marlowe, and of course William Shakespeare.

Spenser's long epic poem *The Faerie Queene* and Sidney's "novel" *Arcadia* mixed medieval knights, classical mythology, magic, adventure, love, and deeper allegorical and symbolic meaning in uniquely Renaissance literary productions. Christopher Marlowe, the Elizabethan bohemian who died young in a tavern brawl, wrote the most admired English plays before Shakespeare. His *Tamburlaine the Great, Doctor Faustus,* and other heroes are all giants of ambition, aspiring to more than human achievements—and struck down like their creator for their arrogant presumption.

William Shakespeare is generally regarded as the most prodigious talent ever to write in English. His three dozen plays—*Richard III, A Midsummer Night's Dream, Romeo and Juliet, Julius Caesar, Macbeth, Hamlet, King Lear, The Tempest,* and the rest—have enriched the Western imagination with a galaxy of living characters. And if you are asked to identify a "familiar quotation," guess Shakespeare and the odds are you will be right, for his poetry has become part of the language. His plots are borrowed, his ideas seldom original, but his words are often perfect, and his characters are still the greatest challenge any actor can face. Will Shakespeare's work, said his friend and fellow playwright Ben Jonson, was "not of an age, but for all time!"[1] So far this estimate has proved accurate: More than three and a half centuries after his death, Shakespeare's plays are still on view any night of the year in the great cities of the English-speaking world.

## THE REFORMATION OF RELIGION

### Decline of the Western Church

The Renaissance began in the fourteenth century and ended somewhere in the sixteenth. But during the sixteenth century it overlapped with another major subdivision of Western history, the Reformation. This great upheaval in the Christian church began not in Italy but in Germany and spread rapidly across northern Europe. The Protestant revolt produced some powerful religious ideas, kindled a great Catholic Counter-Reformation, and led to a wave of terrible religious wars. It is sometimes referred to as Europe's last great age of faith—the last time Western people were willing to die, and to kill, in large numbers for their religious beliefs.

The powerful personality of Martin Luther, the German monk who started it all, looms over the Reformation. Yet it is sometimes said that if Martin Luther had never lived, some sort of reformation of religion must nevertheless have taken place. For the Roman Catholic church was in deep need of reform long before Luther nailed his Ninety-Five Theses to the church door in Wittenberg in 1517.

The Roman church was still wallowing in the aftermath of its great late-medieval collapse as the sixteenth century began. The Babylonian Captivity—the period when the popes lived at Avignon and were widely regarded as tools of the French kings—and the Great Schism—which produced two and then three claimants to Saint Peter's seat—had left the papacy badly demoralized. The popes of the later fifteenth and early sixteenth centuries were more concerned with Renaissance art, humanistic literature, Italian politics, and luxurious living than they were with religion. As we will see, there were more material motives also behind the success of the Reformation. Some, like the German princes who defended Luther or Henry VIII in England, supported the reformers at least partly for political reasons. Some, like the merchants and artisans among the French Huguenots and the trading cities of the Netherlands, may have turned to John Calvin's version of Protes-

---

[1]Ben Jonson, "To . . . Mr. William Shakespeare: And what he hath left us," in Shakespeare's *Complete Works,* ed. Hardin Craig (Chicago: Scott, Foresman, 1961), p. 48.

tantism because they saw it as more friendly to business. Here and there we may detect some early nationalistic resentment of foreign popes and high churchmen.

In the end, however, the condition of the church remained central to the motives of most who demanded a reformation of religion in the 1500s. Simony (buying and selling of offices), nepotism (appointment of relatives to office), clerical concubinage, clerical ignorance, pleasure-loving monks, and high-living cardinals all made ecclesiastical corruption a byword in Europe—and a stench in the nostrils of the pious.

This decadence had stimulated a number of revolts during the century before Luther came on the scene. Jan Hus in the Holy Roman Empire, John Wycliffe in England, Girolamo Savonarola in Italy, and other popular preachers and reformers had defied the Church in the fifteenth century. All had been stigmatized as heretics; all had died for their beliefs.

Then came Luther.

## Martin Luther: Here I Stand

Martin Luther (1483–1546) was a disturbed young man when he entered the Augustinian order of monks in the summer of 1505. Raised by pious middle-class German parents in the duchy of Saxony, he turned his back on law school and entered the cloisters in the grip of a full-fledged religious crisis.

Martin Luther, in a picture by the celebrated German artist Lucas Cranach. Something of the warmth and geniality of Luther's later years shows here, but there is still the haunted look of the young Luther about the eyes, a hint of the spiritual torment in which the Protestant Reformation was born. (The Branch Libraries, New York Public Library, Astor, Lennox and Tilden Foundations)

Like other deeply believing Christians of his time, young Luther was convinced that he was a sinner, hated by God, doomed to hellfire. The Church taught that two things earned a person salvation: faith in Christ and a life of Christian good works. Luther tried a number of Christian works. Entering a monastery was a great work of Christian commitment. He also confessed his sins repeatedly, mortified the flesh with fasting and flagellation, and in the service of his order undertook a pilgrimage to Rome, where he was duly horrified by the worldliness of the papal court and cardinals. He remained, however, convinced of his own sinfulness, his own damnation.

Seeking a deeper understanding of Christian faith, the unhappy monk had meanwhile become a professor of theology, lecturing on Scripture at the University of Wittenberg. He found himself increasingly dissatisfied not only with the official doctrine of salvation through faith *and* works, but with such Church practices as worship of the relics of saints and the sale of indulgences—papal pardons for sins—to raise money for the Church's good works.

In the mid-1510s Martin Luther's rebellious spirit boiled over. While preparing lectures on Saint Paul, he at last found certainty of his own salvation in a new doctrine: belief in salvation through *faith alone,* rather than faith and works. This belief became the cornerstone of Protestantism. Then in 1517, Luther launched the Reformation itself by publicly proposing Ninety-Five Theses (arguments) against the efficacy of purchased indulgences.

The rest of Luther's tumultuous life grew from these two challenges to orthodoxy. He developed other radical doctrines. The only certain source of religious truth, he said, was the Bible—not the Bible plus the accumulated wisdom of popes, Church councils, and Church tradition. Priests had no special powers; all true believers were priests and had as much direct access to God as clergymen could claim. The Roman pope, he finally dared to declare, had no control over him or anyone else: The pope had usurped power; he was, in fact, the Antichrist foretold of old.

When defenders of the orthodox faith spoke or wrote against him, Luther confuted them in print or in public debate. When Pope Leo X at last excommunicated the troublesome German monk, the rebel publicly burned the bull of excommunication. When a council called at Worms by the Holy Roman Emperor Charles V outlawed him, Luther answered that he could not compromise his principles: "Here I stand—I cannot do otherwise."[2]

It was a road of defiance taken by more than one doomed heretic before him. But Luther found many supporters for his rebellion—not all of them impelled by purely religious motives. There were German princes eager to get their hands on the wealth of the German church or to use Luther's crusade to justify their own revolt against the Holy Roman Emperor. There were nationalistic noblemen and knights, angry that German money was building Roman churches or lining the pockets of Italian churchmen. There were peasants who used Luther's name to support their insurrections against the out-of-date manorial exactions imposed upon them by their lords.

Luther accepted the support of German princes and noblemen, rejected that of peasants, and miraculously came through unscathed. Lutheran churches were set up in many North German states, then in Scandinavia. Henry VIII, after authoring an early tract against the Lutheran heresy, took England's religious establishment out of the Roman church for political reasons—and made himself its head. Religious turmoil spread through Europe, and it looked for a while as though all Roman Catholic Christendom might revolt against the pope.

[2]Roland H. Bainton, *Here I Stand: A Life of Martin Luther* (New York: New American Library, 1950), p. 144.

## John Calvin: Building the New Jerusalem

The most famous reformer of the generation after Luther was John Calvin of Geneva (1509–1564), who rose to eminence in the 1530s. Calvin was a very different sort of person from Martin Luther. A cultivated Frenchman, trained in humanism and law as well as theology, Calvin was more famous for his lucid logic and shrewd organizing mind than for eloquence or passion.

In the city-state of Geneva in the Swiss Alps, Calvin set up a Protestant theocracy and preached a militant faith that inspired Protestants all over Europe. His doctrines differed from Luther's more in emphasis than in substance. Calvin put special stress on the omnipotence of God. He set the predestination of each human soul to heaven or hell at the center of his theology. His theocratic state of Geneva was dominated by the Calvinist pastors, and the pastors in turn by the iron will of John Calvin. His great book, the *Institutes of the Christian Religion,* was read by Protestants everywhere, and his Geneva became the sixteenth-century Protestant ideal of a Christian community.

Life in Geneva was rigorous, filled with sermons and narrowly restricted by puritanical moral legislation. Calvin's theology was inflexible, a grim vision of a world divided into the saved and the damned, with the pope as Antichrist and Calvinist Protestants as the builders of a new Jerusalem on earth. This view, and the fervor it produced, became the crusading faith of religious revolutionaries all across Europe. It spread to the Huguenots in France and to the Dutch Reformed church in the rebellious Netherlands, to English Puritans and Scottish Presbyterians. It would leave a mark as deep as Luther's on Protestantism, both in northern Europe and in the New England colonies of America.

## The Catholic Reformation

The Roman Catholic church, meanwhile, had mounted a massive Reformation of its own. Led by a pious new breed of pope, the Church launched a powerful counterattack against the Protestant revolt that had already carried the North German states, England, and Scandinavia out of the Roman fold.

The organizer of the Catholic Counter-Reformation was Pope Paul III (1534–1549). During his pontificate the papal court was reformed and Catholic reformers gained commanding positions in the Church, from which they and their successors were able to guide the Catholic Reformation for the rest of the century.

To deal with the Protestant threat more directly, Pope Paul refurbished the medieval Inquisition and established the board of censors known as the Index of Forbidden Books. He also recognized a militant new order, the Society of Jesus. This order of friars was organized in 1540 by a former Spanish knight—and future saint—named Ignatius Loyola. The Jesuits, as the friars were known, were to become the Church's most militant agents, the shock troops of the Counter-Reformation, as well as one of the greatest missionary orders in church history.

Pope Paul also called the Council of Trent, one of the most important of all Church councils, which met off and on for twenty years during the 1540s, 1550s, and 1560s. The Council of Trent carried the reforming impulse from the papal center to the Catholic church as a whole. Decrees of the council provided stiff penalties for immorality and corruption among the clergy. The council founded new seminaries in order to create a better-educated priesthood. Trent also reaffirmed the traditional Catholic views on all the theological points the Protestants had challenged. From Trent, then, the Roman church entered the second half of the century better prepared for battle and full of renewed fervor for the fray.

## The Wars of Religion

The result of the clash of religious sects was a bloody period in European history. The wars of religion brought the age of the Reformation to a violent climax.

Europe's religious wars began in the early 1500s with revolts such as the Protestant Peasants' War in Germany and the Catholic Pilgrimage of Grace in Henry VIII's England. They petered out in the early 1600s in the Thirty Years' War in Central Europe and the English Puritan Revolution. The height of violence, however, occurred from the 1560s to

## RELIGIOUS POPULATIONS OF WESTERN EUROPE IN THE REFORMATION

the early 1600s. During this period, the Dutch Revolt pitted Calvinist Protestants against Spanish Catholics, the wars of religion in France set Huguenots against the Catholic League, and the Anglo-Spanish naval war blazed from the English Channel to the Spanish colonies in the New World.

During the great religious wars of the latter half of the sixteenth century, the religious passions of Luther's and Calvin's day exploded in decades of propaganda broad-sides, revolutions, wars, atrocities, and assassinations. Protestant mobs vandalized and sometimes looted Catholic cathedrals. The Inquisition broke and burned human bodies. Luther was willing to execute Anabaptists—the radical fringe of the Protestant movement—and Calvin to martyr the religious eccentric Servetus. But Protestant violence was more than matched by the long-established repressive machinery of the Roman church.

By the early 1600s on the continent and the middle of the century in Puritan England, the fires of religious zeal kindled by Luther a century before had burned themselves out. Europeans turned from fruitless crusades to secular state-building and modern science. The second half of the seventeenth century would be the Age of Louis XIV—and of Isaac Newton.

The long-range impact of the Reformation extended beyond the sphere of religion. Calvinism in particular may have inspired the taut, rigorous drive that made Calvinist Huguenots and Puritans the most successful businessmen in France and England, respectively. Calvinist religiosity may thus have been an important cause of the growth of capitalism in the West.

Because of their opposition to popes, archbishops, and bishops in the Church, Protestants frequently opposed hierarchy in the state as well. Calvinist Protestantism could thus be seen as an influence on the emergence of democracy in the Netherlands, in England, and in the New England colonies. Through colonial town meetings and elected assemblies, Calvinists may even have contributed to the birth of the American republic two centuries later.

## THE WEST AND THE WORLD

### Past Contacts

Finally, no survey of the western end of Eurasia at the beginning of the modern era can ignore Europe's relations with the rest of the globe. For these relations would soon become central to Western history—and to world history as well.

Europe, as we have seen, had had its share of contacts with the non-European world in earlier centuries. In ancient times, Greeks had learned from Old World neighbors across the Mediterranean Sea, and Romans had conquered and ruled them. In the Middle Ages, Christian Europeans had fought and traded with Muslim lands in the Near East and North Africa, while Mongol invaders had overrun Russia and raided into Eastern Europe.

Longer-range trade had also linked Europeans to other peoples down the centuries. Arab ships and Asian caravans had brought luxury goods across the Indian Ocean and along the great Silk Road from China. No sea lanes yet connected Europeans with what they would soon be calling the New World across the Atlantic Ocean. But Vikings and European fishermen had already pushed out into the North Atlantic and established isolated or temporary settlements and fishing grounds as far west as Iceland, Greenland, and parts of North America.

None of these contacts, however, had had a transforming impact on either Europe or the rest of the world. And that was about to change.

## The World Had a Problem

The age of the Renaissance and Reformation—to give it its full name—was a tumultuous time for Europeans. Europe, recovered from the collapse of late medieval times, was wealthy—and hungering for more wealth. The kingdoms of the West were strong, contentious, armed and dangerous. The Reformations, Protestant and Catholic, had rekindled the crusading Christian faith of the High Middle Ages.

The rest of the world, blissfully unaware of the powerhouse that was building up at the western end of Eurasia, went on with its own getting and spending, its own wars and politics, its own artistic and religious impulses. But by 1500 the West was already reaching out.

We will have more to say about the relative strength of the Western world and the rest of the world in a later chapter. It is, in fact, a much debated subject. But one thing is clear. By 1500, the Europeans were already appearing among other peoples around the globe. They offered their goods for sale on the rialtos of western India. They thrust deeper into the islands and forests of the New World, swords in one hand and crosses in the other. The world, though it did not know it yet, had a problem on its hands: the rise of the West.

## SUMMARY

Money, politics, art, and religion all exhibited a renewed dynamism in the Europe of the Renaissance and Reformation.

During the fourteenth and fifteenth centuries in Italy, the later fifteenth and sixteenth centuries in Europe north of the Alps, the European commercial economy bloomed once more. Recovering from the wars, plagues, and depression of later medieval times, Renaissance trade made immense fortunes for business families like the Medici of Florence. The Renaissance business revival also completed the work of the commercial revolution of the High Middle Ages in laying the foundations of the dynamic capitalist economy of modern Europe.

Royal power also revived during these early modern centuries. Italian Renaissance despots and the "new monarchs" of other European nations took up the work of building strong central governments for the major European powers. Louis the Spider and chivalric Francis I in France, Ferdinand and Isabella and Philip II in Spain, Henry VII, Henry VIII, and Queen Elizabeth in England all helped build powerful nations in western Eurasia.

Renaissance art and literature established cultural patterns that would influence Western culture through most of modern history. From da Vinci to Shakespeare, they would provide models and inspirations for painters and poets for the next three or four centuries.

The Protestant Reformation and the Catholic Counter-Reformation, finally, revitalized Western Christianity, though at considerable cost in Western lives. Militant Protestant reformers like Luther and rigorous Puritans like Calvin successfully challenged the accumulated abuses of the Catholic church. The popes responded by reforms—and a renewed militance—of their own. The religious conflicts that resulted ravaged Europe through the later sixteenth century and left Western Christendom divided between a Catholic south and a Protestant north.

All told, this brilliant, bloody age generated a renewed European vitality that contributed powerfully to the wave of overseas empire-building that also began during this era of Western rebirth.

# SUGGESTED READING

Asch, R. G., and A. M. Birke. *Princes, Patronage, and Nobility: The Court at the Beginning of the Modern Age c. 1450–1650.* London: Oxford University Press, 1991. Solid collection of essays on this undervalued but key political institution.

Benedict, P., G. Marnef, H. Van Nierop, and M. Venard, eds. *Reformation, Revolt, and Civil War in France and the Netherlands, 1555–1585.* Amsterdam: Koninklijke Nederlandse Akademie van Wetenschappen, 2000. Up-to-date essays on some of the bloodiest of Europe's sixteenth-century wars of religion.

Bouwsma, W. J. *John Calvin: A Sixteenth Century Portrait.* New York: Oxford University Press, 1988. Sees the Reformation leader as a divided personality, reflecting the deep cultural divisions of his century.

———. *The Waning of the Renaissance 1550–1640.* New Haven: Yale University Press, 2000. Intellectual liberation and decline in late Renaissance Europe.

Braudel, F. *Capitalism and Material Life, 1400–1800.* New York: Harper & Row, 1973. A trailblazing French historian's stimulating account of the economic realities of the earlier modern West.

Eisenstein, E. L. *The Printing Press as an Agent of Change in Early Modern Europe* (2 vols.). Cambridge: Cambridge University Press, 1980. Challenging assertion of the larger cultural impact of printing.

Halkin, L. E. *Erasmus: A Critical Biography.* Trans. J. Tonkin. Cambridge: Blackwell, 1993. Deeply scholarly, with extensive quotations.

Hufton, O. *The Prospect Before Her: A History of Women in Western Europe, 1500–1800.* New York: Knopf, 1996. Valuable synthesis, topically organized.

McGrath, A. *The Intellectual Origins of the European Reformation.* New York: Basil Blackwell, 1987. Emphasizes continuity between late medieval and Reformation religious thought. H. J. Hillerbrand, ed., *Radical Tendencies in the Reformation: Divergent Perspectives* (Kirksville, Mo.: Sixteenth Century Journal, 1988) offers a useful collection of papers on the social dimensions of the radical Reformation, by German and American scholars.

Meek, C. ed. *Women in Renaissance and Early Modern Europe.* Portland, Or.: Four Courts Press, 2000. Recent essays with a variety of perspectives on women's lives in this period.

O'Malley, J. W. *The First Jesuits.* Cambridge: Mass.: Harvard University Press, 1993. Stresses the Christian spirituality of the founders rather than their militant defense of the institutional church.

Parker, G. *The Grand Strategy of Philip II.* New Haven: Yale University Press, 1998. Foreign policy goals, successes, and failures of the ruler of the first modern superpower.

Shakespeare, W. *The Complete Works of Shakespeare,* ed. Hardin Craig. Chicago: Scott, Foresman, 1961. The finest writer in English brings the beginning of the modern age to life. His Renaissance men and women, even when they are disguised as ancient Romans or medieval kings, speak with the lusty voices of his age.

te Brake, W. *Shaping History: Ordinary People in European Politics, 1500–1700.* Berkeley: University of California Press, 1998. Popular rebellions in Western Europe in the sixteenth and seventeenth centuries.

 Please refer to the document CD-ROM for primary sources related to this chapter.

# CHAPTER 16

# THE MUSLIM CENTER
## Ottoman Turkey, Safavid Persia, and Mughal India

### (1450–1650)

## A Glance Ahead: Three Islamic Empires Reach Across the Center of Eurasia

The Prophet Muhammad's first followers had constructed a vast Arab empire in the seventh and eighth centuries. By the fifteenth century, that first Muslim empire had fragmented and fallen under the domination of new waves of Muslim converts. Around 1500, however, a new golden age for the Islamic world began, centered on not one but three far-reaching imperial domains.

The largest was the immense Ottoman Turkish Empire, which encompassed sizable tracts of the Middle East, North Africa, and southeastern Europe. East of Ottoman Turkey, Persia—today's Iran—enjoyed a rebirth of wealth and power under the Safavid dynasty. Still farther east, Mughal invaders from the northern steppes unified ancient India for a third time.

Europe was well aware of this massive Islamic presence, as were the Chinese on the other side of the "Muslim center" of Eurasia. Many Europeans feared these Muslim empires, and some admired them. But no one could ignore the resurgent power of the followers of the Prophet at the beginning of the modern age.

## The Abode of Islam

### A Transregional Zone

Europe in 1500 had a truly amazing future. But the present, and indeed the immediate future as well, belonged to Europe's far more powerful neighbor, the vast "Muslim center" of the Old World.[1]

The Arab Prophet Muhammad (570?–632) had called himself the Messenger of God. The message he preached of salvation through submission (*Islam* in Arabic) to the will of God (*Allah*) had spread far across Eurasia and Africa by 1500. The mosque and the minaret, the Quran (Koran), Islamic Law, and mystic Sufi holy men were found everywhere from West Africa to Southeast Asia, from the steppes of Russia to the Indian Ocean. It was a vast terrain, almost four times as far from end to end as Europe was.

The Islamic impact on its zone, furthermore, was much deeper than the Western impact on its emerging colonies would be for several centuries. The Islamic religion—the youngest of the major world religions—had imposed itself deeply upon the lives of all the peoples it touched.

The faith of Islam included an immense body of Muslim law and Islamic tradition that affected every aspect of life. Political organization and business dealings, relations between the sexes, family life, and a multitude of other things were matters of religious concern. All were regulated according to the teachings of the Prophet and the body of tradition that had grown up about his life and work.

Conquest by Muslims or conversion to Islam through the influence of merchants or missionaries brought other cultural influences into a community. As each new region was absorbed, Muslim scholars and Sufi preachers, artists, architects, and artisans, poets and

---

[1] I borrow this usage from the innovative Tufts University world history program, and from Professor Lynda Schaffer, from whom I first heard it.

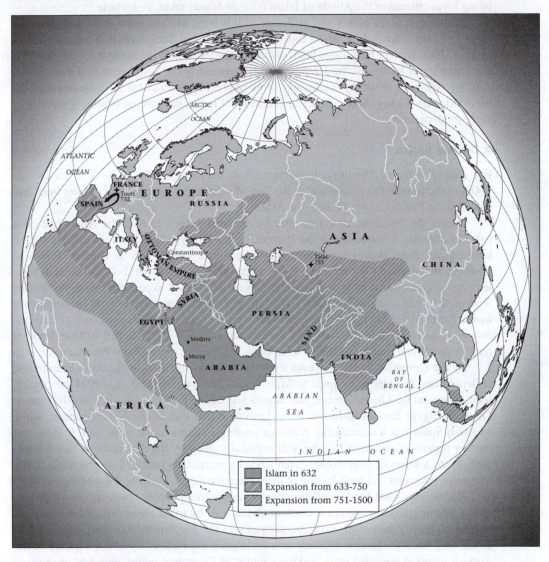

Islam in 632
Expansion from 633-750
Expansion from 751-1500

musicians would be summoned to grace the courts of newly converted local rulers. Mosques would be built, Sufi centers and colleges would spring up, and *qadis* (judges) would sit in every marketplace, settling disputes and decreeing punishment for crimes on the basis of Islamic Law.

Nor were these merely scattered islands of Islamic civilization. Each sector was bound by ties of commercial exchange to all the rest of the Muslim zone. Muslim merchants carried luxury goods along the caravan trails of Eurasia and northern Africa, plied the sea lanes of the Indian Ocean and the Southeast Asian archipelago. Muslim holy men, scholars, and administrators traveled these same routes, seeing large parts of the Old World without ever leaving Islam. It was "a cohesive, growing, and self-replenishing network of cultural communication" that created "a self-conscious, cosmopolitan sense of being loyal citizens of the Abode of Islam (*Dar al-Islam*) taken as a whole."[2]

To understand the power and brilliance of this huge Muslim zone at the beginning of modern history, we will have to look both forward and back from the pivotal period around 1500. We will have to go back several centuries to note the emergence of powerful new peoples as leaders of the Islamic world, particularly the Seljuk and Ottoman Turks. And we will have to survey the history of three great Muslim states in the sixteenth century: Ottoman Turkey, Safavid Persia, and Mughal India, the core of Islamic greatness in early modern times.

## A Divided Realm

For a clear vision of Muslim achievement, then, we must briefly go back as far as C.E. 1000, to the time of the decadence of the first Muslim state, the far-flung empire built and ruled by the Prophet's own people, the Arabs.

During the first three centuries after Muhammad's death in 632, the Arabs had been ruled by *caliphs*, or "successors to the Prophet," of the Umayyad and Abbasid dynasties. Like later caliphs, these leaders were nominally religious as well as secular leaders. Typically, however, they limited their religious duties to the defense of the faithful from foreign foes, leaving religious concerns to scholars and judges, the learned experts on Islam. As secular leaders, they had within a few generations established an impressive Islamic predominance across North Africa and the Middle East, with a touch of southern Europe thrown in. The culture of Abbasid Islam in the ninth and tenth centuries easily outshone that of Christendom, and the power and wealth of the caliphs of Baghdad dwarfed those of any Western ruler.

By the eleventh century, however, even the political authority of the Arab Empire had collapsed into disorder from Spain to Afghanistan. The western subdivisions of the empire, located around the Mediterranean, had largely seceded to form independent Muslim states. Of these, Egypt dominated much of the Levantine east end of the Mediterranean, while Moorish Spain was a scintillating center of medieval culture at the other end. In Asia, the eastern regions of the Arab Empire, still nominally ruled by the Abbasids, in fact disintegrated into a series of hegemonies established by marauding nomad converts to the faith. The most important and long-lasting of these were the Seljuk Turks and the Mongols.

The Seljuks were herders of the steppes, mongoloid peoples speaking an Altaic language that originated somewhere north of China. Led by tribal chieftains and military adventurers, they drifted south from the steppes into the Muslim Middle East, converted to Islam, and became the new military arm of Islamic expansion. By 1000, officers of the Turkish guard at Baghdad were making caliphs, as Praetorian guardsmen had once made Roman emperors, while Turkish chiefs ruled the Persian countryside.

For a brief two centuries—less in some parts of their domain—the Seljuk Turks brought some unity to the Islamic Middle East. But it was at best a tenuous unity. The Seljuks were soldiers and tribute gatherers, not administrators. Their regime was little more than the sort of traditional tribal confederacy that was the highest form of social organization on their native steppes. They fought constantly among themselves. At the same time, enemies came against them repeatedly, from Europe and from Asia.

---

[2]Ross E. Dunn, "The Challenge of Hemispheric History (1000–1500 A.D.)." Paper presented before the American Historical Association (San Francisco: December 28, 1983).

The Mongols of Genghis Khan surged out of the east in the 1200s, built the world's largest empire up to that time, and as quickly faded from the scene. In their glory, however, they were unstoppable. The Mongol cavalry crushed the Seljuks in the 1240s, took and pillaged Baghdad in the 1250s, killing the last figurehead Arab caliph in the process. For a hundred years, the Mongol Ilkhans ruled the Muslim Middle East.

Through these troubled late-medieval centuries of secession and conquest, however, Islamic culture survived, persevered, and prospered. The Seljuks encouraged the further development of the Muslim legal system, especially the essential local authority of the *qadi*. In the end even the Mongol Ilkhans accepted conversion to Islam. And the cosmopolitan cultural and commercial links endured, binding the farthest ends of this politically divided realm.

## A Resurgence of Islamic Power

Political unity was never to come again for the immense and still-growing expanse of Muslim lands. Like the Christian world, Islam was to be fragmented into many nations. But at the beginning of the modern period, the Islamic peoples enjoyed a sudden dazzling resurgence of power.

This revival of Muslim greatness stretched through the sixteenth century, much of the seventeenth, and even beyond in some places. It was led and dominated by three great Muslim empires—those of the Ottoman Turks around the Mediterranean, the Safavids in Persia, and the Mughal dynasty of northern India. All were peoples of Turkish or Mongol background. All were great empire builders and presided over opulent and cultured courts. All three stand out in the history of Islam.

There were many other Islamic lands grouped around the empires of the Mughals, the Safavids, and the Ottomans. Muslim steppe nomads in central Asia, Muslim Kingdoms in West Africa, and Muslim enclaves in Southeast Asia made a formidable Islamic presence. Together, they make Islam central—and not only in a geographical sense—to the history of the time.

# THE POWER OF THE OTTOMAN EMPIRE

## The Ghazi Princes

The Ottoman Turks, like the Seljuks before them, were nomadic clans from the steppes who had drifted down into the Middle East, converted to Islam, and become militant champions of their new faith. Their leaders became military captains and petty princes, carving out little principalities for themselves along the borders of the medieval Byzantine Empire. They were thus lords of the marches on the frontier between Islam and Orthodox Christianity.

Osman (or Othman) I, the founder of the Ottoman dynasty, rose to prominence early in the fourteenth century. He was a *ghazi*, a fighting frontier lord, the Muslim equivalent of a Christian crusader. He won victories, and eager swords from all across the Muslim world flocked to join him in his repeated attacks on what was left of Byzantine power in the Middle East.

Whatever defeats they sustained elsewhere in their long history, the Byzantines, heirs of Roman power in the Middle East, had always been able to fall back behind the huge walls of Constantinople, "the city protected by God," and ride out the storm. On Constantinople,

The Ottoman sultan Muhammad II enters Constantinople as conqueror in 1453. After a thousand years as Christian Europe's most powerful bastion against Asiatic invasion, the Byzantine Empire thus fell to the latest champions of Islam, the Ottoman Turks. This romantic nineteenth-century painting stresses the color and pathos of the moment, emphasizing the oriental costumes, banners, scimitars, and the crescent of Islam, as well as the fallen defenders in the foreground. Fifteenth-century Muslims saw the capture of Constantinople as a great victory for Allah and for God's chosen people, the followers of the Prophet Muhammad for whom the sultan was named. (Painting by Eugene Delacroix) (Library of Congress)

therefore, the Ottomans fixed their eyes. It took them a hundred and fifty years from the days of Osman the *ghazi*, but in the end they succeeded where all others had failed.

They first gobbled up all that remained of the Byzantine lands on both sides of the straits that divided Europe from Asia. Then, in the 1450s, Muhammad II—the Conqueror, as he came to be called—moved against Constantinople itself.

Muhammad mounted the biggest cannon in the world against the impregnable walls. He portaged a whole fleet overland to gain a strategic advantage on the Byzantine fleet in the Golden Horn, the harbor of Constantinople. In the spring of 1453 the Turks broke through. The last Christian emperor of Byzantium—the eightieth in the line since the Roman emperor Constantine—died on the walls. Sultan Muhammad rode in triumph into the city that had been the eastern frontier of Christendom for a thousand years.

Under Muhammad and his immediate successors, especially Selim the Grim in the early sixteenth century, the Ottoman Empire spread far across the Muslim center and into Christian Europe. Like the other empire builders of the age, the Ottomans utilized the new technology of gunpowder and artillery with devastating effect. Their fluttering pennons and flashing scimitars drove deep into the Balkans and swung north above the Black Sea into the Ukraine. Southward from Constantinople (now Istanbul), they imposed unity by force upon Mesopotamia and parts of Persia, the Levant, Arabia. They conquered even Egypt, whose military ruling class, the Mamelukes, had once stopped even the Mongols in their tracks.

By 1500, then, the former *ghazi* princes ruled a considerable swath of territory, extending from southeastern Europe around the eastern end of the Mediterranean, from their capital at Istanbul. It was to this tradition and this heritage that Suleiman the Magnificent, the most renowned of all the Ottomans, was born at the beginning of the sixteenth century.

## Suleiman the Magnificent

Under Sultan Suleiman the Magnificent (1520–1566), the Ottoman Empire became a world power. The Ottomans absorbed new territories in Europe, Asia, and Africa. They put fleets to sea from the Mediterranean to the Indian Ocean. They played the game of power politics with the leading European rulers and dominated the Muslim center as no one had since the Arab caliphs of Baghdad.

Suleiman himself fought a dozen major campaigns, spent a total of ten years in the field, and died in his seventies at the head of his troops. He reclaimed most of the old Umayyad lands along the coast of North Africa and conquered more of western Persia. He advanced still farther into eastern Europe, overrunning Hungary, invading Austria, besieging and barely failing to take Vienna, the capital of the Holy Roman Empire.

Suleiman's commanders on the Mediterranean raided the southern coasts of Italy and France and fought the Spanish fleet to a standstill. In the Indian Ocean, Ottoman squadrons battled the Portuguese on the sea routes to India. On the sea as on land, Ottoman power dominated the heart of the Old World.

By the time he died, Suleiman the Magnificent ruled all or part of what is today Hungary, Yugoslavia, Greece, Albania, Romania, Bulgaria, and southern Russia; Turkey, Iran, Iraq, Syria, Lebanon, Jordan, and Israel; Saudi Arabia, Egypt, Lybia, Tunisia, and Algeria—among others. Unlike the Seljuks and the Mongols, furthermore, the Ottoman sultan really ruled his immense realm. The Ottoman Empire of Suleiman—Suleiman the Lawgiver, as his

# VOICES FROM THE PAST

This contemporary account of the marriage of Suleiman the Magnificent vividly re-creates the splendors of one of Islam's golden ages. Note that Christian knights participated in the festivities—and that this description was in fact written by an Italian banker resident in the Ottoman capital. What does this suggest about the historic rivalry between Christianity and Islam?

*The Grand Signior has taken to himself as his Empress a slave-woman from Russia, called Roxalana, and there has been great feasting. The ceremony took place in the Seraglio, and the festivities have been splendid beyond all record. There was a public procession of the presents. At night the principal streets are gaily illuminated, and there is much music and feasting. The houses are festooned with garlands and there are everywhere swings in which people swing by the hour with great enjoyment. In the old Hippodrome a great tribune is set up, the place reserved for the Empress and her ladies screened with a gilt lattice. Here Roxalana and the Court attended a great tournament in which both Christian and Moslem Knights were engaged, and tumblers and jugglers and a procession of wild beasts, and giraffes with necks so long they as it were touched the sky. . . . There is great talk about the marriage and none can say what it means.*

Leslie P. Peirce, *The Imperial Harem: Women and Sovereignty in the Ottoman Empire* (New York: Oxford University Press, 1993), p. 62.

own people called him—was a far cry from the loose confederations of *ghazi* times. It was a centralized state with an administrative system second to none in that half of the Old World.

## Suleiman's Empire

Sultan Suleiman's empire did not draw its administrative personnel from a single social class, like the European bourgeoisie or China's gentry of scholar bureaucrats. The Ottoman administrative system built upon three groups who already had important functions in society: the *qadis*, the *timariots*, and the *ghulam* system.

The *qadis*, the traditional Islamic judges, had been assigned administrative functions at the village level as far back as the Arab Empire, and they fulfilled similar functions under the Ottomans. The *timariots* were the old *ghazi* cavalry. Rewarded for their military service by tax revenues from recently conquered villages, they also provided police power and protection for these towns. The *ghulam* system was the Turkish practice of appointing men who were nominally slaves to high positions of civil and military authority in the land. Delegating the power to slaves avoided any problems of insubordination, since slaves had no rights against their masters. Christian converts to Islam were incorporated into this system in the fifteenth century, becoming the famous Janissary Corps of elite soldiers and civil servants.

These three groups staffed an impressive administrative structure. At its head was the grand vizier, nominally a slave, but in fact the sultan's right hand. The vizier presided over the royal council, or *divan*, with its many secretaries, scribes, and subordinate bureaus. The provinces of the empire were run by local governors called *pashas* in the cities, *begs* in the countryside. At the local level, *qadis* and *timariots* performed their traditional functions. Janissaries were seeded through the whole system in key administrative and military posts from the capital to the farthest border provinces.

Sophisticated European visitors much admired the empire of Suleiman the Magnificent. Official merit was recognized and corruption punished, they said, as they were not in Europe. Public charity cared for the needy, schools prospered, and the sultan's armies were ever victorious. It was an idealized picture, but there was much truth in it.

Suleiman himself had a clear sense of his own place in the world. "I am God's slave," he caused to be inscribed on a public monument, "and sultan of this world."[3] Ruling in splendor from Istanbul on the Golden Horn, the Grand Turk, as Westerners called him, was the most powerful of Muslim rulers and more powerful than almost any Christian King.

# PERSIA UNDER THE SAFAVIDS

## The Rise of the Safavids

Persia, the Muslim power due east of the Ottoman Empire, was no upstart *ghazi* state. In 1500 the Persians already had two thousand years of history behind them. Many dynasties had ruled there since Cyrus the Great founded the first Persian empire in the sixth century B.C.E. Ever since the Arab conquest in the seventh century C.E., Persia had become in

---

[3]Halil Inalcik, *The Ottoman Empire: The Classical Age. 1300–1600*, trans. Norman Itzkowitz and Colin Imber (New York: Praeger, 1973), p. 41.

many ways the cultural heart of Islam, producing theologians, scholars, and poets in profusion as well as leading schools of art.

Persia had also managed to civilize—and Islamicize—one after another of its subsequent conquerors and foreign rulers. The Seljuk Turks in the eleventh century, the Mongols in the thirteenth, and the terrible Tamerlane and his descendants in the fifteenth had all been schooled in ancient Persian ways. Politically, however, Persia had remained weak and often fragmented among its conquerors.

Persians had not entirely lost control of their own destiny. Turks and Mongols might conquer, but cultivated Persian viziers did much of the governing for them. Persian taste guided one rude warrior after another into magnificent building, lavish patronage of the arts, and Islamic piety. Then, in 1500, a native Persian dynasty seized power once more and set Persian history on an odd new path.

Shah Ismail (1500–1524), the first of the Safavids, was thirteen years old when his devoted religious followers, the *kizilbashi* ("red caps") swept him into power. Safavid Persia would produce another great age in Persian history—and fuel a religious rift in the Islamic world that persists to the present day.

### The Shiite Kingdom

The Safavids were Shiites, members of Islam's largest minority sect. Regarded as heretics by the Sunni majority of Islam, the Shiites rejected the traditional leadership of the caliphs, the acknowledged successors to the Prophet. Shiites insisted that only someone directly related to Muhammad—that is, a descendant of the third official caliph, Ali, and his wife Fatima, the Prophet's daughter—could be the true head of Islam. Such a rightful heir to the Prophet, furthermore, would be an *imam*, a real spiritual head of the faithful—not a mere secular ruler, as most caliphs had tended to be.

Shiites had been martyred for this heterodox faith for centuries. In Safavid Persia they found a homeland of their own at last.

Young Ismail, surrounded by Sufi holy men, swept to power on a wave of religious enthusiasm. He was hailed as shah—secular ruler—and *imam* in Tabriz, the red caps of his supporters thronging about him. By seizing power in Persia, however, Ismail drove a religious wedge into the heart of Islam. To the east and north lay the Sunni Muslims of India and central Asia; to the west and south, those of Ottoman Turkey, Arabia, Egypt, and North Africa. Even more dangerous, Shiite Persia, with its *imam* emperor and its crusading zeal, exerted a powerful attraction on Shiite minorities elsewhere in the Middle East.

As in Reformation Europe at the same time, the sixteenth century saw savage persecutions and wars of religion in the Muslim Middle East. The Sunni champion was the Ottoman colossus, Persia's neighbor to the west. The Safavids compelled Sunni Persians—who were actually in the majority in the early days—to accept Shiite formulations of the faith on pain of death. The Ottomans martyred Shiites, whom they saw as potential rebels, in large numbers. And the armies of the Safavid shah and the Ottoman sultan met repeatedly on the battlefield throughout the century.

In the early days especially, the Ottomans generally had the better of it, adding substantial chunks of Persian territory to their already swollen empire. This is perhaps not surprising, since Ottoman armies were early equipped with firearms and artillery, while Ismail's soldiers were capable of charging bare-chested into battle, calling upon the sanctity of the *imam* to protect them. Around 1600, however, the Safavids produced a ruler who would have considerably more success—the great Shah Abbas.

### Shah Abbas of Isfahan

Shah Abbas I (1587–1629) is in fact generally considered the greatest of all the Safavids. A dark-complected, masterful, immensely energetic man, Abbas, like Ismail before him, came to the throne young, at seventeen. But he reigned much longer than Ismail, and his forty-odd years in power were one of Persia's golden ages.

Shah Abbas came to a throne threatened by encroachment from both sides—by Ottomans occupying western provinces and Uzbek peoples pressing down from Central Asia. He made a temporary peace with the Turks, drove the Uzbeks out of the northeast—and then began to prepare for war on better terms with the Ottomans. By the turn of the century, he had replaced an army of religious enthusiasts with a new military arm composed of paid soldiers trained in the European style. He even armed his new troops with artillery made by English cannon founders he had welcomed for the purpose. Thus equipped, he pushed the Ottoman Turks back out of his western provinces at last.

Shah Abbas also streamlined the royal administration along Western lines. He gladly received European traders and opened diplomatic relations with Western nations. He typically used these Western contacts for his own purposes, however, as when he cooperated with a British naval squadron in forcing the Portuguese out of the strategic island of Hormuz at the mouth of the Persian Gulf.

For his own people, the greatest of the Safavids built roads, dug canals, erected caravansaries to encourage trade. He imported skilled artisans from other lands to expand Persia's ancient store of handicraft manufacturing industries. He fostered the pilgrim trade in Persia by building shrines. But he also distanced himself from the Shiite fanaticism of the *Kizilbashi* and was far more tolerant of other faiths than Ismail had been.

The jewel of Shah Abbas'a Persia was the new capital he built at Isfahan. This ancient town, centrally located for administrative purposes and closer to the Persian Gulf for trade, was soon humming with new industry as Abbas imported artisans and built huge bazaars, the teeming, often roofed markets that still serve the purpose of a shopping mall in old Muslim cities today. Isfahan grew in time to a city of half a million souls, with 160 mosques, 50 religious colleges, 275 public baths—and 1,800 caravansaries! The shah's palace, the imperial mosque, the roofed bazaars, the royal gardens within and outside of the city were things of beauty. Wealthy homes had lovely gardens of their own, and the poor found public charities ready to hand.

Like many masterful men, Abbas could tolerate no rivals, not even potential successors. His failure to prepare his heirs left Persia with a series of much less capable rulers after his passing. But during the four decades of his reign, the nation prospered, art and culture flourished, and even European travelers admired the Sophy, as they called him, as much as they did the Grand Turk.

## THE MUGHALS REUNIFY INDIA

### A Rabble of Adventurers

A journey eastward from Safavid Persia would have brought a sixteenth-century traveler into the third of the great Islamic empires—the realm of the Mughals, comprising most of what is today Pakistan, northern India, and Bangladesh. Mughal India, like Safavid Persia and Ottoman Turkey, was a major exemplar of the transnational, transregional civilization of early-modern Islam.

Two towering individuals shaped the Mughal achievement: Babur, the founder, and Akbar the Great, the true architect of the empire. They were in a sense the Ismail and Shah Abbas of sixteenth-century India.

Like Ismail, Babur (1483–1530) came to precarious power as a youth. He was only eleven when he inherited the throne of the unstable Central Asian kingdom of Ferghana, north and west of India. Half Turk, half Mongol, Babur claimed descent from Tamerlane, who had himself sacked Delhi around 1400.

Babur turned to the conquest of northern India only when the fortunes of war and politics had deprived him of hope for a Central Asian empire. In the middle 1520s, when he was already in his forties, he and his Mughal tribesmen descended through the Afghan passes of the Hindu Kush, India's ancient invasion route along the Northwest Frontier.

He was an exceptional man. Athlete, warrior, poet, and composer of his own memoirs, Babur was relatively humane in an age of massacres. He was also capable of extraordinary heroism, of diabolical practical jokes, and, in the last fateful decision of his life, of remarkable self-sacrifice.

The small army he led down into the Punjab was a typical rabble of Central Asian adventures. But Babur also trundled artillery along in his train, with Turkish gun crews and a mounted force trained in Turkish cavalry tactics. The Mughal realm, like that of the Ottomans, would be a "gunpowder empire." And Babur, like other famous conquerors, earned at least half his victories through skillful preparation.

## Babur's India

The India Babur entered was, like Persia, one of the world's oldest civilizations. Highly developed urban culture had existed for perhaps four thousand years in the Indus and Punjab valleys, where the ancient cities of Harappa and Mohenjodaro rose and fell many centuries before Athens or Rome were dreamed of. The Indian subcontinent as a whole had developed a cohesive culture based on the Hindu religion and the caste system. It was a land of highly developed arts and crafts, many rich commercial cities, and countless peasant villages.

Despite the deep roots of Hinduism in India, however, the subcontinent had found room for many other religions as well. Buddhism had been born in northeastern India and had spread from there across East Asia. The ancient faiths of the Jains and the Parsees still flourished there. Islam had reached northern India some centuries before Babur's arrival, under the aegis of the short-lived Delhi Sultanate. It was a land of many faiths and temples, which could generate its share of internal differences and tensions.

Political unity had also been rare in India's long history. Only under the Mauryas (322–185 B.C.E.) And the Guptas (C.E. 320–540) had a single centralized political order been imposed on most of the vast triangular land mass between the Himalayas and Ceylon (Sri Lanka). Even when there was political power in India, it focused where the Mughals would build theirs—along the wide, brown, sacred river Ganges in the north. Tense relations with southern peoples like the Tamils had repeatedly challenged the traditional dominance of whoever ruled in the north.

In Babur's time, India had collapsed into a particularly messy period of political division. An earlier Muslim regime in the north, the Delhi Sultanate, had crumbled away. Many petty rajas vied for power in the resulting vacuum, imposing extortionate taxes on the people and allowing their armies to live off the land. Lesser princes and nobles felt no loyalty to greater ones. The villagers, who had seen so many invaders stream down from the mountains, remained indifferent to the outcome of any war.

Babur thus arrived at an auspicious time. His artillery, cavalry, and personal heroics combined with this Indian disunity and apathy to give him a series of astonishing victories over larger hosts. Neither the traditional Indian elephant cavalry nor the famous chivalry of the Rajput princes could stop the invader from the north. His first great victory at Panipat in 1526 gave him a kingdom in India. Subsequent triumphs expanded it into a brief and glittering empire.

Then suddenly, still in his forties, worn out by a lifetime of struggle, Babur was dead. According to a perhaps apocryphal account, his oldest and best-beloved son had fallen deathly ill, and Babur offered Allah his own life for that of the young man. In a few months, the youth was healthy once more and the emperor had passed away.

### The Three Lives of Akbar the Great

For the next half century Babur's newly won empire struggled to survive. Then, in Babur's grandson Akbar, the true builder of the Mughal order came at last.

Akbar the Great (1556–1605) reigned for half a century and became for later generations in northern India a figure of legendary benevolence and accomplishment. The greatest and strangest of the Mughals, he lived three very different lives, one after another, each stranger than the last.

Yet another young heir to an unsteady throne, Akbar led an irregular, self-willed life of hunting and revelry during his youth, leaving the conduct of affairs to an overbearing but loyal minister of state. So petulantly pleasure-loving was the young Akbar, and so irregular was his style of life, that he apparently refused to trouble himself even to learn to read. In fact he remained unlettered all his life, an illiterate wise man at the center of one of Islam's most sophisticated courts.

Outbreaks of anarchic violence reaching even into his court finally jolted the young emperor into an awareness of his duties. He reportedly hurled the aristocratic murderer of a royal minister from the battlements of the palace with his own hands—and plunged straightaway into his second life, that of a leader of armies and a rebuilder of empire.

Akbar was an aggressive general, famous for incredibly rapid marches that repeatedly caught his enemies off guard. He aimed not only to reassemble the fragments of the empire his grandfather had won, but to achieve a predominant position in all India. He reconquered the north, going well beyond Babur's conquest to rule from Gujarat in the west to Bengal in the east, from the mountains of Kashmir in the north down into the Deccan, the triangular peninsula of southern India. He thus made the Muslim Mughals heirs of the Hindu Guptas and the Buddhist Mauryas as unifiers of India.

But Akbar was more than a conqueror: He was a pacifier and a conciliator. He humbled the fierce Rajput *rajas* and then made them his vassals and partners in rule, even going as far as to marry a Rajput princess. He launched a Hindu policy, offering equal rights to the Hindu majority among his subjects and opening up high places in his government to high-caste Indians.

He also tried to introduce a number of remarkably far-sighted reforms in the treatment of Indian women. To liberate women from the harem isolation of *purdah*, he urged shopkeepers to introduce special bazaars for ladies. He opposed child marriages and sought to regulate and protect prostitutes. Most strikingly, he tried, at least, to eliminate *sati*, the custom which led some pious Hindu widows to commit suicide by burning themselves at the cremation of their husbands' bodies.

Akbar provided, finally, for a centralized administrative system superior to anything northern India had seen since Gupta times a thousand years before. He divided his realm into a dozen provinces and appointed governors for each. He chose provincial officials from all classes and castes, organized them in thirty-three graded ranks, paid them in cash, and promoted them on a merit basis. He organized the crucial land tax efficiently, fixing a system that lasted for hundreds of years.

Meanwhile, a middle-aged Akbar had undergone another crisis and entered the third of his lives—that of a religious mystic and founder of a new faith. He had listened for many years to the discussions of holy men of various faiths at his court—Muslims and Hindus, Buddhists, Jains, and even Jesuit Christian fathers. By 1580 he had abandoned orthodox Islam in favor of a new cult, an attempt at a universal religion with himself as its prophet. He called it the Divine Faith.

There was a practical side to Akbar's new religion, since the cult transcended the divisive pull of Islam and Hinduism and focused religious veneration upon the head of state. But we may grant him a higher sincerity too when he preached his universal religion:

> O God, in every temple I see people that seek Thee; in every language I hear spoken, people praise Thee; if it be a mosque, people murmur the holy prayer; if it be a Christian church, they ring the bell for love of Thee. . . . it is Thou whom I seek from temple to temple.[4]

Akbar's Divine Faith did not extend far beyond official circles, nor did it long outlast his lifetime. But its overarching tolerance for all religions contrasted strikingly with the bloodshed of Protestant–Catholic and Shiite–Sunni wars in other parts of Eurasia in early-modern times.

Akbar was a great builder and patron of the arts, a man of broad intellectual and spiritual concerns, and a powerful organizer of empire. Like Asoka in ancient India, he comes as close as any earthly monarch to meeting Plato's criteria for a true philosopher king.

## ISLAMIC SOCIETY AND CULTURE

### The City and the Village

The wealth of the Grand Turk, the Sophy of Persia, and the Mughals of India was proverbial in Europe. When they were not fighting, they traded with each other and with the Christian West. All three of the empires of the Muslim center, as we have seen, encouraged crafts and manufacturing. By establishing peace and order, they maximized the potential for both economic and creative endeavor.

In Islamic Asia, as in Christian Europe, wealth gravitated to the cities. Istanbul, Isfahan, and Delhi were among the great urban centers of the world.

---

[4]Steven Warshaw and C. David Bromwell, with A. J. Tudisco, *India Emerges* (Berkeley: Diablo Press, 1974), p. 60.

The metropolises of the Muslim Middle East and of Muslim-controlled India were divided by occupation and by religion. As in Europe, artisans and merchants were organized into guilds, and all practitioners of the same trade had their shops in the same section of the city. There were more likely to be devotees of other religions in the Muslim city than in the West, however: Jews and Christians in Middle Eastern cities, Hindus, Jains, Sikhs, and others in Indian ones coexisted, though they kept to their own quarters of the city. There might also be a foreign quarter for merchants from other places. In India, the many Hindu castes, which were also occupational and religious groupings, were firmly segregated by ancient Indian custom.

The governors, judges, and police commanders who ruled the city, however, were almost always Muslims. In the teachings of the Prophet, they could usually find warrant for a religious forbearance that Christian Europeans sadly lacked. The bloody feuds of Shiite and Sunni were thus rather the exception than the norm in the Islamic world. Even the intermittent wars with Christians or Rajputs were affairs of high policy or wild border raiders—not the concern of civilized city dwellers. In the Muslim metropolis, the Christian merchants had their quarter, the Hindu administrator his high place in government. In the polyglot middle parts of Asia, diversity was simply a fact of life.

The village was much more likely to be homogeneous, however. Villages in the Middle East and in South Asia were physically like villages everywhere: small collections mostly of stone- or mud-walled huts, surrounded by scanty croplands or pasturage. Because Middle Eastern land was less fertile than much of Europe, farm animals were often lean and hungry, and the people burned dung rather than wood. Monsoon India was much wetter, and the Ganges and other streams from the Himalayas provided ample irrigation in the north. Yet villages were meager places, dusty and muddy by turns, and usually poor, even in the subcontinent.

The typical Muslim village was solidly patriarchal. It was run by a headman, and each large household was headed by the father of the family. The authorities expected the headman to keep his village peaceful and productive, the heads of families to be responsible for all their kin. In a period of imperial order, royal armies or authorities from nearby cities would control the lives of villagers. In less orderly times, roving bands of nomads in the Middle East or warring local *rajas* in India would be their masters.

## Women in the Muslim World

The condition of women also had its distinctive features in Islamic lands. Muhammad had allowed polygamy for those who could afford more than one wife, and sixteenth-century Islam was as thoroughly male-dominated as any section of the globe. Muslim women were generally required to wear the veil and to live their lives in a world of women, cut off from the larger world of men by screens, curtains, and high walls. Bare-faced European women, particularly those wearing the low-cut gowns of Renaissance and later times, seemed shockingly immodest to Muslims.

On the other hand, women in the Islamic world enjoyed property rights, control of their own income, and the right to divorce their husbands—none of which was possible, except in exceptional cases, in Christian Europe. Women in the Middle East especially made substantial contributions to the economy, performing farm labor or supervising it on their husband's lands, herding flocks, or weaving many of the famous Persian rugs that found such a large market in the West. Others were shopkeepers, street venders, and artisans of other sorts.

A Persian miniature dating from around 1600. The subject is the archetypal father-son combat of Sohrab and Rustem, based on a tenth-century epic poem, the *Shah Nameh* of Firdausi. The integration of martial figures, flowery setting, and script in a charming composition is typical of the elegant Muslim art of miniature painting. Effective decorative patterning was a key element in Muslim art from its earliest days. (Leah from the Shah-nameh by Firdausi. "Combat of Sohrab and Rustem." The Metropolitan Museum of Art, Gift of Alexander Smith Goderan, 1913. [13.228.16])

In Islamic countries as elsewhere, there were also women who wielded great power. This was most commonly done from behind the scenes: It is much harder to find famous female rulers in the Muslim center than in either Christian Europe or Confucian China. But through political intrigue, especially in the intricate and often critical politics of the royal harem, Muslim women could exert immense influence upon the course of events from "behind the veil."

Some Muslim women, finally, firmly rejected seclusion and the harem life. The golden age of Ottoman power, in particular, produced a number of women widely recognized for their talents and contributions to Ottoman society.

Many of these talented women were intellectuals privately educated by intellectual fathers. There were writers, musical composers, and gifted calligraphers among them. There were also a number of celebrated women doctors, including some attached to the court of Suleiman the Magnificent himself. In addition, women of the aristocracy sometimes organized and ran charitable foundations.

## Literature and Learning: The Influence of Persia

A Book of Verses underneath the Bough,
A Jug of Wine, A Loaf of Bread—and Thou
Beside me singing in the Wilderness—Oh,
Wilderness were Paradise enow![5]

---

[5]*The Rubáiyát of Omar Khayyám*, trans. Edward Fitzgerald (New York: Three Sirens Press, n.d.), p. 175.

These, among the more commonly quoted lines of English verse, are actually a translation from the twelfth-century Persian poet and astronomer Omar Khayyám. Through such poetry, we have direct access to a very different side of Islamic society, a world of sophisticated skepticism rather than religious devotion. *The Rubáiyát of Omar Khayyám* introduces us to a seductive Middle Eastern world where fine wine warms the spirit in spite of the Prophet's prohibition of alcohol, and where all women do not lead secluded lives behind veils and screens.

If the Ottoman Empire was the most powerful of the Islamic states at the beginning of the modern age, Persia was still the cultural heart of the Muslim world. Persian literature, Persian painting, Persian dress and manners, and the Persian language were common among cultured Muslims from Istanbul to Delhi. What Italy was to Renaissance Europe, Persia was to the Muslim center—the predominant force in literature and the life of the mind.

Paradoxically, Persia's own major contributions to literary culture in particular came not under the Safavids, but under the Turkish and Mongol rulers of the later medieval centuries. The Mongol Ilkhanate of the thirteenth and fourteenth centuries produced Persia's most celebrated historical writing, as well as eminent works in astronomy, botany, medicine, philosophy, and theology. This earlier period also produced a vital literature of Sufi mysticism and romantic poetry. Omar Khayyám wrote under the Seljuks, but the Mongol period saw the writing of Sadi of Shiraz, widely admired as Persia's greatest poet as well as a famous Sufi. Under the descendants of Tamerlane in the fifteenth century, Hafiz, also of Shiraz, revived something of Omar's spirit in his odes to springtime and rose gardens, wine and youth, blending Muslim mysticism with a melancholy skepticism that Omar would have understood.

Persian literature of the Safavid sixteenth century, by contrast, was far less vital and original. The puritanical narrowness of the Shiite clerics smothered both the passionate mysticism of the Sufis and the worldly lyricism of the poets. Safavid scholarship had little originality. Safavid poetry sank into a morass of elaborate "poetic diction" and complex verse forms, more a challenge to the professional writer than a pleasure to the reader.

At this time, however, Persian influence spread east and west across the Muslim heartland of Eurasia.

The Ottomans took their theology from the Arabs and borrowed geographical ideas from Europe, but they reserved their highest respect for the history and poetry of their mortal enemies in Safavid Persia. Ottoman scholars wrote exhaustive commentaries on the Persian classics, and Ottoman poets copied them, both in the Persian language and in Turkish. Thus the distinctive mixture of mysticism and romanticism that had taken shape in Persia lived on, in the writing of Persia's greatest foe.

Persian culture was also massively transplanted to India under the Mughals, especially Akbar the Great. Persian architecture and painting, language and literature spread not only across heavily Muslim northern India but down into the Hindu south as well. Educated Rajput princes spoke Persian in polite society, dressed in the Persian style, lounged in Persian gardens. Persian poetry was read in the summer palaces of Indian Kashmir as enthusiastically as it was on the Golden Horn at Istanbul. It was probably read in both places with more appreciation than it could any longer command in the puritanical Persia of the *kizilbashi*. But then, Omar Khayyám of Khorasan had scarcely expected immortality:

Ah, my Beloved, fill the Cup that clears
Today of past Regrets and future Fears:
*Tomorrow*—Why, Tomorrow I may be
Myself with Yesterday's Sev'n thousand Years.[6]

## The Luminous Power of Art

No Muslim nation has left us sculpture or painting like that of Renaissance Europe—living human beings, ready to step down from their pedestals or out of their great gilt frames. The artistic genius of Islam lay elsewhere—in Arabic calligraphy and the decorative arts, in glass, ceramics, and textiles, in the exquisite art of the miniature, and perhaps above all, in architecture, the art of mosques and palaces.

Painting of human or divine figures was frowned upon by Islamic theology as conducive to idolatry, or as an attempt to usurp God's creative function. Yet some lovely figure painting was done in the Ottoman, Safavid, and Mughal empires—on a small scale and for private consumption.

The art of miniature painting flourished first in Persia, as did so much else, and spread from there to the neighboring Turkish and Indian realms. Small in size (Indian miniatures average less than a foot square), these works usually depicted group scenes—famous victories, royal courts, popular festivals—or illustrated well-known myths or famous poems. Simply drawn, delicately colored figures often move against a flat background of trees and flowers. At the court of Akbar, Mughal painters did some striking portraiture: lightly shaded, oddly luminous likenesses of shahs and Muslim saints in silks and turbans. But the classic Persian miniature depicted legendary heroes in action, royal weddings, or emperors in splendor against abstract backgrounds of bright verdure or arched gates and rectangular walls, all glowing like jewels with color and exquisite detail.

The Muslim world's most admired graphic art, however, was calligraphy. Ever since the days of the Arab caliphates, Arabic script had been widely used to decorate mosques, ceramics, metalwork, and textiles, as well as in gorgeous copies of the Quran. Indeed, the universal use of Arabic lettering for religious, commercial, and other purposes helped to bind Muslims of all nations into a single cosmopolitan community.

The decorative potential of Arabic script filled much of the gap created by the taboo on pictures or sculpture in public places. Verses from the Quran mingled with inter-woven abstract patterns to produce a peculiarly Muslim blend of aesthetic pleasure and religious piety. The living word of Allah and the luminous power of art thus mingled in the work of the skilled Arabic calligrapher.

## Architecture: The Most Beautiful Building in the World

But in the days of the Muslim resurgence, as in the original golden age of the Arab Empire, architecture was the most dazzling triumph of Islamic art.

The rulers of the three great Islamic empires lived in a style suitable to the proverbial Oriental potentate. Some of the palaces they built as settings for their elaborate court life survive as evidence of those splendors.

The Topkapi Palace in Istanbul—now a museum—is the example most familiar to travelers. Its sumptuous interiors, polychrome or dazzling blue in color, are brilliant with

---

[6]Ibid., p. 177.

beautifully woven carpets and glazed tiles in floral or leaf designs. Equally splendid, however, are the palaces of the Mughal rulers of India, particularly the Red Forts of Delhi and Agra and the great Akbar's palaces at Fatehpur Sikri. The Fatehpur Sikri complex, built of white marble and red sandstone, enclosed by multilevel galleries and arcades with rows of bell-topped towers in mingled Muslim and Hindu styles, epitomizes the splendid lives of the Mughals. The pleasure gardens of Shalimar in Calcutta and Kashmir in the foothills of the Himalayas, remind us that these sophisticated Muslim monarchs were only a few generations removed from the open steppes and still enjoyed life in the out-of-doors.

Religion, however, remained central to the life of Islam, as the great mosques built during these centuries testify. The first mosques had been in the open style of the Arabs—a large courtyard, a prayer hall with a decorated *mihrab* (alcove) facing Mecca, and tall, slender towers called minarets from which the faithful were daily called to prayer. Two new styles in particular emerged in later times, retaining the basic elements but clothing them in striking new forms.

One of these was the "four-*ivan*" style developed in Persia, featuring four open-ended vaulted halls focusing on a central court or prayer hall. The huge Mosque of Shah Abbas in Isfahan illustrates this form on a colossal scale, its intricately vaulted surfaces rich with tilework and mosaic. Sumptuous carpets, hanging lamps, and ornate *mihrabs* made such imperial mosques fitting sanctuaries for the God who had smiled upon Islam.

It was the Ottoman Turks, however, who developed the more familiar style of huge domes and slender minarets that most Westerners associate with the architecture of the mosque. The dome does go further back, beginning with the earliest of Islamic monuments—the gold-sheathed Dome of the Rock, built by the Arabs in Jerusalem. But it was the Ottomans, impressed by such awesome Roman domes as that over Hagia Sophia in Constantinople, who made the central dome the core of the architectural design of the mosque.

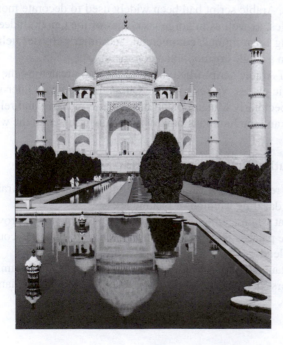

The Taj Mahal at Agra, built by the Mughal emperor Shah Jahan in the early 1600s in memory of his favorite wife, the Mumtaz Mahal. Exquisite in design and setting, the Taj Mahal is one of the jewels of Mughal—and of Islamic—architecture. It also illustrates the subtle interplay of simple masses found in some of the best Muslim building. (Photo Researchers, Inc.)

After surrounding Hagia Sophia itself with minarets, Ottoman architects proceeded to erect similar buildings of their own. These included such wonders as the Mosque of Sultan Suleiman in Istanbul and the Mosque of Selim at Adrianople. These mountainous accumulations of domes and half domes had multigalleried minarets at all four corners and vast courtyards filled with trees and walks, hospitals, caravansaries, the tombs of saints, and other pious structures. They broadcast the greatness of their builders—and their faith in Allah—to the world.

A final brief word must be reserved for the last resting places of the saints and potentates of the Islamic world—for the artistry of Muslim tombs.

There was nothing gloomy about these monuments to the mighty dead, beautifully domed and often set in flowering gardens. The azure dome of Tamerlane's mausoleum at Samarkand looms over walls and towers of exquisite glazed brick and carved marble. The garden where Omar Khayyám lies buried—in the shadow of the tomb of a Muslim saint—blooms with a profusion of blossoms that would have brought a smile to the poet's lips. And the blue reflecting pools, the dazzling white domes, and minarets of the tomb built by the Mughal Shah Jahan for his empress in the early 1600s make the Taj Mahal at Agra quite possibly the most hauntingly beautiful building in the world.

## SUMMARY

The Muslim center of the Old World included parts of all three continents of this half of the inhabited globe. North Africa, Balkan Europe, the Middle East, South and Southeast Asia were among the regions dominated by followers of the teachings of Muhammad around 1500.

The Arab Empire that had established this Islamic hegemony during the earlier Middle Ages had declined and fragmented in later medieval times. First the Seljuk Turks and then the Mongols had replaced the original followers of the Prophet as the predominant people in the central portions of this sprawling Islamic world. Whether ruled by Arabs, Persians, Seljuks, Mongols, or the array of African kings and South and Southeast Asian *rajas*, these Muslim peoples enjoyed a powerful cultural, commercial, and religious unity.

Around 1500, finally, three new empires rose to power in the heart of this Muslim zone. The Ottoman Turks conquered the Byzantine Empire and the Arab states of the Near East and North Africa. The Ottoman sultan, Suleiman the Magnificent, was the most powerful ruler in the western half of the Old World, revered among his own people and respected in Christendom. To the east, meanwhile, the new Safavid dynasty seized power in Persia. Safavid Persia became the militant center of Shiite Islam, a sect as divisive in the Muslim world as Protestantism was in Western Christendom.

Still farther to the east, the Muslim Mughals conquered northern India. Under Akbar the Great, Mughal wealth, administration, and culture gave India another golden age—its last before the coming of the Europeans.

During the centuries of shifting rule in Islam, Muslim culture produced beautiful poetry, painting, Arabic calligraphy, and religious architecture. Persia was the recognized cultural center of the Muslim zone. But the mosques of the Ottoman sultans and the Taj Mahal in Mughal India also revealed the artistic brilliance of the Islamic world at the beginning of modern history.

## SUGGESTED READING

Arjomand, S. A. *The Shadow of God and the Hidden Imam*. Chicago: University of Chicago Press, 1984. Theoretical study of the political influence of Shiite Islam on Iran in medieval and modern times.

Babur. *The Baburnama: Memoirs of Babur, Prince and Emperor*. Trans. W. M. Thackston. Washington, D.C.: Smithsonian Institution, 1996. Memoirs of the Mughal founder.

Barkey, K. *Bandits and Bureaucrats: The Ottoman Route to State Centralization*. Ithaca, N.Y.: Cornell University Press, 1994. Explores controversies over Ottoman history, including assumption of later Ottoman decline.

Blair, S. S., and J. M. Bloom. *The Art and Architecture of Islam, 1250–1800*. New Haven, Conn.: Yale University Press, 1994. Learned and well illustrated, stressing achievements of this period.

Burke, S. M. *Akbar, the Greatest Mogul*. New Delhi: Munshiram Manoharlal Publishers, 1989. See also I. Habib, ed., *Akbar and His India* (Delhi: Oxford University Press, 1997).

Faroqhi, S. *Peasants, Dervishes, and Traders in the Ottoman Empire*. London: Variorum, 1986. Articles on Ottoman social history. See also his *Pilgrims and Sultans: The Hajj Under the Ottomans, 1517–1683* (New York: I. B. Tauris, 1994), on the pilgrimage to Mecca.

Foltz, R. *Mughal India and Central Asia*. New York: Oxford University Press, 1998. The impact of Persian and other Central Asian elites on the culture of the Mughal court.

Greene, M. *A Shared World: Christians and Muslims in the Early Modern Mediterranean*. Princeton: Princeton University Press, 2000. Conflict among Christians as well as between Christians and Muslims.

Grube, E. J. *The World of Islam*. New York: McGraw-Hill, n.d. A beautiful collection of photographs of all forms of Muslim art, from calligraphy to mosques.

Hodgson, M. G. S. *The Venture of Islam: Conscience and History in a World Civilization* (3 vols.). Chicago: University of Chicago Press, 1974. An interpretive account of Islamic history and beliefs.

Inalcik, H. *The Ottoman Empire: The Classic Age, 1300–1600*. London Weidenfeld and Nicolson, 1972. Rise of the Ottoman power through the century of Suleiman the Magnificent.

Mathee, R. P. *The Politics of Trade in Safavid Iran: Silk for Silver, 1600–1730*. New York: Cambridge University Press, 1999. Interaction of political and commercial establishments.

Moosvi, S. *The Economy of the Mughal Empire, c. 1595*. New York: Oxford University Press, 1987. Impressive quantitative study of the Indian economy under Akbar.

Murphey, R. *Ottoman Warfare 1500–1700*. New Brunswick, N.J.: Rutgers University Press, 1999. Revisionist analysis of the power of the Ottomans.

Richards, J. F. *The Mughal Empire*. New York: Cambridge University Press, 1993. Valuable overview.

Savory, R. *Iran Under the Safavids*. New York: Cambridge University Press, 1980. Older but scholarly. See also M. M. Mazzaoui. *The Origins of the Safawids* (Wiesbaden: F. Steiner, 1972).

Singer, A. *Palestinian Peasants and Ottoman Officials*. New York: Cambridge University Press, 1994. Stresses peasant initiatives. See also I. H. Siddiqi, *Mughal Relations with the Indian Ruling Elite* (New Delhi: Munshiram Manoharlal, 1983).

 Please refer to the document CD-ROM for primary sources related to this chapter.

# CHAPTER 17

# MANDARINS AND SAMURAI
## Ming China and the Emergence of Japan

### (1350–1650)

## A GLANCE AHEAD: CHINA AND JAPAN LOOM LARGE IN EAST ASIA

## THE CONFUCIAN ZONE

East Asia: The World beyond the Mountains

China and Its Sphere of influence

## THE MING DYNASTY

The Empire in Disarray

The Pig Emperor: Zhu Yuanzhang

Yongle and the Precious Ships

The Later Ming

## MING CHINA

Government and Society: Mandarins and Peasant Masses

Women in Traditional China

A Land of Sages Confronts the Barbarians

## SATELLITE CIVILIZATIONS— AND EMERGING RIVALS

The Middle Kingdom and Its Neighbors

Influence on Korea and Vietnam

The Emergence of Manchuria

Independent Japan: Land of the Samurai

## CHINA AND JAPAN: CONTRASTING CULTURES

Cultural Differences

Ming Culture: *Fisherman's Flute* to *Golden Lotus*

Japan: From the Pure Land to *Lady Nijo*

**403**

## A Glance Ahead: China and Japan Loom Large in East Asia

Imperial China's domination of East Asia remained immense during the Ming dynasty, which spanned this early modern period from end to end. As they had for many centuries, the smaller peoples of the region feared, admired, and often copied their enormous neighbor. And Ming emperors dispatched fleets of Chinese junks in search of trade and the formal submission of still more foreign rulers to the ancient Middle Kingdom.

But times were changing in the Chinese zone, as elsewhere in Eurasia. The centuries of Ming rule would end with their overthrow by Manchu invaders from beyond the Great Wall. And offshore, the island kingdom of Japan was about to emerge as China's greatest rival in the region.

The Forbidden City in Beijing and most of the Great Wall you will walk on when you visit China were mostly built by the Ming emperors. Perhaps the best-known element of traditional Japanese culture—the *samurai* soldier—flourished in these centuries. And though they could not know it at that time, these two East Asian peoples would be among the last to feel the coming onslaught of Western imperial expansion.

## The Confucian Zone

### East Asia: The World Beyond the Mountains

The hardy, not to say foolhardy, sixteenth-century traveler who wanted to go beyond the Muslim center of Eurasia into the farthest East would have found the last leg of his journey much harder than anything before. Trade routes were no longer what they had been in the classic age of the Roman and Han Chinese empires, or even in the more recent period of Mongol rule across Eurasia, when Marco Polo had made the trip. And basic geography had always cut East Asia off from the rest of the double continent.

The lands and peoples of East Asia were isolated from the world by some of the most formidable barriers in nature. To the north lay barren deserts and the forbidding steppes of Siberia. In the west, the mountains of the Pamir Knot, the Tibetan Plateau, and the five-mile-high wall of the Himalayas barred the way. Southward, the mountains and dense jungles of mainland Southeast Asia were all but impenetrable. Still father to the east, the Pacific Ocean stretched—forever, as it must have seemed in 1500. In addition, the sheer size and wildly varied geography of China itself, with its huge river valleys—especially the Yellow River in the north and the Yangzi in central China—made the East Asian giant an impossible country to know.

The unity of the East Asian world, then, was not like that of either the reborn West or the Muslim center. East Asia was not a system of feuding states with a rough parity of power, like the great powers of Europe. Nor did a common religion, producing cultural similarities among its adherents, bind this part of the globe as it did the Muslim zone. It was rather the historic predominance of a single great nation, warping the history and shaping the culture of all its neighbors, that made the East Asian world a distinct region of Eurasian civilization.

China in 1500 was the largest country in the world, larger in area and population than all of Europe. The very presence of this colossus, with its impressive Confucian civilization and its unified bureaucratic government, had awed the other peoples of the Far East since before the time of Christ. China, vast in its power and influential in its culture, was the great historic fact that imposed cultural unity on the East Asian world.

## China and its Sphere of Influence

China's sphere of influence included a considerable number of peoples around the frontiers of the Chinese Empire. There were steppe nomads to the north, beyond the Great Wall, in Mongolia, Manchuria, and elsewhere, sometimes half sinicized but always a military threat. There were the two peninsular societies of Korea to the northeast and Vietnam in the southwest, both significantly shaped in China's image by 1500. And there was the island kingdom of Japan, which had been accepting some Chinese influences and rejecting others for more than a thousand years.

Chinese influence has in fact waxed and waned over all its huge area of cultural and political predominance down the centuries. When powerful, aggressively expansionist dynasties ruled in China, its influence was all but inescapable. This had been the case particularly after the Qin unification, during the Han (206 B.C.E.–C.E. 220), and again after the Sui reunification, during the Tang (618–906). Over the half-dozen centuries before 1500, however, China's influence had declined, especially under the embattled Song dynasty (960–1279) and during the century of Mongol rule (1264–1368).

By that time, however, the pervasive impact of Chinese civilization had been felt everywhere in East Asia. This Confucian zone had been shaped by a variety of Chinese influences. The Chinese language and its characters, the classical writings attributed to Confucius, and some Chinese-style central government had appeared in a number of neighboring lands. Buddhism, originating in India, had reached China first and been passed on in Chinese forms to Korea, Japan, and elsewhere. Whether they paid formal tribute to the Son of Heaven in Beijing or not, the peoples of East Asia owed a great deal to the land the Chinese called the Middle Kingdom and thought of—understandably—as the true center of the world.

# THE MING DYNASTY

## The Empire in Disarray

The Chinese Empire, the vast central expanse of East Asia, had been unified off and on since Qin and Han times, contemporaneous with ancient Rome in the West. But the Roman Empire fell, and Europe has never been unified since. The Han dynasty in China, by contrast, was by no means the last to rule a united China. In fact, a regular pattern of the rise and fall of central government in China had established itself in the so-called dynastic cycle.

According to this pattern, recognized by Chinese historians since the Zhou dynasty, a particular dynasty ruled China only as long as it enjoyed the Mandate of Heaven, the Chinese equivalent of what was called divine right in Europe (or the will of Allah in Muslim lands). When a regime became corrupt, neglected the ceremonial worship of ancestors and gods, and oppressed the people, Heaven withdrew the mandate to rule. Divine displeasure was manifested through weak and divided government, flood, famine, rebellion, and foreign invasion, climaxing in the overthrow of the regime and the rise to power of a new dy-

EARLY FIFTEENTH-CENTURY CHINESE AND PORTUGUESE VOYAGES

nasty. The latter stages of this cycle were clearly manifested in the fall of the Mongols and the rise of the Ming dynasty in the later 1300s.

The inefficiency and internecine strife of the later Mongol Khans had left dikes untended, the realm ill-governed. In the resulting storm of natural catastrophes and civil discord, the dynasty foundered and fled northward to the Mongolian steppes from which they had come. The immense expanse of China, as so often before in its history, was surrendered to marauding bandits, rebellious peasants, secret societies, and feuding warlords struggling to see which of them would be granted the divine mandate.

But thoughtful Chinese had long since decided that peace, prosperity, and order required political unity under a duly certified Son of Heaven. In the end, then, autocratic order did emerge from anarchy. There was a winner, and once his supremacy was demonstrated, the nation accepted the new dynasty with gratitude for the end of the crisis. Thus began a new cycle in the long history of China. This was the Ming dynasty (1368–1644), which would give China's traditional civilization its final formulation under native rule at the beginning of the modern period.

### The Pig Emperor: Zhu Yuanzhang

The founder of the Ming must have seemed an unpromising beginning to the cultured gentry and scholarly Confucian bureaucrats who ran the provinces and staffed the new government, as they had done for many centuries. Zhu Yuanzhang (1368–1398) was, to put it mildly, a man of the people.

Born of dirt-poor peasant parents, Zhu had been successively a novice in a Buddhist monastery (where he learned to read and write), a beggar, a bandit, and finally a rebel leader. He had a swinish face—he was called the Pig Emperor in later chronicles—was paranoically suspicious, and could be extremely cruel, especially in his later years. But he also had a great capacity for organization, decision making, and plain hard work. He called his dynasty Ming, meaning "brilliant"—and he did his best to make it so.

Zhu Yuanzhang inaugurated a more rigorous personal autocracy than China had seen before. Building on the foundations laid down by the Mongols—who, as foreign rulers, had also had to rule by fiat—Zhu took as much actual power as possible into his own hands. A workaholic, he plowed through piles of official memorials every day. At court, disloyal or inefficient officials were beaten publicly with bamboo as examples to their peers. In the countryside, a system of neighborhood responsibility for labor service and security set neighbors to watching neighbors. Part of the founder's legacy to the Ming dynasty was thus an unprecedented degree of imperial power.

But Zhu's thirty-year reign also saw a number of more positive accomplishments. He provided some economic relief for the peasants after the devastation of the civil war and introduced a more efficient system of taxation. He constructed many schools; reinstituted the civil-service examinations, which had been virtually ignored by the Mongols; and restored Confucianism—the closest thing to a state religion the secular Chinese have ever had—as the nation's official philosophy.

The Ming founder built on a grand scale, especially at his capital at Nanjing, which he made perhaps the largest walled city in the world. While medieval Europe sank into the chaos of the Black Death, the papal schism, and the Hundred Years' War, China thus found unity under a strong dynasty once more.

A Chinese temple in the well-preserved Ming town of Lijiang in China's western Yunan province exhibits such traditional features as the rising series of upward curving "pagoda" roofs. Temples like this may still be seen in some modern Chinese cities, and sophisticated Chinese visitors will still burn a little incense there "for luck." (Anthony Esler)

## Yongle and the Precious Ships

A strong founder has normally been essential to dynastic success in China. Equally important, however, has been the part frequently played by a powerful successor as consolidator and sustainer of the newly established regime. Zhu Yuanzhang was followed on the dragon throne—after a brief power struggle—by perhaps the most powerful of the Ming rulers: the Yongle emperor (1403–1424).[1]

As the consolidator of the Ming, Yongle embarked upon such sizable public works as the renovation of the Grand Canal linking central and north China. He moved whole populations into war-devastated areas to develop these regions once more. He built more schools, honored at least the letter of Confucian doctrine, and commissioned huge scholarly projects for the preservation of Chinese literary culture.

Yongle also moved the capital back to Beijing, the ruined Mongol center in North China. He rebuilt the city on a still grander scale, ringing it with fourteen miles of forty-foot walls. The new Beijing was centered in the administrative section called the Imperial City and the red-walled Forbidden City, where the emperors were to live thereafter in a paradise of palaces and gardens.

Yongle's most startling enterprise, however, was the launching of an unprecedented series of overseas expeditions These were the voyages of the Precious Ships, as they were called in Chinese history.

---

[1]Reign names like "Yongle" (he was born Chengzu) are commonly used by Western historians as if they were personal names, and will often be so used here.

Between 1405 and 1433, a total of seven great fleets of seagoing junks carrying tens of thousands of men sailed from China to explore southern and western seas. Under the command of a shrewd Muslim court eunuch named Zheng He (1371–1433), these huge armadas nosed their way through the islands of Southeast Asia, touching at the rich seaports of western India. They went on to the Persian Gulf and Arabia, up the Red Sea, and down the coast of East Africa. Giraffes, ostriches, and zebras were brought back from Africa. The kings of Ceylon and Sumatra were brought to Beijing in chains. Tributary relations were established with scores of nations. Then, less than sixty years before Columbus inaugurated the great age of European expansion, China's overseas expeditions ceased as abruptly as they had begun.

They were the largest maritime ventures in human history up to that time, some of them involving more than sixty great ships and almost thirty thousand men and traversing thousands of miles of distant seas. The Precious Ships that were the backbone of the fleets were up to four hundred feet long and featured four decks, watertight compartments, and the seaworthiness for which the junk has always been known. They navigated with the help of compasses and detailed sailing instructions accumulated over the centuries in South Chinese trading ports such as Canton (Guangzhou). They were an impressive demonstration of the scale on which China might have operated at sea if this had been its chosen field of endeavor.

But the great maritime endeavors of Yongle were also extremely costly. In addition, they were the special project of the court eunuchs and hence were opposed by the scholar bureaucrats, who were the eunuchs' great rivals in Beijing. Furthermore, China's land frontiers soon preoccupied the Ming emperors. It is also probably fair to say that the emperors of China, with their vast heartland empire, had little sense of the potential importance of seapower in the world.

## The Later Ming

Many problems beset the Ming emperors from the beginning. These included a faction-torn imperial court and a growing population, which put increasing pressure on the government. In later Ming times, a series of ineffective emperors proved increasingly unable to cope with burgeoning difficulties.

More positive achievements included the introduction of new crops to support the rising population. Among these were cotton from India and corn, sweet potatoes, and peanuts from the Americas. China also imported enormous quantities of New World silver through Spain's Asian colony in the Philippine Islands.

One of the most impressive achievements of the Ming dynasty was Beijing itself, the Ming capital. Built around the Mongol ruling city of Cambuluc, the Ming capital city housed the imperial palaces, the offices of central government, and many temples and other official structures. The emperor's personal residence was the collection of red-walled palaces of the Forbidden City, where tourists stroll today.

## MING CHINA

### Government and Society: Mandarins and Peasant Masses

Despite the augmented, sometimes arbitrary powers of the emperor, the organization chart of Chinese government looks much the same under the Ming as it had for centuries previous. Central government fell traditionally into three main divisions: civil administration, the military, and the board of censors. Civil government was carried out through the ancient six ministries for defense and justice, revenues and public works, personnel matters and religious rites. The imperial army, consisting of almost five hundred guards and garrison units of more than five thousand men each, sounded more impressive than it was: In an unwarlike society, under an unaggressive dynasty, the troops got comparatively little practice. The censors, finally, were young officials chosen for integrity and courage, who inspected all bureaus and subdivisions of government and reported corruption and treason directly to the palace.

Ming China, a nation the size of the United States today, was divided into 15 provinces, approximately 160 prefectures, 235 subprefectures, and 1,200 counties. Each province had civil and military administrators, each lower subdivision its prefect, subprefect, or county magistrate, plus a few clerks to carry out the paperwork.

The backbone of this administrative system were the scholar bureaucrats, or *mandarins,* as Europeans came to call them. Chosen by a graded system of nationwide examinations on the Confucian classics, this highly educated ruling class came largely from the landowning gentry. There were problems, of course. The civil service could do little about weak emperors or feuds between officials and court eunuchs. Nevertheless, it seems fair to say that the Chinese government was the closest approximation of a real meritocracy to be found anywhere in the world in 1500.

Much local government was still undertaken on a voluntary basis by prestigious local gentry, especially degree holders, who had passed at least some of the Confucian examinations. These educated landed families organized everything from repairing roads and irrigation ditches to maintaining local schools and temples. Demands upon the peasant masses were limited, consisting of land taxes at harvest time and a variety of compulsory labor.

The Ming centuries were a prosperous time economically. North China, ravaged by the Mongols—who turned large parts of it into hunting parks—was restored to agricultural use under the Ming. Central China, especially the fertile Yangzi valley, produced a prodigious rice crop and flourishing commercial cities such as Nanjing and Hangzhou. The south, finally, remained the most populous and prosperous section of the country, and trade became highly developed at ports such as Canton. From the political capital at Beijing in the north to the economic heartland in the south, from the rice bowl of the Yangzi valley to the endless chilly plains of Xinjiang in China's Far West, the Middle Kingdom of the sixteenth century flourished on a scale unmatched elsewhere.

## Women in Traditional China

Women constituted perhaps half this huge population, and as usual, we know less about them than we would like. There were no great empresses during the Ming period, as there had been in Han and Tang times and would be again under the Manchus. There was an important minority of highly educated women, ranging in social background from court aristocracy and country gentry to imperial concubines, famous courtesans, and Buddhist and Daoist nuns. Some women served as midwives, herb doctors, spirit mediums, silkworm farmers, and tapestry embroiderers. The great peasant majority of women lived lives as limited as the lives of their husbands—the life of unremitting labor that undergirded the wealth of all nations in 1500.

Most women in traditional China were expected to marry and to produce a male heir to carry on the religious ceremonies that bound the living family to the spirits of their ancestors. Because women could not perform these rites of veneration for ancestors, daughters were believed to be inferior to sons.

Young women in traditional China were instructed in the basic female virtues, including fidelity, chastity, and obedience, in a series of moral tales about honored women who had demonstrated these qualities. One such story recounts the heroism of a daughter of the Chan clan who, captured by bandits with her father and brother, won their freedom by offering herself to the bandit chief. As soon as her loved ones were safely away, however, the young woman hurled herself into a nearby river and drowned. She thus both saved her father and brother and preserved her own womanly honor.

Growing girls of the better classes were required to submit to the painful process of footbinding, intended to produce tiny deformed feet These both made it clear that they were wealthy enough not to have to do any active work and produced a stiff, swaying walk that Chinese men found attractive. Marriages were arranged by older relatives and marriage brokers, who considered family interests much more important than the personal inclinations of the bride and groom.

A married woman's duties were many and exhausting. A late Ming woman remembered with affection and respect her own mother, who, though she was sufficiently well off that she had no worry about rice or salt, worked as hard as if her next meal depended on it. As a girl, she had combined daily farm work in the cotton fields with weaving late into the night. As a mother and head of a household, she allowed "no idle hands in her house." And then there were the children: "While the bigger boys and girls clung to her clothes and the smallest sucked at her breast, her hands were still busy with sewing."[2]

Once she had married and borne sons to perpetuate the family, however, a woman could exercise great authority, expecting to be consulted by both her husband and her children on all matters of importance concerning the household. A strong-willed matriarch could thus come to dominate several generations of a large extended family in Ming China.

## A Land of Sages Confronts the Barbarians

When the first Portuguese traders and Jesuit missionaries arrived in China at the end of the sixteenth century, they tended to be impressed by what they saw. Jesuit accounts described China in idealized terms as a land of sages lacking only the Christian Gospel to make it perfect.

In fact, under the Ming emperors of the fourteenth, fifteenth, and sixteenth centuries, China enjoyed another enviably long spell of political stability, relative peace, and general prosperity. The secular cast of mind typical of China spared the Chinese the religious tumults of the Christian West or the Muslim Middle East. The nation's economic well-being was quite comparable even to that of Renaissance Europe, with its new prosperity. And China's central government avoided the endemic warfare of fifteenth- and sixteenth-century Europe.

As mentioned, the Ming emperors built the vast new palace area of Beijing called the Forbidden City. A visit to the Forbidden City of Beijing today is inevitably very touristy. You drift with crowds through spacious courtyards, climb broad staircases you've seen in the movies somewhere, and peer into dimly lit palaces and temples. But even surrounded by Western faces and flashing Japanese cameras, you can get a sense of the Ming achievement.

There is a wonderful symmetry and space to these imperial precincts. The very repetition of red pillars, gilded decorations, and the same sculptured mythic beasts rising from every upward-curving pagoda roof-line reveals a powerful presiding intelligence. It is

---

[2]P. B.Ebrey, *Chinese Civilization and Society: A Sourcebook* (New York: Free Press, 1981), p. 139.

Large Chinese junks like this one preceded European caravels and galleons across the China Seas, the waters of Southeast Asia, and the Indian Ocean. Unwieldy in appearance, they proved seaworthy and capable of carrying large numbers of people and heavy cargoes. The simple sail pattern, rigging, and ease of handling still recommend the "junk rig" to sailors today. (Getty Images, Inc.)

hard to think of the Forbidden City as home, even to the "lord of ten thousand years." But it is a fitting memorial to the power he once wielded as master of the Middle Kingdom, the largest empire in the sixteenth-century world.

The Ming period actually gave traditional Chinese culture what became its final formulation. It was the civilization of Ming China that the Manchu invaders of the seventeenth century would inherit and carry on down into the early twentieth century. It was a massively conservative system of society, heavily oriented toward the past and more famous for stability than for progress. And it had the misfortune to settle into its final, fixed form just when the reborn West was launching into the most dynamic period of Western history.

In hindsight it is easy to condemn China for its rigidity and traditionalism in the face of the coming challenge. Through sixteenth-century Chinese eyes, however, the first Europeans to find their way to south China must have seemed like only moderately subtle barbarians, with their passion for money, their rampant militarism, and their religious fanaticism. What, indeed, did the West have to offer that was better than stability, prosperity, and peace?

## SATELLITE CIVILIZATIONS—AND EMERGING RIVALS

### The Middle Kingdom and its Neighbors

Chinese preeminence, one of the great facts of East Asian life since Han times, continued to be widely recognized under the Ming dynasty. China's political and military power was not as great as it had been under the Han and Tang emperors. But tribute continued to flow into the Middle Kingdom, and China's cultural influence was perhaps greater in 1500 than it had ever been.

The tributary system exemplified China's unique relationship to the East Asian world it dominated. As tributary states, lesser Asian rulers—from tribal chieftains in Manchuria to the emperor of Vietnam—acknowledged the supremacy of the Son of Heaven in Beijing. In return, these lesser potentates got letters patent certifying their right to rule their own lands, a seal to use on official documents, and an intermittent flow of pious exhortations to rule in a true Confucian spirit. More important, perhaps, they got some military protection, the right to trade in the vast Chinese market, and permission to send missions to study the immensely admired Chinese way of life.

Three or four examples of the satellite civilizations that resulted will make clear how great China's influence was. Such an overview will also indicate how vigorous other East Asian cultures were on the eve of European intrusion.

## Influence on Korea and Vietnam

Korea, the peninsular land north of China—or, more accurately, due east of Beijing—is often cited as the model of a Chinese-style Confucian society. Partially Sinicized in earlier centuries, briefly absorbed into the Mongol Empire, Korea emerged as an independent nation once more just before 1400. General Yi, the founder of the new Korea, was, however, strongly pro-Chinese. Yi quickly dispatched the obligatory tribute to the new Ming dynasty, and under his descendants, Korea proceeded once again to import Confucian culture, ideals, and governmental structures wholesale.

Korea was soon divided administratively into provinces and smaller subdivisions on the Chinese model. China's six ministries and board of censors blossomed in miniature in the new Korean capital at Seoul. The Chinese system of Confucian education and state examinations for civil-service posts became still more firmly rooted. Indeed, the fifteenth century was actually a golden age of Confucian scholarship—in the neighboring tributary nation of Korea.

Vietnam, the peninsular country south of China, had a rather rougher long-term relationship with the Middle Kingdom. In the end, however, China's influence played a crucial part here too.

Governed as part of South China for nearly a thousand years, from Han times till the collapse of the Tang, Vietnam gained its political independence in the tenth century—and at once proceeded to send formal tribute to the Son of Heaven to the north. In the centuries that followed, the Vietnamese bitterly resisted Chinese attempts to reimpose their rule by force of arms, fighting off both the Mongols and the Ming. At the same time, however, the sinification of Vietnam continued apace.

During the fifteenth century especially, the Le dynasty modeled Vietnamese government very closely on that of Ming China. The southern nation was divided into thirteen provinces and subdivided into prefectures, counties, and smaller units. A graded system of bureaucratic government, centered in the new Vietnamese capital at Hanoi, was imposed on the land. Chinese culture, dress, and styles of life were cultivated at the court in Hanoi, and the royal chronicles of Vietnam were dutifully compiled in the Chinese style—and in the Chinese language.

This pervasive Chinese influence in Vietnamese ruling circles did have the unfortunate effect of cutting the monarchs off from the masses, who retained their traditional Southeast Asian codes and folkways. But the Chinese model also gave Vietnam a government concerned with public works, the patronage of culture, and other valuable features of the Chinese way in 1500. And Chinese rulers would be intervening in the affairs of their former province as recently as the later twentieth century.

## The Emergence of Manchuria

Northeast of China, another and rather less likely example of the transforming impact of Chinese influence appeared somewhat later, in the sixteenth century. This was the militarized Manchurian state that was to play such a significant part in China's future.

Southern Manchuria, northeast of Beijing, had been part of China under the Han, and the Ming dynasty exercised a loose suzerainty over the area. Chinese emperors sent certificates of authority and honorific awards to Manchu tribal chiefs and accepted their daughters into the imperial harem. Chinese settlers moved into Manchuria, establishing Chinese towns among the seminomadic tribes and exerting a slowly growing cultural influence on their leaders.

But Manchuria lay north of the Great Wall, China's main line of defense against restless steppe invaders. In this no-man's-land beyond the Wall, the unaggressive Ming emperors found the Manchu difficult to control. Then, in the later 1500s, a leader arose who was able to unify the tribes into a roughly centralized state—which suddenly became a threat to China itself.

The new leader in the north was a restless chieftain named Nurhachi (1559–1626) who built state power in Manchuria through a combination of negotiation and war, strategic marriages and tribal alliances. He converted the region from a clan-based society to a bureaucratic state by means of a system of military units called *banners* run by appointed commanders. But he also drew heavily on Chinese models and Chinese personnel. China's six ministries were soon duplicated at the Manchurian capital of Mukden, and literate Chinese-settler administrators were recruited to run the Manchu banners.

In the next century, the Middle Kingdom would regret the strength and order its cultural exports had given to the new Manchurian state. In the 1600s, the Manchu banners would break through the Great Wall itself and come flooding south to overwhelm the ancient civilization that had been their teacher. The establishment of what became China's last historic dynasty was surely facilitated by the influence of Chinese culture on the society of the Manchus before the conquest.

## Independent Japan: Land of the Samurai

The island empire of Japan, stretching northeastward from the coast of Korea, some 120 miles offshore, had absorbed the Chinese model early in its history. A unified Japanese government had first emerged in the sixth century, with a capital at what is today Kyoto in southern Honshu, the large central island of the group. During the formative centuries that followed, Japan had gone to school—like so many others—to the great Tang empire. Japan had copied Tang government institutions, learned the Chinese written language, accepted Chinese Buddhism and Chinese costume and customs.

When the Tang empire fell, shortly after 900, however, Japan had turned inward to shape over the centuries a distinctively Japanese lifestyle and society.

What actually developed were two cultures. At the imperial capital, the Heian culture flourished. Political power slipped away from the imperial government and into the hands

# VOICES FROM THE PAST

These two descriptions of the two sides of Japanese ruling-class training in the age of the samurai come from contemporary sources. Can you see any similarities between literature and arms? Any way in which literary skills could help rulers?

*"From days of old until the present time, military virtue and that of the artist's brush have been regarded as the two virtues comparable to Heaven and Earth. If a man lacks one of them, he cannot administer state affairs. Consequently, noblemen take up the study of literature as a matter of course and are trained in such arts as the composition of poetry and music. But for statesmen, the practice of arms is of supreme importance. They consist of archery, horsemanship and strategy."*

*"Cultural interests and the military arts, archery and horsemanship must be studied constantly. It is an ancient custom to study on the one hand literature and on the other the military arts. They must be studied at the same time."*

L. Frédéric, *Daily Life in Japan at the Time of the Samurai, 1185–1603* (New York: Praeger, 1972), p. 174.

---

of feuding court families. At the same time, however, these courtly Japanese aristocrats cultivated a unique elegance and sensitivity in their personal lives. They developed in their pavilions and palaces a delicate, sensual, and highly aesthetic style of living, delighting in poetry, sophisticated fiction, and the fine art of love.

In the Japanese countryside, however, another culture entirely was growing up. This was the virile, violent lifestyle of the *bushi,* the warrior, with his *bushido* code of Japanese chivalry. From about 1200 on, the bushi—under the more familiar label of *samurai,* "one who serves"—became the real arbiters of Japan's destiny.

From the thirteenth century through the sixteenth, then, Japan underwent a progressive political disintegration. At the top, this process was precipitated by the rise of a military commander called the *shogun.* Appointed by the emperors, nominally as military leaders against barbarian invasion from the northern islands, the shoguns in fact became the feudal overlords of the samurai—and much closer to the true rulers of Japan than the emperors were.

The two early shogunates were those of Kamakura and of the Ashikaga family. The Kamakura shogunate (1185–1333) dominated Japan from a separate court at the city of Kamakura in central Honshu, far to the east of the imperial capital at Kyoto. The Ashikaga shogunate (1336–1603) saw the warriors move into Kyoto itself while the feudal lords of the countryside filled the land with war.

Even at their strongest, the shoguns of these medieval centuries were only paramount feudal lords, never wielders of centralized state power. And even at the top there was conflict—between shoguns and emperors who tried to assert their own long-dormant authority, between rivals for the imperial throne in Kyoto or for the shogunate itself. With central authority thus in disarray, actual power devolved increasingly upon the greatest of the warrior nobles, landed magnates called *daimyo,* or "big names."

Political breakdown, however, was not accompanied by economic decline. Japanese agriculture actually became more productive during these centuries. New strains of rice,

A Japanese Buddhist temple complex. The turned-up pagoda roof lines and the giant statue of Buddha meditating behind the tree on the right recall Chinese influences in earlier centuries. Notice also the lightness of the architectural lines, the openness and airiness of the Japanese center of worship. (The Branch Libraries, New York Public Library, Astor, Lenox and Tilden Foundations)

new farm tools, and more farm animals helped increase Japanese population. Trade expanded, especially with Ming China. The Chinese, however, let very few Japanese into the Middle Kingdom, largely because of the reputation of the Japanese as pirates and brawlers.

By 1500 Japan had thus drifted far from the Chinese model of earlier centuries. While centralized government run by scholarly bureaucrats prevailed on the mainland, the island kingdom had fallen into hopeless anarchy, ravaged by soldiers whose power extended only a short distance beyond their castle walls.

The contrast between the Confucian mandarin of China and the feudal samurai of Japan could scarcely have been greater. The Japanese equivalent of Europe's medieval knights had their code of chivalry too, prescribing such ancient warrior virtues as courage, pride, and loyalty to one's overlord. The samurai was expected to reject wealth, live a hard, strenuous life on the battlefield, and be prepared for death at any moment. Defeat meant certain death by decapitation. Dishonored, the samurai was expected to commit suicide like an antique Roman, by disemboweling himself with his sword in the ritual of *seppuku*. The shogun, as supreme military commander, was seen as the perfect embodiment of these warrior virtues.

They were inspiring qualities for "those who served" in a war-torn age. The samurai, it is said, let go of his life as easily as a cherry blossom falls from the branch in spring. This oddly poetic warrior ideal would live on long after the age that engendered it had passed away. The militant spirit of the age of samurai predominance, from the thirteenth through the sixteenth centuries, would survive and impose itself upon much of the history of modern Japan.

The Europeans who appeared in Japanese waters in the sixteenth century would find their muskets much more welcome than their missionaries. In the nineteenth and twentieth centuries, they would discover that Japan's bushido tradition, equipped with big guns and battleships, could be a formidable rival indeed.

# CHINA AND JAPAN: CONTRASTING CULTURES

## Cultural Differences

A central feature of East Asian history in later modern times would be the conflict between China and Japan. In the nineteenth and twentieth centuries particularly, China's majestic preeminence in East Asia would be challenged by the vigorous, adaptable Japanese. Some of the crucial differences between these two great peoples go back to the cultures that had evolved in China and Japan by 1500, the very beginnings of modern times.

In China, as we have seen, the Ming period saw a final reformulation of the ancient cultural patterns that would survive through the Manchu centuries into the present one. In Japan, whose civilization had begun to emerge more recently, the period of the Kamakura and Ashikaga shogunates saw the first formulation of much of the ethos and artistic tradition that would dominate the modern Japanese spirit. This final section, then, will concentrate on the culture of these two pivotal East Asian nations at the beginning of the modern age.

The most striking thing about the two is the range of differences between them.

Ming China remained, like the China of earlier centuries, an astonishingly secular society, especially by contrast with the religious bent of Hindu India, the Muslim center of Eurasia, or Europe in the Reformation. China was also distinguished by its passion for the culture of the word. It was as profoundly literary a society as any in history, as the intellectual developments of the Ming period make clear.

Japan, by contrast, was as devoted to religion, especially to various forms of Buddhism, as the Hindu, Muslim, or Christian cultures further to the west. The other major aspect of Japanese culture between 1200 and 1600, however—the ethic, art, and literature of the samurai military tradition—makes an equally striking contrast with the literary culture of China—a contrast between sword and pen that is also to be found within the Muslim and Christian worlds.

## Ming Culture: *Fisherman's Flute* to *Golden Lotus*

Ming China was firmly committed to the Neo-Confucian philosophy that had taken shape during the Song dynasty. Buddhism, once so influential in China, was banished to the provinces by Ming times. Under the Ming, hundreds of Confucian schools sprang up to train local collections of scholars and students. And the great Hanlin Academy was established at the capital to undertake, under imperial patronage, truly staggering scholarly projects in the tradition of the Confucian sages. An often cited example is the great *Encyclopedia* produced around 1400 under the most famous of the Mings, Yongle. This immense collection of major Chinese works of the past on history and geography, government and ethics, occupied the labors of 2,000 scholars and ran to more than 1,100 volumes.

The most influential Confucian philosopher of the period was Wang Yangming, a learned official and military commander who experienced a moment of philosophical enlightenment like that of a Buddhist saint. Wang urged self-cultivation as the road to sagehood, but stressed particularly the close relation between right knowledge and moral action. We do not really *understand* the doctrine of reverence for elders and ancestors, he urged, unless we are so convinced of it that we do *in fact* revere them. Knowing and doing are one.

The most famous Ming painters—nature artists in the great Song tradition—blended literary skills into their painting. These "literati" of China's southern school were poets as much as they were painters, and they frequently added a clearly literary dimension to pictorial art.

Executed in the ancient Chinese way, with brushes and ink on hangings or hand scrolls made of paper or silk, these pictures project a sense of reality that would have impressed a contemporary Renaissance artist. Qiu Ying's *Fisherman's Flute Heard over the Lake* vibrates with the reality of leaves and bark, rock and water, a tree-shrouded house on the near shore and misty mountains far off beyond the lake. Tang Yin's *Ink-Bamboo* projects the same sense of reality in the simple shadow of a bamboo branch seen across a window. Other Ming painters went beyond realism, manipulating nature to suit their personal aesthetic canons. They turned mountains into startling architectural forms, or trees into abstract patterns against the sky.

Ming dramatists produced plays composed of dozens of scenes, highlighted by flute music and songs. The most famous Ming playwright, Tang Xianzu, created a series of dream plays. His *Dream of Han Tan,* for instance, is the story of a young man who dreams an entire future for himself and awakens vividly aware of the brevity of this earthly existence—a popular Renaissance European theme as well. These subtle dramas, many of them written by scholarly men, were intended to win the plaudits of fellow sophisticates rather than the cheers of a mass audience.

There was, however, a large popular readership for the stories and novels of the period. Printed on the woodblock press and read by a growing audience of literate common folk, these Ming fictions drew on both history and fantasy for their subjects.

Some of the most famous of Chinese novels date from this period. The universally popular *Romance of the Three Kingdoms* fictionizes the struggles of three rivals for the throne of the dying Han dynasty, while *All Men Are Brothers* recounts the exploits of a band of Robin Hood bandits in the closing years of the northern Song. *Monkey,* by contrast, is the story of the pilgrimage of a real Chinese Buddhist monk to India—accompanied in this version by a mischievous, magical monkey hero assigned by Buddha himself to protect the holy man in his wanderings. *The Golden Lotus,* finally, is a thoroughly erotic novel, still hard to find in uncensored English.

It is a range as wide and human as the age itself. On a smaller scale, the same may be said of the short stories of writers such as Ling Mengqi. Ling's tales of Chinese kings and generals, scandalous Buddhist monks and Daoist sages, strange lands, demons and ghosts, comic incidents, exotic revenges, and properly filial offspring bring the whole of the Ming to life.

## Japan: From the Pure Land to *Lady Nijo*

The thought and art of contemporary Japan focused rather more starkly on two dominant themes: religion and war. But the Japanese expressions of these two ancient concerns of the human race are as rich and vivid as the whole broad spectrum of life revealed in Chinese culture.

Religion in Japan still meant, in part, reverence for the ancient spirits of nature worshiped at simple Shinto shrines. But the shrines were presided over by shamans who were also frequently Buddhist monks. And two forms of Buddhism were even more widespread in Japan than they had been in earlier centuries: the Pure Land sect and Zen meditation.

Believers in the Pure Land—the Western Paradise or heaven of popular Buddhism—believed like many Christians that simply to call with a believing heart upon the Enlightened One was to find salvation. Zen Buddhism, by contrast, required a rigorous monastic life and a personal quest through daily meditation, and only serious adepts were likely to take it up. Masses of common people flocked to the Pure Land and other sects in those violent times. Samurai and great nobles were drawn to the demanding self-discipline of Zen.

Intense vitality and astonishing anatomical realism are main features of Japanese Buddhist sculpture during these centuries. Buddha figures such as the fifty-foot meditating *Buddha of Kamakura* retain traditional poses and proportions, the calm round face and lowered lids, the conventionalized swooping folds of the robe. But the ferocious figures of temple guardians at holy places are carved or cast in metal with an almost supernatural realism. The bulging lifelike muscles and swollen tendons, the menacing gestures, the snarling mouth, bared teeth, and glaring eyes have a ferocity that reflects the savage side of that age of endemic warfare and samurai supremacy. These figures also, incidentally, reflect a mastery of human anatomy that no Renaissance European sculptor could better.

Religious and military themes mingle also in the literature of the early shogunates.

Courtly literature in prose and poetry continued to weave its delicate spell even at the court of figurehead emperors. But now the *Confessions of Lady Nijo,* after detailing her love affairs, conclude with her retirement to a Buddhist convent and a life of chanted prayers and religious rites. The most uniquely Japanese literary development of the period, the *No* drama, reveals a deep sense of the mystery of life behind the gorgeous *No* costumes, the masks, the stylized gestures and choral songs. The typical *No* play features gods and demons, warriors, women—and lunatics.

Warrior tales of the Kamakura period hail the great battles, ingenious ruses, and famous victories of heroes such as the celebrated Yoshitsune, the most famous samurai of them all. But even the great Yoshitsune came to a tragic end, betrayed and driven to ritual suicide by his own brother. Even in their hero tales, the Japanese of the age of the bushido code never forgot the brevity of life and honored above all things the warrior's willingness to cast his own life away.

It was a strange culture and a strange age, at least from a Western perspective. It was an era of seemingly endless warfare, of severed heads and *seppuku.* It was also the period that developed the delicate formality of the traditional Zen tea ceremony, the rich symbolism of Japanese flower arrangement, and the austere beauty of the sand and stone gardens of old Kyoto. The samurai spirit of blazing temple-guardian eyes and flashing swords also found expression in the stillness of Zen meditation and the calm formality of pouring a cup of tea.

The greatness of China was recognized across East Asia in 1500, and even Europeans had heard of the wonders of Cathay. The formidable talents of the Japanese would be a few centuries in emerging to the astonished gaze of Western people.

## SUMMARY

The ancient Middle Kingdom of China continued to dominate East Asia as the modern age began. Cut off from the rest of the Old World by formidable geographical barriers, the world's largest nation exercised a degree of preeminence at its end of Eurasia unmatched by any state in either the Muslim or the Christian zones.

Under the Ming dynasty, China recovered thoroughly from the Mongol conquest of the later Middle Ages. The powerful fifteenth-century Ming emperor Yongle even sent out fleets of junks across island Southeast Asia and the Indian Ocean to the Middle East and East Africa more than half a century before the Portuguese crossed the Indian Ocean the other way. Under the less spectacular later Mings of the sixteenth century, China's unique

Confucian administrative system and prosperous society took on the forms that would prevail in the Middle Kingdom until the Europeans at last forced their way into China hundreds of years later.

The scattered satellite cultures around the Middle Kingdom were closely modeled on Ming China. These sister civilizations in 1500 included the Koreans, the Vietnamese, and even the half-settled Manchurians, who in the seventeenth century would become China's last conquerors before the Europeans came. But the most dynamic of China's neighbors, the island kingdom of Japan, which had owed so much to China in earlier times, developed along contrasting lines in the later medieval and early modern centuries. In Japan, not scholar bureaucrats but soldiers were the leading social class. And strong central government would come to Japan in 1600, not through a divine-right monarchy, but through the victory of the samurai overlord, the shogun.

Chinese culture during the Ming period featured a continuing national commitment to Confucianism, as well as exquisite landscape painting and a range of popular literature from drama to romance. In Japan, Zen and Pure Land Buddhism flourished, and the bushido warrior code of the samurai found its natural home in a war-torn age.

## SUGGESTED READING

Brazell, K., trans. *Confessions of Lady Nijo.* Stanford: Stanford University Press, 1973. Scholarly but readable translation.

Brook, T. *The Confusions of Pleasure: Commerce and Culture in Ming China.* Berkeley: University of California Press, 1998. Cultural impact of commercial development on Chinese society.

Buck, P., trans. *All Men Are Brothers* (2 vols.). London: Methuen, 1957. Translation of the classic Ming novel. See also A. Waley's *Monkey,* an abridged version of *Journey to the West* (London: Allen and Unwin, 1942).

Cass, V. *Dangerous Women: Warriors, Grannies, and Geishas of the Ming.* Lanham, Md.: Rowman and Littlefield, 1999. Women whose life styles liberated them from the limitations imposed on most of their gender.

Farmer, E. *Zhu Yuanzhang and Early Ming Legislation: the Reordering of Chinese Society Following the Era of Mongol Rule.* New York: E. J. Brill, 1995. Reestablishing traditional China.

Gallagher, L. J., trans. *China in the Sixteenth Century: The Journals of Matteo Ricci.* New York: Random House, 1953. A Contemporary European view of late Ming China.

Glahn, R. von. *Fountain of Fortune: Money and Monetary Policy in China, 1000–1700.* Berkeley: University of California Press, 1996. China as an immense independent economic center, especially in the Ming and Manchu periods.

Keene, D., ed. *Twenty Plays of the Nō Theater.* New York: Columbia University Press, 1970. Collection of classic Japanese drama, with drawings to illustrate this highly visual art form.

Marks, R. *Tigers, Rice, Silk, and Silt: Environment and Economy in Late Imperial South China.* Cambridge: Cambridge University Press, 1998. Environmental factors, market economics, and government programs help South China to flourish into the eighteenth century.

Naquin, S. *Peking: Temples and City Life, 1400–1900.* Berkeley and Los Angeles: University of California Press, 2000. Social and political significance of religions in Ming and Qing times.

Needham, J. *Science and Civilization in China.* Cambridge: Cambridge University Press, 1954. A multivolume work still in progress. Volume 4 discusses the Precious Ships, Ming marine design, and technology generally.

Sato, H. *Legends of the Samurai.* Woodstock: Overlook Press, 1995. Training, code, and philosophy come through.

Tong, J. W. *Disorder Under Heaven: Collective Violence in the Ming Dynasty.* Stanford: Stanford University Press, 1991. Uses tools of modern social science to explore rebellions in Ming China.

Tsai, S. H. *Perpetual Happiness: The Ming Emperor Yongle.* Seattle: University of Washington Press, 2001. Politics and foreign affairs of the Yongle ("Perpetual Happiness") reign.

Tsunoda, R., et al., eds. *Sources of the Japanese Tradition.* New York: Columbia University Press, 1960. Valuable collection of materials.

Yang, L. "Female Rulers in Imperial China," *Harvard Journal of Asiatic Studies,* Vol. 23 (1960–1961). Suggestive discussion of the institution and functions of the dowager empress as ruler. On the more traditional place of women, see R. Willier, "Confucian Ideal of Womanhood," *Journal of the China Society,* Vol. 13 (1976).

Please refer to the document CD-ROM for primary sources related to this chapter.

# CHAPTER 18

# POWER BEYOND EURASIA
## Songhai and Great Zimbabwe,
## The Aztecs and the Incas
### (1350–1600)

## A Glance Ahead: Imperial Outreach in Africa and the Americas

Once more, we must combine our coverage of the impressive but less well-documented histories of Africa and the Americas. During this period of rough parity among the world's peoples, Africa produced the sprawling empire of Songhai, the kingdoms of the Guinea coast, and the state we call Great Zimbabwe, which has left us some of the most impressive stone ruins to be found anywhere south of the Sahara.

Across the Atlantic, the two most awesome empires ever constructed by Amerindian peoples took shape in these centuries. The Aztecs and the Incas—sun worshipers, conquerors, organizers of empires—had much in common. They would also share a common fate. As the precarious balance of the world's peoples disintegrated, these American empires would be the first to fall in the new age of the Western predominance.

## From Songhai to Great Zimbabwe

### The Unknown Land

Much closer to Europe than the far reaches of Asia lay the third part of the Old World and the second largest of continents—Africa. And yet, surprisingly, Europeans were just beginning to make contact with many African peoples as the modern period began.

The history of some parts of Africa had been closely interwoven with that of Europe and Asia for many centuries. Africa had been linked by trade and cultural exchange to the Middle East since Egypt and Mesopotamia were the only two centers of civilization in the world. North Africa had interacted with southern Europe since Carthage battled Greece and then Rome for mastery of the western Mediterranean. East Africa had long been part of the Indian Ocean commercial community: African coastal cities exchanged goods with India, Southeast Asia, and even China, usually through Arab or Indian intermediaries.

But neither Europeans nor Asians had much knowledge of what lay behind the coastal lands of Africa. The reality was a great, roughly tapered continent traversed by broad climatic bands running east to west: the green Mediterranean coastal belt, the Sahara Desert, the grasslands of the Sudan, the dense rain forests of the Guinea Coast and the Congo, then more grassy savannas, more deserts, and the plains and hills of South Africa. Broadly speaking, it was Africa south of the Sahara—black Africa—that was unknown to outsiders. And it was over the wide expanses of this region that political growth and development were mushrooming in the centuries around 1500.

### The Western Sudan: Songhai and Kano

The Sudanic belt—grasslands dotted with trees—just south of the Sahara had produced a number of African nations during Europe's Middle Ages Ghana and Mali had developed successively as the largest kingdoms of the Western Sudan in the centuries before 1500. The kings of these states had built their power on the villages of the grasslands. But their wealth had come from trade. Muslim merchants from north of the Sahara had brought salt, manufactured goods, and other things to exchange for gold and slaves from the forest lands south of the Sudan. The Sudanic kings of Ghana and Mali had been the middlemen, managers of the marketplaces of West Africa's commercial cities between the desert and the forest.

# AFRICAN EMPIRES AND TRADE ROUTES

Ghana Empire
Early 11th century

Mali Empire
14th century

Songhai Empire
Early 16th century

**Trade Routes**
●●●● Donkey caravans
━━━ Camel caravans
▥▥▥ Head porterage
······· Lesser routes, head porterage
- - - Portuguese caravels
━━━ Arabian dhows

Typical Sudanic empires had thus developed. They were hereditary monarchies with black elites of the powerful Mande people—known later in the West as the Mandingo—and resident communities of Muslim Arabs and Berber merchants. Appointed officials and standing armies held these states together. Differences of religion and culture divided them: Mande elites became increasingly Islamicized and lived in walled capitals and trading cities such as Timbuktu, while the majority of the people remained animists and lived in agricultural and pastoral communities scattered across the grasslands. There were also feuds over the royal succession and endemic rebelliousness among conquered peoples—problems in imperial cultures everywhere.

The later fifteenth century saw the emergence of the third and greatest West African empire, Songhai, and the rise of the Hausa city-states centered on Kano.

In the days of Mali's greatness, the Songhai peoples dominated the Niger River between its big bend and its juncture with the Benue River in what is today Nigeria. Though subjects of the kings of Mali, the rulers of Songhai—whose capital of Gao was a great trading city too—chafed under foreign domination. In the second half of the fifteenth century, the royal Sonni line of Songhai produced a ruler who could focus this resentment and make it pay: the soldier-king Sonni Ali (1464–1492).

In his nearly thirty years on the throne of Songhai, Sonni Ali overwhelmed a Mali that had declined into a second-class nation, a petty Sudanese state that soon became part of an even larger Songhai Empire. A hard man, he looted Timbuktu and was particularly harsh with resident foreigners, the Berbers and Arabs from north of the Sahara. His followers were drawn from the animist majority of the population, and though he was a nominal Muslim himself, Sonni Ali had little respect for mosques and Islamic scholars.

By the time of his death—in 1492, the year Columbus sailed—Sonni Ali's empire controlled the economic heart of West African commerce—the three great trading centers of Timbuktu, Gao, and Jenne. Under his successors Askia Muhammad (1493–1528), Songhai grew until it commanded the largest sweep of West Africa ever ruled by a Sudanic kingdom.

Askia Muhammad had been one of Sonni Ali's generals. Like his predecessor, he was a fighter and an empire builder, and he completed the edifice of Songhai power that Sonni Ali had begun. He was also an administrative reformer, dividing the enlarged empire into a number of provinces for more efficient governance. He spread the fame of Songhai farther abroad by making a triumphant royal pilgrimage to Mecca and establishing closer relations with the Muslim states of North Africa and the Middle East.

Askia Muhammad's seizure of the throne meant the return to power of the urban elite of Islamicized Mande and northern merchants who had dominated Ghana and Mali. These wealthy, sophisticated communities provided the Songhai Empire with most of its administrators, generals, traders, and thinkers, as they had done for the earlier Sudanic powers. They gave continuity to this succession of West African empires for more than five hundred years.

Under Askia Muhammad, Muslim culture flourished as never before in West Africa. He encouraged the building of mosques and schools. Muslim universities at Timbuktu and Jenne drew scholars and poets from distant places. Songhai was thoroughly integrated into the cosmopolitan world of Islamic peoples that stretched from West Africa to Southeast Asia.

In the late 1500s, however, Songhai faced an invasion unlike anything it had ever confronted before.

The new invaders were Moroccans who had successfully crossed the Saharan barrier into the Sudan in force. They were armed with muskets and artillery, and they soon crushed the armies of Songhai in the field. They did not, however, succeed in establishing

When the Songhai emporer Askia Muhammad posed his queries to the renowned religious scholar al-Maghili, he no doubt sought to strengthen his own claim to the throne by characterizing his seizure of power as a *jihad* against an infidel ruler. Maghili, however, began his response with a ringing assertion of the ultimate power and righteousness of God over all earthly rulers. Many Muslims still value the political views of religious leaders over those secular politicians.

[THE REPLY]. *Know then [sire]—may God aid us and yourself—that all sovereignty belongs to God and that victory comes from God alone, so be a slave to God through obedience to him and God shall be a Lord to you through His preservation and succour. You are but a slave possessed [by God], possessing nothing yourself; and your Lord has raised you up above many another of his servants that you may set aright for them their spiritual and temporal affairs—not that you may be their master and their lord. So over the whole of your domain you are a shepherd, not a master, and every shepherd is responsible for his flock. Look, then, to yourself before you pass away, for unto death you'll surely come one day.*

John O. Hunwick, *Sharia in Songhay: The Replies of al-Maghili to the Questions of Askia al-Hajj Muhammad* (Oxford: Oxford University Press, 1985), p. 61.

their own power south of the Sahara. They merely plunged the Western Sudan into prolonged chaos, a condition from which West Africa would scarcely emerge before the coming of the Europeans in much greater force centuries later.

Hausaland, in the central Sudan just east of Songhai, encompassed much of the well-watered, thickly populated plateau of northern Nigeria. By the fourteenth century, clay-walled towns had sprung up among their scattered farmsteads. Within the walls, Hausa–speaking farmers heaped their produce for sale in the marketplaces. Weavers and dyers of cotton cloth, leatherworkers, blacksmiths, coppersmiths, and other artisans plied their crafts. And merchants began to gather, including growing numbers of Arabs and Berbers from north of the Sahara.

Behind their fifteen-foot walls and iron-bound gates, Hausa merchant and craft communities grew wealthy enough to replace those of Timbuktu and the other trading cities of Songhai as that empire declined toward the end of the sixteenth century. The elites of the Hausa cities accepted a modified Muslim religion and developed a written language based on Arabic. They built many mosques and established schools where their children studied reading, writing, arithmetic, ethics, government, and the Islamic faith.

Kano, eight or nine miles in circumference, with a population of perhaps 75,000—approximately the size of Renaissance Florence—was by 1600 the best-known of the Hausa states. The most famous of Kano's kings, the fifteenth-century ruler Muhammad Rimfa (1463–1499), illustrates the achievements of which this cluster of Sudanic states was capable.

According to the *Kano Chronicle,* this exemplary monarch expanded the city's walls and its caravansaries, enlarged and restructured the army, and reorganized the government, promoting talented slaves rather than hereditary aristocrats to positions of authority. He welcomed Islamic scholars to his capital and presided over a harem of a thousand queens and concubines. Sitting under swaying ostrich fans to listen to the learned Algerian

(a)

(b)

(a) This commemorative head of a sixteenth-century Benin queen-mother was made of a copper alloy with an iron inlay. It features an up-swept hairstyle covered by a cap of coral beads. [cited below] (b) This ivory pendant, carved in exquisite detail and only six and a half inches high, was worn on the belt of the oba of sixteenth-century Benin. The crown is carved in the form of tiny Portuguese heads, a symbol of the royal alliance with the Europeans during the early days of the Western intrusion. ([a] Reproduced by courtesy of the Trustees of the British Museum #38365 [MOPM]: [b] F. L. Kennet; used in Coons, Many Peoples, One Country)

Muhammad al-Maghili read his famed treatise on *The Obligations of Princes,* Muhammad Rimfa represented one more center of urban civilization in the western part of Africa.

### The Guinea Coast: Benin

South of the Songhai Empire and the Hausa city-states lay the rain forests of the Guinea Coast. The forest peoples who dwelt there had learned agriculture and ironworking centuries earlier, at the time of the great Bantu migrations. But the culture of the forest remained one of agricultural villages, loosely linked by clan and tribal ties, until the last few centuries before 1500. Then larger states—Ife, Oyo, and finally Benin—appeared there too, in the deep woods and mangrove forests between the grasslands and the sea.

Limited by the thick rainforests, the kingdoms of the Guinea coast tended to be smaller than those of the open savannas, over which conquering armies could sweep with ease. They may, however, have been commensurately tightly knit and well organized. Perhaps the most famous of the Guinea Coast states was the kingdom of Benin, located in what is today Nigeria, at the great inner angle of Africa.[1]

Flourishing in the fifteenth century, when the first Europeans arrived, Benin was a tightly-knit kingdom lying just west of the mouth of the Niger. The city of Benin was a walled metropolis three miles long with broad avenues and houses in tidy rows, very unlike the close-pressing huts of many African villages. There was a huge palace with many courtyards and long galleries decorated with brass plaques and statues.

Crops grew luxuriantly in the cleared land around the city. Prosperous Benin merchants traded as far away as the Sudan.

The political system was a complex one centering in a political and religious leader, the *oba* (king). But a good deal of power was also dispersed among the *lyoba* (queen mother), the crown prince, a group of leading noblemen or palace chiefs, and the town chiefs outside the capital. The kingdom was divided into provinces with appointed governors, and there was a standing army with a supreme commander and an enviable reputation for winning.

---

[1]The present Republic of Benin lies to the west of the original kingdom.

Ewuare the Great (ca. 1440–1473) was busy building an empire of his own when Portuguese ships first touched at his main port of Gwatto in the 1470s. Ewuare was reputed to have added more than two hundred villages to his domain. Yet he and the other *obas* of Benin had a reputation for mild and beneficent rule, to which European observers would testify in the centuries that followed—even as they themselves proved less than benevolent intruders into African affairs.

## Central Africa: The Kingdom of Kongo

The Congo River winds some 2,700 miles through the deep forests of modern Congo, draining the whole central portion of Africa. It is one of the continent's greatest rivers, comparable in importance to the Nile and the Niger, the Senegal and the Zambesi. Along its banks, a kingdom the size of Belgium or the Netherlands was effectively governed.

Kongo was a developed agricultural society, depending most heavily on a variety of palm trees from which the people made oil, wine, bread, and the fibers they used for everything from clothing to the roofs of houses. The people of Kongo were also stock raisers and worked both iron and copper.

The political organization of this country was based on the immemorial village but was articulated all the way up to the national level. Each village had its head, chosen locally on a matrilineal basis, headship descending through the female side. Villages were grouped into districts, each run by an official appointed from above. The districts in turn were grouped into the six large provinces that constituted the nation of Kongo.

The king was in theory an absolute monarch, governing according to traditional law through a small but centralized bureaucracy in Mbanza. Unlike the rulers of West Africa, the king of Kongo had no standing army, depending instead upon a universal military-service obligation to rally all the men of the kingdom at need. Taxes and tribute were collected by provincial governors, and cowrie shells from an island off the coast were used as coinage. The throne was not directly hereditary: The ruler was chosen by a board of electors, like the Holy Roman Emperor of the Germans.

Kongo was the only one of a number of central African countries emerging about this time, but it was more strongly centralized than most. It was an awkward time to be emerging, just as the imperial expansion of the West was getting under way. Like Japan in later centuries, however, Kongo responded positively, even enthusiastically to the coming of the Europeans. The people of Kongo absorbed some European technology, and Christianity spread among the elite.

After the technicians and the missionaries, however, would come the slavers, and with them a considerable decline in the popularity of things European.

## East Africa: Great Zimbabwe

Great Zimbabwe has been considered one of the mysteries of the African past—"perhaps," as one authority put it, "the greatest in the whole of African history." The mystery of who built this impressive stone city became less mysterious once outsiders stopped trying to ignore the obvious. The huge walls, sprawling palace, conical towers, and looming fort and temple on the hill beyond are a remarkable sight. So remarkable that the first Europeans to see it, in the nineteenth century, wasted a lot of energy worrying about whether it was the work of ancient Phoenician traders, or perhaps even king Solomon's famous African mines.

It was in fact almost certainly the capital of an African trading empire linked to the commercial cities of East Africa. Bits of Chinese porcelain and glass beads that came from India or Southeast Asia show that this great city of the African interior was linked by commerce to the trading community of the Indian Ocean. When the Portuguese sailed up the distant coast around 1500, there were Arab traders in Sofala, probably the main port for Zimbabwe, and in the interior also. But Great Zimbabwe itself, much of it built perhaps two to five hundred years earlier, was no longer an imperial capital in 1500: Its great days were already shrouded in the past.

The empire of the Bantu-speaking Karanga people whom the Portuguese discovered in that part of East Africa in the sixteenth century may, however, have been an offshoot of this earlier Zimbabwe empire. The Karanga kingdom of Zimbabwe was a remarkable state in itself. It had a traditional god-king with a huge court, a powerful queen mother, and nine main wives, all of whom had their own courts. A centralized bureaucracy ruled the nearer districts; appointed governors ran the farther provinces. This government hierarchy maintained order among a diversity of tribes, collected tribute for the royal coffers and conscripts for the royal army. The people cropped the land, herded cattle, made fine textiles, mined and smelted gold. They also traded gold and ivory for luxuries from India and China.

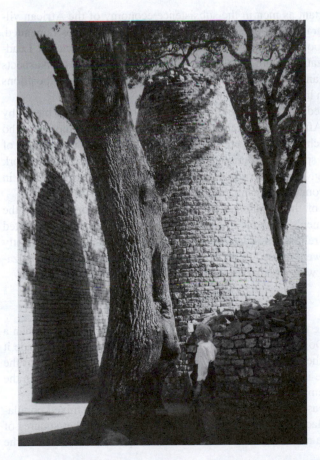

The towers and walls of Great Zimbabwe rise among clustering African vegetation today. This mystery city of East Africa was a flourishing metropolis centuries before Europeans arrived. Probably at its peak between 1000 and 1500, this African kingdom remains one of the world's true "lost civilizations." (Anthony Esler)

But the capital of the Karanga empire, two hundred miles to the north of Great Zimbabwe, was built of wood and thatch. The splendors of their precursors, the builders of the earliest stone city in the south, can only be guessed at now.

You can rebuild Great Zimbabwe in your mind's eye today. From the hilltop Acropolis, you can look down over broken walls and tumbled boulders to the towering grey stone bastions of the Great Enclosure. Imagine all that space between you and those distant walls filled with buildings, crowded streets, the life of that lost African world.

Stretch the causeway across what was then a marsh, rebuild the stone houses, fill the streets with teeming thousands and the air with Bantu voices. Hear the rattle of bullock carts, the clop of donkeys' hooves—you will see both today on the roads around Masvingo. Set drums to beating somewhere, add the clang of ironsmiths' hammers and work songs rising from the labors of a prosperous people long ago. The sense of vanished grandeur will be with you long after you have left these monuments to the birds and lizards who guard ruins everywhere, from ancient Greece to far Peru.

## AFRICAN SOCIETY AND CULTURE

### Queens of the Marketplace

Women were at least as important as men in the subsistence economy of the African village, for they dominated the traditional hoe culture on which many villages depended. Women were important in the political and social organization of village Africa too. Leaders of women's age-set organizations were also the recognized authorities on such aspects of village life as peacemaking and price scales. Women held important religious positions as mediums, diviners, and faith healers.

But women also participated significantly in the new political and economic hierarchy of the evolving kingdoms of Africa. They shared power as queens, queen mothers who were co-rulers, chiefs, and subchiefs. They were sometimes the recognized magistrates of their districts. In the economic sphere, the famous West African women's trading network was probably already emerging. This pattern of female domination is still to be found in West Africa, where powerful women merchants reign as queens of the marketplace.

By 1500, however, some of these high-status positions were being undercut by the spread of Islam in Africa. Women's religious roles were undermined by the more limited part granted women in the new religion. Still later, women's political roles would frequently be ignored by Europeans who were unused to the complexity of African political organization and sought a single "chief" with whom to exchange gifts and negotiate trade treaties.

### The Life of Timbuktu

Timbuktu today is a sandy little town in the West African state of Mali, little more than a side trip for trekkers through Dogon country. It still enjoys the location that once made it great, on the southern edge of the Sahara and only a few miles north of the big bend of the Niger. But it is hard to imagine it as the splendid center of trade and culture it was in the days of the Mali and Songhai empires.

Around 1500, Timbuktu was a walled city of perhaps 25,000 people, a mixed population of Muslim and animist, black Sudanese, Berber, and Arab. In the market squares of Timbuktu, salt from the Sahara and copper, cloth, and metal weapons and tools from the

Mediterranean and Europe were all on sale. They were exchanged for the products of the south—ivory, ebony, ostrich plumes and cola nuts, black slaves and gold.

The sixteenth-century traveller Leo Africanus paints a vivid picture of the city in the days of Askia the Great. Then as now, market women dominated the food marts. And since the desert had not pressed as far south five hundred years ago as it has today, there was plenty of food grown around Timbuktu, a region of cattle and grain and sweet well water. The merchants, Leo assures us, were all very rich, and skilled artisans wove excellent linen and cotton cloth. The houses were unimpressive, thatched roofs on whitewashed wattle-and-daub walls. But there were some famous mosques, and the old palace of Mansa Musa, the most famous of the Malian kings, was still there.

Askia Muhammad, the sixteenth-century patron of Muslim culture, surrounded himself with scholars, doctors, *qadis* (judges), and *imams* (holy men) of his faith. The Sankoré mosque, with its typically pyramidal West African tower, was the center of the most famous university in the Sudan, where learned men taught Muslim law and medicine, Islamic religion, philosophy, and government. The king supported many of these scholars, both native-born and foreign, from his own purse. Manuscripts and books in Arabic, the universal language of the Muslim world, were imported from the Mediterranean. Books, said Leo Africanus, fetched a better price in the markets of Timbuktu than any other merchandise.

## The Benin Bronzes

The widely used term *Benin bronzes* is in fact a bit of a misnomer. Benin sculpture originated, not in Benin, but in Ife to the north. It includes ivory carving and terra cotta objects as well as metalwork—and where metal is used, it is usually brass, not bronze. An artistic phenomenon, however, this art of the West African forests truly is.

Ife was the religious center of a whole section of the Guinea Coast, its famous oracle consulted by many Yoruba peoples. The earliest of all the organized forest states appeared at Ife, probably around 1050. Perhaps as early as the twelfth century, a uniquely naturalistic style of sculpture began to be produced there.

It was perhaps the technical facility revealed by the "bronzes" in particular that first stirred Western viewers. Their great period is the sixteenth century—just in time for the Portuguese to be properly impressed. The castings were made by the classical lost-wax process and are extremely delicate work, no more than two or three millimeters thick. Authorities have compared these sculptures with the metal work of Benvenuto Cellini, the most celebrated bronze caster of the Italian Renaissance.[2]

But once more, as in the art of so many lands, it is the work itself that moves us in the end. A metal rooster, fat and strutting, displays an elegantly formalized patterning of feathers that may remind us of the scales of ancient Chinese dragons. A famous sixteenth-century ivory mask, once part of the royal regalia of a king of Benin, stares at us with deep liquid eyes beneath heavy lids out of the yellowed bone.

In Benin sculpture the naturalism of Ife has been replaced by an exaggerated emphasis on lips and nose and by an increasing stylization, especially of ears, eyes, costume. Yet the life of the people who made them glows from the dark metal of an ancestral head, the smooth skin contrasting with the royal cap and choker of coral beads, the strong features

---

[2]Earlier Western art experts, unable to believe that such delicate work had been done in the African rain forests, credited Renaissance Europeans, ancient Greeks, or even artists from mythical Atlantis.

radiating vitality. One is reminded of something even older than Chinese dragons—of the bronze head, cast more than two thousand years before Christ, of Sargon of Akkad, the first of the historic empire builders. This *oba* of West Africa, whose likeness once stood on the altar of a temple in Benin City, was a builder of nations too.

# THE AZTECS: WARRIOR LORDS OF MEXICO

## A Separate World

Geographically, the New World was a separate world indeed. The two huge continents of North and South America, the narrow isthmus of Central America between, and the archipelagoes of the Caribbean contained all the geographical forms of the world of Eurasia and Africa.

Culturally, the closest parallel is perhaps with Africa. In the Americas as in Africa, some people lived in cities, paid taxes and tribute, and organized their lives according to the will of distant governments. Many others in both places, however, still lived and died in isolated villages, obeying only the traditional mores and taboos of the tribe, clan, and village elders.

Civilization had emerged in two parts of the New World—Mexico and Peru—as early as it had on the mainland of Europe, in ancient Greece—in the first millennium B.C.E.

It was on a solid foundation of twenty centuries of cultural evolution, then, that the great civilizations of the Aztecs in Mexico and the Incas in Peru were built—both, as it happens, not long before 1500. These were the American empires the European conquerors found, and the ones to be dealt with in the pages that follow.

## Mesoamerican Society

Geographically, Mesoamerica is a chain of upland valleys and mountains running between strips of coastal lowlands from Mexico down the length of Central America. Here, by the first millennium B.C.E., civilization in the New World had begun with the development of maize and other food crops and the resulting growth in population density and social sophistication. Olmec culture, the mother culture of Mesoamerica, had taken shape in the Caribbean lowlands, and the most renowned of Middle American societies, that of the Mayans, had also flourished there. But the influence of both had extended into the high plateaus between the mountains also. With the emergence of the metropolis of Teotihuacán in the upland plateau of central Mexico, the Mesoamerican cultural heartland shifted to the high valleys, and Mexico, at the northwestern end of the isthmus, became its power center.

By the year 1000 of the Christian calendar, the classical Mesoamerican civilization of the Mayans and the great city of Teotihuacán had passed away. But the cycles of civilization continued in the area now occupied by Mexico, Guatemala, Honduras, and neighboring states. A well-developed Mesoamerican culture had clearly emerged, one with a capacity for recovering from periodic disasters and for absorbing conquerors comparable to that of India or China.

Mesoamerican culture was built on an agricultural base of maize, beans, chilis, and squash, which supported a comparatively dense population of several million people. Mesoamerican societies were as hierarchical as any in the Old World. Besides the farming majority, they supported many sorts of artisans, a powerful priesthood presiding over large ceremonial religious centers, a fierce warrior caste, and merchants who circulated goods over hundreds of miles. Mesoamericans also had elaborate mythologies and cosmological theories, mathematics and astronomy, and, in some places, forms of writing. Mexico was thus already a thoroughly civilized place when the Aztecs arrived.

## The Rise of the Aztecs

Aztec codices (folded scrolls of picture writing) and information collected by the Spaniards after the conquest tell us a great deal about the history of this last of Mesoamerican Indian civilizations. These sources chronicle, reign by reign, the rise and transformation of the Aztecs, a half-savage people, into great conquerors and rulers during the two centuries preceding the descent of the Europeans upon their coasts.

As late as the fourteenth century, the Aztecs were a small, warlike people, one of the many uncultivated Nahuatl-speaking groups to drift down into Mexico from what is today the United States. They had been nomadic for centuries, following their priests and their god Huitzilopochtli in search of a vaguely promised land in the south. They found it on a muddy island in Lake Texcoco in the high Valley of Mexico, where around 1325 they began to build the city that became Tenochtitlán, the amazing Aztec capital the Spanish found when they arrived in their turn in 1519.

In the early days, the Aztecs were a rude folk, living largely by hunting, by gathering lake creatures, and by trading with the more developed peoples around them. They were said to be given to stealing the daughters of their neighbors for wives, as the most ancient Romans had done, and to forms of human sacrifice that even the sacrifice-prone Mesoamericans found disgusting. Small in numbers and regarded as primitive, the Aztec clans were at first oppressed by their civilized neighbors and generally looked down upon.

But the Aztecs were fierce warriors, in demand as mercenaries and allies in the frequent wars of the Mexican uplands. And they seem to have been very quick learners indeed, picking up techniques of political intrigue, alliance making, and empire-building from the developed zone of urban culture in which they had settled.

They began by freeing themselves from persecution by their neighbors in the Valley of Mexico and ended by conquering them. Under kings with names like Izcoatl (Obsidian Serpent) and Moctezuma (Angry Lord) I, they made warfare a paying proposition, imposing their will by force and collecting tribute over a sphere that extended far beyond the valley of central Mexico. Under more philosophically inclined leaders such as Netzahualcóyotl and his son Netzahualpilli in the fifteenth and early sixteenth centuries, they reared great temples, palaces, and gardens, cultivated such arts as astronomy and eloquence, and ruled severely but impartially over a wide swath of Mexico.

## The Aztec Empire

The Aztecs learned a good deal from the surviving Mayan city-states they conquered in Yucatán. But the hegemony they established in the fifteenth century bore the unique mark of their own society and temperament.

Aztec society was dominated by priests and warriors. Most people were now settled farmers, but all men were liable for the military service necessary to keep subject peoples in awe. Though they did not have money, the Aztecs developed a system of market exchange, even in small provincial cities, that was superior to that of the Mayans. Food flowed into the huge market squares of Tenochtitlán from a hundred miles around. Jade, gold, and silver, feathers and skins, honey, cacao, and other valued luxury items came in tribute from an empire of five million people settled over much of the area of modern Mexico.

Like the contemporary West African kingdoms, the Aztecs had succession problems. Their kings too were not directly hereditary, but were chosen from the males of the more prestigious lineages. The Aztecs compensated for this, however, by considering their monarchs not only as essential intermediaries between the people and their gods, but increasingly as gods themselves, like the pharaohs of ancient Egypt.

As rulers, Aztec kings were able to impose a system of enforced alliances or appointed governors on some sixty provinces and subject peoples. A large scribal bureaucracy kept records of the flow of tributes and the endless wars. Warfare was necessary to maintain Aztec supremacy—and to supply prisoners of war for sacrifice to Huitzilopochtli at his gigantic pyramid temple in Tenochtitlán.

Aztec nobles, high priests, and kings lived in spacious stone houses built in the Mesoamerican style. These flat-roofed buildings were doorless—rigorous laws made thievery rare—and had cool patios and gardens filled with flowers, fruit trees, and pools. The fabled halls of Emperor Moctezuma impressed even the European conquerors with their size, cleanliness, and grandeur.

The average Aztec family had little share in such splendors. Like peasants the world around, they were taught to keep their places and respect their betters. The new order required not only military service but payments to the state in produce and labor. Some peasants were serfs; others were slaves.

Most Mesoamericans, however, lived under the Aztecs as their ancestors had before the conquest. Men worked in the fields, using simple wood and stone tools. They had no beasts of burden to help, since no large domesticatable animals had survived the hunting stage in Middle America.

Women spun and wove cloth made of cotton and other vegetable fibers into the short pants and long mantles or capes worn by men and the long skirts and blouses the women themselves wore. The women also spent many hours a day—as many Indian women still do—grinding corn by hand to make the tortillas that, with beans and chili, were the mainstay of the Mesoamerican diet.

It is hard to associate the sturdy, broad-faced, hard-working people of the surviving codices and paintings with the splendors—and the horrors—of the priestly-military elite who ruled over them, or with the towering, blood-drenched pyramid on the great plaza of Tenochtitlán.

## THE INCAS: EMPIRE OF THE ANDES

### A Land and People Divided

The Andes change color through the day. Driving down through the mountains toward the coast, you crawl like an insect among ridges and peaks that are dark blue in the morning, gray slashed with green and ocher in the dry cold noon, and red in the sunset, sliding through violet and purple toward the dark. The precipitous surge and fall of that miles-high world of angled rock, plunging gorges, and bare, isolated valleys far above the timberline make hard enough driving on a narrow modern road. The thought of traveling through this world before the age of modern transport—let alone living and building here—can kindle an impulse of respect in the most cynical modern spirit.

To unify such a realm in any but the loosest cultural sense would require both immense labor and a kind of genius rare in history. As far as we know, it happened only once before the coming of the conquistadores—in the days of the Sapa Incas, rulers of the largest empire in the history of pre-Columbian America.

Pan-Andean cultural unity was of course achieved long before the Incas conquered the Andes. As in Mesoamerica, the Amerindians of what is today Peru and portions of neighboring nations had perfected a thoroughly workable style of life, with sophisticated forms of art and social organization, centuries and even millennia earlier.

Agriculture was widely practiced. Potatoes were the upland staple, though corn, beans, and various squashes were common here as in Mexico. Hills and mountainsides were terraced, irrigation canals and ditches spread water over arid lowland valleys, and fertilizing was common. Ceremonial centers and even some true cities featured large stone temples and palaces. Many crafts were practiced, including the ancient ceramic and textile industries and more metalworking than in Middle America. Society was acquiring the habits of specialization and hierarchical class divisions characteristic of urban civilization everywhere.

But the Andes divided and subdivided Peru and the peoples who lived there as the mountains and the high central plateaus divided Mexico. If anything, the world's longest mountain range did a more thorough job of breaking up the western side of South America. Peru's rocky spine effectively separated the tropical rain forests of the interior from the coastal deserts along the Pacific. Ecologically, these three zones—jungle, mountains, arid coastland—contrasted as sharply as any in the world. In addition, the ridges and jagged crests subdivided the uplands and the coastal lowlands into many narrow valleys—and separate valley societies—with only the most difficult communication between them.

The economy reflected these geographical and ecological divisions. Amerindian peoples pastured llama and alpaca herds and cultivated potatoes in the higher altitudes. They raised corn in the hills below, took fish from the sea, and gathered coca and other tropical products from the other side of the mountains, where the rain forests of the Amazon basin began. Each separate people, scattered among mountains or hills or forests, also had its unique traditional patterns of ceramic and textile design. Each had a style of life suited to its ecology and its traditions.

## Forces for Unity

To overcome some of these problems rooted in environmental differences, Andean peoples had long since learned to trade with one another, exchanging the produce of one region for that of another. Another solution was to send out "colonies" for seasonal harvesting in a different zone, or even for permanent exploitation of crops available only in a neighboring area. Thus whole regions of this rugged corner of the world attained at least a degree of economic unity. In some cases, as among the areas conquered by the Mochica, there was regional political unity as well.

There had been significant efforts to impose hegemony over even larger tracts of pre-Columbian Peru. During the second half of the first millennium C.E., several sizable empires had divided most of Peru among them. These were the conquest empires of Huari in the north and Tiahuanaco in the south, both flourishing from approximately 600 to 1000, and the Chimu state. The latter flowered somewhat later in the northwestern coastal area earlier organized by the Mochica.

As in Mesoamerica, a key factor behind the rise of these larger political units was the increase in population caused by improved agricultural techniques. The people seem to have needed some higher authority than the usual clan and family structure to deal with the more complex problems of life in their overcrowded valleys. Arguments over water use, landownership, and the conflicting traditional rights of neighboring villages could most effectively be settled by a superior governmental power. And there was never a shortage of ambitious chiefs, priests, and warriors eager to establish such a higher power.

## Pachacuti Inca and the Unification of the Andes

The Incas—the term is a royal title—were the heads of the ruling house of a small kingdom that rose in the upland mountain-ringed valley of Cuzco perhaps as early as C.E. 1200. It was not until 250 years later, however, that a great conqueror came to the throne and became the real founder of the Inca Empire.

The historically significant rulers of Inca Peru thus number no more than half a dozen, from the emergence of the empire around 1450 to its fall to the Spanish in 1532. And the greatest of these Inca empire builders was the first, the famous Pachacuti.

Pachacuti Inca (1438–1471) seized power during a disastrous war with a powerful neighboring people. He first overthrew his father, who had retreated before the enemy, and then executed his brother, who had been so successful against the foe as to seem a threat to Pachacuti's authority. In the process of achieving and assuring his throne, the new ruler also defeated the foreign enemy who had made his rise possible. He then capped his achievement by enlisting his defeated neighbor's armies for a great campaign of conquest up and down the Andes and across the coastal lowlands as well. Pachacuti Inca and his highly competent heir Topa Inca extended their domain north into what is today Ecuador, south as far as the middle of Chile, and inland to include half of Bolivia and even a corner of Argentina.

Topa Inca's successor added little to the empire, and two of Topa's grandsons fought a civil war over the throne, a conflict that was just ending when Pizarro appeared. But the Incas had already earned their place in history. The empire they had assembled was the most impressive—and, among scholars of a later age, the most controversial—in the New World.

## The Inca Empire

The peoples who lived under the Inca emperors found their lives changed significantly by their new rulers. For in their comparatively short tenure of power, the Incas demonstrated an unsurpassed skill at social and political organization.

The Inca Empire stretched for 2,500 miles down the western side of South America, over some of the most difficult terrain in the world. The population may have run as high as six or eight million. To unite this realm and the divided peoples who lived there, the Inca rulers established an awesome hierarchy of officials.

The empire was divided into quarters, each of which was further divided into provinces. There was an appointed or hereditary *curaca,* or leader, for every 10 families, and again for every 50, 100, 500, 1,000, 5,000, and 10,000. There were appointed governors for each of the quarters. There were officials in the central government in Cuzco charged with special functions, from transportation to the military. And all this vast bureaucracy was run by people whose most complicated record-keeping device was the *quipu,* a tangle of knotted strings that served as an all-purpose aid to memorizing both statistics and events!

The great king, or Sapa Inca, at the top of this society lived in splendor in Cuzco. He never wore the same elaborate royal regalia twice, was carried about in a golden litter to a

# AMERINDIAN EMPIRES ON THE EVE OF THE SPANISH CONQUEST

ATLANTIC

OCEAN

GULF OF MEXICO

Oxitipan
Tuxpan
Tenochtitlán
TLAXCALA
Coatza-
coalco

Querétaro

TARASCANS

Chichén Itzá

Uxmal

Petlatlán
Acapulco
Oaxaca
Mitla
Chiapa
Comitán
Ayotlán

MAYAS

Tikal

Copan

Mesoamerica

Indefinite
Eastern
Frontier

CARIBBEAN SEA

Orinoco R.

THE CHIBCHAS

Pasto

Quito

Manta

Tumbez

Equator

Moyobamba

Cajamarca

Chimu

Huanuco

INCAS

Machu Picchu

Cuzco

Amazon R.

CHINCHAS

Peru

Arequipa

Lake Titicaca

Tiahuanaco

Cochabamba

PACIFIC

OCEAN

Iquique

Tarija

Atacama

Tucumán

Copiapó

Coquimpu

Catamarca

ARAUCANIANS

Maule R.

| Aztec Empire (approximate area) |
| Inca Empire (approximate area) |

0        500       1000 Miles

0    500    1000 Kilometers

chanting of hymns, and was generally believed to be descended from the Sun, who was one of the chief gods in the Inca pantheon.

The millions of Inca subjects were expected to provide tribute in produce and were compelled to perform long hours of labor for the state. They were regulated by government edict in everything from care of crops and herds, craftwork, and construction to marriage and religion. In return, the Inca government attempted to provide defense, justice, transportation and communication facilities, food distribution from government granaries in times of scarcity, and at least minimal care for widows and orphans, the old and the sick.


## PARALLEL CULTURES OF MEXICO AND PERU

### Aztec Virtues

Like the civilizations of China and Japan, those of the Incas and Aztecs were very different from each other. The Incas, like the Chinese, demonstrated remarkable skills in the arts of social organization, whereas both the war-like Aztecs and the Japanese of the age of the samurai made martial vigor central to their societies.

In their later years at least, the once barbaric Aztecs mastered many of the traditional Mesoamerican arts and sciences. They possessed considerable knowledge of astronomy, mathematics, and a form of picture writing. They also had great skill in engineering, architecture, and sculpture in stone, and a distinctive style of painting featuring flat colors, heavy outlines, and lively cartoonlike figures. As the ancient Romans learned from the Greeks, or the Arabs from the peoples they conquered, so the Aztecs acquired a sophisticated high culture from their predecessors.

The uniqueness of the Aztecs lay not in art or science, however, but in the rigor of their morality and the extravagance of their religion.

Aztec children were taught from their earliest years to fear the gods and respect their elders. They learned to avoid vice and injustice, work hard, and accept punishment with humility. Courage, self-discipline, justice, and piety were preeminent Aztec virtues. Both parents and a widespread system of village education taught all children these virtues. An equally widespread system of law courts punished misdeeds so rigorously—death for stealing more than four ears of corn—that crime seems to have been all but eliminated among the Aztecs.

Boys were further taught a trade, necessary military skills, and the supreme virtue of standing firm in battle. As young warriors, many proved in fact eager for their first chance to plunge into combat, swinging their obsidianedged war clubs. For girls, marriage was the normal first step into adult life. Some might train to be priestesses in special schools, but the future of most was described in a formal speech commonly pronounced on a girl's wedding day:

> My daughter. . . . it is time that thou didst abandon childish things. . . . Thou wilt have to rise in the night, sweep out the house and light the fire before daybreak. Thou wilt have to leave thy bed every day before sunrise, take care, my child, not to disgrace us. . . .[3]

---

[3]Quoted in Friedrich Katz, *The Ancient Indian Civilizations,* trans. K. M. Simpson (New York: Praeger, 1972), p. 222.

## The Altars of Tenochtitlán

Religion had a powerful grip on all Aztec people. Like other Mesoamericans, the Aztecs were animists. They felt the closeness of the supernatural in earth and rain, the stars and the forests, the sharp edge of the obsidian blade and the burning of the fire. They personified these felt presences in anthropomorphic gods and goddesses, whom they often depicted as hybrid combinations of animals, such as Quetzalcóatl, the feathered serpent with a jaguar's teeth. There were two sorts of divinities: nature gods worshiped by farmers—for example, "your lordship, the corn"—and the great gods of the state, headed by the ancient Aztec sun god, Huitzilopochtli.

In the measured judgment of most historians, it was an intensely felt need to placate the great Huitzilopochtli, the all-devouring Mexican sun, that drove the whole brilliant, brutal machinery of the Aztec state.

Human sacrifice has been practiced at one time or another almost everywhere, usually in order to acquire supernatural powers—or to placate them. The Aztecs believed that the sun above, source of all life, required constant feeding on human hearts. Their unending wars, their stoic warrior ethic, the empire itself was from this perspective but an elaborate way of gathering food for the sun. As long as blood continued to darken the pyramidal temple of Huitzilopochtli on the great plaza—as long as fresh-plucked hearts were held up to the sky—so long would the sun shine, the crops flourish, and the Aztecs rule.

The conquistadores were vastly impressed by the lake city of Tenochtitlán, the Venice of the New World, with its "great towers and . . . buildings rising from the water, and all built of masonry,"[4] with green jungles and purple volcanoes behind it. Five square miles in area, its population perhaps as high as 100,000, it was larger than many European cities. The streets were swept clean daily; even human waste was thriftily hauled away by canoe to be used as fertilizer. The temples, plazas, palaces, and market squares, the sculptured walls, pleasant gardens, and aromatic trees were like something out of a fairy tale to the Spanish intruders.

And then they saw the racks of skulls, thousands upon thousands of them, at the foot of the temple stairs. Europeans, who burned people alive in their own countries to please their God, were, of course, unconvincing champions of humanitarianism. We can lament the destruction of that Venice of the Americas, all gone today beneath the hum and roar of Mexico City. But it is hard to regret the cessation of the rise and fall of that razor-edged obsidian blade, the swiftly probing hand, and the still-pumping lump of flesh thrust up against the sun.

## The Sapa Inca and the Virgins of the Sun

The Incas and their subjects were also polytheistic. They believed in a creator god, Viracocha, who had made all things in heaven and earth, including human beings fully equipped with their tribal languages, traditional music, and textile patterns. Viracocha, however, did not rule the universe: he left that to his chief assistant, Inti, the sun, who was believed to be the ancestor of all the Incas.

The moon, various stars, and Mother Earth were also gods and had earthly responsibilities as patrons of crops, herds, and trades. Numinous power also clustered about many earthbound objects, from the tombs of ancestors to the boundary stones of fields. Even a heap of rocks along the road might be worth a prayer, and might give strength to the traveler.

---

[4]Bernal Díaz del Castillo, *The Discovery and Conquest of Mexico,* trans. Irving A. Leonard (New York: Grove Press, 1950), p. 190.

Religion was as well organized as everything else in the empire of the Incas. There were shrines and temples at the village and provincial-city level as well as at the mountain capital of Cuzco. Priests and priestesses performed rituals and sacrifices punctually. The sacrifices, unlike those in Mesoamerica, were normally guinea pigs or llamas.

Inca priestesses—the "Chosen Women" and "Virgins of the Sun" held a unique place in Inca culture. Selected as girls from their home villages, they were carefully educated in religion, weaving, and ceremonial duties. Chosen Women might become wives for nobles, officials, or the Inca himself. The Virgins of the Sun devoted their lives to religious duties at sun temples in every province. They were among the best educated and most admired women in the empire.

## The King's Highway

But it is in their great public works that this most organized of New World societies excelled. The Incas were above all else great builders.

Inca stonework was probably the best in the Americas, despite the greater flamboyance of Mesoamerican architecture. Inca artisans cut, polished, beveled, and fitted stones with an unexcelled precision. Much of their best work was done at Cuzco, where royal palaces, noble mansions, and the great Temple of the Sun provided a challenge suited to their talents.

The Inca capital was a huge city, containing an estimated 100,000 to 300,000 people. The population of Cuzco represented all the varied populations of the empire, and each was required to wear his or her own brightly colored native costume. The palaces of the Incas and of the noble heads of great clans were complexes of low buildings built around many courtyards, with gardens and store-houses for the clan treasures. There was a great public square for religious ceremonies. And there was the Coricancha, the Temple of the Sun, some of whose walls may be seen in Cuzco today serving as foundations for a Spanish colonial church.

The greatest of all Inca engineering feats, however, was the famous royal road through the Andes. There were apparently almost 9,500 miles of the king's highway, up and down and across one of the world's highest mountain ranges. The roadway was graded, smoothed, frequently paved with stone, and walled where it ran along the edge of a precipice. There were hostels and way stations for the runners who carried the royal

Machu Picchu, the cloud-draped city in the Andes fifty miles from the Inca capital of Cuzco. Poking through the roofless ruins of this walled city on a mountain top 8,000 feet high, you cannot help but be impressed with the genius and determination of this Native American people, and with the ancient South American civilization of which the Inca Empire was the final flowering. (A. Minaev/United Nations Photo)

post. There were hundreds of bridges over gorges and rivers. All of it was built, cared for, cleaned of falling rock, and repaired when heavier slides carried whole sections away, by the corvée labor of the peasants. Amazingly, much of this royal road was kept up by local villagers long after the fall of the Incas who built it, so strong a sense of social responsibility had the Inca regime instilled in its people.

The best place to see Inca urban building today is in Machu Picchu, the famous "lost city" in the clouds north of Cuzco. Here, framed by mist-draped crags high above the valley floor, yellow grass sprouts among the beveled stones, and the characteristic trapezoidal doors open on roofless rooms. The labor, the skill, and the organizing will that shaped this masonry and set it in its place so perfectly that a knife blade still cannot be inserted between the blocks testify to the unique genius of the Incas.

## SUMMARY

As in Europe and Asia, new vitality throbbed in Africa and the Americas in the early modern centuries.

Kingdoms had sprung up in many parts of Africa south of the Sahara by 1500. On the grasslands of the Western Sudan, the Songhai kingdom of Sonni Ali and Askia Muhammad followed in the imperial tradition of Ghana and Mali. In the rain forests of the Guinea Coast, Benin and other kingdoms emerged, impressing the first European mariners as the empires of the Sudan had earlier Arab caravans. The institutional complexities of the kingdom of Kongo in central Africa were less visible to early European visitors. And the civilization of Great Zimbabwe had largely faded by the time outsiders came to marvel at its mysterious stone ruins.

The complexity of evolving African society south of the Sahara was well illustrated by the varied roles played by women in the society: from faith healer to subsistence agriculturalist, from queen-mother to queen of the marketplace.

African culture flourished during the centuries around 1500. Cities like Timbuktu shared in the cosmopolitan interregional culture of the Muslim world, with its mosques, scholars, sophisticated courts, and merchant wealth. Among the most impressive artistic accomplishments of the age are the Benin bronzes and the more naturalistic sculpture of Ife.

In the Americas, as in Africa, urban cultures emerged much earlier than we are used to thinking. In Mesoamerica and the Peruvian Andes, many of the arts of civilization had been practiced for two thousand years when the first Europeans broke in upon this independent stream of social evolution shortly after 1500.

In Middle America, the vigorous and militaristic Aztecs fought their way to power among the peoples of the high valleys of Central Mexico in the fourteenth and fifteenth centuries. Initially regarded as northern barbarians, the Aztecs rapidly mastered a range of traditional Mexican skills, from settled agriculture and city-building to diplomacy and bureaucratic administration. By 1500 they governed the largest empire in Mesoamerican history.

The largest of all pre-Columbian American empires, however, was that of the Incas, which emerged in the fifteenth century in Peru. Pachacuti Inca, the founder of Inca power, demonstrated amazing skill at imposing centralized authority on the historically and geographically divided peoples of northwestern South America.

In both of these highly developed urban-imperial societies of the New World, arts and ideas flourished. They shared a variety of common elements, from sun worship and temple pyramids to a strong sense of social morality. There were, however, striking differences between them.

The Aztecs enforced rigorous moral standards and martial vigor. Their central religious ceremony, human sacrifice on the altar of the sun, was believed necessary to guarantee continued prosperity to the empire. The Incas, though neither literate nor as mathematically inclined as the Mesoamerican peoples, developed other skills. They worked metals on a larger scale and were probably the most expert builders with stone in the Americas. The astonishing Inca royal road through the Andes was one of the great feats of engineering—and social discipline—of the age.

## SUGGESTED READING

Anton, F. *Women in Pre-Columbian America.* New York: Abner Schram, 1973. Good pictures, thorough commentary on Amerindian women before the Europeans came.

Berger, I., and E. F. White. *Women in Sub-Saharan Africa: Restoring Women to History.* Bloomington and Indianapolis: Indiana University Press, 1999. The important role of women in African economics, politics, and society, seen as diminishing under Islamic and later Western influences.

De la Vega, G. *Royal Commentaries of the Incas and General History of Peru* (2 vols.), trans. H. V. Livermore. Austin: University of Texas Press, 1966. Primary source, perhaps too sympathetic to the Incas.

Gibb, H. A. R., ed. and trans. *Ibn Battuta: Travels in Asia and Africa* (2 vols.). New York: Cambridge University Press, 1958–1962. Famous Arab traveler and his observations on the Western Sudan. See also Leo Africanus, *The History and Description of Africa* (3 vols.) (London: Hakluyt Society, 1896).

Hale, T. A. *Scribe, Griot, and Novelist: Narrative Interpreters of the Songhay Empire.* Gainesville: University of Florida Press, 1990. Includes N. Malio's version of *The Epic of Askia Muhammad.*

Hassig, R. *Aztec Warfare: Imperial Expansion and Political Control.* Norman: University of Oklahoma Press, 1988. Analyzes Aztec military tactics and imperialistic motives, questioning the central role of religion.

Huffman, T. N. *Snakes and Crocodiles: Power and Symbolism in Ancient Zimbabwe.* Johannesburg: Witwatersrand University Press, 1996. Roots this African civilization in the culture of local peoples.

Julien, C. *Reading Inca History.* Iowa City: University of Iowa Press, 2000. Ingenious study that extracts the lost Inca historical record from surviving Spanish texts.

Lebeuf, A. "The Role of Women in the Political Organization of African Societies," in D. Paulme, ed., *Women in Tropical Africa* (Berkeley: University of California Press, 1960). Female power on all levels, from African queens and queen-mothers to the village, with a historical dimension.

Nash, J. "Aztec Women: The Transition from Status to Class in Empire and Colony," in M. Etienne and E. Leacock, eds., *Women and Colonization: Anthropological Perspectives.* New York: Praeger, 1980. Marriage and work before and after the conquest.

Rostworowski de Diez Caseco, M. *History of the Inca Realm.* trans. Harry B. Iceland. New York: Cambridge University Press, 1999. A leading authority analyzes Spanish colonial records to deepen our understanding of the preconquest Inca empire.

Saad, E. N. *Social History of Timbuktu.* New York: Cambridge University Press, 1983. Focuses on the role of Muslim elites.

Sahagún, B. de. *General History of the Things of New Spain* (12 vols.), trans. and ed. A. O. J. Anderson and C. E. Dibble. Sante Fe, N.M.: School of American Research, 1950–1969. Basic primary source for the Aztecs.

Salomon, F. *Native Lords of Quito in the Age of the Incas.* New York: Cambridge University Press, 1986. Uses Spanish colonial records as well as archaeological and anthropological evidence to analyze this Amerindian society at the time of the Inca conquest.

Sudarkasa, N. *Where Women Work: A Study of Yoruba Women in the Marketplace and in the Home.* Ann Arbor: University of Michigan Anthropological Papers, 1973. Good study of West African market women, with some account of the historical evolution of their role.

Vansina, J. *Art History in Africa.* New York: Longman, 1984. Sophisticated analysis of African genres and styles.

Wolf, E. J. *Sons of the Shaking Earth.* Chicago: University of Chicago Press, 1959. Evocative portrait of preconquest Mexico.

 Please refer to the document CD-ROM for primary sources related to this chapter.

Salomon, F. *Native Lords of Quito in the Age of the Incas.* New York: Cambridge University Press, 1986. Uses Spanish colonial records as well as archaeological and anthropological evidence to analyze this Amerindian society at the time of the Inca Conquest.

Sudarkasa, N. *Where Women Work: A Study of Yoruba Women in the Marketplace and in the Home.* Ann Arbor: University of Michigan Anthropological Papers, 1973. Good study of West African market women, with some account of the historical evolution of their role.

Vansina, J. *Art History in Africa.* New York: Longman, 1984. Sophisticated analysis of African art and style.

Wolf, E. J. *Sons of the Shaking Earth.* Chicago: University of Chicago Press, 1959. Evocative portrait of precolumbian Mexico.

Please refer to the document CD-ROM for primary sources related to this chapter.

# OVERVIEW V

# THE WORLD
# OF INTERCONTINENTAL EMPIRES
## (1500–1900)

The world had seen empires before, but never empires like these.

Empire-building goes back to the dawn age of human civilization. The city-states of ancient Mesopotamia spawned several empires large enough to encompass the entire Tigris-Euphrates valley, and Egypt for a time extended its power around the southeastern corner of the Mediterranean. During the classic age that followed, empires established in Roman Europe, the Persian Middle East, northern India, and Han China linked all Eurasia commercially. Later periods saw the emergence of other empires across Eurasia, as well as in parts of Africa, Middle America, and South America. Empire-building has thus been a basic pattern of territorial organization from the beginning.

During the centuries immediately preceding the great age of European conquests, there were two particularly astounding waves of interregional empire-building in the Old World.

The expansion of Islam, beginning in the seventh century, created a loose religious and cultural hegemony that stretched from Spain to Southeast Asia and reached well down into Africa as well. And the amazing conquests of the Mongols in the thirteenth century absorbed much of Eurasia, from Russia to China, into a single vast empire, the largest the world had ever seen.

The Mongols had fallen away by 1492. Islam, though still expanding, had long since fragmented into a number of feuding nations no more politically united than Christian Europe. But a third great surge of interregional empire-building began just before 1500—the rise of the West.

Western imperialism would be similar to earlier waves of imperial outreach in the past in some fundamental ways. Like earlier empire builders, Europeans frequently employed military force to impose their will upon other peoples. Like earlier empires, Europe's imperial predominance also commonly took on a political form, converting formerly independent peoples into colonies ruled by Europeans. As in the past, Western political and military power led to economic exploitation, ranging from favorable trade agreements to the massive extraction of natural resources, exploitation of cheap local labor, and large-scale investment—all of greater benefit to Westerners than to indigenous populations. As had frequently happened in the past, finally, military, political, and economic hegemony led to a growing intellectual and social influence by Western society on non-Western societies, a process frequently described as cultural imperialism.

All these features of Western imperial expansion would have been familiar enough to anyone aware of Persian, Roman, Indian, Chinese, Islamic, West African, Peruvian, Mexican, and many other forms of imperialism. But there were unique elements in this new wave as well.

One essential feature was the medium upon which Western imperialism depended from the beginning: sea power, and the resulting mastery of the world's oceans.

This led in turn to a second distinguishing characteristic: the intercontinental reach of the new European empires. By bridging the oceans, European empires brought continents and peoples thousands of miles apart under common Western rule.

The greatest consequence of Western imperialism, finally, may have been to trigger a genuinely global interaction for the first time in human history. The European intercontinental empires, by bringing all the peoples of the world into much closer contact than ever before, fostered an increasing amount of mutual interaction—cultural, economic, demographic, even ecological—sometimes including as much influence of the conquered on the conquerors as the other way around.

The next few chapters, then, will deal with the history of the world in the age of European intercontinental empires—roughly the four hundred years from the sixteenth through the nineteenth centuries. European imperialism is only one of the main strands of modern global history, yet it runs like the proverbial scarlet thread through the history of these centuries, affecting all the other strands.

# INTERCONTINENTAL EMPIRES

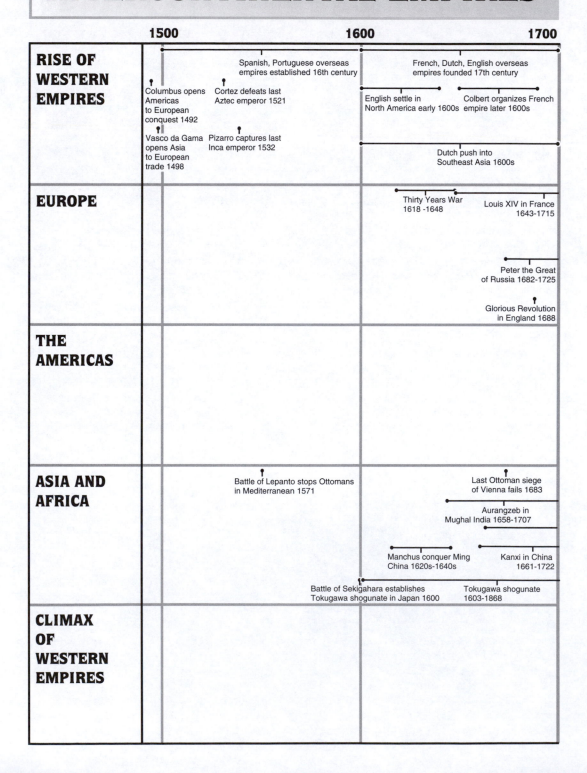

**1500**  **1600**  **1700**

**RISE OF WESTERN EMPIRES**

Spanish, Portuguese overseas empires established 16th century

French, Dutch, English overseas empires founded 17th century

Columbus opens Americas to European conquest 1492

Cortez defeats last Aztec emperor 1521

English settle in North America early 1600s

Colbert organizes French empire later 1600s

Vasco da Gama opens Asia to European trade 1498

Pizarro captures last Inca emperor 1532

Dutch push into Southeast Asia 1600s

**EUROPE**

Thirty Years War 1618 -1648

Louis XIV in France 1643-1715

Peter the Great of Russia 1682-1725

Glorious Revolution in England 1688

**THE AMERICAS**

**ASIA AND AFRICA**

Battle of Lepanto stops Ottomans in Mediterranean 1571

Last Ottoman siege of Vienna fails 1683

Aurangzeb in Mughal India 1658-1707

Manchus conquer Ming China 1620s-1640s

Kanxi in China 1661-1722

Battle of Sekigahara establishes Tokugawa shogunate in Japan 1600

Tokugawa shogunate 1603-1868

**CLIMAX OF WESTERN EMPIRES**

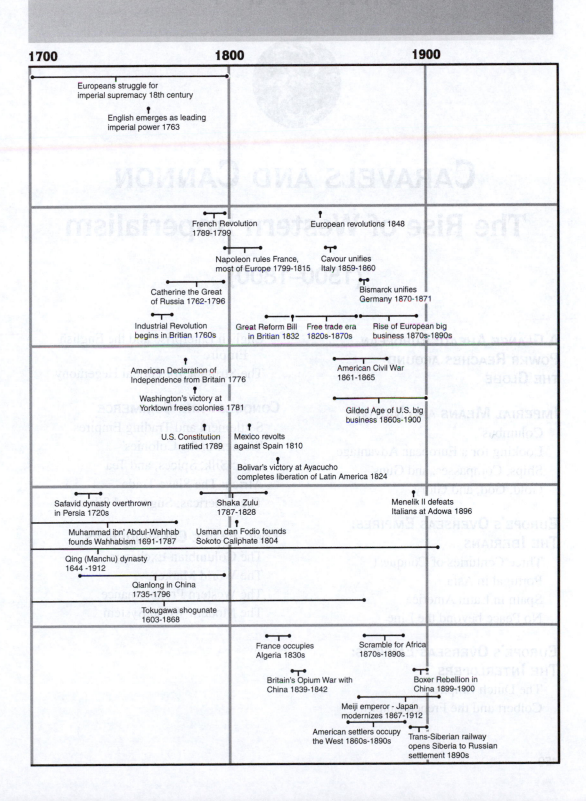

**1700**                                    **1800**                                **1900**

Europeans struggle for
imperial supremacy 18th century

English emerges as leading
imperial power 1763

French Revolution
1789-1799

European revolutions 1848

Napoleon rules France,
most of Europe 1799-1815

Cavour unifies
Italy 1859-1860

Catherine the Great
of Russia 1762-1796

Bismarck unifies
Germany 1870-1871

Industrial Revolution
begins in Britian 1760s

Great Reform Bill
in Britian 1832

Free trade era
1820s-1870s

Rise of European big
business 1870s-1890s

American Declaration of
Independence from Britain 1776

American Civil War
1861-1865

Washington's victory at
Yorktown frees colonies 1781

U.S. Constitution
ratified 1789

Mexico revolts
against Spain 1810

Gilded Age of U.S. big
business 1860s-1900

Bolivar's victory at Ayacucho
completes liberation of Latin America 1824

Safavid dynasty overthrown
in Persia 1720s

Shaka Zulu
1787-1828

Menelik II defeats
Italians at Adowa 1896

Muhammad ibn' Abdul-Wahhab
founds Wahhabism 1691-1787

Usman dan Fodio founds
Sokoto Caliphate 1804

Qing (Manchu) dynasty
1644 -1912

Qianlong in China
1735-1796

Tokugawa shogunate
1603-1868

France occupies
Algeria 1830s

Scramble for Africa
1870s-1890s

Britain's Opium War with
China 1839-1842

Boxer Rebellion in
China 1899-1900

Meiji emperor - Japan
modernizes 1867-1912

American settlers occupy
the West 1860s-1890s

Trans-Siberian railway
opens Siberia to Russian
settlement 1890s

# CHAPTER 19

# CARAVELS AND CANNON
## The Rise of Western Imperialism
## (1500–1800)

## A Glance Ahead: European Power Reaches around the Globe

The first wave of global imperial expansion in the world's history began with the voyages of Christopher Columbus to the Americas and Vasco da Gama around Africa to Asia in the 1490s. It lasted for three centuries, until the tide seemed to turn against the European imperialists in the American Revolution of 1776.

It seems long ago and far away, that era of sailing ships and astrolabes, booming broadsides, and usually not very accurate muskets. But the overseas empires of the Europeans—waves of global colonization and conquest, commercial exchange, missionary activity, migration, and cultural transformation—dwarfed any similar enterprise anywhere in history before that time.

Over these centuries, European nations—Spain, Portugal, the Netherlands, France, and Britain—overran the two American continents and established colonies in parts of Africa, India, and Southeast Asia. Goods, plants, animals, and even diseases traveled around the world as they never had before. The first global market in history emerged, and an economically based "world system" of global domination began to take shape.

## Imperial Means and Motives

### Columbus

On August 3, 1492, Christopher Columbus sailed from Palos, in Spain, on what he called the "Enterprise of the Indies." His goal was to reach the Far East—Cathay (China), Cipangu (Japan), and the Spice Islands of Southeast Asia—by sailing west across the Atlantic. On October 12, his little fleet made its historical landfall—not in Asia but at the island of San Salvador in the Caribbean Sea.

Columbus did not "discover" America: the native American peoples had done that thousands of years before. Nor, though he coasted parts of Central and South America, did he ever set foot in what would become the United States. Yet his achievement was immense. He opened the hitherto isolated Americas to penetration, conquest, and eventual transformation by the peoples of Europe, and subsequently by Africans and Asians as well.

It was not easy. During his four voyages to the New World, as Europeans soon took to calling it, Columbus confronted hunger and thirst, unfamiliar diseases, rotting ships, tropical hurricanes, increasingly hostile Amerindian populations, and the loss of whole settlements. He faced intrigue and mutiny among his own crews and imprisonment by the Spanish sovereigns who had financed his expedition. Obsessed by dreams of wealth and titles, convinced that he sailed under divine protection, a brilliant navigator, efficient seaman, wretched colonial administrator, and enslaver of the Indians, Columbus combined all the qualities of the generations of Western explorers and conquerors who would follow him.

Beyond the Americas, the European impact on the rest of the world would be quite limited for another century or two after 1500. But Columbus and his successors had accomplished something remarkable nevertheless. They had upset the delicate balance of separate centers of power, separate cultures and communities around the world. In the perspective of history, it is possible to see a drift toward "one world," interdependent and increasingly homogeneous, at least, beginning as early as 1492.

## Looking for a European Advantage

The global transformation that began around 1500—from "a world in balance" to one drastically reshaped by Western global predominance—was so remarkable that it has produced a wide range of explanations. Like the fall of Rome, the 'rise of the West' is so impressive a turning point that no single explanation seems adequate to the astonishing event itself.

What historians have been looking for is some sort of detectable "European advantage" that might account for what at least began to happen when Columbus sailed the ocean blue in fourteen hundred and ninety-two. Not surprisingly, Columbus and his voyage have seemed a good place to start. Generations of historians have hailed the Admiral of the Ocean Sea for his commitment to his dream, his determination, his skill as a navigator—a veritable one-man cause of all that came after. More recently, however, students of the period have noted that Vikings had crossed the Atlantic earlier with no earthshaking consequences—that even the much larger Chinese overseas expeditions did not transform India and Africa into Chinese colonies.

From Columbus himself, then, researchers have turned to European society as a whole in search of an explanation for the rise of the West to global dominance. The "specialness" of the western end of Eurasia has been traced to such allegedly unique character traits of Western peoples as curiosity about the larger world, technological ingenuity, relentless determination, and a powerful will to conquer other peoples. Critics have responded that other peoples had all these traits but never became even temporary masters of most of the globe.

Political, military, or economic advantages have also been adduced—and have again been answered with examples of similar institutions in other lands. Economic causes—a vigorous commercial class, for instance—have been particularly popular explanations for European imperial expansion. But again, immensely successful merchant communities can be found in China, India, and on across the Muslim world, to mention only a few.

We must proceed with care, in short, when we try to explain the global spread of western power. One general rule might be that no single explanation is likely to suffice for such an enormous change. It will take a number of factors, a variety of means and motives to make sense out of this turning point in world history. Another general principle might be to remind ourselves that there had been other relatively recent attempts at expansion across regional boundaries. Muslim expansion across North Africa, southern Europe, and the western half of Asia; the Eurasian reach of the Mongol Empire; and the Ming Chinese voyages of the "precious ships" earlier in the fifteenth century suggest that the world as a whole was pushing to break free of regional boundaries when Columbus set sail in 1492.

Still, it was European peoples who broke through, forging the first genuinely global empires, constructing a truly world market, bringing the world's peoples into closer contact than ever before in their history. The next few pages will attempt to outline some of the factors that made this final breakthrough possible.

## Ships, Compasses, and Guns

There was an explosion of white foam under a ship's bow, a scream of gulls overhead, and the gliding shadow of a great fish beneath a sliding wave. Above all, there was the buffeting of the wind about Chinese, Arab, European cheeks, about bare brown Polynesian shoulders or the frozen beards of Vikings. The sea and sea creatures, the push of the wind, and the voyagers who roamed the oceans of the world are all essential elements to the now half-

THE WORLD OF SEPARATE CIVILIZATIONS, CA. 1500

ARCTIC OCEAN

PACIFIC OCEAN

INDIAN OCEAN

ATLANTIC OCEAN

MING CHINESE EMPIRE

MUGHAL INDIAN EMPIRE

SAFAVID PERSIAN EMPIRE

MUSCOVY

FINLAND

SWEDEN

NORWAY

LITHUANIA

POLAND

HOLY ROMAN EMPIRE

OTTOMAN EMPIRE

DENMARK

ENGLAND

NETHERLANDS

FRANCE

PORTUGAL

SPAIN

ITALIAN STATES

SONGHAI EMPIRE

MALI EMPIRE

INCA EMPIRE

AZTEC EMPIRE

| 0 | 1,500 | 3,000 Miles |
| 0 | 1,500 | 3,000 Kilometers |

Columbus's ships and the lands he believed he had reached, as illustrated in the printed version of his report to the Spanish sovereigns who had financed his voyage. (Rare Books Division, New York Public Library, Astor, Lenox and Tilden Foundations)

forgotten romance of the sea. But the key to this daring chapter in the long human venture is the ship itself, and to ships we must turn as we begin the story of the farthest voyagers of all.

Europeans were not the first to venture out upon the oceans of the world. But between the fifteenth and the nineteenth centuries, western humankind mastered the seas as no other peoples had. And by mastering the sea, they opened a watery road to the conquest of all the mainlands and islands of the earth.

The European sailing ships of Columbus's time were not the largest vessels in the world. Any of the huge seagoing junks that China's Yongle Emperor sent east across the Indian Ocean could have carried all the crews of the four ships of Vasco da Gama that crossed the Indian Ocean the other way sixty-five years later. But the Portuguese caravels of the years around 1500—and the Spanish galleons of the later sixteenth century—had advantages that no other vessels could match. And in the seventeenth century, Europeans began to build huge trading vessels themselves. These "East Indiamen," intended for the round trip to the Far East, could carry 1,600 tons of cargo and as many as a thousand passengers and crew.

It was not size, however, that primarily distinguished Western ships of the age of sail. A major innovation was a new combination of the sails themselves. This mix of medieval European square sails and Arab lateen (triangular) ones made it possible for Europeans to develop unprecedented skill at tacking—sailing across or even into the wind. European ships thus became the most maneuverable of sailing vessels, ideally suited for exploring—or for fighting.

European vessels also employed an impressive array of navigational aids for their time. Some of these devices were borrowed, like the magnetic compass, developed first by the Chinese. Some were ancient instruments, like the astrolabe, used for measuring the altitude of the sun above the horizon, and hence the ship's latitude north or south of the equator. There were sand glasses for measuring time, sounding leads for assessing the depth of the water, and the original "log"—a piece of wood flung over the stern at the end of a knotted cord—for estimating speed at sea, and hence longitude east or west.

Improvements in map making also gave Europeans an advantage. Many of the detailed coastal charts drawn by explorers and traders were extremely accurate. The technique of the Mercator projection made it possible to represent the curved surface of the earth on a flat map—a valuable aid for a people embarking on what became a global venture. By the end of the sixteenth century, only a hundred years into the great conquest, Europeans had charted the coasts of all the continents except Australia, which was added more slowly over the next two centuries.

To excellent ships and unexcelled navigational equipment, finally, Western overseas venturers added a range of weaponry and an array of tactics that gave them a powerful advantage wherever they went. The cannon and firearms of European infantry—harquebuses, muskets, and larger powder-and-shot weapons—gave Western soldiers the edge over even the best non-Western troops not so equipped. Above all, the broad spectrum of artillery mounted on European ships made them likely victors in any naval conflict. Fighting to sink ships rather than to board and capture vessels they could not man or use, seamen from the west used their new artillery extremely effectively. With rows of cannon lining gun decks and firing in unison to produce devastating broadsides, the ships of European countries soon became the acknowledged rulers of the waves.

## Gold, God, and Glory

The motives for imperial expansion had also developed among these restless, aggressive peoples of Eurasia's western fringe. Columbus's own dreams embodied most of them.

Wealth was certainly the primary motive for many, as it was one of Columbus's great bargaining points with the king and queen of Spain. Gold and silver, silks and spices, and later the valuable products that could be grown (like sugar) or caught (like furs or fish) in foreign parts all drew the makers of the Old Imperialism to far places.

And they made money too. Columbus may have died a disillusioned man, but the silver and gold that Spain extracted from the Americas over the next century made that nation Europe's richest and most powerful. Vasco da Gama brought home spices enough from India to pay for his long voyage many times over. Many a Dutch or English fortune was founded on a timely investment in the East India Company of Holland or Britain.

Gold was clearly a prime cause of the Old Imperialism. But God also inspired many of these world conquerors. Christopher Columbus himself, after all, claimed that he—like Saint Christopher—was carrying the Light of the World across the water.

The Iberian nations were old Crusaders; Ferdinand and Isabella had in fact just expelled the last of the Moors from Spain when the great overseas conquest began. The sixteenth century was also the century of the Protestant Reformation and the Catholic Counter-Reformation. It was a religiously charged time that saw Jesuits set out to save souls in China and South America as well as in Protestant lands. Seventeenth-century English Puritans and Dutch Protestants were heavy investors in overseas expansion, and their objectives also included the spread of Christianity as well as the extraction of profits from the heathen.

Gold, God, and, dubious as it may seem, glory stand as the three main causes of European empire-building in the early centuries. The glory sought was the sort of public adulation and eternal fame that champions of European chivalry had fought and died for on European battlefields for centuries. The conquistadores of all Western nations were

# VOICES FROM THE PAST

This famous letter from Christopher Colombus to Queen Isabella and King Ferdinand was published soon after his return. Note his belief that he had reached "the Indies," well-known to be the source of rich trade. Note also his description of the Caribbean islands, largely in terms of *potential* value, since there were in fact no prosperous farms or rich cities to be found. Why do you think he describes the people as docile, friendly, and eager to share?

*Sir, since I know that you will take pleasure at the great victory with which Our Lord has crowned my voyage, I write this to you, from which you will learn how in twenty days I reached the Indies with the fleet which the most illustrious King and Queen, our lords, gave to me. And there I found very many islands filled with people without number, and of them all I have taken possession for their Highness, by proclamation and with the royal standard displayed, and nobody objected. . . . Upcountry there are many mines of metals, and the population is innumerable.* La Spañola *is marvelous, the sierras and the mountains and the plains and the champaigns and the lands are so beautiful and fat for planting and sowing, and for livestock of every sort, and for building towns and cities. The harbors of the sea here are such as you could not believe in without seeing them, and so the rivers, many and great, and good streams, the most of which bear gold. . . .*
*The people of this island and of all other islands which I have found and seen, or have not seen, all go naked, men and women, as their mothers bore them, except that some women cover one place only with the leaf of a plant or with a net of cotton which they make from that. They have no iron or steel or weapons, nor are they capable of using them, although they are well-built people of handsome stature, because they are wonderfully timorous. . . . Of anything they have, if you ask them for it, they never say no; rather they invite the person to share it, and show as much love as if they were giving their hearts; and whether the thing be of value or of small price, at once they are content with whatever little thing of whatever kind may be given to them.*

Christopher Columbus, *The Letter of Columbus on His Discovery of the New World.* Edited by Doyce B. Nunis and Charles R. Ritcheson (Los Angeles: University of Southern California Fine Arts Press, 1989), pp. 31–33.

soldiers of a society where soldiering was the most respected of professions, honor the greatest virtue. They wanted crowds to cheer them, crowned heads to honor them with knighthoods and titles, poets and historians to immortalize them. For such insubstantial honors, men such as Hernando Cortés and Sir Walter Raleigh would risk their lives—and sometimes get their hearts' desires.

Money and what it would buy, converts for the Christian God, and a meed of glory to warm a soldier's heart—these were the taut springs that drove the men who manned the remarkable ships of the Western world.

All of these motives, in one form or another, could be found among others of the world's peoples. But in Europe there was a competitive diversity of peoples that perhaps stimulated these passions beyond the normal. There was a freedom for merchant investors, filibustering soldiers, missionary orders, and ambitious princes that was not so common in the centralized empires of the East. Even the most autocratic European rulers, such as the kings of Spain or France's Louis XIV, allowed much of the exploring, trading, and conquering overseas to be done by ambitious private citizens, thereby multiplying the impact by the number of competitors.

China's vast armadas of Precious Ships were an imperial venture and could be stopped forever by a memorial from the Son of Heaven. It is hard to imagine any force powerful enough to restrain the motley hordes of Western conquerors, lusting after golden idols and cargoes of spices, converts beyond the burning line—the equator—and immortal glory when they sailed home again.

## EUROPE'S OVERSEAS EMPIRES: THE IBERIANS

### Three Centuries of Conquest

It was the crash of their great guns that a startled world most vividly remembered. The Chinese had developed gunpowder weapons long before the Europeans did. In 1453, the Ottoman Turks mounted the largest cannon in the world against the walls of Constantinople. But Western gunnery had distanced that of all other peoples by 1500, and Western ships were thereafter converted into floating gun platforms lined with huge "ship-killing" artillery. "They have guns with a noise like thunder," a Ceylonese source wrote of the first Portuguese to come that way, "and a ball from one of them, after traversing a league, will break a castle of marble."[1]

Explorers, missionaries, merchants, soldiers all played important parts in the establishment of the European predominance. But the final arbiter was most often military force.

The three hundred years of the period of the Old Imperialism from the end of the fifteenth century through most of the eighteenth, will be outlined in the sections that follow. The climactic phase of Western imperialism—the so-called New Imperialism of the nineteenth century—will be dealt with in a later chapter.

Century by century, the pattern was something like this. The sixteenth century was the age of Iberian overseas expansion. During this period, the Portuguese set up a primarily commercial empire in the East that encompassed trading posts in Africa, India, and Southeast Asia, an outpost in South China, and a huge territory in Brazil. Spanish power established an even vaster settlement empire in the West, centering in Middle and South America and the Caribbean and extending into North America and across the Pacific to the Philippines.

The seventeenth century was the century of the interlopers, the age in which the North Atlantic powers challenged the monopoly of intercontinental empire enjoyed by the Iberian nations. This was the golden age of the Netherlands, when Dutch traders drove into the Far East, South Africa, and North America. France in the age of Louis XIV established an elaborate edifice of colonies, commercial relations, and mercantilist policies, especially in Canada, the Caribbean, and India. The British staked their claims to colonies in what would become the eastern United States, and in the Caribbean and India also.

There were thus five European powers with holdings on four other continents and many islands by the end of the seventeenth century. In the eighteenth there came a settling out, and a global duel for imperial supremacy. The Dutch gave ground, as the Spanish and Portuguese had before them. And the British shouldered the French aside to emerge as the greatest of European empire builders.

---

[1]C. M. Cipolla, *Guns, Sails and Empires: Technological Innovation and the Early Phases of European Expansion, 1400–1700* (New York: Pantheon Books, 1966), p. 107.

Let us now look in a little more detail at the intercontinental empires established by each of the European imperial powers in these centuries and at the struggle for empire that climaxed the period of the Old Imperialism.

## Portugal in Asia

When Vasco da Gama reached Calicut on the Malabar Coast of India in 1498, the Arab merchants who were already established there sneered at the goods he laid out for sale. "They spat on the ground," one who sailed with him reported, "saying, 'Portugal, Portugal!'"[2] It was war from the beginning between the Portuguese invaders and the Arabs who had dominated the trade of the Indian Ocean for centuries. The architect of Portuguese victory, and of the Portuguese commercial empire that resulted, was one of the greatest of the European empire builders, Affonso de Albuquerque (1453–1515).

Albuquerque, governor-general of the Portuguese Indies in the early sixteenth century, seems to have been a man with an intuitive understanding of the proper deployment and use of sea power to seize and defend key points in Portugal's monopoly of Eastern trade. Instead of basing his operation in far-off Lisbon, Albuquerque captured the wealthy and readily defended island city of Goa off India's west coast to serve as his headquarters. He established a series of lesser bases down the western side of India and others on islands at the entrances to the Red Sea and the Persian Gulf. With Portugal's bases in East Africa, what had once been the Arabian Sea thus became a Portuguese lake.

At the same time, Albuquerque pushed on into Southeast and even East Asia. He seized the rich Southeast Asian commercial center of Malacca on the strait between Malaya and Sumatra through which all Asian trade had to pass. And he dispatched other Portuguese vessels north and still further east to set up a trading port at Macao in South China, just downriver from the great Chinese entrepôt of Canton (Guangzhou).

Portugal thus bestrode crucial waterways and coastlines from East Africa to South China. The profits in silks and spices that had once gone to Arab middlemen now lined the purses of Portuguese merchants. And the little medieval kingdom of Portugal stood taller than ever before in the affairs of Europe.

The Portuguese crown defended this monopoly with savage rigor. European vessels that dared intrude were sunk, their crews thrown into the sea. Muslim spice ships—and sometimes Muslim pilgrim ships bound for Mecca—shared a similar fate. Arab dhows were gutted to the waterline, Arab traders swallowed up by the sea that had once been theirs.

For a time, at least, it worked. In the later sixteenth century, however, the Portuguese monopoly crumbled. Portugal's failure to establish close ties with local *rajas* and an increasingly rigorous policy of religious repression in Goa and elsewhere weakened its position. The smallness of Portugal itself and the comparatively few people Lisbon could put into the Far East further limited Portuguese strength. When the North Atlantic powers—the Dutch, French, and English—burst onto the eastern seas in force around 1600, Portuguese power dwindled rapidly.

## Spain in Latin America

The conquistadores of Spain followed a different path to a very different empire. These military adventurers first occupied the Caribbean islands, including the large central is-

---

[2]E. G. Ravenstein, ed., *A Journal of the First Voyage of Vasco da Gama* (London: Hakluyt Society, 1898), p. 68.

The Spanish conquest in the New World was a bloody business, as this picture shows. The Aztecs, a warlike people themselves, met their match in the conquistadores from Spain. Western beards, shown here, amazed the Amerindian peoples almost as much as the horses and firearms of the invaders. (The Bettmann Archive)

land of Cuba. They then probed westward to the mainland of Mexico, south to Peru and beyond, and north to the American southwest, the Gulf Coast, and Florida. Both the conquest and the organization of Spanish America were models of the vigor—and the cruelty—of the great conquest.

The conquest of Aztec Mexico in the 1520s by Cortés and a few hundred ambitious, out-at-elbows swordsmen is one of the bloodiest epics of the *conquista*. Cortés burned his ships behind him, followed the rumors of a great city on a lake in a high valley beyond the coastal jungles—and found his El Dorado. The Spanish first occupied Tenochtitlán as Emperor Moctezuma's guests. When they converted him into a puppet ruler, the Aztecs revolted and drove them from the city, killing a third of their number in one terrible night. Reinforced at the coast, and supported by a number of other Amerindian peoples who had suffered under the Aztecs, Cortés returned to Tenochtitlán in 1521, captured it, and destroyed it. Aztec power was broken; Spanish rule soon replaced it.

Francisco Pizarro's seizure of the still larger Inca Empire in Peru was an even more unlikely—and equally brutal—feat of arms. Pizarro followed his rumors to Peru with less than two hundred men. But the Inca Empire was just emerging from a bloody civil war, and the Spanish capture of the Inca Atahualpa himself in 1532 further demoralized the ruling elite. The story of that ambush in the village square at Cajamarca, and of the subsequent ransoming and murder of Atahualpa, is another of the gory romantic legends of the New World conquest.

The Europeans had profited from the fact that the realms of the Aztecs and the Incas were both conquest empires that had earned the resentment of their subject peoples. The Europeans, however, wreaked far greater havoc among the Amerindians than any native conquest ever had. Spain had conquered the most heavily populated areas in the Americas. But Western weapons, forced labor in fields and mines, and above all, unfamiliar western diseases to which the Indians had no immunities, reduced the population drastically. It was, in fact, to replace declining Indian labor forces—and to prevent further reduction of their numbers—that African slaves began to be imported soon after the conquest.

The fall of the Inca Empire was essentially accomplished by one bold and ruthless stroke: the seizure of the Inca Atahualpa himself by Francisco Pizarro and his Spanish freebooters at Cajamarca in 1532. The essence of the larger confrontation between these two peoples is conveyed even in this simple drawing. Note the weapons and means of transport employed by the two sides, the seizure of the Inca by a soldier and a priest, and the broadly sketched city on the horizon, evidence that the Western conquerors were aware that they were destroying, not "primitive savages," but a civilized society with roots as ancient as their own. (Anthony Esler)

## No Peace beyond the Line

In 1494, two years after Columbus's first voyage, Spain and Portugal signed the Treaty of Tordesillas, dividing the non-European world up into two zones. The long-term effect of this agreement was to grant the Spanish the right to establish themselves in the Americas, where Columbus had established a Spanish claim, and Portugal the right to exploit Africa and India, which Vasco da Gama would reach in the Portuguese service four years later. The division was not as clear as it seemed. Portugal, for instance, soon got a foothold in Brazil, a colony that would expand to include half of South America, while Spain established a valuable Asian colony in the Philippine Islands. But the line of Tordesillas did appear to give the two Iberian powers exclusive rights to probe and profit from the rest of the globe.

As Spanish and Portuguese vessels began to return from the far places of the earth laden with valuable goods from Asia and precious metals from the New World, however, other European nations sought to shoulder their way into the lucrative business that could be done beyond the line. Seamen from other Atlantic seacoast powers—England, France, and the Netherlands—were soon praying on Iberian galleys or raiding Spanish settlements in the Americas. The Iberian kings called them pirates. Other European sovereigns sometimes honored them as national heroes.

The fighting would go on for three centuries. Whether there was peace or war in Europe, it would be widely said that there was "no peace beyond the line." And meanwhile, these aggressive interlopers, or intruders into the Iberian empires, began to build overseas empires of their own.

# EUROPE'S OVERSEAS EMPIRES: THE INTERLOPERS

## The Dutch Empire

The sixteenth century belonged to the empire builders of Spain and Portugal. The most successful European overseas empire of the seventeenth century, however, was that of the Netherlands. In some ways, indeed, the Dutch seaborne commercial empire was the most efficient of all those established during the period of the Old Imperialism.

The architects and operators of the Dutch Empire were not soldiers like Cortés and Pizarro, or even royal administrators like Albuquerque. They were the solid, stolid Dutch burghers who stare unsmilingly out of their Rembrandt portraits at us. A dull and unromantic lot, one might think—certainly not given to burning their ships behind them or following rumors of El Dorado. But in the seventeenth century, the Dutch East and West India companies dominated trade with the Far East and siphoned off much of the commercial profit from other European colonies in the New World as well.

The Dutch brought to their far-flung trading empire centuries of business experience, manufacturing skills, and accumulated capital. Their ships and their seamanship were acknowledged to be the best. Their trade goods were carefully selected to suit their customers—sultans and *rajas* in Asia, European colonists in the Americas. At need, they could be as ruthless and unscrupulous as any in the great imperialist venture. For a hundred years, they profited exceedingly in the global marketplace that they themselves did so much to create.

The Dutch East India Company shouldered its way into the Spice Islands of Southeast Asia around 1600, expelling first the Portuguese and then the fledgling British East India Company. They paid much more attention than the Portuguese had to the local sultans, giving them the goods they wanted, signing treaties with them, avoiding both rank piracy and religious persecution. From the company's capital at Batavia in Java, they soon controlled not only the European spice trade but much of the profitable regional commerce of Southeast Asia as well.

The Dutch West India Company, meanwhile, set up its trading posts in the Caribbean and in North America, especially along the Hudson River in what would be New York state. Settlers from French, English, and Spanish colonies often preferred trading illegally with the Dutch at New Amsterdam—later New York City—or Curaçao in the Caribbean to dealing with their own more expensive and less efficient compatriots.

For a golden century, hardheaded Dutch merchants handled most of Europe's imperial carrying trade, coasted Australia, settled in South Africa, and took their profits home to build tall houses in Amsterdam and commission Rembrandt or Vermeer to paint their pictures. Then sheer lack of numbers caught up with them, as it had with the Portuguese. Exhausting foreign wars further weakened them. The British expelled them from North America in the later seventeenth century. Dutch predominance survived in the East Indies, but the center of European imperial activity in Asia shifted to the richer pickings of India, where England and France were the prime contenders.

## Colbert and the French Empire

The French were the great organizers of empire. The foremost European exemplars of royal absolutism in politics and mercantilism—government regulation—in economics, seventeenth-century France also took the lead in royal supervision of colonies overseas. It was, as will be evident, a mixed blessing.

In the earlier seventeenth century, French overseas adventures were largely undertaken by daring individuals or by groups outside royal control. Like Spanish conquistadores or Dutch merchants, French fur traders and Jesuit missionaries in Canada, French plantation owners in the West Indies, and French East India Company traders in India had to depend on their own resources and work closely with indigenous peoples. Jesuits, trappers, and traders in the Great Lakes region of North America were better than any other Europeans at living and working with the Native American tribes, learning their languages, marrying and settling among them. In India the French, like the Dutch and English, depended on treaties with and the protection of Indian princes.

In the second half of the seventeenth century, however, the all-encompassing power of Louis XIV and the tidy organizing mind of his first minister, Jean-Baptiste Colbert, reorganized France's overseas holdings. Mercantilistic policies, which most early-modern European governments followed, involved official encouragement and regulation of all branches of the economy—agriculture, handicraft industry, domestic and foreign trade. Under Colbert's direction, colonies overseas became a crucial element in developed French mercantilism.

Colonies provided tropical and other products unavailable in France. They offered a market for French manufactured goods. And they were expected to give plenty of carrying trade to the French merchant marine. Colbert undertook to increase the population of New World settlements and to establish military strongholds there to strengthen French colonies against their English rivals. The French East India Company was heavily financed by the French crown.

By the early 1700s, then, there were French trading and settlement colonies in eastern Canada, their capital at Quebec; in Louisiana at the mouth of the Mississippi; and in West Indian islands such as Martinique and Guadeloupe. There was also a growing French commercial presence in India, headquartered at Pondichéry on the southern coast of the subcontinent. France, the most powerful nation in Europe under Louis XIV, was determined to take a leading role in the building of intercontinental empire as well.

## English Enterprise and the English Empire

The beginnings of English empire-building were not promising. Britain's first colonists in Virginia suffered from the climate and their own helplessness in the wilderness, then from Indian massacres, and for years from financial losses before they discovered in tobacco a crop that would pay. The Dutch ousted early English traders from Southeast Asia, so that they had to fall back on the then less profitable Indian trade.

But English merchants were thirsty for profits. English political history in the revolutionary seventeenth century produced religious exiles in need of new lands to settle in. And the English kings after mid-century proved more willing to encourage colonial development. By the early 1700s, then, Britain's overseas holding were as widely dispersed as those of the Netherlands or France.

Great Britain's major settlement colonies were across the Atlantic in North America and the Caribbean. These included colonies inhabited by Puritan nonconformists in New England, planter settlements in Virginia and surrounding territories, and the plantations of the Lesser Antilles, Jamaica, and the Bahamas. Typically, these colonies were founded by commercial companies having little royal support. In time, however, royal governors were appointed and mercantilistic regulations imposed on England's growing American empire.

The British East India Company was also a private venture. It never had the government support accorded its French and even its Dutch rivals. In the early eighteenth century, however, British traders were well established on the coast of India, having developed bases at Bombay in the northwest, Calcutta in the northeast, and Madras on the southeastern shores of peninsular India.

The English had good relations with the Mughal emperors and were protected by them. As the Mughal Empire declined, however, the British East India Company found it increasingly necessary to fight its own battles. In the middle 1700s, the company would do just that—with spectacular results.

## The Struggle for Global Hegemony

By 1700, then, the Dutch, with too small and embattled a base at home, were losing momentum everywhere to their larger rivals. Spain and Portugal were rapidly declining into backwaters, their overseas empires no longer expanding and much less profitable. In the 1740s, 1750s, and 1760s, therefore, Britain and France fought each other across two oceans and three continents for imperial supremacy.

In India, the French had the advantage in the early years; they even temporarily overran the English settlement at Madras. Thereafter, however, the conflict resolved itself into a feud between the two extraordinary governors of the French and British East India companies, Joseph Dupleix and Robert Clive. Dupleix, by extending judicious French military support to local princes in southern India, had the English base at Madras once more surrounded and in imminent danger of extinction. But Clive, who had worked his way up from genteel destitution through the British India Company, was both a skilled military commander and a superior politician. Instead of Madras, it was the French capital at Pondichéry that fell, and with it all serious hope for a French empire in India.

In North America also, the French began strongly, thanks again to close ties with the indigenous population. With the help of Indian allies, they pushed down the Mississippi Valley, seeking to link up their Canadian colonies with their settlement in Louisiana. They might thus box the British in against the Atlantic shore and at the same time lay out a mid-American empire for themselves. An expedition sent to dislodge them—in which a Virginia colonist named George Washington futilely warned the British commander to beware of French-and-Indian hit-and-run tactics—was cut to pieces in the forest.

But the English prime minister, William Pitt, rose to the challenge to become one of Britain's most famous war leaders. His grand strategy, his choices of leaders and targets all seemed to work like a charm. Clive swept to victory in India. French settlements in West Africa and the West Indies fell to British forces. And in Canada, British armies captured Quebec high on its impregnable bluffs overlooking the St. Lawrence, and then Montreal. All French Canada fell into British hands.

With Britain's victories in India and Canada, English supremacy was unquestionable. Britain had taken a great step forward on the phenomenal march to world empire that would distinguish its history in the following century.

In 1763, when a peace signed at Paris settled the fate of Native Americans and East Indians who had never heard of the City of Light, Western power was entrenched around the world. Europeans held as much of North and South America as they had yet had time to occupy, and the rest was pretty clearly theirs for the taking. They had bases and seaports around the coasts of Africa south of the Sahara, though they had as yet scarcely penetrated inland. They had a number of ports on both coasts of India and had compelled or bought profitable alliances with *rajas* all across the subcontinent. They owned the Caribbean and were masters of the island portion of Southeast Asia.

They had been rudely repulsed from Japan, had made little progress in China, and were only beginning to explore Australia and Oceania. Huge expanses of the interiors of Asia, Africa, and the Americas—protected by difficult geography, disease to which Europeans had no immunity, and other factors—remained to be penetrated. But they would be penetrated in time. A beginning had thus been made in the greatest conquest the world had ever seen.

## CONQUEST AND COMMERCE

### Settlement and Trading Empires

As noted previously, Western empire builders forged two types of overseas dominion during these centuries. In Africa and Asia, Iberians and later interlopers tended to establish commercial entrepots and to concentrate on trade. In the Americas, the invaders took over the land and settled in to live, determined to translate the European way of life to the New World.

*Trading empires* depended on treaties with local kings and paramount chiefs, with *rajas* or the Mughal emperors themselves. Europeans would be needed to build and run trading posts or slave pens, warehouses and harbor facilities, and to garrison the whole operation. But through these early centuries, at least, African and Asian societies would remain largely intact, European imperialists still outsiders in this part of the world.

The *settlement empires* of the Americas brought a much broader and deeper intrusion—indeed, a transforming European presence. In the New World, the Europeans either conquered the Native American peoples or occupied their lands. The settlers cut down forests for European farms and built European-style cities. Frequently they turned the indigenous populations into laborers on the plantations or in the mines run by the conquerors. Their very presence totally reshaped the Native American world.

### Women in the Colonies

Women as well as men settled in the European trading posts or colonies overseas. Among the Iberian settlers in the New World, women often came as relatives of men already established there. Many lived as women did in Spain or Portugal, sheltered by garden walls and heavily shuttered houses. English and other northern European women also came to the Americas in growing numbers, though they were not so carefully sequestered as Iberian settlers were.

Some of these women were imported to encourage male settlers to remain in the colonies. Others were indentured servants for settlers, some of whom would find husbands and found families in the colonies. Still other women, however, were probably expected to aid or replace their husbands in a variety of jobs, working as butchers, blacksmiths, and at other demanding trades.

### Asia: Silk, Spices, and Tea

There were missionaries eager for converts and young men mad for glory among these Western imperialists. But there were probably more who went out to the far places of the earth, as a chronicler who marched with Cortés put it, "to grow rich as all men desire to do."[3] And like empire builders from one end of history to the other, Europeans brought

---

[3]Bernal Díaz, quoted in Robert Knecht, "The Discoveries," in Douglas Johnson, ed., *The Making of the Modern World,* Vol. I (New York: Barnes and Noble, 1971), p. 14.

# World of Expanding Western Empires, 1763

**Legend:**

- Europe in 1492
- European Empires in 1763:
  - British
  - Dutch
  - Russian
  - Portuguese
  - Spanish
  - French
- → European trade routes after 1500

Map labels: PACIFIC OCEAN, ASIA, EUROPE, AFRICA, AUSTRALIA, NORTH AMERICA, SOUTH AMERICA, ARCTIC OCEAN, ATLANTIC OCEAN, INDIAN OCEAN, PHILIPPINE ISLANDS, DUTCH EAST INDIES, BENGAL, CEYLON, CAPE COLONY, MOZAMBIQUE, ANGOLA, GUINEA, PORTUGUESE

Trade goods: FURS, FISH, TOBACCO, COTTON, MANUFACTURES, SLAVES, BULLION, SILK, SPICES, TEA, COFFEE, TEXTILES, MANUFACTURES

Scale: 1000, 2000, 3000 Kilometers; 1000, 2000 Miles

home many things from conquered lands. Asia, Africa, North and South America all paid their tithes to Europe during the early modern centuries.

Asia was the first objective. The original goal of the Western voyagers had been to find a sea route to the spices and luxury goods of the Far East that would be cheaper and surer than the overland routes controlled by other peoples. First the Portuguese, then the Dutch, French, and English broke into the trade of the Indian Ocean and Southeast Asia, and soon they were its masters.

In the holds of caravels and lumbering East Indiamen (large merchant ships), Europeans brought home silk, tea, porcelain, and spices such as pepper, cloves, and cinnamon from China; cottons and precious stones from India; coffee from Arabia and the Middle East; drugs, saltpeter for gunpowder, indigo dye—the list is almost endless. Europe's consumption of pepper doubled in the first half of the sixteenth century. In the seventeenth, coffee and tea became national drinks in Europe. Indian cotton would spawn a whole new industry in Britain and trigger the Industrial Revolution. The long-range consequences of Asian imports were even more incalculable than their immediate impact.

## Africa: The Slave Trade

On the way to Asia, European vessels had to sail around the second-largest continent— Africa. They found profitable commodities here too: pepper and cloves, gold and ivory— and, above all, slaves. Laboring men and women became Africa's primary contribution to the burgeoning wealth of the West. Europeans did not invent the African slave trade. Slavers from the Muslim lands of North and East Africa had raided and traded for slaves in that continent for centuries. It had always been a profitable business for the intruders and a deeply destructive experience for African society. But the European onslaught was to have a much larger impact on the history of the world as a whole.

Perhaps twelve million Africans were bought from slave-raiding African peoples— who of course redoubled their activities once they realized they could get a good price from the Europeans. The victims were transported not to Europe but to the Americas, where they made a very substantial contribution to the labor force of the New World. They thus became part of the famous triangular trade route linking Europe, Africa, and the Americas: manufactured goods to Africa, slaves to the Americas, and agricultural products such as sugar, molasses, and rum back to Europe.

The enslaved Africans who did reach the New World had survived a brutal ordeal. Seized in their inland villages by slave-raiding warriors, they had been roped in long lines and led sometimes hundreds of miles to the coast. After weeks or months in dank dungeons or open pens, they had been crammed into the holds of European slave ships for the westward journey. The horrors of the "middle passage"—Africa to the Americas—were worse still. Broken by disease, filth, brutal treatment, and the shock of the experience, between a tenth and a quarter of the two hundred Africans crowded into a typical slave ship might die.

Those who survived, however, actually made important contributions to the colonial societies of which they became involuntary members. Their skilled hands and sweating backs harvested the crops, built the plantation houses, raised the children, and served the food of Latin American and North American planters. In Latin America particularly, they learned and practiced many urban trades. They also brought African skills to the New World. It was from enslaved West Africans, as one British planter reported, that the colonists "found out the true way of raising and husking rice"—a major money crop in Britain's southern colonies.[4] For the future, they created an African diaspora that would transform the demographics of the globe.

## The Americas: Sugar and Silver

The North American colonies paid tribute to their European rulers in such commercial goods as ships' stores and timber, furs, codfish, tobacco, and sugar. French fur trappers in the sun-dappled quiet of Canadian forests, English fishing vessels laboring in heavy seas off New England or the Newfoundland banks, sweating slaves bending under the watchful eyes of European overseers in the tobacco fields of Virginia or the sugar plantations of the West Indies were also profitable parts of these sprawling European intercontinental empires.

Timber, furs, sugar, fish—it was a stodgy and unromantic contribution compared with the spices and precious stones from the East or the black gold from Africa. Yet by 1776 the North American and Caribbean settlements were probably the most profitable of all the European colonies around the world.

The simplest and most avidly sought form of profit from conquered lands overseas, however, was the silver and gold of Middle and South America. First as booty ripped from the walls of Inca temples, later as ore from mines in Mexico, Bolivia, and elsewhere, hundreds of tons of gold and thousands of tons of silver were shipped across the Atlantic.

All of it was originally destined for the coffers of Spain, but much of it ended up in other hands. Some of it was seized by English or French pirates and privateers. More flooded out over Europe as payment for Spain's huge debts or in salaries and supplies for the armies of Europe's greatest power in the sixteenth century. Much of it, finally, was siphoned off to more industrious peoples like the Dutch, who produced all the good things that Spanish *caballeros*—officers and gentlemen all—were too proud to soil their hands in manufacturing for themselves.

The flood of silver and gold replenished a continent poor in precious metals. It also led to a century of inflation, doubling or tripling prices over the 1500s in various parts of Europe. The new wealth—and the accompanying inflation—benefited the commercial classes, who profited from high prices. But inflation hurt the old nobility who lived on fixed revenues from land. It also hurt the peasantry, many of whom were expelled from their farms to make way for more profitable sheepwalks as their landlords strove to keep up with inflation.

The great influx of precious metals also left Europe with its most enduring memories of that first great surge of intercontinental empire-building—memories of real-life El Dorados found beyond the western seas or the burning line.

# LONG-RANGE CONSEQUENCES

## The Columbian Exchange

In the long run, however, the broader global impact of Europe's intercontinental imperialism would prove even greater than its commercial value to Europe. During the period of the Old Imperialism, there began a great reshuffling of plants, animals, and peoples, a series of economic and political realignments, that would truly transform the world.

---

[4]Quoted in Peter H. Wood, *Black Majority: Negroes in Colonial South Carolina from 1670 Through the Stono Rebellion* (New York: Norton, 1974), p. 61.

The collection of basic ecological changes initiated by Europeans eager to exploit their new overseas holdings to the maximum have been called the Columbian exchange.[5] Europeans transplanted such profitable plants as sugar and coffee and cotton, as well as basic grains such as wheat and large domesticated animals such as horses, cattle, and sheep, from Europe and Asia to the Americas. From the New World they carried potatoes, corn, tobacco, and other crops to the Old. Native American food crops alone would come to feed a large part of the world's population in centuries to come.

Populations also began a shift more dramatic than any since the great prehistoric migrations that had peopled the continents tens and hundreds of thousands of years before. The major population changes in these early centuries of the Western hegemony came in North and South America. Here European germs brought deadly diseases—including malaria, measles, bubonic plague, and above all smallpox—to which the original Amerindian population had no inherited immunities. The result was a catastrophic decline in Native American populations, running perhaps as high as 90 percent in such areas as Mexico, the Caribbean islands, and Peru.

Particularly in South America, however, most of the Native American population did survive. To them were added millions of European settlers and enslaved Africans. This mix of peoples created the most diverse population pattern anywhere in the world. It was a diversity that would grow even more in later centuries.

## The World Market

The profitable exchanges of goods undertaken by Europeans during these centuries had a larger economic impact too. They created the first genuinely worldwide market in human history, inaugurated a global division of labor, and pointed toward the global economic integration and interdependence of later centuries.

Europe contributed manufactured goods to this emerging global economy, Asia contributed luxury exports, Africa labor, and North and South America raw materials and plantation products.

The heaviest flow of goods was across the Atlantic, between Europe and the Americas, where Europeans settled in large numbers and were soon producing the things that Europeans at home wanted. Africa, in return for a large drain in labor, got more European manufactured goods than it had had before and, perhaps most important, American agricultural imports, including Indian corn, which was soon growing in many parts of Africa. The meagerest exchange was between Europe and its ancient trading partner, Asia—due, as in ancient times, to the fact that Europe produced little that the highly developed civilizations of Asia wanted or needed.

The degree of global sovereignty exercised by Western people at this point in history remains debatable. As we will see, many historians detect a systematic European global dominance emerging over these early centuries. Other scholars, however, emphasize the much greater degree of western power achieved during the second great wave of imperial conquest in the 1800s and early 1900s.

Between 1500 and 1800, these specialists assert, most non-Western peoples were still little affected by the long reach of Western ships and guns, soldiers, traders, and mission-

[5]A. W. Crosby, *The Columbian Exchange: Biological and Cultural Consequences of 1492* (Westport, Conn.: Greenwood Press, 1972).

aries. The millions of Native Americans and Africans who became subjects or slaves of Europeans after 1500 would certainly have disagreed with this view. But European intercontinental empires would in fact impact many more peoples during the New Imperialism of the nineteenth and twentieth centuries, when Western predominance turned almost all of Africa and most of Asia into Western colonies, protectorates, or spheres of influence.

One New World product was, however, in real demand in the Far East. This was the silver mined in such immense quantities in Middle and South America. Europe's old trading partner China once more demanded precious metals rather than European products in exchange for the luxury goods the Europeans continued to desire. So much American silver in fact found its way to China that some historians have suggested this demand could be considered an important causal factor in the entire colonial adventure.

## The Western Predominance

The global power balance, however, did shift dramatically between 1500 and 1800. As we have seen, in 1500 the most powerful nation in the world was certainly China. The most dynamic expanding culture was probably that of the Muslim center of Eurasia. In Africa and the Americas, independent centers of empire were developing in the Western Sudan, Mexico, and Peru. Pluralism prevailed, and Europe was by no means the greatest of world civilizations.

As 1800 approached, all this had clearly changed. European power had destroyed the American empires, and the African kingdoms had declined in a welter of wars and slave trading. The Western nations, meanwhile, had repulsed and outflanked the Islamic lands, pushed into an Indian Ocean formerly dominated by Muslim traders, and replaced Muslim power in Southeast Asia with European power. The rulers of India were being slowly sucked into the maw of European dependency. Everywhere except East Asia, the weight of Western political predominance was being felt as the eighteenth century drew to a close.

## The Modern World System

Many historians, finally, feel that the relations between nations and peoples at this time make more sense when they are analyzed in terms of *world systems*. In a world system, the much more developed nations of the economic and political *core* shape and exploit a fringe of less developed peoples called the *periphery*. Immanuel Wallerstein and others see the *modern world system* as the archetypal example of this sort of intricate, changing, yet centrally important structure of international relations.[6]

The modern world system, which emerged at the end of the fifteenth century, was built around the economically developed core of Western Europe. Specifically, as we have seen, it was the economic and political power of a half-dozen Western European "Atlantic powers" that forged the new world system. These nations—Spain and Portugal, the Netherlands, France, and England—poured a vast accumulation of capital into the development of overseas possessions and global commercial networks. They set the terms of trade, the rules under which business would be carried out, wherever their seagoing caravels and galleons and East Indiamen carried them. In many of these places, they also exercised political control over the lands they penetrated, converting a growing portion of the New World particularly into European colonies.

---

[6]Immanuel Wallerstein, *The Modern World-System* (New York: Academic Press, 1974–   ).

As we have seen, relations between the members of the European core changed over the early modern centuries. The Iberian powers, Spain and especially Portugal, declined in importance, becoming part of a semiperiphery of only partially developed states. The Netherlands became the world's most successful global trader in the seventeenth century, but followed Spain and Portugal into second-class status in the eighteenth. Britain and France, meanwhile, dueled for hegemonic power, the preeminent position in the world economy, and Britain emerged victorious in the later 1700s.

The most important regions of the early modern world system's periphery were Latin America, the Caribbean, and—Wallerstein points out—Eastern Europe, which was also economically underdeveloped. In the eighteenth century, India, West Africa, much of the declining Middle East, and a still backward Russia were also sucked into the world system dominated by Western Europe.

In all these areas, the impact of the world system was felt in many ways. The peoples of the periphery commonly contributed not capital but labor to the system. Laboring on the plantations and in the mines of the New World or weaving textiles in Asia, they fed the growing demand of an increasingly wealthy Western European core. Enslaved Africans and Native Americans dragooned into forced labor illustrate the fundamental role of the periphery in the modern world system.

The primary products of the periphery were raw materials and agricultural goods. Gold and silver, sugar and fish, brazilwood, ebony, cotton, and spices were all of central importance to the new economic network. Indian cotton fabrics and Chinese porcelain still found markets in Europe. But by the eighteenth century, Europeans had learned to make elegant "china" themselves and to weave enormous amounts of cotton on machines unheard of in India. Inexorably, an industrializing Europe would convert the rest of the world into raw material suppliers for the peoples of the capitalist core.

## SUMMARY

The Western conquest of the world that began around 1500 is a saga of adventure and brutality, raw greed and raw courage, to match any that history has seen.

The ships, navigational aids, and weapons the European peoples deployed in these opening centuries of the great conquest were among the most advanced of their time. Their motives, however, were not new: a thirst for gold, for converts to their religion, and for the military honor that could only be earned in war. These were old ambitions, though particularly developed in the West at the beginning of modern history. Southern Europeans—Spanish and Portuguese, often with Italian navigators—set the pace in the sixteenth century. In the seventeenth, northern European nations—England, France, and the Netherlands—took the lead in empire-building. By the eighteenth century, Britain emerged as the greatest Western imperial power of all.

The Portuguese, led by daring commanders like da Gama and the brilliant imperial organizer Albuquerque, pushed eastward to India, Southeast Asia, and beyond. They established a cruelly enforced monopoly over the sea trade of the Indian Ocean. The Spanish probed westward.

Columbus discovered a "New World," and Cortés, Pizarro, and their fellows conquered much of South and Middle America, looted the realms of the Aztecs and Incas, and established a continental empire.

The Dutch were the most successful of all the seventeenth-century empire builders. They established trading posts in North America, the Caribbean, South Africa, Southeast Asia, and even East Asia. By the eighteenth century, however, British and French commercial enclaves in India and settlement empires in North America and the Caribbean made them the prime contenders. After the wars of the middle 1700s, British triumphs in India and Canada made Britain master of the greatest of overseas empires.

From their overseas holdings, Europeans brought home spices, silk, cottons, slaves, gold and silver, codfish, sugar, tobacco, and much more. The impact of the so-called Old Imperialism was, however, even greater on the rest of the world. Plants, animals, and human populations were shuffled around the globe on the little European sailing ships. The beginnings of a genuine global economy emerged, and the world power balance began decisively to tilt toward the West.

## SUGGESTED READING

Bieber, J. ed. *Plantation Societies in the Era of European Expansion.* Brookfield, Vt.: Ashgate, 1997. Studies suggest that transformation of the colonized world was not a simple matter of European influences on non-European peoples, but a more complex process of evolving institutions and compromise.

Cook, N. D. *Born to Die: Disease and New World Conquest, 1492–1650.* New York: Cambridge University Press, 1998. A leading proponent of the view that foreign diseases decimated a large Amerindian population makes his case. See also D. Henige's opposite view, *Numbers from Nowhere: The American Indian Contact Population Debate* (Norman: University of Oklahoma Press, 1998).

Crosby, A. W. *The Columbian Exchange: Biological and Cultural Consequences of 1492.* Westport, Conn.: Greenwood Press, 1972. Classic account of the larger results of European contact with the New World. See also his more recent *Ecological Imperialism: The Biological Expansion of Europe, 900–1900.* (Cambridge, England: Cambridge University Press, 1986), which seeks to demonstrate that European colonists brought so many animals, plants, and microorganisms with them that they radically restructured the ecosystems of much of the rest of the world.

Emmer, P., and F. Gaastra, eds. *The Organization of Interoceanic Trade in European Expansion, 1450–1800.* London: Variorum, 1996. Europe's role in the emergence of genuinely global trade seen as building on local trade patterns rather than imposing new ones.

Fernandez-Arnesto, F., ed. *The European Opportunity.* Brookfield, Vt.: Variorum, 1995. Collection of scholarly studies on aspects of European imperial motives, means, and past expansionary momentum at the beginning of the modern age. See also his *The Global Opportunity* (Brookfield, Vt.: Variorum, 1995), explorations of the expansionary potential of other areas besides Europe in the centuries around 1500.

Galloway, C. G. *New Worlds for All: Indians, Europeans, and the Remaking of Early America.* Baltimore: Johns Hopkins University Press, 1997. Depicts early contacts less as a conquest than as a blending of European and Native American cultures.

Grove, R. *Green Imperialism: Colonial Expansion, Tropical Island Edens, and the Origins of Environmentalism, 1600–1860.* New York: Cambridge University Press, 1995. Traces evolving Western views of the non-Western world.

Israel, J. I. *Dutch Primacy in World Trade, 1585–1740.* New York: Oxford University Press, 1989. Global role of the small trading nation that once dominated world trade.

Léon-Portilla, M., ed. *The Broken Spears: The Aztec Account of the Conquest of Mexico,* trans. L. Kemp. Boston: Beacon Press, 1961. The other side of Cortés's victory. For an eyewitness account by a Spaniard, see B. Diaz del Castillo, *The Discovery and Conquest of Mexico,* trans. A. P. Maudslay (New York: Grove Press, 1956).

Manning, P. *Slave Trades, 1500–1800: Globalization of Forced Labor.* Brookfield, Vt.: Variorum, 1996. Larger framework for the Western assault on Africa's coasts.

Phillips, W. D., and C. R. Phillips. *The Worlds of Christopher Columbus.* Cambridge: Cambridge University Press, 1992. Valuable evaluation of the surviving evidence on the man, his times, and his likely views.

Pomerantz, K. *The Great Divergence: China, Europe, and the Making of the Modern World Economy.* Princeton: Princeton University Press, 2000. Widely discussed study seeking to replace a single emerging European economic hegemony in early modern times with several centers of the world economy—mostly in Asia—as late as the eighteenth century.

Reid, A., ed. *Southeast Asia in the Early Modern Era: Trade, Power, and Belief.* Ithaca, N.Y.: Cornell University Press, 1993. Focus on local forces and choices during the first phase of Western economic penetration.

Russell-Wood, A. J. R. *The Portuguese Empire, 1415–1808.* Baltimore: Johns Hopkins University Press, 1998. Topical exploration of the Portuguese overseas empire and its impact on Asia and the New World.

Smith, A. K. *Creating a World Economy: Merchant Capital, Colonialism, and World Trade.* Boulder, Colo.: Westview Press, 1991. World-system analysis of the rise of this first global market.

Smith, R. *Vanguard of Empire: Ships of Exploration in the Age of Columbus.* New York: Oxford University Press, 1993. New standard work, with useful illustrations. See also P. Pérez-Maláina, *Spain's Men of the Sea: Daily life on the Indies Fleets in the Sixteenth Century,* trans. C. R. Phillips (Baltimore: Johns Hopkins University Press, 1998) on the hard life and declining status of seafaring men in early modern times.

Thornton, J. *Africa and Africans in the Making of the Atlantic World, 1400–1680.* New York: Cambridge University Press, 1992. Trailblazing study, challenging orthodox views of African underdevelopment, African slavery, and the role of Africans in the New World. For new perspectives on Africans in the Americas, see S. W. Mintz and R. Price, *The Birth of African-American Culture: An Anthropological Perspective* (Boston: Beacon Press, 1992).

Tracy, J. D., ed. *The Political Economy of Merchant Empires: State Power and World Trade, 1350–1750.* Cambridge: Cambridge University Press, 1991. Essays on the relative importance of government sponsorship, military advances, and business organization in the global expansion of European trade.

Todorov, T. *The Conquest of America: The Question of the Other,* trans. R. Howard. New York: Harper & Row, 1984. Challenging structuralist reading of Spanish perception of the Aztecs. See also I. Glendinning. *Ambivalent Conquests: Maya and Spaniard in Yucatan, 1500–1570* (New York: Cambridge University Press, 1987), a subtle analysis of the conflicting motives and adaptations of Spanish missionaries and Native American peoples.

Wallerstein, I. *The Modern World-System.* New York: Academic Press, 1974–). This challenging and widely debated synthesis is now into its third volume and the nineteenth century. See also C. Chase-Dunn, and T. D. Hall, *Rise and Demise: Comparing World Systems* (Boulder, Colo.: Westview Press, 1997), a critical survey of "world system" analysis of the global economy.

 Please refer to the document CD-ROM for primary sources related to this chapter.

# CHAPTER 20

# BARRICADES, BALLOTS, AND STEAM
## The Transformation of Europe

### (1600–1900)

## A Glance Ahead: A New Europe Emerges

Europe plunged into an era of unprecedented change during the seventeenth, eighteenth, and nineteenth centuries.

During the 1600s and 1700s, European rulers claimed "absolute" power, rationalized their bureaucracies, and expanded their authority. European wealth and population increased rapidly, especially with the coming of the Industrial Revolution in the later 1700s. Radical new notions also spread through the West—the new natural laws of the Scientific Revolution and the political and economic ideas of the Enlightenment. And in 1789, the French Revolution brought radical change to Europe's greatest power.

In the 1800s centralized government continued to grow, while the ongoing Industrial Revolution spread factories and railroads across the West. New ideologies such as liberalism, socialism, and nationalism generated both violent revolutions and waves of social reform. As the century drew to a close, a Europe of strongly centralized yet sometimes more liberal nations commanded more power than the world had ever seen before.

## Europe's Emerging Structure of Power

### The Old Regime in Europe

From a broad overview of the world of intercontinental empire, we turn now to a closer look at some of the major regions of the globe in the centuries before 1900. We begin, because of its significance as well as its familiarity, with the Western world.

Seen as a part of global history, the seventeenth and eighteenth centuries in Europe did two things. They significantly strengthened the power of Europeans to impose their will upon the rest of the world. They also saw the development of ideas and trends that, exported to the world at large in the nineteenth and twentieth centuries, would drastically transform the way many other peoples thought and lived.

European society during the seventeenth and eighteenth centuries is often described as Europe of the *old regime,* Europe as it was before the surge of revolutionary change that began with the French Revolution of 1789 transformed the continent in the nineteenth century. Old regime Europe had inherited much from its medieval and Renaissance past. Most Europeans, like most people around the world, were peasants, living on the land, their lives shaped by seasons and weather, crops and farm animals. European cities were graced by medieval cathedrals and Renaissance palaces, but had their dark warrens of slum streets as well. A landed aristocracy that went back to the Middle Ages still controlled the countryside, while increasingly wealthy middle classes dominated urban life. Politically, hereditary monarchies ruled all large states, but many city-states were governed by oligarchies of merchants, bankers, and other middle-class citizens.

There were five great powers in Europe during the 1600s and 1700s. Three of them—Britain, France, and Austria—were established states with roots deep in the Middle Ages. The other two, Prussia and Russia, were new monarchies shouldering their way to the fore. Much of the history of this age was made by these powerful nation-states and the competitive dynasties that ruled them. For a major preoccupation of all these absolutists was foreign affairs, the relations between the nation-states—and particularly the rivalries between them.

Rivalries between these five powerful nations—and dozens of lesser states—led to a series of bloody wars in the seventeenth and eighteenth centuries. European rulers fought one another for dynastic rights and territory in Europe and for commercial rights and colonies overseas. They fought to maintain—or to upset—the balance of power, the rough parity in war-making potential that alone guaranteed that no one power would ever come to dominate all Europe politically.

The growing power and increasing competitiveness of European rulers would also make them an increasingly powerful threat to the rest of the world. They went at their rivalry for colonies and commerce overseas as aggressively as they fought for territory in Europe. And the impact on less organized, equipped, and rivalrous peoples could be devastating.

## France Under Louis XIV: I Am The State

No ruler of the age embodied the spirit of royal absolutism as did Louis XIV (1643–1715), for whom the age is sometimes named. Who but the Sun King, the Grand Monarch, could have interrupted a diplomat's pompous references to "the French state" with an impatient but quite accurate *"l' état, c'est moi"*—"I am the state"—and have historians nodding sagely ever since?

Building royal power meant undermining local and regional power centers, and this Louis did with a will. The old independent-minded French aristocrats were turned into tame courtiers at Louis's court. Town officials became royal appointees. Royal regulations were imposed upon medieval guilds. Provincial courts called *parlements* were compelled to rubber-stamp royal decrees. The Estates General, France's embryonic Parliament, became a dead letter by virtue of never being summoned to meet during Louis's long reign.

The Sun King himself, Louis XIV, posed in seventeenth-century splendor, from huge wig to high red heels, against an appropriately Roman backdrop. Hyacinth Rigaud's portrait catches much of the magnificence of Europe's absolute monarchs in what has been called the Splendid Century. Though Louis XIV was able to combine hard work with symbolic splendor and ceremony, the lives of his eighteenth-century successors would be swamped by sumptuous living. (Scala/Florence/Art Resource)

In place of medieval regional autonomy, centralized royal institutions grew up. Central councils presided over by the king formulated government policies. Powerful royal ministers such as the Marquis de Louvois, minister of war, and above all Jean Baptiste Colbert (1619–1683), chief minister for finances and many other matters, elaborated and applied these policies. A centralized administrative system of agents called *intendants* then implemented them in the provinces, collecting taxes and army conscripts, regulating the economy, and providing at least some government protection in the countryside.

Perhaps the most impressive achievement of absolutism under Louis XIV, however, was the elaborate system of mercantilist regulation of the national economy developed by Colbert. The traditional goals of mercantilism were to increase national production, secure a favorable balance of trade in the goods produced, and thus guarantee a flow of payments in gold and silver bullion into the country. Bullion, in the mercantilist view, constituted true national wealth. It could also be readily taxed by the state—an additional incentive not lost on Louis's administrators.

Under Colbert, then, an intricate structure of monopolies, chartered companies, protective tariffs, controls on wages, prices, and product quality, and colonial regulations was established to achieve these ends. All major powers practiced mercantilistic regulation of their economies. But few did so as efficiently and wholeheartedly as Louis and his first minister, Colbert.

Louis's war minister, Louvois, presided over the worst fruit of royal absolutism: the four wars fought during Louis's long reign.

They were clearly dynastic wars fought to secure lands Louis claimed for his wife (the Spanish Netherlands—Belgium today), for his grandson (Spain itself), or in his own right (the Rhineland). Louis's immense power and matching ambition elevated France to the position—enjoyed by Spain during the preceding century—of Europe's greatest power, threatening to impose its predominance upon the continent. In the end, only a series of alliances of the other great powers held him in check.

The symbol of Louis's predominance was the biggest palace in Europe, built at Versailles, outside Paris. Versailles provided a regal setting for the most admired of absolute monarchs, a world of formal gardens, glittering fountains, and acres of stately architecture. Here Louis and his ministers, mistresses, and courtiers paraded in their ermines and velvets, living in a style befitting the Grand Monarch, the incarnation of absolute sovereignty whose only fitting symbol was the Sun.

### The Continental Absolutists

Prussia, Russia, Austria, and many lesser countries on the continent of Europe tried to emulate the Sun King's absolutist model. In each case, they strove to increase the central power of the monarchy, with or without an aura of enlightened concern for their people.

Prussia, the ancestor of modern Germany, emerged from the ashes of the Thirty Years' War, fought mostly in the German-speaking states of Central Europe. This bloody conflict began as a last flare-up of the European wars of religion and ended as a struggle for territory involving England, France, Spain, and a number of other powers. Perhaps a third of the population of the German states was killed, wolves prowled the streets of deserted villages, and German development was retarded for generations. It is perhaps not surprising, then, that The Hohenzollern dynasty of Prussia chose to base the new power they built from the rubble on what must have seemed the prime essential of that violent age: military strength.

Their twin goals were to link up the scattered Hohenzollern holdings into a united block of territory stretching across North Germany, and to impose the royal will upon the resulting nation. This they accomplished with the help of the Prussian nobility, the hardheaded Junkers. They staffed the Prussian administration and made it arguably the best in Europe. They also officered the small but powerful Prussian army and ran their landed estates efficiently too.

Frederick II the Great (1740–1786) was Prussia's greatest enlightened despot—and its greatest royal general.

As an enlightened ruler, he wrote volumes of philosophy and history, sponsored reforms of the judicial system, and encouraged religious toleration. He called himself the "first servant" of the state and seems genuinely to have believed that only absolute power in royal hands could bring a better life for his people. But he most captured the imagination of Europe in a more typically Hohenzollern role, as a general and a state builder.

Frederick II fought a long duel with the Habsburg empress Maria Theresa for territory in central Europe. And in the end, by inspired generalship and at considerable cost to his beleaguered homeland, Frederick did detach a sizable chunk from Austria and attach it to the Kingdom of Prussia.

Austria's Empress Maria Theresa (1740–1780) and her son Joseph II (1765–1790), rulers of Europe's oldest great power, were the most dedicated enlightened innovators of all rulers of major powers. A pious Catholic, Maria Theresa nevertheless forced reforms upon her Church. A firm believer in the Habsburg dynasty's power and destiny, she nonetheless drastically reformed both the central and provincial administration of the empire.

Soldiers and bureaucrats were the keys to Central European power in the seventeenth and eighteenth centuries—and particularly to the rise of Prussia, the core of what would become modern Germany.

In Russia, on Europe's eastern frontier, Peter the Great and Catherine the Great faced problems of modernization rather than of unification. But they, like Frederick the Great, depended on royal absolutism and military force to achieve their objectives.

Sixteenth-century czars like Ivan IV the Terrible had imposed a rough form of central government by terror on the growing Eastern European nation in the 1500s. Then, in the decades around 1700, Peter I the Great (1682–1725) determined to redesign his country on the model of Western Europe and make Russia a great power. In so doing, he also made it the most rigidly autocratic of all European states.

Under Peter I, royal power was felt more heavily by more people than ever before in Russian history. Taxes, military conscription, and forced labor were heaped on the Russian peasantry, and the medieval institution of serfdom actually increased in Russia

Peter's accomplishments, however, were as prodigious as his tyrannies. He built the bureaucracy that would be Europe's largest, created a powerful army, founded the Russian navy, and fought long wars with the Turks in the south and the Swedes in the north. The latter conflict won a slice of Baltic seacoast where Peter built a new capital—St. Petersburg—that gave the largely landlocked country a crucial "window on the West" through which trade and Western influences would flow henceforth.

Catherine the Great (1762–1796), Russia's most celebrated *enlightened* despot, was actually not Russian at all. She was a German princess married to an ineffectual young czar who soon died, leaving the throne to his shrewd young widow. Catherine brought the reforming ideas of the European Enlightenment with her to the endless steppes and dark forests of Russia. She also proved to be another of Russia's most colorful rulers, entertaining her court indiscriminately with philosophical letters from Voltaire and her long line of stalwart lovers. Russia proved inhospitable to enlightened reforms—but accepted still more centralized royal power.

## England's Century of Revolution

But there was another line of political development to be detected in the 1600s and 1700s. This was the much rarer liberal line of governmental evolution best illustrated by the rise of Parliament and constitutional monarchy in Great Britain during what has come to be called England's century of revolution. And if royal absolutism pointed ahead to the more authoritarian governments to come, constitutional monarchy would lead in time to the mass democracies of more recent times.

A series of foreign rulers—the Scottish Stuart dynasty—who tried to impose absolute monarchy on England without understanding English traditions undoubtedly helped to precipitate the English Revolution. So did the survival of the strong Tudor Parliament, which served as a rallying point for the enemies of absolutism. So, finally, did unfinished business from the previous century: unresolved Reformation tensions, simmering discontent with the autocratic Tudor style of governance, and the rise of a prosperous and self-confident English gentry class and a merchant middle class ready to defend its interests.

In the seventeenth century, then, resistance to the crown developed among several groups of English people. Puritan Protestants opposed immorality at the royal court and feared creeping Catholicism in the Anglican church. Thrifty merchants resented courtly extravagance and high taxes. Above all, solid country squires rebelled at favoritism shown to a handful of royal courtiers, at the abridgment of their own rights in Parliament, and at the high-handedness of James I and his successors in the Stuart line.

Through the first half of the century, this opposition took the form of famous court cases and courtly scandals, running battles in Parliament, and finally armed revolt. A Puritan country squire named Oliver Cromwell defeated the royal armies in battle, beheaded the second Stuart king, Charles I, in 1649, and ruled the country as Lord Protector for the next decade. Charles II was restored to power in 1660, but his successor, James II, was expelled for good in 1688. A parliamentary faction then imported a new king from the Netherlands: William of Orange, strong Protestant and archenemy of royal absolutism, who with his Queen Mary Stuart became England's first constitutional monarch.

The Glorious Revolution of 1688 gave Parliament a large share in governing the country, including the power to control royal revenues and the rights to free elections and debate. The eighteenth century saw the slow evolution of parliamentary power, especially the authority of the elected House of Commons.

Elections were still far from democratic: Only a handful voted, usually on the basis of property ownership. The kings remained very powerful. But a start had been made on a road that would lead over the next two centuries to genuine democracy in Britain.

## CHALLENGES TO THE OLD REGIME

### Rising Middle Classes and Exploding Population

The prosperity of Europe's commercial middle classes took different forms in different parts of Western Europe. Dutch burghers and shipmasters built on a tradition of trade and seamanship that went back to the Middle Ages. In the seventeenth century, as we have seen, the Netherlands dominated the carrying trade of all Europe and was a leading producer of manufactured goods, as well as perhaps the most successful of the new empire builders. In the eighteenth century, British merchants profited from Europe's largest free-trade zone after the union of England and Scotland. They also benefited from the West's solidest financial institution, the Bank of England, as well as from extensive foreign trade and Britain's own triumphant empire. French merchants had Western Europe's largest population to supply. They also had the West's most elaborate mercantile system, and a sizable empire too, at least until France's imperial duel with England ended in 1763.

In Western European countries especially, capitalist institutions and governmental supports for business growth were thus widespread. Joint-stock companies pooled capital for large-scale commercial projects, and stock exchanges facilitated investment. Mercantilistic governments provided subsidies, monopolies, protective tariffs, and other forms of encouragement for business. Despite these supports, however, the rising middle classes often developed strong resentments of the power and privilege enjoyed by the aristocracy. These resentments would make their contribution to the social and political upheaval that was coming.

The demographic history of Europe took an astonishing and decisive turn around the middle of this period. After stalling in the seventeenth century, population growth turned decisively upward in the middle decades of the eighteenth. We must rely largely on estimates—hard statistical evidence is rare this early—but Europe's total population may have risen by as much as 80 percent between 1730 and 1830. It was, in fact, the beginning of the greatest population explosion in the world's history.

Explanations for this initial take-off are complex and sometimes contradictory. One likely cause for the new numbers, however, is clearly the agricultural revolution of the early 1700s.

Agricultural improvements in the eighteenth century included advances in fertilizer, improved rotation of crops to increase production, and stock breeding to develop heavier beef cattle or pigs. Enclosure of village lands and advanced techniques of land management helped make such improvements possible. More food could feed more people. Life expectancies therefore increased, more people lived to reproduce, and a cycle was set in motion that would multiply the population in the next few centuries.

Most Europeans were still desperately poor. Serfs in central and Eastern Europe and tenants in Western Europe were at the mercy of their landlords or masters. Even free peasants who owned their own land, which many of them did in France and some in England, still lived within reach of starvation in years of bad harvest. Excess rural population, no longer needed on more efficient farms, clogged the cities seeking nonexistent work. The frequent misery of the masses would also contribute to the revolutionary unheaval that would begin at the end of the eighteenth century.

## The Condition of Women

Women, as usual, played many parts in this period. At one end of the scale, there were poverty-stricken peasant women even in such prosperous countries as France. At the other extreme, there were the court ladies, the salon hostesses, royal mistresses such as *mesdames* de Pompadour or du Barry, charming or regal in their velvets and laces. In between there were many middle-class women, thoroughly respectable, managers of households or businesses, readers of novels as well as Scripture.

Scattered generalizations may be made about women in these centuries. They were normally married, at least formally subordinate to their husbands, expected to bear and rear children, both as free labor and as a form of old-age insurance for their parents. In addition, women of the peasant, servant, and other working classes had hard physical labor to do all their lives.

Nevertheless, there does seem to have been some improvement in the feminine condition, particularly during the eighteenth century. There were a number of successful women rulers, including Queen Anne of Great Britain, Empress Maria-Theresa of Austria, and the Empresses Elizabeth and Catherine II, the Great, of Russia. Managing a great house or even a solid middle-class home, with its many servants, was a challenge as it had always been. There were celebrated women novelists such as Mademoiselle de Scudéry in the seventeenth century and women painters such as the famous portraitists Elizabeth Vigée le Brun at the French royal court.

Women also played significant roles in the high politics of seventeenth-century France in particular. Aristocratic ladies were leading intriguers at the Bourbon court. They also founded the first French *salons*, centers for discussion and the arts, to be discussed below. The wives of imprisoned princes were leaders in the *Fronde*, the tangled revolutionary upheaval that ravaged French cities in the mid-1660s. Less aristocratic women rioted in the streets of French towns during this tumultuous time.

## The Scientific Revolution

The remarkable surge of scientific discoveries called the Scientific Revolution of the sixteenth and seventeenth centuries provided the intellectual underpinnings for much of the cultural life of the age.

The physical sciences, as we have seen, flourished in many cultures, including those of China, India, the Islamic center of Eurasia, and the Mayans in the New World. Europe's last significant contribution had come among the ancient Greeks. The Greco-Roman period, however, had left one great error to bedevil later scientific understanding: the astronomer Ptolemy's geocentric (earth-centered) theory of the structure of the universe. It was in correcting this error that the sixteenth-century astronomer Copernicus launched the Scientific Revolution.

Nicolaus Copernicus, a Polish churchman who made astronomy his hobby, first propounded the heliocentric (sun-centered) theory in a book *On the Revolutions of the Heavenly Spheres* in 1543. In Copernicus's view, the sun was the center, the earth merely one of a number of planets. The earth, he said, spins around the sun and rotates on its own axis at the same time, giving the illusion that the universe itself is moving around us. It was a major breakthrough, and the Scientific Revolution is sometimes called the Copernican Revolution in his honor.

Scientists of many lands built on these foundations over the century and a half after 1543. The German mathematician Johannes Kepler proposed the three laws of planetary motion—including the key recognition that planets move around the sun in ellipses rather than circles. The famous Italian astronomer and physicist Galileo Galilei built the first astronomical telescope and observed for the first time the mountains on the moon, sunspots, the rings of Saturn, the moons of Jupiter, and the stellar composition of the Milky Way. Galileo is also celebrated for such terrestrial discoveries as the law of the acceleration of falling bodies and the principle of the pendulum.

The mind that tied all this into a coherent scientific picture of the universe was that of the English mathematician Sir Isaac Newton. The linchpin of Newton's theory was the law of universal gravitation: Every particle of matter in the universe, from planets in their orbits to falling bodies here on earth, attracts every other particle of matter with a force called gravity. This gravitational force, Newton declared in his *Mathematical Principles* of 1687, varies directly with the sum of their masses and inversely with the square of the distance between them.

Copernicus, Galileo, Newton, and the other makers of the Scientific Revolution gave the West—and the world—a new technical language and a new approach to truth. Empirical observation and mathematical calculation replaced ancient authority and abstract logic as the road to understanding the world. Science and its jargon became the core of a new Western world view.

The Scientific Revolution was the beginning of several centuries of progress in pure and applied science that would dwarf all earlier scientific advances. It was also the basis for the equally revolutionary social thought that began during these centuries.

## The Enlightenment

"My trade," the eighteenth century's most famous intellectual is supposed to have said, "is to say what I think."[1] Voltaire was a *philosophe*, one of the intellectual leaders of the Enlightenment, the critical analysis of Western thought and society which climaxed the Europe-wide Age of Reason. A writer of poetry, fiction, drama, history, popular science, political philosophy, and much, much more, François-Marie Arouet, known as Voltaire (1694–1778), was celebrated as much for his radical critique of the society of his time as for his literary brilliance. Of his many books, none is more widely known and imitated than *Candide* (1759), a picaresque, satirical novel about a naive young man who manages to encounter hypocrisy, injustice, and folly in every country and every class of eighteenth-century society.

Voltaire's contemporary, Jean Jacques Rousseau (1712–1778), was a wild man among the coolly witty philosophes, stressing emotional sincerity rather than satirical wit and urging the superiority of the natural world to artificial modern society. Rousseau was given to passionate declarations like "Man was born free, and everywhere he is in chains," which influenced such later revolutionaries as Robespierre.[2]

The French *Encyclopedia*, edited by Denis Diderot and Jean d'Alembert, used this apparently neutral form as a cloak for more subtle attacks on the "old regime," as the society of this age was later called. The influence of such works, particularly in the hands of the educated French bourgeoisie, was inexorably subversive, undermining faith in the major social institutions of the time.

Enlightened philosophes were thus social critics, the most vigorous Europe had known for centuries. Voltaire and his colleagues attacked the churches of their day—Catholic and Protestant—as nests of superstition, fanaticism, and useless logic-chopping. They condemned the European aristocracy as mere decorations rather than pillars of society, daring to suggest that merit might be more important in determining a person's true value than inherited social position. And if kings and queens were less vigorously assaulted, it was primarily because the philosophes hoped to work through duly enlightened absolutists to build a more rational and more just world.

On the positive side, these same often satirical social critics found hope in the Scientific Revolution that a better society was possible once human reason was set to solving social problems. Another century or two of determined *social*-scientific inquiry, they believed, would uncover "natural laws" as valid in society as the laws of planetary motion or the law of gravity were in the material world.

Indeed, such natural laws of history and society seemed to come to light before the end of the Age of Reason itself. John Locke, writing at the time of the English Revolution of 1688, insisted that all people have natural rights, including liberty, equality, and property. In the middle 1700s, the Baron de Montesquieu's monumental *Spirit of the Laws* argued that within governing institutions there were political principles such as "checks and balances" that, properly applied, would guarantee just and virtuous government. And in 1776 Adam Smith, the father of modern economics, declared in his *Wealth of Nations* that the road to prosperity lay in accepting the law of supply and demand as it functioned naturally in the free market economy.

[1]Evelyn Beatrice Hall, *Life of Voltaire*, 3rd ed. (New York: Putnam, 1926), p. 145.

[2]Jean Jacques Rousseau, *The Social Contract*, trans. Maurice Cranstan (Baltimore: Penguin Books, 1968), p. 49.

It was a period of revolutionary social thought that seemed to shed a dazzling new light on the way human society works. The subversive attacks of the philosophes fueled the fires of the impending American and French revolutions. Their social theories would provide support for the social engineering and big government, as well as the more revolutionary creeds, of our own time.

The center of all this radical debate was a unique social institution known as the *salon*. The salon of the seventeenth and eighteenth centuries was not so much a place—an elegant drawing room—as it was a social occasion. The typical salon was a weekly "at home" bringing together witty, cultured people in the drawing room of a witty, cultured and fashionable hostess. The salon brought the aristocratic ruling class and the leading intellectual lights of the age together, advancing intellectual careers and civilizing the aristocracy in the process.

# Voices from the Past

Mary Wollstonecraft (1759–1797), an eighteenth-century writer, teacher, and radical intellectual, was also a pioneer feminist crusader. Inspired by the French Revolution and its ringing assertions of the "Rights of Man," she produced her own <u>Vindication of the Rights of Woman</u> in 1792.

Wollstonecraft's social vision, like that of other Enlightenment radicals, saw human unhappiness and vice as consequences of faulty social organization. What does she here suggest caused the women of her time to be "cunning, mean, and selfish"? What jobs beyond that of wife and mother does she believe women could perform in society? What is Wollstonecraft's view of the history books available in her day?

*"It is vain to expect virtue from women till they are, in some degree, independent of men; nay, it is vain to expect that strength of natural affection, which would make them good wives and mothers. Whilst they are absolutely dependent on their husbands they will be cunning, mean, and selfish, and the men who can be gratified by the fawning fondness of spaniel-like affection, have not much delicacy, for love is not to be bought. . . .*

*But what have women to do in society? I may be asked. . . .*

*Women might certainly study the art of healing, and be physicians as well as nurses. And midwifery, decency seems to allot to them. . . .*

*They might, also, study politics, and settle their benevolence on the broadest basis; for the reading of history will scarcely be more useful than the perusal of romances, if read as mere biography; if the character of the times, the political improvements, arts, etc. be not observed. In short, if it be not considered as the history of man; and not of particular men, who filled a niche in the temple of fame. . . .*

*Business of various kinds, they might likewise pursue, if they were educated in a more orderly manner, which might save many from common and legal prostitution. Women would not then marry for a support, as men accept of places under government, and neglect the implied duties; nor would an attempt to earn their own subsistence, a most laudable one, sink them almost to the level of those poor abandoned creatures who live by prostitution. . . . How much more respectable is the woman who earns her own bread by fulfilling any duty, than the most accomplished beauty!—"*

Mary Wollstonecraft, *Vindication of the Rights of Woman* (London: J. Johnson, 1792), pp. 321–322, 337–338, 340.

The central role in the salon was of course that of the hostess. She had to know enough to guide conversations on everything from the latest play in Paris to German philosophy, from Newton to political reform. She moved with ease and confidence among the best minds of her age, creating among the chandeliers and mirrors an island of intellectuality where ideas could grow, pass from mind to mind, and produce the unique culture of the Age of Reason.

## THE FRENCH REVOLUTION

### Causes of the French Revolution

The complex causes of the French Revolution included some deep-seated social problems, subversive ideas, and a cluster of devastating political and economic crises.

Social discontent in France revolved around an anachronistic social structure. This social order gave special privileges to half a million aristocrats and churchmen and denied them to 23 million members of the "third estate"—the rest of the population. Under this system, the urban poor languished in poverty and frequent hunger in city slums, free peasants grumbled at forced labor and other feudal survivals, and an increasingly aggressive and wealthy bourgeoisie resented the tax exemptions and unearned prestige of the nobility. The nobility clung to their feudal privileges and challenged both the absolute power wielded by the weak heirs of Louis XIV and the demands of the rising middle classes.

Even France's kings helped bring on the revolution. Louis XV (1715–1774) lived for pleasure for most of his sixty-year reign and predicted with a sigh that after him would

The attack on the Bastille, July 14, 1789, France's "Fourth of July." The actual events of that day may not have been so dramatic, but the symbolic significance of the fall of this royal prison to a mob of angry Parisians was not lost on Europe. The fact that the people in arms liberated only seven prisoners, none of them political offenders, did not dim the luster of this potent act of political defiance. (Hulton Deutsch Collection Limited)

come the Deluge. Louis XVI (1774–1792), a well-meaning but weak-willed man, dithered through most of his decade and a half of power—and reaped the whirlwind.

The subversive literature of the Enlightenment further undermined the old order by creating a negative public image of the kings, aristocrats, and clergymen who ran it. Voltaire and his colleagues depicted the clergy as worldly and bigoted, the aristocracy as foppish and feckless, and the monarchy itself as bearing ultimate responsibility for a society far gone in rot and decay.

In the late 1780s a series of linked economic and political crises swept France to the brink of revolution. Bad harvests and industrial depression sent mobs of bread rioters into the streets of French cities and gangs of hungry peasants roaming the countryside, burning and looting. At the same time, a financial crisis, rooted in military expenditures and in the tax exemptions of the nobility and the church, brought the government to the edge of bankruptcy. When all efforts at reform failed him, Louis XVI in desperation summoned an antique political assembly, the Estates General, to meet in the spring of 1789 and vote him the taxing power he needed to save the nation from economic and political collapse.

From that point on, things spiraled out of control. The representatives of the "third estate"—the vast majority of the population who were neither aristocrats nor priests—came to the Estates General with long lists of popular grievances. Once assembled, they shrugged off royal leading strings and announced their intention to undertake a sweeping reformation of the state. In July, the Paris mob stormed the Bastille, a Paris prison notorious for the incarceration of political prisoners, leading Louis XVI to gasp, "It's a revolt!" and a more insightful subordinate to reply: "No, sire—it's a Revolution." In the fall, a mob composed mostly of Paris women marched on Versailles demanding bread and returned with the royal family as virtual prisoners. In between these colorful scenes, the work of the Revolution got under way.

## Course of the Revolution

This archetypal ideological revolution unfolded in four clearly definable stages over a violent decade, 1789–1799. The first and most creative phase of the French Revolution lasted for more than two years, 1789–1791. It produced France's bill of rights—the Declaration of the Rights of Man and the Citizen, including the ideals of Liberty, Equality, and Brotherhood. It formulated a written constitution replacing royal absolutism with limited constitutional monarchy. It saw the surrender of the feudal privileges of the nobility and the nationalizing of the French Catholic church and its vast wealth.

France was now roughly on a par with Britain across the Channel. For many enlightened French, this was quite far enough. But not for others.

Revolutionary clubs, newspapers, pamphlets, and books proliferated in the streets of Paris. Women like Olympe de Gouges and a visiting British intellectual, Mary Wollstonecraft, published books demanding rights for women too. Wollstonecraft urged that women, properly educated, could perform a wide range of socially useful occupations. (See box on page 483.) Olympe de Gouges saw no reason why women shouldn't have equal property rights, a place in the administration of government, and access to justice under law.

Members of the Jacobin Club and their leader Maximilien Robespierre (1758–1794), a dedicated revolutionary known to his followers as "the Incorruptible," demanded still more radical changes, including the abolition of the French monarchy itself. During the second stage of the revolution, the year of the constitutional monarchy (1791–1792), the revolt split into two main factions. The Jacobins and other extremists pushed for the establishment of a republic, while moderates such as the Girondins attempted instead to make the limited monarchy work.

Meanwhile, war hawks among the revolutionaries beat the drums for a great crusade to liberate all Europe from kings and priests. In so doing, they played into the hands of reactionary governments, who were looking for an excuse to extinguish the spirit of rebellion before it spread. In the spring of 1792, then, the Austrian Habsburgs led an invasion of France to rescue Louis XVI and his queen, Marie Antoinette, a Habsburg princess.

The third phase of the French Revolution was the notorious Reign of Terror (1792–1794). During this period of a little less than two years, Robespierre and the Jacobins ruled the beleaguered country through the Committee of Public Safety and the guillotine. Under Robespierre's ideologically impassioned rule, the king and queen were executed, the monarchy itself abolished. Many nobles were also guillotined and their lands confiscated. Attempts were made to abolish the church altogether. Considerable numbers of revolutionaries, too moderate or too anarchistically radical for the Jacobins, also died under the slanting blade of the guillotine.

At the same time, the Jacobins turned the tide of war against the Austrians and their allies. By declaring that the nation now belonged to its people, they mobilized modern nationalism for the first time. Huge revolutionary armies of enthusiastic volunteers drove the invaders out of France and even occupied the Netherlands and the Rhineland. The Committee rallied all the resources, labor, and energies of the nation for this patriotic effort, which is thus sometimes seen as a precursor of the "total wars" of the twentieth century.

But the Square of the Revolution reeked with the blood of traitors, and even revolutionary Paris sickened of the carnage. In the summer of 1794, Robespierre and the Jacobin junta in their turn went under the knife, and the Reign of Terror was over.

The long, grimy final phase of the French Revolution was the rule of the Directory (1794–1799), a grubby period of ideological reaction and political opportunism. Genuine radicals were rooted out, while political careerists got rich. The war was prosecuted with zeal, not for the cause, but for loot, fame, and personal advancement. French armies led by one young general in particular—Napoleon Bonaparte—won famous victories, first and most brilliantly in Italy, then still farther afield, against the British in Egypt. And when General Bonaparte returned from the Battle of the Pyramids, a cabal of Directory politicians tried to use him as a front for their own power.

### Napoleon Conquers Europe—and Meets His Waterloo

But Napoleon Bonaparte (1769–1821) had a vision of his own destiny. A coup in 1799 made Napoleon "first consul" of France. His armies and a seemingly unending string of victories over the great powers of Europe did the rest.

This one-time Corsican artillery officer had learned from brilliant French military innovators. He had risen rapidly in the wide-open revolutionary years, when careers were made by talent rather than by aristocratic names. Napoleon used new light artillery brilliantly and maneuvered with great rapidity over European roads built by generations of enlightened despots. He had the huge, now thoroughly seasoned armies of the French Revolution at his disposal. And he had a rare genius for military command that puts him on any short list of the greatest generals of all time.

For a decade and a half, Napoleon Bonaparte ruled a larger European empire than anyone since ancient Rome. He crowned himself emperor of the French in 1804. By 1810 he, his family, and his generals ruled directly or indirectly over a collection of states that stretched from Spain to the frontiers of Russia, from the English Channel to the toe of Italy. Wherever his armies went, furthermore, Napoleon spread the ideals of the French Revolution. At home he was France's enlightened despot at last, streamlining institutions and modernizing laws with military efficiency.

It looked almost as if Europe might find the unity it had enjoyed in Roman times, under a child of the French Revolution.

But Europe's old regime fought back tenaciously against the "Corsican upstart." Britain, safe on its islands, would not make terms. Napoleon's invasion of Russia in 1812 was a fiasco—his first major setback. He had beaten three coalitions of great powers, but in 1813 a fourth defeated him at Leipzig, in the epochal Battle of the Nations. Temporarily exiled from Europe in 1814, Napoleon returned the following year for the miraculous Hundred Days that ended in 1815 with his final defeat at Waterloo.

It was the end of a great adventure—and the beginning of something even greater. For the revolution and its general had seeded Europe with radical ideas, images, and memories that would bear startling fruit for much of the coming century.

## THE INDUSTRIAL REVOLUTION

### Energy Revolutions

While the drama of the French Revolution and the epic of Napoleon were running their course across the English Channel, events that would prove even more significant were taking place in Britain: the Industrial Revolution.

In the narrowest sense of the term, the Industrial Revolution was the transformation of European industrial production between 1760 and 1830. In a broader sense, the Industrial Revolution continues to this day, a long unfolding of new technologies from steam to petroleum to nuclear power, from the locomotive to the microchip.

To accomplish anything at all—to feed, clothe, house ourselves, to build a pyramid or a skyscraper, to read a book or play a tune—human beings must have access to one thing: *energy*. The amount of energy available to us for all purposes, however, is strictly limited by the sources of energy we have at our disposal. Three stages in the exploitation of energy may be distinguished.[3]

For most of our evolution as a species, it will be remembered, we were hunters and gatherers. Our Paleolithic ancestors depended entirely upon the animals and plants they could collect in the course of each day. Some twelve thousand years ago, in the Middle East, the Agricultural Revolution began. Our Neolithic forebears learned to cultivate grain, domesticate animals, and thus feed substantially larger populations. Cities and em-

---

[3]I follow here Carlo Cipolla, *The Economic History of World Population* (Baltimore, Md.: Penguin Books, 1982), chaps. 1 and 2.

pires developed, with large classes freed from primary energy gathering for more specialized tasks as priests and soldiers, merchants and craftspeople, artists and bureaucrats.

Then, a mere two hundred years ago, came the Industrial Revolution. For the first time, nonbiological energy sources were exploited in substantial quantities. Coal came into widespread use first, then oil and its derivatives, then hydroelectric power, and finally nuclear energy in our own time. Such alternatives as solar and geothermal energy are still to be adequately developed.

The energy locked up in these sources was immense. With this extra energy, we have doubled our life spans, redoubled our population over and over, and built the push-button world of skyscrapers, jetliners, and computers we live in today.

How did this material transformation of human life come about, and why did it happen when—and where—it did?

## Causes of the Industrial Revolution

Attempts to explain the Industrial Revolution that began in the eighteenth century, like explanations of the European overseas empires that emerged in the sixteenth, are many and controversial. Traditional accounts celebrated a handful of English inventors as the heroes of the great transformation. More theoretical economic explanations emphasized the concentration of large amounts of capital to pay for the costly process of industrialization.

Some emphasized character traits seen as typically European, including rationality, individualism, or "industriousness," while others pointed to alleged weaknesses in other societies, from poor tropical soils or unproductive elites to "oriental despotism" in government. One widely discussed recent analysis, on the other hand, could find no major differences between the British and Chinese economies beyond coal and colonial supplies of cotton.

The issue, in short, is still being debated vigorously. Here, we will offer a number of causal factors, all centered in Britain, where the Industrial Revolution did in fact begin. While no one of these factors was unique to eighteenth-century Britain, all of them together may have combined to generate the first industrial "take-off" in history. This complex combination includes natural resources, labor, demand, capital, technology, and entrepreneurship.

Natural resources, especially coal and iron, were essential. So was a substantial labor force free from agricultural labor. An increased demand from a growing population is often cited, as is capital accumulation to pay the huge initial cost of tooling up for industrial production. Invention undoubtedly played a part, though in the more systematic form of an ongoing process of technological development. Perhaps most important, there was the role of the entrepreneur, the catalytic agent that brought all the other elements together, added a touch of factory management and marketing skills—and made the Industrial Revolution happen.

## England and the Age of Steam

The cultural milieu within which this combination first developed was Great Britain in the 1760s. Britain had resources in the iron and coal of the Midlands "black country." The British had surplus labor produced by the eighteenth-century agricultural revolution. They had immense amounts of capital from empire and trade, and a growing population to provide the requisite demand. And Britain had a vigorous middle class, including both skilled technicians and aggressive entrepreneurs.

The process began in textile manufacturing, notably the new cotton industry, which was more willing to innovate than the older, more hidebound woolens business. In the cotton industry, small steam engines bred the factory system, embryonic assembly lines, and rapidly accelerating production. From textiles the new approach spread to heavy industry, transportation, and other central elements of the industrial economy. And from Great Britain the new technology spread to Western Europe, North America, and on around the world. It is spreading still, its transforming effects greater even than the ideologies spawned by the French Revolution.

"Steam," they said in the nineteenth century, "is an Englishman." The importance of steam was summed up in a remark made by the well-known entrepreneur Matthew Boulton. Boulton had just finished showing a visitor around the Soho Manufactury, where he and James Watt produced the first industrial steam engines. "I sell here, Sir," Boulton told his guest, "what all the world desires to have—Power!"[4] Substitute "Energy" for "Power," and few historians would disagree.

---

[4]H. W. Dickinson, *Matthew Boulton* (Cambridge: Cambridge University Press, 1937), p. 73.

## MAIN CURRENTS OF THE NINETEENTH CENTURY

### Revolutions and Political Change

The first half of the nineteenth century—once the French and Industrial revolutions are accounted for—is a short one, historically speaking. It covers the period from 1815 to 1848, from Waterloo to the mid-century revolutions of 1848. In political terms, this was, in fact, Europe's Age of Revolutions, when Europe was as tormented by ideological revolt as the Third World has been since World War II.

At the time of Napoleon's defeat in 1814 and 1815, a great international conclave was held at Vienna to draw up a peace settlement after twenty years of Napoleonic wars. The goals of the Congress of Vienna, however, included not only a lasting peace but also a massive attempt to turn the historical clock back to the old regime, to the way things had been before 1789. To this end, pre-Napoleonic "legitimate" dynasties were restored to power, established churches were reestablished, and the old hereditary aristocrats were encouraged to reclaim their leading places in society everywhere. The primary architect of this Vienna settlement was the intensely conservative Austrian foreign minister, Prince Metternich. Metternich would lead the forces of European reaction for the next thirty-odd years.

You cannot, however, set history back like a clock. Reaction only bred more revolution—three and a half decades of it between 1815 and 1848.

The revolutions of the 1820s were largely on the southern and eastern fringes of the continent, in European backwaters such as Spain, the Italian states, Greece, and Russia. The revolutions of 1830, however, carried the spirit of revolutionary change into the heart of Western Europe, to France again and to Belgium and a number of the German states as well as to Italy and elsewhere.

The revolutions of 1848–1849, finally, saw the great floodtide of the movement—and its ebb. The "springtime of the peoples" in 1848 saw rebellion in France, Austria, Prussia and other German states, various Italian states, and elsewhere. Another French king was overthrown in Paris. The Habsburg emperor and Metternich himself were driven from Vienna by a revolution spearheaded by students and workers. The pope was expelled from Rome by a revolutionary upheaval. "If someone had said, 'God has been driven from heaven and a republic proclaimed there,'" the Russian anarchist Bakunin remarked of those amazing days, "everyone would have believed it and no one would have been surprised."[5]

In 1849 the great tide turned. France got a new monarch to replace its deposed king, the Austrian emperor and the Roman pope returned, backed by bayonets, and the old order was apparently restored once more all across Europe.

Once again, however, pressures for change doggedly forced their way to the surface in Europe—peacefully this time, through continuing reform movements. And rulers, weary of revolutions, began to make concessions. By 1900 all the great powers except Russia had constitutions, elected legislatures, even bills of rights—and France was an established republic at last.

In Western Europe, at least, the revolutionary agenda of the first half of the century had finally been achieved—through reform rather than revolution.

---

[5]P. H. Noyes, *Organization and Revolution: Working-Class Associations in the German Revolutions of 1848–1849* (Princeton, N.J.: Princeton University Press, 1966), p.57.

## The Birth of the Modern Ideologies

The second half of the century saw victories for other ideologies besides the liberal ideals of the French Revolution, however.

A list of the radical seeds sown in the nineteenth century would have a distinctly contemporary ring to it. The first ideologically based student movement erupted in Germany just after 1815. The Italian freedom fighter Garibaldi pioneered the art of revolutionary guerrilla warfare in the 1830s, 1840s, and 1850s, while anarchists brought terrorist bombs to the streets of European cities in the last decades of the century. The women's movement began to make significant numbers of converts in the later 1800s, and the labor movement made substantial headway about this time also. The first stirrings of modern anti-imperialism were felt in the colonies. And so on down a considerably longer list.

Three great ideological trends, however, informed most of these demands for change in nineteenth-century Europe, as they would in the twentieth-century world as a whole: liberalism, nationalism, and socialism.

Nineteenth-century political *liberalism* built on the ideas of the seventeenth-century English thinker John Locke and of French Enlightenment philosophes such as Montesquieu and Rousseau. Liberals believed in Lockean "natural rights" to liberty and equality. They further asserted Locke's contract theory of government—government by consent of the governed—as put into practice in revolutionary France and America. Liberals were thus militantly opposed to hereditary aristocracies, divine-right monarchies, and political oppression in all its forms. They demanded freedom of speech, the press, and religion; equality of economic opportunity and equality before the law; constitutional government, elected legislatures, and bills of rights.

Liberalism had an economic dimension as well, however. Here liberals drew on the theories of Adam Smith, whose *Wealth of Nations* had come out in the revolutionary year 1776. Nineteenth-century liberals believed with Smith in natural laws governing the operation of the economy. These included the key law of supply and demand, which guaranteed that goods would be produced to meet any substantial demand, and that prices, wages, profits,

Karl Marx, the most influential of all the nineteenth-century ideologues, does not look much like the prophet of World Revolution in this picture. Though the great global upheaval he foresaw never came, Marx's theories inspired revolutionaries around the world. Born in Germany, Marx was driven to seek political asylum in other parts of Europe and died in London, where he did most of his writing. (Library of Congress)

and other aspects of the economy would best be regulated by natural market forces. Another basic liberal economic principle was the law of accumulation, which declared that the wealth of nations would grow steadily if supply and demand were allowed to operate freely. Liberal economists therefore opposed mercantilistic regulation of the economy and fought in particular for free trade—another of the great crusades of the first half of the century.

In some ways *nationalism* blazed even more brightly than liberalism across the nineteenth-century sky. Nineteenth-century nationalists built on the teachings of the eighteenth-century German cultural nationalists who preached the importance of each people's national spirit. They also drew on the model of the French Revolution, which had unleashed powerful patriotic energies, both in France and in nations conquered by Napoleon. Nationalists in the nineteenth century dedicated their energies to unifying divided peoples such as the Italians and the Germans. Or they labored to win national self-determination for oppressed minorities such as the Eastern European, mostly Slavic peoples ruled by the Austrian, Russian, and Ottoman emperors. Later in the century, however, nationalism turned chauvinistic. It began to be used to justify the aggressive or expansionist policies of German or French or British governments.

Nationalists believed that common language and literature, history and custom welded a people into a larger whole—the nation. Some of them believed in a folk soul or folk spirit uniting a people spiritually. Many saw a national character that they shared with their fellow nationals: Frenchmen were naturally more civilized and artistic than other peoples, Germans more philosophical or scientific, Britons better at government and more practical, and so forth.

These apostles of nationality preached their patriotic creed in terms of native soil and blood—the black earth of Russia, for instance, or German or Anglo-Saxon blood. They expressed their loyalty with reverence for such concrete symbols as the national flag or the national anthem. They wept when the French Tricolor or the British Union Jack passed by, and they sang the "Marseillaise," "Britannia Rules the Waves," or "Germany over All" with passion.

The last of the major isms to develop was *socialism*. Socialists sought a solution to a uniquely nineteenth-century problem, after all: the problem of wide-spread working-class poverty in the middle of the Industrial Revolution. The new industrial order was producing more goods and services than the world had ever seen before. Yet the laborers who worked in the factories and mines lived in slums, worked long hours under brutal conditions, and were subject to malnutrition, disease, and early death. The socialist solution to this very genuine problem was, quite simply, the transfer of the means of production—the new mines and mills, railroads, banks, and the rest—from private ownership to ownership by the workers themselves.

Several sorts of socialism emerged in the nineteenth century. Utopian socialists urged a rejection of the Industrial Revolution itself and a return to small-scale handicraft production, preferably in small communities in the healthy countryside. Inspired by prophets such as Charles Fourier, Utopians did, in fact, establish a number of socialist country communes—as their successors do, here and there, to this day.

The most influential socialist, however, was clearly Karl Marx (1818–1883), some of whose followers came to call themselves communists in later years. Marx, a German radical thinker who lived most of his life in exile in London, rejected Utopianism as naive. He preached a more violent creed of working-class revolution against the capitalist entrepreneurs and investors who owned the new technology.

According to Marx's widely influential theory, all history had been a chronicle of class struggles between patrician and plebeian, lord and serf, guild master and journeyman. The present class struggle between the proletarians (workers) and their capitalist bosses would lead to a great world revolution. This final class war would end class struggle forever by putting the means of production in the hands of the working people once and for all. In the little tract called *The Communist Manifesto*, which he and his lifelong collaborator Friedrich Engels wrote in 1848, Marx urged the workers of the world to unite, overthrow the bourgeois-capitalist order everywhere, and establish the workers' paradise. Though Marx never fought at a barricade, his revolutionary ideas would inspire radicals around the world to structure the state-socialist, one-party nations of Eastern Europe, East Asia, and elsewhere during much of the twentieth century.

The form of socialism that predominated in Western Europe, however, has been the more moderate type known as social-democratic or (in Great Britain) Fabian socialism. Social democrats drew some ideas from Marx, others from other socialist writers. But they firmly rejected revolution in favor of reform. Social democrats were more practical than the Utopians, more constitutionally minded than the revolutionary Marxists. They were willing to work with labor unions and liberal allies, using the free press and the ballot box to gain their ends. The socialist parties of Western Europe today are of this practical, reform-minded social-democratic sort.

Nineteenth-century ideologues of whatever stripe lived a hard life. Often censored, imprisoned, or driven into exile, they survived on dreams of coming revolutions and utopian futures. And though history seldom bore out their predictions in any detail, they did have a powerful impact on the history of that century—and of the next.

### The Spread of the Industrial Revolution

The middle half of the nineteenth century, from the 1820s to the 1870s, was the heyday of free competition in the simplest sense of the term. Liberal entrepreneurs persuaded many governments that mercantilistic regulation of the economy was a handicap rather than a help to the new technology of the Industrial Revolution. Free trade, freely negotiated contracts between capital and labor, and a decline in government regulation of all sorts resulted.

By mid-century, competition between rival nations, between old and new industries, between countless small or middle-sized producers of the same good or service was widespread in Europe. Cloth making, coal mining, transportation all saw hundreds and even thousands of freely competing firms at work. "Competition," it was widely said, "is the life of trade and the law of progress."

In the last quarter of the century, however, there came a change. It was not a return to government regulation—that would not come on a large scale until the twentieth century. It was rather the rigorous curtailment of free competition by businessmen themselves. These limits on competition were the result of large-scale business combinations—the sort that American law would come to call "combination in restraint of trade."

The move toward monopoly combination that began in the 1870s was in part a defensive measure in the face of the sheer brutality of the fang-and-claw competition of the age. During the periodic depressions particularly, unregulated competition hurt all competitors and drove many into bankruptcy. Under such circumstances, many business leaders began to think that combination, not competition, might be the life of trade and even the law of survival. The result was the most amazing flower of nineteenth-century economic development: the rise of big business.

Some aggressive industrialists merged with or bought out either competitors or related industries to produce giant new *corporations*. Thus Albert Krupp, the German steel-maker, bought up coal and iron mines, ore boats, and even industries which used his steel. When complete, the Krupp family's industrial empire included machine-tool plants, rail-car manufactures, a shipyard, and the arms industries for which his descendants would be most famous.

Another form of combination did not go to the length of actual corporate merger, but simply resorted to working agreements called *cartels*. Cartels, which might be national or even international in scope, fixed prices, assigned quotas, or divided up the market in ways that effectively eliminated competition. A shipping cartel organized first in Britain, for instance, expanded to include major steamship lines in Germany, France, the Netherlands, and even Japan. This single group came close to setting ocean fares and freight rates on the sealanes of the world.

This was the trend as the twentieth century got under way, and it has remained a main current of Western economic history since. Competition and entrepreneurship still play key innovative roles, but big business controls vast swathes of economic activity today.

## Women Challenge the System

The multiple conditions of women remained as diverse as ever, but there seems to have been a new twist: an image of womanhood that would prove a hard cross for subsequent generations of Western women to bear.

Some new lines of work opened up for women, however. Female proletarians shared their husbands' grueling lives in the mills and even in the mines, perhaps suffering more for the lower wages they were paid. But a number of more respectable professions opened up to women, including positions as governesses, elementary schoolteachers, nurses (toward the end of the century), and, for the talented, writing. Novelists such as the three Brontë sisters and Jane Austen, George Eliot and George Sand, and poets such as Elizabeth Barrett Browning and Christina Georgina Rossetti established a place for women at the top of the world of letters.

In the latter part of the nineteenth century, the organized movement for female emancipation emerged in Europe. As early as the 1840s, Utopian socialists had preached female equality, and by mid-century some liberals also spoke up for political rights for women. During the later decades of the century, women in fact gained improved legal status: Married women got control of their own property, for example, and divorce became easier. Contraception began to liberate some women from the burden of large families. Women were admitted to universities and invaded formerly all-male professions such as medicine. They were also increasingly prominent among radical and revolutionary groups in countries such as Russia and France. In England they organized a vigorous, sometimes violent campaign to get the right to vote—the "suffragette" campaign that finally led to women's suffrage after World War I. It was the first wave of a women's movement that still continues.

Most women of all classes, however, still married and reared children duties which were believed to require much tact, training, character, and intelligence. Women were, as the saying went, "put on a pedestal" to be worshiped by their men—who meantime went on running the world. The descent of women from this pedestal would require another psychic revolution in the next century.

# THE CAVALCADE OF NATIONS

## Britain's Age of Reform

The archbishop of Canterbury and several other hoary-headed statesmen woke Princess Victoria up in the middle of the night to tell her the news. At the age of seventeen, she had inherited the throne of the largest empire in the world. After they left, Victoria wrote by candlelight in her journal: "I shall do my utmost to fulfil my duty toward my country. I am very young, but I am sure that very few have more desire to do what is fit and right than I have."[6]

The year was 1837. She would rule the British Empire for the rest of a long and prosperous century, and few would ever accuse her of doing anything that was not "fit and right." She would become the living symbol of the Victorian Age, the century when Brittania ruled the waves and the sun never set on the British Empire. A central achievement of that prosperous and progressive century was the growth of democratic institutions in Britain's age of reform.

The domestic history of Britain in the nineteenth century is in fact usually presented as a chronicle of social and political reform. Queen Victoria (ruled 1837–1901) presided over a parliamentary government that was able to change with the times, to meet the needs of a rapidly evolving industrial society. Politicians of various persuasions, from the Liberal William Gladstone to the Conservative Benjamin Disraeli, both guided and responded to the wishes of a growing electorate to produce the model of a functioning nineteenth-century Western democracy—social change through the ballot box.

Parliamentary reform bills extending the right to vote to one group after another provided the skeleton of Britain's age of reform. The great Reform Bill of 1832 gave new industrial cities such as Manchester and Birmingham—and the business middle classes everywhere—representation in Parliament. Disraeli's reform bill of 1867 granted the suffrage to factory workers, Gladstone's bill of 1884 awarded it to farm laborers, and the 1918 bill climaxed the women's suffrage movement by giving the vote to most women.

Other reform measures included laws designed to render the new industrial system more livable. Laws regulating women's working conditions and child labor were passed, as were factory-safety acts and legislation limiting the length of the working day. Public education began in Britain in the later nineteenth century. During the years before World War I, a Liberal government enacted such socialistic measures—as they then seemed—as the beginnings of public health service and old-age pensions.

There was tension, of course—the massive and sometimes violent demonstrations connected with the Reform Bill of 1832, the (failed) Chartist movement of the 1840s demanding universal manhood suffrage, and the women's campaign for the right to vote in the 1890s and early 1900s. But the system proved flexible and strong enough to contain and channel all such pressures. Change came comparatively peacefully through the democratic process.

## France from Monarchy to Republic

Social change came also to France, the other more liberal great power. But in France, change came as much through revolution as through reform.

---

[6]Quoted in Giles St. Aubyn, *Queen Victoria: A Portrait* (New York: Atheneum, 1992), p. 57.

Revolutionary barricades went up in Paris four times between the late 1700s and the later 1800s: in the great revolution of 1789, in 1830, in 1848, and in the destructive Paris Commune of 1871. New forms of government were established by force five times between 1815 and 1914: three monarchies—the restored Bourbons, the constitutional monarchy of Louis Philippe, and the empire of Louis Napoleon after 1848—and two republics, the Second and the Third, the latter lasting until 1940. Only the French civil service, a centralized structure of administration rationalized and strengthened by Napoleon I, provided basic continuity in government.

Political change thus came to France revolution by revolution. The restored Bourbons felt it expedient to grant France a constitution and a two-house legislature in 1814. Bourgeois voting and political predominance came with Louis Philippe, "the middle-class king," in 1830. Universal manhood suffrage made a brief appearance under the Second Republic, was permanently established by the Third in 1875. Women, however, did not vote till the 1940s. Other social reforms also lagged in the land that had given birth to the Enlightenment. But change did come, and nineteenth-century France saw no more revolutions after 1871.

## Bismarck and German Unification

Chancellor Bismarck, chief minister of the king of Prussia, looked at the faces of this key committee of the legislature with undisguised disdain.

The liberals in the Prussian legislature opposed Bismarck's demand for tax hikes to further strengthen the feared Prussian army. These politicians seemed to think that their endless discussions and disputes determined what the Prussian monarchy was going to do. Looking the assembled political leaders in the eye, Bismarck let them have a dose of hard-boiled realism. "The great issues of the day," he declared, will not be decided "by speeches and resolutions, but by blood and iron!"[7]

Bismarck, Germany's "iron chancellor," would prove the truth of his hardboiled view of history as architect of German unification and as the greatest statesman in Europe during the second half of the nineteenth century.

Austria had dominated the German states since the Middle Ages. Prussia had been challenging that predominance since Frederick the Great's long feud with Empress Maria Theresa in the mid-eighteenth century. In the nineteenth century, Prussia added to its efficient administration and its powerful army a dynamic, rapidly growing industrial machine and close economic relations with other industrializing North German states. Finally, shortly after the revolutions of 1848, Prussia's Hohenzollern king William acquired a chief minister who was also the greatest diplomatic manipulator of his age: Otto von Bismarck (1815–1898).

Bismarck, a huge, powerfully built Junker, was the architect of modern Germany. He was no ideological nationalist, but an old-fashioned royal minister, loyal to the interests of the house of Hahenzollern. He was also not the master planner of later legend. He was rather a brilliant opportunist and manipulator, playing his diplomatic cards as they fell and winning far more often than he lost.

Bismarck demonstrated the power of the Prussian army in the brief Danish War of 1863 and defeated Austria itself handily in the Austro-Prussian War of 1866. He then ral-

---

[7]Quoted in René Albrecht-Carrié, *Europe Since 1815: From the Ancient Regime to the Atomic Age* (New York: Harper, 1962), p. 108.

lied all the rest of the German states in a war of revenge against their common enemy, the victorious Franco-Prussian War of 1870–1871. Intoxicated with their triumph over the French emperor Napoleon III, the German princes gathered in Louis XIV's great Hall of Mirrors at Versailles in the spring of 1871 to swear allegiance to the king of Prussia, now Emperor William I of the new German Empire.

## Italian Unification

The new kingdom of Italy was a more or less pure and certainly enthusiastic product of the new nationalism. Divided like Germany into many small principalities since the Middle Ages, Italy after 1815—again like the German states—was dominated by Austria. For half a century, from the Congress of Vienna to the revolutions of 1848, Italian nationalists such as the ideologue Giuseppe Mazzini and the guerrilla leader Giuseppe Garibaldi worked to overthrow Italy's petty despots and expel the Austrian power that supported them. Garibaldi led rebel forces in 1830, in 1848, and finally in the victorious years 1859–1860.

Success, however, came only when the cause of Italian liberation and unification was taken up by Piedmont, the northernmost, most industrially developed, and most liberal of Italian states. Piedmont's prime minister, Count Camillo di Cavour, threw his boundless energies, his diplomatic skill, and his country's small but efficient army into the struggle in the 1850s. Cavour negotiated an alliance with France for a brief war against its ancient enemy, Austria. Behind this screen of military action in the north, well-organized rebellions in much of Italy and a brilliant campaign by Garibaldi in the south freed the peninsula of its Austrian puppet rulers. Then in a plebiscite the Italians voted for unification as a constitutional monarchy under the royal house of Piedmont.

# EUROPEAN ART FROM CLASSICISM TO REALISM

## The Art of the Old Regime

By and large, literature and the arts during the 1600s and 1700s tended to suit the tastes of the two most prominent elements in the society of those two centuries: the courtly aristocracy and the rising bourgeoisie.

Courtly art produced baroque and classical styles rooted in the art of the Renaissance and the Catholic Counter-Reformation, as well as in the traditional culture of ancient Greece and Rome.

The baroque style emerged first as Catholic church art, intended to awe the faithful into acceptance of religion through the sheer grandeur of churches such as the new Saint Peter's in Rome. But secular rulers of the seventeenth century soon saw that the same baroque qualities of rich color, vitality and movement, gilt, glass, light, and sheer scale could awe their subjects into submission to absolute monarchy also.

The more restrained classical approach in painting, architecture, and sculpture differed from the baroque in many ways. It stressed balance, not movement; drawing, not color; simplicity, not complexity. In literature this approach resulted in the French classical drama at the court of Louis XIV, where writers such as Racine and Corneille shaped powerful emotions to the formal precision of hexameter verse.

Aristocrats also loved the novels of Mademoiselle de Scudéry, who earned wealth and fame and in the process created a national rage for her delicate mapping of the "tender passions" of love. And the comedies of Moliere, France's greatest comic dramatist, showed the court of the Sun king how to laugh at all the pretensions of their age. Solid Dutch burghers, bourgeois members of the French "third estate," and middle-class merchants in England, meanwhile, developed entirely different tastes in art in the 1600s and 1700s.

Painters such as Rembrandt van Rijn could depict the merchant oligarchs of the Netherlands—*The Syndics of the Cloth Guild*, say—with the sober dignity and seriousness of purpose this business elite saw as their great virtues. The French artist Jean Baptiste Chardin could paint a Parisian housewife cutting bread, or a family offering *Grace before Meat* with a simple strength that universalized these aspects of everyday bourgeois life.

In England, the most striking manifestation of middle-class taste was the development of the English novel. In Daniel Defoe's *Robinson Crusoe*, for instance, the bourgeois virtues of industry, ingenuity, common sense, perseverance, and piety that enable Robinson to conquer his island also glorified the virtues with which middle-class Europeans were mastering the material world of their own time.

## New Moods: Romanticism

In the nineteenth century, two overarching world views dominated European cultural life during that century: romanticism and materialism. Romanticism flourished during the first half of the century and enjoyed a revival in the late 1800s. Materialism predominated during the second half of the century.

Romanticism, best known for its artistic expressions, was actually a broad-gauge cultural rebellion. Romantic poets, painters, composers, and other leaders of the movement certainly thought of it as an artistic revolt. It was a demand for movement, color, emotion in the arts, and a rejection of the rigidity and aridity of classicism. It was an enthusiasm for exotic new subject matter, from medieval knights and Renaissance adventurers to Turkish harems and simple peasant cottages. It was a call for freedom, the liberation of the romantic ego from the rules of the academies and the models of the ancients and the old masters.

It was also, however, the beginning of a broad sense of cultural alienation and of a sweeping rebellion against the tyranny of human reason itself. Both of these broader aspects of the romantic revolt have persisted down to our own time.

The romantics' feeling of alienation from the dull, crass bourgeois-philistine society they lived in was very powerful. It led them to turn from society to nature, to draw strength and solace from woods and flowers, from the Alps, the sea, the wild west wind. This romantic sense of alienation drove some artists to flee the West entirely, to explore North Africa, the Middle East, or even the South Seas. And many who were not artists came to feel that they too were out of sympathy with their own time, strangers in their own land.

The romantic revolt against reason has become an even more fundamental part of Western consciousness. Romantics thought that the Enlightenment and the Scientific Revolution provided only thinly cerebral, emotionally unconvincing explanations for things. Since Plato and Aristotle, Western culture had defined humanity as the *rational* animal; now the romantics turned away from reason to glorify the emotions instead.

Love, beauty, suffering, human will, dreams, drugs, enthusiasm for such allegedly nonrational beings as peasants, savages, and children, a fascination with supernatural phenomena, mystic intuitions of God—nonrational elements flooded the romantic consciousness. "All theory, my friend, is gray," said Goethe's *Faust:* "but green is life's glad golden tree."[8] Wordsworth went even further in condemning human reason:

> Our meddling intellect
> Misshapes the beauteous forms of things;
> We murder to dissect.[9]

## New Moods: Materialism

The physical sciences, however, produced some notable advances in the 1800s. As new trends in the arts had fostered the romantic world view in the first half of the century, progress in the sciences encouraged the materialist *Weltanschauung* in the second half.

During this period scientists learned more than ever before about the nature of matter. The modern theory of the atomic and molecular structure of matter, the cellular construction of living matter, the germ theory of disease, Darwinian evolution, and much more first came to light at this time. The prestige of the sciences and the scientific method rose once again, especially after the appearance of Charles Darwin's epochal *Origin of Species* in 1859.

Darwin, an English naturalist, was a life-long student of biology and the natural world around him. His theory of "natural selection" suggested that all species of living things—including human beings—*evolve* from generation to generation. Changes occur because of the immense variety within any species, which gives some individual members an advantage in what Darwin saw as a struggle to survive and reproduce in a changing world. It was a grim theory which had no need of a God, first principle, or other creative force in a bitterly competitive universe.

With the revival of interest in scientific explanations, furthermore, there came a revival of philosophical materialism, which now found more followers than ever before.

This was not the crude commercial materialism that delights in owning material possessions. It was the more profound philosophical materialism that denies the existence of anything *but* matter.

For this school of thought, God was a myth, the human soul an illusion, humanity itself simply a somewhat more complicated ape. Claiming to be realistic rather than sentimental, hard-boiled rather than tenderhearted, materialists turned from religion to science, from poetry to economics. They agreed with the German philosopher Friedrich Nietzsche that God was dead, and with Auguste Comte, the founder of modern sociology, that if there was anything left to worship, it was rational humanity itself.

Romanticism and materialism colored the thought of their respective half centuries. Early cultural nationalists were romantics, revolutionaries of the heart; Bismarck and Cavour, who unified their countries, were hard-boiled realists, manipulators of armies and masters of diplomatic chicanery. Utopian socialists were romantic, back-to-nature communards; Marx was an atheist, a materialist, and a worshiper at the shrine of hard economic facts.

---

[8] Johann Wolfgang Goethe, *Faust, Part One*. trans. Philip Wayne (Baltimore, Md.: Penguin Books, 1949), p. 98.
[9] William Wordsworth, *The Thorn*, iii.

## Art and the Image of the Age

The arts in this divided age had one overwhelming thing in common: a fascination with the age itself, which fostered a longing to portray that age in words or pictures much as it really was.

Romantic painters, with their love for nature and for people who lived close to it, may have made their sowers and harvesters a bit more bronzed and husky, their countryside a little greener or more golden, their ocean bursting into spray a touch more sublime than nature managed. But John Constable surely got the farm wagons right in his *Hay Wain*, or Jean-François Millet the heave and strain of his laboring *Quarriers*. And if J. M. W. Turner's seascapes please us as abstract explosions of color, they also give a vivid impression of real sea and sky ablaze with sunset light.

The realist and even many impressionist and postimpressionist painters of the latter half of the nineteenth century are more likely to show us around the city and the suburbs, the world of the triumphant bourgeoisie. One can wash up at the basin in front of the mirror in the morning with Mary Cassatt (*La Toilette*), spend Sunday in the park with Georges Seurat (*La Grande Jatte*), go dancing at the *Moulin de la Galette* with Auguste Renoir, the bourgeois artist par excellence, or visit the *Moulin Rouge* with the dwarfish nightclub painter Henri de Toulouse-Lautrec. One might end the evening with the urbane Édouard Manet, having a drink at *Bock's* and visiting the celebrated prostitute *Olympia*, her small body reclining a bit stiffly on the bed, an unconvincing flower over her left ear.

The prose and poetry of the nineteenth century also offer up the age in living, breathing, sometimes exhausting detail. Jane Austen's novels of English society bring the world of the country gentry convincingly before us, with their provincial balls and journeyings, their endless concern with property and marriage, family life, common sense, and human individuality. Emily Brontë's *Wuthering Heights* takes us deep into the labyrinthine twists and turns of two tormented human hearts, showing us two passionate lives led in a bleak northern English world of harsh winds and hardened souls.

The urban realities are there too, in the immense canvases of the century's fiction. The many socially realistic novels of Honoré de Balzac give us all Paris in the first half of the century, those of Émile Zola all France in the second half. We can visit the malodorous slums of London with Charles Dickens, explore the unfamiliar world of the Russian serfs in Ivan Turgenev's *Sportsman's Sketches*, or probe with the Norwegian dramatist Henrik Ibsen the corruption behind the frock coats, frilly bodices, and formal manners of the bourgeois drawing room.

The spirit of the age is here, too, the surging emotions of nineteenth-century writers and artists. Aurore Dupin, France's most famous woman of letters, astonished her contemporaries by taking the male name of George Sand, dressing as a man, smoking cigars, and writing some of the century's best-selling novels. Her love affairs with fellow writers and with the composer Chopin were as notorious as romantic novels such as *Indiana and The Haunted Pool* were famous. George Sand hurled herself into everything she did with the passion for life she described to a friend: "To live! how wonderful, how lovely. . . . To live is to be in a state of constant intoxication! To live is happiness! To live is Heaven!"[10]

---

[10]Quoted in Bonnie S. Anderson and Judith P. Zinsser, *A History of Her Own: Women in Europe from Prehistory to the Present* (New York: HarperCollins, 1988), p. 170.

Everywhere you will find awareness of the physical realities of nineteenth-century life. When Balzac describes the boardinghouse where *Old Man Goriot* lives, we see every crack and knickknack, we hear the very boarding-house conversation over dinners a century and a half ago, When Zola takes us through *les Halles*, the vast, heaped, crowded, noisy food markets of old Paris, we can smell the rotting vegetables, see the bloom on the fruit that Paris housewives thumbed and dropped into their shopping bags a hundred years ago. Even the most Romantic poet of the nineteenth century had an eye for concrete detail that many a more modern writer might envy. Keats shows us summer woods as real as Balzac's boardinghouse as he wanders

Through verdurous glooms and winding mossy ways . . .
The murmurous haunt of flies on summer eves.[11]

The flies would never have been there in an Elizabethan sonnet; they might dominate the picture in a twentieth-century production. In the nineteenth, they were simply there, part of the richness of European culture in that last century of Europe's global domination.

## SUMMARY

Change, as we will see, was widespread in the colonized Americas, in Africa, and in Asia during the three centuries between 1600 and 1900. The most consequential changes of all, however, were those that transformed Europe during this middle-modern period.

A half-dozen great powers and dozens of smaller states divided Europe among them during the 1600s and 1700s. The first of these centuries saw the great strengthening of governmental power under royal absolutists like Louis XIV. The following century saw the rationale for royal government shift from simple divine right toward public service and enlightened rule.

During this period, two German-speaking nations, Prussia and Austria, dominated Central Europe. Russia, the sprawling backward giant of Eastern Europe, emerged as a major power for the first time under Peter the Great. And Britain, after a century of revolutionary turmoil and overseas empire-building, emerged as a model for Europe's future: constitutional government with a strong commercial base.

The rise of Europe's commercial bourgeoisie was another major trend of these centuries. Middle-class merchants and handicraft manufacturers dominated the economy and, supported by mercantilistic governments, developed the wealth of the continent. In the eighteenth century, the population also took off, beginning the greatest demographic expansion in history.

The intellectual life of the West was shaped by the Scientific Revolution of the sixteenth and seventeenth centuries and by the Enlightenment of the eighteenth. Philosophes like Voltaire and Rousseau turned the confidence in human reason toward a critique of traditional society that called all inherited institutions into question. Presid-

---

[11]John Keats, "Ode to a Nightingale," in Arthur Quiller-Couch, ed., *The Oxford Book of English Verse* (Oxford: Clavendon Press, 1939), p. 743.

ing over the exciting cultural and intellectual life of these two centuries, the salon hostess epitomized the age as a whole: cultivated, witty, aristocratic, forward-looking, and elegant.

A century of radical change in Europe began in the later 1700s, with the French Revolution (1789–1799) and the Industrial Revolution, which got under way in England in the 1760s.

The French Revolution was rooted in the deep social dislocations of the old regime and in the radical social critique of the Enlightenment. The Revolution accelerated through a series of stages and climaxed with the rise of Napoleon Bonaparte, the "man on horseback" who restored order and directed the new energies unleashed by the Revolution into the brief conquest of most of Europe. The Industrial Revolution, resulting from the coming together in Britain of a number of social, economic, and natural elements, put vast new energy sources at the disposal of the human race. The capacity to exploit these nonbiological forms of energy multiplied the economic output of the Western world many times over in the century that followed.

It was an age of intensely felt revolutionary ideologies—liberalism, nationalism, socialism, and their offshoots—and of ideological revolutions all across Europe. The 1800s spawned industrial corporations and cartels that dwarfed any earlier forms of economic organization. It was a century of expanding population, middle-class predominance, increasing pressure from the proletariat, and the birth of the modern women's movement.

Britain and France emerged as the most liberal of the European powers, Bismarck's Germany as an industrial colossus second only to Britain. Both Germany and Italy were unified in the nineteenth century, and Russia remained the most economically backward and politically autocratic of Europe's great powers.

Art also followed a complex pattern of change through these centuries. The arts of the seventeenth and eighteenth centuries reflected both courtly and bourgeois cultures. Baroque splendor and the classical emphasis on rule and order suited the dominant aristocracy. Dutch painting and the English novel appealed to middle-class audiences with their solid morality and their comfortable middle-class subjects.

The cultural history of the nineteenth century, by contrast, was dominated by romanticism, originating in the arts, and by materialism, rooted in the progress of the sciences. Romantic alienation and materialistic atheism would spread further still in the twentieth century. The arts vividly reflected the social history of the age, from realistic fiction and romantic poetry to painting of all schools.

## SUGGESTED READING

Anderson, B. S. *Joyous Greetings: The First International Women's Movement, 1830–1860*. New York: Oxford University Press, 2000. Studies of early European and American champions of women's rights. See also K. Offen's complex analysis of *European Feminisms, 1700–1950: A Political History* (Stanford: Stanford University Press, 2000) and H. Applewhite, *Women and Politics in the Age of the Democratic Revolution* (Ann Arbor, Mich.: University of Michigan Press, 1990) on women's role in the revolutions of the late 1700s and early 1800s.

Dobbin, F. *Forging Industrial Policy: The United States, Britain, and France in the Railway Age*. New York: Cambridge University Press, 1994. Stresses the role of traditional attitudes and practices in economic change.

Gay, P. *The Enlightenment*. New York: Simon & Schuster, 1974. Authoritative and insightful. See also the thoughtful analysis by one of Europe's most admired intellectual historians, E. Cassirer, *the Philosophy of the Enlightenment* (Princeton, N.J.: Princeton University Press, 1951).

Godineau, D. *The Women of Paris and Their French Revolution*. trans. K. Streip. Berkeley and Los Angeles: University of California Press, 1998. Women's contributions to the French Revolution—and their ultimate rejection by its leaders.

Goodman, D. *The Republic of Letters: A Cultural History of the French Enlightenment*. Ithaca, N.Y.: Cornell University Press, 1994. Emphasis on political culture, role of salons.

Henderson, W. O. *The Rise of German Industrial Power, 1834–1914*. Berkeley: University of California Press, 1975. Expert presentation of the economic growth that accompanied Germany's political unification and military achievements in the later nineteenth century. But see also L. L. Farrar, Jr., *Arrogance and Anxiety: The Ambivalence of German Power, 1848–1914* (Iowa City: University of Iowa Press, 1981).

Hill, C. *The Century of Revolution, 1603–1714*. New York: Norton, 1982. Survey of British history in the century of the Puritan Revolution by a leading authority, with a socio-economic slant.

Hufton, O. *The Prospect Before Her: A History of Women in Western Europe, 1500–1800*. New York: Knopf, 1996. Excellent synthesis of the scholarship.

Jones, E. L. *Growth Recurring: Economic Change in World History*. Ann Arbor: University of Michigan Press, 2000. Sees the Industrial Revolution as only the most recent manifestation of a recurring pattern of "intensive growth."

Madariaga, I. de. *Russia in the Age of Catherine the Great*. New Haven, Conn.: Yale University Press, 1981. Authoritative, with a range that goes beyond standard political treatments to economic, social, and intellectual developments.

Marx, K., and F. Engels. *Basic Writings on Politics and Philosophy*. Boston: Peter Smith, 1975. A good sample of the work of the founders of Marxism. For expert commentary, see G. Lichtheim, *Marxism: An Historical and Critical Study* (New York: Columbia University Press, 1982).

Mill, J. S. *Essential Works of John Stuart Mill*. New York: Bantam Books, 1961. Includes important works of the quintessential nineteenth-century liberal. See also his *On the Subjection of Women* (Cambridge, Mass.: MIT Press, 1970).

Monod, P. K. *The Power of Kings: Monarchy and Religion in Europe, 1589–1715*. Emergence of the nation-state in early modern Europe.

Osler, M. J., ed. *Rethinking the Scientific Revolution*. New York: Cambridge University Press, 2000. Articles exploring recent challenges to the "heroic myth" of scientific geniuses transforming our understanding of the world.

Parker, G. *The Military Revolution: Military Innovation and the Rise of the West, 1500–1800*. New York: Cambridge University Press, 1988. Military developments and their contributions to Western expansion overseas. See also M. S. Anderson, *War and Society in Europe of the Old Regime, 1618–1789* (New York: St. Martin's Press, 1988), a concise but wide-ranging study of evolving military institutions and their place in Western society.

Stearns, P. N. *The Industrial Revolution in World History*. Boulder, Colo.: Westview Press, 1993. Industrialization from the eighteenth century to the present in global perspective.

Sutherland, D. M. G. *France, 1789–1815: Revolution and Counterrevolution*. New York: Oxford University Press, 1986. Solid survey of the revolutionary period in Paris and the provinces, with attention to problems of interpretation.

Tilly, L. A., and J. W. Scott. *Women, Work, and Family*. New York: Holt, Rinehart & Winston, 1979. About women in England and France. On women in Germany, see J. C. Fout, *German Women in the Nineteenth Century: A Social History* (New York: Holmes & Meier, 1983).

Wasserstrom, J. N., L. Hunt, and M. B. Yong, eds. *Human Rights and Revolutions*. Lanham, Md.: Rowman and Littlefield, 2000. Sees the roots of the idea of human rights in the English, American, and French Revolutions—and problems with the doctrine in the twentieth century.

 Please refer to the document CD-ROM for primary sources related to this chapter.

# CHAPTER 21

# LIBERATORS AND ROBBER BARONS
## The Americas from Colonies
## to Countries
## (1770–1900)

## A Glance Ahead: New Western Nations Take Shape in the Americas

As in Europe, major changes came to the two American continents during the three centuries from 1600 to 1900. European colonies for most of this time, they moved in increasingly revolutionary directions, as Europe did. And some went considerably beyond their mother countries across the Atlantic.

During the fifty years from 1775 to 1825, most of the American colonies rebelled against European rule and carved out independent nations. From the United States in the north to Argentina and Chile in the south, the new countries established more democratic political institutions than most European countries achieved.

There were limitations, of course. Even New World democracy did not grant many rights to women, minorities, and other groups. Economically, planters and industrial tycoons flourished while lesser folk too often had to struggle to survive. And a lopsided relationship emerged as the United States grew far more rich and powerful than any of its Latin American neighbors. Nonetheless, the New World in general and the United States in particular had clearly become independent centers of power as the century turned.

## The American Revolution

### The Thirteen Colonies

From sea to shining sea, North America was a thinly settled continent during the period of European colonization. Most of the land, of course, was still inhabited primarily by Amerindian peoples, though their numbers had declined very significantly due to the spread of European diseases. The Spanish claimed much of western North America and the Gulf Coast; the French, Canada and the Mississippi Valley; the Russians, the far northwest. But a scattering of Spanish missions, French fur traders, and the odd Russian Cossack scarcely diluted the life of the indigenous population over most of the continent.

Only in one place were Europeans thick on the ground in the seventeenth and eighteenth centuries. In the English settlements along the east coast, European farms, villages, and cities steadily displaced the Indians who had lived there in 1600. Here on the Atlantic seaboard was born the expansive society that in the nineteenth century would sweep to the Pacific.

The thirteen English colonies differed from one another in important ways. The rocky New England hills of Massachusetts, Connecticut, and Rhode Island bred Puritan clergymen in the early days, flinty Yankee storekeepers, and whaling captains in later centuries. The middle colonies, including bustling New York, New Jersey, and the Quaker haven of Pennsylvania, were the breadbasket of the colonies, producing grains such as wheat and barley. The balmier southern colonies, from Maryland and Virginia down through the Carolinas to Georgia, were the plantation territories, owned by debonair American equivalents of English country squires, worked by black slaves, and producing large cash crops of tobacco and rice for export.

But the thirteen colonies, penned in between the Appalachian Mountains and the sea, had important elements in common too. They had a large population, perhaps two and a half million by 1776—a third of the population of Great Britain itself. They also had a relatively homogeneous society, the Indians having been pushed westward out of English-settled areas, the African slaves thoroughly segregated in the southern plantations. It was in some ways a more prosperous society than that of Europe, thanks to the large amounts of land available for the taking. It was almost certainly a more mobile society, in which the ability to do a job came to count for more than family background. It was even a comparatively well-educated culture, especially in the north, where the first European settlers had been dedicated Protestants, the "people of the Book."

Most important, perhaps, the thirteen English colonies were all used to a significant amount of self-government from the beginning. In Latin America, military commanders and royal officials dominated the *conquista* and the colonies. In the North American colonies, by contrast, all the settlements had assemblies of freemen who debated and determined their own affairs. New England town meetings and colonial legislatures were part of the fabric of colonial life. Royal governors and mercantilistic regulations would run afoul of these colonial assemblies throughout the later colonial period. After 1776 this tradition of self-government would provide the model—and the experience—that would bring the world's largest republic into existence in the United States.

## Washington and the Revolution

The American Revolution may be seen a dozen different ways: as a patriotic struggle for freedom, as an economic revolt against mercantilism, as an ideological clash, as a theater of towering personalities, as part of a larger "age of democratic revolutions" around the North Atlantic, as the first of what would later come to be called national liberation struggles, and on and on. In a global perspective, the primary significance of the American Revolution is perhaps twofold. It revealed the fragility of the political structure of the European intercontinental empires. Its aftermath, however, demonstrated the tenacity of Western society, culture, and interrelations once the Western predominance was firmly established beyond the seas.

Even in retrospect, the Revolution seems to have come on with remarkable suddenness. In 1763, Britain had won the Seven Years' War and stood mistress of the greatest of all the European overseas empires. The American colonies were the jewel of that empire—productive, populous, and full of promise. Almost immediately, however, the British government began an ill-considered series of mercantilist measures. These reforms were designed to increase government revenues from America after the expense of the recent war, much of which had been fought in defense of the colonies. They were also intended to tighten up London's hold on those cities, villages, and farms three thousand miles away.

Mercantilist economic regulation was not new, of course, and the measures did not seem extreme to the royal ministers who proposed them. Taxes on sugar and coffee and tea, stamp taxes on printed matter, and attempts to wipe out smuggling seemed legitimate enough in Britain—but they outraged the colonists. Decisions to quarter troops in the colonies and finally to reorganize colonial governments in order to destroy the power of their assemblies aroused violent opposition.

The colonies responded to a decade of such measures with a series of ingenious—and increasingly subversive—organizations of their own. Like contemporary radicals and revolutionists in Europe, they were endlessly inventive. They held colonial congresses and set up committees of correspondence to coordinate the activities of the colonial leadership. Some of them collected weapons and organized the riotous Sons of Liberty and the paramilitary Minutemen.

A roster of talented leaders emerged during those dozen years of crisis from 1763 to 1775. These included the aging but still witty Enlightenment intellectual Ben Franklin of

Philadelphia, the passionate spokesman Sam Adams of Boston, and his determinedly anti-British cousin John Adams. The new colonial leadership also included a group of Virginia gentlemen, among them the orator Patrick Henry, the young lawyer Thomas Jefferson, and the most impressive of the Virginians, the planter and sometime soldier George Washington.

By the spring of 1775, subversive organization and mob violence had triggered military retaliation. Troops dispatched to seize arms caches in two villages west of Boston confronted colonial militia, and the shot heard round the world was fired on the village green at Lexington.

It was more than a year, however, before the leaders of the colonial revolt, assembled at the Second Continental Congress in Philadelphia, made the break official. On July 4, 1776, Jefferson's Declaration of Independence was formally promulgated, with its ringing Lockean assertion

> That all men are created equal, that they are endowed by their Creator with certain inalienable Rights, that among these are Life, Liberty, and the pursuit of Happiness.
> That to secure these rights, Governments are instituted among men, deriving their just powers from the consent of the governed. . . .

Or, as a veteran put it, "What we meant in going for those redcoats was this: we always had governed ourselves, and we always meant to. They didn't mean we should."[1]

And so they fought. For six long years, ragtag regiments of summer soldiers fought armies of British regulars and Hessian mercenaries up and down the fifteen-hundred-mile strip of land, much of it still wilderness, between the Appalachian Mountains and the Atlantic. The colonial troops were ill trained, ill equipped, inexperienced, and given to desertion around harvest time. The Continental Congress could not supply their armies properly. Most of the colonial population was lukewarm or indifferent, and many were loyal to Great Britain. Freezing at Valley Forge, retreating from many defeats, the Revolution looked much less noble and romantic close up than it has in many a Fourth of July oration since.

But the British were an ocean away from home, the colonials frequently fighting in familiar fields and hills. There were some timely and heartening victories. The snowy midnight crossing of the Delaware to catch the Hessians unaware at Trenton is as much a part of American folklore as the grim winter at Valley Forge. Much more important was the surrender of "Gentleman Johnny" Burgoyne's army, invading from Canada, at Saratoga. On the strength of the Saratoga victory, Ben Franklin was able to negotiate the crucial French alliance that sent arms, money, and a French expeditionary force to aid the rebels against France's old rival, the English.

Above all, perhaps, there was General George Washington (1732–1799). Six feet two, pale-skinned and blue-eyed, he looked good on a horse. He was a prudent man, not imaginative, but resolute once he had decided on action. This single-minded resolution, combined with a southern planter's reserve and a natural dignity, made Washington a perfect symbol for the cause he led, as later for the nation he governed.

Washington was no Napoleon: He seldom commanded ten thousand men (Napoleon could marshal hundreds of thousands), won few battles, and rather wore his enemies out by patience than out-generaled them. British problems and the French alliance were crucial to his final success. And yet when all is said and done, Washington kept armies in the

---

[1]George Brown Tindall, *America: A Narrative History* (New York: Norton, 1984), p. 203.

field for six long years. And when the bands struck up at Yorktown in 1781, the song they played was "The World Turned Upside Down"—for it was a British army, the last of any size left in the colonies, that laid down its arms.

## The Development of Democracy

The nation that evolved over the three quarters of a century after 1781 saw itself as a new beginning in human history. The great seal of the United States proclaimed a *novus ordo seclorum,* a "new ordering of the ages." In a global context, the rise of the United States of (North) America is perhaps better seen as a new surge of Western power—and as a main road toward the climax of the Western hegemony of the world in the twentieth century.

It was, in any event, a spectacular achievement. Three aspects of the growth of the United States between the Revolution and the Civil War will be examined here: the evolution of political democracy, economic growth, and imperial expansion across the continent.

The fruit and in many ways the most important political achievement of the new country was the United States Constitution, the oldest such document in the world today.

After a decade of groping for political stability under the wartime Articles of Confederation, the thirteen United States set a constitutional convention to work, again at Philadelphia, in 1787. Balancing the interests of large and small states, fear of tyranny against the need for unity, the resulting Constitution (1789) created a strong yet flexible central government for the new republic.

Executive authority was put in the hands of an elected president with appointed officials and an army and navy at his disposal. Lawmaking power was vested in a two-house legislature balancing the claims of more and less populous states. There was an appointed but independent federal judiciary. The first ten amendments provided a Bill of Rights protecting the people against governmental encroachments on their liberties as citizens.

The power of this grudgingly accepted central government grew steadily in the hands of the men who filled the offices thus defined for the next few decades. Washington, the first president (1789–1797), brought immense prestige and even a modestly imperial style to the presidency. Alexander Hamilton, the first Secretary of the Treasury, strengthened the crucial

George Washington presides over the last day's deliberations at the Constitutional Convention of 1787. The United States Constitution, built on European liberal ideas, became itself part of the evolving Western liberal tradition. Does the picture seek to convey an impression of passionate political radicalism, flag-waving patriotism, or responsible discussion? (Courtesy of the Library of Congress)

power of the government in financial matters, and John Marshall, Chief Justice of the Supreme Court from 1801 to 1835, emphasized the authority of federal laws over those of the states. The new national capital built at "Washington City" after the turn of the century and strong national leaders such as presidents Thomas Jefferson (1801–1808) and Andrew Jackson (1829–1836) also contributed to the power of the central government in the new country.

At the same time, however, the democratic base of the Republic grew apace. Major spokesmen for popular sovereignty included Jefferson, with his faith in the American "yeomanry," the solid landowning farmers he regarded as the backbone of the nation. A more rudely democratic spokesman was Andy Jackson. A westerner and one of the few heroes of the War of 1812, Jackson became a champion of the "common man," whether he owned land or not, and a vocal opponent of effete eastern aristocrats. In such a climate, taxpayer suffrage and even universal manhood suffrage spread rapidly, till almost all adult white males could vote in America by 1850.

There were limitations to all this political democratization, of course. Millions of black slaves and Native Americans had no part in the political process in the first half of the nineteenth century. The entire female half of the population would remain disfranchised throughout the 1800s. The democratic ideal, however, was firmly established. Its own logic—and rhetoric—would in time carry it to virtually universal application, in the United States as across the Western world.

## Economic Growth and Territorial Expansion

Economic growth was also a striking feature of American history throughout the nineteenth century.

The United States had some distinct economic advantages over the Old World. These included free land in virtually unlimited quantities, which became available as rapidly as it could be taken from the sparsely distributed Indians. The United States also had at its disposal the unmeasurable natural resources of a continent that stretched westward for thousands of miles. Another advantage was a rapidly growing population, rising from less than 4 million at the time of the first census in 1790 to more than 30 million at the beginning of the Civil War—an eightfold multiplication in three generations.

A final advantage, once more, was a relatively open and mobile society, in which it was comparatively easy to move from place to place or up and down the social scale. Particularly in the expanding American West, it was what you could *do,* not who you *were,* that counted. Most people did not make fortunes or rise from rags to riches. But there were enough poor-boy millionaires and shirt-tail western senators to make getting ahead a virtue and a genuine possibility in the United States.

The American economic "miracle," as similar surges elsewhere would be labeled in the twentieth century, was a jumble of lusty work songs and sharp dealings in land, of technological innovation and public-be-damned private enterprise. Its all-encompassing justification was, quite simply, success. That it had. From the Erie Canal boom to flush times in Alabama to the California gold rush, there seemed to be no end to opportunity for Americans.

To bumper crops and burgeoning mines, furthermore, was added the unprecedented eruption of the Industrial Revolution. Crossing the Atlantic from Britain almost as quickly as it crossed the Channel to Europe, the new potential for multiplied industrial production caught the United States at precisely the right moment in its accelerating economic growth. British investment capital, technology, and large numbers of European immi-

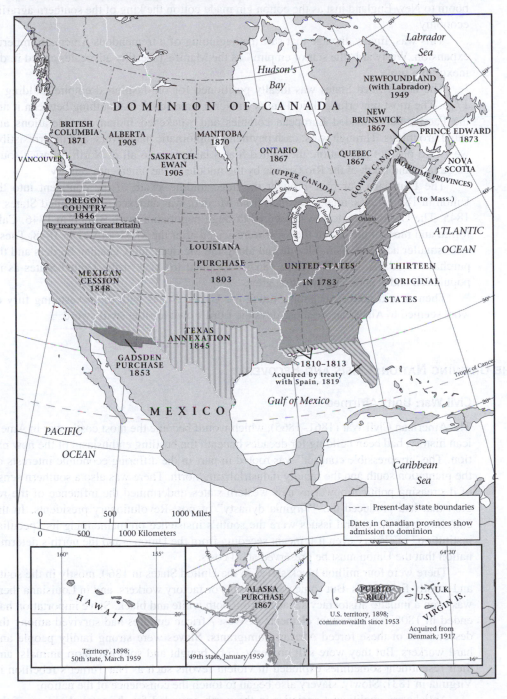

GROWTH OF THE UNITED STATES AND SOUTHERN CANADA

*Labrador Sea*

*Hudson's Bay*

NEWFOUNDLAND
(with Labrador)
1949

DOMINION OF CANADA

NEW
BRUNSWICK
1867

PRINCE EDWARD
1873

BRITISH
COLUMBIA
1871

ALBERTA
1905

MANITOBA
1870

ONTARIO
1867

QUEBEC
1867

NOVA
SCOTIA
1867
(MARITIME PROVINCES)

VANCOUVER

SASKATCH-
EWAN
1905

(UPPER CANADA)

(LOWER CANADA)

St. Lawrence R.

(to Mass.)

Lake Superior

Lake Michigan

Lake Huron

L. Erie

Ontario

OREGON
COUNTRY
1846
(By treaty with Great Britain)

LOUISIANA

PURCHASE

1803

UNITED STATES
IN 1783

THIRTEEN

ORIGINAL

STATES

*ATLANTIC*

*OCEAN*

MEXICAN
CESSION
1848

TEXAS
ANNEXATION
1845

GADSDEN
PURCHASE
1853

1810–1813

Acquired by treaty
with Spain, 1819

M E X I C O

*Gulf of Mexico*

*Tropic of Cancer*

*PACIFIC*

*OCEAN*

*Caribbean
Sea*

- - - Present-day state boundaries

Dates in Canadian provinces show
admission to dominion

0          500          1000 Miles

0     500     1000 Kilometers

H A W A I I

Territory, 1898;
50th state, March 1959

ALASKA
PURCHASE
1867

49th state, January 1959

PUERTO
RICO

U.S.

U.K.
VIRGIN IS.

U.S. territory, 1898;
commonwealth since 1953

Acquired from
Denmark, 1917

grants all made their contributions. The steam engine in the north brought an industrial boom to New England just as the cotton gin made cotton the king of the southern agrarian economy.

This was, finally, the age that saw the beginning of a tremendous American imperial expansion. Westward "the star of empire," as the Manifest Destiny advocates called it, did inexorably move.

The new United States was ideally positioned for old-fashioned empire building in 1776. The most powerful political entity in North America, it had nothing between it and the Pacific but untended European colonies and weakened Indian confederations and tribal groupings. Through wars, cash payments, diplomatic maneuvers, and the irresistible westward push of population, the United States laid claim to all of North America south of Canada and north of the Rio Grande by the middle of the nineteenth century.

The Louisiana Purchase brought the huge middle swath of the continent into the Union in 1803. Texas, after it revolted from Mexico, was annexed to the United States in 1845. The Oregon Territory was secured through negotiation with Britain in 1846. California and most of the rest of the West were seized after the Mexican War in 1848. These, with smaller acquisitions in Florida and along the Mexican and Canadian borders and the purchase of Alaska from Russia in 1867, multiplied the size of the United States as its population and economic production grew.

Then at mid-century, calamity struck the United States with the devastating fury of what seemed to Americans of those days the Lord's own terrible swift sword.

## The Growing Nation: Crisis and Recovery

### Civil War: Unity Affirmed

The American Civil War (1861–1865), which would become the most costly war in American history, had been building for decades beneath the bustling enthusiasm of the new nation. The "irrepressible conflict" was rooted in part in the differing economic interests of the plantation south and the rapidly industrializing north. There was also a southern sense of decreasing political power as new western states undermined the influence of the region that had produced the "Virginia dynasty" of post-Revolutionary presidents. In the end, however, the central issues were the south's insistence on maintaining its "peculiar institution" of slavery even if it meant seceding from the Union—and the north's determination that the Union must be preserved at all costs.

There were four million black slaves in the United States in 1860, mostly in the south and mostly field hands. But some were artisans or factory workers, and in Louisiana there was even a mulatto aristocracy set apart from both white and black. Slave importation had ended in 1808, but important elements of West African cultures had survived among the descendants of these forced African immigrants. Slaves were strong family people and hard workers. But they were still property, to be bought and sold like farm animals; and their resentment sometimes exploded in violent revolts such as Nat Turner's rebellion in Virginia in 1831. Slowly, slavery also began to touch the conscience of the nation.

Antislavery abolitionist societies in the north crusaded for the total abolition of the peculiar institution in the decades before the Civil War. The "underground railway" smuggled runaway slaves north to Canada and freedom. Free-Soilers fought with rifles to keep new states such as Kansas free of slavery. Harriet Beecher Stowe's sociologically unconvincing but morally powerful *Uncle Tom's Cabin* moved the nation, and abolitionist John Brown's bloody raid on Harper's Ferry in 1859 shocked it. Senators and congressmen thundered and maneuvered, seeking to avoid what to many seemed the ultimate catastrophe: southern secession from the Union.

But no crusade or compromise could cut the Gordian knot. The United States, said Abraham Lincoln, could not long endure half slave and half free. "The crimes of this guilty land," John Brown declared on the day he was hanged, "will never be purged away, but with blood."[2]

When Lincoln was elected president in 1860, the southern states began to secede and to organize themselves into the Confederate States of America. In the spring of 1861, southern troops fired on a U.S. fort on an island in Charleston harbor, South Carolina, and the Civil War was begun.

Both sides entered the war confident of victory. The Union under President Lincoln had three quarters of the free population, two thirds of the railways, four fifths of the industry, and most of the nation's wealth. The Confederacy under its hastily elected president, Jefferson Davis, had many of the most experienced military commanders, the patriotic and tactical advantage of fighting in defense of its own soil, and the powerful card of cotton exports, with which it hoped to win crucial support from European textile manufacturing nations such as Great Britain.

Southern generals did, in fact, more than compensate for superior northern numbers in the early years of the war. Robert E. Lee, "Stonewall" Jackson, and the brilliant cavalry commander J. E. B. "Jeb" Stuart repeatedly outmaneuvered and reversed northern advances. Later in the struggle, however, Lee met his match in generals such as the implacable Ulysses S. Grant and William Tecumseh Sherman. And the south, for all its dash and valor, never had a monopoly on courage.

Above all, the north had President Abraham Lincoln (1861–1865). Tall and gaunt, his hair and beard ill combed and his eyes somber and hollow, Lincoln cut an unprepossessing figure in his stovepipe hat and habitual suit of solemn black. But he was a skillful manipulator of people and patronage, a speaker whose eloquence can move us still, and a man in whom confidence in his cause—the salvation of the Union—combined with an immense compassion for all who suffered in that time of national trial.

The war Lincoln fought to a successful conclusion was the bloodiest in the history of the United States, before or since. The basic Union strategy was to blockade the south by sea and cut it off from the west before invading, destroying the southern armies, and ending the secession. Lee and the southern generals fought to defend territory and strove mightily to win victories—especially on northern soil—that might bring them foreign help. In the end, it was the northern strategy that worked.

Lee's greatest effort carried him as far north as Gettysburg, Pennsylvania, where in July 1863 Pickett's famous charge carried across a long and bloody mile to the crest of Cemetery Ridge, to break at last in the acrid powder smoke and the crash of Union guns—and fall away. It was the high tide of the Confederacy—the high tide and the turn.

Ahead lay even bloodier battles in the west and south, and Sherman's notorious scorched-earth march southeast to Atlanta and then on to the sea. Ahead too was the awe-

---

[2]Stephen B. Oates, *To Purge This Land with Blood: A Biography of John Brown* (New York: Harper & Row, 1970), p. 351.

Abraham Lincoln, perhaps America's most admired president, is shown here without the familiar beard. A shrewd politician beneath his legendary folksy stories, Lincoln presided over the costly effort that preserved the Union and freed the slaves. Often described as homely, the tall, gangly Lincoln made a good impression as an orator and debater "on the stump" addressing large outdoor crowds. (Library of Congress)

some silence at Appomattox, where Lee laid down his arms in 1865—and the last shot, less than a week later, when a mad actor put a bullet through President Lincoln's brain.

Six hundred thousand men had died. The Union was preserved, the slaves freed. A nation "conceived in liberty and dedicated to the proposition that all men are created equal" had survived its most terrible ordeal.

## The Gilded Age

The decades that followed the Civil War were perhaps the grubbiest in the history of American politics. Economically, however, the nation boomed as never before. And U.S. expansive energies continued to manifest themselves, filling the American west and reaching out beyond the seas for a share of the world's trade and empire.

After the war to save the Union, the nation as a whole turned its back on political crusades and sank into a period of corruption and cynical disregard for the public welfare seldom matched in its history. Ineffectual presidents, state machines, big-city bosses, and legislators who cheerfully peddled their votes to big business dominated the political scene.

In the south, the old white aristocracy soon re-emerged. Blacks, freed without land, were reduced to share-cropping, working for landowners for a never sufficient share of the crops they grew. In the decades around 1900, hooded terrorists such as Ku Klux Klanners and a series of Jim Crow laws reduced blacks to second-class status at best, segregated, discriminated against, and denied even the basic right to vote.

Farmers' organizations did agitate for reform, and labor unions painfully took shape during the later nineteenth century. Some big-city bosses seem to have served the useful purpose of giving immigrants and other otherwise neglected citizens a bit of patronage in return for their votes. By and large, however, it was a dismal time politically.

Economically, however, the nation grew even faster than it had before the war. Resources were still seemingly limitless, and the population was doubling every quarter century. Vast amounts of capital were available, much of it from Europe, and technological advance was accelerating. What now amounted to a national faith in rags-to-riches entrepreneurship drove the nation to still greater efforts. Under such circumstances, the economic success of the continental republic was perhaps not surprising.

But it was certainly dazzling. In the decades after the Civil War, railroads stretched from sea to sea, till the United States had more miles of track than all Europe combined. The output of U.S. factories tripled from 1877 to 1892 alone. By the end of the century, the United States was both the world's leading agricultural producer and the world's leading manufacturer.

As in Europe, big business developed in the United States at this time. The railroads were the first huge corporations, hiring armies of workers and buying up great expanses of western lands. The names of financial giants such as J. Pierpont Morgan and industrial empire builders such as Andrew Carnegie, the steel king, and John D. Rockefeller of Standard Oil became household words. Master organizers and employers of skilled managers, they learned to cut waste, buy and build in depressed times, and pyramid their holdings. Ruthless competitors, willing to use rebates, stock watering, and other shady or illegal devices, they became greater monopolists than their European contemporaries.

To muckraking reformers, these "robber barons" were symbols of monopoly capital and industrial exploitation. To admirers and would-be imitators, they were embodiments of what Americans were already thinking of as the American success story.

The climax of the westward expansion and the beginning of the nation's reach for empire overseas added to the sense of Yankee progress. It was a gaudy, giddy time, and they called it, if not a true golden age, at least a gilded one.

## The Independence of American Women

Women's lives in this colorful time were as varied in North America as in Europe. Recent research has reminded us of the brutal lives of women in New England mills in the earlier 1800s and in the sweatshops of New York's garment district around 1900. We have learned that pioneer women went west not only with their husbands and children, but on their own or as heads of families. Middle-class American women seem to have earned a particular reputation, especially toward the end of the century, for independence of mind and forthright strength of character. They toured Europe alone, or ran mission stations on isolated Pacific atolls. Europeans found them rather *too* independent; Asians found them inscrutable.

As in Europe, American women were likely to be involved in social causes, from the abolition of slavery to the emancipation of women themselves. They broke into the professions on this side of the Atlantic too, and were soon demanding the vote. There were many women writers in the United States, from Harriet Beecher Stowe before the Civil War to the reclusive poet Emily Dickinson and the great novelist Edith Wharton after it.

As early as 1848—the revolutionary year in Europe—the Seneca Falls Convention of reformist and radical women announced in the words of the American Declaration of Independence: "We hold these truths to be self-evident: that all men *and women* are created equal . . ." They also declared that "all laws which prevent women from occupying such a station in society as her conscience shall dictate . . . are contrary to nature, and therefore of no force or authority."[3]

---

[3]"Declaration of the Seneca Falls Convention" in S.A. Kraditor, *Up from the Pedestal: Selected Writings . . . in American Feminism* (Chicago: Quadrangle Books, 1968), pp. 184, 187.

But American middle-class women also found themselves considered too fine and delicate for politics, business, science, and other careers deemed suitable only for the ruder clay and more rational heads of men. In America even more than in Europe, descending from this unsolicited pedestal would be a problem for the following century.

## Problems of the Growing Nation

Socially speaking, the whole of the nineteenth century in the United States is perhaps best described by that most overworked of historical clichés, an age of contrasts.

Fourth of July speakers tirelessly reiterated that the great republic was the homeland of freedom, equality, opportunity, and hope. Equally impassioned—if rather less numerous—radicals pointed out that these great gifts were distributed quite unevenly among the classes, races, sexes, and other groups that made up the nation. And there was significant truth in both views.

The oldest Americans had essentially no share at all in the benefits of the new democratic-industrial state. Defeated in endless petty wars, betrayed by one broken treaty after another, Native Americans were chivied into "Indian territories" and "reservations" farther and farther west and on increasingly barren tracts of land. Here they lived according to what was left of their old ways, infected by whiskey and guns, tempted either to surrender to the lure of the conqueror's world or to rebel futilely against it.

Black Americans, still clustered very largely in the south, also had little or no part in American growth and self-government. A few blacks did move north to begin building a genuine black bourgeoisie in cities such as Chicago. Others began to construct a base for black advancement in the south itself through educational institutions such as Hampton Institute in Virginia and Tuskegee Institute in Georgia. A start was thus made, though in the nineteenth century it was no more than that.

Another frequently victimized group comprised the millions of new immigrants who poured into the country, primarily in search of economic opportunity but also to escape even more rigidly hierarchical societies in the Old World. Most of these newcomers were still Europeans, still mostly from northern and Western Europe. Some, however, were East Asians, Chinese, and Japanese, many recruited across the Pacific to help build the western end of the transcontinental railroad—while Irish immigrants built the eastern end.

Whether they came to lay rails, to farm the endless western plains opened up to homesteaders, or to practice European trades in the ghettos of eastern cities, the newest comers were likely to be cheated, exploited, and discriminated against. They would typically require a couple of generations to achieve even an uneasy integration into their new country.

Farmers in the United States also had their share of problems in the latter part of the nineteenth century. Declining crop prices, unprotected markets, deflation, and mortgage debt ground them down year after year. Extortionate railway rates and an unfortunate surge of droughts, floods, and blizzards around 1890 added to their miseries. Many farmers were driven into bankruptcy, others into militant farmers' organizations such as the Grange or to radical agitators like "Sockless" Jerry Simpson, "Cyclone" Davis, and Mary E. Lease, who urged farmers to raise "less corn and more hell."

American labor also organized during the closing decades of the century, forming embattled unions, staging strikes that were often suppressed by hired strikebreakers or even the National Guard. Waves of unemployment in the depressions of the last quarter of the century added to the bitterness of laboring people. Organizations such as the Knights

# Voices from the Past

This description of New York "sweat shops" is from an address delivered by Ida Van Etten, a pioneer organizer of women workers, before the American Federation of Labor in 1890. Van Etten's goal was to get the A. F. of L. to undertake the unionization of exploited women workers, whose miserable working conditions she had observed first-hand. What does Ms. Van Etten say about the hours and wages of these workers? What nouns and adjectives communicate her attitude toward this institution? Do you think her partisan attitude may have affected her judgment of the "sweating" system, or would you say it was the other way around?

> *"Any review of the condition of women workers, however brief, would be incomplete without an exposition of the "sweating" system—a system which thrives upon the ignorance of the newly-arrived immigrants, the miseries and misfortunes of the very poor and upon the helplessness of women and little children, which pays no regular rate of wages and has no prescribed hours of work. . . .*
>
> *Neither capital nor skill are requisite for a sweater, only the heartlessness and cunning of a slave-driver. He is usually one of the workmen who saves enough money to hire a room in a tenement house, buys or rents a few machines, for which he charges his employees three dollars a month, obtains a supply of work for some large manufacturer of cloaks or ready-made clothing, secures his 'hands' and begins business.*
>
> *These 'sweater's' dens are always located in the most wretched, overcrowded tenement house districts. He has no scale of wages, but pays the lowest that he can possibly induce his miserable victims to work for. He trades upon the unhappiness and misfortunes of the dwellers in the neighborhood. . . .*
>
> *One of the most frightful features of the "sweating" system is the unchecked employment of very young children. In these districts it is no unusual sight to see children of five, six, or even four years, employed all day sewing on buttons, pulling out bastings, or carrying huge piles of work to and from the 'sweater's' shop."*

Ida Van Etten, "The Sweating System, Charity, and Organization," in Nancy F. Cotti, ed., *Root of Bitterness: Documents of the Social History of American Women* (Boston: Northeastern University Press, 1972), pp. 327–328.

of Labor and the American Federation of Labor and leaders such as the AFL's Samuel Gompers could boast few victories in the 1880s and 1890s. Genuine improvement for factory workers, as for farmers, lay two generations ahead, in the New Deal of the 1930s.

## Reformers and Imperialists

The United States however, enjoyed an impressive political renaissance in the decades around 1900. It was called Progressivism, and it was the first of the great waves of reform that would sweep across the United States during the twentieth century.

The Populist reform agitation of the 1890s, the militance of farmers, and the struggles of organized labor all contributed to the emergence of the Progressive movement. So did a fastidious genteel tradition of disgust at the crooked politics and vulgar greed of America's urban political bosses, corrupt legislators, and new-rich industrialists over the decades since the Civil War. A major source of the Progressive revolt, finally, was a turn-of-the-century surge of investigative reporting by journalists and popular historians called muckrakers.

Beginning on the state and local levels, Progressivism stressed increased democracy, challenges to political bosses and party machines, and greater efficiency in government. Progressives also emphasized regulation of big business through such measures as trust-busting—the breakup of corporations so big that they constituted "conspiracies in restraint of trade." The movement also sought some social legislation, including labor laws, tried to help the poor generally, and renewed the struggles for women's rights and "temperance," the outlawing of alcoholic beverages.

During the first two decades of the twentieth century, the Progressive movement produced two of the most active and influential presidents in American history: the Republican Theodore Roosevelt (1901–1909) and the Democrat Woodrow Wilson (1913–1921).

Roosevelt busted some trusts—including Standard Oil—regulated the worst abuses of the railroads, meat-packers, and others, and passed some legislation designed to improve working conditions in factories. He was an early conservationist, nationalizing large chunks of wilderness and other natural resources to save them from private developers for the nation as a whole. He was no radical, however, and his Progressivism was directed rather toward equalizing competitive opportunities for all than toward government care for the unfortunate.

Wilson also began relatively conservatively. During his first term he reformed the tariff in the direction of free trade, stabilized the banking system by establishing regional Federal Reserve banks, and set the Federal Trade Commission to regulating interstate commerce. In 1916, however, he was caught up in a new surge of Progressive reform activity, including credit for farmers in need of loans, an eight-hour working day for factory hands, and other social legislation.

The other side of the American coin in 1900 was the rise of American imperialism.

American overseas expansion was for many simply a natural extension of the continental expansion of the nineteenth century. Indeed, the United States had already purchased Alaska from the Russians (1867) and taken over Hawaii from its last queen, annexing the islands in 1898. American traders had in fact been jostling Europeans in the "China market" on the far side of the Pacific for the better part of the preceding century.

The Spanish-American War of 1898, however, not only added the Philippines to the scattered Pacific holdings of the United States, it began several decades of aggressive U.S. intervention in the affairs of Middle America and the Caribbean. Teddy Roosevelt encouraged a Central American revolution and then acquired what became the Panama Canal Zone from the victorious revolutionaries in 1903. Woodrow Wilson intervened twice in the great Mexican Revolution that began in 1911. The U.S. Marines also landed to calm troubled regimes and make the Caribbean safer for foreign investors in Nicaragua, Haiti, and elsewhere.

Roosevelt called it the Big Stick; Wilson described it as instruction in democracy; critics labeled it Dollar Diplomacy.[4] In fact, the motives seem to have been a familiar Western imperialist mix of vested economic interests, a missionary zeal for spreading stable democratic government, strategic concerns, and a sense of cultural superiority. Imperial intervention by the United States, as by the other powers, kindled bitter resentment. The Philippines in particular, far from expressing gratitude for liberation from Spain, launched an insurrection against their new American rulers that took years to suppress and cost the United States as much in international approval—and self-esteem—as the Boer War did the British.

---

[4]Teddy Roosevelt made the West African proverb, "Speak softly—and carry a big stick" one of his trademarks.

For Americans, then, the twentieth century began with a mixture of domestic reforms and foreign wars that would become familiar as the decades passed.

# LATIN AMERICA EMERGES

## The Latin American Colonies

The Iberian colonies in the Western Hemisphere were a century older and many times larger than the English colonies on the east coast of North America. Portugal's Brazilian colony alone, occupying half of South America, was almost as large as the continental United States. Spanish America included the rest of South America, the Central American isthmus and most of the Caribbean, Mexico, and much of what is today California, Texas, and Florida, with the southwest and the Gulf Coast in between. By contrast with Britain's compact strip of colonies—a fraction of the future United States—these continental expanses of colonial territory to the south must have strained any early-modern European government.

The population of colonial Latin America was also much more complex than that of the British colonies that would come to master North America. To the large numbers of Amerindians who survived the brutalities of the conquest, the victorious Europeans added masses of African slaves. The result was a tripartite population, like that of colonial North America but less rigidly segregated, peoples of European, African, and Asian descent—the Amerindian population—mingling as they did nowhere else in the world.

This demographic pattern was further complicated by powerfully felt social divisions. There were, in the first place, two groups of Europeans. The peninsulars, primarily officials sent out from Spain or Portugal to govern the colonies, were the ruling elite in the colonial period. *Criollos,* European-descended Latin Americans born in the colonies, composed the provincial aristocracy of mine and plantation owners who would inherit power when the colonies broke free in the nineteenth century.

A final subdivision with a long future were the *mestizos,* Latin Americans of mixed racial background, descended primarily from European and Indian ancestors. This vigorous group belied every racial stereotype of the evils of "race mixing." Minor officials, petty tradesmen, and the like in colonial times, when they were discriminated against, they would emerge as the dominant cultural and political force in twentieth-century Latin America.

This vast expanse and complex population were administered through most of the colonial period in three colonial jurisdictions. These were the viceroyalty of New Spain (from California and Texas through Mexico to Central America), the viceroyalty of Peru (Spanish-speaking South America), and the Portuguese colony of Brazil. Viceroys, captains general, bishops, and other high-ranking officials were sent out from Spain and Portugal to govern, primarily in the interests of the crown. These men, many of whom were bureaucrats with little first-hand knowledge of the huge territories they administered, necessarily depended on local people and lower-ranking officials for the real work of running the colonies.

There were no town meetings or colonial assemblies to resist the authority of the Crown in Latin America, as there were in British North America. But there were the *audencias,* judicial boards whose members also served as advisors to viceroys and sometimes resisted misguided viceregal policies. At the local level there were small town councils usually dominated by the *criollo* elite. And there were local representatives of the Crown, minor officials often more interested in lining their own pockets than advancing any policies, royal or *criollo.*

A more positive view of much of the colonial experience can also be taken, however. The neglect of the colonies by weakened and impoverished mother countries in the seventeenth century may be seen as a form of benign neglect that allowed local people to solve local problems. And in the eighteenth century, the Bourbon kings of Spain in particular embarked upon a campaign of enlightened reforms that had very positive effects. These included efforts at administrative, legal, and financial reform, as well as encouragement of agriculture and local industry and the building of churches and schools. Thanks at least in part to these manifestations of the spirit of the European Enlightenment, there seems to have been a surge of genuine prosperity toward the end of the colonial period, in the later eighteenth and early nineteenth centuries.

Colonial Latin America was indeed a backwater. But in many ways it was a backwater that worked.

## The Spirit of Revolt

Into this somnolent world on the far side of the Atlantic a new spirit intruded around 1800—the spirit of revolution.

Social, economic, and political resentments had been building up for centuries among a variety of colonial groups. Conquered Indians resented the conquest and all the subsequent oppression. Black slaves were never reconciled to slavery. *Mestizos,* cut off by prejudice from all other communities, envied the power of their fathers' European world and resented the oppression of their mothers' non-European people. *Criollos,* the chief builders of the colonial economy, saw no justice in the privileged social position and the political authority enjoyed by peninsular judges, bishops, military commanders, captains general, and viceroys.

In the late eighteenth century, the subversive intellectual influences of the Enlightenment made themselves felt along with the enlightened reforms of the Bourbons. Satirical

This lovely old church in Oaxaca state, southern Mexico, illustrates the appeal of Hispanic colonial civilization. Monastery churches like this one often integrated European architectural styles into picturesque New-World environments. (Anthony Esler)

Voltairian attacks on foppish aristocrats and worldly churchmen applied as well in the New World as in the Old. Rousseauian talk of government by popular consent had as much appeal to colonials in South America as in North America.

Then revolt broke out, in the 1770s in Britain's North American colonies and in the late 1780s in France itself. Under such circumstances, some sort of revolution in Latin America, where there were as many grounds for discontent as in either North America or Europe, is surely not surprising.

The most oppressed rebelled first—Indians in South America and black slaves in the Caribbean.

Tupac Amaru, who claimed descent from the Incas, was Jesuit-educated and wealthy. Nevertheless, he led a 1780 revolt of the brutally exploited Indians of the Peruvian Andes that briefly liberated Bolivia and parts of Peru and Argentina. Toussaint L'Ouverture, grandson of an African king, was a Haitian slave who had made his own fortune. Inspired by the French Revolution, he launched a ten-year rebellion against the French planters in Haiti (1791–1801). Tupac Amaru was captured and executed, many thousands of his followers slaughtered, his insurrection suppressed. Toussaint L'Ouverture freed Haiti but was betrayed to his enemies and died in a French prison. But the flame had been lit, in both South America and the Caribbean, and it would not go out.

## Latin American Wars for Independence

Ironically, it was not the North American or French Revolution that triggered Latin America's fifteen years of revolutionary upheaval, but the great empire builder Napoleon Bonaparte. Napoleon conquered both Spain and Portugal in the early 1800s and put puppet kings on their thrones. Even royalists in the Latin American colonies turned against these usurping monarchs in Madrid and Lisbon.

Three major Latin American Wars for Independence ran their long and often bloody course between 1810 and 1824. There was a revolution in Mexico, pioneered by Father Hidalgo; another in northern South America, led by Simón Bolívar; and a third in southern South America, under the leadership of José de San Martín.

Mexican independence was declared in 1810 by a reforming village priest named Father Miguel Hidalgo y Costilla in the hamlet of Dolores, a hundred miles north of Mexico City. Hidalgo's Sunday sermon on September 16, 1810, before a congregation of poor *mestizos* and Indians, gave the revolution its battle cry, the famous *grito de Delores:* For Freedom and the Virgin of Guadalupe—Death to the Spaniards!

After this inspirational beginning, however, ill-armed and often poorly led hordes of Indians and *mestizos* made little headway against Spanish troops. Father Hidalgo himself was captured and shot. In 1820, however, a liberal revolution in Spain had the paradoxical effect of stimulating wealthy Mexican *criollos* to revolt—against the spreading infection of liberalism from the mother country! At their head was a rich and calculating man—and a formerly successful military commander *against* Hidalgo's rebellion—named Augustín de Iturbide. Iturbide joined the rebels he had once fought, and in 1821 he led a victorious coalition army into Mexico City. Mexico, and with it all of Central America, was liberated at last.

Simón Bolívar (1783–1830), the liberator of northern South America, was an eloquent, dramatic man with a flair for grand schemes and public triumphs. Born to wealthy parents in Caracas, raised by tutors steeped in Rousseau, well traveled in Napoleonic Europe, Bolívar felt himself destined for revolutionary leadership. A rare combination of intellectual and man of action, he was widely read in the Enlightenment and totally committed to freedom in all its forms. He freed his own slaves, promoted members of all classes and races, and tried to persuade his fellow *criollos* to distribute land to peasants and emancipate their slaves.

Bolívar's fifteen-year revolutionary career began with his participation in an abortive insurrection in Caracas in 1810, stimulated by the Napoleonic conquest of Spain. There followed a period of repeated setbacks and exiles in various Caribbean islands—including liberated Haiti. Victories began to come when Bolívar organized the interior of Venezuela and forged an alliance with the *llaneros,* the wild cowboys of the Venezuelan grasslands. He liberated neighboring Colombia first, then swung back to free Venezuela in 1821. Ecuador came next, and the three territories were thereupon united in the short-lived Republic of Gran Colombia.

Thereafter, Simón Bolívar presided over the freeing of Bolivia and Peru. But here the way had already been paved by the liberator of the south—San Martín.

José de San Martín (1778–1850) was a career military officer from Argentina, and a much quieter, more self-effacing man than the mercurial Bolívar. Tall and dark, courteous and simple in his habits, San Martín was a rigorous disciplinarian who cared for the welfare of his troops. He was also a skilled organizer and a general with a rare gift for grand strategy. He clearly ranks with Bolívar as one of the two great leaders of the Latin American revolutions.

Argentina had been in turmoil for years over the same sort of antimercantilist, free-trade issue that had agitated the North American colonies. Napoleon's invasion of Spain led leading citizens of Buenos Aires to declare their independence of the French emperor's puppet ruler in Madrid in 1810.

San Martín took service under the new regime and soon set to work on his grand strategy. The center of Spanish power in South America was in Peru, and San Martín proposed to attack that power base by a great flanking movement across the Andes and north through Chile. Practically single-handed, he organized a military expedition, led his Army of the Andes over the towering mountain barrier, and crushed the Spanish troops in Chile with a series of striking victories in 1817 and 1818. Thereafter he moved with greater caution north to Peru, maneuvered his way into Lima, and then sought an alliance with Bolívar for a final blow at the Spanish military in Peru.

A famous "meeting of the liberators" in Ecuador in 1822, however, revealed personal and political differences between the two men that were too great to bridge. San Martín therefore graciously stood aside, and it was Bolívar's troops who dealt Spanish arms in the Americas a final resounding defeat in the Battle of Ayacucho—Latin America's Yorktown—high in the Andes in 1824.

The independence of Brazil came much more quietly in 1822. The liberation of this largest of Latin American colonies occurred several years after the Portuguese royal family fled to Rio to escape Napoleon. During this period Brazil had gained valued rights, including the right whose denial by the Crown had exercised so many of the colonies—free trade. When an 1820 revolution in Lisbon threatened to countermand these new privileges, events were set in motion that brought full independence to Brazil with a minimum of violence. Alone among the new Latin American nations, Brazil was a constitutional monarchy—under the crown prince of the Portuguese ruling house—rather than a republic.

Paraguay and Uruguay, located between Brazil and Argentina, attained their freedom in a tangle of politics between their powerful neighbors. By 1824 all the Latin American states except a few small colonies around the Caribbean had won their independence. A saga of colonial revolt that began a half century before, in 1776, was ended.

## THE NEW COUNTRIES: *CAUDILLOS* AND PROGRESS

### The Reign of the *Caudillos*

The Latin American revolutions had been more protracted and much more costly in lives and property than the revolt of the thirteen colonies. It had been much closer to a social revolution, pitting *criollos* against peninsulars, and sometimes Indians and *mestizos* against the European power structure as a whole. But the result was no more a social transformation south of the Rio Grande than north of it.

Royal authority had been replaced by republican constitutions in most places, peninsular officials by a *criollo* ruling class, and mercantilistic regulation by free trade. But the basic economic and social structure of the region remained largely as it had been before, as we will see presently.

There were some political changes, however—not all of them for the best. There were, in the first place, a number of other wars and revolutions in the decades following the Wars of Independence. Some of these later conflicts led to major transfers of territory from one new state to another. Other clashes led to the fragmentation of some of the newly independent nations. Still others created a chronic political instability within the new countries.

Among the most important fragmentations of new nations was that of the United Provinces of Central America, which split into half a dozen Central American countries. Bolívar's Gran Colombia was divided into Venezuela, Colombia, and Ecuador. Uruguay also managed to make good its secession from southern Brazil.

Revolutions were common within the new nations of Latin America. Regionalism, which led to the Civil War in the United States, was equally prevalent in the new states to the south. There also, the hinterlands tended to resist the encroaching power of the industrializing cities. Such circumstances led to frequent civil wars and changes of government by force.

Central to this chronic political instability and endemic military conflict was a political phenomenon common almost everywhere in Latin America—the rise of *caudillismo,* the reign of the *caudillo.*

All these new countries had emerged from the Wars of Independence with constitutions, political parties, and civil liberties—at least on paper. In fact, however, political power usually devolved upon local strong men called *caudillos*. These backcountry military chiefs seem frequently to have embodied traditional sources of authority in the countryside: They owned large estates, concluded marriage alliances, performed and received favors. But they also reflected the breakdown of central authority and the burgeoning power of the gun, which were among the by-products of the revolutions. *Caudillos* were above all commanders of military force and beneficiaries of the popular respect for courage and strength that was bred into these descendants of the conquistadores.

Most of the *caudillos* were thus local warlords who championed the autonomy of the regions against the centralizing efforts of the new capital cities. Sometimes, however, a *caudillo* would seize national power himself, bringing the violence and crudity of the backwoods to the center of national life. Examples included the dictatorship of Bolívar's lieutenant José Páez (1830–1848) in Venezuela after the liberator's death; the brutal regime of Manuel de Rosas (1829–1832) and his equally ruthless and Machiavellian wife, Doña Encarnación, in Argentina; and the inept rule of General Santa Anna in Mexico (1834–1855).

As military dictators, *caudillos* were frequently brutal; as country people, many of them were unlearned, even—in the eyes of more polished Latin Americans—barbarous. Secret police, organized mob violence, land confiscations, and executions were notorious adjuncts of many of these dictatorships. On the other hand, *caudillos* were sometimes quite popular with the poor. They shared the values and prejudices of peons and gauchos, and they saw to it that at least some of their patronage filtered down to the village level.

By the end of the century, however, *caudillo* rule was giving way to a new bourgeois class of progress-minded centralizers. These were the architects of the substantial economic advances of the end of the century, to which we now turn.

## Economic Problems: Haciendas and Dependency

Nineteenth-century Latin American economic history is normally divided around 1880. During the half century between independence in the 1820s and the 1870s, the typical Latin American country remained a hacienda economy of separate regions and *caudillo* politics. From the 1880s on, exports and foreign dependency increased, and with these economic changes the authority of central governments and port cities.

Through most of the century, then, the central Latin American economic institution remained the hacienda, the huge plantation or ranch operated by a *criollo* landowner with Indian, *mestizo,* or black labor. Slavery was abolished earlier in South America than in North America—as early as the 1810s and 1820s in Argentina, Mexico, and Central America. Throughout Latin America, however, Indian and *mestizo* workers remained peons, landless laborers bound by unending debt to their masters. The Wars of Independence brought little change to the life of the European-descended hacienda aristocracy, or to that of the laborers on West Indian sugar plantations, Argentine ranches and wheat fields, and in Bolivian mines.

From the 1880s through the early decades of the twentieth century, however, foreign exports increased phenomenally. These exports were largely agricultural products and minerals: sugar, bananas, coffee, wheat, meat, and wool, as well as silver, copper, lead, and tin, all boomed as export products. Swelling profits from the sale of commodities like these stimulated great increases in foreign investment in Latin America and in Latin American imports of foreign manufactured goods. Argentina, Uruguay, and other progressive countries also used some of their earnings from exports for railways, roads, schools, and other reforms. Commodity exports looked to some like the road to progress for Latin America.

Actually, as recent scholarship has stressed, increases in exports also increased the dependency of Latin American countries on more developed nations—Britain especially in the nineteenth century, the United States in the twentieth. The nations of the south borrowed their capital and bought their manufactured goods overseas, while their own industrial production scarcely developed. The end of the century saw boom times for the merchants of port cities and for the landed producers of export products, but the average Latin American worker earned little more in 1900 than in 1800.

In politics too, it sometimes seemed as if the more things changed, the more they stayed the same. Regionalism declined, thanks to the new transportation and communications nets and to the increasing power of large cities. The local power of the *caudillo* thus diminished, and with the loss of his regional base, the chances of his seizing national power also declined.

Yet military rule, political violence, and corruption remained almost as common after 1880 as before. The rough-and-ready *caudillo* was replaced by a spit-and-polish professional military officer—but the latter still felt an obligation to intervene in politics. The goals of the new juntas—Order and Progress—might have a more disinterested ring than the blatant self-aggrandizement of the *caudillo,* but civil government and civil liberties still failed to develop. Corruption at the lower levels of government, finally, remained as common in South America as in North America in the later 1800s.

## Latin American Women

Colonial European standards continued to be urged on Latin American women in the nineteenth century. Religious piety, sexual chastity and fidelity, and obedient dependence on fathers or husbands were enjoined upon them from childhood. Domestic duties filled most of their adult lives, and laws passed by liberal bourgeois regimes sometimes actually increased the husband's power over his wife and her property.

In the later nineteenth century, however, some women escaped the seclusion of the household for work in the larger world. Admittedly, the work often turned out to be brutal sweatshop labor in the new factories of the Industrial Revolution. Few though these were, they were often glad to have women, who would work more cheaply.

A more promising direction was the increase in education for girls in some countries. In relatively progressive nations such as Mexico and Argentina, women began to find work as schoolteachers themselves.

There was even a nascent feminist movement in Latin America in the last decades of the century. Women schoolteachers took the lead in organizing feminist societies and editing women's journals. Feminists worked diligently for the social and intellectual advancement of women and tried to defend their sisters from economic exploitation. As early as the 1850s, Brazil's first woman editor, Joana Paula Manso de Noronha, voiced the aspirations of all these groups when she urged the "social betterment and moral emancipation of women."[5]

One of the most famous Latin American writers—and a leading proponent of education for women—the Argentine Domingo Sarmiento, declared that "the level of civilization of a people can be judged by the social position of its women."[6] By that standard, Latin America was no more civilized than the rest of the world in the nineteenth century. But there were harbingers, at least, of things to come.

## Mexico and the ABC Powers

The histories of several of the major Latin American nations during the decades around 1900 illustrate these many aspects of life in the other half of the hemisphere. Mexico in the north and the ABC countries of South America—Argentina, Brazil, and Chile—will all be glanced at briefly from this point of view.

Mexico, ruled by the modernizing but brutal dictator Porfirio Díaz from 1876 to 1911, epitomized most of these turn-of-the-century trends. The Díaz dictatorship, which began as a popular constitutional regime, had by 1900 become government by and for large landowners, high churchmen, foreign investors, and growing numbers of generals

---

[5]Quoted in E. B. Burns, *Latin America* (Englewood Cliffs, N.J.: Prentice Hall, 1982), p. 223.
[6]Benjamin Keen and Mark Wasserman, *A Short History of Latin America* (Boston: Houghton Mifflin, 1980), p. 241.

and government officials. There were rewards, of course. British, United States, and other foreign capital, combined with Mexican export profits, and operating in the stable social environment produced by repression, had criss-crossed the nation with railroads and made Mexico the world's third largest oil producer and a leader in other mineral and agricultural products as well. But massive land grabs by speculators and hacienda owners, decline in production of ancient food staples such as maize and beans, and widespread peonage left the majority of Mexicans deep in poverty.

Elections were routinely rigged under Díaz, political opposition jailed, peasant discontent suppressed by back-country policemen called *rurales,* and strikers attacked and even killed by troops. Government intellectuals called the *Científicos* ("Scientifics") pointed proudly to zooming production figures and insisted that economic strength must precede political democracy. As the century turned, however, there was growing opposition to the aging Díaz among peasants, proletarians, the liberal middle classes, and nationalistic opponents of foreign economic predominance.

At the other end of Latin America, Argentina illustrated many of these same trends. But Argentine history also revealed the beginnings of both political freedom and radical agitation as the twentieth century began.

Argentina in 1900 was ruled not by a towering individual like Díaz, but by a loose political coalition called the Generation of 1880 (after the period when they came to power), or sometimes simply the Oligarchy. The Oligarchy meant—once more—government by wealthy landowners, export merchants, and foreign capital, especially British. Huge exports of meat and wheat from the rolling pampas made Buenos Aires a modern metropolis and built railways and processing plants. It also led to the usual expropriation of the Indians, land grabs, and peon labor. Argentina's economic boom, the wonder of the south, made it the most industrially developed nation in Latin America. But most of the new wealth stayed in Buenos Aires, where even the hacienda owners now moved to share in the good life.

Politically speaking, Argentina's Oligarchy was more flexible than the Díaz regime far to the north, and even intermittently liberal. In Argentina, education was encouraged, labor unions were made legal, and some political dissent was even tolerated. The principal opposition was the so-called Radical party, really a rather moderate middle-class movement whose major achievement was to induce the Oligarchy to grant the nation universal manhood suffrage in 1912.

Thanks to such piecemeal reforms, Argentina would escape anything like the revolutionary storm that was building in Mexico. And despite the problems of dependency, Argentina was one of the most industrially developed nations outside the Europe–North American axis as the century got under way.

Brazil, Argentina's enormous neighbor to the north, was as strikingly divided, economically, politically, and culturally, as any Latin American land in 1890.

Rio de Janeiro was being built around its perfect harbor and its trademark, Sugarloaf Mountain, into one of the most beautiful and modern cities in the world. Its new corporate offices, banks, and broad avenues matched anything in Europe or North America. The Brazilian "backlands," by contrast, were dark with the poverty of Indians and blacks who had been slaves until 1888, with the feudal power of great landowners, with rampant banditry, and with exotic religious cults that were sometimes cruelly suppressed for their radical social views.

The Brazilian monarchy, headed by a Portuguese prince, had been overthrown in a bloodless coup as recently as in 1889. The alliance of landowners, businessmen, and progressive military officers who had engineered the coup had soon split, and power had fallen largely into the hands of the richest Brazilian landowners, the coffee planters. Brazil produced three quarters of the world's coffee in the early 1900s, and the coffee interests—with the help of foreign bankers—ruled the huge new republic in the decades before 1914.

Foreigners controlled the large banking, transportation, and export-trade businesses. Brazilians—including, however, many new immigrants—built a bustling light-industrial sector, particularly in textiles. In the mills, a Brazilian working class developed—as in Argentina, composed largely of recent European immigrants. Among these workers, labor unions and socialist agitation began, despite police repression.

Chile's economy was dominated by nitrate and copper production, mostly in the northern territories seized from Peru in the War of the Pacific in the early 1880s. The nitrate kings of the north, the owners of the railways, and other economic leaders were British; Germans were powerful in the south. An effort at government stimulation of a Chile-controlled industrial sector had ended with the overthrow of the would-be reformers in the 1890s. Thereafter, foreign capital and foreign influence continued unimpeded into the new century.

Politically, this was the period of Chile's parliamentary republic. Under this regime, the center of power was not in the presidential palace but in the Chilean legislature, where factions representing landowners, priests, business, and foreign interests managed the nation. It was a fundamentally conservative government, but a constitutional and parliamentary one. Growing numbers of factory workers and miners, labor organization, and the beginnings of socialist parties were exerting pressure for social reform.

## PROVINCIAL CULTURE

### Provinces of the Western World

The transformation of the Americas from colonies to countries was slower and more difficult in the cultural realm than in any other area of national development.

An armed revolt and paper constitution could bring political independence. Economic dependency on Europe might drag on, but at least the makers of economic policy now included Americans as well as their European trading partners. Enthusiasm for Old World ways and fashions might continue, but distinctively American social types, Yankee and *criollo,* began to take shape under the influence of New World conditions.

A distinctive American high culture, however, was very slow to develop. Both in the colonial era and during the first century of independence, the art, literature, and intellectual currents of the New World exhibited a character that may best be defined as provincial. American culture, North and South, was like that of a distant province of a more sophisticated metropolitan center. Europe was still the cultural heartland of the Western world; the Americas, culturally speaking, were its provinces.

The provincial nature of American culture during this transitional period came out in several ways. In part, the former colonies remained cultural colonies simply because much of their high culture was clearly derived from the artistic, literary, and intellectual life of Europe. Thus the Americas felt the impact of the eighteenth-century Enlightenment in late-colonial times and nineteenth-century European romanticism in the early-national period, though the forms of both were modified to suit the New World cultural milieu.

American culture was also provincial in its lack of sophistication, and in an occasional air of backwoods crudity that was sometimes quite calculated but nonetheless reflected American realities. This seems to have been particularly true of North America, where a rich vein of "frontier culture" runs from Ben Franklin's *Almanac* and fur cap to Mark Twain's Mississippi days and Jack London's Yukon.

There is, finally, a provincialism that consists simply in a vigorously artistic anatomizing of what constituted the rather far-off and exotic provinces of the Western world. In seeking to understand themselves, Americans—perhaps Latin Americans especially—revealed a distant backwoods world to Europeans.

This world of Indians and gauchos, rain forests and pampas, mining camps and great rivers, was far stranger than any province of the old country, no matter how colorful and old-fashioned. New World intellectual concerns, with *caudillismo* or the "barbarism" of their own life, with transcendentalism or the abolition of slavery, were even more exotic. The books that brought this world and these concerns to vivid life were provincial simply in that their subject matter was the provinces of the considerably expanded Western world of the nineteenth century.

Let us look first at the provincial culture of the United States in the colonial era and the nineteenth century, and then at the cultural life of Latin America over the same period.

## American Culture: Song of Myself

The continuing cultural development between 1600 and 1900 of the new United States and the British colonies from which the new nation was born was a striking combination of European influences and American originality. The influences, not surprisingly, were strongest during the colonial centuries; the originality emerged more strongly during the middle and later decades of the nineteenth century.

The most powerful cultural influence on the British colonies in the seventeenth century was the Calvinist Protestantism that had brought most of the New England settlers there in the first place. Puritan religiosity infused the simple white boxes and pointed steeples of New England churches, the passion of Cotton Mather's sermons, the lyrical intensity of Anne Bradstreet's poetry. This puritanical religious dimension might be partially transmuted into taut Yankee business sense in the next century—as it was among Puritans, Huguenots, and Dutch burghers in Europe. But moralism and religiosity remained important tonal elements in American culture in later centuries.

The most important eighteenth-century European influence all over the North American colonies was the Enlightenment. Benjamin Franklin was not the only colonist to embrace the new interest in science. The political ideas of the Enlightenment found an interested audience among the increasingly disgruntled colonists. John Locke's belief in natural rights and government based on a social contract, Montesquieu's theory of checks and balances in government, and other political beliefs of Europe's Age of Reason influenced the thinking of Franklin, Thomas Jefferson, the Adamses, and other architects of the new American nation.

Europe's Age of Revolutions in the first half of the nineteenth century was an age of fermenting ideas in the new United States. Abolitionism, the crusade against liquor, rights for women, the Mormons and other new sects, utopian socialism imported directly from Europe—all made converts in the United States. These American social movements had a heavier religious and moralistic tone than the liberalism, nationalism, and socialism of the

Old World. But these American ideological gropings also stirred passions and provided background at least for more radical enthusiasms to come.

The later nineteenth century, furthermore, saw more and more individuals and schools of thought whose work was unique, whose concerns were distinctly those of the far fringes of the Western world. The two most strikingly American schools of thought were transcendentalism and pragmatism. Both originated in the intellectual center of the young United States—New England. But they illustrated two strikingly dissimilar aspects of the American mind.

Ralph Waldo Emerson, essayist, poet, and eager proponent of transcendentalism, urged confidence in our own instincts, an inner understanding that transcended reason, authority, even observation. William James, the philosopher who championed pragmatism the most ardently, declared that truth was really a matter of the *usefulness* of an idea, of its "cash value" to us. Emerson's view reflected the spiritual dimension of American thought, which went back to the Puritans, whereas James expressed the practical, this-worldly aspect of the American experience, with its emphasis on getting the job done.

Much of the cultural contribution of the young United States, however, was the work not of schools of thought such as transcendentalism or pragmatism, but of one-of-a-kind individuals.

There is much of the European romantic in the American poet and short-story writer Edgar Allan Poe and in the fiction writers Nathaniel Hawthorne and Herman Melville. Other aspects of their work, however, have few parallels in the Old World. In his obsession with death and beauty, Poe exceeded most European romantics who held similar predilections. Hawthorne's flair for allegory and his immersion in the New England past, Melville's combination of seafaring and symbolism, have no obvious sources in Europe. "The Raven," *The Scarlet Letter,* and *Moby Dick* are all uniquely individual productions.

In the decades after the Civil War, novelist Henry James—William's brother—probed a uniquely American experience in novels such as *The Portrait of a Lady* and *The Ambassadors:* the rediscovery of Europe by Americans, who pitted their strength and provincial innocence against the Old World's sophistication and deeper knowledge of life. Mark Twain, meanwhile, went the other way, exploring the depths of the provinces in the small towns of the American south and west, and produced the novel Ernest Hemingway would call the best ever written by an American: *Huckleberry Finn.*

Among later nineteenth-century American poets, Emily Dickinson stands out in one way, Walt Whitman in another. Dickinson, living a reclusive life in a small New England town, never seeing either Europe or the Far West, came closer than anyone else of her time to capturing glints of the infinite in a few brief, crystalline lines. Walt Whitman, frequently hailed as America's greatest poet, celebrated the democratic heart of the nation and with equal fervor sang his "Song of Myself" in the lush, earthy, exultant lines of his *Leaves of Grass.*

Any attempt to characterize American thought and literature before 1900 would surely include moralism, from the Puritans to Hawthorne; humor, from, Ben Franklin to Mark Twain; and interest in the special North American experience, from the rather unconvincing Indians of Longfellow's *Hiawatha* and Cooper's *Last of the Mohicans* to realist William Dean Howells's chronicle of a nineteenth-century robber baron, *The Rise of Silas Lapham.* But perhaps the outstanding feature of the culture of the new country was an almost exaggerated individualism, a democratic passion for common things, which could find greatness in a runaway slave, a whaling ship, or a slant of light on a New England afternoon.

## Latin American Culture: Gauchos and Indians

The culture of Latin America was also a self-consciously provincial one in these colonial and early-national periods.

The intellectual life of the Spanish and Portuguese colonies was in some ways more religious than that of the English-speaking colonies to the north. But it was a Counter-Reformation Catholic faith rather than a Protestant one, Jesuits its most ardent spokesmen instead of Puritan preachers. The hundreds of churches scattered over the southern continent were not simple New England boxes, but elaborately ornamental baroque cathedrals thick with marble and statuary, color and gilding and rich decoration. The greatest Latin American poet of the seventeenth century was a nun, Juana de La Cruz—who, like her Puritan counterpart Anne Bradstreet, was known as the Tenth Muse.

The Inquisition, still busy in the New World as in parts of the Old, seriously inhibited the spread of the Enlightenment in Latin America. The enlightened despotism of the Spanish Bourbons, however, did lead to an upsurge in scientific studies, particularly in Mexico. Mexico's famous School of Mines taught much more than that—geography and geology, astronomy, mathematics, and other sciences. Jesuits even labored to reconcile the rationalism and empiricism of Descartes, Bacon, and Newton with Catholic theology. On the historical side, an interest in the Indian past developed very early: Missionary fathers and Indian informants were collaborating on chronicles of the Aztecs and Incas as early as the sixteenth century.

The nineteenth century saw a continuing approximation of the cultural history of the Old World unfolding in the new Spanish- and Portuguese-speaking nations. The romantic movement in particular stirred a parallel upheaval across the Atlantic. But Latin American romanticism had especially strong liberal-nationalist overtones. It also exhibited a powerful concern with such strictly Latin American matters as their conquistador and Indian past and the gauchos and *caudillos* of their own century. Mexico and the ABC countries of South America—Argentina, Brazil, and Chile—produced especially powerful literary and historical cultures in the 1800s.

Condemnation of their own Spanish ancestors was common among the Latin American writers and thinkers of the nineteenth century. The Chilean author Francisco Bilbao, writing under the influence of French liberal and socialist ideas, depicted the conquistadors as feudal Catholic holdovers from the Middle Ages. He saw these founding fathers as the source of the slavery, ignorance, and economic backwardness he detested in his own time.

The Indian past was also condemned as barbarous by some, particularly in Argentina. Others, however, especially in Brazil and Mexico, glorified the ancient Indian cultures, seeing them as their true American heritage. Thus in *Prophecy of Cuauhtémoc,* a poem of powerful romantic imagery, the Mexican Ignacio Rodriguez Galván summoned up the ghost of a martyred Aztec king to lead Mexico to new greatness.

Concerned more directly with present problems was the poetry and fiction of young liberal romantic writers who had been swept up in the opposition to the postindependence *caudillo* dictatorships. Esteban Echeverría, the moving spirit behind Argentine romanticism, was also a liberal and a utopian socialist who was driven into exile by the Rosas regime. Echeverría's grim little masterpiece, *The Slaughterhouse,* a realistic yet symbolically intended account of the torment and death of a young man of character and culture in a slaughterhouse reeking of carcasses, guts, and blood, thus figuratively condemned the Buenos Aires dictatorship in a series of vivid images.

Attitudes toward the lawless gaucho, *vaquero,* or *llanero* horsemen of the plains and the backcountry were more varied. Some, like the Argentine romantic leader Domingo Sarmiento, saw the gaucho as the base of *caudillo* power and a symbol of the nation's barbaric past. Others praised the gaucho as the symbol of a wild, free life that was being steadily undermined by the spread of bourgeois urban culture. José Hernández's epic poem *The Gaucho Martín Fierro,* written in the racy language of the Argentine pampas and strongly influenced by gaucho folk songs, condemned officialdom, the military, and civilization generally and glorified the outlaw life of the vanishing gaucho breed.

Groping for a sense of national identity once national independence had been achieved, Latin American writers and thinkers, like their North American counterparts, turned defiantly to the exploration of their own frontier world. They approved of some aspects of what they saw—their Indian past, and frequently the fading gaucho present—and disapproved of others, such as the brutal *caudillo* dictatorships. Whatever their attitude, the result was a vivid depiction of these westernmost provinces of the Western world.

## Summary

During their first century of political independence, the new nations of the Western Hemisphere remained in many ways provinces of the Western world. Both North and South America moved toward a broader future. But both were still rooted in their colonial pasts during the nineteenth century.

The English colonists of eastern North America were numerous, socially mobile, and accustomed to self-government. Attempts to tighten the mercantilistic ties that bound the colonies to the mother country led the generation of Washington, Jefferson, and the Adamses to break those ties entirely in the Revolutionary War (1776–1781). The new nation had its troubles, but strong early leadership and a flexible constitution, combined with the immense resources of the continent, led to a prosperous, increasingly democratic, and territorially expansive first half-century.

The Civil War (1860–1865) nearly tore the nation in half, but determined leadership by Lincoln and superior northern firepower both saved the Union and freed the slaves. The last four decades of the century, however, were a gilded age of political corruption and disregard for the interests of farmers, blue-collar laborers, blacks, Indians, and immigrants. The latter half of the century nevertheless saw substantial additions to the nation's wealth and territory.

By contrast, the Latin American colonies of Spain and Portugal had a much larger admixture of Amerindians and a less rigidly segregated black African component. Colonial rule in Middle and South America permitted much less self-government; but during the later eighteenth century, Enlightenment reform brought many improvements and a surge of prosperity. The Wars of Independence began with ill-fated revolts by the most oppressed: blacks and Indians. Between 1810 and 1824, however, Bolívar in Venezuela, San Martín in Argentina, and the rebellion instigated by Father Hidalgo in Mexico liberated most of Latin America, and Brazil achieved its independence from Portugal.

The governments of the new Latin American republics, however, remained autocratic, though the new leaders were gun-toting local *caudillos* rather than appointed European administrators, and revolutions were far more common. Economically, the new countries were nearly as dependent on European capital, manufactured goods, and markets for their commodities as they had been as colonies. Prosperity and progressive reforms were found only in a few nations, such as Argentina and Chile.

Culturally, North and South America remained provincial in their involvement with European intellectual movements and in their concern with their own exotic provincial worlds of Amerindians and gauchos. North America did produce two original schools—transcendentalism and pragmatism—and a number of rugged individualists in literature. Latin American writers explored their colonial and precolonial past and their often rough frontier present, seeking a sense of national identity that would not emerge until the next century.

## SUGGESTED READINGS

Anna, T. E. *Forging Mexico, 1821–1835.* Lincoln: University of Nebraska Press, 1998. Authoritative study of the formative years.

Amar, A. R. *The Bill of Rights: Creation and Reconstruction.* New Haven: Yale University Press, 1998. Perceptive historical analysis of the changing meanings of a key democratic concept in America.

Axtell, J. *The Invasion Within: The Contest of Cultures in Colonial North America.* New York: Oxford University Press, 1985. Acclaimed analysis of Native American, British, and French cultures in conflict during the colonial era. See also J. Hemming's *Amazon Frontier: The Defeat of the Brazilian Indians* (Cambridge, Mass.: Harvard University Press, 1987), which chronicles the impact of military repression, loss of land, disease, alcoholism, and other consequences of Western intrusion into Amazonia on the Indian population.

Brown, J. S. H., and E. Vibert, eds. *Reading Beyond Words: Contexts for Native History.* Orchard Park, N. Y.: Broadview Press, 1996. Illuminating contrasts between Native American and European-American views of the same events.

Burns, E. B. *The Poverty of Progress: Latin America in the Nineteenth Century.* Berkeley: University of California Press, 1980. Stimulating essay on the theme that economic advance was limited to Latin American elites, seldom trickling down to the masses.

Chasteen, J. C. *Heroes on Horseback: A Life and Times of the Last Gaucho Caudillos.* Albuquerque: University of New Mexico Press, 1995. Frontier studies, emphasizing influence of frontier society.

Chomsky, A., and A. Lauria-Santiago, eds. *Identity and Struggle at the Margins of the Nation-State: The Laboring People of Central America and the Hispanic Caribbean.* Durham: Duke University Press, 1998. Part of a series on the history of the working class around the world.

Durey, M. *Transatlantic Radicals and the Early American Republic.* Lawrence: University of Kansas Press, 1997. European radical views of the emerging American nation across the sea. See also M. Egnal, *New World Economics: The Growth of the Thirteen Colonies and Early Canada* (New York: Oxford University Press, 1998), on how seventeenth- and eighteenth-century Britain and France affected the economic development of the North American colonies.

Eldridge, L. D., ed. *Women and Freedom in Early America.* New York: New York University Press, 1997. Essays on women—and official attitudes toward women—of different social classes. See also C. Berkin's useful survey, *First Generations: Women in Colonial America* (New York: Hill and Wang, 1996).

Flexner, J. T. *George Washington* (3 vols.). Boston: Little, Brown, 1968–1972. Standard account of the revolutionary commander and first president of the United States; makes him more interesting than most of the clichés about the father of his country.

Freyre, G. *The Mansions and the Shanties: The Making of Modern Brazil,* trans. H. de Onis. New York: Knopf, 1963. A classic study of Brazilian social and racial relations. See also E. Viotti da Costa, *The Brazilian Empire: Myths and Histories* (Chicago: University of Chicago Press,

1985), which examines key aspects of Brazil's history from independence in the 1820s to the emergence of the republic in the 1880s.

Gaspar, D. B., and D. C. Hine, eds. *More Than Chattel: Black Women and Slavery in the Americas.* Bloomington: Indiana University Press, 1996. Cultural differences shape the lives of enslaved black women in the United States and Latin America.

Guelzo, A. C. *Abraham Lincoln: Redeemer President.* Grand Rapids, Mich.: William B. Eerdmans Press, 1999. New biography, giving Lincoln more credit for political ideas and policies.

Isenberg, A. C. *The Destruction of the Bison: An Environmental History, 1750–1920.* New York: Cambridge University Press, 2001. Sees new forms of both American and Indian hunting as responsible for the decimation of the herds.

Lynch, J. *The Spanish-American Revolutions, 1808–1826.* New York: Norton, 1973. A thoroughly scholarly survey.

Navarro, M., and V. Sánchez Korrol, with K. Ali. *Women in Latin America and the Caribbean.* Bloomington: Indiana University Press, 1999. Native American, African American, and European American women play key roles within their separate communities.

O'Rourke, K. H., and J. G. Williamson. *Globalization and History: The Evolution of a Nineteenth-Century Atlantic Economy.* Cambridge, Mass.: MIT Press, 1999. An earlier stage of the widely discussed contemporary phenomenon of *globalization.*

Rodriguez, J. E. *The Independence of Spanish America.* New York: Cambridge University Press, 1998. Valuable new overview of the Spanish colonies' struggle for independence, with some emphasis on the Spanish imperial side of the story.

Roy, W. G. *Socializing Capital: The Rise of the Large Industrial Corporation in America.* Princeton: Princeton University Press, 1997. Sociological perspectives on an important subject.

Starkey, A. *European and Native American Warfare, 1675–1815.* Norman: University of Oklahoma Press, 1998. Insights on many aspects of warmaking, from tactics to ultimate outcomes.

Stavig, W. *The World of Tupac Amaru: Conflict, Community, and Identity in Colonial Peru.* Lincoln: University of Nebraska Press, 1999. Vivid account of the lives of Peruvian Indians under Spanish rule.

 Please refer to the document CD-ROM for primary sources related to this chapter.

# CHAPTER 22

# MANCHUS, ZULUS, AND THE CRUMBLING MUSLIM CENTER

## Decline and Disarray
## in Asia and Africa

## (1650–1870)

State-Building and State Power
Evolving Commercial Networks
Interaction with Outside Forces

# TRADITIONAL CULTURES IN AN AGE OF TRANSITION

Society and Community
Art and Life
Development or Disintegration?

## A GLANCE AHEAD: ASIA AND AFRICA BESET BY PROBLEMS

As Europe and the Americas strove to master revolutionary new ideas and material changes between 1600 and 1900, two other continents faced a multitude of old problems.

In Asia, the three great Muslim empires of the sixteenth century had slipped into terminal decline by the nineteenth. Farther east, the new Manchu rulers of China and the Tokugawa shoguns of Japan brought many benefits to those ancient lands. But internal decline and decay opened the door to Western incursions and drastic change in the nineteenth.

Africa also experienced rapid changes during these three centuries. But the changes came too late. The continent was left in disarray, old ways crumbling, new ones not yet in place, when Europeans burst into Africa in the later 1800s.

It was a strange time in these, the two largest continents on earth. Asians sought consolation in memories of their glorious past. Africans plunged into a welter of changes, some also rooted in their past, some quite new. Neither continent was prepared to face the swelling wave of Western imperialism that loomed over their future.

## DISINTEGRATION OF THE MUSLIM CENTER

### The End of Asian Preeminence

While Westerners were exploding in all directions out of their end of Eurasia, the eastern four fifths of the double continent was undergoing a very different process. While Europe was dynamic, aggressive, and expansionist, much of Asia sank into lethargy and decline or simply turned inward, away from the perils of the new age. It was a startling reversal of what had been the norm more often than not; the preeminence of the East in Eurasian history.

Evidence for Asian preeminence is not hard to find. History and civilization began in the Near East. All the Eurasian world religions originated in Asia, not Europe. All but one of the greatest Eurasian empires before 1500 were built in Asia. Trade between East and West almost always drained gold out of Europe because Asians disdained European manufactured items as inferior, while Europeans continually coveted the superior workmanship of the East.

At the beginning of modern times, the situation was pretty much normal. The power of the Ottoman Turkish Sultan Suleiman the Magnificent cast a vast and terrifying shadow over Europe. The new empires of Safavid Persia and Mughal India were wealthy and cultured centers of civilization. Ming China was still by far the world's largest nation, busy working out the final parameters of traditional Chinese culture. Feudal Japan hovered on the edge of unification under the shoguns. Asia, in short, was thriving in the sixteenth century.

As the eighteenth century turned into the nineteenth, the picture looked very different. During this middle period of modern history, large parts of Asia were losing ground while Europe forged ahead.

## ASIAN EMPIRES OF THE EIGHTEENTH AND NINETEENTH CENTURIES

**Legend:**
- Ottoman Empire, 1699
- Mughal Empire, 1700
- Manchu Empire, 1796
- Dutch territory
- Territory lost to Russia
- Territory lost to Austria-Hungary
- Territory lost to Britain
- Territory lost to France
- Boundary of Islamic Zone, 1699

ATLANTIC OCEAN

GREAT BRITAIN

NETHERLANDS

AUSTRIA-HUNGARY

FRANCE

Black Sea

Mediterranean Sea

RUSSIA

OTTOMAN EMPIRE

Serbia (Independent, 1804)

Greece (Independent, 1830)

Caspian Sea

SAFAVID PERSIA

MUGHAL INDIA

Extent of China in 1664

MANCHU CHINA

PACIFIC OCEAN

INDIAN OCEAN

DUTCH EAST INDIES

British

Dutch

British
Dutch

This cultural retreat, or relative decline, took different forms in different parts of Asia during the 1600s, 1700s, and early 1800s. The following pages will look first at predominantly Islamic West and South Asia—the Ottoman Turkish, Safavid Persian, and Mughal Indian empires—where the "Muslim center" failed at last and slid into decline. The chapter will then examine the Manchu conquest of China, the Tokugawa unification of Japan, and the long centuries of intensified isolation that subsequently enveloped both lands. From decline and isolation came the weakened and intensely conservative traditional Asia into which Westerners would finally force their way in large numbers in the nineteenth century. The imposition of the Western hegemony on the largest and most populous of continents was thus facilitated by the relative decline of the East during these centuries of the rise of the West.

## The Ottoman Empire Retreats

Under Sultan Suleiman the Magnificent (1520–1566), the Turkish Empire had attained its greatest extent, stretching from the Persian Gulf to the Atlantic, from Hungary in the north to Egypt in the south. The wealth of the Ottomans was legendary, the efficiency of their government proverbial. And though the sultans at Istanbul made alliances with European rulers in the tangle of Renaissance power politics, the terror of the Turkish scimitar hung heavy over Europe as a whole.

Within five years of Suleiman's death, the situation began to change. The naval battle of Lepanto (1571), a great victory of Spanish and Italian galleys over the fleets of the Ottomans, effectively ended Turkish expansion in the Mediterranean. In the Balkans, too, the Ottoman Empire would make few gains thereafter. In the east, the Ottomans faced the Safavid dynasty of Persia in a series of ultimately indecisive wars during the late 1500s and the earlier 1600s. On all sides, the Ottoman advance was blunted and turned. After one final expansive effort in the later seventeenth century, this halt to Turkish expansion turned into a disastrous retreat.

A series of energetic grand viziers of the Kiuprili family mounted the Ottoman Empire's last great offensives in Europe in the 1660s, 1670s, and 1680s. Turkish arms were victorious from Crete to Hungary, and in 1683 Muslim troops for the last time laid siege to Vienna, the capital of Austria and its German Holy Roman Empire. But Vienna held. The siege was broken by a combined force of German and Polish troops led by the celebrated Polish king John Sobieski. Thereafter, the tide turned relentlessly against the once great power on the Golden Horn.

In the century following the failure of the last siege of Vienna, the Austrian Habsburgs and the Romanov czars of Russia proved more than a match for the Ottomans in Eastern Europe. The Habsburgs took a substantial chunk of the northern Balkans, including Hungary and Transylvania, away from the Turks. The Russians, particularly under Catherine the Great in the later eighteenth century, pushed down to the northern shores of the Black Sea in the Crimea. They even forced the straits linking the Black and Mediterranean seas, bringing Istanbul itself temporarily within range of Russian naval guns. By 1800, Russia seemed quite capable of overwhelming Turkey entirely.

That Russia did not achieve this goal during the nineteenth century was due more to pressure from other European powers than to the dwindling strength of the Ottomans. Turkey was throughout the nineteenth century "the sick man of Europe," ghoulishly observed by Western powers waiting for their shares of the once vast Ottoman inheritance.

The internal decay of the Ottoman Empire was less spectacular but no less inexorable than its decline as a great power. The two were closely related, of course. Turkey's domestic conservatism and decline were reflected in its failure to keep up militarily with the advances of its powerful Western rivals. Turkey, whose big guns had once breached the walls of Constantinople, fell far behind in field artillery during the seventeenth and eighteenth centuries. Its fleets clung to old-fashioned ramming and boarding tactics long after Europeans had turned their naval vessels into floating gun platforms capable of demolishing their foes without ever boarding them at all. The famed Janissary troops, allowed to marry and mingle with ordinary citizens, soon lost their fighting edge and became a sort of Turkish Praetorian Guard, deeply involved in the court politics of Istanbul.

Indeed, corruption sapped the vigor of the entire Ottoman political system in the seventeenth and eighteenth centuries. Weak sultans more interested in enjoying than in running the empire surrendered authority to their grand viziers. Some of these chief ministers were effective rulers, like the Kiuprili clan mentioned previously, but all of them used power to feather their own nests. *Begs* and *pashas* in the provinces and provincial cities followed this example. Military commanders who could no longer be rewarded with new conquests milked the sultan's own subjects instead. A regime envied in sixteenth-century Europe for efficiency and justice became by the nineteenth a byword for corruption.

Economic problems also afflicted the aging empire. There were some advances, notably the great increase in cash-crop agriculture and food production brought about by the introduction of corn and tobacco from the Americas. But manufacturing, dominated by a conservative guild system, did not keep up—a fatal mistake as the Industrial Revolution began in Europe. Fortunes were made in money lending and through political chicanery, but solid economic progress was neglected.

The luxury of the court of the Ottoman Empire is clear from this photographic portrait of "the sultan's favorite," taken in the imperial harem. Notice the water pipe—in which Middle Easterners most commonly smoke tobacco—the lavishly embroidered robes, the sumptuous overstuffed sofa and inlaid table. But note also that the camera that took this picture was a Western invention, and that it had penetrated here to the very heart of the sultan's palace at Istanbul. (Library of Congress)

Division also beset the multinational Ottoman Empire. Various nationalities and religious groups made special arrangements with Istanbul. Greek Orthodox Christians, Jews, Armenians, and others were in effect ruled by their own authorities under the sultan. This tolerance, a virtue in the days of Suleiman, became a decided drawback as later sultans lost the respect of those they ruled.

By the early 1800s, the possibility of fragmentation of the empire was thus as real as that of Russian conquest. Russia had already declared itself official protector of the Christian subjects of the Ottomans. All the southern provinces, from Morocco to Egypt and Arabia, were autonomous or independent. Early in the nineteenth century, the Balkan states of Serbia and Greece successfully rebelled against their Turkish overlords.

The sun that rose over Istanbul still glinted on the masts and spars of the many ships thronging the Golden Horn, flooded the courts of splendid palaces, gilded the domes and minarets of ancient mosques. But the sultans were weak, European traders were many and rich, and the spirit of the Western Enlightenment was penetrating even this far east by the year 1800 of the Christian calendar.

## Safavid Persia Becomes a Cockpit

Safavid Persia had reached its apogee, as we have seen, slightly later than Ottoman Turkey, under Shah Abbas I (1571–1629). Abbas ruled an empire the size of present-day Iran, large enough to fill a sizable chunk of the western United States today. Under Abbas, the Safavids turned back both Ottoman and Central Asian invasions. They also made their capital, Isfahan, one of the most beautiful cities in the world.

The century following Shah Abbas's death, however, was not so splendid.

The seeds of Safavid decay were perhaps planted deep in the brilliant Persian dynasty from the beginning. The warrior tradition of *ghazi* princes smouldered always beneath the cultivated surfaces of beautiful Isfahan, finding violent expression in the many wars of the Safavid period. The militant Shiite spirit was central to the national identity of Safavid Persia from the days of the founder Ismail, but that spirit also made the Shiite state an outlaw among the Sunni majority of Muslim lands. The intrusion of Europeans, finally, was encouraged by even the great Abbas, who wanted their technological and military skills. But those same Western powers would contribute largely to the collapse of the empire into a cockpit of feuding peoples in the eighteenth and nineteenth centuries.

The long wars between the Shiite Safavids and the Sunni Ottomans turned against Persia after Shah Abbas's death. His successors retired to their harems and the sophisticated pleasures of Isfahan. But persecution of Sunni minorities in Persia still exploded from time to time. And the English and Portuguese who had competed for influence and trade in Persia were joined in the later seventeenth century by French, Dutch, Spanish, and Russians, the last a particular threat due to Russia's location just across Persia's northern border.

In the early eighteenth century, a Sunni rebellion in Afghanistan severed the eastern portions of the empire from Persia. In the 1720s, Afghan invaders overthrew the Safavids and precipitated an orgy of massacres and persecutions in Isfahan and elsewhere. Persian independence was restored by the militant Nadir Shah in the 1730s, and this great Persian war leader soon overran both Afghanistan and northwestern India, compelling even the Indian Mughals to pay ransom. But Afghanistan then produced its own great general, and the whole area of modern Iran (Persia), Afghanistan, and Pakistan sank into a welter of unending wars.

Moving dexterously around the fringes of the carnage, vying for influence and encouraging the combatants, were the advance guard of European imperialism. Europeans sold the guns and powder on which all sides depended. Russians pushed down from the north: There were Cossack raids in the 1660s, Peter the Great seized Persian territory in the 1720s, and a long competition with Britain for spheres of influence in Iran filled the following century. The British, meanwhile, pressed for Persian trade and considered influence at Isfahan essential for protecting their growing imperial involvement in India.

Shahs of Iran signed treaties, accepted subsidies and advisors, and continued their squabbles with their Afghan rivals on into the nineteenth century. What had once been a great empire, skillful at manipulating client princes, became itself increasingly a puppet of European powers.

## Mughal India Crumbles

Akbar the Great (1542–1605), the most celebrated of the Mughal emperors, had ruled not only most of modern India but also today's Pakistan, Bangladesh, and part of Afghanistan. As noted in Chapter 27, Akbar's toleration of other Indian faiths and his cultivation of Indian civilization made him popular with the majority of Hindu Indians as well as with his Muslim subjects.

After his death at the beginning of the seventeenth century, there was Muslim power in India still, but never a ruler as popular. And even the political power of Islam in India would disintegrate drastically in the eighteenth century.

The most powerful Mughal ruler of the 1600s was in fact the least popular of all the Mughals: Aurangzeb (1658–1707). Aurangzeb imprisoned his own father and thrust three brothers aside to seize the throne. He reigned long, sometimes cruelly, and generally intolerantly. He persecuted the Hindu majority, pulling down Hindu temples and making it increasingly difficult for any but Muslims to rise in his service. He carried on the military tradition of the Mughals by driving deep into the south, until at his death the Mughal realm encompassed almost the whole of the subcontinent.

Aurangzeb's long reign, contemporary with that of Louis XIV in Europe, was rendered illustrious in seventeenth-century eyes by these many victories. It was also unique in its effort to cut back on courtly magnificence and expenses. But the emperor's reputation for violence and unscrupulousness tarnished all the rest. The traditional history of the Indian countryside attributes everything glorious and admired from these centuries to Akbar the Great, everything dark and terrible to the reign of Aurangzeb.

After 1700, disintegration advanced rapidly. The decay of Mughal power carried India, so seldom politically united, rapidly back to the more familiar plurality of feuding states. And from political disintegration, the subcontinent drifted more rapidly than any other part of the Muslim center into the imperial orbit of the expanding West.

The greatest long-term threat came from the growing numbers of Europeans gathering in trading cities and isolated forts around the fringes of India. By the eighteenth century, the field had narrowed to the British and the French, and after 1763 the British, victorious in the Seven Years' War, were effectively alone in the field.

We have noticed the beginnings of Great Britain's Indian empire above. The British East India Company came to trade in the 1600s. Its officers became involved in princely politics in order to protect their interests. They ended in the 1700s by leading armies of *sepoy* or native Indian troops and signing political alliances with almost all the important *nabobs* (local governors) and independent *rajas* on the subcontinent.

In the 1790s the British crown assumed dual directorship with the company. By 1800 British dependencies stretched the length of the Ganges valley, across northern India from the fringes of the Punjab to Bengal, and down the east coast to the southern tip of the subcontinent.

The once mighty Mughals now had little more than formal claim on the allegiance of their governors and subordinate princes. Most Indian potentates received British "advisors" at their courts, depended on British-officered *sepoy* regiments, and traded liberally in silks and cottons and spices, indigo and precious stones with Britain. The crown and the company in London still railed against political entanglements and costly wars. But in fact the company's "servants" had become the most powerful single force in India as the nineteenth century began.

## THE FAR EAST TURNS INWARD

### The Manchu Conquest of China

The story of East Asia during the seventeenth, eighteenth, and early nineteenth centuries is rather different from that of the Muslim center of Eurasia. Both Manchu China and Tokugawa Japan were in many ways very successful dynasties. But China under its Manchu conquerors and Japan under the unifying Tokugawa shogunate both sought to isolate themselves from the outside world during this period. The result of their efforts to cut East Asia off from the flow of history was a slowing of social change and a relative decline by comparison with the dynamic culture of the West.

The Ming dynasty, which had replaced a regime of Mongolian conquerors in the fourteenth century, fell to a wave of Manchurian invaders in the seventeenth. The end of the Ming era was preceded by the familiar symptoms of dynastic decline: weak emperors, corruption at court and in the administration, drought, famine, and peasant rebellion. The Mandate of Heaven, China's equivalent of the divine right to rule, had clearly been withdrawn by the early 1600s.

Into this decaying order plunged the vigorous new Manchu armies from the north. Nurhachi (1559–1626), the founder of the Manchu state, had welded the Manchurian tribes into a powerful force, combining Chinese bureaucracy with his own system of military organization. The Manchu banner armies, named for the colors of their distinctive standards, were built on companies of three hundred men and included Mongol and Chinese units as well as Manchurians. A total of sixteen bannerman armies—275 companies—participated in the invasion of China two decades after Nurhachi's death.

The conquest was prepared and led by two of Nurhachi's sons, Abahai and Dorgon, between the 1620s and the 1640s. Their success in this unlikely project—victory over a nation twenty times their size—was facilitated by a late Ming peasant rebellion and by the collaboration of a Ming general. The last Ming emperor committed suicide in a capital beset by peasant rebels, and the Ming commander at the Great Wall opened the gates to the Manchu invaders. The Manchu, or Qing ("Pure"), dynasty was formally proclaimed in 1644 and would last until 1912.

South China held out longer, as it had against the Mongols. Chinese generals carved out short-lived kingdoms for themselves in the south. Port cities and seagoing resistance forces fought to the end. But by the 1680s, all China was in the hands of the invaders from the north. The Mandate of Heaven had passed, as it usually did even in this most stable of nations, in blood and violence.

## The Qing Dynasty

Two great and long-lived Manchu emperors divide the history of the century and a half between 1644 and 1800 between them: the Kangxi emperor in the seventeenth century and the Qianlong emperor in the eighteenth. Between them these two Chinese rulers outlived three Louis in France, the later Stuarts and the first three Georges in Britain, and almost the entire rise of the Hohenzollerns in Prussia. And their accomplishments were at least as great.

Kangxi (1661–1722), the longest-reigning emperor in Chinese history, was the ideal monarch. A vigorous outdoorsman, hunter, and leader of armies, like his Manchu ancestors, he was also a Chinese scholar and intellectual and an administrator of endless industry and rigor. At the end of his sixty-year reign, the northern invaders were firmly seated on the throne of China.

Kangxi ruled firmly and fairly, plowing through huge quantities of official reports daily. He preserved most of the Ming structure of government, pairing Chinese provincial governors with Manchu bannermen, combining continuity with the new leadership. He cut taxes and forbade further confiscation of Chinese lands by Manchus once pacification was complete.

As commander in chief of the armies, Kangxi first completed the conquest of South China and then turned his attention to expanding Chinese power westward, into central Asia. He defeated the western Mongols, an ancient threat to China. He turned back the Russian Cossacks, point men for Russia's own expansion eastward to the Pacific. He imposed a pro-Chinese Dalai Lama in Tibet.

As a scholar, Kangxi sponsored a famous dictionary, yet another gigantic encyclopedia, and an official history of the preceding dynasty. He patronized artists and philosophers. He had himself painted, surrounded by art objects, with a Chinese landscape painting and his own portrait on the wall behind him.

A contemporary of Aurangzeb in India and Louis XIV in Europe, Emperor Kangxi combined the Mughal's military prowess with the Sun King's dedication to the art of governance. He has been called not only the longest-reigning but the most successful of Chinese emperors.

Qianlong (1735–1796), Kangxi's grandson, led the Middle Kingdom to new levels of political strength, size, population, prosperity, and international power. Since many of the accomplishments of his reign represent the apogee of the dynasty, they will be developed at length in the survey of Qing society that follows.

Qianlong's personal contribution was particularly visible in his magnificent style of life and his extensive foreign conquests. Under his direction, Manchu Chinese armies pushed westward, as they had in Han, Tang, and Mongol times. Chinese sovereignty was expanded once more across the wastes of central Asia as far as the towering Pamirs.

At home, prosperity and government revenues grew, so that Qianlong was able to live in as grand a style as any European monarch. He built immense palaces and undertook magnificent royal progresses across the empire. His patronage of literature and learning produced a famous collection, *The Complete Library of Four Treasuries*, which amounted in the end to 36,000 volumes!

Qianlong's suspicious nature and absolutist bent led him to censor as well as to sponsor scholarly activity, and he suppressed any book he deemed anti-Manchu. But his splendid style cloaked a work schedule as relentless as Kangxi's, beginning before dawn and exhausting his secretaries. Qianlong piously abdicated in 1796 rather than reign longer than his illustrious grandfather. But his powerful personality continued to dominate the government until death finally stilled his fierce energies in the last year of the century.

## Development and Decline

The power of the Manchus, in numbers a small percentage of the population they had conquered, was imposed on China in a number of ways. Manchu garrisons were stationed strategically across the country. Large tracts of land were set aside to provide revenues for the Qing emperors and for Manchu bannermen. Manchus were forbidden to marry Chinese; Manchu women were discouraged from binding their feet in the Chinese style. All Chinese men, by contrast, were required to shave all but a single braided pigtail from their heads, a symbol of acceptance of the overlordship of the Manchus, who wore their hair this way.

The political organization of China, however, has often been described as a dyarchy, a dual Chinese-Manchu government—and in many ways it looks more Chinese than Manchu. The trend of a historically autocratic government toward royal absolutism, begun under the Mongols and the Ming, continued under the Qing. Manchu emperors made all major decisions and many minor ones personally. But all important imperial bureaus were headed by two officials, one Manchu and one Chinese. Government boards were half Manchu and half Chinese in membership. As noted previously, Chinese provincial governors were matched with Manchu governors-general.

Below the provincial level, however, all officials remained Chinese. Local magistrates and village headmen were chosen on the basis of local prestige, as in earlier periods. For the average peasant, to whom the Son of Heaven had always been a half-mythical being in a faroff capital, foreign rule can have made little difference.

One thing many must have noticed over most of the 1600s and 1700s, however, was the flourishing state of the economy under the Manchus.

Agriculture was basic, as it had always been in China. New types of rice, improvements in irrigation and fertilization, and new crops such as corn and sweet potatoes boosted food production dramatically. Traditional handicraft industries grew steadily—pottery, silk, cotton, mining, and metalwork—practices by ancient guilds in many parts of China. Domestic trade reached new highs, and foreign trade, though comparatively small, produced an inflow of gold and silver steady enough to warm the heart of a European mercantilist. A further result of economic prosperity was a continuing growth in population, which probably doubled over these two centuries to approximately 300 million by 1800.

A final testimony to the success of the Qing emperors during the 1600s and 1700s was the further expansion of the empire. The Manchus brought Manchuria and its suzerainty over Korea with them to China. Once and for all they broke the power of the Mongols, the last of the great steppe nomads, by conquering Inner Mongolia and opening Outer Mongolia to Chinese commercial exploitation. They reconquered and finally incorporated the huge western lands of Xinjiang into the empire. They set up a protectorate over Tibet, garrisoned Central Asia all the way to the Pamirs, and collected tribute from Vietnam, Burma, and other East and Southeast Asian states.

Yet in many ways even the greatest of the Manchus were inward-looking and conservative. As is so frequently the case, the seeds of their ultimate decline were there from the beginning.

To prove themselves more Chinese than the Chinese, the Manchu emperors encouraged the most conservative Confucianism. They stressed China's total self-sufficiency and supremacy, depicting their empire as the one truly civilized land in a barbarous world. Since they did not need the rest of the world, they did nothing to build a navy or a great merchant marine; the nation that had put huge fleets to sea in the fifteenth century was now left far behind in shipbuilding and naval development. Scholars and literati also had no use for mechanical things, and so the nation that had invented printing, gunpowder, and the compass slid steadily further behind in industrial development also.

Contact with the West, reestablished under the later Mings, developed uncertainly and then declined under the Manchus. Jesuit missionaries were welcomed at court in the seventeenth century, mostly for their skills in Western arts and sciences. But later missionaries, who refused to compromise their opposition to Chinese traditional ancestor worship and the veneration of Confucius, were proscribed in the 1720s. Trade developed relatively freely in early Manchu times but was narrowly limited to a section of the southern port of Canton in the later 1700s. Manchu emperors might enjoy learning to play exotic instruments such as the clavichord or dressing up a few court ladies in colorful Western costumes, but they saw little importance in European trade.

When the great decline in Manchu fortunes began around 1800, the Middle Kingdom would pay dearly for having ignored the chance to learn more valuable things from the West while there was time.

## The Tokugawa Shoguns Seize Power in Japan

The Japanese islands were much more open to foreign influences than China was in the early part of this period. In Japan also, a strong new dynasty came to power in the seventeenth century—not foreign conquerors but the unifying Tokugawa shoguns. But in Japan too, an increasingly conservative regime had rejected foreign influences and turned inward before the seventeenth century was over.

Japan, which had learned so much from China in centuries past, was initially much more willing than the Middle Kingdom to deal with the West. From this interaction came a transformation of Japanese feudalism and the reemergence of a strong government—which, paradoxically, proceeded to turn its back upon the West once more.

In the sixteenth century the wealthier Japanese barons, or *daimyo,* were glad to have Portuguese and later English, Dutch, and other merchants come with their goods. To attract the traders, some *daimyo* welcomed Jesuit and other missionaries, who were soon making more converts in Japan than in China. Most important of all in that war-torn age, Western muskets and cannon transformed the art of war in samurai Japan. Firearms gave the military edge to *daimyo* who could build companies of musketeers, artillery, and the huge new castles needed to resist these military innovations in the hands of others.

The suppression of feudal warfare and the political reunification that followed were the work of a series of three of these *daimyo* barons clever enough to exploit both the old feudal rules and the new military circumstances to their own advantage.

Their names were Oda Nobunaga, Hideyoshi, and Tokugawa Ieyasu. These three men shared a knack for manipulating the new weapons with tactical daring. They were also masters of the traditional methods of feudal alliance-building through distribution of rewards, political marriages, and political intrigue. All three first moved to establish themselves as protectors of the ceremonial emperor at the old capital at Kyoto, then turned to overcoming opposition from rival nobles in the countryside.

Oda Nobunaga (1534–1582) established a powerful *daimyo* alliance in the large central island of Honshu, moved on to Kyoto, and overthrew the Ashikaga shogunate, by then moribund and ripe for dispatching. Hideyoshi (1536–1598), a rude peasant who had risen to general's rank under Nobunaga, is usually considered the real unifier of Japan. Hideyoshi expanded Nobunaga's baronial connection to include all the chief *daimyo* in the island empire. He disarmed the peasantry, encouraged trade with the West, and dreamed megalomaniacal—and fruitless—dreams of conquering China itself. Tokugawa Ieyasu (ruled 1603–1616), a vassal of Hideyoshi's, outfought all rivals for his master's legacy at the great battle of Sekigahara in 1600 and was officially named shogun three years later.

Under Ieyasu and his son and grandson, the Tokugawa shogunate was firmly established. They would wield power for the next two and a half centuries (1603–1868). Like the Manchu emperors of China, the Tokugawa shoguns were in many ways a very successful dynasty. But the Tokugawa, like the Manchus, made what became the fatal conservative error of trying to turn their back upon the roaring tide of change.

## The Tokugawa Shogunate

Typical of this tendency was the great event of the immediate postcentralization period: the closing of Japan to Western influences.

By the early 1600s there were Portuguese, Spanish, English, and Dutch merchants in Japan. There were Jesuit and Franciscan missionaries and almost a third of a million Christian Japanese. There was much more interaction between the two cultures in Japan than in China: Jesuits learned the Zen tea ceremony, and fashionable Japanese wore crucifixes and smoked tobacco.

But the seventeenth-century Tokugawa shoguns grew suspicious of European imperialist ambitions. They began to see Christianity as a subversive ideology. Then official persecution set off a short-lived Japanese Christian revolt in one section of the islands. The government reacted with massive martyrdoms that destroyed all but a tiny underground remnant of Christianity in Japan.

Traders also became suspect. One Western trading power after another was expelled, until by the 1640s—a century after the first Portuguese had arrived—only a single Dutch trading post on an island in Nagasaki harbor remained to connect Japan with the Western world.

The fundamental conservatism of the Tokugawa shogunate extended to domestic as well as foreign affairs. Determined efforts were made throughout the seventeenth and eighteenth centuries to revive such traditional elements of Japanese culture as the samurai virtues, class structure, and the agrarian pattern of life.

The most famous such effort to turn the clock back was made by the eighteenth-century shogun Yoshimune (1716–1745). Yoshimune was a model of ancient Japanese rectitude. He issued many decrees on moral and social behavior and urged simplicity, decency, and the military code of the samurai upon his people. Yoshimune's economic reforms, intended to favor agriculture at the expense of trade, succeeded in triggering a major commercial depression, but this has not damaged his reputation as one of the most virtuous of the shoguns.

## Transformation and Tension

The Tokugawa shogunate actually saw an odd amalgam during its first two centuries: an intensely conservative, still semifeudal political regime presiding over a booming urban, commercial economy. Out of this unlikely combination evolved the unique culture of Tokugawa Japan.

The political system of the Tokugawa shoguns was built on the feudal order out of which they had risen. Tokugawa "centralized feudalism" was a structure of power based on the huge landholdings of the shoguns and the substantial allotments of the puppet emperors and the shogun's vassal *daimyo*. The rest of society was fixed by law in a rigid system of classes—peasants forbidden to leave the land, samurai prohibited any but military or administrative careers. There was government support for the traditional agrarian economy. There was also repeated legislation against conspicuous consumption by people of the lower classes. The Tokugawa thus seemed totally dedicated to preserving old Japan in amber, an unchanging perfection in a changing world.

In fact, however, the Japanese islands were in the grip of rapid economic progress during these centuries. The resulting population growth, urban development, and cultural innovation had few points of contact with the conservative ideals of the Tokugawa shoguns.

Agriculture, encouraged by the government, developed steadily. Acreage under cultivation doubled under the impact of new fertilizers and seeds, double cropping, and other improvements in agricultural techniques. The increase in the amount of food available led in turn to considerable growth in population, from perhaps 18 million in 1600 to 30 million in the eighteenth century.

The growth of trade, though it was largely domestic, was even more spectacular, constituting a commercial revolution in Japan during the seventeenth century. Low taxes, a lack of government intervention, and the general lack of interest in business on the part of the country's feudal and Confucian rulers left merchants free to grow as fast as they could. Urban development also contributed by concentrating large numbers of customers for merchants and artisans. Edo—later called Tokyo—reached a population of a million, and the commercial port of Osaka half that. The shoguns required the *daimyo* aristocracy to establish residences in Edo, and samurai collected there and in other cities, creating a growing demand for food, handicraft manufactures, and the luxury trades.

Out of these transformations and tensions in an island kingdom largely cut off from the world, a distinctly Japanese national character evolved. Buddhist and *bushido* traditions, love for art and culture going back to Heian times, the success-worshiping values of the new commercial world, and the pleasures of urban life mingled in Tokugawa Japan. The result was a Japanese temperament combining aesthetic sensibility with a martial sense of duty, a compulsive determination to live up to ancient standards, and an intense drive for personal success.

It was a character that could cling doggedly for hundreds of years to the outdated feudal ideals of the Tokugawa—and then throw itself with equal passion into the modernization and Westernization of Japan in the later nineteenth century.

As in China, however, foreigners pressed in on the self-isolated land of the shoguns. Russian and British traders arrived in the years around 1800, leading to new edicts closing all ports to outsiders. By midcentury, European military victories in China suggested the need for a change in policy. And in 1853, the arrival of an American military squadron in Japan itself would end Japan's isolation, trigger the fall of the Tokugawa shogunate, and inaugurate the amazingly rapid modernization that followed.

## CULTURES OF A TWILIGHT AGE

### A Backward Glance

During these centuries of decline and inward turning, a single note is struck again and again across the diverse cultures of the world's largest continent. It is a tone that may be described perhaps most simply as a backward glance.

New religions did not emerge—only sects. New art modeled itself upon old art, or otherwise reacted to the old masters. Philosophers were much more likely to be commentators on the ancient sages than original thinkers. The sciences were left with a shrug to the Westerners, who, as many Asians saw it, vulgarized everything they touched with the crudest of practical applications.

It was a culture of the twilight, art and ideas conceived by ancient civilizations whose day was drawing to a close. A few examples of this culture of traditional Asia's waning centuries follow.

### Muslims and Hindus Return to the Source

The Wahabi sect that emerged in the deserts of Arabia in the middle of the eighteenth century has at first glance little of a twilight feel about it. Flinty Arab fundamentalists, the Wahabis look more like Puritans building the new Jerusalem than a people at the end of an

# VOICES FROM THE PAST

The Wahabi sect described here by an early nineteenth-century European traveler, harked back to a simpler past and a more rigid "old time religion." The Wahabis described here were bedouin, desert Arabs with little contact with the wealthy and worldly cities of the Islamic world. But Muslims of wealth and sophistication turned to this simpler style of life and religion too, living as they believed the Prophet had.

Do you know of any more recent *jihadists* who returned to the simple wilderness life and attacked Soviet, American, and others they saw as enemies of their faith?

*I think myself authorised to state, from the result of my inquiries among the Arabs, and the Wahabys themselves, that the religion of the Wahabys may be called the Prostestantism or even Puritanism of the Mohammedans. The Wahaby acknowledges the Korán as a divine revelation; his principle is, "The Korán, and nothing but the Korán:" he therefore rejects all the Hedayth or "traditions," with which the Muselman lawyers explain, and often interpolate, the Korán. . . . He reproves the Muselmans of this age, for their impious vanity in dress, their luxury in eating and smoking. He asks them, whether Mohammed dressed in pelisses, whether he ever smoked the argyle or the pipe? All his followers dress in the most simple garments, having neither about their own persons, nor their houses, any gold or silver; they abstain from smoking, which, they say, stupifies and intoxicates. They reject music, singing, dancing, and games of every kind. . . . The Wahaby (as Ibn Saoud, the chief, is emphatically styled) propagates his religion with the sword. Whenever he purposes to attack a district of heretics, he cautions them three times, and invites them to adopt his religion; after the third summons, he proclaims that the time for pardon has elapsed, and he then allows his troops to pillage and kill at their pleasure.*

John Lewis Burckhardt, *Notes on the Bedouins and Wahabys, Collected During His Travels in the East* (London: Colburn and Bentley, 1831), pp. 102–103.

age. Their fundamentalist rigor was actually more than a backward glance: it was a wholehearted rush into the past, a pell-mell plunge back to Islam's beginnings.

The founder of the Wahabi sect, Muhammad ibn' Abdul-Wahab (1691–1787), preached a return to the teachings of the Quran and the Law, the most authentic Sunni traditions of the Prophet. Muslims, he declared, should live as Muhammad had taught them to, and nothing should come between the believer and submission to those fundamental teachings. With rigor worthy of a Martin Luther, Abdul-Wahab rejected all that had come since. The insights of Islam's golden age under the Arab caliphs, the mystical visions of the Sufis, all the accumulated wisdom of the Islamic community since Muhammad had to be rejected. Veneration of Muslim saints, broad interpretation of the Muslim Law, unsanctioned habits such as the drinking of wine—all were cast aside in that long, eager backward reach to the sources of Islam.

Deep in the desert fastnesses of Arabia, in the very area where the Prophet had once walked the earth, the Wahabis lived their vigorous, puritanical faith. Abdul-Wahab accepted the patronage of the ambitious house of Saud—the rulers of Saudi Arabia today—and Wahabism spread rapidly across the peninsula. Wahabis soon dominated both the Muslim holy cities of Mecca and Medina, and pilgrims carried word of the new sect back with them to all parts of the Islamic world.

An Egyptian invasion of Arabia put an end to the worldly expansion of the Wahabi movement. But the reputation and influence of the desert sect spread to pious Muslims as far away as Ottoman Turkey and even India. The Wahabis were *living* as Muslims had in the days of the Prophet! Forbidding as its puritanical rigor might be, this fundamentalist return to the source could not but be appealing in a bewildering time when history seemed to be slowly turning its back on the followers of Allah.

The Rajput painting of seventeenth- and eighteenth-century India, in its very different way, also cast that long, wistful backward glance.

The Rajput painters are normally considered artists in a popular tradition, to be contrasted with the sophisticated realism of the art of the Mughal courts. They actually worked at the courts of provincial princes in central India or in the foothills of the Himalayas. They painted many subjects in a variety of styles. But in both subject and style, there is once more that sense of turning back to the great traditions of the past.

Popular Rajput subjects, for instance, included the heroic deeds of Rajput warriors in earlier centuries; passages from the ancient Indian epics, the *Mahabharata* and the *Ramayana;* and episodes from the timeless myths of Vishnu and Shiva. Rajput artists also painted scenes to illustrate musical modes and the many forms of love—but the latter at least was also a well-established Hindu tradition.

Style, essentially ahistorical, is a harder thing to read in historical terms. But there are elements of earlier schools in the work of most of these painters of the lesser courts. There is a refusal to change, to keep up with the first European influences creeping into the art of the great *rajas*. There is in the painting of one court in Rajastan, where the divine lovers Krishna and Radha were particularly revered, a twilight loveliness that transcends time and space, "a fragile elegance and a wan, neurasthenic refinement that are like an echo of the beauty of Ikhnaton's queen,"[1] the swan-necked Nefertiti—doomed too, like the art of the Rajput princes.

---

[1] Benjamin Rowland, *The Art and Architecture of India* (New York: Penguin Books, 1981), p. 350.

## Han Learning and Genroku Culture

Chinese thought and art had always managed a delicate balance of traditionalism and originality. Under the Manchus, culture seemed to career off to wild extremes, reacting with jarring extravagance to a powerfully felt sense of past greatness and present inadequacy.

Some aspects of Chinese culture continued largely as before. Confucius continued to be revered, sumptuous palaces to be built, immense quantities of traditional chinaware to be produced by government works for export. But scholarship exhibited the odd dichotomy indicated above: There was passion for "Han learning," the wisdom of two thousand years before, yet this same period saw a wave of literary detective work that actually challenged the authenticity of some of the most admired Confucian classics. Painters were divided into two rather different camps: the "orthodox," who followed stylistically in the footsteps of their predecessors, and the "individualists" and "eccentrics" who reacted violently against all earlier schools. Orthodox painters did beautiful work in traditions that went back to the Song. The eccentrics produced wildly assymetrical or whimsical paintings drawn with blunted brushes or—in one case—even with bare hands!

Imitation, however, was probably more common than iconoclasm in this ambivalent preoccupation with the past. The most famous work of literature produced in Manchu times was also China's most loved novel, Cao Xuehqin's *The Dream of the Red Chamber*. It is the story of a great family in decline. Generational conflicts, powerful female characters, and the intricate life of a traditional Chinese family combine against a background of

Two geishas, skilled and cultured Japanese courtesans of two centuries ago, go through their dressing ritual in this colored Japanese woodblock print by Kitagawa Utamaro, a famous eighteenth-century artist. Utamaro was widely admired for his depiction of beautiful women. (Kitagawa Utamaro. "Orian Yososoi Seated at Her Toilet." Woodblock. 14-5/8 × 19-15/16 inches. The Metropolitan Museum of Art, Rogers Fund)

social decay and profound Buddhist and Daoist devotion. *The Dream of the Red Chamber* thus offers a moving vision of yet another Eurasian culture of the twilight centuries.

Tokugawa Japanese culture had its aristocratic casting back to better times too. In particular the court of the figurehead emperor at Kyoto continued to develop a delicate sensibility that harked back centuries to Japan's medieval Heian culture. The shoguns trumpeted the virtues of more recent samurai times. But in Japan, almost uniquely, there was also a surge of originality and vigor under the Tokugawa. It appeared in the new commercial cities, especially in Edo and Osaka, and its finest flowering came in the half century around 1700. It is usually called Genroku culture.

Genroku culture blossomed most brilliantly in the urban subculture of playboys and prostitutes, popular entertainment, gambling, and bohemianism. It created *haiku* poetry, *kabuki* theater, and the Japanese print—an array of cultural innovation that would distinguish any age.

*Haiku* verse, with its deceptive simplicity—seventeen syllables arranged in three lines—deliberately leaves much to the reader's imagination. Typically a series of images drawn from nature is presented in order to stir up a unique complex of associations and echoes in the mind of each reader. Evocative, haunting, sometimes funny, *haiku* can stimulate a sense of spiritual depth as great as that of a misty Song landscape. *Haiku* verse has tempted not only Japanese, but foreigners in many languages since.

*Kabuki* theater, which attracted wildly enthusiastic crowds in Tokugawa Edo, has proved less readily exportable. Begun by a troop of women actors and dancers in the early 1600s, *kabuki* evolved into a popular form of pageantry with gaudy costumes, dazzling scenery, and extravagant passions unleashed in traditional stylized movements. In time, male actors took over the productions. But the most admired of these actors were always the ones who, through a lifetime of training, specialized in playing the female parts.

The Japanese print, finally, is familiar to every Western admirer of the work of Toulouse-Lautrec and other nineteenth-century French painters who were profoundly influenced by the Japanese form. Done in four colors, these wood-block prints were the quintessence of Genroku culture. Beginning as illustrations for "pillow books" (sex manuals), wood-block prints developed as pictures of famous courtesans, theatrical scenes, and representations of city life. These eighteenth-century Japanese prints breathe the sophistication of the very unfeudal pleasure capitals of Tokugawa Japan.

### Women in an Age of Change

Life for Asian women showed both continuities with the past and hints of different things to come.

Across the vast expanse of Asia, from Istanbul to Beijing, most women, like most men, lived according to long-established traditions. Marriage was the normal goal, male children highly valued, and a life of hard work only to be expected. Yet there were exceptions to the routine of family life and physical labor.

In Japan, for example, young women of charm and talent could lead a very different life in the pleasure centers of Genroku culture. Sold by poor parents into this world of eating houses, theatrical entertainment, and bordellos, the more gifted of these courtesans became *geishas* or "accomplished persons." Skilled at witty conversation, music, and dancing, they became arbiters of fashion for society at large. Wealthy patrons sometimes bought them out of the Genroku world and made them official concubines or even wives.

In China, imperial concubines could do well for themselves by producing an imperial offspring. Their contacts with the emperor, however, might be strictly limited—by the empress. It was she who informed a concubine that the Son of Heaven would visit her on a particular night—and without this official notification, complete with the empress's seal, even the emperor would be refused admittance.

In some places, finally, the first touch of Western influence began to change the lives of Asian women. In India, Western objections to the ancient practice of *sati*—a widow's suicide on her husband's funeral pyre—at first only caused pious Hindus to dig in their heels and defend the practice as a traditional ritual guaranteeing endless bliss for the faithful wife after death. An early Indian opponent of *sati*, however, turned to the very ancient religious texts cited by supporters of the practice to challenge it. The Hindu scriptures themselves, wrote Ram Mohan Roy in the early 1800s, told Hindus: "How great is the sin to kill a woman, therein forsaking the fear of God, the fear of conscience, and the fear of Shastrus [religious treatises]."[2]

An age of imperial decline was not always a time of change for the worse for women.

# NEW NATIONS IN AFRICA

## New States South of the Sahara

If ancient empires were crumbling in Asia, in Africa new states were rising, particularly in the later eighteenth and nineteenth centuries. Yet Africa, like Asia, would face the overpowering weight of Western expansion before the nineteenth century was over. And like the declining Asian empires, Africa's new states would be ill prepared to meet that challenge. The rise of new centers of power in Africa and the failure of these structural changes to prepare the continent for what was coming will be the primary themes of the following sections.

Until quite recently, Africa was widely imagined—by outsiders—to have been a continent without a history. The grass-roofed huts of Tarzan's Africa were believed to house primitive folk living much as they had since prehistoric times. We have already seen how mistaken this view of an unchanging Africa was for earlier periods. "To know nothing is bad," goes a West African proverb; "to learn nothing is worse"—and Africans, like other peoples, had in fact been learning, growing, changing throughout their history.[3]

## West Africa: The Jihad States and the Ashanti Confederacy

The term *jihad* is usually translated as a holy war, a Muslim crusade. It also refers, however, to any struggle in defense of the faithful. The eighteenth and nineteenth centuries saw a wave of such struggles and the emergence of a number of *jihad* states across the grasslands of the Western Sudan.

Half a dozen *jihads* founded as many new Muslim states, most of them over the century between 1770 and 1870. The most militant leaders were the Fulani people, zealous Muslims, many of them Islamic scholars or teachers who lived and taught in the towns of the Western Sudan.

---

[2]*On the Burning of Widows,* in L. H. Nelson and P. Peebles, *Classics of Eastern Thought* (New York: Harcourt Brace Jovanovich, 1991), p. 421.

[3]Richard W. Hull, *Modern Africa: Change and Continuity* (Englewood Cliffs, N.J.: Prentice Hall, 1980), p. 82.

# AFRICAN KINGDOMS AND PEOPLES OF THE EIGHTEENTH AND NINETEENTH CENTURIES

States

British territories up to 1880

French territories up to 1880

Centers of Muslim revival in West Africa–
*Jihad* (Holy War) movements in West Africa

Approximate area in which Sanusi
Zawiyas (fortified religious centers) were
situated 1843 to 20th century

Al-Hajj Umar's conquests 1848–1884

Limits of Samori's conquest 1870–1890

Maximum Chokwe expansion 1850s and 1890s

Msiri's kingdom 1856–1891

One of the most important of these Islamic revolutions took place in the Hausa states, the ancient and long-prosperous city-states of what is today northern Nigeria. Here in 1804 the Fulani scholar Usman dan Fodio (1754–1817) led a religious revival and then a political revolt that spread like a prairie fire from one to another of these Muslim trading cities. In half a dozen years, the Muslim revolutionaries had seized power in the Hausa states and had begun to weld them into the empire known as the Sokoto Caliphate with a population of several million people.

The goal of the Fulani rulers of the new empire was a theocratic state governed by its *imams,* religious leaders who would both purify and enforce the faith of the Prophet Muhammad. They established a strongly centralized state in which dan Fodio and his successors took the titles of sultan and "Commander of the Faithful."

In the Sokoto Caliphate, the formerly independent Hausa states were headed by emirs appointed by the sultan in Sokoto City, the new capital the Fulani built for their empire. Officials multiplied, both at the sultan's court and in the emirates. In addition to appointing the emirs, the sultan issued special commissions to provincial aristocrats, whose power thus balanced that of the official governors. The emirs in their turn often gave their slaves, who had no independent source of power beyond their masters' favor, extensive administrative authority over free citizens. Taxation, meanwhile, grew heavier at all levels of government; funds were needed to pay for endless military campaigns against the exiled Hausa aristocracy striving to reconquer power. In the name of religion, in short, a thoroughly modern structure of state power took shape on the African savannas in the first half of the nineteenth century.

Other Mulsim *jihad* states also emerged, ranging from the small principality of Futa Toro, founded in 1776, to the sprawling Tokolor Empire established by al-Hajj Umar in 1862. Founded by scholars and warriors, these new nations were committed both to religious reform and to military crusades to spread the faith. To achieve these thoroughly traditional ends, however, the builders of the *jihad* states organized stronger, more centralized, and more thoroughly bureaucratized governments than Africa had seen before.

In the West African forest belt stretching south from the grasslands of the Western Sudan to the swamps and lagoons of the Guinea coast, other strong centralized states developed during the later eighteenth and nineteenth centuries. Of these, perhaps the best known was the Ashanti Confederacy, located in what was then called the Gold Coast, today's Ghana.

The Ashanti were one of the Akan-speaking peoples of the rain forest region. Eighteenth-century leaders had unified several neighboring peoples into the Ashanti Kingdom. Acquiring firearms, trading in gold, and raiding the villages of other peoples for slaves, the rulers of the new kingdom grew powerful. By 1800, they had absorbed neighbors still farther afield into the Ashanti Confederacy, an African state that in the nineteenth century included 150,000 square miles of tropical forest and grassy plains centered in the capital city of Kumasi.

To hold such a large area together, the Ashanti kings forged a powerful monarchical ideology and a substantial bureaucracy of royal servants. Taking the title of *asantehene,* "king of the Ashanti state," they claimed to rule by virtue of the "golden stool," a royal throne believed to have fallen from heaven. A victorious national army and an elaborate annual festival further focused loyalty on the sovereign.

Sources of administrative strength included a traditional council, originally composed of the kings of the confederacy's member states, which was gradually replaced by an ad hoc advisory council chosen by the *asantehene* himself. The hereditary chiefs of leading

Market day in front of the great mosque at Jenne, in the modern African nation of Mali. The mosque, built entirely of clay, is restored each year by the citizens of the town, each ward or neighborhood working over its traditional section of the structure. (Anthony Esler)

clans and subject peoples were deprived of authority over their own people, which was delegated instead to appointed palace officials and proconsuls. Other royal officials took charge of the profitable mining and slave businesses, both royal monopolies. Muslims from the north served as scribes and treasurers in the Ashanti state.

With a disciplined army and a large taxable population under rigorous royal control, the Ashanti Confederacy dominated the region. Only the restraining power of British coastal settlements established for commercial purposes limited the expansive power of this black African kingdom.

There were other such centralized states in the forests of West Africa. These included the kingdoms of Dahomey and Oyo, the latter tracing its civilization back to the medieval culture of Ife. But no other was as widely known, admired, and feared as the Ashanti Confederacy.

### East Africa: Egypt and Ethiopia

Another pattern of political revival developed in East Africa during the nineteenth century. In Egypt, Ethiopia, and beyond, a calculated process of state-building and the beginnings of modernization emerged on the African scene.

The earliest case was that of Egypt's Muhammad Ali Pasha (1769–1849), who came to Egypt in 1800 as a mercenary in the service of the Ottoman emperor and ended his life as the founder of a ruling dynasty in what was nominally a province of the Ottoman Empire. Over almost half a century of power in Cairo, Muhammad Ali crushed the Mamelukes, the country's long-established military ruling class. He also conquered both Syria in the Near East and the area up the Nile which is today's nation of Sudan. Neither of these conquests lasted; but in preparing for his military campaigns, the pasha brought some changes to his own country.

As khedive or viceroy of Egypt, Muhammad Ali undertook some important reforms. These included major irrigation projects, the encouragement of industry, and a more efficient system of taxation. Some of these innovations were scuttled by the British, who feared his growing strength in the area. Nevertheless, Muhammad Ali Pasha's tenure of power on the Nile did set Egypt on the long road to modernity.

The most successful East African modernization, however, was that of the ancient monarchy of Ethiopia. Here the Christian descendants of the long-vanished empire of Axum had survived in their mountain fastnesses for fifteen hundred years. There had been later flowerings of Ethiopian culture, notably in the thirteenth century, when the unique churches of King Lalibela were carved from the living rock of volcanic mountains. By 1800, however, foreign incursions and domestic division had left the nation little more than a loose coalition of princes with a figurehead king. Then in the later nineteenth century, a series of three rulers reversed this trend toward disintegration with spectacular consequences.

The first of these reforming monarchs, King Tewdoros, laid out an elaborate program of development only to fall victim to a quarrel with Britain, which dispatched a military expedition in 1868. His successor Johannes IV faced several foreign foes before falling in battle with the Sudanese in 1889. Only under the third in this vigorous line, King Menelik II (1889–1913) did Ethiopia, like Egypt, set out on the long, slow path of development often called modernization.

Prince of the autonomous Ethiopian state of Shoa, Menelik II had also served an apprenticeship in government under Yohannes before himself succeeding to the title of *negusa nagast,* "king of kings." From the beginning, Manelik's goals included reestablishing both the authority of the king of kings over the princes and Ethiopian suzerainty over neighboring peoples who had once been tributary states. He was also thoroughly aware of the menace of further European incursions like that which had destroyed King Theodore. To accomplish his aims, however, he found it necessary to begin the modernization of his ancient land by borrowing skills from the West he feared.

Menelik thus imported both Western technicians and Western guns. He built bridges and roads, and, with the help of his European experts, introduced the beginnings of Western postal and educational systems and financial institutions. From his new capital at Addis Ababa, he ruled a united nation by the end of the nineteenth century.

Menelik II's achievements in international affairs were equally impressive. Through a combination of force and diplomacy, he succeeded in imposing his own authority on neighboring peoples. And in 1896, at the high tide of Europe's New Imperialism, Ethiopia's large and well-armed military shattered an Italian invasion at the great battle of Adowa. "If powers at a distance come forward to partition Africa," the Ethiopian emperor had declared, "I do not intend to be an indifferent spectator."[4] He had been as good as his word.

---

[4]Robert W. July, *A History of the African People* (New York: Scribner's, 1970), p. 338.

## South Africa: The Zulus and the *Mfecane* States

Zululand today is a small enclave 10,000 square miles in area on the east coast of the Republic of South Africa. The Zulus who live there trace their ancestry to one of a number of Nguni-speaking peoples who had reached southern Africa by the fifteenth century. Their arrival marked the end of the great Bantu migrations and came only a short time before the first Portuguese vessels touched there on their way to India. The forebears of the Zulus were thus well established when the first Dutch settlers—the ancestors of the nineteenth-century Boers (today's Afrikaners)—arrived in what would become Capetown in 1652. Not until the 1800s, as the Boers began to carve out a state for themselves, did the Zulus emerge as the dynamos of change and of state-building among the black inhabitants of southern Africa.

The original impetus for Zulu expansion seems to have been ecological and demographic. The fertile, disease-free South African plateau produced a steady growth in population, which by 1800 had generated land hunger and conflict among the Nguni peoples. Endemic warfare in turn fostered tighter military and civil organization, replacing the loose clan federations of earlier centuries. Troubled times and an evolving society, finally, opened the way for the most famous African soldier and state builder of the century— Shaka (1787–1828), the "African Napoleon" and founder of the Zulu nation.

The illegitimate son of a war-loving Zulu chief, Shaka revealed little of his innovative genius until he inherited leadership of the Zulus himself in 1817. Throughout his career, he like his father remained above all a military leader. Like state builders elsewhere in Africa—as well as in such European nations as Prussia and Russia—Shaka developed new political institutions primarily as a means of strengthening his army. Both his military and political innovations, however, had far-reaching consequences.

To strengthen his troops, Shaka built upon a reform with which others had already experimented: the conversion of the younger Zulu age grades into permanent military regiments. Shaka's regiments, or *impis,* however, were rigorously trained, rigidly disciplined, and endlessly drilled. Kept under arms for many years, they became experienced and effective forces of veteran fighters. Shaka also revolutionized African tactics by replacing the long throwing spear with the *assegai,* a short stabbing spear used at close quarters by troops advancing in tight formation behind tall cowhide shields. And his "cow's horns" battlefield deployment, with flanking units (the "horns") closing behind their foes, added still further to the effectiveness of his armies. Thus trained, armed, and deployed, operating not as individual warriors seeking personal glory but as groups under officers' orders, Zulu *impis* swept to victory after victory.

As a political organizer, Shaka also showed both shrewdness and rigor. Claiming divine kingship, he made his soldiers completely dependent on him for food—the cattle they won in battle—for clothing, weapons, and for their very lives, since any failure of courage or any act of disobedience was punishable by death. The Zulu nation, furthermore, grew rapidly as Shaka incorporated the youth of each new conquered people into his army, converting each new levy into Zulus too, equally dependent on the king. A precocious Zulu nationalism was thus created, which outweighed—and outlasted—the fear of their leader's iron discipline. "Who are the Zulu?" demanded Shaka:

> They are parts of two hundred unruly clans which I had to break up and reshape, and only the fear of death will hold them together. The time will come when they will be as one nation. In the meantime, my very nature must inspire them with terror.[5]

---

[5]E. A. Ritter, *Shaka Zulu* (London: Hamilton, 1955), p. 319.

By the time of his death in 1828, Shaka's word was law to half a million Zulus spread over 80,000 square miles of South Africa. And a national feeling had been born that is still a political force in the region today.

Shaka was a violent man who died by assassination, struck down by his own brothers. Some of his best commanders had already broken with him, seceding with their regiments to spread both the violence and the discipline Shaka had fostered all across the southern stem of Africa. His former officers also took Shaka's military and political innovations with them, establishing new states wherever they settled. In addition, the Zulu diaspora inspired other peoples to adopt similarly rigorous new social structures to defend themselves against the *mfecane,* the "smashing of peoples" that shook South Africa in the first half of the nineteenth century.

Shaka's successors ruled the Zulu people for half a century, fighting the hardy Boers and winning battles against the British as late as the 1870s. They "washed their spears" in the blood of their enemies and littered battlefields like Rorke's Drift with the bodies of British redcoats before falling victim to superior European firepower in 1879. It was yet another example of the flexibility and growth of which African political organization was capable in that last century before the Western conquest.

## POLITICAL AND ECONOMIC CHANGES IN AFRICA

### State-Building and State Power

As we have seen, in the early nineteenth century, rulers in several parts of Africa embarked upon programs of state-building, or expansion of state power, without parallel on that continent since the fall of the Songhai Empire two hundred years earlier. These leaders included such varied types as the Muslim reformers of the Western Sudan, hereditary monarchs in East Africa, and military conquerors in South Africa. Some general patterns of governmental reform and restructuring were, however, common to many of these emergent powers.

Almost all, for instance, aimed at strongly centralized monarchies. Hereditary rulers built upon traditional attribution of divinity to monarchs, which could provide a strong foundation for claims to enhanced and expanded powers. At the same time, however, they were quick to set aside the element of reciprocal obligation traditionally owed by rulers to the ruled. Rulers also commonly rejected requirements that they consult with councils of elders, subordinate chiefs, or other groups whose countervailing power had once limited the authority of African kings.

Strong central governments entailed the growth of bureaucratic structures, and this too was a feature of these new states. Emperors, kings, and other rulers governed through increasingly elaborate hierarchies of appointed officials, some concentrated at the royal court, others dispatched to execute the royal will in distant parts of the kingdom. Increasingly, efficiency in the royal service, rather than hereditary right or other traditional criteria, determined appointment and promotion. Even royal slaves, completely dependent upon their masters, sometimes held high administrative posts and rose to wealth and power. And as with bureaucracies everywhere, their numbers grew: the Guinea coast kingdom of Oyo, for instance, boasted 15,000 royal officials by the end of the eighteenth century.

It is even possible to detect in some of these new polities the equivalent of a modern sense of national feeling. Some of the new or expanding states drew strength from such preexisting factors as a common language or shared ethnic or clan loyalties. Such allegiances, sometimes dismissed as "tribalism," could in fact involve millions of people, more than some European nationalities could claim. In other places, such as Christian Ethiopia or the Muslim states of West Africa, religion helped to unify a nation and to justify government policies. In still other states, like those of the Zulus in South Africa, efforts were made to expand existing systems of lineage and clan to absorb newly conquered peoples into a unifying structure of loyalties.

All such efforts to create deeper allegiances went beyond anything attempted earlier in Africa. For Mali, Songhai, and other early African empires, like premodern imperial powers in many places, had seldom sought to assimilate the various peoples they ruled into a common framework of cultural affiliation.

## Evolving Commercial Networks

Commercial exchange also evolved in many parts of Africa during the nineteenth century. The majority of Africans remained farmers, herders, and intermittent food gatherers, completely self-sufficient but producing little surplus for sale outside their own villages. But trade did play an increasingly important part in the lives of other Africans as the century advanced.

Long-distance trade had of course existed for many centuries in West Africa and in the coastal trading cities of East Africa. Even in these areas, however, commercial exchange both expanded and changed in this period. In most of Central, South, and inner East Africa, there had been little beyond local trade before 1800. In these regions, a narrow but expanding flow of commerce developed after that date.

A fundamental change was the passing of the slave trade, which had afflicted both coasts and had extended its tentacles far into the African interior ever since European slave traders had made slave raiding a profitable business in the sixteenth century. The eighteenth-century Enlightenment, however, and the accompanying wave of humanitarian concern had led growing numbers of Western people to see slavery as a social evil. The economic imperatives of capitalism may also have made free labor seem more flexible and efficient. Whatever the reasons, over the course of the nineteenth century, one Western nation after another outlawed first the trade in slaves and then slavery itself. And in the later 1800s, the British navy in particular began to hunt down slavers of all nationalities and repatriate slaves found in their holds to the continent if not the region of their birth. First in West Africa, then in East Africa, the trade in human flesh thus finally dwindled.

Commercial exchange among Africa, Europe, and the Americas thereafter took the form of what came to be known as "legitimate trade." New West African export items included timber, peanuts, kola nuts, and palm oil, the latter used to lubricate the new machinery of the Industrial Revolution. East Africa exported luxury products like ivory and cloves as well as a continuing flow of slaves, for which there was still a market in Asia, particularly in the Middle East. In return, Africans imported light cotton cloth from Europe or India, mass-produced utensils, alcoholic beverages, and increasing quantities of firearms, despite the efforts of Europeans to curtail exports of the latter to Africa.

Especially on the coasts, where foreign merchants had long-established commercial enclaves, this legitimate trade—as contrasted with the trade in slaves—grew through the century. On the African side, the lucrative export trade was often a royal monopoly. African kings thus forbade foreign merchants to go directly to local markets, requiring them instead to deal only with royal officials. The latter, though sometimes legally slaves of the king, could become exceedingly wealthy through the administration of such commercial monopolies.

Elsewhere, an energetic new commercial class emerged. Individuals even of lower-class origins rose to commercial prominence on both coasts. Thus the East African Arab-Swahili merchant Muhammed bin Hammad, known to Europeans as Tippu Tip, constructed a vastly profitable string of trading posts reaching deep into Central Africa. Dealing in slaves as well as ivory, Tippu Tip became the virtual ruler of an inland trading empire, though he always insisted that he was "merely a merchant." Similar rags-to-riches stories could be found in other parts of the continent as African traders competed vigorously and often successfully with the Europeans who gathered ever more thickly on their coasts.

## Interaction with Outside Forces

As throughout its history, Africa in the nineteenth century was thus by no means isolated from the outside world. Despite the tendency of Europeans to see it as the "unknown continent" because much of it was not yet on Western maps, Africa continued to relate to the other two continents of the Old World particularly.

Politically, the Ottoman Turkish Empire still claimed parts of North Africa, and Muhammad Ali, even while he built his power base in Egypt, remained nominally the viceroy of the emperor in Constantinople. Also during the earlier nineteenth century, at least some European penetration of the continent occurred. In the 1830s, the French crossed the Mediterranean to begin the occupation of Algeria, in North Africa. In that decade also, the long-established Boer settlers in South Africa, pressured by the British, began the Great Trek into the interior to found the new European enclaves of the Transvaal and the Orange Free State. The vast bulk of the world's second largest continent remained under African control before 1870, but the political presence of these intruders was a reality with which some Africans at least had to deal even in the early 1800s.

Both Muslims and Christians sought converts in Africa with increasing determination in the nineteenth century. We have already noted the emergence of the Islamic *jihad* states, mostly in the first half of the century. In the second half, expanding networks of Christian missionaries would play a significant part in Europe's imperial penetration of Africa.

All this foreign activity had its impact on Africans, stimulating economic, political, and cultural changes. By and large, however, as one authority put it, "the scope and nature of these changes" remained as late as 1870 "matters for African decision and initiative."[6] Only at the end of the century did Western power begin to determine the course of African history.

## TRADITIONAL CULTURES IN AN AGE OF TRANSITION

### Society and Community

Nineteenth-century African views of society and corresponding patterns of social relationships seem to reflect the time of transition that was already under way. An older, more egalitarian view was still preserved in many places, as it is today. In others, sharper dis-

---

[6]John E. Flint, "Introduction," *The Cambridge History of Europe*, Vol. 5, *From c. 1790 to c.1870* (London and New York: Cambridge University Press, 1976), p. 11.

tinctions between social classes had clearly emerged, though they were still softened by an older African sense of community.

Village cultures, particularly in areas of ethnic homogeneity, tended to distinguish between people on traditional grounds, in terms of sex and age group. Different African peoples assigned different social roles and attributed different qualities to men and women, to the old, the mature, and the young.

Women's roles in traditional tribal Africa encompassed a broad range of activities. They often remained subordinate to their husbands and their husbands' families. But they did not have to face *purdah* or the harem, European divorce and property laws, Indian *sati,* or Chinese footbinding. In some places, they shared breadwinning chores with their husbands. And some African women were still chiefs; some were successful traders.

In such traditional societies, status rather than class was the foundation of the ranking system. Where levels of material wealth were uniformly low, distinctions on the basis of material possessions were much less important. Social status meant honor, respect, and social privilege and was assigned to heads of families or clans, to age rather than youth, and to such spiritually powerful professionals as diviners, rainmakers, and priestesses. In these traditional cultures also, an older world view still prevailed. The individual was seen as part of the community, society as embedded in nature, and the natural world itself as part of a larger spiritual order of things.

By contrast, in areas where political and economic changes and outside influences had begun to transform African society, this older view was beginning to change.

Where royalty or rich merchants towered over ordinary people, there were ample grounds for distinguishing one class from another. Where wars of conquest had had their effect, aristocrats were often ethnically distinct from the rest of the population, the heirs of a conquering people. Ordinary peasants, herders of cattle, or cultivators of crops comprised most of the middle range of such a structured society. But there were also often castes or whole villages dedicated to specialized crafts, from iron-working to weaving. There was also likely to be a substantial unfree portion of the population. Technically slaves, these servile elements ranged from field hands and house servants to concubines and even administrative personnel who could wield great power. Despite their unfree status, such people typically felt little of the stigma that was heaped upon slaves in some places.

Moreover, even in these more hierarchically structured societies, traditional attitudes fostered a sense of community. Lineage and clan membership still softened the impact of class differences. Poor relations could confidently call upon more fortunate kinsmen for material help at need. And professional *griots,* or praise-singers, reminded rich and poor alike of the deeds of their celebrated ancestors, veneration for whom bound them all in a larger unity.

### Art and Life

Traditional arts also continued to flourish in nineteenth-century Africa. Indeed, more than any other aspect of African life, the arts tended to preserve the traditions on which the older African order was based and to integrate ancient beliefs with daily life.

Among the traditional arts still widely practiced were distinctive forms of sculpture, literature, music, and dance. Carvers of wood, storytellers, players of drums, flutes, and stringed instruments, and dancers and dance troupes were common in various parts of Africa. In the twentieth century, the work of these practitioners of ancient arts would be collected, analyzed, applauded, and imitated in the West. In the nineteenth century, it was still part of the daily lives of the African people. Carved ritual objects and masks were still the dwelling places of spirits, bards still celebrated ancestral glories, and music accompanied work and play, weddings, births, and deaths.

But the arts also adapted to the evolving political and economic order. In kingdoms and empires like those of West Africa, artists might be sequestered in palace courtyards, reserving the secrets of their crafts for their royal masters. Rich merchants who could afford to hire a *griot* for a traditional family feast combined the honoring of their ancestors with a chance to impress their less affluent kin. On the other hand, singers and dancers had in some places the traditional right to satirize and lampoon as well as to praise the rich and powerful. This privilege they sometimes used as a sharp-edged tool of social criticism, exposing the vanity of the new rich or challenging the untraditional policies of kings.

## Development or Disintegration?

It was a turbulent time of change in Africa. What, however, was the overall impact of these changes on traditional African society? The result, it may be suggested, was a combination of strengths and weaknesses that had the cumulative effect of leaving Africa unprepared for the European onslaught to come.

On the political side, the growth of centralized bureaucratic government in some parts of Africa was certainly a move toward stronger states. At the same time, however, these changes undermined hereditary elites and traditional ethnic and clan loyalties. Appointed officials thrust aside hereditary chiefs and ritual priests. Innovative leaders like Shaka warped age groups into full-time military forces and destroyed their role in traditional society.

Economic changes also had complex and not always beneficial consequences. Wealth channeled into the service of threatened African states, as in the revived Ethiopian kingdom, could pay for the beginnings of a modern society. Accumulation of wealth, however, could also undermine older ways. Both royal trade monopolies and the rise of commoners to great wealth flew in the face of ancient African systems of family ownership and collective use of the means of production.

There had of course been powerful monarchs and rich merchants in Africa before. The more common these became, however, the more subversive they were of older institutions.

Increasing—and increasingly intense—African relations with the outside world brought their share of problems too. Muslim rulers might bring better government, Christian missionaries new skills or medical knowledge. But both Christians and Muslims now sought to uproot older African religions, which both saw as "pagan," down to the village level. In medieval Ghana or early modern Songhai, Islam had been the faith of an urban elite only, leaving the rural majority to the animist faiths of their forefathers. But the Fulani rulers of the new empires of the Western Sudan worked zealously to destroy paganism and to spread a purified Islamic faith to all their subjects. In the colonial order to come, Christian missionaries would further intensify this assault on traditional beliefs.

These political, economic, and ideological changes had one final paradoxical weakness: They were coming too slowly. The drift toward stronger political units, the concentration of wealth, even the spread of a more militant religious faith were simply not proceeding rapidly enough to prepare the continent to face the assault of Western peoples among whom these sources of strength were already well developed. Changes that might have produced a stronger, richer, more militant Africa had time to get under way in the nineteenth century, and to undermine the old order. But they did not have time to produce a new society. The peoples of Africa were thus no better prepared than were the decaying empires of Asia to confront the New Imperialism that swept over them all at the end of the nineteenth century.

## SUMMARY

While Europe and some of its former American colonies underwent major changes and emerged richer and more powerful than ever before, Europe's neighbors in Asia and Africa faced their own changes—with less positive consequences.

During the seventeenth, eighteenth, and nineteenth centuries, the empires of Asia either declined or withdrew into isolation. Asia for the first time lost the position of parity with or superiority to Europe that the larger continent had enjoyed throughout history.

In the Middle East, the Ottoman Empire lost territory to Austria and Russia and sank into political corruption and industrial decay. In Persia, the endless Shiite wars led to fragmentation and increasing British and Russian influence in Isfahan. Mughal India faced Hindu revolts against Muslim persecution and the pressure of growing European power, which climaxed in the ascendancy of the British East India Company after the defeat of the French in 1763.

In East Asia both China's Manchu emperors and the Tokugawa shoguns of Japan adopted isolationist policies toward the West, which, in the long run, did not pay. The long-lived emperors Kangxi and Qianlong led China to renewed power and still greater prosperity under the Manchus. But their intense Confucian conservatism and their rejection of Western influences left China ill prepared for the unprecedented Western onslaught that was to come in the nineteenth century.

The Tokugawa shogun Ieyasu, who seized power in 1600, presided over a prosperous economy and a sophisticated urban culture. But he and his successors also preached conservative *bushido* traditions and expelled the Europeans who had found a foothold in their country.

In withdrawal or decay, Arab Muslims turned to Wahabi fundamentalism, and Rajput painters drew on India's ancient myths and epics for themes and subjects. Manchu Chinese culture went to extremes of conservatism and eccentricity. Only in Japan did cultural development take a dynamic new direction, in the sophisticated urban art and literature of Genroku culture.

In a variety of ways, many parts of Africa were evolving rapidly in the nineteenth century. New nations were emerging, and political and economic changes were occurring that challenged much of Africa's traditional culture.

New kingdoms and empires arose from the grasslands of West Africa to the South African plateau. Muslim crusaders built *jihad* states in the Western Sudan; the Ashanti Confederacy grew in the rain forests back of the Guinea coast; and the Christian kingdom of Ethiopia revived in the northeastern highlands, while Shaka and the Zulu *impis* shook South Africa.

Resulting political changes focused on the growth of strong central government. Economically, commerce expanded as the slave trade gave way to "legitimate trade." Foreign influences intensified, challenging traditional African attitudes and institutions.

Africa on the eve of the last great wave of Western imperialism was thus in the throes of changes that, given time, might have materially strengthened the continent. But lacking such time, these changes left Africa as ill prepared for what was to come as the declining empires of Asia.

## SUGGESTED READING

Blussé, L., and F. Gaastra, eds. *On the Eighteenth Century as a Category of Asian History: Van Leur in Retrospect.* Brookfield, Vt.: Ashgate, 1998. Papers exploring the eighteenth century as a crucial turning point in East and South Asian history.

Boahen, A. A. *African Perspectives on Colonialism.* Baltimore, Md.: Johns Hopkins University Press, 1987. Stimulating summation of the African view that the continent was actually developing rapidly before Western imperialists imposed underdevelopment on their colonies.

Davis, F. *The Ottoman Lady: A Social History from 1718 to 1918.* New York: Greenwood, 1986. Analysis of the lifestyles of upper-class women under the later Ottomans.

Frank, A. G. *ReOrient: Global Economy in the Asian Age.* Berkeley: University of California Press, 1998. Widely discussed study urging reorientation of traditional thinking about the relative economic strength of Europe and Asia on the eve of the Industrial Revolution.

Gaubatz, P. R. *Beyond the Great Wall: Urban Form and Transformation on the Chinese Frontiers.* Stanford, Calif.: Stanford University Press, 1996. Mingling of cultures in frontier Chinese cities.

Gocek, F. M. *Rise of the Bourgeoisie, Demise of Empire: Ottoman Westernization and Social Change.* New York: Oxford University Press, 1996. How Western influences and changes in Ottoman society undermined the empire.

Hamilton, C. *Terrific Majesty: The Powers of Shaka Zulu and the Limits of Historical Invention* (Cambridge, Mass.: Harvard University Press, 1998), on the image of Shaka Zulu as constructed by both Europeans and Africans.

Laband, J. *The Rise and Fall of the Zulu Nation.* London: Arms and Armour Press, 1997. Military history. For a more popular general history, see S. Taylor, *Shaka's Children: A History of the Zulu People* (London: Harper Collins, 1994). For a perceptive analysis of tactics, motives, and backgrounds of Zulu and British commanders and soldiers, see R. B. Edgerton, *Like Lions They Fought: The Zulu War and the Last Black Empire in South Africa* (New York: Free Press of MacMillan, 1988).

Law, R., ed. *From Slave Trade to 'Legitimate' Commerce.* New York: Cambridge University Press, 1995. Essays on the nineteenth-century shift in West African trade. See also P. Manning, *Slavery and African Life: Occidental, Oriental, and African Slave Trades* (New York: Cambridge University Press, 1990).

Mann, S. *Precious Records: Women in China's Eighteenth Century.* Stanford: Standford University Press, 1997. What the work of Chinese women writers tells us about the lives of Chinese women.

Marcus, H. G. *The Life and Times of Menelik II: Ethiopia, 1844–1913.* Oxford: Clarendon Press, 1975. Achievements of the chief architect of modern Ethiopia. See also Marcus's *A History of Ethiopia* (Berkeley: University of California Press, 1994).

Mazumdar, S. *Sugar and Society in China: Peasants, Technology, and the World Market.* Cambridge, Mass.: Harvard University Asia Center, 1998. Probes ways in which Chinese economic development equaled Europe's, as well as ways in which Qing China failed to develop.

McCaskie, T. C. *State and Society in Pre-Colonial Asante.* New York: Cambridge University Press, 1995. Challenging new reading of West African government, based on anthropological rather than political analysis.

McClain, J. L., J. M. Merriman, and U. Kaoru, eds. *Edo and Paris: Urban Life and the State in the Early Modern Era.* Ithaca and London: Cornell University Press, 1997. Parallels between the capitals of Bourbon France and Tokugawa Japan.

Mungello, D. E. *The Great Encounter of China and the West.* New York: Bowman and Littlefield, 1999. Brief account of religious and philosophical exchanges.

Naquin, S., and E. S. Rawski. *Chinese Society in the Eighteenth Century.* New Haven, Conn.: Yale University Press, 1987. Thoroughly researched synthesis of Chinese society in the last century before decline set in, noting early signs of the government's weakening grip on distant provinces.

Okpewho, I. *Once Upon a Kingdom: Myth, Hegemony, and Identity.* Bloomington: Indiana University Press, 1998. Benin's imperial image reflected in an African storytelling tradition.

Romero, P. W., ed. *Life Histories of African Women.* London: Ashfield Press, 1988. Reconstructed lives of African women, including a number from the nineteenth century.

Spence, J. D. *The Search for Modern China.* New York: Norton, 1990. Monumental study of Qing times.

Totman, C. *Early Modern Japan.* Berkeley and Los Angeles: University of California Press, 1993. New standard textbook, with an ecological perspective.

Wrigley, C. *Kingship and the State: The Buganda Dynasty.* New York: Cambridge University Press, 1996. Structuralist analysis of African rulers manipulating traditional religion for political purposes.

 Please refer to the document CD-ROM for primary sources related to this chapter.

# CHAPTER 23

# MAXIM GUNS AND MERCHANT BANKERS

## The Climax of Western Imperialism

### (1870–1900)

## A Glance Ahead: European Mastery of Asia and Africa

What is often called the "new imperialism" exploded across Asia and Africa in the last decades of the nineteenth century. During these years, Europe's enormous technological and organizational superiority turned much of Asia into European protectorates or spheres of influence and almost all of Africa into European colonies. Britain and France emerged as the rulers of the largest intercontinental empires, but others, including Germany, Italy, and Belgium, were not far behind. Elsewhere, huge countries like the United States and Russia poured settlers into areas long claimed but still populated by older indigenous peoples. And all of Oceania, from Australia to Polynesia, came under Western domination in the course of the nineteenth century.

The motives of the imperialists included a lust for profits, land hunger, missionary impulses, and an urge to "civilize"—meaning westernize—the rest of the globe. Colonized peoples often resisted, though seldom successfully in the face of Western artillery and rapid-firing Maxim guns. Colonists, developers, and do-gooders settled in for what they imagined would be a long spell as rightful rulers of the world.

## The Nature of the New Imperialism

### A New Wave of Imperial Expansion

The great revival of Western expansion we call the New Imperialism, running from around 1870 to perhaps 1914, was one of the most astonishing aspects of nineteenth-century world history. The New Imperialism was particularly surprising because during most of the preceding hundred years, imperial expansion had been widely seen as a losing proposition. This feeling was generated by the loss of Europe's most highly developed colonies in the New World between the 1770s and the 1820s, when revolutions cost Britain, Spain, and Portugal their American colonies and France was prevailed upon to sell its substantial sweep of middle North America to the new United States. "Colonies," the philosophe and statesman Turgot declared in a famous aphorism, "are like fruits which cling to the tree only until they ripen."[1]

Still, large parts of the world either remained in European hands or were strongly influenced by European traders, missionaries, and others. Examples would include British holdings in India, Canada, and Australia; the French West Indies and France's conquest of Algeria in 1830; and the Dutch settlements in South Africa and continuing Dutch preeminence in island Southeast Asia. The former colonies in the Americas, furthermore, though politically independent, continued to be ruled by people of European descent and culture and remained closely bound commercially, socially, and intellectually to the Old World.

Then, around 1870, the Western peoples launched a startling new wave of imperial aggression against the rest of the world. This New Imperialism was an explosion of Western conquest that would dwarf the achievements of preceding centuries.

---

[1]F. Lee Benns, *European History Since 1870* (New York: Appleton-Century-Crofts, 1950), p. 13.

## Motives of the New Imperialists

The causes of the New Imperialism have frequently been presented in the most simplistic and unconvincing way. The imperialists themselves claimed that this second great surge of Western colonialism was, in Kipling's phrase, "the white man's burden"—a moral obligation to spread the benefits of a "higher" Western civilization to a backward world. Particularly since the collapse of the European overseas empires after World War II, on the other hand, enemies of imperialism have depicted it as exploitation pure and simple, a cloak for Western capitalist looting of a helpless world. As with most major historical events, however, the New Imperialism seems to have been the product of a considerable variety of factors—economic, political, humanitarian, and even psychological.

As the exploitation theorists emphasize, economic causes played a large part in the new wave of overseas expansion. The Industrial Revolution created new and complex economic and technological demands that in many cases could best be met by the extension of European power into distant parts of the world. One of the most obvious of these needs was the demand for natural resources—many of them exotic commodities such as rubber, manganese, and oil—to feed into the vast hopper of the new industrial machine. There was also a demand for cheap labor, especially as European wages went up in the later nineteenth century. "Coolie" overseas labor would work much more cheaply than unionized Western workers and was therefore hired in large quantities to extract, process, and ship the resources of far-off lands back to Europe.

Another economic motive for expansion was the need for more customers for the fantastic production of the newly industrializing West: New colonies meant new markets for Western goods. The immense profits piling up in Europe also sought new investment areas and often found them in the underdeveloped world. Building a trunk railway line across Asia or Africa could bring in 30 percent interest on an investment, whereas a modest spur line in Europe returned less than 5 percent.

Political and military motives also played a part in empire-building. The need for naval bases or coaling stations for the new steam navies and merchant marines could lead Western powers to seize key harbors or islands. Many strategic straits and strips of land with geopolitical value were targets for annexation. Political determination to out-maneuver a European rival could impel Western governments to acquire large territories having no detectable economic value at all.

Besides economic and political causes, humanitarian impulses played a significant part in the New Imperialism. Protestant and Catholic missionaries thronged to the "mission fields" in Africa and Asia in unparalleled numbers. The flag often followed them, for governments were compelled by pious public opinion to support the spreaders of the Gospel in their good work.

Antislavery societies—formed after the Europeans themselves had given up slavery—urged Western governments to do whatever was necessary to suppress Arab slavers in the nineteenth century. And tidy-minded proconsuls of empire really did go out into what was for them the Heart of Darkness to spread European law, education, and medicine—as well as taxes and compulsory labor—south of the Sahara and east of Suez.

Finally, totally irrational psychological drives may have been at work beneath all of these expressed motives for imperial expansion. A simple but powerful sense of Western superiority, rooted in nineteenth-century progress, prosperity, and racist theories of the biological superiority of caucasoid humanity, was clearly part of the psychological equipment of most imperialists, for instance.

It has also been suggested that instinctive aggressiveness, revealed at home in a range of activities from sports to politics and business competition, may have helped cause imperialism. Europeans may have taken up arms against Zulus and Afghans for the pure primordial joy of "smashing 'em good." Even so simple a human psychological impulse as hero worship was perhaps better met by cavalry charges against the Apaches or skirmishes in the Khyber Pass than by portly politicians fighting election campaigns at home.

Political, economic, humanitarian, and psychological, the motives behind the New Imperialism were thus manifold. To all of these it might be well to add a final reminder that imperial conquest of other peoples is, after all, one of the great givens of history. A pattern of human behavior that can be traced back to the third millennium before Christ perhaps doesn't require too elaborate a scaffolding of explanation in more recent times.

## Means: The World Down the Barrel of a Maxim Gun

The awesome success of the New Imperialism probably requires more explanation than the motives for its undertaking. And here, at least, there is some agreement among the experts.

The new wave of Western aggression may have succeeded in part because of the powerful *esprit* of Western military forces, a total self-confidence generated by many triumphs and by the arrogant sense of racial superiority mentioned above. Another factor was almost certainly the greatly improved governmental organization and efficiency of post-Enlightenment Western administrative machinery. But the major cause of Western supremacy admits of little argument. Once again, the technology of the Industrial Revolution is at the heart of the matter.

Nineteenth-century European empire builders now faced Ashantis and Uzbeks with massed repeating-rifle fire. They confronted the junks and sampans of Eastern potentates with ironclad warships. They reduced the most impregnable strongholds of ancient kingdoms with heavy artillery and explosive shells. For a few brief decades a hundred years ago, the West had a technological advantage over the rest of the world that made Western Foreign Legions and thin red lines, Marines and gunboats well nigh invincible.

There were many differences among cultures, as even the smuggest Victorian had to allow. But the difference that mattered, as a cynical commentator perceptively suggested,

British naval vessels bombarding Canton. This ancient port city in South China surrendered under a rain of shells and rockets—typical prelude to the extraction of unequal treaties from the helpless imperial government in Beijing. "Gunboat diplomacy" was a prominent feature of Western imperial expansion and economic hegemony in many parts of the world in the nineteenth century. (The Bettmann Archive)

was that Western peoples had Maxim guns—an early version of the machine gun—and other peoples didn't.

## Forms of Imperial Control

To most people *empire* means colonies—something like the original thirteen American colonies, perhaps, with royal governors and redcoats. The New Imperialism, however, was a good deal more complicated than that. In fact it took several characteristic forms.

Some of the bastions of Western power overseas were colonies, of course. In a fully developed colony, European administrators set up centralized governmental structures in major cities. They also fanned out through the backcountry, scattering isolated "district officers" among the villages as agents of the new authority. European armies policed the newly acquired region. Marching up and down like Roman legions across Gaul, they often had to carry out several punitive expeditions before the new order was accepted.

A protectorate, by contrast, provided a form of control that was much less than total—and much less expensive. Here the key institution was the European *resident* or *advisor* to the local potentate. The traditional ruler accepted the advice of the European resident on any matter of concern to Europeans—trade, investment, missionary efforts, and the like. Otherwise, he ran his country in his own way. In return, the local sultan or shah or *raja* got financial aid, protection, and perhaps European support in his wars. The European resident was also supported by armed force, of course—commonly a naval squadron, which could patrol a large area and guarantee a number of protectorates.

The sphere of influence, finally, provided a still more diffuse and limited form of European control. The main objective here was almost always economic penetration. Western personnel took over a single institution—say, the customs service—or a limited area, such as a strip of land for a railway or the right to exploit mineral deposits. Spheres of influence commonly developed in regions where European rivals were evenly matched in strength; each would exercise an influence over an agreed-upon portion of the territory in question. The expense to European governments was minimal, the potential for exploitation and development often quite substantial.

There were, of course, many combinations of these three—colony, protectorate, sphere of influence—and bastard versions of each form. The internal imperialism to be discussed in a later section is not a matter of *overseas* empire-building at all, but of absorbing neighboring peoples—a form of imperialism as old as civilization.

There are, finally, those who see any economic relationship in which one party gets the better of another—that is to say, most economic relationships—as forms of imperialism. This concept of informal imperialism will be discussed under the twentieth-century rubric of *neo-imperialism*—though, again, it is anything but new.

Let us turn now, however, to a chronicle of the final phase of the great conquest—the New Imperialism of the later nineteenth century.

## THE SCRAMBLE FOR AFRICA

### First the Treaties, Then the Troops

The partitioning of Africa among the colonial powers of Europe during the last quarter of the nineteenth century was a transfer of sovereignty to rank with the Iberian seizure of South and Central America in the sixteenth century or the Mongol conquest of much of Eurasia

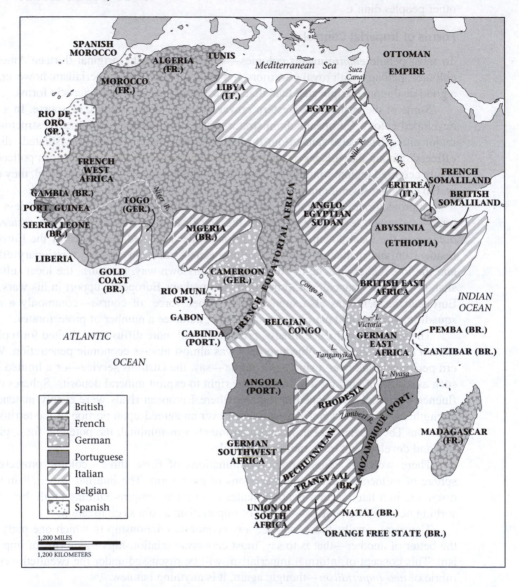

**AFRICA ABOUT, 1910**

SPANISH MOROCCO
MOROCCO (FR.)
ALGERIA (FR.)
TUNIS
*Mediterranean Sea*
Suez Canal
OTTOMAN EMPIRE
LIBYA (IT.)
EGYPT
RIO DE ORO (SP.)
*Nile R.*
*Red Sea*
FRENCH WEST AFRICA
FRENCH SOMALILAND
ERITREA (IT.)
BRITISH SOMALILAND
GAMBIA (BR.)
PORT. GUINEA
SIERRA LEONE (BR.)
*Niger R.*
TOGO (GER.)
ANGLO-EGYPTIAN SUDAN
LIBERIA
NIGERIA (BR.)
ABYSSINIA (ETHIOPIA)
GOLD COAST (BR.)
CAMEROON (GER.)
FRENCH EQUATORIAL AFRICA
RIO MUNI (SP.)
GABON
*Congo R.*
BRITISH EAST AFRICA
*INDIAN OCEAN*
CABINDA (PORT.)
BELGIAN CONGO
L. Victoria
PEMBA (BR.)
*ATLANTIC OCEAN*
GERMAN EAST AFRICA
ZANZIBAR (BR.)
L. Tanganyika
ANGOLA (PORT.)
L. Nyasa
RHODESIA
*Zambezi R.*
MOZAMBIQUE (PORT.)
MADAGASCAR (FR.)
GERMAN SOUTHWEST AFRICA
BECHUANALAND
TRANSVAAL (BR.)
UNION OF SOUTH AFRICA
NATAL (BR.)
ORANGE FREE STATE (BR.)

British
French
German
Portuguese
Italian
Belgian
Spanish

1,200 MILES
1,200 KILOMETERS

in the thirteenth. It was initially accomplished with minimal bloodshed, although holding the Africans in line, even for a few decades, sometimes turned out to be a very bloody business indeed.

The scramble for Africa by competing European powers was carried out by politicians and diplomats in Europe and by explorers, missionaries, military commanders, economic developers, and others in Africa itself. By the end of the century, it had brought nine tenths of the world's second-largest continent under Western rule.

Interest in the unknown interior of the "dark continent" was aroused initially by a handful of colorful individuals. Explorers poking about in search of the source of the Nile and other wonders kindled romantic enthusiasm at home. Increasing numbers of missionaries like Dr. Livingston carried Western religion and medicine into Africa and came back urging government intervention against the slavers.

In Europe, crowned heads and prime ministers began to concern themselves with Africa. Speeches were made about spreading the benefits of French civilization, defending Britain's lifeline to India, acquiring a "place in the sun" for Germany. There was public talk of developing the mineral wealth of inner Africa, suppressing the slave trade, expanding European commerce, and other issues. International conferences were held in Belgium (1876) and Berlin (1884) to lay down acceptable ground rules for carving up the continent.

On the African earth itself, it was first the treaties, then the troops. In the 1870s and 1880s, expeditions set out for the interior from the string of European settlements that had been scattered along the coasts since the heyday of the Old Imperialism. These handfuls of government officials or agents for trading companies negotiated treaties with Muslim monarchs and paramount chiefs, including the rulers of many of the newly evolving states we have visited in an earlier chapter. In return for gifts, protection, and other benefits, African rulers thus accepted a European overlordship that many of them only partly understood.

The misunderstandings were thrashed out later, during the sometimes savage fighting of the 1890s and the early 1900s. The larger states of inner Africa resisted initial penetration. Other African peoples revolted later against the increasingly heavy hand of Western rule.

Recent scholarship suggests that we should not exaggerate the European mastery of the situation. Local rulers often knew the local situation much better than the intruders did and made quite advantageous terms, at least in the short run. In the early 1830s, after a dozen years of mounting British pressure on the Ashanti of West Africa, the Ashanti princess Akyaawa Yikwan negotiated a key peace treaty that brought her people a vigorous revival of trade and postponed foreign rule for most of the rest of the century.

Rarely, however, was either resistance or diplomacy successful for long. The courage of the Africans was great, and their numbers often greater than those of the intruders. But a single Maxim machine gun could make numbers and courage suddenly irrelevant. From Egypt to the Cape, from the tree-studded grasslands of the western Sudan to the green hills of East Africa, European organization, discipline, ruthlessness, and firepower carried the day.

## Britain and Indirect Imperialism

Great Britian's holdings in Africa comprised colonies and protectorates north, south, east, and west.

In North Africa, the Conservative prime minister Disraeli and the Liberal Gladstone between them established a British protectorate over Egypt, despite the bitter opposition of the French, who had just completed the Suez Canal on Egyptian territory. Then trouble arose with a Muslim religious leader called the Mahdi farther up the Nile, and a famous British colonial officer known as "Chinese" Gordon was defeated and killed at Khartoum. British troops responded by pushing up the river, crushing the Mahdi's followers at the Battle of Omdurman, and establishing British authority in what became the Anglo-Egyptian Sudan.

In South Africa, the British faced two tenacious rivals: the Zulus, one of history's great warrior peoples, and the rugged Dutch settlers called Boers. Both were defeated, though at great cost. By 1914 Britain controlled the whole region, rich in gold, diamonds, and farmland. They divided it into the three white-ruled dependencies of Northern and Southern Rhodesia and the Union of South Africa.

On the Guinea Coast of West Africa, British colonies included Nigeria and the Gold Coast (Ghana today), isolated enclaves in the huge French-controlled bulge of West Africa. In East Africa, the British held what are today Uganda and Kenya, reaching from the Sudan to the coast. The western colonies were acquired by treaties with paramount chiefs, the eastern ones through British trading companies and a protectorate over the sultan of Zanzibar.

Almost everywhere in Africa, the British pursued a policy of indirect rule. They left traditional authorities in power at the local level, at least insofar as this was commensurate with British commercial interests and basic values. They intervened to maintain law and order and to support trading companies, railroad builders, and missionary activities. But local chiefs and emirs ruled in most matters and were even allowed to keep a substantial chunk of the taxes they collected to support the colonial regime.

## An Extension of France Overseas

A very different policy was followed by the French in Africa. French colonies were concentrated in the Mediterranean Muslim lands of Tunisia, Algeria, and Morocco, in the great westward sweep of Saharan and Sudanic Africa, and on the huge East African island of Madagascar—twice the size of the British Isles. All were run as if they were provinces of the French nation.

French penetration of North Africa began as early as the 1830s with the bloody conquest of Algeria, due south of France across the Mediterranean. Tunisia was occupied late in the century at the urging of Jules Ferry, France's leading proponent of empire, and Morocco was made a protectorate after a tense dispute with Germany in the early 1900s. Meanwhile, French troops had pushed south across the Sahara, east along the Senegal River from the Atlantic, and north up the Niger into western Sudan. They overcame with considerable difficulty the prolonged resistance of Muslim rulers such as Samori, a Mande leader and heir of the great Mande Sudanic kingdoms of medieval and early-modern times. Madagascar, finally, proved a quagmire for the French. France's intrusion provoked violent revolts and a long pacification campaign, which climaxed in the deposition and exile of the last queen, Ranavalona III, and the declaration of a French colony in the late 1890s.

Because these areas were seized only after prolonged fighting and were ruled for some time by military commanders, a rigidly centralized system of government was established. All of French West Africa—an area roughly the size of the United States—was ruled by a single government in Dakar. French proconsuls did not negotiate with local chieftains or leave the largest share of government in their hands, as the British did. French officials regarded traditional local rulers as subordinates and summoned them to French offices to give them orders.

Arab children in North Africa would soon be memorizing French classical tragedy in their schools. Black Africans from the western Sudan would be studying in Paris—all part of the effort to create an integrated empire that was in every sense an extension of France overseas.

## Other Powers Seek Their Places in the Sun

The main area of British colonial control in Africa ran north and south in a broken strip from Cairo to the Cape of Good Hope. The primary French zone was the whole of northwestern Africa—the states of the Maghreb, French West Africa, and French Equatorial Africa, reaching from the Atlantic to the frontiers of the Anglo-Egyptian Sudan. Most of the rest of Africa beyond these two great blocks was soon absorbed by other European powers, jostling and shoving for their share of the dwindling continent. The most important of these other exploiters of Africa were Belgium, Germany, Portugal, and Italy.

The Belgian king Leopold hired the journalist-turned-explorer Henry Stanley to sign treaties with chiefs all across the dense rain forest of the Congo Basin in central Africa. This gigantic Belgian colony, almost ten times the size of Belgium itself, became a major copper producer—and a byword for colonial cruelty to native peoples.

Germany, filled with national pride and expansive vigor after the unification of 1870–1871, demanded its "place in the sun" rather late. But the new nation soon had three large colonies: Cameroon, at the hinge of West Africa; an East African territory that is today Tanzania; and a southern colony bordering South Africa and composed largely of desert—modern Namibia. The genocidal suppression of the Maji-Maji rebellion in Tanzania became another of the horror stories of the great conquest.

Portugal expanded ancient holdings into the two large colonies of Angola and Mozambique on opposite sides of the stem of South Africa. The new nation of Italy set out with much vigor but mixed success to acquire North African territories. Italians seized the desert sprawl of Libya between French Tunisia and British Egypt, and the northeastern strip of Somaliland on the Red Sea and the Indian Ocean. Italian efforts to conquer Ethiopia, however, met disaster when an Italian army was destroyed at Adowa by the Ethiopians in 1896.

As the twentieth century began, then, only Ethiopia—also called Abyssinia—remained a truly independent African state. All the rest had come under the control, direct or indirect, of the relentlessly expanding West.

## THE EXPLOITATION OF ASIA

### Loans and Rights of Way

In Asia—the four fifths of Eurasia east of the Dardanelles—Europeans confronted a very different situation from that prevailing in Africa. The East, the original home of civilization, had for thousands of years been dominated by powerful Asian empires and complex urban societies. These Asian cultures had successfully resisted or effectively absorbed many invaders over the centuries.

Over much of the East, then, the more direct and brutal methods that had worked in Africa had less application. Military conquest and the establishment of a full-scale colonial administration did happen in Asia, but less often. More common was the protectorate, more common still the sphere of influence.

In Asia, imperialism was thus much less a matter of pith helmets and pacification campaigns. More often it was a dignified affair of bank loans or railway rights of way, of European officers retraining royal armies or European bureaucrats taking over crucial departments of someone else's government.

Warships played their part too, of course, patrolling the coasts of China or "opening up" Japan. There were savage struggles to hold India during the Mutiny of 1857 or to conquer chunks of mainland Southeast Asia. But much of the work of imposing the will of the West upon the East was done in meetings between Europeans themselves, in which they agreed to respect each others' "interests" in other peoples' countries.

There were fewer misunderstandings of the sort that might occur with a paramount chief in West Africa. Highly literate, if not always strong-willed, Asian sovereigns knew the rest of Africa. Beyond these two great blocks was ... absorbed by other European powers, jostling and shoving for their share of the dividing continent. The most important of these other exploiters of Africa were Belgium, Germany, Portugal, and Italy.

The Belgian king Leopold hired the journalist turned explorer Henry Stanley to help ...

## ASIA ABOUT 1910–1926

**Legend:**

- British Colonies
- Protected States in India
- Dutch Colonies
- Ottoman Empire
- Treaty Ports in China
- French
- Portuguese
- Japan
- U.S.A.
- Spain

1,000 MILES
1,000 KILOMETERS

**Map labels:**

EUROPE · AFRICA · RUSSIAN EMPIRE · OTTOMAN EMPIRE · PERSIA (RUSS. INFLUENCE) · AFGHANISTAN (BR. INFLUENCE) · HEJAZ · NEJD · KUWAIT (BR.) · BAHRAIN (BR.) · OMAN · YEMEN · ADEN (BR.) · INDIA · Bombay · Goa (PORT.) · Mahé (FR.) · Pondicherry (FR.) · Calcutta · CEYLON (BR.) · MALDIVE IS. (BR.) · NEPAL · SIKKIM · BHUTAN · TIBET · FEDERATED MALAY STATES (BR.) · SIAM · LAOS · CAMBODIA · COCHIN-CHINA · TONKIN · Rangoon · Singapore (BR.) · BRUNEI (BR.) · BR. N. BORNEO · DUTCH EAST INDIES · PORTUGUESE TIMOR · TIMOR · OUTER MONGOLIA 1912 · INNER MONGOLIA · REPUBLIC OF CHINA · Port Arthur · Hangchow · Shanghai · Canton · Hong Kong (BR.) · Macao (PORT.) · FORMOSA (JAP.) · PHILIPPINE IS. (U.S.A.) · RYUKYU IS. (JAP.) · KOREA · Vladivostok · JAPAN · Tokyo · KURILE IS. (JAP.) · SAKHALIN very well what they were getting into when a treaty was finally presented for their signature. There was simply very little that they could do about it. The benefits of a modernized army or a big loan were too great to be resisted. And the gunboats were always there.

## Great-Power Competition in the Middle East

This was notably the pattern in the Middle East, where France and Germany, Russia and Britain all jockeyed for strategic position and long-range profits.

France was first into the Middle East, in the days of Napoleon's eastern campaign just before 1800. The French victory at the Battle of the Pyramids, which broke the once-feared Mamelukes, attracted respectful attention all across the aging Ottoman Empire. French stock—and interests—rose higher with the opening of the Suez Canal by a French company in 1869. The British pushed the French out of Egypt in the 1880s, but Paris simply turned farther east, investing and building influence in Syria and Lebanon.

Germany developed a close relationship with the center of Ottoman power in Istanbul. German banks lent large sums to Turkey, and German officers worked to modernize the Turkish army. There were negotiations for a German consortium to build railroads in the Ottoman Empire. As the British talked of a Cape-to-Cairo line, the Germans dreamed of a Berlin-to-Baghdad railway with stops in Vienna and on the Golden Horn. Direct trade between the throbbing industrial heartland of Germany and the Far East via the Persian Gulf seemed a distinct possibility to William II, whose father had founded the German Empire in 1871, and who himself dreamed of a larger German empire overseas in the 1890s.

British and Russian imperial interests, finally, clashed in Iran and Afghanistan. These warring fragments of ancient Persia lay athwart the land route to British India—and along expanding Russia's southern frontier. Military commitments were therefore made by London and St. Petersburg to shahs and emirs in Teheran and Kabul. Russia continued to expand in central Asia, and Britain fought several Afghan Wars. Soon after 1900, however, an understanding between the two European powers divided Iran into three spheres of influence: a Russian zone in the north, including Teheran and ancient Isfahan; a British zone in the south, dominating the Persian Gulf; and a large neutral zone in between.

Thus Western governmental efficiency and industrial development began to filter into the ancient Muslim center of Eurasia. With these influences, however, came increasing political and economic dependence on the West.

## Britain and France in India and Southeast Asia

The British in South Asia and the British and French in Southeast Asia were the primary participants in the great drive for a more formal colonial empire east of Suez.

In British India, the subcontinent that constitutes the bulk of South Asia, imperialism took the form of intensification and systematization of the British supremacy established there in the preceding century. This process was particularly accelerated by the Indian Mutiny of 1857.

The mutiny was a consequence of the increased British presence in India in the nineteenth century. Unpopular policies included the dispossession of some Indian princes of their states, campaigns by Christian missionaries against Hindu religious customs, and a tightening up of restrictions on the Indian officials in the employ of the British East India Company, which still ruled India under parliamentary supervision. The famous incident that triggered the great revolt by Indian troops, the greasing of cartridges with pig and cow grease, affronted the most ancient religious taboos of both Hindus and Muslims. In the resulting carnage, hundreds of British men, women, and children were slaughtered—as were thousands of Indians, whose villages were put to the torch by vengeful British soldiers.

After the suppression of the mutiny, the British government took over sole responsibility for governing almost the entire subcontinent. A number of small princedoms continued to exist on sufferance, but a royal viceroy and thousands of British civil servants henceforth guided the colony's destinies. Schools, railroads, harbor facilities were built, and serious attempts were made to root out such unacceptable religious practices as *sati,* the ritual suicide of Hindu widows. India entered the twentieth century as the most glittering jewel in Queen Victoria's crown.

In Southeast Asia, Britain and France found themselves in uneasy competition as they established colonies on the western and eastern sides of the Indochinese peninsula. France pushed into Vietnam as early as the 1860s and subsequently established a protectorate over Cambodia and Laos. Expanding eastward from India, the British invaded and occupied Burma; other British expansionists pushed north from the key port of Singapore up the Malay Peninsula.

In the middle was Siam—Thailand today—the sole remaining independent state in mainland Southeast Asia. An agreement between Britain and France left Siam as a buffer between them. With the islands of today's Indonesia Dutch since the seventeenth century and the Philippines in American hands from 1900 on, Thailand remained, like Ethiopia in Africa, an isolated peak of independence in a sea of expanding Western power.

## The Opening of Japan

Even East Asia, which had flourished so long in comparative isolation from the rest of Eurasia, was in the end sucked into the maelstrom of the New Imperialism. Ancient China became the largest victim yet of Western expansion. And Japan became the first major Asian convert to Western technology—and to Western-style imperialism.

The Meiji Restoration of 1868 was one of the decisive events of modern Japanese history. Its immediate cause was the shattering of Japan's traditional isolation by the West—in this case by the United States.

The Tokugawa shogunate, two and a half centuries old by the middle of the nineteenth century, was an institution—and a dynasty—on its last legs. The Tokugawa clan no longer produced strong leadership capable of meeting crises decisively. Students of Japan's past had already begun to examine the traditional role allotted to the hereditary emperors, a position of religious and ceremonial importance but completely lacking in political power, and to speculate on restoring political authority to Japan's Son of Heaven.

It was at this point that an American fleet appeared. Commodore Matthew Perry arrived with a U.S. naval squadron, including three steam frigates, in 1853, instructed to "open" Japan to diplomatic and commercial exchange. The American ships with their massive artillery much impressed the Japanese. After months of bitter disputes in Japanese ruling circles, Japan signed its first unequal treaty with the United States—and soon after with other Western countries. By these treaties, Japan's rulers agreed to receive Western merchants and diplomats and to allow them special rights in Japan not to be granted Japanese in other countries.

In 1868, in the aftermath of these concessions, a group of outraged *daimyo* compelled the last shogun to resign—and passed political authority not to a new shogun but to the sixteen-year-old emperor, Mutsuhito. Known to history by his reign title—the Meiji ("Enlightened Rule") Emperor—Mutsuhito occupied the Japanese throne for the next forty-five years, widely recognized as a symbol of his country's rise from victim to victor, from an isolated island nation in East Asia to a world power.

The architects of the restoration of imperial power moved the imperial capital from old Kyoto to the shogun's former capital of Edo—renamed Tokyo—and set to work preparing Japan to resist Western penetration in an entirely new way. To this end, they engineered an amazing transformation of their country.

Like Peter the Great in eighteenth-century Russia, this nineteenth-century Japanese emperor and his allies consciously set out to Westernize Japan from the top. Japanese students were sent abroad to learn, foreign experts brought to Japan to teach. Western methods of education and systems of transportation and communications were introduced. Industry, agriculture, banking were all modernized. Above all, Japan's military was updated, the old samurai class deposed, and a modern war machine created, from a steam navy to Western-style uniforms.

Forty years after Perry, Japan was ready to try its new power. In 1894–1895 the Japanese routed their ancient mentor, China, in the Sino-Japanese War. In 1904–1905 they decisively defeated one of the European great powers in the Russo-Japanese War—the first time in this age of the New Imperialism that a Western nation had lost to an Asian country.

From these victories Japan got Korea, the Liaotung Peninsula in North China—and a new status in the world. In the century that followed, the Japanese would play an expanding role in global history.

## The Open Door to China

The destiny of China was final proof of how thoroughly the world was turned upside down by the unprecedented power and unappeasable drive for dominion exhibited by the modern West.

For more than two hundred years, European traders in the Middle Kingdom had been confined to a small section of the port of Canton (Guangzhou) and to the nearby Portuguese port of Macao, in South China. Jesuits might teach European painting styles or techniques of casting cannon in Beijing, but they were not allowed to proselytize much for their faith. When a British ambassador showed up at the capital in the 1790s, he was graciously received and firmly turned away.

Then in the 1800s, Europeans seemed to burst into China from all directions, shattering its immemorial isolation forever.

China was brutally punished in four wars during the nineteenth century. Britain's Opium War (1839–1842) broke out over Chinese attempts to curb opium trading by Britain from British India into China. British naval bombardment, against which the Chinese could do little, compelled the emperor to sign the first of many unequal treaties. China was forced to open a number of ports to Europeans and grant Britain its first slice of Chinese territory, the island of Hong Kong.

A second war (1856–1860), fought by the British and French against China, began with more naval action and climaxed with the temporary seizure of Beijing itself. More "treaty ports" were opened up by the resulting agreements, and more diplomatic concessions made. The Japanese next humiliated the Chinese in the Sino-Japanese War, forcing them to open still more ports to the world and beginning a round of Chinese territorial concessions to foreign imperialist powers.

The "Old Buddha," Dowager Empress Ci Xi, symbol and sustainer of China's ancient civilization. Her defiance of changing times and Western power left China almost helpless at the turn of the century. During her last years, "Old Buddha" lived a secluded life amid the fading splendors at the Forbidden City in Beijing. (Library of Congress)

A final Western invasion, involving not only British and French forces but also U.S., German, and Japanese troops, resulted from the Boxer Rebellion (1899–1900). This revolt was a desperate effort by mobs of Chinese peasants to destroy the by then ubiquitous Western presence in their country. The Boxers were summarily suppressed by a small international expeditionary force—which also brushed aside the Chinese army and took Beijing again in the process.

This disastrous century for the ancient Middle Kingdom was made worse by violent civil discord. The terrible Taiping Rebellion of the 1850s and 1860s was inspired partly by traditional peasant discontents. But it was led by a Christian convert who mixed hazy Christian fundamentalism with Confucian social idealism—and ravaged the land for fifteen years.

At the highest level, China was also divided by the mounting Western pressure. Two factions of officials formed. There were those who favored following the Japanese road and learning modern methods from the West. There were others, including the indomitable Empress Ci Xi, who clung to old methods and prayed to the old gods in this moment of crisis. By and large, the latter prevailed—with unfortunate results for China.

During the last sixty years of the century, then, the Chinese Empire was opened up with a vengeance to Western imperialism. China was forced to open its seacoasts and its great rivers to Western merchants, large areas of its hinterlands to Christian missionaries, and its capital to Western diplomats and embassies. The Chinese government accepted the right of extraterritoriality: All these foreigners could live according to their own laws in China. Beijing also agreed to most-favored-nation clauses, which granted to all foreign countries every concession made to any one of them.

From the 1870s on, furthermore, China surrendered its ancient claims to tributary states in East and Southeast Asia: Vietnam to France, Burma to Britain, concessions in Xinjiang to Russia and in Korea to Japan. In the 1890s the Chinese gave up important slices of China proper to the outsiders: Canton to France, the Shandong Peninsula to Germany, the Liaotung Peninsula to Russia (later passed on to Japan), and coastal territories across from Liaotung and Hong Kong to Great Britain.

Europeans also secured rights to build railways, develop minerals, and otherwise exploit Chinese land. By 1900, Western troops were stationed in China to guard all these concessions, Western gunboats patrolled the coasts and rivers of China, and the Chinese customs service was run by an Irishman.

China's curse and China's preserver during much of this terrible time was the last of its great rulers, Ci Xi (1835–1908). An imperial concubine who clawed her way to power in 1862 and ruled through a series of feckless males through most of her life, Ci Xi was, practically speaking, the last of the Manchus.

In her later years especially, the Dowager Empress—the Old Buddha, as she was called behind her back—was a rigidly conservative, hopelessly superstitious, imperious old woman, determined to make no concessions to the ways of the Western barbarians. She suppressed efforts at reform, pinned much of her hope on a revival of the faithful scholarly bureaucracy, and even supported the Boxers.

Ci Xi built all her hopes on China's immense past, and she lost. Had she been willing to learn, as the Japanese were, China might have been saved many humiliations. On the other hand, a weaker person, less supremely confident in the rightness of all things Chinese, might well have presided over the destruction of the dynasty—perhaps of her country as a whole—half a century earlier.

Driven from her capital by Western armies as the Boxer Rebellion collapsed in a chaos of bloody reprisals in 1900, Ci Xi survived to return to power and make final terms with her enemies. We have photographs of her surrounded by Western diplomatic wives, her aged face a mask of powder and paint, her clawlike fingers glittering with rings. Even in defeat she is the Old Buddha still, a grizzled hawk among doves.

## INTERNAL IMPERIALISM

### Pacifying, Settling, Civilizing

While Europeans partitioned Africa and imposed their will on Asia, another form of imperial expansion was coming to a climax also—the internal imperialism of Western nations whose territorial claims included large portions of the earth's surface still occupied by non-Western peoples. The pacifying, settling, and "civilizing" of such territories had, of course, begun with the first contact between Europeans and non-European peoples. But in several huge areas, this process reached a climax in the later nineteenth century.

Regions that thus came under definitive Western control in this climactic age of the New Imperialism included the Russian Far East, the American Far West, and the British continental territories of Canada and Australia. We will survey in some detail the American and Russian versions of "internal imperialism" in the following sections.

The first comers tended to be peoples from the fringes of the conquering society—mountain men in the American west, Cossacks in Siberia, beachcombers in Oceania. Traders and missionaries frequently followed, beginning the long job of transforming the material and spiritual lives of the peoples thus invaded. Then came farmers, driven by a hunger for land—American homesteaders, Russian peasants, Australian sheepherders—pushing the indigenous populations off their thinly settled territories.

The population of many of these native peoples fell drastically as a consequence of Western intrusion. Typically, these huge casualties were not the direct result of military action by the West. Maoris and Plains Indians, for instance, proved to be powerful antagonists. Drastic declines in population were rather the result of Western disease to which the natives had no immunities, and of starvation as they were driven from the lands where they had gained a livelihood. Ecological changes like the introduction of sheep into Australia or the destruction of North American buffalo herds could destroy old patterns of Aboriginal or Native American life.

Always, however, Western technology lay at the root of the destruction of these preurban peoples. Ships and railways, plows and barbed wire, and everywhere the increasingly devastating firepower of Western weapons destroyed not individual lives alone, but whole societies.

## Russia's Eastward Expansion

Russian eastward expansion across Eurasia paralleled the American westward movement. It was a slower and more deliberate advance, and one that covered even greater distances. But the result was the same: the imposition of a Europe-based culture upon the thinly scattered non-European populations who had once been masters of a substantial portion of the earth's surface.

Prior to 1500, the northern Eurasian steppe had been the homeland of the world's most extensive and formidable nomadic peoples. Semimilitarized, highly mobile, and frequently predatory in their attacks on the urban-imperial cultures to the south, these pastoral nomads were the most dangerous barbarians. The days of the great nomadic offensives in the West ended, however, with the Russian defeat of the Golden Horde in the fifteenth century. And from the sixteenth century on, the Russians themselves began to push relentlessly into Central and East Asia.

The first Russians to cross the Ural Mountains—the traditional boundary of European Russia—were the Cossacks. These bands of free-living horseriders were seminomadic pastoralists themselves, as well as hunters, marauders, and sometime soldiers of the czar. Skilled navigators as well as horseriders, the Cossacks followed a network of rivers eastward across Siberia, reaching the Pacific shortly before 1650.

In 1689, a hundred years before the first British ambassador arrived in Beijing, Russia signed a treaty with Manchu China delimiting their mutual frontier. Some Russians even crossed the Bering Strait to Alaska and worked their way down the Pacific coast into California long before the United States existed to claim it.

Russia's eastward movement was punctuated by a series of southward thrusts toward its Asian rivals south of the steppes. In the eighteenth century, especially under Catherine the Great, Russian armies pushed south against the Ottoman Empire to the Black Sea. In the nineteenth century Russian troops fought their way into the mountainous Caucasus, between the Black and Caspian seas. They also overwhelmed the crumbling Muslim Khanates of Central Asia, east of the Caspian. In the Pacific Far East, Russia pressed south along the Amur River frontier with Manchuria, acquiring the site of its great Pacific port at Vladivostok.

Obtaining land, however, was not occupying it. Modern Russia expanded till it stretched for six thousand miles, a quarter of the way around the world. But most of this land was a vast frontier, only beginning to be settled by Russians in the nineteenth century.

The Cossacks had come in the seventeenth century as fur trappers and marauders. Traders, officials, and tax collectors soon followed, and a number of penal colonies were established in the wilderness. A few landowners took their serfs into western Siberia as early as the eighteenth century. In the nineteenth, increasing numbers of peasants moved east on their own, seeking free land to cultivate. After the emancipation of the serfs in 1861, peasants began to pour into the east, a migration facilitated by the opening of the Trans-Siberian Railway in the 1890s. Three and a half million colonists thus took land in the east during the two decades before 1914.

The impact of Russian eastward migration was in many ways not as devastating as the American colonization of the west or the contemporary occupation of Canada or Australia. Russians had known Turko-Mongol peoples for centuries and felt little racial superiority, and Russian peasants did not expect to live much better than Tatars or Mongols. There was none of the genocidal destruction of native societies that would mark the internal expansion of other continental nations.

Nevertheless, there were inevitable conflicts—and the subject peoples inevitably lost. Cossack depredations made the warning "The Cossacks are coming" feared by Mongol tribes all across Siberia, and official tribute-gathering was almost as burdensome. Tribal resistance to conquest would last for decades in the Caucasus Mountains, and central

# VOICES FROM THE PAST

Two voices from the nineteenth-century North American settlers. The first describes the decimation of a Native American people by disease and alcohol, the second the survival of a pioneer woman and her children after the rest of their party had been killed by Indians. Could you have survived for 53 days of a Canadian winter? How would you have felt about the sale of alcohol to Indians?

*The Indian tribes on Canadian territory are Blackfeet and Piegans. The former used to number over ten thousand, but now are comparatively few. The small-pox, which raged among them in 1870, decimated their numbers; also alcohol, first introduced by Americans who established themselves on Belly River, about 1866, and in which they drove a roaring trade, as Indians sacrificed everything for the 'fire-water,' as they called it, and hundreds died in consequences of exposure and famine, having neither clothes to cover them nor horses nor weapons wherewith to hunt. Luckily in 1874 the mounted police put an entire end to this abominable sale of whisky.*

*I was now at a loss what to do: the snow was deep, the weather cold, and we had nothing to eat. . . . Next morning, after a sleepless night, I wrapped my children in my robe, tied my horse in a thicket, and then went to a rising ground, that overlooked the house, to see if I could observe anything stirring about the place. I saw nothing. [Mrs Dorian managed to find some food amongst the bodies of her husband and his friends, before travelling on:] . . . 'till I and the horse could travel no more . . . I selected a lovely spot at the foot of a rocky precipice, in the Blue Mountains, intending there to spend the remainder of the winter. I killed my horse, and hung up the flesh on a tree for my winter food. I built a small hut with pine branches, long grass, and moss, and packed it all round with snow to keep us warm, and this was a difficult task. . . . In this solitary dwelling I passed fifty-three lonely days.*

Jane Robinson, *Parrot Pie for Breakfast: An Anthology of Women Pioneers* (Oxford: Oxford University Press, 1999), pp. 66, 142–143.

Asian nomads preyed on Russian caravans well into the nineteenth century. Russian Orthodox settlers hated and feared Islam in central Asia, and there were bitter feuds over irrigation water in those dry regions.

## America's Western Expansion

When the Europeans began to push their way into North America, there were perhaps a few million Indians living north of the Rio Grande. Culturally speaking, they were far from homogeneous. In the varied environments of the northern continent, a variety of Native American cultures had been evolving for thousands of years. There were thus hundreds of different tribal societies, including nomadic hunters, agricultural villagers, and some few, like the Mound Builders or the Pueblo Indians, pushing to the edge of settled town life. During the colonial period itself, loose confederacies east of the Mississippi bound tens of thousands of Indians for purposes of peace, war, and trade.

Almost all Indians, however, remained Stone Age toolmakers. Most were organized primarily on the basis of clan and tribe. All were worshipers of animist gods, ghosts, and nature spirits. Like African animists, they frequently believed in the Great Spirit who was the author of all things.

The destruction of these societies took several hundred years. But the process accelerated significantly in the later eighteenth and the nineteenth centuries, reaching a climax during the American westward movement of the half-century after the Civil War.

By 1776, the almost four million English settlers on the east coast may well have outnumbered all the Indian nations on the continent—and their hostility to the Indians was well demonstrated. American land hunger and refusal to mix with the alien culture of the indigenous population thus set a juggernaut in motion. Rolling westward, the expanding United States dislocated, defeated, fragmented, and all but destroyed all the major Amerindian cultures from the Atlantic to the Pacific.

Disease, warfare with Europeans, and involvement in European wars had broken the back of the eastern Indian confederacies before 1800. Even the League of the Iroquois, which for two centuries had bound a half-dozen large tribes into a loose but powerful unit capable of treatment as an equal with Dutch, French, and English colonies, was divided and broken during the American Revolution.

After the Revolution came mounting pressure for Indian "removal" from all the lands east of the Mississippi. This was accomplished by force during the Jacksonian 1830s. Indians such as the Southern Cherokee were rounded up and headed west along the infamous Trail of Tears to Oklahoma, leaving many dead along the road to exile.

After 1865 the restless westward thrust of Americans—gold seekers and other miners, cattlemen, sheepherders, and farmers—shattered the buffalo-hunting Indian tribes of the Plains as they had the woodland confederacies of the East. Their weapons were technological and bureaucratic. Repeating rifles and pistols, railroads, barbed wire, and the steel plow defeated the nomadic "wild Indians" in the field.

The destruction of the Indian cultures was completed by treaties that were never kept, reservations that were always the worst land, exploitative Indian agents, land speculators, and other parasites. The final enemy of traditional Indian society, ironically, turned out to be government reformers who claimed to be the friends of the "vanishing red man." It was these reformers who set out to introduce Indians to private property, modern education, and integration into American society—which meant the disintegration of their own.

Even the reformers, however, sometimes had second thoughts. A woman who had gone out to the Dakota Territory to teach the white man's ways to the Sioux was stunned by the ferocity of a U.S. Cavalry massacre of three hundred Indians, many of them women and children, at Wounded Knee in 1890. "They were pursued up the ravines and shot down indiscriminately," she wrote later. "The killing of women and children was . . . in many cases deliberate and intentional."[2]

The North American tribes had responded to the inexorable advance of the Europeans in many ingenious ways. The woodland Indians acquired firearms, organized large confederations such as those of the Iroquois and the Creeks, and played the power game with the invaders as long as they could. Plains tribes such as the Cheyenne, the Sioux, and the Apache acquired the horse from the Spanish and became as mobile and fierce a nomadic people as any Mongol or Indo-European people of earlier centuries. Defeated once more by the cavalry and by the virtual extermination of the buffalo herds upon which they subsisted, the demoralized Amerindian remnants took up religious movements like the Peyote Cult or the Ghost Dance, until even these were declared illegal.

The westward march of the frontier line, a measure of advance and expansion for most Americans, was a measure of the defeat and disintegration of Amerindian culture in North America. For the real first comers, it was all a Trail of Tears.

## THE WESTERN EMPIRES AND COLONIAL RESISTANCE

### Two Ways to Resist

The rest of the world did not take kindly to the Western predominance. Even in the face of ironclads and Maxim guns, the other peoples of the globe resisted Western aggression. It was a disorganized, usually hopeless resistance, but it was a beginning. Before the next century was done, it would emerge triumphant.

The colonial wars and revolts, the reform movements and embryonic nationalist groups of the late nineteenth and early twentieth centuries were of two types. We may call them traditional and progressive.

The large majority of these anti-imperialist movements were traditionalist rebellions. They were rooted in ancient religions or long-established social structures and political loyalties. Such revolts could mobilize large numbers of ill-organized and poorly equipped native peoples against the new order of things imposed upon them from without. Almost always, they failed.

A few of these nineteenth-century movements, however, were the work of Westernized minorities in colonial areas. These people recognized the necessity of learning some of the organizational, technological, and military skills developed by the West if they were ever to expel the Westerners from their homelands. This approach was progressive not in any moral sense, but simply in that it reflected a determination to master the latest technical advances in order to use them against their inventors. It was an approach that had a much more successful future in the century that began in 1900.

A brief survey of some of the major revolts will at least give some idea of the variety and extent of the resistance even at the high tide of the great conquest.

---

[2]E. G. Eastman, *Sister to the Sioux* (Lincoln: University of Nebraska Press, 1978), p. 164.

## Khartoum and the Little Big Horn

Continent by continent, it was a violent picture. And there were many similarities between the anti-imperialist movements of one colony and those of another.

In Africa the British faced two rebellions in their Egyptian protectorate, the Mahdist movement in the Sudan in the 1880s and 1890s, as well as wars with the Zulus and the Matabele in South Africa and with the fierce Ashanti in the West African Gold Coast (today's Ghana). The French had to deal with rebellions in Tunisia and Madagascar and with insurrections in French West Africa. These latter included a long resistance by the Mande, who in earlier centuries had built some of the most impressive kingdoms of the Western Sudan.

The Germans were challenged by indigenous peoples in almost all their African colonies after 1900. Their savage repression of the Maji-Maji revolt (1905–1907) in what is today Tanzania has lived as one of the most brutal assertions of Western supremacy. The Portuguese, the Belgians, and the Italians also confronted armed resistance in Africa in the late nineteenth and early twentieth centuries.

In Asia the British experienced determined opposition when they invaded Burma in the 1880s, and terrorism in both eastern and western India. The French met decades of armed defiance all over French Indochina. One of their most persistent opponents was the guerrilla Ham Nghi, who fought them from the colony's mountain spine in the 1880s. There were revolts against the Dutch in Java and Sumatra. A bitter guerrilla movement was directed against the American occupation of the Philippines at the turn of the century. The Boxer Rebellion of 1899–1900 in North China, as we have seen, sought the destruction of all Westerners of whatever nationality in that country.

The final stages of United States and Russian continental expansion involved bitter fighting. Russian troops pushing south into the Caucasus faced decades of savage resistance from fierce mountaineers under Shamil, "destroyer of the unbeliever." There was a widespread revolt in Muslim Central Asia against the Russian authorities as late as World War I.

The expanding United States, as noted above, faced recurrent resistance all across the North American continent and overseas as well. In the eastern United States, the most celebrated nineteenth-century fight was probably that of the Seminoles in Florida, who refused to take the Trail of Tears. In the West, the raids of the horseriding Plains Indians also took decades to suppress. In the Philippines, the 1900 insurrection cost tens of thousands of Filipino lives.

Religion provided the impetus and inspiration for many of these resistance movements, including Islam in Africa, the Middle East, and Russia; Hinduism in India; the Ghost Dance among the American Plains Indians; and peasant polytheism in China. Other movements were tribal in origin, such as the resistance of the Mande, Ashanti, and Zulu people in Africa and that of the Moros in the Philippines. Sometimes traditionalist revolts fought doggedly in defense of traditional rulers, such as the emperors in Cambodia and Vietnam.

With spears and machetes and rifles, with ancient prayers and traditional battle cries, they resisted. Homekeeping Europeans could shrug off such manifestations of discontent. It was not quite so easy for the soldiers of empire to ignore.

General "Chinese" Gordon and General George Custer had very little in common besides their unhappy fates. Gordon died at Khartoum in the Sudan at the hands of the Mahdi, Custer at the Little Big Horn in Montana, cut down by Sitting Bull's Sioux. Such victories for the resistance were rare. But the spirit of resistance was not.

## The New Great Power of the East

Modernizing or progressive rebellions were most common in Asia, where structured government, urban environments, and all the skills necessary for a changeover to Western ways already existed. Three of the most striking such modernization movements were initiated by the Indian Congress party as early as 1885, the Persian Revolution of 1905, and the Young Turk revolt in 1908. Both the Persian and Turkish movements were directed against antiquated indigenous governments that seemed likely to surrender their countries to the Europeans. Both movements aimed, with some success, to modernize their nations sufficiently to withstand further Western aggression.

A third early modernizing movement with a long future was the Congress party, organized by professional people in India. In the next century Indian leaders such as Gandhi and Nehru would rise in this party and lead the country to independence after World War II. As we shall see, Mahatma Gandhi's nonviolent methods were rooted deep in Hindu traditions, but his goals included a great deal that was thoroughly Western.

A fourth and much the most successful of the westernizing anti-Western drives began even earlier than that in India—in the island empire of Japan.

Japan at the turn of the century was a nation in rapid and vigorous transition. "Restore the Emperor and expel the Barbarian" had been the cry of the Meiji reformers of thirty years before.[3] The first objective had certainly been accomplished: but by 1900, Western "barbarian" influences were everywhere in the new Japan.

Politically, Meiji Japan had developed a complex constitutional structure that amounted to rule through the cooperation and competition of separate and often rivalrous elites. The emperor himself enjoyed great respect and the power to appoint officials up to and including the prime minister—though he customarily delegated this responsibility to a group of elder statesmen. The political parties of the Diet, the Japanese legislature, passed laws and voted on the budget in a very Western way, but had little of the power exercised by a British-style parliament, whose leader was also the political leader of the nation. The imperial bureaucracy, led by brilliant if conservative Tokyo Law School graduates, also had a good deal of authority in the nation. The army and the navy, finally, had great prestige because of their victories: The military had no civilian superiors in Japan except the emperor himself.

Economically, Japan was in the middle of a boom in 1900, and that surge of economic growth accelerated into the new century. Between 1900 and 1940, Japan's exports or raw materials would triple and its overseas sales of manufactured goods would multiply a dozen times. Its population would also explode once more, from 44 million in 1900 to 78 million in 1940, absorbing at least some of its economic gains. But the direction toward mushrooming growth was clear—and impressive.

The heart of Japan's expanding industrial, commercial, and financial economy was the small group of super-rich business families known as the *zaibatsu*. These equivalents of the German Krupps or the American Rockefellers included such powerful industrial dynasties as the Mitsubishi, Mitsui, Kawasaki, and half a dozen other major firms.

---

[3]Ruth Benedict, *The Chrysanthemum and the Sword: Patterns of Japanese Culture* (Boston: Houghton Mifflin, 1946), p. 76.

Expanding to control a spectrum of ventures from mining and manufacturing to shipping and commerce, *zaibatsu* clans such as Mitsui and Mitsubishi may, in fact, have been the biggest privately owned corporations in the world. They made Japan's economic growth possible. They also had a powerful say in politics, thanks to close ties with the bureaucracy and—as in Europe and America—to substantial contributions to the campaign funds of political parties.

During the turn-of-the-century decades, finally, Japanese imperialism was a central factor in Far Eastern affairs. Japan's decisive victories over the world's two largest land empires—China in 1895 and Russia in 1905—astonished the world. Just as the United States regarded the Western Hemisphere as its bailiwick, so Japan clearly saw the Far East as its own back yard. It was not unlikely that these two dynamic, expansive nations on opposite sides of the Pacific would themselves come to blows sooner or later.

Japan was the supreme example of learning Western ways in order to resist Western encroachments. It learned those ways so well that it was soon challenging the Western imperial powers at their own game across eastern Asia.

# WESTERN IMPACT ON NON-WESTERN PEOPLES

## Material Impact of Imperialism

The New Imperialism had a much more important transforming influence on the rest of the world than the Old Imperialism had had, an impact that was already becoming apparent by 1900. In many parts of the world, this second, more intense and penetrating wave of Western conquest inaugurated a process of social change sometimes called Westernization, sometimes simply modernization.

Materially, the New Imperialism thrust its way into other people's cultures as the Old Imperialism seldom had. The makers of the New Imperialism exploited and developed colonial regions with unmatched thoroughness and intensity. They reaped harvests, tapped trees, dug mines, drilled for oil from Brazil to Borneo. They unrolled barbed wire, strung up telegraph lines, laid rails, constructed harbor facilities. They built processing plants and even manufacturing plants in the colonies to turn raw materials into something closer to the use objects the Europeans, the Americans, and their other customers wanted.

The material impact was vast, cumulative, and accelerating. Irreplaceable natural resources—Congo copper, Arab oil—began to be drained from the land. Patterns of agriculture were drastically changed. Cash crops replaced subsistence farming until populations that formerly fed themselves came to depend on imported food for sheer survival.

Local industries were ruined by the competition of cheap Western machine-made alternatives. The Indian cotton industry was the world's leader in the seventeenth century. It was driven to the brink of extinction by the cotton mills of Manchester and Birmingham in the nineteenth.

Native peoples were often uprooted and forced into new patterns of life. The bright lights of cities built by Europeans lured African villagers away from their old lives and into new ones that were often rootless and demoralizing. European laws were forced on local people by fiat of colonial administrators. European customs spread with the temptation of jobs and contracts that went to those who accepted European ways.

Envious, resentful, filled with righteous wrath or a burning desire to live as these intruders did, the victims of this climactic phase of the Western conquest were drawn as by a great magnet in directions their ancestors could not have imagined.

## Cultural Impact of Imperialism

Intellectually and spiritually, the influence of the West on the rest of the world was perhaps even more astonishing. With the permeating impact of the New Imperialism, old systems of ideas and values began to melt away. It was the beginning of a process that continues today—a process that one expert on twentieth-century non-Western societies has described as "the most totally pervasive example of what historians call cultural diffusion in the history of mankind."[4]

Some of the fundamental features of Western culture—in the intellectual sense of the term—thus spread around the world. European languages, for example, were so widely taught and accepted that they remain the languages of former colonial elites today, decades after independence. Thus, French still flourishes in what was once French West Africa, as English does in India.

Western Christianity spread more widely and deeply than ever before in Asia and Africa as unprecedented numbers of missionaries flooded the non-Western world. Much of the southern half of Africa is Christian today, and there are Christian enclaves from the Middle East to Southeast Asia. China was governed by a Christian—Jiang Jieshi—in the earlier twentieth century, and the presidents of the independent African states of Tanzania and Ivory Coast in the last third of the century were Catholics, Julius Nyerere and Felix Houphouet-Boigny, respectively.

Perhaps more important, the new ideologies of nineteenth-century Europe were broadcast among non-European peoples.

European liberal beliefs were introduced slowly through the gradual democratization of at least some colonial governments. European nationalist notions were seized upon more eagerly as the clamor for independence grew. Though they took the form of anti-imperialist agitation, colonial nationalism soon developed the same preoccupations with national culture, character, mission, and the rights to self-determination that had animated nationalism in the West. Even European socialism, an ideology designed for industrially developed nations with large proletariats, spread to colonial dependencies as the new century advanced. Socialism, especially in its Marxist form, would thus be adapted to the needs of peasant populations in countries having quite limited industrial sectors, most importantly China.

But the most valuable of all Western intellectual contributions to the life of the world was undoubtedly Western science and technology. Western schools run by colonial governments or religious missions began to teach the world according to Newton and transmit technology on the Manchester model. Students from the colonies picked up such up-to-the-minute ideas as Darwinism or the relativistic social theories of modern sociologists and anthropologists in the universities of their imperial masters—and found these notions as disturbing to their Buddhist or Hindu sensibilities as they were to Christian beliefs. Soon elites in other cultures everywhere were compromising traditional religious or philosophical beliefs in order to come to terms with the latest insights of the all-conquering West.

The spread of Western ideas, as well as Western material skills, would direct the course of non-Western development long after the Western structure of political power had collapsed. The pervasiveness of Western techniques and theories would make mod-

---

[4]Paul Harrison, *Inside the Third World: The Anatomy of Poverty* (New York: Penguin Books, 1979), p. 48.

ernization a continuing feature of Third World history long after the great conquest had given way to the great liberation.

## Economic Integration

By the eve of World War I—the historic end of the nineteenth century—the Industrial Revolution and the New Imperialism had also combined to produce a genuinely integrated global economy for the first time in history.

The web of trade was now centered not only in Europe but also in North America. The leading commercial nations were Britain, Germany, the United States, France, the Netherlands, and Belgium. Established trade routes linked all the continents of the globe. The busiest arteries of trade, however, were not between Europe and its colonies but between the two great centers of industrial and commercial development, Europe and North America.

The importance of international commerce in the global economy had also increased greatly. In 1800 only 3 percent of the gross national product of the world was exchanged beyond national frontiers. In 1914 the figure was 33 percent. Fully a third of all the goods produced flowed into the trade routes and sealanes of the world at the beginning of the twentieth century.

Those routes had themselves improved unimaginably over the intervening century. For land transport, the railway had been invented during the interim and had rapidly eclipsed beasts of burden and vehicles drawn by animals as a conveyor of trade goods. By 1914 Europe and the United States were criss-crossed by a mesh of rail lines. Railroads had been built through the Alps and over the Andes, and transcontinental lines spanned the United States, Canada, Russia, and India.

The steamship had also all but replaced sailing vessels for most long hauls. Metal steamers with ten and twenty times the carrying capacity of earlier shipping now dominated the sealanes of the globe. The Suez and Panama canals allowed ships to pass between Asia and Africa and between North and South America, lopping many hundreds of miles off their voyages.

Ceremonies celebrating the opening of the Suez Canal in Egypt in 1869, which provided a short route for shipping from Europe to Asia. Built by French engineers, the canal would later be taken over by the British and only became Egyptian in the 1950s. Such monumental undertakings were major accomplishments of the new industrial technology—and of the New Imperialism of the nineteenth century. (Courtesy of the Library of Congress)

A less visible but equally important force binding the peoples of the world into an increasingly integrated economy was the web of investment, again centered in Europe with a secondary center in the United States. Great Britain had twice the foreign investments of second-ranked France, with Germany, the Netherlands, and the United States following.

Britain's heaviest investments were, once more, not in its colonies but in the United States and the self-governing Dominion of Canada. Thereafter, the pound was deployed most widely in India, Australia, Latin America, and South Africa—a truly global reach. Most of France's smaller total was invested elsewhere in Europe, especially in Russia; lesser amounts of francs financed projects in North and South America, Sudanic Africa, and the Ottoman Empire. And so it went down the line, bankers in London and Paris, New York and Berlin financing much of the large-scale business activity of the world.

This integrated world economy was clearly orchestrated and run by the West, in the interests of Western peoples. Frequently the new web of exchange, investment, and production warped the economies of non-Western nations. Many Latin countries and African colonies, as noted above, became monocultural commodity producers, catering to the international market rather than to domestic needs. For good or ill, however, a global pattern was established that continues to the present day.

## Climax of the Modern World System

As we have seen in earlier chapters, this global economy both grew and changed over the modern age. In the later eighteenth and the nineteenth centuries, the modern economic world system was fully developed and evolving according to clearly established patterns.

During the late 1700s and the 1800s, three separate zones defined the system. A growing *core* dominated the world system economically and politically. A *semiperiphery* provided a source of skilled labor—and sometimes a buffer between the core and the exploited periphery. The rapidly expanding *periphery,* finally, provided relatively unskilled, often coerced labor and contributed basic commodities—agricultural products and raw materials—to the system.

As earlier, the modern world system had an important influence upon all its members in the 1800s. Historians vigorously debate the extent of this impact, but few question its reality. Economic factors may not be as central to human affairs as some world systems theorists have asserted. As critics have suggested, local factors and forces may well have shaped the history of "peripheral" peoples more decisively than the world system did. But the influence of the global economic system was surely an increasingly important element in history. And by the end of the nineteenth century, those involved in the modern world system included virtually all the peoples of the earth.

We will emphasize here the two key elements in the system: the controlling core and the periphery it controlled. Both changed significantly from the later eighteenth century to the end of the nineteenth.

The core of the world system both lost and gained members between 1700 and 1900. Of the original core—Spain, Portugal, England, France, and the Netherlands—several faded into semiperipheral status. These included Spain and Portugal, the original founders of the modern world system in the 1500s, and the tiny Netherlands, the center of the world economy in the 1600s.

New economic powers, however, soon thrust their way into the core. The first of these was the United States, the world's most productive economy by 1900. Two other economic powerhouses also played increasingly important parts in the global economy. The first was Germany, politically unified and Europe's biggest industrial power after 1871. The second was Japan, which began its drive to modernization in 1868 and was Asia's most productive economy by 1900. As a result, New York, Berlin, and Tokyo now commanded as much labor and paid for as much of the periphery's commodity exports as British pounds or French francs did.

The zone of labor and commodity exports called the periphery also continued to expand. The original key peripheral zones had been Latin America, the Caribbean islands, and parts of Eastern Europe. To these the eighteenth century had added India, the Middle East, West Africa, and a still underdeveloped Russia. The nineteenth century, finally, saw East Asia (excluding Japan), Southeast Asia, the rest of Africa, and the far-flung archipelagos of the Pacific added to the global periphery.

## Global Impact of the World System

The impact of overseas empire and world trade on the nations of the core could be political and military as well as economic. As we have seen in this and earlier chapters, the core nations profited exceedingly from their commanding position in the world economy. Even while they grew rich on the rewards of foreign commerce and conquest, however, they also competed bitterly with one another. As William Pitt, British prime minister during the decisive struggle with France in the mid-1700s, said, "When trade is at stake, it is your last retrenchment; you must defend it or perish."[5]

The impact of the modern world system on the peoples of the periphery, as we have seen, could also be very great. The demands of core markets could warp and restructure the economies and societies of peripheral peoples. During the period of the Old Imperialism, for instance, European development changed the basic terms of global trade. Europe learned to manufacture goods of higher quality and technical sophistication—goods that Asians and other non-Westerners coveted. As a result, the West was no longer compelled to pay cash for the products of China, India, and other developed civilizations that had long disdained European goods. By the nineteenth century, the situation was reversed as non-Western peoples clamored for the products of the Western Industrial Revolution.

During this period also, European demand changed. Instead of seeking small but high-value luxury products—spices, gems, precious metals—the European market more and more demanded bulk goods. Cotton, peanuts, palm oil, rubber, coffee, tea, cocoa, copper, petroleum—there was no end to the cargos that flowed into the core from the ends of the earth. The peasantries of the world thus found themselves abandoning subsistence farming to tend export crops or labor underground in mines, using their wages to buy food they had formerly grown for themselves.

## SUMMARY

The resurgence of overseas empire-building we call the New Imperialism brought almost all of Africa and large parts of Asia under Western domination.

The motives of the New Imperialists included a varying mixture of economic, political, humanitarian, and even psychological drives and interests. The elements that made possible so vast a conquest in the generation or two after 1870 included superior Western organization, esprit, and, above all, firepower. The resulting unprecedented global hegemony took several forms, including full-scale colonies, protectorates, and spheres of influence.

---

[5]Quoted in J. H. Plumb, *England in the Eighteenth Century (1714–1815)* (London: Penguin, 1950), p. 71.

The scramble for Africa was the most dramatic theater of imperial expansion at the end of the nineteenth century. There European powers negotiated treaties with local chiefs and other rulers all over the continent and frequently sent in troops later to enforce the new agreements. France's African colonies, mostly in West Africa, were tightly governed as extensions of metropolitan France. Britain's holdings in all parts of Africa were generally run on a system of delegated authority called indirect rule. Germany, Belgium, Italy, and other countries also seized parts of Africa.

In Asia the resistance of long-established and populous urban-imperial cultures was strong. As a result, protectorates and spheres of influence were more common, though there were important new colonies and some old ones as well. Among the areas that came under Western control were British India and the British and French colonies in mainland Southeast Asia. Japan was also "opened" to Western trade and influence, and China became the hapless victim of European gunboat diplomacy from the Opium War to the Boxer Rebellion.

Control of areas already claimed by Western peoples often led to the destruction of indigenous pre-European cultures. Russian Siberia was less violently pacified than some other areas. The Amerindian peoples of the United States, however, were largely destroyed as independent societies.

The Western intercontinental empires were at their height in 1900. Westernization—the restructuring of traditional non-Western societies along modern Western lines—became endemic in the new century as peoples around the world coveted Western material advantages. Non-Western peoples also absorbed the languages, religions, ideologies, and other cultural achievements that had originated in Europe.

## SUGGESTED READING

Boahen, A. Adu. *African Perspectives on Colonialism.* Baltimore, Md.: Johns Hopkins University Press, 1987. By a leading writer and editor on West African subjects.

Brower, D. R., and E. J. Lazzerini. *Russia's Orient: Imperial Borderlands and Peoples, 1700–1917.* Bloomington and Indianapolis: Indiana University Press, 1997. Overview of Russia's eastward expansion across Eurasia. See also S. G. Marks, *Road to Power: The Trans-Siberian Railroad and the Colonization of Asiatic Russia, 1850–1917* (Ithaca, N.Y.: Cornell University Press, 1991) relating the epic construction project to the building and retaining of an empire.

Calder, A., J. Lamb, and B. Orr, eds. *Voyages and Beaches: Pacific Encounters, 1769–1840.* Honolulu: University of Hawai'i Press, 1999. Studies of Polynesian-European interaction, especially of European views of the indigenous peoples of New Zealand and the islands.

Chaudhuri, N., and M. Strobel. *Western Women and Imperialism: Complicity and Resistance.* Bloomington: University of Indiana Press, 1992. Collection of studies on women's roles in empire-building, suggesting that they played larger and more varied roles than commonly assumed. See also L. E. Donaldson, *Decolonizing Feminisms: Race, Gender, and Empire Building* (Chapel Hill: University of North Carolina Press, 1992), on women in imperialist literature.

Cook, S. B. *Colonial Encounters in the Age of High Imperialism.* New York: HarperCollins, 1996. Social and cultural dimensions of European colonization. See also J. A. Clancy-Smith, *Rebel and Saint: Muslim Notables, Populist Protest* (Berkeley: University of California Press, 1994). Muslim spiritual leaders resisting European expansion in North Africa.

Curtin, P. D. *Disease and Empire: The Health of European Troops in the Conquest of Africa.* New York: Cambridge University Press, 1998. New perspectives on the heavy toll taken by disease on the invading imperialist armies.

————. *The World and the West: The European Challenge and the Overseas Response in the Age of Empire.* New York: Cambridge University Press, 2000. Penetrating studies of the imperial relationship and its impact on both the colonizers and the colonized.

Ferguson, R. B., and N. L. Whitehead, eds. *War in the Tribal Zone: Expanding States and Indigenous Warfare.* Santa Fe, N.M.: School of American Research Press, 1992. Impact of imperialism on warfare in areas inhabited by preurban peoples.

Headrick, D. R. *The Tentacles of Progress: Technology Transfer in the Age of Imperialism, 1850–1940.* New York: Oxford University Press, 1988. British technology exported to the colonies.

Mangan, J. A., ed. *Making Imperial Mentalities: Socialization and British Imperialism.* Manchester, U.K.: Manchester University Press, 1990. Papers on the shaping of imperialist attitudes.

Mani, L. *Contentious Trajectories: The Debate on Sati in Colonial India.* Berkeley: University of California Press, 1998. Disputes over the legitimacy of self-immolation by upper-class Hindu women in British India.

Marjomaa, R. *The Military Collapse of the Sokoto Caliphate under the Invasion of the British Empire, 1897–1903.* Helsinki: Finnish Academy of Science and Letters. Balanced case study of the conquest of the West African state by British-officered African troops.

Marshall, P. J., ed. *The Cambridge Illustrated History of the British Empire.* New York: Cambridge University Press, 1996. Balanced essays on the largest of all European overseas empires.

McCaskie, T. C. *Asante Identities: History and Modernity in an African Village 1850–1950.* Bloomington, Ind.: Indiana University Press, 2000. Impact of imperialism on a West African town by a specialist in African thought systems.

Miller, S., A. J. H. Latham, and D. O. Flynn, eds. *Studies in the Economic History of the Pacific Rim.* New York: Routledge, 1997. Pioneering study of Pacific rim peoples in world history. For another aspect of Western penetration, see D. Munro and A. Thornley, eds., *The Covenant Makers: Island Missionaries in the Pacific* (Suva, Fiji: University of the South Pacific, 1996).

Rodney, W. *How Europe Underdeveloped Africa.* Washington, D.C.: Howard University Press, 1984. Sees the roots of Africa's twentieth-century underdevelopment in the slave trade, colonial oppression, and commercial exploitation in earlier centuries.

Salmond, A. *Between Worlds: Early Exchanges Between Maori and Europeans, 1773–1815.* Honolulu: University of Hawai'i Press, 1997. Thoughtful analysis of relations across the cultural divide.

Stanfield, M. E. *Red Rubber, Bleeding Trees: Violence, Slavery, and Empire in Northwest Amazonia, 1850–1933.* Albuquerque: University of New Mexico Press, 1998. The brutal rubber boom in another area of Western "internal imperialism."

Vandevert, Bruce. *Wars of Imperial Conquest in Africa, 1830–1914.* Bloomington: Indiana University Press, 1999. Best available survey of nineteenth-century European military conquest in Africa.

Wallerstein, I. *The Modern World-System III: The Second Era of Great Expansion of the Capitalist World-Economy, 1730–1840s.* San Diego, Calif.: Academic Press, 1989. The founder of world-systems analysis outlines the economic history of the Europe-dominated world of the eighteenth and early nineteenth centuries, stressing growth and change of the global economy.

Wesseling, H. L. *Imperialism and Colonialism: Essays on the History of European Expansion.* Westport, Conn.: Greenwood Press, 1997. Focus on diplomatic and military aspects.

Wilson, G. M. *Patriots and Redeemers in Japan: Motives in the Meiji Restoration.* Chicago: Chicago University Press, 1992. Thoughtful essays on varied motives of the reformers. See also W. G. Beasley, *Japan Encounters the Barbarian: Japanese Travelers in America and Europe* (New Haven, Conn.: Yale University Press, 1995) on Japan's government-sponsored effort to master Western ways.

 Please refer to the document CD-ROM for primary sources related to this chapter.

# OVERVIEW VI

# THE STRUGGLE
# FOR THE GLOBAL FUTURE

## (1900–2000)

The twentieth century since the time of Christ—approximately the fifty-fifth since civilization was born in ancient Mesopotamia—is in some ways a climactic age. This century produced so many *most* and *biggest* things in the long human story: the most people, the longest lives, the biggest wars, the biggest cities, the most polluted environment, the most material wealth. The list of records is endless. From the perspective of the past, this century was certainly the climax of much that had gone before.

From the perspective of the future, however, the twentieth may be seen as a century not of climaxes, but of beginnings.

The century saw many innovations in science and technology. There were beginnings also in major assaults on age-old social problems, from poverty to pestilence. There were breakthroughs in mass culture, in large-scale social organization, and in much else. In that war-ravaged century, there was a more widespread commitment to peace than ever before.

Perhaps most importantly, it was perhaps the first full century of genuinely global history. Many aspects of the history of the second half of the century especially showed the destinies of all peoples of the world to be in a number of important ways inextricably bound up together.

Even a cursory introductory survey of the final section of this book should make clear both the surge of social change that shapes our times and the truly global nature of the response.

A good three-word definition of history might be *History is change.* Everything changes over time, from the geology of planet earth and the biology of its hominid population to the rise and fall of empires, the way we earn our livings, and the fashion in clothes, food, and fun. But there has never been such a rush of change as that which began in the eighteenth century, accelerated and spread in the nineteenth, and exploded into a global surge of change and challenge over the last hundred years.

The changes of the last century in particular involved every area of human life, from technology and economics to government and social mores, from religion and morality to the arts. The rickshaw, horse-and-buggy, railway-train world of 1900 has been replaced by pedicabs and motor scooters, automobiles and jet planes. Agriculture gave way to manufacturing and then to a service economy in much of the world, and the majority of the global population moved from small towns to the city. The European world empires collapsed, and royal governments gave way to a range of much more powerful authoritarian or democratic political forms. Traditional religions reeled under the assaults of secularism—and gave birth to fundamentalist resurgences or bizarre new sects and cults. Sexual freedom and equality transformed the lives of millions, and popular arts, fads, and fashions reached around the globe.

This hectic pace of change, as we will see, generated some startling responses—responses that themselves helped to define the history of the twentieth century. Social change hurts many people. It destroys old elites and leaves people of all classes with a bewildered feeling that the world they knew has disappeared, gone with the winds of change sweeping the globe. Efforts to deal historically with change have been commensurately sweeping.

Politicians and ideologues, revolutionaries and even religious prophets have proposed radical new blueprints for the world we live in. Some have sought to channel the seething tides of change, some to turn them back. Many have resorted to violence and drastic restructuring of institutions, to revolution, war, and dictatorship to build the brave new worlds of their dreams. Painful as historical change has often been, radical responses from left and right have often proved even more agonizing.

The century just ended, furthermore, has seen both challenge and response reach around the earth. Twentieth-century wars and alliances, economic booms and busts, transforming social and cultural trends have all been increasingly global. The following chapters will survey the two world wars and the great global depression of the first half of the century, the Cold War and the colonial liberation movements of the second half. We will see regional divisions based on geography and traditional local institutions, practices, and beliefs give way to divisions of the world into authoritarian and more democratic states, developed and less developed economies—both types scattered across the continents. Local arts, tastes, and lifestyles will give way increasingly to the globally popular culture of film and television, blue jeans, and Coca-Cola™.

As the twenty-first century gets under way, in short, we are all citizens of a rapidly changing world. The twentieth century—to be explored in the following chapters—embarked on a long struggle for the global future. The twenty-first seems to promise more of the same.

# THE TWENTIETH CENTURY

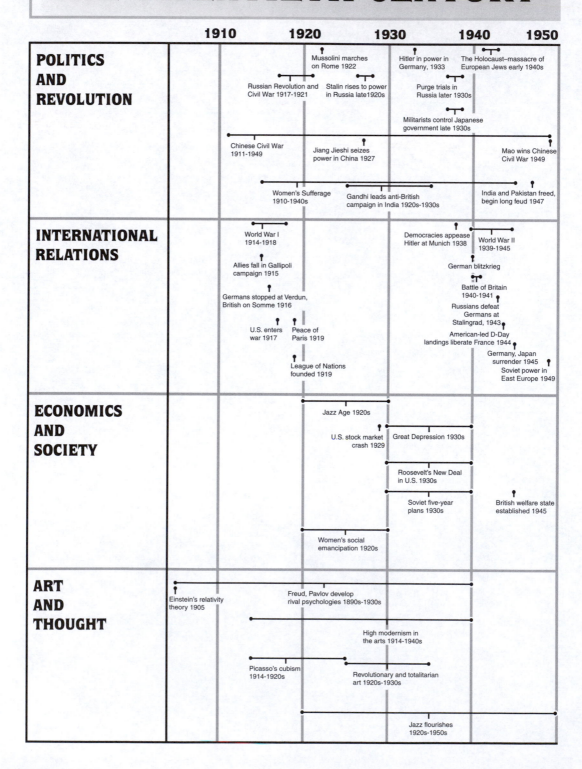

| | 1910 | 1920 | 1930 | 1940 | 1950 |
|---|---|---|---|---|---|

**POLITICS AND REVOLUTION**

Mussolini marches on Rome 1922

Hitler in power in Germany, 1933

The Holocaust–massacre of European Jews early 1940s

Russian Revolution and Civil War 1917-1921

Stalin rises to power in Russia late 1920s

Purge trials in Russia later 1930s

Militarists control Japanese government late 1930s

Chinese Civil War 1911-1949

Jiang Jieshi seizes power in China 1927

Mao wins Chinese Civil War 1949

Women's Sufferage 1910-1940s

Gandhi leads anti-British campaign in India 1920s-1930s

India and Pakistan freed, begin long feud 1947

**INTERNATIONAL RELATIONS**

World War I 1914-1918

Democracies appease Hitler at Munich 1938

World War II 1939-1945

Allies fall in Gallipoli campaign 1915

German blitzkrieg

Germans stopped at Verdun, British on Somme 1916

Battle of Britain 1940-1941

Russians defeat Germans at Stalingrad, 1943

U.S. enters war 1917

Peace of Paris 1919

American-led D-Day landings liberate France 1944

Germany, Japan surrender 1945

League of Nations founded 1919

Soviet power in East Europe 1949

**ECONOMICS AND SOCIETY**

Jazz Age 1920s

U.S. stock market crash 1929

Great Depression 1930s

Roosevelt's New Deal in U.S. 1930s

Soviet five-year plans 1930s

British welfare state established 1945

Women's social emancipation 1920s

**ART AND THOUGHT**

Einstein's relativity theory 1905

Freud, Pavlov develop rival psychologies 1890s-1930s

High modernism in the arts 1914-1940s

Picasso's cubism 1914-1920s

Revolutionary and totalitarian art 1920s-1930s

Jazz flourishes 1920s-1950s

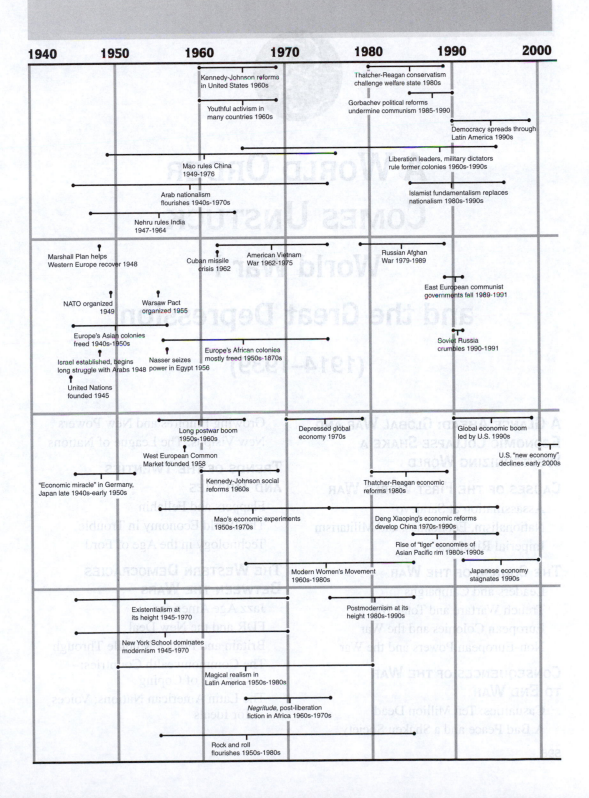

| 1940 | 1950 | 1960 | 1970 | 1980 | 1990 | 2000 |
|---|---|---|---|---|---|---|

Kennedy-Johnson reforms
in United States 1960s

Thatcher-Reagan conservatism
challenge welfare state 1980s

Youthful activism in
many countries 1960s

Gorbachev political reforms
undermine communism 1985-1990

Democracy spreads through
Latin America 1990s

Mao rules China
1949-1976

Liberation leaders, military dictators
rule former colonies 1960s-1990s

Arab nationalism
flourishes 1940s-1970s

Islamist fundamentalism replaces
nationalism 1980s-1990s

Nehru rules India
1947-1964

Marshall Plan helps
Western Europe recover 1948

Cuban missile
crisis 1962

American Vietnam
War 1962-1975

Russian Afghan
War 1979-1989

East European communist
governments fall 1989-1991

NATO organized
1949

Warsaw Pact
organized 1955

Europe's Asian colonies
freed 1940s-1950s

Europe's African colonies
mostly freed 1950s-1870s

Soviet Russia
crumbles 1990-1991

Israel established, begins
long struggle with Arabs 1948

Nasser seizes
power in Egypt 1956

United Nations
founded 1945

Long postwar boom
1950s-1960s

Depressed global
economy 1970s

Global economic boom
led by U.S. 1990s

West European Common
Market founded 1958

U.S. "new economy"
declines early 2000s

"Economic miracle" in Germany,
Japan late 1940s-early 1950s

Kennedy-Johnson social
reforms 1960s

Thatcher-Reagan economic
reforms 1980s

Mao's economic experiments
1950s-1970s

Deng Xiaoping's economic reforms
develop China 1970s-1990s

Rise of "tiger" economies of
Asian Pacific rim 1980s-1990s

Modern Women's Movement
1960s-1980s

Japanese economy
stagnates 1990s

Existentialism at
its height 1945-1970

Postmodernism at its
height 1980s-1990s

New York School dominates
modernism 1945-1970

Magical realism in
Latin America 1950s-1980s

Negritude, post-liberation
fiction in Africa 1960s-1970s

Rock and roll
flourishes 1950s-1980s

# CHAPTER 24

# A WORLD ORDER COMES UNSTUCK
## World War I and the Great Depression

### (1914–1939)

## A Glance Ahead: Global War and Economic Collapse Shake a Westernizing World

The twentieth was perhaps the first full century in which all parts of the world were deeply and powerfully linked at all levels. It began, ominously enough, with a world war and a global economic collapse.

The killing fields of World War I (1914–1918) were largely concentrated in Europe. But people came in large numbers from other continents to die there. The war also redrew maps around the world. Germany lost its recently acquired overseas holdings. Japan gained in East Asia. And three old land empires—those of Russia, Austria, and Ottoman Turkey—collapsed in the chaos engendered by "the Great War."

The 1920s was a decade of frantic pursuit of pleasure for the fortunate few—followed by a worldwide economic collapse in the 1930s. The Great Depression was a genuinely global economic downturn. Everyone shared the pain, from colonial suppliers of raw materials to high-flying New York stockbrokers. It was a lesson the world would learn again and again in the course of the twentieth century: that in an increasingly interdependent world, no man is an island.

## Causes of the First World War

### Assassination at Sarajevo

For many historians, the twentieth century began with two pistol shots on a sun-drenched, crowded street in the ancient Balkan city of Sarajevo. The man who pulled the trigger was a slightly built nineteen-year-old terrorist named Gavrilo Princip, an agent for a Slavic nationalist organization called Union or Death, popularly known as the Black Hand. The chief victim was the archduke Francis Ferdinand, heir to the throne of Austria-Hungary. The consequences of those two shots, fired on June 28, 1914, were the terrible guns of August, the beginning of the greatest war in human history up to that time.

Around that moment in Sarajevo—the excited crowds, the open cars approaching, the man with the plumed helmet and bemedaled chest, the woman in the wide summer hat—swirled a maelstrom of events, deeper causes, and incalculable consequences.

The Black Hand was centered in neighboring Serbia—the core of the postwar nation of Yugoslavia—and was dedicated to the unification of all Yugoslav ("South Slav") peoples into a Greater Serbia. The prime enemy of Slavic unity, as Serbian nationalists saw it, was the Austro-Hungarian Empire. Hence the choice of the Habsburg heir as a symbolic victim. Hence also Austria's violent response to this act of terrorism: accusation, ultimatum, and, a month after the assassination, declaration of war upon Serbia.

Bad news for little Serbia, whose government probably had no part in the crime, and whose dreams of becoming the Prussia of South Slav unification were thus drastically reversed. But worse news for Europe as a whole—and disturbing news for the world at large.

The great powers of Europe in 1914 were locked into two opposing alliances. These treaty obligations were in some cases several decades old. The main coalitions were the Central Powers, Germany and Austria, on the one hand, and the *Entente* ("Understanding") or simply the Allies, comprising primarily Great Britain, France, and Russia, on the other. Established to keep the peace or to defend the legitimate interests of the members, these rival alliances were now to prove a deadly snare, sucking one power after another into a widening war that would quickly engulf all Europe.

Thus Serbia had a patron among the great powers, the Russia of Nicholas II, which announced that it would mobilize in support of its little Slavic brother. Habsburg Austria's strongest ally, William II's Germany, gave Vienna a diplomatic blank check, promising support for whatever action the Austrians took against Serbia. Tension thus mounted through July.

Russia's ally—and Germany's archenemy—France was quickly drawn into the diplomatic tangle. Britain hesitated, hoping to exercise a moderating influence on the increasingly belligerent powers. But when Germany's elaborate war plans led German armies to violate Belgian neutrality on their way into France, London honored its commitments to the *Entente* and declared war on the Central Powers. The guns of August thundered over the Continent.

Bad news for Europe, but strange news also for a larger world that had become used to the monolithic granite face of European mastery. For the peoples of the globe were now about to see that pale, enigmatic effigy of the world-conquering West cracked and fissured by the greatest war in history.

Gavrilo Princip's Browning revolver put a bullet into the Duchess Sophy's stomach and blew a gouting hole in the side of Archduke Francis Ferdinand's neck. But the terrorist of Sarajevo did a great deal more than kill the unhappy royal pair. His were truly shots heard and felt around the world.

## Nationalism, Economics, and Militarism

As is usual with such historic disasters, there were deeper causes for World War I. Among those most often cited are rival nationalisms, economic competition, and militarism—what would later be called an arms race.

Nationalism, perhaps the most powerful of the nineteenth-century European ideologies, had turned chauvinistic in the latter part of the nineteenth century. French patriots dreamed of revenge on Germany for France's humiliating defeat in the Franco-Prussian War of 1870. Russian nationalists aspired to a pan-Slavic sphere in Eastern Europe—dominated by Russia, of course. And the tangled and conflicting nationalisms of the Balkans—Magyar, Czech, Slovak, Serbian, Greek, and others—had already kindled two brief Balkan Wars (1912–1913) before World War I even began. National feeling was thus a Europe-wide problem; when the war began, people danced in the streets of Paris and Berlin, Vienna and St. Petersburg.

The central economic rivalry in Europe at the beginning of the twentieth century was the competition between Europe's two leading industrial powers, Great Britain and the German Empire. Britain had first developed the new industrial-power sources and forms of economic organization of the Industrial Revolution in the later eighteenth century. For a hundred years, "steam," as the popular saying went, was "an Englishman." After the unification of Germany in 1871, however, that nation's already formidable industrial potential had flowered astonishingly. By the turn of the century, Germany's dynamic new industrial plant was pushing past Britain's now antiquated technology to lead Europe in production. Such competition bred bad blood and lent a note of practical national interest to the patriotic fervor of nationalists on both sides.

Militarism was a problem long before nuclear weapons made atomic-age weaponry the transcendent national issue it would become. The new technology and the new wealth of the Industrial Revolution made huge, mechanized military machines affordable even in peacetime. Large military expenditures were soon being built into national budgets, millions of young men conscripted into national armies to be prepared for war if war should come.

Militarism gave special prominence to military leaders—to Germany's famous General Staff, for example, or to admirals in Britain. Arms races also inevitably developed. The most famous of these was the rivalry in fleet construction between a Germany eager for a slice of overseas empire and a Britain determined to maintain its naval preeminence over any conceivable foe. "All this," as a prominent historian of the period pointed out half a century ago, "was done in the name of peace, for it was argued that the best insurance against war was national preparedness."[1] In the end, however, Napoleon's shrewd remark that you can do anything with bayonets except sit on them proved more to the point than slogans about preparedness.

## Imperial Rivalries

But there were still other sources of friction besides the fundamentally European conflicts created by alliances, nationalism, economic competition, and militarism. There was in addition a nexus of intercontinental issues created in large part by the colonial rivalries of the New Imperialism.

Some of the causes already cited were partially rooted in the renewed scramble for overseas territories after 1870. Chauvinistic nationalism fed on imperial conquest. Naval buildups were clearly related to establishing, maintaining, and defending empires beyond the seas.

Specifically, colonial disputes made alliances between imperial rivals such as Britain and France (in Africa and Southeast Asia) and Britain and Russia (in Persia and Afghanistan) particularly difficult. But more divisive imperial competition developed in the early twentieth century between powers on opposite sides in 1914, and these colonial rivalries help to explain the feuds that led to war.

Germany and Britain, for instance, faced significant areas of conflict in both Africa and the Middle East. Britain objected to Germany's rapid establishment of colonies in Southwest Africa (Namibia today) and especially in Tanganyika (Tanzania) in East Africa. The British were also made nervous by Germany's cultivation of the Ottoman Turkish sultan, seeing the German dream of a Berlin-to-Baghdad railway as a threat to Britain's lifeline to India at Suez. The British were especially incensed when William II sent an encouraging message to Britain's rebellious subjects in South Africa during the Boer War.

France's resentment of Germany, rooted in the Franco-Prussian War, was considerably exacerbated by German competition for Morocco. Disagreements over this remaining strip of North African coast produced the two Moroccan crises of 1905 and 1911. The French were also disturbed at the German development of a colony in the Cameroons, which thrust up into the solid block of French West Africa and French Equatorial Africa.

Germany, for its part, grew increasingly angry over these same conflicts. German imperialists and militarists felt that the sprawling British imperial presence blocked German expansion around the world. They believed that France's victory—with British support—in the two Moroccan crises, climaxing in a French protectorate over the area, represented signal diplomatic defeats for Germany. These setbacks would have to be compensated for at the next opportunity.

---

[1] F. Lee Benns, *European History Since 1870* (New York: Appleton-Century-Crofts, 1938), p. 325.

Czarist Russia, the great power of Eastern Europe, also had its share of frustrated imperial aspirations. Russia's ambitions to take control of the Turkish straits from the enfeebled Ottomans was of long standing. Russia felt an increasing need to control the entrance to the Black Sea, where lay Russia's only seaports not closed by ice for a large part of the year. Here, however, Russia's ambitions conflicted with Germany's hopes for German predominance in Turkey.

The Balkan tinderbox itself was part of this larger, extra-European picture. The Balkans and the tensions that divided them were after all part of the legacy left by the decay of the once glorious Ottoman Empire. Russia's support of these new Slavic nations against their old Muslim overlord intensified the feeling that led Turkey to join the Germans and the Austrians in what was then called the Great War.

Conflicts south of the Mediterranean and east of Suez thus played their part in bringing on World War I. These areas, and regions still farther afield, would be importantly involved in the war itself. And the world as a whole would be vitally affected by what Woodrow Wilson would hail as "the war to make the world safe for democracy" and even "the war to end war."

## WORLD WAR I AND THE TERRITORIAL RESTRUCTURING OF EUROPE, 1914–1926

# THE COURSE OF THE WAR

## Leaders and Campaigns

The world supped so full of horrors in the twentieth century that the "frightfulness" of the War of 1914–1918 may no longer shake us as it shook the generations who fought the Great War. It is perhaps hard for people who have grown used to the notion of a nuclear holocaust to empathize with a time that could still see submarine warfare as cowardly piracy and machine guns and barbed wire as atrocities. We have gotten used to the grisly photographs of no-man's-land, and to disturbing verses written by young men who would soon become part of some forgotten battlefield.

As for the impact of the Great War on the world—the very phrase Lost Generation has become a cliché, and the Peace of Versailles has no more resonance than the Congress of Vienna. Nevertheless, an effort must be made to bring both the war and its consequences back to life. Both have left their marks upon all our lives.

The leaders were as varied a lot as the nations they led. The Allies were for the most part the democracies: Britain under the charismatic Welsh reformer David Lloyd George; France under the belligerently nationalistic Georges Clemenceau, sometimes called the Tiger; and the United States under the preacher's son turned Progressive reformer, Woodrow Wilson. But the Allies also included Russia, the most unrelentingly autocratic of the powers, under Nicholas II, and imperialistic Japan, thrusting its way to prominence in the Far East.

The key leaders of the Central Powers in 1914 were thorough autocrats but were otherwise totally different. William II, the German emperor, was an aggressive expansionist who liked to pose, moustache bristling, going over war maps with his generals. Aged Francis Joseph, the Austro-Hungarian emperor, was so opposed to war that he had to be tricked into signing the declaration of war against Serbia by a fake telegram reporting a Serbian invasion.

A traditional way to approach the war these men made is in terms of the great offensives that marked the coming of each new year. A list of some of the more famous of them may stir faint echoes of forgotten heroism. For there was heroism amid the horrors of the Great War.

In 1914, for instance, there was a race to Paris as a new generation of Germans strove to emulate their grandfathers' quick victory in 1870—and failed. This was followed by a race to the sea, French and Germans striving to outflank each other until they reached the English Channel and could go no farther. There was the Gallipoli campaign of 1915, aimed at opening the Turkish straits into the Black Sea—the very name a symbol for futile loss of life.

There was the great German offensive at Verdun in 1916, when Frenchmen fell in unthinkable numbers for the ringing watchword "They shall not pass"—and the Germans did not. There was the colossal British offensive on the Somme, also in 1916, weeks of carnage that began with so many tens of thousands of British casualties in a twenty-four-hour period that it has been described as the blackest day in the history of the British army. There was Caporetto in 1917, the debacle on the Italian front that was Hemingway's *Farewell to Arms*. There was the last great heave of the Kerensky offensive in Russia, again in 1917, which turned beaten Russian soldiers against their own officers, and against the politicians who had sent them off to the front once more.

After such offensives, all sides were exhausted and reeling by 1917. There were mutterings of peace in Austria and even in Germany. There were riots in Italian munitions factories, mutinies in ten divisions of the French army, and revolution in Russia. But 1917 was also a year of startling reversals and renewed hope for both sides, and these developments built toward the climactic battles of 1918.

A British naval blockade, imposed from the beginning of the war, led Germany to respond with something new—a massive submarine campaign against all shipping attempting to reach the British Isles. Both the blockade and the submarine campaign were having their effect by 1917. But the undersea war had an unfortunate side effect: It so outraged neutrals trying to trade with Britain that in 1917 it led Woodrow Wilson to bring the United States into the war on the Allied side—a major setback to German hopes of victory.

This pivotal year, however, also saw the abdication of the Russian czar, the subsequent seizure of power by the Bolsheviks, and their decision to pull battered Russia out of the war unilaterally. Thus if the Central Powers faced the long-run threat of huge American reinforcements, in the short run Germany could all but close down its eastern front and concentrate its forces for crushing offensives in the west.

This Generals Hindenburg and Ludendorff tried to do in the summer of 1918. Three mighty German assaults hurled the Allies back dozens of miles and came as close to breaking through to Paris as Germany ever came. But France's Marshal Foch, enjoying for the first time a unified supreme command of the Allied armies, and reinforced by waves of fresh American troops, stemmed the German tide. As a cold, wet autumn settled over Europe, the war ground to a halt. An armistice was declared on November 11, 1918. The biggest, bloodiest, and, as it increasingly seemed to contemporaries, most pointless war in the history of the world was over.

## Trench Warfare and Total War

An analysis in terms of leaders and campaigns is traditional for great wars. But it is probably not the best approach to this one.

Studies of World War I have generally recognized it as a war of position rather than a war of movement. In military terms, it was a war in which defensive capabilities outperformed offensive ones, so that neither side could achieve significant breakthroughs. In human terms, the result was trench warfare: four dehumanizing years of living and dying half buried in the earth, wet, cold, frightened, and bombarded by the most barbarically ingenious combinations of metal and chemicals the Western mind could invent.

This description applies best to the western front in France. Here the trench lines stretched from Switzerland to the English Channel and moved scarcely at all between late 1914 and early 1918. On the eastern front in Russia, the lines typically swayed back and forth, enormous Russian drives bogging down in a sea of casualties and finally reeling backward in defeat. In northern Italy too—after Italy joined the Allied cause in 1915—advances by one side were likely to be followed by regrouping and successful counterattacks by the other.

Everywhere, the machinery of modern warfare made its true potential felt for the first time in Europe. New weapons were flung into the fray one after another in hopes of achieving a breakthrough: submarines, tanks, airplanes, poison gas. But the most brutally efficient killers were the staples: repeating rifles, barbed wire and machine guns, artillery capable of lobbing explosive shells for miles and burying whole trenches full of soldiers when they hit. The "sacrifices" that patriotic orators liked to make speeches about were,

At the left, French tanks roar toward the front, "eager to strike a blow at the foe." At the right, a shattered tank lies in the mud near Cambrai. Intrigued wartime readers had to have the mechanism of the new weapon explained to them, including "the wide caterpillar tread which . . . ran over the . . . sprocket wheel [and] laid itself down as an ever-renewing road for the monster above" and "the turret from which a deadly fire was directed upon the enemy." But a German shell had broken the sprocket and the tread, leaving the tank a "stationary target" to be destroyed. (Keystone View Co. of N.Y.)

as American novelist Ernest Hemingway put it, "like the stockyards at Chicago if nothing was done with the meat except to bury it."[2] The war was a meat grinder, reducing genera-tions of European youth to hamburger in the mud of Flanders fields.

The other great fact about the war was that it involved national commitment to an ex-tent seldom even approached before. To keep millions of men fed, clothed, armed, and supplied with munitions sufficient for four years of firing at each other over hundreds of miles of front lines required an unparalleled effort by the populations involved. World War I thus became the first total war in history.

Total war meant a total national commitment to, and involvement in, the great strug-gle. Governments took control of national economies as they had never dared do in peace-time. Government boards allocated raw materials, controlled transportation, regulated wages and prices, rationed food and other essentials. All able-bodied males were liable for conscription into the armed services.

Many women went into the war plants to produce the shells and guns their husbands and sons would use. Almost a million English women worked in munitions factories, and well over half a million French women. Others replaced men drafted for the war in other factories, on farms, as railway conductors, as milk deliverers, and in many other jobs.

New taxes, war loans, and a massive increase in the national debt of the warring countries were additional costs. A continual drain of food, fuel, clothing, and other essen-

---

[2]Ernest Hemingway, *A Farewell to Arms* (New York: Scribner's, 1957), p. 185.

War production booms. The industrialized nations of the West turned their formidable energies to manufacturing immense quantities of rifles and artillery, bullets and shells, helmets, gas masks, tanks, planes, warships—the hardware that made the War to End War the bloodiest in human history thus far. Here women munitions workers move casually through endless rows of shells, their fuses still in place, which will soon be on their way to the battle fronts of Europe. (Imperial War Museum, London)

tials from the home front also resulted. Russians froze through icy northern winters, Germans went hungry, Austrians starved. Total war thus ravaged European economies even as it strengthened European governments.

This total mobilization of all the resources of great modern states was in its way as striking a feature of the Great War as the raking machine-gun fire and billowing clouds of mustard gas that turned European battlefields into no-man's-lands. And it would leave as long a legacy in battered economies and in governments with newfound powers.

## European Colonies and the War

"World War I," one historian of the great debacle has written, "was really a vast global enterprise—Europe became an enormous cauldron into which men and resources from Asia, Africa, and America were poured."[3] The war was, in fact, also fought outside of Europe, by peoples from other parts of the globe, and involved extra-European ambitions, resources, and conflicts that had little to do with an assassination at Sarajevo. These larger dimensions of the Great War must be surveyed briefly if the worldwide impact of the struggle is to be understood.

Global involvement in World War I took several forms. Germany had colonies, which of course became targets for the Allies, who controlled the oceans of the world. The Allies also drew upon their own overseas empires for military and support personnel. And important powers from as far away as the Middle East, the Far East, and North America became directly involved in the conflict. World War I thus deserves its global label.

German colonies in East Asia, Oceania, and Africa were cut off from German reinforcement or support by British sea power, and most of them fell easily. The easternmost of the Allies, Japan, laid siege to Germany's base on the Shandong Peninsula of North China and soon captured it. British colonial forces from Australia and New Zealand rolled

---

[3]Jack C. Roth, *World War I: Turning Point in Modern History: Essays on the Significance of the War* (New York: Knopf, 1967), p. 105.

up German island holdings in Oceania. The Boers, who had fought Britain so recently, now led the imperial forces that overran German Southwest Africa, and Anglo-French colonial troops took Germany's West African possessions. Only in East Africa, in Tanganyika, did a skillful and prolonged German defense require years of fighting before a German colony was yielded to the Allies—in this case, Britain.

The European Allies, meanwhile, drew heavily upon their own overseas possessions to augment their forces in Europe. Large numbers of Indian troops fought in the British lines on the western front, and many Africans served in French armies. Both Chinese and Indochinese coolie labor worked behind the Allied lines in Europe in support of the war effort. The bloody Gallipoli campaign to open the Turkish straits was carried out almost entirely by Australian, New Zealand, Indian, and French colonial troops. Indian units also performed yeoman service for the British elsewhere in the Middle East.

The Germans thus lost their empire in the Great War. The British and the French, by contrast, profited immensely from theirs. Either way, colonial peoples far from Europe were significantly affected.

## Non-European Powers and the War

Besides these imperial contributions, the war drew in a number of independent non-European powers. Of these, Turkey, Japan, and the United States were the most importantly involved.

Germany's great influence in Istanbul and the long rivalry between the Ottoman Empire and Romanov Russia brought Turkey into the war on the side of the Central Powers in 1914. It was a disastrous miscalculation for the Ottomans. Turkish troops held heroically at Gallipoli. But British soldiers and rebellious Arab sheiks—urged on by the romantic British agent Lawrence of Arabia—chewed into the Ottoman Empire from the south. By war's end, this Middle Eastern campaign had detached large sections of Arabia, Palestine, and Mesopotamia from the dwindling Ottoman domain.

Japan also entered the war—on the Allied side—in 1914, and much more successfully than Turkey. The Japanese shrewdly exploited Allied support and European preoccupation on the other side of the world to advance their own imperial interests in the Far East, above all in China. After seizing Germany's bases in Shandong and on a Pacific island or two, Japan turned its attention to pressuring the new Chinese republic—established in 1911— into accepting what amounted to protectorate status under Japan. The Twenty-One Demands of 1915, which embodied this claim to imperial suzerainty, had little to do with the war, but they would be the basis for continuing Japanese pressure on China for decades to come.

The United States was the last and most important of the major extra-European participants to enter World War I. The United States had insisted on neutrality through the early years of the war, though Americans sold huge quantities of essential supplies to the Allied side. It was Germany's unrestricted submarine war on shipping destined for Allied shores, along with other manifestations of German resentment, that impelled President Wilson to declare war in 1917.

It was not till the spring and summer of 1918 that a significant number of American troops could be thrown into the struggle. They came at a propitious time, however, to help stem the climactic German offensives of 1918. And as the Germans slowly retreated that last fall of the war, the continuing arrival of fresh American troops undoubtedly helped to convince the German high command that the war was lost.

A famous cartoon of the time showed American doughboys debarking in France with the inspiring remark, "Lafayette, we are here!" There is little warrant for the notion that the United States was repaying a debt of honor that went back to the Revolutionary War when American armies went to Europe in 1918. If it was not a significant echo of the past, however, that first dispatch of U.S. troops to Western Europe was certainly a harbinger of things to come. American soldiers would be back for World War II and again for the Cold War—and they are there still.

## CONSEQUENCES OF THE WAR TO END WAR

### Casualties: Ten Million Dead

A German slogan in the Great War has a resonance of the Crusades of a simpler age: *Gott mit Uns*—God Is on Our Side. For their part, the Allies unleashed a flood of propaganda charging that the Central Powers were twentieth-century barbarians—the Hun come again to Europe—and claiming that the Allied struggle was a war to save civilization. Woodrow Wilson, widely hailed in war-weary Europe as a savior from beyond the seas, called it a "war to make the world safe for democracy" and even "the war to end war."

# VOICES FROM THE PAST

Vera Brittain worked as a British nurse's aide during World War I. This passage from her memoir of her experiences describes the beginning of her war service on the Western Front. Does Brittain's early reaction, conditioned by British war propaganda, seem convincing to you? Does the coolness of the last few lines seem callous—or psychologically convincing? The head nurse, she reports elsewhere, referred to the German wounded as "filthy Huns" but nevertheless did her best to save them. Can you explain this behavior?

*"I was glad to be once more where the work was strenuous, but though I knew that 24 General had a special section for prisoners, I was hardly prepared for the shock of being posted, on the strength of my Malta experience, to the acute and alarming German ward. . . . it was somewhat disconcerting to be pitchforked, all alone into the midst of thirty representatives of the nation which, as I had repeatedly been told, had crucified Canadians, cut off the hands of babies, and subjected pure and stainless females to unmentionable "atrocities." . . . I half expected that one or two of the patients would get out of bed and try to rape me, but I soon discovered that none of them were in a position to rape anybody.*

*At least a third of the men were dying; their daily dressings were not a mere matter of changing huge wads of stained gauze and wool, but of stopping haemorrhages, replacing intestines and draining and re-inserting innumerable rubber tubes. Attached to the ward was a small theatre, in which acute operations were performed all day.*

*I often wonder how we were able to drink tea and eat cake in the theatre—as we did all day at frequent intervals—in that foetid stench, with the thermometer about 90 degrees in the shade, and the saturated dressings and yet more gruesome human remnants heaped on the floor."*

Vera Brittain, *Testament of Youth* (London: Virago Press, 1978), pp. 373–374.

In the outcome, the Great War scarcely seemed to reflect any divine intent, did not make the world safe for either civilization or democracy, and certainly did not put an end to war. It did, however, have significant consequences, on both a European and a global level.

One thing the war produced on an awesome scale, of course, was casualties. At least ten million men in uniform were shot, bayonetted, poisoned, or blown to pieces, and perhaps half that many noncombatants died in the war zones. Millions more were hurt but not killed: Europe after the war was full of walking wounded—armless, legless, blinded, or broken-spirited men who could never seem to get their lives together again.

The figures are numbing. During the worst periods of the war, for instance, the Russians took a quarter of a million casualties *a month*. The casualties in the battle of Verdun alone reached three quarters of a million; in the battle of the Somme they ran well over a million. Whole school classes of English, French, German, and other young men marched off to the front en masse. There, according to one eyewitness, they could look forward to about three more months of life. Statistics like these have shaped the twentieth century's attitude toward one of the most common of human occupations—the making of war—from that day to this.

## A Bad Peace and a Shaken Society

Efforts to estimate the further impact of the war on Europe alone fill volumes. Diplomatically, politically, economically, and in many other ways, the Great War left a smoldering scar across the continent.

Perhaps most obvious, the map of Europe was significantly altered by the war and by the peace the Allies imposed. All three of the great central and Eastern European autocracies that began the war were gone by the end of it, the Romanovs overthrown by revolution in 1917, the Hohenzollerns and the Habsburgs toppled in 1918. Communists clung to power in Russia, and fledgling republics struggled to be born in Germany and Austria as the victorious Allies met in Paris to dictate peace terms. The peace treaties further modified the political map, recognizing the fragmentation of the Austro-Hungarian Empire and the independence of several minority nationalities who had seceded from the collapsing czarist Russian Empire. The result was a band of new or enlarged Eastern European countries running from the Baltic Sea through Poland to the Balkans.

The terms imposed upon Germany by the Treaty of Versailles in 1919 left a bitter political legacy. Worked out in detail by platoons of technical experts, this and the other peace treaties, each dealing with a separate Central Power, reflected uneasy compromises among the three principal Allied war leaders: France's vengeful Clemenceau, Britain's pragmatic Lloyd George, and the perhaps unrealistically idealistic President Wilson. Most important, however, the Versailles Treaty reflected the determination of the British and the French to destroy the German power that had held all Europe in awe since Germany's unification half a century before.

The Versailles peace thus required Germany to acknowledge its "war guilt" publicly and imposed fantastic reparations, by which Germany was to pay for the war it had allegedly caused. The treaty compelled Germany to disarm so thoroughly that it would never again be a threat to its neighbors, stripped it of its overseas colonies, and generally strove to reduce the new German republic to a second- or third-class power. The Germans signed because they had to, seething inwardly at the injustice of the dictated peace. If the Allies had set out to provide Hitler with a list of causes upon which to build his political career, they could not have done a better job.

More subtle social and economic changes also resulted from the war—not all of them as unpromising for the future as the diplomatic and political consequences sketched previously.

Economically, the greatest change was that Europe was left deeply in debt. European investment capital had helped start other nations on the road to industrial development, so that much of the world was in Europe's debt in 1914. The enormous costs of the war, however, had absorbed all this foreign credit and had forced the combatants to borrow huge sums in their turn, particularly in the United States, to pay for supplies and war material. The Allies' war debts were, in fact, impossible to pay, like the reparations imposed on the Central Powers, and the two would contribute to the disastrous economic fluctuations of the interwar period.

Some social groups, though, had done well because of the war. Skilled workers had earned good wages in defense plants. Women had taken a big step toward more flexible patterns of life through their work in war industries. In some places, as in England, women had been widely admired for their war service—British women got the vote on the strength of it.

Aristocrats and middle-class people in general, however, came out of the Great War shaken in status and self-confidence. Hailed as the pillars of the prewar social order, these groups were now widely blamed for the war and all its horrors. The postwar militance of working-class people, plus the menacing power of the newly established Communist Russian power to the east, made many in Europe's ruling classes wonder how long their supremacy might last.

## Growing Empires and New Powers

In the world at large, however, World War I unleashed some wild new dreams indeed. There were new powers moving in the larger world after 1919, new aspirations and new institutions with a genuinely global focus. They were signposts toward a future that would have astonished the most prescient thinker only a few years before.

Expanded empires and emergent world powers were among the more striking larger consequences of the Great War. The peace settlements provided for yet more European protectorates and for colonial possessions enlarged by colonies confiscated from Germany in Africa and the Far East, and from the lands of the rebellious Arab princes of the former Ottoman Empire. Britain got Tanganyika; France acquired German West Africa; the Republic of South Africa received German Southwest Africa; and Japan got Shandong. The modern Middle East—with the crucial exception of Israel—came into being at this time, its southern tier of Arab states from Iraq through Syria and Lebanon to Palestine mostly under the control of Britain or France.

Even in this apparent display of imperial business-as-usual, however, there were differences. The new territories were not taken as of right, in the old way, but mandated to the care of European powers by a new international organization called the League of Nations. Some of these territories, at least, were intended for ultimate independence once they had been adequately "developed." The League at least seemed to be taking seriously some of the more idealistic New Imperialist rhetoric about civilizing missions and grooming for independence.

There was more than rhetoric that was new after 1919, however. Three rising world powers shouldered their way further into the international arena in the aftermath of the war. All three were influenced by Europe, and one was half European geographically, but all were part of an emerging global challenge to the established European hegemony of the world.

Japan, as noted previously, had used the war to further advance its imperial ambitions in the Far East. The Japanese had seized Germany's Chinese holdings and after the war refused to return them to China. Japan's Twenty-One Demands on China, requiring changes in that nation's government and policies that, if accepted, would have made China virtually a Japanese protectorate, did in fact gain some reluctant acceptance from Chinese officials. Japan used this measure of acquiescence as a basis for further aggression against China during the interwar years.

Militarily powerful and victorious in three consecutive wars—two of them involving European nations—Japan was also East Asia's most successful trading and manufacturing nation. By 1919 Japan had thus established the trajectory that would determine its rise to greatness over the rest of the century.

The new Union of Soviet Socialist Republics—still "Russia" to most people—looked much less like a winner in 1919. But the Soviet Union also had an astonishing future ahead of it.

Russia's non-European dimension—three quarters of its territory and much of its population were Asian—had been noted long before the twentieth century. The Bolshevik Revolution, however, put the country in the hands of militant ideological enemies of much that the rest of Europe stood for, from capitalism and democracy to imperial hegemony. The Russia of 1919, still bleeding from World War I, now swept by civil strife, seemed little threat to European predominance. But Joseph Stalin was already prowling in the wings, and the willingness of the Russian Communists to use government power ruthlessly to build up the nation was already amply demonstrated. The Soviet Union too would play a global role in the emerging century.

The United States, finally, stepped definitively onto the stage of world history in World War I. Any attempts to hastily step off again would prove impossible.

The richest nation in the world by the turn of the century, the United States emerged even richer from the war, thanks to European borrowing and to booming American war industries. The United States had also demonstrated in 1917 and 1918 that it could commit its youth to a major war if the nation's interests and ideals were involved. America's President Wilson, whose idealistic Fourteen Points aimed to settle all the world's problems, was for a time hailed as a Messiah on both sides of the Atlantic.

Unaccountably to many, however, the United States drew back from the role thrust upon it in 1919. America refused even to join the League of Nations—Wilson's brainchild—and withdrew into fastidious isolation from the difficulties of the rest of the world. It would take another great war to propel the United States to the position of world leadership it would occupy during the second half of the century. But that direction too was laid down by the war of 1914–1918 and by America's part in it.

## New Visions: The League of Nations

There was, finally, a powerfully felt and growing hope for a larger and more just world order in 1919—one no longer dominated by European intercontinental empires.

Indians and Africans who had fought in Europe and Chinese and Southeast Asians who had served behind the lines went home with an image of the all-conquering Europeans that was rather different from the one they had once had. Woodrow Wilson's talk of "national self-determination of peoples," which had created the new nations of Eastern Europe, seemed equally applicable to the colonies of Asia and Africa. V. I. Lenin's revolutionary charge that imperialism was a stage in the evolution of capitalist oppression had a great appeal to Westernized Asians particularly, as did his call for worldwide revolt. A ferment of new visions and new ideas, none of them conducive to continuing European predominance, was thus abroad in the world after the war.

Most impressive, perhaps, the peace conference at Paris, inspired and urged by Wilson, created a new international forum for such global aspirations: the League of Nations. Even after the United States rejected its own president's dream, the League seemed to point to a different worldwide order. Its Council of permanent and rotating members was empowered to plan for world peace and an end to aggression, by European empire builders as well as by others. Its Assembly gave equal voting strength to all the nations of the world—and most of them were not European. The League of Nations was affiliated with other global organizations, such as the World Court, which also seemed a sign of things to come.

The League had little actual power and would founder after two difficult decades of existence. But it was a beginning, at least, toward recognition of a global system that could conceivably transcend even the interests of the great powers, European or otherwise.

The heritage of the worst of wars thus far was therefore not all danger and depression. The new powers, new visions, new institutions unleashed by that unprecedented conflict pointed down the generations to a wholly unexpected future for the world.

## TRENDS OF THE TWENTIES AND THIRTIES

### Flappers and Fellahin

The stillness that settled over the battlefields of the Great War in November of 1918 triggered a variety of responses around the world. There was exultation in the streets of victorious nations, bitterness among the losers, dull indifference in the eyes of the maimed, the shell-shocked, the walking wounded. On one thing, however, there was general agreement: It was a different world after the war.

In the United States a new freedom emerged in the 1920s, projecting a vivid image of bobbed hair and short skirts, bathtub gin and wailing saxophones. In Europe young moderns got their new dances from across the Atlantic and daringly crossed the Channel by airplane. Older people imitated younger ones, and everybody seemed to drive fast cars.

This is an essentially middle-class image of the age, of course: Mississippi sharecroppers, Sicilian fishermen, and Russian peasants typically had no cars and were unlikely ever to fly in an airplane. But the prosperous bourgeoisie was the heart of Western society still, their lifestyle glorified in magazines and films and admired by many who could not afford to share it. Their image reflects the ideal and much of the reality of the glossy new world of the West after the war.

Most of the rest of the world evidently did not share in this era of automobiles and airplanes that gave a hard-edged new meaning to that overworked adjective *modern*. As we have seen, there were shiny modern cities in South America, but Indians were still making pre-Columbian pottery in the jungles. Modern metropolises were emerging in Africa and the Middle East, but many Arabs were bedouin still, and village Africa was almost entirely intact south of the Sahara. People in Western business suits still swayed along in rickshas in Singapore and Shanghai, and Tokyo's handful of new earthquake-proof skyscrapers towered over a city of bamboo and paper. Yet change would come to these seemingly changeless regions too, just as it did to the Western world, between World Wars I and II.

It will take a chapter and a half to survey the startling, sometimes horrifying trends of the 1920s and 1930s. The sections immediately following will outline the events of the

Jazz Age and the depression decade in the West. The next chapter will deal with special features of the period in various parts of the globe: with the great revolutions that shook Russia, China, and other nations, and with the development of new forms of dictatorship in Germany, Japan, and elsewhere.

A typical American flapper might glory in change and newness, in art-deco modernity for its own sake. Egyptian *fellahin* laboring in the black earth along the Nile, as their ancestors had done since the beginning of history, might never have heard of the modern world at all. But time and change—not always for the better—would come to both of them between that stillness on the November battlefields of 1918 and the roar of Stukas rising into the dawn on September 1, 1939.

## The World Economy in Trouble

It is hard to find two decades that seem to contrast more strikingly than the 1920s and the 1930s. The twenties were frivolity and fun; the thirties were a decade of agonizing social concerns, of taking stands and building brave new worlds. Most vividly, the twenties seem to mean prosperity, boom times; the thirties brought the Great Depression, the biggest economic bust in modern Western history.

On the economic side, however, the contrast seems in fact to have been rather less striking. This is particularly so when the two decades are examined from a global perspective.

The world as a whole seems to have suffered in the 1920s from a vast overproduction, a wartime buildup that could not find peacetime demand to sustain it. Commodity producers in Latin America and in the European colonies of Africa and Asia thus suffered from declining prices through much of the twenties. So did farmers in the United States, coal miners in Britain, and other primary producers within the West.

There were other economic problems as well. There was a postwar depression as hordes of demobilized soldiers swarmed into a job market that was already shrinking because of the end of wartime demand. Inflation soon followed in some parts of Europe, devouring the savings of middle-class citizens in Germany particularly.

Even the apparent prosperity of much of the population of the United States, Europe, and other Westernized lands such as Australia and Canada had an unreal quality about it. The United States, the world's most productive nation before the war, now its foremost trader and exporter of capital as well, was actually responsible for much of the apparent economic health elsewhere. The profits of booming American business, widely available to bolster flagging economies across the West, maintained a material well-being that was in large part artificial.

The central international role of the United States was illustrated most importantly in the nagging problems of reparations and war debt that haunted the twenties.

World War I had left even such prewar economic giants as Great Britain deeply in debt to the United States. To pay these debts, all the Allies depended on the reparations payments from Germany prescribed by the Treaty of Versailles. But Germany, hard hit by the Great War, the inflation of the 1920s, the French occupation of the industrial Ruhr, and other problems, simply could not meet its reparations payments. To handle these obligations, Germany therefore borrowed heavily—from the United States.

Money thus flowed ponderously in a great circle, from the United States to Germany as loans, to the Allies as reparations, and thence back to the United States as war debts. It was a dubious procedure at best. When the American economy began to stagger, it would bring the economies of much of the world down in ruins.

The prosperity of the 1920s has thus been exaggerated in modern memory. The economic misery of the 1930s scarcely could be.

The world depression of 1929–1939 began with the collapse of the American stock market and was sustained by the long years of American economic paralysis that followed. American financiers, hard hit at home, soon cut back on their loans to Europe, putting the fragile structure of European prosperity also under pressure. The failure of Austria's central bank two years after the Wall Street crash triggered a similar wave of economic disaster across the continent. As the depression deepened all across the West, finally, the commodity producers of the rest of the world began to feel the effects of the new poverty of their best customers. Prices of agricultural goods and raw materials, weak through the twenties, spiraled downward in the thirties. By the middle of that bleak decade, much of the world was thus locked in the grip of the Great Depression.

Political and economic leaders tried many expedients during the 1930s to reverse the spiral, prime the pump, get the laws of supply and demand working once more. In the end, paradoxically, it would take another world war to create sufficient demand to get the world economy moving again. In the meantime, as we will see below, the political and social repercussions of the Great Depression were felt all across the Western world.

## Technology in the Age of Ford

Economic dislocation was thus a continuing feature of Western history between the wars, rather than a characteristic of the 1930s only. There were other areas also in which main trends carried on through these two apparently contrasting decades. One crucial aspect of Western life in which change would continue throughout the entire century was technological advance.

In every area, from industrial production, transportation, and communication to modern entertainment, the West and selected areas of the rest of the globe felt the impact of technological change throughout the 1920s and 1930s. The United States had become the recognized leader in many fields of technological development by this time, but the major nations of Europe were not far behind.

The rise of the twentieth century's two main sources of industrial energy, hydroelectric power and petroleum, had actually begun around the turn of the century. Electric lighting and electric railway trains were common in the West by the twenties and thirties. Petroleum production, which had been only 20 million tons at the turn of the century, reached a quarter of a billion tons by the end of the thirties. Refined petroleum products powered ships, automobiles, and airplanes throughout the interwar years.

Technological improvement included key developments in both heavy industry and large-scale agriculture. The industrial assembly line, pioneered by Henry Ford, the American automobile manufacturer, was soon speeding up production in many other industries as well. In agriculture these decades were the age of the tractor. In the United States there were 160,000 tractors already at work in the fields in 1919; by 1939 there were a million and a half of them.

The central innovation in transportation during the twenties and thirties was, of course, the automobile—for this was the Age of Ford. In Britain the number of cars in use multiplied twelve times between 1923 and 1938; in France, twenty times. And in the United States, forty times as many people had cars—almost 50 million of them—by the end of the 1930s as in the early 1920s, in spite of the Depression. Railways remained important, airplanes rare except for military purposes. But the car was king of the road, retiring the working horse in city after city across the West after thousands of years of faithful service to humankind.

Communications, revolutionized by the telegraph in the nineteenth century, was revolutionized again by the telephone in the early part of the twentieth. But it was in the mass media of communications that the interwar decades saw major breakthroughs, particularly in the development of radio and film. Before World War I, radio was used primarily between ships at sea, where wireless communication was essential, and "moving pictures" were little more than an arcade game. Between 1920 and 1940, tens of millions of radio sets came into use in homes across America and Europe, and gaudy modern movie theaters blossomed in every city.

The impact of the automobile on the social life of the West, of the telephone on business and government, of radio and film on popular culture as well as in the hands of a Hitler or a Franklin Roosevelt is almost incalculable. And the take-off time for all these social and technological revolutions was the period between the wars.

## THE WESTERN DEMOCRACIES BETWEEN THE WARS

### Jazz Age America

The United States in the 1920s was Jazz Age America. And thereby hangs a problem. How seriously can you take an age that is named for its popular music? At least the Renaissance was named for its serious culture! But the 1920s were fun times for many Americans, and perhaps it won't hurt to pay a little attention to fun once in a while. There were grimmer times coming.

By 1920, the enthusiasms of the Progressive Era had clearly run their course. Teddy Roosevelt and Woodrow Wilson, the war to make the world safe for democracy, and Wilson's last, most quixotic crusade, the League of Nations, were all consigned to the trash bin of history. "The business of America is business," the new breed declared. It was okay to get rich again, and practically everybody seemed to be doing it.

There were weaknesses even in the American economy—the twenties were still hard times for farmers—but the overall economic trend was intoxicatingly upward. Per-capita income more than doubled between 1914 and 1929. Consumer luxuries such as wristwatches, washing machines, vacuum cleaners, and even automobiles became increasingly common. Technological advances such as the telephone, radio, phonograph, and movie were particularly widespread in America.

There were those who resisted the onward march of progress, of course. Fundamentalist Protestants defended established moral values and the "old-time religion." Intellectuals and literati sneered at the Babbitts who ran America—doltish businessmen with little culture and less sensitivity, named for the central character in a novel by Sinclair Lewis. And many people lamented the passing of the front porch as a social center and its replacement by the automobile, symbol of freedom to youth, "petting parlors on wheels" to disapproving elders.

"Flaming youth," "modern youth," "the younger generation"—the young people of the American 1920s embodied all the vitality and foolishness of the decade. They drank too much, drove too fast, cut their hair and their skirts too short, invented endless fads and new dances every year. They adopted a brassy black style of popular music called jazz and took the gaudy, improvident lifestyle of novelist Scott Fitzgerald and his glamorous wife,

Zelda, as their ideal. For the giddy middle-class American youth of the 1920s, it was always New Year's Eve and no tomorrow.

## FDR and the New Deal

Tomorrow came, of course—a morning-after like few in modern history—in the wake of the New York stock market crash of October 1929.

The causes of the crash of '29 included unwarranted speculation, overcapitalized business ventures, shaky banks, lack of adequate government regulation, and plain fraud. The Great Depression that filled the next decade in America was rooted in deeper problems, however. Continuing hard times for farmers, miners, and others carried over from the twenties. Saturation of middle-class markets for big-ticket items such as autos and houses, a top-heavy income distribution that gave a third of the income to 5 percent of the population, and a "depression psychology" that paralyzed investment for years also contributed to the disaster.

The result was the terrible downward spiral of depression. Business bankruptcies threw people out of work. Unemployed people could not buy goods. More businesses thus closed, throwing yet more people into the ranks of the jobless. And so it went, spiraling down into a seemingly bottomless pit.

It is ancient history now, like scratchy old phonograph records or jittery black-and-white movies. But it was an unbelievable nightmare then.

"Brother, can you spare a dime?" Hoovervilles—tin-and-tarpaper shacks flung up on ash heaps at the edges of cities. Men wrapped in newspapers, sleeping on park benches. Hollow-eyed women and dirty-faced children watching the dry, dead earth of their farms blow away.

"Nothing to fear but fear itself!" Franklin and Eleanor Roosevelt seemed to embody a new self-confidence that many Americans found heartening in the depths of the Great Depression. The ebullient public image displayed here gave credence to the president's confident assertion that his generation had "a rendezvous with destiny." (The Bettmann Archive)

One and one-half million Americans were out of work in 1929. Thirteen million were jobless in 1933.

Yet American democracy survived the decade. The survival expert who carried the nation through was an improbable upstate New York patroon with an aristocratic cigarette holder, a mellifluous voice, and a contagious certainty that "all we have to fear is fear itself"—and a man who could not get out of his wheelchair unaided. His name, perhaps the best-known in twentieth-century American politics, was Franklin Delano Roosevelt—FDR to headlines writers everywhere. An unbeatable politician who was elected president four times—twice as many as any other—and who guided the nation through both the Great Depression and World War II, Franklin Roosevelt (1933–1945) stands with George Washington and Abraham Lincoln on the very shortest list of America's greatest presidents.

At Roosevelt's side throughout the presidential years was his wife, Eleanor, who thereafter became America's most admired woman in her own right. They made an unlikely couple at first glance. Franklin was a handsome, ambitious assistant secretary of the navy and an aggressive governor of New York—condemned to a wheelchair for life by a shattering attack of polio in 1921. Eleanor was plain and shy, the ugly-duckling daughter of an equally aristocratic family. Yet they forged one of the most effective political partnerships in U.S. history. Eleanor Roosevelt was FDR's eyes and ears, his physical presence where he could not go to hearten the people, and a militant champion of social causes.

Roosevelt was a man of action rather than an intellectual, and it was action that the nation wanted in 1933. "I pledge myself," he declared during his first campaign, "to a new deal for the American people. . . . This is more than a political campaign; it is a call to arms."[4] After three grinding years of waiting for the business cycle to turn up again, for the laws of supply and demand to pull the country out of the trough, Americans were finally ready for government involvement in the economy to a degree they had never tolerated before. The result was wave after wave of reform legislation through the 1930s—and a transformed America.

The New Deal meant relief for the hungry, public works projects for the unemployed, loans to help people keep their homes, regulation for Wall Street, insurance for banks, devaluation for the dollar. The Civilian Conservation Corps (CCC) and the Works Progress Administration (WPA) put hundreds of thousands of people to work on government-sponsored projects. The Agricultural Adjustment Act (AAA) raised farm incomes by encouraging cuts in production. The Tennessee Valley Authority (TVA) began the integrated development of an entire region of the country on the basis of cheap electricity and irrigation. The Wagner Act strengthened the bargaining position of labor unions as never before in America. Social Security at last brought national old-age pensions, begun decades before in Europe, to the United States.

Roosevelt's foreign-policy credentials were impeccably liberal also. He broke a conservative Republic front against the Bolsheviks by extending diplomatic recognition to the Soviet Union—and American businessmen as solid as Henry Ford were soon cheerfully trading with Communist Russia. FDR announced a new policy of nonintervention south of the border, a Good Neighbor Policy that at least looked like a significant change from the days of Dollar Diplomacy and sending in the Marines.

---

[4]James T. Patterson, *America in the Twentieth Century* (New York: Harcourt Brace Jovanovich, 1976), p. 158.

Most important, by the end of the thirties Roosevelt was clearly aware of the international danger posed by the rise of aggressive totalitarian regimes in Germany, Italy, Japan, and elsewhere. His efforts to prepare Americans for the possibility of a new world war were handicapped by general disillusionment with the last one. But his estimate of Axis intentions would prove all too accurate as the decade ended.

Franklin Roosevelt could not stop the world depression—it took World War II to do that. But he carried America through it without recourse to totalitarian tyranny and with a renewed sense of national purpose and dignity. And he set the United States at last on the road other Western nations had already taken toward the welfare state—that precarious balance of capitalistic economy, democratic government, and socialist concern for the basic social and economic needs of the people.

## Britain and France Muddle Through

In Europe, democratic governments and capitalist economies survived best in Britain and France, in Scandinavia (Norway, Sweden, and Denmark in particular), in the Low Countries (the Netherlands and Belgium), and in such isolated pockets as Switzerland and Czechoslovakia. In much of the rest of Europe, as we will see, very different tides were rising.

Economically, Britain had lost a quarter of its overseas trade and had been replaced as the greatest foreign investor by the booming United States. The British industrial plant, so vigorously challenged by Germany before the war, remained dated and slow to recover. When the Great Depression came in the 1930s, Britain handled it no better than other Western European countries. The United Kingdom had no FDR to rally the nation against the rising tide of bankruptcies, layoffs, and poverty. A series of more or less ineffectual Conservative leaders cobbled together an array of half measures, from reluctant devaluation of the pound to an inadequate dole intended merely to keep the unemployed from starving.

The British Empire also showed the strains of Britain's anomalous new position in the world. In India, an independence movement led by Mahatma Gandhi and the Congress party gained momentum. Closer to home, England's oldest colony, Ireland, was at last granted its freedom after a brief rebellion in 1916 and a bloody British struggle with the terrorists of the Irish Republican Army in the years around 1920. Northern Ireland, however, with its heavy Anglo-Protestant population, remained part of Britain—and a source of friction for the rest of the century.

A more positive adjustment to new realities was the creation of the British Commonwealth of Nations by the Act of Westminster in 1931. By this act, some of Britain's largest and oldest colonies, including Canada, Australia, and South Africa, gained complete political independence under the symbolic headship of the British crown, while still benefiting from "imperial preference" in trade.

France also seemed to mark time through the interwar decades. The French economy had not surrendered so largely to big-business corporate organization as some other developed nations had. Paradoxically, however, small-scale workshops proved less likely to slip into the devastating downward spiral of bankruptcies and lay-offs, drop in consumer demand and further plant closings that ravaged Germany and the United States.

Internationally, France was deeply concerned with revived German power across the Rhine and with the more distant menace of Bolshevism in Eastern Europe. French leaders moved aggressively if imprudently in the 1920s, occupying the industrial Ruhr district in order to squeeze reparations payments out of Germany. The result was severe economic damage, to France as well as to Germany, and a negotiated settlement.

In the thirties the French spent years and hundreds of millions of francs building an elaborate string of steel-and-concrete fortifications facing Germany—the notorious Maginot Line. While Hitler prepared to fight the next war with highly mobile panzer divisions, France braced itself to fight the last one over again in the grimly defensive spirit of Verdun.

This backward-looking, defensive, Maginot-Line mentality in fact characterized much of French history between the wars. American tourists might enjoy Paris in the springtime, and there was still no better place to be an expatriate. But there was little sense of grandeur along the Seine, and no Napoleons in sight as France's next time of testing came on inexorably.

## The Commonwealth Countries: Capable of Coping

The United States and Europe were the heart of the Western world, as they would be throughout most of the twentieth century. But there were more Western worlds than one by this time. A look at two other areas of Western culture will therefore be necessary to complete this overview.

The nations of the British Commonwealth, scattered around the world geographically, were as much a part of this new, expanded twentieth-century West as the United States was. Domestic autonomy had been granted to Canada, Australia, and New Zealand in the nineteenth century, to South Africa around 1900, soon after the Boer War, and to Ireland around 1920, following the Irish "troubles." The formal grant of independence and equality under the British crown in 1931 completed what had begun a century before—the creation of a British family of nations around the globe.

The nations of the Commonwealth were for the most part as democratic as any in the world, possessing representative legislatures, bills of rights, and lively traditions of political and social reform. South Africa, which contained a huge, totally disfranchised black majority, was the great exception to this tendency.

Economically, most of the Commonwealth countries had been outgrowing their original roles as suppliers of agricultural products and raw materials in return for manufactured goods from the mother country. They continued to produce large quantities of beef, wheat, mutton, wool, gold, diamonds, and other valuable commodities. But the South African mining industries and Australian manufacturing grew apace, and Canada became one of the major manufacturing nations of the world during these decades.

All the nations of the British Commonwealth suffered in the world depression. But all survived it without draconian political measures, as they would survive World War II. For the most part, then, the Commonwealth countries entered the second half of the century as leading examples of successful Western nations, capable of coping with the worst this century could dish out.

## The Latin American Nations: Voices for Ideals

By and large, the twenties were better times, the thirties considerably worse in Latin America, as for most of the Western world. Here, however, general trends stretching over both decades will be stressed.

Economically, a major change was the take-off of a domestic manufacturing capacity in some of the more developed Latin American states. This change was partly the result of the high prices charged for North American and European manufactured goods. These prices were particularly hard for Latin Americans to pay during the Depression, when the prices of their exports of agricultural products and raw materials declined rapidly. All this led some Latin Americans to try to produce at home what they could not afford from abroad.

In part also, the building of new manufacturing plants and the nationalizing of foreign-owned extractive industries was a deliberate policy stimulated by national pride and by a growing awareness of Latin America's relative technological underdevelopment. The result, in any case, was genuine growth in consumer-goods manufacturing—notably in textiles—in Argentina, Brazil, and other nations, and of the oil industry in Mexico, Venezuela, and Andean states such as Peru.

Politically, there was also some striking evidence of progress between the wars, both in political performance and in ideals and social services.

Conservative and military elements did remain prominent in government during the period, but in the 1920s, at least, revolutionary seizures of power dwindled greatly. Some sectors of the civil service, such as the agencies dealing with public utilities and those concerned with irrigation projects, tended especially to be more modern and professional and less exploitative.

Outside groups pressured governments to enact reforms. Liberal, middle-class parties urged more democracy, as did students at Latin America's large universities. The growing working class, reinforced by a new influx of European immigrants bringing socialistic ideas and no tradition of subservience to Latin American establishments, demanded attention to the needs of working people. Furthermore, many Latin Americans of all classes, disturbed by the U.S. military interventions of the early years of the twentieth century, strongly resented foreign influences of all sorts in their countries.

Some genuine though limited progress resulted from the pressures generated by these new groups and by idealistic political impulses. Mexico and the ABC countries—Argentina, Brazil, and Chile—significantly expanded the role of their governments in providing social services for their people. Advanced labor codes regulating hours and conditions of work were passed in some countries. Even some of the more reactionary autocrats prided themselves on educational reforms. Mexico's nationalization of foreign oil wells in the 1930s exemplified a wave of government moves aimed at limiting foreign participation in Latin American economies.

Many of these reforms never reached the peons in the countryside, and others were never put into practice at all. Foreign capital continued to be needed, so that in the end, patriotic fervor frequently gave way to pragmatism, or to a desire for a share of the profits.

Nevertheless, much was accomplished. Domestically owned industries were at last beginning to grow, government's responsibility to the people was broadening, and twentieth-century social idealism had no more ardent spokesmen than in Latin America.

## SUMMARY

World War I and the Great Depression, twin disasters centered in the Western world, jolted the globe during the early decades of the twentieth century.

World War I was triggered by the assassination of the heir to the Austrian throne by a Balkan terrorist. Larger causes, however, turned this local conflict into a global catastrophe. These deeper causes included entangling diplomatic alliances, nationalistic passions, economic competition, and massive military buildups. Imperial rivalries also helped to create the conflicts of interest and the international tensions that led to World War I.

The Great War, as it was called, was the bloodiest in the history of the world up to that time. Major offensives by both the Allies—Britain, France, Russia, Italy, and later the United States—and the Central Powers—Germany and Austria—repeatedly failed. A terrifying array of new weapons, from airplanes and submarines to poison gas, took a heavy toll. And trench warfare, backed by heavy artillery, machine guns, and poison gas, slaughtered millions in a four-year war of attrition. Total commitment was also required on the home front, where governments gained new powers, and economies were drained in the long struggle.

The war also involved non-European peoples. The German colonies overseas were lost, and the British and French colonies participated in the war. Turkey, Japan, and the United States also entered the war, the last two gaining significant imperial and economic benefits from their part in the struggle.

The results of World War I included ten million dead, governments toppled in Germany, Russia, and elsewhere, and economies destabilized by Europe's enormous war debts. More constructive consequences included the founding of the League of Nations—the first political organization to seek genuinely global participation, and a symbol at least of the growing globalization of history.

The decades between the two world wars are often contrasted. The 1920s are seen as the Jazz Age of prosperity, flappers, and fun; the 1930s, as the depression decade, the red decade, the decade of unemployment, suffering, and ideological commitment. In fact, the two decades had much in common. Global overproduction led to poverty among commodity producers in both developed and underdeveloped societies. Technology further transformed the Western world, bringing widespread use of automobiles, telephones, electrical appliances, radios, and moving pictures.

Tensions increased between social classes, and the depression decade in America was dominated by the powerful personality of Franklin D. Roosevelt and the New Deal. Britain muddled through, and France was deeply conservative, building the Maginot Line against foreign enemies. In both Britain and France, however, socialist parties chalked up their first national political victories.

The Commonwealth countries evolved as a loose family of self-governing nations, while Canada became one of the world's leading industrial countries. The Latin American republics revealed new tendencies toward political reform and social welfare—until depression brought increased poverty and a resurgence of authoritarian regimes.

## SUGGESTED READING

Adams, R. J. Q., ed. *The Great War, 1914–1918: Essays on the Military, Political, and Social History of the First World War.* College Station, Tex.: A&M University Press, 1990. Professional papers presented at a military studies institute.

Allen, F. L. *Only Yesterday,* New York: Harper & Row, 1972. Social and cultural trends of the 1920s; lively reading.

Bothwell, R., et al. *Canada, 1900–1945.* Toronto: University of Toronto Press, 1987. Useful synthesis of twentieth-century Canadian history.

Burns, J. M. *Roosevelt: The Lion and the Fox.* New York: Harcourt Brace Jovanovich, 1970. Positive assessment of Franklin D. Roosevelt as leader and political tactician.

Clavin, P. *The Great Depression in Europe, 1929–1939.* New York: St. Martin's Press, 2000. A concise overview of the impact of the Depression on Europe.

Dietmar, R. *The Global Impact of the Great Depression, 1929–1939.* New York: Routledge, 1996. Brief, clear summary of a complex subject.

Edsforth, R. *America's Response to the Great Depression.* Malden, Mass.: Blackwell, 2000. Effective presentation of American capitalism in collapse and revival.

Fussell, P. *The Great War and Modern Memory.* New York: Oxford University Press, 1977. The literary image of World War I and its impact on modern consciousness.

Galbraith, J. K. *The Great Crash.* New York: Avon, 1980. On the American stock market crash that triggered the global collapse.

Grayzel, S. R. *Women's Identities at War: Gender, Motherhood, and Politics in Britain and France During the First World War.* Chapel Hill: University of North Carolina Press, 1999. Covers wide range, from women as objects of war propaganda to women as workers in war plants.

Herrmann, D. G. *The Arming of Europe and the Making of the First World War.* Princeton: Princeton University Press, 1996. Traces the story of the coming of the war from crisis to crisis over the decade before 1914.

Horne, A. *The Price of Glory: Verdun, 1916.* London: Penguin, 1979. Detailed account of one of the great offensives that failed.

Horne, J., ed. *State, Society, and Mobilization in Europe During the First World War.* Cambridge and New York: Cambridge University Press, 1997. Papers discussing the impact of the war on many subgroups in society, from socialists to school children.

Keegan, J. *The First World War.* New York: Knopf, 1999. Solid overview by a celebrated war historian. See also G. Martin, *The First World War: A Complete History* (New York: Holt, 1994).

Melman, B. *Women and the Popular Imagination in the Twenties: Flappers and Nymphs.* New York: St. Martin's Press, 1988. Psychosocial investigation of the multiple meanings of the popular image of the free-wheeling young woman of the 1920s.

Remarque, E. M. *All Quiet on the Western Front,* trans. A. W. Wheen. New York: Fawcett Crest, 1958. Vivid fictional evocation of trench warfare.

Sontag, R. *A Broken World, 1919–1939.* New York: Harper & Row, 1971. Excellent overview of this complex and many-sided era.

Tuchman, B. *The Guns of August.* New York: Macmillan, 1962. Moving narrative of the coming of the war.

Williams, J. *The Home Fronts: Britain, France, and Germany, 1914–1918.* London: Constable, 1972. Comparative study, including emphasis on women and the war effort.

Winter, J., G. Parker, and M. R. Habeck, eds. *The Great War and the Twentieth Century.* New Haven: Yale University Press, 2000. Scholarly essays reconsidering many aspects of the First World War.

 Please refer to the document CD-ROM for primary sources related to this chapter.

# CHAPTER 25

# A SCHIZOPHRENIC AGE
## Revolution and Totalitarianism
## Shake the World

## (1910–1949)

## A Glance Ahead: Revolutionaries and Dictators Menace the World

The 1920s and 1930s, the decades between the world wars, saw governments around the world collapse under the hammer blows of two apparently opposite forces: revolution and dictatorship. Both dictators and revolutionaries, however, reflected a central trait of twentieth century politics: ideological commitment.

The ideologies were extreme versions of the isms formulated in the nineteenth-century West. The roots of Stalinist Communism lay in nineteenth-century socialism, those of Hitler's Nazism in modern nationalism. Both the revolutions and the dictatorships toppled governments and transformed societies in many countries, from Russia and China to Germany, Italy, and Japan.

By 1939, democracies like the United States, Britain, and France faced an aggressively expansionist Axis alliance of Nazi Germany, Fascist Italy, and militarist Japan. And then came the Hitler-Stalin Pact, tilting the odds heavily against the democratic powers as World War II loomed a matter of days away.

## Ideological Revolution—and the Flight from Freedom

### The Central Role of Ideology

The forms of rebellion—even of political revolt—are many and varied, and they are as old as history. As far back as our records run, there have been peasant rebellions, palace coups, civil wars between claimants to the same throne, feuds between factions within the same city. But the ideological revolution, inspired by new social ideas and envisioning a totally new social order, is a modern phenomenon.

Until quite recently, at least, liberalism has perhaps been the weakest of the major modern ideologies in its impact on twentieth-century revolutionaries. Liberal convictions, political and economic, were most potent among rebels between 1776 and 1848. By 1900, many liberal objectives had been achieved in the West.

Nationalism, particularly in the form of anti-imperialism, has been much more of a driving force behind the revolutions of the twentieth century. The European intercontinental empires would be shattered by nationalistic rebellion against foreign domination after World War II. Powerful currents of nationalistic feeling flowed also in the great Mexican and Chinese revolutions of the earlier twentieth century, which will also be dealt with here.

Marxist revolutionary socialism, however, was perhaps more visible than any other ideology in the revolutions of the twentieth century. Since most twentieth-century revolutionary upheavals have come in primarily peasant countries, such as Russia and China, Marxist ideologues have had to do some recasting a theory originally focused on the industrial proletariat to suit the needs of their preindustrial constituencies. But Lenin's turn-of-the-century thesis that imperialism was an extension of capitalism overseas would appeal to revolutionary cadres around the world.

Like the religious motives of earlier times, ideological impulses are frequently mixed with other motives, from political ambition and social resentment to economic needs and desires. But the part played by visions of brave new worlds built on a bedrock of ideas has nonetheless been central.

## Scope and Scale of the Major Revolutions

Between 1911 and 1949, great ideological revolutions shook some of the largest nations in the world, including Russia, the largest in territory, and China, the largest in population. During this same period between the wars, less violent but nonetheless ideologically based independence movements gathered force on the Indian subcontinent—second only to China in population—and in many parts of Africa, the second largest continent.

There would be many revolutions in the second half of the century as well, but these would tend to be in rather smaller corners of the world, in places such as Vietnam, Algeria, and Cuba. These revolutions were significant because of their frequency, cropping up again and again around the globe in the decades after World War II, and because of the part they played in the Cold War. But the big revolutions came in the first half of the twentieth century, especially during the years between the wars.

The Russian and Chinese revolutions in particular had much in common. They were based on Western ideologies and visions of social justice, and they anticipated a better social order. They became models for later generations of rebels in other parts of the world. But perhaps most impressive, they had *scale* in common.

They were fought over hundreds of thousands of square miles by millions of people. Their casualty totals dwarf those of the English, French, and American revolutions of earlier centuries. They changed the lives of hundreds of millions. And they dragged on, sometimes for decades, before a new social order was at last established, a new regime firmly in place.

For the historian, sheer length is perhaps the most striking feature. How long can a revolution be, after all, before it becomes a kind of violent social evolution, consuming whole generations in its quest for a brighter tomorrow?

There was heroism enough for any lover of courage in the face of terrible adversity. There were horrors to turn the sternest of us queasy at the unending violence. There was, finally, social change—though not always the change dreamed of by the founders, many of whom had long been in their graves when the consummation came.

The many revolutions of the years between the wars are historic monuments of our century. They have given us crusaders such as Mahatma Gandhi, men of violence such as Pancho Villa, founders of new nations such as Lenin and Mao, transformers of whole societies by force, such as Stalin. They gave the world new powers—the Soviet Union and the People's Republic of China—which would play central parts in the history of most of the rest of the century.

Idealistic young rebels—and millions of other men and women—fell in hecatombs to bring these things to pass. Too often, once the guns were still, those who survived found their own lives little improved and their new governments at least as authoritarian as those they had overthrown.

In this also, they were typical of their times. For the most revolutionary of centuries was also the most politically authoritarian.

## Defining Totalitarianism

One of the most disturbing things about the upsurge of autocratic, authoritarian, and brutally totalitarian governments was that earlier twentieth-century people seemed to welcome them with open arms. Too many of the new dictators enjoyed widespread popular support among the peoples they tyrannized. There were too many cheering crowds lining the advance of Hitler's Nazis or Mussolini's Fascists to power, too much real enthusiasm for "dear Comrade Stalin" in the Soviet Union.

To many, it looked like what social psychologist Erich Fromm diagnosed as a flight from freedom. The nineteenth century had seen the steady advance of liberal political institutions across the Western world. The early twentieth seemed to be witnessing a widespread rejection of freedom, a disillusionment with democracy. Confronted with economic and social challenges too great for its fragile new liberal institutions, the world seemed to be turning back to cruder, more brutal beliefs in blood and violence, in irresistible force and omnipotent leadership.

The new leaders jeered at the decadence of democracy, the failure of capitalism. They contrasted the flabbiness and degeneracy of the liberal West with their own discipline and strength. "Today," Mussolini declared with total confidence, "the liberal faith must shut the doors of its deserted temples, deserted because the peoples of the world realize that its worship . . . will lead, as it has already led, to certain ruin."[1]

Not all the new dictatorships were of the sort normally described as totalitarian, but the most notorious and powerful of them were. It will therefore be worthwhile to spend some time answering a rather subtle question: What exactly is totalitarianism?

This distinctive twentieth-century ism may be defined most simply as an attempt at total control of society by government. Totalitarian states have attempted to achieve this end by building on ideologically based political parties, powerful bureaucracies, and modern technology.

The party, with its uniforms and parades, its access to power and the perquisites of office, its inspiring ideals and sense of driving purpose, brought many into the totalitarian fold. The omnipresent bureaucracy carried the power of the totalitarian state into the lives of all its citizens as never before. And technology, from propaganda to military and police power, from microphones to machine guns, was always there to deal with doubters and dissenters. The resulting new order subverted all other institutions and ideas, sucking all classes and groups, all ages and both sexes into the new Leviathan state.

A number of explanations have been offered for the rise of this new Leviathan. The economic, social, and political challenges of modernization, the strains of the Great Depression, the humiliations of imperial domination or military defeat certainly played a part. The sheer faceless power of the modern state with its endless hierarchies of officials helps to account for the iron grip of the system. The hypnotic grasp of modern ideologies, comparable to the power of religion in earlier centuries, surely contributed.

Seen as a cast of mind rather than a form of government, totalitarianism involves total commitment to the cause, complete submergence of the individual in the group, unquestioning obedience to the authority of the party or the leader. From this sort of commitment, moral and emotional, comes a sense of inner harmony and collective strength. The petty ego of the individual, submerged in the larger whole of the group, swells with pride, strength, joy, disciplined purpose.

So much for deeper explanations of the jackboot in the face. Now for a look at some historical realities.

---

[1]Benito Mussolini, *The Political and Social Doctrines of Fascism,* trans. Jane Soames (London: Hogarth Press, 1933), p. 9.

# REVOLUTIONS IN RUSSIA AND CHINA

### Lenin and the Bolsheviks

Russia was unique, even in relatively conservative and undeveloped Eastern Europe. Its huge population of peasants, the eternally suffering *muzhiks,* were sunk in poverty and ignorance. Its fairy-tale aristocracy lived the life of the American antebellum South, of Versailles before the Bastille fell, with town mansions and vast estates, lavish balls, and sleigh bells jingling through the Russian night. Its divine-right emperor was a figure out of the Middle Ages, convinced that God had sent him to rule his people. And so he did, with the help of repressive Cossack regiments and the largest bureaucracy and most notorious secret police in the Western world.

In the nineteenth century, revolutionary rumblings had become endemic. Decembrist plotters in 1825, nihilist rioters in the 1860s, and Narodnik terrorists in the 1870s and 1880s had all failed. Then, at the turn of the century, Russia's revolutionary tradition produced its final flower: the generation of Lenin.

There were two main revolutionary organizations, one of them divided into two factions. The older of the two major groups was the Social Revolutionary party—the SRs. Heirs of the Narodniks of the preceding generation, they were convinced that the oppressed peasants would one day rise up to overthrow the man they still called the "dear father czar." The newer group, Russia's first Marxists, insisted that the new and still relatively small Russian industrial proletariat was the wave of the revolutionary future.

The most important Marxist group was the so-called "Majority" or *Bolshevik* faction, which insisted on a tightly knit party of disciplined, full-time revolutionaries. The leader of the Bolshevik wing was a man named Vladimir Ilich Ulyanov, known to history by his alias of Lenin.

Lenin (1870–1924) was a school administrator's son from the Volga region of Eastern European Russia. A student demonstrator in his youth, he was an early convert to Marxism. His older brother had been hanged for plotting to assassinate the czar in the 1880s, and Lenin himself spent time in Siberia for organizing subversive "study groups" among Russian work-

Lenin orates to a Russian crowd in Red Square, Moscow, in the darkest days of the civil war that followed the 1917 revolutions. A committed activist, Lenin believed that revolutions were "the locomotives of history," and that seizing power to effect social change was the point of revolutions. (The Bettmann Archive)

ers. His wife, Nadezhda Krupskaya, was a child of the liberal nobility who moved through workers' education to revolutionary activism and shared Lenin's Siberian years and then his exile in Switzerland, where they and their comrades lived, wrote, schemed, and organized through the opening years of the new century.

Lenin was, said one who knew him, "a man of iron will, of indomitable energy, who combined a fanatical faith in the movement and the cause with no less faith in himself. . . ."[2] He looked old even in youth, with his rapidly receding hairline, broad forehead, narrow Tatar eyes, and small moustache. His fellows in the underground called him the Old Man, honored him for his skill in ideological debate and his twenty-four-hours-a-day commitment to his cause. Many followed him into the Bolshevik faction when the party split in 1903. They were still with him in 1917, when their hour came at last.

## The Russian Revolutions of 1917

There is no question of the dedicated revolutionary zeal of Lenin and his colleagues. There is no doubt either, however, that they did not bring down the czar in 1917. World War I did that.

Romanov Russia's creaky economy, dilapidated administration, and military backwardness made it the least prepared of all the great powers to meet the challenges of total war in 1914. The nation's huge peasant armies were poorly fed, trained, and equipped, their human-wave assaults costly and futile in a modern war. The meager railway system and inefficient administration denied the troops supplies and kept casualties from getting back to medical help. Cities swollen with war workers ran out of food, fuel, even housing in the long Russian winters.

The government of the last czar was a carnival of inefficiency and corruption. Nicholas II himself was at the front with the troops, while Empress Alexandra came under the influence of the "monk" Rasputin, whose ability to ease the suffering of her hemophiliac son Alexis, heir and hope of the dynasty, mesmerized her into thinking he had been sent by God. In fact, Rasputin was an unscrupulous peasant faith healer, devoted to debauchery and influence peddling.

Under such external pressures, a government so thoroughly rotted within simply could not stand. Lenin was still in exile in Switzerland when the Russian government fell.

The February Revolution that brought down the czarist monarchy was guided by liberal Duma politicians and generals who recognized the hopelessness of the military situation. In the depths of that winter of 1916–1917, with mobs surging through the streets of the capital, this group went to Nicholas and persuaded him to abdicate for the good of the country. The nation, they said, would not follow him further.

Nicholas resigned, first in favor of his young son, and then of his brother. But the momentum of the revolution quickly swept the Romanovs aside, and a republic was declared. The new provisional government of Duma leaders, basically liberal in composition, was headed by Alexander Kerensky, leader of a prolabor party in the Duma.

The great failing of the Kerensky government, however, was its inability to take Russia out of the war that had already brought the Romanovs down. Kerensky launched one more vast offensive in the summer of 1917. When this last effort failed, the provisional government followed the czarist one into oblivion. This was the work of the October Revolution of 1917—Lenin's revolution.

---

[2]Bertram D. Wolfe, *Three Who Made a Revolution: A Biographical History* (Boston: Beacon Press, 1948), p. 258.

Beaten soldiers were streaming home that winter of 1917–1918, some of them mutinying, many bringing their rifles with them. The cities were hungry, cold, overcrowded, bitter. The provisional government was in disarray. The peasants were restless, the workers ready to strike.

And Lenin was back in Russia, plotting with the disaffected, haranguing mobs in the streets in order to intensify the disaffection. But the revolutionary who had devoted his life to Marxism had more sense than to try to explain the master's theories to the mob. "Land!" he shouted into the sea of upturned faces, land for the peasantry at last. "Bread!" for the starving cities. "Peace!" and an end to a hopeless war. Land, bread, and peace did the job.

The fighting took place in the cities and was generally brief. Kerensky was driven from St. Petersburg into a long American exile. The walled Kremlin in Moscow fell after a bloodier battle. In other cities, Bolsheviks led workers' militias and squads of mutinous sailors from the Russian navy in quick seizures of power. Lenin replaced Kerensky at the head of the new government.

It was then that the Bolsheviks—soon renamed the Communists—showed what they were made of. For the great Bolshevik achievement lay not in seizing power but in holding on to it.

Through the late teens and early twenties, the new Russian Communist government was beset by enemies on every side. So-called White Russian armies loyal to the czar took the field against the Reds. Subject nationalities—the Baltic states, Poland, and others—rebelled. Invading German armies forced a costly peace upon the new government. The newly independent Poles invaded Russia from the west, Russia's imperial rival Japan from the east. Allied forces—British, French, American—angry at Russia's separate peace and afraid of the Bolshevik virus, established beachheads in Russia and provided logistical support for its enemies. Thus surrounded and attacked from all sides, the Bolsheviks fought back with ingenuity, energy, and ruthlessness that finally carried the day.

Lenin threw a government together and dissolved a constitutional convention when peasant voters gave a majority to his revolutionary rivals the SRs. He hastily nationalized large sectors of the Russian economy, less for doctrinaire reasons than to mobilize the nation's resources for civil war. And he threw together the first Red Army to fight it.

Lenin's right hand in the struggle was a relatively recent convert to Bolshevism named Leon Trotsky. A thin, bespectacled, wild-haired intellectual, shrewd theoretician, and brilliant orator, Trotsky became the unlikely architect of the new Red Army. Roaring about Russia in his famous armoured train, haranguing the troops or terrifying them by rigorous punishment for slackness or failure, Trotsky made a major contribution to the Bolshevik victory.

It was a costly triumph. The largest nation in Europe, already ravaged by the worst war in Western history, bled for more long years in the Russian Civil War. Red and White terrors rivaled each other in ferocity. Lenin himself was shot and badly wounded by an SR terrorist.

Nevertheless, the Bolsheviks won. When Lenin, weakened by his immense exertions and his injury, died in 1924, the members of the renamed Communist party were the masters of Russia.

## The Stalin Revolution

After the immense strains of a decade of war and revolution, the 1920s saw a relaxation and a falling off of zeal in Russia—before the revolutionary drive was renewed once more in the Stalinist 1930s.

The great event of the twenties was a quiet power struggle in the Communist party after Lenin's death. And the winner was not one of the Old Man's close associates in pre-revolutionary days—not even the brilliant late convert Trotsky—but a stolid, ruthless Bolshevik from the south called Joseph Stalin. Stalin—real name Dzhugashvili—was the son of a heavy-fisted cobbler from Georgia, in the bandit-haunted mountainous Caucasus region. While Lenin and Trotsky were arguing the party's future in Switzerland, Stalin was back in Russia, organizing bank robberies to acquire funds for the party—and serving several terms in Siberia.

Stalin's rise to power was a triumph of political savvy, hard work, and the organization-man mentality. He was secretary of the Communist party in the twenties, and he made that post the real center of power in Russia. Running the party machine, he came to know its leaders—who the idealists were, who the opportunists, who needed what and how to get it. Neither a great Marxist theoretician nor a spellbinding orator, he had a much more valuable skill—a talent for manipulating power blocs. By the end of the decade Stalin ruled Russia. His rivals had either joined the chorus of support for "the Lenin of today" or, like Trotsky, were on their way to exile abroad.

As the 1930s came on, then, Stalin set out to win his own niche in history—by taking up the revolution once more. His chosen front was economic development, his method a series of Five-Year Plans for unprecedented economic growth in the most backward of the world's great powers.

During the 1930s the first three Five-Year Plans did, in fact, transform and in key areas expand the Russian economy beyond the wildest dreams of Peter the Great. The Russian government assumed control of industry, agriculture, finance, and trade in the Soviet Union. Government planning commissions worked out schedules of growth for each region, each sector of the economy. Resources were allocated, quotas decreed for every sector, every factory and farm, every worker at his or her desk, lathe, or tractor.

In industry the results were spectacular. Great hydroelectric projects, huge dams, steel mills, tractor factories went up. Whole industrial complexes sprang from the empty steppes. Production goals were reached and surpassed. If there were questions about some of the statistics, the achievement was nonetheless genuine. In a capitalist world still reeling under the hammer blows of the Great Depression, Russia's achievement was particularly impressive.

Agriculture was collectivized under government control. Private farms were merged into large state farms owned by the government, or into farms run collectively by the peasants. Modern agricultural methods and centrally located government machine-tractor stations were introduced to improve production. The increased output was to be used to feed the industrial cities and sold abroad for vitally needed foreign capital. Advances on the agricultural front, however, were slower and much more costly than in the industrial sector, as we will see.

Nevertheless, as World War II came on, Stalin could claim convincingly to have carried Russia's long revolution to something of a climax. Communist-party rule was unquestioned in the vast one-party state, and state socialism had become a reality in the largest nation in the world.

## The Legacy of Sun Yixian

The longest of all the revolutions of the first half of the century was the Chinese Revolution of 1911–1949. And these four decades include only the military phase of this immense upheaval, excluding the enormously costly attempts at social revolution in China that followed the Communist victory in 1949.

Bullied by foreign imperialists and deeply divided over how far to go in learning from the West in order to defeat the West, China was dissolving into a hopeless confusion of conflicting theories, ambitions, and factions as the twentieth century began. The Mandate of Heaven had clearly passed from the battered Manchus: but to whom?

Old realities and new influences collided in turn-of-the-century China. Established court politicians such as the military leader Yuan Shikai, powerful provincial generals, the perennially dangerous Chinese secret societies, and the eternally exploited, increasingly restless peasant masses would play important parts in the coming struggle, as such groups had in the past. New groups with equally important roles included the overseas Chinese community, many of them wealthy merchants scattered over Southeast Asia, the western Pacific, and even the United States; the growing numbers of Western-educated Chinese students trained in Japan, Europe, or the United States, or at the new Chinese university in Beijing; and the emerging Chinese proletariat, exploited products of the rapid industrialization of Chinese cities such as Shanghai.

Out of the tangle, two basic tendencies evolved: a reformist campaign for a constitutional monarchy and a revolutionary demand for a Chinese republic.

The reformers had their day first. In a final effort to save the Manchu dynasty, the Dowager Empress Ci Xi uncharacteristically acquiesced in a series of changes in the old order. The nationwide system of Confucian civil-service examinations, which had served the empire for the better part of two thousand years, was abolished. Provincial legislative assemblies were introduced, and then a national assembly in Beijing. Plans were laid for a gradual transition to a constitutional monarchy like those in Europe or Japan.

But feuds broke out between the powerful Yuan Shikai and the regent for the three-year-old emperor who succeeded Ci Xi in 1908. A rash of abortive popular insurrections made the weakness of the monarchy even clearer. By 1911, the hour of the republican revolutionaries had come.

Sun Yixian (1866–1925) was the best-known revolutionary proponent of a Chinese republic, both in China and abroad. Born near Canton (Guangzhou) in the cosmopolitan south, he was a thoroughly Westernized Chinese. He had studied at a Christian mission school in Honolulu, read for his medical degree in the British colony of Hong Kong, established his first revolutionary organization in Westernized Japan. He had even made a special visit to his native hamlet to break the village idols, a gesture symbolic of his rejection of the old China.

Sun Yixian had already promulgated his famous Three Principles of the People by 1911. The Three Principles are usually stated as nationalism, democracy, and socialism. By nationalism Sun meant opposition to the Manchu conquerors as well as to Western imperialists. By democracy he intended civil rights for all Chinese and constitutional government modeled in part on that of the United States. The socialist (more literally, "people's livelihood") plank was a rather undeveloped economic principle derived not from Marx or any other Western socialist but from the then-popular theories of the American land-tax crusader Henry George, who saw a single tax on land as a panacea for many social ills.

In the broadest sense, these three principles summed up all the European ideological development of the century following the French Revolution. These sweeping social ideals, suitably modified by a much longer indigenous tradition of social thought, would now begin the twentieth-century transformation of China.

Sun Yixian would work for the last fifteen years of his life (like Lenin, he died in his fifties) to make the Chinese republic a democratic reality. His protegé, Generalissimo Jiang Jieshi, would become the maximum leader of China's Nationalist Party through the 1920s, 1930s, and 1940s. And Jiang's great rival, Chairman Mao Zedong, would organize and lead China's Communist Party and the nation through the 1950s and 1960s and into the 1970s. The Three Principles that were China's inheritance from Dr. Sun thus sum up much of the nation's history since.

## Warlords and Student Rebels

The Republic came quickly. Within three years of Empress Ci Xi's death in 1908, the demoralized empire finally collapsed in a welter of peasant rice riots, student agitation, army revolts, court intrigues, and revolutionary outbreaks led by Dr. Sun's own organization, the United League. Sun, who was in the United States rallying support for the cause, read about the revolution in a Denver newspaper. He hurried home in time to be proclaimed first president of the new Republic of China in January of 1912.

But Sun was rather a symbol of the revolution than a ruler. Knowing that he had neither the power nor the support to govern a nation still sliding toward anarchy, he shrewdly used his new position to win to the republican cause the one man who could govern the country. Yuan Shikai, famous general, military reformer, and currently prime minister of the new constitutional monarchy, engineered the final dissolution of Manchu rule in China. Dr. Sun then stepped down and Yuan became the second president of the Chinese republic—and was soon scheming to restore the empire with himself as emperor.

But the old order was finished in China. Sun opposed Yuan's plans. Local rebellions broke out again. And at the outbreak of World War I in 1914, Japan further embarrassed Yuan's government, first by seizing German Shandong, then by imposing the notorious Twenty-One Demands on China itself.

These imperialistic demands included acceptance of Japanese political, military, and financial advisers, further economic penetration by Japan, and recognition of a paramount position for Japan in Manchuria and elsewhere in the north. Such concessions would have made the enormous continental empire little more than a protectorate of the island kingdom. Yuan, hoping for Japanese support for his dynastic ambitions, accepted most of the proposals—and turned the nation definitively against himself before he died in 1916.

With the passing of the old order's strong man, real authority quickly fell into the hands of the local power brokers in the provinces, most of them military leaders with private armies who became known as *warlords*. Through the late teens and early twenties, the anarchy of the warlord era prevailed.

But there was a new force too during this time—the Chinese student movement—and it grew in influence. Westernized yet bitter enemies of Western exploitation of China, the students organized mass demonstrations against foreign exploitation—and the Chinese weakness that made such exploitation possible.

The most important new direction of the 1920s in China, however, was a new interest in Russian Communism. From the postrevolutionary Soviet Union came anti-imperialist assurances, political and military advisors, and the doctrines of Marx and Lenin. Marxism-Leninism explained imperialism as a product of western capitalism. It offered the Bolshevik model of tightly knit organization to challenge the weak government in Beijing.

In 1920 a small group at Beijing University began to study Marxism seriously. In 1921 the Chinese Communist party was organized at Shanghai. Among the organizers was a former Peking University student named Mao Zedong.

## Jiang Jieshi Versus Mao Zedong

The Russian Communists were realistic enough to realize, however, that the only force strong enough to pose a threat to the Beijing government was not the handful of Communists who organized in 1921, but the Nationalist Party, the Guomindang, led by General Jiang Jieshi. To the Nationalists, therefore, they offered help in organizing the Guomindang and military advisors to retrain the Nationalist army.

Jiang Jieshi (1886–1975) was a patriotic, ambitious young soldier with training in both Japan and Russia. His landlord background and the elitist military tradition of the samurai that he had absorbed in Japan had left him with little sympathy for either democracy or socialism. At the Whampoa Military Academy near Canton he trained a generation of officers to unify their country—and to support their teacher in the power struggles to come.

Sun Yixian died in 1925. In 1927 the Guomindang armies, supported by Russian advisors and arms and led by Jiang Jieshi, moved out of South China in the long-awaited Northern Campaign to unify the nation. Scores of warlord armies capitulated or joined the host as it advanced. Propagandists spread out ahead of the troops, convincing many that Jiang was the man who could restore the one indisputable political necessity for peace and prosperity in China: unity.

The Beijing government fell, and Jiang turned to deal with his last opponents—the Communists. He struck swiftly and without warning. Trapped in the cities where they had gathered to organize the workers, the Communist cadres were slaughtered. Their enclaves of proletarian support, isolated in that vast peasant country, were surrounded and crushed, and with them the Communist party in China. Or so it seemed.

Handfuls of the routed Reds fled to the villages. Among the few who had already sought to organize the peasant masses was a now considerably more mature Mao Zedong (1893–1976). A man of peasant stock himself and a former student Communist from Beijing, he never forgot the devastating lesson of the debacle of 1927. No matter what Marx or Lenin said about the vanguard role of the industrial proletariat, in China it was the peasantry, with its incalculable numbers and ancient grievances, that would be the wave of the revolutionary future.

Jiang went on to capture Beijing in 1928. Mao established a Communist base in the interior, in the hills of Jiangxi Province. Here he began to divide large estates among the peasants, to provide education and some health care, and to teach a modified version of Marxist socialism. This Jiangxi Soviet became the model for the basic Maoist tactic thereafter—a tactic as old as guerrilla warfare—which he called "swimming in the peasant sea."

Jiang was head of the Chinese Republic after 1928. He had married an American-educated woman named Soong Mei-Ling, who became an immensely valuable voice for Jiang in the United States. He was also closely linked to Chinese banking families and could depend on cronies and clients within the military. Many of these supporters, however, would require favors and promotions in the years to come—a source of creeping corruption within the regime.

The nation had been badly damaged by the warlord era, and now it faced an even graver foreign threat—a renewal of Japanese imperialist pressure in the 1930s. Thus surrounded by

## CHINA IN REVOLUTION AND WAR WITH JAPAN, 1911–1949

problems, China's foremost general nevertheless found time to launch a series of so-called "antibandit" campaigns to rout the Communists out of Jiangxi in the early thirties.

Driven out of Jiangxi in 1934, perhaps 100,000 Communists escaped the tightening noose. Led by Mao and his right-hand man Zhou Enlai, the survivors of the shattered Jiangxi Soviet fled once more, this time north and west, pursued by the Nationalist armies. The perilous and costly year-long march that followed took them some 6,000 meandering miles to a new sanctuary in the northern province of Shaanxi. Only a few thousand of them made it.

In Chinese Communist history, this is the Long March. The terrible casualties, the desperate river crossings, the frozen mountain passes that Mao's followers traveled through on their northern march have been immortalized in every art since the Communist victory in 1949. In the mid-1930s, however, as Mao and his remnant bands settled into the caves of their new Shaanxi base, ultimate victory must have looked very far away indeed.

In 1931, meanwhile, the Japanese had seized the industrializing northern province of Manchuria. In 1937 they launched a major invasion of China proper. By 1939 most of eastern China was in their hands, and Jiang Jieshi had retreated to the interior, to what became his wartime capital of Chongqing.

Confronted with this massive foreign threat, many Nationalist leaders urged that the final destruction of Mao's Communists be postponed for the duration. The Communists themselves organized guerrilla warfare against the Japanese occupying forces in North China, thus strengthening their image as patriots. Finally, some of Jiang's own officers compelled him to sit down and negotiate a truce with the Communists so that both might concentrate on the war with Japan. Throughout the Second World War—1941–1945 in Asia—this uneasy armistice between the two rivals prevailed.

When World War II ended in 1945, things at long last began to go Mao's way. In the last days of the war, the Soviet Union declared war on Japan and quickly liberated large chunks of North China. Though Stalin had not approved of Mao's peasant-based Communism—had even apparently expelled Mao from the Communist International for a time—he now turned liberated territory and captured weapons over to Mao's forces. Mao was left stronger than ever as the final confrontation approached.

As the later 1940s passed, furthermore, Jiang Jieshi's American friends began to lose patience with him. Envoys from the United States demanded that he clean up the corruption in his government. Like his Russian advisors in the 1920s, his American mentors in the 1940s urged him to work with the Communists to unify the country.

But clashes between Nationalist and Communist troops were already escalating again to full-scale civil war. And this time Mao was on the offensive. Jiang's retreat into the South became a rout, and the roads were littered with abandoned American military hardware.

By 1949 Jiang had withdrawn from the mainland altogether to the large offshore island of Taiwan (Formosa), where he was to survive as president of a Chinese minirepublic protected by an American fleet for the rest of his life. Mao, meanwhile, stood before a crowd of hundreds of thousands in Beijing's Tiananmen Square to announce the new People's Republic of China—which he also would rule until his death.

## RUMBLINGS OF REVOLUTION AROUND THE WORLD

### The Mexican Revolution

No other revolution of the first half of the twentieth century matched the ferocity or longterm impact of those in Russia and China. But violent revolts and revolutionary schemes did reverberate around the world. Among these were the Mexican Revolution of 1910, the rise of India's nonviolent Congress Party, and the beginnings of African anti-colonial organization.

Porfirio Díaz, Mexico's heavy-handed *caudillo* dictator for thirty-five years, was eighty years old in 1910. He had brought the country economic development in the usual Latin American way, through export sales of agricultural and mineral products, especially oil, which was controlled by British and American capitalists. But 90 percent of Mexico's *mestizos* and Indians were still desperately poor peons on the ranches or haciendas of a handful of wealthy landowners. Workers on the new foreign-owned railways and in the mines and oil wells were equally poverty-stricken. The population was 80 percent illiterate, miserably unhealthy, and kept in line by brutal rural police and federal troops.

Then in 1910 began a cycle of revolution that would last, in one form or another, for thirty years.

The violent decade that took the lives of some two million Mexicans began almost casually with outbreaks of revolutionary activity against the aging Díaz in 1910. Three very different men led the opposition to the aging *caudillo*. Francisco Madero, an idealistic, middle-class reformer, called for free elections to decide the nation's future. Pancho Villa, a flamboyant bandit chief, led a motley horde of *vaqueros* (cowboys) in revolt across the large, arid northern state of Chihuahua. And Emiliano Zapata, a peasant horse and mule dealer in the mountainous southern province of Morelos, mobilized a guerrilla force to compel the redistribution of land among his long-suffering Indian and *mestizo* neighbors.

Confronted by real opposition, Díaz abruptly packed up and left for Europe, and Mexico became a battleground for the violent forces thus unleashed.

There is no space here to follow the gaudy, bloody tale of the next decade—roughly 1910–1920—in any detail. The frail Madero was hailed as the Apostle of Democracy, elected president, and murdered by survivors of the Díaz regime who still hoped to recover power. Zapata carried his "land to the peasants" crusade all the way to Mexico City, shared the limelight for a time with Villa, was forced back into Morelos, and finally was killed by troops under a flag of truce. Pancho Villa, after a colorful, bloody time of plundering, was driven back to his bailiwick in Chihuahua, took to killing gringos so as to precipitate U.S. intervention in the chaos, and had a fine time riding rings around General Pershing's expeditionary force. He was finally murdered by a personal enemy in the early 1920s. All three lived on as Mexican folk heroes; none had done much for Mexico.

Meanwhile, however, a succession of other leaders from the dry, spacious northern provinces that abut the American southwest came to the fore. This succession of powerful men, the Northern Dynasty, in time established a reasonably stable regime that at least preached some concern for the welfare of the Mexican people.

A new constitution was promulgated in 1917, promising land to the peasants, decent hours and wages as well as unions for workers, equal pay for women, and at least the possibility of nationalization of the property of the reactionary Mexican Catholic church and of exploitative foreign capitalists.

A unifying, centralizing political party, known as the PRI or Party of the Revolutionary Institutions, came to power in the 1920s and 1930s, restoring order at last. This organization combined all the nation's new leadership cadres—the military, the bureaucracy, business interests and intellectuals, and now the labor unions and the peasantry—in a single structure that would run Mexico for the next fifty years.

In 1934, however, the PRI leadership chose for the next president the most admired of all the leaders of Mexico's long revolution: Lázaro Cárdenas. Cárdenas, an Indian, young and vigorous, carried the revolutionary drive for social justice further than many believed possible.

Cárdenas won over the troops by military reforms, earned the allegiance of much of the business community by supporting Mexican rather than foreign investors, and won the support of young radicals by organizing a huge new labor union and an even larger peasants' union, bringing new spokesmen for these groups into the PRI. And he astonished the world by nationalizing the American- and British-run oil industry, thus breaking the back of foreign exploitation of this key Mexican resource.

## India: Gandhi and the Congress Party

British rule had brought some distinct benefits to India. British engineers had built tens of thousands of miles of railroads, roads, and canals across the subcontinent, stimulating business activity and a new surge in the growth of India's traditionally bustling commercial middle classes. Pressured by Indian demands, the British admitted Indians to higher positions in the colonial administration, including the English viceroy's advisory council. Provincial legislatures—elected by propertied elites—were introduced. Oxford and Cambridge were opened to the talented sons of India's *rajas* and urban business classes.

But British rule had cost Indians dearly. The new transportation networks, for instance, benefited the English economy more than the Indian, facilitating Britain's extraction of a third of India's raw materials and India's receipt of two fifths of her imports from Britain. The Western concept of private property, which undermined traditional family ownership, made some Indians very wealthy—and others poorer than they had ever been. Western education undermined India's traditional culture.

The Indian National Congress, or Congress party, had been organized in 1885 by a group of moderate middle-class reformers, mostly lawyers, teachers, and journalists. A Hindu renaissance of arts and letters had kindled a renewed pride among educated Indians. But India still seemed an unlikely candidate for a popular nationalistic independence movement. The isolation of its countless tiny villages, the traditional lines of social cleavage between the castes, the Hindu-Muslim split, the lack of a common language, and the great distance between the well-off, Western-educated leadership and the Indian masses looked like insuperable obstacles.

The man who bridged these gaps was Mohandas K. Gandhi (1869–1948), who became known to the world as Mahatma Gandhi, the Great Soul of India.

Raised by pious, well-to-do Hindu parents, young Gandhi was shipped off to London to study law. Isolated for years in a London slum, he pored over a potpourri of spiritual sources, from the ancient Hindu *Bhagavad-Gita* (Song of God) and the Christian Bible to nineteenth-century prophets such as Tolstoy and Thoreau. After organizing peaceful protests in South Africa, he returned to India to a hero's welcome from the Congress party.

Building upon the ancient Hindu principle of *ahimsa* (nonviolence), he organized a series of nonviolent demonstrations, first for reform in the administration of the Raj, then for Indian independence. He went repeatedly and peacefully to jail for his cause, frequently turning imprisonment into victory by embarking upon prolonged hunger strikes. As his reputation as a spiritual leader grew, he abandoned his Western clothing and lifestyle entirely, dressed in a traditional costume of homespun, and lived the life of a Hindu guru of an earlier age.

The principles he championed were an odd mix of ancient and modern. His campaign to get Indians to reject British manufactured cloth and spin cotton at home on the old-fashioned spinning wheel put that homely implement on the Indian flag. At the same time, however, he was a firm believer in Western notions of human equality, rejecting India's traditional caste distinctions and preaching the equality of women with men. In Gandhi, then, the Indian National Congress found at last a leader who could bridge the many gaps that divided Indians and who could build a genuine sense of Indian national identity.

Gandhi manipulated the foreign press with as much skill as he moved the hearts of other Indians. Colonial police and soldiers overreacted to nonviolence—or to the riots that sometimes accompanied nonviolent demonstrations—and generated public support for Gandhi abroad, even in Britain. Viceroys learned to negotiate with him—when they were not locking him up. For many in the West as well as for hundreds of millions of Indians, Mahatma Gandhi stood out as the only living saint in a darkening world. And in 1947, in the anti-imperialist aftermath of World War II, Great Britain let his people go.

## Africa: The Anti-Imperialists Organize

World War I and its aftermath had an important impact on colonial Africa during the 1920s and 1930s also. The rise of political idealism that accompanied the founding of the League of Nations and the peace and disarmament conferences of the interwar years affected colonial policies too, even in Africa. The German colonies—most of which were African—were turned over to the victors after World War I as mandates, territories to be governed as much in the interests of the indigenous peoples as for the colonizing Europeans, with regular reports required. Britain's policy of indirect rule through traditional local authorities evolved in the direction of a conscious policy of "preparing Africans for independence" at some admittedly hazy future date. French centralization welcomed African leaders to French educational institutions and political life, where they obtained the skills they would later use against French rule.

Some of the imperial powers with African colonies channeled colonial revenues into modest programs of economic development, health, and education. An air of relatively benevolent rule and an impression of slow but measurable advances along Western lines prevailed over much of Africa. As in India, however, the impression was in many ways deceptive. Tensions were real, and the seeds—in some places, the fact—of militant revolt quite vigorously present.

Westerners saw Africa much as they did Latin America and much of Asia—as a source of raw materials. They utilized cheap African labor to siphon off the cotton of Egypt, the copper of the Belgian Congo, and the gold of South Africa. They put Africans to work on the farms of European settlers in East or South Africa, or along the Mediterranean shores of North Africa. The African middle class was much smaller than that of India, and African economic development proceeded much more slowly.

British indirect rule left local authority in the hands of traditional chiefs, but it did little to advance the few Western-educated Africans beyond clerk status in the colonial administration. French direct rule gave some Africans more power in the colonial government—but only those who were thoroughly transformed by immersion in the French way of life.

Under these circumstances, then, anti-imperialist sentiments, and even a handful of armed resistance groups persisted in Africa between the wars.

Violent resistance was confined largely to North Africa. Resistance by desert sheiks and tribes did flare up during the 1920s, particularly in French Morocco and in Italy's new colony of Libya. Meanwhile, however, a pan-Islamic cultural revival, centered at the Al-Azhar University in Cairo, sent student militants back to their homelands all over Mediterranean and Sudannic Africa. In the 1930s, these highly educated Muslim activists were organizing nationalist political parties to work for independence from their European rulers.

South of the Sahara, African student organizations set up at British or French universities were also a fertile source of dreams and plans for African independence. The pan-African ideal of African independence and unity, preached primarily by African Americans such as the flamboyant Marcus Garvey and the scholar W. E. B. Du Bois, also found eager converts among African students.

In Africa itself, reform-minded African nationalist organizations were set up in the British West African colonies of the Gold Coast (Ghana) and Nigeria and in East Africa in Tanganyika (Tanzania). These groups typically made modest demands. But they used modern Western techniques of organization and newspaper journalism to spread their ideas among Africa's now growing urban populations.

In the later 1920s, the Ibo market women of southern Nigeria reacted violently to British efforts to impose licenses and fees on them. These traditional West African traders launched what came to be known as the "Women's War." They demonstrated in the streets and attacked colonial administration buildings. In the end, the foreign rulers of Nigeria rescinded the fees—and soon the women cloth merchants of Togo were marching and shouting, defying the authorities.

Though the decades between the wars were a comparatively quiet time in Africa south of the Sahara, it was a deceptive calm. The students of the 1920s and 1930s—men such as Kwame Nkrumah, Jomo Kenyatta, Leopold Senghor, and others—would become the leaders of the great liberation movements of the tumultuous years after World War II.

## TOTALITARIANISM IN RUSSIA AND GERMANY

### Stalin's Iron Age

The other major source of savage violence in the world between the wars besides revolution was the rise of totalitarian and authoritarian dictatorships. And one of the most violent of these was the Communist regime in Russia whose revolutionary origins were outlined above.

Historically, relatively rigid authoritarianism went back in Russian history to Byzantine and Mongol models, to the heavy-handed rule of autocrats such as Peter the Great. But there were distinctive ideological sources of Stalinist tyranny too. Lenin, seeking to impose discipline on disputatious Russian ideologues and half-educated proletarians, had developed the key political principles of the *vanguard party* and *democratic centralism*. Communists thus early came to believe that, while democratic debate within the party was all very well while policy was being hammered out, central authority must prevail in the end, and all must close ranks behind the leaders.

The party wanted to increase its power, individual party bureaucrats or *apparatchiks* to advance their careers, by expanding Communist control into more and more areas of life. Stalin wanted to ensure his own authority and to eliminate potential rivals or enemies of his programs. And so, after the lull of the 1920s and the New Economic Policy came the Five-Year Plans of the 1930s—and the sweeping totalitarianization of Russian society.

Communism could boast of some successes in the thirties. Unemployment was virtually eliminated as the state made work for every man and most women in the Soviet Union. Agriculture suffered severe setbacks, in part because of peasant resistance to collectivization. But at least the farms were collectivized and could now develop on a centralized, socialized basis. State-owned heavy industry grew rapidly, overall industrial production expanding at the phenomenal rate of 15 or 20 percent a year. Western admirers who came to Russia in the 1930s to "see the future" were duly impressed by the new industrial cities, the huge dams and factories, the showcase Moscow subway with its dazzling cleanliness and its marble statues.

But there was more to Communism than new dams and the Moscow subway. Politically, party control was unquestioned from the moment Lenin dissolved the constitutional convention in 1918. Stalin gave the nation a shiny new constitution in the 1930s, and elections were held—but in a one-party state there was only a single list of candidates to vote for. And the Soviet Union was a one-party state: Since the Communists were the vanguard of the people, what other party was needed? The real power structure was thus the highly autocratic one of the Communist party.

On the economic side, state planners now allocated resources and set quotas; government-appointed managers ran factories and the huge new farms and directed trade, transportation, and all other aspects of the economy. Comparatively well-off peasants, called *kulaks,* were expropriated outright, and almost all private farms were collectivized. Half the new collective farms were owned by the state; the others, collectively owned by the peasants who worked them, depended on the state for farm machinery and fertilizer and sold their crops to the state at fixed prices. Only tiny private plots and a few peasant markets remained outside governmental control.

Women were thoroughly integrated into the great experiment. Many found jobs and even professions they could never have aspired to under the old regime, working as everything from tractor drivers to doctors. Their labor really was desperately needed to build the new Soviet Russia. On the other hand, most working women found that they were also still expected to do the housework, so that they worked what came to be called "the double shift"—eight hours at the factory and eight more at home.

The Communists, as Marxists, were atheists in matters of religion, and the role of the Orthodox church as a pillar of the old order made it a natural target. Many churches were closed, atheism was taught in the schools, and museums of "church abuses" dotted the landscape. Education aimed at producing hardworking and obedient Soviet citizens, and courses on Marxism-Leninism were required. Communist children's and young people's organizations, beginning with the Young Octobrists and climaxing with the Komsomol, for people in their teens and twenties, filled the new generation with veneration for Marx, Lenin, and Stalin.

### The Stalinist Terror

As the 1930s advanced, the world outside began to become dimly aware of the human cost of Soviet achievements, and of the brutality of which this version of totalitarianism was capable.

The tip of the iceberg was the public "purge trials" of leading Communists in the later 1930s. Once revered party leaders, economic managers, famous generals were accused of crimes against the state. The charges included sabotaging the Five-Year Plans, plotting with Trotsky (then in exile overseas) or with capitalist foreign agents, voicing antiparty ideas, or simply failing to meet assigned quotas. More shocking still, the accused confessed to these crimes, some of which seemed very unlikely even to sympathetic Western observers, and were duly executed.

# VOICES FROM THE PAST

One of the most feared—and widespread—manifestations of totalitarian terror in the earlier twentieth century was the after-midnight arrest for usually unspecified "political offenses." Communists, Nazis, fascists, and authoritarians of all stripes found this an effective way to keep populations properly cowed. Russian writer Alexander Solzhenitsyn, living in exile in the United States, had spent years in the *Gulag*, as the brutal Soviet labor camps operated by the secret police were called. He heard many accounts of the late-night search and arrest while preparing his four volume collection of first-hand testimony, *The Gulag Archipelago*.

> *The traditional image of arrest is . . . trembling hands packing for the victim—a change of underwear, a piece of soap, something to eat; and no one knows what is needed, what is permitted, what clothes are best to wear; and the Security agents keep interrupting and hurrying you:*
> *"You don't need anything. They'll feed you there. It's warm there." (It's all lies. They keep hurrying you to frieghten you.)*
> *The traditional image of arrest is also what happens afterward, when the poor victim has been taken away. It is an alien, brutal, and crushing force totally dominating the apartment for hours on end, a breaking, ripping open, pulling from the walls, emptying things from wardrobes and desks onto the floor, shaking, dumping out, and ripping apart—piling up moutains of litter on the floor—and the crunch of things being trampled beneath jackboots. And nothing is sacred in a search! During the arrest of the locomotive engineer Inoshin, a tiny coffin stood in his room containing the body of his newly dead child. The "jurists" dumped the child's body out of the coffin and searched it. They shake sick people out of their sickbeds, and they unwind bandages to search beneath them.*

Alexander Solzhenitsyn, *The Gulag Archipelago, 1918–1956* Trans. Thomas A. Whitney (New York: Harper and Row, 1974), Vol. 1, p. 5.

Only slowly did the more submerged depths of the Stalinist terror come out. The peasants, it gradually became clear, had resisted collectivization more vigorously than expected, burying their grain and slaughtering their animals rather than surrendering them to the collective. The *kulaks* among them had been sent off to labor camps in the Russian north, where many had died. Other peasants who resisted had had their grain dug up and carried off without compensation. This rigorous government response, coupled with bad weather and small harvests for a couple of years in the early thirties, had cost the lives of millions.

In the later thirties, large numbers of less prominent people, charged with industrial sabotage, spying, or Trotskyite tendencies, were dealt with by the secret police without benefit of public trials. The knock on the door after midnight was followed by months of imprisonment without trial, rigorous interrogation, years of struggling to survive in a forced labor camp, or simply a bullet in the back of the neck at the end of a long dark corridor. Tens of millions were sent off to work camps in Siberia or the Soviet arctic, and millions more were executed or worked to death.

## Failure of the Weimar Republic

One of the greatest challenges of any attempt to deal with the Nazi period in German history is, quite simply, to explain how it could have happened. How could the Germans, best-known in the nineteenth century for philosophy and music, then for science and industry—one of the most civilized of European peoples, in short—have produced the twelve-year Nazi nightmare? How could so many have gloried in it, defended the regime vigorously to foreigners who "didn't understand the *Führer*'s policies" even as the shattered glass of *Kristalnacht* tinkled in the streets?

The origins of Nazism are frequently traced to the notable success of autocracy in German history—and the equally notable failures of democracy. It is a good place to start.

The rise of Prussia to mastery of all Germany was rooted in such autocratic institutions of centralized state power as the Junker bureaucracy and the Prussian army. National heroes such as Frederick the Great and Bismarck had depended on "blood and iron" to advance the interests of the state. Liberalism, by contrast, had never really taken hold and, as we will see, would fail again in the Weimar Republic of the 1920s. By 1933, democracy meant weakness, authoritarianism meant strength to most Germans—and at that time, they desperately needed strength.

The debacle of World War I is another commonly cited cause of the Nazi triumph in Germany. The failure of German arms was a terrible shock to the psyche of a people who had not lost a war since Napoleon's day. The manner of their defeat also—their armies still in the field, strangled by a British naval blockade, tricked by an armistice that somehow turned into an abject surrender—left many Germans feeling betrayed. The harsh Versailles peace terms, stripping Germany of lands, colonies, and military forces, and imposing huge reparations and the unspeakable war-guilt clause, outraged and embittered many Germans. Anyone who would denounce Versailles, give Germans a scapegoat for defeat, and promise victories to come could surely expect a great outpouring of support in Germany.

Adolf Hitler addresses the Nazi party faithful. Hitler's insistence on the Führerprinzip or "Leadership principle" was most vividly validated for most by his hypnotic speaking style. Always intense, as here, he built to shrill climaxes which swept his hearers up in his vision of German greatness and his own destiny to lead his people. Equally effective with beery Rathskeller audiences and the rapt crowds that thronged a stadium, Hitler stormed to power on a wave of passionate words. (National Archives)

The political and economic problems of the Weimar Republic (1919–1933), which succeeded the defeated German Empire, also proved fertile breeding grounds for totalitarian sentiment.

In November of 1918, Kaiser William II was persuaded to abdicate for the good of the nation. The leading party in the Reichstag, the Social Democrats, thereupon took the lead in establishing the German Republic.

The German Constitution adopted at Weimar in 1919 was one of the most liberal in the world, providing for democracy, civil liberties, rights for women. It opened the way for a vigorous opposition press and the brilliant cultural life that distinguished Weimar Germany in the 1920s. The liberals and socialists who ruled through most of that decade were parliamentarians, labor leaders, and constitutional reformers.

Yet within fifteen years, political attacks from left and right and the economic buffeting of alternating inflation and depression had virtually paralyzed the new government— and opened the way for the rise of Adolf Hitler.

Political attacks from the left came first, with the rebellion of a Communist group called the Spartacists in 1919. The Spartacists were suppressed, their leaders Rosa Luxemburg and Karl Liebknecht murdered while in custody. Right-wing attempts to seize power included Hitler's futile Beer Hall Putsch in Munich in 1923—which cost the Nazi leader no more than a few months in prison. Through the rest of the decade, Communists, Nazis, and other political extremists organized paramilitary cadres, fought each other in the streets, and assassinated government officials—while the democratically elected government seemed helpless to do anything about it.

The economic ups and downs of the twenties and early thirties were equally disastrous for the new regime. Inflation unparalleled in modern times ravaged Germany in the early 1920s. The value of the German mark plunged from four to the dollar in 1914 to four billion to the dollar in 1923, wiping out the savings of Germany's once prosperous middle classes. After a brief respite, the Great Depression whipsawed the economy from the other side. Germany, hardest hit of all the European nations, had six million unemployed in the early 1930s.

The Nazis would promise peace in the streets and renewed prosperity, and although what they delivered was the peace and prosperity of the police state, many battered Germans would vote for them. For the Nazis did not seize power, as the Communists had: They were voted into office.

Who supported Hitler? Masses of statistics and elaborate theories have been advanced about the "people behind" the Nazi demagogue, but the point is still being argued. Students supported him noisily and gave him thumping majorities in university straw votes. Big business contributed to his war chest, but gave as much or more to other, more respectable conservative groups. Major support, however, seems to have come from lower-middle-class Germans—shopkeepers, civil servants, old-fashioned artisans—and from farmers; all these groups suffered from the Depression. And a great ground swell of support came from embittered nationalists of all classes.

In large part, fear put Hitler in power. Fear of urban unemployment, of collapsing farm prices, of middle-class loss of status, of Communism, of foreign humiliations, of governmental paralysis—all contributed to Hitler's meteoric rise. The convicted putschist of 1923 got 2.6 percent of the vote in 1928. In 1930 the Nazi total jumped to 18.3 percent. In 1933 the Nazis were the nation's most popular party, commanding 37.3 percent of the vote.

At the beginning of 1933, then, with Hitler clearly the nation's best vote-getter, the politicians around the aging war hero President Hindenburg persuaded him to appoint the

Nazi leader chancellor of Germany. Like the politicos who made Napoleon first consul of France, they thought they could use the strident, vulgar little man with the ridiculous moustache for their own purposes.

## Hitler in Power

Adolf Hitler (1889–1945) was not German but rather Austrian by birth. Failed art student, one-time Munich bohemian, wounded and decorated soldier in World War I, he had found his true career in the extremist politics of the Weimar Republic. He had joined a nationalist sliver group called the National Socialist German Workers party and had quickly come to dominate it, thanks to his fiery oratory and superpatriotic doctrines. As mentioned, the failure of the Beer Hall putsch in 1923 cost him some months in prison, but he spent the time assembling his credo in a famous book, *Mein Kampf (My Struggle),* and emerged as the idolized *Führer* (Leader) of the Nazi party.

Hitler preached German greatness, the superiority of the Aryan or Teutonic "race," and the coming splendor of the Fatherland. He condemned the Versailles treaty, the Communists, and sometimes the very rich. He blamed Germany's troubles increasingly on the Jewish segment of the population, convenient targets of European persecution for centuries and a pathological fixation of Hitler's. He developed a high-pitched but electrifying speaking style and a natural flair for the dramatic—uniforms, swastika banners, night rallies, parades, marching songs. Once in power, he also demonstrated a knack for shrewd political tactics and ruthless manipulation of people.

During the first six months of 1933, the new chancellor made himself absolute ruler of Germany and Nazism its guiding philosophy.

Hitler took advantage of an attempt to burn down the Reichstag building in Berlin, probably undertaken by a feebleminded Dutch Communist, to begin his assault on the structure of the Weimar Republic. Apparently genuinely fearful of a Communist power play, he suspended all civil liberties and arrested the German Communist leadership. Riding the crest of this victory, he held a quick election and won a Reichstag majority large enough to vote the chancellor special powers to make laws on his own authority for the next four years.

Thus strengthened, Hitler turned against the parties. He already had the Communists in jail. He now outlawed the Social Democrats, claiming they also were too far to the left. Then he talked all the other conservative and nationalist parties except the Nazis into dissolving voluntarily in order to promote unity on the right—in other words, to give the Nazis a free hand. Finally, in June 1934, he purged his own party of potential rivals in the gory Night of the Long Knives, when his elite SS troopers seized and executed hundreds of Nazi and other leaders deemed undependable by the Leader.

During the rest of the decade, Hitler turned Nazi Germany into the archetypal totalitarian state. Political and economic institutions, religion, education, recreation, and all other aspects of national life came under the centralized control of the party and its *Führer.*

Totalitarian political structures quickly replaced those of Weimar democracy. The Reichstag became a rubber stamp for the Leader's decisions. The elected governors of the German states were replaced by appointed *Statthalters.* Everywhere, in provinces and towns, power passed into the hands of Nazi strong men called *Gauleiers.*

Totalitarian economic organization also evolved rapidly. In the 1930s, Hitler forged a monolithic alliance of big government and big business with which to run the German economy. Huge cartels were put in charge of industry and agriculture. Massive programs of public works (including the Autobahn highway system) and military rearmament (in defiance of the Versailles treaty) put much of the labor force back to work. At the same time, rigid controls were slapped on wages and prices, small businessmen lost operational control of their businesses, and labor unions were abolished.

The Nazi apparatus reached into every aspect of German life. The Protestant churches were merged into a single German Evangelical church under Nazi control; a concordat gave the party a say in the appointment of Catholic bishops and forbade priests to speak out on political issues. Nazi doctrines were taught in public schools, while university professors were being discharged and books burned for presenting views the Nazis disapproved of.

Young people were quickly enrolled in the Hitler Youth and the League of German Maidens, which replaced the traditional Boy and Girl Scout type of hiking and camping organization. Women were urged to dedicate their lives to the three K's—*Kinder, Kirche, Küche* (Children, Church, Kitchen). They would strengthen Hitler's new Germany best by producing children for the Fatherland. In the early, building years, and then during the Second World War, however, they were also expected to contribute their labor to the cause.

Under Hitler's leadership Germany quickly pulled out of the Depression, boosted production to new highs, and put almost everyone back to work. Hitler unilaterally rejected the Versailles treaty, rapidly built the most powerful army in Europe, and announced a new German empire—the Thousand-Year Reich. Germans stood tall again, proud of their country, contemptuous of the capitalist democracies still floundering in the depths of the Great Depression all around them.

## Nazism and the Holocaust

As in Communist Russia, however, there was a price to be paid.

The chief instruments of the Nazi terror were the *Schutzstafel* (SS), the Leader's black-uniformed private troops, and the Gestapo, the Nazi secret police. The SS, originally Hitler's bodyguard, later an elite military force, were publicized as the perfect Aryans, blond, blue-eyed embodiments of Teutonic racial superiority. They purged the party for Hitler in the early 1930s and ran the concentration camps—the death camps—of the later 1930s and the 1940s. The Gestapo worked much more in the shadows, as a secret political police. It was they who made the after-midnight arrests and ran the most feared torture chambers since the days of the Inquisition.

Millions of human beings died in Hitler's concentration camps—political dissidents, resistance fighters from conquered countries, social "misfits" such as homosexuals, and particularly "inferior" racial groups such as Slavs, Gypsies, and, above all, Jews. The massacre of a large part of Europe's Jewish population by the Nazis is known historically as the Holocaust.

Hitler defined the Jewish "race" as the greatest threat to the German people, blaming them for their success in business and the professions, for Versailles, for the Depression, and for weakening the blood of the German "master race" through "interracial" marriage. Once in power, Hitler passed discriminatory laws against them, expelling them from government service, confiscating their property, compelling many to emigrate. Riotous pogroms were organized against them, including *Kristalnacht,* the Night of the Broken Glass, when the windows of Jewish homes and businesses were shattered in cities all over Germany.

In the later 1930s Jews were herded into concentration camps. In the early 1940s, as we will see, the outbreak of World War II brought the Final Solution to the Jewish "problem." This was the methodical extermination of the Jewish population of Germany and German-occupied Europe. This Holocaust was undertaken at first rather haphazardly with machine guns. Then at camps like Dachau, Belsen, and Auschwitz, the process was systematized in specially constructed gas chambers, followed by cremation of the corpses. Six million European Jews of both sexes and all ages and conditions of life were worked, starved, stripped, gassed, robbed of rings and the gold in their teeth, and trundled off to the crematoria.

The deliberate savagery and the racial dimension of the Holocaust have earned it a unique place in the history of the twentieth century. In fact, it was almost certainly the largest deliberately instigated massacre in human history.

## FASCISTS, MILITARISTS, AND OTHER AUTHORITARIANS

### Mussolini and Italian Fascism

Like the revolutionary pressures building around the globe, authoritarian regimes took many forms in many lands. Two, in Fascist Italy and militarist Japan, would be particularly important in the impending Second World War. But there were many other types of dictatorship too.

The first totalitarian state was neither Stalin's nor Hitler's, but Fascist Italy, which began to take shape when Benito Mussolini seized power in 1922.

Mussolini had begun his career as a left-wing agitator before World War I. After the war, however, he was caught up in Italian demands for "unredeemed" territories held by Austria and Yugoslavia, changed his ideological stripes, and became an ardent nationalist.

Mussolini organized the Fascist Party in 1919. His strong-arm squads of militantly nationalistic war veterans, the black-shirted *squadristi,* were soon breaking up Socialist party meetings, smashing left-wing presses, raiding the headquarters of industrial and agricultural unions. In so doing, Mussolini won the support of many factory owners and large landowners—the very people he had fought in the prewar years.

In 1921 and 1922, Italy's democratic constitutional monarchy went through a paralyzing governmental crisis in which no party or coalition could form a government that commanded majority. During this tense period, the Fascist *squadristi* moved from attacking socialists and unions to seizing control of whole towns. When a Fascist march on Rome itself was announced, Italy's constitutional monarch, Victor Emmanuel III, capitulated and asked Mussolini to form a government.

A mass grave at Belsen concentration camp. Victims of the totalitarian death camps were required to surrender their clothing and any remaining possessions before being shot or gassed. Though most victims were cremated at the death camps, horrifying finds like this, coupled with the skeletal survivors rescued from some camps, brought home the horror of Nazism to the world more forcefully than any other experience of the totalitarian and wartime years. (The Bettman Archive)

Thereafter, through massive propaganda campaigns, roughly engineered electoral victories, constitutional "reforms," and an occasional assassination, Fascist power was institutionalized in Italy. Mussolini would be *il Duce*—the Leader—for the next twenty years, the senior if not the strongest of Europe's totalitarian rulers.

On the political side, Fascism in Italy meant the suppression of all rival parties and the submission of a single list of candidates—prepared by the Fascist leadership—to the voters. Elected officials of provinces and towns were abolished and replaced by appointed *podestàs*. Mussolini was given authority to make law by decree, and in time the legislature was abolished in its turn.

The Italian economy also came under at least nominal party control. An elaborate system of "syndicates" and "corporations" was set up, each representing labor, business, and the government, each concerned with a particular branch of industry, agriculture, trade, finance, or the professions. Labor unions and free enterprise were alike suppressed as outmoded survivors of the liberal past. Tourists, however, were always pleased to see that in Fascist Italy the trains ran on time.

The rest of society also came under the more or less vigilant eye of the party. Politically untrustworthy individuals were taken up by the secret police and bundled off to the Lipari Islands off the coast of Sicily. The press was censored, education regulated, social and cultural organizations dominated by the Fascists. Children's and youth groups, from the Sons of the Wolf to the Young Fascists, were given their first uniforms and set to drilling at an early age. "Everything in the state," trumpeted Mussolini, "nothing outside the state, nothing against the state!"

*Il Duce* was a dictator much photographed, usually on balconies reviewing his troops or his Fascist party, unmistakable with his big jaw and increasingly solid belly. It has been suggested that he was not as massively in control as he seemed. His grab for political power in the twenties may have been almost forced upon him by the restless militance of his *squadristi* Black Shirts. But Mussolini may have hit upon a profound political truth of those merciless years when he declared: "Never before have the nations thirsted for authority, direction, order as they do now."

## The Militarists in Japan: The Day of the Assassins

Japan, like Germany, moved from a period of troubled liberal government in the 1920s to one of strident nationalism, militarism, and renewed imperial expansion in the 1930s. If European-style totalitarianism did not develop in Japan, political tyranny and violence certainly did.

From about the time of World War I through the 1920s, the major political parties in the Japanese Diet enjoyed an enhanced share of political power among the elites that ran the country. The army and navy, though continuing to get large cuts of the budget for the mechanization of the armed forces, were generally prevented from undertaking further imperial adventures. The politicians in the Diet pursued policies of economic expansion instead, investing huge quantities of time and money in establishing close commercial ties with China.

Party power in the 1920s brought mixed results. Western–style laws providing for universal suffrage, legalized labor unions, and health insurance for factory workers were all to the good. The influence of *zaibatsu* big businesses however, made itself felt in the Diet, producing both crackdowns on radicals and a good deal of government corruption.

Military leaders and other nationalists resented the unaggressive tone of Japan's politicians toward Europeans and Americans. And the peasant majority, who did not share in *zaibatsu* prosperity during the 1920s, grew even more bitter when the World Depression of the 1930s further ate away at their dwindling incomes. With so little public support, the political parties rapidly lost control in the thirties.

The decline of party influence began with the totally unauthorized seizure of most of Manchuria from China in 1931 by units of the Japanese army. The annexation was engineered by a cabal of young army officers who ignored civilian orders from Tokyo to cease and desist.

Brought to trial for insubordination, the officers were hailed as national heroes by many Japanese. The "liberated" areas, meanwhile, were reorganized as the Japanese puppet state of Manchukuo.

Other superpatriotic young officers began to raid the headquarters of the political parties, to attack wealthy *zaibatsu* executives, and finally to assassinate important politicians, including the prime minister.

In 1936 a group of junior officers with hundreds of troops under their command seized downtown Tokyo itself, occupied government buildings, and murdered a number of prominent officials. The rebellion was quickly suppressed with the help of the navy, but the military leadership as a whole was only strengthened.

Many were glad to see military men emerge as the new political leaders. The average Japanese did not object when censorship, arrests, and other forms of persecution cut into radical ranks. The ideological void was easily filled by nationalistic propaganda and renewed assertions of absolute loyalty to the emperor.

Young Emperor Hirohito himself, ironically, had more than once stood up to the military. But by 1937, when another "incident" led to a full-scale Japanese invasion of China, there was nothing much even he could do to control the nation's new militaristic masters.

## A Great Authoritarian Tide

Public attention focused on the major totalitarian and militaristic powers in the interwar years. But there were many other examples around the world of the disturbing flight from freedom that some critics noticed.

In Europe, many of the nations in the east and the south proved fertile ground for authoritarian regimes during these two decades. The Mediterranean peninsular states of Europe's southern fringe (Spain, Portugal, Italy, Greece) and the band of Eastern European states from the Baltic (Estonia, Latvia, Lithuania) through Poland and Austria to the Balkans (Hungary, Romania, Yugoslavia, and others) all flirted with or fell to authoritarian regimes.

Many of these were new countries, most of them poor and technologically underdeveloped. Almost all were dominated in 1920 by antiquated social groups and institutions—traditional monarchies, established churches, landowning aristocracies. The strains of economic modernization, the poverty of both urban and peasant masses, the political demands of affluent middle classes, and the increasing appeal of various ideologies—liberalism, nationalism, socialism, communism, anarchism, and fascism—all contributed to tension and disorder in these areas.

In these unstable circumstances, the appeal of authority, direction, and order was obvious. The two groups who most vigorously exploited fear of anarchy or social revolution to create authoritarian regimes were military leaders and fascist ideologues. In some places, military strong men such as Marshall Pilsudski in Poland and Admiral Horthy in Hungary ruled with an iron hand. In other countries, uniformed proto-Fascist parties such as Rumania's Iron Guard or Austria's Fatherland Front broke heads, persecuted Jews, assassinated liberals.

In Latin America, the relatively good times of the 1920s turned definitively sour when the World Depression hit in the 1930s, drastically depressing the commodity prices on which the southern republics still depended heavily. In the early thirties, more than half the twenty independent nations of Latin America responded to the resulting pressures with revolutions. The regimes that came to power followed a familiar pattern. Outside of Cárdenas's Mexico and a few other examples, military leaders, conservatives, and nationalists triumphed again and again.

Thus Argentina's Radical party, which governed the country during the 1920s with policies that ranged from moderate to liberal, was overthrown by a military coup in 1930. The Conservative Republic, as the regime that ruled for the next dozen years is called, accelerated the growth of Argentine industry from small-scale workshops to much larger factories employing hundreds of workers. The new industry was capable of supplying much of the country's needs for manufactured goods without having to depend on foreign imports—a net gain for the economy.

Politically, however, democracy clearly lost ground. The so-called *Concordancia,* an alliance of militarists, nationalists, and conservatives, rigged elections and suppressed political opposition in Argentina as vigorously as any nineteenth-century *caudillo.*

Brazil's maximum leader for fifteen years after he seized power in 1930, and again from 1951 to 1954, was the nationalistic military leader Getúlio Vargas. This long-lived dictator proved to be a skillful administrator who encouraged the growth of domestic industry and, most important, took great strides toward unifying the huge country under the central government in Rio de Janeiro. Besides these administrative reforms, however, Vargas frequently exercised dictatorial powers. He governed by censorship and decree, outlawed opposition political parties, and even deployed military force when necessary. Again, stability and progress were bought at the cost of stunted political liberties.

Some of the smaller Latin American states suffered from more brutal "personalist" dictators, building mass power on the traditional basis of personal followings and personal favors, during the hard times of the 1930s and beyond. The Somoza family seized power in Nicaragua in the mid-thirties and were soon constructing a successful modern sector of the economy while savaging all political rivals. Rafael Trujillo did a brilliant job of modernizing the island republic of Santo Domingo—and turned it into the "dry guillotine" of the Caribbean in the process.

Across the world in the Middle East, much the same sort of procedure was noticeable. Modernizing autocrats such as the Pahlavi shahs of Iran might expand oil output and even sprinkle some schools and hospitals across the land. But political tyranny, extending to imprisonment, torture, and death for enemies of the authoritarian regime, was the perhaps exorbitant price the nation was asked to pay.

Everywhere during those gray, hard, often despairing years, democracy seemed like a lost cause. The strains of modernization, resurgent conservatism, the appeal of ideologies such as nationalism and communism, and the impact of the Great Depression proved too much for many fragile experiments in self-government. A great authoritarian tide seemed to be rising around the world.

# SUMMARY

The twentieth century may have been the most revolutionary—and the most authoritarian—of centuries. Modern ideological revolutions and tyrannies, drawing on nationalist, socialist, anti-imperialist, and other visions of a new social order shook the globe particularly in the period between the two world wars.

The Russian Revolution of 1917 came as a result of the immense pressures of World War I on that huge but underdeveloped land. Lenin and his Bolshevik cadres seized power in a crumbling nation, defended their power in a bloody civil war, and left the country in the hands of the ruthless Joseph Stalin.

Stalin plunged the nation into a new economic revolution in the 1930s. Heavy industry was vastly expanded under Communist state socialism. Agriculture was also largely collectivized, but production still dropped drastically owing to peasant resistance to socialization.

The Chinese Revolution was the largest and longest of the revolutions, the military phase alone beginning before World War I and lasting until after World War II. Both the old empire and the new republic collapsed in turn in the early twentieth century, leaving the country a cauldron of revolution and war until Mao Zedong finally overthrew Jiang Jieshi in 1949.

Revolutionary challenges shook established regimes in many other places, from Mexico's bloody struggle to the rising tide of anti-imperialist feeling in India, Africa, and other areas of Western control.

Ideologically based dictatorships also rose in many lands in these dark years. The most powerful of these governments are often described as totalitarian, vesting total power in a single highly ideological party and appealing to the total commitment of party members to the cause, the movement, and its leader.

Stalin brought Communist party power to a climax in Russia in the 1930s. The new regime built on the czarist tradition of authoritarian rule but developed the bureaucracy, the army, and the secret police far beyond czarist models. Communist repression cost the lives of millions of Russians—officially classified as enemies of the working class—in Stalinist work camps and prisons, or in the famines of the early 1930s.

Hitler's Nazi party rose to power in 1933, capitalizing on German resentment of the Versailles peace, disillusionment with democracy, and economic collapse. Once in power, Hitler suppressed rival parties, free elections, and free enterprise as he remilitarized his country. He bailed the nation out of the Depression with his public works and rearmament programs, and he unilaterally abrogated the Versailles Treaty. He also introduced Gestapo secret-police terror and SS death camps, massacring six million Jews and millions of others deemed biologically inferior to the "master race."

Mussolini's Fascists seized power in Italy in the early 1920s. In Japan, resentment of an unaggressive parliamentary regime and of *zaibatsu* big business allowed the militarists to dominate affairs in the 1930s. Through assassinations and the threat of a military coup, Japanese generals and admirals cowed civilian authorities into accepting increasingly nationalistic, imperialistic, and reactionary policies.

A great authoritarian wave seemed to be sweeping over the world. One-party rule, military dictatorship, and other forms of autocratic government rose to power in many East European, South American, and Middle Eastern nations. Under the pressure of great economic and political problems, people seemed to be turning their backs on democracy.

# SUGGESTED READING

Bergère, M.-C. *Sun Yat-sen.* trans. J. Lloyd. Stanford: Stanford University Press, 1998. Balanced life of the Chinese revolutionary.

Bush, B. *Imperialism, Race, and Resistance: Africa and Britain, 1919–1945.* Good example of evolving Western imperialism and colonial resistance.

Clements, B. E. *Bolshevik Women.* New York: Cambridge University Press, 1997. Two generations of Russian women confront—and contribute to—the Revolution.

Eatwell, R. *Fascism: A History.* New York: Penguin Books, 1997. Historically informed analysis of this form of revolutionary authoritarianism.

Fischer, K. *Nazi Germany: A New History.* New York: Continuum, 1996. Valuable synthesis, aimed at students.

Furet, F. *The Passing of an Illusion: The Idea of Communism in the Twentieth Century.* trans. D. Furet. Chicago: University of Chicago Press, 1999. A leading French intellectual reflects on the appeal of communism to Western intellectuals.

Goldhagen, D. J. *Hitler's Willing Executioners: Ordinary Germans and the Holocaust.* New York: Knopf, 1996. Disturbing, much debated account. But see also P. Hoffman, *German Resistance to Hitler* (Cambridge, Mass.: Harvard University Press, 1988), with some emphasis on the military leaders who opposed the *Führer.*

Guha, R. *Dominance without Hegemony: History and Power in Colonial India.* Cambridge, Mass.: Harvard University Press, 1998. Sees British India as a zone of conflict between foreign and domestic elites, largely ignoring resistance movements among the Indian masses.

Hart, J. M. *Revolutionary Mexico: The Coming and Process of the Mexican Revolution.* Berkeley and Los Angeles: University of California Press, 1987. Analysis of social groups in revolutionary Mexico, from peasants and industrial workers to Mexican elites and foreign businessmen.

Kallis, A. A. *Fascist Ideology: Territory and Expansionism in Italy and Germany 1922–1945.* New York: Routledge, 2000. Takes the expansionist dictators at their word when they demanded "living space."

Katz, F. *The Life and Times of Pancho Villa.* Stanford: Stanford University Press, 1998. A leading expert's life of the Mexican revolutionary leader and the times that produced him. And see S. Brunk, *Emiliano Zapata: Revolution and Betrayal in Mexico* (Albuquerque: University of New Mexico Press, 1995) on the many myths surrounding this revolutionary hero.

Kershaw, I., and M. Lewin, eds. *Stalinism and Nazism: Dictatorships in Comparison.* Cambridge: Cambridge University Press, 1997. A collection of studies seeking to explain the temporary success of these two revolutionary-authoritarian regimes.

Marrus, M. E. *The Holocaust in History.* Hanover, N.H.: University Press of New England, 1987. Historiographical discussion of the genocide of the 1940s. W. E. Mosse's *Jews in the German Economy: The German-Jewish Economic Elite, 1820–1935* (New York: Clarendon Press, 1987) presents a statistically based account of Jewish business and social achievements, depicting Jews not as fringe elements but as leading participants in German society and economic growth.

Mawdsley, E., and S. White. *The Soviet Elite from Lenin to Gorbachev: The Central Committee and Its Members.* New York: Oxford University Press, 2000. Analyzes several generations of Communist leadership.

Mosse, G. L. *The Fascist Revolution: Toward a General Theory of Fascism.* New York: Howard Fertig, 1999. Collected essays of the dean of American students of this ism.

Muhlberger, D. *The Social Basis of European Fascist Movements.* New York: Methuen, 1987. Studies of the roots of fascism in countries where fascists eventually seized power and in others where they failed. But see also T. Kirk, and A. McElligott, eds, *Opposing Fascism: Community, Authority, and Resistance in Europe.* (New York: Cambridge University Press, 1999), documenting sources of opposition.

Schram, S. R. *Mao Zedong: A Preliminary Reassessment.* (Hong Kong: Chinese University Press 1983). Schram has made a life work out of the study of Mao and his political ideas. See also P. Short's more readable recent study, *Mao: A Life* (New York: Henry Holt, 1999), and J. Spence's brief but scholarly and readable *Mao Zedong* (New York: Viking, 1999).

Schrecker, J. E. *The Chinese Revolution in Historical Perspective.* New York: Praeger, 1991. Intriguing interpretation of the revolution in terms of traditional Chinese ideas rather than modern Western ones.

Service, R. *Lenin: A Political Life.* Bloomington: Indiana University Press, 1985. Excellent political analysis. See also his *Lenin: A Biography* (Cambridge: Harvard University Press, 2002), rich in personal detail.

Skocpol, T. *States and Social Revolutions: A Comparative Analysis of France, Russia, and China.* New York: Cambridge University Press, 1979. Challenging theoretical study. See also her more recent *Social Revolutions in the Modern World* (New York: Cambridge University Press, 1994).

Solzhenitsyn, A. I. *The Gulag Archipelago 1918–1956* (3 vols.) trans. T. P. Whitney. New York: Harper & Row, 1974–1978. Personal testimony of the labor camps and prisons of Stalinist Russia, collected by a leading Soviet exile novelist, who was there himself.

Thaxton, R. A. Jr. *Salt of the Earth: The Political Origins of Peasant Protest and Communist Revolution in China.* Berkeley: University of California Press, 1997. Controversial study of twentieth-century Chinese peasant revolts seen as capitalistic struggles for a share of the market.

Yack, B. *The Longing for Total Revolution: Philosophic Sources of Social Discontent from Rousseau to Marx and Nietzsche.* Princeton, N.J.: Princeton University Press, 1986. Sophisticated, controversial analysis of revolutionary philosophical assumptions about true human nature and modern society, the latter seen as impeding the emergence of authentic humanity.

 Please refer to the document CD-ROM for primary sources related to this chapter.

# CHAPTER 26

# BLITZKRIEG AND BURNING CITIES
## World War II

## (1939–1945)

## A Glance Ahead: The Biggest War Leaves a Europe-Centered World Order in Ruins

The last "good war," as World War II (1939–1945) is sometimes called, didn't seem so good to those who were sucked into it. It scattered more death and destruction around the globe than any war in history, leaving cities and nations in ruins, tens of millions dead— and only the United States richer and more powerful than ever.

The Second World War began, like the first one, in Europe, but quickly spread far beyond. The early years saw Hitler's mechanized armies overrun most of Europe and militarized Japan overwhelm much of East Asia. During the second half of the struggle, however, the United States, Britain, and their new ally, Soviet Russia, mobilized massive sea and air power and launched thunderous offensives to crush the Axis powers.

The second global war led to a genuinely global postwar settlement. American aid helped Europe recover, Germany and Japan were turned into modern democracies, and the United Nations seemed to promise peace at last. Such hopes faded, however, as Russia and America, Europeans and their colonies confronted each other menacingly across the world.

## Causes of the Second World War

### Long-Range Causes

Given what has been said about the nature of totalitarian governments, it is easy to see World War II as a splendid illustration of the "devil theory" of history—aggressive dictators on one side, democracies on the other. Certainly, Germany, Italy, and Japan were aggressive, militaristic, and expansionist in the 1930s. On the other hand, Stalin's Russia was as totalitarian as Hitler's Germany, and "Uncle Joe" at least finished the war on the Allied side. Britain still headed the largest empire in the history of the world in 1939. Even the United States, few as its holdings were outside the continent, had made itself so unpopular meddling in the affairs of the Latin American republics that some of them would not side with America against the Nazis.

A related approach having much appeal because it seems to carry a message for our time is to see the cause of the war as Allied appeasement of Axis aggression. Again, there is much truth in this view, as will be apparent when we follow the grim sequence of crises down the thirties to the final confrontation over Poland in 1939. Yet this approach also is incomplete, for it does little to explain why the Axis powers were aggressive and expansionist in the first place.

Deeper, longer-range causes for the Second World War include the World Depression, the Versailles peace after World War I, and perhaps some deeply disturbing features of the global political order.

The Great Depression certainly accounted in significant part for Hitler's rise to power and for the decline of party government in Japan. Military expenditures were also a good way for Hitler and other totalitarian leaders to put people back to work in a hurry. Perhaps most important, however, the Depression left the Western democracies badly weakened in the 1930s. Preoccupied by domestic problems, divided class against class by the new poverty, and unsure of their own future, democratic leaders found appeasement and the avoidance of the confrontation as natural as aggressive rhetoric was to the heads of militarized totalitarian states.

Confrontations there were in plenty—and many of them went back to the unsatisfactory peace settlement signed at Versailles in 1919. The Versailles peace divided the great powers into two camps: the satisfied and the unsatisfied, the supporters of the settlement and those who demanded revisions. Britain, France, and the United States—to the extent that the United States involved itself at all—supported the treaty as signed. Germany, Italy, Japan, and the Soviet Union were among the major revisionists.

Germany and Soviet Russia had emerged from World War I as pariahs among the nations. Germany had been saddled with war guilt and reparations, stripped of its colonies and armies. The Soviet Union had lost large portions of czarist territory in the collapse of 1917–1918 and felt surrounded by capitalist enemies after the civil war that followed. Italy and Japan had seen their imperial ambitions frustrated by the Versailles settlement and by the diplomacy of the postwar period.

The revisionist powers, in the time-honored style of great powers, seized every opportunity to modify the settlement in their favor—and in so doing drew steadily closer to another great war.

Though they didn't know it, then, revisionist dictators demanding justice and defenders of the international status quo pointing to the sanctity of treaties, militarists and appeasers, aggressive politicians, and peoples who were simply too busy with the Depression to care about the international situation all in their different ways contributed to the coming of the biggest war in history.

## Italian and Japanese Aggression

A string of international crises led up to the final explosion. Each crisis pitted revisionists against defenders of the peace, authoritarian states against those that were at least less so. The result was a series of totalitarian and militaristic aggressions met with such tepid responses on the part of relatively democratic states as to give the word *appeasement* a bad taste ever since.

At first the pattern of aggression and appeasement seemed far off and exotic to the Western powers that still claimed to run the world. Japanese aggression in China, Italy's latest plunge into Ethiopia, even a civil war in Spain—land of bullfighters and sunny poverty—did not seem like central concerns to Western democracies struggling for their economic lives. Then it was much, much closer—but still involving unfamiliar names and places: the Rhineland, *Anschluss,* the Sudentenland, the Polish corridor. . . . And then the Panzers were revving up their motors, the Stukas roaring into the dawn.

But at first it was distant thunder on a horizon half a world away. Japan in Asia, Italy in Africa first broke the peace so dubiously established in 1919.

Japan attacked China first in 1931, in Manchuria, and again, in an all-out invasion, in 1937. In both instances Japan's military leaders instigated the aggression while its own civilian government, the Chinese army, and the nations of the world did little but wring their hands in dismay.

Japan had been developing Manchuria, the old Manchu homeland northeast of the Great Wall, as a center of grain, coal, and iron production for decades. A campaign by Jiang Jieshi to regain the political and economic initiative there, plus the revival of Russian power in the Far East under Stalin, aroused the concern of imperialistic Japanese fearful of losing their foothold in Manchuria. In 1931 a handful of Japanese officers stationed in the area staged an attempt to sabotage the Japanese-run railway and used it as an excuse to seize control of the whole region, rechristen it Manchukuo, and install a Manchu puppet there.

Reactions to this first major act of aggression on the decade-long road to World War II were illuminating. The Japanese officers used their trials for insubordination as platforms to explain their patriotic motives, and—as we have seen—were hailed as national heroes in many quarters. In the end it was the current prime minister and cabinet who resigned in disgrace. Jiang Jieshi, preoccupied with his annual campaign against Mao's first base in Jiangxi, could do nothing. The League of Nations appointed a commission of inquiry. When the commission very mildly rapped Japan's knuckles over the incident, Japan simply withdrew from the League. Japan kept its new colony, and was soon expanding its influence into the neighboring provinces of China.

All-out invasion did not come until 1937. By that time Jiang had been compelled by popular opinion—and his own Guomindang colleagues—to make common cause with Mao, now installed in Shanxi, against Japanese power in the north. This united front, encouraged by the Soviet Union, threatened to reverse the Japanese expansionist drive. Another "incident," this one at the Marco Polo Bridge near Beijing, gave Japan the excuse Japanese generals sought for a full-scale invasion of China.

Over the next few years Japan's mechanized, highly trained, and motivated army and navy dominated China's coasts, rivers, and harbors, occupied many Chinese cities, and conquered most of China's east coast. Jiang Jieshi's government, accompanied by large numbers of Chinese fleeing the sometimes savage behavior of the Japanese troops, retreated up the Yangzi valley into the interior to establish a wartime capital at Chongqing.

Jiang's scorched-earth policies as his troops retreated, Mao's guerrilla attacks, and the primitive logistics and transport systems in the interior of China soon turned the triumphant Japanese advance into a grim occupation. But despite strongly worded protests from the United States and some modest continuing Soviet aid, little was done for China. The United States, in fact, went on selling Japan such basic war material as iron and oil right up until 1941.

Italy invaded Ethiopia in 1935, halfway between Japan's aggression in Manchuria and its massive invasion of China proper. Confronted with Italy's African venture, the Western democracies once more reacted inadequately, and the aggressors carried the day.

Mussolini, the oldest of the totalitarian rulers, apparently felt that the younger generation of Fascists needed a great adventure, the party as a whole a new shot of glory. Italy also needed more space to resettle the growing numbers of the unemployed. And Ethiopia, which adjoined Italy's colonies in the Horn of Africa and was the last country on the African continent without a colonial overlord, seemed a logical answer to his needs.

An incident between Italian and Ethiopian troops at an unused water hole on a disputed frontier gave Mussolini his excuse. The Ethiopian king, Haile Selassie, offered to submit the dispute to arbitration. Mussolini responded with shelling, aerial strafing, and mustard gas. The Ethiopians fought a gallant fight, but they could not match the weaponry of the civilizers from the north. By the spring of 1936, King Victor Emmanuel had been proclaimed emperor of Ethiopia.

The international outcry this time was considerably greater. The League of Nations voted economic sanctions against Italy, and the French and British governments worked through diplomatic channels. But the sanctions did not include oil, the one essential that, cut off, could have stopped Italy's war machine in its tracks. And the British and the French were still trying to keep Italy, their ally in World War I, from drifting into Hitler's orbit. So the aggressors rolled on.

## The Spanish Civil War

During the years 1936–1939, the Spanish Civil War gave the self-proclaimed champions of liberty in the world another chance to stand up for freedom. Again, they left the field to the totalitarian powers. It was, by all accounts, the most heart-rending lost cause of a decade that was littered with them.

Spain during the early thirties seemed to be going against the trend of that authoritarian decade—replacing a dictatorship with a budding democracy. In 1930 it had been a European backwater, afflicted by many of the problems of its former colonies overseas: arrogantly wealthy landlords and poverty-stricken peasants, a reactionary and influential Catholic church, and a military-officer caste habituated to interfering in government. In addition, a modest amount of industrial development had created a small, overworked, and underpaid proletariat, a happy hunting ground for anarchists, syndicalists, and communists. Regional nationalisms also flourished, particularly in Catalonia and among the Basques.

Then, in July of 1936, a self-styled Spanish Nationalist movement headed by General Francisco Franco took up arms against the Spanish Republic. Within a few weeks Franco had occupied half the country, the south and west. But the Republic held the capital of Madrid and the industrialized east, including Catalonia. For the next three years, the Spanish Republic and the Nationalist rebels fought each other in a gory civil war.

The liberal powers, Britain and France, trying to avoid escalation of a local conflict into a general war, urged noninvolvement and an embargo on arms shipments. Hitler and Mussolini, however, seeing a brother-in-arms in Franco, sent him tens of thousands of Italian troops and Germany's Condor Legion, whose savage bombing of the town of Guernica was an early warning of the terrible destruction from the air that would be a hallmark of World War II. Of the great powers, only the Soviet Union, fearful of German rearmament under a militant anticommunist such as Hitler, sent advisors, money, and weapons to the Republic.

Large numbers of idealistic young people, however, came to Spain as volunteers to fight for the Spanish Republic and try to stop the further spread of fascist totalitarianism. But the members of the International Brigade, the Abraham Lincoln Brigade, and the rest were going to fight in a lost cause; they were going, in the words of a film made long afterwards, *To Die in Madrid.*

Franco won. What was left of the volunteers, and many Spaniards too, fled across the Pyrenees. The bell went on tolling.

## Hitler's War Begins

Of all the totalitarian leaders, the most successful and in the end the destroyer of the peace was Adolf Hitler.

Having unilaterally revised the Versailles Treaty and begun German rearmament on a vast scale, Hitler was soon demanding modifications of the territorial arrangement of central Europe. A passionate nationalist as well as a racist, he insisted that all German-speaking areas had a right to be reabsorbed into the new German Reich. He also talked about what he

A famous cartoonist's comment on the destruction of Poland in 1939 by her totalitarian neighbors. David Low's caricature of Hitler and Stalin shows the two former archenemies greeting each other with a sardonic parody of the insults they had once exchanged so vigorously. There was, however, no love lost between the two authoritarian rulers, who were at war with each other within two years. (Library of Congress)

called *Lebensraum*—"living space"—for the dynamic and growing German people, meaning a resumption of Germany's historic tendency to push eastward, into the lands of the Slavs.

As steps toward these nationalistic goals, Hitler embarked on a series of aggressive moves in the heart of Europe, against Austria, Czechoslovakia, and Poland. As a preliminary step, however, he remilitarized the Rhineland in 1936.

This German frontier zone between Germany and France was to have remained free of troops so as to discourage border clashes between the two traditional enemies. But this also left Germany open to French invasion. In March 1936, Hitler therefore sent 35,000 German soldiers into the Rhineland, unilaterally revising an international agreement once more and materially strengthening his hand against the liberal Allies. It was his first international aggression. His armies were not ready for war, had apparently even been ordered to withdraw if confronted with force. But the French did not confront them, and the German troops stayed.

In March 1938 Hitler absorbed Austria into the Third Reich. Some of Austria's German-speaking population did, in fact, support what Hitler was doing across the border, and there was an aggressive Austrian Nazi party. Many other Austrians, however, wanted to maintain their historic independence, even of a Germany headed by the Austrian-born Hitler. Nevertheless, the German *Führer* browbeat Austria's leaders into accepting a Nazi chancellor, then dictated a "request" for German troops to "maintain order" in the shaken country. The German army marched in, to be greeted by cheering crowds, and the *Anschluss*—"unification"—of Germany and Austria was completed. Hitler now ruled a country of 80 million Germans—equal to the populations of Britain and France combined, and well over half the population of the United States.

In later 1938 and early 1939, he took over Czechoslovakia. Claiming that that country's German-speaking minority in the Czech Sudetenland was being mistreated. Hitler demanded the surrender of this territory to Germany. France and Russia both had treaty alliances with the Czechs, and Britain supported them publicly. But Hitler again blustered and threatened until the British and French leaders once more agreed to a settlement giving Hitler what he wanted. This final concession, agreed to by British prime minister Neville Chamberlain at Munich in September 1938, made the name of that city synonymous with the bankrupt policy of appeasement.

Most of Europe, however, heaved a sigh of relief: The dead of the First World War were only twenty years in their graves by that time, and many then living remembered. In March 1939, meanwhile, German troops marched into Prague, and most of the rest of Czechoslovakia became a German protectorate.

In September 1939 Hitler moved against Poland, and Europe went to war again at last. Rectification of a dubious Polish-German frontier, the return of the German-speaking port of Danzig to Germany, and a German railway across the Polish corridor that separated Danzig from the Reich were the diplomatic demands that kindled this final crisis. In a broader perspective, the invasion of Poland looked very much like a continuation of the *Drang nach Osten,* Germany's historic drive into Slavic Eastern Europe.

By way of preparation, Hitler astonished Europe by negotiating a nonaggression treaty with his most vocal opponent—Joseph Stalin. The Nazi-Soviet Pact of August 1939 was a triumph of practical self-interest over ideology on both sides. It gave Hitler a free hand in Poland and allowed Stalin further time to prepare for future conflict with his aggressive rival. A secret codicil also agreed on the division of Eastern Europe between them.

Britain and France had given ringing guarantees of Polish rights and territorial independence as the crisis came to a head. Hitler, understandably, did not believe them. A week after the signing of the Hitler-Stalin Pact, German troops invaded Poland.

World War II had begun.


## War Around the World: Axis Victories

### The German Blitzkrieg

The two great alliances of nations that confronted each other in World War II were clearly intercontinental. The major Axis powers were two European nations and one powerful Asian one: Germany, Italy, and Japan. Bound by a series of treaties in 1936 and 1937, the so-called Rome-Berlin-Tokyo Axis involved mutual recognition of one another's spheres of interest and future conquests in Europe and Asia. The Allied Big Five—Britain, France, the Soviet Union, China, and the United States—included two purely European powers, one transcontinental Eurasian power, one purely Asian nation, and one North American state.

Europe, Asia, North Africa, and Oceania were all major battlefields. The war was fought on many seas and islands, from the North Atlantic to the South Pacific, from Crete to Okinawa. Military planners—and armchair strategists at home—filled world maps with colored pins, and everybody learned to pronounce names they had never even seen before, let alone heard spoken over their radios.

World War I was a war of position: There was little change in the trench lines, and the armies swayed agonizingly back and forth, going nowhere. Generalities may suffice to give a sense of that terrible conflict. World War II, by contrast, was a war of movement:

Armies advanced hundreds of miles, fleets struck across even greater distances. Some narrative, then, will be necessary to give a proper sense of this story.

The war began with stunning Axis victories: Hitler's *Blitzkriegs* and the Phony War sandwiched in between.

The first highly mechanized *Blitzkrieg*—"lightning war"—struck into Poland in September of 1939. German motorized Panzer divisions rolled across the frontier, preceded by waves of bombing planes, at 5:00 A.M. on September 1. Western Poland was overrun in two weeks. Soviet Russia, Hitler's ally of one month, then stabbed into the hapless land between them, and Warsaw, Poland's last stronghold, fell before the month was over. It was Germany's first demonstration of what modern mechanized warfare could be like, not in defense, as in the First World War, but on the offense.

The so-called Phony War followed through the winter of 1939–1940. The Soviet Union, triumphant in Poland, turned next on its northern neighbor Finland. But Soviet armies, which had just lost half their officer corps to the purge trials, became bogged down in a sideshow David-and-Goliath struggle with the Finns. The British and the French had declared war on Germany in September. With Poland gone, however, there was little they could do to keep their pledge to defend it. Both Western European powers seemed content to defend themselves, the French in particular barricading themselves behind the steel-and-concrete ramparts of the Maginot Line. They were thoroughly prepared, thanks to massive military outlays during the 1930s, to fight the 1914 war over again. But that was not what was in the cards in 1940.

The reporters who had dubbed the winter lull the Phony War changed their tune when spring came, and with it another *Blitzkrieg*.

Hitler, seeking air and naval bases for himself and intending to cut Britain off from a prime source of foodstuffs, struck suddenly into Scandinavia in April 1940. In a plot so outrageous few thriller writers would attempt it, he dispatched "Trojan-horse" troop ships disguised as freighters and ore barges to pour Germans onto the docks in Denmark and Norway. Denmark, overwhelmed, capitulated. Norway fought—and lasted one month to the day.

The Low Countries came next. Determined to outflank the Maginot Line from the north—the Channel side—Hitler attacked the Netherlands, Belgium, and Luxembourg in May. While their troops flooded over the borders, the Germans made skillful use of paratroopers and brutal bombing of civilian centers to seize key cities well behind the lines. Little Luxembourg fell in one day; the Netherlands lasted five. Belgium, bolstered by desperate French and British help, held out for two and a half weeks. By the end of May it too had fallen.

In June, it was France's turn. But the British were thrust aside first.

The collapse of Belgium exposed the British Expeditionary Force on the continent to disaster. Pressed back against the sea at Dunkirk in early June, the bulk of the British troops were evacuated with the help of a flotilla of private yachts and sailboats. But the "miracle" of Dunkirk was nonetheless a military disaster: The British had been hurled out of Europe.

The German armies, meantime, swung south and west around the end of the Maginot Line and drove for Paris—the great race they had been unable to win in the 1914 war. Before the month of June was out, gray-uniformed German infantrymen were goose-stepping up the Champs-Elysées. Hitler danced a little jig as he received the French surrender—in the same railway car where the Germans had been forced to accept the armistice in 1918.

More than half of France was occupied by the Germans for the remainder of the war. The rest of the country was governed by a puppet French government set up in the south.

# WORLD WAR II EUROPEAN AND MEDITERRANEAN THEATERS, 1939–1945

**Legend:**
- Allies
- Axis countries
- Farthest Axis advances
- Heaviest Allied bombing
- ✴ Sinking of the Bismarck

ATLANTIC OCEAN

SOVIET UNION

FINLAND

SWEDEN

NORWAY

DENMARK

GREAT BRITAIN

IRELAND

NETH.
BEL.
FRANCE 1945

SPAIN

PORTUGAL

FRENCH MOROCCO

ALGERIA

TUNISIA

LIBYA

EGYPT

TURKEY

SYRIA

TRANS-JORDAN

PALESTINE

CYPRUS

GREECE

ALBANIA

YUGOSLAVIA

BULGARIA

ROMANIA

HUNGARY

AUSTRIA

ITALY

SWITZ.

GERMANY

POLAND

EAST PRUSSIA

LITHUANIA

LATVIA

ESTONIA

North Sea

Baltic Sea

Black Sea

Aegean Sea

Mediterranean Sea

Moscow

Volga R.

Stalingrad

Leningrad

Helsinki

Stockholm

Oslo

Sevastopol

Yalta

Istanbul

Ankara

Cairo

El Alamein

Tobruk

Suez Canal

Dublin

London

Coventry

Bordeaux

Dunkirk

Dieppe

Paris

Nice

Marseilles

Vichy

Bern

Cologne

Hamburg

Berlin

Dresden

Prague

Munich

Vienna

Berchtesgaden

Stuttgart

Frankfurt

Torgau

Danzig

Konigsberg

Warsaw

Budapest

Belgrade

Sofia

Bucharest

Kiev

Palermo

SICILY

Naples

Monte Cassino

Anzio

Rome

Florence

Trieste

CORSICA

SARDINIA

BALEARIC IS.

MALTA

CRETE

Bizerte

Tunis

Bone

Algiers

Oran

Gibraltar

Tangier

Casablanca

Lisbon

Madrid

RUHR

NORMANDY

Maginot Line

Border of Vichy France

Siegfried Line

Elbe R.

Oder R.

Vistula

Danube R.

Dnieper R.

Don R.

Loire R.

Ebro R.

Seine R.

English Channel

1939
1940
1941
1942
1943
1944
1945

500 Miles

500 Kilometers

250

0

## The Battle of Britain

The next phase of the war, 1940–1941, saw the fighting still focused on the western end of Eurasia, in the Battle of Britain and the overrunning of Eastern Europe. In this phase too the Axis was generally victorious, though not quite as uniformly as in the lightning thrusts of the preceding year.

Hitler turned his attention particularly to Britain in 1940 and 1941—and met his first setback. Like Napoleon before him, he abandoned plans to invade the British Isles directly because he lacked flat-bottomed barges to transport sufficient troops for the operation. He turned instead to the twentieth century's armory of new war machines—to planes and submarines.

He tried first to break the British by massive bombardment from the air, pounding cities such as Coventry and London with tons of high explosives in almost nightly air raids. Londoners slept in the subways and came up to smoke and ruin. But the Royal Air Force took an unexpectedly heavy toll of the attackers. The rolling oratory of the new prime minister, Winston Churchill, rallied the British people. And Britain did not surrender.

Thereafter the Germans settled down to a submarine siege of the islands, as in World War I. The goal was to cut Great Britain off from overseas supplies, either from the Commonwealth countries or in the form of increasing aid from the United States. For a while it looked very much as though that aim might be accomplished: During the first year after Dunkirk, the Germans sank 1,400 merchant ships in Atlantic waters.

Still, the British did not yield—and the United States began to provide increasingly open support for the last fighting democracy left in Europe. Under a "lend-lease" arrangement Franklin Roosevelt negotiated an aid package that beefed up the British navy, and he announced that although he would not send American boys to fight overseas, the United States could and would become "the arsenal of democracy." In the summer of 1941 Roosevelt and Churchill met secretly at sea to sign an idealistic statement of mutual aims, the Atlantic Charter.

Frustrated in the West, the armies of the totalitarian powers were much more successful in Eastern Europe. During 1940 and 1941, Hitler and Mussolini were mopping up the Balkans, Stalin the Baltic states.

Besides Finland and Poland, former czarist territories lost by Russia in World War I included the states of Estonia, Latvia, and Lithuania on the Baltic Sea. Stalin now seized his chance to reabsorb them into the Soviet Union. Hitler, meanwhile, with some help from Mussolini, overran the countries of the Balkan peninsula. Some—Hungary, Rumania, Bulgaria—were forced to join the Axis alliance. Others—Yugoslavia and Greece—were conquered, though bands of guerrillas remained active in the rugged mountains of both countries.

By the middle of 1941, after almost two years of fighting, the Axis tide was still at its flood. Then, in the latter half of 1941, Germany and Japan made their biggest mistakes of the war.

## Barbarossa and Pearl Harbor

In June 1941 Hitler launched his biggest offensive thus far—and made his largest error of judgment: the invasion of Russia. He seems to have been motivated by simmering disagreements over the spoils of war—especially the division of the Balkans, where Russia's interest went back to the pan-Slavism of the nineteenth century. The German ruler therefore decided on Operation Barbarossa. Named for the famous medieval German warrior-emperor, Barbarossa was planned as a quick campaign to break Russia as the German armies had so many others in those two years.

The invasion began in late June 1941, and in six months Hitler's armies had swept over half of European Russia. By December, German troops were fighting in the suburbs of both of Russia's historic capitals, Moscow and Leningrad (St. Petersburg).

But neither city fell. Long supply lines, the slow Soviet retreat that left only scorched earth behind, and the crushing cold of a Russian winter slowed Hitler's impetuous drive to a crawl, as they had Napoleon's in 1812. Meanwhile, the Soviet Union's newly built factories in and beyond the Ural Mountains farther to the east remained comparatively safe and productive, grinding out war material. And supplies from Britain and the United States began to arrive by sea, through Murmansk in the far north.

There were horrendous battles yet to come in Russia. But by the beginning of 1942, Hitler had reached his limits in the east, as he had in the west. Neither Britain on its tight little offshore islands nor Russia on its endless eastern plains would fall. And by that time a third great power was coming against him—the United States.

While Hitler was knifing into Russia, on the other side of the globe, Japan was carrying Axis victories to a climax by overrunning almost all the Western colonies in the Far East during 1941 and 1942. In so doing, however, the Japanese made the other biggest Axis error of judgment: bringing the United States into the war.

Japanese imperialists and militarists, now thoroughly in charge of Emperor Hirohito's government, saw a golden opportunity for renewed empire-building in the East while the Western imperial powers reeled from Hitler's blows. By the end of 1941, the Japanese had planned a coordinated series of attacks. The first to be hit were the British colony of Hong Kong off the South China coast—and the two American colonies of the Philippine Islands in Southeast Asia and the Hawaiian Islands in the central Pacific.

An American battleship sinks in the smoke and flame of Pearl Harbor on Sunday morning, December 7, 1941. The United States lost 2,400 men and most of its Pacific fleet in the Japanese surprise attack. Ask any American old enough to remember that morning what they were doing when they heard the news, and the odds are they will remember, even half a century later. (Navy Dept./National Archives)

Hawaii, too far away for invasion, was nevertheless hit first from the air so that the American Pacific fleet based there, at Pearl Harbor, could be destroyed. On a quiet Sunday morning—December 7, 1941—carrier-based Japanese planes swept in low over the islands. Shouting into their microphones the prearranged signal for success, *Tora! Tora! Tora!*—Tiger! Tiger! Tiger!—they zoomed along Battleship Row and inland over the airfield, raining down bombs. They sank eight battleships and ten other vessels, leaving the most powerful Western naval squadron in the Pacific dead and smoldering in the water.

Through the following winter and spring of 1942, Japanese forces conquered the American Philippines, British Hong Kong, Malaya and Burma, and much of the Dutch East Indies. They had forced the French to yield to them de facto control of French Indochina—Vietnam, Cambodia, Laos—and absorbed the last independent Asian kingdom, Thailand. In so doing they cut the famous Burma Road, the supply line from British India to China, and brought victory in the long Chinese struggle within sight at last.

The summer of 1942 was thus the high-water mark for Japan in Asia, just as Germany was reaching its limits in Europe. And Japan's error in attacking the United States was already beginning to show.

## War Around the World: Allied Triumph

### The Allied Counterattack: North Africa and Italy

The years 1939 to 1941 were a period of almost unbroken Axis victories. From 1942 through 1945, the initiative shifted to the Allies, and with it the rising tide of victories.

In 1942 the United States, Britain, and the Soviet Union formed what Churchill, with eighteenth-century grandiloquence, called the Grand Alliance. France's government-in-exile under General de Gaulle and what remained of Jiang Jieshi's China were lesser partners. The larger nations of the British Commonwealth joined them, and many other countries around the world found it prudent to cast their lot at least nominally with the Allied cause. The Big Three in particular—Roosevelt, Churchill, and Stalin—met repeatedly through the rest of the war to plan grand strategy and reaffirm their determination to make no terms with their adversaries, to accept only unconditional surrender.

The world's biggest industrial machine, that of the United States, now went into high gear. Factories and men, idle and rusting through the depression, went back to work with a rush. As in World War I, many women took jobs formerly held by men now absorbed by the armed forces. Huge quantities of war supplies were conveyed across the Atlantic to Britain and Russia in the teeth of the German submarines and planes.

In Europe, a massive coordinated air attack was launched against Germany. British and American bombers hit German bases, industrial complexes, and cities, the Americans by day and the British by night. In the Pacific, reinforcements arrived. British raiders began to strike back at the Japanese in the jungles of Southeast Asia. And the U.S. Navy began to raise and repair most of the shattered hulks the Japanese had left behind in Pearl Harbor.

The first major Allied victories, however, came on battlefields not even mentioned yet—in North Africa and Italy.

The deserts of North Africa had been the site of a seesaw tank war between the British and the Germans since 1940. The turning point of the struggle—and one of the turning points of the war—came in the Battle of El Alamein in the fall of 1942. General Montgomery's victory over General Rommel, Germany's celebrated "Desert Fox," saved Egypt and the Suez Canal, Britain's lifeline to the East.

Thereafter the British drove the Germans and their Italian allies out of Egypt and pushed on into Libya, Italy's major North African colony and an Axis stronghold in Africa. In the meantime, an Anglo-American force had landed in the French colonies of Morocco and Algeria and easily overwhelmed the Germans and the collaborationist French forces there. By the spring of 1943, the last Axis armies in North Africa had surrendered.

Hitler had not only been stopped but also had been rolled back. And new Allied victories followed in Italy, later in 1943.

American and British forces leaped from North Africa across the narrow waist of the Mediterranean, first to the island of Sicily, off the toe of the Italian boot, and then to the mainland of Italy itself. The great southern metropolis of Naples fell in the autumn of 1943. The impact of these combined defeats in Libya, Sicily, and southern Italy, furthermore, were sufficient to bring about the fall of Mussolini in July and the surrender of Italy in September of that year.

The German armies in Italy fought on, and the battle for the peninsula turned into a grinding struggle that would drag on through the rest of the war. But one of the Axis powers, at least, had given up. And by the end of 1943, the war had turned against the Axis elsewhere as well.

### Stalingrad and D-Day

The years 1943 and 1944 were years of mounting pressure on the Axis, major breakthroughs for the Allies. In Europe these were the years of Stalingrad and D-Day; in the Far East, the island-hopping war that brought American forces within reach of Japan.

The Battle of Stalingrad, like that of El Alamein, is generally considered a major turning point in the war. The Germans, unable to take either Leningrad in the north or Moscow in the center of European Russia in 1941, had swung south in 1942. They had aimed a great offensive at Russia's huge Baku oil fields and at Stalin's name-city on the Volga. Again, they reached the suburbs but never managed to take the city. The Russians defended Stalingrad street by street, house by house, room by room: "We have fought during fifteen days for a single house," a German officer recorded in his diary.

> with mortars, grenades, machine guns and bayonets. Already by the third day fifty-four German corpses are strewn in the cellars, on the landings, and the staircases. . . . From story to story, faces black with sweat, we bombarded each other with grenades in the middle of explosions, clouds of dust and heaps of mortar . . . fragments of furniture and human beings. Ask any soldier what half an hour of hand-to-hand struggle means in such a fight.[1]

The Russian counteroffensive at Stalingrad ringed the German besiegers, lined up field artillery almost hub to hub, and pulverized the now trapped German forces. What remained of the German Sixth Army surrendered in February 1943—a greater disaster than Dunkirk was to the British.

---

[1]William L. Langer, et al., *Western Civilization,* Vol. II (New York: American Heritage/Harper & Row, 1968), p. 789.

The Russians thereafter launched a series of tremendous offensives on the longest battlefront in a world at war. They attacked summer and winter, even in the Russian snows. By the spring of 1944, the last German forces were staggering out of Russia. Before the year was ended they had been driven out of Poland and the Balkans too, and most of Eastern Europe had been overrun by Russian armies.

The spring of 1944 had worse news for Hitler in the west, however. In June 1944 came D-Day, the invasion of France, and the beginning of the liberation of Western Europe.

The Russians had long been urging the opening of a "second front" that would take some of the German pressure off their own armies. On June 6, 1944, they got it, when Operation Overlord, under the overall command of American general Dwight Eisenhower, breached Hitler's Fortress Europe from the west. The largest invasion fleet in history—3,200 warships, transports, and landing craft—crossed the English Channel from Britain to materialize at dawn off the Normandy coasts. Within twenty-four hours they had put a quarter of a million American, British, and Canadian soldiers ashore, and the battle for Western Europe had begun.

France and Belgium were liberated by the end of 1944, despite a powerful German counterattack in Belgium in the fall, the Battle of the Bulge on all the military maps. In spite of setbacks, then, United States and British troops opened 1945 camped on the Rhine, ready to invade Germany itself.

## Asia and the Pacific War

On the other side of the globe, where the world is mostly water, other landings on equally inhospitable shores were advancing the Allied cause in the Pacific. The Japanese offensive in the Pacific had actually ground to a halt as early as 1942—about the time of the critical German and Italian reversals at El Alamein and Stalingrad. In the East, it was the linked battles of the Coral Sea, Midway, and Guadalcanal that turned the tide.

After their initial victories in Hawaii, Hong Kong, and Southeast Asia, the next likely Japanese targets were the big island of New Guinea and the thinly populated continent of Australia. When they began to move in this direction, from bases already seized in the Solomon Islands, American aid was rushed to these archipelagoes.

Here, in the beautifully named Coral Sea, between Australia and the Solomons, a U.S. naval force intercepted a large Japanese fleet in May 1942, and for the first time in the war won a major victory in this half of the world. In June the U.S. Navy met and defeated another big Japanese naval detachment, this one far to the north, approaching Midway Island, west of Hawaii. Both victories were won by the navy's carrier-based air arm—like Pearl Harbor itself, strong evidence of the crucial part air power would play in naval combat throughout the war.

There was, however, some bloody foot slogging left to do—in the jungles of Southeast Asia and on the islands of Oceania.

In Southeast Asia—the so-called China-Burma-India theater of war—Japanese military power was stretched to its thinnest. By overrunning Burma and cutting the Burma Road in 1942, the Japanese had temporarily severed the line that allowed supplies to reach beleaguered China, Japan's original and always central target. But when Japanese forces pushed still deeper into northeastern India, they were turned back by British, American, Indian, and other allied troops and forced off the subcontinent in 1943.

# World War II Asian and Pacific Theaters, 1941–1945

Area under Japanese domination, Aug. 1942

U.S.–Australian joint drive

U. S. S. R.

MONGOLIA

CHINA

TIBET

British Ladakh Land INDIA Army

BURMA

Lashio

Burma Road

Kunming

YUNNAN

Chungking

Yenan

Szechuan

Peiping

Yellow R.

Yangtze R.

Nanking

Chinese Land Army

Canton

Hong Kong

HAINAN

Gulf of Tonkin

Hanoi

Hue

INDOCHINA

THAILAND (SIAM)

Gulf of Siam

Saigon

MALAYA

SINGAPORE

SUMATRA

BR. N. BORNEO

SARAWAK

BORNEO

JAVA

NETHERLANDS INDIES

CELEBES

Russian Land Army

Russian Land Army

Amur R.

Vladivostok

SAKHALIN

KURILE IS.

1945

1945

MANCHURIA

KOREA

Shanghai

MATSU

FORMOSA (Taiwan)

CHEMOY

RYUKYU IS.

OKINAWA

1945

JAPAN

Tokyo

Hiroshima

Nagasaki

ATOM BOMB—AUG. 6, 1945

ATOM BOMB—AUG. 9, 1945

BONIN IS.

IWO JIMA

1945

PHILIPPINE SEA

LUZON

Manila

CORREGIDOR

PHILIPPINE IS. (U.S.)

MINDANAO

LEYTE 1944

1945

PALAU

YAP

GUAM (U.S.)

1945

MARIANAS IS.

SAIPAN

CAROLINE ISLANDS

TRUK

ADMIRALTY IS.

BISMARCK ARCH.

NEW GUINEA

Lae

AUSTRALIA

INDIAN OCEAN

PACIFIC OCEAN

ATTU I.

KISKA I.

ALEUTIAN IS. (U.S.)

MIDWAY I. (U.S.)

MARCUS I.

WAKE I. (U.S.)

JOHNSTON I.

HAWAIIAN IS. (U.S.)

Pearl Harbor

KINGMAN REEF

PALMYRA I.

LINE IS.

JARVIS I.

SAMOA (Br.) (U.S.)

ENIWETOK

KWAJALEIN

BIKINI

MARSHALL IS.

1943

GILBERT IS.

TARAWA

HOWLAND I.

BAKER I.

PHOENIX IS.

ELLICE IS.

1943

NEW HEBRIDES (Br. and Fr.)

FIJI IS.

NEW CALEDONIA (Fr.)

SOLOMON IS.

GUADALCANAL

1942

CORAL SEA

30°N

180°

150°E

120°E

0   500   1,000 Miles

0   500   1,000 Kilometers

667

The war in this corner of the globe thereafter centered in the steaming jungles and precipitous mountains of Burma. Allied road builders carved a new highway through the rain forest while groups of irregulars with colorful names like Wingate's Raiders and Merrill's Marauders were keeping the Japanese off balance. Weakened by tropical diseases, mired in the monsoon rains, and handicapped by long and uncertain supply lines, the Japanese gradually gave ground. The British pushed east and south, capturing Rangoon and Mandalay and gradually retaking their former colony.

America's westward drive from island to island across Oceania began with the bloody Battle of Guadalcanal in the Solomons in the latter part of 1942. The first of many amphibious landings put U.S. Marines ashore on a jungle island defended by deeply entrenched and determined Japanese. Major air and sea battles roared overhead and in the surrounding waters, and the Japanese launched repeated counterattacks to recover lost ground. The back-and-forth struggle ended with U.S. forces in control, but it was a hard-won victory. Guadalcanal established a pattern of bloody island campaigns that seldom varied thereafter.

The Americans in the South Pacific spent most of 1943 recovering from the losses sustained in the defeats and victories of the first year of the Pacific war, and in regrouping their forces for a major offensive. Then, with ships, planes, and U.S. Marines available in sufficient quantities, and General Douglas MacArthur in overall command, America launched a series of costly but successful amphibious attacks on the Japanese-held islands that formed the outer perimeter of its Asian empire. Through 1944 and 1945, coral atolls and jungle islands such as Tarawa, Saipan, Iwo Jima, and Okinawa became the sites of hard-fought American victories. The Philippines were also invaded and retaken by MacArthur's troops.

Everywhere the Japanese fought with the courage of their samurai ancestors. But 1945 found American arms poised to attack the Japanese home islands themselves.

## Allied Victory: Berlin to Tokyo

Nineteen forty-five was the last year—the year of unconditional surrender.

In Europe, the Russian Red Army had driven German forces back out of Eastern Europe, conquering Hitler's small Axis allies there and liberating the countries that had resisted him. In the latter effort they received important help from partisan leaders such as Marshal Tito in Yugoslavia.

The American, British, French, and Allied forces, meanwhile, after containing the German counterattack in Belgium, pressed in on Germany from the west. The last line of defense, the so-called West Wall, was outflanked and breached, the Rhine was crossed at several places, and the Allies poured into Germany.

From the east, the Russians did the same. With Hitler's Eastern European satellite states firmly in their hands, Soviet forces swept into eastern Germany. Under Marshal Zhukov, defender of Moscow and victor of Stalingrad, the Russians drove for Berlin. In the spring of 1945, Russian soldiers swarmed into the half-ruined capital of the Thousand-Year Reich.

Hitler, in his Berlin command bunker, hands shaking, face twitching as the thud of explosions shook his city, took poison. His body was burned by faithful officers. All across the country, battered German armies gave up. The unconditional surrender of all surviving German forces was signed a week after the fall of Berlin, on May 8, 1945—V-E Day, for Victory in Europe, in American parlance.

A famous photograph shows Russian soldiers planting the red hammer-and-sickle banner of the Soviet Union high on a gutted tower of the German Reichstag. Below them, the wreckage that was left after years of American and British bombing fades into the smoke of the last battle of Berlin.

The fall of Japan was very different. It came after an exclusively aerial bombardment—a further graphic demonstration of the power of attack from the air.

From newly captured island bases, U.S. bombers began to visit the same sort of mass destruction on Japan that Europe, mainland Asia, and Oceania had already suffered. Through the first three quarters of 1945, high-explosive and incendiary bombs gutted large sections of Japanese cities, including Tokyo. Then in August, the war's most terrible secret weapon was deployed against two Japanese urban complexes, Hiroshima and Nagasaki. Atomic bombs destroyed most of both cities—in a matter of minutes. With the majority of its armed forces still intact and occupying foreign lands from Southeast Asia to China, Japan surrendered unconditionally to the Allies.

The surrender document was signed on the deck of the American battleship *Missouri*, anchored in Tokyo Bay, on September 2, 1945—V-J Day. There was no more than a gentle roll on the water, and the hands that signed the document were steady.

But one aspect of that scene was quite similar to the Berlin where the red flag fluttered. The city that ringed the harbor, like Hitler's shattered capital, was a bombed-out ruin as the biggest war drew to a close.

## Consequences of World War II

### Total War

World War II, even more than World War I, required a total commitment from the societies that fought it. To mobilize, equip, and support modern mechanized forces of millions of men, the great powers had to put immense political, social, and above all economic power into the hands of their central governments.

On the political side, this could mean significant increases in the authority of governing officials, even in democratic countries. Government censorship—or self-censorship by the press—of war news was universal, as were the combatants' propaganda campaigns to convince people on all sides that theirs was the righteous cause. Even in a country with an established tradition of civil liberties like the United States, 100,000 Americans of Japanese ancestry were interned for the duration on no better grounds than fear and racial prejudice. In Germany, it was after the beginning of the war that the systematic extermination of six million Jews and several million Slavs and other "inferior races" began.

As in World War I, the governments of the warring states became deeply involved in the economic life of their countries during World War II. Once more, governments allocated raw materials for war industries; regulated wages and prices; set labor policies, generally excluding strikes for the duration; and gave priorities to military production. For the totalitarian states, including the Soviet Union, this could make little difference to peoples already habituated to official control of the economy. Western nations that had hesitated even at some of the welfare legislation of earlier decades, however, were much more willing to accept a strong government role after this wartime experience.

A lone survivor bicycles through the ruins of Nagasaki, Japan, destroyed by an American atomic bomb in August 1945. The wreckage of many other great cities, leveled by more conventional explosives and incendiary bombs, littered Europe and Asia at the end of World War II. For decades afterward, the devastation caused by the atomic bombs dropped on Japan would symbolize the horror of modern technological warfare to peoples around the world. (The Bettmann Archive)

## Women at War

The biggest war in history swept up women as well as men, and the presence of many women at war became one of its most striking characteristics. The heavy bombing of cities, to be discussed below, took its toll on civilians of both sexes, killing and injuring millions of women around the world. Conquering armies preyed on women as they always had, raping, looting, and destroying their homes and families. Women fought back, joining partisan guerrilla bands in conquered lands or serving with underground resistance movements. They carried messages, orders, and bombs. They gathered intelligence for the Allies and helped stranded Allied fliers and other military personnel to escape from Hitler's Fortress Europe. And they, like the men of the resistance, paid a price. "The average 'life' of a female liaison officer," a leader of the French resistance remembered, "was no more than a few months."[2]

Perhaps the most striking social consequence of the war, as in World War I, was the movement of large numbers of women out of the home and into war plants or even into the armed services themselves. In the United States alone, more than 200,000 women served in special units of the U.S. Army, Navy, Marines, and Coast Guard, and six million worked in munitions factories. Some 40 percent of all American aircraft workers were female, a fact that permanently altered old-fashioned notions about the ability of women to acquire mechanical skills. Rosie the Riveter was a label that symbolized another step toward an equal place for women in the Western world.

## Casualties and Destruction: Fifty Million Dead

Not surprisingly, a total war fought with what were then the most up-to-date technological tools available produced vast ruin and unmatched casualty figures.

Years of fighting between huge armies in western Russia and in eastern China cost millions of lives. But the most impressive material destruction, and the most astronomical

---

[2]Henri Michel, *The Shadow War: Resistance in Europe, 1939–1945* (London: Corgi Books, 1975), p. 189.

# Voices from the Past

"Letters from home" meant a lot to soldiers on all sides in World War II. This soldier, who did not expect to live much longer, sends both love and practical advice to the young family he had left behind him. His conviction that he would not be coming home himself was very likely to be correct, since he was a quartermaster in the German Sixth Army at Stalingrad.

*My dearest wife,*

*I am still alive and alright [sic]. Today—Sunday—I attended the funeral of several soldiers of my bakery company. It is cruel what you witness in the cemeteries. Should I ever return home, I will never forget what I have seen. It is an epic second to none. I am sorry that I have not recieved any letters from you since December 5. I would be so happy to read a word of love from you for one does not know what the next hour, the next day will have in store. My dearest wife, come what may, I am prepared for everything. When the time comes I shall die a soldier. . . . God is with us every hour—these were the words of the Protestant minister at the cemetery, which is overflowing. It increases in dimension like an avalanche.*

*With us, Death is a daily guest. He has lost all his horrors for me. . . . In case I fall, move to Schwäbisch Gmünd as soon as possible. Life is cheaper there. There are 1,900 reichsmark on my account at the post office savings bank. My belongings are in a small suitcase, a big handbag, a bootbag and perhaps a small wooden suitcase.*

*Throw away my uniforms. The rest is yours, . . . I wish you and the children all the best for the future. Let us hope that we shall be reunited in the other world.*

---

William Craig, *Enemy at the Gates: The Battle for Stalingrad* (New York: E. P. Dutton, 1973), pp. 313–314.

casualty figures, came with the bombing of cities. Industrial cities, with their heavy concentration of defense plants, transportation junctures, and military facilities, were clearly essential to the enemy's war effort. It was also believed that a rain of destruction from the sky might break an opponent's will to fight on, thus hastening victory. As a result, lavish expenditures of money, scientific ingenuity, labor, and lives were poured into this key feature of the biggest of all wars.

The Japanese in China, the Italians in Ethiopia, and the Germans in Spain showed what could be done from the air before World War II properly got under way. In the early years of the war itself, German bombers began the practice of terror bombing in Warsaw, Amsterdam, Coventry, and London.

But as the war advanced, American and British bombing raids more than matched these German efforts. High explosives and incendiary bombs rained over German and Japanese cities. As many as 100,000 people may have died in a single incendiary raid on Tokyo; the notorious Dresden raid may have cost hundreds of thousands of lives in one night. And in a fraction of a second, in a single flash of light brighter than a thousand suns, Hiroshima was turned into as close an approximation of hell as twentieth-century humanity has thus far managed to achieve.

Total casualties in the greatest and most destructive of wars can only be estimated. Fifty million is a figure frequently advanced.

A million is a hard number to comprehend. As an aid to the imagination, you might note that by the time it sees print, the book you hold in your hand will perhaps contain a quarter of a million words. Multiply that by four, and that again by fifty. Imagine each word as a small white cross on an endless field of green—the military cemeteries of Europe are meticulously cared for—and you will be on your way to appreciating World War II.

# THE POSTWAR WORLD

## A World in Ruins

Every American heard stories after the war. Personal anecdotes, newspaper editorials, vivid journalistic accounts in those last pretelevision years—of what it was like "be there."

A six-foot man, a laconic U.S. Air Corps major said, could see from one side of Hamburg to the other. Graphic photographs showed what had once been the bustling modern Japanese city of Hiroshima, now

> four square miles of reddish-brown scar . . . range on range of collapsed city blocks, with here and there a crude sign erected on a pile of ashes and tiles ("Sister, where are you?" or "All safe and we live at Toyosaka") . . . and in the streets a macabre traffic—hundreds of crumpled bicycles, shells of streetcars and automobiles, all halted in mid-motion.[3]

Some of the people who thought they were "all safe" were beginning to notice burns that did not heal, skin turning patchy, hair falling out.

Britain had "austerity"—more grim, gray years of shortages and digging out of the ruins. In China, a renewal of the long civil war of the interwar years soon convulsed the land once more. From the Far East to central Europe, hollow bellies and empty eyes told a common story of starvation, disease, and human misery.

The world was hungry for peace in 1945. Ironically, the settlement that followed led directly to a new conflict—the long and painful confrontation known as the Cold War.

## The Peace Settlement

There was no great gathering of diplomats and heads of state to rearrange the world after World War II, as there had been at Vienna and Versailles after Europe's last two major military conflicts.

The Big Three met one last time later in 1945, at Potsdam in defeated Germany, but they were strangers already. Roosevelt was three months dead, and a feisty but not overly informed President Truman spoke for the United States. Winston Churchill was defeated for reelection in Britain during the conference itself, and Labor party leader Clement Atlee brought a very different perspective to the meeting. Only Joseph Stalin had been there before.

The Grand Alliance, deprived of a common enemy, rapidly came apart at the seams. Peace treaties were signed with the lesser Axis partners, and eventually with Japan, but not with Germany. Some of the most important consequences of the war simply happened, evolving out of provisional or temporary military agreements that hardened into long-lasting historic realities.

The territorial rearrangements that followed World War II were less complicated than those after World War I, but the dislocation of populations was much greater.

---

[3]John Hersey, *Hiroshima* (New York: Bantam Books, 1959), p. 86.

The chief postwar transfer of territory in Europe involved the westward shift of Poland's frontiers. This shift allowed Russia to keep gains made from the period of the Hitler-Stalin Pact and compensated Poland with a substantial slice of German territory. Even more significant, however, was the division of Germany itself into four separate zones of military occupation. The American, British, and French zones coalesced into the German Federal Republic (West Germany), while the Russian zone evolved into the German Democratic Republic (East Germany). The two Germanies, allied to the rival power blocs of the United States and the Soviet Union, yet never dismissing the possibility of reunification, would be key pieces in the jigsaw puzzle of postwar Europe.

Similarly tangled and unpremeditated territorial settlements occurred in the Far East. The Soviet Union declared war on Japan in the last days of World War II and quickly occupied Manchuria and the northern part of Korea. Manchuria was turned over to the Chinese Communist armies, who thus were strengthened for their final drive to power in China. The Soviets established a provisional government in the northern part of Korea, but the United States sponsored a new government in the southern part of the former nation. Once more, reconciliation between the two proved impossible, and the peninsula entered the postwar period as the two nations of North and South Korea. Within five years the United States would be plunged into a war in Korea, thanks to this division.

World War II generated as many as 25 million refugees, perhaps half of them Germans expelled from the Slavic countries of Eastern Europe. Resettlement was undertaken by the victorious Allies through displaced-persons camps and through an International Refugee Organization. Frequently, however, the refugees themselves settled things with their feet, spreading outward in a great postwar diaspora to West Germany and Britain, the United States, the Commonwealth countries, Latin America, and Palestine.

The United States, finally, occupied Japan in 1945. The vigorous program of demilitarization and democratization that the United States embarked upon at this time, coupled with Japan's rapid economic recovery, transformed that country in an amazingly short time. Here, as we will see, the postwar settlement led to a stable and satisfying outcome.

## Postwar Recovery

Economic recovery for the nations of Western Europe proceeded at first with agonizing slowness. The destructiveness of the war and a series of harsh winters in the mid-1940s slowed things appreciably. The loss of important overseas markets to the United States during the war and the growing rift between the United States and the Soviet Union after the war also contributed to economic sluggishness at the outset. In 1948, however, at the urging of U.S. Secretary of State George Marshall, the nations of the West inaugurated a massive European Recovery Plan combining European cooperation and self-help with substantial American aid.

Food, oil, coal, steel, farm equipment, trucks, electrical gear were soon pouring into Europe. The Europeans themselves negotiated an end to mutually destructive tariffs, balanced their budgets, brought inflation under control, and increased their share of foreign trade. By the 1950s, led by a booming West Germany gripped by what came to be called an "economic miracle," European production and commerce were surpassing prewar levels. Equally important, a successful model for continued economic cooperation had been created among the nations of Western Europe.

Two broad and somewhat contradictory currents transformed the politics of the western half of the continent during the postwar years: the rejection of organized communism and the acceptance of some socialist ideas and reforms.

Domestic Communist parties enjoyed a temporary wave of popularity and electoral success in the years immediately after World War II. Their prestige was heightened by their important role in wartime resistance movements against Nazism. Postwar economic dislocation also brought some votes to the far left. Thanks to vigorous campaigns by conservative leaders such as Charles de Gaulle of France and Alcide de Gasperi in Italy, however, the Communists were defeated in key election campaigns. They soon lost the potential for power they had briefly enjoyed.

Socialist ideas, by contrast, did better in Europe after the war. In Britain, the Labour party under Atlee unceremoniously unseated the great war leader, Tory Winston Churchill, in 1945. Atlee at once proceeded to nationalize large sections of the British economy, including coal mining, iron and steel production, and public transportation. In most Western European countries, government welfare programs were expanded significantly after the war, creating for the first time what British Labourites called cradle-to-the-grave security—the real birth of the modern welfare state.

In Eastern Europe, the Soviet Union played the central economic role filled by the United States in the West. There was, however, a basic difference; whereas the United States had grown richer during the war, the Soviet Union had been one of the most war-ravaged of the combatants. In the immediate aftermath of the war, the Soviets used Eastern Europe primarily as an economic resource for their own recovery. Not only East Germany but also Hitler's former allies in the Balkans were stripped of industrial and other resources. Close trade relationships were established, and joint economic ventures set up, both of which tended to work to the Soviets' benefit. The Russians seemed to be trying hard to encourage most of Eastern Europe to depend on them for manufactured goods, while serving as their source of agricultural products and other commodities.

After Stalin's death in 1953, there was some backing away from too rigid an insistence on the Soviet model in Eastern Europe. Agricultural collectivization, for instance, was cut back in some places, never implemented in others. There was a new stress on consumer goods, in the Soviet bloc as well as in the Soviet Union. Nevertheless, cut off by the Cold War from American aid and from lucrative exchange with the West, hampered by rigid ties to Soviet needs, to Marxist economic theories, and to the Soviet economic model, the Eastern bloc did not achieve even a modest level of economic development until the 1960s.

China had been locked in a brutal war with Japan for eight years by 1945, and had been torn by civil war, as well as by intermittent Japanese intervention, through most of the preceding quarter of a century. Nor did the end of World War II signify an end to China's agony. Under American pressure Jiang Jieshi might clink glasses with Mao Zedong for the photographers: but both men knew that their long duel was not finished. Recovery was thus not possible in China. The war was not over yet.

Recovery was quite possible, however, for China's great East Asian rival, Japan. Japan's war was definitely ended—and ended, as it turned out, in a way that opened the road to decades of even more impressive development for the most Westernized of Eastern nations. During the half-dozen years of the American occupation that followed the surrender in Tokyo Bay, the democratic tendencies that had been submerged by militarism in the 1930s surfaced once more. As in Germany, this second exercise in representative government "took" as the first had not, and in a few years Japan became as stable a working democracy as any in the world.

The Japanese industrial economy also revived with remarkable rapidity, though the nation's impressive economic development over the preceding century made this less surprising than the triumph of democratic institutions. The occupation also imposed some land reform, helping the most miserable of the peasant population, who had not shared in Japan's earlier modernization. By the early 1950s, then, Japan, like West Germany, was embarking on an economic miracle that would contribute substantially to the Western boom years that were coming.

## The United Nations

A peace settlement of sorts had thus been made, and recovery from the war was under way before the end of the 1940s. Even more encouraging, a substantial step had been taken toward keeping the peace in the future: the organization of the United Nations.

The U.N. began as a war-time alliance against the Axis—a cause to which most of the world had nominally pledged itself by 1945. A United Nations Relief and Rehabilitation Administration was set up as early as 1943 to provide basic material necessities to liberated zones as the Allied armies advanced. At the Yalta conference of the Big Three in early 1945, Roosevelt devoted much time to plans for a postwar United Nations Organization, which would both guarantee international peace and open up the world to freer economic exchange.

In the spring of 1945, with Germany and Italy defeated and Japan reeling, representatives of fifty countries met at San Francisco to design a new global organization to replace the League. The United Nations Organization, to be permanently headquartered in New York, was the result.

Like the League of Nations that preceded it, the United Nations had two central deliberative bodies to deal with major international issues, plus a number of special committees concerned with social, cultural, and humanitarian matters.

The most powerful element in the U.N. was the eleven-member Security Council. Five of its members were guaranteed permanent seats: the United States and the Soviet Union, the two most powerful countries in the world; Britain and France, holders of the world's largest empires; and China, the most populous country on earth. Each of these recognized great powers, furthermore, had the right to veto any item of business if it felt that its vital interests might be adversely affected. This special position of the great powers represented a realistic assessment of the fact that some nations *were* politically, economically, and militarily "more equal" than others. It was also necessary simply to get all the major powers into the organization.

The General Assembly grew in time to represent all the nations of the world. This larger body had less power than the Security Council. But it did provide an international forum in which the smallest country could air its grievances, and in which the collective feelings of the entire international community could be expressed by votes on large issues.

The U.N.'s many subagencies and committees concerned themselves with the social ills of the world at large. Under the broad umbrella of the Economic and Social Council were grouped such agencies as the World Health Organization, the United Nations Educational, Scientific, and Cultural Organization, the International Labor Organization, the International Trade Organization, and the Food and Agricultural Organization. In years to come these international bodies would mount campaigns to alleviate hunger, control major infectious diseases, bring literacy to the unlettered, and deal with a wide variety of other problems.

As established in 1945, the U.N. was dominated by the United States, which could normally depend on the votes of its European allies and of the nations of Latin America, where U.S. economic influence was strong. This situation would change over the years, as the Soviet Union acquired satellites of its own and as former colonial territories thronged into the U.N. with no predilection to support the Western powers that had once been their masters.

Global economic problems also preoccupied the Allies as World War II drew to a close. They held less formal, more specialized meetings in order to deal with some long-standing economic difficulties and to avoid some of the postwar economic dislocations that had afflicted the world after World War I.

Key decisions were reached at the Bretton Woods Conference, held in New Hampshire in 1944. Two longlasting international economic organizations came out of this conference: the World Bank and the International Monetary Fund.

The World Bank—officially the International Bank for Reconstruction and Development—would supply loans to poor nations to help them develop their economies. The original function of the International Monetary Fund was to prevent drastic devaluation of major currencies. Later, however, it became essentially a lender of last resort to underdeveloped nations.

Like the United Nations, the Bretton Woods agreements originally did much for American interests. For the next quarter of a century, European currencies were pegged to the dollar at a highly favorable exchange rate. But Bretton Woods also stabilized key aspects of the international economy between the later 1940s and the early 1970s—a boon to all concerned.

There were thus a number of positive consequences to the planetary bloodletting on the Second World War. The world did emerge from the ruins and begin to generate more prosperity and some potentially valuable political reforms at both national and international levels. But even in the earliest postwar years, people began to notice a dark side to the unconditional victory the Allies had won.

The problems, as we will see in the next chapter, had their roots in deep divisions among the victorious Allies themselves. The reemergence of these differences would fill the second half of the century with conflicts as deep and often as violent as those of the first half of the century.


## Summary

World War II, the most terrible of all wars thus far, resulted from the usual tangle of causes. These included the dissatisfactions and ambitions of the more authoritarian powers—Germany, Japan, Italy, and Russia—and the weakness of the leaders of the liberal West—notably Britain, France, and the United States. Through the 1930s, a series of international crises in East Asia, North Africa, and several European countries built toward a final confrontation over Poland in 1939. Hitler's invasion of that country finally led Britain and France to declare war on Germany, beginning the second global conflict of the century.

The war began with a Nazi *Blitzkrieg* of Poland, undertaken in alliance with Communist Russia. After a winter lull, Hitler launched a second series of lightning invasions, this time in Western Europe, resulting in the defeat of France, Belgium, the Netherlands, and most of Scandinavia. German efforts to overwhelm Britain by air and submarine attacks failed, however.

The totalitarian alliance made two crucial errors in 1941. Hitler's armies invaded Russia, only to be stopped at the very outskirts in Moscow. The Japanese attacked the Pacific colonies of the battered Western powers, including those of the United States. The Soviet Union and the United States were thus brought into the war against the Axis powers.

The tide turned in favor of the Allies in 1942. In that year the British stopped the Germans short of the Suez Canal in Egypt, the Russians destroyed a besieging German army at Stalingrad, and the United States shattered two Japanese fleets in the Pacific and began to regain a foothold in the islands. Allied troops also invaded Italy, which became the first Axis power to surrender.

By 1944 the Russians were driving the Germans back across Europe, and the Japanese were in retreat in the Far East. A huge invasion fleet put American, British, and Canadian armies ashore in France. Hitler's Germany was crushed between advancing Russian and Anglo-American forces in 1945. In the Pacific, an American island-hopping campaign put their bombers within range of Japan, and two atomic bombs finally forced the last Axis partner to surrender in August 1945.

Peace was cobbled together without benefit of a major international conference, and a new global organization, the United Nations, replaced the League. Parts of the world at least recovered from the enormous ravages of the war more rapidly than expected. But the victorious Allies soon divided into rival camps, laying the foundations for more conflicts to come.

## SUGGESTED READING

Ambrose, S. *Citizen Soldiers.* New York: Simon & Schuster, 1997. Up-close look at U.S. soldiers in the liberation of Europe.

Beevor, A. *Stalingrad.* New York: Viking Press, 1998. Solid illustrated account of the turning point on the Eastern Front.

Bigelow, B. C., and C. Slovey, eds. *World War II: Primary Sources.* Detroit: UXL, 2000. Brief but representative extracts from sources ranging from diaries to newspaper accounts.

Cole, J. H. *Women Pilots of World War II.* Salt Lake City: University of Utah Press, 1992. Brief account of the Women's Air Service Pilots and their role in the war.

Durnford-Slater, J. *Commando: Memoirs of a Fighting Commando in World War II.* Anapolis, Md.: Naval Institute Press, 1991. Colorful British memoir.

Duus, P. R. H. Myers, and M. R. Peatty, eds. *The Japanese Wartime Empire, 1931–1945.* Princeton, N.J.: Princeton University Press, 1996. Many essays see Japan expanding beyond its capacity to develop and control.

Harrison, M. *The Economics of World War II: Six Great Powers in International Comparison.* New York: Cambridge University Press, 1998. Compares economic performances of three major Allies and Axis Powers.

Hersey, J. *Hiroshima.* New York: Knopf, 1946. The famous book about the first atom bomb, as experienced by those who were under it.

Hough, R. *The Longest Battle: The War at Sea, 1939–1945.* London: Weidenfeld and Nicolson, 1986. Authoritative military history of the naval side of World War II.

Keegan, J. *Six Armies in Normandy: From D-Day to the Liberation of Paris.* New York: Viking, 1982. Vivid account of three crucial months of fighting in France in the summer of 1944.

Large, S. S. *Emperor Hirohito and Shōwa Japan: A Political Biography.* London: Routledge, 1992. The role of Japan's patriotic constitutional monarch in his nation's twentieth-century evolution from militarism to democracy.

Lee, L. E., ed. *World War II in Asia and the Pacific.* Westport, Conn.: Greenwood Press, 1998. Interpretive accounts of broad aspects of the war, including background and consequences. See also his companion "handbook," *World War II in Europe, Africa, and the Americas* (Westport, Conn.: Greenwood Press, 1997).

Liddell Hart, B. H. *History of the Second World War.* New York: Putnam, 1970. Military history of the war by a famous military historian.

Pogue, F. C. *Diaries of a World War II Combat Historian.* Lexington, Ky.: University Press of Kentucky, 2001. Up front on the Western Front.

Read, A., and D. Fisher. *The Deadly Embrace: Hitler, Stalin, and the Nazi-Soviet Pact, 1939–1941.* New York: Norton, 1988. Diplomatic history of the ill-fated alliance, suggesting that Stalin was less Hitler's dupe than is often assumed.

Tanaka, Y. *Hidden Horrors: Japanese War Crimes in World War II.* Boulder, Colo.: Westview Press, 1996. Overview of a long-undiscussed subject, focusing on brutality to Australians. See also G. Hicks, *The Comfort Women: Japan's Brutal Regime of Enforced Prostitution in the Second World War.* New York: Norton, 1995.

Thomas, H. *The Spanish Civil War,* rev. ed. New York: Harper & Row, 1977. Perhaps the best account of this much discussed "little war."

Weinberg, G. *A World at Arms: A Global History of World War II.* New York: Cambridge University Press, 1994. More than 900 pages, but authoritative and extremely readable.

 Please refer to the document CD-ROM for primary sources related to this chapter.

# CHAPTER 27

# THE COLD WAR
# AND THE AGE OF UHURU
# A Half Century of Conflict

## (1945–1994)

## A Glance Ahead: Crumbling Empires and Feuding Superpowers Reshape the Globe

The second half of the twentieth century saw a globalizing planet divided two ways. "East versus West" was the widely perceived reality of the Cold War, the complex struggle between two armed alliances led by the United States and the Soviet Union. "North versus South" saw Europe lose its overseas colonies, most of them in the global South.

It was a much more complex, bewildering, and oddly ambiguous struggle than the two world wars of the earlier twentieth century. The nuclear arms race that attended the East–West conflict made many people more afraid of war itself than of losing one. The much-feared World War III never came—but millions lost their lives in "little wars" around the globe.

The Soviet Union collapsed without firing a shot in the early 1990s. South Africa, the last major area of European rule over non-Europeans, saw a peaceful transfer of power from white settlers to the black majority in the mid-1990s. Once more, many hoped for world peace at last. Once more, it was not to be.

## East versus West: The Two Superpowers

### The U.S.A. versus the U.S.S.R.

The leaders of the two global alliances that confronted each other in the wake of World War II were the United States and the Soviet Union. Commentators were already beginning to call them the "superpowers"—great powers on a scale never before imagined.

It is as easy to point out similarities between these two nations as it is to point out their differences. Both were huge nations, with large populations—250 million for the United States, 270 million for the Soviet Union—and vast natural resources.

Historic differences, however, were even more important. Russia's political tradition has historically been autocratic, from the legacy of the Byzantine emperors and Tatar khans, through the heavy-handed authoritarianism of Peter the Great, to the totalitarian regime of Joseph Stalin. America's history, by contrast, has always included a strong element of representative government, from the colonial legislatures through the federal Constitution and an increasingly democratic suffrage.

The economic development of the two nations also differed significantly. Americans have been a prosperous and in many ways a progressive people. Russia, by contrast, was technologically backward and economically underdeveloped. The United States, furthermore, had inherited the Western European entrepreneurial pattern of economic development. Russia's commercial middle class, by contrast, had been small and comparatively underdeveloped, so that Russia's economic growth had largely depended on government initiatives and subsidies.

Russian interests had for centuries included a need for warm-water ports that would give the world's largest nation access to the world's oceans all year round. Soviet pressure on Turkey, which controlled access to her Black Sea ports, reflected this need. Russia had also had a history of feuding with the Germans that went back to medieval wars. Any Russian government was therefore likely to feel a strong national interest in a weak Germany. A divided Germany and the string of puppet governments that Stalin established in Eastern Europe after World War II satisfied these strategic needs admirably.

The United States, meanwhile, developed a historic set of strongly felt national interests of its own, most of them economic. From the beginning of U.S. history, New Englanders were traders, southern planters exporters. America's late-nineteenth-century foray into empire-building fits this pattern, as does America's eagerness to open all borders to U.S. trade and investment after World War II.

The two most powerful countries in the world, maintaining sharply contrasting world views and possessing national interests that could easily bring them into conflict, thus faced each other across a prostrate Europe in 1945. Paradoxically, however, the rival superpowers would never declare war on each either. All the fighting would take place in other, less developed lands, mostly in what came to be defined as the "Third World"—the nations that were neither East (Second World) nor West (First World).

## Postwar Gains of the Superpowers

Both the United States and the Soviet Union came out of World War II with substantial material advantages: territorial gains for the Soviets, economic ones for the Americans. Both sought to expand these gains still further during the immediate postwar years. In so doing, the two superpowers prepared the way for the decades of Cold War that followed.

Despite the heavy damage the Soviet Union sustained in World War II, territorial rewards were very impressive indeed. For the first two years of the war, Russia fought on the German side, acquiring parts of Finland, the Baltic States of Estonia, Latvia, and Lithuania, and other territories. From 1941 on, fighting on the side of the Allies, Stalin occupied most of the rest of Eastern Europe. And in 1945, he made it clear that he would insist upon "friendly" governments in countries located between the Soviet Union and Germany henceforth. In the case of Hitler's former satellites—Hungary, Rumania, Bulgaria, and of course Russian-occupied East Germany—the Western Allies could hardly object to the establishment of strongly pro-Russian governments. In countries that had allied with the West but had been overrun by the Nazis—Poland and Czechoslovakia—the Soviets proceeded more slowly, promising free elections but offering every aid to Communist candidates. The result, however, was the same; further expansion of the growing Russian sphere of influence in Eastern Europe.

American gains from the war were less obvious but just as real. As we have seen, these gains amounted to further improvement of America's already paramount economic position in the world. By war's end, the gross national product of the United States had nearly tripled, whereas those of its bombed–out European continental competitors had nose-dived. During the war, American enterprise had also pushed into markets and resource areas formerly controlled by Europeans in Latin America, the Middle East, and Africa. Even the Marshall Plan to help Europe recover economically benefitted American business because much of the aid took the form of American products.

After the war, while the Soviets were building closed zones of influence for themselves, America was pushing for an open world in which it expected to prosper. Out of the momentum generated by their respective World War II advances, then, came increasingly tense confrontations between the two superpowers.

The Soviet Union and Eurasia, 1939–1991

## Conflicts after the War

Western objections to the Soviets' emerging sphere of influence became particularly loud only in the case of the two Eastern European states that had been among the most lamented victims of Hitler's aggression a decade earlier: Poland and Czechoslovakia.

In Poland a British-sponsored government-in-exile was rudely shunted aside by a Moscow-sponsored one. Evidence accumulated that the Russians had also massacred thousands of aristocratic Polish army officers during the war. There were less substantiated charges that the Red Army had deliberately halted its advance in order to allow a Warsaw rebellion by supporters of the "London Poles" to be crushed by the Germans.

The takeover in Czechoslovakia in 1948 was an open Communist coup. It involved the seizure of public buildings by Czech Communists, who thereby forced liberal president Eduard Benes to cancel an impending election. And it climaxed with the "suicide" of the country's foreign minister, Jan Masaryk, while he was in the custody of the new regime.

The territorial division of Europe was completed by the division of Germany itself into two nations—the frontline states of the Cold War—in the heart of central Europe. As the Western Allies and the Soviets found it increasingly difficult to get along, these lines hardened. The Western zones were merged and eventually became the Federal Republic of Germany, one of the major Western powers. The Soviet zone became the German Democratic Republic, the westernmost of the Soviet satellites. Berlin remained a zone of conflict and testing in the middle of East Germany.

As these events unfolded, the United States responded with a series of economic, diplomatic, and military moves of its own. As early as 1946, George Kennan, head of the U.S. State Department's policy-planning staff, had described America's policy toward the Soviet Union as "a long-term, patient, but firm and vigilant containment of Russian expansive tendencies. . . ."[1] The first result of this containment policy was to create a massive concentration of American power, anchored in Europe but reaching around the globe, with which to counter Soviet expansive tendencies.

In 1947 President Truman enunciated a new diplomatic principle of American behavior, the Truman Doctrine. He promised United States help "to support free people who are resisting attempted subjugation by armed minorities or by outside pressures." Two years later, in 1949, the key American military alliance came into existence: the North Atlantic Treaty Organization. The NATO treaty guaranteed mutual Western action against any further Russian expansion into Europe. It also stationed American troops in Europe as part of a Western European NATO army in order to block any further Soviet move. In later years the United States supported similar mutual security arrangements in the Middle East, in Southeast Asia, and elsewhere, all aimed at curtailing the further spread of Soviet power.

The Soviet Union reacted by beefing up its own power in Eastern Europe. Economically, a series of bilateral treaties between the U.S.S.R. and its satellites was followed in 1949 by COMECON, an Eastern European equivalent of the Western European Common Market—which followed soon thereafter. Militarily, the U.S.S.R. expanded its army, hastened to develop an atomic bomb of its own, and in 1955 set up the East-bloc military alliance known as the Warsaw Pact to confront the Western NATO alliance.

What Churchill called an "iron curtain" thus divided Europe and the world in the middle of the twentieth century. With World War II barely into the history books, the globe

---

[1] "The Sources of Soviet Conduct," *Foreign Affairs,* 25 (July 25, 1947), pp. 566–582.

was once more divided into two armed camps, the antagonists girding themselves for the complex, involuted struggle known, again in a Churchillian phrase, as the Cold War.

## CONFRONTATIONS AROUND THE WORLD

### Conflict and Rebellion in Europe

In Europe, the first dramatic confrontation between the United States and the Soviet Union was the Berlin blockade of 1948–1949. This dangerous encounter grew out of a dispute over a currency reform introduced in the Western zones of occupied Berlin—part of a series of moves that the Soviets interpreted as an effort to make Berlin a showcase for West German economic recovery. In hopes of forcing the Western Allies out of the old German capital entirely, the Soviets closed all roads and railways across Russian-occupied East Germany into Berlin. The Allies, however, took up the challenge. They proceeded to supply the Western zones of the city entirely by air for almost a year, until the Russians ended their blockade.

In 1961 the Soviets stirred up a new crisis by building a wall dividing the city of Berlin in half in order to close off an embarrassing and debilitating drain of East German emigrants into booming West Germany. In the long run, the Berlin Wall became a propaganda victory for the West, however—a dramatic symbol of the economic and political failures of the East.

The Yugoslav defection from the Stalinist system represented a clear net loss to the new Russian East European empire. Heavy-handed Soviet efforts to reshape Yugoslavia economically and militarily in the image of Stalin's Russia had alienated the Yugoslav Communists. The expulsion of Marshall Tito, Yugoslavia's partisan hero and postwar ruler, from the ranks of international Communism proved to be the straw that broke the Russo-Yugoslav alliance. The Yugoslav comrades responded by rallying around their leader. Tito became the chief international spokesman for the new doctrine of "many roads to socialism"—the view that each Communist country should choose its own path to the classless society rather than blindly following the Soviet model.

Elsewhere in Eastern Europe, continuing postwar poverty and the economic discontents that resulted from collectivization of agriculture, harsh industrial working conditions, and shortages of consumer goods all bred bitterness. Nationalism was also a factor, impelling the peoples who had fought Ottoman Turks, Habsburg Austrians, and Hitler's Germany—not to mention each other—to turn against Stalinist Russia as well.

The first of a series of rebellions behind the Iron Curtain exploded in 1953 with demonstrations in several East European countries. In East Germany, a workers' revolt flared briefly, producing scores of deaths in the streets and hundreds of executions thereafter. Vivid photographs of German youths hurling rocks at Russian tanks symbolized to many Westerners the nature of the Eastern alliance.

In 1956, three years after Stalin's death, an anti-Stalinist reaction stimulated new challenges to Soviet control in Poland and Hungary, both nations with strong nationalistic and anti-Russian traditions. Wladyslav Gomulka in Poland cut back on compulsory collectivization of peasant farms and on police repression, announced a new emphasis on consumer goods—and got away with it. Hungary in 1956 went much further—and didn't get away with it. Imre Nagy had attacked forced collectivization, police power, and shortages of consumer goods, and watched as mobs toppled Budapest's huge bronze statue of Stalin, tore down Russian flags, and attacked secret policemen in the streets. The Soviet

Union responded with a massive military intervention, shelling thousands of buildings, killing several thousand Hungarians, and driving many more into exile.

The 1960s, which saw a surge of youthful dissent around the world, also sparked discontent in Eastern Europe. The major anti-Russian revolt of the decade was the Prague Spring in Czechoslovakia in 1968.

Sources of tension in Czechoslovakia, one of the most highly developed industrial societies in Eastern Europe, included worker resentment of grinding industrial discipline. Equally important, however, were the demands of a new generation of technical experts and government administrators for the freedom to make decisions on a pragmatic basis rather than on the basis of party ideology. In 1968 a repressive older regime was replaced by a new Communist leadership headed by a more liberal party man, Alexander Dubcek. Dubcek cut back on police repression, abolished censorship, called for popular expressions of differing opinions, and unleashed a wave of popular demands for change, including multiparty democracy and withdrawal from the Warsaw Pact.

The Soviets responded with a military occupation of Czechoslovakia by half a million Soviet and other Warsaw Pact troops. Dubcek and the new leadership were removed from power, and more refugees crossed the frontiers, heading West.

Yet another major defiance of Soviet-sponsored Communist rule came in the 1980s. Polish workers erupted, opposing new price hikes with an unprecedented series of strikes, plant occupations, and demands for an new labor union independent of the Communist party. The new union—called Solidarity—also demanded more freedom of religion, an end to censorship, release of some political prisoners, and pay raises. In 1981, however, the Polish Communist general Wojciech Jaruzelski abruptly imposed martial law on the country, smashed Solidarity, and arrested its leaders or drove them underground. No Soviet intervention was required.

### Revolution in Latin America

In Latin America, meanwhile, the postwar period saw a return to the sort of American intervention that had flourished in the first decades of the century. Peasants south of the Rio Grande had long lived with poverty and exploitation, both by their own landowners and military juntas and by the foreign businesses that drew substantial profits out of Central and South America. In the twentieth century. U.S. business replaced European enterprise as the primary developer—and exploiter—of Latin American countries. And in the second half of the century, Soviet patronage and Marxist doctrines inspired a new generation of revolutionaries to challenge the status quo. Nationalistic anti-Yankee feeling and communist ideology thus combined to produce a series of violent confrontations over the decades following World War II.

The Central American republic of Guatemala offered a textbook case of this familiar Latin American syndrome. Dirt poor and dominated by the United Fruit Company, Guatemalans elected a reform-minded—and strongly anti-American—president named Jacob Arbenz in 1952. Arbenz proceeded to redistribute land to peasants and to nationalize foreign holdings, cheered on by a well-organized Communist party in Guatemala. The U.S. Central Intelligence Agency (CIA) thereupon sponsored and equipped a Guatemalan revolution against Arbenz. The president was overthrown, his Communist allies imprisoned or driven into the hills, and a Cold War victory quietly chalked up for the CIA.

Perhaps the most striking case of U.S. political intervention in the affairs of its Latin American neighbors during the Cold War, however, was Washington's long-running feud

Fidel Castro in the Sierra Maestra. The bearded Cuban guerrilla leader opposed not only the Batista dictatorship in his own country, but also U.S. predominance in the Caribbean. To many Latin Americans, Castro symbolized not Communism but opposition to the vast economic and political presence of the United States in the Western Hemisphere. In the 1990s, however, an aging Castro defended Communism after Eastern Europe and the Soviet Union itself had abandoned it. (AP/Wide World Photos)

with Fidel Castro's Cuba—a Communist state and Soviet ally less than a hundred miles off the coast of the United States.

In 1959, Castro, a young Cuban lawyer turned revolutionary, led a ragged guerrilla movement to victory over the dictatorial pro-American government of Fulgencio Batista. The charismatic leader's rejection of Cuba's heavy economic dependence on the American market for Cuban sugar, his nationalization of American property, and his turn to the Soviet Union for trade and aid quickly soured relations with the United States President Dwight Eisenhower thereupon organized and John Kennedy launched an invasion of Cuba by fifteen hundred CIA-trained Cuban exiles in the spring of 1961. Castro's popular support and military organization proved stronger than expected, however, the invaders were captured, and no grass-roots rebellion materialized, as the CIA had believed it would.

The Cuban missile crisis later the following year (to be dealt with later) originated on the island but was carried on over Castro's head, as a military confrontation between the United States and the Soviet Union. Thereafter, affairs settled down to a long-term feud.

The United States imposed diplomatic nonrecognition and an economic boycott on Cuba, and persuaded most of the Organization of American States to go along with these measures. At the same time, however, Cuba served as a base for revolutionary attempts to overthrow governments in other Latin American countries. The United States reacted by providing counterinsurgency training for threatened Latin American states and won a proxy victory of sorts when Castro's right-hand man, the charismatic Che Guevara, was killed leading a guerrilla band in Bolivia in 1967.

A much discussed—if less decisive—instance of American interference was the covert support given to the military revolt that overthrew Latin America's first elected Communist ruler, Salvador Allende, in Chile in 1973. Chile, one of the influential ABC powers of South America (Argentina, Brazil, and Chile), was a functioning democracy with strong leftist parties when Allende was elected president in 1970. By 1973 the Marxists' drive to give Chile state socialism had brought economic chaos, a turmoil encouraged by official U.S. disapproval of Allende's policies. In September 1973, a military coup overthrew Allende, who died in an attack on the presidential palace, as did several thousand of his Chilean supporters. The military regime that followed, headed by General Augusto Pinochet, was widely condemned for brutal political repression, though it did restore Chilean economic prosperity.

In the 1980s, the United States once again intervened in a Central American revolutionary turmoil. Leftist rebels called Sandinistas—after an earlier revolutionary hero—had overthrown the Somoza dictatorship in Nicaragua in 1979. United States leaders at the time saw the new regime as a liberal one and even offered aid and diplomatic recognition to the Sandinistas. In the early 1980s, however, the strongly anti-Communist government of President Ronald Reagan detected an active guerrilla movement in neighboring El Salvador and a Communist regime on the tiny Caribbean island of Grenada, all supported by the Soviet Union and its Cuban ally.

Through the early 1980s, therefore, President Reagan moved to extinguish the revolutionary fires that appeared to be building in Central America. The United States put heavy pressure on Cuba and Nicaragua to stop supporting the guerrillas in El Salvador. The CIA organized an anti-Sandinista guerrilla movement of disaffected Nicaraguans and supported their efforts to topple the new regime. Then in 1984 the U.S. military seized Grenada, overthrowing the divided Communist government there and capturing or killing a number of Cuban military advisors in the process.

As in Eastern Europe, so in Central and South America, a basic pattern of conflict thus seemed firmly established. Clearly, neither of the Cold War superpowers would tolerate revolt in its own back yard.

## American Wars in Korea and Vietnam

In addition to these intermittent rebellions in Eastern Europe and revolutions in Latin America, the postwar decades also saw outbreaks of open war in Asia.

Here China's long civil war came to an end in the late 1940s with victory for Mao Zedong's Communists. Guerrillas challenged Western authority in Malaya and Burma, the Dutch East Indies, and the Philippines in the years immediately after the war. There was a largely American war in Korea in the 1950s and a French struggle in its colony of Vietnam about the same time. In the 1960s the United States launched its own escalating intervention in Vietnam, a bloody conflict that dragged on into the 1970s. And in the latter decade, the Soviet Union sent an army into Afghanistan.

Some of these struggles were fundamentally anti-imperialist rebellions, with or without a veneer of Marxist-Leninist rhetoric. The extent to which these wars were rooted in the Cold War, however, make the Vietnamese and Korean struggles and the Soviet intervention in Afghanistan part of the story of that larger struggle.

America's Korean War was clearly part of the larger Cold War picture. The ancient Korean nation, divided along the thirty-eighth parallel into American and Soviet zones of liberation after World War II, had in less than five years evolved into two countries. Both the Soviets' ally in North Korea, Kim Il Sung, and America's protegé, Syngman Rhee, strongly favored reunification—each under his own rule, of course. It was North Korea that acted, invading South Korea in the spring of 1950.

President Truman therefore responded by sending U.S. occupation troops from Japan, under General MacArthur, to Rhee's aid. The American forces, however, were operating under U.N. auspices with modest contingents from other U.N. members in what was officially described not as a war but as a "police action"—all very typical of the increasingly involuted patterns of the Cold War.

Militarily, the Korean conflict turned into a seesaw struggle up and down the rugged peninsula. In the beginning the well-prepared and well-armed North Koreans almost drove the South Koreans and their American supporters into the sea. MacArthur then recovered, surprised the enemy with large amphibious landings behind North Korean lines, and drove the aggressors back across the thirty-eighth parallel. He did not stop there, however, but pushed on north, overrunning much of North Korea and pressing too close to the Chinese frontier along the Yalu River. The Chinese Communists therefore intervened in their turn, sending massive "volunteer" regiments across the Yalu to help the North Koreans. The front finally stabilized close to the thirty-eighth parallel, where a truce was eventually signed in 1953—a nonpeace to end the nonwar in Korea.

The French Vietnamese war fits only tangentially into the broader pattern of Cold War conflict. The large majority of the Vietminh guerrillas who fought their former French overlords from shortly after World War II until 1954 were simply Vietnamese anti-imperialists. But their leader, Ho Chi Minh, and many of his cadres were Marxists as well as Vietnamese nationalists, and the Communist government they established in North Vietnam was welcomed as a Soviet ally.

Within a few years of Ho Chi Minh's victory over France and his establishment in power in Hanoi, guerrillas appeared in the jungles of South Vietnam. Their goal was the overthrow of the Saigon government headed by the pro-French Ngo Dinh Diem and his ambitious family. Diem was undemocratic and authoritarian, and the initial guerrilla revolt seems to have been the work of South Vietnamese chafing under his rule.

The United States sent advisors, supplies, and finally troops to help Diem resist what American leaders saw as Communist imperialism. North Vietnam sent supplies and then troops to support the South Vietnamese guerrillas, and in time essentially assumed command of the war. The Soviet Union, and to a lesser extent China, supplied war materiel to North Vietnam.

By the later 1960s, the war had become primarily a contest between the North Vietnamese army and a half-million-man U.S. Expeditionary Force, each side with its own South Vietnamese auxiliaries. The Americans carried open warfare into the neighboring states of Cambodia and Laos, which North Vietnam had been using as supply routes to the south. The war cost perhaps a million lives and resulted in brutal devastation in the villages of Vietnam.

In the end, the unpopularity of the long war in the United States led to the withdrawal of its troops in 1973. In 1975 North Vietnamese armies overran the south, and soon thereafter South Vietnam was absorbed into a single unified Vietnam ruled from Hanoi, as in precolonial times.

In the broad perspective of Asian history, Vietnam's reemergence as an important second-level power in South-east Asia was perhaps to be expected. From the point of view of the Cold War, however, the outcome was a clear setback for the West.

### Russia's War in Afghanistan

A major setback for the Soviet side came in the 1980s in the Central Asian nation of Afghanistan. This mountainous, sparsely populated land on the southern fringe of the U.S.S.R. became the target of a major Soviet military incursion at the end of the 1970s.

A Soviet-supported regime in Kabul, the Afghan capital, had pushed modernization—and secularization—too far and too fast for the deeply conservative, notoriously combative Muslim villagers. By the end of the 1970s, a guerrilla revolt led by Muslim fundamentalists threatened to topple the pro-Russian government of Afghanistan. In a swift airborne assault late in 1979, therefore, Soviet troops occupied the capital and engineered a coup that left their own former client ruler in Kabul dead and a new and apparently more moderate pro-Soviet leader in his stead.

The rebellion, however, remained to be crushed—no easy task in the mountains of Afghanistan. Like the American war in Vietnam, Russia's new Afghan war pitted modern firepower against guerrillas who swam in the peasant sea. Although between two and three million Afghans were driven into exile in Pakistan, this war also proved difficult for the superpower to win. And then, in the mid-1980s, the American CIA began to provide covert aid, training, and weapons, including anti-aircraft missiles to the Afghan Mujahedeen. After taking heavy casualties, the Soviets pulled out of Afghanistan as the United States had exited Vietnam, leaving a friendly government in power that—again as in Vietnam—was soon overthrown by its Afghan enemies.

## Confrontation between the Superpowers

The most dangerous conflicts for the world, however, were the Cold War confrontations between the United States and the Soviet Union. Armed with a nightmarish array of science-fiction weaponry, the two superpowers repeatedly seemed to threaten the futures of all peoples with their willingness to risk "Mutually Assured Destruction" in defense of their conflicting interests and ideals. And the tensest of these threatened conflicts was almost certainly the Cuban missile crisis of 1962.

For most of the 1950s, Stalin's Soviet successor, Nikita Khrushchev, and U.S. President Dwight Eisenhower managed to avoid major clashes, allowing their nations to recover from the tensions of the Stalin and Truman years. Then in 1960 the Russians shot down an American U-2 spy plane over the heart of the Soviet Union. When President Eisenhower refused to apologize for this violation of Soviet air space, Khrushchev walked out of a U.S.–Soviet meeting in Paris. It was the beginning of a very tense period in Russo–American relations.

President John F. Kennedy came to office in 1961 with an image of youth and vigor. His first year in office, however, saw a jarring series of American setbacks.

The CIA-organized invasion of Fidel Castro's Cuba failed that year, as the invading Cuban exiles were mopped up on the beaches of the Bay of Pigs. And in beleaguered Berlin later in 1961, the Berlin Wall went up—a challenge that went unanswered by the United States. Kennedy was thus put in the position of having to prove that he could prevent the Soviets from working their will in the world.

Kennedy's chance came the following year, in the Cuban missile crisis of October 1962. Khrushchev, it seems, was also under pressure at home to prove himself as tough with the Americans as Stalin had been. American missile strength was rapidly outdistancing that of the Soviet Union in the early 1960s, and the technological superiority of the West revealed by the U-2 rankled the Soviet leader's Kremlin colleagues. Khrushchev therefore followed up the American humiliation at the Bay of Pigs by responding to Castro's pleas for more support by secretly stationing Soviet missiles in Cuba—only ninety miles away from the American mainland across the Florida straits.

When U-2 reconnaissance photos of Cuba revealed the new Soviet installations, Kennedy took the United States to the brink of war with the Soviets in order to get them out. The American president rallied the Organization of American States and as many Western European allies as he could, put the U.S. military on alert—nuclear bombers in the air, missiles ready to fire—and established a naval blockade around the island of Cuba. More Soviet missiles were already on their way. Kennedy declared that they must be called back, and that those already in place must be removed or face American military action. Privately, he offered assurances that there would be no more invasions of Cuba, and even that some American missiles aimed at the Soviet Union would be redeployed elsewhere.

For a tense week, the world was on the edge. Then the Soviets agreed to remove their weapons from the Western Hemisphere, and the crisis passed. But it left Soviet military leaders determined to overtake the United States in missiles and nuclear warheads—a goal they would achieve in the years that followed that most perilous of Cold War confrontations.

## THE END OF THE COLD WAR

### Coexistence and Détente

Over four decades, then, the Cold War brought the world rebellions, revolutions, wars, and confrontation between the superpowers. The Cold War also, however, turned out to be much more subtle and complicated than a survey of these open clashes might suggest. And in the end, the conflict terminated—dramatically enough, but without the final showdown many had feared.

There was, however, a wide range of nonmilitary contention between the the United States and the Soviet Union. There were propaganda broadsides aimed at their own people and at "world opinion." There was espionage of all sorts, from the most sophisticated electronic gear to old-fashioned spying. There was intense technological and economic competition, ranging from the battle to see who could produce the most tungsten or toothbrushes to the race to the moon. And there was, of course, the unending arms race, to which we will turn presently.

Accompanying these varied forms of competition, however, were repeated attempts to improve relations between America and the Soviet Union. Under such rubrics as "coexistence" or *détente,* these efforts provided a counterpoint of hope that the world could avoid a third global war in the twentieth century.

A number of summit meetings occurred between the two states and a great many consultations between the foreign ministers, ambassadors, and other lesser officials of the two governments. Direct electronic communications between the White House and the Kremlin were set up for easy and quick discussions when problems arose. Trade relations, while fluctuating with other aspects of the relationship, repeatedly provided a splendid opportunity for America to market its habitual agricultural overproduction and for the Soviet Union to import lifesaving quantities of grain when chronically inefficient Russian collectivized agriculture failed to produce. Western Europe also developed lucrative trade connections with Eastern Europe and with the Soviet Union.

An important source of pressure for peace, however, came from the bottom rather than from the top. Citizens—many of them women—in a number of Western countries organized activist peace groups. At each stage of the Cold War, organizations like America's Women Strike for Peace testified, demonstrated, and defied their governments. They expressed hostility to the testing and deployment of nuclear weapons, to the Vietnam War, and to other dangerous confrontations.

And in fact a number of agreements were negotiated limiting arms development in the two superstates—though this proved in the long run perhaps the most difficult problem of all for the two armed camps.

## The Arms Race and Disarmament

The arms race began with advances in conventional—nonnuclear—weapons. In the 1940s the Red Army had overrun Eastern Europe. Under NATO, the United States and its allies established a multinational Western European army, which included large American contingents, to defend Western Europe against any further Soviet expansion. The Soviets responded in the 1950s with the Warsaw Pact and a Russian-led Eastern European army that was soon larger than the NATO force.

The United States, meanwhile, had been seeking to counter the Soviet Union's massive land power in Europe by surrounding that country with a ring of American alliances and bases. After NATO in 1949 came the Southeast Asia Treaty Organization (SEATO) in 1954, the British–run Baghdad Pact in the Middle East in 1955, and its replacement, the Central Treaty Organization (CENTO) in 1959. By 1960 hundreds of U.S. bases were scattered through thirty countries around Russia's perimeter, from West Germany to Japan. The American Seventh Fleet patrolled the far Pacific, the Sixth Fleet the Mediterranean, and others the Indian Ocean, the North Atlantic, and most of the seven seas. Soviet advantages in Europe—still the heart of the conflict—were thus offset by a ring of U.S. bases and allies.

Increasingly, however, the two superpowers came to depend on a range of awesome new weapons involving nuclear warheads delivered by air.

The United States maintained its monopoly of the original Hiroshima atomic bomb for only five years, until the Soviets exploded their first test bomb in 1949. In 1952 the United States exploded the first H-bomb—the vastly more destructive hydrogen or thermonuclear bomb, based on fusion rather than fission. The Russians tested their first H-bomb the following year.

Emphasis then shifted to delivery systems—ways of depositing these terrifying explosives on enemy military installations and cities. By the mid-1950s American Strategic Air Command B-52 bombers had an intercontinental range, as did their Soviet equivalents. The United States, however, had four times as many of these intercontinental bombers as did the Russians.

Then in 1957 the Soviet Union tested the first longrange ballistic missile—a rocket-powered bomb that used its motor to establish a ballistic path and then followed this arching trajectory over thousands of miles to deliver a nuclear warhead without any airplane at all. The United States rapidly overtook the Soviets in this field too, however. By the time of the Cuban missile crisis in 1962, America had more than four hundred targeted missiles to Russia's one hundred, as well as two thousand nuclear warheads to Russia's two hundred.

Through the 1960s the race went on. The United States pioneered in the arming of nuclear-powered submarines with nuclear missiles—an undersea force almost impossible to find and destroy, and one soon emulated by the U.S.S.R. Other new devices included antiballistic missile systems (ABMs) intended to protect cities and cruise missiles, which skimmed the treetops, thus slipping in under enemy radar detection systems. Early in the 1980s President Reagan began to urge the development of a new defensive capability, using the potential of satellites, lasers, and other "Star Wars" weapons as an ultimate defense against surprise attack.

International treaties were negotiated, and some signed, to control the escalating arms race. The first Nuclear Test Ban Treaty was signed by President Kennedy and Russia's Khrushchev in 1963. Two Strategic Arms Limitation Treaties (SALT I and SALT II) were signed in 1972 and 1979, though the second was never ratified by the U.S. Congress. In

1985 arms negotiations began again between the two superpowers, this time focusing on President Reagan's "Star Wars" initiative and on the Soviets' long arms buildup of the 1970s.

As in naval disarmament discussions between the world wars, there were technical disputes over definitions and equivalents, over what to count and how. Questions of verification of compliance also came up, and each side accused the other of violating agreements already in force. In the end, many years of dickering seemed to have done little to slow what to many began to look like a race to Armageddon.

Then, with a suddenness that astonished the world, the implacable Cold War conflict came to an end without a single weapon of mass destruction being fired.

## The Disintegration of the Soviet Bloc

In 1985 a new sort of Communist leader maneuvered his way to leadership of the Soviet Union. Mikhail Gorbachev saw his country confronted by a plethora of problems, from a stagnant economy to a draining intervention in Afghanistan. Vigorous yet flexible, Gorbachev was willing to break with the postwar policies, domestic and foreign, which he saw as responsible for the nation's difficulties. The reforms that he set in motion in 1985, as we shall see in a later chapter, further unraveled the fabric of Soviet society and weakened the structure of the Soviet state. Then, with dramatic suddenness, Soviet economic and political disarray combined with Gorbachev's flexibility to trigger both the collapse of Russia's East European satellite empire and the end of the Cold War itself.

From month to month through the astonishing year 1989, newspaper headlines around the world chronicled the stunning collapse of the Soviet hegemony of Eastern Europe. "Upheaval in the East" intoned *Le Monde* in Paris, and "The People Rise!" blared West Germany's *Die Zeit*. The cover of *U.S. News & World Report* trumpeted a "Communist Meltdown—The Crumbling Iron Curtain—The Soviet Economy in Ruins," while *Time* saw it as "The Big Break—Moscow Lets Eastern Europe Go Its Own Way." The nightly news on television was a sea of moving faces, East Europeans pouring across frontiers to the West or surging up the streets of their own capitals demanding the resignations of their Communist governments. Placards called for democratic elections, agitators urged freemarket economic reforms, and everyone seemed to want the Soviet troops garrisoned on their soil since World War II to pack up and leave.

To the amazement of a watching world, the East European peoples had their way. The borders opened; the governments toppled. First in Poland and Hungary, then in hard-line states like East Germany and Czechoslovakia, finally in the less developed Balkan nations of Rumania and Bulgaria, Soviet puppet regimes disappeared one by one. The opening of the Berlin Wall, symbol of a divided Europe for three decades, convinced most observers that Soviet domination of half the continent had effectively ended.

The Soviet reaction to these popular revolts was of course crucial to the success of the anti-Communist opposition movements. Gorbachev actually had to some degree fostered popular unrest by encouraging fellow Communist rulers to follow his example and attempt the sort of political and economic reforms he was endeavoring to achieve in the Soviet Union. Western analysts pointed out that the Russian leader needed an end to Cold War spending and an infusion of substantial Western economic aid to make his "restructuring" of the U.S.S.R. succeed. And to get this aid, he had to convince the West that the Soviet Union no longer constituted a threat, even to its East European neighbors.

Gorbachev first urged other Communist leaders to meet their peoples halfway with progressive reforms. When such offers failed to placate the mobs of angry demonstrators,

The Berlin Wall begins to come down early in 1990. First opened to free passage late the preceding year, this grim barrier dividing the eastern and western sectors of Berlin was chopped up and sold for souvenirs over the months that followed. Here East German border guards and crowds of civilians watch as the work of demolition gets under way in the shadow of the Brandenburg Gate, Berlin's traditional victory symbol in the center of the city. (German Information Center)

he ordered Soviet garrison troops to stay in their barracks while Communist governments collapsed. Within months, many Red Army units were on their way home, unceremoniously dismissed by the countries they had once dominated.

The "Revolutions of 1989" across Eastern Europe thrust up a bewildering array of new leaders, from the Solidarity labor union leader Lech Walesa in Poland to the avant-garde playwright Vaclav Havel in Czechoslovakia, both former political prisoners who within a year became heads of state. The major villain of the upheaval was Rumania's Nicolae Ceausescu, the only Communist leader to unleash the state security police on his own people. "Nothing short of death," Western journalists opined in November 1989, "is expected to nudge this dinosaur, in office since 1967, toward reform."[2] Two months later, in a still murky combination of palace coup and popular revolt, Ceausescu was overthrown and shot.

Perhaps the most dramatic change of all, however, came in the center of Europe, where the two sides in the Cold War had confronted each other most directly from the beginning. In 1990, the newly liberated German Democratic Republic—East Germany— voted to merge with the Federal Republic—West Germany—re-creating the united German nation after forty-five years of division. From a Soviet security perspective, the reemergence of the powerhouse that had twice invaded Russia in this century was the greatest blow yet. Gorbachev, however, accepted German reunification also—in return for desperately needed economic aid from the new German republic. West German Chancellor Helmut Kohl, who had orchestrated this remarkable coup, had his reward in December 1990, when he was elected to head the first government of the united Germany.

---

[2]*Time*, November 6, 1989, p. 50.

## The Collapse of the Soviet Union

The Soviet Union itself, meanwhile, was on its way into oblivion. This final chapter in the domestic history of Soviet Russia will be explored in more detail in the next chapter. But a brief summary of this definitive end to the long struggle between the U.S. and the U.S.S.R. will be appropriate here.

Essentially, the Soviet Union seems to have been failing when Gorbachev came to power in the mid-1980s. Gorbachev's attempted reforms revealed the economic, social, and political problems that beset the nation without going far enough to cure them. When U.S. President Ronald Reagan piled on the pressure, particularly by launching a costly new round of arms competition, the Soviet system collapsed under the weight of its own many inadequacies.

The Soviet satellite empire disintegrated in 1989. Over the next two years, Moscow abandoned one-part dictatorship and began to stumble toward a free-market economy. Most of the component Soviet Socialist Republics seceded to form independent states, and in 1991 the Soviet Union itself ceased to exist. The Cold War was over.

A great schism that had divided the globe thus came to an end in the final decade of the twentieth century. Another, considerably longer confrontation was also about to reach its climax in the 1990s too. We turn to this other great divide in the second half of the century—the collapse of Western Europe's vast overseas empires—now.

## NORTH VERSUS SOUTH: THE LIBERATION STRUGGLES

### Causes of the Collapse of the Intercontinental Empires

Even a brief survey of the European empires that crumbled, the major new nations that emerged during the decades after World War II, will give some sense of the scope of the liberation struggles that followed World War II.

Great Britain granted independence to many of its colonies in Asia and Africa. In South Asia during the 1940s and 1950s, British India, Pakistan, and Ceylon (Sri Lanka) were liberated, as were Burma (Myanmar) and Malaya in Southeast Asia. In the Middle East, British termination of the Palestine mandate led to the foundation of the new nation of Israel. In Africa, perhaps the most important British colonies to gain their freedom during the 1950s and 1960s were the Gold Coast (Ghana) and Nigeria in West Africa and Kenya and Tanganyika (Tanzania) in East Africa.

France, whose empire was second only to Britain's in size, more reluctantly liberated a number of territorial holdings in both Asia and Africa. In Asia, French Indochina—North and South Vietnam, Laos, and Cambodia—emerged from French rule as four separate nations. In Africa, Algeria led the way to freedom, to be followed by all the colonies of French West and French Equatorial Africa.

Lesser Western imperial powers also surrendered their overseas colonies, usually unhappily. The Dutch East Indies, the Belgian Congo, and the American Philippines were all freed after the war. As late as the 1970s, some imperial holdouts in southern Africa were at last liberated, including the large Portuguese colonies of Angola and Mozambique.

By the 1980s, only isolated enclaves of Western imperial control remained, usually by mutual consent, as in British Hong Kong. The major, much resented exception was the powerful and wealthy state of South Africa, still governed by transplanted Europeans in spite of its large black African majority; but in the mid 1990's, the black African majority attained power there too.

The great liberation dramatically transformed the global political picture. A total of ninety new countries emerged between the mid-1940s and the 1990s. Well over a billion people—a third of the earth's population—gained their independence of foreign rule.

The Swahili word for freedom, used in various East African colonies, was *uhuru. Uhuru!* became a kind of symbol for what was granted—or taken—in these ceremonies repeated in one new country after another across Asia and Africa, particularly during the first two decades after the war.

World War II opened the floodgate of the great liberation in several ways. Most obviously, perhaps, the biggest of all wars sapped the ability of some imperial powers, like France and the Netherlands, to hold their empires in subjection any longer. In other cases, this decline in imperial strength was an outright rejection of the whole imperial mystique. The British Labour Party, sweeping into office on a postwar electoral tide, had for years opposed imperialism. The Labourites were only too happy to undertake what the Conservative Winston Churchill had sworn he would never do—preside over the dismantling of the British Empire.

Even as World War II was weakening the colonial powers, it was encouraging their colonies to move against them. Perhaps it was the example of the Japanese, so easily overwhelming British, French, Dutch, and American troops in Asia in the early months of the war, that stirred the colonial peoples. The Japanese yoke did not prove to be any great improvement, but when they left, the Japanese sometimes left weapons behind—with suggestions for using them. When the Europeans reasserted their supremacy with rude force, their nothing-has-changed attitude further estranged their former subjects.

World War II also produced a basic new set of power relations in the world—one that was essentially favorable to the independence of overseas colonies. The war had put global supremacy in the hands of the two superpowers. Despite their differences, neither the United States nor the Soviet Union aspired to old-fashioned territorial empires. Both of them, in fact, opposed such colonial holdings on ideological grounds.

Finally, there were new winds of opinion blowing over the world in the decades after World War II. Idealistic statements about freedom in wartime documents such as the Atlantic Charter of 1941 and the United Nations Charter in 1945 were expressions of a point of view that was generally hostile to the holding of colonial peoples in bondage. There was also a widespread practical conviction that, in the end, almost all colonies would have to have some kind of independence. Europeans might see autonomy as still generations away, but colonial leaders thought in terms of a few years at most.

Under such circumstances, then, it is not surprising that the great empires began to come apart almost as soon as World War II ended.

## Patterns of the Liberation Struggle

The liberation struggles were a complex, confusing business, but some general patterns can be detected.

The leaders of the various movements for colonial emancipation tended to be both Westernized and charismatic. As Western-educated people, they could deal effectively with their European rulers. The internationally known poet Léopold Senghor of French West Africa and Kwame Nkrumah of the British Gold Coast colony (today's Ghana), educated in France and in Britain and the United States, had no trouble dealing effectively with Westerners. As charismatic figures, flamboyant personalities such as Sukarno of the Dutch East Indies (Indonesia) and saintly ones such as Mahatma Gandhi in India could move their own people to action.

The strength of many colonial revolts also resided in powerful independence parties put together by the new colonial leadership. These intensely nationalistic organizations were strongly centralized on the person of the leader. They helped to overcome regional, religious, tribal, or other differences within the colony, to articulate common demands, and to mobilize mass support for challenges to colonial authority. After independence was achieved, however, these parties tended to become a stronger focus for loyalty than the new nation itself. In some places, they became the core of one-party governments.

In some of the emerging nations, as we shall see, bitter and sometimes long-drawn-out revolutions were fought before independence was achieved. In general, however, a relatively low level of violence—by comparison, say, with the long revolutions of the first half of the century—accompanied the great liberation. This was, in fact, a striking feature of the final disintegration of Europe's huge intercontinental empires.

### Regional and Traditional Sources of Conflict

There were, however, other reasons for war and revolution in the postwar world that had little or nothing to do with the end of imperialism. There were causes rooted deep in the past and vendettas that were still powerful enough to move people to violent action—and sometimes to draw in the great powers too.

China's sense of centrality in East Asia, for example, and the Iranian desire to reassert Persian primacy in the Middle East went back thousands of years before the rise of the European overseas empires. Tribal politics was still important in parts of black Africa and could still spark bitter internecine conflict.

Perhaps most important, however, was the power of ancient religions, particularly the drive of a resurgent Islam. As many as a third of the member states of the United Nations could claim some degree of Muslim predominance. The postwar revival of that crusading faith contributed to clashes with other religions and ideologies from North Africa to Southeast Asia. The conflicts between Pakistan and India, the Iranian Revolution, and the long series of Arab-Israeli wars were all manifestations of this reborn spirit of *jihad* (holy war). Communists, Western powers, and Muslims of differing sects have all suffered at the hands of the new Muslim militance.

These ancient compulsions would also contribute to the tides of violence that swept the postwar world.

## THE WINDS OF CHANGE IN AFRICA

### Ghana and Algeria: Two Roads to Liberation

Africa, the second largest continent, was also the most completely colonized in 1945. Most African colonies, however, were not much more than half a century old, having been seized during the scramble for Africa in the late 1800s. Vigorous campaigns for independence began to bear fruit in the middle 1950s, with the liberation of Ghana in West Africa. By the end of the 1970s, almost all of Europe's African colonies were free.

Kwame Nkrumah, the leader of the emancipation movement in Britain's Gold Coast colony, was one of a brilliant postwar generation of African leaders that included Léopold

## Africa Since 1950

MOROCCO
1956

Ifni

TUNISIA
1956

*Mediterranean Sea*

ALGERIA
1962

LIBYA
1951

EGYPT

WESTERN
SAHARA

*Nile R.*

*Red Sea*

MAURITANIA
1960

MALI
1960

NIGER
1960

CHAD
1960

SUDAN
1956

ERITREA
1993

DJIBOUTI
1977

SENEGAL
1960

GAMBIA
1965

BURKINA
FASO
1960

GUINEA
BISSAU
1975

GUINEA
1958

SIERRA
LEONE
1961

IVORY
COAST
1960

LIBERIA

GHANA
1957

TOGO
1960

BENIN
1960

NIGERIA
1960

CAMEROON
1960

CENTRAL AFRICAN
REPUBLIC
1960

ETHIOPIA

SOMALIA
1960

UGANDA
1962

KENYA
1963

EQUATORIAL
GUINEA
1968

GABON
1960

CONGO 1960

CABINDA
(ANGOLA)

ZAIRE
1960

RWANDA
1962

BURUNDI
1962

TANZANIA
1964

SEYCHELLES
1976

ZANZIBAR
(TANZANIA)

*Congo R.*

ATLANTIC
OCEAN

ANGOLA
1975

ZAMBIA
1964

MALAWI
1964

MOZAMBIQUE 1975

NAMIBIA
1990

ZIMBABWE
1980

MADAGASCAR
1960

MAURITIUS
1968

BOTSWANA
1960

Venda

SOUTH
AFRICA
1966
(Majority rule,
1994)

SWAZILAND
1968

LESOTHO
1977

INDIAN
OCEAN

Member countries of the
British Commonwealth

Member countries of the
French Community

Dates indicate year of
independence

0        500        1000 Miles

0    500    1000 Kilometers

Senghor and Sékou Touré in French West Africa, Jomo Kenyatta and Julius Nyerere in British East Africa, and Gamal Abdel Nasser in Egypt. Like them, Nkrumah was part of the new elite of Western-educated Africans, having lived and studied for years in both the United States and Britain.

The Gold Coast colony to which Nkrumah returned late in the 1940s was already agitated by economic tensions and anti-imperialist sentiment. Strikes in the largest city, Accra, African boycotts of British goods, and criticism of the colonial administration were spreading. Turning his back on the older, more moderate African nationalist organization, Nkrumah set up his own Convention Peoples party (CPP) in 1949.

Nkrumah's CPP demanded drastic change—not administrative reforms in the colonial government but immediate independence—freedom now! Through the militant party newspaper in Accra, vigorous organizing in the villages, and his own charismatic personality, Nkrumah mobilized widespread support for the independence of the Gold Coast. Under this pressure, the British drastically accelerated plans for self-government, filling the colonial cabinet with Africans and holding elections for a parliament. In 1957 Nkrumah's labors were rewarded by independence for the Gold Coast—now renamed Ghana for the ancient West African empire—and by his election as first president of the new nation.

The other major British West African colony, Nigeria, achieved its independence three years later, and Britain's remaining West African colonies received their freedom soon thereafter. The black star on Ghana's national flag, as magazines pointed out at the time, had been the morning star of African independence.

The Africans of the much larger West and North African territories controlled by France gained their freedom in two very different ways. The black African peoples of the Western Sudan and the Guinea Coast won independent statehood much as the British colonies did, through political organization and shrewdly applied political pressure, as did some of the North African Arab populations of French colonies. But in the North African territory of Algeria in particular, France's colonial subjects had to fight for their freedom.

Algeria was politically integrated into the mother country across the Mediterranean. Many of its million or so French settlers had lived in Algeria for generations. But *colon* economic exploitation and political domination fanned the flames of anti-imperialist resentment among the Arab and Berber majority of Algerians. In 1954 the National Liberation Front (FLN) began a campaign of terrorism and guerrilla struggle to oust the French. The French poured in 500,000 troops and resorted to bombing villages, stripping the countryside, and treating prisoners brutally. A *colon* vigilante force indulged in random violence, outdoing the FLN terrorists at their own game.

By the time the struggle ended in 1962, a million Algerian Arabs had been killed. France itself had been painfully divided. General de Gaulle, called back to power and granted virtually dictatorial powers to end the anarchy at home and the long war in Africa, proved himself more a statesman than a nationalist by acceding at last to Algerian demands for freedom.

### Conflict in Kenya

East Africa differed from most of West Africa in that its fertile upland farm country had drawn much larger numbers of European settlers. These British farmers, who had taken over the best agricultural land from native Africans, resisted independence—and black rule—as vigorously as Algerian *colons* did. Two strikingly dissimilar factors, however, turned the tide against the settlers around 1960. One was an upsurge of terrorism by a secret society called the Mau Mau. The other was one man—Jomo Kenyatta—a Kikuyu with a London Ph.D., who became the leader of his people in their struggle.

The Mau Mau depredations, considerably exaggerated in the press, nevertheless led to many thousands of arrests, which further increased African resentment. Kenyatta, head of the Kenya African National Union (KANU), had no connection with the superstitious Mau Mau, though he was imprisoned for refusing to disown them. Between them, however, these two quite different manifestations of Kikuyu power did convince the British to move more rapidly toward freedom for Kenya. In 1963 Kenya became an independent nation, the tall, impressive Jomo Kenyatta its first president.

Other British East African colonies also achieved their liberty in the 1960s. In many ways the most notable of these was Kenya's neighbor to the south, Tanganyika, which became the country of Tanzania under the young African Catholic socialist, Julius Nyerere. Outside of Kenya, however, *uhuru* came without violence. Agitation and organization by leaders such as Nyerere and Kenyatta prodded the colonial administration, and freedom came more rapidly on this side of Africa too.

## Congo Crisis

The worst explosion of violence set off by independence movements in Africa south of the Sahara came in the immense central African colony of the Belgian Congo.

The Congo was totally unprepared for freedom when it came with startling suddenness in 1960. The Belgians had lavished much time and money on developing the hugely profitable copper mines of the Congo's Katanga Province. But they had done almost nothing at all to educate an African elite, train African civil servants, or otherwise prepare residents of almost a million square miles of rain forest and bush villages for life in the modern world. Then, at the first exploratory outburst of anti-imperialist feeling in the Congo, the Belgian government announced the independence of the Congo colony and left the arena to the Africans.

An arena it was through the early 1960s, as Congolese and foreign elements battled for supremacy. The main contenders were Patrice Lumumba, a radical with a broad vision of national unity—and Communist connections; Moise Tshombe, suave ruler of Katanga Province—with close ties to Belgian mining interests; and General (then Colonel) Joseph Mobutu, the military strongman who came out on top in the end. Outside forces involved in the escalating Congolese chaos included the Belgians, who sent troops in to protect their nationals; the United Nations, which authorized several African members to send in armed forces to hold the country together; and various colorful and brutal white mercenary troops, who fought for the highest bidder.

The Congo crisis of 1960 revolved around Tshombe's attempt, supported by the Belgian mining combine, to detach the mineral-rich province of Katanga from the new country. To keep from losing this key source of national wealth, Lumumba, the nation's newly elected prime minister, called for help, first from the United Nations, then from the Soviet Union. At this point, however, a coup led by Colonel Mobutu overthrew Lumumba—and then turned him over to his archenemy Tshombe. Meanwhile, intertribal violence flared in many parts of the country as village people settled ancient rivalries with modern weapons.

In the end Lumumba was murdered, probably by Katanga secessionists. Tshombe was overthrown in his turn, and the Katanga secession was ended by U.N. troops. General

Mobutu emerged as the strongest of the strongmen and ruler of the new country, which he renamed Zaire.

## The Long Struggle in South Africa

"The wind of change," British Prime Minister Harold Macmillan admitted during an African tour in 1960, "is blowing through this continent. . . ."[3] Those winds blew less briskly in southern Africa, however, than in any other part of the continent—indeed, than in almost any other part of the colonial world.

The liberation of the two Portuguese colonies of Angola and Mozambique was linked to the politics of their Portuguese masters. During the postwar years, Portugal was governed by the autocratic Salazar regime, a holdover from the 1930s which offered no concessions, either to liberalism at home or to anti-imperialism in the colonies. It was only in 1974, when Salazar's equally autocratic successor was overthrown in Portugal, that Angola and Mozambique were granted their independence as well.

The two Rhodesias—named for the celebrated nineteenth-century British South African imperialist Cecil Rhodes—reached independence almost a decade and a half apart. Northern Rhodesia won independence as Zambia, ruled by its black African majority under mild-mannered Kenneth Kaunda, as early as the mid-1960s. Southern Rhodesia, with its copper mines and determined English settler community, clung to minority white rule until the end of the seventies. It took an international boycott and a long struggle by two separate guerrilla groups—Robert Mugabe's Zimbabwe African People's Union and Joshua Nkomo's Zimbabwe African National Union—to win majority African rule in the new state of Zimbabwe in 1979.

But no amount of international pressure, guerrilla assault, or domestic resistance seemed to shake the grip of European settlers in the Republic of South Africa. There the winds were blowing all the other way during the postwar decades, for this was the period that saw the imposition of the system of *apartheid* on South Africa.

The colonial and precolonial history of South Africa is a complex story of peoples, rights, and freedoms in conflict. Though British colonists have dominated the state economically in the twentieth century, the Dutch-descended Afrikaners held political power. The condition of the indigenous Africans in South Africa had always been drastically inferior to that of the Europeans. But at the end of World War II the ruling Afrikaner Nationalist party set out to codify that inferiority in a system of discriminatory racial legislation reminiscent of the old Jim Crow laws in the American South.

Apartheid means "apartness," and the physical separation of the ethnic communities was clearly one purpose of the apartheid laws passed in the years around 1950. Europeans, black Africans, Asians, and others were to live in separate areas, be educated in separate schools, work at different jobs, find recreation in separate places. Marriages between Europeans and others were made illegal. Black Africans had to carry passes in white areas.

But it was, of course, more than a matter of separation. Black Africans were confined to the least productive lands, the least pleasant living places; the best jobs were closed to them; they could not be elected to parliament. Apartheid meant separate and *unequal*, and all Africa knew it.

---

[3]Speech of February 3, 1960, in *Vital Speeches of the Day* (March 11, 1960).

For decades after the imposition of apartheid, then, South Africa was caught up in a tragic, brutal confrontation, a struggle of guerrillas and counterinsurgency, of border raids and military incursions. South Africa was pitted against a handful of states on its borders—from Tanzania in the east to Angola in the west.

## Mandela for President!

Liberal foreign governments, however, increasingly excluded South Africa from trade, capital markets, and even athletic competitions to punish it for its racist policies. And a major breakthrough came in the late eighties, when a new president, F. W. de Klerk, offered peace to the black African militants who had resisted apartheid for so long. He repealed the racial laws of apartheid, legalized the outlawed African National Congress, and in 1990 freed the ANC's leader, Nelson Mandela, after three decades in prison.

Mandela had been a young lawyer and leader of the African National Congress's youth wing in the 1950s. After the 1960 Sharpeville massacre of black demonstrators, he had taken a lead in organizing a violent response by the ANC. Arrested and imprisoned, he had grown grey in a South African political detention center. Released in the early nineties by de Klerk, however, he revealed remarkable depths of understanding and strength of character. Under his leadership, the South African freedom fighters negotiated a plan for free elections and an interim regime that would protect the interests of white South Africans. In the spring of 1994, black and white citizens lined up together at polling places for an election that produced South Africa's first black president, Nelson Mandela.

Many problems remained, from widespread black poverty and a soaring crime rate to the need to encourage foreign investment and trade. But the immense potential of Africa's wealthiest and most powerful nation now linked to the rest of the continent by a black African government gave hope of better times to come.

Nelson Mandela, South Africa's first black president, raises a defiant fist. President Mandela's powerful personality won the respect of blacks and whites alike as he carried his country through a tense time of transition. (AP/Wide World Photos)

### Israel and the Arab World

One of the most complex colonial situations was in the Middle East. There anti-imperialist feeling and growing pan-Arab nationalism had led the British to give up control of Egypt and Iraq during the 1930s, though Britain retained control of the crucial Suez Canal. During World War II, Arab princes in the region established the Arab League, which, with British support, compelled the French to liberate Syria and Lebanon in the mid-1940s. In the 1950s, however, a nationalist revolt in Egypt overthrew the pro-British king of that country, and in 1956 the new Egyptian military ruler, Gamal Abdel Nasser, nationalized the Suez Canal.

The most explosive colonial problem in the Middle East, however, had to do with the British mandate of Palestine and the emergence of the modern state of Israel. This strip of Arab land along the eastern end of the Mediterranean Sea, the site of the ancient Hebrew kingdom of David and Solomon, had been the focus of the Jewish nationalist movement called Zionism since the nineteenth century. Encouraged by a British statement of support during World War I, Jews had begun to emigrate from Europe to Palestine in the 1930s. After World War II, survivors of the Nazi Holocaust poured into the British mandate, determined to establish a homeland.

The Palestinian Arab population, strongly supported by the Arab League, resisted these incursions. As violence spread across Palestine, the British attempted to work out a compromise, and the new United Nations voted for a partition of the area between Arabs and Jews. In the spring of 1948, however, Jewish leaders in Palestine, citing the U.N. resolution and depending on strong American support, announced the formation of the new state of Israel. The surrounding nations of the Arab League at once declared war, determined to expel the Jewish immigrants and reclaim all Palestine for its Arab inhabitants.

The 1948 Arab–Israeli conflict, the first of a series of Arab–Israeli Wars, looked to be stacked in favor of the Arab countries. But the Arab princes competed among themselves and were not as familiar with modern weaponry as the Jewish immigrants from Europe and America were. The Israelis, fighting for their existence as a state, unified and determined, not only defended themselves but expanded beyond the U.N. partition line, creating an even larger Jewish nation for the Arabs to deal with.

For the surrounding Arab countries, Israel has been a bitter problem ever since. This problem has been considerably exacerbated by the large number of Palestinian refugees—a million in 1948—who were not absorbed by the neighboring Arab countries and continued to demand the return of Palestine.

The new nation of Israel thus fought no less than five wars with the Muslim states surrounding it during the thirty-five years between 1948 and 1982. Militarily speaking, the earlier of these Arab–Israeli encounters were clear Israeli victories. More recent conflicts, however, proved costly and led to few detectable gains.

The 1948 war with which Israel's history began left the new nation larger than even its founders had expected. The 1956 war, fought by a secret alliance of Israel, Britain, and France against Nasser's Egypt over the Suez Canal, saw more Israeli military successes, though heavy international pressure forced the alliance to evacuate their conquests. The 1967 "Six Day War" was Israel's most smashing success, leading to the conquest of the Sinai from Egypt, the Golan Heights from Syria, and the West Bank from Jordan.

After the 1967 war, however, the leading role in the struggle against Israel was taken over by Palestinian refugee guerrilla organizations. Under the leadership of the Palestine Liberation Organization (PLO), the Palestinians stepped up border raids and terrorist attacks inside Israel. Israeli counterterrorist activities and harsh treatment of Arabs living within Israel's borders cost Israel some international support from this time on.

Later Israeli wars were less successful. The 1973 "Yom Kippur War," so-called because the Arabs attacked Israel on that Jewish holiday, led to Egyptian reconquest of part of the Sinai. Thereafter, peace initiatives by Egypt's new leader, Anwar Sadat, coupled with mediation by U.S. President Jimmy Carter, resulted in a peace treaty and the return of still more conquered territory.

Israel's invasion of Lebanon in 1982, finally, did result in defeats for both Syria and the PLO. But Israel's effort to establish a strong client regime in Beirut failed, and the Israelis eventually withdrew from Lebanon with little but a puppet Christian army in southern Lebanon to show for this latest war with its Arab neighbors. The struggle continued, on the domestic front, as we will see, but it was an underground war between Israel and terrorist groups like the PLO.

## Struggle for Power in the Middle East

Despite postwar Pan-Arab sentiment favoring Arab unity, the Muslim rulers of the Middle East proved to be among the more contentious of the world's leaders. Domestic discord further aggravated the tensions and sporadic violence that made the region one of the world's hot spots.

Two centers of conflict in the 1980s were Iran, power center for the militant Shiite sect, and Iraq under Saddam Hussein.

Iran had been divided into British and Russian zones of influence as late as World War II. Russia had attempted after the war to reach out for paramount influence through a strong local Communist party and the presence of the Red Army in the north. The main result of this effort, however, was to drive the shah of Iran firmly into the arms of the West.

For the next quarter of a century Iran was an American ally, ruled by a modernizing shah who spent his oil money to build up his country to something of its ancient preeminence in the Middle East. He left to his notorious secret police the suppression of both radical opposition and resurgent Islam. In 1979 it was the Muslim *mullahs* who pulled him down, mobilizing huge crowds of militant demonstrators to demand the shah's overthrow and to welcome an exiled spiritual leader, the Ayatollah Ruhollah Khomeini, in his place.

Militant Shiite followers of the Ayatollah were soon running the nation and shaking up the Middle East. Following Khomeini's dictum that "the legislative power in Islam is limited to God alone," the *mullah* leaders purged both American sympathizers and Russian-leaning Marxists.[4] The Ayatollah's supporters embarked upon a national effort to build an "Islamic republic," Women appearing in public were veiled once more, and religious minorities and leftist students alike suffered brutal persecution under the new regime.

In 1980 the new government came into conflict with the United States when a group of Muslim student militants seized the American embassy and held it—and its personnel—for more than a year of increasing tension.

---

[4]Ruhollah Khomeini, *Islamic Government,* in Nikki R. Keddie, *Roots of Revolution: An Interpretive History of Modern Iran* (New Haven, Conn.: Yale University Press, 1981), p. 207.

The Ayatollah's militance disturbed a number of Arab powers almost as much as it did the United States. Khomeini, like Persian Shiites of earlier centuries, talked extravagantly of unleashing a *jihad,* or holy war, against the "corrupt" Sunni states around him. The particularly pious Sunni state of Saudi Arabia, keeper of the holy places at Mecca and Medina, was much disturbed.

But it was Iran's neighbor Iraq that responded with force to the Ayatollah's challenge. This Muslim nation, which also used the Persian Gulf to export large quantities of oil, was run by the Ba'athist Party—dedicated to pan-Arab nationalism and to "Arab socialism," heavily dependent on an alliance with the Soviet Union, and ruled by the brutal and aggressive Saddam Hussein. Saddam, apparently seeking to take advantage of disarray in Iran resulting from Khomeini's Islamic revolution, determined to settle outstanding disputes, including a conflict over the Shatt-al-Arab waterway, by military force. Iraq's strike into Iran late in 1980 at first promised a quick success, thanks to superior equipment and military leadership. But the Iraqi invasion bogged down in a human sea of Iranian fanatics willing to die for the Ayatollah's *jihad.* The war dragged on until 1988, when Khomeini decreed an end to the slaughter and soon thereafter he died. The more moderate government which succeeded the Ayatollah seemed willing and even eager to come to terms with the West.

## India versus Pakistan

Conflict along religious lines also haunted the subcontinent of India during and after its liberation from British rule. After independence, Hindu-Muslim conflict led to a long series of confrontations between the new nations of India and Pakistan.

The Indian Congress party, led by Mahatma Gandhi and Jawaharlal Nehru, had spearheaded the struggle for Indian independence during the interwar years. Gandhi and the Congress party, however, were Hindus, spokesmen primarily for India's 350 million practitioners of that faith. But there were 100 million Muslims in India too. The chief spokesman for this huge minority was Muhammad Ali Jinnah, head of the colony's Muslim League.

When the newly elected British Labour government began to negotiate the final liberation of the subcontinent in the 1940s, bitterness between Hindus and Muslims was wildly inflamed. Rioting flared, civil war threatened, and in the end the huge colony was partitioned. Two nations, Hindu India and Muslim Pakistan, thus came into existence in 1947.

Freedom, however, only exacerbated the rioting between the two religious communities. Some 15 million Hindu and Muslim refugees abandoned their villages and headed for the new frontiers. More than half a million died violently or by starvation and exposure on the road. Gandhi himself was assassinated by a Hindu extremist who hated the Mahatma for his efforts to curb violence between Muslims and Hindus.

During the following decades, three wars were fought between India and Pakistan. Two were over the lovely, high-mountain northwestern Indian province of Kashmir, whose population has a Muslim majority. Despite these wars of 1947–1948 and 1965–1966, the area remains disputed and torn by guerrilla violence.

A third clash, in 1971, was over the isolated north-eastern territory of East Pakistan. This portion of divided Pakistan, almost entirely surrounded by Indian territory, felt exploited and oppressed by the central government in West Pakistan. East Pakistan finally rebelled and, with Indian help, founded the independent state of Bangladesh. During the prewar repression and the conflict itself, casualties mounted over the million mark, and 10 million refugees fled into India.

Tensions continued to sputter and flare. In 1998, first India and then Pakistan tested nuclear weapons—a disturbing development in the light of their long rivalry.

## War in Southeast Asia

Religion counted for less, politics for more in the struggles for independence—and after independence—in East and Southeast Asia. Ceylon achieved independence in 1948 with minimal difficulties and changed its name to Sri Lanka in 1972. Burma, however, freed the same year, was at once faced by revolts led by two distinct groups of Communist guerrillas and by various ethnic minorities, struggles that would drag on for years. In 1990, after a military coup, Burma also changed its name—to Myanmar.

The Malay Peninsula faced both communist-led revolts and ethnic rivalries so serious that independence there was postponed for a decade. British troops stayed on until the Communist guerrillas were defeated. Ethnic and cultural differences between the Malay peoples of the peninsula and the overseas Chinese majority in the great commercial center of Singapore proved harder to deal with. In the early 1960s, the colonial union between the two areas was therefore dissolved, and once more there were two nations where one colony had been: the country of Malaysia (most of the Malay Peninsula plus portions of island Southeast Asia) and the immensely prosperous little city-state of Singapore.

By far the bloodiest struggle for independence in Asia—and the most violent aftermath—was that in French Indochina mentioned earlier in this chapter. This conflict between French armies numbering up to half a million and Vietnamese guerrilla forces under Ho Chi Minh dragged on from 1945 until 1954, producing large casualities for the Vietnamese—defeat for the French—and the divided Vietnam whose conflicts would soon lure the United States into a Vietnamese quagmire of its own.

## China and Its Ancient Sphere

The People's Republic of China concerned itself from the moment of Mao Zedong's victory over other contenders for power in 1949 with reestablishing the Middle Kingdom's ancient frontiers and influence. Most of China's energies also went into domestic affairs: the staggering task of bringing something resembling a modern quality of life to a billion people. But Mao and his successors also found time to remind their neighbors that the old imperial giant was still there.

In 1950, the year after winning control of China, Mao sent the Chinese Red Army to occupy the high, thinly populated plateau of Tibet, which had been dominated by China in earlier centuries. Manchuria, Inner Mongolia, and other large areas were also firmly incorporated into the new China. In 1962 China fought a brief border war with India to readjust some mutual frontiers in the Himalayas; similar disputes were settled peacefully with Burma, Nepal, and Pakistan.

A major continuing territorial dispute was with China's former Communist ally, the Soviet Union, over the region along the Amur River border northeast of Beijing. A crucial sticking point in China's relations with the United States was America's support for the Chinese Nationalist regime on Taiwan, an ancient part of China that in Chinese thinking had to be reabsorbed sooner or later into the Middle Kingdom. And Britain negotiated the return of its colony of Hong Kong, the rich gateway to South China, to Chinese sovereignty in 1997.

Much of China's foreign policy, in short, had nothing to do with ideology, but simply to do with reestablishing the Chinese imperial position in the Far East. China's involvement with

Korea and Vietnam, two peoples who had in earlier centuries been the Middle Kingdom's most successful satellite cultures outside of Japan, illustrated this basic Chinese concern.

In both these countries, as we have seen, China supported northern Communist regimes in wars against large American armies defending governments established in the south of the two peninsulas. But in both cases China's concern was modified by the fact that both North Vietnam and North Korea were much closer to the Soviet Union than to their former overlords in Beijing. Only in this complex context of past Chinese preeminence and present Russo-Chinese rivalry can China's ambiguous role in the Korean and Vietnamese conflicts be understood.

China had no part in North Korea's invasion of South Korea, and the Chinese did not intervene in the struggle until American troops pushed close to China's own frontier along the Yalu River. Then, probably preferring a small Korean neighbor to an outpost of American power, Beijing entered the war and pushed the Americans back as far as the former frontier with South Korea before a truce was signed.

During America's long struggle on the Indochinese peninsula, China did supply North Vietnam with some aid. But Ho Chi Minh depended primarily on the Soviet Union for war material, and Chinese support was apparently always lukewarm.

Then, in the mid-1970s, while South Vietnam fell to the North Vietnamese, Cambodia and Laos were also overrun by their own Communist-led guerrillas. In 1977 Cambodia (renamed Kampuchea and ruled by the brutal Khmer Rouge regime) tumbled into a new civil war—and was then overrun by North Vietnamese troops. Laos also quickly came within Hanoi's orbit.

In 1978, then, the People's Republic of China seized upon the mistreatment of overseas Chinese in Vietnam as a cause for conflict and sent a "punitive" expedition across Vietnam's northern border. The ancient rivalry between the two thus flamed into the open once again. The brief incursion also demonstrated that China could attack a Soviet client state in Asia with impunity. The short Chinese incursion into Vietnam thus served as one more reminder of China's historic primacy in East Asia.

## SUMMARY

Peace was patched together after World War II without a great international peace conference. But the falling-out of the victorious Allies left much of Europe and Asia divided between zones of American and Soviet influence. And the crumbling of the European intercontinental empires, which began soon after the war, further divided the world.

Some aspects of the histories of the United States and the Soviet Union made rivalry between them likely if not inevitable. These two large and populous nations had different political traditions and patterns of economic development, differing interests and very different ideological points of view. The United States came out of World War II with a stronger global economic position than ever before, the Soviet Union with a sphere of influence in Eastern Europe and Asia.

The Cold War involved economic and technological competition between the two superpowers. It led to rival military alliances and economic organizations. It impelled the United States to take covert action against revolutions in Latin America, the Soviets to employ direct military force to suppress rebellions in its satellites in East Europe. It sent American troops into Korea and Vietnam and Russian ones into Afghanistan. And it fueled an accelerating arms race that at least once, over Cuba in 1962, came close to plunging the world into nuclear war.

Then, after forty years of conflict on all fronts, the Cold War ended as suddenly as it had begun. The rise of a new and more flexible leader, Mikhail Gorbachev, to power in the Kremlin and the economic and political deterioration of the Soviet Union, which proved greater than anyone had realized, were apparently the precipitating causes. At the end of the 1980s, Gorbachev reversed the policies of his predecessors, abandoning the Soviet empire in Eastern Europe, permitting the unification of the two Germanies, and seeking closer relations with the United States and Western Europe as his own country slid into chaos.

The decades after World war II also saw the collapse of the vast intercontinental empires constructed by Europeans over the preceding five centuries.

The causes of this collapse included the resentment against foreign domination and economic exploitation that had been building for generations in the colonies. These feelings were strengthened by European weakness of will and resources after the war, and by the fact that both the United States and the Soviet Union opposed old-fashioned territorial imperialism.

The great liberation that followed the war was violent in some places, as in Vietnam and Algeria; it was relatively peaceful elsewhere, as in most British colonies. A third of the world's population thus gained political independence. Asia and Africa thereafter joined Latin America in the vast bloc of politically free but economically underdeveloped countries known as the Third World.

The freedom struggles in Africa and Asia were followed by other conflicts on the two largest continents.

In the Middle East, Israel fought a long series of wars with its Arab neighbors. Muslim militance and the rivalry of Middle Eastern rulers led to a number of armed clashes. In Asia, Hindu India and Muslim Pakistan fought repeatedly. And in East Asia, China reasserted its primacy by limited interventions in Korea and Vietnam, as well as by the occupation of Tibet and continuing disputes with the Soviet Union over their mutual frontier.

## SUGGESTED READING

Ali, A. A., and G. N. S. Raghavan. *The Resurgence of Indian Women.* New Delhi: Radiant Publishers, 1991. Indian women in the liberation struggle and the new India.

Borer, D. A. *Superpowers Defeated: Vietnam and Afghanistan Compared.* Portland, Or.: Frank Cass, 1999. Stimulating interpretation of two key conflicts in the Cold War.

Brogan, P. *A Comprehensive Guide to World Strife Since 1945.* Lanham, Md.: The Scarecrow Press, 1999. Useful continent-by-continent survey of civil strife and international conflicts since the world wars of the first half of the century.

Clough, M. S. *Mau Mau Memoirs: History, Memory, and Politics.* Boulder, Colo.: Lynne Rienner, 1998. Examines memoirs of African combatants to describe the anti-imperialist struggle as they saw it.

Creveld, M. van. *Nuclear Proliferation and the Future of Conflict.* New York: Free Press, 1993. Urges that the nuclear "balance of terror" actually made the world safer during the Cold War and since.

Dupuy, T. N. *Elusive Victory: The Arab-Israeli Wars, 1947–1974.* New York: Harper & Row, 1978. Comprehensive, detailed survey, excluding only the Lebanon incursion of the early 1980s.

Falola, T. *Nationalism and African Intellectuals.* Rochester, N.Y.: University of Rochester Press, 2001. A leading African historian examines the ideas of Westernized Africans and their contributions to the liberation struggle.

Fields, K. *Revival and Rebellion in Colonial Africa.* Princeton, N.J.: Princeton University Press, 1985. African resistance to the Western-imposed social order. See also M. Crowder, ed., *The Cambridge History of Africa,* Vol. 8, *From 1940 to 1975* (New York: Cambridge University Press, 1984), which chronicles the high hopes of the liberation movements and their sometimes disillusioning aftermaths.

Gaddis, J. L. *Strategies of Containment.* New York: Oxford University Press, 1983. Balanced account of American policies in the Cold War.

Garton Ash, T. *We the People: The Revolution of '89.* London: Granta Books, 1990. Brilliant first-hand account of the East European revolts by a journalist who knew the revolutionaries. See also W. Echikson, *Lighting the Night: The Revolution in Eastern Europe* (London: Sidgwick and Jackson, 1990), another concerned journalist's account, featuring encounters with rank-and-file rebels as well as leaders.

Gleason, A. *Totalitarianism: The Inner History of the Cold War.* New York: Oxford University Press, 1995. Emphasis on the concept as it evolved from the 1920s through the Cold War.

Howe, S. *Anticolonialism in British Politics: The Left and the End of Empire, 1918–1964.* Oxford: Clarendon Press, 1993. The contribution of European opposition to the collapse of the empire.

Larson, D. W. *Anatomy of Mistrust: U.S.–Soviet Relations during the Cold War.* Ithaca: Cornell University Press, 1997. Focuses on the degree to which mutual suspicion kept the struggle bubbling along.

Nanda, B. R. *Jawaharlal Nehru: Rebel and Statesman.* New York: Oxford University Press, 1995. Strong defense of the Indian liberation leader's contributions.

Strayer, R. *Why Did the Soviet Union Collapse? Understanding Historical Change.* New York: M. E. Sharpe, 1998. Depicts a complex of forces, from the cost of supporting the satellite states and growing nationalism among the non-Russian soviet socialist republics to Gorbachev's own destabilizing efforts to reform the communist system, as root causes of the debacle. See also A. D'Augostino's more debatable *Gorbachev's Revolution* (New York: New York University Press, 1998), depicting power struggles within the Soviet Union as the primary source of the Soviet collapse.

Stueck, W. *The Korean War: An International History.* Princeton, N.J.: Princeton University Press, 1995. Authoritative diplomatic history.

Suntharalingham, R. *Indian Nationalism: An Historical Analysis.* New Delhi: Vikas, 1983. A synthesis of scholarship on the complex political, social, and economic causes of the emergence of national feeling in India under British rule. See also J. M. Brown, *Modern India: The Origins of an Asian Democracy* (New York: Oxford University Press, 1985), which offers a penetrating study of India's evolution toward democracy under British rule.

Talbot, I. *Pakistan: A Modern History.* London: C. Hurst and Company, 1998. Sees the roots of independent Pakistan's problems in the period of British imperial rule.

Thompson, R. C. *The Pacific Basin Since 1945.* New York: Longman, 1994. Wide-ranging analysis of conflict in the Pacific, rooted in both the Cold War and the anti-imperialist struggle.

Tinker, H. *Men Who Overturned Empires: Fighters, Dreamers, and Schemers.* Madison: University of Wisconsin Press, 1987. Profiles of leaders of the national liberation struggles, including Nehru, Jomo Kenyatta, and Ho Chi Minh.

White, D. W. *The American Century: The Rise and Decline of the United States as a World Power.* New Haven: Yale University Press, 1996. Surveys the views of American elites in government, business, the media, and intellectual circles on America's global role after 1945. See also O. Zunz, *Why the American Century?* (Chicago: University of Chicago Press, 1998).

 Please refer to the document CD-ROM for primary sources related to this chapter.

# CHAPTER 28

# SKYSCRAPERS AND SHANTYTOWNS
## Rich Countries and Poor Countries
## (1945–2000)

Arab Nationalism and Islamic
    Resurgence
Mounting Tensions in Asia

## THE POLITICS OF DEVELOPMENT: AFRICA AND LATIN AMERICA

Black Africa's Struggle
Latin American Revolutions
Political Progress and Economic
    Challenges

## DEVELOPED AND DEVELOPING SOCIETIES

New Technologies: From the Jet Plane
    to the Internet
The Helicopter Economy
Liberated Women, Restless Youth
Village People
Shantytowns
Poverty, Dependency, and Debt

## A GLANCE AHEAD: DEVELOPED AND DEVELOPING SOCIETIES DIVIDE THE WORLD

During the second half of the twentieth century, the domestic histories of the nations were shaped by a wide variety of policies—and saw as many failures as successes. International conflicts unrelated to either the Cold War or colonial liberation struggle also battered the world's peoples.

On the domestic front, Americans, Western Europeans, and a string of Asian peoples from Singapore to South Korea had "never had it so good" economically. Communist Russia and the Soviet bloc, by contrast, wallowed in stagnant economies that contributed centrally to their final collapse. China struggled to survive Maoist "reforms" until new leadership turned to quasicapitalist "pragmatism" late in the century. Latin America never seemed to live up to its promise. And many African and some Asian countries sank into deeper poverty and political chaos.

The world's peoples seemed to be divided between rich countries and poor ones, between a zone of skyscrapers, jet planes, and computers, and a zone where life was limited to villages and shantytowns, where enough food and drinkable water seemed like the limit of reasonable aspirations.

## STRATEGIES FOR PROGRESS: THE UNITED STATES IN THE AMERICAN AGE

### Power Structures

There were two sorts of political power structure in the developed countries after World War II. There were important similarities between them, as social scientists often pointed out. But the differences were real too—and important enough to have generated the Cold War itself.

The most striking similarity was that governments on both sides of the Iron Curtain were performing a great many more services for the governed than governments ever had before. Even in the free-enterprise West, public education, health care, housing, paved roads, streetlights, water and sewers, public transportation, police and fire protection, mail delivery, and a thousand more amenities of modern life were generally provided by national, state or provincial, and local governments. In the state-socialist countries of the East bloc, nationalized economies and central planning meant that all the office staffs of Western private business were government employees too—making big government even bigger.

The skyscrapers of Manhattan dwarf towers of earlier centuries. Built for the most part by great business corporations, these many-storied structures were as typical of the twentieth century as the palaces and temples of earlier centuries were of their times. There were slums, pollution, and poverty below these skyscrapers, but there was grandeur in them too. (AP/Wide World Photos)

Capitalist and communist thus had a basic pyramid of bureaucratic power in common. The significant political difference between them, however, lay in the degree to which the citizens were free of and could regulate the behavior of that power structure.

Western democratic governments came in several varieties. There were multiparty systems, common in Western Europe, in which coalitions of parties governed. There were also two-party versions, especially in English-speaking countries, in which two major parties competed for office.

Looked at another way, there were parliamentary and presidential systems. In the parliamentary pattern, modeled on the British House of Commons, executive and legislative power were merged, the prime minister and his or her cabinet representing the majority party—or coalition of parties—in the elected legislature. A presidential system, such as the varied versions to be found in the United States and France, put much more authority in the hands of a chief executive, who was elected separately and who could be of a different political party from the majority in the legislature.

All Western democracies, however, had two things in common: elected rulers and civil liberties. Periodic elections required political leadership to account to the people for its stewardship. Civil rights limited political repression and prescribed the basic freedom to complain about the way things were going and to organize political opposition to change them. In combination, the freedom to speak one's mind and the requirement that politicians stand for periodic reelection gave the governed at least some control over their governments.

One-party states put power in the hands of a single, usually autocratically run party. With the destruction of most of the fascist states in World War II, almost all the developed one-party states were communist—the Soviet Union and its East European allies.

In Communist countries, dispute over public policy was confined to party members, especially to those in the upper echelons. Elections were held, but since the ballot contained only the names of party-approved candidates, there was little genuine choice and very little public check on the policies and politics of rulers.

These politically authoritarian systems were strengthened by the lack of most of the civil liberties valued in the West. Freedom of the press, of speech, of the right to organize politically was seldom to be found east of the Iron Curtain. In Russia the brutal repressiveness of the Stalin years seemed to recede after his death in 1953. But dissidents were still routinely exiled to the provinces or incarcerated—sometimes in insane asylums, on the grounds that serious opposition to life in the workers' paradise must indicate serious mental disorder.

A survey of these varied—and variously successful—strategies for progress in the global North from the 1940s to the 1990s follows.

## Postwar Problems and Predominance

The United States, between victory in World War II and triumph in the Cold War, was the world's wealthiest and most powerful nation. Both of its chief defeated World War II foes, West Germany and Japan, as well as the once-predominant imperial powers of Western Europe, Britain and France, accepted America's leadership in the postwar period. Much of the rest of the earth fed the hoppers of U.S. industry with their raw materials, enriched America with trade or investment profits, or accepted American largesse in return for political or military commitments of one sort or another.

A distinguished historian called it the American Epoch.[1] Europeans talked about the *Pax Americana*—the American Peace—and some complained about American economic predominance and the "cocacolazation" of their ancient cultures. American influence was certainly greater than it had ever been before.

America's industrial economy was the most productive in history, and its agricultural sector would soon learn that it could feed half the globe. With Europe and Japan temporarily out of the running, the entire world was open to American exports and overseas investments. American democratic government was stable, even if the Republicans did some chafing under the long Democratic control of the federal government by the late Franklin Roosevelt.

Roosevelt's successor, bustling, sharp-tongued Harry Truman (in office 1945–1952), was to all appearances a very ordinary hack politician from Missouri, chosen as vice president merely to balance the ticket, now suddenly confronted with some of the most critical decisions in American history. But Truman managed the early years of the Cold War with vigor. He pushed on with the New Deal program, stressing full employment, higher wages, government-subsidized public housing, more social security benefits, aid to education, even a new campaign for civil rights for black Americans. And when in 1948 he ran for a second term on this expanded New Deal platform, he astonished everyone by winning.

The international tensions of the Truman years, however, generated domestic divisions as well—most disturbingly the wave of anti-communist witch hunting dominated by the ambitious Senator Joseph McCarthy.

The Communist victory in China, the Korean War, the speed with which the Russians built an atomic bomb, and allegations that spies had sold U.S. atomic secrets to the Soviets all contributed to this burst of witch hunting and scapegoating in the early 1950s. Senator McCarthy, generally condemned since as a demagogue seeking to advance his own career, seized upon the theory of an all-powerful "international communist conspiracy" to explain a wide range of disturbing phenomena, from the New Deal to the Cold War.

McCarthy's extravagant charges ruined careers and smeared reputations, especially in the foreign service, with accusations of communist sympathies or affiliation. American courts convicted a handful of Russian agents, and two government employees, Julius and Ethel Rosenberg, were executed for giving atomic secrets to Russia. McCarthy finally overreached himself by claiming that the U.S. Army was full of reds. Censured by the

---

[1]Arthur S. Link, *American Epoch: A History of the United States Since the 1890s* (New York: Knopf, 1955).

Senate, he faded from the political scene while the fires he had kindled expired in the calmer atmosphere of the Eisenhower years.

Dwight Eisenhower (1952–1960), the first Republican president since the New Deal, was a broad-faced Kansan who had become famous as the commanding general of the Allied armies in Europe in World War II. He knew very little about politics, preferred playing golf to reading position papers, and depended heavily on his cabinet, a body dominated by conservative big businessmen.

Nevertheless, as a self-styled progressive Republican, Eisenhower legitimized the New Deal simply by not moving to repeal it. He even made a few modest contributions himself, further expanding social security benefits and committing the country to the Eisenhower highway program, which in subsequent years criss-crossed America with 50,000 miles of superhighways. During Eisenhower's second term he reluctantly sent troops into Arkansas to enforce a crucial 1954 Supreme Court decision requiring racial integration of American schools.

## The Turbulent Sixties

The 1960s combined the social excitement of the 1920s and the political commitment of the 1930s in the most tumultuous American decade of the century. Two Democratic presidents presided: John Kennedy as inspiration, Lyndon Johnson as technician. But much of the demand for change welled up from below, particularly from the most rebellious younger generations in American history.

John Kennedy (1960–1963) was a handsome young Irish-American millionaire from Boston, the first Catholic president, and the embodiment of the youth and energy that America seemed to want in 1960. In fact, he accomplished little, at least in domestic affairs. His more substantive reforms were stalled by a conservative Congress, and he had neither the patience nor the political know-how to push them through. Then in the fall of 1963, Kennedy was shot by a neurotic young man named Lee Harvey Oswald. The new president, Lyndon Johnson (1963–1968), had all the political skills Kennedy lacked, and he used the national grief over the assassination to propel a final flood of New Deal–style reforms through the Congress and into law.

Medical insurance for elderly Americans, aid to education, public housing, aid for rural poor whites in Appalachia, aid for depressed, often largely black inner cities, and a hundred lesser reforms were passed. So was the most sweeping civil rights bill in U.S. history, an act that outlawed racial discrimination in all public places, in employment, and in other aspects of American life.

As a reformer, Lyndon Johnson brought the real climax of the New Deal wave of social change begun thirty years before.

Much of the excitement of "the sixties" in America, however, was the work of the demonstrators and agitators, most of them youthful, who swarmed the streets of the nation. Young Americans demanded further relaxation of already relaxed sexual mores, freer use of drugs, and other youth-oriented changes. In addition, youth organizations launched campaigns against unequal treatment for black Americans, against the "pockets of poverty" still left in affluent America, and against the Vietnam War.

Martin Luther King, Jr., spearheaded the struggle for civil rights for black Americans. A young black minister from Atlanta, King developed and applied the Gandhian principles of "nonviolent direct action" through marches, pickets, sit-ins, and other forms of protest to gain public and government support for black rights. In 1963 he led hundreds of thousands of black and white Americans on a peaceful March on Washington, and in 1964 his efforts were recognized by the Nobel Peace Prize. King was assassinated in 1968, but he had already done more than anyone else to create the climate of opinion that made possible the landmark civil rights legislation of the sixties. These laws and court decisions of the Kennedy-Johnson years forbade racial discrimination in employment, education, housing, transportation, voting, and office-holding.

The other great reform causes of the decade fared less well. Lyndon Johnson declared a War on Poverty, but his efforts to eradicate it fell far short of success. By 1968, John Kennedy' younger brother Robert had been converted to the cause of peace in Vietnam. But he too fell to an assassin's bullet, and peace was finally achieved by the Republican who was elected that year, Richard Nixon.

Other social movements also began in the 1960s and would pursue their ends, generally by less sensational means, in the following decades. In addition to demands for black liberation and black power, other ethnic groups insisted on an end to discrimination, including that against Hispanics from the primarily Spanish-speaking lands to the south and Native Americans. A gay liberation movement, dedicated to ending prejudice against homosexual Americans, burst "out of the closet" in the sixties.

Perhaps most successful would be a new wave of the women's movement, whose crusades went back to the nineteenth century. Politically quiescent since the triumph of the women's suffrage movement after World War I, this new wave of feminist protest dates from the appearance of pioneering books like Betty Friedan's *The Feminine Mystique* (1963). By the end of the decade of protest, new-wave feminists were demanding economic parity and raising women's self-awareness as vigorously as their grandmothers had demanded political rights.

## The Conservative Resurgence

Republican President Richard Nixon (1968–1974), former Vice President under Eisenhower and an established anti-communist politician, succeeded Johnson at the end of the 1960s. Nixon's foreign policy record was impressive, including the revival of American relations with China. But his overreactions to massive, sometimes violent political demonstrations led him to countenance a series of undercover schemes that violated the civil rights of those who opposed him, from street-radicals to the leadership of the Democratic party. In the end, Nixon, his vice president, and a number of his cabinet members and other key officials resigned under fire, many of them serving prison terms as well.

Of presidents Gerald Ford (Republican) and Jimmy Carter (Democrat), little need be said except that both were honest. In 1980 a former actor and two-term governor of California named Ronald Reagan was elected president—the most conservative man to serve in the White House in fifty years.

Reagan tried to repeal large chunks of the liberal legislation of the preceding half century. He sought to cut welfare payments, replacing expensive government programs with volunteer aid, and to cut taxes, putting more money in people's pockets to stimulate national economic recovery. But he also launched the most expensive armament program in U.S. history, pyramiding the national debt beyond anything seen in peacetime before. Nevertheless, economic recovery came on with a rush in the middle of the 1980s. And Reagan's religious supporters, calling themselves the Moral Majority, preached vehemently against such manifestations of the spirit of the sixties as sex without marriage and legal abortion and urged more religious emphasis in the schools.

Ronald Reagan was reelected by a landslide in 1984, and the boom years rolled on. But there were those who noted that, while production figures rose and aggressive entrepreneurs and wheeler-dealers did well under the Republican administration, other Americans did not always share commensurately in the long economic resurgence that began in the 1980s and rolled on through the 1990s. The per capita incomes of the middle classes rose only slowly, however, and the gulf between rich and poor grew.

## STRATEGIES FOR PROGRESS: FROM WESTERN EUROPE TO THE PACIFIC RIM

### Germany: Revival and Reunification

West Germany, the major European loser in World War II, was soon back among the leaders. The Federal Republic became the most successful economic performer among Western European nations and a notably successful democracy as well.

Forged from the Western zones of occupation, West Germany had most of the population and resources of the prewar Reich. With a new capital at Bonn, the new nation soon revived the democratic spirit of Weimar without its deep divisions and weaknesses. West Germany was fortunate too in its leading statesmen in the early decades. The conservative Christian Democratic chancellor Konrad Adenauer, former anti-Nazi mayor of Cologne, guided West Germany through its first fifteen years with skill and dignity. The first Social Democratic chancellor, Willy Brandt, who made his reputation as mayor of West Berlin, eased tensions with the Soviet bloc and kept the door open for future reunification with East Germany.

The Federal Republic's economic miracle, meanwhile, startled the world. It was built on billions of dollars of Marshall Plan aid, millions of German refugees from Eastern Europe and "guest workers" from other countries, and on the proverbial hard work and technical skills of the German people as a whole. The architect of the achievement was Adenauer's free-enterprise economic minister Ludwig Erhard, but there was a good deal of judicious government support for the upwardly mobile economy too.

To cap these achievements, finally, West German leaders engineered an astonishing diplomatic coup in 1990. As the Soviet bloc collapsed in Eastern Europe, the two German states, led by West German chancellor Helmut Kohl, were reunited into a single German nation.

The dream of national unification had burned strongly in Germans on both sides of the Cold War divide. When popular pressure forced the opening of the Berlin Wall in November 1989, champagne corks popped from the Rhine to the Elbe, and crowds from East and West Germany fraternized enthusiastically. Kohl, a big, burly, beer-drinking German with one of the shrewdest political heads of his time, moved quickly to take advantage of the situation. While his gifted foreign minister, Hans-Dietrich Genscher, soothed the nervous apprehensions of the Soviets and the Western Europeans, Kohl used the political and economic weight of West Germany to draw East Germany toward union.

In the spring of 1990, East Germany's first free elections since Hitler's rise to power resulted in victory for the chancellor's supporters in the east. The two nations were politically joined in the fall of 1990, and in reunited Germany's first elections, held in December 1990, Helmut Kohl emerged as the new nation's first head of state.

The years that followed, however, were not a happy time in the newly united Germany. The cost of rebuilding the East German economy along capitalist lines proved much greater than expected. Large numbers of Eastern European immigrants flooded into

Germany in search of jobs and refuge from troubles in their homelands, stirring up violent antiforeign agitation among Germans. Unemployment remained extremely high, and the German welfare state seemed to be raising the cost of labor and undermining German global competitiveness.

Chancellor Kohl's last crusade was to weld the European Community into a genuine Union. When he finally fell from office in 1998, Europe's common currency was about to come into use, and European passports would soon follow.

## Western Europe: Prosperity and Community

Both Britain and France had some wrenching readjustments to make after the war. The loss of the two largest intercontinental empires, the loss of primacy in international affairs to the United States and the Soviet Union, and the dawning realization that their defeated foes, Germany and Japan, were rapidly outdistancing them economically were not easy blows to absorb over the postwar decades. Both nations, however, played major roles in the formation of a new Europe during the second half of the twentieth century.

Britain, under Labour leader Clement Atlee, led postwar Western Europe into the comprehensive system of social services known as the welfare state in the later 1940s. Expanded unemployment insurance, old-age pensions, public-housing estates, new middle-class universities, and above all the much debated British public health service provided cradle-to-grave security for Britons. Soon all Western European nations had similar systems of social welfare for their citizens.

Two postwar French statesmen, Jean Monnet and Robert Schuman, were the architects of another major transformation in Western Europe's economic life during the 1950s and 1960s: the birth of the European Community (EC). Built around a tariff union popularly called the Common Market, the EC coordinated the economic policies of a growing number of Western European nations—fifteen in the later 1990s, with a lengthening line of countries eager to join. The Community was directed by a Commission and a Eurobureaucracy headquartered in Brussels, and by a largely advisory European Parliament meeting in Strasbourg, France. The organization guaranteed free trade between members and a common tariff policy toward outsiders. In addition, the EC and its affiliated institutions regulated the production of coal, steel, and atomic power and encouraged common policies on many matters, from migrant labor to social security. It was a daring experiment that led to unprecedented productivity, trade, and prosperity for all the member nations.

The world recession of the 1970s and 1980s, however, hurt the Western European countries also. Interestingly enough, it was Great Britain, which had led Europe into the welfare state thirty years before, that now set a new trend—toward conservative retrenchment.

Tory leader Margaret Thatcher, first elected prime minister in 1979, faced her very substantial industrial problems with a strongly conservative program. She cut back on services, turned some nationalized industries back to the private sector, and accepted massive unemployment in order to trim Britain's labor bill and make the nation internationally competitive again. Nor was the "Iron Lady" alone in her conservative crusade. The United States in the Reagan years, West Germany under Kohl, Canada, and other nations joined in the rightward drift of the 1980s.

Britain's Prime Minister Thatcher, after serving a record three consecutive terms, fell from power in 1990, rejected by her own party as the nation wearied of her unbending intransigence. But she had made a huge difference in the country she ruled.

## Japan: The New Economic Superpower

Japan emerged in the postwar decades as the most economically powerful nation in the world after the United States.

Democratic political institutions established during the American occupation guided Japan's destinies effectively. The conservative Liberal Democratic party won most elections, despite vigorous opposition led by the Socialist party. Neither violent student demonstrations in the 1960s nor some nasty political scandals in the 1970s and again at the end of the 1980s put any serious strain on the system.

Economically, Japan boomed. The economic miracle of its recovery from the war was only the beginning. The Japanese were early leaders in a system of government guidance of business firms into profitable export markets. This system—sometimes wryly called Japan, Incorporated—plus a hard-working and loyal work force, a frugal population willing to save and reinvest, and the sheer energy and drive of the people made Japan a tough competitor for the older exporting nations.

By 1990, millions of automobiles clogged Japan's roads, virtually everyone had a television set, and Japanese bullet trains were a world's wonder. Tokyo was larger than New York and had a worse smog problem than Los Angeles. Japan was home to the world's largest banks and was both the world's leading creditor nation and the largest provider of foreign aid for less-developed nations.

Japan had its problems. These included the need to import almost all natural resources, an extremely serious pollution problem, and repeated requests from trading partners for "voluntary" limits on Japanese exports—a serious difficulty for a country that prospered by trade. For defense, the island nation still depended above all on America's "nuclear umbrella." But Japan's remarkable postwar success augured well for an equally thriving future.

The 1990s, however, saw a startling and prolonged economic decline in Japan, as we will see.

## The East Asian Rim: South Korea to Singapore

The string of nations curving down the eastern end of Eurasia into Southeast Asia provided the greatest success story of postwar Third World history. The so-called "tiger" economies—South Korea, Taiwan, Hong Kong, Singapore—built productive, prosperous new nations, following Japan in moving from the Third World to the First World. In the early 1990s, southeastern China joined them in an unprecedented surge of economic growth.

South Korea recovered from the devastation of the Korean War of the 1950s. Ruled first by military men, then, thanks partly to the pressure of student demonstrations, becoming more democratic, the Republic of Korea also developed economically from the 1960s on. By the 1990s, industrial growth and export trade made the southern half of the Korean peninsula an enclave of prosperity on the Asian mainland.

Farther south along the China coast, the island republic of Taiwan had also recovered spectacularly from the painful years when Jiang Jieshi's armies, defeated by Mao Zedong, fled to the island from the mainland in 1949. Autocratically ruled, first by Jiang and then by his heirs, "free China" became another beehive of East Asian productivity, its citizens far more prosperous than their fellow Chinese in the People's Republic.

Still farther down the coast of China, Hong Kong, a small island with mainland territories across the bay, remained a British crown colony—and a crucial gateway to the world for Communist China. Chock-a-block with skyscrapers and some of the world's most elegant hotels, Hong Kong epitomized the success of modern business methods in the East.

At the southern tip of Malaysia, finally, the city-state of Singapore achieved the fastest economic growth of any nation between the 1960s and the 1990s. Lee Kuan Yew, for thirty years prime minister of this burgeoning community of overseas Chinese, created a model state. More than half the population owned their own homes. Connected to the outside world by one of the great national airlines and the world's busiest harbor, Singapore also showed what could be done with energy and brains.

All these small countries combined cheap labor with foreign capital, domestic drive with ingenuity, to build up light industry and commerce in order to give them a competitive edge. Then, in the 1990s, the backward Communist nations of China and Vietnam also opened up to capitalism and began to grow economically at double-digit rates. Strengthened by a second generation of "tigers"—Thailand, Indonesia, and Malaysia—the East Asian rim became the fastest-growing economic zone in the world in the 1990s.

### Peoples of Plenty: From Canada to Israel

Scattered around the world, mostly in the global north, there were other nations, smaller in size or population, whose inhabitants were also among the later twentieth-century's peoples of plenty. Most of these affluent countries were European, or were nations dominated by European-descended populations.

Some of these smaller rich nations had higher per-capita incomes than the United States. Switzerland, a world banking center, and Sweden, one of Europe's most highly developed welfare states, both combined capitalist productivity with the benefits of developed welfare states. Sweden in particular was also known for its extensive foreign aid to less-developed peoples.

In North America, Canada had been a major industrial power for much of the century. The huge northern nation depended heavily on trade, especially on massive agricultural exports to China and Russia. Canada also traded extensively with, and imported capital from, its even wealthier neighbor to the south, the United States.

Australia, the other continental nation of the older British Commonwealth, encouraged immigration and foreign investment, especially from the United States and Britain, developed its mineral resources, and inaugurated major water projects to irrigate its arid Outback. As the century drew to a close, Australia also took an increasing part in the economic life of East and Southeast Asia.

Israel benefited from the latest Western technology and from a highly skilled and motivated population, including many immigrants from Europe and America. The Jewish state also received large amounts of foreign aid from the United States and West Germany. Israel thus became the most developed nation in the Middle East, achieving an economic growth rate of over 10 percent annually throughout its early decades.

## DEVELOPMENT AND DISASTER: THE U.S.S.R. AND THE COMMUNIST BLOC

### Soviet Achievements—and Unsolved Problems

The Soviet Union emerged as the second most powerful nation in the world during the second half of the twentieth century. Politically, however, the U.S.S.R. of the post-Stalin decades remained repressive, a one-party state with none of the freedoms common in the West. And economically, the huge country's problems seemed to grow decade by decade.

Joseph Stalin had ended his life in a new wave of state terror, rapidly refilling the prisons and work camps after the heroic fervor of the Great Patriotic War against Germany. His passing in 1953 left no one capable of filling his shoes. But two strong personalities did rise above the sea of faceless *apparatchiks* to guide the nation through the next three decades: Nikita Khrushchev (1956–1964) and Leonid Brezhnev (1964–1982).

Both Khrushchev and Brezhnev were older men, party men, products of the Stalinist pyramid of power established in the 1930s. Both shared final authority with influential colleagues during their rule, and both depended on the machinery of the state and the Communist party. Both, finally, had to face the same recurring problems with the United States and the Eastern European satellites, agriculture, consumer goods, and Soviet dissidents.

Nikita Khrushchev's major political achievement was destalinization, the famous Russian Thaw of the middle 1950s. Soon after Stalin's death in 1953, the current head of the secret police was executed, the vast forced-labor camps closed down, and Khrushchev's famous 1956 "secret speech" to the Communist leadership denounced Stalin's "personality cult" and blamed the purges, the camps, the pounding the U.S.S.R. had taken early in World War II, and other misfortunes on the late Great Leader.

The Thaw did not last long, however. Khrushchev's own government clamped on the censorship again, and dissidents were soon being harassed and imprisoned once more. But their numbers were far fewer now, and the great fear engendered during Stalin's Iron Age would not recur.

The spirit of the Thaw spread to the satellites, however, triggering a revolt in Hungary in 1956. Khrushchev had to send in the tanks, thereby undermining his—and the Soviet Union's—new liberal image. He built up Russia's nuclear-missile armory from a small beginning, but he was still so far behind the United States that he had to back down to Kennedy over the Cuban missile crisis of 1962. In 1964, Khrushchev was quietly and painlessly forced to retire by his colleagues in the Kremlin.

His successor, beetle-browed Leonid Brezhnev, handled problems with methodical pragmatism. He dealt with a bad harvest by buying American grain, with a lack of high tech by contracting with French and Italian companies to build him plants in the Soviet Union. Brezhnev did, however, build up the nation's nuclear arsenal till it rivaled America's. Facing rebellion in Czechoslovakia in 1968, he reacted as Khrushchev had in Hungary—by sending in troops. He even indulged in a foreign adventure or two, including the Soviets' long, drawn-out intervention in Afghanistan, which began in 1979.

But there was more to Russian history from the 1950s through the 1970s than Communist party politics. During these years, the Soviet Union also faced a growing number of economic and technological problems.

As in the Stalin period, the Russia of Khrushchev and Brezhnev did best on large-scale projects. The Soviet Union forged ahead in heavy industry, replacing the United States as the world's leading producer of steel, coal, and oil. Most impressively, the U.S.S.R. was a pioneer in space exploration. A Russian was the first into space in an orbiting earth satellite in 1961.

Agriculture remained the Soviet Union's largest economic bottleneck, requiring the labors of up to half of Russia's work force (compared with 5 to 10 percent in the West). Partly because of peasant inefficiency and compulsory collectivization, inadequate grain supplies frequently required the Soviets to buy large amounts of grain overseas.

Beyond the problems of particular sectors, however, the Soviet economy as a whole suffered from a crushing paralysis rooted in the system of central planning and state control itself. Neither the Soviet Union nor any other Communist country matched the increasing affluence or the quality of life attained in Western Europe, North America, or other free-enterprise societies around the world. A structure of bureaucratic control, assigned production quotas, and fixed prices subsidized inefficiency and discouraged independence, innovation, and entrepreneurial energy. Consumer goods were often unavailable and frequently shoddy; housing remained in short supply; transport and communications were at Third World levels. When the multiplying costs of the Cold War were added to the inefficiency of the system, the Soviet economy declined drastically in the Brezhnev years.

## Gorbachev and the Soviet Collapse

Two old men from the Khrushchev-Brezhnev generation succeeded Brezhnev briefly in the early 1980s. But the subsequent accession of relatively young, vigorous, and thoroughly informed Mikhail Gorbachev in 1985 seemed like a real turning point in Russian history. At age 54, Gorbachev spoke for a post-Stalin generation more flexible and open than any previous generation of Russian leadership.

The new Soviet leader's initial attempts to solve the nation's problems emphasized two tactics: *glasnost,* or "openness," in discussing problems, and *perestroika,* or "restructuring" of Communist institutions to effect change. What this modest program for change mainly succeeded in doing, however, was something very different. Half-way solutions merely exacerbated shortages, bottlenecks, black marketeering, and confusion. And the new tolerance for free expression unleashed a torrent of demands for much more radical changes than the leadership had ever contemplated.

Many changes in fact came about. The Communist party relinquished its monopoly of power, and many local parties and other independent organizations sprang up across the country. The government was reorganized, creating a freely elected and sometimes rebellious legislature. Economic radicals demanded a complete abandonment of the planned economy and a return to private property and capitalist competition, though Gorbachev proceeded more slowly with economic than with political changes. Meanwhile, as we have seen, the Soviet Union abandoned the Cold War and the East European satellite states.

In August of 1991, an attempted communist coup, threatening to topple Gorbachev, failed in the face of popular opposition, and drove Gorbachev into the arms of the reformers led by Boris Yeltsin. Yeltsin became the hero of the hour by climbing atop a tank and denouncing the coup. Troops refused to fire on protesting crowds. Gorbachev was released, and the conspiracy collapsed.

The coup that failed brought down the last vestiges of the Soviet system. Communist party headquarters across the country were padlocked, the Baltic states were allowed to secede, and the centralized Soviet Union was reorganized as a loose confederation of sovereign republics. At Christmas 1991, Gorbachev officially resigned as president of the defunct Soviet Union. Boris Yeltsin, as president of the Russian Republic, was the most powerful individual in the Commonwealth of Independent States, which replaced the U.S.S.R.

## Eastern Europe: From Slow Growth to Rebirth

Eastern Europe did not reach the levels of productivity or per-capita income achieved in Western Europe. But industrial productivity did rise, and compared to Soviet Russia, such nations as East Germany, Hungary, and Czechoslovakia were doing very well.

The standard that East Europeans used to judge their progress, however, was not the U.S.S.R. but Western Europe, which was rapidly becoming the most populous center of affluence on the globe. As the years passed, Eastern Europeans increasingly resented the political authoritarianism, economic inefficiency, and technological backwardness of the Soviet bloc.

As we have seen, the year 1989 was the year of the East European revolutions. First came the Polish government's decision to recognize and deal with the long-out-lawed Solidarity movement, followed by Hungary's recognition of the rebels of 1956 as national martyrs. In the summer of 1989, East European frontiers began to open and refugees poured into Western Europe by the tens of thousands. With autumn came the opening of the Berlin Wall and the fall of the East German Communist government. This was closely followed by the delicately managed and equally bloodless "Velvet Revolution" in Czechoslovakia, propelling an avant-garde playwright named Vaclav Havel to the presidency of his country. At Christmas time, even Nicolae Ceausescu's rigidly autocratic Rumania exploded. The megalomaniacal Rumanian ruler died before a firing squad, perhaps as much a victim of a coup by his fellow Communist rulers as of the popular revolution surging through the streets.

## Looming Problems: Development and Nationalism

Under the leadership of hastily organized dissident groups like East Germany's New Forum or Czechoslovakia's Civic Forum, the successful revolutionaries embarked upon the difficult process of political and economic transformation. As in the aftermath of Europe's earlier waves of revolution in 1830 and 1848, new constitutions, free elections, and other democratic political changes were a first order of business. At least as important, however, the new regimes sought to dismantle the inefficient and unproductive structure of state-run industry and replace it with a free-market system. To effect the transition, they hoped for as much aid from well-off Western countries as possible.

These goals were not easily achieved. Everywhere, economic transformation had inevitably imposed great hardships on East European populations. Inefficient, un-competitive factories had to close, throwing many people out of work. Formerly subsidized prices rose until there was sufficient economic demand to motivate increased production.

Another general problem also loomed. Nationalistic passions, long held in check by the internationalism of class-based Marxism, flared up in many parts of this traditional hotbed of conflicting nationalisms. Czechs and Slovaks soon fell out in democratic Czechoslovakia and divided that country into the Czech Republic and Slovakia.

But the worst casualty of the collapse of Communism in Eastern Europe was the bloody disintegration of the multinational state of Yugoslavia. During the upheaval following the Revolutions of 1989, Yugoslavia's most developed constituent republics, Croatia and Slovenia, seceded and sought economic integration with Western Europe. Slobodan Milosevich, nationalist leader of the majority Serbian population, supported Serbian minorities demanding independence from Croatia and from the Muslim region of Bosnia. The latter soon became the site of a long-drawn-out civil war.

Across that mountainous little country, villages were torn apart by brutal guerrilla strife. Evidence mounted of what came to be known as "ethnic cleansing"—mass expulsions of Bosnians from their homes, systematic rape, brutal imprisonment, and outright massacres. In the end, it took a major military intervention by U.S.-led NATO forces and an American-brokered peace conference to bring an end to the carnage.

## THE POLITICS OF DEVELOPMENT: ASIA

### Patterns of Power: Military Rule, One-Party Rule—and Revolution

The new nations of Africa and Asia, like the older Third World countries of Latin America, tended to alternate between authoritarian regimes and revolutionary upheaval. The authoritarian governments were normally either one-party systems or ruled by military strongmen.

A one-party state would often emerge soon after independence, built on the loyalty of the people to the party that had won the colony its independence. Frequently, however, this party of national liberation would, with the passage of time, no longer deserve the people's support. Failure of grand schemes for development was often the cause of this loss of popular support, but flagrant corruption and high living—considered unsuitable in a tribune of the people—was an even stronger source of disillusionment.

At this point, military dictators would often make use of the other major institution that could command disciplined support—the army—to overthrow the party in power. Such military juntas might, or might not, prove more honest, but they generally lacked the skills needed to run a civilian government, let alone the economic and technical knowledge necessary for nation-building. Thus the country was often no more likely to progress under the military than under one-party rule.

The one-party states with the most capacity for staying in power were those ruled by socialist or communist parties. Such regimes, however, also had their liabilities. They sometimes turned to the ideologically justified but impractical policies explored later, subsidizing benefits for their people that the country was not yet rich enough to afford. Such countries also frequently had to face the hostility of powerful capitalist nations like the United States.

A small number of democratic governments emerged in the Third World. A more common alternative to authoritarianism, however, was revolution. Coups and rebellions,

A third-world village in the rainforests of northern Laos. The wood, bamboo, and palm thatching, like the earthen street, are all local products. The cattle in the streets, the pigs that sleep under the houses, and the vegetables and rice grown nearby provide subsistence for the village—but not much more. (Anthony Esler)

guerrilla wars in the backcountry and terrorism in the cities were widespread across the underdeveloped world. The two great Cold War adversaries also frequently provided moral or material support for the contestants—the United States most commonly for military regimes or the rare democracy, the Soviet Union for one-party governments or guerrilla movements. This outside involvement further complicated Third World politics.

The world grew used to media reports of corruption, military dictatorship, single-party authoritarianism, guerrilla attacks, and "death-squad" repression in the global South. In mitigation, it should be pointed out that these really were very new nations, most of them dating only from the period since World War II. Poverty also might account for many of the difficulties, a poverty rooted in a global economy largely beyond the control of Third World countries.

Underlying all these political gropings for direction, however, there did seem to be a fundamental concern: a search for a viable strategy of economic development, for the modernization of these premodern peoples. Politics throughout the global South was thus fundamentally the politics of development. It is this thread that will unite most of the examples cited below.

## China's Long Road to Development

China's domestic history after the end of its long civil war in 1949 was determined by the Communist party leaders who won that war. For the first quarter century of that period, this meant rule by the leader of the Chinese Revolution, Mao Zedong, or in his later years by the group of revolutionary ideologues who gathered around his iron-willed wife, Jiang Qing. Throughout the years from mid-century to the middle of the 1970s, Mao's round, smiling face and receding black hairline, Mao's "thoughts" in the famous little red book, and Mao's revolutionary legend dominated Chinese life even more than Stalin's personality cult had towered over Russia in his heyday.

The Chinese Communist party and a wide variety of other mass organizations—from the All-China Federation of Trade Unions to the Young Communist League and the All-China Federation of Democratic Women—gave the Communist leadership an unparalleled capacity to mobilize China's hundreds of millions for mass action. Harsher measures were also used to control the nation. Ideological dissenters were given peasant labor that would proletarianize their thinking. Hundreds of thousands, as Mao himself admitted, were "liquidated" in the early years, and more hundreds of thousands, as his successors charged, died during the Cultural Revolution of the 1960s. Most of the time, however, a combination of persuasion and party control was adequate to move the world's largest nation along the paths laid out for it by its new rulers.

Those paths could take some colorful turns as they followed the sometimes erratic thoughts of Chairman Mao and the more moderate insights of those who succeeded him. Early land reforms were soon followed by loose collectivization of agriculture on large peasant-owned farms. Nationalization of heavy industry and government Five-Year Plans followed the familiar Russian model. But in the later 1950s Mao announced a Great Leap Forward involving tightly organized communal farms and small-scale backyard industry on the local level. Peasant discontent with the loss of their private plots and with the compulsory group living, plus a series of bad harvests, led to widespread starvation and a pulling back from some of the extremes of this Maoist reform.

During the latter 1960s, however, the aging Mao decreed a new campaign, the so-called Great Proletarian Cultural Revolution, which came very close to shaking the system to pieces. Mao, his young wife—film actress Jiang Qing—and their allies in Beijing apparently felt that the People's Republic was drifting away from its ideological roots, settling into old bureaucratic ways, and losing its revolutionary zeal. The Cultural Revolution mobilized millions of young people in the new Red Guard units to denounce bureaucrats, compel self-criticism by any and all—up to and including Mao's old comrades in the top leadership—and to reassert the primacy of Marxist-Maoist thought.

The result was a reign of terror that had nearly paralyzed the country by 1968. Large numbers were hounded to death by local vigilantes or killed in clashes between rival factions, including rival gangs of Red Guards. In the end, the Chinese Red Army had to be called upon to regain control.

In the long run, however, pragmatism won the day. By the early 1970s, practical men such as Mao's old colleague Zhou Enlai had even arranged a rapprochement between China and Richard Nixon's America. And after Mao's death in 1976, the pragmatists seized power under another old revolutionary—and victim of the Cultural Revolution—Deng Xiaoping. Under the diminutive but bustling Deng, the new leadership actually brought to trial and convicted Mao's widow and her allies, the now condemned Gang of Four, for the follies of the Great Leap Forward and the excesses of the Cultural Revolution.

China had broken its close relationship with the Soviet Union as early as 1959–1960. After the middle 1970s, the pragmatic new leaders sought closer economic ties with Western nations, including the United States and Japan, in order to help modernize China. In many places, capitalist incentives were introduced to encourage increased production.

Genuine progress resulted. Though general living standards remained at Third World levels, foreign investment and joint ventures with foreign firms stimulated growth rates comparable to those of East Asian "tigers" like South Korea and Taiwan. The People's Republic was able to feed its one billion citizens, and some of its cities were sprucer, its domestic industry developing. A rigorous birth-control program was introduced to deal with what was perhaps the nation's number one problem, massive overpopulation.

In the later 1980s, however, economic changes and increasing contact with Westerners stimulated renewed demands for both political democracy and action against the corruption that had accompanied economic growth. In the spring of 1989 in Beijing, student demonstrations in Tienanmen Square gained the support of a large segment of the population of the nation's capital and sparked sympathy demonstrations in other cities. Deng and the rest of the older Communist leadership, however, refused to open up the political process and finally sent in tanks to clean out the demonstrators. Hundreds were killed in what came to be known as the "Tienanmen massacre," and political freedom was once again suppressed throughout China.

## India: The World's Largest Democracy

India was the second largest Asian nation from the late 1940s on and made significant progress under the leadership of a strong national party and charismatic leadership. But there were crucial differences between the two Asian giants. India's economic growth was somewhat slower, but its politics were democratic, its charismatic leaders elected by those they ruled.

The Republic of India was governed for most of the four decades after independence in 1947 by a "dynasty" of father, daughter, and grandson: first by Gandhi's disciple Pandit

# VOICES FROM THE PAST

Jawaharlal Nehru, the author of this account of his quest for the soul of India, was a Western-educated intellectual who became a leading anti-British agitator and first president of an independent India. Note how Nehru's study of India's past inspired his national feeling in the present.

What evidence of the Indian leader's involvement in Western culture do you see? What aspects of his own country's past does he remember with pride? How does Nehru's view of his people's culture compare with your own view of American history, national character, and achievements? Can you see value to citizens of both countries in these patriotic self-images? Can you see dangers?

*"India was in my blood and there was much in her that instinctively thrilled me. And yet I approached her almost as an alien critic, full of dislike for the present as well as for many of the relics of the past that I saw. To some extent I came to her via the West and looked at her as a friendly Westerner might have done. I was eager and anxious to change her outlook and appearance and give her the garb of modernity. And yet doubts rose within me. Did I know India, I who presumed to scrap much of her past heritage? . . .*

*I stood on a mound of Mohenjo-daro in the Indus Valley in the northwest of India, and all around me lay the houses and streets of this ancient city that is said to have existed over five thousand years ago; and even then it was an old and well-developed civilization. "The Indus civilization," writes Professor Childe, "represents a very perfect adjustment of human life to a specific environment that has endured and forms the basis of modern Indian culture."*

*I read her history and read also a part of her abundant ancient literature and was powerfully impressed by the vigor of the thought, the clarity of the language and the richness of the mind that lay behind it. The mighty rivers of India attracted me . . . and the Ganga, above all the river of India, which has held India's heart captive and drawn uncounted millions to her banks since the dawn of history. The story of the Ganga . . . is the story of India's civilization and culture, of the rise and fall of empires, of great and proud cities, of the adventure of man and the quest of the mind which has so occupied India's thinkers. . . .*

*These journeys and visits of mine, with the background of my reading, gave me an insight into the past. And gradually . . . a sense of reality began to creep into my mental picture of India and the land of my forefathers became peopled with living beings, who laughed and wept; loved and suffered; and . . . built a structure which gave India a cultural stability which lasted for thousands of years."*

---

Jawaharlal Nehru, *The Discovery of India* (New York: John Day, 1946), pp. 38–40.

Nehru, from 1947 till his death in 1964, then by Nehru's daughter Indira Gandhi (no relation to the Mahatma) from 1966 until her assassination in 1984 and finally by her son Rajiv Gandhi for most of the next half-dozen years, until he too died at the hands of an assassin. Their problems were many, their successes significant in this context of endless difficulties.

India, seldom united over its long history, had to be welded into a nation before it could be governed. Institutionally, at least, Nehru accomplished this by compelling all the surviving *rajas* of the so-called princely states to accept absorption into the new country. His personal prestige in the developing world then elevated India to leadership among these new nations.

Indira Gandhi had the harder task of melding the subcontinent's many peoples, languages, traditions, and religions into some approximation of a citizenry. This she at least began to do by a combination of personal appeal, political manipulation, and the occasional use of force. Her effort to crush a separatist revolt by members of the Sikh religious minority in northern India, however, brought her remarkable career to a violent end when her own Sikh bodyguards turned their guns on her. The assassination of her son and successor, Rajiv Gandhi, a reluctant politician, by a Tamil separatist suicide bomber brought an end to this dynasty of political power.

Attempts to develop the country economically encountered similar difficulties. The Indians tried a wide variety of methods to encourage development, from Five-Year Plans to foreign investment, from foreign aid (from both Russia and America) to the agricultural technology of the Green Revolution. In overall production, India achieved a respectable rank somewhere between that of the leading Western and Eastern European nations.

The best efforts of Nehru and the Gandhis, however, repeatedly foundered on India's greatest problem: its burgeoning population. As Nehru said, it was necessary for India to run very hard simply to keep up with the needs of the millions who were added to its citizen body every year.

## Arab Nationalism and Islamic Resurgence

Islamic militance, Arab nationalism, and the dark gleam of oil determined the history of a wide swath of Asia and North Africa in recent decades. Politically speaking, the Muslim nations followed different paths. Some, like Iran under the shah and the oil-rich giant Saudi Arabia, remained anachronistic absolute monarchies in the later twentieth century. Others became military dictatorships, such as Pakistan under General Zia or Libya under the colorful Colonel Qaddafi, often accused of being a patron of international terrorism. Egypt was dominated for decades by a series of former military men of considerable political skill, including the nationalist leader Gamal Abdel Nasser and the internationally admired Anwar Sadat, the first Arab leader to sign a peace treaty with Israel. Two leaders of the Ba'athist Arab Nationalist party came to power. Saddam Hussein in Iraq and Hafez Assad in Syria, and were soon locked in an intense rivalry, like so many of the Arab rulers.

The vast reservoirs of oil that stretch from Iran to the far end of the Sahara gave these recently emancipated sheiks and colonels a powerful new economic role in the world. They used some of their wealth to feud with each other or with their non-Muslim neighbors from Israel to India. Much of it went into lavish living and foreign investments—the petrodollars that flooded the banks of the West. Some of their oil wealth, however, did go into providing agricultural projects, education, health care, decent roads, and housing for the sometimes scanty but rapidly growing populations of these arid lands.

Another powerful force that helped to shape the history of the Middle East was Arab nationalism. Kindled by the anti-imperialist movements of the first half of the century, pan-Arab feeling resembled in some ways the pan-Slav or pan-German movements of the 1800s. All Arabs were brothers, Arab nationalists believed, no matter what country they lived in. The score of postliberation Arab states stretching from Morocco to Iraq were often denounced as products of imperialistic European machinations. For Arabs who believed in the spiritual unity of the "Arab nation," the great enemy was Israel, condemned for occupying Arab land and oppressing its Palestinian Arab minority.

The early 1990s saw a new wave of militance led by Islamic fundamentalists in many lands. Moves toward peace with Israel led by the Palestinian nationalist Yassir Arafat were challenged by "Islamist" organizations like Hamas, who continued to kill Israelis and defy Arafat. In Algeria, Islamist crusaders for Islamic fundamentalism, denied free elections by nationalist army leaders, launched a savage campaign of assassination against modernized Algerians and resident foreigners. In many Islamic countries, meanwhile, people who had been moving toward Western ways turned back toward Islamic customs, costumes, and fervent worship. Muslim fundamentalism, even more than Arab nationalism, seemed to be carving out a widening gap between Islam and the West.

## Mounting Tensions in Asia

In the later decades of the century, mounting tensions still threatened to erupt into open conflict in many parts of Asia, especially in the Middle East.

In the late 1980s, Israel, after repelling so many external attacks, proved unable to control a Palestinian uprising called the *Intifadah* in the occupied territories of Gaza and the West Bank of the Jordan River. Here stone-throwing youths confronted Israeli soldiers, and as months of attempts at suppression turned into years, world opinion began to turn against Israel. In the early 1990s, even the United States, Israel's oldest and staunchest ally, urged discussions with the Palestinian Liberation Organization and supported peace talks between the Israelis, their Arab neighbors, and representatives of the Palestinians. In 1994, Israel signed a peace treaty with Jordan and granted the Palestinians at Gaza and part of the West Bank autonomy under the former terrorist chief, Arafat.

Most explosive of all, however, was the oil-rich region around the Persian Gulf. Here the Iraqi dictator Saddam Hussein, deeply in debt after his long war with Iran, sought once more to advance his interests by a swift military stroke. Literally overnight, his troops occupied the little neighboring state of Kuwait, giving him control of its vast oil resources to add to his own. A world that ran on oil, however, reacted more forcefully than the Iraqi ruler had expected. U.S. President George Bush took the lead in rallying global opposition and military units from Britain. France, and such rival Arab nations as Egypt and Syria joined the coalition. In a rapid and thoroughly high-tech military campaign in the opening months of 1991, the U.S.-led alliance expelled Saddam's troops from Kuwait and devastated Iraq itself.

# THE POLITICS OF DEVELOPMENT: AFRICA AND LATIN AMERICA

## Black Africa's Struggle

In Africa south of the Sahara, political instability and autocratic one-party or military rule alternated in a bewildering kaleidoscope, punctuated by bloody flashes of rebellion. Economically, some of these countries prospered on a combination of commodity exports and foreign aid and investment: others seemed to settle deeper into poverty.

For black Africa, life after the great liberation was a struggle in many ways more difficult than the victorious fight for independence had been. In French-speaking West Africa, for instance, close economic relations with France enabled such liberation leaders as Félix Houphouët-Boigny of the Ivory Coast and Senegal's Léopold Senghor to lead their new nations to relative prosperity. There were paved roads there, bright lights, marketplaces full to bursting, and new skyscrapers in the great African cities of Abidjan and Dakar. But landlocked inner African Sahel states such as Mali, Niger, and Chad remained dusty, poverty-ridden backwaters.

In the former colonies of British East Africa, two of the continent's best-known liberation leaders, Jomo Kenyatta of Kenya and Julius Nyerere of Tanzania, provided an interesting contrast in development styles. Kenyatta opened his doors to Western capital, while Nyerere preached self-reliance and socialism—and got aid from European socialist countries and China. Despite political violence and crime, Kenya, with a considerable colonial head start in development, grew more rapidly, building some industry and an East African metropolitan center in Nairobi. Nyerere's Tanzania provided water, food, some education and health care for his people first—and was on the edge of bankruptcy by 1990.

Terrible famine added to the travail of a number of African nations in the 1970s and 1980s. Drought, government mismanagement, devastating civil wars, and the increasingly rapid spread of the desert into areas bordering the Sahara all contributed to the disaster. In Ethiopia, the Sahel countries, and elsewhere, hundreds of thousands died and whole districts were depopulated by starvation.

Revolutionary struggles and open war came and went in Ethiopia, Somalia, Sudan, in Angola and Mozambique in the south, in Liberia, Ghana, and other parts of West Africa. The Western nations seldom noticed unless a major famine erupted in the war zones, as in Ethiopia and Sudan, or unless Western people were directly involved, as in South Africa. Western involvement, when it did come, took more positive forms than it had in earlier centuries. Substantial international famine relief campaigns were repeatedly launched in the 1980s and 1990s.

## Latin American Revolutions

Development became an all-devouring passion south of the Rio Grande in the decades after World War II. In its name, poor people supported and middle-class businessmen frequently tolerated strong governments of left or right that promised development in return for submission to authoritarian rule. Central planning, import-substitution industries, di-

Jomo Kenyatta, leader of the Kenya independence movement and its first president, was a tall, regal-looking, London-educated Kikuyu. Like other leaders of African liberation struggles, Kenyatta combined Western training with charismatic popular appeal. (The Bettmann Archive)

versification of industrial and agricultural production, continued construction of such essential infrastructures as the new postwar highway systems—all contributed to Latin American economic growth. In some places social services proliferated, though the gulf between rich and poor still remained great in the southern republics.

The 1960s were the boom times. By the early 1970s two large Latin American nations, Brazil and Mexico, ranked with some European countries in overall production. Even in these successful cases, however, poverty remained endemic in the villages where most Latin Americans lived. This poverty of the domestic market choked off the boom in the 1970s and 1980s.

Economic failures also stimulated an increasingly radical ideological opposition to the status quo in Middle and South America.

An early manifestation of the new demand for change was the decade-long personal dictatorship of Juan and Eva Peron (1946–1955) in Argentina. Peron drew his support from the growing Argentine urban working class, the *descamisados* ("shirtless ones"), whom he gave higher wages, social services, and retirement benefits. The magnetic Evita, a former actress, worked for women's emancipation and services for the poor. The Perons, however, also rigged elections, feuded with the Catholic church, and tended to ignore the problems of the peasantry. Three years after Evita's death in 1952, Peron was overthrown by the military.

The most flamboyant and influential revolution in the region during this period, however, was that led by Fidel Castro in Cuba. During his decades of rule in the island country, Castro ran a one-party Communist government. But though many middle-class Cubans fled, the peasant population remained loyal to the revolution, and in many ways benefited from it.

Economic growth was not exuberant under the *Venceremos* regime. Early efforts to diversify the country's one-crop sugar economy did not succeed, and Castro came to depend on selling sugar to the Soviet Union, as his predecessor Batista had on selling it to the United States. A United States–sponsored economic boycott further stunted Cuba's development.

Despite this lack of economic growth, Castro forged ahead with the most elaborate set of social services offered by any of the southern American republics. He built public housing and schools for the poor and provided health care and retirement pensions. A weak economy and impressive social services were thus combined, thanks to substantial economic aid from the Soviet Union—at least until the Soviets' own political collapse and economic problems led to drastic cutbacks in the 1990s.

## Political Progress and Economic Challenges

A regional revolution that attracted fewer headlines was the resurgence of democratic government and free-market economic growth in many Latin American nations during the 1980s and 1990s.

Where authoritarian regimes, frequently military dictatorships, prevailed in the 1950s, elected civilian governments came to power in the 1980s. Older democracies like Mexico and Venezuela were thus joined by the largest South American countries, Argentina and Brazil, as the military gave way to civilian leadership. In the early 1990s, only a single unelected ruler remained in power in Latin America—Fidel Castro.

Economic progress, however, seemed harder to point to as the nineties began. There was still a huge gulf between the prosperity of Latin American upper and middle classes and the poverty of large peasant and working-class segments of society. The former enjoyed their life of elegant cities, while the latter were confined to shantytown slums or dusty rural villages.

Particularly disturbing to many was the deep poverty of the indigenous population of many Latin American countries. Descendants of the original inhabitants, Indians were among the least developed and most exploited citizens of all the American nations, north and south. Middle and South American *indios,* however, lacked the compensations of large government land grants, as in Canada, or the successful gambling casinos that flourished in the United States. Indigenous rights movements grew increasingly vocal in Latin America in the later twentieth century, but indigenous economic progress remained hard to find.

## DEVELOPED AND DEVELOPING SOCIETIES

### New Technologies: From the Jet Plane to the Internet

Much of the technological progress made by the North, beginning in the 1950s, manifested itself in improved—or at least interestingly varied—lives for large segments of the population. This was particularly so in the West, where consumer demand largely determined what got developed and manufactured. From basics such as frozen foods, clothes washers, central heating, and air conditioning to luxuries such as stereo equipment, video recorders, and electronic arcade games, the buying public got its share of the latest technology in capitalist countries.

The peoples of the global North thus created a dazzling new material culture for themselves during the third quarter of the twentieth century. Thousands of later-twentieth-century people walked around with remarkable artificial limbs or electronic pacemakers regulating the beating of their hearts. Decent hygiene, diet, exercise, wonder drugs, and hospital technology doubled the human life span. In industry and government, steady progress in computer technology, robotics, electronics, biological engineering, and energy science continued to reshape the world around us.

In the decades after World War II, regularly scheduled jumbo jets linked the cities of the world, till there was virtually no place more than a few days away from anywhere else, and millions flew the friendly skies of the world every year. Artificial satellites orbited the earth, beeping back a spectrum of information ranging from weather reports to newscasts from the other side of the world—straight to the home television screens of countless viewers.

In 1961 the Russian cosmonaut Yuri Gagarin became the first human being to orbit the earth in an artificial satellite. In 1969 an American, Neil Armstrong, became the first to set foot on the moon. In the mid-1970s Soviet spacecraft landed on Venus, and American ones sent back vivid photographs from the surface of Mars. The peoples of planet earth grew quite blasé about angle shots of the rings of Saturn and fly-bys of the moons of Jupiter. For the developed nations of the North, at least, it seemed as if even the sky was no longer the limit.

To many, the high technology of everyday life seemed even more amazing. The last two decades of the century saw the personal computer and the cellular phone become fixtures of homes, offices, and city streets across the developed world. People used the Internet to communicate around the earth, to market goods across the country, and to educate new generations with an unparalleled access to the rest of the globe. As the vast potential of what the pundits called the Information Age became apparent, the world looked dramatically different, particularly to young people in many lands.

## DEVELOPED NATIONS IN THE 1990s

ARCTIC OCEAN

PACIFIC OCEAN

ATLANTIC OCEAN

ATLANTIC OCEAN

INDIAN OCEAN

PACIFIC OCEAN

UNITED STATES

CANADA

NORWAY
SWEDEN
FINLAND
DENMARK
UNITED KINGDOM
NETHERLANDS
IRELAND
BELGIUM
LUXEMBOURG
SWITZERLAND
FRANCE
GERMANY
AUSTRIA
ITALY
SPAIN
ISRAEL
KUWAIT
UNITED ARAB EMIRATES
SAUDI ARABIA

JAPAN
TAIWAN
SINGAPORE

AUSTRALIA

NEW ZEALAND

| AVERAGE GNP PER CAPITA |
|---|
| $17,000 |

0    2000    4000 Miles

0    2000    4000 Kilometers

## The Helicopter Economy

The economies of the nations of the North also exhibited a tendency to rise at an unprecedented rate during the decades after World War II. Some people called it the helicopter economy—an economy that simply went up and up.

The Western capitalist economy was no longer the fang-and-claw economic jungle of the nineteenth century. The major corporations themselves imposed order—and controlled competition—as efficiently as any medieval city guild in a wide variety of fields, from oil and automobiles to air travel and fast foods. Government also regulated the conduct of business, laying down rules for everything from environmentally polluting by-products to employment practices. Western governments also provided support for industry, agriculture, export trade, and other sectors of the economy by tightening or loosening credit, guiding industry into areas having a strong export potential, and even sharing the cost of research and development.

Such economic "fine-tuning" helped. So did the advantages of cheap immigrant labor and raw materials from the global South. The result was an economic boom of un-precedented proportions through the 1960s and into the 1970s.

In 1973, however, and again in 1979, the oil producers' international cartel, OPEC, drastically hiked the price of petroleum, the single most important source of energy for Western industry. Meanwhile, economic feuds between such rich nations as the United States and Japan intensified. In the 1980s, a wave of "streamlining," "slimming down," and "re-engineering" laid off many workers in order to make the industries that employed them more competitive. And at the end of the 1990s, financial upheaval swept across Asia and menaced the West itself.

Neither the Reagan boom of the middle 1980s nor even the Clinton boom of the 1990s quite matched the across-the-board economic growth of the postwar years. Yet America's 1990s prosperity combined low inflation, low unemployment, and a stratospheric stock market to an unprecedented degree. Europe's money managers also expected the new European single currency to greatly increase the prosperity of that continent. Whatever might lie in wait beyond 2000, the overall performance of the global economy in the later decades of the twentieth century had been genuinely awesome.

## Liberated Women, Restless Youth

During the postwar decades, many women once more took up the crusading spirit of the turn-of-the-century women's suffrage movements—this time primarily in the economic sphere. Again, the results were striking.

In the immediate aftermath of World War II, "Rosie the Riveter" seemed to be content to return to the nineteenth-century ideal career for women—as wives and mothers. What came to be called the "feminine mystique" praised these time-honored social roles, as it urged longer dresses, frillier fashions, and a more feminine image on the female half of the population.

As we have seen, however, the turmoil of the 1960s stirred the movement for what came to be called women's liberation this time around to life again. In the following decade, women's organizations such as the National Organization for Women (NOW) in the United States began a campaign to overcome the remaining forms of discrimination against women.

The main thrust of the revitalized women's movement, however, was economic. Women demanded equal pay for equal work, promotion of more women to executive levels in business, larger representation in the ranks of the professions. In some of these areas, at least, they seemed to be making progress in the last decades of the century. More than half the married women in the United States worked outside the home, and it was no longer difficult to find successful women as role models in all spheres of life.

Recent studies reveal both progress and problems in the world of women and work. Throughout the developed world, women remain less well paid, more likely to get stuck in dead-end jobs, and still most likely to do the housework in addition to work outside the home. Yet these differences seem to be decreasing in industrialized states. More education for women and laws requiring equal treatment raised women's remuneration to three quarters that of men, and the gap seems likely to continue to narrow.[2]

Around the world in the later twentieth century, meanwhile, family size decreased, divorce rates rose, and the number of single mothers grew. These changes in family size and structure seemed to be due to such factors as the need for both parents to work to maintain a high standard of living, the abandonment of the family by husbands, or the departure of husbands to work in distant cities.

The 1990s also saw a renewed restlessness among the young. It began with a surge of new youth culture. Some was as silly as garishly dyed hair or a taste for coffee from Seattle. Some was as serious as increasing psychological disorders and a rash of attacks on their own high schools with automatic weapons.

As the century turned, youth seemed to be once more on the march. Young people filled the streets demanding jobs in France and Germany and violently championed the rights of animals in Britain. In the United States, campus demonstrations forced universities to "deinvest" in foreign "sweatshops." In Asia they overthrew governments. Though they had not perhaps yet found the issues that could galvanize whole generations, the pattern of youthful rebelliousness was once again a factor on the global scene.

## Village People

A Third World village is a cock crowing while it is still dark outside, or perhaps a *muezzin* calling to predawn prayers. It is close-set houses made of wattle and daub, clay brick, roughly whitewashed plaster over stone, roofs of thatch, palm leaves, tile, or tin. It is hard-packed earthern paths and streets, bare feet, sandals, a bike or two. It is water from a village well, vegetables from the back garden, chickens underfoot, goats, sheep, perhaps a sacred cow wandering at will.

It is dirt under your fingernails, in the cracks of your skin, sunshine, insects, and a sore back by noon. It is women slapping wet clothes against the rocks in a stream and laying them out on the grass to dry. It is kids in school uniforms hopping off the school bus at the crossroads, books swinging in straps or satchels, and racing into town. It is dried-up old people without teeth, kids with untreated umbilical hernias, overworked young women ready to drop at the end of the day, young men away in the city, trying to find work.

Village people are still almost half of the human race. They live mostly in Asia, Africa, and Latin America—the three continents of the global South, the world south of the north

---

[2] See H. Kahne and J. Z. Giele, eds. *Women's Work and Women's Lives: The Continuing Struggle Worldwide* (Boulder, Colo.: Westview Press, 1992).

# Developing Nations in the 1990s

ARCTIC OCEAN

PACIFIC OCEAN

ATLANTIC OCEAN

INDIAN OCEAN

**AVERAGE GNP PER CAPITA**
$1900
$300

RUSSIA

MONGOLIA

CHINA

KOREA

JAPAN

BURMA (MYANMAR)

BHUTAN

NEPAL

INDIA

VIETNAM

LAOS

BRUNEI

THAILAND

CAMBODIA

MALAYSIA

INDONESIA

PAPUA NEW GUINEA

SRI LANKA

BANGLADESH

PAKISTAN

AFGHANISTAN

KAZAKHSTAN

KYRGYZSTAN

TAJIKISTAN

UZBEKISTAN

TURKMENISTAN

AZERBAIJAN

ARMENIA

IRAN

IRAQ

OMAN

JORDAN

SYRIA

LEBANON

TURKEY

EGYPT

LIBYA

SUDAN

ETHIOPIA

DJIBOUTI

SOMALIA

KENYA

UGANDA

RWANDA

BURUNDI

TANZANIA

ZAIRE

CONGO

GABON

EQUATORIAL GUINEA

CAMEROON

CENTRAL AFRICAN REPUBLIC

CHAD

NIGER

NIGERIA

BENIN

TOGO

GHANA

IVORY COAST

LIBERIA

SIERRA LEONE

GUINEA

GUINEA-BISSAU

GAMBIA

SENEGAL

MAURITANIA

MALI

BURKINA FASO

MOROCCO

ALGERIA

TUNISIA

PORTUGAL

ALBANIA

MACEDONIA

SLOVENIA

CROATIA

BOSNIA

SERBIA

BULGARIA

ROMANIA

MOLDOVA

UKRAINE

HUNGARY

SLOVAKIA

BELARUS

POLAND

GEORGIA

ANGOLA

ZAMBIA

MALAWI

MOZAMBIQUE

MADAGASCAR

ZIMBABWE

NAMIBIA

BOTSWANA

SOUTH AFRICA

SWAZILAND

LESOTHO

BRAZIL

PARAGUAY

URUGUAY

ARGENTINA

CHILE

BOLIVIA

PERU

ECUADOR

COLOMBIA

VENEZUELA

GUYANA

SURINAME

FRENCH GUIANA

PANAMA

COSTA RICA

NICARAGUA

EL SALVADOR

HONDURAS

GUATEMALA

BELIZE

MEXICO

CUBA

HAITI

DOMINICAN REPUBLIC

4,000 Miles

4,000 Kilometers

2,000

2,000

0

0

temperate zone. They are for the most part non-Western peoples, dwellers in hot lands who wear clothing unlike that worn by Americans, Europeans, or Japanese.

There are important exceptions: Underdeveloped China is not in the geographical south, fully developed Australia is. But by and large, the global South is where village people live.

They may live in an ancient civilization like that of India or China, temporarily relegated to the unfamiliar category of "backward" or "underdeveloped" by the West's sudden leap ahead in industrial technology two centuries ago.

They may be citizens of a new nation, such as Nigeria or Zimbabwe, building from scratch, only decades old, even its name a recent acquisition, all its uncertain history still ahead.

They may be residents of a middle-level developing country such as Venezuela, Mexico, and increasingly China, with resources, cheap labor, and some industry to give them the long-run hope of an industrialized future, with regular elections and a land-reform program that works.

Plenty of books will tell you about their problems: overpopulation, disease, malnutrition, unemployment, illiteracy, one-crop economies, political authoritarianism or instability or both, swollen cities, dying traditional village cultures. It is harder to get a handle on the vitality of many Third World countries. You get a sense of that, perhaps, from watching a West African woman sail regally through the market-day tumult with a fantastic array of things balanced on the tray on her brightly kerchiefed head. Or from the peanuts you buy in India—wrapped in a page covered with quadratic equations, torn from a child's exercise book.

This section deals mostly with the broad problems and the sometimes erratic course of Third World history over the two or three decades since most of these countries gained their independence. But it would be well to remember the human lives that compose those histories, the human vitality that in the long run is surely the best hope for all the village peoples of the globe.

## Shantytowns

The most striking contrast between old and new in the global South, however, was the Third World city—and its surrounding shantytown.

Urban migration, the key to the modernization process in Europe and America in the nineteenth century, reached crisis proportions in Asia, Africa, and Latin America in the later twentieth century. Driven by the lack of land and jobs in the rural areas, drawn by dreams of the high life or by a realistic awareness that education, health care, and job opportunities were concentrated in the city, millions of peasants poured into Third World cities every year.

In the downtown city centers, foreign business outlets and domestically owned emporiums glistened with modernity. But the new immigrant from the country would seldom find his niche in this glittering world of the city center. His world would be the shantytown.

An expert on life among the Latin American poor described the home of a woman named Guadalupe in a Mexico City slum in vivid terms:

The *Panaderos vecindad* where Guadalupe lived consisted of a row of fourteen one-room adobe huts about 10 by 15 feet, built along the left side and across the back of a thirty-foot-wide bare lot. . . . Toward the rear of the yard, two large cement water troughs, each with a faucet, were the sole source of water for the eighty-four inhabitants. Here the women washed their dishes and laundry and bathed their children. In the back of the lot, two broken-down stinking toilets, half curtained by pieces of torn burlap and flushed by pails of water, served all the tenants.[3]

The rent was low, but then Guadalupe and her husband Ignacio earned a total of $5.20 a month between them. When she died, everything she owned in the world was valued at approximately $120.

The majority of those who migrated to the city got no jobs, and the few who did worked as manual laborers, street hawkers, or something less respectable. Many were sucked into the world of the sweatshops, laboring long hours for meager wages assembling clothing or athletic shoes to be sold in the developed nations. Still, entire families came, finding a square of littered earth to call their own in shantytown, and hanging on, hoping that their streetwise, half-educated children would at least find a toehold in the modern world.

## Poverty, Dependency, and Debt

Marshall McLuhan, the media expert, applied the term *global village* to the peoples of the world, linked by television and other media of communication into a single worldwide community. In the last decades of the twentieth century, however, the term seemed equally appropriate for the village peoples of the globe, who despite all cultural differences were united by even more compelling hopes and problems.

The most all-encompassing problem of the developing south then, is poverty. The poverty of the have-not nations is not simply a lack of cars, television sets, or flush toilets. Poverty in the Third World means shantytowns full of the unemployed—and no work back home in the villages either. It means malaria, cholera, typhoid, sleeping sickness, leprosy, hookworm—all the plagues of the Old Testament still killing children and crippling their elders in our century. It means malnutrition even in a decent year: If the crop is bad or nonexistent in arid India or the Sahel countries south of the Sahara, it means swollen bellies, matchstick arms, death under the blowing dust.

Dealing with such fundamental problems requires meeting such basic needs as enough food, drinkable water, access to some sort of clinic. It means selling birth control to people for whom children are a duty, a source of free labor, and the only available old-age insurance. After these needs, the newer nations must find funds for education, roads, capital investment in industrial or agricultural projects that might give their people hope for a better way of life in the future.

The traditional way of acquiring money to pay for development was through the export of what Third World countries had to sell: raw materials or agricultural products. The new nations thus joined Latin America as commodity exporters, shipping overseas vast quantities of coffee, tea, sugar, bananas, copra, palm oil, wheat, beef, cotton, rubber, oil, copper, iron, uranium, bauxite.

When the prices of these products of the southern earth were high, as in the 1960s, the South did passably well—and invested commensurately in new projects. When the prices went down in the world markets, as they did in the 1970s and 1980s, the new countries suffered. Commodity prices, furthermore, were frequently determined not by Third World producers, but by speculators in First World countries or by what Second World governments

---

[3]Oscar Lewis, *A Death in the Sánchez Family* (New York: Random House, 1969), p. xxiii.

were willing to pay. Desperate for foreign exchange, the countries of the global South often cut back even on subsistence agriculture in order to put more land into export crops—and hence had to import food. The result was a very serious set of export-related problems.

Another major category of difficulty was the sort of dependency syndrome that had afflicted Latin America for so long. Third World countries in general depended on other nations for both manufactured goods and energy—meaning mostly oil. Again, a crucial factor in the economic development of the global South was beyond their control, in the hands of oil sheiks and European or American or Japanese manufacturers.

Another fundamental problem for developing nations followed directly from those of commodity exports and dependency. This was the huge debt that many countries in the South incurred, particularly over the 1970s and 1980s, because the other way to capitalize development projects was to borrow the money. This many Third World countries did, negotiating loans from major European or North American banks and from such international agencies as the World Bank and the International Monetary Fund (IMF). When these loans began to come due, the countries of the South found commodity prices still low, the cost of dependency for oil and essential manufactured goods still high. Many of them could not repay the loans or even make interest payments on them—unless they borrowed more money.

Basic tactics for dealing with global markets, dependency, and debt in the early days of the great liberation often involved centralized, controlled economies, development guided paternalistically by the new Third World governments. Government marketing boards, protective tariffs, fixed prices for export goods, subsidized prices for food staples, and long-range development plans were common approaches. Following the precipitous Third world decline of the 1970s, however, many developing nations pinned more of their hopes on free enterprise and market forces rather than on central planning. Pressured to free up the economy by such powerful aid donors as the IMF, Third World governments risked riots and even rebellions in order to cut subsidies that kept food prices low or permitted foreign investments and foreign imports to rise. They could only hope that these risks and sacrifices would be counterbalanced by economic growth comparable to that of the capitalist West, or of the newly developed nations of the East Asian Pacific rim.

## SUMMARY

The United States was the predominate power in the world in the second half of the twentieth century, enjoying general prosperity and political stability for most of these years.

In Europe, Germany loomed as the richest nation, carrying on in its prewar tradition of industrial skill, and was reunified in the 1990s. Britain and France pioneered such advances as the welfare state and European economic integration, while Western Europe as a whole benefited from the Common Market and the evolving European Union. Japan and other nations of the East Asian Pacific rim, meanwhile, forged a productive new center of economic growth at the other end of Eurasia. Other highly developed nations, not all of them in the geographical north, included Canada, Australia, and Israel.

The Soviet Union became the second most massive producer of such basics as steel and oil, but fell drastically behind in agriculture and consumer products, and broke up politically at the beginning of the 1990s.

The material achievements of what is sometimes called the global North—the developed nations of Europe, North America, Japan, and other areas—were truly spectacular during the later decades of the twentieth century. High technology was the secret, a continuation of the Industrial Revolution that produced a range of marvels from frozen foods and television to space science, nuclear power, and the computer revolution. Free enterprise—with some government fine-tuning—produced more goods and services for Western peoples than any people had ever enjoyed.

Horizons expanded once more for women in the developed world, and young people repeatedly took to the streets, compelling the most materially fortunate of societies to raise their sights to a still more dazzling future.

The Third World countries of Asia, Africa, and Latin America, by contrast, faced such basic problems as lack of adequate food, medical care, and education for exploding populations. In addition, Third World countries struggled to develop economically but often remained trapped in an economic dependency on the North that led to cruel suffering when commodity prices, loans, and foreign aid from the global North declined.

Conflicts between the traditional world of the village and the new urban world also threatened Asians, Africans, and Latin Americans with painful cultural up-rooting. Many Third World people who did come up from villages to join the modern world of the city ended up in shantytowns, the slums that ringed the new metropolises from Caracas to Hong Kong.

Politically, many of the countries of the South were one-party governments or military dictatorships, and revolutions and coups were common on all three Third World continents. Even China, with its ancient tradition of central government, was shaken by the social experiments of Chairman Mao and other Communist leaders, including such abortive efforts as the Great Leap Forward and the Cultural Revolution. India managed to preserve its democratic institutions, while struggling with its immense economic, demographic, and religious problems.

A broad swath of Muslim countries, from Iran to North Africa, developed rapidly on the basis of oil wealth, though the gap between rich and poor remained substantial. Much of Africa south of the Sahara struggled with considerably more limited resources and much greater dependency on world commodity prices, bank loans, and international aid. In Latin America, finally, similar economic problems led to a number of revolutions, notably in Castro's Cuba which sought state socialist solutions to the difficulties of development. By the 1990s, however, many Third World leaders were shifting to the free market to bring national prosperity.

## SUGGESTED READING

Allyn, D. *Make Love Not War: The Sexual Revolution: An Unfettered History.* New York: Little, Brown, 2000. Readable account of a much-discussed aspect of the 1960s counterculture.

Chandler, A. D., Jr., F. Amatori, and T. Hikino, eds. *Big Business and the Wealth of Nations.* New York: Cambridge University Press, 1997. America's "managerial revolution" seen as a global phenomenon. See also D.S. Landes, *The Wealth and Poverty of Nations: Why Some Are So Rich and Some So Poor* (New York: W.W. Norton, 1998), which sees long-term cultural difference undergirding the economic success of the Western world.

Coquery-Vidrovitch, C. *African Women: A Modern History.* Trans. B. G. Raps. Boulder, Colo.: Westview Press, 1997. The first full-scale history of modern African women.

Dean, W. *With Broadax and Firebrand: The Destruction of the Brazilian Atlantic Forest.* Berkeley and Los Angeles: University of California Press, 1995. Intensely committed account of the human assault on the Brazilian rain forest.

Dirlik, A. *The Postcolonial Aura: Third World Criticism of Global Capitalism.* Boulder, Colo.: Westview Press, 1997. Challenges "postcolonial" theoretical accounts of the state of the Third World in favor of a return to economic analysis of the Third World's problems.

Domenach, J.-L.*The Origins of the Great Leap Forward.* Trans. A. M. Berrett. Boulder, Colo.: Westview Press, 1995. Blames bureaucrats and opportunists for the Chinese catastrophe. See also Y. Jiaqi and G. Gao. *Turbulent Decade: A History of the Cultural Revolution.* Trans. and ed. D. W. Y. Kwok (Honolulu: University of Hawaii Press, 1996) in which Jiaqi was personally involved. And see R. Baum, *Burying Mao: Chinese Politics in the Age of Deng Xiaoping* (Princeton, N.J.: Princeton University Press, 1994) which sees social and economic changes overwhelming the old Maoist political structure.

Dunn, R., ed. *Democracy: The Unfinished Journey* Oxford: Oxford University Press, 1992. Essays on the history and present advantages of democratic government, with some emphasis on interaction with economic forces.

Fieldhouse, D. K. *The West and the Third World: Trade, Colonialism, Dependence, and Development.* Oxford: Blackwell, 1999. Sees Western exploitation and economic dependency as key causes of Third World poverty, but export-led free-market economics as the hope of the future. See also A. Escobar, *Encountering Development: The Making and Unmaking of the Third World,* (Princeton, N.J.: Princeton University Press, 1995) debunking international agencies and development aid.

Hane, M. *Eastern Phoenix: Japan Since 1945.* Boulder, Colo.: Westview Press of HarperCollins, 1996. Topical survey of Japanese achievement since World War II.

Hicks, A. *Social Democracy and Welfare Capitalism: A Century of Income Security Politics.* Ithaca: Cornell University Press, 1999. Traces the rise of an important component of the modern welfare state. See also J. Klausen, *War and Welfare: Europe and the United States, 1945 to the Present* (New York: St. Martin's Press, 1998), which argues that the roots of the welfare state lie in wartime expansion of the powers of government.

Hughes, H. S. *Sophisticated Rebels: The Political Culture of European Dissent, 1968–1987.* Cambridge, Mass.: Harvard University Press, 1988. A leading historian of European social thought surveys social movements, from the youth revolt of the 1960s to environmentalist Green parties, Soviet dissidents, and others.

Jalal, A. *Democracy and Authoritarianism in South Asia.* New York: Cambridge University Press, 1995. Analyzes authoritarian institutions and traditions that limit democracy.

Keep, J. L. H. *Last of the Empires: A History of the Soviet Union, 1945–1991.* New York: Oxford University Press, 1995. Domestic history of the post-Stalinist U.S.S.R. See also M. Lewin, *The Gorbachev Phenomenon: A Historical Interpretation* (Berkeley and Los Angeles: University of California Press, 1988), which puts the Gorbachev reforms into a context of other attempts at changing Soviet Russian society. For Gorbachev's years in power, see a thoughtful account by two journalists, D. Doder and L. Branson, *Gorbachev: Heretic in the Kremlin* (New York: Viking, 1990).

Killick, J. *The United States and European Reconstruction, 1945–1960.* Edinburgh: Keele University Press, 1997. Brief but perceptive evaluation of the U.S. Role in European recovery after World War II.

Lewis, B. *Islam and the West.* New York: Oxford University Press, 1993. Essays by a leading scholar, critical of Islamist fundamentalism.

Mandela, N. *Long Walk to Freedom.* Boston: Little, Brown, 1994. Nelson Mandela's own story of a life of resistance and imprisonment. See also F. Meer, *Higher Than Hope* (New York: Harper, 1990), an authorized biography.

Marah, J. K. *The African People in the Global Village: An Introduction to Pan-African Studies* (Lanham, Md.: University Press of America, 1998). Sees African nations savaged by imperialism and neo-imperialism—but in need of "African solutions to their African problems." But see G.B.N. Ayittey, *Africa in Chaos* (New York: St. Martin's Press, 1998), which sees Africa's development problems as rooted primarily in the failings of postliberation African leadership.

McNeill, J. R. *Something New Under the Sun: An Environmental History of the Twentieth-Century World* (New York: W. W. Norton, 2000). Balanced survey of the damage humans have done to land, water, air, and other species while building the richest civilization in history. See also M. V. Melosi, *Coping With Abundance: Energy and Environment in Industrial America* (Philadelphia: Temple University Press, 1985) and V. Smil, *China's Environmental Crisis* (New York: M. E. Sharpe, 1993).

Miller, F. *Latin American Women and the Search for Social Justice.* Hanover, N.H.: University Press of New England, 1991. Historical overview, emphasizing the twentieth century and such ongoing concerns as democracy, revolution, education, and feminism.

Mitter, S. S. *Dharma's Daughters: Contemporary Indian Women and Hindu Culture.* New Brunswick, N.J.: Rutgers University Press, 1991. Modern Indian women come to terms with ancient Indian traditions.

Pino, J. C. *Family and Favela: The Reproduction of Poverty in Rio de Janeiro.* Westport, Conn.: Greenwood Press, 1997. Focuses on midcentury Rio, but illuminates the grimly rational motives of shanty-town dwellers around the world today.

Thébaud, F., ed. *Toward a Cultural Identity in the Twentieth Century.* Cambridge: Belknap Press of Harvard University Press, 1994. Vol. 5 of the *History of Women in the West* series, with essays tracing the great changes in women's lives in this period.

 Please refer to the document CD-ROM for primary sources related to this chapter.

# CHAPTER 29

# FROM ELIOT TO AFRO-POP

## Art and Thought
## Around the World

### (1900–2000)

## A GLANCE AHEAD: THE ROCKY ROAD TO GLOBAL CULTURE

The rocky road to global consciousness made some remarkable strides in the course of the tempestuous twentieth century. High culture and popular culture, globe-trotting local cultures and global culture icons mingled as international arts and ideas spread around the world.

A modern scientific world view found acceptance among educated people virtually everywhere, and many Western intellectuals looked gloomily on the world around them as a meaningless human construct. Experimental modernist and postmodernist arts sometimes supported, sometimes challenged the conflicting political and social ideologies of the century. Separate trends still manifested themselves in different parts of the world, of course, from Latin American "magical realism" to Africa's search for cultural identity in a changing world. But popular arts and ideas—from American movies to African music, from Buddhism to the Beatles—found an audience in many lands.

Some at least of these complex trends and currents pointed to an emerging global life of the mind and spirit. And as we will emphasize in the final chapter of this book, there were other, more concrete social, economic, and political aspects of the century that also brought the peoples of the world together. But—as we must also stress—there were also many who rejected the whole five-centuries-long drift toward one world. And some of these antiglobalizers pointed with particular dismay at the crumbling of ancient local cultures as global culture spread.

## A DISINTEGRATING WORLD VIEW

### From Atoms to Outer Space

The cultural history of the twentieth century clearly reflected its place as a turning point in the human story. This first century of genuinely global history seemed to be stumbling toward a truly global culture as well. The result was a century of art and thought perhaps fuller of changes, challenges, and new directions than any other in human history.

One source of this confusion of fundamental convictions was a transformation of the primarily scientific world view that the Western world had been cultivating for the preceding three or four centuries. Since the days of Copernicus and Newton in the sixteenth and seventeenth centuries, science had increasingly seemed to educated Western people to provide answers to the riddles of the universe that philosophy and religion had once attempted to explain. Around the turn of the twentieth century, however, scientists began to uncover evidence and to develop theories that brought much of the Newtonian world view into question. By the 1920s and 1930s, disturbing questions were being asked about the ultimate nature of matter, the validity of natural law, and the very possibility of scientific truth—doubts that soon reached elites in the rest of the world as well.

The distinctive qualities of matter had been clearly defined since the seventeenth century. Matter possessed mass and extension in space; it was solid, made of tiny concrete particles called atoms. But around 1900, the work of Marie Curie with radium—which disintegrated from matter into pure radiant energy—and the discovery of cosmic rays and X-rays caused some scientists to question the solid materiality of all physical phenomena. The researches of H. A. Lorenz and of Ernest Rutherford and Niels Bohr showed that the allegedly solid atom was in fact composed largely of space between subatomic particles

Albert Einstein, the most famous genius of the "Second Scientific Revolution." This was the man whose theory of gravitation upset Newton's and who introduced relativity into the exact sciences. His genial humanity also helped to give science a "human face" just as the increasing abstractness and complexity of the modern physical sciences rendered them almost incomprehensible to most nonspecialists. (The Bettmann Archive)

orbiting around a nucleus. In time, even these particles were discovered to be composed not of matter, as it had once been defined, but of pure charges of energy.

Natural laws, the linchpins that had held the material world together since Newton, were also reinterpreted in disturbing ways in the decades after 1900. Evidence accumulated that there were exceptions to these allegedly absolute principles. These exceptions might be rare, and they might occur largely at the microscopic level. But they led scientists to think more and more that natural "laws" were statistical probabilities rather than absolute truths.

The very possibility of scientific truth, finally, was called into question. The relativity of truth invaded pure science after the turn of the century with Albert Einstein's famous theory of relativity in physics. Einstein demonstrated that both space and time, the absolute givens of Newtonian physics, were in fact always relative rather than absolute. Einstein defined time as a form of perception rather than as something "out there." Time, he declared, was relative to the position of the observer, to his motion, through space. Space also was far from fixed and absolute. The size of an object moving at velocities approaching the speed of light would actually decrease, whereas its mass would increase as the velocity did. Einstein's general theory of relativity redefined the universe as a whole as a four-dimensional continuum in which time and space were relative to each other—and in which the queasy layperson might feel that he or she had nowhere solid left to stand.

Werner Heisenberg put the capstone on the confusion at the end of the 1920s by announcing in his notorious principle of indeterminacy that there were definable limits to human knowledge. Even the introduction of a scientific measuring instrument, Heisenberg asserted, would so alter the reality being measured that the complete truth about the behavior of even an electron could never be known.

Yet twentieth-century researchers did not give up the search for scientific truth. In fact, as the century advanced, discoveries came so thick and fast that the later 1800s and the 1900s were increasingly hailed as a "second scientific revolution." Perhaps most sensational and sweeping in their impact were developments in nuclear energy, cosmology, and space technology.

The American atomic bombs over Japan, which brought an end to World War II, launched the world as a whole into what quickly became known as the atomic age. Those relatively primitive bombs based on nuclear fission—the "splitting" of the atom—were soon replaced by much more powerful hydrogen bombs based on nuclear fusion. Nuclear fusion, as it turned out, could also be generated in a controlled fashion, which produced a limitless flow of power for peaceful as well as military uses. In the second half of the twentieth century, then, many nations switched to nuclear power for a large part of the energy they needed.

Even more amazing breakthroughs came in the previously science-fiction realm of space travel. Beginning around 1960, space scientists began to explore the universe beyond the earth's atmosphere. Soviet cosmonauts orbited the earth and spent months in space. The United States sent astronauts to the moon, landed unmanned spacecraft on Mars, and photographed other planets close up.

New theories about the origin, structure, development, and possible future of the universe also emerged in the midcentury decades. In the later 1900s, the so-called "big bang" theory predominated among cosmologists. In this view, all the matter and energy in the universe had at one time been condensed into a single incredibly dense sphere. Then, a few billion years ago, this primal fireball exploded. The result was the cosmos we know—an expanding universe in which galaxies, stars, planets, and smaller fragments propelled by this cosmic explosion continued to fly apart at incredible speeds.

Almost all the behavior of this expanding universe proved to be explainable in terms of three basic forces. These were gravity, redefined as a field of force linking all matter; the electromagnetic force that holds atoms together; and the strong nuclear force that binds the core particles of the atom.

## Psychology and Sociobiology

The biological sciences also experienced drastic changes during the twentieth century.

The middle decades of the century in particular saw a remarkable series of medical discoveries. Penicillin, discovered in the 1930s, was only the first of a number of "wonder drugs" that curbed infections and cured once fatal diseases. Vaccines were developed that virtually wiped out such plagues as polio. Medical science also developed pills that controlled the psychological tensions and depressions generated by the pressures of modern society. For a time, it looked as if there might be a pill for every ill, with lengthening life spans, health, and happiness a virtual birthright for citizens of an industrializing world.

There were problems, however. The global influenza epidemic that followed World War I killed more millions than the war itself. Late in the century, once "eradicated" diseases began to take a toll once more. And at least one new major plague haunted the world in the 1990s. AIDS—Acquired Immune Deficiency Syndrome—was an invariably fatal disease commonly transmitted sexually, for which no cure was known. As the number of those infected grew, the world whistled past the graveyard, ignoring a pestilence that, if not contained, could match the Black Death of the Middle Ages in its consequences.

Early in the century, meanwhile, a number of new theories concerning human psychology also emerged. Sigmund Freud's concept of the human mind emphasized sexuality, childhood, the repression of our basic impulses, and the dominant role of the unconscious mind.

For Freud the human psyche resembled an iceberg. The conscious portion of the mind is only the tip of the iceberg; the unconscious mind, nine tenths of the whole, is in-

Even in the Western nations with the strongest traditions of freedom, some groups felt oppressed in the twentieth century. Feminists urged that patriarchy—domination of society by the male sex—was still a real and painful problem for women. As they saw it, the socialization process that perpetuated patriarchy warped the attitudes of both little girls and little boys. In this passage, the leading French intellectual Simone de Beauvoir links this process to childish impressions of history.

What effect does de Beauvoir think history as taught has on a young girl's view of the relative importance of men and women in the world? Note that the historical (and journalistic) accounts mentioned here focus on individuals—history as the story of "great white men." Do you think a type of history that emphasized social trends or material culture would be less male-centered?

*"Everything helps to confirm this hierarchy in the eyes of the little girl. The historical and literary culture to which she belongs, the songs and legends with which she is lulled to sleep, are one long exaltation of man. It was men who built up Greece, the Roman Empire, France, and all other nations, who have explored the world and invented the tools for its exploitation, who have governed it, who have filled it with sculptures, paintings, works of literature. Children's books, mythology, stories, tales, all reflect the myths born of the pride and the desires of men; thus it is through the eyes of men the little girl discovers the world and reads therein her destiny.*

*The superiority of the male is, indeed, overwhelming: Perseus, Hercules, David, Achilles, Lancelot, the old French warriors Du Guesclin and Bayard, Napoleon—so many men for one Joan of Arc.*

*The goddesses of pagan mythology are frivolous or capricious, and they all tremble before Jupiter. While Prometheus magnificently steals fire from the sun, Pandora opens her box of evils upon the world.*

*Reality confirms what these novels and legends say. If the young girl reads the papers, if she listens to the conversation of grown-ups, she learns that today, as always, men run the world. The political leaders, generals, explorers, musicians, and painters whom she admires are men; certainly it is men who arouse enthusiasm in her heart."*

Simone de Beauvoir, *The Second Sex*, trans. H. M. Parshley (New York: Random House, 1974), pp. 324–326.

visible beneath the surface. But it is the drift of that submerged nine tenths that determines where the visible tip will go. This unconscious mind beneath the surface is driven by what Freud called *libido,* primal psychic energy consisting originally of sexual desire—which thus becomes the central motivating force in human life.

Another psychological pioneer was the Russian Ivan Pavlov, the first proponent of the school of behaviorist psychology. Working primarily with animals in his laboratories, Pavlov developed the concept of the conditioned reflex as the central explanation for human as well as other animal behavior. Discovering that animals could be conditioned by positive or negative responses to their behaviors, he argued that accidental or deliberate conditioning in a given social environment determined how all human beings behave.

## From Existentialism to Deconstruction

Like the new scientific world view, the most striking new philosophies of the twentieth century took shape in Europe and spread slowly to the rest of the world. Existentialism emerged in the first half of the century, structuralism and its spin-offs poststructuralism and deconstruction in the second half. Both streams of thought provided philosophical underpinnings for the increasingly negative view of the human condition that prevailed in much of the world as the century drew near its end.

*Existentialism* saw the world and human life as simply existing, lacking all higher meaning, significance, or point. Developed by German and French thinkers between the 1930s and the 1960s, this materialistic view declared that all philosophical or religious explanations for our existence were mere human inventions. In Jean-Paul Sartre's telling phrases, "the heavens are empty" and "hell is other people."

On the positive side, existentialists claimed the most radical freedom ever asserted—the right to *invent* values, to *impose* meaning upon a meaningless universe. But even existential freedom brought its share of *Angst,* or anguish—the terrifying obligation to make up the meaning of life.

*Structuralists* were more likely to be students of language, literary critics, or anthropologists than philosophers. Their world view, far from dismissing theories, seemed to assert that *only* systems of thought and structures of language were real. Structuralist anthropologists like Claude Levi-Strauss studied the *patterns* of myths, not their social or historical references. What mattered about a book, structuralist critics declared, was not its content but the patterns of language it revealed. Structuralist thinkers also expanded the concept of language to include all systems of "signs" or symbols. They insisted that only these systems of meaning mattered—not the "real world" that the words, images, or other symbols claimed to represent.

*Poststructuralists* argued that the establishment brainwashed the public into accepting the status quo by controlling the "discourse," the permissible forms of expression and lines of argument. They rejected the literal meanings of the "text," as they called a book, a picture, a political speech, or a style of clothing. Instead, they sought to expose the real

Existentialist Jean-Paul Sartre and feminist Simone de Beauvoir, Europe's leading intellectual couple during the postwar decades, wait for a meal at an outdoor cafe. Their novels, plays, and books of philosophy and social commentary helped set the agenda for the intellectual life of the West in the second half of the twentieth century. (Photographer Giansanti: Corbis/Sygma)

significance of the "subtext" beneath the official text—and to show how this system of signs really functions as a tool of social control.

*Deconstructionists* sometimes seemed to go even further. In deconstructionist analysis of a book, the author, the author's intent, even the text itself do not exist. Only the *reader's perception* of these things is demonstrably there at all.

## Creeds, Cults, and Fundamentalisms

Religion in the twentieth century, as we have seen, at one level faced vigorous intellectual challenges. But at a popular level, cults, creeds, and religious convictions of all sorts showed an impressive degree of vitality.

Religious ideas, like so much else on the twentieth-century cultural scene, flowed back and forth from one culture to another. The century began with a new surge of Christian missionary activity spreading the Gospel message to non-Christians from China to Africa. At the other end of the century, evangelical Protestant groups were carrying their version of the Word to formerly Communist Eastern Europe and even Catholic Latin America. Throughout the century, meanwhile, Asian faiths were making increasing numbers of converts among Western peoples. Popularized versions of Hinduism, Buddhism, and some forms of Islam touched the hearts of spiritually empty Americans and Europeans for whom traditional Christianity had little appeal.

For those who sought the supernatural in zones still more and more remote, the century provided an increasing variety of religious cults. Some of them were dangerous, like the Japanese Aum Shinrikyo cultists who attempted to spread poison gas through the Tokyo subway. Others were a menace only to themselves, like the California group who committed mass suicide under the impression that they were on their way to a space ship in the wake of a passing comet. Most seemed to reveal a genuine hunger and thirst for the sort of simple faith that still filled many Latin American churches or moved the poorest Southeast Asian villagers to drop a daily bit of rice into the begging bowls of Buddhist monks.

A notable trend of the religious life of the world's peoples as the century drew to a close, finally, was a resurgence of fundamentalist doctrines. *Fundamentalist* religion called for a return to the basic principles of ancient faiths—to belief in the literal truth of the Christian Bible, for instance, or to rigorous application of the Muslim Law. Fundamentalists also emphasized traditional practices and customs, from dietary regulations and distinctive costumes to traditional caste or gender roles. They were often aggressively militant, ready to fight for their beliefs. Hindus, Muslims, and Sikhs fought in the streets of northern India; Muslim extremists fought their fellow Pakistinians as well as Israelis in the Near East. In the United States, evangelical Christians attacked secular humanism, crusaded against pornography and abortion, and urged prayer in the schools.

How successful this fundamentalist counterattack might be in the long run remained in doubt. Western Europe's churches did not seem to be refilling, and Japan continued to celebrate Christmas without Christianity, as a marketing device. Muslim Pakistan twice elected a woman, Benazir Bhutto, prime minister—a distinctively untraditional role for a woman in Muslim lands. And even fundamentalist Americans appeared to feel that religion was a private matter, not a requirement for citizenship. On the other hand, astonishing numbers also believed that the end of the world was near as the century turned.

## ART AMONG THE ISMS

### The Rise of Modernism

The arts in the twentieth century reflected the same sort of conflict and confusion that was shattering traditional world views. In particular, twentieth-century literature, painting, sculpture, architecture, music, and other arts displayed two basic tendencies in many parts of the world. One of these was the modernist enthusiasm for artistic experimentation. The other put art at the service of revolutionary social movements or authoritarian political regimes.

Early twentieth-century modernism generated a host of new schools and individual experimentation. Modernists operated in an atmosphere of militant manifestos and defiant "little magazines," grubby studios, and bohemian cafes. They shrugged off the censors who found their subject matter obscene and ignored the general public, who could not understand them. For some, popularity itself was evidence of "selling out," pandering to the vulgar taste of the mass market. To all modernists, what mattered was originality and self-expression.

In the arts, modernism quickly replaced Renaissance naturalism and its close study of anatomy, perspective, and nature with a new passion for pure form. Modern artists gave themselves over wholeheartedly to exploring the formal elements of which all art is made: color, line, shape, volume, texture, movement, tone. They also glorified the quest itself; novelty, exploration, and innovation in the arts became ends in themselves. Originality in art, a cult since the romantics, became the high god of the modernists.

New schools of art thus proliferated during the early decades of the present century. Futurism in Italy and Russia came to terms with the speed and power of modern technology, worshipping at the shrine of the locomotive, the automobile, and the airplane. Cubism in France, led by the expatriate Spaniard Pablo Picasso, broke nature up into its component geometrical shapes and reassembled them in barely recognizable forms on the canvas. Surrealist artists such as Salvador Dalí tried to liberate the Freudian unconscious by painting a dream world of sexually suggestive figures, melting clocks, and technicolor skies. Mavericks such as Paul Klee, Vasily Kandinsky, and Piet Mondrian abandoned subject matter completely, painting purely abstract patterns and brightly colored shapes that were dazzlingly decorative but totally without content.

Modernism raged happily through the arts. Architects such as Frank Lloyd Wright insisted that modern buildings should not imitate traditional Gothic or Greek styles but should follow function and integrate their structure into their natural surroundings. The twelve-tone scale invented by Arnold Schönberg revolutionized modern music, and Igor Stravinsky's *Firebird, Rite of Spring,* and other ballets scandalized Paris with their bizarre themes, staging, and rhythms, and their apparent abandonment of melody and harmony. American dancer and choreographer Martha Graham developed modern dance as an expression both of deep human emotions and of great themes in human life and myth.

Pablo Picasso (1881–1973), the king of modern art, was in his heyday between the wars. A lifelong experimenter—he lived into his nineties, changing every decade, sometimes every year—Picasso most disturbed the art world with his development of cubism before, during, and after World War I. Pictures such as *Les Demoiselles d' Avignon* and *Les Trois Musiciens* broke their subjects up into their component shapes, simplified these shapes into geometry, and then rearranged them for artistic effect, much as you might arrange flowers in a vase or rocks in a Japanese garden. Yet he could use Cubist techniques to make a powerful point, as in his attack on the horrors of war in *Guernica.*

Western writers also expressed their sense of artistic vocation—and their disinterest in a large readership—by a growing emphasis on self-expression as the point of art. This approach led in turn to a deliberate obscurity cultivated through the use of unfamiliar allusions, private symbols, and even foreign languages and references to details of the author's personal life that no reader would be likely to understand. Thus T. S. Eliot, perhaps the most famous Western poet of the century, was able to squeeze three languages and references to an Elizabethan dramatist, a French romantic poet, Dante, and the Hindu Upanishads into half a dozen lines of his poem *The Waste Land.*

Yet wonderful work could come from writers and artists working in these modernist modes. In novels like *To the Lighthouse,* Virginia Woolf pioneered the "stream of consciousness" technique, widely used since, which views events entirely through the eyes, hearts, and minds of characters in the story. James Joyce's notorious novel *Ulysses* follows not a Greek hero but an ordinary Irish advertising solicitor through a single unexceptional day in Dublin, making that day emblematic of the whole of modern culture at its most various and dehumanizing. Franz Kafka's strange and sometimes terrifying parables of modern life, including short stories like "Metamorphosis" and "In the Penal Colony" and such enigmatic novels as *The Trial,* suggested haunting, even horrifying depths beneath the surfaces of modern life.

## Modernism Around the World

Modernism was born in the West, but it soon spread much farther. It became the true high-international style of the twentieth century—particularly after World War II.

As early as the years between the wars, non-European artists such as the enigmatic Argentine short-story writer Jorge Luis Borges and the Japanese painter Togo Seiji were

Pablo Picasso's famous painting of an attack on a Spanish town, <u>Guernica</u>, used Cubist techniques of breaking up, simplifying, and reassembling images to present a deeply disturbing view of modern war. The painting, which was kept in the United States throughout the years of the Franco dictatorship, has been sent to Spain since the restoration of democracy in that country. (Pablo Picasso, <u>Guernica</u> 1937. Oil on canvas. 11′5 1/2″ × 25′5 3/4″) Museo Nacional Centro de Arte Reina Sofia/© 1998 Estate of Pablo Picasso/Artists Rights Society (ARS), New York producing widely admired work in the modernist vein. The Mexican painter Frida Kahlo used a highly personalized surrealist style to express both her own suffering and that of her people. And the Egyptian novelist Naguib Mahfouz depicted his own country's twentieth-century transformation in a range of modernist techniques that won him a Nobel prize.

In the decades after World War II, however, modernism's determination to break with the Western cultural tradition made the modernist style highly appealing to non-Western peoples in many parts of the world. The modernists' reduction of art to its fundamental formal elements made their work uniquely comprehensible as a purely aesthetic experience, as culture-free as art could be. Experimental art, it seemed, was truly free of cultural limitations—and hence it was the ideal international style.

Modernist architecture in particular traveled with ease and appropriateness around the globe during the post-World War II years. Developed especially by European architects such as Mies van der Rohe or le Corbusier, these distinctively twentieth-century styles of building were based on exploiting the possibilities of new building materials and modes of construction: reinforced concrete, glass, steel, plastics, the high-rise block, and the geodesic dome. The result was a vocabulary of basic shapes and sweeping contours that was as free of associations with any particular culture as any art could be.

Modernist techniques and styles were thus applied with equal success to public buildings and business blocks, hotels, and universities in many countries. Chinese-born American architect I. M. Pei could design with equal ease the Mile High Center in Denver and the glass pyramid added to the Louvre art museum in Paris.

Entire national capitals for countries as culturally diverse as Brazil, Arabia, and India were built in the modernist mode. A roughly representational mural on a local theme, a decorative band of Aztec hieroglyphics or Arabic script seems to have been enough to make modernist architecture fit into any tradition around the world.

## Revolutionary and Totalitarian Propaganda in the Arts

Two examples of earlier-twentieth-century revolutionary culture will be touched on all too briefly here: the diverse culture flowerings that occurred in Mexico and India.

In Mexico, painting was the predominant art in the remarkable renaissance that followed the revolution there. A militant "Indianism" infused much of this work. As part of their effort to elevate the long-oppressed peasantry, the Mexican revolutionary governments of the 1920s and 1930s celebrated the Native American as the most down-trodden of all prerevolutionary groups. And the broadest human ideals, as epitomized in the rendering experience of the revolution, captured the imagination of the new artists.

The most admired builders of Mexico's revolutionary culture between the wars were its internationally known group of mural painters, José Orozco, David Siqueiros, and above all Diego Rivera. In huge modernistic paintings on the walls or ceilings of public buildings, these artists celebrated the greatness of pre-Columbia Mexican culture and of the revolution, the nobility of the peasant and the factory worker, Mexican patriotism and human achievement. Rivera's poetic, massively simplified, formally composed murals of *Earth and the Elements,* and *Man in Four Aspects* (laborer, scientist, philosopher, rebel) bring years of training in European modernism to the service of the Mexican Revolution.

On the other side of the world, in India, continuing developments in Hinduism combined with a surge of Indian literary creativity. The result was vigorous cultural support for the nationalist political movement spearheaded by the Congress party. On the religious side, traditional Hinduism was taught in seclusion by gurus. On the literary side, the Indian flowering grew through a fertile fusion of Indian and European elements. The influences of Western romanticism and realism contributed to the emergence of the modern novel and short story in India. Romantic and historical subjects persisted, but there was more attention than before to realistic description and modern psychological portraiture. Social problems, ranging from the caste system to the condition of women, became important subjects.

The leading light of this self-confident, self-conscious Indian cultural revival was Rabindranath Tagore, whose Nobel prize for literature in 1913 earned him world-wide renown. Tagore's poems, plays, stories, and novels were rooted in a deep love of his native Bengal, of the river Ganges that flows through it to the sea, and of the peasant villagers among whom he lived much of his life. His vision had a deep spiritual dimension as well, and he worked for both religious and secular education in India.

The forms of totalitarian culture were as diverse as the cultural traditions from which these new and extreme forms of twentieth-century authoritarianism sprang. Yet there were some similarities too.

Nazi propagandists tirelessly preached the greatness of the *Führer,* the party elite, and the Aryan master race. Nazi art attempted to communicate this message with an eclectic array of romantic nineteenth-century and glossy modern imagery. Paintings of Hitler accoutered as a knight in shining armor illustrated his role as defender of his people. The monolithic, square-pillared Nazi public buildings, sometimes described as "totalitarian gothic," projected the sense of monumental power that was central to the Nazi self-image. Nazi regalia itself—the military uniforms, medals, weapons, the death's heads and lightning-shaped SS insignia, the flapping blood-red banners with the hooked-cross swastika emblem—all radiated the barbaric strength the Nazis clung to.

The great party rallies were carefully staged so as to embody all these core qualities of Nazi totalitarianism. One, at least, has been preserved: the Nuremberg rally of 1934, which the gifted film-maker Leni Riefenstahl made into the artistically acclaimed *Triumph of the Will.* It is all there, living still on film: the German gothic architecture of the old city and the new Leader descending in a shiny modern airplane to his people. The blond, clean-cut Hitler Youth, the packed stadium, and the *Führer* leaning toward them with his rising off-key rhetoric, his voice shaking with passion, fist slamming the podium. Below him, the rigid military formations greet every chopping point with right arms shooting up, voices rising in the rolling *Sieg heil!*—"Hail, victory!"—of the Nazi salute.

Many talented people were filled with genuine enthusiasm for the Russian Revolution in the early years. The symbolist poet Aleksandr Blok produced an evocative vision of the most violent days of the Revolution in *The Twelve,* the lusty, sometimes brutal epic of a Bolshevik platoon—led by the symbolic figure of Christ!

The glorification of the working masses, the proletarians and peasants who were the chosen people of the Communist promised land, was another salient aspect of Soviet totalitarianism. The art and literature that embodied these concepts went by the label of *socialist realism.* It was, as the Communist Union of Soviet Writers declared, an art "saturated with the heroic struggle of the world proletariat and with the grandeur of the victory of socialism ... reflecting the great wisdom and heroism of the Communist Party . . . ."[1] The socialist realist paintings of those days show brawny factory workers or bronzed farmers toiling for the motherland, Lenin Speaking to the People, or heroic incidents from the Russian past.

---

[1]Gleb Struve, *Soviet Russian Literature 1917–1950* (Norman: University of Oklahoma Press, 1951), p. 239.

Even within this framework, however, some impressive art could be produced. The internationally celebrated films of Sergei Eisenstein, in particular, grappled with the artistic problem of the collective hero posed by Communist doctrine with remarkable success. Eisenstein's masterwork of the 1920s, *Battleship Potemkin,* immortalized the 1905 naval mutiny that Communists saw as a forerunner of their own revolution. Art-film fanciers in the decadent West were soon lining up to revel in Eisenstein's surging crowd scenes and searing montage effects—the shattering cuts from cheering crowds to charging police, and then to the unforgettable close-ups—a baby carriage jolting down the wide cement stairs, a screaming face, broken glasses, blood gushing from an eye.

## The Rise of Postmodernism

Hovering behind these cultural problems of the later twentieth century was a new tendency in the arts increasingly labeled *postmodernism.* Like the structuralists, poststructuralist, and deconstructionists considered above, postmodernists challenged even twentieth-century culture to justify itself. For postmodernists, modernist giants like T. S. Eliot or Frank Lloyd Wright were as much elitist enemies of the new, free art as any earlier classic or academician.

Postmodernism erupted first in architecture, where modern tower blocks of glass and concrete were rejected as soulless. Postmodernist architects added bright colors, playful details, and architectural touches borrowed from earlier styles, though the latter were deployed with a knowing wink as joking allusions to the dead past. Postmodernism affected many other aspects of twentieth-century culture too, from journalism, photography, and motion pictures to music, the dance, television videos, and fashion in clothing. Everywhere a tongue-in-cheek sense of playfulness and artificiality dominated the postmodern cultural scene.

Postmodernist writers turned their backs on realism, emphasizing instead word play, extravagant or intrusive styles, and story lines that were impossible or outrageous. Rejecting the traditional hierarchy of literary genres, they were as likely to turn their hands to detective stories or science fiction as to esoteric poetry or ponderously obscure novels. And though they claimed no exalted artistic vocation, they constantly put themselves at the center of their "self-reflexive" works, tirelessly reminding readers that what they were reading was, after all, "only a story."

Literary conventions and traditional subject matter thus crumbled once more in the hands of the postmodernists. American novelist John Hawkes firmly declared that "the true enemies of the novel" were "plot, character, setting, and themes."[2] The "real world" was dismissed, and fantasy enjoyed free reign. In *Invisible Cities,* the Italian writer Italo Calvino offered an incredible travelogue of physically impossible but philosophically intriguing urban complexes as they might have been described by a postmodern Marco Polo to a very gullible Kublai Khan. Postmodern critics followed poststructuralists and deconstructionists in asserting that it was "impossible any longer to see reality as something 'out there,' a fixed order of things which language merely reflected."[3]

## Postmodernism Around the World

Outside Europe and North America, postmodern modes gradually infected other late twentieth-century cultures as well. Much Latin American magical realism has a post-

---

[2]Quoted in "John Hawkes: An Interview," *Wisconsin Studies in Contemporary Literature,* Vol. 6 (1965), p. 143.

[3]Terry Eagleton, *Literary Theory* (Minneapolis: University of Minneapolis Press, 1983), p. 108.

modern ring, mixing fact and fantasy in self-conscious artifacts. The same could be said for much African and other art that commingled often gritty realism with supernatural legendry, history with myth. And the most developed of Asian societies produced full-fledged post-modern literature whose medium of expression was at least as important as its message.

Among the writers of Latin America's literary "boom," Manuel Puig produced a series of postmodern novels and plays like *Betrayed by Rita Hayworth* and *Kiss of the Spider Woman.* His work drew heavily on such popular culture icons as mystery stories and romance fiction, glamour magazines, sports, and above all the movies. In works like *Hopscotch,* Julio Cortázar, an Argentine writer based in literary Paris, produced works that read like wrestling matches with language itself.

African writers who aroused interest as postmodernists included Sony Labou Tansi, weaver of intricate webs of "suprareal fiction." Nigerian writer Ben Okri mingled African folk beliefs with the realities of African village and shantytown life in his prize-winning *The Famished Road.* Here compassionately described characters mingle with hallucinatory, often terrifying creatures out of African legend.

In Asia, Japan's rapid postwar plunge into an affluent consumer society dominated by foreign cultural imports produced some sophisticated postmodern work. Tanaka Yasua's novel, *Somehow, Crystal,* was a plotless adolescent daydream of glittering shops and brand-name products, American or European words, and unrelated feelings. From Bombay came Muslim novelist Salman Rushdie, mixing India's real past with its ancient religions in *Midnight's Children.* Rushdie earned a death sentence from Iran's Ayatollah Khomenei for his blasphemous treatment of the Prophet Muhammad in his international best-seller, *The Satanic Verses.*

Wherever postmodernism spread, it raised disturbing questions about what was real, what was important, and what values ought to dominate our lives. In a world in the grip of surging change, readers in many lands found relief in realms of fantasy and games, in pop culture, and in radical challenges to the way things were.

## CONTINENTAL CULTURES

### European Literature Bears Witness

As we have seen, both modernism and postmodernism had international appeal. You could find "French modernist" painting done by Vietnamese artists decorating the walls of a cafe in old Hanoi, and international-style architecture bloomed from South Africa to Singapore. But the arts of the twentieth century did differ significantly from one part of the world to another. We will look next at the unique or distinctive contributions of each of the major inhabited continents to global culture during this tumultuous century.

In the decades after 1945, many European writers sought to use literature to turn a searchlight on the dark side of the century's history. Ironically, many of these targets were the totalitarian regimes that had seemed to offer hope to many during the first half of the century.

An internationally known example was George Orwell, a British socialist author who vividly depicted the suffering of the masses during the Great Depression before World War II—and then exposed the communist solution to the problem of poverty after the war. Orwell's novels *Animal Farm* and above all *1984* warned of a totalitarian future where some are "more equal" than others and a Stalinist "Big Brother" rules an enslaved population through propaganda and terror.

Survivors of continental totalitarian regimes also testified to the nightmare underside of the century's dream of a brave new world. In West Germany, Günter Grass's *The Tin Drum* forced the German generations who had plunged into two world wars and cheered Adolf Hitler to face their past. In the Soviet Union, Boris Pasternak's *Dr. Zhivago* offered an epic and deeply moving account of the collapse of Russian society during the Revolution. Alexander Solzhenitsyn's writings, especially the brief but powerful *One Day in the Life of Ivan Denisovitch* and his multivolume compilation of prisoners' memoirs, *The Gulag Archipelago,* vividly exposed the brutality of Stalinist labor camps.

## America's Cultural Critique

In the United States as in Europe, writers chipped away throughout the century at American society's faults and failings. Between the wars, the experimental plays of Eugene O'Neill tried virtually everything, from Greek tragedy set in rural New England in *Mourning Becomes Electra* to using voodoo drums to involve us in the decline and fall of a Caribbean dictator in *The Emperor Jones.* William Faulkner created his own world in the deep south, setting many of his novels and stories in the imaginary Yaknapatawpha county, Mississippi, and novels like *The Sound and the Fury* entirely in the minds of its highly disturbed characters.

After World War II, the writings of such widely admired novelists as Normal Mailer and Saul Bellow seldom presented an orthodox "good guy" hero. Sylvia Plath's poems and autobiographical novel, *The Bell Jar,* revealed the psychological anguish of growing up sensitive and a woman in mid-century America. The plays of Arthur Miller probed deeply into the American psyche, exposing the witch-hunting mentality of the McCarthy years in *The Crucible* and the hollowness at the heart of a typical American family in *Death of a Salesman.* Novels like Ralph Ellison's *Invisible Man* and *Beloved* by Pulitzer prize winner Toni Morrison drew upon the African-American experience to forge complex and powerful works of art.

Both world wars and the Vietnam War triggered floods of antiwar writing. And some young Americans in each generation turned their backs on middle-class society altogether and followed Ernest Hemingway to the bull-fights in Spain where *The Sun Also Rises* or Jack Kerouac *On the Road* across America.

## Latin American Magical Realism

Latin America bloomed somewhat later but in an equally dazzling display of literary experimentation and social criticism. Some Latin American writers became leading modernist voices in the earlier 1900s; but it was after 1945 that Latin American magical realism began to generate books with a global appeal.

Leaders in the glittering galaxy of Latin American writers included Jorge Luis Borges, Carlos Fuentes, and Gabriel García Márquez. Borges, an Argentine writer who spent many years in Europe, became internationally known between the wars for his short fictions, tales that seemed to combine the charm of anecdotes or Arabian nights' entertainments with deeper meanings, philosophical mazes without exits.

Carlos Fuentes, a Mexican author educated in the United States, and the Colombian novelist Gabriel García Márquez became leading practitioners of the unique combination of realism and fantasy called *magical realism.* Fuentes's mingling of naturalistic detail and dream-like surrealism won him an international reputation for such novels as his study of the corruption of a Mexican Revolutionary hero, *The Death of Artemio Cruz.* García

Márques's worldwide best-seller, *One Hundred Years of Solitude,* carved out his private universe in the jungle-girt Colombian village of Macondo. Whether it is the discovery of ice in the tropics or the arrival of a flying carpet over the rooftops, life is always full of wonders in Macondo. Like Faulkner's county, García Márques's village turned local color into high art.

## Africa's Search for Cultural Identity

Like other regions overrun by Western imperialists in the nineteenth century, liberated twentieth-century Africa faced a problem of cultural identity. Africa writers and artists inevitably felt the influence of Western, particularly European culture. But they also sought eagerly to recover their precolonial roots in the traditional African past. Out of this mixed heritage and the traumatic experience of the great liberation itself, Africa forged new forms of cultural expression in the second half of the century.

Some of the most widely known African literature was produced in two of the world's international languages, English and French. French-speaking West African poets like the Senegalese Léopold Senghor—later president of his country—celebrated the mysterious essence of Africa in the poetry of *négritude,* or "blackness." English-language writers such as Chinua Achebe won global renown for novels like *Things Fall Apart,* dealing with the shattering impact of imperialism, and *A Man of the People,* vividly evoking the chaotic results of liberation. In southern Africa, a galaxy of black and white writers, including Nadine Gordimer and J. M. Coetzee, made the world conscious of the dehumanizing consequences of apartheid.

Other creative spirits used African rather than European languages, among them another major international language, Arabic. The Egyptian writer and critic Taha Hussein knew both Europe and his homeland well despite blindness from an early age. Taha wrote of his own life in two beautiful volumes, *An Egyptian Childhood* and *Stream of Days,* while his later critical writings urged modern Egyptian culture to find its place in a Mediterranean context.

South of the Sahara, excellent writers in languages from Wolof to Zulu gave western and southern Africa rich regional literatures in the postcolonial period. In modern Nigeria, for instance, Yoruba folk opera mingled traditional myths and history in a medley of forms including silent mime and spoken dialogue, song and dance, and powerful African music.

Independent Africa's search for cultural identity has often found vigorous expression in music and dance. Traditional black African music combined polyphony and percussion in complex rhythms that intrigue modern musicologists. Drums, xylophones, and the hand piano, or *mbila,* produced an intricate yet intoxicating outpouring of sound that was distinctively African.

African dances, widely preserved and developed, continued to play a key part in rural African society. Line and round dances were common, and sensational stilt dances never failed to awe visitors. The integration of old and new come home vividly when you see stilt dancers celebrating a ritual occasion in a West African village—and later opening a new supermarket in town.

## Asia's Confrontation with Cultural Change

In Asia as in Africa, a variety of peoples confronted social change in the second half of the twentieth century. The impact of Western influences, economic growth, war, and politics brought sweeping changes to established forms of Asian literature and art.

In India, writers in English and in a number of historic Indian literary languages produced fiction that focused on Indian problems yet found an international audience. R. K. Narayan, author of many books about the fictional south Indian village of Malgudi, was particularly well-known and widely read outside his own country. Kamala Markandaya surveyed a broad spectrum of Indian life, from dusty villages to teeming cities, in such novels as her widely admired *A Handful of Rice*. Perhaps the most famous of all "Indian" writers, however, was "Indian" only by ancestry. V. S. Naipaul, born of immigrant parents in the West Indies and a resident of Britain for most of his life, traveled the world to write novels and travel books about the Caribbean (*Guerrillas*), Africa (*A Bend in the River*), the Middle East (*Among the Believers*), and the India from which his ancestors came (*India: A Wounded Civilization*).

In China, student culture had opened wide to Western influences in the earlier decades of the century, welcoming Western lecturers and devouring Western classics. After the triumph of the Communists in 1949, however, the cultural life of the Middle Kingdom was dominated by Mao Zedong's dictum that "Politics Takes Command!" in the arts. As in Soviet Russia under Stalin, literature in Mao's China set out to chronicle the victories of idealized workers and Communists over evil capitalists, landlords, and other oppressors. Chinese drama and opera also hailed the achievements of the People's Liberation Army and Chairman Mao, the "great helmsman." Only in the last decades of the century, under the more pragmatic regime of Deng Hsiaoping and his successor, Jiang Zemin, did a few writers begin to expose the grimmer side of the Great Leap Forward and the Red Guard era in first-person narratives like Gao Yuan's *Born Red: A Chronicle of the Cultural Revolution*.

Japan, as we have seen, absorbed many Western social and cultural influences during the later nineteenth and earlier twentieth centuries. Its military ambitions shattered in World War II, a new Japan rose to the economic heights in the following half-century. Japanese culture vividly expressed the impact of these dramatic changes.

Postwar Japan preserved many of its traditional arts, including print making, calligraphy, and the classic Japanese theater, honoring skilled practitioners of these arts as national treasures. At the same time, however, Japanese architects like Tange Kenzo, designer of the Hiroshima Peace Memorial, won international prestige for building in the modernist style.

Emblematic of these conflicting traditions was the career of Mishima Yukio. Mishima's brilliant postwar novels glorified Japan's traditional past, including samurai militarism, and condemned the new, Westernized Japan—yet combined sensuous Japanese prose with Western psychological analysis. Torn between two traditions, Mishima turned the last volume of his masterpiece, *The Sea of Fertility,* over to his publishers—futilely urged Japanese troops to overthrow their government—and then committed *sepukku,* ritual suicide in the ancient samurai tradition.

## POPULAR CULTURES WITH A GLOBAL REACH

### Folk Art Goes Cosmopolitan

On the popular level as well as in modernist and postmodernist circles, the arts displayed a tendency toward convergence and the beginnings of some sort of genuinely global taste in the later twentieth century. Both traditional folk art and contemporary popular art exhibited these trends toward common patterns of development.

Aboriginal dancers in the Australian Outback perform traditional dances near Alice Springs. The dance mimics the hunt–and–peck movements of a local game bird and symbolizes the oneness of the Aboriginal people with their natural environment. These particular dancers, however, are preparing for a European tour on which they will soon be embarking. (Anthony Esler)

Traditional arts would seem at first glance the least likely to contain such a global dimension. Artistic traditions, after all, are typically the defining features of separate regional cultures. From patterns on pots to the symbolic forms of temples (the cross, the mandala), traditional styles have historically distinguished one culture from another, heightening each people's sense of its own uniqueness. Styles in African masks, Andean textiles, Appalachian folk tales, and the folk dances of many lands are all cultural products that—it is often suggested—only a native can completely appreciate.

As it happens, however, the present century has seen a steadily growing appreciation for the traditional arts of all peoples. Interest in other peoples' cultural traditions spans an astonishing range today, from arts as demanding as Japanese Kabuki theater to those as accessible as African drumming and Cossack dances.

This international smorgasbord of traditional art has had its limitations and weaknesses. The very popularity of foreign culture could lead to the proliferation of "airport art"—mass-produced copies of authentic village art intended to separate tourists from their travelers checks. Even the most sensitive nonnative, furthermore, is unlikely to grasp the full social and spiritual significance of traditional art removed from its place in a living culture and hung like a trophy on a museum wall.

On the other hand, interest in other peoples' traditional art forms did mark a very considerable broadening of the world's taste. When whole museums were dedicated to "primitive" art, when sophisticates from New York, Paris, Berlin, New Delhi, Tokyo, or Mexico City could look at one another's traditional art with some understanding and with genuine admiration, the world's peoples were clearly closer to mutual respect than they had ever been before.

## Popular Arts, from Music to the Movies

Modernism was in a sense *the* first global style, the inter-continental style par excellence. But it was also high culture, an art for elites. People with education, money, and power stayed in modernist hotels, worked in modernist commercial, cultural, or government buildings, read Borges and Joyce, and covered their living room walls with abstract expressionist art. Recent years, however, have seen the birth of an international popular culture as well.

Popular arts having an international appeal were perhaps most noticeably those of music and film. Jazz, blues, and other forms of African-American music had a global appeal between the two world wars, as did such Latin American dances as the samba, the conga, and the rhumba. American rock 'n' roll, West Indian reggae, and the performances of intercontinental superstars such as the British Beatles and Rolling Stones continued this tradition of internationally adored popular music. A group hadn't "arrived" until it had toured Australia, and hotel musicians in Communist Yugoslavia were belting out international favorites such as "Itsy-Bitsy Teeny-Weeny Yellow Polka-Dot Bikini" in the depths of the Cold War years.

Perhaps the most dazzlingly successful form of popular art internationally, however, was the motion picture. The films of Hollywood's dream factories also went back to the interwar years in their popularity, and it was a popularity that continued throughout the second half of the century. Worldwide taste for American television—also a film medium—was overwhelming. Despite the ideological objections of some governments, despite the clucking of people with more sophisticated sensibilities in many countries, mass audiences around the world took enthusiastically to American television series.

The taste for American films and television shows was not a passion for things American so much as for things *modern*. American television had the urban feel and the smell of money, the violence, slickness, professional precision, and glitter of the century itself.

Classic Japanese films like Akiro Kurosawa's *Seven Samurai* fascinated Western audiences as much as American cowboy movies did people from other lands. The Japanese samurai warrior thus entered the global army of heroic types, from Indian and Greek epic heroes to European knights and Muslim *ghazis*. This particular film, in which these Japanese warriors join the peasants in their struggle against the bandits, inspired such Hollywood epics as *The Magnificent Seven*. (Photofest)

Television series such as "Dallas" were the dream of all the world—an unrealistic fantasy of a global Texas symbolized by the gleaming new skyscrapers and fabulous wealth of that quintessentially twentieth-century city.

Over the postwar decades, other nations also developed major motion picture industries. Artistic film-making flourished from France and Italy to India, China, and Japan. But other countries also produced their share of movies intended as popular entertainment. India's film industry evolved from musical comedies to three-hour historical epics which also included their share of impressive mass song-and-dance numbers. Hong Kong contributed Bruce Lee and the martial-arts movie to the world's menu of popular film fare.

## Counterflow: The Rest and the West

One final category of cultural exchange was the varied array of arts and ideas which flowed the other way—from the rest of the world to the Western world. For increasing numbers of Western peoples not only enjoyed non-Western performing arts and art shows but accepted non-Western ideas and art forms as part of their own culture. A strong counterflow was thus set up which contributed substantially to the drift toward a genuinely global culture.

Among the non-Western faiths that found followers in the West were all three of the major Asian religions—Hinduism, Buddhism, and Islam.

In many cases, of course, all of these religions came to Western countries with growing numbers of Asian and African immigrants. Muslims flocked into France from what had been French North Africa, and both Hindus and Muslims flooded into Britain from formerly British India. Practitioners of all three faiths arrived in growing numbers in the United States, Canada, Australia, and other traditional immigrant destinations.

But other citizens of Western countries also felt drawn to Hindu, Buddhist, or Islamic sects. Indian gurus set up meditation centers in Switzerland or Colorado and reaped rich harvests of seekers. By translating traditional Hindu concepts into modern Western-sounding terms like "vibrations" or "meditation," these spiritual guides were able to reach at least an educated segment of Western populations.

Buddhist monks also showed up in America and Europe, establishing ashrams and monasteries and organizing retreats, workshops, and seminars which drew many visitors. Islam found a particularly committed constituency among black Americans. The Nation of Islam and various Black Muslim institutions, from restaurants to religious houses, preached an unorthodox faith that combined self-reliance with a very un-Islamic racism.

The flow of non-Western religious ideas seemed endless. Many Westerners turned to yoga exercises to improve their physical and mental health. Some found mystic depths in the lamaism of Tibet. Others pored over Sufi devotional literature or learned the vigorous dances of Sufi "whirling dervishes." The more absorbed in material things Western culture seemed to become, the more eagerly some Western people turned to other civilizations for the sort of spirituality they could no longer find in convincing form at home.

Non-Western arts also found increasing numbers of admirers in Europe and America.

Popular music and dance drew heavily on African and Afro-Caribbean influences throughout the century. One younger generation after another gyrated to the rhythms of Latin American music or admired the vigor and later some of the subtleties of African–American jazz.

To this array, we should add the rich contributions of non-Western practitioners of arts that had at least originated in the West. African popular music—Afro-Pop—found a growing audience as Ghanian High Life or French West African bands performed in clubs in Western cities. And Asian film makers like the Indian Satyajit Ray and the Japanese master Akira Kurasawa were admired and studied by Western directors. The medium might be the product of Western technology, but the themes and stylistic qualities of the work of these artists vividly reflected their own non-Western cultural backgrounds. And the emerging global culture of our times was the richer for this fertile mixture.

## SUMMARY

The influence of Western culture on the rest of the world remained great throughout the twentieth century. Yet by the end of that century, a genuine, if varied and multifaceted, global culture did seem to be emerging.

Western art and thought themselves underwent a serious crisis during this period. Religion, philosophy, and science all faced powerful challenges from the spread of secularism, materialism, and various kinds of relativism. Yet the sciences added greatly to our understanding of the universe we live in. Existentialism, structuralism, and their offshoots transformed the way many people saw their world. And resurgent fundamentalism mobilized some of the world's great religions to reassert their basic values in the world. In the arts, modernist experimentalism combined with revolutionary political and social commitments to make the first half of the century a turbulent one for the West and the rest of the world. The cultural history of the second half of the twentieth century continued to reveal strong social and political influences on artists and writers in many lands. The period since 1945 also saw late modernism give way to even more experimental postmodern writing and art.

Popular art in particular, meanwhile, developed a global reach in the course of the twentieth century. Western peoples learned to admire the traditional arts of many cultures. Peoples around the world absorbed and imitated Western, especially American film, television and music. Though there were still strange and exotic things to be seen in many lands, the makings of a global civilization seemed to be coming together by the year 2000.

## SUGGESTED READING

Achebe, C. *Things Fall Apart.* New York: Heinemann, 1981. A disturbing novel of the new Africa by a leading African writer.

Appleby, R. S. *Spokesmen for the Despised: Fundamentalist Leaders of the Middle East.* Chicago: University of Chicago Press, 1997. Substantial essays on eight leaders.

Calvino, I. *Invisible Cities,* trans. W. Weaver, New York: Harcourt Brace Jovanovich, 1974. Enigmatic vignettes of unreal yet intellectually challenging cityscapes.

Cohen, R., ed. R. *Film: An International History of the Medium.* New York: Abrams, 1993. Solid and detailed, perhaps strongest on the first half of the twentieth century.

Eliot, T. S. *The Waste Land and Other Poems.* New York: Harcourt, Brace, 1955. The poems that defined the cultural despair that underlay much of the frivolity of the 1920s.

Feuer, L. S. *Einstein and the Generations of Science.* New York: Basic Books, 1974. A close look at the people and ideas that launched the twentieth-century surge in the sciences.

Floyd, S. A. *The Power of Black Music: Interpreting Its History from Africa to the United States.* New York: Oxford University Press, 1995. Technical study of links between African and Afro-American traditions.

García Márquez, G. *One Hundred Years of Solitude,* trans. G. Rabassa. New York: Harper & Row, 1970. Epic of the Latin American backlands, written in the neosurrealist "magical realist" style of many postwar Latin American writers.

Grass, G. *The Tin Drum,* trans, R. Manheim. New York: Random House, 1971. One of the leading postwar German writers looks back scathingly at his country's experience in this century.

Green, C. *Cubism and Its Enemies.* New Haven, Conn.: Yale University Press, 1987. Highlights the differences between Cubism and other modernist movements, especially surrealism.

Joyce, J. *Ulysses.* New York: Random House, 1967. The archetypal modernist novel, challenging both the ethical and aesthetic values of the time.

Kuhn, T. *The Structures of Scientific Revolutions.* Chicago: University of Chicago Press, 1962. Valuable insight into the workings of the scientific mind in a century that has learned more about the material world than any other.

Manuel, P. *Popular Musics of the Non-Western World.* New York: Oxford University Press, 1988. By a leading expert on Caribbean and Latin American music.

Mishima, Y. *The Temple of the Golden Pavilion,* trans. I. Morris. New York: Putnum, 1981. Passionate and profound novel built around the destruction of Kyoto's Golden Pavilion after World War II.

Narayan, R. K. *Under the Banyan Tree.* New York: Viking Press, 1985. Stories of traditional village India.

Okri, Ben. *The Famished Road.* New York: Doubleday, 1992. An African "spirit child" moves effortlessly from reality to magic.

Rushdie, S. *Midnight's Children.* New York: Knopf, 1981. Post-modern novel of Anglo-Indian cultural disarray.

Senghor, L. *The Collected Poetry,* trans. M. Dixon. Charlottesville: University of Virginia Press, 1991. English versions of the poetry of *négritude*.

Woolf, V. *To the Lighthouse.* New York: Harcourt Brace Jovanovich, 1964. Masterpiece by one of the giants of the high modernist period between the wars.

 Please refer to the document CD-ROM for primary sources related to this chapter.

# CHAPTER 30

# THE AMERICAN AGE AND ITS FOES

## America, Globalization, and Terror (1990– )

# A Glance Ahead: The Problem of American Power

As the twentieth century wound down and the twenty-first began, the United States loomed large on the world scene. During the years after the end of the Cold War and the colonial liberation movements, America boomed and then skidded into recession, but still remained the world's richest nation. Europe continued to inch its way toward a more perfect union. Parts of Asia moved toward first-world status, while Africa, Latin America, and the far-stretching Muslim zone continued to face many problems. The sole superpower inevitably became involved in all these regions and their difficulties—an involvement that many resented.

America also stood at the heart of the major world-historical trend of modern times: the ongoing process of *globalization*. Some peoples supported such aspects of globalization as global free trade, international organizations, or universal human rights. But there were others who demanded protection for their local economies, their national interests, or their traditional values-and blamed the United States for pressuring them to change. The most disturbing of these opponents of American power were the international terrorists and "rogue states" who achieved global prominence as the new century began.

# The New World Order

## America at the Head of the Table

As after World War II, the United States emerged from the Cold War further strengthened. The United States was "the sole superpower" now. American military bases girdled the globe. The "almighty dollar" was the hardest of hard currencies. American social and cultural influences drenched the planet in fast food, blue jeans, and whatever Hollywood was doing this year. And wherever the nations of the world met to discuss their common affairs, America sat at the head of the table.

As the twentieth century drew to a close, rich people around the world invested their petrodollars in Wall Street stocks or U.S. Treasury bills. Poor people voted with their feet, migrating to the United States in growing numbers, hoping to follow in the footsteps of earlier generations of rags-to-riches immigrants. Rich and powerful behind its two oceans, the United States looked as solid as the skyscrapers of the New York skyline in the 1990s.

America had a liberal president through the nineties, but his two terms were an uphill struggle against an increasingly conservative public mood. Bill Clinton and his politically active wife, Hillary Rodham Clinton, failed in an attempt to legislate a national health service for Americans and lost control of both houses of Congress. Clinton thereupon abandoned large-scale liberal programs, declaring that "the era of big government is over" and focusing on "niche" reforms in areas like education and crime prevention.

Economically, however, he committed the United States to a new era of free trade by engineering an international agreement that replaced the creaky postwar General Agreement on Tariffs and Trade (GATT) with the new, more effective World Trade Organization (WTO). He also negotiated the North American Free Trade Agreement (NAFTA) with Mexico and Canada.

The economic growth of the next few years flooded federal coffers with taxes that turned long-running budget deficits into surpluses. Unemployment sank to record lows. Real wages, long stagnant, began to rise. And the Dow Jones stock market index soared, tripling during the 1990s.

America's position at the head of the global table was symbolized by the location of the headquarters of the United Nations in New York City. The second global organization has long outlasted the first and made important contributions to the international community. (Michael Kagan)

Clinton's personal integrity quotient was another matter. Sexual scandals clouded his two terms. But even when morally outraged Republicans in the House of Representatives actually impeached the president—charged him with lying under oath and other offenses to cover up his philandering—the Senate refused to convict him and his ratings rose still higher in the polls.

The Clinton years ended in a cliffhanger disputed election in which his Vice President Al Gore won the popular vote but lost in the electoral college to George W. Bush—the son of the man Clinton had defeated eight years before.

"W's" administration was strongly business-oriented—both Bush and his vice president Dick Cheney were former CEOs of large corporations. It was also supportive of the "moral majority" of conservative Christians. Bush also passed sizable tax cuts despite growing demands on the federal budget.

The American economy, meanwhile, skidded downward in Bush's early years. The recession that followed the long Clinton boom began with the bursting of the "dot-com" bubble and the collapse of many of the apparently much overvalued electronics firms of the nineties. This blow was followed by a series of big-business scandals and bankruptcies involving major firms. The stock market spiraled downward, unemployment rose, and, particularly as America girded for a new round of military action, huge federal deficits loomed once more.

## Europe Inches toward Unity

The rest of the world also had its troubles as the century turned. In Western Europe as in the United States, liberal leaders had everywhere to come to terms with conservative trends in the 1990s.

Britain's "iron lady," Margaret Thatcher, who had led the Conservatives to victory in three consecutive elections, finally fell from power in 1990. But the dynamic young Labor Party leader Tony Blair who dominated British politics in the later 1990s was no radical. He firmly disciplined the party's traditional labor union support, and concentrated on winning the votes of middle-class Britons. Once in power, he worked to expand the economy as a whole rather than focusing on government help for the lower classes.

Across the Channel, French Socialist President Mitterand died in office, to be replaced by a divided administration led by conservative President Jacques Chirac and a socialist

Premier Lionel Jospin. This divided administration faced such common European problems as swelling immigration, growing antiforeign feeling, and substantial unemployment, particularly among the young. In Germany, Europe's wealthiest nation, Conservative Chancellor Helmut Kohl gave way to moderate Socialist Gerhardt Schroeder, another Clinton-style apostle of compromise. He too dragged his party and its environmentalist "Green" coalition partners from the left toward the center. Again, the more liberal end of the political structure seemed to have found a way to power by borrowing policy positions from the conservative right. At the end of the 1990s, then, nominally left-wing parties controlled most of the governments of Western Europe—and seemed committed to only the mildest of reforms. The center was clearly where politicians felt most at home at end of the millennium.

Farther east, Yeltsin's new Commonwealth of Independent States had replaced the once monolithic Soviet Union. Despite Western aid, steps toward capitalist reform, and its own vast population and natural resources, Yeltsin's Russia sank into economic chaos. Russians suffered grievously from unemployment, inflation, "robber baron"-style profiteering, and an unprecedented crime wave. Boris Yeltsin proved less democratic than many had hoped: The hero who had defied the tanks at the time of the anti-Gorbachev coup sent tanks himself to shell the parliament building when it defied his authority.

By the mid 1990s, however, the once widely-feared Red Army proved unable to suppress a bloody rebellion in the tiny breakaway province of Chechnya.

In the late 1990s, Russia's awkwardly emerging capitalist economy seemed to be on the verge of collapse. Russia, unable to enact workable economic reforms, pay back wages owed government employees for years, collect taxes, or control massive corruption began to devalue the ruble and default on debts.

Help came from a partial Western economic bail-out-and a new political leader. Vladimir Putin, who became president in 2000, was a career KGB officer with foreign experience, Putin came across as a cool customer. He responded to a new challenge from Chechnya with a massive offensive that at least drove the rebels into the hills. He then concentrated on reasserting his country's place as a great power. To do so, he had to accept closer ties between Western Europe and former Soviet satellites and American plans for resuming ballistic missile development. But he got Russia a seat at the G-7 meetings of the richest capitalist countries and a consultative relationship with NATO, Russia's former foe.

The great achievement of the period in Europe, however, seemed to be the increase in European unity. France, Germany, and other supporters of the European Union pushed through the Maastricht Treaty in 1993, requiring members to recognize a uniform set of social rights for all citizens. Economically, borders were opened to a freer flow of capital and labor as well as goods. And in January 2002, the *euro* became the common currency of most of Western Europe. The successes were striking. But a growing gap seemed to be opening between leadership dedicated to a stronger European Union, perhaps with a common foreign policy and multinational military force, and many ordinary citizens, whose loyalty to their separate countries remained strong.

## Asia and the Islamic World on Different Paths

The largest of the continents, Asia, and the transcontinental Islamic zone stretching from North Africa to Southeast Asia seemed to be following different paths in the 1990s and early 2000s. A number of Asian nations appeared to be well on the road to economic progress and social change. Even the richest Muslim lands, on the other hand, clung to institutions as old-fashioned as hereditary monarchy and state religion.

For Japan, the nineties were a deeply frustrating period. The number two economy in the world sank into a period of paralysis and contraction, riddled with cronyism, bad debts, and a refusal to open the country up to foreign competition. Even the end of the Liberal Democratic Party's decades-long tenure of power and the election of the colorful and innovative Prime Minister Junichiro Koizumi failed to turn the economy around.

China, by contrast, barreled ahead economically through the 1990s. Led by Jiang Zemin and other pragmatic Communists who had clearly abandoned Marxist economic policies, China achieved double-digit growth rates through the decade. Such cities as Shanghai and Beijing boomed with Hong-Kong style high-rises and a luxury-loving business elite.

Problems still abounded. Masses of peasants were falling behind again and streaming into the cities in search of nonexistent jobs. As the modernizing Communist government closed down hopelessly inefficient state-run enterprises, millions of laid-off workers were added to the ranks of the unemployed. But the Peoples Republic was admitted to the World Trade Organization in 2002, and China's new leadership headed by Hu Jintao dedicated itself to more of the same

India, the giant of South Asia as China was of East Asia, moved more hesitantly toward open markets and grew more slowly in the 1990s and early 2000s. Some economic sectors, such as electronics, flourished. But vast numbers of Indians still lived in dusty villages and urban slums. On the political side, the strongly Hindu Bharatiya Janata Party (BJP) came to power in the nineties. Under BJP leadership, India was soon threatening both non-Hindus in India and another war with Muslim Pakistan in the long-running Indo-Pakistani dispute over India's Muslim-majority province of Kashmir.

In other parts of Asia, continuing economic progress was the main story of the 1990s. South Korea, Taiwan, Hong Kong, and Singapore continued to flourish. A new generation of Asian "tiger" economies joined them as real progress was made in Thailand, Malaysia, and Indonesia. The late nineties saw an economic downturn in some of these small states, triggered by such factors as a student-led revolt in Indonesia and the depredations of foreign speculators in Malaysia. Despite such setbacks, however, the Asian model of economic development still looked like a shining beacon to poor countries around the world.

The Muslim zone, by contrast, showed much less progress over this period. The hereditary rulers, generals, and one-party leaders who still governed many Islamic nations lived in splendid palaces while the majority of the citizens struggled with deep poverty. Muslim wealth often came from the exploitation of resources like petroleum. The Muslim poor turned increasingly to an Islamic religious revival led by aggressively "Islamist" scholars and preachers who urged political reform based on religious rule and Islamic law.

There were many thoroughly modern Muslims, skilled at business and the professions, both in their own countries and living in Europe, North America, and elsewhere. Most of the Islamic religious resurgence, furthermore, was a matter of traditional, often private, devotions. But it was fundamentalist *mullahs* with a bitter hatred for everything modern—and the young terrorist bombers they inspired—who shaped the Western image of Islam. And neither group contributed to the economic and political modernization of the Islamic zone.

## Africa and Latin America Beset by Problems

The two continents of Africa and South America seemed to be at opposite ends of the spectrum of developing countries as the century turned—but both faced many problems.

Longhaul Pakistani trucks on the Karakoram Highway that links Pakistan's Northwest Frontier Province with western China. The road, winding hundreds of miles through the towering Karakoram Mountains, is a major engineering feat that well illustrates what developing countries are capable of even in first-world terms. The elaborate painting, added to after each successful journey, is a point of pride with the longhaul drivers. (Anthony Esler)

Despite the achievements of South Africa and the potential of such resource-rich countries as Nigeria and Congo, large parts of Africa ranked at the bottom of global poverty statistics. Repeated famines and a horrifying AIDS epidemic further seared life on the second-largest continent. Western observers blamed corruption and state-controlled economies for Africa's economic problems. Africans pointed to the protectionist policies in developed countries, who defended their own producers by excluding imports from developing nations.

On the political side, many African nations still lived under military rulers or the autocratic legacy of ageing liberation leaders who couldn't bring themselves to lay down power, like Robert Mugabe in Zimbabwe. The alternative, however, was too often violent revolt, as in Rwanda and Sierra Leone. In Rwanda, the Hutu majority rebelled against rule by the traditionally dominant Tutsi, whose position had been strengthened by the region's former colonial rulers. Perhaps half a million Tutsis were slaughtered and large numbers of Hutus driven into exile as the Tutsis regained control. On the other side of the continent, a rebellion in the small West African country of Sierra Leone reached a new level of savage violence.

The worst international conflict on the continent was the war that engulfed Zaire—soon renamed Congo—in the early 2000s. Half-a-dozen Central African nations were sucked into the bloody struggle for the mineral wealth of the Congo basin.

One hopeful step came in 2002, when leaders from across the continent gathered in South Africa to replace the old, liberation-era Organization of African Unity with a new African Union. The new organization, broadly modeled on the European Union, was dedicated to furthering development and pledged to democratic and free-market methods. How successful the new organization would be in curbing authoritarianism and corruption and in limiting conflict remained to be seen. But the African Union did offer hope to a continent sorely in need of it.

Latin American nations began a renewed quest for democracy and economic growth with considerably more experience than most of the developing world. Political democracy had spread to many countries in the region in the 1980s. Economically, countries like Argentina, Brazil, and Chile certainly looked more advanced than their counterparts elsewhere.

Latin America's democratic leaders of the 1990s, furthermore, broke with a pattern of protective tariffs and government direction of their economies that went back to colonial times. Leading industrial powers like Mexico, Brazil, and Argentina turned to free trade and free market forces to solve their economic problems. They began to lower tariffs, sell off government industries to the private sector, trim government spending, and curb the inflation that had been Lain America's particular bane. The NAFTA treaty opened Mexico to further economic stimulation from the United States and Canada, while a South American free trade zone, Mercosur, linked Argentina, Brazil, and two smaller states.

The transition, however, proved extremely painful, generating widespread unemployment and much hardship among peoples who had depended on protective tariffs and government subsidies. Some, such as Brazil, seemed to be moving ahead as the century turned. Argentina, on the other hand, collapsed economically in the early 2000s. Again, some blamed a local culture of corruption and dependence on government handouts, while others condemned unrealistically rigid International Monetary Fund prescriptions.

## Global Boom, Global Bust

The global boom of the 1990s certainly looked awesome at the time. The Clinton years in America saw the longest period of uninterrupted economic growth in U.S. history. The Western European countries of the European Union, China and the tiger economies of East and Southeast Asia, and even parts of Latin America also experienced remarkable economic progress.

The later nineties and the first years of the new century, however, saw a scarifying economic downturn. The decline that began in 1997 swept emerging economies in Southeast Asia, Russia, and Brazil. Then, in the early 2000s, the American high-tech boom collapsed, threatening to trigger a global economic recession.

The U.S. stock market had tripled in value in the nineties. From Dow-Jones numbers in the 3000s at the beginning of the decade, the Dow had risen into the 10,000s in the later 1990s. Much of this growth, however, had apparently been illusory, based on fantastic overvaluing of stock, particularly that of the new electronic-communications firms widely known as "dot-coms." In 2001, then, shares of these so-called "new economy" firms began to plummet. The shocking financial scandals and stunning bankruptcies that followed involved some of the nation's largest corporations and led to yet more sell-offs of stock and a further vertiginous decline in the stock market. Around the world, meanwhile, other stock markets plunged in synch with Wall Street, sometimes shrinking by 50 percent or more.

The economic question with which the new century began was whether this was merely another "down" in the business cycle or something deeply structural, a major economic decline. One thing was clear to both sides, however. No one watching the gyrations of stock markets in London, Paris, Frankfurt, Tokyo, and Hong Kong, following Wall Street up and down like an echo, could fail to recognize the global economic centrality of the United States.

## GLOBALIZATION AND THE ANTIGLOBALIZERS

### America's Global Foreign Policy

The central role of the United States was also clear in international relations. And though U.S. foreign policy typically included a strong assertion of principles and ideals, it also involved the sort of aggressive pursuit of national interests that has motivated great powers down the centuries.

On the principled side, American leaders shared with many Americans a commitment to democratic political institutions, human rights, and a free-market capitalist economy. The United States therefore opposed political dictatorships like Castro's in Cuba, government-run economies in such unrepentant Communist countries as North Korea, or violations of women's freedoms in some Muslim countries.

America's sense of national interest, however, was also far reaching. Access to the oil of the Middle East and to military bases in the Far East were thus of central concern to American foreign policy planners. Foreign trade issues generated endless diplomatic negotiations and disputes as America put pressure on other capitalist countries like Japan to open their borders to U.S. agricultural and industrial exports. Yet strong ties with the allies, from Western Europe to isolated Israel, Japan, or South Korea were traditionally matters of great practical concern in Washington.

A national interest of mounting concern to American foreign policy planners in the post–Cold War years was usually summed up as "nuclear proliferation." The new, post-Communist Russia was no longer perceived as a nuclear threat, and the United States had no objections to the smaller nuclear arsenals of its European allies Britain and France. But mounting evidence that "rogue states" like Iraq or North Korea, dictatorships known to be hostile to the United States, might be developing nuclear or other weapons of mass destruction created a growing American interest in preventing this from happening.

In pursuit of these disparate goals, America's global foreign policy involved the United States in a series of unexpected little wars over the years between 1990 and the early 2000s.

### America's Wars in Central America, the Balkans, and the Persian Gulf

Clever commentators called them "television wars," spectacular displays of science-fiction firepower that could almost have been designed for living room watching. Highly trained troops armed with the latest in precision weaponry routed their foes. The conflicts were short, one sided, and made it increasingly clear that no nation could match the sole superpower militarily. With American military bases and military alliances ringing the globe in the aftermath of the Cold War, crises virtually anywhere seemed capable of triggering an American military response.

An early post–Cold War instance of the use of this unprecedented military capability came in Panama. The first Bush administration accused the president of that country, General Noriega, of involvement in the drug trade. American troops, utilizing some of the newest weapons in their armory, swept into the country in 1989, overthrew and captured Noriega, and brought him back to the United States for trial and imprisonment.

A far larger enterprise was Bush's war in the Persian Gulf against the Iraqi dictator Saddam Hussein. Iraq, deeply in debt after its long war with Iran, launched a lightning occupation of its oil-rich little neighbor, Kuwait. The United States responded by organizing a large international coalition, devastating Iraq with a massive bombing campaign, and then crushing the Iraqi armed forces in a ground assault that drove them out of Kuwait in a matter of days.

The next challenge to America's military might came in an unexpected place—Europe, a continent that had not seen an open war since World War II. During the upheaval following the anti-Communist revolutions of 1989, however, Yugoslavia's most developed constituent republics, Croatia and Slovenia, seceded, seeking economic integration with Western Europe. Slobodan Milosovich, nationalist leader of Yugoslavia's majority Serbian population, supported Serbian minorities demanding independence from both new countries. And a third would-be secessionist republic, Bosnia, soon became the site of a long-drawn-out civil war.

Across that mountainous little country, villages were torn apart by brutal guerrilla strife. Evidence mounted of what came to be known as "ethnic cleansing"—mass expulsions of Bosnians from their homes, systematic rape, brutal imprisonment, and outright massacres. In the end, it took a major military campaign by United States–led NATO forces and an American-brokered peace conference to bring an end to the carnage.

Soon thereafter, furthermore, further fighting broke out in the Kosovo province of Serbia itself, where Serb military forces fought to suppress a separatist movement by the Albanian majority. The Serbs expelled hundreds of thousands of Albanians, but a rain of NATO bombs compelled them to withdraw in their turn. Milosovich himself was subsequently overthrown and wound up on trial for war crimes in the Hague.

America's little wars of the 1990s were impressively successful. Fought on far-flung battle fronts, from Panama to the Balkans and the Persian Gulf, they were short, low on U.S. casualties, and high in technological sophistication. America spent more than the next dozen countries combined on its unique military machine—and it showed.

## The Ties that Globalize

A broader form of conflict in the American Age was that between the long-term trend toward globalization and the many adversaries who challenged that trend. This section will serve as a reminder of some of the ties that have been globalizing our world at an accelerated pace for the last two centuries. The following section will highlight the many forms of opposition to globalization that have sprung up around the world.

A striking embodiment of the evolving international order around 2000 was a growing number of what we might call *global people,* true citizens of the world whose lives and labors were helping to weld the world's many communities into one. These new global citizens included business people, diplomats, military personnel, representatives of international agencies and charitable organizations, American Peace Corps volunteers, overseas Chinese merchants in Asia, and Indian computer experts who swarmed to California's Silicon Valley. Global people were immigrants and expatriates and compulsive travelers. They were all the people who staffed the institutions and mobilized the trends discussed below.

A major globalizing structure was the web of *technological links* which brought the peoples of the planet closer together. In the nineteenth century, the age of steam and telegraphy had strapped the continents across with rail lines, bound one continent to another with shipping lanes, and provided instantaneous telegraphic communication around the world. In the twentieth century, the automobile and the airplane, the super-tanker and the high-speed train had further revolutionized transport, while the telephone, radio, television, computer, and world wide web had transformed communications. Never had the world's peoples been physically so close as they were as the new millennium dawned.

Closely related to these technological links were the growing *economic ties* that bound the nations of the world more closely with every passing decade. When the European empires crumbled after World War II, the economic relationships between the western nations and their former colonies forged in earlier centuries survived. Raw materials and industrial products, investment capital and labor in search of employment flowed with increasing freedom around the globe. Critics stressed the exploitative dimension of these ties, dubbing them "economic imperialism." But the growing global economy bound both parties. A third-world country that negotiated a development loan incurred an immense debt which it might find desperately hard to repay. But default on a loan large enough to help a whole nation could put the biggest western bank in jeopardy.

Besides global people, technological links, and economic ties, *similarly structured societies* seemed to be bringing the nations into greater harmony politically, economically, and socially in the years around 2000. One-party states, military dictatorships, and other forms of authoritarian regime seemed to be giving way to democratically elected governments in many places. Free-market capitalism was widespread after the collapse of Communist and other state-run economies. And socially, most modern nations seemed to accept the need for a tax-financed public sector, providing some degree of such services as police and fire protection, public education and public health care, unemployment compensation, and retirement benefits.

An immense proliferation of *international organizations,* finally, clearly linked the world's peoples by the year 2000. As early as the nineteenth century, organizations relating to peace and war between nations had been established, including the Red Cross shortly after mid-century and the World Court (Permanent Court of Arbitration) at the century's end. The twentieth century saw two major attempts at global organization intended to keep the peace—the League of Nations after World War I and the United Nations growing out of World War II. The latter became the apex of a pyramid of global institutions, including the World Health Organization (WHO), the World Bank (International Bank for Reconstruction and Development), and the International Monetary Fund (IMF). Important regional organizations also proliferated, such as the European Common Market—today's European Union—the Organization of American States, the new African Union, and the economically powerful Organization of Petroleum Exporting Countries (OPEC), as well as the annual economic summits that brought together the heads of the seven richest nations, nicknamed the G-7.

The United States played a prominent part in all these globalizing trends of our times. Not surprisingly, then, opponents of these trends often became opponents of the United States as well. A survey of this resistance will thus also suggest something of the range of opposition to American power that seemed to be emerging at the beginning of the new millennium.

## The Antiglobalizers

*Defend the local!* became one of the watchwords of turn-of-the-century antiglobalization protesters. Defend local economies, values, and ways of life, resistence movements urged, against all external pressures. Whether it was economic pressure from the International Monetary Fund, secular challenges to the religious traditions of Muslim clerics, or modernizing challenges to the lifeways of surviving food-gathering societies, everything traditional, familiar, and locally approved should be protected against the onslaught of global change.

None of these challenges to globalization was more surprising than the new enthusiasm for *indigenous peoples* around the world. Canadian Indians, Australian Aborigines, and Maoris in New Zealand demanded and got increasing control over traditional lands and respect for traditional culture. In the Mexican province of Chiapas, rebellious Mayans attacked police and soldiers and found a charismatic leader in ski-masked "Subcomandante Marcos," who became an international celebrity from his Chiapan jungle base. There was even talk of a global alliance of indigenous peoples, the original inhabitants of many lands, against exploitation and oppression by local governments or multinational corporations. Conservatives might urge these ancient peoples to cut their hair and join the modern world, but the liberal anthropologist June Nash was deeply moved by the spectacle of a torch-lit international festival of indigenous peoples in the Middle American jungle, complete with drumming, dancing, and incense curling upward into the triple-canopy rainforest overhead.

Among the most powerful of the movements that opposed globalization were *environmental protests* against pollution, exhaustion of resources, and other destructive side effects of global technological growth. Environmentalists strove to protect wetlands, forests, and oceans from mining and lumbering, oil drilling and overfishing. They joined animal rights activists in campaigns to "save the whales," tropical game animals, rare birds, and other endangered species. In Europe, "the Greens" organized political parties and protest organizations like Greenpeace. Viewing globalization as violation of the planet in the name of development, they warned of "greenhouse gasses" produced by factory and automobile emissions and the resulting "global warming" already melting earth's ice caps and causing droughts in Africa, forest fires in America, and floods from Europe to China. Swarming to international conferences held at Rio de Janeiro, Tokyo, and Durban, South Africa, they urged stricter regulation of global technology in the interests of saving the environment for our children.

Environmentalists found strong allies in a more economically focused protest, often called simply *"the antiglobalization movement."* The antiglobalization alliance targeted the commercial and financial institutions behind globalizing economic and technological forces. But member groups tended to focus on global poverty, demanding an end to sweat shops in poor countries, cancellation of third-world debt, and a drastic narrowing of the economic gap between developing and developed nations. Some in the antiglobalization movement opposed capitalism itself, insisting once more that, though the European empires had been dismantled, economic neo-imperialism—the exploitation of the poor by the rich—still flourished.

Much more violent in their opposition to the forces of globalization, however, were the linked forces of *nationalism and ethnicity.* Many nationalist or ethnic movements of the later twentieth century seemed to generate maelstroms of violence in their struggles for autonomy or independence. The Tamil rebels of southern India and Sri Lanka fought a long and bloody guerrilla war to liberate the ancient Tamil lands. Kurdish liberation movements in the Middle East fought for an independent Kurdistan which would have to be carved out of at least three separate countries—Iraq, Iran, and Turkey. The Basque liberation movement in Spain (ETA), and the Irish Republican Army (IRA) won many concessions for their peoples but went on bombing and shooting, demanding independence.

Another form of loyalty often seemed to generate even more fanatical resistance to the global drift. This was the resurgent commitment of many of the world's peoples to ancient and *contentious religious faiths.*

In India, activists affiliated with the militantly Hindu Bharatiya Janata Party (BJP), which came to power in the 1990s, vigorously rejected that country's tradition of religious pluralism. Insisting that the only "real" Indian was a Hindu, they attacked Muslims and other religious minorities. Even more disturbing was the resurgence of the *jihad* or holy war tradition among some Muslim groups. The struggle between India and Pakistan was rooted in the desire of many Muslims in India's Kashmir province for unification with Muslim Pakistan. In Palestine, Islamist terrorist organizations like Hamas and Hezbullah resisted Israeli occupation of Palestinian land by sending suicide bombers to blow themselves up in crowded Israeli streets. On across North Africa, Islamist terrorists attacked the tourists in Egypt, rioted against beauty contests in Nigeria, and decimated whole Algerian villages in their determination to establish a religious republic. And many of these crusaders saw a secular, materialistic America as the Great Satan behind all their foes.

## Opposition to America's Role in Globalization

The United States in fact had a finger in so many pies around the world that it was almost bound to kindle resentments in many places. Every time the U.S. came down on one side or the other anywhere on earth, it inevitably made enemies on the other side.

As we have seen, a hostile analysis could trace every global problem, from third-world poverty to environmental decay, to America's door. Globalization itself, in all its forms, could be seen as a plot to "Americanize" the world. And some went still further, suggesting that the United States was becoming the center of the first truly global empire, threatening the beliefs, economies, and political independence of other peoples around the globe.

American tourists were usually still welcome, and the world still gobbled up American popular culture. European radicals cheerfully toured the United States selling books with titles like *Why Do People Hate America?* and *Rogue State*—the United States, of course. But opposition to many American policies seemed to be more widespread than ever at the beginning of the twenty-first century.

Then came 9/11.

# AMERICA'S WAR ON TERRORISM

## The Road to 9/11

Most Americans, safe behind their nation's wealth, power, and immense military clout, paid little attention to what foreigners thought of them at all. One thing they might have learned from other peoples, however, was more about something others had been living with for a long time: the menace of global terrorism.

A leading authority on this grisly subject defines terrorism as "the use of violence by a group for political ends."[1] All the formal essentials are here: violence, small groups, broadly defined political goals.

---

[1]Walter Laqueur, *The New Terrorism: Fanaticism and the Arms of Mass Destruction* (New York: Oxford University Press, 1999), p. 46.

Another key feature of historical terrorist movements, however, has been intense, even fanatical commitment. Terrorists have usually been ideologues or religious true believers like the militant groups mentioned above. Terrorism as a tactic has also normally been the weapon of the weak, of true believers without sufficient support to force political changes, topple governments, or otherwise impose their will. Thus, despite impassioned commitment, the expert cited above declares that "the impact of terrorism on history has been slight . . . it is difficult to think of a single case in which the policy of a country has been radically changed as the result of a terrorist campaign."[2]

As the same authority also points out, however, operating in complex and delicate modern societies and wielding immensely destructive modern weapons, even the weak can be dangerous. Targeting the most vulnerable nexes in complicated social structures, a handful of suicidally determined terrorists could do a horrendous amount of damage. Which is what they did to New York, the commercial capital of the United States, in the fall of 2001.

The man and the terrorist organization behind the attacks of September, 2001, seem to have understood these new realities. Osama bin Laden was a wealthy Saudi whose commitment to *jihad* had been kindled by participation in the struggle to drive the Russians out of Afghanistan in the 1980s. After the war, he had used his family wealth to support the Islamist Taliban movement in its seizure of power in Afghanistan.

From his hideaway in the Afghan mountains, bin Laden cultivated a Wahhabi image, communicating with true believers via video tapes of himself sitting in the rocky wilderness in flowing robes, Kaleshnikov always within reach. He had become the acknowledged leader of *al Qaeda*—"the Base" in Arabic. Al Qaeda was a loosely structured group providing training, financial support, and at least some direction for terrorist activities in many lands.

Al Qaeda's hostility toward the far-reaching power of the United States had grown steadily through the 1990s. The most obvious cause for this enmity was America's unswerving support for Israel in its long conflict with its Arab neighbors. As a Saudi Arabian, however, bin Laden nursed a particular resentment of the continued U.S. military and economic presence in that country. Arabia, homeland of the prophet and the destination of millions of Muslim pilgrims, had in Osama bin Laden's eyes been transformed into an oil supplier for the United States and a launching pad for the American jets that held the Middle East in awe.

Al Qaeda operatives had apparently been behind the bombing of two American embassies in Africa and of an American naval vessel in a Near Eastern port. In the fall of 2001, its agents attacked the United States itself.

## Twin Towers Down

On September 11, 2001, nineteen terrorists funded by Osama bin Laden launched an attack on the nerve centers of American power. Boarding four airliners in different eastern American cities, they seized control of the planes, installed one of their own (who had had flight training) at the controls of each jet plane, and turned the planes and their passengers toward New York City and Washington D.C. No explosive devices were needed: The big jetliners themselves, filled with fuel for long transcontinental flights, were flying bombs.

Random cameramen caught the chilling pictures as two of the hijacked planes passed over neighboring skyscrapers and disappeared with a burst of flame and a swelling cloud of smoke into the twin towers of the World Trade Center in New York. The whole world

---

[2]*Ibid.*

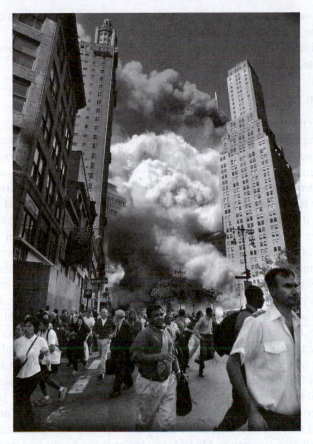

The most devastating terrorist action in history—the destruction of the World Trade Center in New York City—left a lasting scar on the American psyche. Supported by an avalanche of popular fear and anger, the U.S. launched a "war on terrorism" that sought to put an end to a plague of political violence that had long afflicted the modern world. (AP/World Wide Photos)

watched through that endless morning as billowing black smoke spread over the famous skyline and first one and then the other tower crumbled, gouging a gigantic smouldering hole out of lower Manhattan.

The other two attacks that day were much less successful. One slammed into the Pentagon in Washington, headquarters of the American armed forces, but the damage there was limited, and most of the building was soon back in use. And passengers on the fourth hijacked airliner actually resisted the terrorist take-over, causing the plane to crash in a forest in Pennsylvania, far from its intended target in Washington.

Nevertheless, the deaths of three thousand people and the destruction of the twin towers in New York, symbols of America's economic predominance around the globe, constituted the biggest terrorist hit in history.

The perpetrators were soon identified from passenger lists and airport surveillance cameras, their possessions searched, and their American neighbors—and flight instructors—interviewed. Most of the nineteen turned out to be young, educated, and well enough off to have lived for some time in Europe or America. Their short lives had left them embittered at western and particularly American supremacy and in love with martyrdom. U.S. President George W. Bush condemned them and their supporters abroad as "evildoers." But he also visited a D.C. area mosque to make clear that he was not tarring either American Muslims or their one billion plus coreligionists around the globe with any responsibility for the crime of terrorist fanatics.

Meanwhile, it was time to think about a counterattack. While sympathy poured in from many lands, the United States declared war on terrorism.

## Lashback in Afghanistan

The road ahead was by no means clear.

In the wake of 9/11, the world's greatest power was declaring war on a radical tactic that the world had been wrestling with for a good century and a half. Police and secret services in many lands had tracked terrorists patiently for years. They had captured or killed some, as the Germans had the leaders of the Baader-Meinhof gang and the French had Carlos the Jackel, but they had never eliminating the threat. This seemed to be what the United States was proposing to do when it declared itself to be at war with terrorism in the fall of 2001.

Active terrorists were usually organized in small, isolated cells. To function effectively, however, the cells often depended on networks of supporters to manage recruiting and training, provide financial and other material support, and to offer refuges and safe havens in time of need. Some of the logistical and financial support came from governments who sympathized with terrorist causes or used terrorist groups to advance their own ambitions. They allowed such groups to organize, recruit, and train volunteers within their borders. Financial support also came from charitable organizations established to collect contributions for oppressed peoples from Ireland to East Timor. At the purely local level, you could see supporters of the Egyptian Islamic Brotherhood or the Indonesian Lascar Jihad darting in and out of traffic in the chaotic streets of Cairo or Jakarta, passing out leaflets or thrusting contribution boxes under the noses of drivers trapped in traffic jams.

In the long run, America's counter-terrorist fighters would have to penetrate and destroy all these networks if they were to defeat the many terrorist organizations that blew up buses in Israel, vans full of policemen in Madrid, an airport in Sri Lanka, a department store in London, or the prime minister of India.

The American goals, however, went beyond uprooting underground terrorist cells. The al Qaeda organization which had attacked the United States was of course a primary concern. But al Qaeda's headquarters and training camps were known to be located in the mountains of Afghanistan, where they operated openly under the protection of the fundamentalist Taliban. Afghanistan itself therefore became the first target.

Veterans of Russia's long struggle in Afghanistan warned their American colleagues that they were in for a long, hard campaign in Central Asia. It didn't turn out that way.

America's war in Afghanistan was much more like the "little wars" of the 1990s. Operating from hastily negotiated bases in neighboring Pakistan, from a couple of former Soviet states, and from U.S. naval vessels offshore, American special forces and sophisticated air power poured pinpoint strikes into Taliban and al Qaeda bases. Local enemies of the Taliban—rival warlords and minority ethnic groups in the north—were recruited to do most of the ground fighting. In a matter of months, a pro-American government ruled in Kabul and both the Taliban and al Qaeda had been routed from their Afghan sanctuaries.

Many al Qaeda fighters slipped out of the country. Bin Laden himself disappeared into a cloud of guesses and rumors to re-emerge as a voice on tape threatening death to the Great Satan in the years that followed.

Nevertheless, a pro-American government reigned in Kabul. The United States had lost two skyscrapers—the terrorists had lost a country. The last video cassettes of Osama bin Laden showed cheeks a lot hollower, beard a lot grayer than they had been before the American counterattack began.

And the United States turned its attention elsewhere.

## Regime Change in Iraq

The brutal Iraqi dictator Saddam Hussein had invaded two neighboring Muslim countries—Iran and Kuwait—deployed biological and chemical weapons against rebellious Kurds in his own country, and crushed all political opposition with an iron fist. But he had never been as clearly associated with the region's proliferating terrorist groups as authoritarian rulers in Iran, Syria, or Libya had been.

Bush administration hawks, however, saw Saddam as a long-time enemy secretly arming himself with biological, chemical, and possibly nuclear weapons. The president's men suggested that he might in the future turn such weapons over to terrorists for use against the United States. The president declared "regime change" in Iraq to be a new goal of the war on terrorism, and planning began in earnest the year after 9/11.

Many of the same nations who had heaped sympathy on the United States at the time of the terrorist attacks on New York and Washington, however, now expressed opposition to military action against Iraq. They pointed out that there was no evidence linking Saddam Hussein to the events of 9/11. And they opposed a "preemptive" U.S. attack on Iraq—that is, an attack without clear evidence of an impending Iraqi assault on America.

The United States sought and got a United Nations Security Council vote in favor of some sort of action against Saddam's Iraq. UN arms inspectors fanned out over the country to search again for weapons of mass destruction—chemical, biological, or nuclear. European political leaders and demonstraters around the world loudly opposed any further action. But President Bush, supported by British Prime Minister Tony Blair, forged ahead with preparations for the conflict. And in the spring of 2003, American and British troops, planes, and missiles plunged into Iraq.

It looked like and in many ways was another of the half-dozen "little wars" America had fought since the last days of the Cold War. American and British casualties were light—no more than a couple of hundred dead—Iraqi deaths probably in the low thousands. Saddam and other leaders disappeared, his military formations disintegrated, and Baghdad surrendered without a fight. The war was over in less than a month, and many Iraqi citizens cheerfully helped pull down heroic statues of their former maximum leader. Perhaps most important, the latest round of new American weaponry proved its worth, shattering Iraqi communications, fortifications, and government buildings while largely avoiding mosques, historic ruins, and civilians.

Many problems remained as the United States set to work to organize the rebuilding of a once relatively developed Middle Eastern state ravaged by Saddam's tyranny, two decades of war, and a decade of international economic sanctions. Critics of the war emphasized the difficulties of holding a divided population—Sunni and Shiite, Arab and Kurd—together without the iron fist of an authoritarian regime. But some in Washington confidently expected to see a democratized, free-market Iraq become a model for change throughout the region.

## Rogue States in the Crosshairs?

The Bush administration, however, seemed to have even broader ambitions. Even before the successful attack on Iraq, President Bush and others had repeatedly condemned a number of other "rogue nations" or "rogue states" who must also change their ways or face the consequences. Without specifying military means, U.S. leaders made it clear that the consequences could be dire.

The term "rogue state" had come into widespread usage in the late twentieth century as a label for nations that egregiously flouted the norms of international conduct. The label apparently came from a perceived parallel with "rogue elephant," meaning a vicious elephant driven out of the herd. Specific characteristics differed from one definition to another, but commonly cited features of rogue states included brutally repressive government, callous unconcern for the sufferings of one's own people, and military attacks on neighboring nations. They also included such specific policies as efforts to build up arsenals of nuclear or other weapons of mass destruction and covert support for international terrorism.

Rogue states were outlaw countries, nations beyond the pale of civilization. And with the end of America's long struggle with the Soviet Union, the United States seemed to become increasingly concerned with these lesser threats.

Candidates for rogue state status, as defined particularly by United States policy makers, had included Cuba under Fidel Castro, seen at least for a time as a threat to Latin America; Qaddafi's Libya, condemned for involvement in terrorist attacks and eagerness to acquire nuclear weapons; Syria under Haffez al Assad, angling for regional power and supportive of violence in Lebanon and Israel; and Afghanistan under the Islamist Taliban dictatorship. In 2001, President Bush listed three rogue states in particular as an "Axis of Evil": Saddam Hussein's battered but still brutal Iraq, an Iran still heavily dominated by the reactionary Shiite heirs of the Ayatollah Khomeini, and one of the few surviving Communist states, North Korea, believed to have at least a few nuclear weapons and to be preparing to produce more of them.

In the wake of 9/11, then, the United States urged once more that some rogue states at least provided support for terrorists like al Qaeda and were guilty of "nuclear proliferation," the stockpiling of nuclear or other weapons of mass destruction. Worse yet, American leaders argued, these outlaws among the nations might turn such weapons over to terrorists for use in their irrational assaults on civilized nations like the United States.

The rise of the rogue states, then, provided another and much more visible target for America's war on terror.

# A NEW GLOBAL ORDER—OR A NEW GLOBAL EMPIRE?

## Reactions to America's Global Power

While everyone had expected an American victory in Iraq, this most recent in the series of half-a-dozen "little wars" around the world—Panama, Bosnia, Kosovo, Kuwait, Afghanistan, and Saddam's Iraq—seemed to jolt world opinion in a way that went far beyond its apparent historical importance. "No issue has so divided the world since the end of the Cold War," said United Nations Secretary General Kofi Annan. "It is vital that we heal that division now. The world cannot afford a long period of recrimination."[3] To judge by the moving masses of demonstraters in the streets, the Iraq conflict had stirred up public opinion as nothing had since America's Vietnam War.

Responses varied in various parts of the world. America's old allies in Europe, particularly France and Germany, and her nearest neighbors, Canada and Mexico, all of whom had opposed the war, moved to mend fences with the United States once it was over. Arab countries and many other Muslim lands saw the brief struggle in the context of the much longer conflict between the Arab Middle East and America's closest ally in the region, Israel. The Arab street, at least, sided with Iraq. Farther east, India's Hindu leadership wondered if the U.S. would ever turn its anti-terrorist crusade against its Asian ally Pakistan, long suspected of supporting terrorists in India's disputed Kashmir province. And an increasingly nationalistic China saw the "shock and awe" bombing of Baghdad as more American aggressiveness. Websites and newspapers compared it to the American bombing of a Chinese embassy in the Balkans or the accidental knockdown of a Chinese fighter and its pilot by an American spy plane over the China Seas.

Everywhere, local contexts shaped reactions to America's latest demonstration of power. But there were larger and more long-range possible consequences too, consequences on a global scale.

## Consequences of America's Global Power

Even while leaders around the world scrambled to avoid further friction with Washington, long-range changes in the familiar post-World-War-II structure of the community of nations seemed like a very real possibility.

The European Union, the economic alliance that had grown out of the postwar Common Market, would expand from fifteen to twenty-five members in 2004. For the leaders of such European great powers as France and Germany, an important advantage of expansion would be that the larger European Union would achieve economic equality with the United States. In the global debate about the war in Iraq, however, many of the new members had sided with America, which they credited with liberating them from Soviet domination. The paradoxical result looked like being an *expanded* European Union with *less* loyalty to the traditionally dominant European powers.

The North Atlantic Treaty Organization that had stood firm against the Communist Warsaw Pact now also faced serious structural problems. NATO's basic reason for existing seemed to be in question when there was no rival alliance to confront on the other side of Europe. And as America's series of dazzling little wars demonstrated, the alliance was deeply divided at a basic level between a United States equipped with the latest high-tech firepower and the rest of the members, who preferred to spend tax money on the benefits of the welfare state.

The future of the United Nations itself, however, seemed to many to be most significantly in doubt. The UN had not given the US as much support as it wanted on the issue of war with Iraq, and President Bush had responded by dismissing the global institution as "irrelevant" to the great issues of our time. The UN had actually tried to play a more active political role since the end of the Cold War. Now the United States seemed to wish to

---

[3]Felicity Barringer, "The Future of Iraq: 'Intense Dialogue' Comes Next," in *The International Herald Tribune* (April 19–20, 2003), p. 4.

# VOICES FROM THE PRESENT

This foreign policy address by United States President George W. Bush before the United Nations in New York was widely praised as an eloquent expression of America's case for "regime change" in Iraq. In it, Bush accuses Saddam Hussein's Iraq of defying UN resolutions, violating human rights, and "likely" possession of weapons of mass destruction.

In this segment, Bush also attacks underground terrorist cells in America and elsewhere. Does he seem to link these to Iraq? In general, what sort of world does he seem to see around him in 2002? Would you say that the tone of his speech—as well as its concluding sentences—suggests an aggressive or a defensive approach to the dangers of this world?

*Our common security is challenged by regional conflicts—ethnic and religious strife that is ancient, but not inevitable.*

*Above all, our principles and our security are challenged today by outlaw groups and regimes that accept no law of morality and have no limit to their violent ambitions. In the attacks on America a year ago, we saw the destructive intentions of our enemies. This threat hides within many nations, including my own. In cells and camps, terrorists are plotting further destruction, and building new bases for their war against civilization. And our greatest fear is that terrorists will find a shortcut to their mad ambitions when an outlaw regime supplies them with the technologies to kill on a massive scale.*

*In one place—in one regime—we find all these dangers, in their most lethal and aggressive forms, exactly the kind of aggressive threat the United Nations was born to confront.*

*We must choose between a world of fear and a world of progress. We cannot stand by and do nothing while dangers gather. We must stand up for our security, and for the permanent rights and the hopes of mankind. By heritage and by choice, the United States of America will make that stand. And, delegates to the United Nations, you have the power to make that stand, as well.*

George W. Bush, "Remarks at the United Nations General Assembly," 12 September 2002 (http://www.whitehouse.gov/news/releases/2002/09/20020912-1.html)

strip it of its political functions, limiting it instead to humanitarian and other uncontroversial activities. With even its supporters suggesting that it needed serious reforms—two of the three richest countries in the world, Germany and Japan, were not even permanent members of the Security Council—the United Nations clearly faced an uncertain future. And again, the opposition of the sole superpower looked like being the determining factor.

## World Views in Conflict Threaten a Globalizing World

But there were deeper levels of discord in the world of the early twenty-first century. There were two fundamental world views in conflict. And the global reach of these two views seemed to threaten the future of the globalization process which had been central to global history for the past five centuries.

One view, held most prominently by American leaders, began with the grim assertion that the world was a jungle out there. The "events of 9/11" had greatly strengthened their long-standing view that what the world needed was stronger, more assertive American leadership. In a world menaced by terrorists who struck without warning, the best defense

Ramesh Thakur, the author of this personal comment from the *Herald Tribune*, the international English-language newspaper, is rector of the United Nations University in Tokyo—a "global person" if there ever was one.

How does the view of the world's problems expressed here differ from President Bush's on the preceding page? Does Thakur seem to see the US as the solution to these problems—or as part of the problem? How dangerous does this comment suggest Iraq is to the world at large? Thakur fears international "anarchy" and a global "authority vacuum" if international rules and institutions are not maintained. According to this view, who might step in to fill that vacuum? Finally, how would you contrast Thakur's emphasis on discussion, agreement, and "amending existing rules and institutions" with Bush's stress on taking "a stand"?

*Is the world ready to accept the doctrine that the United States decides if a country's leader is to be toppled?*

*To ask this question is not to deny that present institutions and systems are often out of date and incapable of meeting today's real challenges. Such challenges include widespread poverty, obstacles to economic development and the spread of weapons of mass destruction. But there is also the growing disparity between U.S. power and that of all others, and the challenge that this poses to the Westphalian fiction of sovereign states equal in status and legitimacy.*

*The solution lies in amending existing rules and institutions. Otherwise, in the resulting authority vacuum, anarchy will prevail. If regime change is to be a legitimate goal, let us argue for that, agree on what constitutes legitimate statehood deserving of sovereign rights, such as market democracy, and amend or replace the UN Charter accordingly.*

*Saddam Hussein is insignificant. The real issue is: What sort of world do we wish to live in, who do we wish to be ruled by, and do we want to live by rules and laws or by the force of arms?.*

Ramesh Thakur, "Let's Decide what kind of world we want," *International Herald Tribune* (17 April 2003). p.8.

---

was a good offense. And if antique international rules and institutions inhibited direct action, they should be more or less politely thrust to one side.

Leaders of some other nations shared this increasingly activist view that only the vigorous application of power could solve the world's problems. But they saw themselves—not the United States—as empowered to take direct action to achieve their goals. Some old-guard European leaders, for instance, dreamed of a much more unified European Union, equipped with a common foreign policy and even a European army, which might serve as a "counterweight" to the United States in world affairs. Hardliners in China, India, and Israel talked of taking vigorous unilateral action to achieve national objectives in Taiwan, Kashmir, and Palestine.

It was what a hundred years before had been called a "forward policy" by ambitious European imperial powers. In the early 2000s, some in Washington talked about a "forward leaning" approach to foreign relations.

The second widely-held global view adopted a more defensive stance. It saw a significantly different set of problems confronting the world and a very different sort of solution.

This second world view agreed that it was a jungle out there. But it saw aggressive governments—especially that of the United States—not as offering a solution, but as part of the problem. "What," a British commentator asked, "if the sophisticated U.S. missiles that rain down on Baghdad, Belgrade [Yugoslavia], or the Hindu Kush [in Afghanistan] were to be aimed toward London, Paris, or Berlin?" The danger, in this view, lay not in scattered terrorist attacks—many nations had lived with terrorism for decades—but in the massive power at the disposal of aggressive nation states. If the United States felt it had a right to overthrow Saddam Hussein's government in Iraq, how long would it be before India decided it must attack Pakistan preemptively to end that nation's alleged support for terrorists in Kashmir? Might not China assert its ancient claim to Taiwan militarily in years to come—again, acting unilaterally, with no regard for the opinion of the community of nations? Or might not Israeli hardliners move at last to solve the problem of Palestinian terrorism by expelling all the Palestinians from the West Bank and Gaza in the teeth of U.N. resolutions?

The world was littered with flashpoints, this view of things urged. Even such diplomatic fictions as the equality and legitimacy of all nations might be better than a resurgence of the kind of direct, unilateral, preemptive action that had so often shattered the peace of the globe in centuries past.

Proponents of vigorous action in Washington talked about turning a liberated Iraq into a model of democratic capitalism for the entire Middle East. They suggested that further challenges by rogue states could be handled by American-led "alliances of the willing." Sometimes they went so far as to advocate a future American "moral empire"—not a territorial one—guaranteeing democratic government, free-market economies, and security from tyranny and terrorism around the world.

Opponents of such an American-dominated world feared both American imperialism and the global anarchy of a world where might makes right. They also saw a broader range of global problems, including world poverty, environmental degradation, and aggressive governments as well as tyranny and terrorism. Their solutions, however, were more multilateral and institutional, building on the positive achievements of recent centuries of globalization. Proponents of this world view urged maintaining such traditions as the integrity of all nations and the prohibition of attack by one nation on another. To accomplish these ends, they urged more—not less—authority for international law and strengthening—not weakening—of global institutions like the United Nations.

### Globalization, Peace, and the Frightened Dutchman

Globalization in some familiar forms still rolled on. Immigrants from poor countries still flooded into rich ones, people of all nations into their neighborhood McDonalds. English was the world's second language still, and you could usually find a cyber café to put you in instant touch with home wherever you might be.

But the process looked less sure and more dangerous to people on both sides of the global divide on which way globalization should go. A distinguished Harvard authority could summarize the situation quite simply by saying that "the U.S. today has become an imperial power, bent on forging a global pax Americana"—an American peace.[4] And an equally distinguished Yale historian could write: "Just a few days ago. I was shocked when a Dutch journalist told me that many of his countrymen were now 'scared' of America."[5]

---

[4] Andrew J. Bacevich, "We Have the Power. Now, How Do We Use It?" *The Washington Post* (20 April, 2003), p. B03

[5] Paul Kennedy, "The Perils of Empire," *The Washington Post* (20 April, 2003), p. B01.

As usual, the end of the story remained to be written. But whether the go-for-broke activists or the steady-as-she-goes approach to global change carried the day, everyone on planet Earth would have to live with the results.

## SUMMARY

American preeminence in global history took many forms in the last decade of the twentieth century and the first years of the twenty-first. The regions and nations of the world continued to follow their own trajectories on many matters. The European Union drew closer together and parts of Asia boomed, while Latin America, Africa, and the Muslim zone faced serious economic and political problems. But America—rich, militarily unmatched, and vastly influential politically—sat at the head of the table whenever global concerns were discussed.

With the great Cold War and colonial struggles of the later twentieth century ended, America's foreign policy seemed to grow at least intermittently more aggressive. In a series of one-sided little wars, the United States settled problems in Central America, Balkan Europe, the Middle East, and Central Asia.

To many people, the United States also seemed to play a leading role in the onward march of globalization, a historic trend that had been gathering steam for at least five centuries. Globalizing forces included globe-girdling technology and economic ties, international organizations, and similar social structures around the world. Opposition came from rising concern for indigenous peoples and the environment, resistance to global economic combines, and from aggressive defenders of ideological and religious traditions in many parts of the world.

A major engagement in these struggles came when one of these latter—the Islamist terrorist group known as al Qaeda—destroyed the World Trade Center in New York in 2001. The United States responded with a rapid and devastating military campaign that shattered the Taliban Islamist government in Afghanistan, which had sheltered al Qaeda, and scattered the al Qaeda organization. President George W. Bush then declared the anti-American regime of Saddam Hussein, the Iraqi dictator, to be a stockpiler of weapons of mass destruction and a potential sponsor of terrorism and overthrew the Iraqi government in another shatteringly high-tech assault.

As other "rogue states" began to feel American pressure to disarm and sever ties with terrorists, the rest of the world looked with new alarm at the dominant position of the United States in world affairs. Two views of the twenty-first century contended for the global future: an aggressive "forward" policy that sought to solve problems by vigorous direct action and a more restrained view that sought to defend the existing world order.

## SUGGESTED READING

Appadural, A. *Modernity at Large: Cultural Dimensions of Globalization.* Minneapolis: University of Minnesota Press, 1996. Exploration of the jargon-rich new visions of globalization that have emerged in recent decades.

Attali, J. *Millennium: Winners and Losers in the Coming World Order,* trans. L. Connors and N. Gardels. New York: Times Books, 1991. International relations in a post–Cold War world. See also C. W. Kegley and E. R. Wittkopf, eds., *The Future of American Foreign Policy* (New York: St. Martin's Press, 1992) for essays on America's place in the new world order.

Bacevich, A. *American Empire: The Realities and Consequences of U.S. Diplomacy*. Cambridge, Mass.: Harvard University Press, 2002. Sees the United States as already an imperial power.

Crenshaw, M., ed. *Terrorism in Context*. University Park: Pennsylvania State University Press, 1995. Collection of scholarly articles on left-wing terrorism. For right-wing terrorists, see articles in T. Bjorgo, ed, *Terror from the Extreme Right* (London: Frank Cass, 1995).

Huntington, S. P. *The Clash of Civilizations and the Remaking of World Order*. New York: Simon & Schuster, 1996. Controversial theoretical study predicting conflicts involving three major world civilizations of our times.

*Jane's World Insurgency and Terrorism*. Alexandria, Va.: Jane's Information Group, 1999. Gives a sense of the vast range of terrorist movements. For further information on the broad picture, see *International Encyclopedia of Terrorism* (Chicago: Fitzroy Dearborn, 1997).

Juergensmeyer, M. *Terror in the Mind of God: The Global Rise of Religious Violence*. Los Angeles: University of California Press, 2000. Political utopianism gives way to religious imperatives.

Kramer, M. *Hezbollah's Vision of the West*. Washington, D.C.: Washington Institute Political papers, 1989. Explores the mindset of the terrorists.

Laqueur, W. *The New Terrorism: Fanaticism and the Arms of Mass Destruction*. New York: Oxford University Press, 1999. By a leading scholar of the phenomenon.

Meyer, B., and P. Geschiere, eds. *Globalization and Identity: Dialectics of Flow and Closure*. Oxford: Blackwell, 1999. Studies of the cultural impact of globalization—and of resistance to it.

Meyer, K., and T. Parssinen. *Webs of Smoke: Smugglers, Warlords, Spies, and the History of the International Drug Trade*. Lanham, Md.: Rowman and Littlefield, 1998. Global drug trade seen as a skillfully managed international business.

Robertson, R. *Globalization: Social Theory and Global Culture*. London: Sage Publications, 1992. A leading sociological analyst of the globalization process summarizes sociological explanations for the increased interaction between peoples.

Stiglitz, J. *Globalization and Its Discontents*. London: Allen Lane, 2002. A former chief economist at the World Bank explores the failures of global economic institutions to live up to their promises of global economic development.

Toblas, M. *World War III: Population and the Biosphere at the End of the Millennium*. Santa Fe, N.M.: Bear and Co., 1994. Massive study of the impact of overpopulation on the environment.

Tomlinson, J. *Globalization and Culture*. Oxford: Polity Press, 1999. Examines the "deterritorialization" of local cultures under the impact of globalization.

Von Laue, T. *The World Revolution of Westernization: The Twentieth Century in Global Perspective*. New York: Oxford University Press, 1987. Controversial but stimulating account of the impact of globalism on regional cultures around the world.

Wagenleitner, R., and E. T. May, eds. *Here, There, and Everywhere: The Foreign Politics of American popular Culture*. Hanover, N.H.: University Press of New England, 2000. Essays on the global reach of U.S. culture, with some awareness of the modifications imposed on cultural imports by other peoples. See also H. Fehrenbach and U. G. Poiger, eds., *Transactions, Transgressions, Transformations: American Culture in Western Europe and Japan* (New York: Berghahn Books, 2000).

Warren, K. B. *Indigenous Movements and Their Critics: Pan-Maya Activism in Guatemala*. Princeton: Princeton University Press, 1998. Case study of indigenous Native American organizations, often cited by students of contemporary antiglobalization struggles.

 Please refer to the document CD-ROM for primary sources related to this chapter.

# Index

Omar (Muhammad's patron), 256
Opium War, 577
Orozco, Jose, 750
Orwell, George, 753
Osiris, 47, 60
Osman, 387
Ottoman Empire
    administrative operations, 390
    corruption, 538
    decline, after Suleiman's death, 537–539
    Ghazi princes, 387–389
    origins, 387–388
    Suleiman the Magnificent (see Suleiman the Magnificent)
Oyo, 554

Pacific islands
    geography, 339
    migrations, 339
    prehistoric migrations, 341–342
Pakistan, India, conflict with, 704–705
paladins, 247
Paleolithic period, 16–20
Palestine Liberation Organization, 703, 782
Panama invasion, 769–770
Pasha, Muhammad Ali, 554
patriarchy, description of, 26
Pavlov, Ivan, 745
Pax Americana, 712, 782
Pearl Harbor, 664
Pei, I. M., 750
Peloponnesian War, 84–85
Pelstinian issue, 702–703
Pentateuch, 67
Pericles, 82–84
Peron, Eva, 729
Peron, Juan, 729
Perry, Matthew, 576
Persia
    Achaemenids (see Achaemenids)
    art of imperial age, 156–157
    classes, 154
    decline following Shah Abbas's death, 539–540
    diversity, 154
    dynasty of Cyrus (see Cyrus the Great)
    dynasty of Darius (see Darius the Great)
    empires vs. small politics, 152–153
    gender relations, 154
    Safavids, rise of, 390–392
    Sassanids rule, 153–154
    Zoroaster faith (see Zoroaster)
Persian Empire, 80–82
Persian Gulf war, 770
Persian Gulf, tensions in, 727
Peru
    Andean ruins, 139–140
    art, 140–141
    Chavin culture, 138–139, 140–141, 211–212
    Chimu (see Chimu)
    civilizations, vanished, 212–213
    geography, 138–139
    Mochica culture, 212 (see Mochica culture)
    postclassical period, 330
    religion, 140–141
    stone terraces, 139, 140
    worship centers, 328
Peter the Great, 478
Peter, Saint (See Saint Peter)
Petrarch, Francesco, 374
pharoahs, 47
    Akhenaton, 52–53
    god powers (people's belief in), 47, 48
    Hatshepsut, 50–51
    hereditary lineages, 46
    power of, 53
    pyramid tombs, 48

Ramses II, 53
    Thutmose III, 51–52
Philip Augustus, 232, 233
Philip II, 369
Philip of Macedon, 85
Phoenicians, 65–66, 66
phonograms, 55
physics, Newtonian, 743
Picasso, Pablo, 748
pictograms, 54–55
Pilgrimage of Grace, 379
Pitt, William, 463
Pizan, Christina de, 367
Pizan, Christine de, 367, 374
Pizzaro, Francisco, 459
plague, the, 241
Plath, Sylvia, 754
Plato, 87
    ethical teachings, 88
    morality, 88–89
    universe, view of, 88
PLO (see Palestine Liberation Organization)
Poe, Edgar Allen, 529
Poland, 721
polio, 744
polis, 78–79, 83. See also Greek Civilization
Polish Solidarity, 685
Polo, Marco, 347, 348, 752
Pompey, 161
popes, power of, 234, 235. See also Roman Catholic Church
Populist reform, 1890s America, 517–518
Portugal
    Asian exploration, 458
    treaty with Spain, 1494, 460
postmodernism, 752–753
poststructuralism, 745, 746–747
poverty, Third World issues, 723. See also economics; shanty-towns; Third World
prehistoric world
    human development (see human development)
    Old Testament version of, 7
    origins of earth, scientific, 8
Princip, Gavrilo, 599
Progressivism, 517–519
Prussia
    German unification, 496–497
    Hohenzollern dynasty, 476, 477
Ptolemy, 90
Pueblos
    at Chaco Canyon, 326
    culture, of the Anasazi, 326
    description, 326
Puig, Manuel, 753
Putin, Vladimir, 765
pyramids
    age of, in Egypt, 45–46
    Aztecs, 135
    Chavin, 139
    Mayan, 135, 215–216
    size, 57
    Teotihuacan, 214
Pythagoras, 89

Qaddafi, Colonel, 726
Qian, Sima, 197
Qianlong, 542
Qing, Jiang, 724
Quran, 262, 263, 264. See also Islam

Rabelais, Francois Shakespeare, William, 374374
racial diversity, 15–16
Rajputs, 548
Rama, Prince, 103, 104
Ramadan, 252
Ramayana, 103